W9-CTW-094

Twentieth-Century Literary Criticism

Guide to Gale Literary Criticism Series

For criticism on	Consult these Gale series
Authors now living or who died after December 31, 1959	*CONTEMPORARY LITERARY CRITICISM (CLC)*
Authors who died between 1900 and 1959	*TWENTIETH-CENTURY LITERARY CRITICISM (TCLC)*
Authors who died between 1800 and 1899	*NINETEENTH-CENTURY LITERATURE CRITICISM (NCLC)*
Authors who died between 1400 and 1799	*LITERATURE CRITICISM FROM 1400 TO 1800 (LC)* *SHAKESPEAREAN CRITICISM (SC)*
Authors who died before 1400	*CLASSICAL AND MEDIEVAL LITERATURE CRITICISM (CMLC)*
Authors of books for children and young adults	*CHILDREN'S LITERATURE REVIEW (CLR)*
Dramatists	*DRAMA CRITICISM (DC)*
Poets	*POETRY CRITICISM (PC)*
Short story writers	*SHORT STORY CRITICISM (SSC)*
Black writers of the past two hundred years	*BLACK LITERATURE CRITICISM (BLC)*
Hispanic writers of the late nineteenth and twentieth centuries	*HISPANIC LITERATURE CRITICISM (HLC)*
Native North American writers and orators of the eighteenth, nineteenth, and twentieth centuries	*NATIVE NORTH AMERICAN LITERATURE (NNAL)*
Major authors from the Renaissance to the present	*WORLD LITERATURE CRITICISM, 1500 TO THE PRESENT (WLC)*

ISSN 0276-8178

Volume 83

Twentieth-Century Literary Criticism

**Criticism of the
Works of Novelists, Poets, Playwrights,
Short Story Writers, and Other Creative Writers
Who Lived between 1900 and 1960,
from the First Published Critical
Appraisals to Current Evaluations**

Jennifer Baise
Editor

Thomas Ligotti
Associate Editor

The Gale Group
DETROIT • SAN FRANCISCO • LONDON • BOSTON • WOODBRIDGE, CT

STAFF

Jennifer Baise, *Editor*

Thomas Ligotti, *Associate Editor*

Maria Franklin, *Interim Permissions Manager*
Kimberly F. Smilay, *Permissions Specialist*
Kelly A. Quin, *Permissions Associates*
Sandy Gore, *Permissions Assistant*

Victoria B. Cariappa, *Research Manager*
Michele P. LaMeau, Andrew Guy Malonis, Barbara McNeil, Gary J. Oudersluys, Maureen Richards, *Research Specialists*
Tamara C. Nott, Tracie A. Richardson, Cheryl L. Warnock, *Research Associates*
Corrine Stocker, *Research Assistant*

Mary Beth Trimper, *Production Director*
Deborah L. Milliken, *Production Assistant*

Christine O'Bryan, *Desktop Publisher*
Randy Bassett, *Image Database Supervisor*
Robert Duncan, Michael Logusz, *Imaging Specialists*
Pamela Reed, *Imaging Coordinator*

Library of Congress Catalog Card Number 76-46132
ISBN 0-7876-2738-0
ISSN 0276-8178

Printed in the United States of America
10 9 8 7 6 5 4 3 2 1

Contents

Preface vii

Acknowledgments xi

Preface

Since its inception more than fifteen years ago, *Twentieth-Century Literary Criticism* has been purchased and used by nearly 10,000 school, public, and college or university libraries. *TCLC* has covered more than 500 authors, representing 58 nationalities, and over 25,000 titles. No other reference source has surveyed the critical response to twentieth-century authors and literature as thoroughly as *TCLC*. In the words of one reviewer, "there is nothing comparable available." *TCLC* "is a gold mine of information—dates, pseudonyms, biographical information, and criticism from books and periodicals—which many libraries would have difficulty assembling on their own."

Scope of the Series

TCLC is designed to serve as an introduction to authors who died between 1900 and 1960 and to the most significant interpretations of these author's works. The great poets, novelists, short story writers, playwrights, and philosophers of this period are frequently studied in high school and college literature courses. In organizing and excerpting the vast amount of critical material written on these authors, *TCLC* helps students develop valuable insight into literary history, promotes a better understanding of the texts, and sparks ideas for papers and assignments. Each entry in *TCLC* presents a comprehensive survey of an author's career or an individual work of literature and provides the user with a multiplicity of interpretations and assessments. Such variety allows students to pursue their own interests; furthermore, it fosters an awareness that literature is dynamic and responsive to many different opinions.

Every fourth volume of *TCLC* is devoted to literary topics. These topic entries widen the focus of the series from individual authors to such broader subjects as literary movements, prominent themes in twentieth-century literature, literary reaction to political and historical events, significant eras in literary history, prominent literary anniversaries, and the literatures of cultures that are often overlooked by English-speaking readers.

TCLC is designed as a companion series to Gale's *Contemporary Literary Criticism,* which reprints commentary on authors now living or who have died since 1960. Because of the different periods under consideration, there is no duplication of material between *CLC* and *TCLC*. For additional information about *CLC* and Gale's other criticism titles, users should consult the Guide to Gale Literary Criticism Series preceding the title page in this volume.

Coverage

Each volume of *TCLC* is carefully compiled to present:

- criticism of authors, or literary topics, representing a variety of genres and nationalities

- both major and lesser-known writers and literary works of the period

- 6-12 authors or 3-6 topics per volume

- individual entries that survey critical response to each author's work or each topic in literary history, including early criticism to reflect initial reactions; later criticism to represent any rise or decline in reputation; and current retrospective analyses.

Organization of This Book

An author entry consists of the following elements: author heading, biographical and critical introduction, list of principal works, excerpts of criticism (each preceded by an annotation and a bibliographic citation), and a bibliography of further reading.

- The **Author Heading** consists of the name under which the author most commonly wrote, followed by birth and death dates. If an author wrote consistently under a pseudonym, the pseudonym will be listed in the author heading and the real name given in parentheses on the first line of the biographical and critical introduction. Also located at the beginning of the introduction to the author entry are any name variations under which an author wrote, including transliterated forms for authors whose languages use nonroman alphabets.

- The **Biographical and Critical Introduction** outlines the author's life and career, as well as the critical issues surrounding his or her work. References to past volumes of *TCLC* are provided at the beginning of the introduction. Additional sources of information in other biographical and critical reference series published by Gale, including *Short Story Criticism, Children's Literature Review, Contemporary Authors, Dictionary of Literary Biography,* and *Something about the Author,* are listed in a box at the end of the entry.

- Some *TCLC* entries include **Portraits** of the author. Entries also may contain reproductions of materials pertinent to an author's career, including manuscript pages, title pages, dust jackets, letters, and drawings, as well as photographs of important people, places, and events in an author's life.

- The **List of Principal Works** is chronological by date of first book publication and identifies the genre of each work. In the case of foreign authors with both foreign-language publications and English translations, the title and date of the first English-language edition are given in brackets. Unless otherwise indicated, dramas are dated by first performance, not first publication.

- Critical excerpts are prefaced by **Annotations** providing the reader with information about both the critic and the criticism that follows. Included are the critic's reputation, individual approach to literary criticism, and particular expertise in an author's works. Also noted are the relative importance of a work of criticism, the scope of the excerpt, and the growth of critical controversy or changes in critical trends regarding an author. In some cases, these annotations cross-reference excerpts by critics who discuss each other's commentary.

- A complete **Bibliographic Citation** designed to facilitate location of the original essay or book precedes each piece of criticism.

- Criticism is arranged chronologically in each author entry to provide a perspective on changes in critical evaluation over the years. All titles of works by the author featured in the entry are printed in boldface type to enable the user to easily locate discussion of particular works. Also for purposes of easier identification, the critic's name and the publication date of the essay are given at the beginning of each piece of criticism. Unsigned criticism is preceded by the title of the journal in which it appeared. Some of the excerpts in *TCLC* also contain translated material. Unless otherwise noted, translations in brackets are by the editors; translations in parentheses or continuous with the text are by the critic. Publication information (such as footnotes or page and line references to specific editions of works) have been deleted at the editor's discretion to provide smoother reading of the text.

- An annotated list of **Further Reading** appearing at the end of each author entry suggests secondary sources on the author. In some cases it includes essays for which the editors could not obtain reprint rights.

Cumulative Indexes

- Each volume of *TCLC* contains a cumulative **Author Index** listing all authors who have appeared in Gale's Literary Criticism Series, along with cross references to such biographical series as *Contemporary Authors* and *Dictionary of Literary Biography.* For readers' convenience, a complete list of Gale titles included appears on the first page of the author index. Useful for locating authors within the various series, this index is particularly valuable for those authors who are identified by a certain period but who, because of their death dates, are placed in another, or for those authors whose careers span two periods. For example, F. Scott Fitzgerald is found in *TCLC,* yet a writer often associated with him, Ernest Hemingway, is found in *CLC.*

- Each *TCLC* volume includes a cumulative **Nationality Index** which lists all authors who have appeared in *TCLC* volumes, arranged alphabetically under their respective nationalities, as well as Topics volume entries devoted to particular national literatures.

- Each new volume in Gale's Literary Criticism Series includes a cumulative **Topic Index,** which lists all literary topics treated in *NCLC, TCLC, LC 1400-1800,* and the *CLC* yearbook.

- Each new volume of *TCLC,* with the exception of the Topics volumes, includes a **Title Index** listing the titles of all literary works discussed in the volume. In response to numerous suggestions from librarians, Gale has also produced a **Special Paperbound Edition** of the *TCLC* title index. This annual cumulation lists all titles discussed in the series since its inception and is issued with the first volume of *TCLC* published each year. Additional copies of the index are available on request. Librarians and patrons will welcome this separate index; it saves shelf space, is easy to use, and is recyclable upon receipt of the following year's cumulation. Titles discussed in the Topics volume entries are not included *TCLC* cumulative index.

Citing Twentieth-Century Literary Criticism

When writing papers, students who quote directly from any volume in Gale's literary Criticism Series may use the following general forms to footnote reprinted criticism. The first example pertains to materials drawn from periodicals, the second to material reprinted from books.

[1]William H. Slavick, "Going to School to DuBose Heyward," *The Harlem Renaissance Re-examined,* (AMS Press, 1987); excerpted and reprinted in *Twentieth-Century Literary Criticism,* Vol. 59, ed. Jennifer Gariepy (Detroit: Gale Research, 1995), pp. 94-105.

[2]George Orwell, "Reflections on Gandhi," *Partisan Review,* 6 (Winter 1949), pp. 85-92; excerpted and reprinted in *Twentieth-Century Literary Criticism,* Vol. 59, ed. Jennifer Gariepy (Detroit: Gale Research, 1995), pp. 40-3.

Suggestions Are Welcome

In response to suggestions, several features have been added to *TCLC* since the series began, including annotations to excerpted criticism, a cumulative index to authors in all Gale literary criticism series, entries devoted to criticism on a single work by a major author, more extensive illustrations, and a title index listing all literary works discussed in the series since its inception.

Readers who wish to suggest authors or topics to appear in future volumes, or who have other suggestions, are cordially invited to write the editors.

Acknowledgments

The editors wish to thank the copyright holders of the excerpted criticism included in this volume and the permissions managers of many book and magazine publishing companies for assisting us in securing reproduction rights. We are also grateful to the staffs of the Detroit Public Library, the Library of Congress, the University of Detroit Mercy Library, Wayne State University Purdy/Kresge Library Complex, and the University of Michigan Libraries for making their resources available to us. Following is a list of the copyright holders who have granted us permission to reproduce material in this volume of *TCLC*. Every effort has been made to trace copyright, but if omissions have been made, please let us know.

COPYRIGHTED EXCERPTS IN *TCLC*, VOLUME 83, WERE REPRODUCED FROM THE FOLLOWING PERIODICALS:

The Centennial Review, v. XXIII, Spring, 1979, for "*Native Son* and *An American Tragedy*: Two Different Interpretations of Crime and Guilt" by Yoshinobu Hakutani. © 1979 by *The Centennial Review.* Reproduced by permission of the publisher and the author.—*The Dreiser Newsletter,* v. 9, Spring, 1978. © 1978 *The Dreiser Newsletter.* Reproduced by permission.—*The Eastern Buddhist,* v. XIV, Autumn, 1981, for "Views and Reviews: The Diary of a Zen Layman, The Philosopher Nishida Kitaro" by Shibata Masumi. Translated from the French "Vie d'un Laic selon le Zen by Frederick Franck. Dans les Monastere Zen au Japan, Hachette, Paris, 1972. Copyright © 1981 by The Eastern Buddhist Society, Kyoto, Japan. All rights reserved. Reproduced by permission of the translator.—*Essays in Criticism,* v. 6, 1956, for "The Prisoner of *The Prisoner of Zenda*: Anthony Hope and the Novel of Society" by S. Gorley Putt. Reproduced by permission of the Editors of *Essays in Criticism* and the author.—*ETC: A Review of General Semantics,* v. 43, Summer, 1986. Reproduced by permission.—*Hispania,* v. 59, May, 1976, for "This World and Beyond: Mário de Sá-Carneiro's Struggle for Perfection" by William W. Megenney. © 1976 The American Association of Teachers of Spanish and Portuguese, Inc. Reproduced by permission of the publisher and the author.—*Human Studies,* v. 16, 1993. © 1993 Kluwer Academic Publishers. Reproduced by permission.—*International Philosophical Quarterly,* v. XXX, June, 1990, for "Experiential Ontology: The Origins of the Nishida Philosophy in the Doctrine of Pure Experience" by Andrew Feenberg and Yoko Arisaka; v. XXXII, September, 1992, for "'Inverse Correspondence' in the Philosophy of Nishida: The Emergence of the Notion" by Masao Abe. Both reproduced by permission of the publisher and the respective authors.—*Luso-Brazilian Review,* v. 12, Summer, 1975. © 1975 by the Board of Regents of the University of Wisconsin System. Reproduced by permission of The University of Wisconsin Press.—*Modern Fiction Studies,* v. 23, Autumn, 1977. Copyright © 1977 by Purdue Research Foundation. Reproduced by permission of The Johns Hopkins University Press.—*Modern Language Quarterly,* v. XXIX, December, 1968. Copyright © 1968 by the University of Washington. Reproduced by permission of Duke University Press.—*Monumenta Nipponica: Studies in Japanese Culture,* v. XX, 1965; v. XXI, 1966; v. XXII, 1969. All reproduced by permission.—*The New Yorker,* v. 35, October 3, 1959. © 1959 by The New Yorker Magazine, Inc. All rights reserved. Reproduced by permission.—*Papers on Language and Literature,* v. 27, Spring, 1991. Copyright © 1991 by The Board of Trustees, Southern Illinois University. Reproduced by permission.—*Philosophy East and West,* v. XIX, October, 1969; v. 40, July, 1990; v. 41, April, 1991; v. 44, April, 1994; v. 45, April, 1995. Copyright © 1969, 1990, 1991, 1994, 1995 by The University of Hawaii Press. All reproduced by permission of the publisher.—*Prospects: An Annual Journal of American Cultural Studies,* v. 1, 1975, for "*An American Tragedy*: A 50th Anniversary: Dreiser's Tragedy: The Distortion of American Values" by James T. Farrell. © 1975 Burt Franklin & Co., Inc. & Jack Salzman. All rights reserved. Reproduced by permission of the author.—*Scribner's Magazine,* v. LXXIX, April, 1926. Copyright 1926, renewed 1954. Reproduced by permission of Scribner, a Division of Simon & Schuster, Inc.—*Studies in the Novel,* v. 22, Winter, 1990. Copyright 1990 by North Texas State University. Reproduced by permission of the publisher.—*Thought,* v. XLVII, Winter, 1972. Copyright © 1972 by Fordham University Press. Reproduced by permission of Fordham University Press, New York.

COPYRIGHTED EXCERPTS IN *TCLC*, VOLUME 83, WERE REPRODUCED FROM THE FOLLOWING BOOKS:

Algeo, Ann M. From *The Courtroom as Forum: Homicide Trials by Dreiser, Wright, Capote, and Mailer.* Peter Lang, 1996. © 1996 Ann M. Algeo. All rights reserved. Reproduced by permission.—Davis, Joseph K. From "The Triumph of Secularism: Theodore Dreiser's *An American Tragedy*" in *Modern American Fiction: Form and Function.* Edited by Thomas Daniel Young. Louisiana State University Press, 1989. Copyright © 1989 by Louisiana State University Press. All rights reserved. Reproduced by permission.—Elwin, Malcolm. From *Old Gods Falling.* Collins Publishers, 1939. Copyright 1939 by Collins Publishers. Reproduced by permission of William Collins Sons & Co., Ltd.—Guest, David. From *The American Novel and Capital Punishment.* University Press of Mississippi, 1997. Copyright © 1997 University Press of Mississippi. All rights reserved. Reproduced by permission.—Harter, Carol Clancey. From "Strange Bedfellows: *The Waste Land* and *An American Tragedy*" in *The Twenties: Fiction, Poetry, Drama.* Edited by Warren

An American Tragedy

Theodore Dreiser

(Full name Theodore Herman Albert Dreiser) American novelist, essayist, autobiographer, journalist, short story writer, dramatist, and poet.

INTRODUCTION

As one of the principal American exponents of literary Naturalism at the turn of the century, Dreiser led the way for a generation of writers seeking to present a detailed and realistic portrait of American life. Widely considered his most important work, *An American Tragedy* (1925) was a departure from traditional American stories in which hard work and perseverance inevitably yield success and happiness, instead portraying the world as an arena of largely random occurrences. While the novel has often been criticized for its awkward prose style, inadequately conveyed philosophy, and excessive length and detail, it retains critical regard for its powerful characterizations and strong ideological convictions.

Biographical Information

Dreiser was born in Terre Haute, Indiana, into a large and impoverished family. While Dreiser did not excel as a student, he received encouragement from a high school teacher who paid his tuition when he entered the University of Indiana in 1889. Acutely self-conscious about his poverty and his appearance, Dreiser left the university after his first year and pursued a journalism career in Chicago. After several years as a reporter in Chicago, he began writing for newspapers and magazines in St. Louis, Pittsburgh, and New York. With the disappointing reception of his first novel, *Sister Carrie*, in 1900, along with marital difficulties, Dreiser's physical and mental health began to fail. After not working for several years, Dreiser was sent by his brother to a health resort to recuperate. In 1905 he resumed magazine writing and editing and over the next two years rose to the editorship of three prominent women's magazines. He lost this position in 1907 because of a scandal involving his romantic pursuit of a co-worker's teenage daughter. The same year, *Sister Carrie*, which had been received favorably in England, was reissued to positive reviews and good sales in the United States. Over the next eighteen years Dreiser published a succession of novels to widely varied but rarely indifferent critical notice; the publication of *An American Tragedy* in 1925 established him as the country's foremost living novelist. He went to Russia in 1927 to observe the results of the revolution, publishing his findings in *Dreiser Looks at Russia*, and he joined investigations of labor conditions in Kentucky coal mines in 1931. At the time of his death in 1945 Dreiser was better known as a social and political activist than as a novelist.

Plot and Characters

An American Tragedy is based on the real-life murder case in 1906 of Chester Gillette, who was executed in the newly-invented electric chair for the drowning of his pregnant working-class girlfriend Grace Brown in Big Moose Lake in New York's Adirondack Mountains; Gillette's motive was allegedly that he hoped to advance socially by pursuing relationships with members of the upper class, and he believed that his impending fatherhood would impede that. Dreiser had been fascinated by the case for years when he decided to fictionalize it in a novel. In Dreiser's version Chester Gillette became Clyde Griffiths, the son of fanatical evangelist parents in Kansas City whose attempt to "spiritualize" their son as much as possible makes the boy dangerously rebellious. When Clyde takes a job as a bellhop in a large hotel, he becomes intoxicated by the idea of pleasure, material wealth, and the American ideal of success. He leaves his position when the car he is riding in with drunken friends kills a little girl, and eventually moves to upstate New York to work in his wealthy uncle's collar factory. There he meets Roberta Alden, the daughter of a very poor farmer, to whose trusting and loving nature Clyde is attracted. At the same time, Clyde attracts the attention of Sondra Finchley, the daughter of a wealthy vacuum cleaner manufacturer. Clyde is torn between the two women until Roberta tells him she is pregnant and wishes to marry him. Wanting to impress Sondra's family and move into her circle of friends, Clyde decides his only way out is to kill Roberta. He takes her rowing on Big Bittern Lake and, rather than murdering her, allows her to drown when she falls out of the boat after he accidentally hits her in the head with his camera. He is arrested for her murder, tried, and sentenced to death. The novel ends in a scene with Clyde's young nephew sitting through a family prayer service similar to those that strongly impressed upon Clyde as a child.

Major Themes

An American Tragedy is considered by most critics to be a powerful indictment of the gulf between American ideals of wealth and influence and the opportunities available for their realization. The entire American system is blamed for the destruction of Clyde Griffiths, from his militant religious upbringing to the ambition of the local district attorney and the unfeeling jury who send Clyde to his death. Additionally, Clyde accepts everything he is told, never questioning the values of his parents' religious convictions or of the American ideals he later kills Roberta in order to obtain. Clyde's—and the rest of society's—blind allegiance to the pursuit of high social status and material wealth are ultimately, according to Dreiser, to blame for Roberta's death, as the American culture of consumption robs the human spirit of an ethical stance as well as the ability to express genuine feelings and beliefs, and dooms individuals like Clyde to destruction and decay.

CRITICISM

H. L. Mencken (essay date 1926)

SOURCE: "Dreiser in 840 Pages," in the *American Mercury,* Vol. 7, No. 17, March, 1926, pp. 379-81.

[In the following essay, Mencken praises the second volume of An American Tragedy, *but calls the first "vast, sloppy, chaotic."]*

Whatever else this vasty double-header [*An American Tragedy*] may reveal about its author, it at least shows brilliantly that he is wholly devoid of what may be called literary tact. A more artful and ingratiating fellow, facing the situation that confronted him, would have met it with a far less difficult book. It was ten years since he had published his last novel, and so all his old customers, it is reasonable to assume, were hungry for another—all his

old customers and all his new customers. His publisher, after a long and gallant battle, had at last chased off the comstocks. Rivals, springing up at intervals, had all succumbed—or, what is the same thing, withdrawn from the Dreiser reservation. The Dreiser cult, once grown somewhat wobbly, was full of new strength and enthusiasm. The time was thus plainly at hand to make a ten strike. What was needed was a book full of all the sound and solid Dreiser merits, and agreeably free from the familiar Dreiser defects—a book carefully designed and smoothly written, with no puerile clichés in it and no maudlin moralizing—in brief, a book aimed deliberately at readers of a certain taste, and competent to estimate good workmanship. Well, how did Dreiser meet the challenge? He met it, characteristically, by throwing out the present shapeless and forbidding monster—a heaping cartload of raw materials for a novel, with rubbish of all sorts intermixed—a vast, sloppy, chaotic thing of 385,000 words—at least 250,000 of them unnecessary! Such is scientific salesmanship as Dreiser understands it! Such is his reply to a pleasant invitation to a party!

By this time, I suppose, you have heard what it is all about. The plot, in fact, is extremely simple. Clyde Griffiths, the son of a street preacher in Kansas City, revolts against the piety of his squalid home, and gets himself a job as bellboy in a gaudy hotel. There he acquires a taste for the luxuries affected by travelling Elks, and is presently a leader in shop-girl society. An automobile accident, for which he is not to blame, forces him to withdraw discreetly, and he proceeds to Chicago, where he goes to work in a club. One day his father's rich brother, a collar magnate from Lycurgus, N. Y., is put up there by a member, and Clyde resolves to cultivate him. The old boy, taking a shine to the youngster, invites him to Lycurgus, and gives him a job in the factory. There ensues the conflict that makes the story. Clyde has hopes, but very little ready cash; he is thus forced to seek most of his recreation in low life. But as a nephew to old Samuel Griffiths he is also taken up by the Lycurgus *haut ton.* The conflict naturally assumes the form of girls. Roberta Alden, a beautiful female operative in the factory, falls in love with him and yields herself to him. Almost simultaneously Sondra Finchley, an even more beautiful society girl, falls in love with him and promises to marry him. Clyde is ambitious and decides for Sondra. But at that precise moment Roberta tells him that their sin has found her out. His reply is to take her to a lonely lake and drown her. The crime being detected, he is arrested, put on trial, convicted, and electrocuted.

A simple tale. Hardly more, in fact, than the plot of a three page story in *True Confessions.* But Dreiser rolls it out to such lengths that it becomes, in the end, a sort of sequence of serials. The whole first volume, of 431 pages of small type, brings us only to the lamentable event of Roberta's pregnancy. The home life of the Griffithses in Kansas City is described in detail. We make intimate acquaintance with the street preacher himself, a poor fanatic, always trusting in the God who has fooled him incessantly, and with his pathetic, drab wife, and with his daughter Esta, who runs away with a vaudeville actor and comes home with a baby. There ensues a leisurely and meticulous treatise upon the life of the bellboys in the rococo Green-Davidson Hotel—how they do their work, what they collect in tips, how they spend their evenings, what sort of girls they fancy. The automobile accident is done in the same spacious manner. Finally, we get to Lycurgus, and page after page is devoted to the operations of the Griffiths factory, and to the gay doings in Lycurgus society, and to the first faint stirrings, the passionate high tide, and the disagreeable ebb of Clyde's affair with Roberta. So much for Volume I: 200,000 words. In Volume II we have the murder, the arrest, the trial and the execution: 185,000 more.

Obviously, there is something wrong here. Somewhere or other, there must be whole chapters that could be spared. I find, in fact, many such chapters—literally dozens of them. They incommode the action, they swamp and conceal the principal personages, and they lead the author steadily into his weakness for banal moralizing and trite, meaningless words. In *The "Genius"* it was *trig* that rode him; in *An American Tragedy* it is *chic*. Did *chic* go out in 1896? Then so much the better! It is the mark of an unterrified craftsman to use it now—more, to rub it in mercilessly. Is Freudism stale, even in Greenwich Village? Ahoy, then, let us heave in a couple of bargeloads of complexes—let us explain even judges and district attorneys in terms of suppressions! Is the "chemic" theory of sex somewhat fly-blown? Then let us trot it out, and give it a polishing with the dish-rag! Is there such a thing as sound English, graceful English, charming and beautiful English? Then let us defy a world of scoundrels, half Methodist and half æsthete, with such sentences as this one:

> The "death house" in this particular prison was one of those crass erections and maintenances of human insensibility and stupidity principally for which no one primarily was really responsible.

And such as this:

> Quite everything of all this was being published in the papers each day.

What is one to say of such dreadful bilge? What is one to say of a novelist who, after a quarter of a century at his trade, still writes it? What one is to say, I feel and fear, had better be engraved on the head of a pin and thrown into the ocean: there is such a thing as critical *politesse.* Here I can only remark that sentences of the kind I have quoted please me very little. One of them to a page is enough to make me very unhappy. In *An American Tragedy*—or, at all events, in parts of it—they run to much more than that. Is Dreiser actually deaf to their dreadful cacophony? I can't believe it. He can write, on occasion, with great clarity, and even with a certain grace. I point, for example, to Chapter XIII of Book III, and to the chapter following. There is here no idiotic "quite everything of all," and no piling up of infirm adverbs. There is, instead, straightforward and lucid writ-

ing, which is caressing in itself and gets the story along. But elsewhere! . . .

Thus the defects of this gargantuan book. They are the old defects of Dreiser, and he seems to be quite unable to get rid of them. They grow more marked, indeed, as he passes into middle life. His writing in *Jennie Gerhardt* was better than his writing in *The "Genius,"* and so was his sense of form, his feeling for structure. But what of the more profound elements? What of his feeling for character, his capacity to imagine situations, his skill at reaching the emotions of the reader? I can only say that I see no falling off in this direction. *An American Tragedy,* as a work of art, is a colossal botch, but as a human document it is searching and full of a solemn dignity, and at times it rises to the level of genuine tragedy. Especially the second volume. Once Roberta is killed and Clyde faces his fate, the thing begins to move, and thereafter it roars on, with ever increasing impetus, to the final terrific smash. What other American novelist could have done the trial as well as Dreiser has done it? His method, true enough, is the simple, bald one of the reporter—but of *what* a reporter! And who could have handled so magnificently the last scenes in the death-house? Here his very defects come to his aid. What we behold is the gradual, terrible, irresistible approach of doom—the slow slipping away of hopes. The thing somehow has the effect of a tolling of bells. It is clumsy. It lacks all grace. But it is tremendously moving.

In brief, the book improves as it nears its shocking climax—a humane fact, indeed, for the reader. The first volume heaves and pitches, and the second, until the actual murder, is full of psychologizing that usually fails to come off. But once the poor girl is in the water, there is a change, and thereafter *An American Tragedy* is Dreiser at his plodding, booming best. The means are often bad, but the effects are superb. One gets the same feeling of complete reality that came from *Sister Carrie* and especially from the last days of Hurstwood. The thing ceases to be a story, and becomes a harrowing reality. Dreiser, I suppose, regards himself as an adept at the Freudian psychology. He frequently uses its terms, and seems to take its fundamental doctrines very seriously. But he is actually a behaviorist of the most advanced wing. What interests him primarily is not what people think, but what they do. He is full of a sense of their helplessness. They are, to him, automata thrown hither and thither by fate—but suffering tragically under every buffet. Their thoughts are muddled and trivial—but they can feel. And Dreiser feels with them, and can make the reader feel with them. It takes skill of a kind that is surely not common. Good writing is far easier.

The Dreiserian ideology does not change. Such notions as he carried out of the experiences of his youth still abide with him at fifty-four. They take somewhat curious forms. The revolt of youth, as he sees it, is primarily a revolt against religious dogmas and forms. He is still engaged in delivering Young America from the imbecilities of a frozen Christianity. And the economic struggle, in his eye, has a bizarre symbol: the modern American hotel. Do you remember Carrie Meeber's first encounter with a hotel beefsteak in *Sister Carrie?* And Jennie Gerhardt's dumb wonder before the splendors of that hotel in which her mother scrubbed the grand staircase? There are hotels, too, and aplenty, in *The Titan* and *The "Genius";* toward the end of the latter there is a famous description, pages long, of the lobby of a New York apartment house, by the Waldorf-Astoria out of the Third avenue car-barn. It was a hotel that lured Jennie (like Carrie before her) to ruin, and it is a hotel that starts Clyde Griffiths on his swift journey to the chair. I suggest a more extensive examination of the matter, in the best Dreiser-Freud style. Let some ambitious young *Privat Dozent* tackle it.

So much for *An American Tragedy.* Hire your pastor to read the first volume for you. But don't miss the second!

John Cowper Powys (essay date 1926)

SOURCE: "*An American Tragedy,*" in *The Dial,* Vol. LXXX, 1926, pp. 331-38.

[*In the following review, Powys praises the scope and vision of* An American Tragedy.]

The fact that Theodore Dreiser's new novel [*An American Tragedy*] seems likely to leave many readers repulsed and many critics confounded does not detract from its value. Its cold Acherontic flood pursues its way, owing little, if anything, to the human qualities that disarm, endear, or beguile, owing nothing to the specious intellectual catchwords of the hour. The pleasure to be derived from it is grim, stark, austere, a purely aesthetic pleasure, unpropitious to such as require human cajolery in these high matters.

To use the expression "objective" with regard to it is only illuminating if what one means is that the writer's energy is so powerful that his vision of things is projected to a certain distance from himself; to such a distance, in fact, that there are no trailing and bleeding fringes left to tug at his vitals or to hinder him from taking up his load and going on his way. In this sense the book is certainly a planetary projectile. It lives, if it lives at all, by its own revolution on its own axis. Its creator has written no *apologia,* no consolatory interpretation, on the sky of its orbit.

But what chasms and crevasses, what dark cavities worse than lunar craters, have we to enter, in order to geologize and botanize among the lava-cracks and the grey mosses of this scarcely congealed metallic microcosm! One reads somewhere that certain aboriginals of North America used to murmur of mysterious presences they named *manitou, wakanda, orenda.* The Bantu Africans whisper too of an invisible essence called *mulungu.* These primordial emanations do not appear to have been exactly divine or exactly diabolic. Rather do they present themselves as diffused magnetic dispersions, thrown off by the motions of primal Matter, as it stirs in its sleep, groping forward from the inanimate towards the organic. Some such *orenda,* some such *mulungu* seems to be the motive force and indeed the subject-matter of *An American Tragedy;* only in this case the mysterious effluence is given off rather by psychic than by physical forces. But to catch, out of the "palpable obscure," these secret stirrings and to follow them in their furtive motions a writer has to break many rules of language.

Perhaps the *Introibo ad altare* of any scrupulous initiation into the Dreiserian cult is to put one's finger upon the "blind mouth" of the historical method and wash one's hands clean of all rules, standards, conformities, traditions.

An American Tragedy certainly justifies its title. It is not merely American in its external stage-sets and the superficial idiosyncrasies of its characters. Plenty of American novels offer these allurements and yet remain as much afloat and deracinated as drifting seaweed. This extraordinary creation is American in its bones and blood and entrails. It is American in the heave of its breath, in the swing of its stride, in the smoke of its nostrils. Its Atlantean shoulders are American; so are its portentous buttocks. Its solemn wink, its shameless yawn, its outstretched, nonchalant limbs, all betray the sardonic sentiment, the naïve brutality, the adamantine stoicism of that organized chaos whose event is "in the hands of God."

The greatness of this work lies in the fact, among other things, that it covers so much ground. Some of the most arresting of Mr Dreiser's contemporaries are vigorous and convincing enough when on their own particular native soil. But where these "localists" lose their plumage is when they leave home and like all ill-advised migratory birds settle and chatter upon alien roof-tops. No one except Dreiser seems strong enough to swallow the whole chaotic spectacle and to disgorge it into some form of digested brain-stuff. His alone is the sprawl and the clutch, his alone the gullet and the stomach, competent to make away with such a cantle! On their own immediate ground these other writers can be suggestive enough. Off their ground they are nothing at all. But to be off the American of Dreiser's saturation you would have to take ship; and even then you would be miles out at sea ere that voice of Polyphemus fell upon silence or that Cyclopean eye, along with the light-ship of Sandy Hook and the search-light of Alcatraz, sank below the horizon!

An American Tragedy begins in Kansas City, the geographical navel of the land, moves thence to upper New York State, and terminates with the execution of its hero in Sing-Sing; but the psychic chemistry, of which it captures the *mulungu,* has its body and pressure in every portion of this country, and needs no map nor chart. This would hardly have been the case had what interested Dreiser most been those particular idiosyncrasies of our common nature that require a local habitation for their richest efflorescence. His Ygdrasil, his occult World-Ash-Tree, straddles its roots from coast to coast; finds nourishment as easily from the sands of Arizona, as from the red soil of the Carolinas; and it can do this because its roots are not really in the earth at all but in a vast diffused life-illusion, rising up like a thick mist out of a multitude of defrauded souls. This accounts for the fact that *An American Tragedy* is so lacking in what is soothing and healing to the mind, so sombrely naked of the kind of charm which pastures upon old usages, grows sweet and mellow upon the milk of ancient fields. Bell-hops, store-keepers, drummers, lawyers, sheriffs, politicians, factory-owners, factory-managers, factory-hands, stenographers, policemen, ministers, waiters, crooks, doctors, newspaper-men; all these, together with their counterparts in the residential sections, are perpetually throwing off, from Portland, Oregon to Portland, Maine, from Duluth to Miami, a cloud of invisible eidola, airy images of their grosser desires; and these are the filmy bricks of which Dreiser builds his impregnable dream-world.

It needs something thaumaturgic in a writer to enable him to separate this *mulungu* of accumulated life-illusions from the rest of the cosmic spectacle. But what Dreiser has done is nothing less than this; and we are compelled to accept as reality the "grim feature" thus starkly presented; although we cry to it in our dismay—"Hence, horrible shadow, unreal mockery, hence!" For it is as if, in Dreiser's work, *America itself*—the "commensurate antagonist" of the old civilizations—*saw itself* for the first time; cast a sly, shrewd, exultant, inquisitive look at itself; and turned away with a sardonic shrug.

Why is it that agriculturists and sea-faring people play so small a part in Dreiser's books, though both Witla in *The Genius* and Clyde in this story find their friendliest sweethearts in a farmhouse? Is it not because the doom is on him to recreate just that particular life-dream which cannot co-exist with any close contact with earth or sea? The traditions of earth-life and sea-life surround the persons committed to them with all manner of magical encrustations such as have the power to reject and ward off that garish hubbub, that crude hurly-burly, of an existence dominated by "modern improvements."

The very fatality of this spectacle, as Dreiser half discovers and half creates it, is something that sets its rhinocerus-horn, rampantly and blindly against all that is quaint, delicate, subtle in human nature. And yet throughout those scenes in the Kansas City hotel, throughout the coarse duplicities of the boy's first infatuation, throughout the scatter-brained jovialities in brothel, wineshop, and automobile, throughout the rough-and-tumble on the frozen river—so like a picture by Teniers or Jan Steen—throughout these pathetic struggles of Clyde and Roberta to outwit the vulgar respectability of Lycurgus, New York, one grows increasingly conscious that, rank and raw as it all is, there is something in the relentless and terrible *gusto* of the author's relish for what he is about which rises to the height of a monstrous sublimity.

It seems a strange use of the word "realistic" to apply it to this stupendous objectification of the phantasmal life-

dreams of so many tin-tack automatons of a bastard modernity; but when one grows aware how Dreiser's own Deucalion-like mind murmurs, weeps, laughs, and gropes among them, a queer oppression catches at the throat and a kind of grim hypnosis—as if a beast-tamer were luring us into his cage of snouts and tails and hungry nonhuman eyes—makes us almost ready to cry out, in kindred delusion, "It's the truth! It's the truth!"

An American Tragedy is the other side of the shield of that "plain democratic world" whereof Walt Whitman chanted his dithyrambic acceptance. And we may note that just as Whitman took ordinary human words and made them porous to his transcendent exultations, so Dreiser has invented a style of his own, for this monody over the misbegotten, which is like nothing else in literature. I think it is a critical mistake to treat this Dreiserian style as if it were a kind of unconscious blundering. If it is unconscious it certainly could find a very sophisticated defence; for who is not aware to-day of many recondite craftsmen who make use of the non-grammatical, the non-rational, and even of the nonsensical, to most refined aesthetic results?

It is much easier to call Dreiser naïve than to sound the depths of the sly, huge, subterranean impulses that shape his unpolished runes. The rough scales and horny excrescences of the style of *An American Tragedy* may turn out to be quite as integral a part of its author's spiritual skin as are the stripes and spots and feathered crests of his more ingratiating contemporaries.

The subject of the book, this tragedy that gathers and mounts and accumulates till it wrecks the lives involved, is the tragedy of perverted self-realization, the mistaking of the worse shadow for the better. All are shadows; but the art of life is still in its infancy when we make the mistake that this poor Clyde Griffiths made. But, after all, such in its own day and place was the tragedy of Macbeth; such, with yet insaner convolutions, the tragedy of Raskolnikoff. One has to take refuge in a different world altogether, in a world that has vanished with the philosophy of the ancients, to find an ignoble mistake of this kind unworthy of the ritual of Dionysus. Certain it is that with the exception of the unfortunate Roberta, not a character in this book wins our deeper sympathy. Clyde is pitiable, if we renounce all craving for mental and moral subleties, but we pity him as we would pity a helpless vicious animal driven to the slaughter-house, not as we pity a fully conscious human intellect wrestling with an untoward fate. And yet the book produces a sense of awe, of sad humility, of troubled wonder. How has this been achieved?

No one but Dreiser, as far as I know, could take a set of ragamuffin bell-hops, scurvy editors, tatterdemalion lawyers, greedy department-store wenches, feather-weight society chits, "heads without name, no more rememberéd than summer flies," could thrust into the midst of these people an ill-starred, good-looking weakling like Clyde; and then, out of such material—surely more uninspiring than have ever been selected by the brain of man or art-ist—set up a colossal brazen-ribbed image, which the very wild geese, in their flight over the cities of men, must suppose to be fathom-based upon reality!

To taste the full flavour, the terrible "organic chemical" flavour, like the smell of a stock-yard, which emanates from this weird book, it is necessary to feel, as Dreiser seems to feel—and, indeed, as we are taught by the faith of our fathers—that the soul of the most ill-conditioned and raw-sensed of our race, gendered by man, born of woman, has a potentiality of suffering equal with the noblest.

Thus in place of the world we know there rises up before us Something towering and toppling and ashen-grey, a very *Balaena Mysticetus* of the abyss, riddled with de-vouring slime-worms. And we ourselves, so great is this writer's power, become such worms. It is a formidable achievement, the creation of this "empathy," this more than sympathy, in the case of such unfortunates; and to have brought it about is, say what you please, a spiritual as well as an aesthetic triumph. To watch the death-hunt of the faltering Clyde is to watch a fox-hunt in the com-pany of some primordial Fox-god, who knows as you cannot know, both the ecstasy of stealing into the hen-roost and *what it is* to feel the hot breath of the hounds following your flying tail!

Balzac used to throw his protean magnetism into the urge of the most opposite obsessions, becoming sometimes an angel and sometimes a demon; but Dreiser does some-thing different from this. He overshadows his herd of hypnotized cattle in the totality of their most meagre and petering-out reactions, meditating upon them in an ubiq-uitous contemplation that resembles the trance of some "astral body" of iron and steel and paving-stone, some huge impalpable soul of the inanimate, yearning in som-bre tenderness over its luckless children. And yet it is not really out of the elements of the earth that Dreiser—moving like some vast shepherd of Jotunheim-flocks, among his rams and ewes—erects his sorrowful sheep-fold, but rather out of the immaterial hurdles and straw of their own turnip-tasting dreams.

The portion of the story that deals with the murder itself is so imaginatively heightened as to cast a Janus-like shadow backwards and forwards over the rest of the book. What the boy sees and hears as he sits in the train that is bearing him towards his victim; the "supernatural soliciting" that calls to him out of the air; the spasm of panic-stricken weakness that distorts his purpose at the supreme moment; his convoluted doubts, after the event, as to his actual guilt; these passages, like the dark waters of the lake where the girl is drowned, possess so much poetic porousness and transparency that they make the earlier and later portions of the work seem like an opaque face, of which they are the living and expressive eye.

Dreiser has always been a mystic. Only a mystic could capture the peculiar terror of *Matter become a ghost to the mind,* as he captures it, so as to be a veritable con-federate with the Chthonian divinities. Only a mystic could ponder so obstinately upon the wretched pulse-beats of a scamp like Clyde, till they respond to the rumble of Erebus, till they rise and sink in ghastly reci-procity with the shadow-voices of Typhon, of Loki, of Azazel, of Ahriman!

We can protest—and here, as I pen these lines in the very hotel where Clyde served his transients, I do most heart-ily protest—that there are aspects of human nature en-tirely obliterated from this gregarious shadow-dance. But such protests must conform to aesthetic intelligence. *An American Tragedy* is the tragedy of only such aspects of mortal consciousness as can get themselves objectified in such a psychic panorama. An artist, a mystic, a prophet if you will, must be allowed to *isolate his phenomena.* Dreiser's phenomena are not lacking in their own inher-ent contrasts. Compare the letters of Roberta, for ex-ample, so poignant as to be almost intolerable, with the baby-talk in the letters of Sondra, so intolerable for the very opposite reason! Sondra is one stage further re-moved from nature than Roberta; but the genuineness of her infatuation for Clyde is not lost in her queer jargon. Infatuated young persons, of both sexes, do babble in this unpleasant way when they are devoid of all critical alter-egoism. Like some gigantic naturalist studying the twitchings and turnings of a crowd of shimmery-winged dung-beetles Dreiser has been put to it to invent human sounds such as shall represent the love-cries and the panic-cries of these husks of inane rapacity.

Had any of his rampaging bell-hops, his crafty lawyers, his sly department-store ladies, his bouncing society-chits, shown too marked a tendency to emerge into a more appealing stratum of consciousness, a certain formi-dable unity of "timbre" would have been lost to the book, a consistency of rhythm broken, a necessary pressure removed. Composed of everything that prods, scrapes, rakes, harrows, and outrages an intelligent organism the environment, to which these creatures of Dreiser's con-templation respond, itself mingles with their lamentable response. It is out of this appalling reciprocity of raw with raw, that the mass and weight and volume of the book proceed. And this accumulated weight—so terribly mortis'd and tenon'd by its creator's genius—has its own unparal-leled beauty, as pure an aesthetic beauty (almost mathemati-cal in the rigidity of its pattern) as the most purged and exacting taste could demand. Thus is brought about through the mediumship of this omophagous intellect, the only es-cape from the impact of a certain horrible dream-world which a lost soul can find; the escape, namely, of giving to the Chimaera itself the lineaments of a work of art. To the unhappy wretch by the wayside whom Zarathustra found with a snake in his gullet was uttered the magic formula—"Bite and spit!" This is what Theodore Dreiser has done; and the result is *An American Tragedy.*

In *Plays Natural and Supernatural* this same author bestowed an articulate voice upon that thundering ox-bellow of the American Locomotive (so different from the thin whistles of European trains) which, reverberating across a continent, sounds the modern tragic chorus to so many broken-hearted vigils. In this same book there reaches the brain of a patient under laughing-gas a monstrous voice, repeating the syllable Om! Om! Om!

Such, it seems to me—that moan of the freight-train as you hear it in the night and that *other sound* which few have the ears to hear—is the only adequate commentary that can be made upon the temptation and crime and punishment of Clyde Griffiths, bell-hop of Kansas City! Not for nothing has this unique book gathered itself about the mystery of evil.

Every imaginative writer is doomed sooner or later to become a scape-goat; doomed to take upon himself, in a strange occult fashion, "the Sins of the World." And as one ponders upon the figure of Dreiser, moving in sombre *bonhomie,* humming and drumming, across the literary arena, one cannot fail to note that he also has had to balance that pack upon his shoulders.

His vision of things blames no one, lets no one off, reduces all "benevolence and righteousness" to sorrowful humility; pitiful, patient, dumb. For at the back of the world, as he sees it, is neither a Devil nor a Redeemer; only a featureless *mulungu,* that murmurs forever "Om! Om! Om!"

William Lyon Phelps (essay date 1926)

SOURCE: "As I Like It," in *Scribner's Magazine,* Vol. LXXIX, No. 4, April, 1926, pp. 431-38.

[*In the following review, Phelps dismisses* An American Tragedy *as a second-rate novel, concluding "I cannot believe that this work, hampered by such clumsy composition, will be read in the next century."*]

And now let me tackle that two-handed engine of naturalism, Theodore Dreiser's *An American Tragedy,* where we follow the fortunes of a nincompoop from childhood to the chair. What A. E. Housman told in a page Mr. Dreiser tells in two volumes. Yet his steam-roller method gains, I suppose, by crushing out all this accumulated mass of detail. The style is clumsy and awkward; it has as much grace as an ichthyosaurus in a quagmire. But it is all true, unanswerably true. It is the naturalistic method of Zola. And if the novelist chooses to select from life a hero without brains or backbone or charm, and depict his unimportant career with patient microscopy, and bring in hosts of other characters none of whom one would ever wish to know in real life, that is his own affair. There are plenty of such persons and I suppose they spend their days in the manner herein described. One may justly admire Mr. Dreiser for sticking to his own theory of art, and for his dogged and truth-loving patience not in writing jewels five words long, but in scraping together pebbles and more pebbles.

It is properly called an American tragedy not because of the unfortunate career of this particular protagonist, but because he represents many Americans who lead equally tragic lives although not meeting an equally tragic end. The very commonplaceness of the vast number of characters in this story makes their representative quality more depressingly impressive. They are, alas, samples.

Yet it is strange that in this work and in others of the same author there should apparently be no hint that every town in America contains individuals of nobility, unselfishness, and idealism, people of intellect, resolution, and charm, who find and help to make life a splendid adventure.

The last thing Mr. Dreiser would wish to be called is a moralist or a preacher; yet this vast book resembles not a little the obvious sermon of Hogarth's Idle Apprentice.

It is quite easy for me to see and feel the qualities emphasized by his adorers, such as Mr. H. L. Mencken, Mr. Burton Rascoe, and the latest convert, Mr. Stuart Sherman. I remain outside this kneeling group, sceptical and unconvinced. For two reasons:

First, all great novels should have the element of transfiguration. People who are poor in health and brains and money may still be rich in significance. It would not be fair to compare Mr. Dreiser with Dickens; but it is easy to imagine how splendidly Dickens, with a knowledge of the seamy side of life fully equal to the American's, and with as much studiously realistic detail, would nevertheless have breathed into this ash-heap such a glow of life that it would have made a conflagration unquenchable by time. It would not be fair to compare Mr. Dreiser with Dickens, because Dickens was a man of genius. Let us then compare him with Mr. Arnold Bennett, who has perhaps no genius, but who is a literary expert, who has mastered the art of the novel, who is a shrewd, hard-bitten man of the world, and who loves life with a fervor both chronic and passionate. Compare *An American Tragedy* with *The Old Wives' Tale,* or with *Riceyman Steps.* Mr. Bennett has transfigured the lives of the commonplace and of the downtrodden with a veritable glow of creative power, with the gift that belongs only to the true artist. Now if Henry James complained that Arnold Bennett's novels were simply an accumulation of bricks without ultimate significance, if what should have been the means had become the end, what would he say to *An American Tragedy?*

Furthermore, the great preservative is *style.* There *is* a literary standard, there is a difference between good writing and bad. I cannot believe that this work, hampered by such clumsy composition, will be read in the next century. To use William Sharp's phrase, it will float around awhile, a colossal derelict on the ocean of literature, and will eventually sink.

John J. McAleer (essay date 1972)

SOURCE: "*An American Tragedy* and *In Cold Blood,*" in *Thought,* Vol. XLVII, No. 187, Winter, 1972, pp. 569-86.

[In the following essay, McAleer contrasts An American Tragedy *with Truman Capote's crime novel* In Cold Blood.*]*

When Truman Capote's *In Cold Blood* was published in 1965 the *London Sunday Express* hailed it as "one of the stupendous books of the decade." The *New York Review of Books* agreed. Capote's book was "the best documentary of an American crime ever written." And in *Harper's* Rebecca West wrote: "Nothing but blessings can flow from Mr. Capote's grave and reverend book." Yet the editor of the *Atlantic Monthly,* Edward Weeks, who might be supposed to know something about fact-based novels since Nordhoff and Hall wrote the Bounty trilogy at his behest, demurred: "In *In Cold Blood,*" he wrote, "Truman Capote is providing the readers with a high-minded, aesthetic excuse for reading about a mean, sordid crime." In the pages of the *New Republic* Stanley Kauffman supported him: "It is ridiculous in judgment and debasing of us all to call this book literature. Are we so bankrupt, so avid for novelty that, merely because a famous writer produces an amplified crime feature, the result is automatically elevated to serious literature?"

While contending critics framed their avowals with matching ardor and indignation, only one, Granville Hicks, thought to praise *In Cold Blood* at the expense of another crime novel—Theodore Dreiser's *An American Tragedy*—which on its appearance forty years earlier likewise met a divided critical response. Applauding Capote's restraint in limiting "himself to ascertainable facts," Hicks told readers of the *Saturday Review:* "If Dreiser had done the same sort of thing with the Gillette-Brown case . . . *An American Tragedy* might have been a better book."

Although Dreiser, unlike Capote, unabashedly had fictionalized his source, critics berating *An American Tragedy* picked grounds similar to those Capote's detractors would occupy when they denounced *In Cold Blood.* Russell Blankenship, for example, had dismissed it as "simply a mammoth example of the reporter's art." No one suggested, however, that Dreiser had exploited a lurid situation for mere sensationalism. Unlike Capote, Dreiser had a thesis that went deeper than a demonstration of form. Critics could and did dispute Dreiser's thesis yet there could be no pretending that he lacked one.

To Joyce Cary *An American Tragedy* was "a great book," to H. G. Wells it was "one of the great novels of this century," to Joseph Wood Krutch, "the greatest American novel of our generation." Anderson, Lewis, Bennett, Fitzgerald, Agee, Dos Passos, Wright, Warren, Bellow, Mailer—to seek for commentary only among Dreiser's fellow novelists—also have lauded Dreiser's achievement. Just lately C. P. Snow has written: "*An American Tragedy* has its place among the 'great' novels in a sense, and to an extent, that no other American novel has, and, I might add, in a sense not possessed by any English novel since *Little Dorrit.*" If, then, *In Cold Blood* is a better book than *An American Tragedy,* Capote's

success has been notable. To determine if it has been, let us see his book in overlay to Dreiser's.

Basing a literary work on an actual murder is not a twentieth-century innovation. The sixteenth-century play, *Arden of Feversham,* once attributed to Shakespeare, was based on a real-life murder. So were Poe's "Mystery of Marie Roget," Dostoevsky's *Crime and Punishment,* and Browning's *Ring and the Book.* Yet in literature, to draw from life, even a life that deals in death, is no sure guarantee of merit. What is crucial is the writer's success in transcending the meanness of his materials to give them universal significance. As Goethe expressed it: "The artist has a twofold relation to Nature. . . . He is her slave, inasmuch as he must work with earthly things, in order to be understood; but he is her master, inasmuch as he subjects these earthly means to his higher intentions, and renders them subservient."

Capote's own account of why he wrote *In Cold Blood* centers on one fact—he wanted to give the nonfiction novel status as an art form. He had, he admits, "no natural attraction to the subject matter," choosing it on the theory that "Murder is a theme not likely to yellow with time." Even then he was ready to abandon this topic if he found another that suited his purpose better. Since Capote makes no declaration of intention in writing *In Cold Blood* beyond stating his desire to illustrate the feasibility of his form, we must wonder if his announced resolve really took him beyond the goal of achieving a dramatic ordering of facts, in felicitous prose, to serious consideration of how the potentials of his materials might be utilized to express a true, universalizing experience. Capote seems to have mistaken craft for art.

Dreiser did not write *An American Tragedy* to establish a literary method, nor was murder incidental to his purpose. Like Capote he did have trouble choosing his starting point, like Capote, it took him five years to complete his book once it was under way. But he had no doubts about the area in which he intended to work. He believed that murders such as the one Chester Gillette had committed were indigenous to America and his book was to be about the typicality of such a murder—murder carried out under the auspices of the American Dream. He researched "ten or fifteen" such murders and weighed their narrative potential before he chose the Gillette-Brown case [1906]. He was not interested in the crime as a crime but in the social pressures which fostered it. He tells us:

> I had long brooded upon the story, for it seemed . . . so common to every boy reared in the smaller towns of America . . . so truly a story of what life does to the individual—and how impotent the individual is against such forces. My purpose was . . . to give, if possible, a background and a psychology of reality which would somehow explain, if not condone, how such murders happen. . . .

An American Tragedy, then, has a social direction. Its author wishes to identify and condemn a social evil which, under the pretext of opening the way to self-realization, lures men to ruin. This therapeutic aim does not mean that *An American Tragedy* is a tract; that is hardly better than calling it an expanded exercise in journalism. Art is not always vanquished by preachment, and in his ultimate handling of his subject Dreiser detaches himself from society and its failings to write with insight and power of problems of the human condition which transcend time and place—and to chronicle the history of a cosmic hunger found in every human heart, though beyond man's reckoning in common hours. *"An American Tragedy,"* says Robert Penn Warren, "is conceived as a drama involving both the individual and the universe."

Regardless of the reason each author gave to explain his choice of subject, any record of the parallels between *An American Tragedy* and *In Cold Blood* must begin with awareness of how each author quarried from his own past, episodes which let him identify with his protagonist and, through such identification, draw upon an inner store of psychic perceptions. Neither author was new to the practice. *The 'Genius'* (1915), with its near *American Tragedy* ending (its protagonist, Eugene Witla, actually wishes his wife, Angela, dead, so that he might marry a young girl with whom he is infatuated), fictionalized Dreiser's own unhappy life up till the age of forty. Capote admits that *Other Voices, Other Rooms* (1948) is "all about" himself.

Both Dreiser and Capote have insisted that, in childhood, they never were wanted enough. In his own early poverty and aspirations Dreiser found a pattern that paralleled the history of Chester Gillette, whom he fictionalized as Clyde Griffiths. Warren says of Dreiser's autobiographical volumes: "In *Dawn* and in the first twenty-two chapters of *A Book About Myself,* not only the basic personality and life pattern of Dreiser himself have been presented and analyzed, but the basic characters, situations, and issues of *An American Tragedy* have been projected." Warren concludes that "in the strange metabolism of creation" Dreiser's source materials, both personal and derived, "are absorbed and transmuted into fictional idea, fictional analogy, fictional illusion." Thus: "This book is 'created,' and therefore generates its own power, multiplying the power implicit in the materials."

Dreiser then refashioned his own experiences to give verisimilitude to portions of Clyde's history. Although fealty to facts would not allow Capote to interpolate such data into his novel, it could not keep him from seeing himself in one of his protagonists—Perry Smith. Novelist Harper Lee, who was at Capote's side during those months when he made a final assessment of the materials he had gathered for *In Cold Blood,* relates: "I think every time Truman looked at Perry he saw his own childhood." The early years of both Smith and Capote were nomadic. Both hungered to escape from poverty and obscurity. Both were estranged from their fathers, neglected by their mothers. Both had talents which went unrecognized and therefore unencouraged. Although these are riches that go unclaimed, there is fully as much of Truman Capote in

Perry Smith as there is in the autobiographical child-protagonist of *Other Voices, Other Rooms*—Joel Knox.

As a boy in Vincennes, Indiana, Dreiser had shared the same living quarters with a youth, Jimmie Dooney, executed later for murder (1901 or 1902) by the State of New York. Without success Dreiser had petitioned the governor for commutation of sentence. It required no great force of imagination for Dreiser to see himself in Dooney's place. Neither Dreiser nor Capote propose that the Dooneys, Gillettes, and Smiths of this world could have been Dreisers and Capotes had they made of their talents and opportunities a wiser use. On the contrary, their anguish and compassion seem rooted in their conviction that what they are recording might have been, save for the caprices of fortune, their own destiny.

To turn from the authors to their protagonists, Clyde, Perry, and Perry's companion in crime, Dick Hickock, both Dreiser and Capote incorporate the reader into their lives at a level of compassion and sympathy which deplores not only the treatment which society dispenses but what Dreiser identifies as "the substance of the demands of life itself"—those circumstances which are the soil in which tragedy ripens toward its season of reaping. All three have experienced poverty, inequality, lack of success in satisfying basic needs, insecurity, frustration, and futility of quest. Clyde and Dick had godfearing parents. Perry's father, as well as his institutional keepers, tried to instill moral lessons. Yet both books insist that powerful moral influences are actual incentives to rebellious behavior when blind authority and emotionalism would try to enforce them.

Now consider how society deals with these protagonists as transgressors. Although in both books the crowds—society made visible—are amazed that such well-appearing boys could have committed the crimes they are charged with, no one thinks to investigate this paradox. We become aware, instead, of the morbid curiosity of a public which, despite its alleged Christian adherence, is titillated by the unfolding drama. A carnival atmosphere takes over as Roberta's letters are hawked in the street at Clyde's trial, along with peanuts, hotdogs, and popcorn. A local church sponsors a gala auction of the effects of the Clutter family. Hotdogs and soda pop are sold to the crowd gathered to see Dick and Perry arraigned. Though the defendants want a change of venue, their lawyers dissuade them on the theory that the community is religious-minded and will deal leniently with them. Yet, in each instance, the prosecution calls down Old Testamental wrath on their heads. Defense attorneys, in both books, ultimately ask the court if a fair trial is possible in a community so emotionally aroused. The limited mentality of the jurors is stressed. Farm people are the victims and farm people sit in judgment on the accused. In *In Cold Blood,* when the verdict is reached the judge himself has to be fetched from his farm. The governor, who refuses clemency, is, like the murdered man, a rich farmer. Both books disclose that forthcoming elections influence the conduct of the trials. For Orville Mason, in

An American Tragedy, and Al Dewey, in *In Cold Blood,* stalwarts of the law, a verdict of guilty becomes an epic obsession. And in Kansas, as in New York, the aristocracy of the community holds aloof from the trial.

The post-trial phase of legal justice, in the reversal of public interest which occurs, becomes society's subtlest barbarism. Legal postponements in the death house are excruciating. Dreiser deplores the "unauthorized cruelty and stupidity and destructive torture" which these delays constitute. Capote finds that the state exacts a thousand other deaths besides the one which the sentence calls for. In *An American Tragedy* Dreiser relates that the dimming of the prison lights as a man is electrocuted, is a psychological ordeal for other occupants of the death house.[1] In *In Cold Blood* Capote says that the sound of the floor dropping on the gallows constitutes mental torture for others, confined within earshot, who await hanging. In both books the point is made that money keeps people from execution. One recalls that on June 25, 1906, two weeks before Chester Gillette killed Grace Brown, Harry Thaw, in the same State of New York, with impunity shot Stanford White.

Concerning the underlying causes of the crimes—what Dreiser speaks of as "the substance of the demands of life itself"—both books convey an "only in America" emphasis—a strong sense of America as the logical environment sponsoring these murders. As Margaret Mead has noted, the title itself records Dreiser's intent "to make it [*An American Tragedy*] universal, at least for the American scene." The Dream of Success is paramount. Hence Alfred Kazin's remark: "Roberta's rival is not just a rich girl; it is, literally, the American Dream." And Leslie Fiedler's conclusion: "Clarissa is seduced here not by Lovelace but by Horatio Alger." Dreiser and Capote, indeed, each strikes a blow at the "bootstrap myth." In *An American Tragedy* a boy comes out of the West, into the East, seeking material fulfillment, only to find that conditions responsive to his expectations no longer exist. The Clutter murders truly appall because the crime occurs within the premises of paradise. Clutter himself says: "an inch more of rain and this country would be paradise—Eden on earth." The mythic Garden of the World is violated. In this context, observe that a condition of happiness, an archetypal situation as ancient as Eden, is imposed. Clyde is told that he must, under no circumstances, fraternize with girls working in the Griffiths' factory. Perry and Dick are forbidden to fraternize with former convicts. In each case the tragedy becomes possible when this injunction is flouted. That Dreiser appreciates this fact is affirmed by Clyde's Adamic lamentation, after his condemnation, that his failure to heed the mandate had cost him paradise. For Capote, it is simply another fact, stored among an array of facts, and left unevaluated. It is, as we shall see, this misguided reluctance on Capote's part to make functional use of his facts, save at the most literal level, that causes the two books to cleave apart. This point can be illustrated in another way. Corollary to the loss-of-Eden theme, in both books, estrangement from Nature is basic

to the misfortunes of the protagonists. Dreiser illustrates it in that memorable episode in which Clyde drops on all fours to run through a barren field, again in Roberta's death scene, the spot enclosed by dead trees with the weir-weir bird hovering and, finally, in causing Clyde to be taken by the posse at the margin of a woodland which beckons as a refuge—a classic ameliorative retreat to the wilderness situation. Capote, for his part, is satisfied to allude vaguely to Perry's lost Cherokee heritage and abortive Alaskan frontier adventure. A further parallel use of Nature offers additional illustration. In *An American Tragedy* water lilies equate with purity and death. Roberta's courtship begins and ends with them. A latter-day Persephone, Roberta, in Milton's parlance, gathering flowers is herself gathered. In *In Cold Blood,* Mrs. Clutter looks at her flower garden and sighs for bygone innocency. Dreiser functionally assimilates details from the Gillette-Brown case, making himself responsive to their mythic potential. Confronted with comparable riches, Capote ventures a grace note.

Although Capote, unlike Dreiser, makes an elaborate use of flashbacks to cover the early histories of Perry and Dick, thereby precipitating the reader at once into a gory drench, he pays a steep price for the dramatic appeal gained. Emphasis falls on effect rather than cause, a predictable consequence for an operational plan which gives to method precedence over matter. That Capote recognized an obligation to do something more may be inferred from the several efforts he made to provide a context for the crime. Among his notations, a principal instigating cause for the murder of the Clutters leaps to prominence. But Capote himself does not see it. He tries to mask his bewilderment by offering a succession of probable causes, creating for the reader a veritable solve-it-yourself packet. And that, of course, gives head to chaos.

When the film version of *In Cold Blood* was made, the moviemakers proffered one of Capote's implied secondary causes—Perry's Oedipal frustrations—as chief cause of the murders. When Perry cut Mr. Clutter's throat, Hollywood suggested, he thought he was butchering his father. When he climbed the gallows he saw his father as hangman. These Freudian revelations do not appear in Capote's book. When, however, the evidence is evaluated as Capote ought to have evaluated it, but failed to do, the cause of the murders of the Clutters proves to be identical with the cause of Roberta Alden's death, that is, blind pursuit of the American Dream. That is the theme Capote gropes for throughout *In Cold Blood* and which, despite his floundering, he most nearly proved valid. Ironically, someone in Hollywood sensed this. As Dick and Perry drive to Holcomb to commit the murders, they pass a theater the beckoning marquee of which announces its feature attraction—"A Place in the Sun," a movie version of *An American Tragedy.*

Capote says that when he saw the completed film of *In Cold Blood* he was "increasingly gripped by a sense of loss," as he viewed it. Since he himself did not know what it was that he had tried to say through his book, Capote's complaint was without focus. It did not occur to him that Hollywood, possibly because it did not want to march to Dreiser's music, had eschewed the one theme that held together his narrative. Nor were matters improved by the effort Hollywood made to bolster the fragile theme it had built the film around by tagging on to it the adjunctive notion that the book mounts an assault on capital punishment. Even Capote would not go along with that. After the film was released he told an interviewer that he believes in capital punishment and wishes only that it could be evenly enforced and used more generally.

In truth, in his preoccupation with form, Capote did not give enough thought to what conclusions his materials would lead to. Perhaps he believed that if he kept serving up facts they would supply their own logic—make their own gravy—with no assistance from him. As fiction writer Dreiser was free to deal with the uncut gem in his possession in whatever way best served his aims so long as he took into full account its natural planes of cleavage. As documentary-novelist, Capote was shackled by commitments which permitted him neither to release fully the potentials of his materials nor to concentrate their power for maximum effectiveness.

Capote's topic of prime focus is, like Dreiser's, the destructive encroachments of the American Dream. Although preoccupation with his experiment in form caused him to look on this theme and other lesser themes as intrusive, it surfaces too often not to be recognized. We have his word for it. He assures us: "The arbitrary act of violence springs from the poverty of Perry's life. . . . " Perry's resentment of those making good is illustrated in his attitude toward his sister, Bobo: "One fine day he'd pay her back . . . spell out in detail the things he was capable of doing to people like her, respectable people, safe and snug people, exactly like Bobo." In striking down the Clutters, Perry is striking at the embodiment of the American Dream—not, however, because he disapproves of it, but because he cannot get in on it. In a revealing statement, Perry confesses: "They [the Clutters] never hurt me, maybe it's just that the Clutters were the ones who had to pay for it." Capote says that the key to Perry's personality is "self-pity."

Dick's thinking parallels Perry's. At the trial a psychiatrist explains: "He secretly feels inferior to others . . . and dissatisfaction with only the normal slow advancement he could expect from his job. . . . These feelings seem to be overcompensated for by dreams of being rich and powerful . . . spending sprees when he has money." The Christmas following the killings, Dick and Perry are in Miami. "'Didn't I promise you we'd spend Christmas in Miami, just like millionaires?'" Dick asks Perry. But they are not millionaires and Dick soon shows the same kind of resentment that caused Perry to kill the Clutters. They see a shapely blonde masseuse hovering over a wealthy racketeer, at poolside at the Fontainebleau. We are told that Dick mused: "Big-shot bastards like that had better be

careful or he might open them up and let a little of their luck spill on the floor." Capote sees the key to Dick's personality as "envy." Self-pity and envy—defects of character which Clyde Griffiths shares and which impel him in pursuit of the American Dream.

Consider the trip to Mexico, the dreams of sunken treasure, a hill of diamonds, of Cozumel, the island paradise. Contrast with these things the ignominy which Perry feels wriggling on his belly beneath Nancy Clutter's bed, in pursuit of a keepsake silver dollar. The disparity between his hopes and his gains, produces a rage and shame which leads directly to the killings. In prison, awaiting execution, Perry whimpers: "'I was better than any of *them.*'" Why should the "haves" have while he has not? This thought makes a murderer of him.

Perry's last thoughts, at the foot of the gallows, are of his father and his father's "hopeless dreams." Here is the point about Perry's father which Capote must have wanted to implant in the reader's consciousness. The failure of the elder Smith to attain the American Dream, yet his relentless quest for that Dream, contributed much to Perry's discontent. Perry could and probably did hate his father for the false hopes he had engendered. Yet he could not rid himself of the habit of hoping which his father had implanted in him. He did not reject his father's goals, only his idealistic methods of pursuing them. When he killed Herbert Clutter he was not cutting his father's throat, he was splitting open a money bag.

When the Clutters were murdered their neighbors sensed at once that they had been killed because they emblemized the American Dream. One such neighbor laments: "'Feeling wouldn't run half so high if this had happened to anyone except the Clutters. Anyone less admired. Prosperous, secure. But that family represented everything people hereabouts really value and respect, and that such a thing could happen to them—well, it's like being told there is no God. It makes life seem pointless.'" Capote himself has described the Clutters to an interviewer as "a perfect embodiment of the good, solid, landed American gentry." Their neighbors wonder, indeed, if a wealthier family, living near the Clutters, had not been the intended victims, since they were even more representative. Perry's and Dick's dreams of riches are, after all, the dreams of the community that judges them. That really is why it had admired the Clutters. Accordingly the community is outraged not so much by the murders as by the assault on the American Dream which the murders signify. The community hates the persons who have sullied that Dream and, by implication, challenged its validity. An ironic feature of the tragedy is that the Clutters were not that much to be envied. Imagine winning, as a prize, a weekend with the Clutter family! Clutter himself, perched in his chair, as on the night of the murders, reading *The Rover Boys,* trying to escape back into the untroubled days of his boyhood. The Clutter children, Nancy and Kenyon, restively testing their father's fundamentalist authoritarianism. Daft Mrs. Clutter shut away in her room, as she has been for years, her neuroticism a likely by-product of her husband's obsessive concern with piling up riches. To pursue the American Dream he had neglected her emotional needs. Even on the eve of his death plans for newer and greater business ventures jostled for place in his head with new plans for her rehabilitation. Here, indeed, is a household the occupants of which are leading "lives of quiet desperation." Thus, both Perry and Clutter are double victims of the American Dream. Pursuing the Dream and persuading his son to pursue it, Perry's father had destroyed his home life. In pursuit of the Dream, Clutter, too, had destroyed his family life, and was slain, at last, by someone pursuing the Dream who envied him his apparent attainment of it. This game had no winners.

At the close of *In Cold Blood* a reporter opines that the only good that came of the Clutter case was that a lot of newspapers had been sold. The final irony: the Clutter murders had been good for business, good for someone's pursuit of the American Dream. Inevitably, critics would say that Truman Capote's dream had come true, also, when *In Cold Blood* brought him a fortune amounting to millions. Dreiser had known the same opprobrium, if not the same rewards.

A further dilemma faced Truman Capote as author of a nonfiction novel based on the Clutter case. He had dual protagonists. Now Chester Gillette had been the protégé of not one but two uncles. He had courted not one but three society girls. Not committed, as Capote was, to presenting facts without variance, Dreiser was able to merge the uncles into one, and to alloy the three belles. As co-protagonist, alleged instigator of the Clutter killings but not the actual killer, Dick Hickock is an incumbrance to Capote as storyteller. He "doesn't fit," as Capote himself has owned. Capote's narrative would have gone better if he could have dispensed with him entirely. His rapport was with Perry. It was Perry who wrote him a ten thousand word farewell letter and kissed him goodby before ascending the gallows. Capote lavished every attention on him. That is not surprising if, as Harper Lee surmises, Capote saw himself in Perry, just as Dreiser saw himself in Clyde. Dick's role, on the other hand, seems like something thrown in to strike the bargain. Since Dreiser sifted through at least ten American tragedies before he settled on Chester Gillette as the representative victim of the American Dream, it might be supposed that other victims of the same illusion, insofar as they approach typicalness, would resemble Clyde Griffiths. Dick does not. Perry does, in numerous particulars.

Dick's get-it-easy attitude and good looks remind us of Clyde. Otherwise he is nonrepresentative—an unwanted excrescence. Had Dreiser found such a personage bulking on the landscape of the Gillette-Brown case, he would have excised him without a pang, or telescoped his salvageable parts into a single characterization, just as he did with the dual uncles and triad of society girls. A good artist must have the surgical touch and apply it as needed. Capote's attempts to handle Hickock peripherally show that he realizes this. But he had to retain him because the scheme he had bound himself to demanded it. Hickock

further illustrates, then, the quagmire the writer steps into who supposes that a work of art can be shaped from uninterpreted facts.

The parallels between Perry and Clyde, unlike those between Dick and Clyde, are both intimate and sustained:

Neither has a father with whom he can identify.

Both seek mother surrogates.

Both are unable to establish lasting and meaningful relationships.

Both despise religious rigorism.

Both are rootless, nomadic, and in flight from failure.

Both envy prosperous relatives.

Both are quick to excuse the conduct of sisters who have shared in their hardships.

Both are described as following a "mirage."[2]

Both dream of coming into possession of fabled riches—Aladdin's treasures; a hill of diamonds.

Both have in their natures a strain of tenderness, vivid but ephemeral—a by-product of their own hardships and disappointments.

Both are sentimentalists and betrayed by their sentimentalism.

Both morbidly hoard memorabilia touching on their emotional ties with others.

Both antagonize those whom they might look to for help: Gilbert won't help Clyde or let his father help him; Bobo won't help Perry or let her husband help him.

Both are wary prior to the crimes, reluctant to proceed, eager to call them off.

Each must assume a new personality to be capable of killing: Clyde joins forces with the afrit; Perry fuses his personality with Dick's.

Both think they have been shrewd but leave damaging clues behind.

Both attract comforters to them in prison.

Both see someone in the courtroom who reminds them of their victims and are haunted by that fact: Clyde, a girl who looks like Roberta; Perry, a brother of Clutter's who resembles Clutter.

Both are superstitious: For both a bird is harbinger of death; both regard Kansas City as "a place of bad luck."

Both are specifically charged in court with having murdered "in cold blood."

Both are perplexed by the role they have played: Clyde, legally innocent, feels morally guilty; Perry, legally guilty, feels morally innocent.

Both go to their deaths believing they have not received justice.

Granting the reality of coincidence, we must none the less concede that many of these parallels go beyond chance. Certainly if an anthropologist turned up so many matching bones we would not hesitate to concede that they probably came from creatures of the same species. Yet even if we did not know that Capote was working from facts alone, it would be unwise to conclude that he had plundered *An American Tragedy* for confirming touches for his narrative. On the other hand, if Dreiser's fictionalization had postdated Capote's nonfiction novel, how many critics would have been ready to bring in an indictment against him, charging plagiarism! Actually, when two authors are mining the same vein such duplications are inevitable. What is unforgettable is the realization that much of what Capote dug from the bedrock in his role as documentarian, Dreiser, through a remarkable use of the creative faculty, was able to provide out of his own intuition. Dreiser's sense of the American Tragedy type of individual was so unerring, he was able to identify with such a personage so totally, that he summoned up, out of his own innate sense of what was probable about such a man, a wealth of details which find actual substantiation in Capote's true-life record of Perry Smith.

Dreiser met none of the principals involved in the Gillette-Brown murder case, but he rowed to Moon Cove on Big Moose Lake where the murder occurred and lingered there for two hours; he sat in a cell on Death Row with a man awaiting execution, he went to a shirt factory and studied the process of shirt manufacturing, all in preparation for writing *An American Tragedy.* And he went beyond these physical preparations, beyond a scrutiny of the trial record and newspaper accounts, to take on an actual sense of the identity of Chester Gillette. In doing that he created as honestly as Michelangelo did when he summoned David from his marmoreal cerements. Only a wraith of the Clyde Griffiths whom Dreiser created exists in the Chester Gillette of the trial record, yet in the truth of the characterization we are given an archetypal grasp of the American Tragedy type of protagonist, and of his dilemma, such as no dossier ever has been ample enough to hold. And all future portrayals of him, to the extent that they correspond to the facts, must resemble that archetype.

In 1838 William Ellery Channing wrote:

> You must have taken note of two classes of men, the one always employed on details, on particular facts, and the other using these facts as foundations of higher, wider truths. . . . One man reads a

history and can tell you all its events, and there stops. Another combines these events, brings them under one view, and learns the great causes which are at work. . . . So one man talks continually about the particular actions of this or another neighbor; whilst another looks beyond the acts to the inward principle from which they spring, and gathers from them larger views of human nature . . . strives to discover the harmony, connection, unity of all. . . . To build up that strength of mind, which apprehends and cleaves to great universal truths, is the highest intellectual self-culture.

By fictionalizing his material Dreiser gained vastly more in truth of nature than Capote did when he deployed his material without creative intervention. Capote's nonfiction novel format kept him from sorting out his major theme from secondary ones. It shackled him to petty data, kept him from soaring, from taking creative possession of his material. Lacking a viable artistic alternative, he let a debilitating morbidity, sponsored by his closeness both to the events and personages involved, and perhaps by his own narcissistic needs, inundate the resultant vacuum. The result is a work which avoids what Warren calls "the dreary factuality of an old newspaper account" solely by its dependency on an exalted style and on an emotionalism which combines Gothicism and sentiment in equal measure.

Dreiser's liberating method lets us enter into a bona fide relationship with Clyde. Chester Gillette admitted murdering Grace Brown. By qualifying Clyde's guilt in Roberta's death, Dreiser lays stress on society's role in the failure of his protagonist. By making Clyde a situational criminal impelled by circumstances, rather than an habitual criminal whose conduct is complicated by a twisted psyche, as is true of Dick and Perry, Dreiser is better able to convince us of the compelling force of the American Dream. After *An American Tragedy* was published Dreiser received letters from many readers who told him—"Clyde Griffiths might have been me." Readers could, in fact, identify with Clyde. Rare is the reader who will see himself as Dick or Perry. By the time he has read of Perry's Oedipal anxieties, his paranoia, his pathological drives, his craving for notoriety, of Dick's checkbouncing mentality and feelings of sexual inadequacy, he must be able to relate to them about as well as he could to *Australopithecus robustus.*

As a shaper of materials who does not have to answer to any person or pattern of events, Dreiser can place his emphasis where it will best support his thesis. Clyde reaches his decision to kill Roberta because of his wish to safeguard his American Dream prospects. Perry kills out of frustration at not attaining them. It is easier to relate to Clyde in his efforts to preserve his hopes than to Perry in his exasperation at not attaining his. Clyde's actions are consistent with his aspirations, Perry's a gesture of spite which negates the whole thrust of his ambitions—an acknowledgment of defeat. Dreiser thus is able to keep a positive emphasis, consistent with pursuit of the Dream, but Capote is compelled to deal with an act which repudiates it, with a protagonist who, at the start of his quest, has forsaken his goal. What is to be said of the Horatio Alger hero who loses faith when he experiences a setback in his progress toward success?

Not committed to rote delivery of hard facts, Dreiser is able to make the pace of his narrative less deliberate than Capote, to convey better a sense of Clyde's stumbling progress through life, with things falling out for him, as they do, by caprice rather than calculation. Against this pattern the pathos of his own petty scheming is better grasped and the reader prepared both for the ineptitude which characterizes his plan of murder, and the irony which lets chance make of it a foolproof vehicle for his destruction.

Dreiser is able to speak openly, too, of the inadequacies of the law. Capote, dealing with actual people, many of whom will be searching his narrative for grounds for libel, has to report on their shortcomings inferentially. Recognizing, also, that the appeal of his book is blunted by the absence of a love plot, Capote patches on an extraneous account of Nancy Clutter's lost love. Indeed, because Capote does not know how to tie together his facts, the whole final portion of *In Cold Blood* is fragmentary. He might have assured harmony, as Dreiser did, with the use of a relay character, like the Reverend Duncan McMillan, who could carry on the protagonists' quest and help them to order their thoughts on their ordeal. Dreiser was free to invent McMillan to serve this end and to invent little Russell whose role, at the close of the book, is to affirm that the action of the novel is about to unwind itself again, and will continue to do so, *ad infinitum,* until society itself alters. Wanting such characters, Capote loses his final chance to force an assessment of the true meaning of the Clutter murders.

Lilies, seasons, sports, the dance, cars, birds, boats, trees, colors, all intrigue at the level of the symbol to give *An American Tragedy* expanding dimensions of subtlety and strength. Some are supplied out of Dreiser's creative imagination, others germinated by some actual circumstance of the Gillette-Brown case which Dreiser's imagination could restructure without reproach. By such measures was Dreiser able to enlarge the scope of his thesis and produce what Sergei Eisenstein would salute as an "epic of cosmic veracity." Moreover, while Capote must grind under foot anything that looks like an undocumented assumption, Dreiser is free to give to his material a mythic sweep by invoking in Roberta the image of Persephone, and in Clyde, the transgressing Adam.

We have remarked that in *An American Tragedy,* Dreiser, without being on the scene as Capote was, or privy to confessional disclosures, again and again accurately intuited what was classic in such instances. The documentation which Capote provides on an American Dream sponsored murder in *In Cold Blood* confirms Dreiser's extraordinary instinct for the relevant in crimes of this specific kind. *In Cold Blood*'s chief value then—the real blessing which flows from it—may well be its

affirmation, as an accurate but uninventoried stockpile of American Tragedy details, of the soundness of Dreiser's intuitions and methods. It is striking proof of the timeless integrity of *An American Tragedy.* What Dreiser saw as true in 1925, is shown by Capote's documentation forty years after to be true still. Capote has reported on an event. Transcending time (and, indeed, as Mason Gross has observed, there is by design little in *An American Tragedy* to confine it to an era), Dreiser has reported on the truth of human nature. After all, materialism is, as E. M. Forster long ago noted, "the old, old trouble which eats the heart out of every civilization."

Dreiser's achievement confirms the essential role of the creative faculty and its generosity in supplying authenticating detail when the author acts from an understanding of the human condition founded on genuine responsiveness to the universe. By its very amplitude, it affirms the pity of a creative faculty stifled by limiting forms, of which the nonfiction novel, at least in Capote's understanding of it, is a repelling example. Capote's facts adorn him like leg irons. He is, in turn, jailer to imprisoned archetypes, myths, and symbols, inherent in his material, but denied liberty. They stare out at us like bugs in amber. Through Dreiser's method they could gorgeously soar. Even when style approaches the luminosity of Holy Writ, and Capote's sometime does, that is not enough if the facts strain for release, without avail, against the membrane of words enclosing them.

"Fact," says Norman Mailer, "is nothing without nuance." These words hint at a larger truth which Dreiser saw. In his edition of *The Living Thoughts of Thoreau,* Dreiser expresses admiration for this statement of Thoreau's:

> When facts are seen superficially, they are seen as they lie in relation to certain institutions, perchance. But I would have them expressed as more deeply seen, with deeper references; so that the reader or hearer cannot recognize them or apprehend their significance from the platform of common life, but it will be necessary that he be in a sense translated in order to understand them. . . . A fact truly and absolutely stated is taken out of the region of common sense and acquires a mythologic or universal significance.

As author of *An American Tragedy,* Dreiser can cite this passage with the authority of someone who has confronted truth and been caught up in its vastness. In the failing light of the void we live in, Capote, footloose amid the lovely lawns of his lyricism, is merely the most fragrant of the ineffectual angels who woo us. To see facts wholly, to be enveloped in verities that are eternal, we still must go to Dreiser.

NOTES

[1] The notoriety Dreiser's book gave to this circumstance eventually brought the desired reform. Electric chairs now are powered by a dynamo separate from those which supply prisons electricity for normal use.

[2] *Mirage* was Dreiser's original choice of a title for *An American Tragedy.* Clyde's aspirations are twice spoken of as a mirage.

James T. Farrell (essay date 1975)

SOURCE: "*An American Tragedy*: A 50th Anniversary: Dreiser's Tragedy: The Distortion of American Values," in *Prospects: An Annual Journal of American Cultural Studies,* Vol. 1, 1975, pp. 19-27.

[*In the following essay, Farrell contends that it is the loss of American values and an uncaring society that represent evil in* An American Tragedy.]

Dreiser seems to have thought for years about the book that eventually became *An American Tragedy.* For years he had wanted to write about a crime. He kept clippings of various murder cases, and before the Chester Gillette-Grace Brown case in upstate New York in 1906 he had clippings about other murders, including one about a minister who committed a murder.

An American Tragedy has been compared to *Crime and Punishment.* But in *Crime and Punishment* the crime is committed by an intellectual who does a lot of thinking about whether or not he's justified. His was the crime of an intellectual and entirely different from the crime in *An American Tragedy.*

Dreiser was deeply concerned with good and evil, about which he had a relativistic concept. In *An American Tragedy,* and in Dreiser's thinking in general, good and evil are related to the instincts and desire. In *Sister Carrie,* he had mentioned several times the conflict between instinct and convention. And his final attitude about morals is that they are relative, that what others consider evil does not seem evil to the person who does it. One acts under the compulsion of desire, out of impulses which one does not understand or know. Dreiser did not accept the notion of free-will, and in *An American Tragedy* he spells out in slowly presented, careful detail his notions of the relativity of good and evil. In this way he explains the motivation of Clyde Griffiths' crime.

Dreiser slowly and carefully motivates his character, and he establishes the responsibility of society in the fate of Clyde Griffiths (this is one of the reasons why it is an *American* tragedy) through his presentation of the ideals of society, the way in which Clyde fastens on them, and the way in which they appear to Clyde as the only ideals he seems able to understand. *An American Tragedy* would be a tragedy even if there were no deaths in it. It would be a tragedy in this sense: that Clyde Griffiths abandons and thinks to murder a girl, Roberta Alden, because she is pregnant and interferes with his getting on in life by marrying a much more trivial though rich girl, Sandra Finchley, who seems to have much less capacity to develop, is less warm and human than Roberta. And that is tragic. The tragic distortion of values is the heart of the tragedy. Fundamentally, *An American Tragedy* is a tragedy because of the play of false values; and the consequence of Clyde's effort to live by these false values establishes, documents, and drives home the tragedy.

Clyde Griffiths' development is such that it seems almost inevitable that he pick up these false values. He grows up in what is a socially abnormal atmosphere. His parents are good people, small, itinerant religious peddlers; but they are, in contrast to most people, bizarre, a little bit freakish. They do not convey by example or by instruction much to him about living other than that he should live in terms of the tenets of their religion. "They tried to dent the apathy of life," is the way Dreiser puts it. And we quickly see that Clyde is embarrassed by it all. He doesn't understand why he's embarrassed, except he doesn't like the fact that he does not live a socially normal life, that his family doesn't live in one fixed place, that he doesn't go to one school and have companions, and that his parents' occupation is in no way similar to the occupations of the parents of other children. They move from city to city in the early course of the book while Clyde is growing up. By the time they settle in Kansas City at a little mission, he has an undefined sense of shame about his parents and about their difference from other people.

Clyde's first job is as a bellboy in a large and, to him, magnificent hotel in Kansas City. Hotels are grand and magnificent palaces, particularly to a boy like Clyde Griffith, who has known nothing in his own life to prepare him to realize what a hotel is like. At a hotel everybody is equal if he can pay the bill. (And those who can pay the bill better than others may be more equal.) And there's a kind of an anonymity about hotels. Many people use hotels for purposes that are immoral in terms of Clyde's background, or in terms of the values of his parents. People at a hotel drink, have sexual affairs. There's a certain looseness with money. And this hotel culture is, outside of the home, Clyde's first school of values. It's the beginning of the formation of his desires and of his branching out into the world. He is very simple and naive. He's not shocked, but he is surprised that money comes easily. He sees people drinking and men with expensively dressed wives or mistresses or women. It's a kind of a luxury, a luxuriousness, that was unimaginable to him before. The other bellboys are more knowing and more sophisticated in a superficial way. They know what to do to get tips, and he doesn't. He learns from his peers, and what he learns are false values based upon luxury and desire.

The knowledge he picks up is superficial and more or less related to an expansion of his desires. Dreiser says about Carrie Meeber in *Sister Carrie* that "she expanded not in knowledge but in desire," and in a sense the same thing happens with Clyde. He wants better clothes. He doesn't want to give up all his money at home, where it is needed, because he wants to use some of it for his pleasure, to go out with the other bellboys. And he does go out with them. He meets a girl, for the first time meeting a member of the opposite sex outside his own family, or other than in the most superficial or casual way. After a few weeks he begins to cut down on the amount of money he brings home. He learns how to dress, and he learns how to drink. He learns how to go out with those of his own age and have a good time; and he acquires a desire for a richer life, defined in terms of what he sees in the hotel and what he can do with the bellboys when they go out on a party.

In the hotel culture Clyde learns a completely new life. He doesn't realize that it demoralizes him in the sense that it gives him false values, false in terms of the worth of human beings and of the things that make for human growth. He begins to see worth in terms of what is luxury to him.

Clyde and some others go out once in a borrowed automobile, and there is an accident. And Clyde, out of fright, runs away and goes to Chicago. There he has a few jobs. For a while he works for a laundry, and then as a bellboy in an athletic club in Chicago. For a considerable period he doesn't even communicate with his parents, and he even takes a different name. He's afraid. He's so unknowing of the processes of society that his fright is an exaggeration of what might have happened to him. He was scarcely culpable. He wasn't driving the car, and the probability is that nothing would have happened to him. At most he would have been given a lecture. But he's so unknowing of the ways of the world that he runs away in fear.

Up to this point there continues to be a kind of social abnormality about Clyde's life. He feels that he's committed a crime and that he's liable to arrest, so he still feels alienated from the normal stream of life where he could satisfy his desires, where he could have a better or richer, more satisfactory material way of living. Nevertheless, he has what could be called the ambition of his desires. While he's working in the Chicago athletic club, where rich, well-to-do people stay, he meets his uncle, a successful manufacturer from New York. He's heard of his uncle, and he recognizes that this is his uncle when he serves him. Clyde is clever and ambitious enough to want to impress the uncle, and he succeeds. The uncle brings him to the town of Lycurgus, in upstate New York, to work in his shirt factory. Although Clyde is given a job, they start him at the bottom. Immediately, of course, he runs afoul of the snobbish attitudes of his cousins. The Griffiths family is one of the prominent families in Lycurgus. To them he's a poor relation. But to those with whom he works he is the nephew of the owner. He cannot have casual or normal relationships with either his co-workers or his relatives.

Clyde proves himself capable in his work, as capable as his cousin, the son of Mr. Griffith. But opportunity through capability is closed to Clyde. He was as capable as his cousin to be an executive, but there was no chance for success on the basis of his capabilities.[1] He does not have a job in which he could advance in the normal way.

In any case, Dreiser's view of the world is not the same as that of Horatio Alger. Alger died in 1897, and between the last decades of the nineteenth century and the first decades of the twentieth century there had been much stratification of society; the chances of taking a shoeshine box as a starting point and ending up a person of wealth were diminished. Clyde apparently wouldn't have known how to go out with a shoeshine box anyway. It seems almost an accident that he got even a job as a bellboy.

The abnormality in Clyde's life makes it likely that he would see success, the aim for his life, in terms of advancing through connections. When he goes to Lycurgus and begins to work in the factory, he is still as much on the outside as he was in Chicago, as he was in Kansas City, and as he was in San Francisco where the novel opens. He's traveled all the way across the country, and still he is bewildered. He has the desire, the ambition to live like those who are materially better off then he is. His work does not tax him, but it leaves him lonely because of his ambiguous position. And his ambiguous position is parallel to his ambiguous position as a boy, when he did not grow up like others of his generation. He did not have the same pattern of school life, he did not have the same kind of home—all of that was another world to him. He is still a bewildered figure.

When he finally takes up with Roberta Alden, one of the girls in the factory, their relationship starts off on a secretive footing which gives a kind of falseness to it and prevents Clyde from entering into a completely honest relationship with her. First they exchange notes. Then, when he goes out with Roberta, they have to go to another town. He doesn't want to be seen. It's dangerous to his position. Eventually she gives herself to him out of love, and she becomes pregnant. By this time an affair has developed, but there has been no talk of marriage or anything else. Now something has to be done, but both of them are so unknowing of urban life that they don't know what to do.

Roberta is only a farm girl, though her background is more normal than Clyde's. She has experienced a more normal family, a family with love. She's had some responsibility in her family. There's less strangeness between her and her family, although they are simple people and their moral ideas based upon religion are as rigid as those of Clyde's parents. But Roberta Alden really feels, more than Clyde does, that she belongs someplace in the world. Clyde is alienated from society in a way that she isn't. Dreiser has a phrase that perfectly fits the character of Roberta Alden. He says she is a young girl of "troubled modesty." The very fact that she has an affair with Clyde suggests that she feels a real depth of emotion, because her upbringing, her attitudes would not have permitted her to do a thing like this lightly. She does it out of fear of losing him, because Clyde insists on a sexual relationship and threatens otherwise to leave her.

In the meantime Clyde has been very much ignored by the Griffiths. He has been invited only once or twice to their house. He is invited around Christmas time, and he goes alone. Sandra Finchley happens to visit the Griffiths and she notices Clyde. At first she doesn't pay him much heed, but she has a feeling of rivalry with the Griffiths' son, Clyde's cousin, and her developing interest in Clyde comes largely out of spite. She picks him up, and they begin to go out with the young people in the town. Clyde finds their life ideal, the thing towards which he thinks he has been moving. It is more or less consistent with the life of people who had tipped him in the hotel. In Sandra's company he is attractive, and he seems to fit in. He begins to lie to Roberta, not to see her; his name begins to appear in the society column of the newspaper. In the meantime a crisis is building up—something has to be done.

Through all this, Dreiser has consistently detailed the social determination of Clyde's conduct. It centers on values, on what Clyde wants to do, and on what he understands in relation to values and desires. There is nothing in his experience to open up a different perspective on life. His perspective is fixed—formed by moral conceptions that are black and white, right and wrong, good and evil. Roberta Alden's is also a black and white moral world, but at least in her world there are more emotional and more affectionate family relationships. For Clyde all of that is absent. Not that his mother has no emotional depth; but she is given to saving the souls of people who are apathetic to the appeal that she and her husband make, preaching the true religion on street corners and singing hymns. Clyde simply drifts along, much as Carrie Meeber did. He takes the easiest course. But the world that has opened to him, the world in which he wants to believe, is a world of superficial richness, vulgarity, and material things—a world of easy leisure and a world which he endows with a kind of illusory value. He sees Sandra Finchley's name in the society column, and he thinks this all-important. Very superficial things characterize the world which he wants to enter, the world that means success to him. He is almost completely entranced and infatuated, and he doesn't know what to do about Roberta.

After failing to bring her around with some medicine, he agrees to marry her. They have a pathetic practical ignorance about life. They knew nothing about contraception, and he doesn't know how to find a doctor. Today all this would seem unlikely; there are still Clyde Griffiths and Roberta Aldens, but there are fewer of them. In an earlier period they would not have seemed unusual. People just grew up, and it was thought that the tenets of religion and morality were enough to keep them on the straight and narrow path; if not, they deserved their fate. That was the prevailing attitude, and this was the plight of many youths in an earlier period of American life. Ultimately, Clyde in his desperation thinks to kill Roberta.

Dreiser was a determinist and didn't believe in free-will, but what is important is that he carefully, patiently, and solidly builds up a motivation which is so definitely socially established that Clyde appears a victim. Clyde emerges from the book as a victim of false, shallow, and superficial values. Whether Clyde does right or wrong is irrelevant to what Dreiser is attempting to establish with the character. What he has established is a character with false or shallow values rather than more human values. *An American Tragedy* is made more awesome by the fact that it ends with death in the electric chair. But the tragedy is in the false values and in the way Clyde comes to see no other values for him, no other possibilities. After his early bewilderment, his chances come. He is about to attain what he wants, what has been evolving and developing in him since he was a bellboy and saw the rich and shallow life and behavior of people in the hotel culture. The hotel was a school of values for him, and these values are built up slowly and patiently, almost solemnly in Clyde.

Dreiser was a determinist. Logically, you can prove or disprove determinism. Considering determinism versus free-will is too all-conclusive a question to be subsumable to empirical evidence. It can only be answered logically or in terms of wish-fulfillment or prejudice. But there is one sense in which we can say that determinism is something that exists. If through a tendency towards action, through repetition of the play of thought and fancy and aspiration, the actions of a person become a kind of habit, so that they are a fixed orientation, a fixed goal in life, and if a person cannot then see any other alternative, and there is no intervention of some force, some problem, some impulse which enables that person to see a different alternative, then in that sense the person's actions become determined. Other possibilities are blotted out. This is the sense in which Clyde Griffiths' life is determined. There is a responsibility of society, insofar as he lives in the kind of a society where boys like him are not paid any attention. They are individuals floating in a sea of forces and powers stronger than they are, and they cannot contend with their own impulses and with the problems they face in giving satisfactory expression to those impulses.

Clyde is characterized almost in terms of his lack of having any function, of his drifting. He has no importance. His estimation of himself is partly set in the future when he can associate with rich people, when he will be on their level—the same as rich if not rich. He is alienated, he is socially outside, and he is seeking a kind of an identity and fulfillment in a world to which he must come by connections, to which he must come through his social presence. And his desire, the impulsion of his desire, is so strong that he actually thinks he will solve the problem of Roberta's pregnancy by murdering her. Here again Dreiser is characterizing a relationship to society and a relationship to social function. This is why he gives Clyde Griffiths a past where socially normal feelings are not within his intimate, personal, direct experience. Clyde has not known the kind of feelings and experiences that come with a consistency of family life and school life, and in relationships with those of his own age. His life has been abnormal and somewhat bizarre, and out of his own experience he doesn't gain the understanding or the habit of feeling and response that one gets from a consistent, regular, and seemingly motivated pattern of living in family and society and work and school.

The alleged murder of Roberta Alden becomes a sensational case, and is written up in the newspapers. It's the subject of national attention. Much social energy—the time of trained men at great cost—is spent in ferreting out every detail, every discoverable fact about the life of Clyde Griffith. Up until this point he has been a waif, just one of the vast anonymous population of the country. He has been one of millions seeking to feel more free, seeking to feel that life is getting better than it has been, or that it's better than the lives of others. But after the death of Roberta attention is focused on Clyde Griffith. There's irony in that. Only because of a death, and presumably a murder, is any attention given to this individual. Before that, he's unguided, uncounseled, uninstructed, unknown; he's drifted to a point where he seems to be emerging out of this anonymous mass, out of this anonymous, unspoken, unwritten destiny to which he and many like him seem predestined. Dreiser was not an ironist, but the repetition of Clyde's life through the investigation as it is brought out in the chapters on the courtroom has an ironical and deepening effect. Mencken felt that this book was too long, and that this repetition wasn't necessary. I don't agree with him. I think it gives a depth to the book, and that the repetition of so much about Clyde's life, put into this new context of the investigation and the uncovering of this murderer Clyde Griffith, as he's conceived to be, gives an added dimension to the book.

In the first part of the book we focus directly on Clyde as he goes from Kansas City to Chicago, as he drifts from job to job and into various relationships, we see him partly struggling, partly drifting, wanting something better, wanting to be free and freed in the sense in which he conceives freedom, which is a life richer in an obvious, shallow, material sense. And then his whole life is presented to us again in the context of an investigation uncovering motives and reasons to show that he is a killer and that he has a past which is consistent with his indictment for murder in the first degree and which gives added substantiation to a verdict of guilty and a sentence of electrocution for the murder of Roberta Alden. We read the story of his life in two contexts: first as it happened, and then as it is presented in consequence of the investigation, the ferreting out of his past, the examination of witnesses, the picking up of detail by detail leading to the conviction.

Clyde, after his conviction, is really dulled, bewildered; he scarcely knows what has happened. This has all been rather sudden. One minister finally reaches him, and he goes through a process of reconversion or conversion, of finding religion. It's a simple religious conception, and it's a means of appeasing his guilt, so that he goes to the electric chair feeling that he has done wrong.

At the end of a Dreiser novel my feeling is often one of wonder about the irreconcilable, irrefragable aspects and characteristics of different destinies: rich and poor, strong and weak, the contrast of grandeur and misery, failure and success. There have been many youths in American life like Clyde Griffith. They may have been a little more or a little less sophisticated. They may not have ended in the electric chair. They possibly lived out their lives in what Thoreau called quiet desperation. But they lived for false values. They lived for aspirations similar to Clyde Griffith's, and their lives were more or less marked by the same emptiness.

[1] This differentiates Clyde from some of the earlier main characters of Dreiser. Sister Carrie's success is due to her emotional nature. In Dreiser's *The Genius,* the material success of the principal character, Eugene Witla, is due to the fact that he has talent, that he is more or less of a genius as a painter. In Dreiser's trilogy about the financier Cowperwood, again, Cowperwood shows from his early teens that he has a genius in manipulating stocks. He becomes a millionaire in his early twenties. In each of these cases where there is material success, it is related to the capacity within the personality and the organism of these characters.

Carol Clancy Harter (essay date 1975)

SOURCE: "Strange Bedfellows: *The Waste Land* and *An American Tragedy,*" in *The Twenties: Fiction, Poetry, Drama,* edited by Warren French, Everett/Edwards, Inc., 1975, pp. 51-64.

[*In the following essay, Harter argues that despite being antithetical in most ways, T. S. Eliot's* The Waste Land *and* An American Tragedy *share a similar view of the human condition "as it is manifested in the modern world."*]

It is difficult to imagine any two contemporary men of letters more dissimilar than Theodore Dreiser and T. S. Eliot. They are not merely unlike by virtue of ethnic, religious and economic background, professional interests, education, philosophy, and temperament; as artists they represent antagonistic—even irreconcilable polarities: Dreiser epitomizes the naturalist, journalist-fictionalizer, while Eliot remains the quintessentially allusive metaphysician, aesthetician-poet. Indeed, despite the fact that *The Waste Land* was published only three years prior to the publication of *An American Tragedy,* the dissimilarities between the two works are so profound they are rarely discussed in relation to one another. But that would not surprise either writer, for neither Dreiser nor Eliot seems to have been particularly aware of the other's artistic existence or impact on the literary scene, and there is no evidence whatever (in either his biography or letters) that Dreiser was in any way either impressed with or directly influenced by the publication of *The Waste Land.* Nevertheless, it seems remarkable that two monumental literary works such as *The Waste Land* and *An American Tragedy* were given the world within three years, and as yet have not been seriously discussed in the same critical context. Antithetical as they are, both works emanated from the rich artistic, socio-economic and cultural milieu of the twenties; and along with *Ulysses, The Sound and the Fury,* and *The Great Gatsby,* belong to an era of English and American letters as abundant and opulent as that of the Elizabethan theatre or the American Renaissance. Perhaps because of the distinctive quality of the milieu from which they evolved, both embody—however much they are diametrically opposite as literary forms—many of the same themes, symbolic motifs, and views of the human condition as it is manifested in the modern world. Each creates a metaphoric fabric whose design ultimately reveals the barren landscape of man's spiritual and moral wasteland. Frederick J. Hoffman notes some of the differences between Eliot and Dreiser's use of the wasteland landscape, but the similarities are equally apparent: "Since naturalism is, in literary terms at any rate, an extension of realism, the naturalist landscape incorporates not only the sordid detail used for a very much more complex purpose by Baudelaire, Eliot, and their contemporaries, but the scene itself in which social disparities can easily be imaged. Dreiser's concern with cities, hotels, clothes, and interiors helps to identify this landscape as a *social record of moral deficiencies.* But the landscape does not record merely despair over the disabilities of the modern world; it is asked as well to express externally the inner dispositions of its heroes" (my italics, "The Scene of Violence: Dostoevsky and Dreiser," *Modern Fiction Studies,* Summer 1960).

It would not, I think, be unfair to him to suggest that the particular American tragedy Dreiser so memorably delineates through Clyde Griffiths is a projection of human loss and hopelessness conceived by (and in turn re-nourishing) the same wasteland that Eliot symbolically creates in his poem. For every landscape Dreiser paints—the natural, the "civilized," the urban, the psychological and moral—presents the bankruptcy of values and debasement of spirit which Eliot so forcibly perceived and made immanent in *The Waste Land.* However, while Eliot's panoramic view of human experience encapsulates all time, history, and culture, and filters it through the virtually omniscient consciousness of an androgynous Tiresias who despairingly contemplates the entire cosmos, Dreiser refracts the cosmic view and counterpoints it against the puny, never fully conscious sensibility of the lost Clyde Griffiths. The state of man and his universe is, nevertheless, strikingly similar in both works even though our vision of that universe is controlled by antipodal points-of-view. In *The Waste Land* we are behind the camera scanning the desolate ruins of the ash heaps, merely invited to identify with our brothers: "'You! hypocrite lecteur—mon semblable—mon frere!'" In *An American Tragedy,* however, we are drawn inside immediately vis à vis the internalized controlling consciousness of Clyde Griffiths. (Perhaps this is Dreiser's most masterful technical accomplishment in *An American Tragedy,* one which he failed to perfect in *Sister Carrie.* In the later novel we are rarely exposed to the heavy-handed intrusions of the all-wise narrator who shapes the world from

the outside as he did in *Sister Carrie.* As a result, Dreiser achieves in *An American Tragedy* a dramatic narrative which embodies his view of the wasteland of modern life. In its own way, *An American Tragedy* is as dramatic in form as *The Waste Land.*) If Eliot had chosen to present a fuller characterization of his "young man carbuncular," we would perhaps also experience *The Waste Land* from the inside, from the pathetic half-consciousness of a Griffiths-like sensibility. In both poem and novel, however, we the *hypocrites lecteurs,* are left with an overwhelming sense of futility and horror: institutions are hopelessly corrupt, Christianity is atrophied, nature is debased by industrialization, and the spirit of man is imprisoned: the secularization of the world and its values has resulted in an overriding materialism which leads, in both works, to death by drowning, death which offers little or no possibility for resurrection. Paradoxically, the "death by water" which Madame Sosostris warns against becomes the ultimate embodiment of human experience in both *The Waste Land* and *An American Tragedy.*

Ellen Moers is one of the few critics of Dreiser's work who articulates a symbolic link between *The Waste Land* and *An American Tragedy.* Referring to the novel in *The Two Dreisers,* Moers remarks: "From its opening paragraph—an opening pared down to schematic starkness through the many stages of Dreiser's revisions—the novel unfolds as a fable of the 'Unreal City.'" She further suggests that the fable-like quality of Dreiser's city is emphasized by a "purposeful vagueness about time and place," a vagueness, I might add, resembling Eliot's own. While Moers does not pursue the comparison she introduces, one can trace the metaphors of urban life and landscape throughout each work and discover how analogous Eliot and Dreiser's views of the modern city were: each used the city as a metaphor for man's abuse of his resources, for his materialistic and destructive compartmentalization, and for his spiritual prison. While the image of the city as prison is symbolically suggested in *The Waste Land,* it is a literal reality for the convicted Clyde Griffiths, and is eventually transformed into an actual deathhouse. The city-as-prison-as-deathhouse in *The Waste Land,* while never literal, is invoked through Eliot's allusions to *The Inferno.*

> Unreal City,
> Under the brown fog of a winter dawn,
> A crowd flowed over London Bridge, so many,
> I had not thought death had undone so many.

Likewise, in *An American Tragedy* the Dantesque texture of the city is rendered imagistically in the opening paragraphs: "Dusk—of a summer night. . . . And the tall walls of the commercial heart of an American city of perhaps 400,000 inhabitants—such walls *as in time may linger as a mere fable.* . . . Having reached an intersection this side of the second principal thoroughfare—really just an alley between two tall structures—*not quite bare of life of any kind,* the man put down the organ . . ." (my italics, Modern Library, 1953, p. 15). This imagistic suggestion of an earthly Inferno, however, becomes explicit as Clyde awaits execution on murderer's row: "And in the meantime Clyde was left to cogitate on and make the best of a world that at its best was a kind of inferno of mental ills—above which—as above Dante's might have been written—"abandon hope—ye who enter here'" (p. 824). What Clyde's limited awareness cannot grasp is that the literal deathhouse he inhabits is simply an extension of the "unreal cities" to which he was continuously drawn. The difference is merely of degree: "The 'death house' in this particular prison was one of those crass erections and maintenances of human insensitiveness and stupidity principally for which no one primarily was really responsible. Indeed, its total plan and procedure were the results of a series of primary legislative enactments, followed by decisions and compulsions as devised by the temperaments and seeming necessities of various wardens, until at last—by degrees and without anything worthy of the name of thinking on any one's part—there had been gathered and was now being enforced all that could possibly be imagined in the way of unnecessary and really unauthorized cruelty or stupid and destructive torture. And to the end that a man, once condemned by a jury, would be compelled to suffer not alone the death for which his sentence called, but a thousand others before that. For the very room by its arrangement, as well as the rules governing the lives and actions of the inmates, was sufficient to bring about this torture, willy-nilly" (pp. 815-816).

Eliot's narrator, blessed with acute consciousness, sees and records the Styx-like quality of the "glorious" Thames; he recognizes his Inferno:

> The river sweats
> Oil and tar
> The barges drift
> With the turning tide
> Red sails
> Wide
> To leeward, swing on the heavy spar.
> The barges wash
> Drifting logs
> Down Greenwich reach
> Past the Isle of Dogs.

But Clyde, given the same opportunity to perceive the abuse of the Mohawk River and the town of Lycurgus, seems to be oblivious to the ramifications of what he sees: "The depot, from which only a half hour before he had stepped down, was so small and dull, untroubled, as he could plainly see, by much traffic. And the factory section which lay opposite the small city—across the Mohawk—was little more than a red and gray assemblage of buildings with here and there a smokestack projecting upward, and connected with the city by two bridges—a half dozen blocks apart—one of them directly at this depot, a wide traffic bridge across which traveled a car-line following the curves of Central Avenue, dotted here and there with stores and small homes" (pp. 197-198). These very bridges, evocative of the entrances and exits to various circles in the Inferno, become the dreary paths to and from the monotonous and uncreative work at the factory which lulls both Clyde and Roberta Alden into a lethargy only temporarily alleviated by sensuality.

Like "those hooded hordes swarming / Over endless plains, stumbling in cracked earth / Ringed by the flat horizon only," Roberta and other factory workers partake of endless and meaningless journeys to and from the factories: "And immediately after breakfast joining a long procession that day after day at this hour made for the mills across the river. For just outside her own door she invariably met with a company of factory girls and women, boys and men, of the same relative ages, to say nothing of many old and weary-looking women who looked more like wraiths than human beings, who had issued from the various streets and houses of this vicinity. . . . And at night the same throng, re-forming at the mills, crossing the bridge at the depot and returning as it had come" (p. 273). Eliot's "hooded hordes swarming" are not unlike Dreiser's equally abstract and symbolic women "more like wraiths than human beings," mindlessly and hopelessly participating in (and hence in part creating and sustaining) the nightmare landscape of a world dominated by materialism.

Often in Dreiser's work, that world committed to materialistic values crystallizes in the urban hotel, essence of vulgarity, pretentious display, and garish pseudo-art to which Dreiser's romantic seekers are magnetically drawn. For Clyde Griffiths, the colorless poverty of his family's life and religion is easily superceded by the ersatz splendor of an American hotel. Kansas City's Green-Davidson, for example, represents to Clyde a palpable manifestation of the privileged life; it is a bower of bliss, a garden of earthly delights and a gauche monument to worldly success: "Under his feet was a checkered black-and-white marble floor. Above him a coppered and stained and gilded ceiling. And supporting this, a veritable forest of black marble columns as highly polished as the floor—glassy smooth. And between the columns which ranged away toward three separate entrances, one right, one left and one directly forward toward Dalrymple Avenue—were lamps, statuary, rugs, palms, chairs, divans, tête-à-têtes—a prodigal display" (pp. 41-42).

But like the sensuously stifling display of jewels, perfumes, colored glass, and "coffered ceiling" in Eliot's "A Game of Chess," Clyde's world of luxury masks a realm of boredom, frustration and meaningless activity. "'What shall I do now? What shall I do?'" is echoed in *An American Tragedy* by Sondra Finchley and her circle as they continuously seek satiation in superficial pleasures to vitiate their idleness. Here, for the first time, in his voyeuristic initiation to the world of the Sondra Finchleys, Clyde becomes converted to the religion of materialism: the hotel and its occupants play heaven to Clyde Griffiths' novitiate. Spying a young woman engaged in frivolous party conversation, Clyde imagines that "this sight was like looking through the gates of Paradise." At this early point in his development, Clyde makes the facile transition from the non-remunerative faith of his family to the cult of the rich and idle, and in so doing, naively imagines that freedom can thus be achieved: "Such grandeur. This, then, most certainly was what it meant to be rich, to be a person of consequence in he world—to have money. It meant that you did what you pleased. That other people, like himself, waited upon you. That you possessed all of these luxuries. That you went how, where and when you pleased" (p. 58).

Dreiser's Green-Davidson has its symbolic analogues in Eliot's Cannon Street Hotel and Metropole. For Eliot, the corrupting forces of materialism inevitably lead to the perversion of human relationships, and Mr. Eumenides's invitation to the reluctant narrator to join him for a weekend at the Metropole is suggestive of the debasement of sexual experience.

It appears, therefore, that in both works the hotel serves as a microcosm for the alienation, randomness, rootlessness, and lusts of 20th century man. H. L. Mencken perceived the importance of the hotel as symbol in Dreiser's work and suggested its relation to secularization and materialism, a relation Dreiser clearly shares with Eliot: "[Dreiser] is still engaged in delivering Young America from the imbecilities of a frozen Christianity. And the economic struggle, in his eye, has a bizarre symbol: the modern American hotel" ("Dreiser in 840 Pages," in *The Merrill Studies in AN AMERICAN TRAGEDY*, Columbus, Ohio, 1971).

The perversion of sexual relationships resulting from and contributing to spiritual and moral bankruptcy is at the center of both *The Waste Land* and *An American Tragedy*. For Eliot, the sources of fertility and creativity are dormant: "here is no water but only rock," "sweat is dry," and the sky reverberates with "dry sterile thunder without rain." The landscape of sterility forcefully mirrors the perversion of love that dominates the world in the shapes of lust. "The change of Philomel, by the barbarous king / So rudely forced," becomes an emblem in the poem for sexual uncreativity and the absence of love. The couple at the game of chess, the secretary, the young man carbuncular, and Lil, pathetically seeking abortion, are all variations on the theme of human sterility—for Eliot, the physiological and emotional consequences of the debilitation of spirit.

While Dreiser's brand of naturalism tends to ascribe overwhelming drives and instincts to man over which he has little control, and Clyde seems to be cursed with a preter-naturally powerful sexual "chemism" (similar to that which Dreiser attributed to himself), Griffiths is nevertheless responsible for the debasement and abuse of other human beings through misguided sexuality. Roberta Alden becomes a Philomel-like creature "rudely forced" by Clyde's emotional blackmail and eventually she fills the desert of Clyde's world with an "inviolable voice" of pain, isolation and love that simply sounds "jug, jug" to Clyde's dirty ears. But Clyde is not wholly without conscience; indeed, while he refuses to respond to the pathetic voice of Roberta's suffering, he does respond to the "weird, haunting cry" of an "unearthly bird" at Big Bittern. "What was it sounding—a warning—a protest—condemnation? The same bird that had marked the very birth of this miserable plan. For there it was now upon

that dead tree—that wretched bird. And now it was flying to another one—as dead—a little farther inland and crying as it did so. God!" (p. 529). But because he is unable to translate that cry (a warning—a protest—a condemnation?), it remains an ominous and mysterious "jug, jug," merely filling the unresponsive desert places of Clyde's soul.

Roberta Alden's weakness, on the other hand, while similarly originating in the rejection of her family's poverty and despair, is not due to tyrannical sexual impulses or to a destructive romanticism. Her need is for affection and approval, qualities which Clyde at first willingly provides in exchange for sexual intimacies. But Roberta's genuine potential for a creative relationship is immediately thwarted by Clyde's rejection of love and creative sexuality. Like the young man carbuncular, "his vanity requires no response," and when it receives one in the form of an unborn child, Clyde's immediate reaction is to conceive a means to induce abortion. And he naively proceeds to seek that abortion with utterly no consideration for the moral or human questions involved in the act. The thunder in Clyde's world is dry indeed, and like Lil in Eliot's poem, he views the potential birth of his child as a burden and an obstruction to life rather than as an indispensable projection of it: "And so disturbed was he by the panorama of the bright world of which Sondra was the center and which was now at stake, that he could scarcely think clearly. Should he lose all this for such a world as he and Roberta could provide for themselves—a small home—a baby, such a routine work-a-day life as taking care of her and a baby on such a salary as he could earn, and from which most likely he would never again be freed! God! A sense of nausea seized him" (p. 449).

This acute sense of nausea which seizes him whenever he imagines a mundane family life with Roberta and their child is symptomatic of Clyde's conversion to the religion of materialism—a cult over which Sondra Finchley rules as a pagan priestess. For Clyde never relates to Sondra as a man to a woman: he worships her as a goddess, much as he did Hortense Briggs, the first Sondra in his life. "For apart from her local position and means and taste in dress and manners, Sondra was of the exact order and spirit that most intrigued him—a somewhat refined (and because of means and position showered upon her) less savage, although scarcely less self-centered, Hortense Briggs. She was, in her small, intense way, a seeking Aphrodite, eager to prove to any who were sufficiently attractive the destroying power of her charm, while at the same time retaining her own personality and individuality free of any entangling alliance or compromise" (p. 350).

His Aphrodite is not so much an object of lust as an *object d'art* and Clyde's desire is "to constrain and fondle a perfect object" (397). In Clyde's consciousness, in fact, Sondra comes to represent a degree of perfection that utterly removes her from the world of mundane human experience of which Roberta is so much a part: "He lifted his hands as though to caress her gently, yet holding them back, and at the same dreamed into her eyes as might a devotee into those of a saint . . ." (p. 398).

This destructive idol worship is not unfamiliar to Eliot, and in "A Game of Chess," he presents us with a woman who, like Sondra Finchley, occupies the throne of a traditional love goddess and appears to embody the passions which have the potential to re-vitalize the arid landscapes of the wasteland.

> The Chair she sat in, like a burnished throne,
> Glowed on the marble, where the glass
> Held up by standards wrought with fruited vines
> From which a golden Cupidon peeped out
> (Another hid his eyes behind his wing)
> Doubled the flames of seven-branched candelabra
> Reflecting light upon the table as
> The glitter of her jewels rose to meet it,
> From satin cases poured in rich profusion; . . .

But also like Sondra's, this imitation Cleopatra's allure is based on the illusions of her "strange synthetic perfumes" which "troubled, confused / And drowned the sense in odors." And, of course, Clyde, prisoner of his senses and his fantasies, associates the "synthetic perfumes" of Sondra's world with genuine passion: "Sondra, Twelfth Lake, society, wealth, her love and beauty" (460). For Clyde, this ingenuous linking of society, wealth, and love ultimately focuses on life at Twelfth Lake, for it is there that Clyde experiences his most splendid moments with Sondra amidst the frivolous activity of the resort population: "And then this scene, where a bright sun poured a flood of crystal light upon a greensward that stretched from tall pines to the silver rippling waters of a lake. And off shore in a half dozen different directions the bright white sails of small boats—the white and green and yellow splashes of color, where canoes paddled by idling lovers were passing in the sun! Summertime—leisure—warmth—color—ease—beauty—love—all that he had dreamed the summer before, when he was so very much alone" (p. 482).

This lake country becomes symbolic of the possibilities of a new life for Clyde; he imagines a veritable rebirth occurring there. In Clyde's obsessive pursuit of that new life, however, it becomes clear to him that in order to achieve it, he must dispose of all remnants of his past. Having already deceived Sondra and her peers concerning his family and their life in the West, Clyde gradually concludes that Roberta and his unborn child are the only remaining links with what he considers his sordid past. They too must be destroyed. It is not surprising then that the very lake country which seems to symbolize the new life becomes the means to the destruction of the old. The lake, previously evocative of love, is transformed into a symbol of death: "And as they glided into this, this still dark water seemed to grip Clyde as nothing here or anywhere before this ever had—to change his mood. . . . And yet, what did it all suggest so strongly? Death! Death! More definitely than anything he had ever seen before. Death! But also a still, quiet, unprotesting type of death into which one, by reason of choice or hypnosis or

unutterable weariness, might joyfully and gratefully sink. So quiet—so shaded—so serene" (p. 527).

The same strange sense of peace in death which mesmerizes Clyde as he gazes on the waters in which Roberta will momentarily sink in horror and incomprehension, accompanies the death by drowning of Phlebas the Phoenician in the "Death by Water" section of *The Waste Land.*

> A current under sea
> Picked his bones in whispers. As he rose and fell
> He passed the stages of his age and youth
> Entering the whirlpool.

But the ostensible peace in the death by drowning is a superficial and transitory peace; it precedes the final descent into the churning whirlpool and gives no hint of resurrection. If Phlebas is a corrupt version of the fertility god, and if his death signals finality with little or no hope of regeneration, then it is clear that Dreiser uses the death of Roberta Alden analogously in *An American Tragedy.* For Clyde Griffiths, Roberta and her child should represent fertility and its fruits. But he destroys them in order to procure his own "resurrection" into the new life which Sondra Finchley—as idol—represents. However, that destruction by drowning results merely in death for Clyde Griffiths—Roberta's, his child's, his own. Water, potential symbol for love and creativity in both poem and novel, becomes the emblem of sterility and death. For both Eliot and Dreiser "there is no water" imminent to quicken the "dried tubers" of the modern landscape.

While the cleansing and rejuvenating waters of spiritual rebirth are not immediately forthcoming for Eliot, there are nevertheless signs that the forces of creativity are not altogether lost: the thunder brings hope that self-control, giving, and compassion can re-awaken the deadened spirit of humanity; and, the narrator sits upon the shore, fishing, with the arid plain behind him, seeking the means to regeneration. There is guarded optimism in *The Waste Land* and hope that "these fragments I have shored against my ruins" (perhaps the poem itself) will prevail against the ubiquitous forces of destruction.

But for Clyde Griffiths there is no such promise. He has shored up no fragments against his ruin. He has changed little, understood less. Indeed, his last-minute conversion from a worship of the material to the religion of his mother and the Reverend McMillan is ironically undercut by the tone and texture of the imagery Dreiser uses to describe Clyde's last moments. "And his feet were walking, but automatically, it seemed. And he was conscious of that familiar shuffle—shuffle—as they pushed him on and on toward that door. Not it was here; now it was being opened. There it was—at last—the chair he had so often seen in his dreams—that he so dreaded—to which he was now compelled to go. He was being pushed toward that—into that—on—on—through the door which was now open—to receive him—but which was as quickly closed again on all the earthly life he had ever known" (p. 870).

Even the potentially purgative "fires" of the electric chair seem destined to work utter confusion on Clyde Griffiths. Reverend McMillan himself appears to recognize the desperation of Clyde's situation and remembers his final forlornness with horror: "He walked along the silent street—only to be compelled to pause and lean against a tree—leafless in the winter—so bare and bleak. Clyde's eyes! That look as he sank limply into that terrible chair, his eyes fixed nervously and, as he thought, appealingly and dazedly upon him and the group surrounding him" (p. 871).

Indeed, the minister's profound fear that Clyde died with no genuine understanding and no faith to transcend his earthly experience is reinforced by the barren images which Dreiser creates to describe Clyde's death. While his mother and the minister offered Clyde the opportunity to embrace religious acceptance (" . . . how easy it was—if Clyde would but repeat and pray as he had asked him to—for him to know and delight in the 'peace that passeth all understanding'" [p, 784]), his response to their zeal was mechanical, half-hearted acceptance.

But as Eliot suggests, the state of "shantih"—"the Peace which passeth understanding"—is far more difficult to achieve than Reverend McMillan would like to believe. And for Dreiser, traditional modes of Christianity simply cannot lead man to that achievement; he makes his rejection of Christian salvation eminently clear with the masterful last chapter of *An American Tragedy* in which the cycle of Clyde's life is about to be repeated by another restless and lost boy.

Where there is hope in *The Waste Land,* there is despair in *An American Tragedy.* All Dreiser seems to leave us is "the vast skepticism and apathy of life."

Paul A. Orlov (essay date 1977)

SOURCE: "The Subversion of the Self: Anti-Naturalistic Crux in *An American Tragedy,*" in *Modern Fiction Studies,* Vol. 23, No. 3, Autumn, 1977, pp. 457-72.

[*In the following essay, Orlov posits that, despite Dreiser's well-known devotion to literary naturalism,* An American Tragedy *is actually anti-naturalistic in its treatment of the idea of the individual.*]

Various critics have pointed out that Dreiser's fiction does not consistently conform to techniques and beliefs common to naturalism (which the literary histories have traditionally assumed to be fundamental to Dreiser or even the only reason for discussing him); his fiction, according to these critics, reveals characteristics in the mode of transcendentalism as well as humanism.[1] Criticism of *An American Tragedy,* liberated from the assumption that the work is a mere naturalistic depiction of man objectively viewed as a helpless victim of heredity and environment, has begun to examine the novel in ways that imply a humanistic orientation—in particular, a con-

cern with Dreiser's artistic treatment of the idea of individual identity. The story of Clyde Griffiths has been discussed by Lauriat Lane as an ironic view of identity in terms of the double motif[2] and by Richard Lehan as the effect of interaction between accident and determining forces on one side and the protagonist's "essential self" on the other.[3] And Robert Penn Warren and Robert Elias have analyzed the novel's conception of "tragedy," announced in its title, in relation to Dreiser's fictional handling of the theme of the self.[4]

In their different ways, these critics seem to me to have been moving toward—without having yet reached—a radical conclusion about the *Tragedy:* that for all its manifest quality of naturalism, the novel is, nevertheless, fundamentally, not naturalistic at all. My interpretation attempts to demonstrate that the ultimate level upon which the novel actually becomes anti-naturalistic is the crux of Dreiser's implicit ideas concerning the meaning of identity. I will argue, too, that such ideas, discoverable in the text viewed as an object of literary art, may well be our best key to understanding why Dreiser conceives of the stories of Clyde and Roberta as tragic.

While Warren and Elias reach different conclusions about the *Tragedy* from those I hope to document, their approaches to the novel are based upon some perceptions about Dreiser's vision of the nature of selfhood and of relations between individuals which anticipate aspects of my discussion. Elias' recent essay in *Prospects* sees the novel as Dreiser's statement about the tragic consequences of a society in which the individual believes his self-realization is possible only in emotional disengagement from others, in the isolation of unfettered self-reliance, and in which the banishing of differences rather than the clash of wills is the accepted ideal. Intensely alone and removed from actuality, Clyde, Elias writes, "moves amid abstractions . . . and in the view of others is ultimately an abstraction himself. Clearly Dreiser intends it to be this way."[5] Since he is bringing the perspective of the cultural historian to bear upon the novel in order to define how the book and Clyde Griffiths pointedly reflect assumptions of the twenties, Elias finds the significance of Dreiser's rendering of individuality in these terms in the novelist's final germination of a long held fictional idea during a decade marked by self-defeating notions of fulfillment sought through self-insulation. Yet Elias' reading of the *Tragedy* seems to me at least obliquely to suggest a new recognition concerning Dreiser's artistic premises on the topic of individuality that criticism has been evolving toward and that is waiting to be articulated. And Warren's elaborate study of the theme of identity in the novel serves, precisely by virtue of what it does *not* conclude, to put the recognition to which I refer—that Dreiser's masterpiece is at bottom anti-naturalistic—in focus for us.

Clyde's pursuit of his dreams, says Warren, entails an attempt to repudiate his own identity and to create a dream-self possessing wealth and social distinction. But having analyzed the novel's study of lost or ambiguous identity in the life of Clyde, Warren concludes that the work reflects Dreiser's "final subject," the "illusion of the self," and derives its "tragedy" from the idea that man is a mechanism with consciousness.[6] At the end of a discussion concerned with the loss of self and of life in the quest after illusory materialistic goals, Warren decides that this theme in the novel is grounded in Dreiser's conviction that individuality itself is an illusion. This is to say, of course, that Warren first treats the novel as a work of art written by a humanistic author who believes in the meaning of the self and who finds tragic the protagonist's misguided aspirations, and then reverts from the outlook implied by his interpretation to the assumption that the Dreiser who has written the novel is Dreiser the mechanistic theorist. To be sure, mechanistic thought and especially the influence of Jacques Loeb inform the *Tragedy;* Clyde *is* a victim of physicochemical laws and an exemplar of tropistic effects—at least, he is in part. A novel's intentions, however, are not necessarily the same as its author's. And in Dreiser's treatment of the idea of the self in the novel, we find the most quintessential evidence that the imaginative artist fundamentally rejects his own overt "philosophical" beliefs.

If this contention initially appears to be just another echo of the long since commonplace view that Dreiser is an "inconsistent mechanist," it is meant to lift that view out of the critical morass of statements about Dreiser's compassionate emotional bond with his characters onto a solid ground of recognition that Dreiser's artistic achievement in his most famous novel rests upon (notwithstanding Lionel Trilling and a host of earlier critics) an idea about human identity and social experience. This idea, let me assert at once, is that man does have a genuine individuality—a true selfhood—and that the intrinsic reality and importance of identity in Clyde and in Roberta Alden is the source of the tragic import of their lives and deaths. Examination of the premises necessary to make belief in the concept of the self meaningful quickly forms a bridge to carry us from Dreiser's explicit ideas as mechanist or naturalist toward the ideas implicit in the world-view in the *Tragedy.*

In much of his polemical writing, Dreiser proclaims (to use the title of one of his best-known essays) the "myth of individuality"; a representative quotation permits us to scrutinize his mechanistic assumptions about the matter of identity:

> Even now chemists and physicists are at work upon the balances and equations involved in the mechanical and chemical construction of man, the leverage by which he moves, the combinations which control his form or aspect, as well as the chemical combinations which can induce motion or self-propulsion. Even as to his so-called thought how close are the Behaviorists to the material mechanics which produce it? His thoughts also are apparently little more than compelled reactions of one chemical upon another which he can no more escape than can he his form or motions. The one unsolved mystery apparently is why a machine so easily made and controlled should be able to speculate as to the reason for his being. . . . [7]

The main point to be made about the perspective on man expressed in this passage is that it shows an extreme philosophic commitment to empiricism. While Dreiser the theorist thinks that the "essential tragedy of life" (as he calls the essay from which I am quoting) is that man is a mechanism with a basically ineffectual consciousness, Dreiser the novelist projects a vision of life that pivots upon a very different perspective. A work that has no overt relevance to Dreiser or his fiction, Hugh Kenner's *The Counterfeiters,*[8] can be used as an incisive critical tool with which to probe Dreiser's divergent ideas on the question of identity: Kenner's study of the peculiar impact of the empirical point of view upon life and literature since the late seventeenth century helps to cast light upon the premises underlying a naturalistic view of the world and will subsequently prove quite illuminating of the contrary premises implied by *An American Tragedy.*

Men in the age of Swift, notes Kenner, began to think that terms such as *humanitas* were to be viewed as suspect—that the "stable essence" of that which makes man uniquely man does not in fact exist:

> When analysis has not yet disclosed how a watch knows what time it is, the watch is mysterious; and men were perhaps only mysterious in that way. Observe their behavior, according to the best empiric disciplines, as you observe a watch's behavior; and when you have observed thoroughly you will know all there is to know about man. (pp. 9-10)

Reducing all phenomena including "manness" to the observable realities of appearances and behavior, empiricism denied the actuality of human identity: man could be as thoroughly understood as a machine and being understood, could be effectively simulated—"counterfeited." Sharing the empiricists' way of seeing, Dreiser the mechanist asserts that man is a machine, a watch-like phenomenon, all the workings of which can be described and comprehended by the chemists, physicists, and behavioral psychologists. Like the men whom Kenner reveals to have been the progenitors of the modern era with its synthetic objects and increasingly clever (man-like) machines, Dreiser holds all that is not outward or scientifically verifiable to be illusion.

Now since the self is nothing but its "traces" in the empirical view, why call it a self at all? Individual identity has no real meaning, unless one grants that there is some essence or quiddity to which these appearances belong. The empirical emphasis on observable data precludes the possibility of belief in such an essence, and naturalism in literature—following the empirical bent of science—involves the same problematic denial of the reality of the self and of the possibility of true individuality. Thus Dreiser would seem to have brought to the writing of his naturalistic story of Clyde acted upon by heredity and environment a clear conviction that the "self" is an illusory concept. Yet the *Tragedy* offers enduring evidence of the fact—a fact hinted at by the mechanist's admission that the human machine's speculations upon his own being remain a mystery—that Dreiser finally sees man as more than the empirically understandable "workings of the watch."

If we believe that *An American Tragedy* is a naturalistic novel, our belief includes the supposition that Dreiser assumes the reality of the social environment that so decisively shapes the life of Clyde. In effect, that is, the empirical view leads Dreiser to the premise that Reality is either in mind or in matter, either "in here" or "out there"—and to conclude (having chosen the latter alternative) that the rest is illusion. Yet as Alfred North Whitehead's classic *Science and the Modern World* demonstrated upon its publication in 1925, just a few months before the *Tragedy* was published, reality is not an "either-or" proposition but an ongoing coalescence of mind and matter, subject and object, finite and infinite. Thus Dreiser's own metaphysical speculations as a mechanist are self-refuting indications of man's capacity (his reality thus indirectly granted) to give meaning and reality to the material and social worlds beyond himself through his perceptual and philosophical responses to them, though they also have an existence essentially independent, quite as he does. And in the novel, the art of which is the reason Dreiser's thought is important in the first place, Dreiser transcends his empirical premises to affirm the reality of the self and the importance of selfhood. Not Dreiser, but Dreiser's major characters and their social realm deny the reality of individual integrity; and Dreiser, as his instinctive or artistic views can be inferred from the actual effect of the novel, in fact construes the subversion of the idea of self as the core of their tragic experience. Ultimately, therefore, *An American Tragedy* turns upon the very antithesis of its apparent naturalistic premises concerning individuality and despite all its actual naturalism becomes an anti-naturalistic statement about the self's intrinsic importance.

At the first Now and Then Club gathering to which he is invited, Clyde is reminded by cynical Gertrude Trumbull that "[p]eople like money even more than they do looks" (I, 328).[9] Her remark is a blunt appraisal (from within the social sphere to which Clyde aspires) of the values and views of upper-class Lycurgus—which represents the materialistic society at large that shapes his attitudes. A parallel outlook on a lower scale of society is symbolically conveyed through the conduct of gold-digger Hortense toward Clyde during his adolescent worldly education in Kansas City. And his friend Ratterer subsequently chides Clyde for showing so much eager interest in girls, rather than holding himself aloof and making them pursue him and earn his regard: Ratterer notes that Clyde "possesse[s] the looks—the 'goods'—" (I, 303) that can enable him to be rather exacting in relations with girls. Although Ratterer's attitude is obviously typical of an adolescent sense of the basis for "popularity," it should by no means be dismissed as nothing more; his

statement corresponds to that of the Lycurgus socialite in an important way that helps to expose a perspective prevalent in the society the novel tacitly criticizes. The emphasis upon looks and money implicitly suggests that the world in which Clyde absorbs beliefs and goals subscribes to a way of seeing that discovers meaning only in the surfaces of things and people. Identity consists of the external and extrinsic—that is, of people viewed empirically as bearers of appearances, literal as well as figurative possessions, and (as we shall see) approved behavior forms.

"Clyde had a soul," writes the narrator, "that was not destined to grow up" (I, 174). But in the frame of reference of assumptions concerning the worth of individuals, Clyde is not any more immature than the society whose standards he all too thoroughly accepts. An adolescent emphasis upon perceptible qualities as a means of defining others' significance has become the adult norm in a society in which ambitions obliterate interest in or responsiveness toward the complex, impalpable substantiality of other human beings. Stimulated to fantasize about a possible relationship with Sondra by the chance encounter in which she mistakes him for his cousin/double Gilbert, Clyde reflects,

> Ah, to know this perfect girl more intimately! To be looked upon by her with favor,—made, by reason of that favor, a part of that fine world to which she belonged. Was he not a Griffiths—as good looking as Gilbert Griffiths any day? And as attractive if he only had as much money—or a part of it even. To be able to dress in the Gilbert Griffiths' fashion; to ride around in one of the handsome cars he sported! Then, you bet, a girl like this would be delighted to notice him,—mayhap, who knows, even fall in love with him. (I, 317)

From the detached point of view in which the reader's experience is primarily rooted, of course, the opportunities for Clyde to marry a girl like Sondra are a "mirage," and the differences between Clyde and Gilbert are too crucial and elemental to be obscured, let alone surmounted, by any hypothetical acquisition (on Clyde's part) of the rich cousin's material manifestations of status. Such recognitions—in that we derive them from Dreiser's omniscient narrative—clearly indicate the novel's underlying assumption that people outwardly alike are, nevertheless, to be significantly distinguished in terms of substantive individualizing qualities. Yet it is precisely the key point that neither Clyde nor his society (in its dominant aspects) share any assumptions of the kind.

Rather, the very idea that possessions and trappings appended to one's person can effect a true transformation of one's identity—one's individual import in the eyes of society as well as in one's own—is integral to the ethos of the ambition-ruled America portrayed in the *Tragedy*. Thus in the perspective from within the world of the novel, Clyde's reflections after his encounter with Sondra, far from being tragically misguided as in objective terms, are not only justified; they reveal the most profound idea behind the success dream. With reference to prevailing values, Clyde is quite right that with the addition of money, clothes, and a car—all "in the Gilbert Griffiths fashion"—he would be "as attractive" to the most desirable of girls as Gilbert—in effect, equal or tantamount to him. Dreiser's use of the double motif emphasizes that Clyde's extreme physical resemblance to the cousin whose family name he shares could make him virtually indistinguishable from Gilbert, once he possesses Gilbert's accessories. Implicit in Clyde's thoughts is the notion that he *will be,* and, therefore, be taken as, a different person when equipped like Gilbert from what is in the unfulfilled present of his poverty. Clyde, like those to whom he wants to be "attractive," puts appearing and having before being and in the final analysis fails to distinguish them *from* being. Once we realize how pervasive this theme is to the novel's whole story of Clyde's life and quest, Dreiser's foremost fictional purpose in exploiting the double theme in relation to the Clyde/Gilbert connection (and its impact upon Sondra's responses toward Clyde) appears to be to extend to its most trenchant degree a developing ironic commentary upon the attempt of the protagonist to falsify his identity.

The first two chapters of Book One of the novel indicate Clyde's alienation from his family and its way of life: inherently convinced that he is (or at least, should be) a person of distinction in the social context, he is humiliated by the cheapness and eccentricity of his parents' image in the eyes of others. He resents not only his parents' failure to provide him with material advantages but also their failure to "give" him a public character conducive to belonging in the world of the crowds who ignore their street-corner prayer meetings. He begins early in life to emphasize the visible shell of himself; a normal adolescent concern about "looks" and clothes (I, 15) becomes in him an obsession with that facet of identity that can be conclusively discovered in the nearest mirror. That Dreiser's references to mirrors at several key moments in Clyde's life (see I, 15; I, 308; I, 322; II, 348) are meant to suggest the boy's inclination to confuse outward characteristics with the inner self becomes evident as soon as Clyde finds his first real job. From behind the drugstore soda fountain, he observes the pretty girls and the fine clothes worn by them and their male escorts with delight and awakening desire. And one passage in particular at this point in the text is very revealing:

> And very often one or another of these young beauties was accompanied by some male in evening suit, dress shirt, high hat, bow tie, white kid gloves, and patent leather shoes, a costume which at that time Clyde felt to be the last word in all true distinction, beauty, gallantry and bliss. To be able to wear such a suit with such ease and air! To be able to talk to a girl after the manner and with the sang-froid of some of these gallants! What a true measure of achievement! No good-looking girl, as it then appeared to him, would have anything to do with him if he did not possess this standard of equipment. It was plainly necessary—the thing. And once he did attain it—was able to wear such clothes as these—well, then was he not well set upon the path that leads to all the blisses? All the joys of life would then most certainly be spread before him. The friendly smiles! The secret handclasps, maybe—an arm about the waist of some one or another—a kiss—a promise of marriage—and then, and then! (I, 26)

Clyde's unconscious premises here are paradigmatic of his peculiar orientation toward himself and the world in all his subsequent experience. He sees the correct "standard of equipment" as a requirement for an identity that can make him interesting and worthwhile to girls who (the syndrome is circular) are "good-looking"—and presumably, therefore, intrinsically good or admirable.

This passage at the start of Clyde's quest alerts the reader to the novel's full delineation of a society's distorted view of identity taken by the youth as a philosophy for the conduct of life. Clothes are significant to his mental set in figurative as well as literal terms: his soda fountain observations stress the idea of having the proper manner and speech patterns as well as the fashionable attire. The underlying meaning of his alienation from his own family and social class, in his disposition to dreams of personal grandeur, is that he is alienated from his own genuine identity: he does not like or accept the self he is and is unequipped, in every sense of the word, to become the being he feels he can be. And since individual import is defined by material possessions and socially approved forms, he feels that his family is a group of ciphers. He must clothe an identity, symbolically as well as literally, to be and be received as "someone" in the world whose pleasures become *his* objects of "religious" idealism. Otherwise, he is convinced, he will lack any worth as a person and thus naturally fail to deserve the love or affection of any girls worth having. In sum, the representative social scenes in the drugstore strike him as a revelation that hardens into a resolve: shunning his parents' world, he will "work and save his money and be somebody" (I, 26). In his view, the final words of this resolution are not a mere figure of speech; they have a tragic literalness of meaning to him.

After the auto accident and his flight from Kansas City, Clyde gives up his name and resorts to a series of aliases to protect himself against possible pursuit by the police. But the shedding of his name during this transitional phase of his life has symbolic point, too: escaping the ruins of the structure of identity he had sought to build upon a position in the Green-Davidson Hotel and a relationship with Hortense Briggs, he is in a condition to which he cannot bear to see his name connected, a limbo through which he must move uncertainly toward some new scene of possibility for self-creation. Somewhat like Joe Christmas in Faulkner's *Light in August,* Clyde (as Chapter III of Book Two tells us) moves through the streets of a succession of towns and cities, a man without an identity awaiting a person and a set of circumstances that will give meaning to his life. In contrast to Christmas, whose nightmare state of nameless nullity surrounds him throughout his entire life (as that life appears in his own consciousness), Clyde thinks he discovers an opportunity for self-actualization once he has reencountered Ratterer in Chicago. Appropriately, he resumes the use of his own name in time for his promising contact with the Union League Club and with his rich uncle Samuel, who (as if in a genie-produced answer to his Aladdinish wishes) materializes there to open the path to a future in Lycurgus and perhaps to dreams fulfilled. In the reality that with time overwhelms all his most cherished illusions, however, Clyde is quite similar to Faulkner's protagonist even during—indeed, especially during—the climactic part of his story. Just as Christmas' ambiguity in racial terms as perceived both by himself and by others leads those he meets to assign him various roles or pseudo-identities rather than to grant him an authentic identity, so does Clyde's ambiguity in socio-economic status shape all his relations and experience in Lycurgus into a vise that crushes his true self. And as with Christmas in his fateful encounters with Joanna Burden and Percy Grimm, the manner of Clyde's death will become the most dramatic expression of the failure of a person and his world to recognize or affirm his integrity of individual being. Paradoxically, in the reader's perspective, the death of Clyde (like that of Faulkner's character) produces the most profound illumination of the genuine individual import of the subverted self.

As the whole pattern of Clyde's experiences in Lycurgus shows, self-betrayal is inextricably bound up with the betrayal of the self by others—as we should expect from the fact that his distorted ideas about identity stem from those at the heart of society. His own self-conception fluctuates between the two contrasting states of mind, both radically unwarranted in different ways, in play when he stands before his rich uncle's impressive home in Wykeagy Avenue for the first time:

> What member of his own immediate family had ever dreamed that his uncle lived thus! The grandeur! And his own parents so wretched—so poor, preaching on the streets of Kansas City and no doubt Denver. Conducting a mission! And although thus far no single member of this family other than his chill cousin had troubled to meet him, and that at the factory only, and although he had been so indifferently assigned to the menial type of work that he had, still he was elated and uplifted. For, after all, was he not a Griffiths, a full cousin as well as a full nephew to the two very important men who lived here, and now working for them in some capacity at least? And must not that spell a future of some sort, better than any he had known as yet? For consider who the Griffiths were here, as opposed to "who" the Griffiths were in Kansas City, say—or Denver. (I, 194)

Here again a figure of speech conveys a destructive literal idea about identity—about "who" certain people are, including himself—in Clyde's thoughts. Viewing himself

as an extension of the Lycurgus Griffiths, he elatedly feels that he is (or has definite prospects of being) quite "somebody"; as soon as he ponders the possibility of being seen by those in Lycurgus as a member of his own immediate family (and as a person with sordid past associations), Clyde is utterly dejected by the conviction that he is "very much of a nobody" (I, 194). These opposed apocryphal self-estimates thereafter correspond to the contrary interpretations of Clyde on the part of different segments of his community that augment his basic uncertainty about his identity and further contribute to his specious conclusions about himself.

Clyde quickly discovers the magical power of his face and family name to elevate his apparent consequence as a person in the eyes of all of Lycurgus except its patrician class. When the rude receptionist at the Griffiths factory learns "who" he is, her altered manner toward Clyde shows him that in his new environment it is "no small thing to be a Griffiths . . ." (I, 192). She accords him "a form of deference that never in his life before had been offered him. . . . To think that he should be a full cousin to this wealthy and influential family!" (I, 185). For as such, he is treated as a distinguished individual; to Kemerer, Dillard, the people at the church social, his landlady, and diverse others including Rita and then Roberta, Clyde is defined as "a 'Griffiths'" whose present or imminent share of his relatives' money and status automatically earns him their friendly regard. In the view of his rich uncle and cousin themselves, meanwhile, Clyde is to be condescended to and largely neglected since he is defined as the poor relative with embarrassingly humble antecedents. To them (and their social peers) "Clyde" *is* his set of external qualities—his looks, clothes, ambitions, empty wallet, unassertive manner, and reliance upon them for elevation from an inferior rank. Gilbert's special hostility combines with this dehumanizing attitude to lead him to decide that Clyde is a nondescript even before (here Dreiser works an ironic twist upon the overriding empiricism involved) he has ever *seen* his western cousin.

Clyde's relatives do not acknowledge or care about the intrinsic particularity of his being, or the lonely insecurity of his position in Lycurgus: in deciding how to act toward him as in evaluating him, appearances are their sole concern. Samuel Griffiths, like a thorough empiricist, forgets about the nephew he has consigned to the factory's shrinking room (so apt a symbol of his implicit reduction of Clyde's human importance) until he accidentally sees Clyde at work looking like a disconcerting version of Gilbert garbed in old clothes and bathed in sweat (I, 230-231). The manufacturer then gives his nephew an ostensible promotion so that Clyde "can wear a decent suit of clothes and *look* like somebody" (I, 232; emphasis mine). Then, since he does not truly regard Clyde as "somebody"—as a person deserving sympathetic attention—the uncle eliminates his nephew from his mind again. Months later, Samuel Griffiths suddenly invites Clyde to his home for Christmas dinner because he has learned of his nephew's increasing inclusion in social events organized by Sondra and her friends: appearances must be satisfied again; it will not do if the youth's own kin do not welcome him into their personal parties while the children of other eminent families extend social acceptance to him (I, 360-363). Upon Clyde's arrival in Lycurgus, his relatives dictate where he should live; later, they tell him in various ways what to do and whom not to see in his personal life, never either telling him or enabling him to do *anything* except work, never indicating whom he *may* properly see socially. In sum, indifferent to his reality as an individual, Clyde's relatives are concerned about his behavior, not his mental and emotional state, about the appearance he presents, not the life he leads, about how well he does at preserving their dignity as "the Griffiths," not who he is as "Clyde."

When he receives the chance to assume a foreman's position, Clyde decides that he is "going to be all that his uncle and cousin obviously expected of him . . ." (I, 239). As a matter of fact, Clyde attempts throughout his brief career in the world to do and be whatever is demanded by those whose approval he seeks. The *Tragedy*'s protagonist, in Dreiser's conception of him, is in many respects an anticipatory example of the "other-directed" type of person subsequently made familiar through the analysis of David Riesman in *The Lonely Crowd* (1950). Given the values and the premises about identity he absorbs, it is natural that Clyde should be very sensitive to the ideas—especially the tastes and expectations—of significant others in his life, and should be entirely prepared to fabricate the self required by others to the best of his ability. Like the "other-directed" man in the abstract, Clyde seeks to be not himself but what others *are* like or *will* like.

Mirroring the mode of "other-direction," Clyde carries role-playing to such an extreme that his various roles virtually become his identity. The true self is distorted and buried beneath an accumulation of consumption preferences and behavior forms adopted either in imitation of others or in response to the demands made by others or their lifestyles, for the sake of "becoming" a person with all the accouterments that are supposed to indicate success and individual distinction. Chameleon-like, Clyde repeatedly manipulates himself into shapes intended to make him fit into his surrounding: by such contortions of his true character, he seeks to gain acceptance, affection, or respect from others whose opinions or positions have unquestioned authority in his view. Applying for a job at the Green-Davidson, Clyde contrives an ingratiating smile and a line of diplomatic talk to win the approval of Squires: "it occurred to him that if he wanted to get on he ought to insinuate himself into the good graces of people—do or say something that would make them like him" (I, 31). Quite in the way Clyde will later carefully imitate the style of dress of his double Gilbert (see I, 318), he selects Eddie Doyle from among his fellow bellhops as a model of good looks and social success whose clothes are to be studied and duplicated on his own person as fully as possible (see I, 48; I, 54). On the outing

with the boys from the hotel, Clyde learns which drink he should order and in which restaurant; he overcomes his moral crisis about drinking by following a conservative example made acceptable by Ratterer (I, 57-59), and then takes Hortense to Frissell's on dates because of its evident reputation. Having heard that "women [like] fellows who [do] things for them" (I, 82), Clyde begins by buying flowers for Hortense and then seeks to obtain her sexual favors through the purchasing of gifts of mounting value that she in effect demands. Working in the Union League Club in Chicago, Clyde feels "himself different from what he really was—more subdued, less romantic, more practical, certain that if he tried now, *imitated* the soberer people of the world, and those only, that some day he might succeed . . ." (I, 173; emphasis mine). Such self-deception about his authentic identity is naturally joined to the deceit that results from his characteristic approach to significant others: in his very opportune meeting with Samuel Griffiths in the club, Clyde portrays his parents' economic circumstances in exaggerated terms to make a good impression, claims that he has always thought he would be suited to the shirt and collar business, and makes his most direct appeal by describing his intense eagerness to "get in with some company where there [is] a real chance to work up and make something of [him]self" (I, 179). Clyde, of course, does not wish to "work up" at all, but rather magically to attain some superior position that will (in his literal sense of the phrase) "make something" of him as a person. Thus, he feigns an interest in shirts and collars so that he may play roles which will permit him to *wear* such articles as part of the "clothing" of an achieved ideal identity.

Irving Howe has observed that what results from Clyde's quest to create a fantasy-self is "not, in any precise sense, a self at all, but rather the beginning of that poisonous fabrication which in America we call a 'personality.'"[10] This, of course, calls to mind *The Great Gatsby*, the Fitzgerald novel which most readily suggests itself when we seek analogies between the fiction of Fitzgerald and Dreiser's *Tragedy*. But Howe's remark can be usefully expanded upon—in a manner that helps to illuminate Dreiser's anti-naturalistic perspective on the import of the self—by connecting it to a similar idea found in another Fitzgerald novel, *This Side of Paradise* (1920), before it is applied to Clyde's story. What Howe refers to as a "personality" appears to be fundamentally the same as what Monsignor Darcy means by the term "personage" as he offers Amory Blaine, the novel's young hero-egotist, one of his personal "courses" in spiritual and intellectual education as friend and advisor:

> (Mons.) " . . . we're not personalities, but personages."
>
> (Amory) "That's a good line—what do you mean?"
>
> (Mons.) "A personality is what you thought you were, what this Kerry and Sloane you tell me of evidently are. Personality is a physical matter almost entirely; it lowers the people it acts on— I've seen it vanish in a long sickness . . . Now a

personage, on the other hand, gathers. He is never to be thought of apart from what he's done. He's a bar on which a thousand things have been hung—glittering things sometimes, as ours are, but he uses those things with a cold mentality back of them."[11]

Thayer Darcy's comment on a "personage" can serve as a curiously apt account of the manner of self-creation pursued by Clyde "with a cold mentality": Clyde works painstakingly to make of himself a "bar on which" myriad "things" are "hung," in particular "glittering things" meant to enhance his value as an individual and apart from which he hopes never to be "thought of" or defined.

The pertinence of this idea of an identity forged through a mechanical addition of surface traits as if they are attachments for a machine becomes clearer when we examine Clyde's conduct in the light issuing from Hugh Kenner's discussion of "counterfeiting." Kenner notes that "the principle on which counterfeiting rests," derived from strict adherence to empiricism, is "that a man is knowable only in his behavior, and, when he is dead or otherwise out of sight, only in the traces his behavior has left" (p. 17). And Clyde's monomaniacal, misguided purpose throughout the novel is to adopt forms of behavior—especially ostensible interests and skills—calculated to compose a socially successful counterfeit self. Lacking free will as much as he does, Dreiser's protagonist is still by no means the passive subject of processes of destiny or forces of environment that naturalistic interpretations of the *Tragedy* have often termed him; and the most essential way in which Clyde asserts his will is by his active attempt to *be* through belonging. To his mind, the person is synonymous with the persona. His initial experiences in Kansas City teach Clyde not only the importance of dressing, drinking, and even talking (in popularized colloquialisms) in a given manner, but also the crucial call for "skills" such as dancing. Spurned by Hortense because of his inability to dance, Clyde is upset with himself and acquires the ability to dance as a prerequisite for her acceptance of him as one of her beaus. Whereas Clyde in Lycurgus enjoys dancing with Roberta and then Sondra, there is nothing in the first phase of his story to suggest that he finds dancing intrinsically enjoyable. He responds to the activity as something he should do to fit in with his peer group and must do to attract a girl like Hortense, to whom it is a major concern. Dancing is a means to the ends of social success, and perhaps sexual satisfaction, and dance, therefore, he will—as diligently and proficiently as possible. It need not be objected that Clyde has no "personal" inclination to dance: such an idea is irrelevant to his entire orientation toward the world and quite meaningless in the wake of his total obliviousness toward his authentic self.

In Clyde's behavior toward dancing Dreiser gives us an introduction to a pattern woven throughout the novel that implicitly expresses the soul-deadening impact of an emphasis upon appearances without reference to the being behind them. During his career in Lycurgus, Clyde is joylessly intent upon affixing activities and skills which are conducive to inclusion in his dream world to that surface which is to be presented as "Clyde Griffiths." Despite his strong rejection of his own religious background, he starts attending the principal church to which his uncle's family sometimes goes, in order to "raise him[self] in their esteem" (I, 241)—and perhaps in their scale of employees and associates. Even before the start of his relationship with Roberta, Clyde is "always thinking that if by chance he should be taken up by the Griffiths, he would need as many social accomplishments as possible . . ." (I, 262). Thus he learns to swim, dive, and canoe; notably, even the pleasure he finds in canoeing in itself is based upon "the picturesque and summery appearance he ma[kes]" in doing it and in wearing outing clothes (I, 262). His outlook in this regard shows how thoroughly he has absorbed the point-of-view central to the social world to which he aspires: Sondra, we learn, revels in outdoor exercise for its own sake, yet she is "fairly dizzied by the opportunity all this [her various sports] provides for frequent changes of costume and hence social show, which [is] the one thing above all others that [does] interest her. How she looked in a bathing suit—a riding or tennis or dancing or automobile costume!" (I, 336) Delight in costumes that inflate the individual's stature in social terms follows from the stress upon role-playing. And later, to encourage Sondra's interest in himself, Clyde imitates all her athletic enthusiasms: during the winter he simulates a motivation toward horse-back riding (I, 333) and tennis (I, 336) in conversations with her; in the summer following, before the death-trip to Big Bittern with Roberta, he engages in those sports as well as in golf to share Sondra's time. Once he has been tentatively welcomed into the Now and Then parties of the younger members of his relatives' rank, Clyde reacts to the "college chatter" that marks the conversations around him with the determination to invent a past association with some university and then to "look up afterwards what, if anything, he was supposed to know about it—what, for instance, he might have studied" (I, 326).

Against the background of these deliberate steps by Clyde to construct an identity from the sum of apparently necessary visible parts, Kenner's witty analysis of the counterfeiters' methods can be used as a mirror reflecting unmistakably Dreiser's tacit rejection of empirical premises concerning the self in *An American Tragedy*:

> Observe one appearance with care, and record the observation: you have a Fact. A dog with eighteen ounces of water pumped into its thorax grew short-winded. Record another: a dog injected with opium, brandy and water, died. Another: a die swallowed by a dog was excreted after twenty-four hours, its weight halved but its shape and spots retained. All these things were noted at the Dublin Philosophical Society in the 1680's, when Swift was an undergraduate. Do they help us know what a dog is? A dog is perhaps partially defined as that animal which is inconvenienced in one way by water in the thorax, but in another way by brandy in the

jugular, and has the power of halving the bulk of dice. Or granted that these conditions . . . are insufficient to specify dogginess, what conditions are? . . .

We can easily devise a mechanism which water will slow, and brandy halt, and through which dice will pass at the cost of half their volume; and if these are the necessary and sufficient specifications for a dog, we who have abandoned faith in a hovering *caninitas* must agree that that machine will be a dog. Let no one object that they are outrageous specifications: experiment has shown that common dogs meet them, so they must be met. True, although necessary they are not sufficient. Experience calls also for a bark: well, we can add one; and for a wagging tail: nothing simpler. It is easy to think of more and more and more criteria, but not to think of any the mechanician could not simulate. . . . (pp. 7-8; 13)

The satirical point made here, as well as in Kenner's account of the remarkably "lifelike" mechanical ducks complete with simulated indigestion made by a counterfeiter named Vaucanson, helps to underline his implied explosion of the pretensions of the counterfeiters to having created the equivalent in each case of the *Ding an sich*. A parallel denial of the empirical stance toward *humanitas* emerges from Dreiser's novel's illumination of the fact that Clyde's elaborate effort to "counterfeit" an individuality equipped to satisfy all the specifications of Sondra and her world, based on forms of self-delusion linked to his society's illusory values, is a gathering of qualities (necessary but never sufficient) for a self he cannot possibly be. And in the process, Clyde's quest is exposed as an experiment in self-production (in method resembling the counterfeiters' approach to creating "a dog" or "a duck" in preparation for the twentieth-century simulations of human behavior by infinitely clever machines) that leads first to the destruction of his identity and then to the literal extinction of his being.

Clyde's "counterfeiting" project can take him as close to his goals as it does, of course, because those who must credit his pseudo-identity are all committed to the empiricist point-of-view, so to speak. If one believes in the counterfeit thing, its reality is empirically evident. So if Clyde can make himself a convincing enough specimen of a Lycurgus Griffiths, a sort of extension of Gilbert, his background history and its meaning for his true identity will be irrelevant; indeed, for all intents and purposes it will be nonexistent. Clyde's most difficult task in thus fictionalizing a self before Sondra and her friends, central to this attempt to be seen as "somebody," is to convince them that he has never been a "nobody." He must convince them of the authenticity of his origins, as Kenner's comment on the first principle of counterfeiting might suggest:

[T]he counterfeiter is never doing what we think. . . . We see him bent over his table, and imagine him bent on the manufacture of an object, resembling a twenty dollar bill as closely as his craftsmanship will permit. We suppose that his work is an exercise in craftsmanship. It is not. It is an exercise in creative metaphysics. What the counterfeiter is imitating is not the bill but the moment when that bill was (we are to suppose) issued by the Treasury of the United States: not a visible thing but an invisible event: perfectly invisible: it never happened. In the same way the logical term of Vaucanson's simulations was a nonexistent necessary egg. (pp. 72-73)

Dreiser's depiction of Clyde at a key moment—the first Now and Then party which initiates his acceptance by Sondra and her class—reveals Clyde's own exercise in "creative metaphysics."

He announces that his father has a small hotel in Denver, that he has come to Lycurgus at the suggestion of his uncle, and that he will remain only if he finds the collar business worth his while. He, therefore, causes Sondra and the others to conclude that "Clyde must possess some means and position to which, in case he did not do so well [in Lycurgus], he could return" (I, 332). And the narrative stresses the importance of this moment to Clyde's future; ironically, it relieves his listeners of their skepticism that Clyde (although good-looking and a Griffiths) is a "mere nobody, seeking . . . to attach himself to his cousin's family, which [is] disquieting" (I, 332). In short, his pseudo-information about his background suddenly means that Clyde is "proving more acceptable" than Sondra has expected—and that she is, consequently, "inclined to *make more of him* than she otherwise would have done" (I, 332; emphasis mine). The symbolic reverberations in the phraseology of the text's closing remark here indicate the novelist's capacity to use just the right words to realize his fiction and intimate that Dreiser's artistic conception of the way society undermines the self is a thematic clue to the novel's informing idea.

Just as Clyde evaluates himself in terms of the appearances and possessions he can present, so does he judge the worth of the girls in his life—in association with whom he perceives a key basis for self-definition. Even before meeting Hortense Briggs, he is utterly "determined that, girl or no girl, he would not have one who was not pretty. . . . The thought of being content with one not so attractive almost nauseated him" (I, 80). Having learned to equate sexual satisfaction with the possession of money and popularity in the relationship with Hortense, Clyde feels himself to be a "nobody" until a pretty girl yields herself to him. So after Roberta's surrender to his demands, Clyde adopts a new complaisant manner and sees himself as "an individual of import" at last. Revealingly, he begins to "[look] at himself in his mirror from time to time with an assurance and admiration which before this he had never possessed" (I, 308). Yet he considers the ideal surface quite incomplete: possessing a pretty girl, he still aspires to be a "Clyde" deemed worthy of the affections of a beauty who also has money and position.

Clyde responds to Roberta and Sondra in the same terms as those by which he has always expected to *be* responded to: their identity is adjudged solely upon extrinsic criteria of merit. The contrasting allure of Sondra and her world and the concentration of his deepest desires upon the actualization of a prospective dream-self in conjunction with her reduce the identity of Roberta in Clyde's eyes even during their first weeks of rapturous intimacy: "For after all, who was she? A factory girl! The daughter of parents who lived and worked on a farm and one who was compelled to work for her own living. Whereas he—he—if fortune would but favor him a little!" (I, 309). "Who" she is, once her beauty no longer sufficiently commends her, must be gauged in these terms alone; the prevailing point-of-view denies the reality of intangible qualities that might supposedly give her other or greater value as a person. Conversely, Sondra's status enhances the worth of her beauty itself, offers Clyde a ladder to his own idealization of self, and apotheosizes her identity in his eyes in a way that gives her import beyond everything common or carnal.

If Roberta appears to Clyde to be even less than the sum of her commonplace parts, Sondra "is" much more than the sum of *her* parts or observable qualities. A burning glass radiating meaning outward, Sondra is for Clyde the Word of his worldly religion Made Flesh. Behind Clyde's need to remove the demands of a pregnant Roberta from his life is his overpowering sense of the "difference between the attitudes of these two girls— Sondra with everything, offering all—asking nothing of him; Roberta, with nothing, asking all" (II, 57). In view of his perspective toward her identity, it is no surprise that on Big Bittern, Roberta has only the significance for him of "a shadow or thought really, a form of illusion more vaporous than real" (II, 74). Tellingly, Clyde seems to think that once Roberta has drowned, it will be as if she has never existed. If his plot could succeed (with him avoiding all legal responsibility for her *dis*appearance and happily marrying Sondra), his story would not be one of crime unpunished but of the ultimate triumph of the empiricism whose rules he blindly adheres to!

Dreiser re-emphasizes the tragic implications of society's attitudes subversive of individual integrity by showing that Roberta is less a victim of Clyde's than a victim of the same misconceptions that finally destroy him. For "Roberta, after encountering Clyde and sensing the superior world in which she imagined he moved . . . , was seized with the very virus of ambition and unrest that afflicted him" (I, 256). She relates to him as he does to Sondra, that is, shares his distorted premises concerning individual worth. Roberta's reflections on Clyde while waiting for him to call her forth from Biltz with her pathetic trousseau for the marriage she has demanded, coming after all his mistreatment of her for months past and at a time when she knows he desires only Sondra, clearly indicate the intensity of her idealized vision of him and her readiness to sell herself very cheaply in order to touch her dream:

> And, strangely enough, in spite of all the troubled and strained relations that had developed between

them, she still saw Clyde in much the same light in which she had seen him at first. He was a Griffiths, a youth of genuine social, if not financial distinction, one whom all the girls in her position . . . would be delighted to be connected with in this way—that is, via marriage. He might be objecting to marrying her, but he was a person of consequence, just the same. And one with whom, if he would but trouble to care for her a little, she could be perfectly happy. And at any rate, once he had loved her. (II, 17)

Her view confers "distinction" upon Clyde as "a Griffiths"—not as a person whose thoughts and feelings, and capacities, comprise his "consequence." If her thoughts imply one aspect of Roberta's self-betrayal, her agreement with Clyde's own orientation toward her does so more strikingly. "As contrasted with one of Sondra's position and beauty," thinks Clyde, "what had Roberta really to offer him?" (I, 345). Ironically, Roberta's thoughts (II, 10) and impassioned statements to him during their Christmas Night quarrel (I, 369) reveal her own view that relative to Sondra she is a nonentity with nothing to offer Clyde.

Roberta's figurative and then literal death as a self parallels, as well as crucially ties in with, Clyde's: her story amounts to a tragic subplot that extends the novel's idea of the distortions of identity prompted by false values. In Book Three of the novel, Clyde's own victimization by premises destructive of the authentic self and of the self's intrinsic image of dignity finds its grim, if logical, culmination in the distorted versions of his identity fabricated by those who vilify him, those who prosecute him, those who would purify him before his death. But the anti-naturalistic impetus of the treatment of selfhood in *An American Tragedy* finds its climactic expression in the reader's tragic vision of the scene at Big Bittern. Given her premises concerning individuality, Roberta would theoretically agree that Clyde should deny her existence and marry Sondra, and thus she appears finally as a symbolic accessory to the crime of her own drowning. And Clyde's conduct in the scene—and before it—unwittingly reasserts his own underlying self in a manner that soon unleashes forces that give transfigured meaning and harrowing reality to his very being.

NOTES

[1] See David Brion Davis, "Dreiser and Naturalism Revisited," in *The Stature of Theodore Dreiser*, eds. Alfred Kazin and Charles Shapiro (Bloomington: Indiana University Press, 1955 [1965]), pp. 225-236; Charles Child Walcutt, *American Literary Naturalism, A Divided Stream* (Minneapolis: University of Minnesota Press, 1956), pp. 180-221; Roger Asselineau, "Theodore Dreiser's Transcendentalism" in *English Studies Today*, ed. G. A. Bonnard (Bern: Francke Verlag, 1961), pp. 233-243; Donald Pizer, *Realism and Naturalism in Nineteenth-Century American Literature* (Carbondale: Southern Illinois University Press, 1966), pp. 11-14, 19-24; and Jack Salzman, "Introduction" to *Sister Carrie* (Indianapolis, IN: Bobbs-Merrill, 1970), pp. xix-xx.

[2] Lauriat Lane, Jr., "The Double in *An American Tragedy*," *Modern Fiction Studies,* 12 (Summer 1966), 213-220.

[3] Richard Lehan, *Theodore Dreiser: His World and His Novels* (Carbondale: Southern Illinois University Press 1969), pp. 142-169.

[4] Robert Penn Warren, *Homage to Theodore Dreiser: On the Centennial of His Birth* (New York: Random House, 1971), pp. 96-139; Robert Elias, "Theodore Dreiser and the Tragedy of the Twenties," in *Prospects, I,* ed. Jack Salzman (New York: Burt Franklin, 1975), pp. 9-16.

[5] Elias, p. 12.

[6] Warren p. 131; see p. 138.

[7] Theodore Dreiser, *Hey, Rub-a-Dub-Dub* (New York: Boni and Liveright, 1920), p. 247.

[8] Hugh Kenner, *The Counterfeiters: An Historical Comedy* (Garden City, NY: Anchor Books/Doubleday, 1973); all subsequent references are from this edition and shown in parentheses in the text.

[9] Theodore Dreiser, *An American Tragedy* (New York: Horace Liveright, 1925), 2 vols. All page references are cited from this edition of the novel.

[10] Irving Howe, "Dreiser and Tragedy: The Stature of Theodore Dreiser," in *Dreiser: A Collection of Critical Essays* [20th-Century Views], ed. John Lydenberg (Englewood Cliffs, NJ: Prentice-Hall, 1971), p. 150.

[11] F. Scott Fitzgerald, *This Side of Paradise* (New York: Scribner's, 1920), p. 104.

Mona G. Rosenman (essay date 1978)

SOURCE: "*An American Tragedy*: Constitutional Violations," in *The Dreiser Newsletter,* Vol. 9, No. 1, Spring, 1978, pp. 11-19.

[*In the following essay, Rosenman examines the violations of the United States Constitution committed in the trial of Clyde Griffiths and of Chester Gillette, the man on whom Dreiser based his protagonist.*]

Theodore Dreiser's **An American Tragedy** was first published in 1925. Nineteen years earlier, on July 11, 1906, Chester E. Gillette, the prototype of Clyde Griffiths, the main character of the novel, allegedly drowned a young woman named Grace Brown in Herkimer County, New York. On March 20, 1908, Gillette was electrocuted for this crime. Clyde Griffiths, his fictional counterpart, accused of drowning his pregnant girlfriend, Roberta Alden, also received the death penalty, although there was no witness to the occurrence and the accused claimed the drowning was accidental. Thus, Clyde was convicted on what seems purely circumstantial evidence. But was the circumstantial evidence really "pure"? To Dreiser the answer to this question must have been an emphatic "No."

Since Dreiser based Clyde's trial on the Gillette records, to the extent even of using several parts of the Court's transcript practically verbatim, the American tragedy in his mind must have contained elements *dehors* the record; and these elements must have consisted of practices prohibited by the Fourteenth Amendment but resorted to repeatedly during the Gillette/Griffiths trial. Such practices, abhorrent, illegal, and unconstitutional—and not the fact of the murder of a real or fictional person—are what Dreiser thought constituted an American tragedy. By an ironical coincidence, the same year (1908) that Gillette was executed, the United States Supreme Court, ruling on its own power to determine the scope of the Fourteenth Amendment, held that such practices violated the fundamental principles of liberty and justice which are inherent in a free government and are the inalienable right of a citizen of such a government.[1] Later it further ruled that such practices offended the canons of decency and fairness which express the traditions of English-speaking peoples even toward those charged with the most heinous offenses.[2]

Such "practices" are governed by Section One of the Fourteenth Amendment, which provides that no State shall deprive any person of life, liberty, or property, without due process of law. As guardian of the State criminal justice systems, the Supreme Court of the United States has decided that the Due Process Clause cannot be limited to those specific guarantees spelled out in the Bill of Rights, that it even contains protection against practices which may be unfair without the violation of any *specific* provision. (An example is Justice Harlan's holding that despite the absence of a specific Constitutional provision requiring proof beyond a reasonable doubt in criminal cases, such proof is nonetheless a Due Process requirement.[3]) Another clause of Section One provides that the State cannot deny to any person within its jurisdiction the equal protection of the laws, and the Supreme Court has interpreted this to mean that no agency of the State, or of the officers or agents by whom its powers are exerted, can deny equal protection of the law to anybody, the reason being that since such a person acts in the name of and for the State and is clothed with the State's power, that his act is that of the State.[4] Yet both of these Constitutional prohibitions were violated in the Gillette/Griffiths trial. Had the defense attorneys been competent and experienced trial lawyers capable of comprehending fully the implications of the Fourteenth Amendment, the death penalty probably would not have been imposed; or had it been, another trial would have been won upon appeal. But, as Dreiser described so well in his fictionalized account, Clyde Griffiths had neither adequate counsel nor a fair trial.

What is meant by a "fair" trial? The provisions of the Bill of Rights applicable to State procedures contain certain basic guarantees: right to counsel, right to speedy and public trial, right to be free from use of unlawfully seized evidence and unlawfully obtained confessions, etc. But these are not the only requirements: "Due process of law requires that the *proceedings* shall be fair . . ."[5] and "as applied to a criminal trial, denial of due process is the failure to observe that fundamental fairness essential to the very concept of justice. In order to declare a denial of it . . . [the Court] must find that the absence of that fairness fatally infected the trial; the acts complained of must be of such quality as necessarily prevents a fair trial."[6] Thus, in *Lisenba v. California,* the Court ruled that there are some Constitutional rights so basic to a fair trial that their infraction can never be treated as harmless.[7] One such infraction is bias or prejudice, either inherent in the structure of the trial system or imposed by external events.[8] Obviously, then, bias and prejudice on the parts of the prosecuting attorney, the judge, and the jury would be violations of the Due Process provision and grounds for an appeal. Bearing this in mind, let us scrutinize the motivations and actions of Orville W. Mason, the district attorney who prosecuted Clyde Griffiths' case, of Frederick Oberwaltzer, the presiding judge, and of the jury which returned a verdict of guilty.

At the time of Clyde's arrest, Mason had been district attorney for two consecutive terms and knew that unless he were fortunate enough to be nominated and elected to a county judgeship which was vacant, "defeat and political doldrums loomed ahead." What he needed to insure achievement of that judgeship was a "really important case" in connection with which he would be "able to distinguish himself and so rightfully and hopefully demand further recognition from the people."[9] Moreover, because Mason's boyhood "had been one of poverty and neglect," he had a tendency to "look on those with whom life had dealt more kindly as too favorably treated" (p. 546); therefore, when informed that Clyde was the nephew of the wealthy Samuel Griffiths, he automatically assumed that the boy was a member of "The wretched rich! The indifferent rich!" (p. 559). Bringing such a criminal to justice would not only reward Mason emotionally but also promised him much favorable publicity "in view of the state of public opinion, which was most bitterly and vigorously anti-Clyde" (p. 623). Consequently, because the election in which he hoped to be nominated for the judgeship was fast approaching, Mason "decided to communicate with the governor of the state for the purpose of obtaining a special term of the Supreme Court [in New York the "Supreme Court" is the court of first instance] . . . with its accompanying special session of the local grand jury, which would then be subject to his call at any time" (p. 622). Yet, according to the Supreme Court, whenever a grand jury is utilized, it must be fairly constituted and free from prejudicial influences.[10] But because Mason's political ambitions demanded a speedy trial, he was willing to deny Clyde his right to Due Process and equal protection of the laws as guaranteed in the Fourteenth Amendment.

When Belknap and Jephson, attorneys for Clyde, learned of Mason's request to the governor, they immediately

asserted that he was endeavoring to railroad Clyde to the electric chair "merely to achieve a victory for the Republican party in November." Mason's reply to this charge is very revealing, particularly inasmuch as "it was listened to with proper gravity by the representatives of the various newspapers":

> What reason have I, a representative of all the people in this county, to railroad this man anywhere or make one single charge against him unless the charges make themselves? Doesn't the evidence itself show that he did kill this girl? (p. 663)

Such remarks not only prove Mason to have been dishonest about his own motivations, but also constitute a bias or pre-judgment on his part and show him to be absolutely partial. The rule of law operative in the United States and in New York has always held that a person is presumed to be innocent until he is proved guilty and this means the finding or verdict of a jury *after* it has heard all the evidence.[11] Furthermore, because Mason went on to ask the question, "And has he ever said or done one thing to clear up any of the suspicious circumstances? No! Silence or lies" (p. 663), it is obvious that he was trying to influence the press; for, as an attorney admitted to practice in New York, he must have known that in accordance with the rules of law operative in that state, or in any state, it is not incumbent upon the accused to say *anything* prior to the actual trial. His innocence is presumed until the testimony at the trial disproves it.[12]

Mason then said, "and until these circumstances are disproved by these very able gentlemen [Belknap and Jephson] I am going right ahead" (p. 663). The rule of law is that the *state* must prove beyond a reasonable doubt that the accused is guilty before the jury can convict him; therefore, the burden of proof is on the state and *not* on the accused, who is never required to disprove his guilt although he may do so.[13] What Mason's statement shows is that he did not consider the rules of law applicable to the Griffiths case because he had shifted the burden of proving or disproving guilt onto the defendant. And his next remark, "I have all the evidence necessary to convict this young criminal now" (p. 663), indicates that he had already arraigned, tried, and convicted Clyde without the latter's having had the benefit of a hearing before judge and jury. Of course, Dreiser deliberately introduced this material for the purpose of showing just how unfairly Clyde was treated. Any attorney could have told Dreiser then, as he would now, that Mason's remarks not only disqualified him as prosecuting attorney but also guaranteed—should he insist on prosecuting the case—that the next highest court would reverse any decision made by the trial court adverse to the accused.

Belknap's formal protest and personal argument to the governor against Mason's request for a special term of the Supreme Court were denied. Yet neither he nor Jephson then filed a motion to be heard by the presiding judge—and not by the governor—asking that because of Mason's obvious prejudice, he be removed from the case;

and this is a typical example of their fumbling. They knew that statements of the kind Mason made to the press would tend to prejudice the people in the community and make impossible the selection of an "impartial" jury, particularly since a jury's verdict must be based on evidence received in open court and not from outside sources.[14] Moreover, they should have known that collaboration between counsel and press as to information affecting the fairness of a criminal trial is not only subject to regulation but is also highly censurable and deserves disciplinary measures (Syllabus 14). The irony of the situation is twofold: not only did Mason broadcast his own bias and prejudice, but he also indicted the community where the trial was to be held for similar bias and prejudice when he stated that he was "a representative of all the people."

Now let us examine the conduct of Frederick Oberwaltzer, justice of the eleventh judicial district, who was designated to preside over Clyde's trial. Belknap and Jephson's first move was to approach Oberwaltzer for a change of venue, "on the ground that by no possible stretch of the imagination could any twelve men residing in Cataraqui County be found who, owing to the public and private statements of Mason," would not be "already vitally opposed to Clyde and so convinced of his guilt that before even such a jury could be addressed by a defense, he would be convicted" (p. 664). Unfortunately for Clyde, Oberwaltzer was "a slow and meticulous man inclined to favor conservative procedure in all things"; therefore, the legal precedent that should have determined his decision seemed less weighty to him than Mason's argument that a change of venue would saddle Cataraqui County with an enormous expense. (The Supreme Court might have considered this to be a bias imposed by an external event on Oberwaltzer that resulted in his denying Clyde the right to a fair trial. However, what constitutes influencing the impartiality of the presiding judge has often divided the court.[15]) At any rate, although Oberwaltzer knew that there was a reasonable likelihood that the prejudicial news prior to trial would prevent a fair trial, and that under the circumstances he should either have continued the case until the threat abated or transferred it to another county not so permeated with publicity (Syllabus 11), he decided, "after five days, in which he did not more than muse idly upon the matter" (p. 665), to deny the motion.

Moreover, had Oberwaltzer had doubts concerning the existence of prejudicial publicity—and there is no evidence in the book that he did—they should have been immediately dispelled by the conditions prevalent on the first day of Clyde's trial. By his careful depiction of the atmosphere that day, Dreiser shows us once again just how unfairly Clyde was handled by the court. Despite the presence of hundreds of people eagerly buying peanuts, popcorn, hotdogs, and the "story of Clyde Griffiths, with all the letters of Roberta Alden," which had been issued "in pamphlet form together with an outline of 'the great plot' and Roberta's and Clyde's pictures" (p. 679), Oberwaltzer failed to do his duty as a state trial judge in

a murder prosecution. He made no efforts at all to protect the defendant from the inherently prejudicial publicity which saturated the community (Syllabus 15). Nor did he order a new trial when publicity during the proceedings threatened the fairness of the first trial (Syllabus 12). Even when the "solemn, vengeful voice" of an irate woodsman resounded throughout the courtroom, "'Why don't they kill the God-damned bastard and be done with him?'" (p. 776), Oberwaltzer did not declare a mistrial. (Mob domination of a trial so as to rob the jury of its judgment on the evidence presented is a Due Process violation: "And if the State, supplying no corrective process, carries into execution a judgment of death or imprisonment based upon a verdict thus produced by mob domination, the State deprives the accused of his life or liberty without due process of law."[16] But despite the fact that Oberwaltzer's failure to control such disruptive influences deprived the defendant of due process (Syllabus 15), Oberwaltzer was not particularly concerned: "If he were wrong, there was the Appellate Division to which the defense could resort" (p. 665).

However, just as finding the woodsman guilty of contempt was not enough on Justice Oberwaltzer's part, so was acceptance of this ruling not sufficient action on the parts of Belknap and Jephson. Again they proved themselves astonishingly inept by not orally moving for a mistrial and asking the court for an immediate recess during which their motion could be argued in the absence of the jury. Even had Oberwaltzer refused such a motion in any particular, except to declare a mistrial, Belknap and Jephson should have taken exception to such ruling and have had the record show what had transpired; they then should have filed a formal written motion for a reconsideration of Oberwaltzer's decision and again, in writing, renewed their request for a mistrial. And, if this motion and request were overruled by the judge in any particular, Belknap and Jephson should have insisted that such be noted in the record of the trial as an exception to the court's ruling; for any such ruling on the judge's part would instantly have beclouded the correctness of his trial procedure, and the record of Belknap and Jephson's exceptions to the ruling would have implied error on his part. Unfortunately, neither Jephson nor Belknap thought to move for a mistrial; consequently, when they did seek recourse to the Appellate Division, which ironically had been Oberwaltzer's rationale for his shabby performance, they had no record of one ground which probably would have won Clyde a new trial—an implication of error on Oberwaltzer's part. The reasons Jephson and Belknap did present were, to the Court of Appeals, of insufficient moment to justify the granting of a new trial; the decision of the lower court was therefore unanimously confirmed; and Clyde, the victim of a horrible miscarriage of justice, was sentenced to die.

There can be no doubt that Dreiser intended to portray Clyde as such a victim, for, besides making it plain that the boy was actually innocent of deliberate murder and showing the parody of justice accorded him, he also included other factors in the combination which defeated

Clyde. For instance, Burton Burleigh, Mason's assistant and therefore an officer of the court, deliberately and with forethought threaded "two of Roberta's hairs in between the door and the lens of the camera" (p. 622) because he knew that without such incriminating proof Clyde might very well go free. That such hair could reasonably have been expected to be there is of no significance: Burleigh could not possibly have known this *prior* to the trial; consequently, his action in falsifying evidence made him guilty of conspiring against the life of another. Indeed, he is symbolic of all of the State forces allied against Clyde because he misused power that he possessed by virtue of state law and that was available to him only because he was clothed with the authority of state law. Such action is construed by the Supreme Court to be action taken "under color of" state law.[17] Then there was the mob who screamed for Clyde's life and thus displayed the kind of hatred and ruthlessness that he himself had been unable to generate at the fleeting moment when he had thought to kill Roberta. And last, there was Reverend McMillan, whose word the governor would have taken to spare Clyde's life. Because of his conviction that committing murder in the heart made one a murderer, McMillan found it impossible to give that word even to save a life. Like all the others, he, too, violated the very laws of justice, mercy, and compassion that he professed to uphold.

It was in 1868 that Congress ratified Constitutional Amendment Fourteen, Section One of which guaranteed Chester Gillette/Clyde Griffiths that which in 1906 Mason, Oberwaltzer, and the people of Cataraqui County so summarily refused to grant—due process and equal protection of the laws. These provisions were finally vindicated and sustained, although it took another and similar case, which received nationwide publicity and discussion, to bring this about. In a similar trial (1954), Samuel H. Sheppard, a young Ohio osteopath, was found guilty of bludgeoning his pregnant wife Marilyn to death and ultimately served a number of years in the Ohio Penitentiary. Sheppard tried several times in one way or another to obtain his freedom. He finally engaged the services of attorney F. Lee Bailey, who was more successful; the result was that the Supreme Court decided that the community where Sheppard had lived had been so inflamed by the newspapers, especially *The Cleveland Press,* that he could not have had a fair trial. The Court therefore reversed the decision of the jury and ordered a new trial, at which Sheppard was defended by the able and aggressive Bailey, who won an acquittal for him.

The Sheppard case was not decided until June of 1966; therefore, the Syllabi that have been cited herein would not have been available at the time of the Gillette trial. However, the Sheppard case is based on the same Fourteenth Amendment; had Gillette's lawyers used it as did F. Lee Bailey, a court of last resort no doubt would have rendered the same decision that it rendered in the Sheppard case. In fact, the *Griffiths* case is even stronger for the defendant than the Sheppard case because Mason told the newspapers, reporters, and the public generally that the defendant was guilty long before the trial. In the Sheppard case this did not happen because the prosecuting attorney knew that this could not and should not be done. What actually happened was that the newspapers and other news media made such a sensation out of the murder that in the opinion of the United States Supreme Court, a fair trial could not be had. Justice Clark delivered the opinion of the Court: "We have concluded that Sheppard did not receive a fair trial consistent with the Due Process Clause of the fourteenth amendment and therefore reverse the judgment. . . ." Had the appeal in the Gillette/Griffiths case been handled properly, some other Supreme Court Justice would have had to say much the same thing.

NOTES

[1] *Twining v. New Jersey,* 211 U.S. 78, 106 (1908).

[2] *Rochin v. California,* 342 U.S. 165, 169 (1952).

[3] *In re Winship,* 397 U.S. 358 (1970).

[4] *Ex parte Virginia,* 100 U.S. 339, 346-347 (1880).

[5] *Snyder v. Massachusetts,* 291 U.S. 97, 116, 117 (1934).

[6] *Lisenba v. California,* 314 U.S. 219, 236 (1941).

[7] *Ibid.*

[8] *Tumey v. Ohio,* 273 U.S. 510 (1927).

[9] Theodore Dreiser, *An American Tragedy* (Cleveland: World Publishing, 1948), p. 543. All subsequent references to this edition will appear within the text.

[10] On prejudicial publicity, see *Beck v. Washington,* 369 U.S. 541 (1962).

[11] See article in *American Jurisprudence,* Second Edition, Volume entitled "Evidence." (Rochester, N.Y.: The Lawyers Cooperative Publishing Co., 1967), paragraphs 225 et. seq.

[12] *Ibid.,* Volume XXX (Paragraphs 1170 et. seq.).

[13] *Ibid.,* Volume XXI. See article entitled "Criminal Law." (Paragraphs 409 et. seq.).

[14] *Sheppard v. Maxwell,* Warden of the Ohio Penitentiary, 384 U.S. 333 (1966). 86 *Supreme Court Reports,* 1508. Syllabus 3. The Syllabi of a case are like synopses and appear at the beginning of the report. All subsequent references to Syllabi in the Sheppard case will appear within the text.

[15] E.g., *Ungar v. Sarafite,* 376 U.S. 575 (1964); *Holt v. Virginia,* 381 U.S. 131 (1965); *Mayberry v. Pennsylvania,* 400 U.S. 455 (1971).

[16] *Frank v. Mangum,* 237 U.S. 309 (1915).

[17] *United States v. Classic,* 313 U.S. 299, 326 (1941).

Yoshinobu Hakutani (essay date 1979)

SOURCE: "*Native Son* and *An American Tragedy*: Two Different Interpretations of Crime and Guilt," in *The Centennial Review,* Vol. XXIII, No. 2, Spring, 1979, pp. 208-26.

[*In the following essay, Hakutani discusses the influence of* An American Tragedy *on Richard Wright's crime novel* Black Boy, *noting similarities in the two writers' views of crime and punishment.*]

I

Theodore Dreiser is, among modern novelists, one of the most influential predecessors of Richard Wright. In an episode from *Black Boy,* Wright tells us how he was inspired by Dreiser's *Jennie Gerhardt and Sister Carrie:* "It would have been impossible for me to have told anyone what I derived from these novels, for it was nothing less than a sense of life itself. All my life had shaped me for the realism, the naturalism of the modern novels, and I could not read enough of them."[1] Such acknowledgment must have convinced critics that the primary source of his best-known work, *Native Son,* was Dreiser's *An American Tragedy.* In fact, several early reviewers of *Native Son* pointed out that the two novels shared the same theme and technique. And both novels convince their readers that the crimes they dramatize are inevitable products of American society and that both protagonists are morally free from guilt.[2]

Except for the obvious problem of race, Wright and Dreiser shared quite similar experiences before they became novelists. Since their boyhood both had been economically hard pressed; they were always ashamed that they had grown up on the wrong side of the tracks. As boys they witnessed struggling and suffering and felt excluded from society. They grew up hating the fanatic and stifling religion practiced at home. In both lives, the family suffered because of the father's inadequacies as a breadwinner; the son inevitably rebelled against such a father, and the family was somehow put together by the suffering mother. Under these circumstances, their dream of success was merely survival; they tried to hang on to one menial job after another. As a result, both had nurtured a brooding sensibility. At twelve, Wright held "a notion as to what life meant that no education could ever alter, a conviction that the meaning of living came only when one was struggling to wring a meaning out of meaningless suffering" (*Black Boy,* p. 112). This statement indeed echoes what Dreiser recorded in his autobiography:

> In considering all I have written here, I suddenly become deeply aware of the fact that educationally speaking, where any sensitive and properly interpretive mind is concerned, experience is the only true teacher—that education, which is little more than a selective presentation of certain stored or canned phases of experience, is at best an elucidative, or at its poorest, a polishing process offered to experience which is always basic.[3]

But this close kinship between the lives of Wright and Dreiser need not necessarily have resulted in the similarities between *Native Son* and *An American Tragedy.* Although both novels are obviously concerned with the crime and guilt of a deprived American youth struggling to realize his dreams of success, the characterization of the hero fundamentally differs in the two novels. Clyde Griffiths in *An American Tragedy* is seen by Dreiser as a representative type, and the novel's psychological focus serves to delineate the frustrations of not only an individual, but a class. Bigger Thomas in *Native Son,* on the other hand, is presented as a particular individual in Wright's imagination. Wright's essay "How Bigger Was Born" suggests an extension of Bigger to include all those rebels the author had known in the South, and even white victims of the system who actively fought against it. Nevertheless, within the confines of the novel itself, we find no other character remotely like Bigger once the murder triggers the creation of his personality and no similar identification between character and author. It is significant in this regard that, as *Black Boy* demonstrates, Wright always considered himself unique, an outsider, not only from whites but also from most of the blacks with whom he grew up.

It would seem that both authors, being literary naturalists, used authentic court records. Dreiser drew on the Gillette murder case in upstate New York; Wright on the Leopold and Loeb kidnap-murder as well as the Robert Nixon murder trial and conviction in Chicago. Both titles strongly imply that Clyde and Bigger are the products of American society and that society, not the individuals involved in the crimes, is to blame. But doesn't a naturalistic novel *always* create tensions in the life of the hero, growing out of an environment over which he has no control and about which he understands very little and, therefore, by which he is *always* victimized? If so, *Native Son* does not appear to fit into this genre. Bigger's transcendence of the type of defeated, determined protagonist of which Clyde in *An American Tragedy* is a good example provides the clearest distinction between the two works. Despite the obvious parallels between *Native Son* and *An American Tragedy,* the comparison is of limited value, and the purpose of this essay is to demonstrate significant differences between the two books.

II

It is true that both novels employ crime as a thematic device. In *Native Son,* the murder of Bessie is the inevitable consequence of Mary Dalton's accidental death; in *An American Tragedy,* Clyde's fleeing the scene of the accident which kills a child leads to his plotting of murder later in the story. Without the presence of crime in the plot neither author would have been able to make significant points about his protagonist. But the focus of the author's idea differs in the two books. Wright's center of interest, unlike Dreiser's, is not crime but its consequences—its psychological effect on his hero. Before committing his crime Bigger is presented as an uneducated, uninformed youth; indeed he is portrayed as a victim of white society who grew up in the worst black ghetto of the nation. We are thus surprised to see him gainidentity after the murder. The crime gives him some awareness of himself and of the world of which he has never been capable before. When Bigger and his friend Jack went to see a bourgeois movie called *The Gay Woman,* they were both puzzled by certain words used in the dialogue:

"Say, Jack?"

"Hunh?"

"What's a Communist?"

"A Communist is a red, ain't he?"

"Yeah; but what's a red?"

"Damn if I know. It's a race of folks who live in Russia, ain't it?"

"They must be wild."

"Looks like it. That guy was trying to kill somebody."[4]

We are surprised to learn that after the murder Bigger is well versed in world affairs. "He liked to hear," Wright tells us, "of how Japan was conquering China; of how Hitler was running the Jews to the ground; of how Mussolini was invading Spain" (*Native Son,* p. 110). By this time he has learned to think for himself. He is even proud of Japanese, Germans, and Italians, because they "could rule others, for in actions such as these he felt that there was a way to escape from this tight morass of fear and shame that sapped at the base of his life" (pp. 109-10).

Book I of *Native Son* is entitled "Fear," and ironically Wright's characterization of Bigger makes his stature deliberately smaller and less courageous than we might expect of a fighter against oppression. No small wonder that Mary Dalton's death is caused by Bigger's fear of whites and their world. His killing of Mary is an accidental homicide. In *An American Tragedy,* on the other hand, Clyde is placed in a situation so oppressive that only violence can provide him with the hope of dignity. But the oppression for Clyde has a corollary of hope, not fear, on his part. Clyde is an optimistic character, always seeking opportunities for success in life. While Bigger can only kill accidentally, Clyde in the same position can consciously plot murder. Even though the boat into which Clyde lures Roberta overturns when he has not planned it, and her actual death may legally prove accidental, Clyde is not entirely innocent. On this ground alone the interpretation of the death of a girl as a central episode vastly differs between *Native Son* and *An American Tragedy.*

Throughout the story Dreiser implies that Clyde's aspirations to rise in the world are not matched by his abilities. Near the beginning Dreiser makes known that Clyde, overly impressed by every sign of success in his future,

"lacked decidedly that mental clarity and inner directing application that in so many permits them to sort out from the facts and avenues of life the particular thing or things that make for their direct advancement."[5] This is why whatever he does is so inept that he is easily caught after the crime. At the trial, Clyde after such a harrowing experience is called by the prosecutor "a loose, wayward and errant character" (p. 525). Before execution Clyde remains "a mental and moral coward," as his defense attorneys have presented him. Not only has he become a puppet of his own lawyers for their political purposes but he ends his life as an immature youth without a sense of remorse, let alone a conviction.

In contrast, Bigger after committing two crimes has for the first time redeemed his manhood. Max, Bigger's defense attorney, argues that the actions leading to the death of Mary and Bessie were "as instinctive and inevitable as breathing or blinking one's eyes. It was an act of *creation!*" (*Native Son,* p. 366). Bigger tells Max:

> But really I never wanted to hurt nobody. That's the truth, Mr. Max. I hurt folks 'cause I felt I had to; that's all. They was crowding me too close; they wouldn't give me no room. Lots of times I tried to forget 'em, but I couldn't. They wouldn't let me. . . . (p. 388)

Bigger's earlier evasion of life has been converted to participation. The fact that he had killed a white girl, a symbol of beauty for white society, made him "feel the equal of them, like a man who had been somehow cheated, but had now evened the score" (p. 155). Bessie's murder also marks a new development in Bigger's manhood. For the first time he desires to be at peace with himself. Bigger is no longer a slave but a free man who claims his right to "create." Bessie's murder results from a willful act, a clear departure from the accidental killing of Mary Dalton.

Despite a death sentence handed down by his white rulers, Bigger now proclaims his own existence. Even Max, who has taken a sympathetic attitude towards the oppressed, is bewildered by Bigger's deep urges for freedom and independence. "I didn't want to kill," Bigger tells Max. "But what I killed for, I *am!*" (pp. 391-92) Having overcome white oppression, Bigger now stands a heroic exemplar for the members of his race. His brother Buddy, he realizes, "was blind . . . went round and round in a groove and did not see things." Bigger sees in Buddy "a certain stillness, an isolation, meaninglessness" (p. 103). His sister Vera, too, was a tired and fearful girl who "seemed to be shrinking from life in every gesture she made" (p. 104). Alcohol was what sustained his girl friend Bessie as religion was what obsessed Mrs. Thomas. All his mother could do after Bigger's capture was kneel on the floor at Mrs. Dalton's feet to beg for sparing her son's life. "Bigger," says Wright, "was paralyzed with shame; he felt violated" (p. 280). Finally, in both *Native Son* and *An American Tragedy* a preacherappears before the trial to console the accused. But in *Native Son* the black preacher is described in derogatory terms. Bigger immediately senses that the Reverend Hammond possesses only a white-washed soul and functions merely as an advocate of white supremacy. Wright offers this explanation:

> The preacher's face was black and sad and earnest. . . . He had killed within himself the preacher's haunting picture of life even before he had killed Mary; that had been his first murder. And now the preacher made it walk before his eyes like a ghost in the night, creating within him a sense of exclusion that was as cold as a block of ice. (p. 264)

During his act of liberation, too, Bigger is consciously aware of his own undoing and creation. A successful naturalistic novel often creates tensions in the life of the hero and they often crush him. To survive in this state of being, Bigger is forced to rebel, unlike Clyde, who remains a victim of the tensions. In rebelling, then, Bigger moves from determinism to freedom. Bigger knows how to escape the confines of his environment and to gain an identity. Even before he acts, he knows exactly how Mary, and Bessie later, has forced him into a vulnerable position. No wonder he convinces himself not only that he has killed to protect himself but also that he has attacked the entire civilization. In *An American Tragedy*, Dreiser molds the tragedy of Clyde Griffiths by generating pity and sympathy for the underprivileged in American society. In *Native Son*, however, Wright departs from the principles of pity and sympathy which whites have for blacks. In "How 'Bigger' Was Born," Wright admits that his earlier *Uncle Tom's Children* was "a book which even bankers' daughters could read and weep over and feel good about."[6] In *Native Son*, however, Wright would not allow for such complacency. He warns the readers that the book "would be so hard and deep that they would have to face it without the consolation of tears."[7]

The meaning of *Native Son* therefore derives not from crime but from its result. Dreiser's interest in *An American Tragedy*, on the other hand, lies not in the result of crime but in its cause. While Bigger at the end of his violent and bloody life can claim his victory, Clyde at the end of his life remains a failure. *Native Son* thus ends on an optimistic note; *An American Tragedy* as a whole stems from and ends on the dark side of American capitalism. F. O. Matthiessen is right in maintaining that the reason for Dreiser's use of the word *American* in his title "was the overwhelming lure of money-values in our society, more nakedly apparent than in older and more complex social structures."[8] Furthermore, Helen Dreiser seems to confirm Dreiser's central thought in interpreting materialism as the cause of Clyde's tragedy. Commenting on Dreiser's choice of the Chester Gillette murder case for fictionalization, Helen Dreiser writes:

> This problem had been forced on his mind not only by the extreme American enthusiasm for wealth as contrasted with American poverty, but the determination of so many young Americans, boys and girls alike, to obtain wealth quickly by

marriage. When he realized the nature of the American literature of that period and what was being offered and consumed by publishers and public, he also became aware of the fact that the most interesting American story of the day concerned not only the boy getting the girl, but more emphatically, the poor boy getting the rich girl. Also, he came to know that it was a natural outgrowth of the crude pioneering conditions of American life up to that time, based on the glorification of wealth which started with the early days of slavery and persisted throughout our history.[9]

Dreiser's fascination with this subject resulted in his treatment of Clyde as a victim of the American dream. Bigger, too, a product of the same society, cherishes a dream of his own. Like anyone else, he reads the newspapers and magazines, goes to the movies, strolls the crowded streets. Bigger is intensely aware of his dreams: "to merge himself with others and be a part of this world, to lose himself in it so he could find himself, to be allowed a chance to live like others, even though he was black" (*Native Son*, p. 226). Unlike Dreiser, Wright must have clearly recognized his hero's sense of alienation from the rest of the world. It is an alienation that Wright himself, not Dreiser, often experienced as a boy and as a man. But it never occurs to Bigger that he can pursue such a dream. Indeed, throughout the book Wright amply documents the prevailing social mores, economic facts, and public sentiments to prove that Bigger's actions, attitudes, and feelings have already been determined by his place in American life. It is understandable for James Baldwin to say of *Native Son* that every Negro has "his private Bigger Thomas living in the skull."[10] Given such a determined state of mind, Bigger would not be tempted to pursue his dreams. Ironically, the racial oppression and injustice in fact enhance his manhood. To Clyde Griffiths, however, the flame of temptation is brighter and more compelling. He is easily caught, and he thrashes about in a hopeless effort to escape the trap. Under these circumstances, "with his enormous urges and his pathetic equipment."[11] as Dreiser once characterized the plight of such an individual in America, there is no way out for Clyde but to plot murder.

The central meaning of *An American Tragedy* thus comes from the economic and social forces that overpower Clyde and finally negate his aspirations. Where a Bigger Thomas before liberation must always remain an uninformed, immature youth, a Clyde Griffiths is the one whose mind is already ingrained with that glorious pattern of success: one must climb the social ladder from lower to middle to upper class. Money is necessarily the barometer of that success. At the beginning of the story Dreiser directly shows how the family's mission work in which Clyde is compelled to take part looks contrary to his dreams. Dreiser at once comments that "his parents looked foolish and less than normal—'cheap' was the word. . . . His life should not be like this. Other boys did not have to do as he did" (*An American Tragedy*, p. 12). A basically sensitive and romantic boy, he cannot help noticing the "handsome automobiles that sped by, the loitering pedestrians moving off to what interests and comforts he could only surmise; the gay pairs of young people, laughing and jesting and the 'kids' staring, all troubled him with a sense of something different, better, more beautiful than his, or rather their life" (p. 10). This scene functions in the story as a great contrast to a similar scene in *Native Son*. Near the beginning Bigger goes to the movies and sees double features. *The Gay Woman,* portraying love and intrigue in upper-class white society, quickly loses his attention, and *Trader Horn,* in which black men and women are dancing in a wild jungle, shows him only life in a remote world. Bigger is thus placed in no man's land; he is only vaguely aware that he is excluded from both worlds. Unlike Wright, however, Dreiser places his hero in **An American Tragedy** at the threshold of success and achievement.

Clyde is also a victim of sexual forces. Early in the story his family is confronted by his older sister Esta's elopement, pregnancy, and desertion. Although Clyde is aware that sex leads to exploitation and misery on the part of the girl, he does not blame the whole problem upon the seducer. This ambivalence in his attitude towards sex has a foreshadowing effect on his own affair with Roberta. For Bigger, sex is merely a biological force and it plays a minor role in his life. For Clyde, however, sex is not only viewed materialistically but weighed in the gradations of the economic and social scale. Clyde is first attracted to the incipient whore, Hortense Briggs, because her eyes remind him of an alcove in the hotel hung with black velvet. To her suggestion that "fellows with money would like to spend it" on her, Clyde boasts: "I could spend a lot more on you than they could" (p. 79). To win her love he must buy her an expensive fur coat beyond his means. Sondra Finchley, his ultimate love, for whom he is forced to sacrifice his second girl friend Roberta, is called "the most adorable feminine *thing* he had seen in all his days" (p. 219, italics added). Dreiser can make us feel what Clyde feels: "Indeed her effect on him was electric—thrilling—arousing in him a curiously stinging sense of what it was to want and not to have—to wish to win and yet to feel, almost agonizingly that he was destined not even to win a glance from her" (pp. 219-20). In short, sex becomes not a romantic force of love but a symbol of material success in the American dream.

Thus Clyde is presented as a helpless victim of society. Characterized by the defense attorneys as "a moral and mental coward," he is not strong enough to oppose the system, nor is he well equipped to transcend his spurious dreams. On the contrary, Bigger in *Native Son* is represented to his disadvantage by the defense attorney. A more convincing argument in that courtroom would have been for the defense to plead insanity rather than to demonstrate that Bigger is a victim of society. Such representation does not occur in Clyde's defense in **An American Tragedy**. Jephson most faithfully equates Clyde's infatuation with Sondra with a "case of the Arabian Nights, of the ensorcelled and the ensorcellor. . . . A case of being bewitched, my poor boy—by beauty, love, wealth, by things that we sometimes think we want very, very much,

and cannot ever have" (p. 681). Dreiser's theme therefore becomes the baffling problem of Justice. Jephson, Dreiser's mouthpiece during the trial, tells Clyde and the court: "Clyde—not that I am condemning you for anything that you cannot help. (After all, you didn't make yourself, did you?)" (p. 675). This pronouncement is later echoed by Clyde's own reflections in the prison:

> Was it not also true (the teaching of the Rev. McMillan—influencing him to that extent at least) that if he had led a better life—had paid more attention to what his mother had said and taught— not gone into that house of prostitution in Kansas City—or pursued Hortense Briggs in the evil way that he had—or after her, Roberta—had been content to work and save, as no doubt most men were—would he not be better off than he now was? But then again, there was the fact or truth of those very strong impulses and desires within himself that were so very, very hard to overcome. (p. 784)

Other naturalists who often show their characters being destroyed by overwhelming forces always remind us how small and helpless human efforts are. "Men were nothings," says Norris towards the end of *The Octopus,* "mere animalcules, mere ephemerides that fluttered and fell and were forgotten between dawn and dusk."[12] Dreiser never does this because he is always seeking the possibility of magnitude and self-determination in human existence. No matter how small and weak a man like Clyde may prove to be, Dreiser never gives up searching for his humanity and individual worth. In an interview in 1921 Dreiser flatly stated his predilection for little men that was to explain his treatment of Clyde Griffiths: "I never can and never want to bring myself to the place where I can ignore the sensitive and seeking individual in his pitiful struggle with nature."[13]

Both Wright and Dreiser are intensely concerned with the forces in society which man must battle for survival. Most naturalist writers are clearly pessimistic determinists who observe that man is destroyed either by competition or submission. And his fate is often death. But Wright stands at the opposite end of this human struggle, for his hero is victorious over the brutal facts of experience. True, Bigger is condemned to die as a murderer, but this defeat is really a triumph for Bigger, who has rejected society's rules and values and established his own. Dreiser, on the other hand, stands between defeat and triumph. If naturalism faces the tension between will and determinism, Dreiser is content to keep the tension unresolved. Despite Clyde's destruction in the end, Dreiser refuses to indict life. Instead he has tenaciously sought its beauty and exaltation till the end.

III

The two novelists' divergent attitudes towards the problem of guilt are reflected in the style and structure of their books. *Native Son* is swift in pace and dramatic in tone, and displays considerable subjectivity, involving the reader in experiences of emotional intensity. The thirties were hard times for whites as well as blacks, and it was not possible to take a calm and objective view of the situation. Wright himself was a victim of the hard times and he could speak from his heart. Moreover, Bigger Thomas is a conscious composite portrait of numerous individual blacks Wright had known in his life. As indicated in "How 'Bigger' Was Born," all of them defied the Jim Crow order, and all of them suffered for their insurgency. "So volatile and tense," Wright observes, "are these relations that if a Negro rebels against rule and taboo, he is lynched and the reason for the lynching is usually called 'rape,' that catchword which has garnered such vile connotations that it can raise a mob anywhere in the South pretty quickly, even today."[14] As in the novel, Wright had lived in a cramped and dirty flat. He had visited many such dwellings as an insurance agent.[15] In Chicago, while working at the South Side Boys' Club, he observed other prototypes of Bigger Thomas—fearful, frustrated, and violent youths who struggled for survival in the worst slum conditions.[16]

The twenties, the background of Dreiser's novel, however, had not of course erupted into the kind of social strife witnessed a decade later. Unlike the hostile racial conflicts dramatized in *Native Son,* what is portrayed in *An American Tragedy* is Clyde Griffiths' mind, which is deeply affected by the hopes and failures of the American dream. A later reviewer of *An American Tragedy* accused Dreiser of scanting, "as all the naturalists do, the element of moral conflict without which no great fiction can be written, for he fobbed the whole wretched business off on that scapegoat of our time, society."[17] But the depiction of such a conflict was not Dreiser's intention for the novel in the first place. Rather the poignancy of Clyde's tragedy comes from his helpless attraction and attachment to the dream which society had created. Dreiser defines this essential American psyche in an essay:

> Our most outstanding phases, of course, are youth, optimism and illusion. These run through everything we do, affect our judgments and passions, our theories of life. As children we should all have had our fill of these, and yet even at this late date and after the late war, which should have taught us much, it is difficult for any of us to overcome them. Still, no one can refuse to admire the youth and optimism of America, however much they may resent its illusion. There is always something so naive about its method of procedure, so human and tolerant at times; so loutish, stubborn and ignorantly insistent at others, as when carpetbag government was forced on the South after the Civil War and Jefferson Davis detained in prison for years after the war was over.[18]

In contrast to Bigger's violent life, Clyde's mind can only be conveyed by a leisurely pace and undramatic tone. Dreiser's approach is basically psychological, and this allows us to sympathize with the character whose principal weakness is ignorance and naiveté. Consequently we become deeply involved with Clyde's fate. Above all, the relative calmness and objectivity in which Clyde's experience is traced stem from a mature vision of the tribulations shared by any of us who have ever dreamed.

The lack of dramatic tone in *An American Tragedy* is also due to change of setting. Dreiser's restless protagonist begins his journey in Kansas City, flees to Chicago, and finally reaches his destiny in upstate New York. In contrast, Wright achieves greater dramatic intensity by observing a strict unity of setting. All of the action in *Native Son* takes place in Chicago, a frightening symbol of disparity and oppression in American life. Wright heightens the conflict and sharpens the division between the two worlds throughout the book. In the beginning, the Thomases' apartment is described as the most abject place imaginable, while the Dalton mansion suggests the white power structure that ravages blacks and destroys their heritage. The conflict is obvious throughout, and the descriptions of the two households present ironic contrasts. Whereas everything at the Thomases' is loud and turbulent, at the Daltons' it is quiet and subdued. But the true nature of the oppressor is later revealed: Mr. Dalton, real estate broker and philanthropist, tries to keep blacks locked in the ghetto and refuses to lower the rents. During the trial, the prosecutor, the press, and the public equally betray the most vocal racial prejudice and hatred. Thus the central action of Book III is for the defense to confront and demolish this wall of injustice before Bigger could be spared his life.

The narrative pattern in *An American Tragedy* is entirely different. Although the novel is divided into three parts as is *Native Son,* Dreiser's division is based upon change of time and characters. Each part has its own complete narrative, and one part follows another with the same character dominating the central scene. Each unit is joined to the other not only by the principal character but by the turn of events that underlies the theme of the novel. Book I begins with Clyde's dreams of success but ends in an accident that forebodes a disaster. This narrative pattern is repeated in Book II, beginning with a portrayal of the luxurious home of Samuel Griffiths in Lycurgus and ending with the murder. Book III opens with a depiction of Cataraqui County, where Clyde is to be tried and executed. Clyde's defense, resting upon the most sympathetic interpretation of his character as a moral and mental coward, clearly indicates the possibility of hope but nonetheless ends on a note of despair. The death of a child caused by an automobile accident at the end of Book I does not make Clyde legally guilty, but his fleeing the scene of the accident makes him morally culpable. This pattern is also repeated at the end of Book II, where he willfully ignores Roberta's screams for help, an act of transgression for which he is tried and punished. Such a narrative pattern is not given to the death of Mary and Bessie in *Native Son,* since one murder is necessarily caused by the other. Despite the fact that Bessie's death is caused by a premeditated murder, Bigger's crime does not raise the same moral issue as does Clyde's.

There are also many other parallels that thread the three parts together in *An American Tragedy.* Esta's seduction and abandonment by a travelling actor earlier in the story foreshadows what happens to Roberta. Clyde's attraction to Hortense Briggs has a great deal in common with his helpless enticement to Sondra Finchley with her beauty and wealth. Roberta and Clyde, in fact, come from similar backgrounds, both trying to extricate themselves from the past in order to realize their dreams of social and economic success. Further more, the entire book is enclosed, in the beginning and in the end, by almost the same vignettes. The novel opens with Clyde and his family preaching in a street of Kansas City at dusk of a summer night and closes with an almost identical scene in San Francisco, with Russell, Clyde's nephew, now taking his place. Dreiser's implication is unmistakable: given the same temperament and circumstance, Russell will grow up to be another Clyde Griffiths and encounter another American tragedy.

Such parallels and ironies not only dominate Dreiser's narrative structure but also constitute the naturalistic detail that characterizes a Zolaesque experimentation. A literary naturalist first establishes a milieu taken from life and, into it, projects characters who then act in accordance with that milieu. In *An American Tragedy,* unlike his earlier novels such as *Sister Carrie,* Dreiser conducts his experiment with the characters not once but twice to prove the process of a natural phenomenon. What underlies the plot development in this novel is Dreiser's constant reminder for us to form our own flashbacks and reflections. In *Native Son,* Wright allows us as little interruption of the action as possible. Unlike *An American Tragedy,* Wright's book has no chapter divisions and only an occasional pause to indicate a transition or change of scene. Before Mary's murder, for example, Wright gives us only three brief glimpses of Bigger's life: his relations with his family, his gang, and his girl friend. Before Roberta's murder, on the other hand, which occurs at the end of Book II, Dreiser provides a comprehensive background of Clyde's life: his relationship with his family including Esta, with all his friends and associates, and with all the girls with whom he has attempted to make friends. Whereas Dreiser's presentation is complete and direct, Wright's is selective and metaphorical.

In *Native Son,* Wright thus differs from the traditional naturalist who piles detail upon detail to gain verisimilitude. He is more akin to his contemporaries like Faulkner and Steinbeck in using the devices of the symbolic novel. He writes with great economy, compressing detail in small space and time; the reader must supply the rest. But his ideas are scarcely misinterpreted, because *Native Son,* as James Baldwin aptly points out, is a protest novel with the author's voice dominating the narrative.[19] Bigger is therefore meant not so much to be a character but to be a symbol, though some critics consider this a confusion in the book.[20] In *An American Tragedy,* the author's voice is relatively absent. In *Sister Carrie,* for example, Dreiser is noted for a lengthy philosophical commentary inserted at every turn of event, as well as for a strong tendency to identify with his characters throughout the

story. But in *An American Tragedy* Dreiser's comments are not only few but short. Despite Clyde's resolution to work hard and steadily once he has reached the luxurious world of the Green-Davidson, Dreiser's comment is devastatingly swift: "The truth was that in this crisis he was as interesting an illustration of the enormous handicaps imposed by ignorance, youth, poverty and fear as one could have found" (p. 384).

In contrast to *Native Son,* Dreiser in *An American Tragedy* also reduces the author's omniscience by relying upon the method of indirect discourse. When Clyde is helplessly trapped between his loyalty to Roberta and his desire for Sondra, the insoluble dilemma is rendered through his dreams involving a savage black dog, snakes, and reptiles. About the possibility of Roberta's accidental murder, Dreiser depicts how Clyde is trying to dismiss the evil thought but at the same time is being enticed to it. His actual plot to murder, suggested by the newspaper article, now thrusts itself forward, as Dreiser says, "psychogenetically, born of his own turbulent, eager and disappointed seeking" (p. 463). This crucial point in Clyde's life is explained in terms of a well-known myth:

> . . . there had now suddenly appeared, as the genie at the accidental rubbing of Aladdin's lamp—as the efrit emerging as smoke from the mystic jar in the net of the fishermen—the very substance of some leering and diabolic wish or wisdom concealed in his own nature, and that now abhorrent and yet compelling, leering and yet intriguing, friendly and yet cruel, offered him a choice between an evil which threatened to destroy him (and against his deepest opposition) and a second evil which, however it might disgust or sear or terrify, still provided for freedom and success and love. (pp. 463-64)

The immediate effect of such a passage for us is to create compassion for the character whose mind is torn between the two forces with which he is incapable of coping. Given Clyde's weaknesses, then, we are more likely to sympathize with than despise such a soul.

On the contrary, Bigger's manhood—which is as crucial a point in his life as Clyde's dilemma in his—is rendered through direct discourse. It is not the narrator's voice but the character's that expresses his inner life—the newly won freedom. His murder of a white girl makes him bold, ridding him of the fear that has hitherto imprisoned him. In the midst of describing Bigger's intoxication over his personal power and pleasure, Wright shifts the tone of the narrative to let Bigger provide a lofty voice of his own. While preparing a ransom note, Bigger utters: "Now, about the money. How much? Yes; make it ten thousand. *Get ten thousand in 5 and 10 bills and put it in a shoe box.* . . . That's good" (*Native Son,* p. 167). Even more remarkable is Bigger's final statement to Max:

> "What I killed for must've been good!" Bigger's voice was full of frenzied anguish. "It must have been good! When a man kills, it's for something. . . . I didn't know I was really alive in this world until I felt things hard enough to kill for 'em. . . . It's the

truth, Mr. Max. I can say it now, 'cause I'm going to die. I know what I'm saying real good and I know how it sounds. But I'm all right. I feel all right when I look at it that way. . . . " (p. 392)

Bigger's utterance, in fact, startles the condescending lawyer. At this climactic moment Max, awe-stricken, "groped for his hat like a blind man" (p. 392). Interestingly enough, Dreiser's presentation of Clyde in the same predicament is given through indirect discourse:

> He walked along the silent street—only to be compelled to pause and lean against a tree—leafless in the winter—so bare and bleak. Clyde's eyes! That look as he sank limply into that terrible chair, his eyes fixed nervously and, as he thought, appealingly and dazedly upon him and the group surrounding him.

> Had he done right? Had his decision before Governor Waltham been truly sound, fair or merciful? Should he have said to him—that perhaps—perhaps—there had been those other influences playing upon him? . . . Was he never to have mental peace again, perhaps? (p. 811)

In contrast to this portrait of Clyde, who is largely unaware of his guilt and his manhood, the final scene of *Native Son* gives the ending its dramatic impact. Despite his crimes and their judgment, Bigger's final utterance elicits from us nothing but understanding and respect for the emerging hero.

IV

The sense of ambiguity created by Dreiser's use of portraits, dreams, and ironies throughout *An American Tragedy* is thus suited to the muddled mind of Clyde Griffiths. Bigger Thomas, however, can hardly be explained in ambivalent terms, for he has opted for the identity of a murderer. Clyde is presented as a victim of the forces over which he has no control, and Dreiser carefully shows that Roberta's murder—the climax of the book—has inevitably resulted from these forces. The principal interest of the novel, centering upon this crime, lies in Clyde's life before the murder and its effect on him. In Book III, Clyde is depicted not merely as a victim of society but more importantly as a victim of his own illusions about life. In the end, then, he still remains an unregenerate character as Dreiser has predicted earlier in the story.

Like Clyde, Bigger in *Native Son* is presented in the beginning as an equally naive character, and his life is largely controlled by fear and hatred. He kills Mary Dalton because he fears his own kindness will be misunderstood. He hates in turn what he fears, and his violence is an expression of this hatred. But unlike Clyde, he has learned through his murders how to exercise his will. Each of the three books in *Native Son* is built on its own climax, and Book III, "Fate," is structured to draw together all the noble achievements of Bigger's life. Significantly enough, each of the changes in Bigger's de-

velopment is also measured by his own language. The difference in characterization between the two protagonists is therefore reflected in the style and structure of the novels. Granted, both writers deal with similar material, but their treatments of a young man's crime and guilt in American society vastly differ in theme as well as in technique.

NOTES

[1] Richard Wright, *Black Boy* (New York: Harper and Row, 1963), p. 274.

[2] Clifton Fadiman, for instance, wrote, "*Native Son* does for the Negro what Theodore Dreiser in *An American Tragedy* did a decade and a half ago for the bewildered, inarticulate American white," *The New Yorker,* 16 (March 2, 1940), 52. Also see Peter Jacks, "A Tragic Novel of Negro Life in America—Richard Wright's Powerful 'Native Son' Brings to Mind Theodore Dreiser's 'American Tragedy,'" *New York Times Book Review,* March 3, 1940, p. 2.

[3] Theodore Dreiser, *Dawn* (New York: Liveright, 1931), p. 586.

[4] Richard Wright, *Native Son* (New York: Harper and Row, 1966), pp. 34-35. Later textual references are to this edition and appear in parentheses.

[5] Theodore Dreiser, *An American Tragedy* (New York: The New American Library, 1964), p. 169. Later textual references are to this edition and appear in parentheses.

[6] Richard Wright, "How 'Bigger' Was Born," in *Native Son,* p. xxvii.

[7] Ibid., p. xxvii.

[8] F. O. Matthiessen, *Dreiser* (New York: William Sloane, 1951), p. 203.

[9] Helen Dreiser, *My Life with Dreiser* (Cleveland: World, 1951), pp. 71-72, 76

[10] James Baldwin, "Many Thousands Gone," in *Notes of a Native Son* (New York: Bantam Books, 1968), p. 33.

[11] Quoted by F. O. Matthiessen in *Dreiser,* p. 189.

[12] Frank Norris, *The Octopus* (Garden City, N.Y.: Doubleday, 1956), p. 343.

[13] Matthiessen, p. 189.

[14] Richard Wright, "How 'Bigger' Was Born," in *Native Son,* p. xii.

[15] See Richard Wright, "The Man Who Went to Chicago," in *Eight Men* (Cleveland: World, 1961), pp. 210-50.

[16] See Richard Wright, "The Negro and Parkway Community House," Chicago, 1943 [a four-page pamphlet].

[17] J. Donald Adams, "Speaking of Books," *New York Times Book Review,* February 16 and April 6, 1958.

[18] Theodore Dreiser, "Some Aspects of Our National Character," in *Hey Rub-A-Dub-Dub* (New York: Boni and Liveright, 1920), p. 24.

[19] Baldwin argues that although this authorial voice records the Negro anger as no Negro before him has ever done, it is also, unhappily, the overwhelming limitation of *Native Son.* What is sacrificed, according to Baldwin, is a necessary dimension to the novel: "the relationship that Negroes bear to one another, that depth of involvement and unspoken recognition of shared experience which creates a way of life . . . it is this climate, common to most Negro protest novels, which has led us all to believe that in Negro life there exists no tradition, no field of manners, no possibility of ritual or intercourse, such as may, for example, sustain the Jew even after he has left his father's house." *Notes of a Native Son,* pp. 26-28.

[20] Edward Margolies, for instance, in *The Art of Richard Wright* (Carbondale: Southern Illinois University Press, 1969), p. 113, observes an inconsistency of tone in Book III, "where the reader feels that Wright, although intellectually committed to Max's views, is more emotionally akin to Bigger's." What Margolies regards as inconsistent might more profitably be interpreted as a thematic juxtaposition of points of view, the personal (Bigger's) and the ideological (Max's), with both of which Wright is sympathetic.

Lee Clark Mitchell (essay date 1989)

SOURCE: "The Psychopoetics of Desire in Dreiser's *American Tragedy,*" in *Determined Fictions: American Literary Naturalism,* Columbia University Press, 1989, pp. 55-74

[*In the following essay, Mitchell examines* An American Tragedy *as a deterministic novel in which repetition forces the characters to submit to events beyond their control.*]

The death of Roberta Alden forms the dramatic crisis of ***An American Tragedy.*** Having journeyed to Big Bittern Lake with the intention of drowning her, Clyde Griffiths recoils from the act itself. Only her impulse to rise up and touch him impels him to strike out in thoughtless resistance, then to rise up himself to her aid in a series of movements that capsize their boat.

> And the left wale of the boat as it turned, striking Roberta on the head as she sank and then rose for the first time, her frantic, contorted face turned to Clyde, who by now had righted himself. For she

was stunned, horror-struck, unintelligible with pain and fear—her lifelong fear of water and drowning and the blow he had so accidentally and all but unconsciously administered.[1]

The scene has a powerful dramatic energy, evoked by a disjointed syntax that masks nonetheless a surprising inconsistency: Roberta's last appearance alive is described quite precisely as only a "first time." Yet nothing can form a first until a second time occurs, when memory is able to create repetition from resemblance. For Roberta to rise to the surface of the lake "for the first time" requires a re-surfacing that does not occur. In a novel replete with repetition, death itself would appear to be the only experience that remains starkly singular.

Two days and as many chapters later, however, another kind of rising does take place when the appropriately named woodsman, John Pole, finally drags Roberta to the water's surface. It is as if this successful repetition of the novel's most critical event was meant to accentuate the special function in this novel of repetition itself—as a narrative resurrection of the past, a kind of recitative "raising of the dead."[2] Indeed, our attention is drawn to the very power of the narrative act through the long delay in providing a referent for the earlier implied repetition. This suspension of repetition's promise denies our common faith in a natural sequence of events by bridging, even effacing the effects of represented time. The referential illusion is subverted, that is, as Roberta surfaces a second time in the text, not the lake—through the immediate re-presentation of a "first time" whose autonomous status is deferred until the woodsman's successful poling.

The idea that repetition might have such a complex effect is profoundly ironic in a novel whose multiple repetitions have seemed to most readers all too excessive, and even whose staunchest admirers have been heard to lament the lack of a ruthless editor.[3] Those same readers have nonetheless occasionally been heard to confess to the sense of "entrapment" so aptly described by Robert Penn Warren: "We live in Clyde's doom, and in the process live our own secret sense of doom which is the backdrop of our favorite dramas of the will."[4] Few, however, have sensed that this feeling is largely an inadvertent response to stylistic excesses they have otherwise shrugged off or scorned. They fail to consider, in other words, that the novel's echoing structure itself is responsible for its "sense of doom," or that the text's determinism largely depends on its multiple recurrences.[5] Given this lack of attention, few have thought to suggest that the repetitions in the novel form an interconnected pattern—that, for instance, the prefigurements and flashbacks which disrupt the narrative help to structure its ironic mode, or that in turn they shape the rhythm by which characters differ from each other and divide from themselves.

PSYCHOLOGICAL DOUBLES

Strangely enough, the lively characterization that everyone acknowledges in Dreiser's novel results from the kind of psychological doubling that few have admitted is important—a doubling more subtle than most have even thought to suspect.[6] Customarily, narratives of the double establish an aura of inevitability by posing alter-egos that deprive the central figures of a sense of agency. *An American Tragedy* presents the double less obviously than such an identification suggests by paradoxically directing attention to what seems to be its most obvious occurrence: Clyde's uneasy relationship with his wealthy, look-alike cousin, Gilbert.[7] The plot of book 2 is generated by the resemblance between the two young men—a resemblance that spurs Samuel Griffiths's initial invitation to visit Lycurgus, Sondra Finchley's later interest in Clyde, and his subsequent rise to social acceptance. Indeed, according to Freud, Gilbert would seem the perfect double for Clyde, the personification of "all those unfulfilled but possible futures to which we still like to cling in phantasy, all those strivings of the ego which adverse external circumstances have crushed, and all our suppressed acts of volition which nourish in us the illusion of Free Will."[8] True as this seems at first, at least for Clyde, the cousins soon discover that the features they share ironically suggest how fully at odds they are. As no more than "manifest" doubles, their physical similarities merely mask far more significant psychological differences.

Their first meeting establishes the contrast between a "soft and vague and fumbling" Clyde and his "dynamic and aggressive" counterpart: "he entered and faced a youth who looked, if anything, smaller and a little older and certainly much colder and shrewder than himself— such a youth, in short, as Clyde would have liked to imagine himself to be."[9] Clyde desires Gilbert's Princeton education, his wealth, and easy assurance, viewing his cousin less as a distinct personality than as a fortunate set of circumstances. Gilbert with a sneer responds likewise to Clyde, dismissing him as a mere interloper raised above his station by the sheer accident of family connections. Still, the very strength of his unexplained resistance to someone who so closely resembles him suggests a fear of the double that is complemented by Clyde's own uneasiness. Each seems the other's alter-ego, as revealed most clearly in the mutually exclusive pattern of their separate inadequacies: Clyde fails to control his conflicting desires by hardening his will; Gilbert fails to escape a will that has grown inflexible and overbearing. For both, the other becomes something like an involuntary repetition, embodying not "strivings of the ego" but what Freud described elsewhere as a return of the repressed.

The strength of that repression is revealed in the depth of their mutual resentment, evident in their parallel efforts to gain revenge upon the other. At a trivial level, Gilbert simply delights in keeping Clyde waiting, perversely delaying his cousin's appearance before him when they are scheduled to meet; Clyde similarly gloats in the knowledge that he has inadvertently disrupted Gilbert's life.[10] Yet behavior is shaped by repression and revenge far more fully than this, as confirmed in the dual plot mo-

tions of book 2: the Griffiths' casual neglect of Clyde encourages his secret dalliance with Roberta, while Sondra later befriends him merely in order to irritate Gilbert. The Griffiths slight Clyde out of nothing other than social embarrassment, hoping thereby to avoid imputations that they share his lower-class origins. He nonetheless keeps reappearing before them in dramatic enactment of a return of the repressed, and finally disrupts their lives more disastrously than even their worst fears had suggested. On the other hand, Sondra intentionally wins the affection of his double against Gilbert's will, and achieves in the process a revenge as well as self-punishment far exceeding her expectations.

Much as the cousins seem doubles of each other, their relationship lacks a daemonic power that is generally considered characteristic of psychological twinning. For that notably absent quality, we need to look elsewhere— most obviously, at the tension between Clyde and Roberta. More than is ever possible with Gilbert, she allows Clyde to project certain aspects of himself onto her—a displacement producing a burden of guilt that shapes their self-defining, self-denying relationship. As Otto Rank first noted, "the most prominent symptom of the forms which the double takes is a powerful consciousness of guilt which forces the hero no longer to accept the responsibility for certain actions of his ego, but to place it upon another ego, a double."[11] The double emerges, in other words, out of a regressive need for self-perfection—a narcissistic process that at once issues from and fosters a disposition toward paranoia. "The literary representations of the double-motif which describe the persecution complex," Rank observed further, "reduce the chief pursuer to the ego itself, the person formerly loved most of all" (74). Little as this description matches Clyde's relationship to Gilbert, it exactly fits his affair with Roberta, an affair that eerily dramatizes the fuller implications of doubling in terms of narcissism and guilt, persecution and pursuit.[12]

Roberta hardly fits a traditional conception of the double, in part because she is so much more distinctively a character in her own right than the fictional avatars imagined by Dostoevsky, Conrad, Melville, and Poe. Still, from Clyde's point of view she comes to seem a "secret sharer," an Other that represents to the self desires at once fulfilled and frustrated. Her tacit identification with him is made through a chronological equation with his physical twin; like Gilbert, she is twenty-three, exactly two years older than Clyde. And because of the opposite sex, their psychological doubling results not from physical similarity, but from a social and economic resemblance. Her parents are virtual carbon-copies of Clyde's, "excellent examples of that native type of Americanism which resists facts and reveres illusion" (249). Both fathers are inept and fog-bound, each one the youngest and least forceful of three sons; and given equally strong wives, both Titus Alden and Asa Griffiths produce children with nearly identical dispositions. Her "warm, imaginative, sensuous temperament" (250) prompts Roberta, like Clyde, to escape a dull life at home, only to grow similarly dissatisfied at work. She too aspires to a better future, revealed in a "wistfulness and wonder" that strikingly resembles Clyde's predominant mood, and her dreams have the force of conviction that he recognizes in himself, as "a kind of self-reliant courage and determination" (246).

Similar circumstances create emotional drives that affect them alike, against their wills.[13] Caught in a whirl of helpless impulse, Clyde looks and speaks "in spite of himself," just as Roberta is "seized with the very virus of ambition and unrest that afflicted him" (247-48, 256). Spurred by loneliness and mutual desire, they can do nothing other than discover their own self-images in the other. Indeed, their first encounter alone at Crum Lake allows them successfully to conjure the other into life. In a canoe, a solitary Clyde pictures Roberta's "bright eyes" and soft face at the same time that, "looking down in the water," she strives to imagine him. Suddenly, they are together: "Almost before he had decided, he was . . . looking up at her, his face lit by the radiance of one who had suddenly . . . realized a dream. And as though he were a pleasant apparition . . . she in turn stood staring down at him, her lips unable to resist" (265). Looked down on by others ever since childhood, uncomfortably stared at from the novel's opening pages (as he will also be through its entire last third), Clyde finds that that condition is momentarily transformed in his surprised confrontation of Roberta. Likewise she, Narcissus-like, with lips "parted in careless inquiry," has discovered a wished-for version of herself in the act of staring up at her. The uncanny embodiment of their imagined longings, the setting on water, and the joining "so intimately" in a ride that prefigures their final trip: all coalesce to suggest a deep psychological kinship.

The lake lends a fluid familiarity to a relationship that can only falter when on land, and their step from the traditional psychological setting of water onto the social shore abruptly changes their new-found ease. Nevertheless, the bond is established, leaving them both unable to think of anything but the other, both acting counter to original intentions. The pressure of psychic need, not considered volition, dictates their first walk together, then their first kiss, and finally sexual consummation. Neither one is able to control a relationship shaped so fully by desire, and at last each "yielded to the other completely. And dreamed thereafter, recklessly and wildly" (307). Now, as if to recover selves so newly and entirely displaced, the lovers separately develop the habit of staring into their bedroom mirrors, attempting to consolidate intention and desire with a self-image the other has helped to create. Two months of mutual self-abandonment have led them finally to depend on each other for a sense of self.

By the time Clyde starts to rise in the social circles of Lycurgus, Roberta has become his alter-ego. Her days and nights repeat his own early experience in town, as his indifference to her repeats society's former neglect of him.[14] Left to her room, she now embodies a part of him-

self rejected and cast out—that part of the ego once "loved most" and, in the usual double pattern, become the pursuer. Roberta's determination quickly grows to equal Clyde's, as the two develop into what seem like opposing fragments of a psychological whole—she expressing what he knows he should feel in the way of honorable obligation.[15] Despite lost love, Clyde cannot break free, which makes it less than ironic that Roberta should find herself pregnant only after both have finally decided to part. The pregnancy now seems not merely a natural result of their sexual union, but a kind of psychosomatic response in which psychic energies have been bonded, with a physical consequence that symbolizes at once a mockery of love and a fulfillment of their relationship. The fetus that is destined never to become a child embodies their inability to create another outside the confines of a joint-self, a life beyond the projected other.

In his resentment of Roberta's demands, Clyde at one point silently exclaims: "Oh, why had he ever been so foolish and weak as to identify himself with her in this intimate way? Just because of a few lonely evenings! Oh, why, why couldn't he have waited and then this other world would have opened up to him just the same? If only he could have waited!" (2:12) Unusual as is this backward view, Clyde characteristically misrepresents his passion, assuming that it had resulted from a mere accident of bad timing and the pressures of loneliness. Yet his words themselves belie the very disavowal he wants to make, in the double meaning they unintentionally but nonetheless clearly convey. His euphemistic circumlocution ("identify himself with her") suggests not simply irritation at himself for having given way to sexual desire, but a larger regret that he could only achieve the assurance of a full identity by "identifying" with Roberta.

Clyde's inability to acknowledge how fully he displaces himself onto Roberta—much like her own inability to admit having projected similar desires onto Clyde—later causes his resentment to become overpowering. He cannot face up to the implications expressed in his fear of direct confrontation: "as he knew, her steady, accusing, horrified, innocent blue eyes would be about as difficult to face as anything in all the world" (2:22). What he does not realize here is that the two of them have become fundamentally one, and that Roberta's increasingly desperate pursuit of him simply reflects the energy of self-abandonment doubled. Rejecting her, in other words, Clyde seems to be rejecting himself. And as if to make the pattern clear, the murderous plan he will finally adopt incites a dream of self-destruction that anticipates his own later death: a nightmare of snakes and beasts that everywhere block his path and prevent his escape.

Perhaps unsurprisingly, therefore, emotional state more than physical events seem to dictate the closing days of book 2, where the estranged pair are reduced to little more than psychological essences. Provoked beyond measure by Roberta's importunate and finally threatening letters, Clyde listens as the "genii of his darkest and weakest side" (2:49) suggests her murder. He feels pressed by "her crass determination to force him in this way" (2:66), and sets about luring her once again to a solitary boat on a deserted lake, where reminders of their first meeting appear in the same cloud shapes, the same fingers trailing in water, the same desultory search for water lilies. Again, that search turns inward and psychological, as the two float aimlessly along in "an insubstantial rowboat upon a purely ideational lake."[16] But now, Clyde's revulsion from Roberta becomes an all-absorbing self-revulsion, as the water seems transformed into an eerie fluid that no longer even reflects their images. Apparently oil or molten glass, it separates them both from the "substantial earth" of customary social identity. "This still dark water seemed to grip Clyde as nothing here or anywhere before this ever had—to change his mood. For once here he seemed to be fairly pulled or lured along into . . . endless space where was no end of anything . . . And the water itself . . . seemed bottomless as he gazed into it" (2:74). Roberta grows ever more shadowy and insubstantial as the scene progresses, while "he seemed to slip away from the reality of all things."

Critics have often observed that Clyde's "murder" of Roberta seems a curious non-action. Despite his reiterated plan to hit her with the camera, the event seems fully deprived of intent by what the narrative describes as a sudden "aboulia" (or "palsy of the will," 2:76). Some claim the murder is self-committed, others that Roberta abets the crime, still others that she kills herself, with Clyde as a mere accessory.[17] Yet while all agree that her death seems the product of forces beyond the individual will, none of the explanations sufficiently reveals the scene's striking inevitability; each one resurrects categories of innocence and guilt that the scene itself radically undercuts. Clyde is *not* in fact innocent from a legal point of view, since a consequence occurs that he had admittedly once intended. As the trial judge explains, the jury must find him "constructively" guilty if it lacks contrary evidence that might prove a change of heart. Likewise, Clyde is implicated from a moral perspective: no matter how his intention may have changed, he did indeed callously fail to swim to her rescue once he realized she was drowning.[18] Legal and moral terms differ, however, which ironically leads to a series of fateful interpretations. Despite the judge's instructions, an appalled jury convicts Clyde for having refused to help Roberta; the Reverend Duncan McMillan, on the other hand, later refuses to encourage the Governor's pardon because he thinks Clyde has "sinned in many ways" (2:392). In each of these cases, the narrative draws attention to the categories by which judgment is made, categories of agency that introduce considerations altogether irrelevant to the novel. Only the reader can know that the scene of Roberta's drowning enacts a death of the double—since other than Clyde, only the reader has been present at the scene itself. The point is that such deaths resist attributions of guilty by inviting a psychological determinist interpretation.

Rank, who argued that the double originated in narcissistic guilt, understood the paradox that "it is nourished by

a powerful fear of death and [yet] creates strong tendencies toward self-punishment, which also imply suicide" (77). Exaggerating his attributes and abilities, Clyde rejects desires that do not fit his ideal, and conveniently transfers onto Roberta what he would otherwise deny in himself; that impulse helps explain why her demands express so effectively his own sense of guilt. The uncanny power of the scene at Big Bittern emerges not in Clyde's hesitant failure to help, or even in Roberta's apparent assistance in her own destruction, but in the silent acknowledgment that he is destroyed in the process of her death. More precisely, he cannot prevent the annihilation of what he cannot see: his own displaced self. Wanting first on the lake to withdraw from Roberta, then impelled by the need to "recapture her," Clyde is consumed by paralysis and ends by not acting at all. Since the demise of the double always destroys the self, Roberta's death becomes Clyde's deathknell. He too dies psychologically, unable thereafter to move beyond that moment, condemned in perpetuity to recall the lake vision, and thereby denied any comfort in even the fragments of a self he might shore against his ruin. The loneliness troubling him before he met Roberta, a loneliness assuaged only in their year-long relationship, significantly returns to plague him only after her watery death.

NARRATIVE REPETITIONS

The principle most clearly apparent in psychological doubling structures the novel throughout. Repetition, that is, distinguishes every other aspect of the characters' lives, including the language used to describe them. Yet no less immediately apparent than the iterative cadences of its prose is the effect of the novel's compulsive representation of scene and event.[19] To begin with, the physical activities that organize the three separate sections of the novel are each mechanically repetitive: bellhops jump up to identical requests for equivalently measly tips in the first book; collars are stamped one-by-one, day-by-day through long stretches of the second; and in the third, Clyde's relationship with Roberta is recounted over and over without variation, first in the woods, then in the courthouse, and finally in prison. The opening and closing scenes of the novel depict street preachers trailed by boys, while the parallel conclusions of books 1 and 2 describe Clyde's panicked flight from "accidents." Stark scenes of death end both these books, both of which nonetheless follow the duration of pregnancy (Esta's first, then Roberta's), suggesting in turn the powerful, ongoing rhythm of biological repetition. Life and death simply repeat themselves while things persist as they have in the past, constraining everyone willy-nilly to recurrences of which they remain unaware.

Yet these examples are far too brief to suggest the complexity of Dreiser's use of scenic repetition. When Esta leaves home in chapter 3, for example, the event is presented twice: synoptically first and then in a detailed rendition of background, motive, and consequence. That narrative pattern of summary, description, and iteration characterizes other episodes as well: Clyde's job at the soda fountain; his deception of his parents; the bellhops' dinner and drunken whorehouse visit; and countless other occasions that lead to the Governor's final refusal to grant a pardon. This stammering technique effectively establishes an aura of inevitability, by making events seem fully concluded from the beginning, before narration has even begun.[20]

Descriptions likewise offer a double view, as if by moving from outside to inside, the narrative can fix the specific context that determines an emotional response. This stress on material contexts, moreover, renders psychology secondary, since it is so dependent upon the world as to seem fully predictable. Well before his resentful impressions are given, for example, Clyde appears to an unnamed street denizen as a beleaguered child; pages prior to the account of his precocious sexual and social development, the bellhop Ratterer leers at a passing blonde. Most major characters—and in particular, Roberta and Sondra—are likewise introduced through a cinematic technique that first pans an outer perspective before zooming in on the private sensibility idiosyncratically shaped by a past. Even settings appear this way, whether the opulent Green-Davidson Hotel (and its bellhop system) or the Lycurgus Griffiths' mansion.[21]

The effects of scenic and descriptive repetition are further compounded by the narrative technique of prolepsis. Indeed, prefigurement and foreshadowing in this novel might best be thought of as anticipatory repetitions that likewise instill a sense of inevitability by linking events in the future to present expectations. The car crash that concludes book 1 has been anticipated by the fur salesman's hypothesis to Hortense Briggs: "But supposin' the next day after you take the coat an automobile runs you down and kills you. Then what?"[22] Squire warns Clyde of the fate of irresponsible bellhops and the warning is literally enacted; similarly, Gilbert cautions him of the consequences of flirting with factory girls, and his prediction is borne out. On their first chance encounter, Roberta asks, "Is it safe?" before stepping into Clyde's canoe—a question that ironically anticipates the event toward which the entire novel is pointing. Even though her hesitation is innocent, it too contributes more than a predictably unsettling atmosphere to the perils implicit in a romance on water. Just as the account of the boating accident is prefigured, so are the possibilities of a trial and a lynch mob.

Repetition, in other words, profoundly characterizes the novel's crucial event, structuring a narrative that looks forward to and repeatedly recalls Roberta's drowning. In the process, the contingency of that scene comes to seem denied, as openness, uncertainty, and possibility are gradually leached from narrative expectation. Prior to her death, Clyde entertains the various alternatives, thereby anticipating risks that will be elaborately described in the event itself. Book 3 then opens with the telephone account to Coroner Heit that initiates a series of recountings, including Mason's explanation to Clyde's landlady, his pointed confrontation of Clyde, and Clyde's

separate descriptions to the lawyers Smillie, Belknap, and Jephson. Later, the actual trial testimony atomizes the event once again, in the process adding aspects unknown to either Clyde or the reader. Witnesses previously absent from the text come forward to testify to their impressions, as Roberta's death increasingly seems beyond Clyde's will, outside the possibility of change or alteration.

Each retelling of the story fixes Clyde more fully in the past, enmeshing him in a drama written by various, incomplete memories—including the reader's own. The trial testimony complicates any true recollection of the incriminating events, compelling some readers to return to book 2 in order to establish the account they have read—even as the later conflicting reports confirm Clyde's inability to do the same. At the end, he has a lonely "feeling in his heart that he was not as guilty as they all seemed to think," but he too is finally impelled to accept his past as no longer his. Repetitions compounding repetition have enabled the community successfully to appropriate Clyde's history, first by co-opting elements of his experience to their limited terms and then by reiterating those elements into a pattern of certainty.

Likewise, the novel's recapitulations and flashbacks put Clyde at the behest of time, and reveal in the process the fundamentally ironic tenor of his life. In the transition between books 1 and 2, for instance, the narrative shifts from Kansas City to Lycurgus, New York, revealing neither the consequences of the automobile accident nor the amount of time that has since elapsed. For the duration of two whole chapters, we know only that Clyde is once again a bellhop, this time in Chicago. Although the next three chapters describe the intervening three years that bring him to Lycurgus, the proleptic narrative structure itself forcloses the realm of contingency. This narrative pattern is predictably repeated in the two days that elapse between books 2 and 3, between Roberta's death and the coroner's notification. More compellingly than in the earlier shift, the novel fills the temporal gap that separates public discovery from private torment by alternating the plot of Clyde's pursuers with that of his escape. Five chapters describe the chase, followed by three depicting his nervous flight, before chapter 9 unites the two plots in Mason's arrest of Clyde.

Time is thoroughly fragmented by this unusually doubling narrative motion, but with an equally unsettling effect: instead of thereby intensifying possibility, it tends paradoxically only to confirm what we know has already happened. Just as Mason at the very beginning of book 3 quickly identifies Clyde, so Samuel Griffiths had announced his nephew's imminent arrival early in book 2; subsequent chapters provide a host of further details, but they cannot generate any tension over a foreclosed future. Both revelations permit an ironic perspective on a Clyde who is already trapped without knowing it; denying suspense to his escapes, they reduce his plight to a sequence of forces.

At a more general level, scenic repetition weaves together the three books. Some critics think they move in terms of cause, effect, and reprise; others, that each one forms an examination into the terms of the preceding.[23] But the three can also be seen as narrative recapitulations of one another, leaving Clyde faced each time with less secure consequences to similar actions. Freud spoke of this pattern as a "compulsion to repeat," and invoked the example of "people all of whose human relationships have the same outcome." According to him, "this 'perpetual recurrence of the same thing' causes us no astonishment when it relates to *active* behavior on the part of the person concerned . . . We are much more impressed by cases where the subject appears to have a *passive* experience, over which he has no influence, but in which he meets with a repetition of the same fatality."[24] Notwithstanding Clyde's intentions to resist sexual entanglement—first with the prostitute, then with Hortense, and lastly with Rita and Roberta—he keeps experiencing similar crises as if they were somehow different. Moreover, he never recognizes what Lycurgus shares with Kansas City, or how Roberta's accident resembles the car crash, or the way so much of his behavior passively, self-destructively repeats itself. "Behind the realm of accident," Richard Lehan observes, "is the realm of causal sequence and inevitability."[25] For the reader, if not for Clyde, the sheer repetition of event exposes that realm.

In thus presenting events, descriptive reiteration delays their course, with the effect once again of calcifying them unalterably in time. No matter how expansive the novel's review of Clyde's growth from twelve to twenty-two, each book focuses tightly upon only a few representative moments. Spanning Esta's pregnancy, for instance, from April to the January car ride, book 1 nonetheless concentrates on the dozen days when Hortense frustrates Clyde. Twice as many months are covered in book 2, which is considerably more than two times as long, but it also concentrates on representative scenes of Clyde's relationship with Roberta—on their June meeting, October consummation, December altercations, and July drowning. Book 3 is nearly as long again and documents the longest period (of nineteen months), but it attends even more narrowly to Clyde's two-month trial and incarceration. Despite the chronologically expansive rhythm of the novel, in other words, the narrative focuses on a series of experiences that seem merely more of the same. Similar episodes recur from scene to scene, book to book, in a process compounded by the narrative's separate recapitulation of the separate events themselves. The cumulative effect of these various repetitions is to brake the plot's onward flow.[26]

This retardation of temporal process grinds down everyone in the novel. In making their actions seem unnaturally slowed by a process beyond their control, it puts them at the behest of forces clearly greater than any individual will. Clyde in particular seems constrained by narrative as well as historical forces precisely because he is caught unaware in moments that figuratively and literally repeat. His perpetually unabated enthusiasm confirms an inability to learn from experience, to master it by recognizing its repetitions and thereby possibly alter-

ing them. Unable to break from a temporal circle that tends to conflate the past with the future, he lacks the simple powers of memory that would allow him to exert intentional control. Only by recognizing the past as past, that is, might Clyde have begun to diverge from it and in the process have defined an alternative to the novel's deterministic pattern.

Against the slowed chronological rhythm of a narrative in which events and scenes endlessly recur, Clyde's obliviousness to recurrence only further imprisons him, condemning him to treat as new what the reader can see is clearly not. In book 1, for instance, he looks ever forward with an eerily frightening enthusiasm as he moves from home to soda fountain to hotel. He never recalls his first job (nor even gives notice of his departure) and forgets his family's plight as easily as Carrie Meeber does her own. Like Carrie as well he looks backs on former relationships only rarely, only out of extreme anxiety. One occasion alone in book 1 prompts any form of reconsideration: his fear that Esta will require money he has saved for Hortense. In book 2, he unreflectively moves from a Chicago hotel lobby to Lycurgus prospects, from Walter Dillard to Rita, then to Roberta and Sondra, all without a backward glance. Myra Griffiths, then Bella, disappear from the novel as easily as they slip from his consciousness.[27]

The death of Roberta therefore has a singular effect on Clyde, since it brings involuntary memory for the first time alive, and does so with a vengeance. The past now begins to assert itself in a dramatically powerful way, and when book 3 compels Clyde to reconstruct his life, he learns to fear the drowning as an episode he will never be allowed to forget. With his lawyers, he is forced to recall one past, on the witness stand to invent another, and in prison to invoke a third (by wildly imagining those who might help him to escape). Earlier, his perspective had been focused exclusively on the future—vague, unrealized, dreamy.[28] Yet the novel turns him not forward, but backward, until hope itself ends with Sondra's final letter: "the last trace of his last dream vanished. Forever" (2:383). Coercing him gradually from his desires, the narrative at last entraps Clyde through the repetitive strategy it has enforced from the beginning.[29]

That strategy even characterizes the double edge of the narrative voice, which identifies with Clyde at one point only to hector him at another. The pattern resembles the narrator's stance toward the unnamed man in "To Build a Fire," except that the hectoring tone disappears in the second half of Dreiser's novel. Donald Pizer concludes that the narrator shifts "from contempt toward compassion" (285), although the narrator expresses no overt sympathy with Clyde's predicament and continues to mock his clear "lack of wit" (2:314). The abatement in narrative bullying, however, marks less a softened perspective toward Clyde than merely growing silence. The omniscient voice slowly disappears, refusing to declaim any more against "all religionists" (20), or "the illusions of youth" (55), or "every primary union between the sexes" (304). It no longer gleefully divulges information clearly unknown to Clyde, as it had earlier revealed the secret of Hortense's lost virginity, of the Green-Davidson's dangerous "influence," and of Sparcer's unsuspected fondlings. That voice fades, moreover, because Clyde's increasingly divided sensibility has displaced the narrator's voice in a gradual shift to free indirect discourse. Looking backward more than ahead, now turned from diminished dreams to the ineluctable consequences of a misspent past, his own double vision keys the narrative with ever greater clarity. Earlier, the narrator confirmed the inevitability of events through a sardonic ironic tone. Now, instead of a narrator's patsy, Clyde is the victim of his own perspective. It is one of the novel's consummate ironies that his characteristic vision emerges most fully and his voice is most clearly heard only as he begins to sense how little his life is finally his own to articulate.

Still, whether at the service of an omniscient voice or of Clyde's, the novel's language is patently as repetitive as everything else about it. Just as characters, events, and descriptions all overlap, so the prose itself divides and doubles, saved from utter fragmentation by a sequence of conjunctions and participial clauses that link separate phrases into parallel structure. Much as this repetitive technique suggests an uninterrupted stream of thought, the description of Clyde's sexual initiation reveals a more telling effect:

> And now, seated here, she had drawn very close to him and touched his hands and finally linked an arm in his and pressing close to him, inquired if he didn't want to see how pretty some of the rooms on the second floor were furnished. And seeing that he was quite alone now . . . and that this girl seemed to lean to him warmly and sympathetically, he allowed himself to be led up that curtained back stair and into a small pink and blue furnished room, while he kept saying to himself that this was an outrageous and dangerous proceeding on his part, and that it might well end in misery for him. . . . And yet he went, and, the door locked behind him . . . (68)

No decision has here been made, as one action leads ineluctably to another in a prose of endlessly linking copulatives (that here ironically matches the subject represented). More generally, that syntactical pattern shapes what Ellen Moers called the novel's "sense of relentless inevitability."[30] Clyde seems deprived of personal control over his life less by events themselves than by the way those events are described. Behavior is dictated not by a conscious, predicating will, but by grammatical forces outside his self. It comes as little surprise, therefore, that the charged moments prior to Roberta's death offer more frequent syntactical repetitions than any other passage. Those moments end, of course, with the very scene in which she rises "for the first time," a scene presented through a grammar that achieves a pitch of willless inevitability.

MAKING ONESELF?

Repetition collapses time and forecloses memory in *An American Tragedy* by dislocating language itself, much

as occurs in "To Build a Fire" and other naturalist texts. But it weaves a special aura of necessity by putting Clyde in a double bind, one where sameness paradoxically ends by yielding difference. Contexts with similar characteristics, calling for apparent consistency of behavior, nonetheless require contradictory responses that challenge the concept of identity itself. Clyde's resemblance to Gilbert prompts both his uncle to offer him a job and Sondra to extend her invitations; yet his fellow-workers and Gilbert shun him because of that very similarity, which in turn leads to his critical misjudgment of assuming an elevated social status. As a Griffiths, Clyde clearly benefits from his uncle's legal advisors; yet because a Griffiths, he cannot submit the obvious plea of insanity that would gain an acquittal. In a novel that relentlessly exposes a life that can only fall as it rises, Clyde finds himself everywhere affirmed yet denied, with a social definition that leads to incompatible consequences. Instead of confirming identity, the repetitions in his life only unsettle it, as desire becomes intertwined with fear, the potentially advantageous with the inherently self-destructive.

Involuntary repetition reverberates with more profound implications than this, however. Whether the repetitions of one's self occur in another, fragmenting the will, or in a series of mirroring others, thus reducing one to part of a set; whether they consist of repeated events and scenes that prove one's helplessness, or of verbal iterations that instill an aura of inevitability: collectively, these shape Clyde's narrative context as a realm of psychological constraint. Yet this series of repetitions more than merely determines him; as others have noted, they seem to make him disappear altogether. Robert Penn Warren has claimed that Clyde "always sought to flee from the self"; Richard Lehan, that he "lacks consciousness"; and Philip Fisher, most radically, that "Clyde has no self to which he might be 'true'."[31] The novel, in other words, deprives Clyde of the kind of coherent, conscious self we customarily assume for each other. Or as Ellen Moers has stated, "the thoughts that pass through Clyde's mind take up, at a guess, about half the wordage of Dreiser's long novel"—but only to establish "the thinness, the accidental indefiniteness of Clyde's consciousness."[32]

These characterizations certainly speak to our overwhelming sense of Clyde, but they also sneak into his narrative world a conception of consciousness denied by the text. Its multiform repetitions void the category of a "self" by revealing how irrelevant anything other than needs and desires are to behavior. Because Clyde lacks a will that might organize the chaos of his inner life, he thereby lacks any semblance of a self. Thus, in denying that he had *intended* to strike Roberta, he is in a way doubly correct (and this despite the fact that he had certainly *desired* her death).[33] At one level, of course, his blow with the camera was unaccompanied by an active intention, which is all that Clyde means in his testimony. But more comprehensively, he seems incapable of any larger intention, of taking a deliberate course of action in the service of a guiding purpose. Lacking the structure of character we usually associate with an independent self, he seems merely a reflexive function of his conflicting desires. Indeed, his desires in some sense cannot ever be consistently mediated, caught as he is between the equal appeals of "pagan" and "religious" realms (5). Neither one ever puts him at ease, a mood characteristically expressed in the repeated construction "And . . . yet." Although he is fully aware of his life, his consciousness itself is curiously thin since unable to stand outside itself, beyond the dictates of the immediate present. Because unable to reflect on the past, or to direct the present, or decide on the future, his consciousness seems little more than a window on desire.

It is the novel's involuntary repetitions that contribute to this reading of Clyde's voided self. Yet no one else is any different—any less self-divided or any more able to order conflicting impulses. Hortense Briggs, for instance, acts like Clyde when she exclaims, "'Oh, what wouldn't I give for a coat like that!' She had not intended at the moment to put the matter so bluntly" (113). Similarly, Roberta misstamps a set of collars and unconsciously encourages Clyde's attention even as she resists the exposure it entails: "in the face of all her very urgent desires she hesitated, for this would take her direct to Clyde and give him the opportunity he was seeking. But, more terrifying, it was giving her the opportunity she was seeking" (275). These are only two among many instances that call responsibility into question, preparing us to ignore that category in such major "accidents" as the automobile crash, Roberta's pregnancy, and the boating scene. In each, Clyde is unfortunate, but he is much like everyone else he meets, whether his family or New York relatives, Kansas City bellhops or bar girls, Lycurgus factory workers or the various participants at his trial. They too respond to events with no greater sense of volition or self, unaware of how much they resemble the character they assume is so different from them.

Responsibility dissipates from the novel via involuntary repetition, largely because consequences loom so much larger than any intentions one may have had. Yet those repetitions have a further, more significant effect in denying that one can choose the kinds of choices one wants to make. Clyde's lawyer, Jephson, comes closest to identifying this dilemma in his courtroom confrontation of Clyde: "And it was because you were a moral and mental coward as I see it, Clyde—not that I am condemning you for anything that you cannot help. (After all, you didn't make yourself, did you?)" (2:268). The issue indeed is one of "making oneself"—of choosing the kind of desires one wants, and thereby taking responsibility for the kinds of actions we can attribute to a self. Because Clyde cannot judge what he wants to do, his actions seem simply impersonal events outside any realm of responsibility. His very inability to resist the things and people that express his longings means he becomes what he "identifies" with, absorbed into the world only somewhat more dramatically than everyone else.[34]

"Clyde" represents a locus of urges whose very repetition increasingly reveals how little responsibility he bears.

Indeed, when desire for Roberta's demise grows so strong as to threaten his moral reflexes, it can only find expression as a voice that somehow speaks through him. The supposed "Efrit" or genie that persuades him to the "way of the lake" arrives "in spite of himself" from a part of consciousness he cannot admit as his own. Consisting as he does of alternating impulses and contradictory desires, the person that is Clyde can only at last fall apart. That means, of course, that descriptions of him also become incoherent. Listen to the depiction of the act that will supposedly define Clyde for the jury, immediately prior to the passage with which this chapter opened:

> And then, as she drew near him, seeking to take his hand in hers and the camera from him in order to put it in the boat, he flinging out at her, but not even then with any intention to do other than free himself of her—her touch—her pleading—consoling sympathy—her presence forever—God!

> Yet (the camera still unconsciously held tight) pushing at her with so much vehemence as not only to strike her lips and nose and chin with it, but to throw her back sidewise toward the left wale which caused the boat to career to the very water's edge. And then he, stirred by her sharp scream . . . rising . . . (2:77)

Instead of actions straightforwardly linked by a simple copulative construction, the events now form a torturous series joined by oppositional conjunctions ("but" and "yet") that keep turning clauses back against one another. As the subject of each of these sentences, Clyde is grammatically overwhelmed by clauses, lost in the shuffling movements of a countermarching prose. He disappears as a coherent, directive force in the very dissipation that occurs in the shift from predicate syntax into an attributive mode. Sentences rely on either participial, infinitive, orappositional constructions that refuse to link Clyde at any given time and place directly with the action. He merely, so it would seem, happens to be in the same vicinity.

When Roberta dies, leaving Clyde bereft of an Other, he is left adrift both psychologically and physically. In fact, the process of the rest of the novel is one of finding in society a literal and figurative place for him. The "tragedy" of the novel (as much as is possible in any naturalist text) is that society finally does succeed in enforcing a coherent "self" upon the body that is his. Roberta's death is accounted for by a trial that constrains his desires and actions within the social construct all construe as "Clyde." That construct may not account for any of the contradictory impulses he feels, but in giving him a past and a (curtailed) future, it serves the community's available categories.[35]

In a world already "in place," with its fixed categories of selfhood, will, and desire, the unfocused energies that constitute Clyde can hardly survive. The problem is a difficult one, in part because *An American Tragedy* consistently questions the efficacy of a will that might coordinate the self's energies. Instead, Clyde finds himself repeatedly acting with repeated others in a narrative that everywhere repeats. Unable to control desire any more than he can constrain repetition, he finally is able to do nothing other than submit to execution. In the deterministic world depicted by Dreiser, life is equivalent to repetition and narrative a matter of "raising the dead." Freedom, itself always singular, lies well beyond the grave.

NOTES

[1] Theodore Dreiser, *An American Tragedy.* 2 vols. (Garden City: Sun Dial Press, 1925), 2:78. Subsequent references to this edition occur directly in the text, with only the second volume indicated by number.

[2] J. Hillis Miller has made this claim for Virginia Woolf's *Mrs. Dalloway,* in *Fiction and Repetition: Seven English Novels* (Cambridge: Harvard UP, 1982), p. 178. Significantly, the raising of Roberta from the lake is also a literary repetition of the recovery of Zenobia's drowned body near the end of Hawthorne's *Blithedale Romance.*

[3] Ironically, Dreiser did in fact omit actual historical recurrences in fictionalizing the 1906 Chester Gillette-Billy Brown murder. As well, he dropped chapters from an early draft that described what he thought was the excessively repetitive background of Clyde's parents.

[4] Robert Penn Warren, *"An American Tragedy,"* *Yale Review* (1962), 52:8.

[5] For one dismissive example, see Charles Thomas Samuels, "Mr. Trilling, Mr. Warren, and *An American Tragedy,*" *Yale Review* (1964), 53:629-40. More sympathetically, Richard Lehan has observed that "as in Zola's novels, Dreiser's fiction takes place in a world of limits, controlled by what Dreiser called the 'equation inevitable.' This is the term Dreiser used to convey his belief in the circularity and repetitiveness of life which stemmed from antagonistic forces canceling each other out." See "American Literary Naturalism: The French Connection," *Nineteenth-Century Fiction* (1984), 38:553. Lehan anticipates some of my observations on repetition in his earlier full-length study, *Theodore Dreiser: His World and His Novels* (Carbondale: Southern Illinois UP, 1969), ch. 10, pp. 142-69. For other explanations of Dreiser's view of life (in terms of his style), see Ellen Moers, *Two Dreisers* (New York: Viking, 1969), p. 204; and Donald Pizer, *The Novels of Theodore Dreiser: A Critical Study* (Minneapolis: U of Minnesota P, 1976), pp. 235, 243, 259.

[6] Readers have not tended to notice how often characters from doubles of Clyde and Roberta, or pursued Robert Penn Warren's observation that even "apparent digressions are really mirrors held up to Clyde's story, in fact to Clyde himself: in this world of mirrors complicity is the common doom" ("American Tragedy," 12).

As in London's "To Build a Fire," repetition has an erosive effect upon identity, making the two lovers disappear in the multiple reflections offered by others. The self's characteristics proliferate, making them no longer characteristically the self's. Among secondary figures, the bellhops at the Green-Davidson; the fellow-boarder, Walter Dillard; the haberdasher, Orrin Short; the prosecutor, Orville W. Mason; the defense attorney, Alvin Belknap; the Reverend Duncan McMillan; and Clyde's nephew, Russell: all repeat characteristics and experiences that Clyde thinks of as uniquely his. Similarly, Roberta is mirrored by Mrs. Elvira Griffiths, Esta Griffiths, Hortense Briggs, even Sondra Finchley. Their varying relationships with Clyde anticipate and repeat each other, despite all his attempts to avoid "the danger of repeating" (303). His and Roberta's doubles end by driving them only closer, into mutual self-annihilation.

For discussion of these other "doubles," see Richard Lehan, *Dreiser,* pp. 153-55; Donald Pizer, *Novels,* pp. 252-53; and Strother B. Purdy "*An American Tragedy* and *L'Etranger,*" *Comparative Literature* (1967), 19:264. René Girard provides a broader context for understanding the dynamics of the novel in his claim: "This disconcerting return of the identical exactly where each believes he is generating difference defines this relationship of the doubles, and it has nothing to do with the *imaginaire*. Doubles are the final result and truth of mimetic desire, a truth seeking acknowledgement but repressed by the principal characters because of their mutual antagonism. The doubles themselves interpret the emergence of the doubles as 'hallucinatory.'" See "The Underground Critic" in *"To Double Business Bound": Essays on Literature, Mimesis, and Anthropology* (Baltimore: Johns Hopkins UP, 1978), p. 41.

[7] Donald Pizer finds this resemblance "one of the few discordant melodramatic devices in the novel," an instance where "melodrama moves in the direction of allegory" (*Novels,* p. 246). Ironically, however, as Richard Lehan points out, Chester Gillette resembled his nephew, Harold Gillette, quite strikingly (*Dreiser,* p. 147; see also p. 163). Lauriat Lane, Jr., first analyzed this relationship in "The Double in *An American Tragedy,*" *Modern Fiction Studies* (1966), 12:213-220.

[8] See "The Uncanny" (1919), p. 41, in *Studies in Parapsychology,* trans. Alix Strachey, *Collected Papers* (New York: Collier Books, 1963). On "manifest" doubles, see Robert Rogers, *A Psychoanalytic Study of the Double in Literature* (Detroit: Wayne State UP, 1970), p. 19; also Ralph Tymms, *Doubles in Literary Psychology* (Cambridge: Harvard UP, 1949); Albert J. Guerard, "Concepts of the Double," in *Stories of the Double,* ed. Guerard (Philadelphia: Lippincott, 1967), and Claire Rosenfield, "The Shadow Within: The Conscious and Unconscious Use of the Double," in *Stories of the Double,* pp. 311-31.

[9] 1:186. The first contrast is made by Gilbert's mother (221), but the judgment is more or less shared (and repeated) by the prostitute Clyde visits (67), Clyde's mother (122), and Roberta (259).

[10] Compare Hortense Briggs' and Rita Dickerman's similar success in delaying Clyde (80, 208), which likewise

suggests a need to control and subdue. In these cases, however, the tactic of delay occurs not because he is Clyde, but because he is any swain to be kept dangling.

[11] Rank goes on to state: "This detached personification of instincts and desires which were once felt to be unacceptable, but which can be satisfied without responsibility in this indirect way, appears in other forms of the theme as a beneficent admonitor . . . who is directly addressed as the 'conscience' of the person." See *The Double: A Psychoanalytic Study* (1925) trans. Harry Tucker, Jr. (Chapel Hill: U of North Carolina P, 1971), p. 76 (also p. 33).

[12] In a footnote, however, Rank resisted describing cross-sexual doubling: "The significance of the pursuer's possibly being of the other sex in the picture of paranoia cannot be discussed here" (74). Irving Howe is nearly alone in having detected this bond between Clyde and Roberta: "The part of him that retains some spontaneous feeling is doubled by Roberta, thereby strengthening one's impression that Clyde and Roberta are halves of an uncompleted self, briefly coming together in a poignant unity." "Afterword," *An American Tragedy* (New York: New American Library, 1964), pp. 824-25. But Howe does not develop this observation. See also Richard Lehan, *Dreiser*, pp. 164-65.

[13] Like the automobile crash and accidental meeting with his uncle that result in Clyde moving to Lycurgus, Roberta arrives in town through a series of similarly fortuitous events: a younger sister's marriage, the closing of the Biltz factory, and Grace Marr's casual invitation.

[14] The sole exception to his consistent blindness occurs when Clyde at one point can "almost see himself in Roberta's place" (369).

[15] Robert Rogers has defined the double as an "opposing self" (*Psychoanalytic Study*, p. 62). In this sense, my reading of Roberta implicitly denies Donald Pizer's claim for her increased "emotional maturity" (*Novels*, p. 258).

[16] 2:70. Ellen Moers not only claims that the world of the novel grows increasingly unreal, but that Big Bittern Lake absorbs all the waters of the novel (*Two Dreisers*, p. 283).

[17] For statements expressing each of these three, see: Robert Elias, *Theodore Dreiser: Apostle of Nature* (1948; rev. ed. Ithaca: Cornell UP, 1970), p. 222; Strother B. Purdy, *"An American Tragedy* and *L'Etranger,"* *Comparative Literature* (1967), 19:257; Paul A. Orlov, "The Subversion of the Self: Anti-Naturalistic Crux in *An American Tragedy,"* *Modern Fiction Studies* (1977), 23:472; Ellen Moers, *Two Dreisers*, p. 285; and Philip Fisher, "Looking Around to See Who I Am: Dreiser's Territory of the Self," *ELH* (Winter 1977), 44:747. Fisher incorporates most of this essay verbatim into *Hard Facts: Setting and Form in the American*

Novel (New York: Oxford UP, 1985), but does not include its last four pages.

[18] Donald Pizer has laid out nicely the legal and moral terms of Clyde's involvement in Roberta's death (*Novels*, pp. 271-72). For a more speculative analysis, see Leo Katz's discussion in *Bad Acts and Guilty Minds*, pp. 201-9. He first compares the case with an account of a man "out driving thinking about how to kill his uncle [and whose] intention to kill his uncle makes him so nervous and excited that he accidentally runs over and kills a pedestrian who happens to be his uncle" (204). Since the man isn't guilty of murder, Katz argues, neither is Clyde. Katz then develops the problem of intention, pointing out that "the act triggering Roberta's death was not merely noncriminal but *commendable*—it was aimed at saving Roberta's life" (206).

[19] This has been partially described by Richard Lehan, "Dreiser's *An American Tragedy,"* *College English* (1963), 25:188, 191; Lehan, *Dreiser*, pp. 164-65; and Donald Pizer, *Novels*, pp. 282-83.

[20] Richard Lehan has further described the novel's structure: "*An American Tragedy* employs the familiar block method with a great mass of accumulated material being arranged into blocks or units, each scene repeating and then anticipating another. Each individual scene parallels the structure of the novel as a whole . . ." Lehan then adds in a footnote: "We spiral down on Clyde, and movement of each scene, as of the novel, is from the general to the particular" (*"An American Tragedy,"* p. 191).

[21] For a description of Dreiser's borrowing from the cinema, see Moers, *Two Dreisers*, p. 232, and Pizer, *Novels*, pp. 286-87.

[22] See p. 117. The car crash is also recalled by Clyde, and by Mason at the trial; see 2:50, 267. Of a somewhat different order of repetition, Mason tells Titus Alden of his daughter's death, reminding us of Clyde asking directions on that same doorstep only weeks before.

[23] See Richard Lehan, *"An American Tragedy,"* p. 191; Donald Pizer, *Novels*, pp. 234-35; and Philip Fisher, "Looking Around," p. 747.

[24] Sigmund Freud, *Beyond the Pleasure Principle* (1920), trans. James Strachey (New York: Norton, 1961), p. 16.

[25] *"An American Tragedy,"* p. 164.

[26] No one, to my knowledge, has commented on the fact that the novel's time scheme is not merely vague, but actually confused—which also has the effect of slowing time. Since days and dates are given at various points, a universal calendar can confirm certain years for the course of the narrative; but there still remain too many vivid internal conflicts. Roberta, for instance, dates one letter to Clyde, "Saturday, June 14th," which places the year of her death as 1919 or 1924 (given the style of

automobiles, the slang, and other identifying details of the period). Yet she dates a letter two weeks later, "Wednesday, June 30th," which occurred only in 1920 and 1926. As well, Clyde's December datebook allows too few days between his Christmas party with Sondra and his meeting with Roberta. The novel's time scheme, in other words, is as fictional is everything else—and this is true whether one attributes the confusion to Dreiser's sloppiness or his deliberate intention (categories that simply reinscribe the novel's concerns back into any critique of it).

[27] Brief exceptions to this general pattern do occur, as when Clyde fears his past will become known, or wonders "What had become of Hortense?", or dwells in Lycurgus on "happier scenes," the "few gay happy days he had enjoyed in Kansas City" (200, 209, 263). Near Big Bittern, he and Roberta will independently recall their walk of a year before. Yet these rare recollections encourage Clyde only once to change his mind, when having first considered running from Roberta—"as in the instance of the slain child in Kansas City—and be heard of nevermore here" (2:13)—he resists flight and steels himself to remain: "No, he could not run away again." Ironically, his one attempt to avoid repetition becomes the major instance in which he courts it.

[28] Clyde had notably attempted to escape the possibility of repetition when he telephoned Roberta during her last month out offear of the evidenciary impact of her letters. The reading of her letters at his trial does in fact convince the jury to convict. By bringing her lonely anguish alive once again, they throw both Clyde and the reader back into an earlier time and thereby make its process seem slowed.

As many critics have remarked, "dream" is repeated over a hundred times, more often than any other word in the novel. See William L. Phillips, "The Imagery of Dreiser's Novels," *PMLA* (1963), 78:580-81; Lehan, *"An American Tragedy,"* p. 189; and Moers, *Two Dreisers,* p. 277.

[29] Haskell M. Block has claimed: "The relentlessness and inevitability of the sequence of events in the courtroom are an analogue on a smaller scale of the coercive movement of the novel as a whole." See *Naturalistic Triptych: The Fictive and the Real in Zola, Mann, and Dreiser* (New York: Random House, 1970), p. 69 (also pp. 71-72). My conclusion disagrees with two of Pizer's judgments: that "the trial is not fictionally repetitious . . . The details therefore contribute to a sense of ironic density rather than to an effect of repetition"; and that "the closing section of *An American Tragedy* is the weakest of the novel" due to its "repetitious detail" (*Novels,* pp. 274, 276).

[30] Moers, *Two Dreisers,* p. 276. Donald Pizer usefully analyzes the prose, but interprets its effect differently (*Novels,* pp. 287-89). See also Lehan, *"An American Tragedy,"* p. 191.

[31] Warren, *"An American Tragedy,"* p. 14; Lehan, *"An American Tragedy,"* p. 190; and Fisher, *Hard Facts,* p. 140.

[32] Moers, *Two Dreisers,* p. 230.

[33] He is, in Harry G. Frankfurt's term, a "wanton." See ch. 1, n. 18. Warwick Wadlington argues a contrary interpretation of Clyde, in identifying the novel with the mode of pathos. "Pathos and Dreiser," *Southern Review* (1971), 7:414.

Leo Katz helps unpack the problem of action by offering hypothetical cases where "the intention that caused the action doesn't really 'explain' the action." As he imagines: "Suppose Clyde's real intention had been to push Roberta to the ground and then to shoot her. He would still have been seized by panic, his hand would still have jerked, Roberta would still have stumbled backwards, the boat would still have careened, and she would still have drowned. Again, by changing his intention, Clyde would not be changing the action that it brings about. Because of this, it makes more sense to say that the actor's action happens to coincide with his intention that then fulfills it. And without such fulfillment, one would be loath to speak of an intentional action" (*Bad Acts and Legal Minds,* pp. 207-8).

[34] Philip Fisher has nicely observed that "Clyde is never intimatelysculpted by his actions. He does not seem to do them. Every decisive event in his life is an accident, a mistake or a confusion. In the existential sense, he does not 'do' his life. For that reason his acts are not essential to who he is" (*Hard Facts,* p. 148). My claim, however, is that no "essential" Clyde exists outside the events of his life. Richard Lehan likewise describes Clyde's "mechanistic" appearance (*"An American Tragedy,"* p. 188), while Ellen Moers outlines "the gradual desubstantiation of Clyde himself" (*Two Dreisers,* p. 280). See Charles Thomas Samuels ("Mr. Trilling," p. 635) for another version of this will-versus-psyche dilemma.

[35] Strother B. Purdy claims that "though society is the villain of both novels, it is also the victor. It organizes chance into something resembling determinism" (*"An American Tragedy,"* p. 264). From a different angle, Warwick Wadlington observes that "pathos is imprisoning, leading to a vision of a series of inescapable, concentric prisons—the self, society, nature" ("Pathos," p. 415).

Joseph K. Davis (essay date 1989)

SOURCE: "The Triumph of Secularism: Theodore Dreiser's *An American Tragedy,*" in *Modern American Fiction: Form and Function,* edited by Thomas Daniel Young, Louisiana State University Press, 1989, pp. 93-117.

[*In the following essay, Davis argues that both Clyde and Roberta are victims of American culture, which cre-*

ates in its citizens an insatiable desire for material things rather than nurturance for their souls.]

In 1900, in his first novel, **Sister Carrie,** Theodore Dreiser shows the impact of the modern city upon the lives of his major characters. Twenty-five years later, in **An American Tragedy,** he broadens his theme to comprehend the influence upon individuals of all aspects of American civilization. **An American Tragedy** is emphatically Dreiser's critique of civilization in the United States.[1] Underscored in this critique is how contemporary American civilization distorts values, twists the patterns of individual growth, and nurtures in the unsuspecting person an excessive desire for things and pleasures. Dreiser's true interests in this 1925 novel, consequently, are less in the personal traits and actions of his two victims, Clyde Griffiths and Roberta Alden, than in their typicality and helplessness before the powerful forces of American society, chief among which is its thorough secularization.[2]

That the outcome of the narrative is genuinely tragic for Roberta Alden and Clyde Griffiths may be debated; that, for Dreiser, American civilization had come to tragedy is absolutely certain. In particular, Dreiser wants his characters to bear witness to the complex of ugly, destructive forces that he himself had come to identify with modern America, specifically those forces generated by religious fundamentalism and the pursuit of money and pleasure. By 1925 Dreiser's own thinking had moved from a narrow focus on the individual in confrontation with a limited urban environment to a larger view of the network of influences and interactions between any typical individual and American civilization. The outcome of Dreiser's changing concerns is **An American Tragedy,** a major work that marks the culmination of his career as a novelist.

The line of development in Dreiser's fiction from 1900 until 1925 has critical impact upon his effort in **An American Tragedy.** In **Sister Carrie, Jennie Gerhardt,** and **The "Genius,"** Dreiser stresses the impact of the new commercial-industrial order upon the lives of his characters. He wishes to show, in particular, how typical people meet the difficulties and the challenges of their environment, specifically the modern secular city. In these initial novels Dreiser's characters exemplify his own experiences and views: they attest to the author's personal conviction that the individual is so situated in this world that he must constantly struggle for existence, even if his efforts are finally unsuccessful and tragic in outcome. The pivotal characteristic of this general theme is the implied quest for some unifying principle of life, even some transcendental force, that suggests a pattern and a meaning inherent in the scheme of things. Thus, the characters evidence a desire to move beyond the secular values of their culture because those values are unable to provide them with such a sense of life's meaning.

Dreiser's personal fascination with the plight of the modern individual led him, between 1911 and 1915, to write two novels toward what he then projected as "A Trilogy of Desire." His central character, Francis Cowperwood, is the ultimate individualist, a tycoon of finance. Yet in working with the materials of the Cowperwood story, Dreiser came to see that a ruthless individualism not only violates the interests of the vast majority but also is inconsistent with what he himself then acknowledged as nature's system of harmony and balance. Dreiser still believed that strength and brute force were ever present in the affairs of men, yet he had come to recognize that Darwin's "survival of the fittest" and the so-called Nietzschean "will to power" express only secondary, not primary, laws of nature. At the end of **The Titan** (1914), Dreiser argues that rapacious, aggressive individualism constitutes an inadequate explanation of human existence, that "even giants are but pygmies" when one surveys life fully and completely.

In the decade between 1915 and 1925, Dreiser turned to exploring the American scene. He came to feel very strongly about what he regarded as the materialistic bias of the urban-industrial civilization then rapidly coming to dominate the United States. Through various public activities, he came to know and to admire such men as Max Eastman and John Reed, with whom he joined forces in denouncing privileged individuals, commercial-industrial trusts, and all similar instances of exploitation of the masses.[3] He also developed a keen interest in the work of Dr. Abraham Brill, prominent psychiatrist and the American translator of Sigmund Freud. Finally, and more significantly for the development of his personal views, Dreiser became attracted to the ideas of Jacques Loeb, whose mechanistic interpretation of human motivation and behavior influenced his thinking.[4] Yet above all, Dreiser determined that the promises of America, the ideals of personal freedom and universal equality, were largely illusions. In his view there was no genuine freedom, real equality, or sustained public morality. Dreiser increasingly professed to see around him outrageous instances of injustice, sham, and hypocrisy, with the average individual everywhere controlled and manipulated by the privileged few. Money was king, Dreiser concluded, and actual conditions for the average citizen were much worse than even he himself had heretofore imagined. In particular, he believed that the possibilities for the healthy development of individuals were far less capable of realization than anyone might think. Thus, in his own investigations of the role society plays in the life of every individual, Dreiser arrived at several rather grim conclusions about American civilization.[5]

His principal conviction at this time was that a society devoted to manufacturing and trade runs contrary to the true needs of its citizens. In the volume of travel and reminiscences, **A Hoosier Holiday** (1916), Dreiser makes his position clear:

> This matter of manufacture and enormous industries is always a fascinating thing to me, and careening along this lake shore [Lake Erie] at breakneck speed, I could not help but marveling at it. It seems

to point so clearly to a lordship in life, a hierarchy of powers, against which the common man is always struggling, but which he never quite overcomes, anywhere. The world is always palavering about the brotherhood of man and the freedom and independence of the individual; yet when you go through a city like Buffalo or Cleveland and see all its energy practically devoted to great factories and corporations and their interests, and when you see the common man, of whom there is so much talk as to his interests and superiority, living in cottages or long streets of flats without a vestige of charm or beauty, his labor fixed in price and his ideas circumscribed in part (else he would never be content with so meager and grimy a world), you can scarcely believe in the equality or even the brotherhood of man, however much you may believe in the sympathy or good intentions of some people.[6]

Then, in 1920, Dreiser published *Hey Rub-A-Dub-Dub,* a collection of essays and sketches growing directly out of his investigations of life in the United States. The basic tenet underlying these pieces is that American civilization has fallen hopelessly into an all-consuming drive for money: "Here in America, by reason of an idealistic Constitution which is largely a work of art and not a workable system, you see a nation dedicated to so-called intellectual and spiritual freedom, but actually devoted with an almost bee-like industry to the gathering and storing and articulation and organization and use of purely material things."[7]Comparing American society with that of the trading Carthaginians and Phoenicians, Dreiser argues that the entire structure of a commercial-industrial civilization is designed for the privileged few at the expense of the mass of its citizens.

In a final, summary essay in *Hey Rub-A-Dub-Dub,* **"Life, Art and America,"** Dreiser characteristically attempts to use his own life as an illustration of what he believes American society does to the average youth. He stresses that the typical individual in America emerges from a naive, optimistic youth to become at maturity quite disillusioned and anxious to imitate secular standards. For Dreiser the fundamental reality of life in the United States is best described in terms of its threatening, even its destructive, manipulation of the unsuspecting average citizen: "The darkest side of democracy, like that of autocracy, is that it permits the magnetic and the cunning and the unscrupulous among the powerful individuals to sway the vast masses of the mob, not so much to their own immediate destruction as to the curtailment of their natural privileges and the ideas which they should be allowed to entertain if they could think at all."[8] Such pointed descriptions of the powers of the urban-industrial order foreshadow the unequal contest between the contemporary American secular city and Dreiser's next fictional character, Clyde Griffiths.

By 1922 Dreiser's views about America were sufficiently clarified for him to begin work in earnest on a novel he had planned for some years. The shape of this projected work was determined by his growing conviction that the average citizen is by and large controlled by his social environment, and Dreiser wanted to construct a story that would set forth precisely how American life in all its various, diverse ways conditions and manipulates its typical members. Especially did he intend to show that the pursuit of money and a narrowly moralistic point of view—both so characteristic to him of the deepest patterns of American life and its essential secularism—are instrumental in destroying the person to whom democracy traditionally guarantees equality and justice. He chose as his principal subject an average individual of poor background and inferior opportunities. Such a person, Dreiser felt, is particularly susceptible to the compulsive forces of modern, urban-industrial society. In an interview in 1921 Dreiser declares his support of such an individual: "I never can and never want to bring myself to the place where I can ignore the sensitive and seeking individual in his pitiful struggle with nature—with his enormous urges and his pathetic equipment."[9]

With that struggle as theme, Dreiser determined also that his fictional narrative would be taken from real life and that it would involve a crime of passion and violence. The nucleus of his novel, he believed, should be an actual story and, preferably, one that was well documented and something of a public drama. Yet the conscious purpose behind this plan was not simply his wish to construct a social diatribe but his deep conviction that crimes of passion and violence are perfectly in keeping with the innercontradictions of American society. Since his newspaper days Dreiser had been keenly interested in the sensational crimes frequently publicized in the press. He often, in fact, clipped out these stories and filed them away. To Dreiser these crimes were basically the same in their general pattern: behind each one were the forces of social pressures—in particular, social aspirations—and the deep yearning for wealth and power.[10]

When he turned to write what eventually became *An American Tragedy,* however, Dreiser had uppermost in his mind not simply the reconstruction of an actual crime but a fictionalized study of the underlying bases for the crime. As in his "Trilogy of Desire," he was intent upon the investigation of circumstances, of social environments, and above all else of character—not upon the presentation of facts of the construction of a true-to-life plot. Throughout this work, Dreiser intended to emphasize how his characters are victims of a social system that by bitter paradox creates them and yet denies them full access to its promises and benefits. Indeed, Dreiser's conceptualization and artistic rendition of characters as victims are similar to what such writers as Dostoevsky, Kafka, and Camus achieve in certain of their novels—namely, the portrayal of an innocent who is thoroughly defined, if not in effect created, by his intimate relationship with an assailant. In Dreiser's mind, the "assailant" is clearly the secularized civilization of modern America.

After examining many actual crimes, Dreiser settled upon the case of Chester Gillette, a young man who had drowned his sweetheart Grace Brown in Big Moose

Lake, in the state of New York, in July, 1906. This particular case seemed perfect for Dreiser's artistic purposes. First, in even the obvious facts of the case the enormous tensions of love and social pressures were clearly evident, and these tensions were exactly the subjective and the objective ingredients Dreiser knew and understood best. Second, the crime had been an international public sensation because the defendant seemingly had no guilty feelings and displayed only cold indifference throughout the lengthy legal proceedings of 1906-1908. A final bonus for Dreiser lay in the fact that fully documented records of the crime and the trial were available in numerous public sources.

Yet the narrative that Dreiser at last produced differs in major ways from the actual Gillette-Brown case. Dreiser well understood that his work was an artistic rendition, not a factual reporting; he constructed an entire first section of the novel largely out of his imagination, giving here a thorough treatment of his hero's family background and early years. Like Dreiser's own, Clyde's formative years are highlighted by narrow religious pietism and conditions of abject poverty. Similarly, Dreiser so alters the drowning of his fictional Grace Brown that legal, perhaps even moral, guilt is almost impossible to prove. The criminal lawyer Clarence Darrow concluded after reading the novel that Clyde Griffiths could never have been convicted in real life on the basis of the evidence given.[11] Finally, Dreiser ends his narrative by means of a short epilogue in which he constructs for the reader a parallel to the opening scenes in Kansas City and the mission work of the Griffiths family. Now in San Francisco, with Esta's natural son Russell in the place of Clyde, the Griffiths are continuing their shabby street singing and preaching. The brief scene projects Dreiser's story into the future, both visually and morally, suggesting that as long as conditions such as those depicted in the novel are allowed to exist, there will be other Clydes and Robertas.

Dreiser completed *An American Tragedy* on November 25, 1925, in time for publication late in December of the same year. Within a year of publication, the novel became a best seller. Book royalties were higher than on any previous Dreiser work. When the motion picture rights were sold, together with various schemes for editions and reprintings, Dreiser found himself financially comfortable for the first time since his days with the Butterick publications twenty years earlier.

An American Tragedy is not, of course, a tragedy in the classical sense of the term. Certainly the narrative does not purport to show the acts of a great man or his fall from a high place.[12] Dreiser originally planned to call his novel *Mirage,* a title suggesting that reality is not all that it appears to be and that life itself is finally impossible to comprehend. The word *American* and the term *tragedy* were later accepted for the particular meanings conveyed: *American* because it defines the action as particularly connected with the culture of the United States, and *tragedy* because it reveals, at least in Dreiser's mind, the far-reaching, cruel nature of the events and acts he wanted to present.

As a work of fiction, however, the story does have a center, and that center is Clyde Griffiths, who carries the burden of Dreiser's message. Dreiser divides his narrative into three books, each of which concentrates on a particular aspect of Clyde's story. Book One treats Clyde's background and early years; Book Two, his activities in Lycurgus, New York, terminating with his participation in the drowning of Roberta Alden; and Book Three, his trial and execution. If the reader occasionally loses sight of Clyde in the mass of details, analyses, and incidental descriptions, Dreiser never allows the narrative itself to deviate long from its theme: the conflict between Clyde and the social and moral forces by which he eventually is destroyed. All elements of the novel are clustered around this conflict. Noticeably absent from the narrative are Dreiser's characteristic authorial interpolations and digressive comments. He was determined that this piece, above all his other novels, would tell its own story.

In Book One, Dreiser establishes in full, clear dimensions the background and the early years of his protagonist, a history much like Dreiser's own. Certainly many of the circumstances of Clyde's early years were all too familiar to Dreiser.[13] Two of these common circumstances shape Clyde's childhood and pervert his natural development: the narrow religious pietism of his parents and the poverty their urban evangelism forces upon them. The opening chapters of *An American Tragedy,* in fact, depict with stark realism the shabby and degrading occupation of Asa Griffiths, characterized by Dreiser as "one of those poorly integrated and correlated organisms, the product of an environment and a religious theory, but with no guiding or mental insight of his own, yet sensitive and therefore highly emotional, and without any practical sense whatsoever."[14] Modeled on a man Dreiser had worked for in Chicago during the 1890s—and no doubt endowed with many of the traits Dreiser identified with his own father—Asa Griffiths operates the Bethel Independent Mission, a hopeless religious enterprise that offers "the Door of Hope" to countless men who are without food or shelter. His wife, who is portrayed with more sympathy by Dreiser, is devoted to her husband's evangelism. Both parents are ignorant, nearly illiterate, and engaged in a futile and unrealistic religious crusade. The effect of such religiosity upon their children is devastating, committing them to a grinding daily existence of poverty, ignorance, and social ostracism.

According to Dreiser, the religious doctrines advanced by Asa and his wife are divorced from reality and thus, especially when combined with the daily hardships the family must endure, have only an adverse influence upon the lives of their children. To the sensitive and observant Clyde, their twelve-year-old son, the religious creed of his parents is devoid of any viable or useful truth. So embittered is he against the conditions that his parents' religion brings upon them all, that when Hester, his sister, runs off with an actor "he could not see that her going was such a calamity, not from the *going* point of view, at any rate" (I, 23).

This religious pietism and accompanying narrow moralism of Clyde's parents, manifest in their every utterance and act, thwart and stunt the boy's development. Dreiser points out again and again how Clyde is alienated from his neighbors and even from youths his own age who live about him. Forced to participate in the daily singing and preaching conducted on the streets of Kansas City, Kansas, Clyde feels humiliated and dishonored before his peers. In great anger he thinks: "His life should not be like this. Other boys did not have to do as he did. He meditated now more determinedly than ever a rebellion by which he would rid himself of the need of going out in this way" (I, 8). Clyde thus rejects the parents as total failures whose religious zeal has forced him to live amid poverty and daily personal humiliations. He has, in his own eyes, been denied the companionship of other young people and the normal social pleasures enjoyed even by the poor. Clyde therefore comes to young manhood badly confused and disoriented, especially with regard to basic questions of right and wrong. Deeply insecure and all too aware of his own social inferiority, he rebels against his parents and their way of life. He sees how the majority live around him, and he wants to be like them. At one point he exclaims, "Oh, the fine clothes, the handsome homes, the watches, rings, pins thatsome boys sported; the dandies many youths of his years already were!" (I, 15). Clyde has learned at an early age to identify success and happiness in this world with the urban-secular way of life—in particular with exterior appearances and the power of money.

In young adulthood Clyde begins to interact with his urban environment, the world of Kansas City. Time and time again, in fact, Dreiser points out how Clyde's surroundings overpower and corrupt him. Sensitive to all that is around him in the city, Clyde recognizes that the conclusions he reached as a youth hold true, that a person's esteem and worth are associated with appearances—with clothes, houses, cars, women—and thus, in essence, with all that money can buy. The menial labor and inferior status of his first job in a drugstore only serve to intensify the bitterness that he feels toward his lot in this world. By chance, he gets a second job as bellboy in the city's most fashionable hotel, where he is daily brought into contact with the other side of life—a world of material opulence and fashion he scarcely dreamed existed. Dreiser emphasizes that this environment operates as a formative influence upon the youth: "And so, of all the influences which might have come to Clyde at this time, either as an aid or an injury to his development, perhaps the most dangerous for him, considering his temperament, was this same Green-Davidson [Hotel], than which no more materially affected or gaudy a realm could have been found anywhere between the two great American mountain ranges" (I, 46).

Not only the luxury and splendor of the hotel but also the other bellboys greatly influence Clyde. Dreiser observes that Clyde "was now daily in contact with a type of youth who, because of his larger experience with the world and with the luxuries and vices of such a life as this, had already been inducted into certain forms of libertinism and vice even which up to this time were entirely foreign to Clyde's knowledge and set him agape with wonder and at first with even a timorous distaste" (I, 53). Quickly accepting the values of these young people, Clyde learns to drink, smoke, curse, steal, and run with slatternly women. "So starved had been Clyde's life up to this time," Dreiser writes, "and so eager was he for almost any form of pleasure, that from the first he listened with all too eager ears to any account of anything that spelled adventure or pleasure" (I, 53). At every turn Clyde finds occasions to curse his parents for depriving him of things that his companions have been given. He feels that he must now race throughout the remainder of his life in an attempt to make up for what his parents and early home environment have denied him.

Beautiful women play an important role in Clyde's newfound life. But when he is in the company of women, Clyde usually falters in his efforts to attract them. As he had in previous novels, Dreiser shows in *An American Tragedy* that a man's yearning for the feminine is a manifestation of his own deep insecurities and alienation. His evaluations of these women are usually faulty. When Clyde, forexample, begins to pursue a girl named Hortense Briggs, Dreiser informs us that Clyde's so-called love for her is in reality only "conscious lust" (I, 101). In his infatuation he is blind to her vain, petty nature. He scrimps and saves to give her presents and to take her to places where she can impress other boys whom she wishes to attract, thus allowing her selfishly and viciously to manipulate him.

The outcome of this first romantic episode serves as the conclusion of Book One and foreshadows Clyde's role in the death of Roberta Alden in Book Two. Returning in an automobile from an excursion in the country, Clyde, Hortense, and four other young people hit a pedestrian. Since the car they are in has been secretly borrowed from the rich employer of the father of one of the boys, they cannot stop and accept their guilt. Pursued by the police, the group are themselves the victims of an accident when their car overturns. Afraid of criminal charges and moralizing parents, Clyde runs away; thus he begins three years of wandering from job to job, after which he settles in Chicago. Dreiser emphasizes that Clyde's action is typical of his nature; he is simply unable to face any personal crisis. Blinded by fear, motivated by the instincts of a cornered animal, and prey to a malevolent environment, Clyde acts without thinking or even clarifying the nature of his dilemma.

Book One of *An American Tragedy* contains, then, not only the most important material for an understanding of Clyde Griffiths but also the most significant statements by Dreiser on his attitude toward his fictive hero. Yet critics often pass too lightly over specific criticisms Dreiser makes of Clyde. While revealing that Clyde is a victim of religious fundamentalism and an ugly environment, characterized by poverty and daily humiliations, Dreiser points out repeatedly that the youth is an especially *willing* victim. Early in the narrative Dreiser remarks that "Clyde was as vain and proud as he was poor" (I, 14). Because of good looks and a sensitive nature, he feels that he is better than most people. When he decides to get a job, for example, his parents suggest various honest types of labor, but he haughtily resents the implication that he is to resign himself to a life of menial employment. His expectations, which are based on personal dreams and not on actual possibilities, constitute for Dreiser the typical American illusion of "unlimited opportunities for all." Dreiser puts the matter this way: "For true to the standard of the American youth, or the general American attitude toward life, he felt himself above the type of labor which was purely manual" (I, 14). Dreiser also criticizes his hero for his contemptuous attitude toward his parents. Although scornful of Asa and his wife for their zealous pietism, Dreiser cannot accept Clyde's total rejection of his parents and his disavowal of all filial obligations. When Clyde spends forty dollars on whiskey and prostitutes, Dreiser offers the comment: "And his mother and sisters and brother at home with scarcely the means to make ends meet" (I, 66). Similarly, when Hester, now deserted by her lover, returns home to have her baby, Clyde must give money to help provide for her. Angered by this additional burden, he complains bitterly that this is "typical of all that seemed to occur in his family. . . . It made him a little sick and resentful" (I, 96). Dreiser never agrees with this attitude, and he shows that Clyde is partly to blame for his misfortunes.

Later in Book One, Dreiser points out that Clyde has no basis for his pretensions and inflated ambitions. Ill prepared for life, without training or education, Clyde possesses badly distorted tastes and values: his "ideas of luxury were in the main . . . extreme and mistaken and gauche—mere wanderings of a repressed and unsatisfied fancy, which as yet had had nothing but imaginings to feed it" (I, 33). At the beginning of Book Two, Dreiser comments: "For to say the truth, Clyde had a soul that was not destined to grow up. He lacked decidedly that mental clarity and inner directing application that in so many permits them to sort out from the facts and avenues of life the particular things that make for their direct advancement" (I, 174). Hence, Dreiser's portrait of Clyde contains a basic ambiguity—namely, presenting him as not only a helpless victim of his environment but also as a free individual who is partly to blame for his selfish and cowardly nature. Clyde's pathetic early years in Kansas City may have largely determined him, but he is nevertheless personally involved in his own nature—in particular, he is involved in his actions, and thus if he is not literally culpable for these actions, he is at least morally responsible for them and what they produce.

Book Two moves the story to Lycurgus, New York, which Dreiser presents as a microcosm of the social and psychological patterns of life in twentieth-century America. Although Dreiser depicts it as a small town, Lycurgus is thoroughly secular and urban.[15] In this second section Dreiser portrays Clyde as being hopelessly involved in the class struggle of the town and forced to contend against its ignorance, prejudice, snobbery, and class values. Again partly a victim of his environment, he is caught between two levels of existence—that of the workers and that of the socially and financially prominent. Dreiser reveals the loneliness, frustration, and demoralization that the opposition of these forces exerts on Clyde. The rigid class stratification in Lycurgus forces him to struggle to better himself in terms of the values and social codes accepted by the people of Lycurgus. Above and behind all standards in the town is the pervasive power of money, both as fact and as symbol, money is the center of the culture of Lycurgus. It is Clyde's efforts to achieve success in terms of the values and codes of the town that lead to his destruction.

When Clyde Griffiths arrives in Lycurgus, he immediately sees that life is structured by visible symbols of status—homes, cars, parties, and the like. Brought to town by his rich uncle Samuel Griffiths, whom he accidentally has met in Chicago, Clyde is from the first an outsider. He has no place in any social group, and he cannot fit into the rigidly class-ordered life of the town. Because of his connections with the rich and powerful Griffiths, he is an object of suspicion and envy among the laboring class with whom he must live and work. Similarly, because of the reluctance of his rich benefactors to associate with him, he is denied entrance into the circle of the ruling elite of the town. In both groups he is an interloper, hopelessly caught between the two social forces.

Despite the fact that he is all but ignored by the Griffiths family, Clyde cannot bring himself to associate with his so-called inferiors: "'What!' he exclaims to himself. 'Mix with people so far below him—a Griffiths—in the social scale here and at the cost of endangering his connections with that important family. Never! It was a great mistake'" (I, 218). Often he stands outside the Griffiths' mansion, to him "the symbol of that height to which by some turn of fate he might still hope to attain. For he had never quite been able to expel from his mind the thought that his future must in some way be identified with the grandeur that was here laid out before him" (I, 309). In the novel the house represents the security and social respectability for which Clyde so desperately yearns. With an impulse close to frenzy, he covets everything that wealth and position represent. Dreiser suggests that Clyde would eagerly sell his soul to the devil for a place in this opulent social order.

Yet such aspirations are never to be realized. Lonely and confused by his ambiguous position in the town, Clyde at last enters into an illicit relationship with Roberta Alden, a working girl in the department he supervises at the Griffiths factory. Recognizing all too well the immense dangers to which he is exposing himself by his union with Roberta, he nevertheless cannot resist, for as Dreiser comments: "His was a disposition easily and often intensely inflamed by the chemistry of sex and the formula of beauty. He could not easily withstand the appeal, let alone the call, of sex" (I, 244).

Dreiser characterizes Roberta Alden as not merely sweet and innocent but also clever and socially ambitious: "And so it was that Roberta, after encountering Clyde and sensing the superior world in which she imagined he moved, and being so taken with the charm of his personality, was seized with the very virus of ambition and unrest that afflicted him" (I, 256). Roberta is drawn to Clyde because she is possessed of the same hopes, because she dreams the same dreams of security and love, of position and happiness, that animate Clyde. Behind her willingness to give herself sexually to Clyde is the firm conviction that he will marry her, a hope that represents for her the pinnacle of happiness and worldly success.

When, however, Clyde is accidentally given a chance to impress the rich Sondra Finchley, he quickly loses interest in Roberta. Earlier at the Griffiths home, where he had first met Sondra, Clyde had identified her with all that he felt to be beautiful, feminine, and socially desirable. Dreiser points out that she is hardly an ideal, describing her, in fact, as "a seeking Aphrodite, eager to prove to any who are sufficiently attractive the destroying power of hercharm" (I, 329). Her social status alone, however, is enough to recommend her to Clyde. Because he flatters her and expresses an idealized affection for her, Sondra permits Clyde to see her. Gradually there develops an unusually strong feeling between the two, and Clyde discovers that at last he has achieved his goal—admittance to the inner circle of Lycurgus society. In the initial stage of his relationship with Sondra, Clyde continues to see Roberta. But when he is eventually faced with a choice, his decision is obvious. Clyde's love can ultimately be focused only on an object that is a part of the society he desires. "For Clyde," explains Dreiser, "although he considered himself to be deeply in love with Roberta, was still not so deeply involved but that a naturally selfish and ambitious and seeking disposition would in this instance stand its ground and master any impulse" (I, 304).

Caught between the mounting demands of the now pregnant Roberta and the dazzling prospect of his hope to marry Sondra, Clyde loses the slight degree of self-possession he has heretofore shown. To him, complete success and great failure are separated only by a narrow margin; he must now take decisive action or all will be forever lost. Dreiser observes that "the mind of Clyde might well have been compared to a small and routed army in full flight before a major one" (II, 40). Thus, when he reads in a local newspaper how a young couple has been drowned in a nearby lake, Clyde sees that the death of Roberta is a possible answer to his dilemma. Dreiser emphasizes that the presence of such a thought in Clyde's mind is a great shock to the youth, and he tries constantly to clear his mind of all such dark schemes. He cannot do so, however, and his inner voice counsels him to action: "Paw—how cowardly—lacking in courage to win the thing that above all things you desire—beauty—wealth—position—the solution of your every material and spiritual desire. And with poverty, commonplace, hard and poor work as the alternative to all this" (II, 51).

From this moment until Roberta Alden is drowned, Dreiser constructs his narrative so that Clyde never fully acknowledges to himself the murderous impulses in his heart. Dreiser cautions that "never once did he honestly, or to put it more accurately, forthrightly and courageously or coldly face the thought of committing so grim a crime" (II, 52). A final ominous warning from Roberta forces Clyde to act. He now resolves to murder Roberta. Taking her to a lake, he rents a boat and the two paddle to the middle of the lake. Even now, however, he cannot execute his plan. When she excitedly comes toward him, he carelessly pushes her, she stumbles, and the boat overturns. Despite her cries for help, Clyde swims to shore, leaving Roberta to drown. Even the most thoughtful reader may find in these circumstances cause to ponder just how guilty Clyde Griffiths finally is of the act of murder.[16]

Book Three presents an even more direct indictment of the society that has produced a Clyde. Here Dreiser stresses how petty politics, self-interest, and the moral laxness of the general system of government prevent a truthful inquiry into the guilt orinnocence of Clyde. Fred Hiet, the county coroner, and Orville Mason, the district attorney, use the crime for their own political and economic advancement. A member of their coterie actually constructs false evidence in order to prove his own abilities as a detective. Jephson and Belknap, the attorneys hired by Samuel Griffiths to defend Clyde, refuse to allow Clyde to tell the truth, since that truth would hardly win the case. Instead, they concoct a fictitious, highly sentimental yarn for Clyde to tell. At every stage of the complicated proceedings, histrionics, local and state politics, mass media, and the public mood are used and manipulated by both sides.

Against the immediate background of lies, distortions, and personal interests, Dreiser places the larger forces of the community and the nation itself. Merchants, politicians, clergymen, and newspapermen use the sensational aspects of the story for personal gain. While Clyde is being tried, magazine stories and pulp-book accounts of the case abound. The business world misses no chance to make money on the criminal proceedings. Even the opening day of the trial itself is depicted by Dreiser as a local event that conveyed "a sense of holiday or festival, with hundreds of farmers, woodmen, traders, entering [town] in Fords and Buicks—farmer wives and husbands—daughters and sons—even infants in arms" (II, 222). The whole affair smacks of travesty and circus. Outside the courtroom are the cries of the barkers: "'Peanuts!' 'Hot dogs!' 'Get the story of Clyde Griffiths, with all the letters of Roberta Alden. Only twenty-five cents!'" (II, 222).

Blended with this materialism is an inflated, false sense by the community members of their own powers of judgment. Inside, the gentlemen of the jury gather to begin hearing testimony: "And with but one exception, all religious, if not moral, and all convinced of Clyde's guilt before ever they sat down, but still because of their almost unanimous conception of themselves as fair and open-minded men, and because they were so interested to sit as jurors in this exciting case, convinced that they could pass fairly and impartially on the facts presented to them" (II, 231). However, the public is incensed at the murder of a seemingly hapless, poor, and innocent girl. Despite their moral obligation to objectivity, the jurors simply must find Clyde guilty. When one juror refuses to vote against Clyde because he personally likes the defending attorneys, the others threaten him with commercial ruin.

Finally, Clyde is found guilty and sentenced to death in the electric chair. Clyde spends his final days in the state prison at Ossining, New York. He is absorbed by fumbling, pathetic attempts to discover the nature of his guilt and to seek the forgiveness of God. According to Dreiser, Clyde's mind has been too thoroughly confused by his past to be able at this point to achieve any inner sense of religious atonement: "Tortured by the need of some mental if not material support in the face of his great danger, Clyde was now doing what every other human in related circumstances invariably does—seeking, and yet in the most indirect and involuteand all but unconscious way, the presence or existence at least of some superhuman or supernatural personality or power that could and would aid him in some way—beginning to veer—however slightly or unconsciously as yet,—toward the personalization and humanization of forces, of which, except in the guise of religion, he had not the faintest conception" (II, 379). Dreiser sees Clyde's attempt to find solace in religion during these final days as a search for "an easy way out."

Dreiser introduces a last note of irony into the story in the person of the Reverend Duncan McMillan, a nonsectarian minister who visits Clyde daily. Hoping to save the soul before the material body is lost, this man of God encourages Clyde to tell his story. McMillan probes more and more into past events, fascinated by the sheer confusion and complexity of Clyde's life. Eventually he becomes convinced that the condemned man, though perhaps not guilty of actual murder, is guilty in the sight of God for the death of Roberta Alden.[17] McMillan's unselfish desire to help the youth to spiritual peace is frustrated by Clyde's inability to understand the fundamentals of right and wrong. With his courage momentarily strengthened by McMillan's sincerity and piety, Clyde appears to develop religious faith. He even issues a written statement to the youth of America, warning them of his error and challenging them to Christian ideals. To McMillan, these professions of Christian belief are dubious, for he understands that genuine religious belief is beyond Clyde's resources. Perhaps this inability of Clyde's to develop sincere religious convictions constitutes the real tragedy of his life. Dreiser sustains this ironic interplay between McMillan and Clyde until the very end. As Clyde prepares to leave his cell for the electric chair, he speaks a final word to his mother: "'Mama, you must believe that I die resigned and content. It won't be hard. God has heard my prayers. He has given me strength and

peace.' But to himself adding: 'Had he?'" (II, 404). This last note of inner doubt is sufficient to convey Dreiser's point that Clyde dies confused, bewildered, and without genuine religious faith. He dies, in fact, much like the cornered animal that he has been from the beginning of the novel.

Any critical analysis of *An American Tragedy* must necessarily offer an interpretation of Clyde's character. The most generally accepted critical evaluation of Clyde holds that he is a weak, amoral, will-less creature whose fate is pathetic rather than tragic because he manifests neither human choice nor human will. Robert Spiller, for example, finds Clyde completely "passive" and therefore concludes that "by removing the only opposition that the individual can supply, the force of his own will for mastery, Dreiser here descends to the lowest possible plane of pure mechanistic determinism."[18] Similarly, F. O. Matthiessen, though more cautious than Spiller, first points out that "a crucial element in our final estimate of this novel is how far he [Dreiser] can enable us to participate in his compassion." Later, after an examination of the novel and of Clyde's role, Matthiessen concludes that "the shallowness of a Clyde prevents his history from everreaching the transfiguration that Dostoevsky dwells upon in the closing pages of *Crime and Punishment.*"[19]

Other critics sympathetic with the basic views of Matthiessen regard the novel as an example of Dreiser's adherence to philosophical naturalism.[20] To some, Dreiser's mechanistic or deterministic assumptions undermine whatever value and meaning he might otherwise have given to the fictional work. Robert Shafer, for one, feels that Dreiser's "difficulty is that his mechanistic naturalism compels him so to select and manipulate facts of experience as to deny, through his narrative, that human life has any meaning or value." Shafer continues, in fact, with the assertion that "precisely for this reason it [the novel] contains no single element of tragedy in any legitimate sense of the word, and it impresses thoughtful readers as a mere sensational newspaper story long drawn out."[21] This problem of the value and meaning of an artistic work that contains elements of philosophical naturalism has also been considered by Charles Walcutt. Writing about *An American Tragedy,* he states:

> And by what right do we call a naturalistic novel tragic, when its premises strip the protagonist of will and ethical responsibility? The answer lies, surely, in the fact that will is not really absent from the naturalistic novel. It is, rather, taken away from the protagonist and the other characters and transferred to the reader and to society at large. The reader acknowledges his own will and responsibility even as he pities the helpless protagonist. But the protagonist is not an automaton: His fall is a tragic spectacle because the reader participates in it and feels that only by a failure of his will and the will of society could it have taken place.

Walcutt also points out that the naturalistic novelist has some personal views that are an important part of his work: "The naturalistic novelist while he portrays with loathing and bitterness the folly and degradation of man is also affirming his hope and his faith, for his unspoken strictures imply an equally unspoken ideal which stimulates and justifies his pejorative attitude toward the world about him."[22]

Thus, for Walcutt, *An American Tragedy* can have positive meaning, even a moral and ethical message. Although its hero, Clyde, is largely passive and not assertive, the world in which he moves, and the world in which his reader moves, may possess both moral order and ethical values. It is therefore the total world of the novel, not a limited approach to the central character, that finally determines the artistic impact. The significance of Clyde's last days, then, needs to be viewed against the larger implications of the novel. And clearly, the power of the narrative suggests that Dreiser has achieved in *An American Tragedy* a credible if not an absorbing rendition of that world.

That the novel itself is actually concerned with what Walcutt terms "unspoken strictures" and that it implies "an equally unspoken ideal" are all-important aspects of its ultimate significance. Arguing some years ago that the work is purposeful and "profoundly moralistic," George F. Whicher comments:

> If such a book as *An American Tragedy* is read as an ordinary novel about an individual hero, it is tedious and practically unreadable. But it is not intended to be so taken. Its subject is not the fortunes of the wretched Clyde Griffiths, but the nature of modern materialism which drives men like sensate particles to their doom. The author of such a work no more looks for special qualities in the individual who illustrates his thesis than a physicist looks for wisdom and self-control in the ions he is observing. Dreiser regards the spectacle of human behavior as the recording angel might view it if he possessed an exceptionally powerful microscope. All distinctions of strong and weak, good and evil, wise and foolish are obliterated by the immensity of the cosmic perspective, and there is no need to focus on a Macbeth or a Lear when any specimen of the race will do as well.[23]

Indeed, Dreiser's fundamental aim in *An American Tragedy* in showing "the nature of modern materialism" is to portray its impact on the typical, if weak, modern individual.

Writing in a similar mood but addressing in particular Book Three of the novel, Karl Heinz Wirzberger, an East German critic, points out that Dreiser's novel is an attack upon the American system.

> We are constantly comparing Mason's fragmentary description with the real facts and come to the realization that not Clyde but the American bourgeoisie should stand trial. It is not a unique case of a youthful murderer that is here being tried before the eyes of the law but rather the failure of an established society which has set the dollar as a measure of value, which constantly infects youth with the poison of an unnatural greed for money and power, without feeling guilty when one of these young people becomes a criminal because his implanted ideals bring his miserable existence to an unsurmountable contrast with reality.[24]

Money and money-oriented patterns of behavior, for Wirzberger (and for Dreiser), are the underlying values and goals of modern American society.

The world of money in twentieth-century America is of course the world of the secular city. To Whicher's and Wirzberger's evaluations, Blanche H. Gelfant adds her critical opinion: "In denying responsibility to the individual Dreiser makes it impossible to condemn him as a moral actor. Yet Dreiser's position is profoundly moralistic, for he is indicting a whole society. . . . His novels carry a mass condemnation for all of modern urban society—for its inequalities that evoke inordinate desires for money; for its spiritual confusion and desolation; for its cultural barrenness and its failure to show man beauty in any form otherthan that of material things. Thus, his real villain is the city itself. It has created Hurstwoods and Carries, Cowperwoods and Witlas, and weaklings like Clyde."[25]

More recently, in *The Novels of Theodore Dreiser*, Donald Pizer argues that in *An American Tragedy* "Dreiser depicts the falseness and destructiveness of such American illusions as the faith in moral abstractions, the implicit virtue of small-town or rural life, and the association of one's noblest dreams with a wealthy girl." Aware of Dreiser's proclivity toward ideas and positions associated with literary naturalism, Pizer demonstrates that "Dreiser's account of Clyde in the opening chapters of *An American Tragedy* is not a doctrinaire study in hereditary and environmental determinism. It is rather a subtle dramatization of the ways in which a distinctive temperament—eager, sensitive, and emotional, yet weak and directionless—interacts with a distinctive social reality which supplies that temperament with both its specific goals and its operative ethic." Pizer's detailed examination of the novel stresses Dreiser's ability to give his readers a

> sense of oneness with a figure who, though weak and ineffectual, desires with a deepening need to be understood. These themes and effects are not coherently related to any single describably tragic theme, either traditional or otherwise. But they and other characteristics of the novel do move us deeply because we sense in them a mature vision of the most poignant strains in the lives of any of us who have ever dreamed. . . . A work which had its origin in Dreiser's fascination with a distinctively American crime now speaks above all to the "mental, physical, and spiritual suffering" which all men have shared.[26]

Pizer's judgment of Dreiser's vision accurately identifies the author's consistent view of the individual as the wistful, suffering creature who must play the central role in the cosmic scheme of existence.

Implicit in this view of the individual, particularly in *An American Tragedy*, is Dreiser's conviction that modern man is thoroughly urbanized and secularized. The essential success of this 1925 novel, in fact, is its dramatization of the typical individual in his quest to discover and to sustain himself by secular standards and values that are hostile to him and his true needs. A passage near the end of the novel well illustrates this theme. Waiting to die in the electric chair, Clyde Griffiths thinks of his early years in Kansas City.

> He had longed for so much there in Kansas City and he had had so little. Things—just things—had seemed so very important to him—and he had so resented being taken out on the street as he had been, before all the other boys and girls, many of whom had all the things that he so craved, and when he would have been glad to have been anywhere else in the world than out there—on the street! That mission life that to his mother was so wonderful, yet to him, sodreary! . . . She would never understand his craving for ease and luxury, for beauty, for love—his particular kind of love that went with show, pleasure, wealth, position, his eager and immutable aspirations and desires. She would not understand these things. (II, 401)

If we find it difficult to sympathize with Clyde in his moment of self-pity, we cannot fail to appreciate the deep import of his words. They reveal the terms of his true dilemma; namely, "his craving for ease and luxury, for beauty, for love." Thoroughly conditioned and compelled by desire, Clyde is Dreiser's exemplification of what any secular-urban citizen may become.

Writing of Dreiser's characters in general, David Weimer renders a critical judgment especially indicative of Clyde Griffiths' status: "Dreiser's individual is always at bottom adrift in the metropolis. He can only salvage some part of what he is born with, his emotive nature, and hope to give it spasmodic expression. His desire is not to be self-reliant but to be free; not to fulfill himself through adventure, in the manner of the Romantic hero, but to preserve some passional identity."[27] Clyde cannot achieve, much less preserve, a "passional identity," because he required a creative framework in which to develop. He earlier needed, as a child in Kansas City, purposeful traditions and familial security and love. In his quest for that of which he senses he has been deprived, he finds only the illusory promises of the city: the fake standard that appearance is reality; the proposition that success and money will bring true happiness; and, perhaps quite crucial for Clyde, the compulsive desire to indulge constantly in pleasure. In his analysis of *An American Tragedy*, Robert Penn Warren says of Clyde: "His 'tragedy' is that of namelessness, and this is one aspect of its being an American tragedy, the story of the individual without identity, whose responsible self has been absorbed by the great machine of modern industrial secularized society, and reduced to a cog, a cipher, an abstraction."[28]

Not surprisingly, Clyde ends his life hapless and bewildered, although still possessed by the early desires born in him long ago in Kansas City. He never understands why his pursuit of the golden images of the Green-Davidson Hotel and of the rich Sondra Finchley have failed. He cannot grasp why his life has so soon come to grief, to despair, and to death in the electric chair.

The significance of the story of Clyde Griffiths, however, lies finally in Dreiser's novel as decisive comment on the patterns of America's new commercial-industrial civilization. In unmistakable ways Dreiser shows that twentieth-century attitudes, values, and life-styles result from an urbanized, secularized world view that has displaced an older way of life. Entirely modern in temperament and character, Clyde Griffiths eagerly conforms to urban values and standards, hoping there-by to overcome his deep insecurity and sense of meaninglessness. Empty of beliefs and devoid of the personal means of generating convictions, he is a vessel to befilled by whatever means and for whatever ends the secular-urban world dictates. His life and death suggest conclusively Dreiser's view that modern American civilization is in decline. Expressed another way, Dreiser contends that key American institutions—family, religion, education, government—are not capable of supporting and assisting the average individual in either informing and gratifying his basic needs or providing him with satisfying, creative life roles.

In a broadly defined way, the enduring value of *An American Tragedy* can only be determined against the truth or the falseness of Dreiser's depiction of American civilization in this century. A nineteenth-century realist in artistic approach and conviction, Dreiser has created a novel that represents the way people live and how they confront the world in which they live. Dreiser emphasizes neither the rational nor the irrational in his characters, neither the good nor the bad in their behavior. Perhaps unfortunately for Dreiser, as for other realists, this honest, faithful accommodation to perceived conditions does not result from a new vision of man and his world. Still, the portraits and stories of American life captured by Dreiser's realism contain informative, even highly valuable, examples that are meaningful today.

An observation of the American literary critic and comparist Harry Levin suggests an approach to evaluating the continuing importance of realistic novels such as *An American Tragedy*. Although writing about myth, he speaks thoughtfully about the redeeming value of "a fiction": "Now there are two ways of looking at a fiction: we can consider it as a deviation from fact or as an approximation to fact. Fact is always the criterion; and when the facts are under control, we emphasize the degree of deviation; but when we are out of touch with the facts, we utilize fiction to explain the unexplainable by some sort of approximation to it."[29] Dreiser's secular city, with its devastating influence on the individual, is his dominant image of society—a society that had become, for Dreiser, one of those that, in Levin's phrase, is "out of touch with the facts." In using Levin's comment, then, to suggest an approach for evaluation of Dreiser's *An American Tragedy,* the question to ask is simply this:

Did Dreiser have the facts under control, and did he give in this novel a proper approximation to them? If the answer is yes, today's readers and critics need to look very carefully at the fabric, condition, and future of civilization in the United States.

NOTES

[1] The notable critics of Dreiser's fiction agree on this point. See, for example, the treatments of the novel by the following authors: Dorothy Dudley, *Forgotten Frontiers: Dreiser and the Land of the Free* (New York, 1932); Robert H. Elias, *Theodore Dreiser: Apostle of Nature* (New York, 1949); Philip L. Gerber, *Theodore Dreiser* (New York, 1965); Richard Lehan, *Theodore Dreiser: His World and His Novels* (Carbondale, 1969); Francis O. Matthiessen, *Theodore Dreiser* (New York, 1951); John J. McAleer, *Theodore Dreiser* (New York, 1968); Ellen Moers, *Two Dreisers: The Man and the Novelist as Revealed in His Two Most Important Works* (New York, 1966); Donald Pizer, *The Novels of Theodore Dreiser* (Minneapolis, 1976); W. A. Swanberg, *Dreiser* (New York, 1965); Charles Shapiro, *Theodore Dreiser: Our Bitter Patriot* (Carbondale, 1962); Robert Penn Warren, *Homage to Theodore Dreiser on the Centennial of His Birth* (New York, 1971); Karl Heinz Wirzberger, *Die Romane Theodore Dreisers* (Berlin, 1955).

[2] The use throughout of *secular* and *secularization* follows the American theologian Harvey Cox. *Secular* (from the Latin *saeculum*) denotes "this present age," that which is entirely contemporary. *Secularization* denotes, in Cox's words, "the liberation of man from religious and metaphysical tutelage, the turning of his attention away from other worlds and toward this one." See Harvey Cox, *The Secular City* (Rev. ed.; New York, 1966), 1, 15.

[3] See Swanberg, *Dreiser*, 180-233.

[4] See Moers, *Two Dreisers*, 240-70, and Pizer, *The Novels of Theodore Dreiser*, 206, 212-13.

[5] Dreiser's conclusions about American civilization are really part of that larger, better-known disenchantment with Western civilization widely in evidence following World War I and perhaps typified by the volume edited by Harold Stearns and others, *Civilization in the United States* (New York, 1922)

[6] Theodore Dreiser, *A Hoosier Holiday* (New York, 1916), 180.

[7] Theodore Dreiser, *Hey Rub-A-Dub-Dub: A Book of the Mystery and Wonder and Terror of Life* (New York, 1920), 258.

[8] *Ibid.*, 257.

[9] Dudley, *Forgotten Frontiers*, 407.

[10] Dreiser's interest in crimes of violence and passion may be seen in a play he wrote in 1916, *The Hand of the Potter*, the theme and central character of which foreshadow Clyde Griffiths and his story. Isadore Berchansky, son of poor, ignorant New York immigrants, is a sickly youth with a perverted desire for young girls. After sexually attacking an eleven-year-old girl, he is tracked down, tried, and convicted. Dreiser's play argues, however, that Berchansky is not a criminal, but merely a very sick individual, and that society itself is to blame for his condition because of the awful urban slums that create him and the cruel laws that arrogate his punishment.

[11] Elias, *Theodore Dreiser*, 222.

[12] From 1926 until the present, critics have debated Dreiser's use of the term *tragedy*. Good discussions may be found in Matthiessen, *Theodore Dreiser*, 207-209; Warren, *Homage to Theodore Dreiser*, 131-32; and Pizer, *The Novels of Theodore Dreiser*, 280-81.

[13] See Elias, *Theodore Dreiser*, 222, and Warren, *Homage to Theodore Dreiser*, 102-12.

[14] Theodore Dreiser, *An American Tragedy* (2 vols.; New York, 1926), I, 10. Subsequent references to the novel are to this edition and will appear in the text.

[15] Warren, *Homage to Theodore Dreiser*, 101.

[16] Critics do not agree on the fact or the degree of Clyde's guilt or innocence. In *Theodore Dreiser*, for example, Lehan thinks that "Clyde is really innocent of murdering Roberta," since he strikes her unintentionally (168). In *Theodore Dreiser*, McAleer sees Clyde as not guilty legally of the specific crime of which he is convicted (144). Gerber, however, in *Theodore Dreiser*, points to "the idea of the distribution of guilt," which he feels Dreiser writes into the narrative (144-47). Warren, in *Homage to Theodore Dreiser*, first alluding to "shadowy complicities" in the world in which Clyde acts, stresses the theme of "ambiguity—of complicity and responsibility" as Dreiser's basic message, not the emphatic either-or literality of guilt or innocence (123-25).

[17] Warren takes exception to several interpretations of McMillan, rejecting Lehan's view that the minister is a bigot. In a lengthy note cited for page 137 of the text of *Homage to Theodore Dreiser* and appearing on pages 159-66, Warren argues that Dreiser's intention, and thus the meaning of McMillan in the novel, is to show the minister as "a man committed to absolutes but doomed to live in a world of complex definitions and shadowy ambiguities" (163).

[18] Robert E. Spiller, "Theodore Dreiser," in Spiller *et al.* (eds.), *Literary History of the United States* (3rd ed. rev.; New York, 1963), 1203.

[19] Matthiessen, *Theodore Dreiser*, 205, 210.

[20] It is interesting today to read Stuart P. Sherman's notable attack on Dreiser—"The Barbaric Naturalism of

Mr. Dreiser," *Nation,* CI (December, 1915), 648-51—and then to read his very positive later estimation, centered on *An American Tragedy*—"Mr. Dreiser in Tragic Realism," in Sherman, *The Main Stream* (New York, 1927), 134-44.

[21] Robert Shafer, "*An American Tragedy:* A Humanistic Demurer," in Alfred Kazin and Charles Shapiro (eds.), *The Stature of Theodore Dreiser* (Bloomington, 1955), 124.

[22] Charles E. Walcutt, *American Literary Naturalism: A DividedStream* (Minneapolis, 1956), 27, 29.

[23] George F. Whicher, "The Twentieth Century," in Arthur Hobson Quinn (ed.), *Literature of the American People* (New York, 1931), 850.

[24] Wirzberger, *Die Romane Theodore Dreisers*, 188-89.

[25] Blanche H. Gelfant, "Theodore Dreiser: The Portrait Novel," in Gelfant, *The American City Novel* (Norman, 1955), 88-89.

[26] Pizer, *The Novels of Theodore Dreiser*, 218, 240, 281.

[27] David R. Weimer, "Heathen Catacombs: Theodore Dreiser," in Weimer, *The City as Metaphor* (New York, 1966), 75-76.

[28] Warren, *Homage to Theodore Dreiser*, 129.

[29] Harry Levin, "Some Meanings of Myth," *Daedalus,* LXXXVIII (Spring, 1959), 225.

Sally Day Trigg (essay date 1990)

SOURCE: "Theodore Dreiser and the Criminal Justice System in *An American Tragedy*," in *Studies in the Novel*, Vol. 22, No. 4, Winter, 1990, pp. 429-40.

[*In the following essay, Trigg examines Dreiser's portrayal of the American criminal justice system as inherently unfair in* An American Tragedy.]

At the end of Book Two of *An American Tragedy*, the central character, Clyde, and we, the readers, feel a sense of completion. For over 500 pages (1948 edition) Clyde's life has built to the event that caps Book Two: the drowning (maybe murder) of Roberta. Theodore Dreiser has taken the reader through all the stages of Clyde's "education": his youth in an evangelical family, his years as a bellhop learning the values of that materialistic group, his slow ascent into management in his uncle's collar factory, his intimate relationship and gradual boredom with Roberta, his involvement with Lycurgus society, and his love for the rich Sondra. And then there is the discovery of Roberta's pregnancy and Clyde's plot to drown her, ending in their trip to a lonely lake and Roberta's (maybe accidental) drowning. The events of Clyde's life seem to hurtle one after the other, culminating in his efforts to murder. When Roberta drowns and Clyde hauls himself on shore, the reader senses an ending, a climax.

Yet the book continues for over 300 more pages, detailing the investigation of the murder, Clyde's capture, the trial, and Clyde's final days on Death Row awaiting execution. Robert Penn Warren points out that some readers have found this split in thenarrative to be "a grave flaw in the structure."[1] The account of the trial is exhaustive. Opening and closing arguments are reproduced word for word, as are numerous letters presented in evidence. As F. O. Matthiessen states, "For some readers interest breaks down under the sheer weight of details."[2] Yet these details serve a purpose: they show the "remorseless web of events in which Clyde was caught."[3]

In Books One and Two Dreiser explores the influences and internal characteristics that shaped Clyde and the directions his life takes in response to these forces. In Book Three Dreiser details the response of society to Clyde's actions. And in his mountains of specifics Dreiser not only describes, he condemns. His target is the American criminal justice system. Dreiser points out the inherent injustice of its underlying structures: the win-lose system of courtroom adversaries, the use of juries to determine guilt, and the assumption of criminal law that the defendant determines his own actions. But Dreiser does not stop with the mechanisms of the criminal system; he also explores the other social forces intertwined with this system that heighten its unfairness: the courtroom participants intent on political gain and the Press that sensationalizes the case, convicting Clyde before the first minute of his trial. And finally, Dreiser saves his strongest criticism for the death penalty and the harrowing psychological torture of Death Row.

The goal of the ideal trial is to accurately determine the facts of an event so that a fact-finder can decide if the actions of an individual fulfill the requirements of a statute. Yet Dreiser points out that the structure used to "objectively" discover these facts often results in inaccuracy and distortion. The adversarial system accents winning, not objective fact determination. In their drive to win, not to depict facts accurately, the lawyers on each side think nothing of fabricating evidence or withholding it from the opposition. The DA's assistant, Burton Burleigh, is disappointed that the camera the police fish from the lake of the murder, a camera Clyde allegedly used to strike Roberta, contains no blood, so he weaves two of Roberta's hairs into the mechanism. And the District Attorney, Orville Mason, fails to disclose to the defense the incriminating camera and much other evidence, including a card from Clyde in Roberta's trunk and a witness who heard Roberta's last cries.

The accent on winning affects not only the existence and availability of evidence, but also the way in which the evidence is presented in court. Dreiser describes how the adversarial system encourages the parties to portray the disputed acts to reflect favorably on their argument, not to show how the event actually occurred, always overstating and exaggerating to balance the overblown claims of the opposition. In his opening address Mason paints Clyde as a black-hearted monster. He focuses not on the crime, but on what he knows will sway the jury: Clyde's sexual relationship with Roberta, what he calls in his opening address"'the secret and intended and immoral and illegal and socially unwarranted and condemned use of her body outside the regenerative and ennobling pale of matrimony!'"[4] Mason depicts Clyde as "a murderer of the coldest and blackest type," (26:791) "'a wolf'" (20:696). As Clyde listens to Mason's opening argument, he notes "how much of exaggeration and unfairness was in all this" (20:694).

And it is not only the prosecution who exaggerates. To counteract the black picture Mason paints, Clyde's lawyers fabricate a completely false defense that represents Clyde more positively than do the actual facts. In his opening argument, Alvin Belknap, Clyde's attorney, denies that Clyde plotted to murder and describes Clyde as "'clean and energetic and blameless and innocent'" (23:717). Even Clyde is "a little amazed by this frank program of trickery and deception on his behalf" (15:653). But does not this two-sided exaggeration cancel itself out? Do not the facts emerge in the balance? Unfortunately, what usually emerges is the personalities of the adversaries, not the facts. In this contest atmosphere, the trial becomes focused on the drama in the courtroom and on the performances of the players—the lawyers. Who seems the most sincere, the most genuine? Who seems to believe what he claims? The jury believes the attorney who argues the most vehemently, the one who seems the most personally involved. And this quality of authenticity depends far more on their personal responses to Clyde and to the crime than on any rational determination of fact.

Dreiser contrasts the prosecution and the defense in their reaction to Clyde. Mason hates Clyde before he sees him because of biases arising from Mason's background. He resents Clyde's connections with wealth. Coming from a childhood of poverty much like that of Roberta, Mason "look[s] on those with whom life had dealt more kindly as too favorably treated" (3:546). To him the rich are "wretched" and "indifferent" (4:559). And he hates Clyde's good looks and easy way with women. Rendered unattractive by a broken nose, Mason avoided women as a young man, gaining what Dreiser calls "a psychic sex scar" (3:547). What Mason sees as Clyde's "sly, evil seduction" (4:560) of Roberta plays as prominent a part in his "enormous personal hatred for the man" (5:562) as does the murder. And Mason, raised in a rural area, considers city folk like Clyde inherently suspicious. Even before meeting Clyde he desires revenge against him. Dreiser describes Mason's perception: "born . . . of religion, convention and a general rural suspicion of all urban life . . . and . . . its ungodly ways, there sprang into his mind the thought of a city seducer and betrayer . . . The scoundrel! The raper! The murderer!" (4:556).

In all his contacts with Clyde, Mason harries him, treating him with contempt and coercion from their first encounter. When Clyde is captured, Mason approaches him like "an angry wasp or hornet" (9:603). Mason badgers Clyde into admitting his connection with Roberta, shifting from aggression to persuasion to threat to elicit the statement he wants, During his cross examination of Clyde,Mason's mood is "that of a restless harrier anxious to be off at the heels of its prey—of a foxhound within the last leap of its kill" (25:756). His manner is "snarling, punitive, sinister, bitterly sarcastic" (25:783).

As with Mason, Belknap's reaction to Clyde is based on individual attitudes originating in Belknap's background. Belknap's response, however, is sympathy, not hatred. Like Clyde, in his youth Belknap also seduced a girl he did not love who became pregnant. Yet, with the help of his father and his father's money, he extricated himself from the situation. He sees Clyde as "emotionally betrayed or bewitched" (14:640). Dreiser portrays Belknap as "capable of grasping any reasonable moral or social complication" because the "sex-inhibitions and sex-longings" of someone like Mason have been dealt with and absorbed (14:639). Belknap's argument defending Clyde's decision not to marry Roberta echoes an idea central to Dreiser's philosophy: a forced marriage without love in which the spouses "hate and despise and torture each other forever after" is a greater sin than unwed motherhood (23:721). Instead of hating Clyde, Belknap "felt intensely sorry for him" (14:641). Yet Belknap cannot totally convince himself of Clyde's innocence and so lacks the force of the single-minded Mason.

Reuben Jephson, Belknap's partner, emerges as a more effective attorney than Belknap because he does not apply his individual attitudes to Clyde and is unconcerned about his guilt. As Clyde observes, "he was so shrewd and practical, so very direct and chill and indifferent and yet confidence-inspiring, quite like an uncontrollable machine of a kind which generates power" (15:654). It is to Jephson's eyes that Clyde turns for strength when he is on the witness stand. And Jephson is the one who fabricates Clyde's false defense. Jephson lacks *any* moral judgment; to him the courtroom is a giant, fascinating game.

Or maybe it is a stage. It is the performances of the lawyers that determine which side wins. Dreiser describes Mason's performance in the District Attorney's opening argument: "it was as if some one had suddenly exclaimed: 'Lights! Camera!'" (20:689). He turns "dramatically" toward Clyde, pointing his finger at him as he accuses him of murder, and the audience "crowd[s] and lean[s] forward, hungry and thirsty for every word he should utter" (20:690). Mason intends drama "in connection with every point in [the] trial" (21:701). He repeatedly reads the most dramatic evidence: Roberta's emotional letters to Clyde pleading with him to marry her soon. And as Mason movingly reads the letters, "the moist eyes and the handkerchiefs and the coughs in the audience and among the jurors attested their import"

(22:712). After Mason's closing argument, even Clyde believes that "no jury such as this was like to acquit him in the face of evidence so artfully and movingly recapitulated" (26:791).

So the verdict depends on the performance ability of the lawyers as much as on the facts. But the best lawyers are not free. Even in this day of public defenders, a top quality lawyer usually costs money, and lots of it. In Clyde's case, Samuel Griffiths, Clyde's rich uncle, pays for Belknap and Jephson. But he also hamstrings them by refusing to allow them to claim the defense of insanity, an argument that most closely fits Clyde's actual mental state during the crime. Griffiths does not want his family associated with mental illness. So the defense is forced to concoct a lie that "condemn[s] Clyde when the truth might have saved him."[5] Further, Griffiths refuses to finance an appeal for Clyde. Only when Clyde's mother goes on the lecture circuit with her story is the money found to finance Clyde's last futile defense.

The adversarial structure is not the only standard component of the American criminal justice system that Dreiser attacks. He also criticizes an institution surrounded by populist mythology and traditions of truth and justice: the jury. Juries are popularly conceived of as expressions of the innate justice and insight of the common man. Dreiser paints another picture, one of a group who "convicts Clyde as much for his sex offense as for murder," twelve people who have "been unduly influenced by public opinion and their own prejudices and emotions."[6]

Instead of a group of inspired truth-finders, a jury is just a collection of normal people who reflect the biases and prejudices of the community from which they were drawn, in Clyde's case a rural town of fundamentalist religion. The jury's job is to objectively determine the facts of the crime and to decide if these facts fit the requirements of the statute. Dreiser points out the absurdity of expecting cool, impartial judgment from common people untrained in such logic and influenced by pressures from many sources, including public opinion and their own personal biases. Instead of considering only the facts of the crime, the jury, with constant prodding from Mason, becomes caught up in the personal types Roberta and Clyde represent and in their sympathy or animosity towards these types. As H. Wayne Morgan states, the trial becomes "a conflict between morality and immorality, religion and godlessness, slick city life which Clyde supposedly represented and the bitter rural element from which Roberta came."[7]

Mason depicts Roberta as a poor, innocent country girl who comes to the big city only to be deceived by the slick city seducer. In his opening address Mason speaks of the "true and human and decent and kindly . . . generous and trusting and self-sacrificing" Roberta (20:693). He brings in Roberta's trunk to ask her father about its homely contents—handmade dresses and hats, pictures of her family, an old cookbook. The trunk is irrelevant to the crime, and the evidence is struck from the record, but

"its pathetic significance by that time [is] deeply impressed on the minds and hearts of the jurymen" (21:701). And her sad letters, to which Mason returns again and again, produce a "wave of passing pity" in the jury (25:758). In his closing argument, again he "retell[s] the bitter miseries of Roberta—so much so that the jury . . . [is] once more on the verge of tears" (26:791). Even Belknap's warning in his closing argument that "no generous impulse relating to what this poor girl might have suffered in her love-relation with this youth be permitted to sway them to the belief . . . that for that this youth had committed the crime . . . stated" does no good (26:790). Along with Mason, the jury is convinced that anyone who would use or neglect or harm in any way such a girl is a monster. Whether Clyde committed the acts and harbored the intent required by the statutory definition of murder is not important; the community and its representatives on the jury want revenge for all the sins committed against this pure, innocent, sweet girl.

As with the portrait he paints of Roberta, Mason frames a picture of Clyde centered around the biases of the jury. Clyde is from the city; the jury are rural folk. Clyde seduced and impregnated a single girl, a horrible sin to the religious jurymen, but even worse, he then refused to marry her, unthinkable to the uniformly married jury members. And, as Mason states in his opening argument, Clyde has had "social and educational advantages" (20:692). His uncle is wealthy; most of the jurymen are poor or grew up in poverty. As Dreiser states, the jury are "all convinced of Clyde's guilt before ever they sat down" (20:689).

Instead of promoting accurate determination of fact, the jury system encourages moral judgments of personality based usually on biases, prejudices, and emotion. Yet Dreiser goes beyond the question of jury impartiality to an issue even more central to criminal law, the assumption that a fact-finder can objectively determine criminal intent and that man has the free will necessary to form intent in the first place.

Clyde is convicted of first degree murder, a crime traditionally punishable by death. A typical murder statute is Section 19.02 of the 1978 Texas Penal Code: "A person commits [murder] if he: (1) intentionally or knowingly causes the death of an individual; [or] (2) intends to cause serious bodily injury and commits an act clearly dangerous to human life that causes the death of an individual."[8] And Section 6.03 defines intentionally as having a "conscious objective or desire to engage in the conduct or cause the result."[9]

The jury must find intent in the defendant to judge him guilty. Yet Dreiser questions the ability of anyone to determine, with certainty, the intent of the defendant. On the lake with Roberta, Clyde is caught in a kind of "trance or spasm," balanced in combat between "fear (a . . . revulsion against death or murderous brutality that would bring death) and a harried and restless and yet self-repressed desire to do—to do."[10] Only when Roberta draws near to him does Clyde push out at her in reaction, hitting her face and causing the boat to capsize. And then he does not rescue her, watching her struggle and go under. Even though Clyde planned to kill Roberta, at the actual moment of the crime, does he intend to cause her death? Even Clyde is not sure. In the Death House, he is unable to "demonstrate to himself even—either his guilt or hislack of guilt" (33:853). According to Robert Penn Warren, Dreiser depicts the worlds inside and outside Clyde as uncertain and unknowable. Nothing is certain in the outside world of the case: the facts can be explained by many different scenarios, and the jury's understanding of them is tainted by their individual biases. But even less certain is the "shadowiness of [Clyde's] inner world."[11] Intent is an idea, not a reality.

Dreiser does not stop his questioning at the issue of how to determine amorphous intent; he explores the assumption that justifies punishment for intentional acts: that man acts from free will. If man's actions are totally determined by society, by his background, and by his nature, then individuals do not freely choose to do what they do; they are just victims of inexorable forces. If Clyde is, in effect, "overpowered" by "sexual and social forces," then Dreiser's theme becomes "the terrible and baffling problem of justice."[12] Most critics believe that Dreiser sees Clyde as a victim, a pawn of forces that determine his every move. However, one critic claims that Dreiser, to his own surprise, discovered that he believed in individual responsibility as he wrote *An American Tragedy*.

Most critics agree with Richard Lehan that Clyde was "an innocent victim of his own nature and a world he does not understand."[13] Clyde's education and moral training ill prepares him to deal with the world. He lacks any education and feels embarrassed when his society friends speak of college experiences. The rigid, old-fashioned morals of his evangelical parents have little impact on him since he recognizes that they deny the reality he sees around him every day. So early in his life he turns elsewhere for his standards: to the "material lushness" he sees in the luxurious hotel where he works as bellhop. There the wealthy spend freely and often live immorally, even as they mouth the conventional standards of conduct.[14] "The hotel is his college," where he learns the values of "cheap desire and false gratification."[15] Clyde becomes an "Everyman of desire," representing the yearning members of a materialistic society.[16] As Irving Howe states, Clyde represents "our collective smallness, the common denominator of our foolish tastes and tawdry ambitions."[17] Clyde's insatiable desire combines with his own weak nature and ignorance to set him up for his inevitable downfall.

Dreiser paints Clyde as "the very image and prisoner of our culture."[18] After teaching Clyde to yearn for every pleasure he sees, society limits him at every turn. After finding himself uncontrollably attracted to Roberta at the collar factory, he must meet her in secret because rules at that institution forbid social contact between male management and female employees. And after he moves

higher in society and his desire shifts from Roberta to a new object, the beautiful and wealthy Sondra, Roberta insists that he marry her when she discovers her pregnancy. After acquiring the idea of drowning from a news account, Clyde seems inexorably fated to plot Roberta's murder. As Lehan states, "the conflicting forcesboth inside and outside him create the context that lead to his destruction."[19] Even his last-minute hesitation seems to be part of this process since it arises from his weak nature. H. Wayne Morgan points out that Dreiser himself wrote of the book that "it seemed so truly a story of what life does to the individual—and how impotent the individual is against such forces."[20]

Clyde is "a mechanism."[21] He simply reacts to forces; he does not determine his own actions. He is "essentially helpless."[22] To Matthiessen, Clyde is "below" tragedy because he is such an "overwhelmed victim" that he lacks free will.[23] Lehan sees Clyde's will as "negated" by "conflicting impulses and conflicting forces."[24] So who should be held responsible for his actions? Charles Child Walcutt argues that "society is responsible, as the immediate cause, for Clyde's action."[25] But Clyde, along with the others on Death Row who "responded to some heat or lust or misery of [their] nature[s] or [their] circumstances," is the one who pays (30:824). As he awaits execution in the Death House, Clyde questions the understanding of those who judged him: "They had not been tortured . . . by Roberta with her determination that he marry her and thus ruin his whole life. They had not burned with that unquenchable passion for the Sondra of his beautiful dream . . . They had not been harassed, tortured, mocked by the ill-fate of his early life and training" (33:857). Clyde disputes the right of the jury to condemn him without understanding the forces that determined his behavior. Similarly, Dreiser is pointing out that the criminal justice system fails to acknowledge the reality of modern life, where behavior is often determined by the inexorable "great machine of modern industrial secularized society."[26] The criminal justice system justifies prosecution on the basis of the free actions of the defendant. If defendants have no control over their actions, the courts do not have the right to condemn and punish them.

Lawrence E. Hussman, Jr. acknowledges that one of Dreiser's goals was to "shift the largest measure of guilt from Clyde to society."[27] Yet he argues that Dreiser could not, in the end, fulfill this purpose: "although Dreiser may have originally intended to fully absolve Clyde from guilt . . . , he could not finally do so."[28] Clyde himself is never sure of his own innocence. In the closing lines of Book Two, after he climbs out of the lake where Roberta drowned, he thinks, "He had not really killed her." But a second later, he doubts: "And yet . . . had he not refused to go to her rescue, and when he might have saved her, and when the fault for casting her in the water . . . was . . . his? And yet—and yet—."[29] Even after the trial he is not sure. He realizes that he would have struggled to save Sondra or the Roberta of the previous summer had she been tossed into the water. In his confession to Reverend McMillan in the Death House he can not say with certainty whether he is innocent or guilty. Even in the last hours before his execution he is still studying "the puzzle of his own guilt" (34:867).

Hussman argues that Clyde's uncertainty reflects Dreiser's own searching. In the end Dreiser is confused about Clyde's measure of guilt. Hussman contends that McMillan, the minister who tries to convince Clyde to accept Christ and confess his guilt, "becomes in part a spokesman for Dreiser, who ultimately shared his confusion about Clyde's measure of guilt."[30]

Perhaps, as Hussman claims, in the end Dreiser did discover a personal belief in individual guilt and responsibility and a consequent justification for punishment by the criminal justice system. Yet he clearly condemns the way the prosecution is carried out. Too many influences irrelevant to the facts of the case prejudice the outcome, sometimes to the point of determining the final verdict. In Clyde's case politics determine the timing of the hearings and the motivations of the attorneys. Furthermore, the Press manipulates the minds of the spectators and of the jury members, and ensures the trial will be a circus.

As Matthiessen states, "the question of Clyde's guilt or innocence becomes a mere incident in the struggle between rival politicians."[31] Mason is running for county judge and has aspirations to the governorship. But he is concerned that his previous cases have been routine, none pushing him into the limelight. Clyde's case, with its sensational elements of sex and wealthy families, is "just what he needed to revive a wavering political prestige and . . . perhaps solve the problem of his future" (3:547). He asks the Supreme Court to push up the date of the trial so the case can be heard before the election. He plays to the jury and the audience in the courtroom, striving to appear as a "dynamic and electric prosecutor" for "the eyes of all the citizens of the United States [are] on him" (20:689).

Yet Clyde's lawyers are no better. Alvin Belknap also seeks the same county judgeship and feels confident of his election until Clyde's trial. The main reason he takes Clyde's case is so that he can "at least [construct] a series of legal contentions and delays which might make it not so easy for Mr. Mason to walk away with the county judgeship" (14:640). Politics even enters the jury room. Ironically, the one juror who temporarily dissents does so not because he doubts Clyde's guilt, but because he is "politically opposed to Mason and taken with the personality of Jephson" (26:792).

Another force that Dreiser condemns for how it influences, perhaps determines, the outcome of the trial is the Press. Grabbing at the most sensational aspects of the crime—the sexual immorality. Roberta's poverty and country background versus Clyde's wealthy family—the papers trumpet Clyde's guilt long before the trial in their headlines: "BOY SLAYER OF WORKING-GIRL SWEETHEART INDICTED" (17:670). Articles focus on the seduction of the poor, innocent country girl. Excerpts from Roberta's let-

ters are published. Roberta's mother is interviewed. As Hussman states, "Clyde is convicted by newspaper coverage before the jury is assembled."[32]

Hundreds attend the trial, lured by their desire for revenge and their thirst for scandal. The trial acquires the air of a "holiday or festival" (19:679), down to the hawkers outside the courthouse selling peanuts, hot dogs, and pictures of Clyde and Roberta. The animosity of the spectators is palpable. Clyde shrinks under the pressure of their hatred, sometimes fearing he may be attacked. On the first day of the trial, before any evidence is heard, the crowd swarms around him as he is led to jail, one woman pushing in for a good look with the words "I just want to get a good look at you, young man. I have two daughters of my own" (19:688). On the stand, Clyde feels the pressure of the hatred of the crowd: "this it was that most . . . painfully and horribly weakened him—the eyes of all these people" (24:745). As Mason cross examines him, Clyde feels "the strong public contempt and rage that the majority of those present had for him from the start—now surging and shaking all. It filled the room" (25:774). At one point in Clyde's testimony a man in the audience announces "Why don't they kill the Goddamned bastard and be done with him?" (25:776).

As a result of sensational newspaper accounts that tug at emotions and feed biases, the judgment of guilt is made before the first word of testimony, and the trial becomes a ritual of public persecution. And the criminal justice system does nothing to prevent this result. The judge refuses to change the venue of the trial. Multiple motions for mistrial are rejected. The courtroom is never cleared. And Clyde's appeal is denied.

Dreiser's criticism of the trial system and its influences is scathing, but he saves his most damning indictment for the final chapters of the book, where he condemns the death penalty itself, especially for the cruel way it is carried out.

Only defendants convicted of first degree murder receive the death penalty; conviction of second degree murder is not enough. Typically, second degree murder requires the "immediate influence of sudden passion arising for an adequate cause."[33] Yet, like intent, how easy is "sudden passion" to determine? Was not Clyde's cause, given his nature, "adequate"? And is not all passion, in essence, sudden? But this statutory distinction between degrees of murder is rarely what determines which crime the defendant is charged with and found guilty of. Far more often the public sympathy or hatred of the defendant is the determining factor, as is the case with Clyde. Just as often the key is race. On Death Row Clyde meets members of many minorities: a Chinaman, a Jew, a Hispanic, an Italian. So the distinction between who is condemned to death and who receives a prison term is rarely the crime itself.

However, the aspect of the death penalty Dreiser has the harshest words for is how it is carried out, the "sanctioned slaughter"[34] of the condemned men. The members of the criminal justice system with closest contact to the death penalty, the warden and guards at the penitentiary, are all against it. They see the reality of Death Row, especially the "unnecessary and unfair" emotional torture of the condemned men (29:818). Dreiser states: "[Death Row] was . . . all that could possibly be imagined in the way of unnecessary and really unauthorized cruelty or stupid and destructive torture. And to the end that a man, once condemned by a jury, would be compelled to suffer not alone the death for which his sentence called, but a thousand others before that" (29:815-16). Forced to watch each other as they await execution, the men on Death Row decline mentally, some into madness. As Dreiser states, they are "tortured to death, maybe, by being compelled to witness these terrible and completely destroying—and for each—impending tragedies" (30:826). Pasquale Cutrone, convicted for the murder of his brother for trying to seduce his wife, is reduced to mumbling prayers as he crawls on the floor of his cell after he loses his mind from worry.

Before an execution some pray, others mutter, and still others "scream from time to time" (30:829). Then they are forced to listen as the condemned man shuffles—and is pushed—to the electric chair. Even Reverend McMillan is shaken after watching Clyde's execution. As McMillan walks back through the prison, he remembers how he "had all but fainted beside [Clyde] as that cap was adjusted to his head—that current turned on—and he had had to be assisted, sick and trembling from the room." The horror of the place and of the death penalty reverberates as he thinks "The law! Prisons such as this" (34:870).

As McMillan staggers from the death chamber, Dreiser's indictment of the American criminal justice system is complete. The trial he describes is a travesty. The men who direct the proceedings are adversaries focused more on victory and political prizes than on truth. The jury, primed by sensational press accounts, is the epitome of partiality, basing their judgments on biases, emotions, and public opinion. And the defendant is a mechanism, constructed by the forces of society and by his own nature, and lacking the free will assumed by the law. He cowers in the face of the crowd that craves his death because they despise his immorality and his association with wealth. And finally, Dreiser damns the cruelty and inhumanity of Death Row, the condemned man's last stop before society slaughters him.

NOTES

[1] Robert Penn Warren, "An American Tragedy," [First published in *The Yale Review* 52 (1962): 1-15] in *Dreiser: A Collection of Critical Essays,* ed. John Lydenberg (Englewood Cliffs, NJ: Prentice-Hall, 1971), p. 138.

[2] F.O. Matthiessen, *Theodore Dreiser,* American Man of Letters Series (USA: William Sloane Associates, 1951), p. 198.

[3] H. Wayne Morgan, *American Writers in Rebellion: From Mark Twain to Dreiser,* American Century Series (New York: Hill and Wang, 1965), p. 177.

[4] Theodore Dreiser, *An American Tragedy,* Introduction by H. L. Mencken (Cleveland: The World Publishing Co., 1945), bk. 3, ch. 20, p. 693. Subsequent references to *An American Tragedy,* Book 3, will be incorporated into the text, with chapter number followed by page numbers.

[5] Richard Lehan, *Theodore Dreiser: His World and his Novels* (Carbondale: Southern Illinois Univ. Press, 1969), p. 151.

[6] Lawrence E. Hussman, Jr., *Dreiser and his Fiction: A Twentieth-Century Quest* (Philadelphia: Univ. of Pennsylvania Press, 1983), p. 138.

[7] Morgan, *American Writers in Rebellion.* p. 177.

[8] Texas Penal Code Ann. Sec. 19.02 (Vernon 1979).

[9] Ibid., Sec. 6.03.

[10] Dreiser, bk. 2, ch. 47, p. 530.

[11] Warren, p. 138.

[12] Matthiessen, p. 192.

[13] Lehan, p. 149.

[14] Morgan, p. 176.

[15] Irving Howe, "Dreiser and Tragedy: The Stature of Theodore Dreiser," [First published in *The New Republic* 25 July 1964, 19-21, and 22 Aug. 1964, 25-28], in *Dreiser: A Collection of Critical Essays,* ed. John Lydenberg (Englewood Cliffs, N.J.: Prentice-Hall, 1971), p. 148.

[16] Ellen Moers, *Two Dreisers* (New York: The Viking Press, 1969), p. 228.

[17] Howe, p. 147.

[18] Ibid., p. 148.

[19] Lehan, p. 165.

[20] Morgan, p. 179.

[21] Moers, p. 244.

[22] Morgan, p. 181.

[23] Matthiessen, pp. 205-206.

[24] Lehan, p. 159.

[25] Charles Child Walcutt. "Theodore Dreiser and the Divided Stream," [First published in *The Stature of*

Theodore Dreiser: A Critical Survey of the Man and his Work. ed. Alfred Kazin and Charles Shapiro (Bloomington: Univ. of Indiana Press, 1955), pp. 246-269], in *Dreiser: A Collection of Critical Essays,* ed. John Lydenberg (Englewood Cliffs, N.J.: Prentice-Hall, 1971), p. 122.

[26] Warren, p. 140.

[27] Hussman, p. 131.

[28] Ibid., p. 133.

[29] Dreiser, bk. 2, ch. 47, p. 534.

[30] Hussman, p. 134.

[31] Matthiessen, p. 202.

[32] Hussman, p. 138.

[33] Texas Penal Code Ann. Sec. 19.04 (a) (Vernon 1979).

[34] Hussman, p. 139.

Philip Gerber (essay date 1991)

SOURCE: "'A Beautiful Legal Problem': Albert Lévitt on *An American Tragedy*," in *Papers on Language and Literature,* Vol. 27, No. 2, Spring, 1991, pp. 214-42.

[*In the following essay, Gerber explores the reaction of the legal community to the questions raised in* An American Tragedy, *particularly the question of whether or not Clyde Griffiths was guilty of first-degree murder.*]

When in July of 1906 ambitious young Chester Gillette, then of Cortland, New York, invited his pregnant, working-class lover, Grace Brown, on a supposed romantic trip to the isolated waters of Big Moose Lake high in the Adirondacks—intending there to drown her and thereby free himself for a new and more advantageous alliance with the daughter of a local society family—he set in motion a chain of events that has affected American literature ever since. Two decades after the fact there appeared Theodore Dreiser's monumental *An American Tragedy,* transmuting the Gillette-Brown case into fiction. In its outlines the fictional story hews to the facts: the protagonist, now renamed Clyde Griffiths, escorts the burdensome Roberta Alden to Big Bittern Lake; there she drowns; Clyde is hunted down, tried, and like Gillette, is convicted of her murder. He ends in the electric chair. At the same time, Dreiser's additions, deletions, and other alterations in the record produced a tale considerably different, much more complicated, ambiguous, and provocative than its prototype.

The immediate response to *An American Tragedy* was overwhelmingly favorable, and for sixty-five years critical esteem has effectively disproved the opinion of the few contemporary dissenters, such as William Lyon Phelps, who ventured to predict that Dreiser's novel would "float around awhile, a colossal derelict on the ocean of literature and [would] eventually sink" (Salzman 487). Aside from the massive completeness of Dreiser's realism, what accounts for the survival of *An American Tragedy?* Surely, much of the appeal of the story hinges on the ambiguity which Dreiser painstakingly built into its central scene, the drowning of Roberta Alden, and the questions which that event pose concerning Clyde Griffiths's relative guilt and innocence. He was executed in Auburn Prison as a cold-blooded murderer—but was he really a killer? On that basic question, reviewers and critics of Dreiser's day were in disagreement, and perceptive readers became acutely aware of the many doubts and ironies which clouded the issue.

Opinion ranged over a considerable spectrum. At one extreme stood molders of opinion such as H.L. Mencken, who suggested that Dreiser's hero was indeed guilty as charged: "Clyde is ambitious and decides for Sondra. But at that precise moment Roberta tells him that their sin has found her out. His reply is to take her to a lonely lake and drown her. The crime being detected, he is arrested, put on trial, convicted, and electrocuted" (Salzman 477). Writing for the *Atlantic Monthly,* R.N. Linscott also accepted the murder as indisputable fact. In Massachusetts, reviewer W. Elsworth Lawson expressed his basic concurrence: "Dreiser makes it perfectly plain that personal responsibility and capacity to act remained with the boy. . . . [It] is no mere accident. . . . Responsibility still remains with Clyde Griffiths" (Salzman 479). T.K. Whipple was almost clinically precise in advising readers of *New Republic* that "on page 78 of the second volume Clyde commits the murder which really ends his story" (Salzman 487).

Others were less certain. In a surprisingly favorable review, Stuart P. Sherman, arch-enemy of Dreiser from past years, straddled the guilt fence rather adroitly: "[Clyde] is held criminally responsible, though perhaps he is technically innocent, yet not without murderous malice aforethought" (Salzman 474); and in Columbus, Ohio, Julia Collier Harris described the drowning of Roberta as "a disaster for which [Clyde] is only partly responsible since [Roberta] not only yielded to him in love but was a woman full two years his senior" (Salzman 445). Robert L. Duffus, in an important notice in the *New York Times Book Review,* took something of the same tack in analyzing the drowning scene: "At the last there is a moment of hesitation. Did [Clyde] mean to strike her with the camera? Did he commit murder? Perhaps no jury of readers would vote to acquit him, and yet there remains a doubt" (Salzman 453). And Charles R. Walker in the *Independent* forthrightly inquired, "But wasn't it half an accident?" (Salzman 469).

Another group of critics pleaded Clyde's technical innocence more directly, Burton Rascoe among them: "To be accurate, Clyde did not actually commit the murder he premeditated but allowed the girl to drown in an accident without going to her aid" (Salzman 469). On the West Coast, the reviewer for the *Sunday Oregonian* agreed precisely, citing the legal distinction between intent and act, and concluding that Clyde "goes to his abject and miserable death in the electric chair for having plotted a cold-blooded murder, [that] he never actually committed" (Salzman 459). Now and again reviewers perceived the novel as being consistent with the broad societal dimensions so characteristic of Dreiser's view of life, Donald Davidson advancing the environmental theory rather directly by calling *An American Tragedy* "a moral and spiritual allegory depicting man as the victim of the complicated civilization he himself has made" (Salzman 459). Herbert S. Gorman cast Donaldson's thought into phrases considerably more Dreiserian in tone: "[Clyde] is a victim of circumstances induced by a weak will and so we see him finally like some pathetic and cornered little rat fighting in a bewildered manner against a gigantic juxtaposition of the Fates" (Salzman 467).

In all this welter of disputation, one fact stood out: the popular success of *An American Tragedy* was immediate and unprecedented. Despite its having been issued in two volumes (at a whopping five dollars a set), by the end of 1926 the novel had sold more than 50,000 copies, and its publisher, Horace Liveright, had negotiated the sale of screen rights to Famous Players for $90,000, in that day a startling sum for residuals. Suddenly "opulent," Dreiser took a lease on a fashionable duplex apartment in the Rodin Studios on Fifty-seventh Street in Manhattan, where he entertained lavishly when not being lionized by others. A stage adaptation of *An American Tragedy* by Patrick Kearney opened on 11 October 1926 at the Longacre Theater and soon was grossing $30,000 per week. The output of Dreiser's pen was sought as never before. New stories and articles brought sums to which he was unaccustomed, and the Hearst newspapers offered him $5000 for the syndication rights to the *Tragedy.* Requests for autographs, photographs, and speeches became numerous enough to require employment of a full-time secretary (Swanberg 302-16).

Among the mail that deluged Dreiser from around the world came a letter of a somewhat different sort, not from a book reviewer but a young Professor of Law at Washington and Lee University, Albert H. Lévitt. He praised Dreiser's story of Clyde and Roberta as "thrilling, excellently well written" and as constituting "a most poignant picture of certain aspects of our national life" (Lévitt). In further remarks he became more intriguingly specific:

> As a lawyer, and a teacher of law, I wish especially to commend the legal aspects of your story. I know nothing in all of Anglo-American literature which gives so fine a description of criminal procedure as your book does. I have commended it to my class in criminal law, and they have all taken to reading yourbook. The legal problem presented by the facts, as you give them, surrounding the drowning of Roberta, is fascinating and subtle. I expect to put the bare facts . . . as a question

> dealing with homicide on the examination I shall set my class at the end of this term. It will test their knowledge of the law as no other question I can think of. It is a beautiful legal problem.

Seizing the moment of Dreiser's ascendancy, his publishers, Boni and Liveright, conceived the notion of sponsoring a nationwide essay contest on the topic: "Was Clyde Griffiths guilty of murder in the first degree?" The prize for the winning entry would be $500. The judges would be Heywood Broun, Arthur Garfield Hays, and Bishop William Montgomery Brown. This trio of liberal thinkers could not have been more judiciously selected to coincide with Dreiser's own lifelong inclinations regarding contemporary social issues ("'American Tragedy' Essay Contest"). The youngest of the three was Broun, a Harvard-educated journalist who had written for three New York newspapers. Even as he sat as judge, Broun was engaged, with Margaret Leach, in composing his book *Anthony Comstock: Roundsman of the Lord,* a scathing biography of America's prime censor; Comstock's New York Society for the Suppression of Vice had successfully blackmailed the John Lane Company into withholding Dreiser's *The "Genius"* from circulation in 1915. Only after eight years of seemingly endless struggle in which Dreiser refused to capitulate did Boni and Liveright dare to issue the novel in a new edition. In their attitudes toward freedom of expression, Dreiser and Broun were soulmates.

Hays was a forty-seven-year-old Jewish attorney with a collection of degrees from Columbia University. His liberal credentials were impeccable. He had served as defense counsel in any number of civil-liberties cases, helped to open up company-shuttered towns to the workers during the 1922 coal strike in Pennsylvania, and played a role on the team of lawyers headed by the great Clarence Darrow in the notorious 1925 Scopes "Monkey Trial" in Tennessee, that same year entering the Sweet Case in Detroit, involving racial segregation. At the time of the Boni and Liveright contest, Hays was heavily involved in the defense of Nicola Sacco and Bartolomeo Vanzetti, who were condemned to death in the most notorious and far-reaching civil liberty case of the decade. The title of Hays's book, *Trial Prejudice* (1933), suggests its author's basic cynicism about the plight of equity in the American judicial system.

The choice of Bishop Brown was perhaps the most interesting of all. A man of seventy-two, he had just been deposed from his office by the House of Bishops of the Protestant Episcopal Church at its convocation in New Orleans. The charge was heresy. The bishop had been convicted by a church court which based its charge upon twenty-one paragraphs taken from Brown's *Communism and Christianity* (1920), paragraphs construed to assert that he accepted the Bible, miracles, the immaculate conception, and the birth and life of Jesus Christ as symbols merely. Brown had requested that the church reconsider his conviction in its 1925 general convocation and alsothat it spell out precisely what "heresy" meant, requests which created nationwide interest via the news media ("Bishop Brown to Appeal"). At the Community Church on Park Avenue, the Reverend Dr. John Haynes Holmes had alluded to Bishop Brown as a "saint," albeit one of a distinctly unorthodox stamp, one whose reading of Darwin's *On the Origin of Species* and Marx's *Das Kapital* had simultaneously wiped out his faith in both Christianity and the prevailing political-economic order ("Holmes Praises Brown"). Dreiser did not always agree with Horace Liveright, but what choice could have been better calculated to delight his nonconformist soul?

When the three judges had read the entries and agreed on their decision, a fourth prize was given to Arnold Weissberger of Cambridge, Massachusetts. A third prize went to Ross M. Barrett of Philadelphia, and a second was shared by Edward Rohrback of Passaic, New Jersey, and Byron L. Gifford of Sioux City, Iowa. In a decision concurred with by two of the three judges, the grand prize was awarded to none other than Albert Lévitt. Lévitt (1887-1968), already primed for the event by his fascination with the legalities of the fictional Gillette-Brown case, stood in an enviable position for writing a winning paper. Then thirty-nine years old, he was Phi Beta Kappa, Columbia University, from which he graduated *cum magnis honoribus* in 1913, and was well into an impressive career; he had taken an LL.B. from Harvard and a J.D. degree from Yale Law School, and served apprenticeships on the faculties of Columbia and Colgate as well as positions teaching law at George Washington University, the University of North Dakota, and Johns Hopkins Medical School. While at Washington and Lee, he also held the post of associate editor on the *Central Law Journal.* Yet his background was not exclusively academic. As a much younger man he had served in the hospital corps of the U.S. Army and had been stationed in the Philippines in 1906-1907. During World War I he held a chaplain's post, going overseas in 1918 to serve during the Meuse-Argonne offensive, where he was wounded and gassed.

He was a man possessing one of the sharpest legal minds in the nation, whose training, career, and natural inclinations toward liberal ideas and humanitarian causes—as well as his life experience—placed him in a position to compose a brilliant analysis of Dreiser's story. But why? With all the many claims upon his time and attention, why should one such as Albert Lévitt use his precious hours dissecting a popular novel in a contest that might be construed as being no more than a cheap publicity stunt concocted by a clever publishing house? Surely it was more than the possibility of winning $500, impressive a lure as the sum might have been in 1926, for an artfully conceived and expertly written analysis of 10,000 words cannot be composed as an overnight lark. A good portion of the answer to this question, I believe, is to be found in the expertise of Dreiser's novel itself, a powerful stimulus to a legal mind. Clearly, Lévitt enjoyed writing his essay, primarily, it would appear, because of his passionate espousal of the issues underlying the story of Clyde Griffiths.

In this effort, on another level, Lévitt would have been abetted by his wife, a prominent feminist—Elsie Mary

Hill, a graduate of Vassar, student of law to Enrico Ferri in Rome, and a thoroughgoing advocate of women's rights. Four years Lévitt's senior, Hill by the time of their marriage in 1921 had held the presidency of the Equal Suffrage League and was a member of the committee which secured passage of the Kenyon Bill, abolishing the vice district in Washington, D.C. After serving on the National Committee of the Congressional Union for Women's Suffrage (1914-1917), she became an organizer for the National Women's Party and was three times imprisoned for her aggressive efforts to obtain the vote for women. A member of the Lucy Stone League, Hill retained her maiden name after marriage and made herself available for political office in Connecticut. In all, her credentials were ideally attuned to her husband's tendencies. There seems little doubt that Albert Lévitt's eventual turning in his essay from the surface issue of guilt or innocence to subterranean texts—first to the controversial and then-suppressed topic of birth control, then to the even more-to-be-avoided issue of abortion, and finally to the question of capital punishment itself—can be connected intimately with the impact on his thinking of Elsie Mary Hill's crusading efforts. These two active intellects experienced a fusion of thinking that was, indeed, a marriage of true minds. Lévitt relished unloading at last some deeply-felt principles that cried out for public utterance.

The facts concerning Boni and Liveright's intention as to the ultimate dissemination of the prize essay(s) remain in doubt. The publisher may well have speculated about periodical publication or even the issuance of a timely volume. The Lévitt essay by itself, arranged in an appropriate format, could have made an impressive little book, but if any such plan were contemplated it seems not to have materialized. However, Lévitt's work does appear to have enjoyed a certain modest circulation. Preceded by the legend: "Boni and Liveright announce winner in 'The Essay Contest on Theodore Dreiser's An American Tragedy'" and the list of judges and prize winners, it was mimeographed (on twelve legal-sized papers of predictably cheap paper, fastened by staples) to serve what would appear to be a relatively modest distribution, perhaps no more than a press release.

Whatever the intended use, practically no copies have survived. The title is not, for instance, listed in the otherwise inclusive Pizer, Dowell, Rusch Dreiser bibliography (1975). Surely Dreiser himself received a copy, but he (who saved everything, even laundry lists and receipts for overcoats) appears not to have preserved Lévitt's effort, for no copy is on deposit in the Dreiser Collection at the University of Pennsylvania. One copy of the essay did eventually come to the Library of Congress, probably during the early 1930s. But even the circumstances surrounding this acquisition are not altogether clear of ambiguity. Apparently not intended as a copyright deposit, the LOC copy is accompanied by a notice of sale from Merle Johnson, specialist in rare books, then located at 65 East 53rd Street in New York City (the same Merle Johnson whose *American First Editions* remains a standard source for collectors). The authenticity of the essay is attested to in Johnson's invoice by a quotation from Vrest Orton's 1929 bibliography, *Dreiserana:*

> In 1927 [1926?] in connection with publicity for the book, Boni and Liveright offered a prize of $500 for the best essay to be entitled *"Was Clyde Griffiths Guilty of Murder in the First Degree?"* The prize was won by Prof. Albert H. Lévitt, Prof. of Law at the Washington and Lee University, Lexington, Virginia.

> Three pieces of interesting Dreiserana are concerned with this prize contest. A—Boni and Liveright first issued four pages of typewritten copy on white paper announcing the contest with details and conditions. These four pages were stapled together and issued without wrappers. B—When the contest had been won and the prize awarded to Prof. Levitt, his essay was issued in a 12 page stamped and typewritten folder . . . and bound in tan paper covers. On the front cover of the wrappers the following appeared: Essay No. 10, Submitted November 22, 1926. WAS CLYDE GRIFFITHS GUILTY/OF MURDER IN THE FIRST DEGREE? Albert Lévitt/Lexington, Va./ November 15, 1926. C—At the same time Boni and Liveright issued a printed one sheet broadside entitled ANNOUNCING THE WINNER OF THE ESSAY CONTEST ON THEODORE DREISER'S/AN AMERICAN TRAGEDY/(Text)/Boni and Liveright. (52-53)

The price quoted (for all three pieces, it would seem): $9.00

Although he does not mention it in his praising letter to Dreiser (18 November 1926), Lévitt seems already to have completed and mailed his contest essay to Boni and Liveright. Its publication here, to our knowledge, constitutes its first formal appearance in print, an act made possible through the courtesy of the LOC, which has made an exception to its ruling that the essay at this point is too fragile for indiscriminate reading or even for photocopying. That the essay is worthy of preservation in its entirety almost goes without saying. Not only will it be of considerable use to the increasing number of scholars engaged in Dreiser studies, but the prescient quality of the essay suggests that it will be of interest and value to the general reader concerned with topics of societal controversy—birth control, abortion, capital punishment—which have continued to receive attention and which loom even larger in the public consciousness today, perhaps, than in Dreiser's time.

WAS CLYDE GRIFFITHS GUILTY OF MURDER IN THE FIRST DEGREE?

I.

The facts in the case are entirely clear. Clyde Griffiths induced Roberta Alden to be his mistress. Then he met Miss X. He falls in love with Miss X. She appears to reciprocate. He thinks that she will marry him. He determines to break relations with Roberta. Roberta becomes pregnant. She tells Clyde. She insists that he either abort the foetus or marry her. Clyde gives her an abortifacient. It fails

to work. He sends her to a physician. The physician refuses to perform a criminal operation. Clyde then promises to marry Roberta. But he does not really intend to marry her. He plans to drown her. He determines to take her to a lonely lake in the woods, row out to a secluded spot, upset the boat and then swim to shore leaving Roberta, who cannot swim, to drown. He begins to carry out this plan. Under pretense of taking a prewedding trip he induces Roberta to accompany him to the lake he has chosen to be the scene of the drowning. They register at an hotel, hire a boat, row out to a secluded spot on the lake and drift about. But Clyde does not have the courage to upset the boat. He sits there brooding on his plan. He clutches a small camera in his hand. Roberta is startled at the expression on his face. She crawls along the bottom of the boat to approach him. She seeks to take his hand. He flings out his hand with the intention of freeing himself from her touch. The camera strikes Roberta. She is thrown to the bottom of the boat. The boat careens. He rises and reaches forward to assist her and apologize. The boat upsets. Both are thrown into the water. She calls for help. He swims ashore. Roberta drowns. Clyde is suspected, arrested, tried and convicted of murder in the first degree. He is executed. The question is this: Was Clyde Griffiths guilty of murder in the first degree?

Four answers can be given to the question. 1. The answer given by the law governing murder in the first degree. 2. An answer based upon a system of Christian ethics. 3. An answer based upon the facts as the jury saw them. 4. An answer based upon the societal conditions under which Clyde Griffiths lived.

II.

The Law

1

A crime consists of an act, or omission, which is not permitted by law, plus an intent to do the act, or fail to do that which has been omitted.

An act is a doing. An omission is a failing to do. An act is not an omission. But both act and omission are treated in the same way by the law. Thus X may open the window of a warehouse in order that Y, a confederate, may enter the warehouse and steal. Or, X may permit an open window in the warehouse to remain open, though it is his duty to shut it, in order that Y, his confederate, may come into the warehouse and steal. It is obvious that opening the window is physically different from letting the window, already open, remain open. The first is an act. The second is an omission. But the law will deal in the same way with X, if he is indicted for burglary. The consequences of the act or the omission would be the same. Y is enabled to enter and steal. The distinction between an act and anomission must be kept clear. It is of prime importance in the Griffiths case.

The act, or omission, must be forbidden by law. Thus if X punches Y in the nose and Y draws a knife and stabs

X, the act of stabbing is forbidden by law. Y may punch back, or appeal to the police for protection, but he cannot redress his own wrongs by using a knife on his assailant. But if Y is a prison guard and X is a prisoner and X is trying to break out of prison, Y may shoot and kill X, if the killing is the only way to prevent the prison breach. In the first case the act of Y is forbidden by law. In the second case the act of Y is permitted. In the first case there is a crime. In the second case there is a justified act, and no crime eventuates.

The prohibition may be imposed by statute or by common law. Thus, a city ordinance may prohibit the operation of automobiles in certain sections of the city at a rate of speed greater then eight miles an hour. That is a statutory prohibition. Or, there may be no ordinance regulating the speed with which automobiles may be driven, but the driver may drive through a crowded city street at a speed of sixty miles an hour. This would be the basis of a criminal charge. It is such great carelessness, such disregard of possible injury to human beings, that the law would deem such conduct to be prohibited. The technical term for such driving would be either negligence or recklessness. Both are forbidden. The prohibition is imposed by common law. The prohibited act, or omission, must be the cause of an injury to a person, which injury it is the function of the law to prevent. That is, the injury would not have eventuated if the act had not been done, or that which omitted had been done. Thus, if X is driving down a city street at a rate of speed forbidden by ordinance, and Y is walking on the sidewalk, and Y slips on a banana peel and breaks his leg, X cannot be arrested for assault and battery on Y. It is true that X violated the law in regard to speeding. But this violation did not cause Y to break his leg. It was slipping on the banana peel which did that. X did not produce the slipping. But, suppose, that X, in driving at an illegal rate of speed, comes so close to Q that Q, in order to save himself from injury, leaps on the sidewalk where Y is walking, bumps into Y with sufficient force to throw Y to the ground and breaks Y's leg. Here X would be the cause of the injury to Y. He could be indicted for a criminal assault and battery upon Y.

Furthermore, the forbidden act, or omission, must be the "proximate cause" of the injury sustained by the victim. It is difficult to define "proximate cause." Many courts have tried it but none have succeeded entirely. But some illustrations will make the concept clear.

A direct application of force is always considered to be a proximate cause of any injury which the directly applied force produces. Thus, if X stabs Y and Y dies, the stabbing is deemed to be the proximate cause of the death. This is so even while it isrecognized that, medically speaking, death is due to stoppage of heart action which is produced by various causes which intervene between the stabbing and the death. But difficulties arise where, as in the Griffiths case, we deal not with a direct application of force but with an intervening force of nature, that is the element of water which really killed

Roberta. In such a case the legal rule is that if a direct application of force brings the victim into contact with the natural force which inflicts the injury, the one who applies that force is said to be the proximate causer of the injury to the victim. Or, if one fails to deflect a natural force, when it is his duty to deflect it, and the natural force continues on to injure the victim, the omission is the proximate cause of the injury and he who fails in his duty is the proximate causer of the injury. The natural force is a cause of the injury to be sure. But the natural force cannot be forbidden to operate; it cannot be an illegally acting force; it cannot be held accountable for injuries it does. So the law turns to the human being who is accountable for the operation of the natural force in the direction of the victim, and holds him responsible for the injuries sustained.

But the forbidden act, or omission, is not in itself a crime. It must be accompanied by a criminal intent. The legal maxim is: *Actus not facit reurn nisi mens sit rea.* (The act does not become evil unless the mind is evil.) The notion is that there cannot be a crime committed unless the perpetrator of the injury has an evil mind. Wickedness is the basis for punishment.

By "intent" is meant the will to do that which is done or the desire to bring about that which the forbidden act, or omission, causes. The intent must exist at the *same time* that the act, or omission, operates. It is not enough that the intent existed before the act or omission. It is not enough that the intent exists *after* the act or omission. They must be contemporaneous. Thus, if a man finds some sheep and takes them into his fold, intending at the time of the taking to keep them for the true owner, and thereafter, determines to appropriate them to his own use, and does so, he is not guilty of larceny. The act of taking and the intent to steal were not contemporaneous. But, if a pickpocket takes a purse intending, at that instant of taking, to deprive the true owner of the purse of his property, he is guilty of larceny from the person. The intent and the act concurred in space and time. The crime is deemed committed.

The habitat of an intent is, of course, the inside of a man's cranium. The law cannot get there to see if the intent really existed at the time the act was done. But there are several presumptions of law which operate to aid the law. A man is presumed to intend to do that which he does, or omits to do. He is also presumed to intend all the natural and probable consequences of his acts or omissions. Sometimes the phrasing used by the courts leads to the idea that a person is responsible for all the criminal acts which are the natural and intended results of his actions. Other phrasings indicate that one is guilty of the necessary consequencesof his acts, and that, where injury is caused, the intent to injure will be presumed. It is further held that the law presumes a criminal intent from the willful commission of an unlawful act; that the willful violation of a law is evidence of unlawful intent; that malice may be inferred from any deliberate and unlawful act against another; and that when one acts maliciously he is presumed to have intended the consequences of his act.

Of extreme importance is the legal fact that an evil mind without an act, or omission, which is forbidden to accompany it is not a crime. Mere intent is not a crime. Blackstone makes this clear when he says:

> To make a complete crime cognizable by human laws there must be both a will and an act. For though in *foro conscientiae,* a fixed design or will to do an unlawful act, is almost as heinous as the commission of it, yet, as no temporal tribunal can search the heart, or fathom the intentions of the mind, otherwise than as they are demonstrated by outward actions, it therefore cannot punish for what it cannot know. For which reason, in all temporal jurisdictions, an overt act, or some open evidence of an intended crime, is necessary in order to demonstrate the depravity of the will, before the man is liable to punishment. And as a vicious will without a vicious act is no civil crime, so on the other hand an unwarrantable act without a vicious will is no crime at all. So that to constitute a crime against human laws, there must be first, a vicious will; and secondly, an unlawful act consequent upon such will.

By the word "consequent" Blackstone means *produced* by the will. He does not mean that the act must be *subsequent, following after,* the operation of the will. Neither the act nor the intent standing alone constitutes a crime. Both are needed, existing at the same time, to make up the crime. A crime consists of an act, or omission, plus a wicked intent.

> Murder existed, at the Common Law, "When a person of sound memory and discretion unlawfully killeth a reasonable creature in being, and under the king's peace, with malice aforethought, either express or implied." The Criminal Code of the United States provides that: "Murder is the unlawful killing of a human being with malice aforethought. Every murder perpetrated by poison, lying in wait, or any other kind of willful, deliberate, malicious and premeditated killing . . . is murder in the first degree." The Penal Law of New York defines murder in the first degree as "The killing of a human being, unless it is excusable or justifiable . . . when committed (1) From a deliberate and premeditated design to effect the death of the person killed, or of another; or, (2) By an act imminently dangerous to others, and evincing a depraved mind, regardless of human life, although without a premeditated design to effect the death of any individual.

The penal codes of the several other states of the Unioncontain provisions similar to the above. The general principles governing murder in the first degree are the same in all the states. Murder in the first degree is killing a human being with malice aforethought. Malice may be express or implied. It is express when the killer actually has a hatred of the person he kills. It will be implied by the law from the mere fact of the killing.

Where malice is implied by law, that is inferred to have existed because of the killing itself, the accused may show, if he can, that malice did not actually exist. It is for the jury to determine if he has negatived the existence of the malice which the law has inferred.

The foregoing principles of criminal law are accepted by all criminal lawyers without doubt or question. They form the background for every criminal prosecution for murder. It now remains to apply them to the Griffiths Case.

2.

That Clyde had planned to kill Roberta is clear. But the plan to murder is not murder. That there was premeditation is established. But the premeditation is not the killing. There must be an act, or omission, which leads to the death of Roberta and an intent to kill or produce the killing of Roberta which act and intent must coexist at the same time. Did they so exist? The only evidence is what the novelist gives us. We cannot go behind his statements. We cannot presume an intent if the novelist definitely tells us that the intent we wish to presume did not exist. Where facts are Unknown the law will permit inferences of fact. But where facts are established, then no inferences at variance with the facts can be made.

What is the mental state of Clyde as Roberta approaches him? The novelist says:

> And then, as she drew near him, seeking to take his hand in hers and the camera from him in order to put it in the boat, *he flinging out at her,* but *not even then with any intention to do other than free himself of her—her touch—her pleading—consoling sympathy—her presence forever—God!* [Lévitt's emphasis]

It was "the flinging out at her" which brought the camera into contact with her and threw her back into the boat. But the blow was given with no intent to hurt her in any way. IT WAS A PURE ACCIDENT. There was no criminal intent present at the time of the act which started the causal sequence that led to the two being plunged into the water. Nor was the act forbidden. Accidents cannot be forbidden. Neither a forbidden act nor a criminal intent existed at the time the camera struck Roberta. Murder in the first degree cannot be predicated upon an accidental act accompanied by a non-culpable intent. At the most manslaughter may be charged, which is an *unintentional* killing, but murder in the first degree cannot be charged, for that means intentional killing.

> The next activity of Clyde is given by the novelist thus: And then he, stirred by her sharp scream (as much due to the lurch of the boat as the cut on her nose and lip), *rising and reaching half to assist or recapture her* and half to apologize for *the unintended blow*—yet in so doing *completely capsizing the boat* himself and Roberta being as instantly thrown into the water. . . . [Lévitt's emphasis]

The "rising and reaching" with the purpose and intent which accompanied them are not activities which the law condemns. They are acts which the law would commend. There can be no possible harm done by going to the rescue of one who is in danger. Nor is it legally wrong to apologize, or intend to apologize, for a blow accidently given. And the capsizing of the boat was the result of a series of blameless acts. The capsizing cannot be the foundation of a charge of murder in the first degree. The contemporaneous act and intent were not criminal. The capsizing, although planned for, hoped for, came, when it did come, not as a result of a willful act, but as the result of a series of accidental activities. The capsizing brought Roberta into contact with a force of nature which killed her. But the capsizing was not willful. It was accidental. No one can be held criminally liable for accidentally bringing another into contact with a force of nature that kills that other. The capsizing was not the proximate cause of the death of Roberta.

Then the novelist again reiterates that the blow struck by Clyde was accidental. He says, Roberta being then in the water,

> For she was stunned, horror struck, unintelligible with pain and fear—her life-long fear of water and drowning and the blow he had so *accidentally* and all but unconsciously administered. [Lévitt's emphasis]

Whatever the premeditation and the design, ironical as the situation is, none-the-less Roberta was brought into contact with the force of nature which killed her by accident. Murder in the first degree does not legally exist.

One fact more and the law is done. Clyde does not go to the aid of Roberta. The novelist puts it thus:

> And then Clyde, with the sound of Roberta's cries still in his ears, that last frantic, white, appealing look in her eyes, swimming heavily, gloomily, and darkly to shore.

Here we have, on the part of Clyde, an act of omission. Was the omission culpable in law? Was there a legal duty on Clyde to swim to the aid of Roberta? The answer to both questions is, No! Had Roberta been the daughter or the ward of Clyde, then he would have been under such a duty. The law imposes upon the parent or guardian the duty to succor and aid an infant. In some jurisdictions husband and wife owe each other mutual duties of care and support. But the law nowhere puts a duty upon a man to go to the aid of his mistress when she is in danger. At the most there was a moral duty on Clyde to help Roberta. But a moral duty cannot be made the basis of a criminal prosecution. Bishop, the leading authority on criminal law in America, has well put the law. He says:

> An act which is simply wrong in morals, but is not taken cognizance of by the law as a violation of any civil or criminal obligation or duty, if from it the death of a human being casually results, will

not sustain an indictment for felonious homicide. Indeed, we are here reasoning in a circle; for if the law made the force punishable, whether under the name of felonious homicide or any other, it would not be lawful.

> If one neglects to do an act the doing whereof would save life, in violation of a social and moral but not a legal duty,—as where he knows a murder is about to be committed, or witnesses its commission, yet takes no steps to prevent it—he does not become a felon though the death of a human being results from his neglect.

Roberta drowns. But the failure of Clyde to go to her aid is not legally the proximate cause of her death. The omission was brutal, cruel, callous. But it was not forbidden by law. Clyde did not murder Roberta.

The first answer to our question is clear and direct. From the point of view of criminal law Clyde Griffiths was not guilty of murder in the first degree.

III.

Christian Ethics

Christian ethics is founded upon the Holy Bible. Both the Old and the New Testaments are properly appealed to when ethical standards are sought by which human conduct is to be judged as innocent or culpable. The highest authority in the Holy Bible is Jesus Christ. His words are definitive. The standards He sets cannot be impeached or criticized. The noblest of His sayings are found in The Sermon on the Mount. It is here that we find the answer to our question concerning Clyde Griffiths.

> Jesus Christ said:

> Ye have heard that it was said by them of old time, Thou shalt not kill; and whosoever shall kill shall be in danger of the judgment:

> But I say unto you, That whosoever is angry with his brother without a cause shall be in danger of the judgment.

> Ye have heard that it was said by them of old time,

> Thou shalt not commit adultery;

> But I say unto you, That whosoever looketh on a woman to lust after her hath committed adultery with her already in his heart.

These sayings give the highest sanction to the principle laid down by the writer of the Book of Proverbs when he said,

> Eat not the bread of him that hath an evil eye, neither desire thou his dainty meats;

> For as he thinketh in his heart, so is he; Eat and drink, saith he, but his heart is not with thee.

Not only what a man does, but the spirit in which he does determines his guilt or innocence. Saint Augustine makes this very clear in his sermon on perjury. This sermon is the starting point for the maxim which was afterwards incorporated into the criminal law in the principle that every crime must have been done with a criminal intent.

Saint Augustine is dealing with certain cases of perjury. He puts this case. A certain man is asked if it rained in a designated spot. The man believes that it *did not* rain. But it is to his interest to testify that it *did* rain. He, therefore, says that it did rain. In fact, it did rain in that place, but the man was ignorant of the fact. Saint Augustine says that the man is a perjurer. He testified to that which he thought was not true. His heart was not clean. *"Ream linguam non facit, nisi men sit rea."* The tongue does not do evil if the mind is not evil. But if the mind is evil, there is evil done even by an innocent act.

Applying the foregoing principles to the facts in the Griffiths Case, there can be no doubt that Clyde was morally guilty of the death of Roberta. One cannot say that it was "murder in the first degree" for the simple reason that that is a strictly technical term in substantive criminal law. It is not a term to be used out of its context. But the death of Roberta can be justly laid upon the soul of Clyde. He had bitterness and hatred in his heart for her even at the moment, when he reached out impulsively to help her. He accepted the opportunity offered by the accident. He made no move to undo that which his plan had made possible. Had he started to rescue Roberta and failed even, morals would have held him guiltless. There is always room for the *locus poenitentiae*. The vilest sinner may repent and be forgiven. But Clyde did not repent. There was no remorse. Coolly and calmly he swam ashore leaving Roberta to drown.

I can see no excuse for Clyde in morals. It might be argued that Clyde was so obsessed with an *idée fixe,* with the desire for her death, that he was not responsible in morals for his acts. But the argument would be fallacious. When a man deliberately fastens his mind on murder with such intensity that his activities become most automatically evil without conscious effort, he must stand the consequences of his unconscious acts. His obsession was voluntarily induced. His subconscious reactions were consciously attached to an evil thing. He is the author of his own "irresistible impulses." He cannot plead them in morals, or in strict law for that matter, as a defense to the charge of homicide.

The second answer to our problem is definite. Clyde Griffiths was guilty of the death of Roberta Alden.

IV.

As the Jury Saw the Case

A jury must base its verdict upon the facts as presented to them and upon the law as given by the Court. The charge given by the court was unimpeachable. It went straight to the heart of the case. Was Roberta drowned as the result of an accident or not? If so, the jury must find Clyde "not guilty." If not, then the jury must find Clyde "guilty." The fact that Clyde made no effort to rescue Roberta is immaterial in law. There was no duty upon him to rescue her. If Clyde *intentionally* did anything to contribute to the drowning then there was no accident, and Clyde was guilty of murder in the first degree.

The facts as presented by the prosecution were clear. There was a plan devised by Clyde, to get rid of Roberta; there were activities following this plan which brought Clyde and Roberta to the place where the death of Roberta occurred; there was a blow struck by Clyde which precipitated Roberta into the water; there was the desertion of Roberta in her peril, just as was planned, and the subsequent drowning. Even the most thoughtless man could see the causal chain in these series of facts. There was nothing subtle about them.

The defense was centered on two things. One, that there was an accident. Two, that there was no intent to kill, because there had been a change of heart on the part of Clyde. If the jury believed that either claim was true they should find Clyde, and would have to find Clyde, not guilty.

The first claim was true. The second was a lie. The jury did not believe that either was true. Nor were they unreasonable in so believing. After all if a man does repent of his evil plans, truly repent, he stops them from going forward. Clyde did nothing to show he was repentant. He went ahead with his plans. He himself said that Roberta was still above water when he saw her, after the boat had upset. But he made no move to save her. It was hardly reasonable for ordinary jurors to believe that Clyde could have really repented and had a change of heart if he made no move to save Roberta. He seemed quite willing to take advantage of the consequences of the accident. He did nothing to stop its consequences. The jury naturally wondered if there was an accident or not. It seemed rather a queer coincidence that an accident should bring about just what Clyde had deliberately planned and acted to produce. Was it not likely that Clyde had carried out his plan and then claimed that there was an accident to escape punishment? He was rather unconvincing in his story. He did not give the impression, while he was on the stand, that he really had had a change of heart. He did not show that he had abandoned his plan to kill. He could not seem to make clear just why he had struck Roberta with the camera, nor why he had not gone to her rescue. Of course, he was under no legal duty to go to her rescue, but if he had there would have been *something* human to show that he really did not intend to murder her. It was beyond a reasonable doubt, in the minds of the jury, that Clyde planned the death, worked to bring the death about, and actually got what he planned to get. The verdict was inevitable. He was guilty of murder. And as a matter of law, it was murder in the first degree.

Our third answer, therefore, is that the jury was justified in finding Clyde Griffiths guilty of murder in the first degree.

V.

The Social Background

The societal question in the Griffiths Case is this: was the social organization of which Clyde Griffiths was a part to blame for the death of Roberta Alden? The answer to this question must inevitably be a personal one. Organized society, by keeping on the statute books prohibitions against murder, and allowing no defense based upon weakness of will, unless such weakness amounts to insanity, and by imposing punishment upon weak-willed killers, has definitely given the answer that it is not to blame for such activities as Clyde Griffiths carried out. Furthermore, it does very little, if anything, to prevent such situations from arising. But the fact that organized society has given an answer to this question does not establish the validity of that answer. Nor need each member of the social group make that answer his own. I think that the answer given by society is wrong. I believe that the state (the social organization, the groups that are in control of the governmental machinery, the individuals who actually make the laws what they are), in spite of a theory of democratic control of human conduct, is to blame for the death of Roberta and the weakness of Clyde.

1. The starting point of the tragedy is the desire to gratify sex impulses. Both Clyde and Roberta felt, and yielded to, the sex urge. They were not to blame for that. It seems to be a Universal force, driving and expressing itself in every aspect of life. It cannot be denied. But it can be controlled. Clyde was never taught to control it. He was never told anything about it by either his family or the authorities of the state. For this the state is to blame. The state does not instruct growing children in matters of sex. It leaves this most important phase of existence to be picked up casually, filthily, sordidly, from dirty-minded men and women, who themselves have had no other approach to the problem than that of the beast and, often, the pervert. Occasionally a boy or girl is fortunate enough to have some rational, clean-minded discussion of sex problems. More recently the topic has been aired somewhat. But even now, most growing boys and girls do not get any information in a clean, sensible way. And yet the sex impulse, the urge to procreation, is the tenderest and sweetest and purest of all human impulses. It is only when it is perverted that it becomes a degraded thing. The state does degrade it.

In doing this the state accepts the ideas of orthodox Christian theology. Mark that I say *theology* and not *religion*. The Christian religion is founded upon Jesus. Christian theology is based upon Paul and Augustine. There is a vast difference between the two. It is the difference between beauty and purity and ugliness and filth. Jesus dealt with sex problems from the point of view of spiritual holiness. Paul and Augustine deal with them from the point of view of physical depravity.

It must never be forgotten that Paul was an oriental. In sex matters he had the harem point of view. Women were meant for physical gratification. That was all. They were excellent cooks, handmaids and mistresses. But they were snares and traps for men. They were potent instruments of the devil for keeping men out of heaven. Given the frailties of men, it was better that men "should marry rather than burn." But the state of true celestial purity was found only in total abnegation of the sex impulses. Furthermore, childbirth was an unholy thing. Men were conceived in sin and born in iniquity. Conception was evil. Childbirth called for a ceremonial purification of the mother. Otherwise men were defiled who came into any sort of contact with her. This position which Paul took was logically consistent with his notions of man's depravity. When Adam sinned in the Garden of Eden, all of mankind was eternally damned. The damnation was transmitted to all human beings until the Vicarious Atonement on the Cross at Calvary. It was inevitable that procreation was an evil and wicked thing. Woman seduced Man in the Garden of Eden by making him disobey God. She has been seducing him ever since, with her sex appeal, to the continued disobedience of God. The only thing for man to do, if he would truly save his soul, is to treat his sex impulses as coming from the devil, and to fight them to the point of utter negation.

Nor must it be forgotten that Augustine was a reformed Roman rake. He had gone through every form of sexual experience and perversion. His confessions make this quite clear. It was inevitable that his reactions to sex relations should be strongly antipathetic. Extremes lead to extremes. It is not to be wondered at that he accepted with great avidity the Pauline conceptions of sex relations. Following Paul's lead, also, he does, in his treatise on marriage, give some commendation to the marriage relation. But it is far inferior to the value and holiness of celibacy which he never tires of preaching.

Orthodox theology accepts the point of view of Paul and Augustine. This point of view has been given the sanction of the organized community. Our entire education system bars discussion of sex matters. If a teacher dares to discuss these things he is deemed immoral. The public schools cannot even teach sex matters as part of courses in physical hygiene. The whole subject is taboo. Prudery drives out modesty. Smut destroys knowledge. Ignorance parades as innocence. A fearsome and cowardly theology bars the doors of our educational institutions. Wisdom remains outside because theology is entrenched within.

There are thousands of Clydes and Robertas in the country. At the age of puberty they are gripped by the forces of sex. They are told nothing about them. They experience the urge. They yield to it. They find an indescribable ecstasy in its consummation. Nothing is told them of its value and purpose, as a matter of social welfare. Self-control is not taught. Attempts to discuss it are frowned down by parents, teachers and clergy. But they will have information. And they get the wrong kind.

So long as children are permitted to grow up in ignorance of the most driving force they will ever experience in life,

Robertas and Clydes will continue to do in the darkness and by stealth what they might not do if they knew what sex impulses were all about. So long as the policy of suppression and ignorance continues, the state will be to blame for the results of such ignorance. The state should kick Paul and Augustine out of the schools and put Jesus there. "Except ye become as little children ye cannot enter the kingdom of heaven." He could not have intended to people heaven with those who were conceived in sin and born in iniquity. Little children are not the depraved outcome of devilish impulses. They are the flowering of noble and uplifting physical and spiritual communion between men and women.

2. This brings us to the second point in the tragedy. It is the problem of birth control. The federal governments and most of the governments of the several states make it a criminal offense to disseminate contraceptive appliances or information. Abortion is a crime in every state in the Union. No reputable physician will perform an abortion except when absolutely sure that childbirth will be dangerous to the mother. The result is that whatever abortions are performed must be done under cover, by unscrupulous physicians or ignorant midwives and practitioners who should not be permitted to handle such cases at all.

This to my mind is wrong. If children are not wanted they should not be born. It is not fair to them. Every child is entitled to being born into social relations and conditions which make for its proper development and nurture. If the state does not provide for such proper opportunities it ought not to interfere with those who wish to abort the birth of children. On the contrary they should provide means both for preventing the birth of children, and for stopping the birth, in proper time, of those organisms which if permitted to develop will become children, if the natural parents of the fetus do not want the child to be born. Both men and womenshould be instructed in contraceptive methods and principles. Clinics should be established and supported by the state where those who had failed in carrying out the information they had could be helped if they did not want the children to be born. The very best physicians should be authorized, under the same type of safeguards which now govern their admission to the practice of medicine, to abort any conception which came without the wish of the mother, and her continued desire to give birth to the child. Birth control for the sake of the general welfare is sound in principle and inevitable, to my mind, as a matter of law.

If there had been some place where Roberta could have gone legally and without social stigma when first she found herself pregnant and been relieved of the fetus she had conceived, there would have been no need for Clyde's plotting and planning. There would have been no murder. A life not yet in being, but only in process of becoming, could have been stopped. But two lives already in being would have been conserved. Furthermore, the life which it is the function of the abortion laws to conserve, that of the unborn child, was also destroyed.

The purpose of the law was thwarted. The law was ineffective. It failed in action. The state did not save the life it was trying to save. It lost two lives it had. It snapped at a shadow and lost the substance.

The opposition to birth control is based upon two concepts. All arguments come back to them.

(a) The first is that birth control would tend to an increase in immorality. And by immorality is meant sexual intercourse between the sexes. This is the theological argument we have already discussed. It is Paul and Augustine once more. But there is nothing inherently wicked about sexual intercourse. The wickedness comes in thinking that it is evil. Granting, for the sake of the argument, that there would be an increase in sexual intercourse, one may ask; Well, why should there not be an increase? Where is the inherent wrong in having the functioning of the strongest of the human impulses increased? The instinct itself is not evil. It is only its perversion or abuse which is evil. If the instinct itself is socially inimical then all human beings should be treated the way some of the insane and epileptic are treated in some of the states. They should be sterilized. It is a commonplace of medicine that sterilization reduces the sex urge to a minimum. It does not utterly destroy the sex impulse or sex desire, but it comes as close to doing that as human science can get.

But the ones who are most insistent that birth control is evil are equally insistent that the gratification of the sex urge is proper and valid within the marriage relation. For married people the instinct is not evil. For unmarried people the instinct is evil. And when you ask them: Why is sexual intercourse right when the pair are married, and wrong when they are not? you get no sensible answer. They always come back, in some form or other, to the notion that children will be born, and that the children will beillegitimate. But that notion is utterly stupid. It loses sight of the whole subject matter of the discussion. Birth control will prevent children from being born. If they are not born they cannot be illegitimate. They are nonexistent. And at this point in the argument the opponents of birth control usually switch to the second fundamental concept.

(b) This concept is that neither individual nor state has the moral right to interfere with the development of life, once life has started to exist. Hence from the moment that the ovum is fertilized by the spermatozoa nothing should be done to hinder the potential child from coming into being. Life has started. It must be permitted to continue.

It is difficult for me to listen to the enunciation of this concept with any degree of patience. And for this reason. The most dogmatic proponents of the conception are the staunchest advocates of war and the bitterest foes of social legislation, the purpose of which is to alleviate the lot of little children. The same forces that fight the birth control movement fight the child labor laws and the peace movement. And for the life of me I cannot see the value of letting an impregnated ovum develop into a human being when that human being is to be destroyed by slow stages, as happens in child labor, or is to be wiped out in the flicker of an eyelash as happened to millions during the World War. It seems to me that if the choice could be exercised, the ovum would rather not be born than be born to misery and suffering. Furthermore, if life *is* sacred why permit thousands of lives to be destroyed yearly by industrial conditions which are a disgrace to civilization? Sweatshops, mines, steel mills, cotton mills, and oil refineries daily take their toll of human lives. And yet any attempt to ameliorate conditions in industry so that industry may become less dangerous to workers meets determined resistance on the part of those who raise the cry of socialism, paternalism, bolshevism and communism. And those persons are also found to be opponents of birth control. They are not really interested in maintaining the sanctity of life, but in maintaining the sanctity of life until *they* can use life for their own purposes. Life is sacred, until it becomes the life of a child, who can be kept in a cotton mill until its body is twisted and broken and its soul is stunted beyond development. Life is sacred, until it becomes the life of a man working in a coal mine. Then it can be destroyed, without compunction, by permitting the mine to cave in, although proper shoring would prevent the loss of life. Life is sacred, until it is placed in the scales to be weighed against profits in industry. Then life becomes as small dust in the balance. Life is sacred until the business and political rivalries of ambitious and self-seeking men develop wars. Then life becomes cannon food and nothing more. Life is sacred until *they* wish to destroy it. Then it is sacred no more. When the opponents of birth control put the full weight of their power behind a program of social legislation which will conserve life in industry and politics, enact that program into law, and see to it that they and others obey the law, it will be time enough to listen to their arguments which are based on the sanctity of life. Until then they must be deemed users of words without meaning and mouthers of phrases without sense. Emerson's phrase comes pat. What they are speaks so loud, we cannot hear what they say.

Sometimes the concept is altered. The argument is made in this fashion. If birth control is permitted, women would be unwilling to suffer the pangs of childbirth and men would not want the annoyance of providing for children when it would be simple to prevent children from being born. Hence, the human race would soon die out. And they point to France as an example of what birth control will do. Ignoring for the time being the utter absurdity of thinking that the desire for children would vanish utterly from the present generations of men and women, and accepting the argument as made, we may well raise the question; What of it? Why should the human race not vanish from the face of the earth? Why should it persist? Why should human beings be born?

The answers given to such questions by the opponents of birth control all come back to a theological basis. This is, that God has planted the procreative instinct in the human

spirit and to abort that instinct is to attempt to thwart the will of God. Such an attempt is a sin and, therefore, wrong.

It is an odd fact that the chief opponent of birth control, the Roman Catholic Church, stresses this answer. Yet, at the same time, it commends and fosters the most perfect type of birth control, celibacy and utter continence. It wants all men and all women to be married only to the Church. The highest type of human perfection is attained by entering into a monastery or nunnery. This calls for the total negation of the procreative instinct. This ought to be a sin. But it isn't. Such inconsistency would be ludicrous were it not so beautifully human. And, paradoxical as it may sound, the inconsistency is not illogical. The conclusions are predicated upon different premises. Starting with the Augustinian position that sex impulses are immoral, the monastic ideal of celibacy is inevitable. But starting with practical considerations such as, that most folks won't negate their sex impulses, that no church can exist if its adherents practice race suicide, and that the civil power of the church will increase as the number of its adherents will increase and these adherents attain to civil power, one can easily avoid looking at inconsistencies of position and solemnly aver that the sex impulse is God-given and must under no circumstances be interfered with under penalty of sin.

When the state liberates itself from the thrall of these two concepts it can claim to be guiltless of the death of Roberta and Clyde. Until then the state must bear the onus of their destruction.

3. The third point in the tragedy brings up the question of capital punishment. Should Clyde have been executed for the death of Roberta?

(a) As a matter of fact and law he should not have been. He was not guilty of murder in the first degree.

(b) Upon the facts as the jury saw them the execution was legal and justified. This is not the place for a discussion of the value and defects of trial by jury. I wish simply to state that I believe that trial by jury is the best means yet devised by organized society for the settling of disputes between men and for the determination of the guilt or innocence of those who are accused of crime. Defects exist. Miscarriages of justice do occur. But the benefits of trial by jury outweigh its defects. Until a system of perfect justice is found, trial by jury is as good as one can expect any human institution to be.

(c) Does capital punishment deserve a place in modern criminology?

1. Speaking generally, I think it does. The modern state has no high regard for human life. One need but to recur to the present industrial situation within which thousands of innocent lives are destroyed yearly, by swift or slow means, and to the maintenance of war as a legal institution to prove this. I cannot get excited about the execu-

tion of weaklings or evil-doers. There are times when human beings act so that they become unendurable menaces to organized society. There is no reason why they should be conserved. I have no hesitancy about shooting a mad dog or killing a rattlesnake. Some men are as dangerous as both of these. I see no reason why they should be permitted to exist. So long as he exists he is a potential menace to other human beings. In balancing out the value of a human being who is a potential menace against the value of having the community live in safety and freedom from fear, I decide against the individual life. There is no inherent validity to my decision. If I thought that an individual life was of more value than the general peace and security, I should decide the other way. Nor can I see it as a kindness to the malefactor that you spare his life but shut him up for life in prison or penitentiary. A swift death is better than a lingering one. Such is my belief. I am keenly aware of the possible fallibility of my judgment. But such as it is I stand upon it. There are times when the safety of the state calls for the death of an individual. Because of this, capital punishment has its place in any system of criminology.

2. Speaking specifically, I cannot see any reason why Clyde should have been permitted to live. He was a spiritual weakling with criminal susceptibilities. A study of recidivism leads me to believe that offenders of Clyde's type never repent of their acts, become repeaters in crime, can never be rehabilitated and cannot be made safe for societal existence. As the novelist paints Clyde, there is nothing which can contribute to the social welfare which will outweigh the social danger he represents. If he had some qualities of genius, could paint a picture, or write a book, or discover a principle of science which could be utilized by society, one might be justified in sparing him for the social gain that might come of it. But so far as I can see Clyde was a noxious weed. I see no reason why he should not be destroyed. Technically he was not guilty of the death of Roberta. Morally, socially, he was guilty of her death and of other offenses against the law. He managed to escape detection for the other offenses, at the time they were committed. That is all. Circumstances convicted him for a crime he wanted to commit but was too cowardly to consummate. It is immaterial, to my mind, how the law got him. Once the law had him, it was justified in ridding the world of him, so far as death can rid the world of any species of life. He was a bit of poison ivy. There is no reason, so far as I can see, for letting him continue to grow in the field of human life, or on a prison wall.

But I cannot exculpate the state. It is to blame for the need to put Clyde to death. Had social conditions been better, had society done its part with the child that Clyde once was, he might have been if not a flower, at least, perhaps, a less noxious weed.

The fourth answer to our question, then, is this: The state is primarily to blame for the death of Roberta, Clyde and their unborn child. Organized society should mend its ways. It should reduce to a minimum the possibility of the recurrence of such a tragedy. How should this be done? I do not know.

WORKS CITED

"'American Tragedy' Essay Contest." *Publishers' Weekly* 3 (1927): 1338.

"Bishop Brown to Appeal." *New York Times* 20 Sept. 1925: 26.

"Holmes Praises Brown." *New York Times* 3 Aug. 1925: 18.

Lévitt, Albert. Letter to Theodore Dreiser. 18 Nov. 1926. The Theodore Dreiser Papers, Special Collections, Van Pelt Library, University of Pennsylvania. The Trustees of the University of Pennsylvania. Quoted with permission.

Orton, Vrest. *Dreiserana: A Book About His Books.* New York: Chocorua, 1929.

Pizer, Donald, Richard W. Dowell, and Frederic E. Rusch. *Theodore Dreiser: A Primary and Secondary Bibliography.* Boston: Hall, 1975.

Salzman, Jack, ed. *Theodore Dreiser: The Critical Reception.* New York: Lewis, 1972.

Swanberg, W.A. *Dreiser.* New York: Scribners, 1965.

Kathryn M. Plank (essay date 1991)

SOURCE: "Dreiser's Real American Tragedy," in *Papers on Language and Literature,* Vol. 27, No. 2, Spring, 1991, pp. 268-87.

[*In the following essay, Plank traces the nonfiction sources of* An American Tragedy.]

In the early 1930s a series of events led Theodore Dreiser to write several articles explaining the historical background of *An American Tragedy.* Dreiser had based much of the novel, which was published in 1925, on Chester Gillette's murder of Grace Brown in 1906. In 1931 the New York Supreme Court ruled against Dreiser, who had complained about Paramount's film version of the novel. The court held that *An American Tragedy* was the story of Chester Gillette and therefore was in public domain. That same year, Elisha Kane, a professor at the University of Tennessee, was accused of drowning his wife. Supposedly a copy of *An American Tragedy* was found in his hotel room. Kane was acquitted, but in 1934 and 1935 two more murders were noted by the press for their resemblance to the crime depicted in *An American Tragedy.* Newspapers commonly referred to them as the "American Tragedy" murders and invited Dreiser to comment on the cases. In 1934 he wrote a series of articles for the *New York Post* on the trial of Robert Allen

Edwards, and in 1935 he wrote another article in the *Los Angeles Examiner* on the Newell Paige Sherman case. Together, these four events raised two important questions about *An American Tragedy*. Had Dreiser merely copied the story of Chester Gillette for his novel? And was the novel responsible for the "American Tragedy" murders which occurred afterward? Partly in answer to these questions, and partly to capitalize on the renewed interest in his novel, Dreiser wrote several articles explaining the composition of *An American Tragedy*. In addition to the newspaper articles on the Edwards and Sherman cases, he also wrote two versions of an unpublished article titled "American Tragedies."[1] Later he revised "American Tragedies" and used it as the introductory portion of **"I Find the Real American Tragedy,"** a much longer article on the Edwards case published serially in *Mystery Magazine* from February to June 1935. In these articles he discusses the philosophical and historical sources of the novel.

Because it outlines the sources of *An American Tragedy*, **"I Find the Real American Tragedy"** has become a major document for Dreiser critics studying the composition of the novel. Dreiser's article clarifies and elaborates the themes of the unpublished "American Tragedies" manuscripts and of the published newspaper articles, drawing from them a paradigm of the socially and economically motivated murder—such as the one depicted in *An American Tragedy*. In **"I Find the Real American Tragedy"** Dreiser states that the numerous murder cases he studied form a specific pattern, which he describes as "That of the young ambitious lover of some poorer girl, who in the earlier state of his affairs had been attractive enough to satisfy him both in the matter of love and her social station. But nearly always with the passing of time and the growth of experience on the part of the youth, a more attractive girl withmoney or position appeared and he quickly discovered that he could no longer care for his first love" (6). Dreiser supports this pattern by listing the "many related cases which had occurred before" (9), suggesting that the kind of crime depicted in *An American Tragedy* was a national phenomenon. By describing the details of some of these other murders, Dreiser establishes a pattern which supports his conclusion that Clyde Griffiths was a victim of a society that demanded success without giving him the means of attaining it. With this argument Dreiser answers the questions regarding the relationship between *An American Tragedy* and these historical cases. Since the Gillette case was only one example of a specific kind of crime, Dreiser argues, the novel is not a report of one case but a portrayal of a sociological phenomenon. The more recent murders were only two more manifestations of this pattern. According to Dreiser's argument, *An American Tragedy* is not journalism or fiction but is instead social criticism, detecting and illuminating a serious fault in American culture.

Understandably, Dreiser critics have accepted the model in **"I Find the Real American Tragedy,"** basing their studies on the "type" of murder which so clearly structures it.[2] The novel is assumed to be based on historical events which Dreiser, as a former journalist, had investigated. However, close study of the composition of **"I Find the Real American Tragedy"** reveals that the article should be regarded as an extension of the fiction of the novel, not as historical research. The first drafts of the article, the "American Tragedies" manuscripts, were written by Dreiser in anger and haste. After the Edwards murder in 1934, he responded to charges that he had indirectly caused this murder by referring for the first time to a long tradition of similar murders. The style of the surviving manuscript is informal, with Dreiser inventing this tradition of crime as he writes. He is unsure of the details of the cases, of names and dates, and acknowledges possible errors—"he seduced a poor young girl, a nurse, I believe, but I am not sure." Later he writes, "A certain young Orton or Orpenor—I forget which" ("American Tragedies" B 7, 8). Furthermore, Dreiser's clippings file reveals not an organized survey of "a certain type of crime," but a scattered collection of interesting murders involving insurance fraud and insanity, sex crimes and revenge, and even hexes and witchcraft. Dreiser is not recording the results of years of study, but is spontaneously pulling names from his memory to create what he needs—a pattern of similar crimes.

"American Tragedies," never published, is an important artifact in the post-publication history of *An American Tragedy*. The ideas of this article, written in anger and defensiveness, were the basis for a myth which would eventually be accepted as fact. Dreiser recognized that this myth reinforced the theory behind *An American Tragedy*, so he refined his ideas in a second version of the article and developed them further in **"I Find the Real American Tragedy,"** adopting a more confident tone in this final version. The cases he hastily seized from his memory in "American Tragedies" werereshaped to form a definite pattern in **"I Find the Real American Tragedy."** Consequently, when Newell Paige Sherman was convicted in 1935 of drowning his wife, Dreiser refers confidently to the tradition of crime as if it were a long-established fact. The myth Dreiser had created had taken on a reality of its own.

However, these are not a series of "chillingly similar crimes" (Fishkin 117), but a varied collection of murders with only occasional similarities. Dreiser did not derive the pattern from a study of the murders; rather, he imposed the pattern upon them. The murders described in Dreiser's articles are very different from their historical counterparts. Dreiser alters the cases to fit the pattern of motivation he had already established, a pattern that supports his own theories about American society. The real sources of the paradigm—Dreiser's own life and his observations of American society—are deeply rooted and complex. The crime in the novel is truly the creative product of the author's philosophy and experience. In order to add a sense of historical verifiability to the social and economic forces that he offers as the motivation for crime in *An American Tragedy*, Dreiser creates a tradition of similar crimes. Although this tradition is not factually accurate, it is a valuable extension of the novel.

The errors in **"I Find the Real American Tragedy"** are not evidence of a careless researcher, but of an imaginative writer who borrows from history to support his fiction. It reveals that Dreiser depended less on historical events and factual details than many people have argued. Evidence of inaccuracies may prevent scholars from continuing to use it as verification of Dreiser's reliance on historical fact, but the article is still valuable (perhaps even more valuable than before) when seen as a fictional creation. It is the pattern Dreiser creates through this fiction, and not the historical truth, which illuminates the themes of *An American Tragedy.*

Dreiser creates this pattern by altering the facts of a number of historical murder cases. As Dreiser indicates, his interest in sensational public murders began over thirty years before the publication of *An American Tragedy,* when, as a young reporter in St. Louis in 1892, he heard about a perfume dealer in that city who had murdered his lover. Dreiser claims in 1935 that this case was followed by more than seventeen similar murders, and that "between 1895 and this present year there has scarcely been a year in which some part of the country has not been presented with a crime of this type."[3] He then proceeds to discuss several of these crimes, demonstrating how they fit his pattern.

Of the cases mentioned in **"I Find the Real American Tragedy,"** Dreiser seems to have investigated most closely the trial of Roland B. Molineux in 1899-1902. The Molineux case, which filled newspapers for four years, was at least as well known as the Gillette murder. The New York papers regularly carried several pages of daily stenographic reports, even as the proceedings dragged on to include a lengthy inquest, several hearings before the grand jury, and two trials with long weeks of repetitive testimony by handwriting experts. On 14 January 1915 Dreiser began writing *The "Rake",* a novel based on the Molineux case, which was in many ways his first attempt at *An American Tragedy.* After gathering clippings from the *New York World* Dreiser completed six chapters of the manuscript before abandoning the project. Because of the sheer volume of evidence generated by this complicated case, Dreiser scholars have often reduced it to the story of a man who kills his rival for "the charms of an actress," a simplification which can be made to fit Dreiser's pattern (Swanberg 178). While such a story may have been the intended plot of *The "Rake",* the actual case is much less easily defined, and even less easily presented as a direct source for *An American Tragedy.*

The Molineux case centers around the Knickerbocker Athletic Club, where Molineux was a member and an officer.[4] The victim was Mrs. Kate Adams, the fifty-two-year-old aunt of Harry Cornish, physical director of the club. On 28 December 1898 Mrs. Adams swallowed cyanide of mercury, disguised as a sample of bromo-seltzer that had been mailed anonymously to Cornish. Mrs. Adams's death brought about renewed interest in the sudden death of Henry C. Barnet, another club member,

who had died of diphtheria a month earlier after he too had received a sample of a patent medicine in the mail. Cornish, the intended recipient of the medicine which killed Mrs. Adams, blamed Roland Molineux, a chemist and color maker in a paint factory. Two years earlier, Molineux had complained about Cornish's management of the club, and Cornish had retaliated by spreading malicious rumors about Molineux, causing Molineux to resign and join another club. The prosecution, claiming that Barnet had had an affair with Molineux's wife, Blanche Chesebrough Molineux, attempted to prove that Molineux had committed both murders. He was tried and convicted of the Adams murder but was later acquitted in a second trial. After his release Blanche divorced him. Later he suffered from mental illness (spending time at Muldoon's Sanitarium, where Dreiser had recovered from his own illness in 1904) and died of paresis fifteen years later.

In writing *The "Rake"* Dreiser eventually found that the Molineux case did not provide an historical basis for the kind of crime he wanted to portray. Molineux was a young socialite who had already achieved the kind of success for which Clyde is willing to commit murder. His mother was "of an excellent family," and his father, "brave, heroic General Molineux," was "reputed to be a millionaire or nearly so," and was respected and revered by the public, the press, and even the prosecution.[5] Molineux's manner reflected his background and position; he was "so suave, so well balanced, so perfectly master of himself" (*New York World* 28 Feb. 1899: 3). He charmed the public, who greeted his acquittal with an ovation and carried him home in a triumphal procession. With family, money, education, and popularity, Molineux had already realized Clyde's ambitions. He could not very well have served as the model of the striving young man who murders to achieve such ambitions. Although a novel based on a case as sensational as Molineux's would probably have attracted a wide audience, it did not provide Dreiser with a vehicle for his ideas about society, marriage, ambition, and murder.

Although Dreiser found that the Molineux case did not conform with the ideas he wanted to express, he later cites it as evidence of those very ideas in **"I Find the Real American Tragedy."** Curiously, however, despite all his work on *The "Rake",* in **"I Find the Real American Tragedy"** Dreiser does not discuss the Molineux case. He merely notes, "In 1907 or 1908 the Roland Molyneux case of New York City"—thus misstating both the name and the date (8). In the earlier article, "American Tragedies," he supplies a slightly more detailed but still erroneous account: "He—somewhat differently, sought to poison a male rival who had taken his best girl away from him, but by accident, killed a woman whom he did not know—the housekeeper of his rival, who took the poison by mistake and died instantly" ("American Tragedies" B 11). Such major errors in describing a case Dreiser had studied so closely and had begun to write a book about are puzzling. Faulty memory does not seem to be a sufficient explanation. Since Dreiser omitted all discussion of the case from the final draft of **"I Find the Real American Tragedy,"** one possible conclusion is that he knew, both from his troubles in writing *The "Rake"* and from the changes he had to make in describing the case in "American Tragedies," that the Molineux case would not fit his paradigm convincingly. Instead, Dreiser retreats to merely a passing mention of the case that at one time was to be the basis of *An American Tragedy.*

In discussing some of the other murders, however, Dreiser gives longer descriptions in order to fit them into his paradigm, although most of them are in reality as dissimilar to the crime in *An American Tragedy* as is the Molineux case. The first case that he names as a source for the novel is that of Carlyle Harris, who was executed in 1893 for the murder of his wife, Mary Helen Neilson Potts.[6] In February 1891 Helen Potts died of an overdose of morphine, presumably contained in the sleeping pills that Harris, a medical student, had prescribed for her. Harris and Potts had been secretly married, under false names, the previous February. During the summer of 1890 Helen Potts's uncle, one Dr. Treverton, performed an abortion on Helen and accused Harris of making two unsuccessful attempts to abort this same pregnancy. Helen's mother, the only one who knew they were married, wanted to make the marriage public. Shortly before Helen Potts died, Harris finally promised to acknowledge the marriage, which he had kept hidden because it might have endangered his status in medical school.

The Harris case bears a superficial resemblance to the murder in *An American Tragedy:* a young man is convicted of murdering his lover (in this case a secret wife) who has become pregnant. But beyond this framework, there are few similarities. In **"I Find the Real American Tragedy"** Dreiser alters his account of the case to make it resemble *An American Tragedy* more closely. According to Dreiser, Harris "seduced a young girl poorer and less distinguished than he was, or at least hoped to be. No sooner had he done this than the devil . . . presented Carlyle with an attractive girl of much higher station than his own, one who possessed not only beauty but wealth" (**"I Find"** 7). Based on this plot, Dreiser blames Harris's mother "for her urgency and insistence on what was the proper type of life for him," and he blames America for "its craze for social and money success" (**"I Find"** 7). Dreiser depicts the case as a simple conflict between "Miss Poor" and "Miss Rich," a crime arising from the American dream of success at any cost ("American Tragedies" B 7).

But the actual case does not fit so neatly into Dreiser's pattern. Harris, like Clyde Griffiths, had been poor in his youth and had been forced to leave school and begin working to support his family (Ledyard 9). But Harris succeeded where Clyde failed. Harris did not need to resort to murder to achieve success; he succeeded within the rules of society. With the financial assistance of his maternal grandfather, Harris entered the Columbia College of Physicians and Surgeons, where he demonstrated his ability by winning first place in a competitive examination for an appointment to Charity Hospital. Furthermore, Harris's marriage to Helen Potts actually improved his prospects for the future. Harris's father was an alcoholic incapable of providing for his family, but Helen's father was an upper-middle-class railroad engineer. In addition, Helen's mother had promised to give Harris and Helen $5000 for a trip to Europe after he completed medical school.

In view of these facts, the prosecution was never able to establish a convincing motive for the murder. Since Helen Potts was destined to inherit a fairly large amount of money, and Harris would most likely become a successful physician, money was not a plausible motive. Neither was the pregnancy a problem, for the abortion had been performed successfully several months prior to the murder. The other young woman, "who possessed not only beauty but wealth" (**"I Find"** 7), was in reality an actress of questionable reputation named Queenie Drew, with whom Harris had had a brief affair. Although she was also from a wealthy family, Queenie was not a serious threat to Helen Potts. She freely participated in her affair with Harris and seems not to have expected him to marry her. The prosecution attempted in vain to find another woman who could have replaced Helen in Harris's desires, but no motive was found to explain why Harris would want to murder Helen, who was by all accounts beautiful, intelligent, and financially secure.

Although he met Harris's mother, Hope Ledyard, in 1894, Dreiser was probably only casually familiar with this crime.[7] However, as recently as 1915 he would have been reminded of the problematic lack of motive in the case. The newspaper reports of the Molineux trial in both the *Times* and the *World* compared the current case to the Harris poisoning several times. On the same page from which Dreiser copied information about cyanide of mercury for *The "Rake"*, the *World* reporter asked Francis C. Wellman, the district attorney who convicted Harris, to comment on both cases. Wellman emphasizes the lack of motive: "We never could discover the motive for taking the life of Helen Potts, because he was poor and was offered support and a European medical education at the hands of her father if the marriage were made public, and there seemed every reason why he should accept the proposition" (*New York World* 8 Jan. 1899: 2). Although Dreiser very likely read this statement, he contradicts it in his own account. In fact, Dreiser takes advantage of the lack of motive to supply his own. Whereas the prosecution could not discover the reason behind the murder, Dreiser invents a motive of ambition and desire. It is this motive, of course, which is important in establishing the roots of *An American Tragedy;* the actual case is merely used as a name for the fictionalized version of the crime which Dreiser describes in **"I Find the Real American Tragedy."**

Dreiser alters the motive in another case to provide an historical parallel for Clyde's crime. In **"I Find the Real American Tragedy"** he mentions a case in San Francisco in 1899. Although he gives no more details, in the revised version of "American Tragedies" he says that one of the murderers he studied "lured a girl to a belfry and was hopeful that her body would never be discovered! In that case, circling buzzards and carion [sic] crows exposed the crime" ("American Tragedies" A 3). This description, in conjunction with the reference to a murder in San Francisco, points to the case of Theodore Durrant, whom Dreiser also mentions in *Hey Rub-A-Dub-Dub* (126). Although Dreiser added the buzzards and crows, this 1895 murder was lurid and bizarre enough to have captured the fancy of the young journalist in New York. On 13 April 1895 a group of women entered the Emanuel Baptist Church to decorate it for Easter services, only to find the horribly butchered body of Marian Williams in the church library.[8] The young woman had worked as a domestic and was an active member of the church. While searching the church, police discovered the strangled body of Blanche Lamont, another church member, who had been reported missing ten days earlier. Since the day of her disappearance, Lamont's body had been lying undetected in the belfry of the church, stripped nude and laid out with some care and respect in the position of a body during an autopsy. Suspicion fell almost immediately on Theodore Durrant, a young medical student and secretary of the Young People's Society of the church.

Dreiser apparently found in Durrant an interesting demonstration of his belief in the failure of conventional religion to suppress sexuality. Both girls were noted for their extremely high morality and sexual innocence. Durrant, who knew the women through their participation in the church, had a reputation as spotless as those of his victims. He had "a moral character so high that he chose most of his companions from the Sunday school of which he was assistant superintendent. Tobacco, liquor, profanity and vulgarity were vices in which he never indulged" (*San Francisco Examiner* 15 April 1895: 4). Yet this model of Christian virtue also had a less righteous reputation in other circles. Fellow students commented on his tasteless boasting about sexual conquests and about his visits to brothels. The two sexually naive, religious young women had unexpectedly incited a violent, uncontrollable passion in this seemingly upright young Sunday school teacher.

Appropriately, Dreiser cites the Durrant case in *Hey Rub-A-Dub-Dub* when discussing the nation's "profound and even convulsive interest in any case involving a sex crime or delusion" (126). Since no other motive could be found, and since Minnie Williams had been raped shortly before she was strangled and stabbed, the prosecution charged that Durrant murdered Blanche Lamont when she would not submit to his sexual advances. In support of this theory, another woman testified that Durrant had tried to lure her into the church to conduct a "medical examination." The newspapers depicted Durrant as a monster and said he suffered from "psycho mania sexualis" (*San Francisco Examiner* 16 April 1895: 2). The public reacted violently against this "fiend" of sexuality. The verdict of guilty was received with an "inarticulate, half savage, half rejoicing cry from the body of

the room" (*San Francisco Examiner* 2 Nov. 1895: 1). The simultaneous horror and fascination provoked by this case proves Dreiser correct: "Our conviction is apparently that sexuality is essentially wrong and debasing," he writes, "and yet we do not really think so, as our intense national interest in every phase of sex proves" (*Hey Rub-A-Dub-Dub* 131).

However interesting a study of social psychology or sexual repression this case may be, it is not a good example of the type of crime in *An American Tragedy*. Durrant's violent lust, which leads to rape and brutal, bloody murder, is very different from Clyde's rather naive sexuality. Furthermore, money was not a factor in these crimes. Blanche Lamont, a student in a normal school, was of approximately the same class as Durrant; she "was not an heiress about whom dark plots might be hatched" (*San Francisco Examiner* 13 April 1895: 8). Minnie Williams, who was forced to work when her parents divorced, could be construed as the "Miss Poor" of the paradigm, except that Durrant was not trapped by her—he barely knew her. He was engaged to Flo Upton, but she was a governess, not an heiress, and was not likely to raise the social position of a future dentist enough to warrant murder. Dreiser does not offer a description of the case in any of the articles, but he includes it in his list of similar crimes. By placing this murder within the pattern, he implies that it is a source for the crime in *An American Tragedy*.

Dreiser does discuss in more depth the case that was the basis for another attempt at *An American Tragedy* after the failure of *The "Rake"*. He reports in "American Tragedies" that he had written six chapters of a book based on Clarence Richeson's murder of Avis Linnell before he decided to base his novel on the Gillette case ("American Tragedies" B 9). This time he was working with a source which closely resembles the murder he would finally depict in *An American Tragedy*. Clarence Richeson was a minister in Avis Linnell's hometown of Hyannisport, Massachusetts.[9] He was a friend of the Linnell family, and eventually he and Avis Linnell became lovers. Later, Richeson was transferred to a more prestigious church in Boston, where he became engaged to Violet Edmands, the daughter of one of his wealthy parishioners. Yet he continued to see Avis Linnell, who had also come to Boston in order to attend the New England Conservatory of Music. Eventually she became pregnant, and on 14 October 1911 she died of cyanide poisoning. When her connection with Richeson was revealed, the police discovered that on 10 October he had bought cyanide, supposedly to kill a pregnant dog, and that he had had lunch with Linnell the afternoon she died. Although Richeson at first denied the charges, he finally confessed "that he had wronged an innocent girl, and that he had finally murdered her that he might satisfy his own selfish and proud desires by marrying another" (*New York Times* 7 Jan. 1912: 1). In his confession, Richeson describes a motive that fits, fairly closely, the model Dreiser sets forth in **"I Find the Real American Tragedy."**

Not only does Richeson's crime resemble *An American Tragedy*, but Richeson himself is a likely model for Clyde Griffiths. Richeson, whose good looks gained him the attention of a young heiress, physically resembled the pale, dark-eyed Clyde. Richeson was also abnormally nervous, subject to nervous "fits" that could incapacitate him both physically and mentally. He personifies Dreiser's theories on sex and morality, for he was apparently unable to control either his sexual impulses or the guilt accompanying such desires. In prison, out of remorse and guilt for a murder resulting from his sexuality, he tried to castrate himself with a jar lid. He immediately called for help, and doctors were able to save his life, but, according to the *World*, only by performing "an operation that left the man emasculated" (*New York World* 21 Dec. 1911: 7). "Alienists" spent several days examining Richeson as his attorneys unsuccessfully tried to prove insanity in order to prevent execution. The image of Richeson as a "mentally weak" man who was forced to murder in order to realize his financial and sexual ambitions is strongly reminiscent of the depiction of Clyde Griffiths (*New York Times* 3 Jan. 1912: 8).

Clarence Richeson and Clyde Griffiths are not the same man, however. Richeson was not wealthy, for example, but neither was he a product of poverty like Clyde. Dreiser asserts that Richeson "was a man of poverty-stricken background" (*Los Angeles Examiner* 23 July 1935: 2), but in fact, Richeson's father was "a substantial, though not wealthy farmer" in Virginia and "one of the most prominent residents of the county" (*New York Times* 21 Oct. 1911: 1). Richeson, unlike Clyde, was also relatively well educated; he had attended both William Jewell College and Newton Theological Institution. Furthermore, Richeson's affair with Avis Linnell was only the last in a series of similarly awkward situations. A few years earlier, three women had forced him to resign his post at a Kansas City church after they discovered that they were all three engaged to him simultaneously. Members of his church in Hyannisport accused him of exercising hypnotic powers over women, and the newspapers claimed that he was engaged to a total of nine women. Even allowing for the inevitable exaggerations of the press in a sensational case, the evidence still suggests that Richeson was not a naive youngster trapped in an incomprehensible situation. He was instead a thirty-year-old man with a history of sexual adventuring. Still, Richeson's case, alone among those listed by Dreiser, follows fairly closely the model of American crime set out in **"I Find the Real American Tragedy."** Dreiser does not say why he abandoned his novel on a case that fit his intentions so well. Whatever the reason, he left the Richeson novel unfinished and a year or two later began to write *An American Tragedy*.

Another example which Dreiser cites in **"I Find the Real American Tragedy,"** the case of William Orpet in 1916, also resembles some aspects of the plot of *An American Tragedy*. Orpet, a junior at the University of Wisconsin, was accused of poisoning Marian Lambert, a high school student in Lake Forest, Illinois.[10] Orpet was engaged to marry Celeste Youker when Marian told him that she was pregnant. She either mistakenly believed she was pregnant, or else she claimed to be in order to prevent Orpet from marrying Celeste Youker. On 9 February 1916 he secretly left Madison, Wisconsin, and met Marian Lambert by prearrangement in the woods near Lake Forest, bringing with him a bottle that he later said contained a placebo of molasses and water to calm Marian's anxieties about pregnancy. In the woods, Orpet, who claimed to know that Marian was not in fact pregnant, told Marian that he still intended to marry Youker. Orpet later stated that after he turned to go, Marian swallowed cyanide crystals that she herself had brought to the woods. The prosecution claimed that the bottle Orpet brought actually contained liquid cyanide, which he offered to Marian Lambert as an abortifacient. Since both persons had easy access to cyanide—Orpet at the greenhouse of the estate where his father worked, and Lambert in her high-school chemistry class—both stories were plausible. However, when the defense proved that the cyanide from the greenhouse could not have been the cyanide that killed Lambert, their argument that Lambert was depressed and suicidal succeeded, and Orpet was acquitted.

Although this case again involves the murder of a pregnant (or seemingly pregnant) girlfriend, it does not fit the major premise of **"I Find the Real American Tragedy."** Even if one assumes that Orpet did murder Lambert, one cannot automatically attribute the crime to social or economic pressures. Orpet was not rejecting a poor girl in favor of a rich one: both Lambert and Youker were members of his own class. In fact, he had grown up with both young women. Youker, a chemistry teacher at a normal school, was of no higher social station than Orpet, who was attending a university. Likewise, Lambert was no poorer than Orpet, for her father, superintendent of the Kuppenheimer estate, held a position identical to that of Orpet's father, who was superintendent of the McCormick estate. In **"I Find the Real American Tragedy"** Dreiser presents us with the prototype of the American fortune hunter, who will resort to murder if an impediment such as a pregnant girlfriend stands in the way of his aspirations. This theory is the basis of Dreiser's model of murder which these historical crimes are supposed to reflect. The Richeson case is a fair example of the model, but the Orpet case is not. If Orpet did murder Lambert, he did not do so for money or for social status.

The murder case closest in time to the composition of *An American Tragedy* occurred when Dreiser was beginning work on the novel. Although Dreiser does not specifically mention Harry New in **"I Find the Real American Tragedy,"** he does discuss this case in "American Tragedies." This murder, which occurred in Los Angeles, would probably have caught Dreiser's attention, for he and Helen Richardson were living there during the trial in late 1919. Furthermore, New was the illegitimate son of Harry S. New, a United States Senator from Dreiser's home state of Indiana, which Dreiser had visited just prior to the time of the murder. The paragraph discussing the New murder in "American Tragedies" shows that

Dreiser must have followed this latest case of a young man killing his lover.

On 4 July 1919 Harry New drove up to a Los Angeles police station with the body of Freda Lesser, the daughter of a German spy, in his automobile.[11] He had shot her at Topango Canyon and then had driven around aimlessly for four hours, trying to decide what to do. Freda Lesser, like Marian Lambert, mistakenly thought she was pregnant. New and Freda had planned to be married on 5 July, but apparently she had wanted to postpone the wedding and have an abortion. New tried to persuade Freda to marry him immediately, and when she refused, he shot her. New described the matter very simply when he brought the body to the police: "We didn't understand each other . . . and so I shot her and here I am. There she is too" (*Indianapolis Star* 6 July 1919: 1). When he was arrested, New told the police that he was the son of Senator New, who, he claimed, had divorced his mother many years before. Senator New immediately denied any marriage; later he admitted that he had had an affair with New's mother thirty years earlier. He knew about his son and had paid for him to go to college.

In "American Tragedies" Dreiser states that New did not know the identity of his father until after he had become involved with Lesser: "Then came my old friend the devil or Mephistopheles and soon New was surprised to learn that his father was going to do something for him—give him money to help him get up, etc. But just at that time the girl was pregnant. A poverty marriage was ahead of him as Doctor Mephistopheles had most carefully planned. Was he going to marry and be nobody when he could stay single and do so much better?" ("American Tragedies" B 9). This description conforms approximately to Dreiser's model in **"I Find the Real American Tragedy,"** with a rich father replacing the rich young woman. In actuality, however, New had always known his father's name, had received financial support from him, and had even grown up believing that his parents had been married at his birth. He was not facing an unexpected chance at wealth and success; he knew his position when he asked Freda Lesser to marry him, and he knew that his opportunities were not likely to change. Furthermore, he was not another young man trying to escape marriage. Even Freda Lesser's mother admitted that her daughter was the one who wanted to postpone the wedding, while it was New who was pressing for marriage. Owing to the lack of any rational motive, the crime was blamed on New's unbalanced mind. He was therefore convicted only of second-degree murder and escaped execution. Once again, Dreiser uses the framework of this case, supplying his own motive in order to defend his novel. Since a full account of the case exists in all the versions of the article until the final published account, one can guess that, perhaps here too, as in the Molineux case, Dreiser knew that the facts would not support his paradigm and therefore he did not include this case.

The actual cases, then, when considered together, do not form any kind of pattern. Although some share common elements, they are not a series of similar crimes. They are simply cases with which Dreiser was familiar and in which he was interested. When he began to explain the sources of *An American Tragedy* he called upon these cases for their historical reality, but he rewrote them to create the pattern he needed as a background for his novel. In "American Tragedies" he tries to revise each case so that it has the same motive as the murder in the novel, but later, in **"I Find the Real American Tragedy,"** he describes only the three cases—those of Harris, Richeson, and Gillette—which most closely fit the pattern, leaving his reader to infer that the other cases mentioned also follow this pattern. Except for being able to name actual, historical cases, Dreiser is not interested in the real circumstances of the crimes, but in the paradigm he is creating. This paradigm, which foreshadows *An American Tragedy* so well, is his own invention, added to these other cases in 1935 in order to unite them as a documented sociological trend.

"I Find the Real American Tragedy" and the other articles written in 1934 and 1935 lead to a greater understanding of *An American Tragedy,* although not in the way that Dreiser intended. Dreiser's account of studying a series of similar murders is false, but his method of creating fiction from historical fact in **"I Find the Real American Tragedy"** parallels the method of composition of *An American Tragedy.* Dreiser used the Gillette case as a framework for a fiction which expresses his own themes and ideas in the same way that he altered the other cases in order to create an historical background for the novel. After the failures of *The "Rake"* and the Richeson novel, Dreiser finally found in the drowning of Grace Brown a murder which he could use to express the ideas about American society which he had been developing over many years.

John F. Castle has analyzed Dreiser's use of this case in his dissertation, "The Making of *An American Tragedy,*" and more recently Craig Brandon has investigated the Gillette-Brown murder in *Murder in the Adirondacks.* Both Castle and Brandon demonstrate that Dreiser used the details of the Gillette case, borrowing the characters, plot, and setting of the actual murder. Dreiser also lifted entire passages from the account of the trial in the *New York World,* quoting directly from the attorney's speeches and Grace Brown's letters and incorporating verbatim Chester Gillette's final written statement. Although Dreiser copied these details, he created the larger issues of his novel imaginatively. The sociological conditions that cause Clyde to commit murder are fictional additions to the actual crime.

By expanding the range of social classes present in the original story, Dreiser created the "dreadful economic, social, moral and conventional pressures" that lead to the murder ("I Find" 11). The actual Gillette case includes neither Clyde's great poverty nor Sondra's great wealth. Gillette's parents were middle-class members of the Salvation Army, not destitute street preachers.[12] Unlike Clyde, Gillette also had the advantages of attending college and learning a trade. At the other extreme, Gillette's uncle was not nearly so wealthy as is Samuel Griffiths in the novel. Gillette's Cortland, the Lycurgus of *An American Tragedy,* was not the glittering world of the Jazz Age but rather the middle-class society of church socials. The closest equivalent to Sondra Finchley was Harriet Benedict, a student at the normal school in town with whom Gillette had no more than a casual relationship. The vision of wealth that leads Clyde to murder was not present for Chester Gillette.

Without this financial conflict, the Gillette case lacks the universal implications of *An American Tragedy.* Gillette was not a victim of society as Clyde is. He was an enigmatic character who laughed and chewed gum during the trial, who hung photographs of pretty girls in his cell, and who gave flip, sarcastic answers to the prosecutor's questions (Franz 92, 94; Castle 92). In order to provide a comprehensible structure for the crime, Dreiser created a motive that reflects a larger concern than merely the case of one young man and his pregnant girlfriend. As Brandon states, "In transforming a careless and thoughtless pleasure seeker like Chester into a victim of society and his own dreams and ambitions, Dreiser used more imagination than history and had to leave out key facts" (344). Using his knowledge of various philosophical and psychological theories, as well as his own experience, Dreiser constructed a pattern of economic and social motivation for Clyde's crime. As Dreiser's comments during the Paramount case reveal, this paradigm of motivation, and not the Gillette case, is for him the subject of the novel.

Dreiser's account of the other murders in **"I Find the Real American Tragedy"** underlines the importance of the novel's indictment of society. The factual inaccuracies of Dreiser's descriptions in **"I Find the Real American Tragedy"** are more than mere carelessness. Dreiser has fictionalized these murders, just as he did the Gillette case, in order to prove his social theory. As Dreiser states in his newspaper coverage of the Edwards murder in 1934, he was concerned not with the factual details of the case, but with the psychology of the crime (*New York Post* 2 Oct. 1934: 1). In truth, he meant a psychology which he had himself devised long before he began to study the Gillette case. While this psychology may not actually have its roots in the murders listed in **"I Find the Real American Tragedy,"** it is even more important as an expression of what Dreiser saw wrong in American society. He borrowed the details of the Gillette murder to provide realism for his story, but he created the whole apparatus of motivation in *An American Tragedy.* The paradigm in **"I Find the Real American Tragedy"** is not just a summary of historical facts; it is Dreiser's creation of history to explain America. And his fictional history reflected reality so well that it outlasted the true facts. The pervasiveness and longevity of the myth Dreiser created in **"I Find the Real American Tragedy"** fulfills Abraham Cahan's statement in 1926: "A work like Dreiser's is not merely true to life. It conveys the illusion of being Life itself" (3).

NOTES

[1] Two versions of "American Tragedies" exist in the Dreiser papers at the University of Pennsylvania: Manuscript B, the original article with a carbon copy; and Manuscript A, a heavily revised version. Chapter 8 in Helen Dreiser's *My Life With Dreiser* follows Manuscript B almost exactly.

[2] For example, see Elias 221; Moers 195-201, 210; Fishkin 100, 112-17.

[3] "I Find the Real American Tragedy" 7. The number of cases varies in different articles. Since Dreiser names only a relative few, the number of cases that he actually studied is uncertain.

[4] Facts of the Molineux case have been derived from reports in the *New York Times* 29 Dec. 1898-19 Nov. 1902, and from reports in the *New York World* 29 Dec. 1898-March 1900.

[5] *New York World* 28 Feb. 1899: 3; *New York Times* 15 Feb. 1900: 12; *New York World* 28 Feb. 1899: 3.

[6] Facts of the Carlyle Harris case have been derived from Boswell and Thompson; from *The Trial of Carlyle W. Harris for Poisoning His Wife, Helen Potts, at New York;* and from reports in the *New York World* 2 Feb. 1891-31 May 1891.

[7] "I Find the Real American Tragedy" 7. Frances McCready Harris, author of children's stories and books on homemaking and child rearing, used the pen name of Hope Ledyard.

[8] Facts of the Durrant case were derived from reports in the *San Francisco Examiner* 13 April 1895-13 Dec. 1895; and from reports in the *New York World* 30 April 1895-2 Nov. 1895.

[9] Facts of the Richeson case were derived from reports in the *New York Times* and the *New York World* 18 Oct. 1911-24 May 1912.

[10] Facts of the Orpet case were derived from reports in the *New York Times* and the *New York World* 13 Feb. 1916-16 July 1916.

[11] Facts of the New case were derived from reports in the *Indianapolis Star* 6 July 1919-24 Dec. 1919, and from reports in the *New York Times* 6 July 1919-30 Jan. 1920.

[12] Facts of the Gillette case are derived from Castle, Brandon, and reports in the *New York World* 14 July 1906-1 August 1906.

WORKS CITED

Boswell, Charles, and Lewis Thompson. *The Carlyle Harris Case.* 1955. New York: Collier, 1961.

Brandon, Craig. *Murder in the Adirondacks: 'An American Tragedy' Revisited.* Utica: North Country, 1986.

Cahan, Abraham. "Dreiser's New Novel and What the Critics Say About It." *Jewish Daily Forward* 24 Jan. 1926, sec. 1: 3.

Castle, John F. "The Making of *An American Tragedy.*" Diss., U of Michigan, 1952.

Dreiser, Theodore. "American Tragedies." TMs. The Theodore Dreiser Papers, Special Collections, Van Pelt Library, University of Pennsylvania. The Trustees of the University of Pennsylvania. Quoted with permission.

————. "Crime Analyzed by Dreiser." *Los Angeles Examiner* 23 July 1935: 1-2.

————. *Hey Rub-A-Dub-Dub.* New York: Boni & Liveright, 1920.

————. "'I Find the Real American Tragedy' by Theodore Dreiser." Ed. Jack Salzman. *Resources in American Literary Study* 2 (1972): 3-74. Reprinted with commentary by Jack Salzman from *Mystery Magazine* 11 (Feb.-June 1935).

————. "Theodore Dreiser Describes 'American Tragedy.'" *New York Post* 2 Oct. 1934: 1, 6; 3 Oct. 1934: 3; 4 Oct. 1934: 23; 5 Oct. 1934: 12; 6 Oct. 1934: 3. Also published in the *Philadelphia Record.*

Elias, Robert H. *Theodore Dreiser, Apostle of Nature.* 1948. Ithaca: Cornell UP, 1970.

Fishkin, Shelley Fisher. *From Fact to Fiction: Journalism and Imaginative Writing in America.* Baltimore: Johns Hopkins UP, 1985.

Franz, Eleanore Waterbury. "The Tragedy of the 'North Woods.'" *New York Folklore Quarterly* 4.2 (1948): 85-97.

Ledyard, Hope, ed. *Articles, Speeches and Poems of Carlyle W. Harris.* New York: Ogilvie, 1893.

Moers, Ellen. *Two Dreisers.* New York: Viking, 1969.

Swanberg, W.A. *Dreiser.* New York: Scribners, 1965.

The Trial of Carlyle W. Harris for Poisoning His Wife, Helen Potts, at New York. New York, 1892.

Barrie Hayne (essay date 1991)

SOURCE: "Dreiser's *An American Tragedy,*" in *Rough Justice: Essays on Crime in Literature,* edited by M. L. Friedland, University of Toronto Press, 1991, pp. 170-86.

[*In the following essay, Hayne examines the ways in which* An American Tragedy *is a "peculiarly American" tragedy.*]

Theodore Dreiser is the first major American novelist of 'ethnic' background and name (following on the Browns, the Hawthornes, the Jameses, the Clemenses), a member of a deprived minority looking in on a world not hitherto his own. In *An American Tragedy* (1925), his masterpiece, he wrote a novel which was strongly doctrinaire, showing its hero as the victim of that world not his own. He wrote a novel which drew heavily on the contemporary people's (and immigrants') art of the cinema, and then gave that novel, rather less than willingly, back to the cinema. And he wrote a novel which was based in a real crime, committed by a young man, not 'ethnic', but determined to rise above his own more or less predetermined lot. In this clash of deprived and blessed, not having and having, especially as Dreiser dramatized it, was the stuff of crime, and crime of a kind peculiar to a country where rising through class lines was possible, though fraught with danger—a peculiarly *American* tragedy.

The first thing to do with *An American Tragedy,* therefore, is to set it in its literary-historical context, and see it as a naturalistic novel—perhaps the best, the copybook, example of that genre produced on this side of the Atlantic. While we must, therefore, begin with a working definition of naturalism,[1] we shall pass by here the preference American fiction has always had for the romantic over the real. This is a preference that naturalism itself cultivated; and European naturalism—we will take it for granted—found, when it crossed the Atlantic, a very congenial soil for its growth.

The earliest exponents of naturalism conceived their fictional writings as essentially laboratory examinations: the central character is placed in a controlled environment so that the novelist-scientist may observe and analyse what becomes of him. Coming, moreover, after Darwin, naturalism in fiction assumes thatthe character—he is generally too commonplace to be called a *hero*—will survive in that environment only so long as he adapts to it; and only the fittest survive. The world in which he struggles is a deterministic world, so deterministic as finally to deny him any freedom of will; and as he adapts he moves from one role to another. A player of pre-ordained parts, he loses himself when he loses his social role. The characters of naturalistic fiction are thus presented *as* their roles rather than as individuals: in Dreiser's first novel, *Sister Carrie* (1900), the heroine is 'the little battler' 'the waif amid forces'; Hurstwood, who steals money lest he lose her, is 'the manager,' and, when at the nadir of his fall he is asked if he is a motorman on strike, he replies, 'No, I'm nothing.' The people of naturalistic fiction are indeed nothing when their adaptations have failed, and their roles are gone.

Yet lest naturalism become even more dreary, dull, and dark than it is, the hero is not uncommonly given a humanistic value, an aspiration which, so long as he does adapt, may leave him undefeated at the end. The relentless determinism is certainly realistic, and grimly so; the aspiration is romantic, and characteristically American, if we allow Howells' famous *obiter* about 'the smiling aspects of life.'[2] One of the leading critical commentators on American naturalism, Charles C. Walcutt, describes the genre as both 'a shaggy apelike monster' and a 'godlike giant.' 'Whereas,' he goes on, 'one authority describes it as an extreme form of romanticism, another counters that it is the rigorous application of scientific method to the novel. When others say it is desperate, pessimistic determinism, they are answered by those who insist that it is an optimistic affirmation of man's freedom and progress.'[3] All are correct, as Walcutt says in summarizing; and Frank Norris, whose novels include such finely balanced treatments of realism and romance as we find in *McTeague* (1899), which became Stroheim's famous film *Greed,* and *The Octopus* (1902), claims Emile Zola as the apostle of that balance. Naturalism represents the transcendent synthesis of the dialectics of romance and realism. Realism, as Norris says, is what happens between lunch and supper; romance takes the whole wide world for range, 'the unplumbed depths of the human heart [with its distinct echo of his compatriot Hawthorne], and the mystery of sex, and the problems of life, and the black, unsearched penetralia of the soul of man.'[4] Since Norris' catalogue does not omit a great deal, we need not be surprised to find him claiming Zola, an accumulator of realistic detail of Dreiserian proportions, as a naturalist—whose naturalism underscores the romantic elements in the school:

> These great, terrible dramas no longer happen among the personnel of a feudal and Renaissance nobility, those who are in the fore-front of the marching world, but among the lower—almost the lowest—classes; those who have been thrust or wrenched from the ranks, who are falling by the roadway. This is not romanticism—this drama of the people, working itself out in blood and ordure. It is not realism. It is a school by itself, unique, sombre, powerful beyond words. It is naturalism.[5]

It is clear that Dreiser's whole *oeuvre* belongs to naturalism, from Sister Carrie, who comes from the provinces to Chicago, and adapts to make her fortune there, to Frank Cowperwood, who becomes, from *The Financier* (1912) to *The Titan* (1914), a millionaire by surviving and thriving in a very Darwinian way. And beneath the relentless beat of factual detail in *An American Tragedy* is a strong strain of romance—Clyde's whole drive towards success is motivated by his dreams (an insistent metaphor in the novel); but those dreams, because of their very romantic, Arabian Nights quality, are doomed to pre-ordained defeat. As the tips pour into the hands of the bellhops at the hotel in Kansas City, 'He could scarcely believe it. It seemed fantastic, Aladdinish, really.'[6] His uncle, before he meets him, 'must be a kind of Croesus living in ease and luxury.' Ultimately, Clyde's dreams of romance come to be centred upon the dream figure of Sondra Finchley. (The dream is also Dreiser's: could anyone real bear such a name?) When his desire for her leads him to plan murder, he is even denied free will itself; and this young man is executed for a crime he did not, technically, commit—for he suffers at the moment of Roberta's drowning a 'palsy of the will.'

If dream is associated with the world of film, the repository of so many individual dreams as well as the collective one, put out by the 'Dream Factory' itself, then we are reminded again of the strength of the connections between Dreiser's novel and the new 'democratic art.' But there are other indications of the affinity, most notably the insistently visual quality of *An American Tragedy.*

The whole story is enclosed within the dusks of two summer nights, vividly brought before our eyes, with the tall walls of the two cities, the little group of salvationists, the immediate sense of seeing what is described. And there is emphasis throughout on Clyde's vision, his 'seeking eyes', a point of attraction to all who meet him, the eyes that the Reverend Macmillan cannot get out of his mind at the end when Clyde sinks limply into that terrible chair.

Now Dreiser's life-span was almost exactly the same as that of D.W. Griffith, the moving spirit of early American film; and the American naturalistic novelists (Norris, David Graham Phillips, Dreiser himself) provided many of the literary bases of the American silent film. *An American Tragedy* was published in 1925, when the silent film was at the peak of its achievement and its popularity; and Dreiser, whose contacts with Hollywood over the years were many, was at this time fascinated by film, the people's art; was living, for much of the writing of the novel, in and around Hollywood; and was living with the woman he later made his second wife, who was working in the film industry.

It is therefore not surprising to find many references to film in the novel. As Clyde casts about for an escape from the pregnant Roberta, 'he drifted—thinking most idly at times of some possible fake or mock marriage such as he had seen in some melodramaticmovie' (2:6). (It is distinctly possible here that Dreiser may have been thinking of the central scene in Griffith's 'melodramatic movie' *Way Down East,* the most popular of his pictures, which had appeared on the screens of America in 1920.) As Roberta projects in her mind the very marriage Clyde is trying to avoid, she envisages 'a flowered grey taffeta afternoon dress, such as she had once seen in a movie, in which should Clyde keep his word, she could be married' (2:16). And looking over the crowded courtroom at his trial, Clyde whispers to his lawyers, 'quite a full house, eh?' (2:226). While this metaphor might suggest only the legitimate theatre, Orville Mason, rising to open the prosecution, is described in terms which move the *mise en scène* more directly into the cinema: 'This was his opportunity. Were not the eyes of all the citizens of the United States upon him? He believed so. It was as if someone had suddenly exclaimed: "Lights! Camera!" ' (2:231). Indeed, isn't there even a reference to film in the murder weapon Clyde uses? Chester Gillette hit Grace Brown, in the event which inspired *An American Tragedy,* with a tennis racquet. Clyde hits Roberta, albeit unintentionally, with a camera.

The principal effect of these filmic references and analogies is both to enforce the naturalistic point and remind the reader yet again that these characters are locked into a world of dreams and illusions, and also to underline the fact that they are all speaking parts written for them by other people, other forces outside themselves. When Clyde walks to his execution, his voice emerges as though spoken by somebody else, 'another being walking alongside of him' (2:405). He is the role as well as the actor; his part has been assigned by his director. The yellow, unimposing door that the small company enters at the end of the first chapter and which they enter again at the end of the novel, without Esta's Russel, who seems to be on the way to becoming another Clyde, predicts and looks back on the door that opens for Clyde as he enters the death chamber. His uneasiness at being a part of the opening group, his two protectors shouldering closer and closer to him while he shrinks down within himself mentally on the way to his trial (with the cameras clicking and whirring in the background)—these are dress rehearsals for the 'shuffle' as they push him toward the execution chamber at the end. But the sense, more widely, has been there from the beginning of the novel that here is a group of actors—Clyde, his parents, Roberta and hers, Sondra, even Mason, Belknap, and Jephson—playing roles written for them by forces located in their genes, in their psyches, in their upbringings, and above all in their society, *American* society, itself. It is appropriate, therefore, that the metaphors used are not those of the theatre, such as Dreiser used in *Sister Carrie,* but those of the distinctively *American* art of the cinema.

But the Americanness of Clyde's tragedy asserts itself in other ways as well. Dreiser for years studied (and clipped from newspapers) accounts of actual cases in which young men, rising in the world, aspiring to young women above them in social status, murdered girls who would hold them back in their original class. This effect of upward mobility Dreiser saw as essentially American. Writing in 1935, he put it like this:

> It was in 1892, at which time I began as a newspaperman, that I began to observe a certain type of crime in the United States. It seemed to spring from the fact that almost every young person was possessed of an ingrowing ambition to be somebody financially and socially. In short, the general mood of America was directed toward escape from any form of poverty . . . In the main, as I can show by my records, it was the murder of a young lady by an ambitious young man . . . What produced this particular type of crime about which I am talking was the fact that it was not always possible to drop the first girl. What usually stood in the way was pregnancy, plus the genuine affection of the girl herself for her lover, plus also her determination to hold him.[7]

After the publication of *An American Tragedy,* Dreiser noted the number of letters he received from people who said 'Clyde Griffiths might have been me'; and certainly there is a large amount of Dreiser himself in Clyde—the deprived background, the stern religious upbringing, the yearning for social advancement and sexual conquest, the dominating mother of mixed motives, the father for

whom, though for reasons other than Clyde's, he felt contempt. This American tragedy takes the nineteenth-century Horatio Alger myth[8] which was still the basis of much contemporary fiction (not to say the blueprint for many a successful career) and turns it on its head. And the lesson it teaches is just as exemplary as Alger's *Making His Way* or Herrick's *The Memoirs of an American Citizen,* and the hero is just as much an authorial surrogate. The difference between *An American Tragedy* and the school of Horatio Alger lies in the degree of criticism to which the society itself is subjected, the extent to which it is actually blamed for the tragedy.

But if there is much of Dreiser in Clyde Griffiths, there is a good deal of another young man as well—Chester Gillette;[9] and *An American Tragedy* is based fairly closely on the famous murder and trial that had taken place in upstate New York some fifteen years before. Rejecting other versions of this 'certain type of crime in the United States,' where the murderer had been a medical student, or a clergyman, Dreiser chose the nomadic Chester Gillette, the son of Salvation Army parents, and supplied him with his, Dreiser's own, seduced and abandoned elder sister. He then gave him a two-fold defence that Gillette's lawyers never considered, of 'mental and moral cowardice' and 'change of heart.' He also reduced Gillette, in transforming him into Clyde, to a lower social status. Chester's parents had travelled as far as Hawaii; and he himself was a fairly sophisticated Westerner who left the mission background of his parents to seek the favour of his uncle, who owned a skirt factory in Cortland; he had already passed through a series of minor service jobs. But he had never known true poverty, was given a supervisory position in the factory, of which his cousin was superintendent, and used his authority to seduce one of the factory girls, the daughter of poor country farming people, whose name was Grace—'Billy'—Brown. Gillette had a taste of high society in both Cortland and around Lake Skaneateles, and laid siege to a local debutante, who was quite amenable to his courtship, and who did in fact give evidence, though for the prosecution, at his trial. Billy, now pregnant, pursued him; he took her on a lake tour—they travelled as man and wife, and one of his false names was Carl Graham, keeping his initials—hit her over the head with a tennis racquet, and swam away as she drowned, leaving a second straw hat floating in the lake to establish his own drowning. There were in the background of his trial a number of small-town political squabbles (the district attorney was running for country judge on the Republican ticket, and the defence counsel were Democrats); he was convicted, his mother tried without success to overturn the verdict, and he was executed in 1908, two years after the crime.

What Dreiser made out of these relatively unaltered facts, transforming Chester Gillette's life and character, and his own, into that of Clyde Griffiths, was this his sixth novel, and his most successful, artistically as well as commercially. It sold twenty-five thousand copies in its first six months, was banned (only) in Boston, and was hailed by two reigning naturalists on the other side of the water, H.G. Wells and Arnold Bennett, as one of the greatest novels of the century.[10] That judgment has been confirmed, if somewhat shaded, over sixty years.

The immediate effect of its great popularity, joined with what I have insisted upon as its visual qualities, was to ensure a film version. But there would be delays: the basic theme seemed too raw for the mass medium, and there were long wrangles between Dreiser and his publishers over their shares in the proceeds of the sale of the film rights. D.W. Griffith, Erich Von Stroheim, even Ernst Lubitsch, the master of sophisticated film comedy, have recorded plans to turn the novel into film.[11] But it was not until 1930 that Paramount brought Sergei Eisenstein, no less, to Hollywood to make a version.[12] This version, of which Dreiser whole-heartedly approved, for it placed the blame for Clyde's tragedy firmly on the shoulders of the capitalist society, was rejected by the studio for that same reason. The next version was actually realized, directed by the very pictorial Josef von Sternberg in 1931. This version Dreiser whole-heartedly deplored, and sued the studio for misrepresenting his novel. He lost his case. Twenty years later there was a third version, much admired and much honoured, *A Place in the Sun,* directed by George Stevens, with two of the most glittering stars of the day, Montgomery Clift and Elizabeth Taylor.

Let us then take the cue for the structure of our present inquiry from Eisenstein, who wrote in 1933—two years after his dismissal by Paramount—that he had prepared a script according to 'the formula of a sociological treatise,' when all the studio wanted was 'a strong, simple detective story,' or 'a love affair between a boy and a girl.'[13] To varying extents, *An American Tragedy* belongs to all three genres Eisenstein mentions—sociological treatise, detective story, love affair—and each of the three film versions emphasizes one generic aspect. But leaving the films aside, let us read the novel in each of these three ways.

Predominantly, it is true, it is a sociological treatise; hence Dreiser's approval of Eisenstein's script. In writing his inverted Horatio Alger story, Dreiser is deeply critical of the society which produced and destroyed Clyde. It is also, however, true that some of Clyde's failures come from within, from his own chemic compulsions and just plain temperamental weaknesses. His defence at the trial is that of mental and moral cowardice; and his attempts to plan Roberta's murder and then cover up his role in it are all extremely inept ('What a dunce you are!—what a poor plotter' (2:150), as Mason tells him in the courtroom). Clyde's sexual urges might appear to be a major internal factor in his downfall, but they are really a part of his romantic yearning, thrust upon him by a hostile society. Thus women, from Hortense and her yen for a fur coat, to Rita and Roberta to Sondra herself, are an essential part of Clyde's paradisiac dreams. A work with which *An American Tragedy* has many affinities is *Great Expectations,* which with a more conscious irony

of title makes the same link between sexual and social ascent, and yet perceives the dream as just as tainted, the hero just as self-deceived. With Dickens' greater skill, the girl and the fortune are both shown as springing from the same source, the convict; the final difference between the two novels lies in Pip's escape from the dream, and his consequent reformation; his 'murder' (of Mrs Joe) is done for him by another. And to see the sexually charged nature of much social aspiration one need stray no further than the box watched nightly by so many, whether 'goin' down with Pepsi,' or turning Fortune's wheel (a debased invocation of naturalistic determinism!) with Vanna.

The three deterministic strands, of social, sexual, and hereditary determinism, are finely interwoven in the opening pages of the novel. Clyde is clearly 'outa place' (1:7) in this group of evangelical zealots, as of course is Esta, whose dereliction, in sexual terms, will shortly predict his own; he is admiring of his mother, yet ashamed of both her and especially his father, the ineffectual. The family presents anomalies 'of psychic and social reflex and motivation such as would tax the skill of not only the psychologist but the chemist and physicist as well, to unravel,' as Dreiser says. Clyde, 'a thing apart,' is marked by 'a certain emotionalism and exotic sense of romance' (1:10), and in the next few years as they are surveyed in the second chapter, 'the sex lure or appeal had begun to manifest itself and he was already intensely interested and troubled by the beauty of the opposite sex' (1:15)—this at the very same time 'the fact that his family was the unhappy thing it was . . . was now tending more and more to induce a kind of mental depression or melancholia which promised not so well for his future': sexual and psychological determinism, the latter associated particularly with the family, go hand in hand.

Yet the dominant note in these opening pages, for all the attention given to that family background, is of Clyde's yearning for a life beyond the confines of this one, and that yearning calls attention to the way his life is already being predetermined by *social* forces. The tall walls of the city, the canyon-like ways, their path 'just an alley between two tall structures,' predict the narrow path of his life. His parents' poverty prevents them from giving him a car of his own, as other parents do; and the main vision in Clyde's mind—his first dream—is also one that predicts the course, and the destruction, of his life: 'The handsome automobiles that sped by, the loitering pedestrians moving off to what interests and comforts he could only surmise; the gay pairs of young people, laughing and jesting and the "kids" staring, all troubled him with a sense of something different, better, more beautiful than his, or rather their life' (1:6).

There are two characters in the novel who are primary registers or indices of Clyde's progress and downfall: Gilbert Griffiths, his cousin, and Orville Mason, his prosecutor or persecutor. Both are in some sense his alter egos,[14] and both are used by Dreiser for commentary on the social forces at work in the novel. Dreiser goes out of his way to underline the physical similarity between Gilbert and Clyde, which fuels Gilbert's jealousy of his cousin, and his fear of being supplanted, since it is perhaps that similarity which has persuaded Samuel Griffiths to employ Clyde in the collar factory in the first place. The likeness also prompts Sondra to take up Clyde when they meet in town, at the beginning of what Dreiser calls 'a chain of events,' 'destined,' which leads, immediately following as it does Clyde's seduction of Roberta, to the catastrophe. She takes him up—having momentarily mistaken him *for* Gilbert—because Gilbert has wounded her pride by his indifference to her. She initiates the fatal relationship with Clyde to get back at his double. And the chain of events associated with Gilbert's likeness to Clyde ends at last with Gilbert's persuasion of his father to drop the family's support for Clyde at the end of the trial.

Of primary importance, too, is the role Gilbert plays in warning Clyde against the very course of action which ultimately brings him to the execution chamber. It is Gilbert who lays down to Clyde the rule that those who hold responsible positions in the factory must have nothing to do with the female employees. Drawn by his sexual urges to the factory girls like Hortense, Rita, and now Roberta, and by his aspirations of wealth and romance to such as Sondra, Clyde is destroyed by the class system and by the vested interests of the social order.

When Clyde first sees Gilbert, he sees 'a youth who looked, if anything, smaller and a little older and certainly much colder and shrewder than himself—such a youth, in short, as Clyde would have liked to imagine himself to be . . . deep down in himself he felt that this young man, an heir and nothing more to this great industry, was taking to himself airs and superiorities which, but for the father's skill before him, would not have been possible'(1:186). As he muses when approaching dinner with his wealthy relatives: 'Think of being such a youth, having so much power at one's command!' (1:223). Dreiser's implication is clear that were there no class system based upon money and the inheritance of it, the roles of Clyde and Gilbert might be interchangeable: all that locks Clyde out of wealth and leisure is the chance fate that has bestowed these gifts on Gilbert. That Gilbert is the Eastern cousin while Clyde is the Western one, aside from its probably ironic allusion to Aesop, does not carry the point that Fitzgerald was making the same year (1925) in *The Great Gatsby,* that a strength and continuity belong to the Westerners like Nick and Gatsby himself, and only a decadence attaches to Daisy and Tom, the destructive Easterners. Rather, Dreiser presents the ironical obverse, that even the Western, characteristically American values are being subverted by Eastern metropolitan values—the novel ends in San Francisco, with the cycle of determinism perhaps about to begin again. And that the Western Griffiths show absolutely none of the enterprise or independence associated with the West, which is here given to Samuel, shows a further subversion of the American way, another facet of the *Americanness* of the tragedy.

Orville Mason, on the other hand, the district attorney, is Clyde's double in a different sense, another poor boy with romantic yearnings who, unlike Clyde, lacks the good looks which seduce women and open social doors: 'in his late youth [he] had been so unfortunate as to have an otherwise pleasant and even arresting face marred by a broken nose, which gave to him a most unprepossessing, almost sinister, look. Yet he was far from sinister. Rather, romantic and emotional. His boyhood had been one of poverty and neglect, causing him in his later and somewhat more successful years to look on those with whom life had dealt more kindly as too favorably treated' (2:91-2). His disfigurement 'had eventually resulted in what the Freudians are accustomed to describe as a psychic sex scar.' Mason hounds Clyde to the electric chair, pursuing him like 'an angry wasp or hornet' (2:147), ignoring Clyde's similarly poor background in favour of delivering to justice the seducer and killer of the equally impoverished Roberta, with whom and her family Mason feels the greater affinity. His jealousy of Clyde's sexual conquest leads him to prosecute him with more than professional enthusiasm.

If this suggests that Mason is Clyde's double or mirror image, there is a further dimension, and a further reason for Mason's prosecution of the case. He wants a quick conviction to further his political ambitions, and this too blinds him to Clyde's humble origins. Clyde's adoption by the Finchley set 'suggested all the means as well as the impulse to quiet such a scandal as this. Wealth. Luxury. Important names and connections to protect no doubt . . . [M]ight it not be possible that long before he could hope to convict him, he himself would automatically be disposed of as a prosecutor and without being nominated for and elected to the judgeship he so craved and needed' (2:145).

Mason too is a part of the social order, another representative of the society that destroys Clyde Griffiths. He is a Republican politician running for county judge, which transcends considerations of justice or even his prosecution of the case against Clyde: Clyde's lawyers, Belknap and Jephson, are Democrats, and a large part of their being chosen to represent him is to prevent Mason from making too much political capital out of the case: 'Fate seemed too obviously to be favouring the Republican machine in the person of and crime committed by Clyde' (2:182). Clyde thus becomes a pawn in a political battle, his guilt or innocence less important than the outcome of the next local election. The judge too, a Democrat, but one appointed by the previous administration, perhaps rules against Belknap and Jephson on political lines of self-preservation, and even after the trial, the newly installed governor must decide Clyde's fate primarily on political grounds. Belknap's youthful peccadillo, exactly the same as Clyde's, did not end as Clyde's does, but in marriage to *his* Sondra, for he belongs to a class who can buy off *his* Roberta. These are the members of the legal and social order who now, in the trial, combine to destroy Clyde Griffiths. Even the jury represents that order: the one juryman who holds out, 'pretending that he had doubts,' is 'politically opposed to Mason and taken with the personality of Jephson' (2:329), and is brought round to a guilty verdict by threat of a public exposure which would endanger his drug business.

Such, then, is the case for seeing *An American Tragedy* as Eisenstein most emphatically saw it, as a sociological treatise in which society is ultimately indicated for its destructive power. 'The essential tragedy of life,' as Dreiser had written,[15] is that man is 'a waif and an interloper in Nature' (for which we may also read *society* and other environmental factors), which seeks only 'to work through him,' so that he has 'no power to make his own way.' As a matter of course, we may note in passing, Eisenstein's film treatment deepens Dreiser's more or less Marxist view of American society, and this was why Paramount rejected it; for them it really did represent what Eisenstein ironically called 'a monstrous challenge to American society.'[16] No less truly, this was why Dreiser whole-heartedly approved of it.

One of the most memorable scenes in Eisenstein's script comes at the end of reel twelve, when we hear and see a series of telephone bells ringing in succession, as the political influence necessary to keep Sondra's name out of the trial moves upwards through the echelons of power. 'The last light is turned on in the house grandest of all, and from this house can be heard the wanted promise.'[17] Though Eisenstein eliminated everything from the novel that did not go towards Clyde's victimization by a bourgeois society, in doing so he remained faithful to Dreiser, adding nothing that was not already implicitly there.

Eisenstein's statement that the studio wanted a detective story or a love affair, rather than what he gave them, is certainlyhyperbole, though *An American Tragedy* has elements of both. However, though it is a story dealing with crime, it hardly belongs to the genre of detective fiction. That genre, which reached its apogee of popularity at the very time Dreiser was writing his novel, has always at its centre a percipient and analytic detective, with whom the reader is asked to identify, and who unmasks the hitherto unidentified criminal one step before the reader at the end and who in doing so restores the social order upset by the original crime: Dupin, Holmes, Father Brown, Hercule Poirot; all but the first were alive and well at the time Dreiser was writing. But Orville Mason (despite, perhaps, his invocation of one of the famous early fictional detectives, Randolph Mason, and perhaps even his anticipation of Perry Mason) does not belong in that family, any more than *An American Tragedy,* with its revelation of the criminal from the beginning, belongs in that genre; as F.O. Matthiessen has noted, 'As Clyde plots murder in spite of himself, Dreiser goes to the opposite extreme from the writer of a detective story.'[18] Certainly what is restored at the end of *An American Tragedy* looks much more like the continuation of chaos. Indeed, Clyde's ineptness makes him almost a parody of the criminal of detective fiction who matches wits with the percipient detective—he plans nothing effectively, he leaves a train of clues behind him which will convict and execute him with or without a

'change of heart' or a 'palsy of the will'; he lies in the face of evidence proving him a liar. It is true that one reads *An American Tragedy* with something of the compulsiveness that many readers bring to detective fiction, with what John Berryman has called 'the febrile, self-indulgent eagerness Dreiser is apt to induce,'[19] but the essential sense of a world built upon logical principles, and therefore amenable to the detective's analysis, is missing, has, indeed, been replaced by a highly illogical and unpredictable one.

There are certainly some elements of the police procedural genre in *An American Tragedy,* as Mason, Kraut, Sissel, and Swenk gather evidence for the prosecution, and Belknap and Jephson try to forestall their efforts; one official even fabricates evidence, attaching some of Roberta's hair to the camera which Mason has dredged from the lake. But primarily the novel is the psychological study of a murderer, a crime novel rather than a detective story, as Julian Symons defines that form, in terms which apply uncannily well to *An American Tragedy:* character is the basis of the story, setting is frequently an integral part of the crime itself, and the social attitude is 'often radical in the sense of questioning some aspect of law, justice, or the way society is run.'[20]

The classic crime novel is no doubt Dostoevski's *Crime and Punishment,* a work which transcends mere social discontentment to attain a level of *tragedy* which most critics have denied to Dreiser's novel because of Clyde's triviality and the mental and moral cowardice which prevent him from accepting the full moral responsibility for his crime. But Dreiser once told an interviewer that Raskolnikov was his favourite character in fiction—this was about the time he was finishing his own novel—and he urged theinclusion of *Crime and Punishment* in the Modern Library, which was put out by his own publishers. Raskolnikov and Clyde Griffiths are, however, worlds apart, the Russian an intellectual post-Nietzschean man who kills a woman he hardly knows, not for the money, but for the rather abstract good of society. Four years after he made Dreiser's novel into a film (and brought on Dreiser's suit for distortion of his work), Josef von Sternberg put *Crime and Punishment* on the screen. The difference is there to see: despite Dreiser's protest, the essentials of his novel have been captured in the picture, but no picture could capture the complexities of Dostoevski's novel.[21]

Another feature of the detective, or even crime, novel is its paucity of social detail; except where the social purpose transcends, as sometimes occurs in the crime novel, only such details as are necessary for the solution or understanding of the crime are provided. This paucity of detail is certainly not a feature of *An American Tragedy!* Dreiser is writing a case history in the naturalistic mode, a tremendous amassing of facts and even figures which more than amply illustrate the reasons for Clyde Griffiths' rise and fall. Roberta's and Sondra's backgrounds are detailed, as are Mason's, Belknap's, even such minor figures as Sheriff Heit and Catchuman. We know how much a shirt costs as well as the price of an abortion or the pills to secure a miscarriage. And we are taken laboriously through the testimony of the 127 witnesses who appear at Clyde's trial.

As to the third characterization by Eisenstein of the novel, a love affair between a boy and girl, it would hardly be worth consideration were it not for the romantic strain in the novel, as in American naturalism generally. And it is, predominantly, the interpretation given to the novel in the most successful of the film versions. But it is absurd to suggest that Clyde's love affair with either girl transcends the social aspects, or even the criminal elements in *An American Tragedy*. It is adjunct to both—his attempt to abandon the girl of one class for the girl of another leads him to commit the crime for which the class system combines to destroy him. Sondra, and even Roberta, like Hortense and Rita before her, are all in the novel to suggest Clyde's increasingly romantic dreams of Paradise, his Aladdinish pursuit of the beautiful princess. They are the reasons for his crime, and the reasons for his destruction.

So that the final view of *An American Tragedy* as an example of crime in literature is that it follows the standard pattern of the crime novel, an amorphous but fairly formulaic genre, governed by the presuppositions of naturalism. A contemporary analogy might be found not in the novels of the most famous current practitioner of the genre, Patricia Highsmith, whose interest is in the Maileresque exploration of, and perverse sympathy with, the psychotic criminal mind, but in the novels of John Bingham, who, from *My Name is Michael Sibley* (1953) on, has been seeing the forces of legally constituted order as being often as reprehensible as the criminal, a view which may derive from Dickens via Dostoevski. Is Clyde's *crime* worthy of his *punishment?* A lawyer-reader of *An American Tragedy* may find the leading interest in the trial, which indeed takes up a third of the novel. (A literary colleague of mine once admitted to having skipped this section!) Without justifying such a reading, and noting that Dreiser went out of his way to take advice in grasping the legal questions involved, one may reasonably point out that the trial pits Clyde's defence of mental and moral cowardice, and therefore diminished or even non-existent responsibility, against the determination of the eager bloodhounds of the legal establishment. In doing so, it merely confirms the struggle enacted throughout the novel. Clyde has no defence because his society leaves him with none. His society made him, and it is finally free—freedom being something reserved to the state rather than the individual—to break him. And Dreiser, while he buttressed his argument with both supporting legal evidence and what he read into the Gillette case, was leading, and loading, the case against that society.

NOTES

[1] The best accounts of *American* literary naturalism, which is the main concern here, may be found in Charles

C. Walcutt *American Literary Naturalism: A Divided Stream* (Minneapolis: University of Minnesota 1956), and Donald Pizer *Realism and Naturalism in Nineteenth-Century American Literature* (Carbondale: Southern Illinois University Press 1966). For the practitioner's view, see Frank Norris *The Responsibilities of the Novelist* (London: Grant Richards 1903), and Emile Zola *The Naturalist Novel* ed Maxwell Geismar (Montreal: Harvest House 1964).

[2] William Dean Howells' familiar, and much derided, reference to 'the smiling aspects of life, which are the more American,' is contained in his *Criticism and Fiction* (Boston: Harper and Brothers 1891).

[3] Walcutt 3

[4] Norris 220; see as well 215: 'Zola has been dubbed a Realist, but he is, on the contrary, the very head of the Romanticists.' Hawthorne's definitions of Romance are to be found throughout his writings; the most familiar phrases occur in the preface to *The House of the Seven Gables* (1851): 'When a writer calls his work a Romance, it need hardly be observed that he wishes to claim a certain latitude, both as to its fashion and material, which he would not have felt himself entitled to assume had he professed to be writing a Novel. The latter form of composition is presumed to aim at a very minute fidelity, not merely to the possible, but to the probable and ordinary course of man's experience. The former—while, as a work of art, it must rigidly subscribe itself to laws, and while it sins unpardonably so far as it may swerve aside from the truth of the human heart—has fairly a right to present that truth under circumstances, to a great extent, of thewriter's own choosing or creation.'

[5] Frank Norris 'Zola as a Romantic Writer' in *Novels and Essays* ed D. Pizer (New York: Library of America (1986) 1108.

[6] Theodore Dreiser *An American Tragedy* (New York: Liveright 1925) 2 volumes, 1:51. All subsequent references to the novel are to this edition, and are included in the text of this article.

[7] See Ellen Moers *Two Dreisers* (New York: Viking 1969), especially 192-205. This, along with Matthiessen's, is the best critical biography of Dreiser.

[8] Alger wrote well over a hundred self-improving fictions in the second half of the nineteenth century. Though his vogue, which sold some two hundred million copies, was spent by the time Dreiser was writing *An American Tragedy,* he has received some attention, largely patronizing and nostalgic, in recent years. Perhaps the new vogue begins with *Struggling Upward and Other Works* ed Russel Crouse (New York: Bonanza Books 1950).

[9] Two examinations of the facts surrounding the Gillette case have been published in the last few years: Joseph W. Brownell and Patricia A. Wawrzaszek *Adirondack Trag-*

edy: The Gillette Murder Case of 1906 (Interlaken, NY: Heart of the Lakes Publishing 1986), and Craig Brandon *Murder in the Adirondacks: An American Tragedy Revisited* (Utica: North Country Books 1986).

[10] F.O. Matthiessen *Dreiser* (New York: William Sloane Associates 1951) 94, 127, 210

[11] For an account of the film versions, projected or executed, see my article 'Sociological Treatise, Detective Story, Love Affair: The Film Versions of *An American Tragedy*' *Canadian Review of American Studies* 8:2 (Fall 1977) 131-53.

[12] Eisenstein's 'treatment,' which is in fact a rather full scenario, without dialogue, is printed in Ivor Montagu *With Eisenstein in Hollywood: A Chapter of Autobiography* (New York: International Publishers 1969). For Eisenstein's own account, see *Close Up* 10:2 (June 1933), and as reprinted (in different translation) in *Film Form: Essays in Film Theory* ed Jay Leyda (New York: Harcourt, Brace 1949).

[13] *Close Up* 110

[14] For a discussion of the theme of the double in *An American Tragedy* as it relates to Gilbert Griffiths, see Lauriat Lane, Jr 'The Double in *An American Tragedy*' *Modern Fiction Studies* 12 (Summer 1966) 213-20.

[15] Matthiessen 204-5

[16] *Close Up* 110. Dreiser wrote to Eisenstein on 3 January 1938 urging him to produce his scenario; see *Letters of Theodore Dreiser* ed Robert Elias (Philadelphia: University of Pennsylvania Press 1959).

[17] 'Scenario' *With Eisenstein in Hollywood* 312-13

[18] *Dreiser* 203

[19] John Berryman 'Dreiser's Imagination' in *The Stature of Theodore Dreiser* ed Alfred Kazin and Charles Shapiro (Bloomington: University of Indiana Press 1955) 150

[20] Julian Symons *Bloody Murder: From the Detective Story to the Crime Novel: A History* (London: Faber and Faber 1972) chapter 14, 'Crime Novel and Police Novel' 163

[21] See both von Sternberg's own account in *Fun in a Chinese Laundry: An Autobiography* (New York: Macmillan 1965) and Andrew Sarris *The Films of Josef von Sternberg* (New York: Museum of Modern Art 1966).

Donald Pizer (essay date 1993)

SOURCE: "American Naturalism in Its 'Perfected' State," in *The Theory and Practice of American Literary*

Naturalism, Southern Illinois University Press, 1993, pp. 153-66.

[*In the following essay, Pizer discusses the ways in which Dreiser's naturalism in* An American Tragedy *compliments the naturalism in Edith Warton's* The Age of Innocence.]

Naturalism has been a significant literary movement in America for almost a century. From the early work of Stephen Crane and Frank Norris to the recent novels of Robert Stone and William Kennedy, the subject matter and fictional form of naturalism have continually attracted writers of stature.[1] Of course, given the problematical philosophical base of naturalism, and given as well the often sensationalistic contents of a typical naturalistic novel, the movement has also been subject to intense attack. Indeed, one common assertion by those who would deny significance to naturalism in America is to claim that the movement failed to survive its high point in the 1890s—this despite the powerful thread of naturalistic expression in most major American writers, including Hemingway and Faulkner, from the nineties to our own time.

But naturalism, despite this critical hostility, refuses to go away, and thus, willy-nilly, has attracted a historiography over the last thirty or forty years—a historiography that contains several seemingly permanent and irrefutable assumptions about the movement. The difficulty presented by these assumptions, of course, is that they may serve to hinder rather than aid in the identification of works that can usefully be discussed as naturalistic. This screening role often played by the conventional historiography of American naturalism is nowhere more evident than in the almost complete neglect of Edith Wharton in discussions of the movement. In an effort to locate Wharton's major work more clearly and fully within American naturalism, I will initially discuss those beliefs about the history of American naturalism that have prevented a close examination of her most finished novel, *The Age of Innocence,* as naturalistic fiction. I will then take up *The Age of Innocence* and Theodore Dreiser's *An American Tragedy* as "companion" novels, using the more readily identifiable naturalism of Dreiser's work to confirm the naturalism of Wharton's.

. . . . .

One of the major assumptions about American naturalism is that it is a literature that is closely attuned to, and indeed derives from, "hard times."[2] The naturalist, it is believed, grounds his fiction in the social realities of his historical moment and he therefore cannot help being especially responsive to social reality when that reality impinges cruelly on the fates of most men. Or, to put the matter somewhat differently, the naturalistic ethos, which views man as circumscribed by conditions of life over which he has no control, appears to be confirmed during periods of social malaise and individual hardship. The history of American naturalism seems to support this interpretation of the movement. Naturalism first took hold in America during the economic hard times and social turmoil of the 1890s; it achieved a second major flowering during the 1930s depression; and it appeared as a significant force for a third time during the difficult political conditions occasioned by the onset of McCarthyism and the Cold War in the late 1940s and early 1950s. Indeed, many of the archetypal scenes of American naturalism—of futilely looking for work, for example, as do Hurstwood and Studs Lonigan, or of being killed by a bullet or club that is the symbolic equivalent of an all-powerful economic or political force, as are Annixter and Jim Casy—derive from the contemporary social immediacies in which these works are set. Naturalism, in this assumption about its periodicity, is thus like a dermatological condition. Its appearance usually signifies a disturbance elsewhere in the organism. When the patient gets better, the spots disappear.

A second major belief about naturalism is that it is, to use Dreiserian slang, a young man's game, with both modifiers—young and man—operative. A moment's reflection produces evidence that appears to bear out this view. Frank Norris, Stephen Crane, and Theodore Dreiser were all in their twenties when they wrote important naturalistic novels, and John Dos Passos, James T. Farrell, and John Steinbeck were hardly much older when they published major naturalistic fiction in the 1930s. During the years following World War II, it was the very early fiction of Norman Mailer, William Styron, and Saul Bellow—novels such as *The Naked and the Dead, Lie Down in Darkness,* and *The Adventures of Augie March*—that are amongthe most naturalistic of their works. Two observations arise from these facts. The first is that naturalism appears to attract writers in their youth and then fade as an interest. Crane and Norris of course died when still very young, but otherwise all the writers I have named moved on to other kinds of fiction as their careers advanced. Even Dreiser, who wrote naturalistic novels in his 40s and 50s, went on to a very different kind of fiction in his last years in the semimystical allegories of *The Bulwark* and *The Stoic.* The second observation is that naturalism appears to be entirely the province of male authors. Together, the two observations constitute an implicit indictment of the quality and importance of naturalism. The naturalistic novel, it seems, is the product of a masculine late adolescence frame of mind that has overreacted both to the physical in life and to the deep disappointment that life as found is not as it was promised. An underlying premise of this indictment is that writers within the naturalistic movement lack the fine tuning of the imaginative temperament that women authors presumably have from birth and which the male author will gradually achieve, though some—like Dreiser—show an arrested development well into their careers. Naturalism is thus principally the expression of crass, youthful, male authors. To demonstrate the force of this assumption one need only recall the distaste that naturalism as a literary form occasioned among the followers of Henry James once James assumed—in the early 1940s—his position as the consummate artistic and moral sensibility.[3]

A third—and last—major assumption about naturalism as a literary movement is closely related to its presumed origins as a form of social realism written largely by young men. Naturalism, it has been believed for almost its entire history, is not conducive to artistic expression. Initially it was often denigrated as art by claims that it was a kind of photography in verbal form. But when photography itself emerged as a major art, the notebook took its place as a metaphor of the naturalist's unmediated documentation of external experience. The naturalist might have an accurate sense of how to butcher a hog or of the workings of a Model T, but was the expression of this knowledge art? The answer was usually "no." Norris's often heavy-handed symbolism or Dreiser's disastrous ventures into purple prose were also frequently cited as sure evidence of the inadequacy of the naturalist when he sought to push beyond a documentary style. Thus a kind of naturalism/art inverse ratio was established in the historiography of American naturalism. Writers who were obviously self-conscious and innovative literary craftsmen—a Crane or Faulkner—could not be naturalists, while writers who appeared most clearly to have plowed the dull furrows of documentary realism—a Dreiser or Farrell—were consummate naturalists. And in the critical analysis of any one novel, the less naturalism found by the critic the more likely was he to praise the novel for its artistic strength. Naturalism, in brief, was not a technique but a literary bludgeon. And though bludgeons might create an effect, that effect was a different and lesser thing than the one obtained by a genuine work of art.

These historical and critical platitudes about naturalism that I have been describing do indeed have a certain truth. Naturalism has flourished among difficult social conditions, much naturalistic fiction is written by young men, and naturalism of the poorer sort does have its dull and blatant reaches. But the movement is also—and this is my central point—a far more complex critical and historical phenomenon than is implied by these clichés. The naturalistic novel, in other words, can also emerge during good times; it can be written by mature male *and* female authors; and it can express naturalistic themes with great fictional artistry.

Theodore Dreiser's *An American Tragedy* and Edith Wharton's *The Age of Innocence* are major examples of naturalistic fiction that lie outside of these clichés.[4] Both works appeared during the comparatively flush times of the 1920s—*The Age of Innocence* in 1920, *An American Tragedy* in 1925—and both were written when their authors were in full maturity. (Wharton was fifty-eight, Dreiser fifty-four.) And both works illustrate the highest fictional craftsmanship.

. . . . .

Given their obvious differences in subject matter and fictional form, it is perhaps difficult to recall that both *The Age of Innocence* and *An American Tragedy* are also historical novels of a special and essentially similar kind.

Wharton's novel is set in upper-class New York of the 1870s. And *An American Tragedy,* though set in the 1920s, is based on a 1906 incident and, even more pertinently, was grounded in Dreiser's preoccupation since the 1890s in a distinctively late nineteenth-century configuration of the American dream of success.[5] Through the dramatization of an unconsummated love affair on the one hand and a sensational murder case on the other, Wharton and Dreiser seek to depict some of the limitations placed on human freedom by the social and moral nature of late nineteenth-century American life.

One way to begin describing what Wharton and Dreiser wish to say about American life of their youth is to realize that beneath the urbane wit of Wharton and the discursive expansiveness of Dreiser the two novels contain a striking similarity of plot. In *An American Tragedy,* Clyde Griffiths, a young man of poor and uncultured background, makes his way to the upstate New York town of Lycurgus, where he is given employment in his uncle's collar factory. There he falls in love with and has a secret affair with Roberta, a fellow worker in the factory who is from an equally impoverished background. But he also meets and attracts Sondra, the daughter of a wealthy local manufacturer. Desperately anxious to push his way upward, and seeing a marriage to Sondra as a means of doing so, Clyde is about to break off with Roberta when she announces that she is pregnant. In *The Age of Innocence,* Newland Archer, a young man from one of the best and oldest New York families, believes himself in love with May Welland, an equally well-bred girl of his set. Their courtship proceeds placidly until Archer encounters Ellen Olenska and finds himself deeply drawn to her. Ellen, though originally from Archer's world, has disgraced herself in an unfortunate foreign marriage and now is merely tolerated in upper-class New York society. Despite the increasing attraction of Ellen, Archer goes through with the marriage to May. But he is restless and bored in the marriage, he and Ellen express their love for each other, and he is about to tell May that he is leaving her for Ellen when May announces her pregnancy. It is on this fulcrum of an unexpected and undesired pregnancy that both novels balance. Roberta's pregnancy forces Clyde into a series of actions with fatal consequences for them both, and May's pregnancy forces Newland into the inaction of an acceptance of his marriage to May. The themes inherent in these events can be examined for signs of a common naturalistic ethos shared by the two novels, an ethos that can also constitute evidence of the existence of a naturalistic fiction that transcends the limitations placed on the movement by its conventional historiography.

By the 1920s, the naturalistic impulse had refined itself into a more subtle representation of the qualifications placed on man's freedom than was true of naturalistic works of the 1890s. Here are no degenerate parents causing foul hereditary streams to run in the veins of their children, as in Norris's *McTeague.* And here, too, are no such melodramatic renderings of social constraint as an East Side slum or the "moving box" of a military unit in

combat, as in Crane's *Maggie* and *The Red Badge of Courage.* Rather, the theme of constraint is dramatized within more domesticated and everyday phases of life, and those constrained within these phases are more like the common run of humanity. Both Dreiser and Wharton, in short, have chosen to push American naturalism away from the direction represented by *McTeague* and *Maggie* and more toward that implied by Dreiser's own *Sister Carrie,* in which largely commonplace characters are drawn toward their destinies within the largely commonplace world of American city life.

In *An American Tragedy,* the capacity of the individual to be shaped by the ordinary world in which he lives can best be illustrated by Clyde's early experience as a bellhop in the Green-Davidson Hotel. Young, inexperienced, and eager for the pleasures and excitement of life, Clyde finds in the gauche luxuriousness of an American middle-class hotel of the 1920s a potential fulfillment of all he desires. In pursuing this fulfillment, he encounters and absorbs codes of behavior and belief that will condition his own actions and values for the remainder of his life. This process begins with his interview for the position of bellhop and his realization that he must make himself pleasing to his superiors within a hierarchical social structure if he is to climb within that structure. "For the first time in his life, it occurred to him that if he wanted to get on he ought to insinuate himself into the good graces of people—do or say something that would make them like him. So now he contrived an eager, ingratiating smile. . . . "[6]

Clyde also quickly encounters another condition of social power—that those in positions of strength exploit those beneath them. So Clyde is confronted during his first day by the convention of kickbacks that runs through the hotel's economic structure—that he must pay a portion of his tips to his watch captain, another portion to those who supply ice water and drinks, while he himself receives money from hotel merchants to whom he brings trade. Yet these instances of hypocrisy and corruption are not questioned by Clyde, despite his moralistic upbringing, because they are a means toward the winning of a secular Eden far more immediate and desirable than any heavenly reward promised by his parents' faith. "What a realization of paradise!" (1, 37), Clyde cries, when he comes to understand that even a tiny part of the opulence of the Green-Davidson can be his.

The Green-Davidson as a microcosm of that aspect of American life in which power functions as deception and exploitation is even more sharply portrayed in the sexual ethic operative in the hotel. Well-to-do perverts and rich society women prey on the usually willing bellhops, and Clyde also learns of "a guy from St. Louis" who brings a young girl to the hotel, runs up a large bill, and then both deserts the girl and fails to pay the bill. In these instances, Clyde can still recoil with shock because of his sexual inexperience. But so powerful is the controlling ethic of the hotel that Clyde will eventually, in his relations with Roberta and Sondra in Book Two of the novel, act out this precise model of deception and exploitation, one in which Sondra now constitutes the Green-Davidson of his desires. For as he said to himself after his full absorption of the meaning of the hotel, "This, then, most certainly was what it meant to be rich, to be a person of consequence in the world—to have money. It meant that you did what you pleased. That other people, like himself, waited upon you. That you possessed all of these luxuries. That you went how, where, and when you pleased" (I, 45).

In *The Age of Innocence,* a parallel metaphor of entrapment within a powerful social institution is provided by the wedding ceremony of Archer and May. The right church for an upper middle-class New York wedding, the perfectly attired and correctly seated guests, the elaborately rehearsed and precisely orchestrated sequence of events—all constitute an acceptance by those participating in the occasion of a rigid code of life. Yet it is a code that is dead and meaningless—both in itself and in particular as it represents for Archer a death of the spirit that is about to engulf him. Whatever is fresh in the spring day is smothered by the smell of camphor from the "faded sable and yellowing ermines" of the "old ladies of both families."[7] Archer has contributed "resignedly" to the gestures that make up the ceremony, gestures that make "a nineteenth century New York wedding a rite that seemed to belong to the dawn of history" (1157). He has provided flowers and presents for the bridesmaids and ushers, has thanked his male friends for their gifts, has paid the necessary fees, and has prepared his luggage—and each of these seemingly inconsequential acts constitutes his tacit acceptance of the more consequential rites and taboos that are at the heart of a middle-class marriage in his culture. For the remainder of his life, in short, he will be expected to play various prescribed roles and make various conventional provisions.

Unlike Clyde's imprisonment within the ethic of the Green-Davidson, Archer is aware of the enclosed world of behavior and value that is about to shut its doors upon him. But despite the pain and confusion of this realization, he is too much a part of this world to even imagine at this point a rejection of it. And so, at the right moment, he provides the ring, repeats the formula of the marriage vows, and is married to May—a girl he does not love because he is now in love with Ellen. And in the carriage, after the ceremony, a "black abyss yawned before him and he felt himself sinking into it, deeper and deeper, while his voice rambled on smoothly and cheerfully: 'Yes, of course I thought I'd lost the ring; no wedding would be complete if the poor devil of a bridegroom didn't go through that'" (1163).

There are, of course, major differences between these two instances. The Green-Davidson is a gross representation of American middle-class life, and Clyde is both oblivious to its excesses and completely taken in by them. The wedding at Grace Church, on the other hand, is subdued and decorous, its social nuances expressed in a low key, and Archer himself is fully conscious both of

his own feelings and of the world that is about to enclose him. But the occasions nevertheless also contain an essential similarity, one which constitutes the distinctive character of naturalistic expression in the more sophisticated stage of its development. In both, there are no authorial declamations about the power of environment, and environment itself is rendered not in melodramatic excess but in the form of commonplace institutions at the heart of American middle-class life—a hotel and a wedding. Yet these seemingly neutral institutions, neutral because they are so commonplace, have the power to hold and imprison the individual—to shape his actions, beliefs, and feelings in ways that control his destiny.

Clyde Griffiths is an archetypal example of an individual of this kind. Indeed, his experiences in ***An American Tragedy*** can be described metaphorically as his immersion in a series of walled social institutions, from the formalized religion of his early youth to the prison where he is executed, institutions that Clyde ineffectually seeks either to escape from or to enter. One such institution is the collar factory of the Lycurgus Griffiths, a factory that, as Dreiser dissects its controlling principle early in Book Two, comes to represent as well the controlling nature of the American economic system as a whole. Clyde, despite being a member of the family, is to learn the business from the bottom up in the basement shrinking room as a factory hand at a low salary. The Griffiths believe that "the nearer the beginner in this factory was to the clear mark of necessity and compulsion, the better" (I, 180). Better because it was of great importance for those starting out on the road of life to gain "a clear realization of how difficult it was to come by money." Within this formula of working hard for little reward, youthful aspirants to success would "become inured to a narrow and abstemious life. . . . It was good for their characters. It informed and strengthened the minds and spirits of those who were destined to rise. And those who were not should be kept right where they were" (I, 181).

It is this bastardized version of a puritan ethic that contributes greatly to Clyde's destruction. He indeed wishes to "come by money"—to be a true Griffiths, to marry Sondra, and to ascend to the paradise of identity and wealth. But he is also driven by the immediate human needs of companionship and love, by needs that take him outside the confines of a "narrow abstemious life" into a relationship with Roberta. And so he eventually finds himself in a terrible dilemma in that he must somehow dispose of Roberta in order to gain the crowning symbol of success, Sondra. He is torn, in other words, between a confining and imprisoning form of duty represented by a pregnant Roberta and a seemingly liberating fulfillment of desire represented by a marriage to Sondra. Unable to find a way out of this dilemma acceptable both to Roberta and himself, he begins to plan her death, a plan that will eventually lead to his own death. Put another way, Clyde is fatally constrained by the moral climate of Lycurgus both as it restricts his freedom within the ladder of success construct and as it limits him to a single acceptable response to Roberta's pregnancy. He seeks in both instances to break out of these constraints—to make love to Roberta and then not to marry her when she becomes pregnant—but his failure to do so successfully is a token both of his own weaknesses and of the power of the institutionalized moral and social walls he is seeking to breach.

Newland Archer's world is as much a system of limitations and prohibitions as is Clyde's. And though Archer in the end chooses to accept rather than to break through these barriers, the effect of the novel, as with *An American Tragedy,* is to demonstrate the power of the socially constraining over individual desire and destiny. Archer's world, as I have noted, is one in which tribal custom, discipline, and taboo are as prohibitive as engraved tablets of the law. But though little is permitted, even less is said. Communication rather—in what is perhaps the first fully intended semiotic novel—is by a system of signs. They all live, Archer reflects, "in a kind of hieroglyphic world, where the real thing was never said or done or even thought, but only represented by a set of arbitrary signs" (1050). The "real thing" in *The Age of Innocence* is Archer's discovery of his love for Ellen Olenska during the course of his courtship, engagement, and marriage to May Welland.

Within the poles of duty and desire in *The Age of Innocence,* May is all that Newland's breeding and world deem most acceptable. She is young, pure, of excellent family, and—for good measure—attractive. She is also, Archer begins to realize, indescribably dull, conventional, and predictable. Ellen, on the other hand, is a thoroughly suspect commodity within tribal values. With a dissolute husband and a rumored love affair behind her in Europe, she is clearly shopworn and is available principally as a mistress—as indeed she is so pursued by the wealthy philanderer Beaufort. Moreover, she is bohemian and artistic and emotionally deep. Archer, seeing the long dull road before him which May represents, and fully engaged emotionally for the first time in his life by the pathos and beauty of Ellen's nature, contemplates escape from duty and fulfillment of desire. But at every turn he is silently but effectively anticipated, forestalled, and thwarted. His marriage to May is advanced, Ellen's divorce is blocked by family pressure, and—at a climactic moment—May uses her just-discovered pregnancy to drive off Ellen and hold Newland.

In one of the principal ironic devices of *The Age of Innocence,* Archer and Ellen serve as the major spokesmen for and agents of the system of moral and social taboos that keeps them apart. Neither wishes to descend to a clandestine affair; there must be a complete break with their world or nothing. And a complete break, Newland realizes, though it may gain love, will also mean the loss of "habit, and honour, and all the old decencies that he and his people had always believed in" (1259). And so, in the end, when Newland is driven by the imminent loss of Ellen to project a possible escape—to find at last the emotional equivalent of the fresh air he is constantly seeking in stuffy drawing rooms and closed carriages—

the "old decencies" he speaks for exert their greatest power in the compelling commitment represented by May's pregnancy.

The Age of Innocence, as I have noted, is a novel of inaction rather than, as is true of *An American Tragedy,* one of doing. Newland and Ellen never consummate their love. And though, in a scene remarkably evocative of *An American Tragedy,* Newland at one point wishes May dead (1251), he does not harm her but rather settles into the placid but empty life with her that he had foreseen. But though it seldom expresses itself either in open prohibition or direct punishment, the social and moral world portrayed in *The Age of Innocence*—the world that Archer describes as a "silent organization" of habit, custom, and assumption—exerts a web of compulsion that powerfully shapes and controls individual belief and behavior in the most vital areas of human experience.

An American Tragedy and *The Age of Innocence* share another major characteristic of American naturalism in its fully mature form. In both works, the central figure consciously accepts the premise that he is free. For Clyde, freedom is expressed in his belief that he can fulfill the American dream—that he can move from the basement of the Griffiths factory to the ideal world of an unending summer with Sondra at Twelfth Lake. Indeed, much of the action of the novel emerges out of Clyde's effort to translate his sense of himself—that there is a better life than he has had and that he can gain it—into actuality in the face of his own limitations and an intractable world. In *The Age of Innocence,* Newland even more than Clyde accepts the proposition that he can mold his own life. It is his to choose, he believes almost to the end, whether he will elect to live with May or run away with Ellen. But both Clyde and Newland come to realize that their destinies were shaped outside of their conscious volition. In prison, awaiting execution, Clyde understands—as the world has not—how much his nature had been conditioned by "the ill-fate of his early life and training." And he realizes as well how devoid of any true freedom of choice was the seeming choice between Roberta's "determination that he marry her and thus ruin his whole life" and "the Sondra of his beautiful dream" (II, 392). And Newland, in Paris some thirty years after seemingly freely choosing to remain with May, is told by his son that May, on her deathbed, had spoken of the crisis represented by Newland's attraction to Ellen and of how May had asked Newland not to leave her, had asked him to give up "the thing [he] most wanted." After a long pause, Newland responds to his son, "She never asked me" (1298). May did not have to ask, and Newland was not given a choice, because—with the announcement of her pregnancy—the choice was made for Newland, as May well knew and as Newland now fully realizes, so powerful were the constraints that all of them—including Ellen—fully accepted.

Both novels, therefore, dramatize not only that we live in a contingent universe, that our lives are largely shaped and conditioned by the distinctive social context in which we find ourselves, but also that we continue to share in the myth of the autonomous self that is capable of realizing and choosing its own fate. And in both works as well, though each in its own way, the dynamic aesthetic center of the novel is the tragic irony inherent in the conflict between a character's felt belief in his autonomy and a social contingency that does indeed shape his destiny. Clyde, thinking that he can somehow get out of his scrape and still have Sondra, Newland reaching out for a self-acceptance of his love for Ellen and what this requires of him—both figures are pursuing life as though it were malleable when it is they who have been and are being shaped.

Clyde and Newland are thus neither dumb brutes nor unthinking victims of grossly determining conditions. They are rather close to life as many of us suspect it is. They are less than strong figures who nevertheless wish to believe that they can control their lives and who discover that the ordinary worlds in which they exist—a commonplace factory town and an upper-class community—subtly but nevertheless powerfully are the controlling agents of their fates.

. . . . .

Novels such as *The Age of Innocence* are seldom discussed as naturalistic fiction because of the critic's assumption that if a novel is naturalistic in its central impulse it cannot be a successful novel and because *The Age of Innocence* is clearly successful. But another tack would be to recognize that most literary movements produce in their opening stages ungainly and awkward expressions of the movement—much pre-Shakespearean Elizabethan tragedy, for example—and that American naturalism is no exception to this general rule. The major naturalistic novels of the 1890s are indeed often crude and melodramatic both in theme and form. But in *An American Tragedy* and *The Age of Innocence* the movement comes to maturity both in the discovery of a fuller range of experience available for the representation of naturalistic themes and in the skill of the dramatization of these themes.

NOTES

[1] For an effort to assert this position, see Don Graham, "Naturalism in American Fiction: A Status Report," *Studies in American Fiction* 10 (Spring 1982): 1-16.

[2] I myself adopt this approach to the history of American naturalism in my *Twentieth-Century American Literary Naturalism: An Interpretation* (Carbondale: Southern Illinois Univ. Pr., 1982).

[3] For a characteristically antinaturalistic position by a Jamesian, see Charles T. Samuels, "Mr. Trilling, Mr. Warren, and *An American Tragedy*," *Yale Review* 53 (Summer 1964): 629-40.

[4] *An American Tragedy* has of course been frequently discussed as a naturalistic novel. For a representative

sampling of such commentary, see *Critical Essays on Theodore Dreiser,* ed. Donald Pizer (Boston: G. K. Hall, 1981). Wharton's work, including *The Age of Innocence,* is far less frequently linked with naturalism. Two somewhat limited such efforts are Larry Rubin, "Aspects of Naturalism in Four Novels of Edith Wharton," *Twentieth Century Literature* 2 (January 1957): 182-97 and James A. Robinson, "Psychological Determinism in *The Age of Innocence*," *Markham Review* 5 (Fall 1975): 1-5. In addition, Alan Price has briefly compared two earlier novels by Wharton and Dreiser in his "Lily Bart and Carrie Meeber: Cultural Sisters," *American Literary Realism* 13 (Autumn 1980): 238-45.

[5] See my *Novels of Theodore Dreiser: A Critical Study* (Minneapolis: Univ. of Minnesota Pr., 1976), pp. 203-4.

[6] *An American Tragedy* (New York: Boni and Liveright, 1925), I, 31. Citations from this edition will hereafter appear in the text.

[7] *The Age of Innocence,* in *Edith Wharton: Novels* (New York: The Library of America, 1985), p. 1157. Citations from this edition will hereafter appear in the text.

Ann M. Algeo (essay date 1996)

SOURCE: "Theodore Dreiser's *An American Tragedy,*" in *The Courtroom as Forum: Homicide Trials by Dreiser, Wright, Capote, and Mailer,* Peter Lang, 1996, pp. 9-39.

[*In the following essay, Algeo explores Dreiser's nonfictional sources for* An American Tragedy.]

Theodore Dreiser, introduced to the world of crime as a young reporter in St. Louis, became especially interested in unusual homicide cases. Dreiser collected clippings of these cases as they appeared in the newspapers. He was not alone in his fascination. Murder trials "dominated public attention in the twenties in a way rivaled by no other category of public or private events except sports and the movies" (Brazil 163). Dreiser had for some time considered writing a book about a murderer, and eventually used his collection of unusual homicides to develop "a paradigm of the socially and economically motivated murder" which became the crime at the core of *An American Tragedy* published in 1925 (Plank 269, 284).

An American Tragedy tells the story of Clyde Griffiths from the age of twelve to his execution at twenty-one. The son of poor religious parents who run a street mission, he wants to escape his restrictive environment and takes a job as a bellboy in a hotel, where he learns about the life-style of the rich, about drinking, and about women. One day Clyde is riding with friends and their dates in a borrowed car when they strike and kill a child. Even though he was not driving, Clyde is afraid he will be implicated in the death and runs away. After wandering for two years, he takes a job as a bellboy at the Union

League in Chicago, where a chance meeting with his rich uncle, the owner of a collar factory in New York, results in a job offer, and Clyde goes to Lycurgus, New York, to learn his uncle's business. On the job Clyde meets Roberta Alden, who has left the family farm to earn a living in the city. Clyde begins to meet with Roberta outside of work in violation of company policy. At the same time he is drawn into the world of wealth and social status that his uncle's family inhabits. He is invited to dinner at the Griffiths' home and meets the rich Sondra Finchley, a friend of the family. As Clyde begins a physical relationship with Roberta, he is also developing a romantic relationship with Sondra. Clyde falls in love with Sondra and is encouraged by her. He prepares to leave Roberta, but by now she is pregnant. He attempts to obtain an abortion for her, but without money or connections he is unsuccessful. Finally, Roberta demands that he marry her or she will reveal the relationship to their families. Clyde reads a newspaper story about an accidental drowning and considers killing Roberta to escape the situation. He plans a trip for the couple, and they travel under assumed names to a hotel on a lake in the mountains. The couple decides to have a picnic lunch on the lake, and Clyde takes his camera. Once in the rowboat, Roberta, sensing something wrong with Clyde, crawls toward him. As she approaches, Clyde thinks about how he hates himself and her, and he is afraid to act and unable even to speak. Roberta attempts to take the camera from his hand and he lashes out at her, smashing the camera into her face and causing her to fall backward. Clyde rises to reach her—half to assist her, half to apologize—and capsizes the boat, throwing them both into the water. The boat strikes Roberta on the head and she is stunned but manages to yell to Clyde for help. At this point the proverbial voice whispers in Clyde's ear that this was a mishap, that if he tries to rescue her they both might drown as she thrashes about, that if he hesitates a moment she will be gone forever as the result of an accident. As Clyde waits, Roberta sinks from view. Clyde swims to shore, leaving a straw hat behind to convince searchers that he too is dead, buries the camera and tripod in the woods, and hikes to the next town. Once Roberta's body is found, an investigation ensues, and Clyde is arrested, indicted, tried, convicted, and executed for Roberta's murder.

Dreiser described the genesis of *An American Tragedy* in a series of articles published in 1935.[1] As a newspaperman he observed that "almost every young person was possessed of an ingrowing ambition to be somebody financially and socially." "Fortune hunting became a disease" according to Dreiser (qtd. in Saltzman 5, 6). As evidence of this disease Dreiser lists cases of "murder for money" that attracted his attention: Carlyle Harris (1894), Roland Molyneux [Molineux] (1899), Chester Gillette (1906), and Clarence Richesen (1911) (Saltzman 7-8; Lingeman, *Gates* 402; Pizer *"American Tragedy"* 45). Plank argues persuasively that Dreiser did not derive a pattern from the study of these murders as he claimed, but rather he imposed a pattern on crimes only superficially similar in order to support his "paradigm of the

socially and economically motivated murder" (269). It is true that Dreiser said it was the psychology of these cases that fascinated him, and he made several aborted attempts to write about a murderer, first Molineux and then Richesen (Saltzman 4; Pizer *"American Tragedy"* 47). He also read the morgue clippings on the William Orpet case and clipped stories on the Gillette case while searching for the "right" murder trial on which to base his narrative (Lingeman, *Journey* 175-76). Barrie Hayne, writing about *An American Tragedy* in *Rough Justice: Essays on Crime in Literature,* tells us that Dreiser rejected a medical student [Carlyle Harris] and a clergyman [Clarence Richesen] as murderers and instead finally chose "the nomadic Chester Gillette" (175).

The most thorough summary of the facts of the Gillette case, based on court records and newspaper stories, has been compiled by John F. Castle in his unpublished dissertation "The Making of *An American Tragedy*" submitted at the University of Michigan in 1952 (14-27). A more concise summary is the entry in *The Murderers' Who's Who.*

> GILLETTE, Chester. American factory worker from humble family background who wanted to join high society. He worked in his uncle's garment factory, made steady progress, but had grandiose ideas.
>
> The 22-year-old Gillette's liaison with an 18-year-old secretary, Billie Brown, at the factory resulted in her pregnancy and she begged Chester to marry her.
>
> After unsuccessful pleading she threatened to tell Chester's uncle. Panic-stricken, Chester took her on a hastily arranged holiday, and on 11 July 1906 he rented a boat for a picnic on Big Moose Lake in New York State. Later Chester was seen drying his clothes by a lakeside bonfire at Eagle Bay. Billie Brown's body, with the face battered, was washed up the following day. Chester Gillette, who had inquired at a local hotel whether there had "been a drowning reported in Big Moose Lake", was arrested.
>
> His trial lasted 22 days, and created considerable public interest. He said the girl had committed suicide. Then that the boat had capsized and Billie was drowned accidentally. From his cell Gillette sold autographed pictures of himself in order to earn money to buy special meals in prison. Found guilty of murder, he was sentenced to death, and appeals lasted for a year. Finally he was electrocuted at Auburn prison on 30 March 1908. Theodore Dreiser based his novel *An American Tragedy* on this case. (Gaute and Odell 137)

How much of *An American Tragedy* is based on the Gillette case has always been of interest to critics.[2] Castle's work contains the most complete discussion of the issue, including fifty pages of comparisons between Dreiser's text and the documentary sources (32-82).[3] It may be useful, however, to keep in mind Plank's assertion that "this paradigm of motivation, and not the

Gillette case, is for [Dreiser] the subject of the novel" (286).

Dreiser's material came from a variety of sources: newspaper accounts of the Gillette trial; discussions of case histories with a prison psychiatrist, Dr. A. A. Brill; a visit to the Adirondacks to trace Gillette's journey, to observe the scene of the crime, and to view the courthouse; interviews while on location with a neighbor of the victim's family, the rowboat attendant at the lake, and the widow of the prosecuting attorney; advice from attorneys J. G. Robin and Arthur Carter Hume; and the work of Clarence Darrow, especially the trial of Leopold and Loeb in 1924 (Lingeman, *Journey* 177, 224-28, 239, 257; Dunlop 387).

There is no agreement over whether Dreiser saw the official transcript of the Gillette trial. He wrote to the District Attorney of Herkimer County, New York, to inquire about the transcript as early as 1920 (Pizer *"American Tragedy"* 49). The "abstract" of the transcript that Castle refers to, not the complete transcript, is made up of 2,109 pages in three volumes (Castle 87). Castle observes that Dreiser would have been able to get several hundred pages of transcribed testimony in Herkimer "just for the asking," but he does not indicate whether Dreiser ever asked. Castle correctly points out that a summary of the trial testimony (which he also calls an "abstract") would have appeared in the published Court of Appeals opinion available at state and law school libraries (12).

Dreiser depended heavily on morgue clippings from the *New York World* newspaper (Castle 32-82; Lingeman *Journey* 227-28). Pizer does an excellent job of delineating what the newspaper provided that the trial transcript could not:

> The account in the *World* summarized such matters [jury selection, medical evidence, minor witnesses] in favor of full coverage of sensational evidence and emotional moments in the trial and much material on such vital concerns for a novelist as Gillette's background, his Cortland love affairs, the atmosphere in the court, the appearance and actions of participants in the trial, and the circumstances of Gillette's execution. . . . The *World*, in short, supplied a good deal of grist for the novelist's mill not available elsewhere and gave this material, by means of emphasis and selection, a kind of preliminary fictional expression which Dreiser had the good sense to recognize as invaluable. (Pizer *"American Tragedy"* 57-58)

Castle says Dreiser transformed all of the documents into a novel by (1) creating a structure of motivation; (2) adding the social background of the 1920s; (3) using the traditions of naturalistic fiction—the element of chance, nature as a conditioning force, frankness about sex; and (4) changing the material by amplification—picking up on hints and suggestions in the documents (98, 119, 129, 135). Examining the material that Dreiser selected to support his themes and seeing how he organized that material for the maximum dramatic impact give us insight into the process of creating an effective trial scene in a narrative.

The themes of *An American Tragedy* include the destructive effects of the American Dream on one who is socially and economically outside the reigning class and the inability of the legal system to deal with such a person and the societal issues he represents. "In this clash of deprived and blessed, not having and having, especially as Dreiser dramatized it, was the stuff of crime, and crime of a kind peculiar to a country where rising through class lines was possible, though fraught with danger—a peculiarly *American* tragedy" (Hayne 170). Dreiser stated his thematic concerns as follows:

> I concluded that there were too many elements of a social and economic, as well as moral and religious, character to permit a jury (themselves the representatives, one might even say the victims, of these same financial conditions and social taboos) to judge fairly the guilt or innocence of the alleged murderer [Gillette]. . . . this was really not an *anti-social* dream as Americans should see it, but rather a *pro-social* dream. *He was really doing the kind of thing which Americans should and would have said was the wise and moral thing for him to do had he not committed a murder.* . . . Not Chester Gillette . . . planned this crime, but circumstances and laws and rules and conventions which to his immature and more or less futile mind were so terrible, so oppressive, that they were destructive to his reasoning powers. (qtd. in Saltzman 9, 10, 12)

Pizer believes Dreiser was expressing "an archetypal American dilemma" (*"American Tragedy"* 45). Lingeman calls it "the American nightmare, a vertiginous fear of falling, of social extinction, of being a nobody" (*Journey* 265). This concept of the outsider with whom the system cannot effectively deal recurs in each of the texts under examination. If anything, the outsiders become more alienated as the century progresses.

An American Tragedy is an excellent example with which to begin our discussion of trial scenes in narratives because it covers the entire trial process from arrest through conviction. Criminal procedure in state courts is governed by state statutes and court rules that can vary from state to state, but the basic principles are similar. To arrest a person for a felony, like homicide, one must have probable cause, that is, evidence that there has been a violation of the law and that the person to be arrested committed the crime. All states allow the police to make a felony arrest without an arrest warrant. The exact pretrial processes and the names of the judicial bodies differ from jurisdiction to jurisdiction, but, in all cases, once the individual is arrested, he [the defendants in our four narratives all happen to be male] will have a preliminary arraignment before a magistrate, usually within 72 hours. The purpose of the preliminary arraignment is to put the defendant on notice of his rights, of the upcoming preliminary hearing, and of the availability of bail if applicable. Usually the accused will be represented by counsel at this stage or will be advised of his right to counsel—a public defender if necessary—at the preliminary arraignment.

Next is either a grand jury hearing or a preliminary hearing before a judge at which evidence is heard to determine probable cause to hold the defendant for trial; if probable cause is found, the grand jury, made up of members of the community, issues an indictment, or the judge has the accused bound over for trial.

The purpose of the next stage, the arraignment, is to formally advise the accused of the charges against him and to allow him to enter his plea of guilty or not guilty. If the plea is not guilty, the accused is held for trial; if the plea is guilty, the accused is scheduled for sentencing. During this pretrial process, plea bargaining may be going on between the prosecutor and the defense attorney. The prosecutor is elected or appointed to represent the state in criminal prosecutions and has a title, such as "district attorney" or "state's attorney," depending on the jurisdiction. In a plea bargain, the prosecutor may offer to lower the charge, from first degree homicide to second degree homicide for example, or to recommend a lenient sentence in exchange for a guilty plea from the defendant that guarantees a conviction and saves the taxpayers an expensive trial.

Prior to trial, the lawyers have the opportunity to file pretrial motions with the judge. These motions may include a motion to exclude evidence, such as a confession; a motion for severance, that is, that two defendants accused of the same crime be tried separately; a motion to suppress evidence that was illegally obtained; a motion for pretrial discovery of the evidence held by the prosecutor; and a motion for a change of venue because a fair trial cannot be held in this particular jurisdiction (Cole 350). Cole cites a Houston defense lawyer who listed the following strategic advantages to aggressive use of pretrial motions:

> 1. It forces a partial disclosure of the prosecutor's evidence at an early date.
>
> 2. It puts pressure on the prosecutor to consider plea-bargaining early in the proceeding.
>
> 3. It forces exposure of primary state witnesses at an inopportune time for the prosecution.
>
> 4. It raises before the trial judge early in the proceedings matters the defense may want called to his or her attention.
>
> 5. It forces the prosecutor to make decisions before final preparation of the case.
>
> 6. It allows the defendant to see the defense counsel in action, which has a salutary effect on the client-attorney relationship. [note omitted] (350)

Pretrial procedure is described in some detail in *An American Tragedy.* By the time the trial starts, we have covered 126 pages that include the introduction of the district attorney and his investigation; Clyde's arrest and the retention of defense counsel; and the indictment and pretrial motions (Dreiser 503-629). Some of this material

reveals the strategies employed by the attorneys and emphasizes the economic and social barriers among the characters.

The District Attorney, Orville Mason, hates Clyde for the wealth and social status he believes Clyde possesses. Hayne argues in addition that "[Mason's] jealousy of Clyde's sexual conquest leads him to prosecute him with more than professional enthusiasm"—an understatement (180). Mason is determined not only to convict Clyde but to use that conviction for his own gain. He asks the governor for a special term of the Supreme Court, the trial-level court in the state of New York, along with a special session of the local grand jury. With these requests granted, Mason is in a position to present evidence to the grand jury, gain an indictment against Clyde, and proceed to trial within four to six weeks, well before the upcoming election in which Mason hopes to become a county judge. He justifies his action by noting the ferocity of public opinion against Clyde:

> And in view of the state of public opinion, which was most bitterly and vigorously anti-Clyde, a quick trial would seem fair and logical to every one in this local world. For why delay? Why permit such a criminal to sit about and speculate on some plan of escape? And especially when his trial by him, Mason, was certain to rebound to his legal and political and social fame the country over. (Dreiser 576-77)

Mason uses the power of his office to gain not justice for Clyde but an advantage for himself. Dreiser included an impending election in his narrative to emphasize the pervasiveness of the corrupting power of the American Dream. (At the time of the actual Gillette trial, the local election had already been held.) Clyde murders to get ahead; Mason uses Clyde's suspected crime for personal and professional gain. And Mason views that gain *not* just as legal and political, but also social, as quoted above. Mason may despise the social status of the Griffiths family, but at the same time that status is the height to which he aspires. In other words, he is driven by envy.

Not only does Mason manipulate the judicial calendar, but he also withholds evidence from the defense, and, unknown to him, the evidence has been tampered with. Up to this point in the interrogation, Clyde has denied having a camera with him in the boat. But Mason has recovered the tripod and camera and believes the camera to be the murder weapon. (Dreiser's change from the tennis racquet of the actual case to a camera adds to the ambiguity of what happens on the boat. A camera on a boat at a scenic location is more plausible [Pizer *"American Tragedy"* 62].) Under the rules of evidence Mason must reveal the finding of the camera to the defense. He chooses instead to withhold the information. In an even more sinister turn of events, the withheld evidence has been tampered with, unknown to Mason, by his assistant, Burton Burleigh, who plants two of Roberta's hairs on the camera in order to seal the state's case. Burleigh "was convinced that Clyde had murdered the girl in cold blood. And for want of a bit of incriminating proof, was such a young, silent, vain crook as this to be allowed to escape?" (Dreiser 575). Burleigh has already made a decision of guilt that, in our system, is supposed to be left to a jury. That lack of a "bit of incriminating proof" is meant to protect the innocent from being found guilty. If that philosophy sometimes means that a guilty man goes free, that is the choice we have made as a society, not a choice to be tampered with by an individual. Mason's reaction to this incriminating evidence is to keep it from the opposition:

> . . . deciding for the present, at least, not to say anything in connection with the camera—to seal, if possible, the mouth of every one who knew. For, assuming that Clyde persisted in denying that he had carried a camera, or that his own lawyer should be unaware of the existence of such evidence, then how damning in court, and out of a clear sky, to produce this camera, these photographs of Roberta made by him, and the proof that the very measurements of one side of the camera coincided with the size of the wounds upon her face! How complete! How incriminating! (Dreiser 576)

How gleeful is Mr. Mason! His thoughts here remind us of the 1950s television character who always legally managed a surprise ending in court and who shares Mason's surname. In reality Mason has improperly withheld evidence from the defense.

The selection of defense counsel is not without its own political component. Samuel Griffiths, Clyde's uncle, knows that the family must provide an attorney to represent Clyde. Griffiths's personal attorney advises him that there are criminal lawyers in the larger cities of the state "deeply versed in the abstrusities and tricks of the criminal law" (Dreiser 588). These lawyers could probably save Clyde from the electric chair, but the process would expose the family to extensive publicity and to ridicule from an already incensed public. Griffiths chooses local counsel instead and thus deprives Clyde of the best representation that money could buy were Griffiths not so worried about his social standing. The local lawyer chosen is the political counterpart to the district attorney Mason. Alvin Belknap, a former state senator and assemblyman, is the Democrats' future hope for high office and a worthy courtroom opponent for the politically ambitious Republican Mason. In fact, Belknap is being considered for the same county judgeship nomination as Mason. Belknap acknowledges that the case cannot hurt him politically—at the very least he may be able to delay the proceedings until Mason is out of office and deprived of the publicity the trial will bring (Dreiser 591-93). "[Clyde's] guilt or innocence [becomes] less important than the outcome of the next local election" (Hayne 180). No one in the process is devoid of ulterior motives.

Once the attorneys are retained, Dreiser allows the reader to eavesdrop on several realistic defense strategy-planning sessions, where all of the options for defending Clyde are explored. One argument that could be made on behalf of Clyde would be that of insanity or "brain storm," but the Griffiths family will not permit such a defense, and, after all, they *are* paying the legal fees. Here Dreiser is emphasizing the influence that money can exert on the legal system, and the money is being used not in Clyde's best interest but to protect the Griffiths family. The lawyers determine that Roberta's letters are the most damaging part of the prosecution's case and that Clyde must testify in his own defense. Belknap's partner, Jephson, willing to consider any option in order to save Clyde, ultimately fashions the story Clyde tells on the stand. Though this may be viewed as merely aggressive lawyering, there is a difference between crafting a story and suborning perjury. Clyde himself is not entirely comfortable with Jephson's tactics, but he is willing to embrace the "change of heart" defense Jephson creates. As Strychacz notes, "Jephson . . . 'stories' in such a way as to undo the criminality of Clyde's plot" (103). "Storying" plays a major role in Dreiser's trial scene just as it does in any trial where each side constructs a version of events most favorable to its position.

Dreiser handles the grand jury proceeding in a single sentence, and then describes the pretrial motion of Belknap and Jephson for a change of venue, which is denied. Mason continues to investigate and to withhold what he has found from the defense.

Just as he chose to emphasize the backgrounds and planning sessions of the attorneys and to deemphasize the grand jury proceeding, Dreiser selects carefully when describing what goes on in the courtroom. The trial, covering 112 pages or approximately fourteen per cent of the narrative, begins in Chapter 19 of Book Three (Dreiser 629-741). Dreiser describes the circus-like atmosphere: "'Peanuts!' 'Popcorn!' 'Hotdogs!' 'Get the story of Clyde Griffiths, with all the letters of Roberta Alden. Only twenty-five cents!'" (630). At this point the lawyers and the author are engaged in a very similar process. The district attorney and staff are arranging the order of evidence and directing or instructing the various witnesses, and the defense attorneys are coaching Clyde on his demeanor and his "change of heart" testimony to marry Roberta after all. The district attorney must tell a story that will persuade the jury that Clyde is guilty of murder. The defense attorney must tell a story that will convince the jury that Clyde is not guilty. The author must tell a story in the courtroom that supports the major themes of the text. Dreiser too is deciding who will speak at the trial, what they will say, and in what order.

In an actual trial the next step is jury selection. A panel of jurors, drawn by the procedure mandated by the jurisdiction, is brought into the courtroom and questioned, either individually or as a group, by either the judge or the attorneys. Jurors are asked questions about their age; address; marital status; occupation; affiliations; and any physical or mental disabilities that would disqualify them from serving. They may be asked whether they or any member of their family has been the victim of a violent crime. They are usually introduced to the attorneys and the defendant and asked if they know any of the parties. They are read a list of potential witnesses and asked if they know any of them. Each side gets a number of challenges for cause to dismiss a particular juror, for example, if a potential juror demonstrates racial or religious prejudice, and a number of preemptory challenges that can be used for any reason, for example, if the attorney simply has a "bad feeling" about a particular juror. Nowadays in serious cases where the defendant can afford it, a jury consultant, often a psychologist, is brought in to advise the defense attorney on the selection of jurors who will be sympathetic to the defendant's case.

In *An American Tragedy* the courtroom and the jury selection are described through Clyde's eyes. Clyde's mind wanders as he tries to distract himself during the tedious process of picking a jury. As his eyes roam around the room, he uses physical landmarks such as"next to the wall," "five rows from them," and "this side of that third window from the front" to ground his thoughts. We hear Clyde's thoughts at this point because they are more interesting and more relevant to the narrative than the often boring process of jury selection. Dreiser tells us jury selection takes five days but, except for the first day in court, he sums up the experience in two sentences at the beginning of Chapter 20. He is assuring dramatic pace by eliminating a less important aspect of the trial to move quickly to Mason's opening statement.

Opening statements are to advise the jurors of the theory and main points of each side's case. In opening statements the lawyers introduce themselves and try to establish a rapport with the jurors. The attorneys are not supposed to argue their positions or present their personal opinions, but to give an overview of the evidence that their witnesses will be presenting. Naturally, each attorney presents the facts in the light most favorable to his case. Each may also choose to highlight the statutory elements of the offense for which the defendant is being tried. The defense usually has the choice of presenting its opening statement after the prosecution or of reserving that statement for presentation at the beginning of the defense case-in-chief. Belknap's opening is reserved until the defense case-in-chief begins later in the narrative.

The prosecutor's opening in *An American Tragedy* covers eight pages (Dreiser 639-47). "It was as if some one had suddenly exclaimed: 'Lights! Camera!'" (Dreiser 639). Mason asserts that his motive is to have justice done, a questionable assertion from the reader's perspective, knowing what the reader knows about the pretrial maneuvering. He reviews the facts of the case, emphasizing Roberta's humble background and Clyde's royal Griffiths blood. Dreiser has Mason employ all of the tactics taught to first-year law students: the finger pointing at the defendant for emphasis, the repetition of a key word ("the people *charge*"), a scornful smile when speaking about the defendant, and a reverential tone

when mentioning the victim. Even the unsophisticated Clyde sees through the tactics being used, but his response can only be one of fear: "Clyde, terrorized by the force and the vehemence of it all, was chiefly concerned to note how much of exaggeration and unfairness was in all this" (Dreiser 644). Since Clyde has more information than the jury and knows the real story, he has good reason to worry that they will accept this exaggerated version of events. For his finale, Mason promises to produce an eyewitness: "Mason had no eye witness, but he could not resist this opportunity to throw so disrupting a thought into the opposition camp" (Dreiser 647). Belknap's response to the announcement of a surprise witness is to assure his client that Mason is bluffing, but Belknap also notes alternative approaches the defense can use if Mason is telling the truth, including buying time by cross-examining witnesses "by the week" in order to delay the trial until Mason is out of office.

It is unclear whether or not Dreiser knew that "surprise" witnesses are not permitted under the rules of most jurisdictions. Both sides must supply a list of witnesses in advance to the opposition. This rule is based on a principle of fairness in trial preparation. In Dreiser's scenario, it would be unfair to produce a witness for which defense counsel could not have prepared. The rule against surprise witnesses is also a way to avoid any conflicts of interest between the jurors and the witnesses. The list of witnesses is usually read to a prospective juror so he or she can state any potential conflict before being sworn.

Once Mason has completed his opening statement, he is ready to begin his case-in-chief. In the case-in-chief the prosecutor questions his witnesses on direct examination and the defense attorney questions those witnesses on cross-examination. On direct, the lawyer may not ask leading questions. On cross, the attorney may ask leading questions but only within the scope of the direct examination; he may not introduce any new topics. Once cross-examination is completed, the prosecutor has the opportunity to ask questions on redirect, but only within the scope of cross-examination; opposing counsel may then ask questions on recross, but again only within the scope of issues covered in redirect testimony. In theory, the examination of witnesses is a self-limiting endeavor.

To those readers who find Dreiser's prose long-winded, the first sentence of Chapter 21, introducing the prosecutor's case-in-chief, must be especially daunting: "And then witnesses, witnesses, witnesses—to the number of one hundred and twenty-seven" (648). We are told these include doctors, hiking guides, and the woman who heard Roberta's last cry. But Dreiser carefully selects the witnesses whose testimony will be heard in part or in full. Titus Alden, Roberta's father, is called by the prosecution to elicit sympathy for the victim's family and used by Dreiser to illustrate this trial tactic and how the defense can counter with a series of objections to a witness of this type. Dreiser does not present the testimony word for word but alternates questions and answers with summarized portions of the testimony that details Roberta's move to Lycurgus. Finally Mason has Roberta's trunk brought into the courtroom and her possessions are paraded before the jury. Is this information relevant? The defense objects at the beginning of the testimony, but Mason promises to "connect it up." Relying on the district attorney's word, the judge allows the prosecution to proceed, but when Mason cannot "connect it up," the judge is forced to sustain the defense's objection and order the testimony stricken from the record. A useless foray on the part of the prosecution, you say? To the contrary. The jury has seen the victim's grief-stricken father and heard the victim's story whether or not that story remains a part of the official record. This is the infamous "unringing the bell" principle—once the bell is rung and the testimony has been heard, the damage has already been done, despite the repeated objections of the defense. The district attorney has scored points. But Belknap is not to be so easily outdone. He questions Mason's tactics, and Mason asks who is running the prosecution. Belknap replies, "The Republican candidate for county judge in this county, I believe!" The audience laughs, Mason accuses Belknap of trying to inject politics into the trial, and the judge reprimands both sides (Dreiser 649-50). It is Dreiser who has reminded us of the political motives of the characters.

Next the district attorney calls a series of witnesses to set the scene for Roberta's life in Lycurgus and her relationship with Clyde: Roberta's friend; Roberta's landlords; supervisors at the factory; Clyde's landlady; Roberta's mother; Clyde's society acquaintances; the druggist from whom Clyde sought information about an abortion; the doctor to whom he was referred; the neighbor of Roberta's parents whose telephone she used to contact Clyde; and the local mailman. Dreiser presents the testimony of these witnesses and those who saw Clyde and Roberta on their mountain trip in summary form. At the end of the tenth day of the trial, Belknap protests Mason's withholding of evidence as to the trip—guest registers with false names in Clyde's handwriting as verified by handwriting experts (Dreiser 651-55).

Dreiser's decision to use the summary technique for many of the witnesses could have been based on his judgment that the testimony of minor witnesses would not serve his thematic purposes and would dilute the dramatic quality of the trial, and he would certainly have been correct that listening to testimony from minor and expert witnesses is often tedious. But the decision may also have been more practical. Pizer points out that the 2,000 page Gillette transcript contained the testimony of many minor and expert witnesses that was merely summarized in the *New York World,* the main source of Dreiser's information (*"American Tragedy"* 57).

The eleventh day of the trial begins with Dreiser presenting summaries of the testimony of more witnesses to Clyde's actions before the crime. The existence of the camera is revealed, along with Clyde's reaction to that revelation. Over the next few days five doctors who ex-

amined Roberta's body testify as to their findings, and Mason puts Burleigh on the stand to perjure himself by testifying that he found Roberta's hairs on the camera. The woman who heard Roberta's last cry also testifies (Dreiser 655-60). Mason's final evidence, the love letters of Roberta to Clyde, is carefully calculated to elicit the greatest emotional response from the jury at the end of the prosecutor's case. As he reads the letters into the record, he cries, and as he rests his case, Roberta's mother faints.

Dreiser is at his best here in creating an effective trial scene. In the Gillette trial the letters of Grace Brown were read into the record by the district attorney as they occurred in the chronology of events, that is, *before* the testimony concerning the final trip and the medical testimony. There could have been many reasons for this sequence, including the unavailability of the doctors or a miscalculation on the part of the district attorney or merely the desire for a chronological structure to the case, but surely the most effective use of the victim's "voice," or her story in her own words, is as a climax to the prosecution's case. Dreiser used the letters in *An American Tragedy* for dramatic effect, and some of the letters are in whole or in part the letters actually written by Grace Brown. Pizer tells us that Dreiser used some letters in the body of the narrative—at the time Roberta wrote them and Clyde received them—and has Mason read only six carefully chosen passages at trial for the greatest emotional impact. "Dreiser mixed verbatim quotations, loose paraphrase, and new material—yet maintained the emotional texture of alternating pleading and recrimination, and hope and fear, of the original letters" (Pizer *"American Tragedy"* 66-67).

Defense counsel, having reserved his opening statement, is now ready to open and present his case-in-chief. The procedure for the defense case will be the same as for the prosecution except that the roles of the attorneys will be reversed: the defense counsel will examine on direct and the district attorney will cross-examine the witnesses.

Belknap faces a hostile audience as he makes his opening statement. The jury and the audience have heard three weeks of prosecution evidence. Belknap emphasizes that only the defense knows the truth and cautions the jury not to be swayed by circumstantial evidence. He makes a passing remark on the "politically biased prosecution" and asks that the male jurors remember "we were once all boys." He admits that Clyde loves "Miss X," as the parties have agreed to call Sondra in order to protect her reputation, but states that Clyde and Roberta were never formally engaged. Instead Clyde offered Roberta the opportunity to be supported but to live apart; she insisted on marriage. Now what was he supposed to do? Belknap labels Clyde a mental and moral coward. He is afraid of the social mistake and the sin of pursuing the relationship with Roberta, and he fears the consequences of his behavior. Finally, it is mental and moral cowardice that makes Clyde conceal Roberta's death. Belknap ends his statement by indicating that the person from whom the jurors need to hear the story is Clyde.

Dreiser does the best he can in crafting an opening when Belknap is denied the use of the strongest argument in favor of Clyde's actions, that of diminished capacity or insanity. Belknap is right to admit some of the prosecution's contentions but vehemently to deny that Clyde intended to kill Roberta. The "mental and moral fear complex" argument seems risky since the jury can decide that cowardice is no excuse for crime, as Belknap admits, but here the writer rather than the lawyer takes over the speech. Dreiser needs to reinforce the idea that society's rules have a negative effect on the less privileged. Through Belknap Dreiser can emphasize that, after getting a co-worker pregnant, Clyde has good reason to be afraid of the social system to which he aspires. Clyde can imagine what his wealthy relatives will think of his conduct. He will be ostracized. He will certainly lose the woman he loves along withher lifestyle. And he will bring shame on his parents. Dreiser wants to highlight the fact that these are dire consequences for having sex.

In a change of plans, Jephson rather than Belknap conducts the direct examination of Clyde (Dreiser 673-702). Clyde begins with his birth, his life as a bellboy in Kansas City, his two years of wandering after he and some friends are in a car that strikes and kills a child, and his work in Chicago, where he meets his uncle who offers him a job. Just as he did for Roberta's father, Dreiser chooses a question-and-answer format for the beginning of Clyde's testimony. Mason objects repeatedly and his objections are usually sustained by the judge. Through frequent objections early in the direct examination that interrupt the flow of testimony, Mason is attempting to fluster either the examiner or the witness.

Dreiser alternates between summarizing Clyde's testimony and presenting it in question-and-answer format. This method serves several purposes. It allows Dreiser to move quickly through parts of Clyde's life with which the reader is already familiar and to dramatize the sections of testimony that support the "mental and moral cowardice" theory of the defense and support Dreiser's themes. For example, the events of Clyde's life after his arrival in Lycurgus are summarized, but the question-and-answer format is used on the issue of Clyde's feelings for Roberta and Sondra. In addition Dreiser interjects the conflicts between the attorneys during the question-and-answer portions of the text. At one point Mason and Jephson argue over whose witnesses are being led like parrots. A scuffle is about to break out and the attorneys must be restrained by court personnel.

Clyde begins to tell the story, created for him by Jephson in Belknap's office, about what happened on the lake. This is also a story created by Dreiser; no information about what happened in the boat appeared in the evidence presented at trial in the Gillette case (Lingeman, *Journey* 245). By including this information, Dreiser illustrates the ambivalence of someone trapped by personal desires and social forces. Clyde says he still had no plan as to Roberta, and *she* suggested the trip to the Adirondacks. She said she just wanted to get married to

give the baby a name and then she would go away. Clyde testifies that he had a change of heart and decided that he would marry Roberta, but he did not tell her yet. He was going to tell her that day on the lake. Then he describes the accident:

> "I called to her to try to get to the boat—it was moving away—to take hold of it, but she didn't seem to hear me or understand what I meant. I was afraid to go too near her at first because she was striking out in every direction—and before I could swim ten strokes forward her head had gone down once and come up and then gone down again for a second time. By then the boat had floated all of thirty or forty feet away and I knew that I couldn't get her into that. And then I decided that if I wanted to save myself I had better swim ashore." (Dreiser 700)

Jephson has coached his client well. The story blends fact and half-truths in a way that makes it plausible to the jury and psychologically satisfying to Clyde by resolving his personal doubts. This version of events is really a retelling of the little voice in Clyde's head that counseled him to save himself. He did save himself that day on the lake, and he hopes to do so again on the witness stand. When questioned by Jephson, after affirming that he understands what it means to tell the whole truth, Clyde denies striking Roberta in the boat, throwing her into the lake, willfully upsetting the boat, or causing her death. Then comes the last question on direct examination:

> "You swear that it was an accident—unpremeditated and undesigned by you?"

> "I do," lied Clyde, who felt that in fighting for his life he was telling a part of the truth, for that accident was unpremeditated and undesigned. It had not been as he had planned and he could swear to that. (Dreiser 701-2)

Mason's cross-examination of Clyde fills the next thirty-one pages of text (Dreiser 702-33). Dreiser uses a question-and-answer format for this testimony as Mason jumps from topic to topic in an attempt to unnerve Clyde (Pizer *"American Tragedy"* 65). Both Lingeman and Pizer note that Dreiser writes a more effective cross-examination for Mason than the prosecutor at the Gillette trial actually performed (*Journey* 251; *"American Tragedy"* 66). The result is a devastating attack on Clyde, substantively and psychologically. Obviously Mason focuses on the weaknesses in the defense case such as registering in three different hotels under three different names, the expectation of marriage in Roberta's letters, and the fact that Clyde originally lied about not having a camera with him. Belknap objects frequently during the cross-examination. At one point he is successful, and Mason's thoughts sum up the tactic being used: "'Well, to go on,' proceeded Mason, now more nettled and annoyed than ever by this watchful effort on the part of Belknap and Jephson to break the force and significance of his each and every attack, and all the more determined not to be outdone . . ." (Dreiser 717). But if anyone can be annoying it is Mason with his sneers and his sarcastic tone of voice. He frequently manages to rephrase Clyde's answers or to denigrate what Clyde has said. He often makes speeches in the guise of asking a question, to which Belknap properly objects:

> "Remember her writing you this?" And here Mason picked up and opened one of the letters and began reading. . . . "Does that seem at all sad to you?"
>
> "Yes, sir, it does."
>
> "Did it then?"
>
> "Yes, sir, it did."
>
> "You knew it was sincere, didn't you?" snarled Mason.
>
> "Yes, sir. I did."
>
> "Then why didn't a little of that pity that you claim moved you so deeply out there in the center of Big Bittern move you down there in Lycurgus to pick up the telephone there in Mrs. Peyton's house where you were and reassure that lonely girl by so much as a word that you were coming? Was it because your pity for her then wasn't as great as it was after she wrote you that threatening letter? Or was it because you had a plot and you were afraid that too much telephoning to her might attract attention? How was it that you had so much pity all of a sudden up at Big Bittern, but none at all down there at Lycurgus? Is it something you can turn on and off like a faucet?" (Dreiser 704)

Dreiser stage-manages the cross-examination very effectively. Early in the cross, Mason has the rowboat brought into the courtroom, hands Clyde the camera, and asks him to demonstrate exactly what happened on the lake. (This reenactment never occurred at the Gillette trial.) Belknap objects but after argument his objection is overruled. Someone plays the role of Roberta, and Mason tells Clyde to "direct" her actions. Belknap continues to object on the basis that the demonstration cannot possibly be conducted under the same circumstances in a courtroom as on a lake. Mason asks, "'Then you refuse to allow this demonstration to be made?'" (Dreiser 706). Mason has forced Belknap into a corner, and Belknap now has a tough decision to make. If he refuses to permit the demonstration to go forward, it will seem as though his client has something to hide. If he allows Mason to proceed, Belknap has no way of knowing or controlling what will happen. Belknap feigns indifference: "'Oh, make it if you choose. It doesn't mean anything though, as anybody can see,' persisted Belknap, suggestively" (Dreiser 706). The impression left at the end of the demonstration is that, based on the evidence of injuries to Roberta, Clyde must have hit her harder than he did in court. Mason's second bit of showmanship occurs when he hands Clyde a lock of Roberta's hair "more to torture Clyde than anything else—to wear him down nervously. . . . " Clyde recoils. "'Oh, don't be afraid,' persisted Mason, sardonically. 'It's only your dead love's hair'" (Dreiser 713).

But Mason's strength is his ability to catch Clyde in lies, especially concerning whether or not Clyde had a plan in mind all along. Mason asks Clyde to account for the twenty dollars Clyde claims to have spent on the trip. Clyde cannot account for every cent, and Mason points out that Clyde has forgotten the cost of the boat rental at Big Bittern. Instead of relying on the answer "I didn't notice" that he uses elsewhere in his testimony, Clyde makes up an answer and is trapped. Mason is able to show not only that Clyde does not know the cost of the boat because he neverasked—since he never expected to return—but also that he has just lied about it on the stand. For his last line of questions, Mason is equally effective in demonstrating that Clyde lied when he said he got the maps and brochures about the Adirondacks at the hotel in Utica. Mason passes the brochures, stamped with the name of a hotel in Lycurgus, to the jurors. Once again this evidence is doubly damaging—a lie and proof of premeditation. Mason knows a powerful conclusion when he sees one, and he ends his cross-examination.

Dreiser summarizes the testimony of the eleven remaining witnesses, seven for Clyde and four for Mason. Mason's witnesses are presumably called as rebuttal witnesses after the defense has rested. Dreiser does not go into this procedural detail but does indicate that the prosecution witnesses contradict defense testimony, the purpose of rebuttal witnesses.

Closing arguments are just that, arguments that summarize the testimony and present the conclusions to be reached based on that testimony. Unlike opening statements, an attorney here may give his own opinion and characterize the evidence to fit his theory of the case. The attorney points out subtleties and connections that may not have been apparent to the jurors. The jurors decide the facts of the case, but the lawyer's job in closing argument is to help the jurors see *his* version of the facts.

Dreiser presents the closing arguments in summary form, a choice that seems odd at first because in many cases these speeches provide some of the most dramatic moments of the trial. When considering Dreiser's purpose, however, one sees that Clyde's reactions have been the focus of the trial scene, and Clyde is already exhausted by the process culminating in his intensive cross-examination. To Clyde the closings are merely to be endured. And it takes endurance because we are told that each side speaks for an entire day. Belknap closes first, retracing much of his opening statement. Pizer tells us that since Dreiser took material from the defense attorney's closing argument at the Gillette trial and used it in Belknap's opening statement, the reader has already heard that information (*"American Tragedy"* 65). Belknap reiterates his theme of mental and moral cowardice and warns the jurors not to allow their sympathy for the victim to sway them to convict Clyde for a crime of which he is not guilty. He goes on to cite again the circumstantial nature of the evidence and repeat that only Clyde knows what happened, and Clyde has clearly explained the events.

Belknap explains away such evidence as the brochures, the price of the boat, the burying of the tripod as either "accidents of chance, or memory," and Clyde's failure to rescue Roberta as a result of Clyde's confusion—"'hesitating fatally but not criminally.'" Mason's closing argument for the prosecution focuses on Clyde's lies, reiterates the testimony of the witnesses, and plays on the jurors' sympathy for the victim. After hearing Mason, Clyde decides "no jury such as this was likely to acquit him in the face of evidence so artfully and movingly recapitulated" (Dreiser 734-35).

Just as the jurors are responsible for determining the facts of the case, the judge is responsible for providing the law that the jurors are to apply to those facts when deliberating. In his instructions the judge normally reads the applicable criminal statute to the jury and reviews the elements of the crime. He reminds the jurors that the burden of proof is on the prosecution and that they must be convinced "beyond a reasonable doubt" that the defendant is guilty in order to convict. The judge, of course, covers any other point of law that may be relevant in the case. The judge in *An American Tragedy* instructs the jury that circumstantial evidence is often more reliable than direct evidence, that proof of motive is not necessary for conviction, and that the defendant had no duty of rescue toward the drowning Roberta. Only if the defendant intentionally brought about or contributed to the accident can he be found guilty (Dreiser 735-36).[4] These instructions are reasonable if a bit brief considering a man's life is at stake, although Dreiser's version is almost identical to the charge in the Gillette trial (Fishkin 119).

The judge and the lawyers retire to a nearby hotel for dinner and drinks as the jury deliberates. In Dreiser's world we are privy to information about the deliberations that would never be found in a transcript. We are told that one man, politically opposed to Mason and sympathetic to Belknap and Jephson, holds out for five ballots. He is then persuaded, however, that it would be in his own best economic interest as the owner of a local drugstore not to be discovered as the one responsible for a hung jury, and he goes along with the majority. Belknap believes in the theory that a jury that won't look you in the eye when it reenters the courtroom after deliberations is one that is about to convict your client, and no one looks at Belknap, Jephson, or Clyde as the jurors return. The verdict is guilty of murder in the first degree. Clyde asks that a telegram be sent to his mother. Later, as he listens from his cell, the crowds cheer for Mason.

The Griffiths family refuses to fund Clyde's appeal, and Belknap and Jephson are also unwilling to bear the cost of what they see as an expensive undertaking (Dreiser 745-46). In order to fund her trip east for the sentencing, Clyde's mother hires herself out as a reporter for a Denver paper. While in New York, she is encouraged by Belknap and Jephson to give speeches in defense of her son in order to raise money for his appeal. She manages to raise about half the money necessary before her husband becomes ill and she must return to Denver. Ironically, it is a fellow inmate at Auburn penitentiary, Nicholson, a lawyer convicted of poisoning a wealthy elderly client, who advises Clyde on the best argument for his appeal:

> [T]hat the admission of Roberta's letters as evidence, as they stood, at least, be desperately fought on the ground that the emotional force of them was detrimental in the case of any jury anywhere, to a calm unbiased consideration of the material facts presented by them—and that instead of the letters being admitted as they stood they should be digested for the facts alone and that digest—and that only offered to the jury. (Dreiser 775)

Clyde's attorneys agree to pursue the appeal, including this argument, but to no avail. The Court of Appeals affirms the decision of the lower court. The appellate court notes the circumstantial nature of the evidence, "'But taken all together and considered as a connected whole, [the facts] make such convincing proof of guilt . . . '"(Dreiser 799). Clyde has one last hope: a commutation of his sentence from death to life in prison by the governor. His mother arrives to plead personally for her son's life, and she is accompanied by the Rev. Duncan McMillan, to whom Clyde has confessed his true, confused feelings about what occurred on the lake. When the governor asks McMillan if he knows of any "material fact" that would invalidate or weaken the testimony presented at trial, McMillan responds, "'As his spiritual advisor I have entered only upon the spiritual, not the legal aspect of his life'" (Dreiser 803). McMillan does not take advantage of this final opportunity to describe Clyde's obsession with Sondra, which was withheld from consideration at trial. The governor rejects this appeal as well as another by telegram just two days before Clyde's execution in the electric chair.

Was Clyde Griffiths guilty of murder in the first degree? This question was the topic of a national essay contest sponsored by Dreiser's publishers Boni and Liveright in 1926. Appropriately, a lawyer supplied the best answer. Law professor Albert H. Lévitt of Washington and Lee University won the five hundred dollar prize. His essay, formally published for the first time in a 1991 article by Philip Gerber, presents an excellent overview of the law of the case as well as addressing the many social issues involved. To Lévitt there is no single answer to the question of guilt but a series of answers based on the perspective from which one views the events: "1. The answer given by the law governing murder in the first degree. 2. An answer based upon a system of Christian ethics. 3. An answer based upon the facts as the jury saw them. 4. An answer based upon the societal conditions under which Clyde Griffiths lived" (qtd. in Gerber 222). It is easy to understand why Lévitt won the contest. He crafted a response that would satisfy every reader of the novel.

As for guilt as it accrues outside of the courtroom, Lévitt finds Clyde guilty under Christian ethics. "I can see no excuse for Clyde in morals" (qtd. in Gerber 231). Society also bears some responsibility for its failure to adequately address issues of sex education, birth control and abortion, and capital punishment. While Lévitt agrees that Clyde should be executed, he declares that the state shares blame for the social conditions that produced Clyde (Gerber 241).

Lévitt understands completely why the jury found Clyde guilty, based on the facts as they were presented by the attorneys and the law as it was presented by the judge. The jury did not believe that the capsizing was an accident or that Clyde had changed his mind and therefore had no intent to commit a crime, and their beliefs were reasonable. Under these circumstances, the jury had no choice but to convict Clyde. For Lévitt moral guilt can be imputed to Clyde for his failure to save Roberta, to society for its failure to properly raise Clyde, but not to the jurors for their reasonable conclusions.

Lévitt's answer to the question of legal guilt is one of the clearest presentations of the law as it applies to this case. A crime consists of an act or omission that is the proximate cause of the injury and the concurrent intent to commit that act or omission. Clyde may have planned a murder, but, based on his thoughts at the time of the capsizing, he lacked the requisite intent to commit the crime at the time of the act. In other words, the capsizing was an accident that caused Roberta's death (Gerber 228). As to the omission of not saving Roberta from drowning, Lévitt points out that without a legal duty of rescue, of which none exists under these facts, there can be no legally culpable omission (Gerber 229). Clyde had no duty to rescue Roberta and therefore cannot be held legally responsible for her death. The correct answer to the question of whether Clyde was legally guilty of murder in the first degree is no.

Based on Dreiser's purpose of examining societal issues both in and beyond the courtroom, it would be unfair to demand any more than a reasonable representation of what happens during a trial. Dreiser gives a reasonable representation; he effectively describes both the strengths and the weaknesses of our legal system. Mona G. Rosenman in her article on *An American Tragedy* holds Dreiser to a constitutional standard within which to make his thematic point. She is correct that the conduct of the district attorney at Clyde's trial, including his prejudicial statements and his efforts to hold the trial as quickly as possible, would constitute reversible error on appeal. But the most Dreiser can be accused of here is exaggerating what goes on to a certain degree in at least some of the trials held every day in this country. Yes, Dreiser illustrated violations of due process under the Fourteenth Amendment—that was his point, not something for which he should be condemned.

Rosenman admits that Dreiser deliberately introduced material not present in the accounts of the actual case:

Of course, Dreiser deliberately introduced this

material for the purpose of showing just how unfairly Clyde was treated. Any attorney could have told Dreiser then, as he would now, that Mason's remarks not only disqualified him as prosecuting attorney but also guaranteed—should he insist on prosecuting the case—that the next highest court would reverse any decision made by the trial court adverse to the accused. (14)

Yet Rosenman in her argument seems to demand that Dreiser should have presented a case without constitutional error. She cites the case of Sam Sheppard, where a 1954 conviction was overturned when an appeals court ruled that the trial court had improperly denied a change of venue in a situation where the community had been inflamed by the extensive press coverage of the case, as Clyde's attorneys also alleged in their denied motion for a change of venue. Rosenman credits a young F. Lee Bailey with winning the reversal and Sheppard's later acquittal in the death of his wife. We should all be so lucky to be able to afford F. Lee Bailey as our attorney; Bailey costs money. Sheppard was an affluent neurosurgeon who had access to his own source of funds, unlike Clyde, whose uncle provided the funds but acted in his own best interest, not in Clyde's best interest. Rosenman states that if Clyde's attorneys had used a Fourteenth Amendment due process argument and claimed that Clyde had not received a fair trial, as was argued in the Sheppard case, then Clyde's conviction would have been overturned. Rosenman is probably right, but that result would not have served Dreiser's larger purpose of bringing to the reader's attention the issue of whether society was placing unreasonable burdens on individuals in pursuit of the American Dream.

Sally Day Trigg is more in tune with Dreiser's purpose. She concludes her article on the criminal justice system in *An American Tragedy* with the following summary:

The trial he describes is a travesty. The men who direct the proceedings are adversaries focused more on victory and political prizes than on truth. The jury, primed by sensational press accounts, is the epitome of partiality, basing their judgments on biases, emotions, and public opinion. And the defendant is a mechanism, constructed by the forces of society and by his own nature, and lacking the free will assumed by the law. He cowers in the face of the crowd that craves his death because they despise his immorality and his association with wealth. And finally, Dreiser damns the cruelty and inhumanity of Death Row, the condemned man's last stop before society slaughters him. (438)

Trigg is right: "The goal of the ideal trial is to accurately determine the facts of an event so that a fact finder can decide if the actions of an individual fulfill the requirements of a statute" (430). This would be an *ideal* trial. Instead, in Dreiser's account and in our courts, we have an adversarial system where winning counts, where shading the facts is the lawyers' job, and where the "performance ability" of the lawyers counts more than the facts (Trigg 430-432).

Our system is not perfect, but even Dreiser, who spent much of his life questioning the system, could not offer a better alternative. The fact that critics like Rosenman and Trigg, and a lawyer like Lévitt, take Dreiser's depiction so seriously is itself testimony to the effectiveness of his trial scenes.

Why does Dreiser give us the trial in such detail? Certainly he iscriticizing the criminal justice system in which Clyde is enmeshed. Hayne believes "what is restored at the end of *An American Tragedy* looks much more like the continuation of chaos" (182). McWilliams notes that as Dreiser was writing *An American Tragedy,* Roscoe Pound, the legal scholar and writer, was lecturing against the flaws in American criminal procedure, such as prejudiced jurors, ambitious prosecutors, the tendency of the media to turn a trial into a circus, and monetary motivation in a trial, all of which occur in Dreiser's narrative (93). Both *An American Tragedy* and *Native Son* show "politically ambitious district attorneys, inept lawyers, an aggressive press, and hostile public opinion as features of the American criminal justice system of the time. In [neither case] is there a change of venue or effective control of the press" (Friedland xxii). Dreiser mirrors the concerns of his time, but he goes beyond the flaws in the system to highlight the flaws in society as a whole—a society that tempts everyone equally with the American Dream of wealth, success, and social acceptance at the same time that it denies a large segment of the population the means, through education and employment, to attain that dream.

David Guest (essay date 1997)

SOURCE: "Theodore Dreiser's *An American Tragedy*: Resistance, Normalization, and Deterrence," in *The American Novel and Capital Punishment,* University Press of Mississippi, 1997, pp. 45-74.

[*In the following essay, Guest explores the ways in which Dreiser raised questions about the nature of criminal responsibility in* An American Tragedy.]

Twenty-six years after the publication of Frank Norris's *McTeague,* Theodore Dreiser published *An American Tragedy,* a novel likewise inspired by a well-publicized capital murder case. Dreiser's real-life subject was Chester Gillette, a young man executed by the state of New York in 1908 for the murder by drowning of Grace "Billie" Brown. Gillette came from a poor family and had supported himself by doing odd jobs and menial labor for six years after his parents abandoned him at fourteen. He eventually found work in a factory owned by a wealthy uncle, and although his position and pay were modest, the family connection allowed him some social contact with high society. At the time of the murder, Grace Brown, a secretary at the Gillette factory, was pregnant with Gillette's child, and he apparently planned the murder as a way of avoiding scandal and an undesirable marriage.

After persuading Brown to elope with him in upstate New York, Gillette carried out his plan. Gillette took Brown for a ride in a rowboat on Big Moose Lake and then threw her from the boat. Her face, arms, and hands were bruised and lacerated, and authorities concluded that she had been beaten with a tennis racket that Gillette took along on the outing. Gillette, who had been traveling under an assumed name, soon registered at a nearby hotel, perhaps believing that he would be presumed drowned and that his crime would go undiscovered. He was arrested within hours but contended to the last that Grace Brown had committed suicide after he refused to marry her.

For a few months in the summer of 1906, the trial was a sensation, at least in the regional press. Gillette proved a photogenic murderer, and the newspapers reported that the crowds attending his trial included numerous young female supporters. From jail he sold dozens of autographed photos of himself for five dollars apiece. The proceeds paid for catered meals that were served in his cell. Newspaper accounts stressed Gillette's utter lack of remorse. A disturbing self-portrait emerged even from his own account of Grace Brown's death. Gillette, himself a strong swimmer, stated that he had watched Brown drown from a few feet away without attempting to help her. His heartlessness fueled interest, as did his connection to one of the region's most wealthy families, but after his electrocution on March 30, 1908, the case received little attention. Sixteen years later, when Dreiser retold the story in a novel of more than eight hundred pages, he was reconstructing an obscure chapter in the history of capital punishment.

The novel's dependence on the Chester Gillette murder trial for plot, character, and circumstance is well documented. Dreiser's retelling, however, raises many questions about criminal responsibility and irresistible impulse that did not figure in the Gillette case.[1] Criminal responsibility and irresistible impulse did stand at the very center of two far more sensational murder trials from the period. These other proceedings, because of their spectacular notoriety, shaped the public debate over the death penalty in the early decades of the century.

Both cases involved extremely wealthy defendants who were guilty by all accounts. Both received tremendous publicity and trials prolonged by well-financed, aggressive defense strategies. In the first, in 1906, millionaire Harry K. Thaw was found innocent by reason of insanity of the murder of architect Stanford White. In the second trial, which unfolded in 1924 as Dreiser was writing *An American Tragedy,* Nathan Leopold and Richard Loeb avoided the death penalty and were sentenced to "life plus ninety-nine years" after pleading guilty to the premeditated kidnaping and murder of fourteen-year-old Robert Franks.

The outcome was widely criticized in both cases, and protests voiced many of the same arguments against capital punishment that surface in Dreiser's novel and, much later, in the U.S. Supreme Court's majority opinion in

Furman v. Georgia. In 1926, Dreiser's readers did not need to be reminded that the very wealthy could dodge the death penalty. Clyde Griffiths, bewildered, a child of poverty and a puppet of deterministic forces that he could not understand, contrasted starkly with the arrogance and willfulness of wealthy, cold-blooded murderers like Leopold, Loeb, and Thaw. As Dreiser's readers followed Clyde to the threshold of the deathchamber, they would likely know that Leopold and Loeb were living in prison like exiled kings and that Harry Thaw was squandering inherited millions on a tour of European capitals.

Like *McTeague, An American Tragedy* has often been described as an exercise in objective realism. One early reviewer contended that Dreiser had written his book "with no thesis whatever, with no ulterior purpose beyond the complete uncovering of all the intricate network of causes which led to the event." This same reviewer argued that such scrupulous objectivity represented a dramatic change from Dreiser's earlier work: "Mr. Dreiser has changed both his method and his point of view. He has withdrawn to a position of far more complete artistic 'detachment.' He gives me now for the first time an impression of 'impersonality,' 'objectivity,' 'impartiality.' He appears to me now for the first time in his fiction to be seeking sincerely and pretty successfully to tell the truth, all the relevant truth and nothing but the truth—and with such proportion and emphasis that every interest involved shall feel itself adequately represented" (Sherman, 21).

Another reviewer considered the novel so scientifically accurate that it constituted a kind of criminological treatise: "No one can question either the ring of truth in the incidents or the adequacy of the motives assigned. Thus and for these reasons are murders done" (Krutch, 10-11). Clarence Darrow, who as the nation's most famous trial lawyer had kept Leopold and Loeb from hanging, praised the book for its meticulous accuracy and realism. He wrote, "Dreiser carries the story straight, honest and true to its inevitable end" (9).

If there are superficial similarities between Norris's project and Dreiser's, however, there are also very important differences. Each novel creates an aura of disinterested scientific inquiry, but in their representations of capital murder and capital punishment, the two are rhetorically opposed. Norris's account of hereditary degeneracy and congenital criminality strengthens the state's case for execution and reinforces the dominant discourse. To allow McTeague to live would be to risk more murders and the continuance of his degenerate line. Dreiser counters *McTeague* with a narrative apparently designed to refute the dominant discourse and to undermine the state's case for execution. Clyde may have murdered—the novel is vague on this point—but he was certainly not biologically destined to murder. The forces that shaped Clyde's life are located not in his body but in his environment, and under different circumstances he might have become a law-abiding citizen.

As if to emphasize that Clyde's fate was not preordained, several incidents show that the course of Clyde's life was profoundly shaped by unlikely and arbitrary circumstance. The automobile accident in Kansas City forces Clyde to live the life of a fugitive while still an impressionable teenager. The chance meeting with the uncle he had never known brings him to Lycurgus, where he finds himself supervising the department in which Roberta works. The twoare attracted to one another from their first meeting, but the fatal affair begins only after a chance encounter at a local lake. Another unlikely encounter marks the beginning of Clyde's affair with Sondra Finchley; Sondra offers Clyde a ride because she mistakes him for his cousin Gilbert. Without this unlikely chain of coincidences, Clyde's life would not end in the electric chair.

By emphasizing the role of chance in Clyde's life, Dreiser undermines important elements of the typical diagnostic biography of an executable offender. Chance, however, forms but one part of the novel's resistant strategy. Dreiser's response to Gillette's crime is also shaped by the debate, which reached fever pitch in the 1920s, between environmental and biological determinists. As we saw in the previous chapter, *McTeague* endorses and naturalizes the tenets of biological determinism in a way that promotes the criminal justice system's power. By demonstrating that McTeague's murderous nature is congenital, the novel asserts that McTeague will always be dangerous regardless of his environment. In the world of *McTeague,* biological forces determine criminality, carceral power, and class divisions.

Dreiser's Clyde Griffiths, in contrast, appears to have no inherent, biological nature. Rather his identity reflects his experience and his immediate social environment. Unlike McTeague, Clyde is not constitutionally unsuited for life among the upper class. In the world of *An American Tragedy,* class divisions are accidents of birth rather than expressions of biological plan. The ultimate source of McTeague's murderous nature may lie within him, but the ultimate source of Clyde's desire to kill Roberta lies in the interaction of social pressures, unconscious motives, and sheer chance. From various strands of environmental determinism—including the Marxist critique of social class, the Freudian paradigm of human behavior and personality, and Boasian cultural determinism—Dreiser weaves a resistant discourse.

Dreiser's use of environmental determinism to plot a resistant strategy complements the novel's detailed critique of the criminal justice system. When Norris reconstructs the Collins case, he removes all evidence of the criminal justice system and creates a fable of biological destiny. In contrast, Dreiser devotes roughly a third of his novel to examining the criminal justice system's response to Roberta's death. He finds a system rife with bias and corruption and swayed by the influence of money, social class, personal prejudice, and inflammatory press coverage. The judge and the lawyers for both sides view the trial as an opportunity for political gain, and the press sensationalizes the case for profit. The judicial ritual that culminates in Clyde's execution stands revealed as both arbitrary and corrupt.

Dreiser seems especially alert to diagnosis as it is used to identify executable offenders. Norris's novel minimizes the pitfalls of diagnosis; an omniscient, clinically detached narrator finds McTeague to be a born murderer in the same way that anaturalist distinguishes a toad from a frog. Dreiser takes the opposite approach. He introduces so many variables and so many opportunities for error that diagnosis seems hopelessly complicated. The narratives of Roberta's death presented at Clyde's trial prove inadequate, and even willfully inaccurate, when compared to the one produced by the novel's narrator, and even the narrator's version highlights the ambiguities of the case. Dreiser's reader knows that Clyde kills for reasons both more complex and more elusive than those specified at the trial or in the press.

Moreover, Dreiser's narrative reproduces some of the rhetorical strategies used by defense attorneys to argue against death sentences for their clients. Clyde's defense team, for example, considers the strategy used to save Harry Thaw from the electric chair: "Well, I'll tell you, Jephson, it's a tough case and no mistake. It looks to me now as though Mason has all the cards. If we can get this chap off, we can get anybody off. But as I see it, I'm not so sure that we want to mention that cataleptic business yet—at least not unless we want to enter a plea of insanity or emotional insanity, or something like that—about like that Harry Thaw case, for instance" (599).

Although Thaw is mentioned only briefly, Dreiser's audience would likely be more familiar with the case than with Gillette's. Within weeks of Gillette's murder of Billie Brown, Thaw, a wealthy socialite, shot and killed Stanford White in front of dozens of witnesses during a performance at a dinner theater atop Madison Square Garden. White was New York's most famous architect—his designs included the Washington Square arch and the building in which he was murdered—and also one of the city's most notorious womanizers. His design for Madison Square Garden included a private penthouse apartment that permitted him to pursue his extramarital interests. Thaw, the son of a Pittsburgh man who had amassed a fortune in the coke market, had a history of bizarre and sometimes violent behavior. He had never worked and spent his allowance, reportedly more than eighty thousand dollars a year, on travel, parties, and prostitutes. When he married Evelyn Nesbit, a member of the famed Floradora Chorus burlesque show and former mistress of Stanford White, his father cut off his allowance, but his mother surreptitiously restored it.

On the night of the murders White was, uncharacteristically, dining alone. Thaw excused himself from the table where he was dining with Evelyn Nesbit Thaw, his wife, and another couple, walked to White's table, withdrew a handgun from his coat pocket, and fired three bullets into the architect's head. Thaw immediately surrendered, claiming that he had acted to avenge White's rape of Evelyn in the years before the Thaws married. He was eventually found not guilty "on the ground of his insanity at the time of the commission of the act" (jury's verdict quoted in Nash, 545). In delivering its decision, the jury endorsed the position, advanced by Thaw's attorneys, that Thaw suffered from *Dementia americana*, "a singularly American neurosis among males in the U.S. who believed that every man's wife was sacred" (Nash, 545).

Thaw's was arguably the most celebrated and publicized murder case the nation had yet produced. Interest did not end when Thaw was admitted to the New York State Asylum in 1906 for the Criminally Insane in Matteawan. He escaped from the asylum briefly in 1913 but was soon captured in Canada and returned. In 1915 he was declared sane and released. He took control of the family fortune, estimated at forty million dollars, and divorced his wife, who had conceived and given birth to a child during his institutionalization. In 1916 he was again arrested, this time for flying into a rage and horsewhipping a teenage boy named Fred Gump. The arrest led to another stint at Matteawan, but in 1922 Thaw was again declared sane and released. He spent the remaining twenty-five years of his life in an extended, well-publicized, and dissipated tour of European capitals.

Clyde Griffiths may bear little resemblance to Harry Thaw, but Dreiser's novel suggests that they shared a compulsion to murder. Like the Harry Thaw depicted by Thaw's defense team, Clyde kills during a fit of temporary insanity or delirium. Just before the drowning, Clyde is in "a confused and turbulent state mentally, scarcely realizing the clarity or import of any particular thought or movement or act" (485). Throughout the scene Clyde seems dissociated from his own actions, and the journalistic, naturalistic tone that characterizes most of the narrative turns suddenly disjointed and expressionistic. Clyde hears disembodied voices urging him through the steps of his plan, and the repetitive call of a bird becomes a hallucinatory incantation. Later, awaiting execution, Clyde will recall that, during the death scene, "there had been a complex troubled state, bordering, as he now saw it, almost upon trance or palsy" (793).

Clyde's case is also like Thaw's in that both defendants are represented as enacting a peculiarly American pattern. Dreiser's account of the writing of his novel stresses that he saw Gillette's case as but one of many possible forms of American murder. That genre contained many variations on a basic plot:

> In the main, as I can show by the records, it was the murder of a young girl by an ambitious young man. . . . [One variation] was that of the young ambitious lover of some poorer girl, who in the earlier state of affairs had been attractive enough to satisfy him both in the matter of love and her social station. But nearly always with the passing of time and the growth of experience on the part of the youth, a more attractive girl with money or position appeared and he quickly discovered that he could no longer care for his first love. What produced this particular type of crime about which I am talking was the fact that it was not always possible to drop the first girl. What usually stood

in the way was pregnancy, plus the genuine affection of the girl herself for her love, plus also her determination to hold him. [Quoted in Fishkin, 106]

Dreiser claimed familiarity with numerous cases fitting this pattern, and he settled on the Gillette case as his model only after starting two other novels based on similar murders. The parallels between the forms of temporary insanity that drive Clyde's and Thaw's actions heighten the contrast in the outcomes of the two trials.

The cumulative effect of Dreiser's rhetorical strategies is to call into question Clyde's responsibility for Roberta's death. If Clyde's actions follow a common pattern, then perhaps the ultimate source of those actions lies in his circumstance and not his inherent nature. If the judicial process that hands down Clyde's death sentence is a corrupt one, then the sentence itself may be unjust. If his actions spring from mental illness, then his responsibility for them is diminished. Beneath the apparent objectivity of Dreiser's novel there lies a kind of political allegory.

The two points of view represented by Norris and Dreiser may be regarded as sides in a debate over the causes of crime and the legitimacy of correctional authority. Norris naturalizes police power and the social hierarchy by equating them with biological law, while Dreiser depicts police power and class divisions as imposing unnatural restrictions on Clyde's natural instincts. Norris, like many biological determinists, envisions a continuum of power in which the police abet natural selection and evolutionary progress. Dreiser, siding with the environmental determinists, takes a less generous view; in *An American Tragedy,* crime is shown to be a product not of our animal past but of our human present.

In adapting Gillette's story, Dreiser saw his task as a corrective one. He perceived mistakes in the way the crime had been interpreted and reported, and he sought to correct those mistakes. He would later say that his study of the Gillette case convinced him "that there was an entire mis-understanding or perhaps I had better say misapprehension, of the conditions or circumstances surrounding the victims of that murder *before* the murder was committed" (quoted in Fishkin, 110). This misapprehension as depicted in the novel recalls the biological determinism of *McTeague* as well as the newspaper reports on the Patrick Collins case. Clyde is represented to the public as a "reptilian villain" (502) and a "murderer of the coldest and blackest type" (735).

While the prosecution labors to cast Clyde as a cold-blooded monster, the defense counters with a strategy more consonant with the events surrounding Roberta's death as the reader knows them: "Gentlemen of the jury, the individual on trial here for his life is a mental as well as a moral coward—no more and no less—not a downright, hardhearted criminal by any means. Not unlike many men in critical situations, he is a victim of a mental and moral fear complex" (669). The defense attorney's contention that Clyde is "not unlike many men in critical

situations" signals one of the novel's central rhetorical strategies: the novel defends Clyde by blurring the distinction between the normal and the criminal.[2] This strategy places the novel squarely in conflict with the dominant discourse, which identifies a gap between normalcy and criminality. *McTeague,* in line with the dominant discourse of its time, portrays the capital murderer as an evolutionary throwback and radically different from normal humans.

An American Tragedy undermines the facile distinction between the normal and the criminal in a number of ways. The novel's corrective retelling of the Gillette case, for example, first alters some basic facts of that case that would make it more difficult to place Clyde within the spectrum of normalcy. The most significant change involves the manner of death. Gillette told several conflicting stories of Billie Brown's death and testified at his trial that she had leaped from the boat in order to commit suicide. The medical evidence demonstrated, however, that she had been violently and repeatedly struck about the head and shoulders while she drowned. In Clyde's case the medical evidence is much more ambiguous. Roberta's relatively minor injuries do not disprove Clyde's claim that the blow he struck was accidental. Dreiser's transformation of the alleged murder weapon likewise obscures Clyde's culpability. Gillette could offer no unincriminating explanation for taking a tennis racket along on the rowboat, but Clyde strikes Roberta with a camera. The camera, which could be used on a boat, is less damning as circumstantial evidence.

By introducing the possibility that Clyde struck Roberta accidentally, Dreiser changes the entire complexion of the case and eliminates many of the questions that typically dominate crime narrative. The reader knows who was in the boat with Roberta and what his motives were. The reader knows that Clyde struck Roberta and that Roberta was conscious when she went into the water. The reader even knows that although Clyde plotted cold-blooded murder, he found himself, momentarily at least, unable to carry out the plan. By reconstructing the Gillette case in this way, Dreiser shifts the reader's attention from the usual questions and toward diagnostic questions about state of mind. Whether or not Clyde struck the blow is less important than whether or not his actions were voluntary, involuntary, or accidental. The question of guilt is thus narrowed to the legal question of intent, of *mens rea.*

The novel does not answer the question directly. The blow, we are told, was "accidentally and all but unconsciously administered" (493). Even Clyde seems uncertain about Roberta's final moments. In prison, he "sat there, trying honestly now to think how it really was (exactly) and greatly troubled by his inability to demonstrate to himself even—either his guilt or his lack of guilt" (795). The confusion regarding Clyde's guilt may indicate Dreiser's belief that complex factors produce murder, and it certainly raises questions about the certainty with which judge and jury render their verdicts. There is simply no way for the court to prove or disprove Clyde's story.

The question of intent may also—appropriately—be considered in relation to Dreiser's well-documented interest in Freudian psychology. While writing *An American Tragedy,* Dreiser frequently discussed Freudian interpretations of murder and murderers with Dr. Abraham Brill, Freud's American translator. During this same period Brill completed and published his translation of Freud's *The Psychopathology of Everyday Life* (1924).

Freud's book purports to reveal the psychological underpinnings of everyday "accidents" and "absent-minded" behavior. Freud argues, of course, that there are no true accidents, and this idea provides us with perhaps the best context within which to consider Clyde's "accidental" killing of Roberta. Brill and Freud offer Dreiser a way to depict Clyde killing Roberta while simultaneously affirming his status as the puppet of deterministic forces. When Clyde strikes Roberta, he unconsciously carries out the plan concocted by his own poorly restrained id: "Indeed the center or mentating section of his brain at this time might well have been compared to a sealed and silent hall in which alone and undisturbed, and that in spite of himself, he now sat thinking on the mystic or evil and terrifying desires or advice of some darker or primordial and unregenerative nature of his own, and without the power to drive the same forth or himself to decamp, and yet also without the courage to act upon anything" (463). The novel figures the id as malevolent genie to Clyde's Aladdin, and as "the very substance of some leering and diabolical wish or wisdom contained in [Clyde's] nature" (463-64).

The rewriting of Gillette's premeditated, brutal act of murder as ambiguous accident prepares us to understand Clyde as normal, and Dreiser's use of the Freudian paradigm furthers this purpose. Freud helps Dreiser establish that Clyde is extraordinary not because of his psychological structure but because of his circumstance. In fact, Clyde's motives and desires, when compared with those of the novel's other characters, prove quite ordinary. Like many Americans of humble origin, Clyde dreams of great wealth and high social station. Dreiser suggests that this cultural obsession with money and material success provides the true context in which we should understand cases like Gillette's. Dreiser would later comment that Clyde "was really doing the kind of thing which Americans should and would have said was the wise and moral thing to do . . . had he not committed a murder" (quoted in Fishkin, 110).

Having recast the most troublesome facts of the Gillette case so as to make it at least possible that Clyde struck Roberta accidentally, Dreiser was left with the still daunting task of portraying the plotter of cold-blooded murder as an ordinary boy victimized by circumstance. While the novelist was immersed in this task, the Chicago trial of Nathan Leopold and Richard Loeb for kidnaping and murder began receiving national attention. Clarence

Darrow's eloquent defense of the two young men employs many of the rhetorical strategies that Dreiser uses to tell the story of Clyde Griffiths.

The story of Leopold and Loeb, like Clyde's, unfolds against a backdrop of money and privilege. The two teenagers, children of wealthy Chicago socialites, seemed destined for lives of luxury and success. At eighteen, Leopold, who had a prodigious intellect, became the youngest person to receive a B.Ph. from the University of Chicago. He was an avid student of philosophy, ornithology, and botany and spoke nine languages fluently. Leopold's friend Loeb was likewise a precocious student, the youngest ever to graduate from the University of Michigan at Ann Arbor. On May 20, 1924, apparently in an effort to prove themselves Nietzschean supermen, the two attempted to commit the perfect crime. Their plan required them to kidnap, murder, and then collect ransom for a child of a wealthy family in their neighborhood. They chose as their victim Bobbie Franks, who was fourteen years old and a distant cousin of Loeb's.

After murdering Franks and hiding his body, the two delivered the ransom note. The perfect plan of the boy geniuses, however, proved full of holes. Several different trails leading to Leopold and Loeb were discovered almost immediately, and the boys soon confessed. Leopold's father reportedly got down on his knees and promised Clarence Darrow one million dollars if he would take the case and save young Leopold from execution. Darrow, knowing that a jury would be inflamed by the sensational press coverage of the case, advised his clients to waive their right to a jury trial and plead guilty. In the month-long bench trial that followed, Darrow argued that his clients should be spared. He was successful. The judge sentenced each of the boys to life plus ninety-nine years.

Darrow's lengthy defense of his clients, and especially his widely reprinted closing remarks, may have been an important source for the defense of Clyde Griffiths. Richard Lingeman in his biography of Dreiser reports, "Dreiser had followed the Leopold-Loeb trial closely in 1924 while he was writing the *Tragedy*" (288). Lingeman contends that Dreiser "was more interested in the psychology of the murderers than in Darrow's tactics" (288), but the novelist's strategy clearly parallels Darrow's in a number of ways. Both emphasize environmental determinants of criminal behavior, and both plead for mercy on the basis of immaturity and mental disease. Just as Dreiser opposes the portrayal of his client as a reptilian monster, Darrow argues against claims, put forth by the prosecution and in the press, that his clients are cold-blooded "thrill-killers." He claims instead that his clients are relatively normal boys caught up in extraordinary circumstance.

Although the details of the two crimes differ, Darrow and Dreiser describe the social and economic contexts in similar terms. Both men, for example, depict accumulated wealth as a corrupting influence on everyone near it, particularly the young. When Darrow closes his defense of Leopold and Loeb, he blames wealth for their crimes: "We have grown to think that the misfortune is in not having [money]. The great misfortune in this terrible case is the money. That has destroyed their lives. That has fostered theseillusions. That has promoted this mad act" (*Attorney*, 63). Dreiser later echoed this interpretation of the link between wealth and crime in an essay written after *An American Tragedy* had been published: "Yet even prosperity itself, the prosperity that takes too much for the few and gives too little to the many, foments outlawry. The madness of material things (most of which are hideously inartistic, and yet in America encouraged by every sort of price reduction and installment payment plan) makes people run amuck, hooting and snorting to heap up more and more possessions, mostly worthless, and lawfully or otherwise" (**"Crime and Why,"** in *Tragic America*, 299). In both examples, wealth and prosperity—which are fundamentally good in most versions of the American Dream—are linked to criminality.

In his mad quest for wealth, then, Clyde differs in degree but not in kind from the American norm. In his desire for prosperity and social advancement, he resembles most of the other characters in the novel. When Hortense Briggs schemes to lure Clyde into buying her a fur coat, and when the bellhops carouse at expensive restaurants and brothels, they seek the trappings of wealth. By the same token, the hope of a "newer and greater life" (245) causes Roberta to leave her small hometown for the wider prospects and higher salaries available in Lycurgus. The same hope enters into her attraction to Clyde: "Roberta, after encountering Clyde and sensing the superior world in which she imagined he moved . . . was seized with the very virus of ambition and unrest that afflicted him" (250). In all of these examples, the lure of prosperity seduces the young into some form of transgression. The gap between Clyde and his peers thus grows smaller.

Neither Darrow nor Dreiser, however, suggests that the desire for prosperity corrupts only the young. Darrow accuses state attorneys of sensationalizing the Leopold and Loeb case to inflate their reputations and further their careers (*Attorney*, 27). He also calls the testimony of Dr. Krohn, the state's psychological expert, "the cold, deliberate act of a man getting his living by dealing in blood" (39). Similar considerations of money and social standing animate the individuals involved in Clyde's prosecution and sentencing. As soon as the coroner sees Roberta's body, his thoughts turn to the upcoming elections. He notes that such a case could benefit the incumbent district attorney, "a close and helpful friend of his" (501). With a conviction in so infamous a case, the district attorney might carry his party's entire ticket—Coroner Heit included—to victory.

In the world of Dreiser's novel, even jurors are not free from such pragmatic considerations:

> And in the meantime the twelve men—farmers, clerks and storekeepers, re-canvassing for their own

mental satisfaction the fine points made by Mason and Belknap and Jephson. Yet out of the whole twelve but one man—Samuel Upham, a druggist— (politically opposed to Mason and taken with the personality of Jephson)—sympathizing with Belknap and Jephson. And so pretending that he had doubts as to the completeness of Mason's proof until at last after five ballots were taken he was threatened with exposure and the public rage and obloquy which was sure to follow in case the jury were hung. "We'll fix you. You won't get by with this without the public knowing exactly where you stand." Whereupon, having a satisfactory drug business in North Mansfield, he at once decided that it was best to pocket this opposition to Mason and agree. [736-37]

Thus Dreiser, echoing Darrow, discredits the judicial process as an unbiased, clinically detached search for justice. He also resists the mainstream tendency to draw a hard and fast line between the normal and the criminal. The motives of the jurors, the attorneys, and the judge are strikingly similar to Clyde's motives, and in most matters Clyde embraces the values of his culture.

After indicting wealth and the pursuit of wealth as both the culprit in Bobbie Franks's murder and the motive behind the state's case for execution, Darrow's defense strategy focused on two factors that he considered mitigating. He said, "I think all of the facts of this extraordinary case, all of the testimony of the alienists, all that your honor has seen and heard, all their friends and acquaintances who have come to enlighten the court—I think all of it shows that this terrible act was the act of immature and diseased brains, the act of children" (79). Leopold and Loeb deserved mercy, Darrow argued, because of their age and because they were mentally ill. This same general approach informs Dreiser's treatment of Clyde's story.

The task of portraying Leopold and Loeb as children was not as straightforward as it might seem. One was eighteen and the other nineteen, and both were college graduates. Nevertheless, Darrow described his clients as "two minors, two children, who have no right to sign a note or make a deed" (*Attorney*, 25). He also suggested that the prosecutors, eager to mislead the court, had portrayed the boys as more mature than they really were: "Here is Dickie Loeb, and Nathan Leopold, and the State objects to anybody calling the one 'Dickie' and the other 'Babe' although everybody does, but they think they can hang them easier if their names are Richard and Nathan, so we will call them Richard and Nathan" (25).

Similar exchanges occur during Clyde's trial. The prosecutor argues that Clyde is "not a boy" but a "bearded man" and insists that his "mind is a mature, not an immature one" (642). The defense counters by charging the prosecution with deliberately misrepresenting Clyde's level of maturity: "The foolish and inexperienced, yet in every case innocent and unintentional, acts of a boy of fifteen or sixteen have been gone into before you gentlemen as though they were the deeds of a hardened criminal, and plainly with the intention of prejudicing you against this defendant, who . . . can be said to have lived as clean and energetic and blameless and innocent a life as any boy of his years anywhere. You have heard him called a man—a bearded man—a criminal and crime-soaked product of the darkest vomitings of hell. And yet he is but twenty-one" (665). The mitigating aspects of immaturity help explain why Clyde is a year younger than Chester Gillette at the time of the drowning and also, perhaps, why Roberta is five years older than Billie Brown.

Dreiser's narrator, although not as hyperbolic as Clyde's attorney, sides with the defense team when it pronounces adolescence a fundamental determinant of Clyde's character: "For to say the truth, Clyde had a soul that was not destined to grow up. He lacked decidedly that mental clarity and inner directing application that in so many permits them to sort out from the facts and avenues of life the particular thing or things that make for their direct advancement" (169). Even Darrow, who reviewed *An American Tragedy* for the *New York Evening Post Literary Review,* saw adolescence as the key to understanding Clyde's fate: "Without the slightest preparation, he faces puberty, with all its new emotions and luring calls" (reprinted in Salzman, 6).

The defenders of Clyde, Leopold, and Loeb, by portraying their clients as adolescents, hope to gain from judge and jury the sort of sympathetic understanding that adults reserve for children. In addition, however, they participate in a larger public debate over adolescence, and some elements of this debate seem to have left their mark upon Dreiser's novel. In the United States in the mid-1920s, adolescence stood at the center of the dispute between biological and environmental determinists. Both sides conceded that adolescence was commonly marked by turbulent and even criminal behavior, but they disagreed regarding the reason. The biological determinists and the eugenicists cited widespread reports of adolescent turbulence as proof that human personality and behavior acted out inherited scripts. Proponents of environmental determinism claimed that adolescent turbulence was guided by cultural forces and further hypothesized that members of some cultures would show no signs of adolescent turmoil.

During the very years that Dreiser spent writing *An American Tragedy,* Franz Boas, the nation's most prominent cultural determinist, was planning for a graduate student some research into the relative importance of hereditary and environmental factors in determining adolescent behavior. The student was Margaret Mead. The book describing her research and conclusions, *Coming of Age in Samoa* (1928), became one of the most widely read and influential texts in modern anthropology. In it, Mead argued that Samoan adolescents showed no signs of the turbulent, antisocial behavior common in their Western counterparts. The Samoan example, Mead argued, offered proof that cultural factors far outweigh hereditary ones in determining human personality and behavior.[3]

Mead's method—to compare the behavior of biologically similar subjects in very different environments—also forms the basis of Darrow's 1925 essay "The Edwardses and the Jukeses." Darrow's essay responds to Richard L. Dugdale's *"The Jukes": A Study in Crime, Pauperism, Disease, and Heredity* (1877). Dugdale, an inspector of jails for the state of New York, tells of his discovery that several members of the same extended family were simultaneously serving time, for various crimes, in a rural jail. Dugdale uses a genealogical history of the family to demonstrate that crime is a form of biologically determined behavior prevalent in certain bloodlines. His essay is often cited in the writings of hereditarians and eugenicists, so much so that Darrow chooses it for public rebuttal.

The rebuttal compares two family histories: one beginning with Jonathan Edwards, the other with Max Jukes. The descendants of Edwards became college presidents, doctors, and clergymen, while those of Jukes became burglars, thieves, and prostitutes. Darrow counters the hereditarian analysis of the two histories, which emphasized inferior and superior bloodlines, by explaining the divergence in terms of political, economic, social, and geographical circumstance. In closing his defense of Leopold and Loeb, Darrow contended that adolescents were especially susceptible to just such circumstantial factors: "The whole life of childhood is a dream and an illusion, and whether they take one shape or another shape depends not upon the dreamy boy but on what surrounds him" (*Attorney,* 63).

Like both Darrow and Mead, Dreiser hews to the tenets of cultural determinism by comparing the lives of biologically similar individuals in vastly different surroundings. His novel documents a controlled experiment in which two boys of the same bloodline are raised in very different settings and meet with very different ends. The narrator often comments on the resemblance between Clyde and his cousin Gilbert, and the physical likeness heightens the contrast in their backgrounds. Clyde is born into near poverty. His ineffective parents afford him little education, and by the time adolescence strikes he is virtually alone in the world. He begins working in a somewhat disreputable environment at an early age and begins living as a solitary fugitive in his midteens. Without the safety net provided by a strong family or by a secure position in a stable social group, Clyde is defenseless against adolescence and its accompanying turbulence. Gilbert's parents, in contrast, provide him with a secure and ordered home life, an expensive education, and a well-salaried position in the family business. He is guided through adolescence by stern, loving parents and protected from its pitfalls by social and financial buffers. Had Clyde taken Gilbert's place, Dreiser seems to tell us, he would have turned out as well or better.

The stress of Clyde's adolescence nicely accommodates the argument that he is relatively normal. It also helps resolve an apparent contradiction in Dreiser's defense strategy. The effort to depict Clyde as normal conflicts with the view that he suffered from temporary insanity.

How can Clyde be both normal and insane? The answer, as Darrow notes, is that adolescence and insanity are linked: "Both these boys are in the adolescent age. Both these boys, as every alienist in this case on both sides tells you, are in the most trying period in the life of a child—both these boys, when the call of sex is new and strange; both these boys, at a time of seeking to adjust their young lives to the world, moved by the strongest feelings and passions that ever moved men; both these boys, at the time boys grow insane, at the time crimes are committed" (*Attorney,* 65). The volatile nature of adolescence in our society, then, helps Dreiser locate the source of Clyde's insanity in his circumstances rather than in his identity. If Clyde's motives and desires resemble those of many of his peers, his extraordinary situation most certainly does not, and adolescence makes Clyde all the more susceptible to its stress.

Clyde's situation is extraordinary because, unlike most of his working-class peers, he has a chance to move rapidly up the social scale. Like the other killers of whom Dreiser speaks, Clyde is caught between social classes. His blood tie to the Griffithses of Lycurgus gives him temporary access to high society, and marriage to Sondra Finchley would bring wealth enough to make this access permanent. The promise of prosperity, however, is attended by a tremendous amount of stress, stress perhaps best understood in terms of Dreiser's reading of Freud.

Clyde's sex drive may be typical for an adolescent, but as his social prospects widen, his opportunities for sexual release are proportionally restricted. When Clyde is promoted to foreman in his uncle's factory, Gilbert warns him that his new position is precarious and makes it clear that the chief obstacle to Clyde's success is a sexual one:

> "This plant is practically operated by women from cellar to roof. In the manufacturing department, I venture to say that here are ten women to every man. On that account everyone in whom we entrust any responsibility around here must be known to us as to their moral and religious character. If you weren't related to us, and if we didn't feel that because of that we knew a little something about you, we wouldn't think of putting you up there or anywhere in this factory over anybody until we did know. But don't think that because you're related to us that we won't hold you strictly to account for everything that goes on up there and for your conduct. We will, and all the more so because you are related to us." [232]

Gilbert ends by admonishing Clyde: "Not the least little thing must occur in connection with you that any one can comment on unfavorably" (233).

Clyde's precarious position between social classes thus places him under such relentless scrutiny that he is cut off from sexual release far more completely than his unmarried peers in either the upper classes or the lower. This atmosphere of surveillance is most apparent in the scenes depicting Clyde working at the head of the stamping department. Clyde is intensely aware of the women in the room and entertains sexual fantasies about several of them. Yet he is always aware that his every move is being watched. The feeling is not mere paranoia; every woman in the department studies Clyde for signs of sexual interest in one or another of the workers. Also, because he bears the Griffiths name and resembles his cousin Gilbert, Clyde finds this atmosphere of surveillance extended to every aspect of his life in Lycurgus. Initially, Clyde resolves to meet the challenge: "So elated was he at the moment that he bustled out of the great plant with a jaunty stride, resolved among other things that from now on, come what might, and as a test of himself in regard to life and work, he was going to be all that his uncle and cousin obviously expected of him—cool, cold even, and if necessary severe, where these women or girls of this department were concerned. No more relations with Dillard or Rita or anybody like that for the present anyhow" (234). Clyde later pursues an affair with Roberta but only in secrecy and only while his prospects for social advancement seem dim. He ends the affair when he realizes that he might actually be able to marry Sondra.

Clyde's predicament separates him from his counterparts, whose social status is unlikely to change. If Clyde were a factory worker with no hope of social advancement, any sexual indiscretion would go virtually unnoticed. The novel's descriptions of the other workers make it clear that they engage in sexual activity without significant risk to their social positions or jobs. As a career factory worker, Clyde might visit a brothel, just as he does while working as a bellhop. He would also have little reason to avoid marrying Roberta and easier access to birth control and abortion: "If only he could get her out of this! If only he could. But how, without money, intimates, a more familiar understanding of the medical or if not that exactly, then the sub rosa world of sexual freemasonry which some at times—the bell-hops of the Green-Davidson, for instance, seemed to understand" (408). If, on the other hand, Clyde were born to wealth, if he were Gilbert's brother and not his cousin, then he would likewise be allowed some form of sexual release. He could, presumably, visit a brothel, or perhaps "trifle" with some young woman from the lower classes, and he could do so without risking banishment.

When sons of the novel's wealthy do get in trouble with daughters of the underclass, there are ways to rectify the situation without severing family ties. Alvin Belknap, one of Clyde's attorneys and the son of a prominent politician, was once extricated from a situation much like Clyde's:

> In his twentieth year, he himself had been trapped between two girls, with one of whom he was merely playing while being seriously in love with the other. And having seduced the first and being confronted with an engagement or flight, he had chosen flight. But not before laying the matter before his father, by whom he was advised to take a vacation, during which time the services of the family doctor were engaged with the result that for a thousand dollars

and expenses necessary to house the pregnant girl in Utica, the father had finally extricated his son and made possible his return, and eventual marriage to the other girl. [592-93]

For most members of society, Dreiser seems to be telling us, the social structure permits the controlled release of sexual tension and also provides remedies when "problems" arise. But for those few members of the underclass who are offered the possibility of rapid, effortless elevation to the aristocracy—the common ingredient in Dreiser's American genre of murder—intense scrutiny and precarious social standing combine to prohibit sexual activity, with the result that libidinal pressure builds to intolerable levels.

Unlike Belknap, Clyde cannot expect anyone to solve the problem of Roberta's pregnancy for him. His ties to the Lycurgus Griffithses are so weak that he finds himself living on a kind of probation. The family might rescue Gilbert from such a situation, but Clyde, a nephew and a virtual stranger, would likely be abandoned. This same probationary status prevents Clyde from finding help among the working class. As a Griffiths living in Lycurgus, Clyde is so widely recognized and so visible that by revealing his predicament to anyone he would risk gossip and exposure. Clyde's pathology, then, is not in his soul but in his situation.

The extraordinary pressures brought to bear on Clyde produce a mental illness much like the one said to have driven Leopold and Loeb. The two were portrayed in the press and by the prosecution as intellectual giants, and Darrow was able to turn this characterization to his advantage. He does so by demonstrating, at great length, that the plan concocted by the two supposed geniuses was dangerously ill conceived and destined to fail:

> The State says, in order to make out the wonderful mental processes of these two boys, that they fixed up a plan to go to Ann Arbor to get a typewriter, and yet when they got ready to do this act, they went down the street a few doors from their house and bought a rope; they went around the corner and bought acid; they went somewhere else nearby and bought tape; they went down to the hotel and rented a room, and then gave it up, and went to another hotel, and rented one there. And then Dick Loeb went to the hotel room, took a valise containing his library card and some books from the library, left it two days in the room, until the hotel took the valise and took the books. Then he went to another hotel and rented another room. He might just as well have sent his card with the ransom letter. [Darrow, *Attorney*, 33]

Premeditation, which should serve the interests of the prosecution, is thus transformed into a mitigating factor: "But we are told that they planned. Well, what does that mean? A maniac plans, an idiot plans, an animal plans, any brain that functions may plan; but their plans were the diseased plans of the diseasedmind" (Darrow, *Attorney*, 41).

Clyde's plan to murder Roberta proves to be similarly flawed. Despite his elaborate attempts at secrecy, authorities discover Clyde's identity almost immediately. As soon as Roberta's body is found, incriminating evidence begins to surface. A man matching the description of the drowned woman's companion is seen later that night walking furtively through the woods, dressed in a suit and carrying a suitcase. The bruises on Roberta's face suggest violence. An examination of the items Roberta left at the inn reveals further reason for alarm. Clyde and Roberta do not register under their true names, but in Roberta's coat investigators find a letter addressed to her mother detailing her plans to marry. A subsequent conversation with Roberta's mother leads the authorities directly to Clyde. Even if Roberta had not told her mother Clyde's name, the local postman could have provided it; he remembers that Roberta had mailed as many as fifteen letters to Clyde Griffiths in Lycurgus during the weeks preceding her death. When the letters are found in Clyde's room—along with letters from Sondra—they provide a narrative account of his motive for murder. In Roberta's suitcase, left at the inn, authorities find a toilet set with a card that reads "For Bert from Clyde—Merry Xmas" (519).

The incriminating clues accumulate so quickly and in such number that the district attorney wonders, at least momentarily, whether Clyde is innocent. "Would a man contemplating murder fail to see a card such as this, with his own handwriting on it? What sort of plotter and killer would that be?" (520). Dreiser, perhaps following Darrow's lead, suggests that Clyde's plan fails miserably because it was conceived during a fit of temporary insanity. "There are moments when in connection with the sensitively imaginative or morbidly anachronistic—the mentality assailed and the same not of any great strength and the problem confronting it of sufficient force and complexity—the reason not actually toppling from its throne, still totters or is warped or shaken—the mind befuddled to the extent that for the time being at least, unreason or disorder and mistaken or erroneous counsel would appear to hold against all else" (463). Dreiser characterizes Clyde not as insane but as normal, a young man temporarily unbalanced by environmental stress. Mental disease deprives Clyde, like Leopold and Loeb, of the ability to reason—both intellectually and morally. Like Harry Thaw, Clyde comes temporarily under the spell of an irresistible impulse whose shape bears the peculiar, even unique, stamp of American culture.

In *An American Tragedy*, Dreiser dismantles the diagnostic biography of an executable offender with remarkable thoroughness. Gillette is portrayed in the press as a cold-blooded killer, but Clyde is a mentally ill coward who may even be innocent of the crime for which he is executed. In the press accounts, Gillette, like McTeague, is described as biologically programmed to murder; Clyde, however, is a victim and the product of circumstance. The state argues that Clyde is fundamentally criminal, a moral imbecile or reptile. Thenovel shows that his character was determined by the values of his society. Had Clyde been born into a more hospitable environment, his life need not have ended in the electric chair. Had society not teased him with wealth and power while simultaneously condemning him to mindless labor and low pay, he need not have killed. Had the officials charged with evaluating Clyde's life and crime not been blinded by their own greed, they would not have delivered a sentence of death.

It is clear, then, that the novel declares its opposition to the dominant carceral discourse, but assessing the effectiveness of such opposition is a complex task. Careful examination may reveal that Dreiser's narrative is built on assumptions about criminality and normalcy that, while overtly opposed to the dominant carceral discourse, nevertheless serve the interests of carceral power.

In *Discipline and Punish,* Foucault makes the arresting observation that the modern criminal justice system has been attacked, virtually from its inception, in ways that paradoxically call for strengthening and extending the power to imprison. Again and again, in a pattern that persists to this day, critics have complained that prison does nothing to reduce crime and in fact encourages delinquency. And yet the "answer to these criticisms was invariably the same: the reintroduction of the invariable principles of penitentiary technique. For a century and a half the prison had always been offered as its own remedy: the reactivation of the penitentiary techniques as the only means of overcoming their perpetual failure; the realization of the corrective project as the only way of overcoming the impossibility of implementing it" (268). By identifying failures in the criminal justice system, critics may call, directly or indirectly, for the very reforms that ensure its continued operation and expansion.

Dreiser's novel can likewise be seen to criticize certain elements of our criminal justice system in ways that potentially serve the interests of the power it embodies. The tragedy of Clyde's case, for example, results from a diagnostic failure. Clyde is deliberately misdiagnosed so that attorneys, judges, and jurors can further their careers. He differs greatly in personality and type from the other inmates of Death Row.

The other condemned men are described in language that recalls both the racism that underlies much biological determinism and the sensationalized coverage of crime in the popular press. The first inmate whom Clyde notices is "a sallow and emaciated and sinister-looking Chinaman in a suit exactly like his own, who had come to the bars of his door and was looking at him out of inscrutable slant eyes" (755). Other inmates are described in similar terms:

> The two dark-eyed and sinister-looking Italians, one of whom had slain a girl because she would not marry him; the other who had robbed and then slain and attempted to burn the body of his father-in-law in order to get money for his wife! And big Larry Donahue—square-headed, square-shouldered—big of feet and hands, an overseas soldier, who, being ejected

from a job as night watchman in a Brooklyn factory, had lain for the foreman who had discharged him—and then killed him in an open common somewhere at night, but without the skill to keep from losing a service medal, which had eventually served to betray and identify him. . . . And Thomas Mowrer . . . a man who had killed his employer with a pitchfork . . . a rude, strong, loutish man of about thirty, who looked more beaten and betrayed than as though he had been able to torture or destroy another. [768]

Clyde's case is tragic because he is improperly diagnosed and placed on Death Row with born murderers. The novel attacks not so much capital punishment, then, as the mistakes made in administering it. The misdiagnosis of Clyde on which his execution rests in no way fundamentally challenges the idea that executable murderers can be distinguished from nonexecutable murderers through a scientifically informed diagnosis. Instead, the narrative seems to reaffirm the importance of the diagnostic task. If people so very different from one another can be convicted under the same statute, then the only hope for appropriate sentencing is a more painstaking and more accurate diagnostic procedure. Only through heightened vigilance and increased attention to diagnosis can tragedies like Clyde's execution be avoided.

Attempts to distinguish dominant from resistant discourse are further complicated by the fact that the social significance of the discourse surrounding capital punishment is not limited to the task of diagnosing executable offenders. Only a tiny fraction of the felons eligible for the death sentence actually receive it, but the diagnostic narratives used in selecting the condemned have wide-ranging implications. Diagnostic biographies naturalize various categories of criminal—including the executable offender—but as we have seen, they also naturalize the normal, law-abiding citizen. By defining both the normal and the criminal, these narratives legitimize regulatory powers that extend far beyond prison walls. Furthermore, because the two functions may operate independently—the one focused on the individual offender, the other broadcast toward the general population—texts that openly disagree on a particular diagnosis may nonetheless share assumptions about criminality and normalcy.

In sum, narrative can overtly declare its opposition to the dominant discourse and nevertheless support the penal project. In addition, the diagnostic biography used to identify the executable offender can also serve to police the normal. Critical evaluations of the execution novel might accommodate these facts by focusing on the way in which a novel manipulates the images of danger associated with crime. Execution novels, like the diagnostic biographies from which they derive, trace brutal crimes to their antecedents in a broad range of "abnormal" behaviors and characteristics. These behaviors and characteristics may themselvesbe legal and even harmless, but when linked to capital crimes they acquire an aura of danger.

An American Tragedy uses the rhetoric of danger to promote normalization partly in its treatment of sexuality.

When Clyde carouses with the other bellhops from the Green-Davidson, and especially when he accompanies them to a house of prostitution, he takes the first in a series of steps that will lead him to the death house. Later, when he seduces Roberta, the encounter is marked by an almost palpable sense of impending doom: "And Clyde feeling, and not unlike Roberta, who was firmly and even painfully convinced of it, that this was sin—deadly, mortal—since both his mother and father had so often emphasized that—the seducer—adulterer—who preys outside the sacred precincts of marriage. And Roberta, peering nervously into the blank future, wondering what—how, in any case, by any chance, Clyde should change, or fail her" (299). Clyde's plan to kill Roberta stems directly from an illicit affair that significantly offends both Christian decency and his company's policy. The link between illicit sexuality and crime, professional failure, and danger is also evident in the novel's suggestion that people who lead successful lives avoid sexual impropriety. When Clyde begins working as a bellhop at the prestigious Union League Club of Chicago, he is struck by the fact that the men who frequent the club (no women are allowed) betray no interest in sexual matters. Clyde concludes that "one could not attain or retain one's place in so remarkable a world as this unless one were indifferent to sex" (169).

Illicit sexuality is only one source of danger identified in the novel. The danger represented by people like Clyde is also linked to failures within the family and departures from traditional family values. Clyde's weak, vacillating character is largely a product of his early family life, and the novel seems to single out Asa, his father, for special blame: "To begin with, Asa Griffiths, the father, was one of those poorly integrated and correlated organisms, the product of an environment and a religious theory, but with no guiding or mental insight of his own, yet sensitive and therefore highly emotional and without any practical sense whatsoever" (13). Asa's inability to provide a stable, financially secure environment for his family causes Clyde to develop in two ways that will eventually lead him to plot murder. From a very early age, Clyde becomes "conscious of the fact that the work his parents did was not satisfactory to others,—shabby, trivial," and he dreams of bettering himself. These dreams take no practical form, however, because Clyde's parents "did not understand the . . . necessity for some of practical or professional training for each and every one of their young ones" (14). Lacking a practical education, Clyde attempts to achieve his dreams of wealth through marriage and through murder.

Had Clyde been raised in a more "normal" family, he might not have yielded so easily to the temptations of murder and illicit sex. Thenormal counterpart to Clyde's abnormal family is embodied by the Lycurgus Griffithses, a branch of the family headed by a man characterized as Asa's exact opposite. When Clyde first meets Samuel Griffiths, he notes that "his uncle appeared to be so quick, alert, incisive—so very different from his father in every way" (171). Samuel Griffiths is a shrewd

businessman and a stern, effective father. As a result his children grow into law-abiding citizens. By suggesting that weak fathers like Asa can produce children capable of capital murder, the novel polices family life. Individual failures to live up to the ideals of middle-class morality and Christian decency are exposed as dangers to the entire society.

The novel's treatment of adolescence complements this tendency to link familial abnormality to crime and dangerous behavior. Dreiser's narrative criminalizes adolescence by portraying it as the time in our lives when we are most apt to give in to criminal urges and temptations. The novel thus suggests that both society and the family have the responsibility of policing and disciplining adolescents. Clyde needed, and did not get, the stern tutelage of a strong father. He should never have been exposed to the easy money and seedy life enjoyed by bellhops working in luxury hotels. Roberta should never have been allowed to leave her parents' farm for factory work in another town, nor should she have been allowed to rent a room in a bad part of town, away from the watchful eyes of older friends and relatives. The inherently turbulent and even criminal nature of puberty in American society demands that adolescents be held under strict supervision.

In identifying the antecedents of dangerous criminality, however, the novel designates extramarital sex, abnormal family life, inadequate education, and adolescence as significant but secondary. The primary focus is on the American dream of success and social advancement. Because the doors to America's aristocracy are not entirely closed, and because all American schoolchildren are taught that wealth and luxury are both desirable and generally available, people like Clyde will be placed in stressful situations that they would not have to endure in societies with more clearly defined social boundaries. The American dream may provide a blueprint for success for a tiny fraction of the nation's youth, but accepting that dream also means that a normal working life, the life that the vast majority of Americans must lead, is tragically devalued. For Clyde, working-class existence is so onerous that he will attempt anything—even murder—to escape it.

The novel's critique of the American dream seems intended to mitigate Clyde's responsibility for Roberta's death. Clyde plots murder not because he is inherently evil but because he is born into poverty, raised by incompetent parents, and forced to make his way alone during adolescence. Dreiser may have been calling for a more humane approach to crime, but the underlying assumption is nevertheless that the uneducated poor are the most dangerous members of society. Darrow, whose arguments about the nature ofcrime provided an important source for Dreiser, treats the underclass with a similarly paradoxical mix of fear and sympathy:

> What we call civilization has moved so fast that
> the structure and instincts of man have not been

able to become adjusted to it. The structure is too cumbersome, too intense, too hard, and if not breaking down of its own weight, it is at least destroying thousands who cannot adjust themselves to its changing demands. Not only are the effects of this growing body of social and legal restrictions shown by their constant violation, generally by the inferior and the poor, but indirectly in their strain on the nervous system; by the irritation and impatience they generate, and which, under certain conditions cause acts of violence. [*Crime*, 43]

Clyde cannot withstand the strain of his situation because his background and his childhood experience leave him with no stable identity. He remakes himself to match each new environment and thus lacks the moral fortitude to resist temptation. Even as the novel shows why Clyde should not be blamed for his actions, it demonstrates that he is hopelessly dangerous.

Dreiser traces the danger associated with capital crime back to its various sources. In so doing, he advertises his novel as a humane countermyth that corrects fatal errors in the diagnostic biography of the executable offender. As *An American Tragedy* works to discredit the fundamental assumption of diagnostic biography, however—that some people are inherently and immutably criminal—it naturalizes a new, situational model of the dangerous individual. The source of Clyde's crime may lie outside his body, but it lies within aspects of the social structure that are absolutely fundamental to American culture. Dreiser's narrative suggests that when the poor are allowed access to affluent communities, they may be possessed by irresistible criminal urges. As long as some Americans are rich and others are poor, as long as the borders between social classes remain semipermeable, some number of people in Clyde's situation will be driven to act as he does. Social contact between the poor and the affluent, then, is the novel's most dangerous circumstance.

An American Tragedy illustrates just how easily a dissenting text can be made to serve the interests of the opposing viewpoint. As demonstrated above, the novel interprets crime in a way that encourages people of low social status to engage in "normal" behavior: they should avoid extramarital sex, learn a trade, adhere to company policy, maintain traditional families, and vigorously discipline their adolescent children. Otherwise social advancement may escape them. By supporting a "scientific" criminology that naturalizes criminal activity in poor populations, the novel also discourages social contact between rich and poor and justifies the residential and social segregation of social classes. The novel's comingling of dissent and complicity suggests that overtly resistant discourse must be evaluated on the basis of what it does, not what it claims to do.

NOTES

[1] Detailed accounts of the composition of *An American Tragedy* can be found in Robert Elias's *Theodore Dreiser:*

Apostle of Nature, Ellen Moers's *Two Dreisers*, and Donald Pizer's *The Novels of Theodore Dreiser: A Critical Study*.

[2] Shelley Fisher Fishkin, in "From Fact to Fiction: *An American Tragedy*," makes a similar claim, although in a somewhat different context, about the way Dreiser blurs the line between the normal and the criminal.

[3] It should be noted that Mead's assessment of Samoan culture has been challenged, most notably by Derek Freeman.

FURTHER READING

Bibliography

Pizer, Donald; Richard W. Dowell; and Frederic E. Rusch. *Theodore Dreiser: A Primary Bibliography and Reference Guide*. Boston, Mass.: G.K. Hall & Co., 1991, 308 p.
    Comprehensive primary and secondary bibliography of sources, including a section on *An American Tragedy*.

Criticism

Bloom, Harold, ed. *Theodore Dreiser's "An American Tragedy."* New York: Chelsea House, 1988, 152 p.
    Collection of essays exploring major themes in *An American Tragedy*.

Eby, Clare Virginia. "The Psychology of Desire: Veblen's 'Pecuniary Emulation' and 'Invidious Comparison' in *Sister Carrie* and *An American Tragedy*." *Studies in American Fiction* 21, No. 2 (Autumn 1993): 191-208.
    Examines Dreiser's view of the self in terms of desire for material objects in his two major novels as delineated by Thorstein Veblen in his theory of "person-object relations."

Funk, Robert. "Dreiser's *An American Tragedy*." *Explicator* 51, No. 4 (Summer 1993): 232-34.
    Briefly explicates a chapter of *An American Tragedy* in which Dreiser alludes to Franks Norris's novel *McTeague*.

Gammel, Irene. "Two Odysseys of 'Americanization': Dreiser's *An American Tragedy* and Grove's *A Search for America*." *Studies in Canadian Literature* 17, No. 2 (1992): 129-47.
    Discusses "significant differences in Canadian and American conceptions of personal and national identity" as found in *An American Tragedy* and Canadian novelist Frederick Philip Grove's *A Search for America*.

Kazin, Alfred. "*An American Tragedy* and *The Sound*

and the Fury," in *An American Procession*, pp. 334-56. New York: Alfred A. Knopf, 1984.

> Examines Dreiser's and Faulkner's respective places as novelists of the 1920s.

Salzman, Jack, ed. *"An American Tragedy,"* in *Theodore Dreiser: The Critical Reception*, pp. 439-500. New York: David Lewis, 1972.
> Collects reviews of *An American Tragedy* upon its publication.

Spindler, Michael. "Class and the Consumption Ethic: Dreiser's *An American Tragedy,"* in *American Literature and Social Change: William Dean Howells to Arthur Miller*, pp. 135-49. London: The Macmillan Press, 1983.
> Attempts to place the novel in the "conflict of values characteristic of twenties America," marked by class status and the emerging culture of consumption.

The following sources published by Gale Research contain additional coverage of Dreiser's life and career: *Contemporary Authors*, Vols. 106, 132; *Contemporary Dictionary of American Literary Biography*, 1865-1917; *Dictionary of Literary Biography*, Vols. 9, 12, 102, 137; *Dictionary of Literary Biography Documentary Series*, Vol. 1; *DISCovering Authors*; *DISCovering Authors: Canadian*; *DISCovering Authors Modules: Most-Studied* and *Novelists*; *Major Twentieth-Century Writers*; *Twentieth-Century Literary Criticism*, Vols. 10, 18, 35; and *World Literature Criticism*.

Ernst Haeckel

1834-1919

(Ernst Heinrich Philipp August Haeckel) German natural scientist, philosopher, essayist, and nonfiction writer.

INTRODUCTION

As a zoologist at the University of Jena in Germany during the 1860s, Ernst Haeckel became an early and vocal proponent of Charles Darwin's Theory of Evolution. Haeckel, however, took evolution further than Darwin had, and posited an evolutionary explanation of man's origins. Raised as a practicing Christian, Haeckel renounced his faith and ultimately adopted a belief system he called Monism, based on the idea that there is only a physical realm and not a spiritual one as "dualists" throughout history had believed. Haeckel's ideas about evolution, challenging as they were to belief in the Biblical story of creation, made him a controversial figure; writings such as *Natürliche Schöpfungsgeschichte*, (1868; *The Natural History of Creation*) and *Die Welträtsel* (1899; *The Riddle of the Universe*) made him enormously popular around the world. Many of his notions have since been discredited, among them the so-called "biogenetic law," which holds that in growing from a seed to a fully developed organism, a creature reenacts the stages of its evolutionary development. Haeckel's primary importance to the history of science lay in his popularization of Darwinism, and his critique of the once-prevalent idea that religious faith should govern science.

Biographical Information

Haeckel was born in Potsdam in 1834. From an early age, he was interested in science, and the high school he attended in Merseburg was known for its experiments in chemistry and physics. After graduating in 1852, he embarked on an education in medicine that took him to Berlin, Würzburg, and Vienna. Haeckel actually wanted to be a botanist, but he pursued his medical studies with vigor. During this time, he studied under the scientist Rudolph Virchow, whose materialistic view of the universe would have a great influence on Haeckel. Raised as a Christian, Haeckel had begun to question his beliefs, and when he read Darwin's *On the Origin of Species* in 1860, he renounced Christianity entirely. In 1862, he received an appointment as a zoology instructor at the University of Jena, in Thuringia, a position he would hold for most of his remaining life. Haeckel, who was noted for the enthusiasm with which he took part in sports and other pursuits, was soon ready to announce his newfound beliefs to the German scientific community, and at an 1863 conference in Stettin, he had an

opportunity to do so. His speech on Darwinism spawned controversy, but this remained a matter of interest mainly to scientists until the mid-1860s, when he began publishing the first of his many popular books. In 1892, he inaugurated a second phase of his career with another public speech, which would become the basis for *Der Monismus als Band zwischen Religion und wissenschaft* (1893; *Monism as the Bond between Religion and Science*). In it he presented his "new" philosophy of Monism, which rejected existing dualistic interpretations of reality in favor of a more or less strictly materialistic one. Within Haeckel's dualism, however, there was room for "spirit" inasmuch as such a term described phenomena whose origin could theoretically be described in physical terms. Hence he is usually considered not an atheist per se, but a pantheist, or one who believes that the entire universe is imbued with a single spirit resident in all things living and non-living. These concepts he developed in another enormously popular book, *The Riddle of the Universe*. His ideas would ultimately become institutionalized through the Monistic Association, founded in Germany in 1906.

Major Works

Haeckel's most significant works were his popular expositions of his ideas about evolution and Monism. Starting with *Generelle Morphologie der Organismen* (1866; *The General Morphology of Organisms*), Haeckel published a series of booksthat made his a household name for the next half-century. *General Morphology* outlined, in simple language that any reasonably educated person could understand, Haeckel's theories as to the origins and development of life—particularly human life. He further explored these ideas, including the formation of life from inorganic substances and the descent of man from lower animals, in *The Natural History of Creation*. In *Anthropogenie* (1874; *The Evolution of Man*), he made the case for his biogenetic law. *The Riddle of the Universe* would become perhaps his most popular book, and would ultimately be translated into some twenty-five languages. In the last two decades of his life, Haeckel published *Lebenswunder* (1905; *The Wonders of Life*), an addendum to *The Riddle of the Universe*, along with several books in which he combined his studies of nature with his drawings of plant and animal life. During his lifetime and afterward, several volumes of Haeckel's correspondence would appear as well.

PRINCIPAL WORKS

Die Radiolarien [*Monograph on the Radiolaria*] (essay) 1862

Generelle Morphologie der Organismen [*The General Morphology of Organisms*] (nonfiction) 1866

Natürliche Schöpfungsgeschichte [**The Natural History of Creation*] (nonfiction) 1868

Anthropogenie [*The Evolution of Man: A Popular Scientific Study*] (nonfiction) 1874

Freie Wissenschaft und freie Lehre [*Free Science and Free Teaching*] (essay) 1878

Das System der Medusen [*Monograph on the Medusa*] (essay) 1879

Indische Reisebriefe [*Indian Letters*] (letters) 1883

Der Monismus als Band zwischen Religion und Wissenschaft [*Monism as the Bond between Religion and Science* or *The Confession of Faith of a Man of Science*] (essay) 1893

Die Welträtsel [*The Riddle of the Universe*] (nonfiction) 1899

Kunstformen der Natur [*Art Forms in Nature*] (journal and drawings) 1899-1904

Der Kampf um den Entwicklungsgedanken (nonfiction) 1905

Lebenswunder [*The Wonders of Life: A Popular Study of Biological Philosophy*] (nonfiction) 1905

Wanderbilder (journal and drawings) 1905

Last Words on Evolution: A Popular Retrospect and Summary (nonfiction) 1906

The Story of the Development of a Youth: Letters to His Parents, 1852-1856 (letters) 1923

*This work is sometimes called *The History of Creation* or *Natural History of Genesis*.

CRITICISM

The Monist (essay date 1895)

SOURCE: A review of *Systematische Phylogenie der Protisten und Pflanzen,* by Ernst Haeckel, in *The Monist,* Vol. V, No. 3, April, 1895, pp. 451-52.

[*In the following essay, a critic assesses* Systematische Phylogenie.]

The fundamental idea of a general phylogeny of the world of organic forms was broached by Professor Haeckel in 1866 in his **General Morphology,** and shortly afterwards developed in a more popular form in his **Natural History of Creation.** As the phylogenetic materials were scanty at that period, the author's researches were limited to the merest outlines of a history of the race; in the necessity of the case a rigorous scientific demonstration was impossible. The author now attempts such a demonstration [in **Systematische Phylogenie der Protisten und Pflanzen.**], in the light of the materials recently furnished by palæontology, ontogeny, and morphology. Thus, the reader will find incorporated here the results of thirty years of fruitful research.

Professor Haeckel's point of view has remained practically the same as when he first promulgated the idea. It is his aim to reach a scientific knowledge of the organic forms and of the causes that produce them by a study of the causalrelations obtaining between phylogeny and ontogeny, the history of the race and the history of the individual. As is well known, he vigorously opposes the new theories of embryology and heredity, upholding in contradistinction to the latter the doctrine of progressive inheritance. There is much philosophical discussion and speculation in the work, as must be, for phylogeny, like historical biology, is a hypothetical science and can never hope to gain access to all the materials that would verify its conjectures. The tables of descent and the genealogical trees which Professor Haeckel has traced out are for this reason not put forward as perfected and rigid plans, but are to be taken simply as attempts at a reconstruction of ancestral history, and as indicating the way in which, according to our present knowledge, future phylogenetic research is perhaps to be best conducted. In cases of doubt, parallel hypotheses have been suggested.

The present work is not a text-book, but presupposes considerable knowledge of natural history on the part of its readers. Nevertheless, Professor Haeckel's style is delightfully lucid, and what with his explicit explanations of new terms and his profuse use of diagrams and counter-references, the intelligent reader who has access to a good compendium of natural history will not only have no difficulty, but will experience considerable pleasure, in the perusal of portions of this work. The volume before us treats of Protists and Plants, and is to be followed before the close of the year by the two other parts on vertebrate and invertebrate animals. A number of the most important sections of the present volume have been translated and are appearing in the current numbers of *The Open Court.*

T. D. A. Cockerell (essay date 1905)

SOURCE: "A Monistic Trinity," in *The Dial,* Vol. 38, No. 451, April 1, 1905, pp. 232-34.

[*In the following review of* The Wonders of Life, *Cockerell critiques Haeckel's account of man's origins, and treats Monism as a form of religious faith.*]

The veteran professor of Jena gave us to understand that *The Riddle of the Universe,* published in 1899, was his last book; but it had such a wide circulation, and raised so many questions, that the author felt obliged to prepare the work now under review [*The Wonders of Life*]; in order to make clearer his views on biological questions and their relation to the monistic philosophy. Being quite unable to answer the letters—more than five thousand—addressed to him, or to acknowledge adequately the many documents, flowers, and other gifts addressed to him on his seventieth birthday, Professor Haeckel gracefully begs his admirers to receive his new book as an expression of his thanks, the best gift in return he is able to make. Perhaps, in recognition of the fact that this latest product shows no sign of diminishing vigor, we may still refuse to believe that Professor Haeckel has retired from the stage; and may be allowed to remind him that another distinguished evolutionist, Dr. A. R. Wallace, though some fifteen years his senior, is still active.

The Wonders of Life is, of course, a little handbook of monism; that is to say, monism according to Professor Haeckel. It is postulated that throughout the whole universe, 'in every atom and every molecule,' are found three fundamental attributes: matter, force, and sensation. This is what Professor Haeckel himself calls 'a monistic trinity,' a trimonism not less mysterious than that of the theologians.

The scientific philosophers of the nineteenth century, Professor Haeckel and his contemporaries, did a great service in unifying and therefore simplifying human thought. At the beginning of the century, facts were being recorded rapidly, and it might have been expected that science would at length become a vast storehouse of miscellaneous information, quite beyond the power of man to utilize or comprehend. In biology, there was the unceasing discovery of new species, some thousands of them described by Professor Haeckel himself; and of course this outpouring of new material has continued to the present day, yearly increasing in volume. Yet, notwithstanding all this, science becomes continually more intelligible and rational; the pattern of things is gradually made clear as hitherto missing parts are supplied; and, in short, we are daily more assured of the fundamental unity and harmony of the universe. Thus, in a sense, all scientific men are monists; all believe that their smallest contributions possess value for the very reason that they help toward an understanding of the totality of things, so far as this may be grasped by the human mind.

In another sense, however, it may fairly be maintained that all sane men are dualists. The fundamental dualism is that of the I and the not-I; our lives are made up of the actions and reactions between these two. Regarding things objectively, and as a mere matter of logic, it is possible to argue that our very consciousness is but a part of the nature of things, free will being no more inherent in human beings than in gases or crystals. This is really Professor Haeckel's position, and yet it is impossible to read his very human work without a keen sense of his personality as a consciously free agent. There used to be at Maskelyne and Cook's, in London, an automaton which played chess, and was able, it was said, to beat nearly all comers. The proprietors of the device declared that it was a mere mechanism, and indeed inspection seemed to preclude the possibility of someone being concealed within. Nevertheless, it was the general opinion that there *was* a free agent somewhere, and a clergyman of my acquaintance, baffled in the attempt to furnish a more ordinary explanation, really believed that the conjurors were in league with the devil. In much the same way, we must be permitted to discount Professor Haeckel's assurance that even he himself is an automaton,—a mere result of blind preexisting causes,—leaving it, however, to our clerical friends to offer the diabolical hypothesis!

It is not fair to say that Professor Haeckel is unaware of this difficulty. He overcomes it, to his own satisfaction, by adding sensation to force and matter as a third universal attribute of being. There is the 'sensation' of atoms, that is, the affinity of the elements in chemical combinations. The 'sensation' of protoplasm is what is often spoken of as its 'irritability.' So passing upward through twelve defined stages, we reach the sensation of civilized man, producing the arts and sciences. This 'sensation' is one in the sense that force is one, and matter is one, and is indestructible in the same sense. Thus it is not necessary to postulate that the human consciousness is the outcome of any metamorphosis of matter or force; on the contrary, this is denied, and it is said to be merely the highest type of another universal attribute, 'sensation.' We reach a sort of pantheism rather than atheism.

It is likely to be claimed by materialistic monists, that this is giving away the whole monistic position; that the 'monistic trinity' is a contradiction in terms, notwithstanding Haeckel's arguments in its defense. It may be so, but that is merely a question of words, and it is much more interesting to investigate the merits of the Haeckelian doctrine than to dispute about its label. It is not very easy to understand what is meant by an unconscious sensation, though we are reminded of the photographer's use of the word 'sensitive' in connection with his plates, and of the chemist's 'sensitive reaction.' At all events, letting the term pass, it is not shown that consciousness and sensation (in the Haeckelian sense) are the same thing, even in the sense that light and heat are the same. It is rather assumed because philosophy requires it; and if one cannot so believe as a matter of faith, there is no resort to actual demonstration.

Accepting the 'monistic trinity,' it does not seem to me that it is necessary to reject the immortality of the soul, or even a personal God. Professor Haeckel rejects these, but for other reasons; practically, because they seem to him totally unproved and unlikely. If 'sensation' is a universal attribute, and human consciousness is a phase of it, does it not seem reasonable to suppose that it reaches similarly high development in many places and ways in this vast universe? That it should be otherwise, would seem as improbable as that elaborate chemical compounds or combinations of forces should be restricted to one or a very few places. This on the Haeckelian hypothesis, merely.

The book is translated into good English, but there are various slips or misprints in names and technical terms, and the printing and paper are both very poor—or rather, the printing is poor chiefly because of the paper.

W. P. Pycraft (essay date 1905)

SOURCE: "Man in Nature," in *The Academy,* Vol. LXVIII, No. 1722, May 6, 1905, pp. 489-90.

[*In the following review of* The Evolution of Man, *Pycraft presents Haeckel's work as a complement to that of Darwin and Huxley.*]

The problem of the origin of life, and of man in particular, has always exercised a peculiar fascination over the human mind. In these latter days, while many have contrived to satisfy their thirst for information on this subject by the adoption of ancient and venerable traditions, others have ventured to push their inquiries further, though in so doing, they bring down upon themselves the charge of impious curiosity.

Our great countryman, Darwin, did more in his lifetime to lift the veil of this great mystery than had been done in all the centuries before him. But so firmly had the old traditions established themselves that the gift of his labours to the world caused his name and all that it stood for to become *anathema* to the multitude. Execration poured from the throats of well-nigh the whole civilised community of the world. A few, however, of the more advanced minds grasped the immense importance of the new revelation, and among these Huxley in our country and Haeckel in Germany stand out conspicuously. It became evident to them that the old idea of creation must give place to the scheme of evolution propounded by the Master. And they ceased not, day nor night, to insist on this fact.

Professor Haeckel did for Germany what Huxley did for this country; and now, thanks to the work of the translator, [*The Evolution of Man*] Haeckel's contributions to this tremendous issue are almost as familiar among us as those of Huxley. But there is a great difference in the attitude of these two men with regard to the interpretation of the now famous Darwinian theory. Huxley, while convinced of the truth of evolution, never adopted Darwin's principle of "Natural Selection" which accounted for this evolution. For him the evidence, irresistible in so far as evolution was concerned, was not strong enough to support the hypothesis of selection. With Haeckel it was otherwise. Gifted with an exuberant and fertile imagination he has, in the minds of the more cautious, not seldom outrun the bounds of legitimate inference: he has pushed his conclusions further than the evidence warrants. This criticism applies, however, rather to matters of detail than to broad principles.

Like Huxley, Haeckel has spared no effort to place the fruits of the new learning before the lay public, believing that the right conception of this earth and its inhabitants, even though it may clash with preconceived notions, is far more likely to make for righteousness than to bring about the evils which the timid prophesied.

When the hypothesis propounded in the *Origin of Species* first saw the light, a thrill of horror ran through society. But when the *Descent of Man* appeared, it was felt indeed that the foundations of morality and religion would be undermined if the propagation of ideas so blasphemous were tolerated: and bell, book, and candle were vigorously used. After a while, when the excitement had subsided somewhat, and men began to examine this ogre that had excited such alarm, they found him surprisingly comely. To-day even those who occupy our pulpits are not a little proud of displaying the fact that they are on speaking terms with him.

Just now we are entering on an acute phase of this consequence of the invasion of the Darwinian theory. All the outer forts were captured long since, but the inner citadel yet remains in the hands of a few irreconcilables. While admitting defeat on the main issue, they still refuse to allow the application of the evolution theory to man himself. They are goaded into action by a sword of their own forging, to wit, that they cannot bring themselves to admit their descent from apes. This very exclusive attitude is really quite unnecessary, for the evolution theory demands no such admission. The human race, *and* the apes, have both come from the same common stock. Whether they accept this or not is after all immaterial.

With a view to the hastening of their capitulation, the great siege guns of Professor Haeckel have been modified, so to speak, so as to become available for the bombardment of that portion of the fort held by the English-speaking defenders. Huxley long since initiated the attack in a series of crushing arguments familiar to most of our readers under the title of "Man's Place in Nature." Haeckel's work adds nothing to this of any importance, but it amplifies the evidence. He gathers the public into one vast lecture-room, so to speak, and there unfolds the story of evolution piece by piece: beginning with the lowest of living animals and leading up to man himself; he shows them the warp and woof of life, and demonstrates the working of the looms.

The two handsome volumes before us have been admirably translated from the fifth (enlarged) edition of the German work. The abstruse and puzzling phenomena of embryology occupy the whole of the first volume; and this will be found hard reading indeed to those who have no practical acquaintance with the subject. The second volume is devoted to the vexed problem of our ancestry—beginning with the lowest forms of life and working upwards through "Our Worm-like Ancestors," "Our Fish-like Ancestors," "Our Five-toed Ancestors," and "Our Ape-like Ancestors." But besides these we have some luminous chapters on the evolution of the nervous system, sense organs, vascular system, and so on. A summary on the "results of anthropogeny" closes the book.

In spite of the infinite pains which the author and translator have taken, it is open to question whether the vast mass of information here collected will prove capable of assimilation by those for whom it is prepared. There are, however, a large and rapidly increasing number of people who, if they cannot digest the contents of these tomes in their entirety, will at least find in them not only a source of unfailing interest, but also a mine of facts, the bearing of which they can fully grasp.

Haeckel, as we have already remarked, differs markedly from Huxley in his mental attitude towards this great question, and this is painfully evident in his aggressiveness. He is not content with proving the sweet reasonableness of the Evolution theory: he makes no secret of the fact that he desires at the same time to deal a death blow to the Creed of Christendom. Having succeeded, he proposes to give the world a new dogma—Monism!

The monistic or mechanical philosophy of Nature:

> "holds that only unconscious, necessary, efficient causes are at work in the whole field of nature, in organic life, as well as in inorganic changes."

For Professor Haeckel the monistic is the only possible philosophy. It is the soul of these two ponderous volumes; it crops up in the most unexpected places, and jostles arrogantly against the prevailing creed of to-day as though it were already dispossessed. While the triumph of Evolution is assured, it is by no means so certain that this new cult of Professor Haeckel's will achieve a like success. To our thinking these volumes would have lost nothing by the suppression of his philosophy. A little of the leaven of speculation can do no harm when introduced into the magma of scientific fact, but in excess the whole becomes so extremely vacuolated as to be too frail for service. Monism at present can only be looked upon as a sort of nebulous philosophy, and this does not come within the pale of Science.

In the first of these two volumes Professor Haeckel refers very briefly to the study—yet in its infancy—of experimental embryology: and to the very remarkable phenomena of parthenogenesis, or virgin birth. The latter is a subject which maywell have stimulated the desire of the reader for more facts. For the very latest discoveries, then, in these subjects we would refer him to two volumes just published by Professor Jacques Loeb (*Studies in General Physiology*: Unwin). In many respects Professor Loeb reminds us of Haeckel. He deals with the most complex problems, and the most obscure phenomena of life, as though but one interpretation were possible. Thus in a chapter on Geotropism and another on the Heliotropism of animals he appears to regard his subjects as automata. Many of the phenomena he describes are capable of quite another interpretation, however. Most of us, for example, could regard the light or shade seeking proclivities of these creatures as the result of the operation of natural selection: that is to say, whether they shun the light or seek it has been determined by the nature of the food they live upon or the enemies they have to avoid. Nocturnal animals are generally regarded as the descendants of those who sought shelter by day to escape persecution, those of their kind who persistently roamed about having become wiped out of existence. The positively heliotropic animals of Professor Loeb are, however, positively heliotropic because the pangs of hunger compel them to be so; they have no choice between being positively heliotropic or positively starved. Professor Loeb contends that these creatures are either heliotropic or the reverse because they are, so to speak, born so. The protoplasm of their bodies is controlled absolutely by the presence or absence of light: and willy nilly they must hide or come abroad, as 'tis their nature to.

But these essays, which deal with a variety of questions of a similar kind, are all of the highest value; and by the biologist, at any rate, they will be read and re-read with genuine pleasure. They form a solid contribution to our knowledge of the phenomena of life.

Science (essay date 1905)

SOURCE: A review of *The Evolution of Man,* in *Science,* Vol. 22, No. 553, August 4, 1905, pp. 137-39.

[*In the following review of* The Evolution of Man, *a critic faults Haeckel for making broad and often unsubstantiated claims.*]

In the two stately and richly illustrated volumes before us we have a translation of the fifth edition of Haeckel's **Anthropogenie,** and coming as they do from the pen of one who may now be regarded as a Nestor of zoology and the most vigorous exponent of the historical method of investigation, they present not a little interest. They profess to give in their course of some nine hundred pages an account of the embryological and comparative anatomical evidence bearing on the origin of man, a subject of perennial interest not only to the laity, but also to professional zoologists, since it involves the problem of the origin of the vertebrates.

The work [**The Evolution of Man**] opens with a chapter upon the biogenetic law, or, as it is termed, 'the fundamental law of organic evolution,' and then follow five especially interesting chapters devoted to a history of the development of embryology and phylogeny. To these succeed an extended account of the principal embryological stages of the vertebrates and a discussion of their significance, in which the germ cells, segmentation, gastrulation, the germ layers, metamerism, the fetal membranes and the development of the general form of the body, are all considered from the standpoint of their bearings on the ancestral history. This completed, the author passes on to a consideration of the recent representatives of the ancestral stages and concludes with several chapters devoted to the phylogeny of the various organs of the human body.

It would require much space to consider adequately the entire contents of the volumes, and the purpose of this review will, perhaps, be best served by indicating briefly the line of descent which Haeckel advocates. It is essentially the same as that presented in earlier editions, of which the third has appeared in an English translation, but differs in the greater detail and precision with which the various stages are defined.

It starts with the Monera, non-nucleated masses of protoplasm which 'stand exactly at the limit between the organic and the inorganic worlds' and have originated by spontaneous generation. Of these, two varieties existed, differing in their physiological activities; the one group, the phytomonera, being plasmodomous, building up protoplasm from unorganized material, and the other, the zoomonera, being plasmophagous, finding their nutrition in already organized material. The phytomonera were the more primitive of the two, the zoomonera arising from them by metasitism or metatrophy, the reversal of the mode of nutrition, a process which may have occurred several times independently and among cytodes as well as moners. Hence not only have zoomonera been derived from phytomonera, but nucleated unicellular plasmophags have arisen from similar plasmodomes, and so Haeckel takes as his second stage of the ancestry the Algaria, represented to-day by such unicellular algæ as the Palmellaceæ. From these he derives the third stage, that of the Lobosa, represented by Amœba and having corresponding to it the ovum stage of ontogeny.

The line of descent is then traced through the moræa, blastæa and gastræa, familiar to all readers of Haeckel's writings, and then passes to the Platodaria and Platodinia, two groups of turbellarian worms represented today by the so-called Acœla and the Rhabdocœla. The ninth stage is that of the Provermalia, represented by such recent forms as the Rotatoria and Gastrotricha, and presenting an advance upon preceding stages in the possession of a body cavity and an anal aperture; and to these succeed the Frontonia, a group which many will regard as decidedly heterogeneous, since both the Nemerteans and the Enteropneusta are regarded as being its modern representatives. Then follows the Prochordonia stage, characterized by the possession of a definite notochord and branchial slits and by the absence of a well-defined metamerism; its nearest representatives among recent forms are the copelate ascidians and the appendicularia larvæ.

Haeckel thus omits metamerism as a fundamental and primitive condition whose existence in several groups of animals implies a community of descent; for him it is merely a mode of growth and as such has been independently acquired in different phyla. He regards the metamerism of the annelids and arthropods as something quite different both structurally and phylogenetically from the metamerism of the vertebrates, and consequently excludes the annelids from the line of descent.

The next stage ushers in the vertebrate phylum and is that of the Prospondylia, which finds its modern representative in the larval *Amphioxus,* and then succeeds a stage corresponding to the adult *Amphioxus,* then the Archicrania, represented by the Ammocœtes larva, and then a stage corresponding to the adult cyclostome. The line then passes through the Proselachii, Proganoidea and Palædipneusta, thence through the stegocephalous Amphibia to the Proreptilia represented most nearly by the modern Hatteria, and so to the Monotremes, which represent the Pro-mammalian stage. Then follows the Prodidelphian stage and then that of the Prochoriata or Mallotheria, represented by an extinct group of placental mammals which included the stem-forms of the rodents, ungulates, carnivores and primates and, perhaps, finds its nearest recent representatives among the Insectivora. From the older Mallotheria the Prosimiæ are descended and of these Haeckel recognizes two ancestral stages, the Lemuravida and the Lemurogona, both belonging to Eocene times. From these the Simiæ with a true discoidal placenta are descended, but a discrepancy occurs between the general text, which is identical with the earlier edition in passing directly to the catarrhine forms, and the table given on p. 551, in which the line of descent is taken through primitive platyrrhines and thence through the Cynopitheca. However, the twenty-eighth stage is that of the Anthropoides, most closely approached by Hylobates among recent forms, and then succeeds the Pithecanthropi or Alali, which included forms similar to, but not identical with, the gorilla and chimpanzee and finally, as the thirtieth stage, comes man.

Without attempting either a general or particular criticism of such a scheme, it may be said of the work that while clearly and interestingly written, it will hardly carry conviction to the mind of the reader. The gaps in the plan are tooevident and too lightly passed over; conflicting theories, if mentioned, are treated too summarily; similarities between forms are frequently exaggerated; and, in short, the entire tone of the work is too dogmatic to be convincing. Sentences such as the following are by no means rare: 'In their first stage of development . . . the embryos of all the vertebrates, from the fish to man, are only incidentally or not at all different from each other,' 'Comparative evolution leads us clearly and indubitably to the first source of love—the affinity of two different erotic cells, the sperm cell and ovum (*erotic chemotropism*).'

On the other hand, one looks in vain for many facts which would have added strength to the general argument, and especially is this so in the chapters dealing with the phylogeny of the organs. Much that is highly pertinent has been omitted from the chapters on the muscular and nervous systems, and it is disappointing to find merely a mention of the recent important researches of Schwalbe and Klaatsch on the Neanderthal and Pithecanthropus remains.

But, notwithstanding these imperfections, the book is exceedingly interesting and contains a wealth of information on the questions under discussion. One can not help feeling, however, that it would have gained in value and authority if it had been limited to a discussion of the more general question of the descent of man, without attempting to define some thirty ancestral stages. It is especially in connection with the details that the dogmatism offends.

Finally, it may be remarked that it is unfortunate that more care has not been taken with the translation and proof-reading, in the latter especially with regard to proper names. Thus one finds Dreisch for Driesch, Moll for Mall, Ralph for Rolph, Dalton for D'Alton and Wiederscheim. Numerous terms are employed in the translation which are unfamiliar to English-speaking zoologists, and so much so as to indicate a lack of familiarity with the science on the part of the translator. It is possible to recognize the earthworm in the designation 'rainworm,' but to speak of a Turbellarian as a 'coiled-worm' can not be said to have the authorization of usage; 'tinting and dissection' mean staining and sectioning in ordinary parlance; and it is rather amusing to find one of His's reconstructions described as 'invented' by him. The rabbit is throughout transformed into a hare; *Echidna* is labeled a 'sea-urchin,' and a plate showing variations in the form of the pinna of the ear has for its legend 'ear muscles' (cf. Ohrmuscheln). On the whole, however, the translation is readable and set forth in idiomatic English.

Christian Gauss (essay date 1907)

SOURCE: A review of *Last Words on Evolution*, in *North American Review*, Vol. 186, September, 1907, pp. 130-34.

[*In the following essay, Gauss combines a review of* Last Words on Evolution *with an assessment of Haeckel's career.*]

Ernst Haeckel has now reached the biblical years of three-score and ten, and tells us that his age will prevent him from again appearing in public. The pronouncement has its pathos, for the veteran professor has for nearly half a century carried on in Germany the battle for Darwin and Evolution. He has been perhaps its ablest champion; he has certainly been its boldest. Since the beginning of that great intellectual combat in Germany, he has made himself the target for the shafts of its opponents. They have attacked his science, and with the peculiar bitterness engendered by that conflict, they have attacked his personality. Unlike the gentle Darwin, he could not allow such attacks to pass unanswered and he has replied occasionally in no measured terms. It may be said in his praise, however, that he has never descended to invective and abuse. He has fought fairly, with unwavering conviction, with undaunted courage. He had a genius for titles, *The History of Creation, The Riddle of the Universe*. Age has not robbed him of this talent, and the present volume is sent out into the fray under the ringing caption, *Last Words on Evolution.* After reading his book onemay find oneself in accord with much that is told or retold therein; with the *justesse* of the title, however, neither scientist nor philosopher will agree. Haeckel's last words, if you will, but the last words on evolution they certainly are not. Some years ago many thought that the Synthetic Philosopher had already pronounced those last words; today you could count his adherents among philosophers of note on the fingers of one hand. If, by his title, the author intended to convey the idea that his book has in it anything really approaching finality, he doubtless believed it to lie in that philosophy of monism which is so highly lauded by his translator. But of this more anon.

His book is interesting for many reasons. Not the least of these will be its excellent presentation by a scientist of the first rank of a question that is in itself somewhat abstruse. It has been made more so by incompetent and unscrupulous popularizers who here, as elsewhere, have taken advantage of the modern fret for information of whatever sort. Professor Haeckel avoids phraseology that smells of the laboratory, yet his meaning is everywhere clear. In his own words, the work of his life has been "the advancement of knowledge by the spread of the idea of evolution." Occasionally he has done more than this. He has spread the idea of evolution in advance of present knowledge. Thus he has, with great pains, with much acumen, and no little conjecture (which is not knowledge) built the genealogical tree of the human race, going forward unabashed through those barrens in which data are lacking, and down the troubled paths where the evidences of geology and biology do not as yet entirely correspond and occasionally even contradict. He traces our descent from the acrania, a skull-less form somewhat similar to the living lancelet, through the cyclostoma, to fishes, dipneusts, amphibia, reptiles, mammals. Among the last our immediate ancestor is the pithecanthropus, or ape-man. All this is done with much circumstantiation, and in its completeness his tree reminds us somewhat of the similar tree of a certain Austrian house which carries us all the way back to the Flood. The family has in addition a portrait which shows us Noah taking off his hat to the founder of their line. One wonders what the illustrious ancestor did when Noah turned on his heel and entered the Ark. Occasionally similar doubts perplex us here. Though we all of us go back as far as Noah, it takes much patient research and a strong sense of family pride to establish beyond cavil such a genealogy. Certain advocates of the dignity of our genus have protested against some of these bars sinister in our past, and Haeckel's tree has proved a fruitful subject of controversy among biologists and palaontologists. If his tree is still very largely a matter of conjecture, for his main thesis, the mutability of species, Haeckel has adduced practically irrefutable evidence through his researches on radiolaria, and this is no mean service to the cause of evolution.

Haeckel will doubtless be remembered as one of the greatest scientists of his time. He has helped to do for Germany what Darwin did for England, and this in the face of an opposition which, if not more virulent, has at least been more lasting. As his scientific theory approached completeness he began to see in it the solution of all great fundamental problems. He began to substitute a system of science for a philosopher's theory of the universe, and from being a very excellent scientist he has become a very mediocre philosopher. Under his clairvoyant gaze, the original nebulous mist which the earth was, or was not, resolves itself into a world of perfectly developed species, even as the Milky Way under the telescope resolves itself into stars. The idea of evolution has become a sort of conjuror's hat out of which, with a little sleight-of-hand, Haeckel and his followers extract answers to any kind of question, if they do not, as sometimes happens, cavalierly deny the existence of any problem at all. Thus we are told that memory is a function of certain compounds of carbon; free will is not only an illusion, it is a delusion. We are made to feel that we have it when in reality we do not. He has sometimes been called an atheist, but denies the allegation; yet if there is a god in Haeckel's world he adheres so rigorously to his policy of non-intervention that it is impossible to be aware of his presence, and we cannot see how he comes into it unless it be *ex machina,* an hypothesis which Haeckel's scientific attitude forbids him to admit. He is a mere haggard abstraction, and the logical principle of economy would exclude him. He is nothing more than La Place's useless hypothesis.

All this is part of the much-vaunted philosophy of Monism, usually spelled with a capital. What these monists have to say on free will we had already learned from the determinists; their contribution lies almost entirely in the magic word, process. This is the solvent which erodes and swallows up all old-fashioned difficul-

ties. An objector might suggest that it makes of them only a saturated solution. Haeckel's main thesis is "the mechanical character of all physical and psychic activity, the unity of organic and inorganic life." This once established, we can disregard all distressing questions of metaphysic, all pettifogging epistemology, and all chimerical teleology. Previous philosophers had merely been battling with the mists. We have had philosophies based on numbers, like that of Pythagoras, or on history, like that of Hegel, but the monism based on the evolutionary process possesses the cardinal advantage of being immensely more simple. There are but two main categories, time and quantity. There can be no differences except of quantity. His intelligence man shares with the beasts, and in the end, as Goldwin Smith has said, "he lies down and dies like the dog."

How rapid the evolution of ideas occasionally is, we can see when we remember that Novalis, who has been dead little more than a century, could say that Philosophy bakes us no bread, but gives us God, freedom, and immortality. The three boons which the master science once conferred have been taken away. In Novalis's definition they have allowed her to retain only her inability to bake us bread.

One must distinguish carefully between Haeckel's monism and the monism of such other thinkers as Professor Royce, for example. As a system of philosophy the idea is not new, though the word may be. There is, too, the older monism of Spinoza, if we but choose to call it so, for his doctrine of substance is every whit as monistic and much more philosophical than this later creed. There is, too, a very nice problem, which, in spite of his monism, Spinoza thought it worth while to consider Standing off, and looking at a heated plate of metal, we perceive it as white. As a matter of fact, it is hot, and its prepotent and important attribute is not its whiteness, but its heat. Before setting up a philosophy, might it not, therefore, be well to investigate the relation and correspondence, or lack of correspondence, between our world of ideas and the external world of reality? To say that psychic activities are merely functions of compounds of carbon would, in this case, explain nothing. We still have no guarantee that the thing we remember is the record of anything that actually happened.

It would likewise be wrong to imply that there is any close similarity between Spinoza and Haeckel. The real congeners of Haeckel's philosophy are to be found largely in the Eighteenth Century. To us there is no fundamental difference between the present philosophy and Holbach's "System of Nature" and Helvetius's *"De l'Esprit."* Where Haeckel says process, Helvetius and Holbach said chance or necessity, and where there is no aim to the process we do not see that there is any particular difference. Perhaps we are old-fashioned, but it does seem as if Haeckel's philosophy were inadequate in its conclusions, and what is more serious, restricted in its outlook upon life. For him, reality, at its best, can be measured with a yardstick; at its worst, with the micrometer calipers. It considers, after all, but a single set of phenomena, but one aspect of the truth. He has carefully circumscribed a system of facts, leavened them with a conjecture to make them a unit, and then explained them with an "Eureka." This is as easy as setting up a man of straw and knocking him down again. We will not say that it is as unprofitable, for on Haeckel's part it has been an earnest endeavor to solve problems that deeply concern us all. His training as a scientist has stood in his light as a philosopher. That part of his work which deals with science shows him an investigator who will stand with the foremost of his century. He has the rare distinction of having contributed materially to the sum of human knowledge. But all this science has here become only the stair to his philosopher's tower of ivory. To us this tower is a mere castle in Spain, and the last words on evolution are still unuttered.

Irving Wilson Voorhees (essay date 1910)

SOURCE: "A Synopsis of Evolution," in *The New York Times Book Review,* Saturday, July 2, 1910, p. 371.

[*In the following review of* The Evolution of Man, *Voorhees offers a positive appraisal of the work, in spite of what he considers Haeckel's penchant for digression and speculation.*]

The venerable author of this exhaustive work (*The Evolution of Man*) is one of the most interesting figures in contemporary scientific thought. It is fair to say that no other biologist, save perhaps the famous Metchnikoff, has been more widely read. We might add that no one has been more generally assailed for the free expression of his extremely radical views. It cannot be gainsaid that Prof. Haeckel is most interesting when he deals with established facts, possessing as he does a wide knowledge of several related sciences and the ability to set forth what he has to say in a graphic and convincing manner. He possesses the noble enthusiasm of the devoted student, the tireless energy of the painstaking investigator plodding almost pitifully along his tortuous pathway toward the goal of truth, and the undaunted and fairly defiant attitude of the propagandist. He is a thinker who is also, however much one dislikes to say it, a good deal of a pedant. A stickler for exact knowledge in science, he leaps with all the confidence and assurance of the dogmatist into fields which must remain largely speculative.

The first edition of the present work appeared in Germany in 1874. At that time the theory of evolution was by no means established on a firm basis. It was suffering from the attacks not only of the theologians, but of the conservative men of science, who could not yet be made to consider the successive chain of facts determined and brought together from many departments of knowledge. It is noteworthy that a few famous scientists, including the renowned Virchow, have disbelieved to the very end

of their lives Darwin's theory of descent as set forth by Huxley and promulgated by his contemporaries. Virchow declared that it would be just as well to say that man came from the sheep or elephant as from the ape— an opinion which was concurred in by his assistant, Ranke of Munich. That a great philosopher or poet is simply an outcome of the development of a tiny speck of protoplasm was to them unthinkable, and was considered to be a blot on the fair escutcheon of scientific thought. To-day, however, the main contentions of evolution are well established and are believed in not only by biologists, but by all educated people who have taken the pains to study the foundations of the theory in a candid and unprejudiced manner.

As a materialist Haeckel necessarily has little sympathy with the work of Louis Agassiz, whom he characterizes as "famous and gifted, but inaccurate and dogmatic." Naturally enough he has no patience with the sentimentalist or the religionist who yields blindly to the faith of sects.

Haeckel's chief claim to greatness as a biologist must rest upon his determination and enunciation of the so-called "biogenetic law." In brief, this law states that:

> The evolution of the foetus (or ontogenesis) is a condensed and abbreviated recapitulation of the evolution of the stem (or phylogenesis); and this recapitulation is the more complete in proportion as the original development (or palingenesis) is preserved by a constant heredity; on the other hand, it becomes less complete in proportion as a varying adaptation to new conditions increases the disturbing factors in the development (or cenogenesis).

The main purpose of this work is to prove this law by a process of induction. The first five chapters of the first volume describe in entertaining fashion the history of evolution from the standpoint of embryology, which Haeckel considers synonymous with ontogeny. The sixth and seventh chapters give a clear account of the sexual elements and the processes of reproduction. These are the most readable in the book. The succeeding chapters, dealing with mattersunfamiliar to the general reader who is not a biologist, will offer some difficulty, in spite of the 240 illustrations. The facts in support of the evolutionary hypothesis have been drawn from the sciences of paleontology, geology, embryology and comparative anatomy.

The main theme of the work is that, in the course of their embryonic development, all animals, including man, pass rapidly through a series of forms which represent stages in the development of their ancestors from the beginning of organic creation. The beginning of organic life upon the earth did not take place until the vapors surrounding the earth cooled and permitted the formation of water, for without water there cannot be, and could not have been, any life. "It is an astonishing but indisputable fact," says Prof. Haeckel, "that the science of the evolution of man does not even yet form part of the scheme of general education. In fact, educated people even in our day are for the most part quite ignorant of its important truths." He is amazed that people do not know that every human being is developed from an egg or ovum, and that this egg is a simple cell like any other plant or animal egg; while, on the contrary, everybody knows that the butterfly emerges from the pupa and the pupa from the larva and the larva from the butterfly's egg. But with the exception of medical men, who are expected to have an interest in the formation and transformation of the individual, the world at large knows little of the wonders of human life. The last chapter of the first volume carries the story of evolution to the point where man at last parts company with the anthropoid ape. It gives a full account of the membranes that envelop the embryo.

The second volume is much more difficult of comprehension, because it adduces a large number of scientific facts in the endeavor to trace the line of man's ancestry from the primaeval microbe to the ape-man of Java. It is, however, important to understand these matters if one would arrive at an independent conclusion. The duration of time necessary for the development of the individual is insignificant as compared with that required for the development of the race—a fact which Huxley made famous in his statement that the differences in structure between man and the anthropoid apes are less than between the anthropoids and the rest of the apes. In four weeks of embryonic life the human being goes through a cycle which it has taken the race millions of years to complete.

Coincidently with the process of physical evolution there has been likewise an evolution of languages, says Haeckel, in supporting the statement by reproducing Schleicher's table of the derivation of the Indo-Germanic languages. "This evolution of language was simply an outcome of the evolution of human speech. The evolution of language also teaches us (both from its ontogeny in the child and its phylogeny in the race) that human speech probably was only gradually developed after the rest of the body had attained its characteristic form. . . . The third and last stage of our animal ancestry is the true or speaking man (Homo), who was gradually evolved from the preceding stage by the advance of animal language into articulate human speech."

Whatever we may think of Prof. Haeckel as a scientific investigator and a lover of truth, we are bound to judge him also as a philosopher, for much of his published work, whether purposely or otherwise, seems to have been written from the standpoint of the enthusiastic controversial materialist. But as a philosopher he can never appeal to the mass of mankind because he is too didactic, too fond of drawing inferences where inferences are scarcely warranted. He would reduce everything in heaven and earth to a physical basis. Even the human soul he conceives of simply as a function of mind which perishes utterly and absolutely with the

death of the body. To quote his own words, "Personal immortality of the human soul is scientifically untenable." Incidentally he takes a fling at the modern psychologist who describes "the human soul . . . merely the soul of a learned philosopher who has read a good many books, but knows nothing of evolution and never even reflects that his own soul has had a development." Haeckel believes that the human spirit or soul is merely a force or form of energy inseparably bound up with the material substratum of the body.

To students of philosophy Haeckel is chiefly known as the expounder of the doctrine of Monism, which "affirms that all the phenomena of human life and of the rest of Nature, for that matter, are ruled by fixed and unalterable laws; that there is everywhere a necessary causal connection of phenomena, and that therefore the whole knowable universe is a harmonious unity, a Monon." In the light of this gospel even love is the mainspring of heterogeneous and altogether remarkable processes, and "its source is considered to be the attractive forces of two erotic cells." There is a note of disappointment at the end of this second volume which seems to declare that the prejudices both of the learned and unlearned against "natural anthropogeny" are responsible for the inability of Monism to secure a permanent foothold as a widely recognized system of rational philosophy.

Prof. Haeckel's work compels admiration for the industry, energy and perseverance of the aged author (he is now seventy-six), who has drilled his own little shaft through the great sphere of knowledge by dint of tremendous effort and with very little aid from his colleagues. But we should have felt more at ease with him, more inclined to praise his splendid achievements as a student, if he had adhered in this book to the scientific and discursive. All the side lights and speculative interpretations which so irresistibly engage his mind might well have been published in a separate volume for the edification of those whose conclusions must be of the ready-made variety. One feels that there is little occasion for their intrusion here.

Edwin E. Slosson (essay date 1914)

SOURCE: "Ernst Haeckel," in *Major Prophets of To-Day,* Little, Brown, and Company, 1914, pp. 242-99.

[*In the following excerpt, Slosson presents a wide-ranging biographical sketch of Haeckel, by turns laudatory and critical, which views his work and thought in the context of his personal life.*]

Monistic investigation of nature as knowledge of the true, monistic ethic as training for the good, monistic æsthetic as pursuit of the beautiful— these are the three great departments of our monism: by the harmonious and consistent cultivation of these we effect at last the truly beatific union of religion and science so painfully longed for by so many to-day. The True, the Beautiful, the Good, these are the three august Divine Ones before which we bow the knee in adoration; in the unforced combination and mutual supplementing of these we gain the pure idea of God. To this triune Divine Ideal shall the twentieth century build its altars.—Haeckel's **"The Confession of Faith of a Man of Science."**

The geographical distribution of German universities is such as to shock the orderly mind of our General Education Board, which, like a trained forester, believes in weeding out, or rather, in not cultivating, institutions growing close together. But in Germany the soil is so rich as to support three great universities—Leipzig, Halle, and Jena—planted within a circle of twenty miles radius, and nevertheless all thriving. Even the overweening development of Berlin University since that city has become the imperial capital has not yet overshadowed the smaller institutions. For, curious as it seems to us Americans, students in Europe are not influenced in the choice of a university chiefly by its size, the splendor of its buildings, or even its athletic record. They seem rather to consider the personality of the professors as the important thing, and will often travel considerable distances, at a cost of one and sixteen hundredths cents per mile, third class, in order to put themselves under the instruction of a particular man they have taken a fancy to, quite ignoring some other university which from our point of view had a claim upon their allegiance, from the fact that it was nearer or had been attended by their fathers. Jena, the least of the three in the matter of numbers, is not by reason of that willing to confess inferiority to any of its rivals, not even to big Berlin. On the contrary, Haeckel, in his famous controversy with Virchow, apologized with satirical politeness for his opponent's ignorance of zoölogy, on the ground that he couldnot be expected to keep up with the advance of the science when he had left the little institute of Würzburg for the luxurious appliances and the political and social duties of Berlin. In fact, Haeckel, with his fondness for formulation, laid down a law on this point thirty-five years ago which, he says, has yet to meet with contradiction, that "the scientific work of an institution stands in inverse ratio to its size."

Certainly, if seclusion and scholarly traditions are conducive to intellectual achievement, Jena is the place for the thinker. The university, with one thousand eight hundred and seventeen students, is about a third the size of the University of Wisconsin. The population of the city is about the same as that of Madison. But while Madison has other interests, political especially, Jena is absorbed in the university. Its chief industry, the glassworks, is the offspring of the university, for it was through the fortunate collaboration of Ernst Abbé, a professor who could figure out indices of refraction, with Carl Zeiss, a glassmaker who was willing to put money into queer formulas, that the new lenses were discovered which make possible our modern photography and microscopy. Generously has the debt that the

industry owed to science been repaid, for the Zeiss company has borne a large share of the expenses of maintaining the university and erecting its new buildings, besides giving to the city many public buildings, among them a splendid bathhouse, an auditorium and a free library and reading room, where are on file one hundred and fifteen daily papers and three hundred and sixty periodicals (American librarians, take notice).

From this it may be seen that Jena is an up-to-date town. Yet at the same time it retains more of medieval picturesqueness than most, mingling the new and the old as none but Germans know how to. *"Das liebe närrische Nest,"* as Goethe called it, is hidden away among the Thuringian hills so that the railroad was a long time finding it. The cobble-stoned streets stroll out from the market place in a casual sort of a way and change their minds about where they are going without notice, twisting about Gothic churches, diving under old towers, wandering slowly along the banks of the Saale, or starting suddenly straight up hill. The gossipy gables of the old houses lean toward each other like peaked eldritch faces in fluted red caps. So close they stand sometimes that you can touch the walls on either side, and you have to walk with one foot on the sidewalk and the other on the pavement, like the absent-minded German professor who thought he had gone lame. When I saw Jena, I understood something which had long puzzled me, that is, how the dachshund originated. It is manifestly a product of evolution according to the principle of the survival of the fittest, for only a creature constructed according to the specifications "dog and a half long and half a dog high" could make his way with convenience and celerity through this maze of narrow streets. But all sorts of vehicles and beasts of burden get around somehow, too; oxen and horses, automobiles and bicycles, dog carts and women carts. Most in evidence everywhere are the students, who swagger through the town with the consciousness of owning it, their bright-colored corps caps at a cocky angle, and their faces looking like advertisements of the dangers of not using safety razors, for the Jena student has three hundred and fifty years of university tradition to live up to, and he realizes the responsibility of it to the full.

The ancient and honorable history of Jena is unescapable. It is woven into the very fabric of the place, and he who runs may read it from the street signs. The Volkshaus, which I have mentioned, is very appropriately approached through Ernst Abbé Strasse and Carl Zeiss Strasse. On the other side of it is Luther Strasse, for Jena harbored the great reformer for two years at a critical period in his career. This leads to Goethe Strasse—Goethe composed the "Erlkönig" at Jena. The next turn brings us into Schiller Strasse—Schiller was professor of history in the University for ten years, carrying an active side line of poetry the while. A big stone in the old garden marks the spot where he wrote "Wallenstein," 1798. At the garden gate is Ernst Haeckel Platz, from which Ernst Haeckel Strasse leads us to our destination, the Villa Medusa.

What other town could give a ten-minute walk so rich in names worth remembering?

The Villa Medusa, mind you, is not named from the Greek gorgon, but from the beautiful jellyfish with the long trail of waving threads, one of the livingcomets dredged up by the *Challenger* which Haeckel depicted and described thirty years ago. The house is a square-built, white, two-story dwelling, half hidden by the tall trees. The furniture is of the conventional German type. The room into which I was shown was not small, but it seemed so when Professor Haeckel entered it, for the first impression one gets is largeness. He really is a large man any way you take him; tall, heavy-limbed, large-featured; his hair is now white but thick, and his beard broad and bushy. He moves with some stiffness now, but otherwise his fourscore years have not impaired his vigor. His bearing is erect and his handclasp strong. His laugh is hearty and his blue eyes twinkle as he relates some amusing incident in the controversies of which his life has been full.

For Haeckel has been a storm center of the cyclonic movements that have swept over the whole earth during the last century. His name has been a battle-cry in the scientific, religious, and political wars of more than one generation, and never more than at present, when a new religion with many thousands of adherents has set out to conquer the world under the sign, "There is one Substance and Haeckel is its prophet." I inferred from what he said to me and still more from what he did not say that he was not very enthusiastic over the semi-ecclesiastical form which the propaganda is now taking in Germany, but is more interested in the quieter and wider acceptance of his ideas which he regards as virtually complete in scientific circles. He disclaimed emphatically any intention of establishing a cult or ritual, like Comte. I fancy that the sentence with which he ended his chapter on "Our Monistic Religion",

> Just as the Catholics had to relinquish a number of churches to the Reformation in the sixteenth century, so a still larger number will pass over to the free societies of Monists in the coming years,

was, like many another paragraph in the book, put in more to irritate the clergy than with any serious intent. But it is curious to observe how rapidly the Monist locals are assuming the forms of the non-conformist congregations. They celebrate Christmas—that is, the winter solstice—with trees, candles, and gifts. They have a weekly sermon by Ostwald and a Sunday-school paper, *Die Sonne.*

To see Haeckel at his best one should get him to talk of his beloved Jena, which indeed is not difficult to do, for he is ever ready to speak with enthusiasm of its beauty, its freedom of thought, and its leadership in many of the great intellectual movements of German history. When I remarked upon the many delightful roads and pathways upon the hills round about the town, he explained Jena was the last of the university towns to be reached by railroad. Professors and students were poor, and they had to walk, so they learned to walk well and to take pleasure in outdoor exercise and to appreciate fine views. That Haeckel himself is a great lover of landscape as well as of the beautiful in all forms of life is well known to readers of his travel sketches. For this he gives credit to his mother, who, as he says in dedicating to her his *Indian Letters,*

> Aroused in me in my earliest childhood a sense for the infinite beauty of nature and taught the growing boy the value of time and the joy of labor.

His skill as a draftsman and colorist appears in his zoölogical works, and besides this professional work he has in his portfolios more than a thousand original sketches in oil and water colors of scenery from Norway to Malay; in fact, of every quarter of the globe except America. When he was twenty-five he was so captivated by Sicily that he almost gave up science to adopt landscape painting as a career.

The freedom of instruction which Jena has enjoyed to an exceptional degree, even for Germany, Haeckel ascribes in part to the fact that the university is located in one of the minor States, remote from the great political centers, and derives its support from several sources. "We had four masters," said Professor Haeckel to me, "and so we remained free." He closes his address of 1892 on **"Monism as the Bond Between Religion and Science"** with a grateful eulogy of the Grand Duke Karl Alexander, who, he says,

> has during a prosperous reign of forty years constantly shown himself an illustrious patron of science and art; as Rector Magnificentissimus of our Thuringian university of Jena, he has always afforded his protection to its most sacred palladium—the right of free investigation and the teaching of truth.

We see that Haeckel has reason to be grateful for the protection accorded him when we realize that he first championed the cause of Darwin in 1862, only three years after the publication of *The Origin of Species,* and that twenty years after that professors were being dismissed from American universities or were viewed with suspicion for believing in evolution. Even to-day a man of Haeckel's views on religion and his blunt way of expressing them would find it difficult to retain his chair in most American universities. In Germany a professor may be almost anything he pleases—except a Socialist—and hold his job.

A song of the Jena students contains the couplet

> "Wer die Wahrheit kennet und saget sie nicht,
> Der ist fürwahr ein erbärmlicher Wicht!"

But according to Haeckel the students of Berlin University have a different version:

> Wer die Wahrheit kennet und saget sie frei,
> Der kommt in Berlin auf die Stadtvogtei![1]

The grand duchy of Saxe-Weimar-Eisenach, of which Jena is one of the chief cities, has about the same area as Rhode Island and fewer inhabitants. It was the first of the German States to acquire a constitutional government, in 1816. The community is rather rigidly orthodox in the evangelical Lutheran faith, which it was among the first to espouse. How well the Grand Duke Karl Alexander maintained the Jena tradition of *Lehrfreiheit* is shown by an incident that happened when Haeckel first scandalized Germany by championing the cause of Darwinism. A prominent theologian came to the palace of the Grand Duke at Weimar and begged him to dismiss the heretic professor. Karl Alexander asked: "Do you suppose that he really believes the things he publishes?"

"Most certainly he does," was the prompt reply.

"Very well," said the Grand Duke, "then the man simply does the same as you do."

It was about this time, when Haeckel, perceiving that the University was suffering from the attack made upon him, approached Seebeck, the head of the governing body, with an offer to resign his professorship in order to relieve the tension. Seebeck, who had little sympathy with his theories, replied: "My dear Haeckel, you are still young and you will come yet to have more mature views of life. After all, you will do less harm here than elsewhere, so you had better stay."

It may be well to add that while Haeckel did not change his views except to become more radical as he grew older, the University did not suffer in the long run by his presence. On the contrary, his fame as an investigator and teacher drew students from all over the world and brought to the University several large endowments.

Near to Ernst Haeckel Strasse and facing the park called Paradise there is a unique building, the Phyletic Museum, established by Haeckel to house collections illustrating the theory of evolution. On the wall is painted the genealogical tree of the greatest family in the world, embracing the whole animal kingdom, and over the central arch is inscribed a quotation from the poet whom Haeckel most admires, Goethe:

> Wer Wissenschaft und Kunst besitzt
>   Der hat Religion;
> Wer diese beiden nicht besitzt
>   Der habe Religion!

Which Lange puts into English as

> He who Science has and Art
>   He has Religion too;
> Let him who in these has no part
>   Make his religion do.

Nowadays, when evolution is generally accepted, when it is preached from the pulpit as well as taught in the school, it is hard for us to realize the scorn and incre-dulity that greeted the theory on its first formulation. We who see about us laboratories of experimental evolution where new species of plants and animals are produced at will, according to specifications drawn up in advance, can hardly put ourselves in the position of those who fifty years ago believed that to question the immutability of species was to induce intellectual confusion and invite moral chaos. So we can scarcely appreciate the courage and perspicacity of the young Haeckel in openly championing Darwinism at a time when that theory was regarded as an absurdity, not alone by theologians, as one would infer from Andrew D. White's "Warfare of Science with Theology", but by most of the leading authorities in all fields of science. But we may picture him on that memorable Sunday evening of September 19, 1863, as he rose to give the opening address of the Scientific Congress at Stettin; a tall, handsome young man, blond-bearded, bright-eyed, sun-browned, hard-working, athletic (that same year he won a laurel crown at the Leipzig festival for a record-breaking jump of twenty feet). It was certainly presumptuous in a zoölogist of only twenty-nine years, who had just secured a position in the university circle as Extraordinary Professor at Jena (which means below the Ordinary in Germany); who had just published his first book, the **Monograph on the Radiolaria,** so to attack the convictions of his elders and masters there assembled. Haeckel was no halfway man. As soon as he espoused Darwinism—which was barely a month after he had laid eyes on *The Origin of Species*—he drew from it conclusions that Darwin himself hesitated to suggest; on the one hand that life originated in inorganic matter, on the other that the human race originated from the lower animals. He at once drew up a pedigree not only of the radiolaria but of mankind. Here is a passage from the very beginning of his Stettin speech:

> As regards man himself, if we are consistent we must recognize his immediate ancestors in the apelike mammals; earlier still in kangaroo-like marsupials; beyond these, in the secondary period, in lizard-like reptiles; and finally, at a yet earlier stage, the primary period, in lowly organized fishes.

and this, be it remembered, was eight years before Darwin published his *Descent of Man*.

"Without Haeckel there would have been Darwin, but no Darwinism," says one of his enthusiastic disciples. But this immediately suggests the question of whether it was altogether an advantage to have made an "ism" out of Darwin. As a mere question of taxonomy his theory would have been regarded by the lay world as harmless and uninteresting. But heralded by Haeckel as evidential of materialism, as antagonistic to the Church and as destructive to Christianity, Darwinism raised up foes on all sides who would not otherwise have concerned themselves with it. This, however, is a question of what-might-have-been like to that of whether the slaves might not have been freed without bloodshed *if* the abolitionists had not been so extreme and if the Southerners had not been so intolerant. So in this case; Haeckel was extreme, his opponents were intolerant, so the war had to be. The gentle-natured Darwin more than once had to caution his ardent German champion to be less violent and sweeping in his attacks upon those who held the older views. They were more to be pitied than blamed, said Darwin, and they could not keep back permanently the stream of truth. In England Huxley at the same time, with quite as sharp a pen as Haeckel's, was waging a similar warfare against clerical antagonists.

It may be said that Haeckel spent the rest of his life in filling in the outlinehe had sketched at the Stettin Congress of 1863, for, however detailed the work on which he was engaged, he never afterward lost sight of the guiding clew to the labyrinth of life evolution. We are here not concerned with the zoölogical studies on which his fame securely rests, but only with the philosophical views to which they led him. His convictions were very definitely established in early manhood, and he occupies to-day essentially the same point of view as fifty years ago. During this time his efforts have been increasingly directed toward reaching a wider audience. In 1866 he developed the fundamental principles of his monistic philosophy in the two large volumes of his *General Morphology of Organisms.* This gained few readers outside the circle of savants, and little acceptance there. In 1868 he put his theory of evolution into more popular form in *The Natural History of Creation.* This had an unusual sale for a book of its kind, but Haeckel was dissatisfied to see that the general public remained indifferent and unaffected by the new conceptions of the world and man arising from the discoveries of modern science. Worse still, he observed with alarm a rising tide of reactionary thought at the close of the century and a growing dominance of the clerical power in German politics. So he determined to make a final effort to influence his generation, an appeal to the court of last resort, the Cæsar of to-day, the people. He packed his science and philosophy into one volume of moderate size, filled in the chinks with *obiter dicta,* and published it in 1899 under the title of *The Riddle of the Universe.* This time he hit the mark. The success of the book was immediate and amazing. An author of a detective tale or a Zenda romance might have envied him. Ten thousand copies were sold within a few months, one hundred thousand within a year, and by this time the sale of the German and English editions has doubtless passed the half million mark, not to speak of the fourteen other languages into which the book has been translated. Since a book like this usually has several readers for each copy, it is probable that those who have been directly reached by Haeckel within fifteen years must be numbered by the million. Besides this, of course, the spread of his views has been further extended by a similar volume, *The Wonders of Life,* five years later, and by the widely circulated pamphlets of the Deutscher Monistenbund. *Haeckels einheitliche Weltanschauung,*[2] then, whatever one may think of it, is undeniably an important factor in the thought of to-day.

I found Professor Haeckel not altogether pleased that he owed his popular reputation to that one of his works in which he took the least pride. He seemed to hold it in almost as light esteem as his opponents and was frank in acknowledging its defects of style and content. "But," he said in substance to me, "I had set forth my philosophy with due dignity and order in my *General Morphology* more than thirty years before and nobody read it. Nobody reads it now, even when they criticize my ideas. So what could I do but put them forth in a way that would secure attention?"

We must observe that to secure this wider audience he did not resort to any of the ordinary expedients, such as palliating unpopular views, skipping dry details, and avoiding technical terms. *The Riddle of the Universe* is not the sort of writing that goes by the name of "popular science" and that is commonly regarded as necessary to catch the attention and reach the understanding of the lay reader. Haeckel discusses questions of physiology, zoölogy, botany, paleontology, and astronomy, each in its own tongue, the bare facts stated without any poetic disguise or flowery adornment. Far from dodging long words when necessary, he invents them when unnecessary. Few men have done so much word coinage. In his work on the radiolaria alone he had to christen more than thirty-five hundred new species, two names apiece. So it is no wonder that when he comes to talking metaphysics and religion he sticks to the habit of making up his language as he goes.

In the case of other authors of this series I have had to distill the essence of their philosophy from the leaves of many volumes. I have had sometimes to translate poetry into prose and sometimes to piece together scattered suggestions and faint allusions into a coherent and compact doctrine. But in the case of Haeckel my task is easy, for nothing of the sort is necessary. He has himself expressed his views in succinct form and the plainest of language. He takes as much delight in creeds and dogmatic statements as any scholastic theologian, andhe has the same implicit faith in formulas as capable of expressing all things in heaven and earth. One reason why his conflicts with the clergy have been so sharp and bitter is because he has much the same type of mind and uses similar language. Ordinarily, in the so-called warfare of religion and science, the adversaries revolve hopelessly around one another, like double stars, without ever coming into contact.

The most convenient formulation of Haeckel's philosophy for our purpose is that which he prepared as a sort of confession of faith for his lay church, the Monistenbund. It is here translated entire and for the most part literally, though in a somewhat condensed form.[3]

. . . . .

THE THIRTY THESES OF MONISM

I.—*Theoretical Monism*

1. Monistic Philosophy. The unitary conception of the world is based solely upon the solid ground of scientific

knowledge acquired by human reason through critical experience.

2. Empiricism. This empirical knowledge is attained partly by sense observations on the external world and partly by conscious reflection on our mental internal world.

3. Revelation. In opposition to this monistic theory of knowledge is the prevailing dualistic conception of the world, that the most profound and important truths can be gained through supernatural or divine revelation. All such ideas are due either to obscure and uncritical dogmas or pious frauds.

4. Apriorism. Equally untenable is the assertion of Kantian metaphysics that some knowledge is acquired *a priori* independent of any experience.

5. Cosmological Monism. The world is one great whole, a cosmos, ruled by fixed laws.

6. Cosmological Dualism. The idea that there are two worlds, one material or natural and the other spiritual or supernatural, arises from ignorance, cloudy thinking, and mystical tradition.

7. Biophysics. Biology is only a part of the all-embracing physical science and living beings are under the same laws as inorganic matter.

8. Vitalism. The so-called "vital force", which is still believed by some to direct and control physical and chemical processes in the organism, is just as fictitious as a "cosmical intelligence."

9. Genesis. Organic beings and inorganic nature alike have been developed by one great process of evolution through an unbroken chain of transformations causally connected. Part of this universal process of evolution is directly perceptible; its beginning and end are unknown to us.

10. Creation. The idea that a personal creator made the world out of nothing and embodied his creative thought in the form of organisms must be abandoned. Such an anthropomorphic creator exists as little as does a "moral world order" ordained by him or a "divine providence."

11. Theory of Descent. That all existing beings are the transformed descendants of a long series of extinct organisms developed in the course of millions of years is proved by comparative anatomy, ontogeny, and paleontology. This biogenetic transformation is established whether we explain it by selection, mutation, or any other theory.

12. Archigony. When the earth's crust had cooled sufficiently, organic life came into existence through the katalysis of colloidal compounds of carbon and nitrogen in the form of structureless plasma globules (Monera) represented to-day by the Chromoceæ.

13. Plasmic Metabolism. The innumerable forms of plant and animal life arose from the ceaseless transformation of the living substance in which the most important factors are the physiological functions of variation and heredity.

14. Phylogeny. All plants and animals form a single genealogical tree rooted in the Monera.

15. Anthropogeny. The position of man in nature is now fully understood. He has all the characteristics of the vertebrates and mammals and developed out of this class in the later tertiary period.

16. Pithecoid Theory. Man is most nearly related to the tailless apes, but is not descended from any of the existing forms. On the contrary, the common ancestors of all the anthropoid apes and man are to be looked for in the earlier extinct species of old world apes (Pithecanthropus).

17. Athanism. The soul consists of the totality of cerebral functions. This soul or thought organ in man, a certain area of the cerebral cortex, acts in accordance with the same laws of psychophysics as in the other mammals. This function of course ceases at death, so it is nowadays utterly absurd to believe in "the personal immortality of the soul."

18. Indeterminism. The human will, like all other functions of the brain (sensation, imagination, ratiocination), is dependent upon the anatomy of this organ and is necessarily determined by the inherited and acquired characteristics of the individual brain. The old doctrine of "free will" is therefore seen to be untenable and must give way to the opposite doctrine of determinism.

19. God. If by this ambiguous term is understood a personal "Supreme Being", a ruler of the cosmos who, after the manner of men, thinks, loves, generates, rules, rewards, punishes, etc., such an anthropomorphic God must be relegated to the realm of the mystical fiction, no matter whether this personal God be invested with a human form or regarded as an invisible spirit or as a "gaseous vertebrate." For modern science the idea of God is tenable only so far as we recognize in this "God" the ultimate unknowable cause of things, the unconscious hypothetical "first cause of substance."

20. Law of Substance. The older chemical law of the conservation of matter (Lavoisier, 1789) and the more recent physical law of the conservation of energy (Mayer, 1842) were later (1892) by our Monism united into a single great universal law, for we recognized matter and energy (body and spirit) as inseparable attributes of substance (Spinoza).

II.—*Practical Monism*

21. Sociology. The culture which has raised the human race high above the other animals and given it dominion

over the earth depends upon the rational coöperation of men in society with a thoroughgoing division of labor and the mutual interdependence of the laboring classes. The biological foundations of society are already perceptible among the gregarious animals (especially the primates). Their herds and groups are kept together by the social instinct (hereditary habits).

22. Constitution and Laws. The rational arrangement of society and its regulation by laws can be attained by various forms of government, the chief object of which is a just Nomocracy, the establishment of a secular power based upon justice. The laws which limit the freedom of the citizen for the good of society should be based solely upon the national application of natural science, not upon venerable tradition (inherited habits).

23. Church and Creed. On the other hand, all means should be used to fight the hierarchy which cloaks the secular power with a spiritual mantle and makes use of the credulity of the ignorant masses to further its selfish aims. The confessional obligation as a particular form of superstition is especially to be attacked, since it only serves to evoke the distinction between those of other beliefs. The desirable separation of Church and State is to be accomplished in such a way that the State leaves equally free all forms of belief while restricting their practical encroachments. The spiritual power (Theocracy) must always be subordinate to the secular government (Nomocracy).

24. Papistry. The strongest hierarchy which today exercises spiritual domination over the greater part of the civilized world is papistry or ultramontanism. Although this mighty political organization stands in sharp contradiction with the original pure form of Christianity and wrongfully employs its insignia to obtain power, it nevertheless finds strong support even from its natural opponents, the secular princes. In the inevitable *Kulturkampf* against papistry it is, above all, necessary to abrogate by law its three strongest supports, the celibacy of the clergy, auricular confession, and the sale of indulgences. These three dangerous and immoral institutions of the neo-Catholic church are foreign to original Christianity. So also is the strengthening of superstitions dangerous to society through the cult of miracles (Lourdes, Marpingen) and of relics (Aix la Chapelle, Trèves) to be prevented by law.

25. Monistic Religion. If we understand by religion, not a superstitious cult and irrational creed, but the elevation of the mind through the noblest gifts of art and science, then Monism forms a "bond between religion and science" (1892). The three ideals of this rational monistic religion are truth, virtue, and beauty. In all civilized states it is the duty of the representatives of the people to see that the monistic religion is officially recognized and its equal rights with other confessions assured.

26. Monistic Ethics. The rational ethics which forms a part of this monistic religion is derived, according to our modern theory of evolution, from the social instincts of the higher animals, not from a dogmatic "categorical imperative" (Kant). Like all of the higher gregarious animals, man strives to attain the natural equilibrium between the two different obligations, the behest of egoism and the behest of altruism. The ethical principle of the "Golden Rule" has expressed this double obligation twenty-five hundred years ago in the maxim: "Do unto others as you would that they should do unto you."

27. Monistic Schools. In most civilized countries, and especially in Germany, the instruction of youth in upper and lower grades is still largely bound in fetters which the scholastic tradition of the Middle Ages has retained to the present day. Only the complete separation of Church and school can loose these fetters. The prevailing confessional or dogmatic religious instruction is to be replaced by comparative religious history and monistic ethics. The influence of the clergy of any confession is to be removed from the school. The inevitable school reform must be accomplished upon the basis of modern natural science. The greater part of education should be devoted, not to the study of the classical language and history, but to the various branches of natural science, especially anthropology and evolution.

28. Monistic Education. Since the sound development of the soul (as a function of the cerebral cortex) is closely connected with that of the rest of the organism, the monistic education of youth, free from the dogmatic teachings of the Church, must strive to upbuild soul and body equally from earliest youth. Daily gymnastics, baths and exercises, walks and tours, must develop and strengthen the organism from early youth. Observation and love of nature will be thus awakened and intensified. Through public libraries, continuation schools, and popular monistic lectures will the more advanced be provided with mental nourishment.

29. Monistic Culture. The admirable height of culture which mankind in the nineteenth century has attained, the astonishing progress of science and itspractical applications in technology, industry, medicine, etc., gives grounds for expecting a still greater development of culture in the twentieth century. This desirable progress will then however be possible only if the beaten paths of the traditional dogmas and of clerical superstition be abandoned and a rational monistic knowledge of nature attain the mastery instead.

30. The Monistenbund. In order to spread the natural unitary theory of the universe to the widest circles and to realize practically the beneficent fruits of theoretical monism, it is desirable that all efforts in this direction find a common point of application through the founding of individual monist societies. In this universal monist association not only all free thinkers and all adherents of the monistic philosophy find place, but also free congregations, ethical societies, and free religious associations, etc., which recognize pure reason as the

only rule of their thought and action and not belief in traditional dogma and pretended revelations.

There is a strong resemblance in form between this creed of the monistic religion and the creeds that have been formulated by many other religions in the history of the world; the same juxtaposition of cosmogony and ethics without any apparent connection; the same mixture of the fundamental and trivial, the permanent and ephemeral; the same affirmation of idealistic aims mingled with attacks upon what is assumed to be the beliefs of the opposition.

It is not my purpose in this book to criticize the views I present or to obtrude my personal opinions, so I shall not discuss this monistic confession of faith except to point out the striking contrast between the theoretical and practical sections of the statement. The second is in no sense a deduction from the first, and they are so different in character as to give the effect of an anticlimax. Haeckel's fundamental principles are bold and revolutionary. His practical conclusions are timid and conventional. It would be a dull faculty meeting which did not bring out more heretical views on education than Haeckel expresses. Why is it necessary to storm the battlements of heaven and create a new earth in order to make Greek optional and get the students to take baths and walks?[4] Any session of the American Sociological Society will bring out more suggestions for the radical reorganization of society from professors in good and regular standing than are to be found in all of Haeckel's works. He seems blind to what would appear to us the glaring evils of his country, the burden of militarism, the oppression of government, the conflict of classes, the monopoly of land, the injustice of hereditary rank, the superstition of royalty, and the like. If he touches on these at all, it is in mild and cautious terms. His gratitude to the Grand Duke who was kind enough to let him alone is expressed in language that sounds sycophantic to American ears. All his fury is directed against the Church, Protestant and Catholic alike, yet he remained until the age of seventy-seven a member of the orthodox Lutheran Church. Of course, to be radical in thought and conventional in practice is not peculiar to Haeckel. It is common to most thinkers, but is especially conspicuous in his case.

The reforms he advocates in social customs are for the most part very moderate. He is himself no smoker, and he thinks that the German students devote too much attention to beer and dueling. This is sensible but not startling. He declaims against the tyranny of fashion and denounces corsets as injurious to the health.[5] In this, however, most men and not a few women would agree with him. He asserts that marriage is not a sacrament, but a civil contract, and as such may be dissolved.[6] This is a doctrine common to Hebrew and Puritan. One of the chief objects of the founding of the Monistenbund was to force the separation of Church and State and the secularization of the schools. This seems so obviously just and desirable that it is hard for us to realize on what

grounds it should be opposed. And as for the demands expressed in Article 25 it is almost inconceivable to us that a government could refuse a man the right to declare himself a Monist, instead of a Lutheran or a Hebrew, if he wants to.

In our own free land anybody can get up a church of his own if he find disciples, and if he prefers to belong to no church it is nobody's business but his own. Not so in Germany, where a man has to give his religion together with his age and occupation at every turn. Even if he wants nothing more than a permit to a building or a rebate on his railroad fare, he is called upon to make a confession of faith. And it must be one of the few religions officially recognized by the State; none of the "fancy religions" will pass muster. A man who declares himself not a member of an established church, *konfessionslos,* is looked upon with suspicion as a sort of outlaw. Under these circumstances, of course, a large proportion of the adherents of the State churches never attend the services and have no belief in the creed they profess.

There is now going on in Germany what might be called an "anti-Christian revival." Protracted meetings are being held in the cities at which Monist missionaries exhort the people to leave the Church, and at the conclusion the converts are called upon to stand up and be counted. In 1913, during a whirlwind campaign in Berlin at Christmas time, sixteen meetings were held and attended by thirteen thousand persons, of whom twenty-three hundred and forty-three announced their intention of formally separating themselves from the churches of which they are nominally members. The Monist locals, the independent congregations, and the free-thinker societies have joined forces under the management of a central *Komitee Konfessionslos.* Very curiously the Social Democratic party, which in its early days was so fiercely anti-clerical, stands aloof from the movement and appears to view it with disfavor.

This *Kirchenaustrittsbewegung,* or church-exit-movement has for its aim to effect the complete separation of Church and State and to secure for the individual freedom of religious choice. It does not, therefore, indicate so great an increase of irreligion as appears on the face of it. It will on the contrary tend to reduce the percentage of hypocrisy and to allow the growth of new forms of religious association better adapted to the times than the established churches. Already it has stimulated a useful reflex. The "Go-to-church Sunday" has been introduced from America, and the State churches are showing more signs of life than for a long time.

It would obviously be an injustice to Haeckel to assume that, because the practical reforms he advocates seem trite and timid to us, they do not require both perspicacity and courage in Germany. The fact is that Germany, advanced though it be intellectually, is still medieval in government and usages. If, for instance, a German clergyman should visit this country and stay in the home of an American minister, the latter would probably be distressed by the views held by the visitor on the inerrancy of the Scriptures and the value of beer, while, on the other hand, the German would be equally shocked to hear his reverend friend advocate secular schools and ridicule the divine right of kings.

Haeckel practically takes over intact the fundamental principles of Christian ethics, making the Golden Rule the basis of his system, although characteristically refusing to give Jesus any credit for it by saying that it had a "polyphyletic origin." He attacks, indeed, certain extreme forms of it, asceticism, belittlement of family life, absolute self-sacrifice, etc., but he adopts substantially the moral standards which the Christian men of his time and environment profess and endeavor to practice. I do not say that he is wrong to borrow ethics from Christianity. I do not suppose he could do better. But he would have done the world great service if, instead of taking a ready-made ethical system, he had worked it out from his fundamental principle of evolution, as Spencer, Drummond, and Kropotkin have tried to do. If, having done this, he had arrived at the same conclusions as the Christian moralists, his aid would have been invaluable just now, when, almost for the first time, attacks are made not so much on the theology as on the ethics of Christianity, and this, too, in the name of science. The air is filled with questions which arise in Haeckel's peculiar field. Is, for example, Nietzsche justified in preaching ruthless egoism as the logical lesson of evolution? Or is it true, as many now say, that the preservation and protection of the weak in body and mind necessarily lead to the degeneration of the race? In the incidental references he makes to these questions,[7] he condemns Nietzsche, but advocates euthanasia for the hopelessly diseased, reaching the first conclusion from his "own personal opinion" and the second from "pure reason." As the individual views of an evolutionist, these are interesting and even valuable, but they can hardly be regarded as established principles of the science of evolutionary ethics.

Haeckel's politics may be summed up by saying that he is anti-clerical and not much else. He concerns himself little about the form of government or economic conditions, regarding them indeed as comparatively unimportant matters.

The monistic and the socialistic movements in Germany are closely associated, but chiefly, it seems to me, because both are anti-clerical rather than because the evolutionary philosophy necessarily leads to either democracy or socialism. Many Social Democrats profess themselves Monists, and doubtless a large proportion of that party would agree with Haeckel in the matter of religion. But on the other hand, they can derive little if any support for their doctrines from the monistic literature. Haeckel states his opinion with his usual frankness in a contribution to Maximilian Harden's magazine, which concludes with the words:

> I am certainly no friend of Herr Bebel, who has attacked me repeatedly, and among other things has slandered me in his book on Woman. Besides, I hold the utopian aims of the official social democracy to be impracticable and its ideal future state to be a big workhouse. That, however, cannot prevent me from recognizing the kernel of justice in the great social movement. That this can be overcome by the repressive acts of the Berlin council, by the power of the police and of the State prosecutors can be believed only by one who knows neither the history nor the natural history of mankind.—*Zukunft*, 1895, No. 18. Quoted in the introduction to *Freie Wissenschaft und freie Lehre*, p. 9.

The immense popularity of *The Riddle of the Universe* is, I think, largely to be accounted for by the personality of the author. The man behind the gun was what gave it power. I do not mean that the reception given to the book was due to Haeckel's standing as a zoölogist. The outside world knows little and cares less for scientific reputation. It was rather that the book revealed a man tremendously in earnest who had made up his mind on questions of the most vital interest to all and who said what he thought in the plainest and most emphatic language, without regard to whose feelings he hurt. *The Riddle of the Universe* and *The Wonders of Life* are, it seems to me, more valuable as contributions to the psychology of genius than to philosophy. The personal interest he aroused is evinced by the thousands of letters he received and is still receiving about these books, ranging in tone from the warmly sympathetic to the furiously antagonistic. He years ago had to give up the task of answering them save by a printed slip.

Few books have ever excited so much heated controversy. Hundreds of criticisms and replies have been published, and new ones appear frequently yet, fifteen years after. The book was intended to draw the fire of the enemy, clericalism, and it did. Nor did the philosophy of the chair receive it any more favorably. It will be sufficient on this point to quote the sharp criticism of Professor Friedrich Paulsen, of Berlin University, whose idealistic monism comes into direct contact with Haeckel's materialistic monism:

"I have read this book with burning shame for the state of general culture and the philosophical culture of our people. That such a book was possible, that it could be written, printed, sold, read, admired, believed by a people which claims a Kant, a Goethe, a Schopenhauer, is painful."

It is one of the curiosities of controversy that the Church should often be found defending with desperation, not her own positions, but some of the old, abandoned redoubts of Science. This was largely the case in the evolution controversy. The real "origin of species" was in the scientific mind. It was Science that discovered that all the multifarious forms of plant and animal life could be classified into distinct types, which, it too hastily assumed, were absolutely separate and fixed. When later Science came to revise that view, it discovered that the immutability of species had somehow in the meantime become a theological dogma, to be zealously defended by curates who could not tell a species from a genus.

It was the same in regard to the theory of spontaneous generation or the production of living beings from non-living matter. This was formerly good Christian doctrine, accepted by St. Augustine and taught by the medieval schoolmen, and when in 1674 the Italian physician, Francisco Redi, showed that the maggots that appeared in dead matter came from eggs, he was persecuted for unbelief. But it was still maintained that microscopic living forms could arise spontaneously in bouillon and infusions of hay until Pasteur proved that this was false, for in sealed and sterilized tubes no trace of life appears. Such negative experiments are, of course, not competent to prove that at some time and under other conditions life might not be produced from the non-living. Yet, strangely enough, Haeckel's theological opponents voluntarily adopted this untenable position and waged war against him especially on account of his belief that when the earth's crust cooled down, compounds of cyanic acid were transformed into globules of albumin, from which developed unicellular organisms.

The only alternative hypothesis to this which has been brought forward is the one advocated by Arrhenius, that the germs of life might have been brought from some other planet in meteorites or floating free in space and propelled by radiant energy. This is apparently not impossible, but it seems a very violent assumption, much harder of acceptance than the other, that of abiogenesis. For the wall between the organic and the inorganic has been broken down completely, and that between the living and non-living is being tunneled into from both sides. On the one hand we have been able to construct artificially such complex organic molecules as sugar and protein. On the other hand, it has been found possible to produce in siliceous and metallic solutions mimic cells which grow, move, put forth pseudopodia, select their food, propagate by fission, and assume many of the characteristic forms of vegetable and animal life. In more than one laboratory experiments in the generation of life are still being hopefully carried on, and an announcement of their success at any time would not amaze biologists in general. But even though abiogenesis should forever remain impossible as a laboratory experiment, it would not be untenable as a hypothesis of the origin of life under the exceptional conditions of some earlier stage in the world's history. Such a supposition, whether true or not, is at least no more irreligious than is a recognition of the fact that non-living matter is being continuously transformed into living within our own bodies.

The volume invited attack because it was not only intentionally provocative, but unintentionally vulnerable. One does not have to be very learned in order to discover in it occasional errors as well as many extravagant and questionable statements. The fact that few people could treat of such a wide range of topics without making more mistakes than Haeckel did not, of course, protect him from criticism. Huxley, who enjoyed crossing swords with the clergy as much as Haeckel, was more careful to guard himself from counter attack. If a discussion of demonology led unexpectedly to the question of the exact status of the district of Gadara in the Roman Empire, he was prepared to meet his opponents on that ground as well as in biology. Not so Haeckel. He picks up his church history from infidel pamphleteers[8] and recklessly caricatures Christian beliefs. In attacking the dogma of the Immaculate Conception of Mary he confuses it with that of the Virgin Birth of Christ, and at the same time uses language needlessly offensive to those who regard the Mother of Jesus with adoration.[9]

A more serious charge than ignorance of ecclesiastical history was later brought against Haeckel by Doctor Brass, namely, that he had fabricated evidence in support of his theory of evolution by falsifying his drawings of embryos, that he had, among other things, taken away vertebræ from the tail of a monkey embryo and had extended the backbone of a human embryo in order to enhance the resemblance. Since accuracy is the soul of science, this is as serious as it would be, for instance, to charge a minister with preaching miracles when he does not believe in them. In his reply Haeckel acknowledged

> that a small part of my numerous embryo pictures (perhaps six or eight per cent) are actually "falsified" (in the sense of Doctor Brass), all those in fact in which the material at hand for observation was so incomplete or unsatisfactory that one was forced to fill up the gaps by hypothesis and to reconstruct themissing members by comparative synthesis in order to produce a connected chain of evolution.

Haeckel emphatically denies any deception or misrepresentation, and calls attention to the fact that such diagrammatic and reconstructed drawings are common to all physiological works and are necessary to bring out the desired points. As to whether Haeckel has transgressed the permissible limits of such schematization of material I should not be competent to decide. Thirty-six German men of science signed a condemnation of Haeckel; forty-seven German men of science, "though they did not like the kind of schematizing which Haeckel practiced in some cases", signed a condemnation of Brass and the Keplerbund. The numbers have no significance, since majorities never decide anything except the balance of opinion, but the group that stood by Haeckel contained more embryologists and zoölogists than the other.

So I will dismiss the subject by quoting the opinion of a biologist and evolutionist who is thoroughly appreciative of Haeckel's contributions to science. Professor V. L. Kellogg, of Stanford University, in reviewing the *Evolution of Man* in *Science,* says:

"Biologists are likely to be of two minds concerning the advisability of putting Haeckel's *Evolution of Man* into the hands of the lay reader as a guide and counselor on this most important of evolution subjects. Haeckel is such a proselytizer, such a scoffer and fighter of those who differ with him, that plain, unadorned statement of facts and description of things as they are cannot be looked for in his books. Or, if looked for, cannot be found. But this very eagerness to convince; this hoisting of a thesis, this fight for Haeckelian phylogeny and Haeckelian Monism, all make for interest and life in his writings."

This whole affair is a striking illustration of Huxley's observation that a controversy always shows an unfortunate tendency to slip from the question of what is right to the relatively unimportant question of who is right. Haeckel's critics have rarely attempted to controvert his scientific work and in fact would not in most cases be competent to discuss it. Even if he were guilty of all the mistakes alleged, it would not materially affect his scientific conclusions.

In noting Haeckel's faults, we are in danger of failing to appreciate the marvelous constructive genius of the man; the creative imagination which is characteristic of the great scientist even more than of the great poet. It was this gift that enabled him to discern in a handful of slime dredged up by the *Challenger* from the depths of the sea an orderly system of living beings wherein each microscopic skeleton of silica found its natural niche. It was this power which enabled him to assist so largely in the transformation of zoölogy from a purely observative and descriptive science, as it was when he began his labors, to a rational, experimental, and prophetic science, as it was when he closed them. As Cuvier from a few bits of bone could construct a whole animal, so Haeckel from scattered species ventured to construct, as early as 1865, a family tree, including all living forms from monera to man. Faulty it is from the standpoint of our present knowledge, but yet it must command our admiration because of the insight he showed in perceiving natural relationships and the skill with which he bridged the gaps in his living chain by hypothetical forms. Just as the great Russian chemist Mendeléef was able to describe in advance elements then unknown, but which were discovered later and found to fit into the vacant places he had assigned to them in his periodic law, so Haeckel's anticipations have been in many cases confirmed by later science. It was his good fortune to be able to hold in his hand the skullcap and femur of the "missing link" which had for years been the jest of the anti-evolutionists. The ape-man, or Pithecanthropus, which he had in 1885 described and named, was in 1894 discovered by Dubois in Java. The mind of Haeckel has such high tension that it leaps over the gaps in a demonstration like a ten thousand volt current.

His account of how he was led to doubt the dogma of the immutability of species must be quoted because it is an excellent illustration of the wisdom of the laboratory adage: "Study the exceptions. They prove some other rule."

The problem of the constancy or transmutation of

species arrested me with a lively interest, when, twenty years ago, as a boy of twelve years, I made a resolute but fruitless effort to determine and distinguish the "good and bad species" of blackberries, willows, roses, and thistles. I look back now with fond satisfaction on the concern and painful skepticism that stirred my youthful spirits as I wavered and hesitated (in the manner of most "good classifiers", as we called them) whether to admit only "good" specimens into my herbarium and reject the "bad", or to embrace the latter and form a complete chain of transitional forms between the "good species" that would make an end of all their "goodness." I got out of the difficulty at the time by a compromise that I can recommend to all classifiers. I made two collections. One, arranged on official lines, offered to the sympathetic observer all the species, in "typical" specimens, as radically distinct forms, each decked with its pretty label; the other was a private collection, only shown to one trusted friend, and contained only the rejected kinds that Goethe so happily called "the characterless or disorderly races, which we hardly dare ascribe to a species, as they lose themselves in infinite varieties", such as rubus, salix, verbascum, hieracium, rosa, cirsium, etc. In this a large number of specimens, arranged in a long series, illustrated the direct transition from one good species to another. They were the officially forbidden fruit of knowledge, in which I took a secret boyish delight in my leisure hours.—Bölsche's *Life of Haeckel*, p. 38.

Ernst Heinrich Philipp August Haeckel, to give him for once his full baptismal name, was born in Potsdam, February 16, 1834. He has a double inheritance of talent, for both the Haeckels and the Sethes, his mother's family, have contributed prominent names to German history, and the two families have intermarried more than once. It is a curious fact that Gustav Freytag, in his series of "Pictures from the German Past", should have chosen for his representative men of the nineteenth century two of Haeckel's ancestors: his mother's father, Christopher Sethe, Privy Councilor and defender of Prussia against Napoleon, and his father, Karl Haeckel, State Councilor.

But Ernst did not follow the family tradition and take to the law. He showed an unmistakable bent for natural science, so, as a compromise profession, his father had him trained as a physician. He took the medical course, and in obedience to his father's wishes consented to practice the profession for a year to see if he could make a success of it. During the year only three patients came to him, owing perhaps to the fact that Haeckel in order to get time for his biological researches had fixed his consultation hours from five to six in the morning. His father then gave up trying to make a doctor out of him and allowed him to go to Messina in 1859 to study marine animals. Haeckel straightway became engaged to his cousin Anna Sethe, and as soon as he got his appointment at Jena married her. Their happiness was brief. Two years later she died, leaving Haeckel, then thirty, so stricken that he felt that he could not long survive the blow, so he plunged with feverish haste into the preparation of his *General Morphology* in order to leave to the world his science and philosophy in a systematic form. It was written and printed, two thick volumes of more than twelve hundred pages, in less than a year, during which Haeckel lived like a hermit, working all day long and half the night, getting barely three or four hours sleep out of the twenty-four.

Haeckel immortalized his wife by giving her a living monument instead of one of marble or brass. He named for her one of his beloved medusæ, a fairy-like jellyfish, whose mass of long, trailing tentacles reminded him of his wife's blond hair. The Mitrocoma Annæ is described in his *Monograph on the Medusæ,* published in 1864, and a note states that it was so named[10]

> in memory of my dear, never-to-be-forgotten wife, Anna Sethe. If it is given to me to do something during my earthly pilgrimage for science and humanity, I owe it for the most part to the blessed influence of my gifted wife, who was torn from me by a premature end in 1864.

Three years afterwards he married again, Agnes Huschke, daughter of a Jena anatomist. They have three children, two daughters and a son, who has inheritedhis father's artistic talent and has devoted himself to art in Munich.

Haeckel's æsthetic taste is shown not merely in the thousands of paintings and drawings that fill his monographs, but especially in his *Art Forms of Nature,* which consists of ten portfolios of large color plates depicting strange and beautiful creatures from all realms of animal life but particularly in little known lower forms, fishes, crustaceans, corals, radiolaria, diatoms, and desmids. Here are to be seen real gargoyles, more grotesque than a sculptor's unaided imagination can create. Here the designer and decorator can find hundreds of suggestive themes for almost any purpose, so they have no excuse for repeating the trite and traditional forms as they do.

A large part of these "art forms" Haeckel discovered in the course of his investigations of deep-sea life on the material gathered by the *Challenger,* which was commissioned by the British Government in 1872-1875 to explore the ocean. The results of this expedition, published in fifty large volumes, constituted the greatest contribution to oceanography that has ever been made. Haeckel contributed the volumes on the medusæ, the siphonophora, the keratosa, and the radiolaria. To the radiolaria Haeckel devoted ten years, 1877-1887, and described 4318 species and 739 genera, from the curiously complicated siliceous skeletons deposited on the bottom of the ocean by these minute one-celled creatures.

Although Haeckel's life was largely devoted to the closest study of the minutest forms of life, yet he never lost sight of the broader aspects of his science. It seems as though he felt the need of resting his eyes by raising them from the microscope and looking out of the win-dow to focus on infinity. Haeckel is essentially a specialist with a fondness for generalization. He welcomed the change in the current of thought that set in at the close of the nineteenth century, the effort of the new century to get at the inner meaning of the mass of miscellaneous facts that the old century had heaped up. It was with intent to assist in this movement that he produced, at the age of sixty-five, his *Riddle of the Universe,* intending this to be the final expression of his view of the world, a fragmentary sketch instead of the complete "System of Monistic Philosophy" which he had projected many years ago and could not now hope to complete. But five years later he supplemented this with a similar popular volume, *The Wonders of Life,* in which he replies to certain criticisms and explains the biological principles on which his philosophy is based. This, unlike the *Riddle,* was not composed at various intervals in the course of many years, but was written uninterruptedly during four months spent at Rapallo, on the Italian Riviera, when he was

> stimulated by the constant sight of the blue Mediterranean, the countless inhabitants of which had, for fifty years, afforded such ample material for my biological studies; and my solitary walks in the wild gorges of the Ligurian Apennines and the moving spectacle of its forest-crowned altars, inspired me with a feeling of the unity of living nature—a feeling that only too easily fades away in the study of detail in the laboratory.

Professor Haeckel retired from active service as teacher and investigator in 1909 at the age of seventy-five. "Indeed I am wholly a child of the nineteenth century and with its close I draw the line under my life's work," he said, and the publication of *The Wonders of Life* in 1904 confirms rather than contradicts this, for it shows that he maintains his position altogether unshaken by the revolution that has taken place in philosophic thought. Like Herbert Spencer he lived to see a reaction against many of the opinions for which he fought most earnestly.

The nineteenth century was cocksure of so many things about which the twentieth century doubts. We are not so certain that, as Haeckel says, everything can be reduced to the motion of the atoms. The atom itself is crumbling, and as for motion, what is it? The ether in the reality of which Haeckel puts implicit faith is to us a doubtful, perhaps an unnecessary, hypothesis. Vitalism and teleology are coming back again into biology in new forms. Pluralism, not monism, is the fashion of the day, and some carry it almost to polytheism. Indeterminism finds more advocates nowadays than determinism. Haeckel makes the first law of thermodynamics (conservation of energy) one of the corner stones of his philosophy, but has little regard for the second (degradation of energy). Modern thought considers the second law more important than the first.[11]

And what shall we say about the "Law of Substance", which is Haeckel's contribution to the fundamental principles and which he apparently regards as of equal importance to the discoveries of Lavoisier and Mayer?[12] Speaking for myself, the reason I cannot accept it is because it is absolutely meaningless to me. We know what the law of the conservation of matter means. It means, among other things, that 12 pounds of carbon when burned make 44 pounds of carbon dioxide, which we may decompose and get back 12 pounds of carbon again. The law of the conservation of energy means, among other things, that when we burn 12 pounds of carbon we produce 135,305,600 foot pounds of energy. But what does it mean when we say that matter and energy, or body and spirit, are somehow the same substance? Have we said more than when we affirmed the two laws separately? Even if true, does it make a bit of difference to anybody or anything; or to put the query into the pragmatic form, can it be true if it does not make a bit of difference to anybody or anything? But we must bear in mind that the rigid application of this formula to many historic attempts to solve the "riddle of the universe" would leave less of them intact than in the case of Haeckel.

The Christian reader is likely, in his irritation at what appears to him to be willful misrepresentation of his beliefs, to be too sweeping in his condemnation of the ideas of Haeckel. Even in the matter of religion Haeckel is not nearly so heretical as he assumes or is presumed to be. Many of the things he attacks are almost unrecognizable caricatures of modern religious views. It should be remembered that the *Riddle* and the *Wonders* were written at a time when he saw the German Government coming under the domination of the Blue-Black Block, and when it seemed to him that this coalition of conservatives and clericals threatened to suppress free speech and to check the advance of science. In his earlier writings his views are expressed in much more conciliatory language. Indeed, his pantheism is hardly distinguishable at times from theories of divine immanence such as are now held very commonly in orthodox churches. Wherein lies the magic of the word "Monism" if not in our ingrained prejudice in favor of unity, inherited from the fierce monotheism of the Jews? Is not Haeckel then borrowing the thunders of Sinai to enforce his new religion?

His *General Morphology* of 1866, which, as he told me, he prefers to his later works as an expression of his philosophy, concludes with the following passage:

> Our philosophy knows only one God, and this Almighty God dominates the whole of nature without exception. We see his activity in all phenomena without exception. The whole of the inorganic world is subject to him just as much as the organic. If a body falls fifteen feet in the first second in empty space, if three atoms of oxygen unite with one atom of sulphur to form sulphuric acid, if the angle that is formed by the contiguous surfaces of a column of rock-crystal is always 120°, these phenomena are just as truly the direct action of God as the flowering of the plant, the movement of the animal, or the thought of man. We all exist

"by the grace of God", the stone as well as the water, the radiolarian as well as the pine, the gorilla as well as the Emperor of China. No other conception of God except this that sees his spirit and force in all natural phenomena is worthy of his all-enfolding greatness; only when we trace all forces and all movements, all the forms and properties of matter, to God, as the sustainer of all things, do we reach the human idea and reverence for him that really corresponds to his infinite greatness. In him we live, and move, and have our being. Thus does natural philosophy become a theology. The cult of nature passes into that service of God of which Goethe says: "Assuredly there is no nobler reverence for God than that which springs up in our heart for conversation with nature." God is almighty: he is the sole sustainer and cause of all things. In other words, God is the universal law of causality. God is absolutely perfect; he cannot act in any other than a perfectly good manner; he cannot therefore act arbitrarily or freely—God is necessity. God is the sum of all force, and therefore of all matter. Every conception of God that separates him from matter, and opposes to him a sum of forces that are not of a divine nature, leads to amphitheism (or ditheism) and on to polytheism. In showing the unity of the whole of nature, Monism points out that only one God exists, and that this God reveals himself in all the phenomena of nature. In grounding all the phenomena of organic or inorganic nature on the universal law of causality, and exhibiting them as the outcome of "efficient causes", Monism proves that God is the necessary cause of all things and the law itself. In recognizing none but divine forces in nature, in proclaiming all natural laws to be divine, Monism rises to the greatest and most lofty conception of which man, the most perfect of all things, is capable, the conception of the unity of God and nature.

. . . . .

HOW TO READ HAECKEL

The Riddle of the Universe (Harper) is the best popular presentation of science and philosophy from Haeckel's point of view. This may be supplemented by *The Wonders of Life* (Harper), in which he develops more fully the biological side and defends himself against certain criticisms. To these should be added the very interesting life of Haeckel by W. Bölsche (Jacobs). Cheap editions of these three are published by the Rationalist Press Association, London. They, as well as other works of Haeckel, are translated by Joseph McCabe.

The Natural History of Creation (Appleton) and *The Evolution of Man* (Appleton or Putnam) are both intended to explain in a way comprehensible to the general reader the fundamental principles of the theory of evolution and the biological facts on which it is based. Special addresses by Haeckel are translated under the titles of: *Monism as Connecting Religion and Science* (Macmillan) and *Last Words on Evolution* (New York). Of his *Indische Reisebilder* there are two versions in

English; one by Mrs. S. E. Boggs entitled *India and Ceylon,* which is neither literal nor complete, and one by Clara Bell, *A Visit to Ceylon* (Eckler), which is better. On the personal side may be read Herman Schauffauer's sketches, "Haeckel, a Colossus of Science" (*North American Review,* August, 1910), and "A Talk with Haeckel at Home", in *T. P.'s Magazine,* 1912; Elbert Hubbard's "Little Journeys to the Homes of Great Scientists", and Joseph McCabe's "A Scientist's Sunset Years", in *Harper's Weekly,* August 7, 1909. A few of the more noteworthy of the books and articles on Haeckelism in English are: *Life and Matter,* by Sir Oliver Lodge, a criticism from the standpoint of a spiritualist; the discussion between Lodge and McCabe in *Hibbert Journal,* Vol. III, pp. 315 and 741; "The World View of a Scientist", by Frank Thilly in *Popular Science Monthly,* Vol. LXI, pp. 407-425; "Ernst Haeckel, Darwinist, Monist", by V. L. Kellogg, in *Popular Science Monthly,* Vol. LXXVI, pp. 136-142; "Haeckel and Monism", by J. Butler Burke, in *Oxford and Cambridge Review,* 1907; "Lucretius and Haeckel", by F. B. R. Hellems, in *University of Colorado Studies,* Vol. III, 1905; "Religion as a Credible Doctrine", by W. H. Mallock; "Haeckel's Monism False", by Reverend F. Ballard; "The Old Riddle and the Newest Answer", by Father Gerard; "Haeckel's Critics Answered", by Joseph McCabe (London: Rationalist Press); "Haeckel's Answer to the Jesuits" (New York: *Truthseeker*); Haeckel·and His Methods", by R. L. Mangan, in the *Catholic World,* May, 1909. The monism of Doctor Paul Carus, of Chicago, is a different variety from Haeckel's as he has pointed out in the *Monist,* Vol. II, p. 498; Vol. IV, p. 228; and Vol. XVI, p. 120.

Of the immense body of literature in German on Haeckel it is impossible to give more than a few selected titles. The bibliography appended to *Ernst Haeckel: Versuch einer Chronik seines Lebens und Wirkens* by Walther May (Leipzig: Barth, 1909) devotes fourteen pages to the titles of Haeckel's writings, four pages to a list of biographical books and sketches, and thirteen pages to a list of criticisms and discussions of Haeckelism.

Die Welträtsel and *Die Lebenswunder* are published by Alfred Kröner, Leipzig. The epitome of Haeckel's philosophy, which is given almost entire in the preceding pages, is to be found in "Der Monistenbund", *Thesen zur Organisation des Monismus* (Neuer Frankfurter Verlag). Other works of Haeckel of a general and philosophical character are: *Natürliche Schöpfungs-Geschichte* (Berlin: Reimer); *Anthropogenie oder Entwickelungs-geschichte des Menschens* (Leipzig: Engelmann); *Generalle Morphologie der Organismen* (Reimer); *Systematische Phylogenie* (Reimer); *Der Kampf um den Entwickelungs-Gedanken* (Reimer); *Der Monismus als Band zwischen Religion und Wissenschaft* (Kröner); *Freie Wissenschaft und freie Lehre,* the reply to Virchow (Kröner); **"Das Weltbild von Darwin und Lamarck",** the centenary address on Darwin's birthday (Kröner).

Haeckel's travel sketches are to be found in *Indische Reisebriefe* (Berlin: Paetel) and *Aus Insulinde* (Kröner).

Even one who reads no German will find enjoyment and gain an appreciation of the artistic side of Haeckel by looking over the color plates in *Kunstformen der Natur* (Leipzig: Bibliographisches Institut) or *Wanderbilder* (Gera: Köhler).

A remarkable tribute of world-wide affection is the volume issued on his eightieth birthday, *Was wir Ernst Haeckel verdanken* (Leipzig: Verlag Unesma), to which one hundred and twenty-five men and women contributed,—savants, artists, workingmen, officials, and businessmen.

The monistic movement may be followed by the pamphlets of the society which may be obtained ordinarily from the Verlag Unesma, Leipzig. Some of the more interesting of these *Flugschriften* are: "Friedrich Paulsen über Ernst Haeckel", by Albrecht Rau; "Reinke contra Haeckel", by Heinrich Schmidt; "Eine neue Reformation vom Christentum zum Monismus", by Hannah Dorsch and Arnold Dodel; "Monismus and Christentum", by Heinrich Schmidt; "Monismus und Klerikalismus", by J. Unold; "Das Einheit der physikochemischen Wissenschaften", by Wilhelm Ostwald; "Die einheitliche Weltanschauung", by Ernst Diesing: this last urges the Monists to support the peace and conservation movements. The official organ is *Das monistische Jahrhundert,* a weekly edited by Ostwald and published by the Verlag Unesma, Leipzig. The issue for February 14, 1914, is, in honor of his eightieth birthday, devoted to Haeckel. For the history of monistic philosophy in general from the Greeks to the present time see *Der Monismus,* by various authors, under the editorship of Arthur Drews (Jena: Diederich, 1908) or *Geschichte des Monismus,* by Rudolf Eisler (Leipzig: Kröner).

Of the expository and controversial literature, pro and con, it must suffice to mention the following titles: *Die Weltanschauung Haeckel,* by Max Upel (Berlin-Schoenberg; Buchverlag der Hilfe), a brief and fairminded critique; *Ernst Haeckel, ein Bild seines Lebens und seiner Arbeit,* by Wilhelm Breitenbach (Brackwede i. W.: Verlag von Breitenbach & Hoerster), a tribute to the master on his seventieth birthday; *Haeckel's Welträthsel nach ihren starken und ihren schwachen Seite,* by Julius Baumann (Leipzig: Diederich, 1900); *Anti-Haeckel,* by F. Loofs, Professor of Theology in Halle; *Philosophia Militans* by F. Paulsen, Professor of Philosophy in Berlin. A good account of the Haeckel-Paulsen controversy by Theodor Lorenz may be found in *Deutsche Literaturzeitung,* March 12, 1910, and later.

NOTES

[1] An undergraduate friend of mine to whom I referred these verses for translation into the vernacular of the campus gives me this version:

Who knows the truth and speaks not out
He is indeed a sorry lout!
Who knows the truth and speaks too loose
In Berlin gets in the calaboose!

[2] This is *not* to be translated, as I once heard a student give it, "Haeckel's one-sided showing-up of the universe."

[3] *Thesen zur Organization des Monism.*

[4] *Riddle of the Universe,* p. 363.

[5] *Wonders of Life,* p. 430.

[6] *Ibid.,* p. 248.

[7] *Wonders of Life,* pp. 115 and 119.

[8] President Thomas, of Middlebury College, exposed the source of his theory that the father of Christ was a Roman officer named Pandera in *The Independent,* Vol. 64, p. 515.

[9] Some of the more offensive of these passages are modified or eliminated in the later editions of *Die Welträtsel.*

[10] Another medusa also named for his wife, Demomema Annasethe, will be found on one of the color plates of the New International Encyclopedia (Vol. XII, p. 68).

[11] The significance of this change of emphasis in its bearing on metaphysical, religious, and ethical ideas I endeavored to explain in the preceding chapter.

[12] See Number 20 of the thirty theses given above.

Clara Millerd Smertenko (essay date 1923)

SOURCE: "Letters of a Scientist," in *The Nation,* New York, Vol. 117, No. 3044, November 7, 1923, pp. 527-28.

[*In the following review of* The Story of the Development of a Youth, *Smertenko considers the book as a key to understanding the later Haeckel.*]

"Exactly that which people despise and tread under foot as contemptible, inferior dirt, the green slime on old wood lying in the water, the turbid foam on the surface of the mire, does not my microscope prove these things to be just the most magnificent and most marvelous forms of creation? Never, by the way, have I missed my beloved microscope so painfully as in those days when the waters of the mountains offered me so much and such new material, animal and vegetable, for my microscope. So, thereupon, I took a solemn oath never, no matter how great the possible difficulty in the way, even on journeys, to let the dear companion of my life, which opens to me an infinitude of organic life where the unassisted eye sees nothing but rubbish and rottenness, out of my sight."

Such rapturous outpourings as this from the pen of a university student of twenty-one years do not often reach the eyes of parents, especially concerning so unromantic a theme as a microscope. They express, however, not the exalted mood of a moment, but a profound and permanent passion for nature, given lyric utterance with a hundred variations, intermixed with a minute account of daily happenings, meals, expenditures, and ailments, as well as with reflections upon life, upon God, and upon human destiny.

During the four years of his student days at Würzburg, the period covered by these letters, Ernst Haeckel sketched microscopic forms and preserved mosses and insects, "my hay and vermin," with an ardent devotion incomprehensible to ordinary minds. The gift of Berghaus's Physical Atlas made of his eighteenth birthday an exciting adventure among geographical plates. Literature, too, was no *terra incognita* to him. He read Goethe and Lessing for pleasure, and Homer in the original. A letter dated New Year's eve, 1853, contains the following postscript: "When I asked you to send Homer to me, I meant the original in Greek, which affords me quite another pleasure than the translation. However, I am quite fond of reading it once more in that form." For painting and sculpture he had an enthusiastic appreciation, but, an unusual thing in a German of culture, little enjoyment of music. "My musical sense is in reality equal to zero. The only music in which I take any interest is the popular song."

It would be a mistake to assume that this youth was an average German university student of the early fifties. His isolation from most of his fellows is evident. In their jollifications, their *Studentenspritze,* their drinking bouts, he wasboth unable and unwilling to join. He recounts some pathetic attempts to enter with ease into general social life. Concerning an excursion at which young ladies were present, he comments: "I have learned how to navigate safely around such rocks [namely the task of entertaining these ladies] so I did not speak a single word to one of them throughout the day." After two years of residence in Würzburg he remarks that he is "not conscious of knowing, with the exception of Frau Professor Schenk and Frau Dr. Gsell-Fels, any female soul in the whole of Würzburg, even by sight." He has nevertheless quite enough in common with the life around him to make the letters valuable as a picture of the university life of the time. They are still more important to the psychologist for the revelation they contain of a growing mind, and in particular the growing mind of a man of undoubted genius. No laboratory could furnish data half so significant, and none of the many recent studies of youth in fictional form escapes the unconscious distortion which mature reflection inevitably gives. As literature, neither in the original nor in this fairly good translation does the book quite merit Professor Schmidt's enthusiastic preface. For, in range of ideas and experience, in variety and richness of expression, many collections of letters are superior to these, though few equal them in candor, in depth of feeling, and in the completeness with which the heart is "shaken out."

Possibly, however, the chief interest of the volume lies in the light thrown upon the career of the mature Haeckel, the impassioned apostle of Darwinism, the poet-prophet who made materialism a religion, the zealot who led the German professors in their pronouncement regarding Germany's innocence in the Great War. Haeckel's American friends apologized for his war hysteria on the score of his advanced age and failing powers. But he had earlier shown the same docility in making his powerful intellect the servant of an intolerable governmental policy. In 1870 he cut from one of his books a passionate protest against militarism with its waste of precious human life, and during the *Kulturkampf* he inserted an attack on Catholicism. The real explanation is based upon that combination of indifference to politics with deep-seated respect for authority which was the price consciously or unconsciously paid by many German university professors for their boasted *Lehrfreiheit.*

When Haeckel first read Darwin's *Origin of Species,* he remarked that he could have written much of it himself. In these letters it is evident that for him the dividing line between plant and animal life is already growing dim. Indeed the final step in this process of thought, a completely monistic philosophy in which all nature is regarded as the working out of uniform laws, a step which Darwin himself seems never to have taken, is already present to his mind. In the letters, Monism, which ultimately became a religion to Haeckel, is in continual conflict with a devout pietism that had been deeply instilled by parental training, and evidently was as nearly native to his temperament as religious feeling can be. Like many other devout souls, he staved off the crisis of the conflict by separating the spheres of religion and science. "Also I myself can only find comfort and peace in this Christian belief, which is contemplated by so many and such important minds to be mere ridiculous foolishness, by my admitting this life of faith as a sphere quite apart from the life of knowledge and understanding based on the evidence of our five senses, which is not only possible side by side with it but also necessary, just as justified, and even infinitely more important." This twofold truth subterfuge begins to wear thin in the latter part of the correspondence, and only a few years subsequently the open break with Christianity came. We actually find him in middle life issuing a challenge upon the subject to his former teacher and friend, the great scientist Virchow, against whose materialistic views he had struggled throughout his university years, but who in later life turned apologist for institutional Christianity.

The less unusual traits of personality revealed in the letters: artistic sensitiveness, eagerness and impatience of temper, passionate loyalty to family and friends, susceptibility to partisan prejudice, sincere concern for human welfare, emotional fervor in the discussion even of abstract subjects, add greatly to the reader's interest and are by no means unimportant in explaining the extent and specific character of Haeckel's influence throughout hisremarkable career.

Frank Harris (essay date 1924)

SOURCE: "Ernst Haeckel," in *Contemporary Portraits,* Grant Richards Ltd., 1924, pp. 84-92.

[*In the following excerpt, Harris offers his personal recollections of an encounter with Haeckel, as well as a chance meeting with the latter's translator.*]

> "Knowledge is unattainable, in Man's State,
> We at best may only see some little part;
> After short purblind visions of Man's thought,
> Wisdom; our heritage, lies within our might,
> Time past, our fathers' was; this day that is,
> Is ours; the Future, we ourselves beget."

These lines are taken from a book with the secondary title of "The Riddle of the Universe," by Charles Doughty, an English poet of to-day, and as Haeckel's book with the same title is his most popular work, and has been translated into half a dozen languages and had an enormous sale, I thought the poetry might well introduce what I have to say about the thinker. For, strange to say, Haeckel thought he had solved the riddle, and his reputation as a prickly and aggressive disputant was due in great part to his profound belief in his own insight.

The publication of Darwin's *Origin of Species* in 1859 changed the whole course of Haeckel's activities. He went to Sicily a German naturalist, and came back from Palermo a scientific observer and student with a mass of data; Darwin's work made him a thinker; showed him how to use the vast stock of scientific knowledge he had been accumulating. In his ***Last Words of Evolution*** he tells with simple directness the revolution which Darwin's work caused in him:

> Darwin's work appeared in 1859, and fell like a flash of lightning on the dark world of official biology. I had been engaged in a scientific expedition to Sicily and given myself to a thorough study of the graceful radiolarians, those wonderful microscopic marine animals that surpass all other organisms in the beauty and variety of their forms. The special study of this remarkable class of animals, of which I afterwards described more than 4000 species, after more than ten years of research, provided me with one of the solid foundation-stones of my Darwinian ideas. When I returned to Berlin in the spring of 1860, I knew nothing of Darwin's achievement. I merely heard from my friends that a remarkable work by a crazy Englishman had attracted great attention, and that it turned upside down all previous ideas as to the origin of species.

> I was deeply moved by the first reading of Darwin's book, and soon completely converted to his views. In Darwin's great and harmonious conception of Nature, and his convincing establishment of evolution, I had an answer to all the doubts that had beset me since the beginning of my biological studies.

Haeckel set to work at once in the light of the new knowledge, and five years later published his *Mor-*

phologie; that formed the complement and chiefest corroboration of the Darwinian theory. It was all very well for Darwin to fix upon the simplest form of life and then construct an ascending ladder, each rung of which was more complex than the preceding one, and to tell us that this was how mankind came to the birth by gradual development from the tadpole to reason, and from undefined feelings and instinctive reactions to thoughts that wander through eternity. But Haeckel showed in the *Morphologie* that the individual embryo is like a tadpole and the foetus in the womb passes through the chief metamorphoses already predicted of the race by Darwin. Never was there corroboration of a theory at once so unexpected and so complete. And in many other ways Haeckel showed himself to be rather the collaborator than the disciple of Darwin. Haeckel published his *History of Creation* before Darwin published *TheDescent of Man,* and Darwin, with the rare generosity which distinguished him, declared that he would never have written his *Descent* if he had known that Haeckel was at work on the same subject. The truth was though Darwin had elaborated his theory quite fifteen years before he published his *Origin of Species,* yet he shrank for some time from applying his theory to man, fearing the hatred and malice of English puritanism. But, explain the matter how you will, the fact remains that Haeckel was the first boldly to apply the theory of evolution by natural selection to mankind.

That fact, and the biogenetic theory first discovered and demonstrated by Haeckel in the *Morphologie,* makes him the peer of the great Englishman. Haeckel, too, was the first to popularise the theory by lecturing on the new biology. In bare justice, one must admit that he never feared to push his thought to the furthest.

He was a controversialist by nature, and waged unsparing, if only verbal, war on whosoever differed with him. He took Virchow to task for a careless phrase, and, indeed, at one time or other crossed swords with all the ablest thinkers of the time.

Here is a passage which reveals a great deal of the man:

"I do not belong," says Haeckel boldly, "to the amiable group of 'men of compromise.' I am in the habit of giving candid and straightforward expression to the convictions which half a century of serious and laborious study has led me to form. If I seem to you an iconoclast, a fighter, I pray you to remember that the victory of pure reason over current superstition will not be achieved without a tremendous struggle."

The truth is that Haeckel delighted in controversy, and was always too combative to be a disinterested lover of science.

. . . . .

When I was a student in Munich about '79 or '80, I took up the *Morphologie* by chance, and simply devoured the biogenetic theory, while leaving untouched all the scientific paraphernalia.

Without help, I had already come to the conclusion that the individual man had stored up in himself all the chief stages of feeling and thought which the race had passed through in countless generations. Time and again, when reading this or that philosopher, I had closed the book, saying to myself, "You had these very thoughts as a cowboy on the Trail." And, more than once, I was able to guess what speculation would come next in the history of metaphysics. From this fact, I had drawn conclusions that outran Haeckel's theory.

The complete agnosticism of my youth had begun to change into a sort of Pantheism. As force and matter are indestructible, I saw that spirit was everlasting, and the spirit of man one and universal.

A new vision and a new reward came to me from this understanding. In measure as you grow, I said to myself, so your ideas and feelings will become a forecast of the future of the race, and just as you embody in yourself today the chief experiences of the long-forgotten past, so you will be able from your own growth to divine what is to come thousands of years after your death.

This comparative immortality filled me with new hope and unexpected exultation. I felt that it lay with me and in my power to become a sort of beacon for generations of men yet to be born; if I chasten myself, if I live to the highest in me, if I seize every opportunity of extending my knowledge and thought, if I school myself to feel the joy and suffering of others as deeply as my own, I too may yet become one of the sacred guides and, in spite of all insufficiency, help to steer humanity across the unpath'd waters to the undreamed-of shores. Swinburne's great hymn to the Earth-mother took on a new significance to me:

> "But what dost thou now
>   Looking Godward to cry
> 'I am I, Thou art Thou,
>   I am low, Thou art high.'
> I am Thou whom Thou seekest to find,
>   Find Thou but thyself, Thou art I.

> "I the seed that is sown
>   And the plough-cloven clod
> And the plough-share drawn thorough
>   The germ and the sod.
> The seed and the sower, the deed and the doer,
>   The dust which is God."

No wonder I wanted to meet Haeckel, and in my first long vacation I made a pilgrimage to Jena.

I had written to Haeckel, telling him I was an Irish-American student who wished to see and thank him for his "epoch-making addition" to "Darwinismus." He replied, saying he would be glad to see me and to have a talk, and a talk we had that lasted ever so many hours.

He was very affable, ingenuously eager to know what was thought of him in America; "did they regard him as a mere pupil of Darwin? or as a worker beside him in the same field?" I told him the truth, that his embryological knowledge and biogenetic discovery had given him, with Alfred Russel Wallace, rank as an independent thinker among the followers of Darwin.

Reassured in this respect, he let himself go, and gave me a sketch of his monistic philosophy, in which he appeared much more interested than in his scientific discoveries. In the course of this lecture, he spoke with passionate contempt of all who disagreed with, or even sought to modify, his materialistic view. Virchow even, who was a teacher of mine at Berlin, came under the whip for a mere phrase; but I must admit that, when I asked him about Virchow's cell-theory, he admitted his high worth as an independent observer and spoke of him as a fellow-student.

The man was eminently fair-minded, broad-minded even; but he was of his time and thought that the demolition of the superstitions and spiritual guesses of the past was much more important than it in reality was. Like Huxley, he was an iconoclast and expositor of the new biology, rather than an original thinker; and laid stress rather on the ancillary benefits of the new thought than on its hidden spirit content.

When I ventured to extend his creed and show the inferences to be drawn from it and its implications as regards the future, and consequent influence on man's conduct and hope, he listened, it is true, but with courteous, patient inattention. Though in the prime of life, his blue eyes as bright at 45 or 46 as they had been twenty years earlier, his development seemed to be arrested. He talked of the great book he had in mind (which afterwards appeared as *The Riddle of the Universe*), and spoke as if he would solve all problems in it, satisfy all doubts, never dreaming that he had got on a side-track and was neglecting the inspiring vision to be drawn from his own discovery. He didn't seem to realise that the new knowledge brought new questionings of sense and outward things, and that the riddle of man's existence was never to be answered. An English poet of our time, whom I have quoted at the beginning of this article, knew better. He wrote:

> "The sum of all is; there be many paths
> Of human goodness, and the blameless life;
> Wherein a man may walk towards the Gods,
> Till some be found new aspect of Man's mind.
> Until a candle light exceed the sun;
> Can none read Riddle of the Universe,
> It passeth Man's understanding; and shall pass."

It is well for us, no doubt, that we cannot as yet, at any rate, grasp the whole and comprehend the ultimate purpose.

. . . . .

Some incidents of our talk stuck in my mind. Haeckel mentioned the English translator of his *Morphologie*

with great respect, Mr. Ray Lankester. I knew nothing of him; but I could not help telling Haeckel that the translation was disgracefully bad. "To judge by that," I said, "Ray Lankester knows little English and less German."

"You surprise me," Haeckel exclaimed, reprovingly. "I've been assured by English friends that it was well done and Ray Lankester is a man of very considerable scientific attainments."

I could only stick to my guns and, at the same time, modify the disagreeable impression by expatiating on the incredible difficulties of translation and so forth. Some fifteen or twenty years later, I got to know Ray Lankester in London, and had from him the solution of that riddle, at least.

I told him of Haeckel's touching belief in the excellence of his translation, and asked him without more ado how he came to put his name to such 'prentice work. It was during a dinner at the Athenæum Club, I remember, and the big man (all the three or four Lankester brothers were big men) burst into a peal of laughter.

"I couldn't possibly afford the time," he said, "and so I wrote to Haeckel, telling him at the same time I'd supervise it if he wished. He wrote effusively, and I happened to know a girl at the time who wanted work and had some understanding of German, and so I passed it on to her. The price offered was not enough even for a beginner, and naturally I could give but little time to such ungrateful labour. I looked over a few pages, and thought it fairly done. Haeckel's German is anything but good; if I remember rightly, he coins neologisms by the score, but I thought one could understand the gist of it in its English dress. I'm sorry if it's rotten, but all translators are traitors—you know the Italian—*tradutore-traditore*."

There is a good deal of truth in what Ray Lankester said; Haeckel's German is appalling to anyone with a sense of style, and it would have taken years for a master to turn it into acceptable English. Still—I was a little indignant with Lankester, not realising even then how badly most of the world's work is done.

I came away from my visit to Haeckel with high appreciation of the man's ingenuous honesty and kindliness; a real student and scholar, his unremitting industry as a youth had enabled him to complete Darwin's work and to bracket his name for ever with that of the great Englishman. As a populariser, too, of the new knowledge, he did most useful work, and as an iconoclast cleared the ground for the new Temple of Science. But, comparing him with Russel Wallace, or even with Thomas Huxley, he seemed to me of smaller stature, though his discovery placed him on a loftier pedestal. I never wrote to him after leaving, because he told me his correspondence had become enormous; he spoke of answering thousands of letters; and I could see no object in wasting his time or my own. In 1914 Haeckel celebrated his 80th birthday, and has since gone to his long home, unwitting of the misfortunes that have befallen his fatherland. In this, at least, he was fortunate.

The great discovery of Haeckel is an excellent example of what international competition and work may produce of benefit to humanity. Darwin's work fell on receptive ears, not in England, but in Germany; and Haeckel added as much to the Darwinian theory as he received from it. All the nations of Christendom are children of the household of God.

James M. Gillis (essay date 1925)

SOURCE: "Ernst Haeckel," in *False Prophets,* The Macmillan Company, 1925, pp. 102-24.

[*In the following excerpt, Gillis critiques Haeckel's Monism and his presentation of it, treating the former as a variety of religious dogma and the latter as an often dishonest attempt to make facts conform to theory.*]

I

It is odd that a man like Charles Darwin should have for champion a man like Ernst Haeckel. No two men could be more opposite in character. Darwin was diffident about himself and about his doctrine; Haeckel was arrogantly certain. Darwin knew his limitations; he made few if any incursions into the foreign field of philosophy. Haeckel, not content with his reputation as a scientist, persistently encroached upon the ground of philosophy and of theology. Darwin said, humbly enough, that though he might claim to know something about the origin of species, he knew nothing about the origin of life. Haeckel claimed to know the solution of the riddle of life—and of all the other world-riddles. Darwin loved seclusion; Haeckel was over-fond of the limelight. Darwin was deferential to the opinions of others; Haeckel was truculent toward those who disagreed with him. Darwin sought peace; Haeckel reveled in controversy. In the few recorded utterances of Darwin about theology, he seems to speak with regret, and even with pathos, of his inability to profess the Christian faith. Haeckel, on the contrary, was an exultant atheist, and took malicious delight in loud-mouthed blasphemy. In fine, Darwin was always the scientist; Haeckel was sometimes a scientist, but frequently a demagogue and dogmatist.

Consequently, men of science have almost universally expressed disgust with Haeckel. Professor His said of him, "He has forfeited, through his methods of fighting, the right to be counted an equal in the company of serious investigators." Dr. Dwight[1] records that Agassiz's tone in dealing with Haeckel was "not that of one arguing with an equal, but of one exposing a knave." Dwight himself says, "The hero (Haeckel) is but a quack." Alfred Russel Wallace, codiscoverer with Darwin of the theory of natural selection, says, "I have no sympathy with Haeckel's unfounded dogmatism of combined negation and omniscience, more especially when the assumption of superior knowledge seems to be put forward to conceal his real ignorance of the nature of life itself."[2]

But if Haeckel is recognized by scientists as something of a charlatan, he is held by the mass of believers in evolution to be something of a prophet. He is incomparably more "popular" than Darwin. Probably for every one reader of Darwin's difficult and painstaking *Origin of Species,* there are fifty thousand readers of Haeckel's fascinating—and fallacious—*The Riddle of the Universe.* Indeed, that volume is one of the world's "best sellers." It has been translated into a score of languages, and its sale has run to millions of copies. Not only in Germany, therefore, but in all the world, Haeckel and not Darwin is the popular apostle of "Darwinism." True, Haeckel's Darwinism varies greatly from Darwin's Darwinism, but Haeckel's is the brand that is known to the multitude. Speaking broadly, when the man in the street mentions "evolution" he has Haeckelism, not Darwinism, in mind. Semi-educated men, who form the bulk of our population,—and of every population,—are not interested in minutely reasoned biological or anthropological treatises, but they are captivated by sensational philosophical and theological theories such as those of Haeckel. They have not the capacity for following a rigidly scientific discussion. But they are easily interested and beguiled by a man who, in the name of science, declares that "evolution" has done away with God, free will, and moral responsibility.

Man is naturally religious, that is, he is instinctively interested in religion,—whether he be for it or against it,—but his interest in "science" must be artificially produced and generally remains superficial. Men are interested in evolution, not because of its scientific importance, but because of its religious importance. Generally speaking, they have neither the patience nor the ability to follow Darwin's meticulously laborious reasonings from observed phenomena; they know only his principal thesis, and that none too accurately. But Darwin's phrases, "the struggle for existence," and "the survival of the fittest," make an appeal to the imagination—and fascinate the unscholarly. "Evolution" to the ordinary man means, not the origin of species by natural selection, but the development of man from the monkey!

Hence the wide popularity of such a book as Haeckel's *The Riddle of the Universe.* That title itself captivated the fancy of the ordinary reader. The volume, in substance, had been published under the title *General Morphology,* but the public whom Haeckel sought to interest didn't even know the meaning of the word "morphology." So he adroitly revised the work, popularized it, made it spectacular, rhetorical, sensational, gave it the catchy title, achieved a prodigious popular success, and garnered enormous royalties. But in so doing, he sacrificed much of his reputation as a scientist. Stepping out of his character to play the part of a propagandist of infidelity, he became, not only obnoxious to religious-minded people, but ridiculous and hateful in the eyes of his fellow scientists.

II

Ernst Haeckel was born in Potsdam, Prussia in 1834. He was, therefore, a young man in 1859, when Darwin's revolutionary treatise appeared. Immediately he became an enthusiastic Darwinian. Gradually he developed a mania against religion. He seems to have considered himself possessed of two vocations—the one, research in the fields of biology and zoölogy; the other, controversy in the realm of theology. It is always risky for a scholar to step out of his own province. Darwin was aware of that danger. His Christian faith had slowly slipped away from him. He became, however, not a militant atheist, but a "gentle skeptic." And he declared his opinion that "a man ought not to publish on a subject to which he has not given special and continuous thought." He might have said, with equal justice, that a man ought not to publish on a subject unless it be his life's work.

Men of science, tempted to think themselves philosophers, need above all men to be reminded of the homely maxim, "Shoemaker, stick to your last." When, for example, Thomas A. Edison is in his laboratory, experimenting with electricity, he is the incomparable "wizard." When he stops for a few minutes to grant an interview for a Sunday newspaper, on the immortality of the soul, he is rash and becomes ridiculous. Likewise, when Mr. Henry Ford prophesies that he will turn out of his factory a "flivver a minute," we say, "How wonderful!" When he says that he "would not give a nickel for all the art in the galleries of Europe," we say, "How asinine!" It is said that Edison spends eighteen hours a day in his workshop. That—together with his genius—is why he is a great inventor. It is also the reason why he is not, and cannot be, a theologian. One who spends three-quarters of every twenty-four hours in one kind of study has no time for another study. Philosophy and theology (contrary to the common view) do not come to a man by instinct or inspiration, but by labor and the expenditure of time. Consequently, the opinion of an electrical engineer on immortality is no better than the opinion of a blacksmith, and probably not so good as the opinion of a cobbler. Mr. Edison should cling close to his dynamos and eschew theology.

So of Mr. Ford: he is a good tinsmith, but no one who sees the product of his factory would consider him an artist. A sign-painter, or a sand-sculptor, is a better judge of art. Indeed, the poorest and raggedest son of little Italy knows more than Mr. Ford about Rubens and Titian and Michelangelo. The uneducated and uncultured manufacturer would be wiser if he knew his limitations.

Ernst Haeckel is no exception to the rule. He knows much about Radiolaria, and Siphonophora, and deep-sea Ceratosa, but he is not thereby entitled to speak with authority on the Trinity, the Incarnation, and the Immortality of the Soul. Science deals with facts and phenomena, or at the most with secondary causes; it has nothing authentic to say about the First Cause. It deals with matter; spirit is beyond its ken.

Curiously, however, there are multitudes of persons who prefer to take theirtheology from almost any one rather than a theologian, as there are multitudes who take medicine recommended by a chauffeur, or a bricklayer, rather than by a doctor. Still more curiously, there are great numbers of those who love to be told that there is no God and no soul; that human life is only animal life, and human love only animal passion. Even if these calamitous statements were true, it would seem decent to communicate them reluctantly and to receive them with disappointment. But the apostles of materialism and "scientific" atheism seem to take a wild delight in their unholy vocation of ruining the ideals and aspirations of mankind. And the recipients of the melancholy evangel of despair are unwarrantably and incomprehensibly gleeful over the news that their ancestors were anthropoid apes, and that they themselves are only highly organized beasts. With an air of triumph as if he were proclaiming the news of the Resurrection, Haeckel cries out, "Man who exalted himself to the heavens, man who claimed to be the offspring of gods, and demigods, is found to be only a 'placental mammal,' of no more value in the scheme of things than the microscopic Infusoria." And for these inspiring words he is rated as the prophet of a new and better dispensation.

Surely it is one of the most curious of all psychological phenomena that man should rejoice at having a pair of beasts rather than a man and woman for his first parents. A man will furiously resent what has been called "the imputation of canine maternity." But the same man will consider with equanimity, and accept without proof, the statement that his ancestors were apes.

Man on occasion, seems glad to be rid of his dignity. "Who steals my purse, steals trash," says the poet; "but he that filches from me my good name, robs me of that which not enriches him, and leaves me poor indeed." But when Haeckel, in the most high-handed manner, robs man of his good name and tells him that he is of no more value to the universe than bugs which live in a puddle of mud and die in a day, man strangely swells with pride and satisfaction. Just so, there are men who, revolting from the doctrine of the divine dignity of the human race, love to be told that we are only ants and that this planet is only an ant-hill in the infinite cosmos.

Not content with debasing man, Haeckel insults God with the utterance, "God is only a gaseous vertebrate." Millions of men read the coarse blasphemy, not only without indignation, but apparently with pleasure and satisfaction. True scientists, like Professor Conklin of Princeton, protest against the grossness of such a statement, but apparently there are other scientists, and surely there are non-scientists, who welcome an insult to God as enthusiastically as an insult to the human race.

III

However, these crimes against God and man are of lesser importance, in the eyes of scientists, than Haeckel's deliberate "scientific" falsifications. Here we come upon one of the most surprising and disedifying facts in all the history of modern science. In a lecture at Jena, on **"The Problem of Man,"** Haeckel drew skeletons of a man, a gorilla, a chimpanzee, an orangoutang, and a gibbon. Wherever dissimilarities occurred he minimized them; similarities he magnified. Also, he drew a human head upon the embryo of an ape. Likewise, in his *Natural History of Creation,* he printed three cuts, representing the ova of a man, a monkey and a dog, and three other cuts representing the embryos of a dog, a fowl, and a tortoise. He then pointed out that in no instance could a difference be found between one and another of the ova, or of the embryos. But Professor Rutimeyer of Basel discovered that Haeckel had in each case merely printed the same cut three times, and called the pictures, in one instance, man, monkey, dog, and, in the other, dog, fowl, tortoise. When the diagrams were published, Dr. Brass accused Haeckel of fraud. "Not only," he said, "has Professor Haeckel falsely represented the various evolutionistic changes of man, the monkey, and other mammifers, but he has even taken from the work of a scientist the figure of a macaco, cut off its tail, and made a gibbon of it."

Thereupon commenced a controversy as acrimonious as any sixteenth-centurytheological debate. Haeckel's most telling retort was by epithets and doubtless the most insulting of all his epithets (in his own mind and in that of his adversary) was when he called Dr. Brass a "Protestant Jesuit."

Not content with falsification, he perpetrated downright falsehood. He wrote: "In the last twenty years a considerable number of well-preserved fossil skeletons of anthropoid and other apes have been discovered, and amongst them are all the important intermediate forms which constitute a series of ancestors connecting the oldest anthropoid ape with man." If this were true, the "missing link" would be no longer missing. But Alfred Russel Wallace was writing, at about the same time, "There is not merely one missing link, but at least a score of them" and Father Muckermann declares, "Haeckel's curious 'Progonotaxis,' or genealogy of man, is pure fiction. It consists of thirty stages, beginning with the 'moners' and ending with *homo loquax.* The *first fifteen stages have no fossil representatives.*"[3]

Perhaps even more startling then Haeckel's dishonesty in fabricating drawings, is the fact that he ultimately admitted the fraud. He confessed: "Six or eight per cent of my drawings of embryos are really falsified. We are obliged to fill the vacancies with hypotheses." But immediately he declared, in his own defense, that it is customary for scientists to make use of fraudulent designs. "I have the satisfaction," he says, "of knowing that side by side with me in the prisoner's dock, stand hundreds of fellow culprits, many of them among the most esteemed biologists. The majority of figures, morphological, anatomical, histological, which are circulated and valued in students' manuals, and in reviews and works of biology deserve in the same degree the charge of being falsified. None of them is exact. All of them are more or less adapted, schematized, reconstructed."

This is interesting, if true. Obviously we cannot consider it true on Haeckel's authority. A liar will lie about men as well as about embryos. But, on the other hand, a liar sometimes tells the truth. A criminal, undergoing the "third degree," will lie, and continue to lie for hours or even for days. But if he is suddenly cornered and admits one lie, it is a well-recognized psychological fact that he will probably break down and tell all the truth he knows. Indeed, he may tell so many true things as not only to incriminate his companions, but to embarrass his investigators. I suspect that it is so in Haeckel's case. Angered at being caught in a fraud, he "peaches" on his fellow scientists. He admits the lie, and then proceeds to "spill the beans."

Indeed, there is not a little deception among scientists about the larger question of the certainty attached to the hypothesis of evolution. So reliable and careful an authority as Dr. Dwight says: "Very few of the leaders of science dare to tell the truth concerning the state of their mind. They would not tell an untruth, yet they write and speak as if evolution were an absolute certainty as well-established as the law of gravitation." And he accuses some of them of "cringing to public opinion." The theory of evolution has won its place in the universities. Hardly any one in the world of learning dares to oppose it or even seriously to criticize it. Dr. Thomas Hunt Morgan of Princeton says: "Biologists have many doubts which they do not publish. The claims of the opponents that Darwinism has become a dogma contains more truth than the nominal follower of the schools finds pleasant to hear."[4]

The entire subject of fraud in natural science, especially in connection with the theory of evolution, is so important— so much more important than Haeckel—that it may be well to digress for a moment or two, and call attention to the fact that there has been a vast amount either of conscious deceit, or of unconscious but blameworthy misrepresentation, amongst biologists, anatomists, and anthropologists overeager to convince the public of the truth of evolution. Even Huxley is not blameless in this matter. In his well-known summary of the evolution of the horse, he records the steps of the progress as follows: "First, there is the true horse, as we now know him. Next we have the American Pliocene form, Pliohippus. Then comes Protohippus, having one large toe and two small ones on each foot. Next, Miohippus, with three complete toes. Then the older MioceneMesohippus, with three toes in front and one large splint-like toe immediately behind. Last (most remote) we have Orohippus with four complete toes on the front feet and three toes on the hind feet."[5]

These are offered as the steps in the progress of the horse as discovered in America. It is disconcerting, therefore, to learn that "the true horse," the horse as we know him, was not found in America by the first white men, but was introduced from Europe, in the time of Columbus. The fossil remains found in America may perhaps be those of ancestors of the European horse, but the fact that the American horse was extinct is a detail not mentioned by Huxley.

Sir J. W. Dawson declares that the "existing American horses, which are of European origin, are descendants of Paleotherium, and not of Eohippus," and he brushes away Huxley's carefully constructed theory with the abrupt statement, "Such genealogies are not of the nature of scientific evidence."[6] That is to say, Huxley, like Haeckel, was drawing upon his imagination.

Apropos of the evolution of the horse, I am sure that Dr. James J. Walsh's humorous description of the process that is alleged to have taken place will be entertaining and instructive: "The little ancestor of the horse, about the size of the rabbit, or probably a little smaller to begin with, wanted to be bigger and to run faster. He wanted so much to run fast that he touched the ground in his eager haste only with the middle toe of each foot, and did this so constantly that gradually the other toes began to atrophy, and eventually disappeared. His anxiety to get larger made him lift himself up ever more and more, until, finally, he began to run on the toe nail of this middle toe, adding at least a part of a cubit to his stature, and this middle toe became a hoof. See how easy it is for the horse to create himself."[7]

Professor Henry Fairfield Osborn, I may add, has said, "It would not be true to say that the evolution of man rests upon evidence as complete as that of the evolution of the horse." Father LeBuffe quotes Bateson, Ranke, Virchow, Steinmann, and Vernon Kellogg in support of the statement that "the evolution of the horse is scarcely more than a very moderately supported hypothesis." You may draw your own conclusion about the certainty of the evolution of man.

Unfortunately the habit of "adapting, schematizing, and reconstructing,"—of calling upon the imagination to fill up the gaps in the record of evolution,—of drawing fanciful pictures of "missing links" that, of course, have never been seen,—is not confined to textbooks of biology. The newspapers have caught the habit. In particular, the screechingly sensational Sunday Supplements are addicted to pseudo-science.

In the New York Sunday *American* for August 7, 1921, there is an entire page of "faked" illustrations—of men with tails like monkeys, with the legs, hands, and feet of monkeys, and with bodies entirely covered with monkey-like hair. The picture is described in an accompanying article, written by an alleged famous "scientist." To the ignorant readers of that sheet (their name is millions), the picture is proof sufficient of the truth of human evolution. Naturally, one does not expect the editors of a popular Sunday supplement to have scruples about scientific accuracy. But it is to the shame of science that sensation-mongers can claim to take their cue from scholars who know better. The bad example was set by Haeckel and Huxley. It is not strange that it should be followed by such as William Randolph Hearst.

IV

To return to Haeckel. I have contrasted him with Darwin, and have called him a dogmatist. Some painstaking student of Darwin (apparently having plenty of leisure) counted the phrase, "we may well suppose," over eight hundred times in Darwin's two chief works, *The Origin of Species* and *The Descent of Man*. But in Haeckel there is no such timidity of expression. His favorite phrases are: "It must have been," "it is impossible to doubt," "it is inconceivable," "we are compelled to assume," and the like.

To give just a sample or two of his scientific method. He is enumerating his famous thirty stages in the evolution of man, "fifteen of which have no fossil representatives." He says: "The vertebrate ancestor, number fifteen, akin to the salamanders, *must have been* a species of lizard. There remains to us *no fossil relic* of this animal. In no respect did he resemble any form actually existing. Nevertheless comparative anatomy and ontogeny authorize us in affirming that he once existed. We will call this animal Protamnion." This, be it remembered, is science, not poetry. But was there ever a better example of the poet's truth that "Imagination bodies forth the form of things unknown . . . turns them to shapes, and gives to airy nothing a local habitation and a name!"

Let us suppose that a Biblical historian were to argue thus: "In regard to the genealogy of Christ, we have decided *a priori* that from Joseph to King David there must have been twenty-eight generations. We have the record of the second fourteen generations from Joseph back to the transmigration of Babylon. The records of the first fourteen generations, from the transmigration of Babylon back to King David are missing. But our theory of twice fourteen authorizes us in affirming that there were fourteen from Jechonias to David, and we will name them Josiah, Ezechias, and so on." One can imagine with what contempt Haeckel would spew upon such calculations. But he, wishing to trace the genealogy of Homo sapiens back to the anthropoid ape, declares *a priori* that there were thirty stages, admits that the first fifteen are missing, but *assumes* them, and *names* them. And this is science.

It is, however, quite on a par with the procedure of every scientist who claims to be able to trace the genealogy of man back to the ape. As Alfred Russel Wallace says, in that genealogy there is, not one, but at least a score of "missing links." The unsophisticated layman, not knowing the use of hypothesis and imagination in biology, would imagine that "science" would refuse to *imagine* a stage in the process of which there is no evidence. Therein, of course, the layman would show his ignorance. Science builds upon imagination and hypothesis quite as much as the theologian builds upon faith. The natural sciences, like the mental sciences, are not halted by *lacunae,* or missing links. Indeed, if there were as many missing links in theology as there are in biology, no theologian would be bold enough to ask a hearing, and no theologian would expect anything but ridicule for his theories. But every evolutionist knows that you may ridicule theology because it does not prove its every step with mathematical precision. But you must not ridicule biology for making use of hypothesis. You must not even find fault with Haeckel when he "assumes" fifteen out of thirty links in the chain that binds man to the anthropoid ape.

Haeckel is not only dogmatically certain of evolution. He is dogmatically certain of monophyletic evolution; that is to say, he insists upon the theory that all animals and men have derived from one, and not several original species. With his customary cocksureness, he declares: "It is impossible to doubt that all reptiles, birds, and mammals had a common origin, and constitute a single main division of kindred forms. To this division belongs our race."[8] Again: "It is inconceivable that all existing and extinct mammals have sprung from several different and originally separate root forms. We are compelled, if we know anything, to assume (!) the monophyletic hypothesis. All animals, including man, must be traced from a single common mammalian parent form."[9] And he calls this an "irrefutable proposition."

So he dogmatizes against those of his fellow scientists who believe in evolution, though not monophyletic evolution, as truculently as against the imbeciles who will not believe in evolution at all.

Let us, however, comment no more on the blatant dogmatism of those two passages. Let us pause only for a moment to make sure that the significant phrase, "We are compelled to assume," does not go unnoticed. In our simplicity, we may have held that "science" was not compelled to assume anything, but was prepared to prove everything. We stand corrected—and chastened. And if, also in our guilelessness, we imagined that no one could be compelled to assume "the monophyletic hypothesis" or any other hypothesis—that there was only one thing ascientifically-minded person is compelled to assume—a fact,—again let us confess that we are duly castigated and corrected.

But, being compelled to assume, not only evolution, but evolution of all reptiles, birds, and mammals, including man, from *one* root form, we cannot but lament that this makes evolution even harder to accept than we had anticipated. For there are limits, after all, to the power of the human imagination. It is not so hard to imagine that a hawk or an eagle had the same ultimate ancestor. But it is hard to imagine that an eagle and a humming

bird are from the one same primary species. It is not hard to imagine that a dog and a wolf are from one stock. But the imagination is strained a bit when called upon to picture one common ancestor of the dog and the cat. A shark and a wren, a camel and a Pomeranian poodle, an elephant and a canary, a rhinoceros and a dachshund, a hippopotamus and a butterfly, a kangaroo and a tree toad may all be descended, not from various original species, but from one and the same original pair of progenitors. But the theory staggers the imagination. Ask me to believe that the zebra, the donkey, and the horse had a common ancestor, and I say, "Quite probably!" Tell me that the race horse, the draft horse, and the cab horse are brothers, and I can believe you. Tell me even that the tiger and the pussy cat are of one species, and I will smother my rebellious imagination and believe. But when you fulminate the dogma that a hen is only a degraded dinosaur, or that a cow is a walrus that took to the land, you must pardon me if my mind balks a little before it will submit. Scientific faith makes a greater demand upon me than theological faith. Yet, of the score of millions who have read all these things in Haeckel, millions seem to believe him without a struggle. But we simple folk who are not overly scientific cannot understand why people who believe all that, should hold up their hands in scandal and horror when we say that we believe in the Trinity or the Incarnation, or in life after death. A man who can accept the brain-dizzying dogmas of Ernst Haeckel should see no difficulty in a few little theological mysteries.

Haeckel, though an unbeliever, has a creed of his own. "The Universe," he says, "is eternal, infinite, and illimitable." The devout evolutionist answers "Credo!" "It evolved from a vast nebula of infinitely attenuated material revolving upon its own axis." "Credo!" "Its substance fills infinite space." "Credo!" "It is in eternal motion." "Credo!" "Its movement is innate." "Credo!" "Every living cell has psychic properties." "Credo!" "Every cell has volition." "Credo!" "The development of the universe is a monistic mechanical process." "Credo!" "In that process we discover no aim or purpose whatever." "Credo! Amen!"

Since we Christians must choose between this creed and that of the Apostles, we prefer the Apostles' Creed—"I believe in God the Father Almighty, Creator of heaven and earth," and the rest. It is simpler, less arbitrary, more reasonable, easier to believe.

Haeckel, however, is not the only dogmatic evolutionist. When an international council of scientists met at Cambridge, Mass., in 1922, a committee presented, by way of preliminary to the proceedings, the dogma of evolution: "The council affirmed" (note the dogmatic tone) "That so far as the scientific evidence of the evolution of plants, animals, *and man* are concerned, there is no ground whatever for the assertion that these evidences constitute a 'mere guess.' No scientific generalization is more strongly supported by thoroughly tested evidences than is that of organic evolution. The *evidences in favor of the evolution of man are sufficient to convince every scientist of note in the world.*" Remember that this proclamation was made before the discussion, as if to intimidate any delegate who might feel inclined to cherish any little scientific skepticism about the certainty of the evidence for evolution. To all intents and purposes the declaration was a dogmatic formula. It might have been worded: "If any one shall say that organic evolution of plants, animals, and man is not a scientifically established fact, let him be anathema." Naturally the Biblical word "anathema" is avoided. But, in effect, a scientist who should say that evolution is still only a "shrewd guess" (or to speak more accurately an "hypothesis") is excommunicated from the body of the learned. He is no longer a member of the society of the "scientists of note in the world." "To doubt evolution," says Professor Marsh, "is to doubt science."

Now this may all be quite true. But we laymen would like to see it put just a little less dogmatically. We should be more highly edified by the religion of science if its popes and prelates would say—and mean it: "Nothing is ever definitely settled in science. Science is always open to new information. It is contrary to the scientific method to promulgate any doctrine or dogma." But, to tell the truth, it would ruin the reputation of any but the greatest scientist in the world if he now questioned evolution.[10] His name would be anathema-maranatha. Let not the scientists accuse theologians of intolerance.

Finally, since this discourse on Haeckel has led, logically enough, to the discussion of the offensive dogmatism of some scientists, let us Christians take warning and be on our guard against undue dogmatism and intolerance. The Catholic Church has not issued any dogmatic definition upon the question of evolution. Catholic scientists are free to accept it or reject it.[11] Members of the Catholic Church ought not to usurp the prerogative of making infallible decisions, nor should we who are laymen in science prejudge the findings of science. Let us take the only truly scientific position, that is, let us form our judgments strictly on the evidence presented. Let us call an hypothesis an hypothesis. If the hypothesis becomes an established fact, we shall gladly recognize the fact. We will not anticipate. There is no need of hurry. Between now and the time when, if ever, the evolutionary theory shall be demonstrated, so many modifications of its meaning may take place that it will be acceptable even to the most orthodox. Meanwhile, any theory of evolution that leaves us the right to believe in God and to call our souls our own, is welcome to a hearing. But if an evolutionist, forgetting the limitations of his science, tells us that evolution abolishes God and makes man not an immortal soul, but a chemical compound, or a mere animal, we shall repudiate him. If he tells us that our body is dust, we shall say, "We have that in our Bible." If he tells us that through the body we have kinship with the beasts, we shall say, "We know that too." But if he tells us that there is no strictly human soul animating his flesh, or if he declare

that no First Cause is necessary to explain the origin of either body or soul, we shall tell him that by supposing an effect without an adequate Cause, he undermines the primary law of science, and incidentally he stultifies himself. For reason and religion and science all combine to demonstrate that, though man is kin to the animals, "A man's a man for a' that"; and that whether this dust of the body came to us directly from mother earth, or indirectly through the beasts, there is a "spark that animates the dust." The whole mystery of man is that he is at once a brother to the animals and a child of God.

NOTES

[1] *Thoughts of a Catholic Anatomist.* By Thomas A. Dwight, M. D., Parkman Professor of Anatomy, Harvard, 1883-1911. Longmans, N. Y., 1912.

[2] *The World of Life,* p. 7.

[3] *Catholic Encyclopedia,* Art. "Evolution."

[4] Quoted in Dwight, *Thoughts of a Catholic Anatomist,* p. 43.

[5] Quoted in Dwight, *Thoughts of a Catholic Anatomist,* p. 43.

[6] Quoted in Gerard, *The Oldest Riddle and the Newest Answer,* p. 246.

[7] Walsh, *The Comedy of Evolution,* in *The Catholic World,* October, 1922.

[8] *Evolution of Man,* Vol. II, p. 136.

[9] *Ibid,* p. 142.

[10] It is worthy of note that the illustrious Virchow, anatomist, archæologist, anthropologist and founder of the science of cellular pathology, objected to the teaching of evolution in the schools of Germany on the ground that the hypothesis was unproven. Those who vituperated Bryan, and ridiculed the Kentucky Legislature, for taking substantially the same stand, might well take notice.

[11] See Dorlodot, *Darwinism and Catholic Thought* (Benziger Bros., New York, 1923).

Harry Thomas and Dana Lee Thomas (essay date 1941)

SOURCE: "Ernst Heinrich Haeckel," in *Living Biographies of Great Scientists,* Nelson Doubleday, Inc., 1941, pp. 233-44.

[*In the following excerpt, Thomas and Thomas offer an account of Haeckel's professional and personal life.*]

"In a recent microscopical lecture," wrote Haeckel to his parents during his college days at Würzburg, "Professor

Leydig suddenly stopped and pointed to me with the greatest astonishment. 'I've never seen the like of it in my life!' he cried. 'This young man can look through the microscope with the left eye while with the right eye he can draw what he sees . . .' This curiosity in my physical make-up," continued Haeckel, "is of the utmost importance in the study of natural history."

Together with his double physical vision Haeckel was blessed with a double mental vision. One half of him was an observant scientist; the other half, an imaginative artist. He was equally adept at sketching a human muscle and at painting a rural landscape. It was this combination of the seeing eye and the aspiring heart that made him one of the outstanding German personalities of the nineteenth century.

II

His stock was a mixture of nobility and peasantry—with the peasant element in the ascendant. He never to the end of his days acquired the refined artificialities of the aristocracy. In his youth he describes himself as "a wild lad with chubby red cheeks and long blond hair . . . careless in my dress and frequently forgetful of my table manners." Shy in the presence of other people, he was passionately fond of walking, swimming and collecting all sorts of curious plants. Always on his holidays from school he went off adventuring into the forest in quest of "new specimens of growing and living things." When his elders asked him what he wanted to become he answered, "I will be a *Reiser*"—a childish form of the word *Reisender,* a traveler.

He was destined, however, to do most of his traveling on the mental rather than on the physical plane. His father, a government official, moved his family from Potsdam to Merseburg and from Merseburg to Berlin. But Ernst did not accompany his parents to Berlin. Instead, he matriculated at the University of Würzburg. Here he hoped to specialize in botany with a view to following "the footsteps of Humboldt and Darwin into the tropical forests." His parents, however, had other hopes for him. They wanted him to specialize in medicine.

His entire university career was a struggle between his distaste for medicine and his passion for botany. "I am convinced," he wrote again and again to his parents, "that medicine is not my field." . . . "The study of disease fills me with an unconquerable disgust (which is due probably to weak nerves and hypochondria) and I shall never be able to adapt myself to it." On the other hand, he experienced the keenest delight whenever he discovered a new plant. "The day before yesterday I took a walk on the shore near the Main where the ships unload their cargoes. Suddenly I found among the shrubbery a strange, yellow-colored, cruciferous plant, related to the *black cabbage* but still quite unknown to me . . . Can you imagine my ecstasy!"

But his parents couldn't imagine his ecstasy. They told him to forget about his plants and to stick to his medicine. And Haeckel dutifully complied with their wishes.

He bought a microscope—having saved up the money for it by subsisting for a time on "sour kidney and buttermilk soup"—and plunged faithfully into his anatomical studies. He successfully completed these studies and absorbed his *materia medica*—"the most terrible instrument of torture ever devised for the intellect of man"—and passed his examinations for the doctor's degree. "And now, my dear parents, here I am—Herr Doktor Haeckel—a lanky, dried-up lath of a young medico, with shaggy, yellow-brown hair, a mustache and a beard—only three or four inches long—of the same color, and with a long pipe in his mouth." But when he comes home, Haeckel warns his parents, he will bring along with him something besides his microscope and his medical books. "You will have to reserve an extra room for a beautiful haycock (of plant specimens). This will become a pleasant addition to my botanical treasure house."

Even though he was now licensed to practice medicine, he looked upon "the hit-or-miss art of healing" as a high class form of quackery. "When you get sick," he said, "you can choose one of two courses. You can leave it to nature if you want to recover, or you can go to a doctor if you want to die."

Nevertheless he was "reconciled," as he told his parents, "to the thought of a medical career." For several weeks he served as an interne at the Würzburg Hospital, attending to the births of "those rascally babies who insist upon coming into the world at an hour when all honest people ought to be sound asleep." His "obstetrical duties" came at a most inopportune time—precisely nine months after the Würzburg Carnival. "During the period of my service at the lying-in hospital the babies arrived literally in shoals, so that I was awakened several nights in succession."

And yet, "since medicine is to be my career, I will try my best to endure it." Indeed, with the scientific nonchalance of the "finished" medical student he began to look forward to his first post mortem—"the most interesting, yea the *only* interesting part of medicine." And then he got his initial post mortem—an autopsy upon the body of a fellow interne "to whom I had been talking intimately only a few days ago." This episode cured him of his medical ambitions for the rest of his life.

In deference to the wishes of his parents, however, he continued his medical practice for one year. But during this entire period he had only three patients—owing principally to the fact that he fixed his consultation hour from five to six in the morning. By the end of the year he had succeeded in proving to his father that he was not "cut out" for the medical profession.

What to do now? Unfit for medicine in spite of his training, he felt equally unfit for botany because of the *inadequacy* of his training. For a time he played with the idea of devoting his life to landscape painting. But he realized that as an artist he was merely a gifted imitator and not a creative genius. Good enough for an amateur—he painted in his lifetime more than a thousand landscapes—but woefully incompetent (he confessed to himself) for a professional.

And so at twenty-five he found himself confronted with a dark wall. Yet somewhere, he believed, an opening would rise unexpectedly out of this impenetrable darkness. For he had an eager faith in God—this young man who later was to deny His existence. In a letter to his parents he expressed his determination, under the guidance of heaven, to face the future unperturbed: "Fear God, do that which is right, and be afraid of no man."

III

Just as he had expected he found his opportunity—or rather, he *seized* his opportunity—in the field of natural science. He had wheedled his father into allowing him a year's vacation "for travel and general study." He spent the greater part of the year in fishing for "rare forms of sea life" at Messina. Among other interesting specimens he discovered and studied and classified those "pure and beautiful snowflakes of the sea"—the *radiolaria*. He prepared a monograph on this subject and on the strength of it secured a professorship in zoölogy at the University of Jena.

And then came the first of his two tragic romances. He fell in love with his cousin, Anna Sethe, a young woman "of rare gifts of mind and soul." They were married and lived happily—for just two years. It was precisely on his thirtieth birthday that his young wife died.

For a time his friends feared that he wouldn't survive the blow. "Work alone can save me from going mad." And so he plunged into his work and prepared within a single year a twelve-hundred-page summary of his scientific ideas—the **General Morphology of Organisms**. Throughout the writing of this manuscript Haeckel lived like a hermit, working eighteen hours a day and getting about three or four hours' sleep out of the twenty-four.

Haeckel dedicated this book as a living monument to his wife. He named after her one of his favorite *medusae*— a fairy-like jellyfish "whose long, trailing tentacles remind me of her lovely golden hair."

Three years later he married again—this time not out of love but out of a desire for companionship. He moved into a "roomy" cottage which he named the *Villa Medusa* and settled down to a lifelong study of the mystery of life. For exercise he took long walks—he was always a good athlete, having established a record in the broad jump—puttered around in his garden, and pounded on his chest with his fists "to make it breathe deeply" as he stood at the open window of his bedroom. Sometimes he resorted to this chest-pounding on his way from his house to the college— to the great amusement of his students.

In the lecture-room, however, his students felt nothing but the highest admiration for their teacher who "talked like the devil and sketched like a god." Sitting at a small table, except when he got up to draw a diagram on the blackboard, he delivered his lectures in a voice that was "perfervid, scintillating, assured." He expressed his ideas with deference to few and with apologies to none. He suffered from no sense of false modesty. One day when a friend asked him, "Who is your favorite author?" he promptly replied, "Ernst Haeckel."

But if his favorite author was Ernst Haeckel, his favorite scientist was Charles Darwin.

IV

It was in 1866 that Haeckel met "the genealogist of the world's greatest family tree." This meeting with Darwin, Haeckel tells us, was one of the supreme moments of his life. "The carriage stopped before Darwin's pleasant ivy-covered and elm-shaded country house. Then, emerging from amidst the creepers which surrounded the shadowy porch, I saw the great scientist advancing towards me—a tall and venerable figure, with the broad shoulders of an atlas supporting a world of thought . . . The charming, candid expression of the whole face, the soft, gentle voice, the slow, deliberate speech, the simple and natural train of his ideas, took my whole heart captive during the first hour of our conversation, just as his sublime words had taken my whole mind by storm at the first reading. It was as if some exalted sage of Hellenic antiquity, some Socrates or Aristotle, stood in the flesh before me."

Haeckel became the champion of Darwin in Germany just as Huxley had become his champion in England. ("The heresy of Darwinism," remarked an English clergyman, "has now entered upon an unholy alliance of three H's—Haeckel, Huxley and Hell.") Unlike Darwin, Haeckel announced himself aggressively as a missionary of free thought. "There is no God," he said. "And," added a facetious adversary, "Haeckel is His prophet." He attacked the "fanaticism of religion" with an equally vehement fanaticism of irreligion. He wrote book after book to disprove the divinity of God and to establish the divinity of Nature. And with the appearance of each book a new avalanche of vituperation fell upon the head of the author. At the turn of the century, when evolution had become somewhat respectable, a visitor at the University of Jena spoke to the janitor about the popularity of Haeckel's courses. "Yes," replied the janitor, "but I have seen him stoned down that street there." When he delivered one of his early lectures on Darwinism to a great assembly of naturalists, the audience rose in a body and left him to expound his ideas to an empty room. On another occasion when he came as a delegate to a Freethinkers' Convention at Rome, the Pope ordered a "divine fumigation" of the entire city.

The name of Haeckel was anathema everywhere—except in the little University of Jena. Here he remained undisturbed for fifty years. More than once he offered to resign from the university in order that "it may escape the stigma of harboring an infidel." But Dr Seebeck, the head of the governing body, always refused his offer. "I don't like your ideas, and that is why I insist upon your remaining here. In a little university you have but a little influence. In a bigger university, however, you can do a great deal of harm . . . Besides, the older you get, the less radical you'll become."

And Haeckel grew older and became *more* radical—and still remained at Jena. As time went on and his ideas became popular, he received numerous offers from larger universities at more attractive salaries. But he turned them all down. Here at Jena Goethe had written some of his finest lyrics. Here Schiller had taught history for ten years. Haeckel loved the traditions of the college. And he loved the atmosphere of the town—*das liebe närrische Nest,* with its meandering cobble-stoned streets, its Gothic towers, its fragrant little gardens and its gossipy houses whose gables, like the faces of beldames in fluted red caps, leaned toward one another "in a perpetual whisper." Above all, he loved the Thuringian Mountains that ringed the little city and kept away from it the noises and the traffic of the outside world. "Here I have everything I want, everything I can use. Why should I think of uprooting my life?"

In this quiet fruit-bowl of a valley nestled under the inverted bowl of the heavens he took his long walks and delivered his lectures and wrote his books and formulated the outlines of a new scientific credo—"the irreligious religion of *Monism.*"

V

The *Monism* of Haeckel is the *Pantheism* of Spinoza translated into the scientific language of the nineteenth century. *Monism* (from the Greek *monos,* which means *single* or *alone*) is the doctrine that the entire universe is a single unit. This doctrine is opposed to the *Dualistic* theory that the universe consists of two parts—the *Creator* of the World and the *Created* World.

The world, according to Haeckel, has not been created by an external God. It is the result of "one great process of evolution operating through an unbroken chain of transformations that are causally connected."

In this causal and unbroken chain of connections all plants and animals form a single genealogical tree from the primordial cell to the modern man.

The soul of man is no different from the soul of the lower animals. Both in men and in animals the soul is nothing more than "the totality of the cerebral functions." These living functions of the brain are ended at death, and so it is absurd—declares Haeckel—"to believe in the personal immortality of the soul."

Just as there is no soul distinct from the body of man, so too there is no God distinct from the body of the world. God is the sum total of the matter and the energy—the body and the spirit—that compose the inseparable unit of the world's substance.

So much for the theoretical side of Monism. Let us now take a brief glance at the practical side. In the evolutionary struggle for existence—asserts Haeckel—the law of competition among the lower animals gives way to the law of coöperationamong men. The human individual can best survive through the application of the social instinct of reciprocal interdependence. The most effective form of government for human society is *Nomocracy*—the rule of justice in accordance with the laws of nature. These laws of nature, as applied to human conduct, require mutual respect for one another's opinions, tolerance in religious matters, and freedom for the individual up to but not beyond the point where his freedom would interfere with the freedom of other individuals.

This scientific approach to human ethics brings Haeckel—and he admits it—very close to the religious approach. In summarizing the "rational morality" of his monistic religion he concludes that "man, since he is a gregarious (social) animal, must strive to attain the natural equilibrium between his two different obligations—the behest of egoism and the behest of altruism. The ethical principle of the *Golden Rule* has expressed this double obligation twentyfive hundred years ago in the maxim: *Do unto others as you would that they should do unto you.*"

And thus we find in Haeckel the paradox of a man who denies God and accepts Jesus. After all, Haeckel was not a *freethinker* but a *free thinker.* Released from the shackles of prejudice he had chosen a new path to the heart of the world's mystery. And he had found there the selfsame truth that had been discovered by the prophets of the old religions. The old prophets had said, "God is love." Haeckel merely paraphrased these words into the scientific dictum, "Nature is friendly toward the noblest aspirations of man."

VI

At the age of sixty-five he put all his scientific and philosophic thought into a single volume—*The Riddle of the Universe.* It became an immediate best seller and remained so for a quarter of a century. But he derived little joy from his success. For in the course of the writing of this book he had entered upon the second of his tragic romances. One day in 1898 he received a letter from an unknown young woman. "Please forgive this intrusion from a stranger, and be a little patient. I will write as briefly as a woman can . . . By accident one of your books, *The Natural History of Creation,* fell into my hands. What a new world rose before me! . . . Is it any wonder that I require more after having read your book? . . . Will you reach me your hand, my esteemed Professor, and tell me what to read? . . ." Signed, *Franziska von Altenhausen.*

Haeckel sent her a list of books to read. After a few more letters they exchanged pictures, and then they exchanged hearts. Haeckel was unhappy at the Villa Medusa. His life had been embittered by the incessant nagging of a feeble-minded daughter and an invalid wife. Here was a young woman—she was only thirty—who soothed his "wounded old heart" with the balm of adoration. For five years they kept up a clandestine and passionate correspondence. "What an amazing thing"—he wrote—"that a young girl like you and an old man like me should have fallen so desperately in love with each other!" And Franziska wrote back: "Don't call yourself an old man. In spirit you are a young god."

They had several secret trysts, in various parts of Germany. "From the depths of my heart," he wrote to her after their first meeting, "I thank you for the two memorable days that brought me the happiness of your personal acquaintance . . . You must surely have perceived from my awkward behavior how completely your kind visit has upset the ordinary composure of my prosaic existence—the radiance of a sweet spring fairy who brings fragrant blossoms to the dungeon of a poor, lonely captive."

After another meeting—"How enchanting was our bridal journey yesterday!"

And Franziska to Haeckel, after still another meeting—"Our dear days together seemed to me like a beautiful dream too lovely to endure. Its memory still enfolds me so magically that it is difficult for me to express in words what moves my heart. Only be sure of this—in those few hours you grew far, far dearer to me than ever before."

Age, wrote Haeckel in one of his letters to Franziska, is no guard against folly. Torn between his disloyalty toward his own wife—he deceived her, he said, for her own peace of mind—and his infatuation for Franziska, he entertained for a time the idea of committing suicide. "The important question of self-destruction (the very term is nonsense—it should be called self-deliverance) has occurred to me very often in recent weeks." He gave up this thought in favor of another avenue of escape—a trip to the Indian Ocean. "Franziska, dearest, best beloved wife of my heart—I depart for the tropical seas to escape from you and from myself—two rare and extraordinary souls made for each other—who, separated, must wander lonely through life . . ." He traveled to India, Singapore, Buitenzorg, Sumatra, Java—but wherever he went he carried along his sorrow. "Man," he wrote to Franziska from Port Said, "escapes himself nowhere."

And so he returned home and waited—for what? "We must agree never to see each other again," wrote Franziska, "as long as your wife lives." Haeckel gave his consent to this agreement. And then they met again—and again.

Ardently they both yearned for the day when his wife would leave them free. But they expressed this yearning only by innuendo. "The poor thing," writes Haeckel, "has been in bed again for the past eight weeks. I assure you that I am doubly patient and attentive now." And Franziska, in reply—"You must be very careful of your poor, dear wife. How is her heart? Is there any hope?"

Every day, indeed, the doctors expected his invalid wife's heart to flicker out. . . .

But it was Franziska's heart that gave out. One winter morning Haeckel received a telegram from Ursula Altenhausen. "My sister Franziska died suddenly last night."

VII

Haeckel lived on for another sixteen years—tragically alone. And then, on a midsummer night in 1919, he fell mercifully asleep. "The riddle of man's life," he wrote a few days before he died, "remains unanswered. But—*impavidi progrediamur,* let us go forward unafraid!"

FURTHER READING

Bibliography

Bölsche, Wilhelm. "Bibliography." In *Haeckel, His Life and Work*, pp. 323-24. London: T. F. Unwin, 1906.
  A list of Haeckel's published works, with the exception of articles that appeared only in scientific periodicals.

Biography

Haeckel, Ernst. *The Story of the Development of a Youth: Letters to His Parents 1852-1856*, translated by G. Barry Gifford. New York: Harper and Brothers, 1923, 420 p.
  Haeckel's letters home to his parents from medical school, translated—according to Gifford's preface—in such a way as to "render into English *as literally as possible* [italics his] the exact words of the writer."

Zeitlin, Ida. Review of *The Love Letters of Ernst Haeckel*. *Times Literary Supplement* (11 September 1930): 714.
  Tells the story of the married Haeckel's relationship, via correspondence, with a young woman who went by the name of Franziska von Altenhausen, and lauds the volume as "a remarkable revelation of the conflict of love and duty. . . ."

Criticism

Jacobs, Joseph. "Man and Evolution: The Advance in Scientific KnowledgeSince Darwin's Day—Prof. Ernst Haeckel's Recent Books." *New York Times Saturday Review of Books* (2 February 1905): 1-2.

Review of *The Evolution of Man* and *The Wonders of Life* which places Haeckel's work in a historical context with Darwin's.

Review of *Die Lebenswunder/The Wonders of Life*. *The Monist* XV, No. 2 (April 1905): 308-09.
    An extremely laudatory review of Haeckel's popular book, "a stately volume of 500 pages" in a "translation well done."

Routh, H. V. "Chapter XVIII." In *Towards the Twentieth Century*, pp. 278-93. New York: Macmillan, 1937.
    Chronicles the steps by which Darwin, Thomas Huxley, and Haeckel "explain[ed] man's relation to the universe, thereby leaving him to discover his relation to himself."

Will, Allen Sinclair. "Haeckel's Own Evolution: Early Religious Faith of the Famous Expounder of Darwinism." *New York Times Book Review and Magazine* (15 July 1923): 1, 24.
    A review of *The Story of the Development of a Youth* which begins by announcing that Senator William Jennings Bryan, a well-known opponent of Darwinism, "has an ally"—the youthful Haeckel, who in his letters to his parents shows repeatedly his belief in God.

Anthony Hope

1863-1933

(Pseudonym of Sir Anthony Hope Hawkins) English novelist, dramatist, short story writer, and autobiographer.

INTRODUCTION

The author of more than thirty novels, Hope gained the most attention for his first adventure romance, *The Prisoner of Zenda* (1894), a novel recognized as the progenitor of the "sword and cloak" genre. Set in the fictional European kingdom of Ruritania, *The Prisoner of Zenda* combines such traditional swashbuckler elements as court intrigue, chases on horseback, chivalry, and swordplay from such novels as Alexander Dumas's *The Three Musketeers* and *The Man in the Iron Mask* with more contemporary touches, including firearms and railroads. The success of *The Prisoner of Zenda* prompted Hope to write a sequel, the novel *Rupert of Hentzau* (1898), and a collection of short stories, *The Heart of Princess Osra, and Other Stories* (1896), which serves as a history of Ruritania before the events recounted in *The Prisoner of Zenda*. Although Hope published several other adventure romances, none achieved the enduring popularity of his inaugural effort, which was adapted into a long-running stage play. He also published several novels satirizing English society and manners.

Biographical Information

Hope was born in London, the son of Reverend Edward C. Hawkins, the headmaster of London's St. John's Foundation School for the Sons of Poor Clergy. Hope graduated from Balliol College, Oxford University, in 1885, and began practicing law in 1887. He also mounted an unsuccessful campaign for public office in 1892. At first unsuccessful in business, Hope filled his plentiful spare time with writing, including his first book, *A Man of Mark* (1890), a collection of short stories that he published at his own expense, political novels, and social satires contributed to the Westminster *Gazette*. Because of his career as a lawyer, Hope adopted his middle name as a pseudonymous surname for his literary career. While celebrating his first major success as a barrister, Hope was inspired to write *The Prisoner of Zenda*, which he finished in four weeks. The popularity of this novel and *The Dolly Dialogues* (1894), a novel compiling his satires from the Westminster *Gazette*, enabled Hope to abandon his law practice to pursue a full-time career as a writer. He subsequently made frequent lecture tours of America, where he met Elizabeth Somerville Sheldon, his future wife. His non-military work for the British government during World War I earned him a knighthood in 1918. He settled in Surrey,

where he continued to write novels, short stories, and pamphlets until his death in 1933.

Major Works

Hope's early work includes the short stories collected in *A Man of Mark* and the political novel *The God in the Car* (1894), as well as several other novels with historical, social, and political themes. Critics noted that the events and characters in *The God in the Car* paralleled the career of real-life politician Cecil Rhodes, who is depicted as conniving and amoral. A series of articles lampooning British society, *The Dolly Dialogues* won Hope moderate public and critical attention, including favorable notice from George Meredith. *The Dolly Dialogues* concerns a flighty and superficial young woman's observations on upper-class culture and manners. Hope returned to a story he had written in *A Man of Mark* concerning an adventure in the fictional South American country of Aurentland for the inspiration for Ruritania, the setting for *The Prisoner of Zenda* and subsequent fiction. Narrated by Rudolph Rassendyll, a descendent of

Ruritanian royalty who excels in swordplay and horsemanship, the story is admired for Rudolph's refusal to take the fantastic elements of his story too seriously, a comedic quality most critics agree is missing from the sequel, *Rupert of Hentzau,* and the short stories detailing Ruritania's distant past collected in *The Heart of Princess Osra. The Prisoner
of Zenda,* however, became the standard by which the adventure romances of Rider Haggard and Robert Louis Stevenson were judged. Hope created the Balkan country of Kravonic for *Sophy of Kravonia,* another adventure romance that became instantly popular. The novel's heroine is a scullery maid who becomes queen of Kravonia, is deposed, and mounts a campaign of vengeance against her husband's assassins. Hope continued to be a prolific writer, publishing plays, novels, short stories, and political tracts until his death. Most critics agree, however, that Hope's decision to pursue a full-time writing career imposed commercial demands on his literary output that had a profound negative effect on the quality of his prose.

PRINCIPAL WORKS

A Man of Mark (novel) 1890
Father Stafford (novel) 1891
Mr. Witt's Widow (novel) 1892
A Change of Air (novel) 1893
Half a Hero (novel) 1893
Sport Royal, and Other Stories (short stories) 1893
The Dolly Dialogues (novel) 1894
The God in the Car (novel) 1894
The Indiscretion of the Duchess (novel) 1894
The Lady of the Pool (novel) 1894
Lover's Fate, and a Friend's Counsel (short stories) 1894
The Prisoner of Zenda (novel) 1894
The Chronicles of Count Antonio (novel) 1895
Frivolous Cupid (short stories) 1895
Comedies of Courtship (short stories) 1896
The Heart of Princess Osra, and Other Stories (short stories) 1896
Phroso (novel) 1897
The Adventure of Lady Ursula (drama) 1898
Rupert of Hentzau* (novel) 1898
Simon Dale (novel) 1898
When a Man's in Love (drama) 1898
A Cut and a Kiss (short stories) 1899
The King's Mirror (novel) 1899
Captain Dieppe (novel) 1900
Quisanté (novel) 1900
Tristam of Blent (novel) 1901
The Intrusions of Peggy (novel) 1902
Double Harness (novel) 1904
A Servant of the Public (novel) 1905
Sophy of Kravonia (novel) 1906
Helena's Path (novel) 1907

Tales of Two People (novel) 1907
The Great Miss Driver (novel) 1908
Love's Logic, and Other Stories (short stories) 1908
Second String (novel) 1910
Mrs. Maxon Protests (novel) 1911
A Young Man's Year (novel) 1915
Beaumaroy Home from the Wars (novel) 1919
Lucinda (novel) 1920
English Nell** (drama) [with Edward Rose] 1925
Little Tiger (novel) 1925

*This novel was adapted into the drama *Rupert of Hentzau* in 1899.
**This drama is an adaptation of the novel *Simon Dale.*

CRITICISM

Sarah Barnwell Elliott (essay date 1894)

SOURCE: A review of *A Change of Air,* in the *Sewanee Review,* Vol. 3, No. 1, November, 1894, p. 98.

[*In the following review of* A Change of Air, *Elliott admires Hope's characterizations, but finds the novel less satisfying than* The Prisoner of Zenda.]

[In] **A Change of Air,** we find a short biographical sketch, a picture of Anthony Hope, and the fact that his full name is Anthony Hope Hawkins. Mr. Hawkins was born in 1863, is the son of a clergyman, a graduate of Oxford, a lawyer with chambers in the Middle Temple, stood as Liberal candidate for Parliament, was defeated by Viscount Curzon, and wrote his first book in 1890. *A Change of Air* is his seventh and latest story, and is in marked contrast to **The Prisoner of Zenda.** It is clever, but not as clever; it is humorous, bright, cheerful, and pathetic, but all in a less degree than the former book. Perhaps we think this because we are so accustomed to English country life as shown in books and so unaccustomed to the Kingdom of Ruritania. Perhaps it is because we read possible stories constantly and fairy stories never, that we are so charmed with **The Prisoner of Zenda.** Be that as it may, thereseems to be a glamour over the one that does not rest on the other. The characters in **A Change of Air** are admirably drawn, Philip Hume being the best, perhaps, the Mayor, Mrs. Hodges, and Johnstone coming very close on his heels. Tora Smith is better done, we think, than either Janet or Nellie, save at the end, where Nellie makes her confession. Roberts is put in as well as a Radical grown too radical, in short, a lunatic, can be, and the would-be murder and actual suicide grow well nigh humorous in his hands. The story moves easily, carries the reader along, and ends happily, so that, perhaps, it fulfils better than its companion volume the whole duty of the novel, for *The Prisoner of Zenda* ends with a touch of pathos that is rather keen to be amusing.

Frederic Taber Cooper (essay date 1912)

SOURCE: "Anthony Hope," in *Some English Story Tellers: A Book of the Younger Novelists,* Henry Holt and Company, 1912, pp. 232-51.

[*In the following excerpt, Cooper praises Hope's literary technique, and his ability to write well consistently in different genres.*]

It is a sufficiently pleasant task to undertake to write a brief appreciation of Mr. Anthony Hope. The prevailing urbanity of his manner, the sustained sparkle of his wit, the agreeable expectation that he arouses of something stimulating about to happen, largely disarm criticism. Besides, he does not seem to demand to be taken too seriously; he is not a preacher or reformer, he is not trying to revolutionize the world; he is too well pleased with men and women as they actually are, to desire to make them something different. In short, he is a suave and charming public entertainer, and like all wise entertainers he alters the character of his program in accordance with the fluctuations of public taste. And being both versatile and farsighted he is usually in the van of each new movement. *The God in the Car,* his story of gigantic land speculations in South Africa, with the Herculean figure whom he chooses to disguise under the name of "Juggernaut," appeared in 1894, thus antedating by five years *The Colossus,* by Morley Roberts. *Phroso,* with its romantic setting among the islands of modern Greece, anticipated by a year Mr. E. F. Benson's analogous attempts, *The Vintage* and *The Capsina.* When the revival of the English historical novel was at its height, he succeeded once more in coming in ahead of his competitors, and *Simon Dale,* which appeared in 1898 and is a study of Restoration manners, with Nell Gwynn for its central interest, led the way for *The Orange Girl* by Sir Walter Besant, issued in 1899, and F. Frankfort Moore's *Nell Gwynn, Comedian,* which was not published until 1900.

But although he so cleverly adapts himself to the trend of public taste, Mr. Anthony Hope is not an innovator; he adapts but does not originate. Yet it is no uncommon thing to hear him erroneously praised for having created two new and widely popular types of fiction, the *Zenda* type and that of *The Dolly Dialogues.* Now, *The Prisoner of Zenda,* as we remember at once when we stop to think, is not the first up-to-date sword and buckler story of an imaginary principality; it was preceded, by nearly a decade, by Stevenson's *Prince Otto;* and the only reason that it so often gets the credit of being the forerunner of its class is simply because it was done with a defter, lighter touch, a more spontaneous inspiration. Similarly, *The Dolly Dialogues* are not the first attempt to imitate in English the sparkle and the piquancy of the Gallic

dialogue in the form that "Gyp" and Henri Lavedan have made familiar. Although it is quite likely that at that time Anthony Hope had never even heard of it, *The Story of the Gadsbys* had at least three years the start of *The Dolly Dialogues,* and even though it was done with a heavier hand, it succeeded in getting a greater effectiveness out of the type.

But, after all, statistics of this sort, while interesting to a person of precise and inquiring mind, have little or no bearing upon the sources of enjoyment which a surprisingly large number of people undoubtedly find in Mr. Hope's writings. And there is variety enough among them to suit all tastes. He began in a spirit of blithe and irresponsible romanticism; he has gradually come, in his later years, to look upon life in a rather matter-of-fact way and to picture, by choice, the more serious problems of life in the social world to which he belongs. Yet his novels, even the most ambitious of them, never suggest the ponderousness of a novel-with-a-purpose; he never forgets what is expected from a conscientious entertainer. And one reason why he so uniformly succeeds is that he is an exceedingly good craftsman; he has mastered the sheer mechanics of his art. It is never wise for a novelist, whatever his literary creed may be, to be wantonly scornful of technique. There are just a few erratic geniuses who, because they have in them certain big thoughts that are struggling for utterance and apparently cannot be uttered in the simple usual way, boldly break the established rules and make new ones to suit their needs. To draw an offhand parallel, they are somewhat in the position of a man who, although untrained in public speaking, is listened to indulgently because of the importance of what he has to say. But your public entertainer enjoys no such license; and the lighter and more irresponsible his theme the more perfect must be his execution. And it is because Mr. Hope possesses that magic touch of the born story teller, that such delightful triflings as *The Dolly Dialogues* and *The Indiscretion of the Duchess* seem to linger in the memory with perennial youth, while many another weightier volume has faded out with the passage of years.

Accordingly, Mr. Hope belongs to that order of novelists about whom it is not only more enjoyable but more profitable to gossip genially than to weigh strictly in the balance. It is so easy to become garrulous over volumes that have worn well and afford many a pleasant hour of relaxation. It would be purposeless to take up serially each one of his many volumes, analyze and pigeonhole it according to its relative value. The better and the franker thing to do is to admit that there are certain volumes by Mr. Hope which gave the present writer genuine pleasure, and certain others that gave him no pleasure at all, and that those falling under the first division are the only ones which it seems worth while to discuss. In his earlier period the mere mention of Anthony Hope conjured up scenes of spirited adventure, reckless daring, gallant heroes combining the good breeding, the patrician ease, the assured manner of the better class of young Englishmen possessing the double advantage of birth and education, who, nevertheless, despite their studied reserve and immaculateness of dress, are plunged by a whim of fate into adventures of extraordinary daring and sublime audacity,—adventures that would have taxed the prowess of Dumas's Immortal Three. It is a clever formula, this trick of taking certain types of familiar everyday people straight out of prosaic actuality and compelling them, whether they will or no, to perform romantic deeds against a romantic background. This peculiar combination was certainly a happy thought. It appealed to that latent thirst for adventure which we almost all possess; it unconsciously flattered the reader with a new sense of daring, a feeling that he too, if thus suddenly and surprisingly transported into Zendaland, might similarly rise to the occasion and achieve great deeds. There is no purpose served by analyzing once again the story of *The Prisoner of Zenda.* It is one of those stories the artificiality of which stands out glaringly the moment one starts to lay its bones bare. Any story which depends upon the chance resemblance of two human beings, a resemblance so close, so misleading, that even the wife of one of the two is at a loss to distinguish them, takes on, when stated briefly, apart from the glamour of the tale itself, an air of palpable falsity to life. And yet the fact remains that tens of thousands of readers have lost themselves, forgotten time and space, in their utter absorption in the dilemma of the Princess Flavia, who finds in Rudolph Rassendyl all the qualities which might have made it possible for her to love her husband, if only he had been as close a replica of Rassendyl morally as he was physically.

I do not mind admitting that personally I revert more frequently to *The Dolly Dialogues* than to any other volume by Mr. Hope. This is not merely because of the delicate touch and epigrammatic neatness for which they have been so universally praised. Superficially considered they are a series of encounters between a sparkling and fascinating little lady and a sedate and nimble-witted gentleman, whom it is insinuated that the Lady Dolly has jilted. Now, the real fascination about these brilliant exchanges of repartee lies chiefly in the subtle and yet elusive implications that we are always on the point of reading between the lines, and yet never quite get in their entirety. That Mr. Carter has long been a worshiper at the shrine of Lady Dolly, that he has many a time felt a pang of regret that his fortune in life has made him ineligible, that he considers her husband not half grateful enough to Providence and that his own assumed air of sentimental resignation has in it a little touch of genuine regret,—all this we get pretty clearly. And yet, we are well aware, all the time, that Mr. Carter,in spite of an occasional twinge of envy, would not change his condition if he could; that, although he may not be precisely aware of it, he is already confirmed in his bachelor habits; that he likes his freedom from responsibility, his harmless, unprofitable daily routine, his favorite corner in his favorite club, his innocent philandering with various young women, married and unmarried. He may, at times, deceive the Lady Dolly into commiserating him and blaming herself as a thoughtless coquette,—but never for very long at a time. The whole thing is a sort of grown-up game of make-

believe in which the players get a curious transitory, almost illogical enjoyment in feigning broken hearts and blighted lives. And yet there is just enough truth underlying it all to suggest that Mr. Hope was capable of more serious work than he had yet done. There was, for instance, everywhere a pervading suggestion of the infinite number of contradictory motives and impulses that determine every human action, and the impossibility which every man and woman must admit to themselves of deciding just how much gladness and how much regret is entailed in every least little thing that they do.

Almost without warning Mr. Hope proved that the vague promise of more serious work was well founded, by producing what, I think, the sober judgment of posterity will recognize as his most ambitious and most enduring work, *Quisanté.* Alexander Quisanté, from whom the volume takes its name, is not an Englishman either by birth or ancestry. He comes of antecedents almost unknown beyond the fact that they are a mixture of French and Spanish. With scanty means he comes, an absolute outsider, preparing to lay siege to the political and social world of London. In every way he finds himself handicapped. The foreordained course of education through which the English ruling classes pass as a matter of course and by which their prejudices and points of view are determined, has not been his privilege. In addition to this he lacks that inborn refinement which sometimes makes up for good breeding and social experience. His taste is often exceedingly bad; his manner is alternately too subservient and too arrogant. Of the higher standards of morality he has no perception; he is the typical adventurer, unscrupulous, insincere, monumentally selfish. But, to offset all this, his intellect is quite extraordinary; his brain is an instrument marvelously under control, and he uses it at his pleasure, to bring the lesser intellects about him under his dominion. Above all, he has the gift of eloquence; and when he chooses to give full rein to his rhetorical powers, he can sway his audience at will, and thrill and sweep them with him through the whole gamut of human emotions. Of the men and women whom he meets, fully one-half are antagonized and repelled; the others give him an unquestioning, almost slavish devotion. But he has a personality which cannot leave negative results; it must breed love or hate.

The other character in the book who shares the central interest is Lady May Gaston, a woman who, by birth and training, participates in all those special privileges of rank and caste, all the traditions of her order from which Quisanté is shut out. There isanother man, one in her own class, who would be glad to make her his wife. He is in all respects the sort of man whom she is expected to marry; and she is not wholly indifferent to him. But she meets Quisanté, and, from the first, comes under the spell of his dominant personality. There is much in him from which she shrinks. His social ineptitude, his faculty for doing the wrong thing, or the right thing at the wrong time, makes her shudder. Although fascinated, she is not blinded. She sees his vulgarities, she questions his sincerity, she even doubts whether he is deserving of her respect. Nevertheless, the spectacular, flamboyant brilliancy of the man dominates her better judgment, and in spite of her relatives' remonstrances, in spite of warnings from a member of Quisanté's own family, she marries him, unable to resist the almost hypnotic spell cast over her by this man, who is something of a charlatan and something of a cad. The greater part of the book concerns itself with the story of the married life of this curiously ill-assorted couple; of his success in the public eye; of her gradual disillusionment, which, bitter though it is in its completeness, finds her somewhat apathetic, unable to feel the resentment that she knows she ought, unable to acknowledge that she regrets her choice. This, indeed, is the most interesting aspect of the book, the domination, mentally and morally, of a woman of rare sensitiveness and infinite possibilities by a man with whom companionship inevitably means deterioration.

The next of Mr. Anthony Hope's volumes, which personally appealed to the present writer, is entitled *A Servant of the Public,* and is enjoyable chiefly because of the tantalizing witchery of its heroine. Ora Pinsent is a young actress, who has taken London by storm. She has a husband somewhere, it is said, "whose name does not matter"; indeed, it matters so little that it does not prevent her from letting Ashley Mead make ardent love to her, one Sunday afternoon, though all the while she "preserves wonderfully the air of not being responsible for the thing, of neither accepting nor rejecting, of being quite passive, of having it just happen to her." Thus with a single pen-stroke Mr. Hope has set the woman unmistakably before us. Throughout the book she practises the art of having things just happen to her, the art of dodging responsibility. With Ashley she drifts, dangerously one thinks, at first, until one sees how easily she checks his ardor when she chooses, with a nervous laugh, and a low whispered "Don't, don't make love to me any more now." She talks much solemn nonsense about her duty to the husband whose name does not matter, and about her intention to renounce Ashley, although one realizes that there is really nothing to renounce, nor ever will be. And when the time comes for her company to leave London and start on their American tour, here also she plays the passive rôle, neither accepting nor rejecting. It is only when the weary months of her absence are over and she comes back as the wife of her leading man, that Ashley begins to see her as she really is; only then that he feels her power over him has ceased; only then that he can say, "I no longer love her, but I wish to God I did!" It is not easy to convey an impression of a woman's charm, when it lies not in what she says, but in the way she says it; not in what she does, but in the way she does it. But this is precisely what Anthony Hope has done triumphantly in his portraiture of Ora Pinsent,—Ora, with her upturned face, with its habitual expression of expecting to be kissed, is one of the heroines in contemporary fiction that will not easily be forgotten.

Helena's Path deserves something more than a passing word of commendation, for it is an excellent example of Mr. Hope's deftness in doing a very slight thing ex-

tremely well. It has an outward framework of actuality, the atmosphere of present day English country life; yet into this he has infused a certain spirit of old-time chivalry and homage that gives to his whole picture something of the grace and charm of a Watteau landscape. The whole theme of the volume, which is scarcely more than a novelette, concerns itself with a right of way. The hero's estates lie somewhere on the east coast of England; but between his land and the strip of beach where he and his fathers before him have for generations been in the habit of bathing lies the property which the heroine has recently purchased; and, unaware of any right of way, she closes up the gate through which it is his habit to pass for his daily swim. He writes courteously but firmly, insisting on his right. She answers in the same spirit, emphatically denying it. He refuses to be robbed of his legal rights, even by a pretty woman; she refuses to yield, at a command, what she would have graciously granted to a prayer. As neither side chooses to adopt legal measures, a state of mimic war ensues, in which he continues to invade the enemy's territory, while she continues to barricade and intrench. And all the while, although they have not once met face to face, each is quietly falling in love with the other, so that when finally honorable terms of peace are concluded, it is already a foregone conclusion that the whole dainty little comedy will end with oaths of fealty and bestowal of favors worthy of a knight and a lady of the olden times.

With the passage of years, however, the author of *The Dolly Dialogues* has tended to give us fewer and fewer of these dainty trifles and more and more of his serious and careful social studies. In this class belongs *The Great Miss Driver,* and there is no exaggeration in saying that since the publication of *Quisanté* it is easily the biggest, best-rounded, and altogether worthiest book he has written. And yet, the first thing you are apt to think of is that the germ idea of the story goes straight back to *The Dolly Dialogues;* that in a superficial way, yes, and perhaps in a deeper way, too, there is a certain rather absurd similarity between them; just as though the author, having once made a pleasant little comedy out of a certain situation, had ever since been turning over in his mind the possibility of using it in a bigger and more serious way, until eventually he evolved the present volume. Not that Jennie Driver, heiress to Breysgate Priory, bears any close resemblance to Lady Mickleham beyond the very feminine desire for conquest,—any more than the Mr. Austin of the one story is a close relative of Mr. Carter in the other. The resemblance lies in this, that both stories are told in the first person by the man who in his secret heart loves the woman of whom he writes, but knows that because he is poor, because he has the natural instinct of an old bachelor, because, also, she has given her heart elsewhere, he must remain content to look upon her joys and sorrows in the capacity of a friend, and not that of a lover. To this extent *The Great Miss Driver* may be defined as *The Dolly Dialogues* rendered in a different tempo.

Yet, such a definition gives no hint of the strength, the variety, the vital interest of this story. In the character of Jennie Driver Mr. Hope has given us a woman whose ruling passion is to hold sway, to fascinate and bend to her will every one who comes within her sphere. And because of this desire she can never bear to lose the allegiance of any man, no matter how mean and unworthy he has proved himself; and herein lies the source of her life's tragedy. She is not content to be merely the richest woman in the county, to play the part of Lady Bountiful, and build memorials and endow institutions with fabulous sums; she wants also to be a social leader with undisputed right to take precedence over all the other ladies of the community,—and this she could do if she married Lord Fillingford, whom she respects, and who badly needs her fortune; but not if she should marry Leonard Octon, big, brusque, rather brutal, who is cut by the whole county, and whom she happens to love. It is a rather unique situation in fiction for a woman to be forced into publicly slighting the one man on earth that she cares for; still more unique for a woman who is pledged to marry one man to be secretly meeting the other man, and thus atoning for deliberately cutting him whenever they meet in public. And, surely, it was a rather audacious thing for Mr. Hope to attempt to make us feel that in spite of her double-dealing Jennie Driver is a rather big and fine and splendid sort of woman; that she would have kept faith with Fillingford had he been big enough to trust her when appearances were heavily against her; and that in defying convention and scandalizing the little world she lives in by fleeing with Octon to Paris, she is doing the one big, brave, inevitable act. Yet, that is precisely what the author does succeed in making us feel; and when because Fate intervenes and wrecks the last chance of Jennie's happiness through the death of Octon, we not only sympathize with her bitterness toward the narrow-minded social circle that had forced her lover into exile, but we also glory with her in the big, carefully planned and altogether adequate revenge by which she forces the county to pay tardy homage to the name of Octon.

Notwithstanding the statement made at the beginning of this chapter, to the effect that Mr. Anthony Hope does not write problem novels, the volume entitled **Mrs. Maxon Protests** comes critically near the border-line. Mrs. Maxon is simply one more young woman who has discovered marriage to be something vastly different from what she had imagined; and her difficulty is of the variety which she regards as almost humiliatingly commonplace—namely, incompatibility. Her husband happens to be one of those narrow, self-satisfied, dictatorial men, with old-fashioned ideas about women in general and a rooted conviction that a man has a high moral responsibility for his wife's conduct and must mould her in all fashions to his own way of thinking. Mrs. Maxon bears the strain for five years; then she consults a lawyer. She learns that while she cannot get a divorce in England, she can leave her husband and he cannot force her to come back. At the time of their separation, or to be more accurate, her desertion of him—for Maxon refuses to

take the matter seriously—there is no other man in her life; but in the weeks that follow during which she stays at the country home of some friends with lax ideas of life and a houseful of curious and often irregular people, she suddenly surprises herself by falling in love with a certain Godfrey Ledstone and promptly scandalizes society by eloping with him openly and unashamed. The rest of the book traces, with a clear-sightedness that Mr. Hope has not always shown in his books, the subsequent career of a woman who thinks that by the force of her own example she can bring the whole world over to her way of thinking. He does not spare us any of her disillusions, her humiliations, her heartache and loneliness. But through it all she is learning, strangely and cruelly learning, much that is exceedingly good for her. She is learning, for instance, that charity and sympathy and understanding are often found where least expected. She is learning, too, that there are many other standards in this world as well as her own and that they are just as reasonable and perhaps nobler. She learns that one of the best men she has ever had the good fortune to meet, loving her, pitying her, utterly disapproving of her, would nevertheless have made her his wife in spite of the scandal that had preceded and followed her divorce—but for one reason: he is an army officer, and a woman with a taint upon her name would lower the social tone of his regiment and be in some degree a menace to the moral tone of the younger set. It is a temptation to analyze at some length the separate episodes of this rather unusual book throughout the years while Mrs. Maxon is slowly finding her way out of the quagmire of her own making into a belated peace and happiness. Yet, after all, what the book stands for is so admirably summed up in the concluding paragraph that one cannot do it a greater service than to close with one brief quotation. It is a satisfaction to find a book written upon this theme which, while recognizing that there is much to be said on both sides, shows neither vindictiveness toward the woman nor a misplaced championship that would exalt her into a martyr.

> In the small circle of those with whom she had shared the issues of destiny she had unsettled much; of a certainty she had settled nothing. Things were just as much in solution as ever; the welter was not abated. Man being imperfect, laws must be made. Man being imperfect, laws must be broken or ever new laws will be made. Winnie Maxon had broken a law and asked a question. When thousands do the like, the Giant, after giving the first comers a box on the ear, may at last put his hand to his own and ponderously consider.

Such are the volumes chosen as a matter of personal preference, out of the generous series that Mr. Hope has so industriously turned out, during a score of years. Another reader's choice might be different, and who shall say whether it would not be as well justified? Because, the first duty of a public entertainer is to entertain; and, taking this for a criterion, the most that any one can say of his own knowledge is, such-and-such volumes have entertained me. It is obvious that Mr. Hope's own preference is for his more serious work, that with the passage of years he has grown more willing to allow the books of his romantic period to fade from sight. Yet, by doing this, he challenges a harder competition, a stricter measurement against a host of rivals. There has been no one to give us a second *Prisoner of Zenda,* excepting Mr. Hope himself,—notwithstanding that many another writer has tried his best. But it would be easy to name a dozen contemporary novelists who could give us the annals of another *Servant of the People,* or chronicle some further *Intrusions of Peggy,*—and one or two who, perhaps, could do it better. Mr. Hope is not one of the great novelists of his generation; but he is never mediocre, and even in his uninspired moments never dull. His *Prisoner of Zenda* and his *Dolly Dialogues* were both gems of the first water; his *Quisanté* certainly suffers nothing by comparison with George Gissing's *Charlatan,* separated from it by barely a year. As a chronicler of English manners he is certainly of rather more importance than Mr. E. F. Benson or Mr. Maarten Maartens, although not in the same class with Galsworthy, Bennett, or W. H. Maxwell. He will be remembered, I think, somewhat as William Black and Marion Crawford are remembered, as having preserved a wholesome optimism, an unshaken belief in human nature, and as having done his part to keep the tone of the modern novel clean and wholesome.

A. St. John Adcock (essay date 1923)

SOURCE: "Sir Anthony Hope Hawkins," in *Gods of Modern Grub Street: Impressions of Contemporary Authors,* Sampson Low, Marston & Co., Ltd., 1923, pp. 123-30.

[*In the following excerpt, Adcock favorably assesses Hope's work after* The Prisoner of Zenda, *a novel that Adcock believes overshadowed unfairly Hope's other fiction.*]

The dawn of the present century brought with it what critics, who like to have such matters neat and orderly, delight to call a romantic revival in fiction. As a matter of fact, it also brought with it a revival of realism, and both had really started before the century began, and have continued to advance together ever since on pretty equal terms. In the 1890's Gissing was nearing the end of his career, but the torch of realism was being carried on by Hubert Crackanthorpe (who died too soon), by Arnold Bennett, Arthur Morrison, Pett Ridge, Edwin Pugh, George Moore, Oliver Onions, Kipling, Wells (who divided his allegiance between both movements), George Egerton, Elizabeth Robins, Mrs. W. K. Clifford, and many another.

The romantic revival, which had started earlier, was well afoot during the same period. Stevenson died in 1894. Rider Haggard's best romances were out in the 1880's; Doyle's *Micah Clarke* and *The White Company* belong to 1888 and 1890; Sir Gilbert Parker came soon after; Stanley Weyman and Anthony Hope arrived in the movement together, when the century was still in its infancy.

All these were in the same boat but, to adopt Douglas Jerrold's pun, with very different skulls; how they are to take rank in the hierarchy of letters is not my concern at the moment—I am only saying they were all romantics. That Weyman might have been something else is indicated by the strong, quiet realism of his second book, *The New Rector,* and the much later novels he has written, after an inactive interval of ten years, *The Great House,* and *Ovington's Bank;* and that Anthony Hope Hawkins might have been something else is the inference you draw from nearly all his work after *The Intrusions of Peggy.*

His father was the Vicar of St. Bride's, Fleet Street, and he was a nephew, or some other near relation, of the famous "hanging judge," Sir Henry Hawkins. From Marlborough he passed to Balliol, Oxford, where he took his M.A. degree and was president of the Oxford Union Society. He seems to have set out with an eye on a career at the Bar which should lead him into the House of Commons. But though he was, like Stanley Weyman, duly called to the Bar, like Weyman, he did not do anything much in the way of practising. Once he put up as a Parliamentary candidate, but was not elected; yet one can imagine him as an ideal Member—he has the distinguished presence, the urbane, genially courteous manner, the even temper and nimbleness of mind that ought to but do not always go to the making of an Attorney General and, as any who have heard him take part in after-dinner discussions will know, in addressing an audience he has all the gifts of clarity, ease and humour that make the successful public speaker.

But law and politics piped to him in vain, and his ambition took the right turning when he wrote his first novel, *A Man of Mark.* It was a deft and lively enough tale; it was read and talked about, and was considered promising, but caused no particular excitement. The excitement was waiting for his next book. When *The Prisoner of Zenda* burst upon the town, in 1894, it leaped into success at once. Stanley Weyman's *Under the Red Robe* was issued almost simultaneously and the two ran a wild race for popularity and both won. Both were dramatised promptly, and repeated on the stage the dazzling success they had enjoyed between covers. Each inspired a large school of imitators, which increased and multiplied until the sword and cloak romance, and stories of imaginary kingdoms were, in a few years, almost as plentiful as blackberries and began to become a drug in the market. But, meanwhile, the spirit of romance was awake and abroad, and any capable novelist who rode into the library lists wearing her favours was pretty sure of a welcome.

In that same bustling year, 1894, we had from Anthony Hope *The God in the Car,* a tale of a South African Company promoter, and *The Dolly Dialogues.* These were not in a direct line of descent from *The Prisoner of Zenda,* and were possibly written before that; they were, at all events, written before the enormous vogue of that could prompt the author to follow it with another of the same desirable brand. But *The Dolly Dialogues* soared to an independent success of their own. Those crisp, neat, entertaining chats of that adroitest of flirts, Dolly Foster, with her husband, with Mr. Carter, and others of her fashionable circle, were not without a certain distant likeness to the bright, irresponsible talk of "Dodo", and repeated the triumph that had been "Dodo's" a decade earlier. The *Dialogues* set another fashion, and generated another school of imitators. Whether people ever talked with such consistent brilliance in real life was of no consequence; it was amusing, clever talk, it was often witty, and when it was not it was crisp and smart and so like wit that it could pass for it. And in so far as such acute remarks and repartee were too good to be true they only brought the book into line with the airy, impossible romance and inventive fantasy of *The Prisoner of Zenda.*

With *Rupert of Hentzau* Anthony Hope was back in his imaginary kingdom next year; if the sequel was not so good as *The Prisoner* it had as good a reception; and *The King's Mirror,* and a romantic comedy, *The Adventure of Lady Ursula,* not dramatised from one of his books but specially written for the stage, followed in quick succession. For those were days when he was working strenuously and systematically at his art; to cultivate the habit of work he left home every morning, like any lawyer or stockbroker, and went to a room off the Strand—wasn't it in Buckingham Street?—where he wrote steadily for a fixed number of hours without interruption. The notion that an author can only do his best by fits and starts as the mood takes him is a romantic convention dear to the dilettante, but Hope was never that; he kept his romance in his books as sedulously as Scott did and was as sensibly practical as Scott in his methods of making them.

But he had to pay for his first popular success, as most novelists do. Jerome has more than once complained that the public having accepted *Three Men in a Boat* with enthusiasm and labelled him a humorist would never after allow him to be anything else. His *Paul Kelver* is worth a dozen of the other book, but it has withdrawn into the background and *Three Men in a Boat* is still selling freely. *Quisante* (1900) marked a new departure, suggested that Hope was turning from romance to reality. That study of the political adventurer and the aristocratic wife who realises she has made a mistake in marrying out of her order, is, as literature and as a story, a stronger, finer piece of work than any Hope had done before, but it was not what his readers had expected of him, and it did not win the new reputation it ought to have won for him, though the critics did not fail to recognise its quality. To the general world of readers he was the author of *The Prisoner of Zenda;* that was the type of novel they wanted from him; they continued to ask for it and would not willingly take any other. He humoured them at intervals with *The Intrusions of Peggy,* and *Sophy of Kravonia,* but on the whole he had done with such light entertainments and settled down to the serious interpretation of modern life and character. Next to *Quisante,* I would place his poignant and dramatic handling of the marriage problem in *Double Harness,* the study, in *A*

Servant of the Public, of a temperament that is only baffling by reason of its elemental simplicity; the masterly realistic presentment of a capable, courageous, unconventional, attractive woman in *The Great Miss Driver,* and the brilliant treatment again of the problem of marriage and disillusion in *Mrs. Maxon Protests.* These five—subtle in characterisation and fashioned of the comedy and tragedy of actual human experience—these and not his more notorious trifles are the true measure of Anthony Hope's achievement as a novelist.

But they are obscured by the flashier glory of *The Prisoner of Zenda* and *Rupert of Hentzau,* which are now renascent and appealing mightily on the films to the romantic susceptibilities of a new generation of admirers.

The novels he has written since the honour of knighthood was conferred upon him in 1918 are sufficient to show that his invention and skill in narrative are by no means failing him, though neither *Beaumaroy Home from the Wars* nor *Lucinda* reach the level of *Quisante* or *Mrs. Maxon Protests.* But *Beaumaroy* has touches of humour and character that are in his happiest vein, and if I say that *Lucinda* is an abler and more notable piece of work than is either of the dazzling fairy tales that established his position, it is not that I would belittle those delightful entertainments but would emphasise that, so far from representing his capacity, they misrepresent it; they stand in the way and prevent his better work from being seen in its just proportions, so that though at first they may have secured a prompt recognition for him, it looks as if, at last, they will, in a larger sense, prevent him from being recognised.

Malcolm Elwin (essay date 1939)

SOURCE: "The Romantics," in *Old Gods Falling,* Collins Publishers, 1939, pp. 279-89.

[*In the following excerpt, Elwin presents a critical overview of Hope's body of work.*]

Sir Anthony Hope Hawkins, who wrote under the name of Anthony Hope, provides another instance of a novelist whose success denied him fair consideration by the critics. The son of a London clergyman, he won a scholarship at Marlborough and an exhibition at Balliol, took a double first at Oxford and was President of the Union at a time when Archbishop Lang, Lord Cecil of Chelwood, Gilbert Murray, Sir Michael Sadler, and Quiller-Couch were contemporaries, and having been called to the bar in 1887, for a time devilled for Asquith. Like Haggard, he beguiled his leisure in waiting for briefs by writing, and in 1890 published at his own expense his first novel, *A Man of Mark.* The story is a political skit somewhat after the manner of W. H. Mallock, the flippant satire of which was pompously pronounced by the *Spectator* to be cynicism "nothing less than repulsive" and "not far off deserving the epithet of immoral." His second book, *Father Stafford,* though seriously treating the tragedy of a priest's falling in love, was also rebuked by the *Spectator* for cynicism and betraying "the prevailing tendencies of modern English fiction" in the year of the publication of *Tess* by the iniquitous Hardy.

Though only two hundred copies of **Father Stafford** were sold in the year of publication, and in addition to his work in the courts, he unsuccessfully contested a parliamentary seat as a Radical, he continued to write, and published three novels in eighteen months, **Mr. Witt's Widow, A Change of Air,** and **Half-a-Hero. Mr. Witt's Widow,** an amusing satire on fashionable society, had been out for fifteen months when Andrew Lang stumbled upon it, and remarking that he did not remember having seen any reviews of it, pronounced it "an extremely clever and capable novel" and thought the author "a little like" W. E. Norris, the popular society novelist of the day, with "a touch of Trollope." Lang's notice came out appropriately on the eve of the publication of **Half-a-Hero,** a political novel on the Parnell theme, which drew from Henley's *National Observer* an appreciation which applies to most of Hope's books: "Mr. Hope has humour, character, insight, the sense of fitness; he writes clean English; he is often witty; he is nearly always agreeably intelligent; so that you read him for himself as well as for his story." The sales of his novels continued slight, but the praise of Lang and Henley, allied with the amusing **Dolly Dialogues** which Hope began to contribute to the *Westminster Gazette,* attracted the notice of the shrewd Bristol publisher, Arrowsmith, who had started his "Bristol Library" of shilling shockers with Hugh Conway's *Called Back* in 1884, and his later series of three-and-sixpenny fiction with the equally successful *Three Men in a Boat* of Jerome K. Jerome. He offered Hope a royalty of twopence in the shilling for either a shilling or a three-and-sixpenny book, and Hope sent him **The Prisoner of Zenda,** the first draft of which, before revision, he wrote in a month.

Arrowsmith published **The Prisoner of Zenda** in the spring of 1894 as No. 18 of his three-and-sixpenny series, which included, besides *Three Men in a Boat,* two early books by Eden Phillpotts, *The End of a Life* and *A Tiger's Cub,* Grant Allen's *Recalled to Life,* and George and Weedon Grossmith's *Diary of a Nobody.* Its success was assured when Andrew Lang described it at the Royal Academy banquet as "the type of story he loved"; the immensity of Lang's influence was such that probably nobody else ever created a vogue for an author with an after-dinner speech till a late Prime Minister achieved as much for Mary Webb. Most of the critics, except Le Gallienne and the *Yellow Book* circle, followed Lang and Henley, and the book was the great success of the season, seven thousand copies being sold in the first six weeks after publication.

No account is necessary of the romance of Rudolf Rassendyll, the gallant red-haired English gentleman who is persuaded to impersonate temporarily the unsatisfactory King of Ruritania, a state somewhere between Ger-

many and the Balkans, and falls in love with the King's affianced bride. Nearly everybody who has ever subscribed to a circulating library has read the story, or if they have not, they have seen the stage play, originally produced by George Alexander, or one of the several films featuring Messrs. Henry Ainley and Gerald Ames, Lewis Stone, and Ronald Colman. By the time of Hope's death, over half a million copies had been sold in England alone—probably more than twice as many in America—and the sales still continue. "Ruritanian" has become the appropriate descriptive adjective for romances of imaginary kingdoms such as those so popular in post-war musical comedy. Probably the name of Anthony Hope will be always remembered simply as the author of **The Prisoner of Zenda,** like Blackmore for *Lorna Doone,* Thomas Hughes for *Tom Brown's Schooldays,* Lewis Carroll for *Alice in Wonderland,* and James Payn for *Lost Sir Massingberd.*

Yet Hope wrote many books after **The Prisoner of Zenda**—many that aimed at much higher achievement and cost him more pains and labour. Within three months of the appearance of **The Prisoner of Zenda,** he resigned his practice at the bar to devote himself entirely to writing—a step which he sometimes regretted in later years. For he was never able to escape from **The Prisoner of Zenda.** Just as the public expected more of *She* from Haggard, more *Lorna Doone*s from Blackmore, so it demanded Ruritania everlastingly from Hope, and was disappointed when it did not get it. When, in the summer of 1894, he published **The Indiscretion of the Duchess** and **The God in the Car,** Quiller-Couch's review in the *Speaker* represented the sort of review he was to receive for the rest of his life; it talked of "a touch of Dumas" and "more than a touch of Sterne," it found a chapter of **The God in the Car** comparable with a similar chapter in *The Ordeal of Richard Feverel,* both novels were "most entertaining books by one of the writers for whose next book one searches eagerly in the publishers' lists," but—though "the telling of **The Indiscretion of the Duchess** is "firmer, surer, more accomplished, . . . story for story, it falls a trifle short of **The Prisoner of Zenda.**"

He tried hard to escape from Ruritania. **The God in the Car** is a serious character study of an empire-builder, in whom contemporaries recognised an obvious likeness to Cecil Rhodes, though Rhodes himself, on reading the book, remarked shortly, "I'm not such a brute as that." In **The Chronicles of Count Antonio** (1895) he followed Conan Doyle in attempting mediaeval romance, and in 1898 achieved a much better historical romance in **Simon Dale,** drawing an idealised portrait of Nell Gwyn which despoils her of her charm of vulgarity. **Phroso** (1897) is what Arnold Bennett called a "fantasia", a satirical treatment of improbable people behaving improbably under a semblance of reality, which sustained Hope's reputation for wit and humour created by the **Dolly Dialogues.** Having adopted writing as a means of livelihood, he would have beenfoolhardy to resist the demand for more Ruritania, and the advisability of a sequel to **The Prisoner of Zenda** was proved when he sold the serial rights of *Rupert of Hentzau* for nine hundred pounds. The story of Rassendyll's return to Ruritania to fight the battles of his lady against the gay scallywag Rupert, whose character obviously derives from the popular legend of the historical Rupert as the dashing young victor of cavalry skirmishes in the Civil War, was followed breathlessly by thousands through its serial course in the *Pall Mall Magazine,* like Lang, who publicly confessed that he pined to know "whether Rudolf set up as a king for good and all," but feared that the story would not "end well."

With much skill Hope sought to compromise with his Ruritanian popularity by combining his styles. In *The Heart of Princess Osra* (1896) he set the scene in Ruritania of the eighteenth century, but the stories of the beautiful Elphberg princess's flirtations and courtships are told with the flippancy of the *Dolly Dialogues.* In *The King's Mirror* (1899) he created another Ruritania, but it was only a background for a character study of a young king, on the lines of the empire-building hero of *The God in the Car,* showing his progress from boyhood, through loves and intrigues and struggles between duty and inclination, to maturity and a political marriage. Some sound critics acclaimed *The King's Mirror* as his best book, though most, as Hope complained, would "not *follow* the writer, I mean, try to see what he was at: they always want him to have been at something else." Most of them, finding themselves in Ruritanian surroundings, hoped for more cloak-and-sword stuff like the adventures of Rassendyll and Rupert, and felt aggrieved when they received instead a brilliantly conceived study in the making of a monarch, the imagined autobiography of a young king, who was probably suggested by Louis XIV. Lang was probably exasperated by its "preachments":

> "I feel that I give involuntarily a darker colour to my life than the truth warrants. When we sit down and reflect we are apt to become the prey of a curious delusion; pain seems to us the only reality, pleasure a phantasm or a dream. Yet such reality as pain his pleasure shares, and we are in no closer touch with eternal truth when we have headaches (or heartaches) than when we are free from these afflictions. I wonder sometimes whether a false idea of dignity does not mislead us. Would we all pose as martyrs? It is nonsense; for most of us life is a tolerable enough business—if we would not think too much about it. We need not pride ourselves on our griefs; it seems as though joy were the higher state because it is the less self-conscious and rests in fuller harmony with the great order that encircles us."

But Lang must have recognised some scenes of fine drama, like the death of old Prince von Hammerfeldt, the statesman and mentor who perhaps owed a little to Mazarin, a little to Metternich, and more to Bismarck and Baron Stockmar:

> "An old man struggling hard for breath; gasps now quicker, now slower, a few words half-formed, choked, unintelligible; eyes that were full of an impotent desire to speak; these came first. Then

the doctors gathered round, looked, whispered, went away. I rose and walked twice across the room; coming back I stood and looked at him. Still he knew me. Suddenly his hand moved towards me. I bent my head till my ear was within three inches of his lips; I could hear nothing. I saw a doctor standing by, watch in hand; he was timing the breath that grew slower and slower. 'Will he speak?' I asked in a whisper; a shake of the head answered me. I looked again into his eyes; now he seemed to speak to me. My face grew hot and red, but I did not speak to him. Yet I stroked his hand, and there was a gleam of understanding in his eyes. A moment later his eyes closed; the gasps became slower and slower. I raised my head and looked across at the doctor. His watch had a gold front protecting the glass; he shut the front on the face with a click."

The King's Mirror was followed in 1900 by another ambitious novel, *Quisanté,* the study of an opportunist adventurer in English politics, whose conception was generally reckoned to have been suggested by Disraeli's career. The tale of his tragedy, and the tragedy of the noble woman he married, represents perhaps Hope's highest achievement; certainly he wrote nothing better afterwards, and none of his books more lucidly reflects the command of language which was Hope's major gift and charm.

The charm of the unscrupulous Quisanté fascinates the reader as it fascinated Lady May Gaston:

> "That strange, intolerable, vulgar, attractive, intermittently inspired creature, who presented himself at life's roulette-table, not less various in his own person than were the varying turns he courted, unaccountable as chance, baffling as fate, changeable as luck. Indeed he was like life itself, a thing you loved and hated, grew weary of and embraced, shrank from and pursued. To see him then was in a way to look on at life, to be in contact with him was to feel the throb of its movement. In her midnight musings the man seemed somehow to cease to be odious because he ceased to be individual, to be no longer incomprehensible because he was no longer apart, because he became to her less himself and more the expression and impersonation of an instinct that in her own blood ran riot and held festivity."

Lady May is as good as Quisanté himself, and her sacrifice of herself and her feeling for the decent and worthy Marchmont to the fascination of the brilliant cad, though conscious of his failings and repelled by his vulgarities, affords a subtle study of feminine psychology.

In *The Intrusions of Peggy* (1902) Hope returned to the vein of light social satire, in which he had already scored his greatest success with the *Dolly Dialogues.* These dialogues between Dolly, Lady Mickleham, a "bright young thing" of the 'nineties, and the man she has jilted were considered as "clever" in their day as the works of Mr. Noel Coward and Mr. Michael Arlen in the nineteen-twenties; they were praised by Meredith, and retain the curiosity to-day of a period piece.

> "'Besides, it's awfully *bourgeois* to go to the theatre with one's husband.'
>
> '*Bourgeois,*' I observed, 'is an epithet which the riff-raff apply to what is respectable, and the aristocracy to what is decent.'
>
> 'But it's not a nice thing to be, all the same,' said Dolly, who is impervious to the most penetrating remark.
>
> 'You're in no danger of it,' I hastened to assure her.
>
> 'How would you describe me, then?' she asked leaning forward, with a smile.
>
> 'I should describe you, Lady Mickleham,' I replied discreetly, 'as being a little lower than the angels.'
>
> Dolly's smile was almost a laugh as she asked— 'How much lower, please, Mr. Carter?'
>
> 'Just by the depth of your dimples,' said I thoughtlessly. Dolly became immensely grave.
>
> 'I thought,' said she, 'that we never mentioned them now, Mr. Carter.'
>
> 'Did we ever?' I asked innocently.
>
> 'I seemed to remember once: do you recollect being in very low spirits one evening at Monte?'"

The success of the dialogues naturally suggested the potentialities of a playwright, and Hope enjoyed several successes on the stage, though several of his novels were adapted for the theatre by other hands.

In the ten years following *The Prisoner of Zenda* in 1894, Hope published sixteen books, besides writing several plays, and his earnings for the period totalled seventy thousands pounds. In addition he was lionised in London society and much courted by fashionable hostesses. The strain of these strenuous years told its tale, and at forty-two he found that he had virtually written himself out. After *Sophy of Kravonia* (1906), a first-rate romance of an adventuress who rises from the situation of a domestic servant to become queen of a Ruritanian state, obviously suggested by the career of the Empress Catherine I. of Russia, Hope published only six novels during the remaining twenty-seven years of his life. These were all stories of social and domestic life, except *A Young Man's Year* (1915), in which he drew upon his own recollections of early days at the bar and in the theatre for the romance of a young barrister's struggles through vicissitudes to success. *Mrs. Maxon Protests* (1911), like the earlier *Double Harness,* deals with matrimonial problems and preaches the practical, perhaps cynical, philosophy that contentment and happiness depend on compromise.

During the war he worked hard on pamphlets in counteraction against German propaganda, and received a knighthood. He was "tickled" when he heard a young critic's remark that, if he was to receive a knighthood, it should have been from Queen Victoria, but when Haggard died, he wistfully envied that fertile romancer's retention of his inventive faculty through forty years. Hope's books in his fruitful years reveal all the equipment of the accomplished novelist—vivid imagination, shrewd observation, skill in devising plot and character, the sense of drama, an easy, cultured, and flexible style. Yet when commercial success had removed the immediate need for pot-boiling and he might have been expected to produce at leisure the polished work of maturity, the well of his creative gift unaccountably dried up. It seems simply that the vital germ of genius was lacking, and he is to be remembered gratefully as a competent, delightfully readable craftsman, who produced, besides the famous romances of Ruritania, two such satisfying novels as *The King's Mirror* and *Quisanté.*

Ruritania found many imitators, the ten years following *The Prisoner of Zenda* witnessing the creation of a whole continent of imaginary states. Sir William Magnay (1855-1917), a Hampshire baronet, wrote a good story called *The Red Chancellor,* telling the adventures of an Englishman in a state somewhere in east central Europe, ruled over by an intriguing chancellor endowed with the personality of a Richelieu. Another story of Magnay's, *The Master-Spirit,* tells of how Paul Gastineau, a barrister as brilliant and unscrupulous as Quisanté, being crippled in a railway accident, allows himself to be thought dead and becomes the secret mentor of a young barrister, helping him to a great career till his *protégé* becomes the favourite suitor of the society beauty whom Gastineau himself had hoped to marry.

Novodnia, on the lower Danube, was the scene of *The Garden of Lies,* an able romance which made the mark of Justus Miles Forman as a popular storyteller. If that voluminous romancer, William Le Queux, never invented an imaginary state, many of his secret-service stories had a Ruritanian colour, and Mr. E. Phillips Oppenheim, who began his prolific output of popular stories in the 'nineties, added at least one item to the imaginary map of Europe by setting most of the action of *The Black Watcher* in Bergeland. Memory does not recall if any Ruritania figured in the works of C. N. and A. M. Williamson, who wrote probably the first romance of motor-car travel in *The Princess Passes,* and whose husband-and-wife collaboration inevitably calls to mind two other pairs of collaborators, Alice and Claude Askew and Agnes and Egerton Castle. The Castles wrote some historical romances—one was called *Incomparable Bellairs;* the Askews specialised in sensational tales of society. Their books are now even more utterly lost in the basements of second-hand booksellers than those of such minor writers of a former generation as Florence Marryatt, Percy Fitzgerald, and George Augustus Sala, but their seven-penny editions offered entertainment on every railway station boasting a bookstall in 1914.

One of the best writers of popular romance who created a Ruritania was Guy Boothby (1867-1905), who wrote a tale of adventure and intrigue in an imaginary South American republic called *A Maker of Nations,* an able story combining something of Merriman's manner—his Spielman is a cosmopolitan in the mould of Merriman's Steinmetz and Paul Deulin—with the more obvious debt to *The Prisoner of Zenda.* Boothby was an Australian, who personally courted adventure in his unfortunately short life, penetrating the Australian bush to cross the continent from north to south in 1891 and travelling widely in the East. In seven years between 1894 and 1901 he published no fewer than twenty-three books, many of which enjoyed great popularity and maintained big sales in the old seven -penny reprints till the war in 1914. His best known books were *A Bid for Fortune* and *Dr. Nikola,* which had several sequels like *Dr. Nikola's Experiment* and *Farewell Nikola,* all relating the daring adventures of a megalomaniac scientist thirsting for knowledge and power, and incorporating much of Boothby's intimate knowledge of the East. *The Kidnapped President* was another romance of an imaginary South American republic, but his best Ruritanian essay was *The Fascination of the King,* the story of a white man who made himself the sovereign of a state in the Malay peninsular—a fiction suggested by fact, as an adventurer named de Mayrena actually established himself as king of a province in Annam during the late 'eighties, and was for some time recognised by the French government.

Boothby wrote a good story in a bald, clipped style, which has the merits of simplicity and swiftness, but a much better writer was E. W. Hornung (1866-1921), who provides one of the most inexplicable omissions from the *Dictionary of National Biography.* On leaving Uppingham, he spent three years in Australia, but returned to take up a journalistic career and published his first novel, *A Bride from the Bush,* in 1890. He wrote several Australian stories, one of the most successful of which, *Stingaree,* he adapted for the stage, and competently attempted the romance with a problem in books like *Peccavi* (1900), but his name is inevitably associated, like Conan Doyle's with Sherlock Holmes, with his creation of Raffles, the debonair gentleman-burglar whose adventures are related in *The Amateur Cracksman, The Black Mask, Mr. Justice Raffles,* and *A Thief in the Night.*

When Hornung died, Anthony Hope wondered if he had ever realised "what a low scoundrel his Raffles was." A scoundrel he was, and a cad, too, not only in his graceless habit of acceptingcountry-house hospitality to steal the valuables of fellow-guests, but in his luring of his friend and biographer into the career of an accomplice. But Raffles was not low; he never invites contempt, like Casanova or Cellini or Mr. Meyerstein's *Terence Duke,* but remains ever the most winning of rascals, such as

have wrought havoc with the hearts of women since the beginning of time, though Raffles has nothing of the bounder about him like most men successful with women, but, on the contrary, possesses the graces of a prince of good fellows, ever welcomed with a glad hand in club or tavern. We are sad at the wanton sacrifice of his brilliant gifts, sadder still when he becomes an outcast from society as a result of his crimes, causing his exile from his rooms in the Albany and his cricketing triumphs at Lord's—when he has to resort to disguises and live, hunted, as a pretended invalid or in lodgings on Ham Common. With his subtlety and resource, what a bowler he must have been! Never does he lose our sympathy and admiration, for he has the irresistible charm of genius, and when he commits his meanest crime by deluding poor Bunny into helping him to rob the house of his former fiancée, the reader echoes the feelings expressed by Bunny in deciding that, even though he had been tricked into the sacrifice of love and honour, he could not desert his friend.

> "It was Raffles I loved. It was not the dark life we
> led together, still less its base rewards; it was the
> man himself, his gaiety, his humour, his dazzling
> audacity, his incomparable courage and resource."

Like Sherlock Holmes, Raffles was killed and brought to life again; his second death, on a field of battle in the Boer War, was so fitting that Hornung did not again revive him, but resorted in later books to his biographer's reminiscences of earlier exploits.

S. Gorley Putt (essay date 1956)

SOURCE: "The Prisoner of *The Prisoner of Zenda*: Anthony Hope and the Novel of Society," in *Essays in Criticism,* Vol. 6, No. 1, 1956, pp. 38-

[In the following excerpt, Putt examines Hope's transition from a writer of adventure novels to novels commenting on contemporary British society.]

I

One day in November, 1893, a young barrister of thirty was walking from Westminster County Court to his chambers in the Temple, when the idea of Ruritania came into his head. He smoked a pipe on it, and the next day wrote the first chapter of *The Prisoner of Zenda.* This young man had already published three novels with only moderate success; a fourth novel was about to appear, and he was meditating a fifth. He was torn (as many werebefore and have been since) between the safety of his profession and the nagging itch to make more time for his writing. He made time. Within one calendar month the new novel was finished. It appeared in April 1894—for in those unenlightened days it was possible to see your book on sale within three months of completing the manuscript. (For biographical material I have relied solely on Anthony Hope's *Memories and Notes* (1927) and the authorized life by Sir Charles Mallet: *Anthony Hope and his Books* (1935).)

The creation of Ruritania made one reputation and has ruined another. Both reputations belonged to Ruritania's creator, Anthony Hope Hawkins (he used a ready-made *nom de plume* by docking his surname). The first, a reputation for a 'rattling good story', for romance larger than life and refreshingly unlike life, has had a sturdy survival. Three years ago, a Hollywood film company found it worth while spending a fortune on the fifth film version of *The Prisoner of Zenda*—a Technicolor version in which, to the distress of purists, the Elphberg red hair was overlooked. The second, a reputation for social and political comedy of a high order, barely survived the author's death in 1933. Its duration may be gauged by the ease with which it is possible to collect a library of Anthony Hope novels by scouring the less-favoured shelves of secondhand bookshops, at an average price of perhaps one shilling and sixpence per volume.

II

Zenda or no *Zenda,* it would have been difficult for the critics of the 1890s to forecast Anthony Hope's future as a novelist. All they could learn from the pre-*Zenda* books was that the young writer was remarkably versatile and productive. His first novel, *A Man of Mark* (1890), was published at the author's expense. It is a carefully contrived unambitious little tale of Aureataland, a South American republic—and the first step towards Ruritania. The plot includes a small-scale revolution with stagey late-Victorian 'effects' of horses' hoof-beats and presidential yachts; the dialogue is in the main stiff, with only occasional gleams from the future author of *The Dolly Dialogues,* such as the reference to 'a sum of money too small to mention but too large to pay'. The second novel, *Father Stafford* (1891), ushers in Hope's long series of novels of courtship, the common quality of which is a combination of quite astonishing naivety of motivation (as we say nowadays) and a singular aptness in conveying observed behaviour. Here, for example, is a sample of his commentary on Lady Julia: 'She had a considerable, if untrained and erratic, instinct towards religion, and exhibited that leaning towards the mysterious and visionary which is the common mark of an acute mind that has not been presented with any methodical course of training worthy of its abilities.' The jolt from this sort of urbanity to horrible fustian must strike a modern reader with an almost physical shock and reminds us of Anthony Hope's divided view of himself, his art and his public. 'Be it good or evil, she was his! Who forbade his joy? Though all the world, aye, and all heaven, were against him,nothing should stop him.' It is hardly possible to believe that the man who wrote the two passages could, when he sat down to dash off this sort of thing, wilfully mistake fustian for emotion, tale-telling for art, day-dreaming for psychology. The plot of *Father Stafford* is equally bedevilled. At first, all is pleasantly witty in the leisured world in which Eugene Lane, a wealthy young M.P., happily engaged to one damsel and mildly flirting

with another, turns aside for a moment to entertain his old friend Stafford, an ascetic but fashionable Anglo-Catholic priest. Stafford is charmed by the flirtatious Lady Julia, but only recognizes his own feelings when he sees them staring from the portrait of himself painted by an artist, another of Lane's house-guests. Horrified, he flies to the embrace of the Church of Rome, leaving Lady Julia to that of Lane. The amiable old cynic who in so many of Hope's novels stands aside in the wings muttering the author's own commentary, ends the novel with the observation: 'I think, Lady Julia, you have spoilt a Saint and made a Cardinal.' *Father Stafford* had grace and wit in plenty, but the young novelist was still willing, sometimes with insulting abruptness, to fob off his readers with archness, melodrama, or (as in the absurd revelation of Stafford's true passion *via* the portrait) downright drivel.

Mr. Witt's Widow (1892), the third pre-*Zenda* novel, offered a simple reversal of fortune' theme, an easy familiarity with the world of fashion, and a more consistent tone of light intrigue. Gerald, son and heir of Lord Tottlebury, is engaged to marry the widow of Mr. Witt. His cousin George recognizes her as a pauper whom he had defended years ago in an obscure courtroom—her crime being the theft of a pair of shoes. George must save the family honour, but his reluctant mud will not stick because he cannot bring himself to substantiate his hints and charges. He himself, of course, falls in love with Mrs. Witt. When, by another hand, Mrs. Witt's past history is confirmed and Gerald dutifully drops her, the reversed championship now undertaken by George brings him in turn into the social shadow. The whole enterprise is competent, novelette-ish, readable; once again the reader is kept firmly in his place, and wonders quite what to do, in the contrived pantomime, with such bonus gems as this: 'It was Mr. Blodwell's practice to inveigle people into long gossip, and then abuse them for wasting his time.'

Here is a sentence from the first page of *A Change of Air* (1893), the most successful of the pre-*Zenda* novels: 'Manners and etiquette are first the shadowed expression of facts and then the survival of them, the reverence once paid to power, and now accorded, in a strange mixture of chivalry and calculation, to mere place whence power has fled.' This is the world of Henry James—and it is true that in their shocking lapses into melodrama no less than in their set-pieces of social and moral 'placing', Hope's novels do remind us that his writing career overlaps, for much of its course, that of The Master. Yet two other qualities, one to Hope's advantage and the other sadly hampering, were already present in these earlytales to indicate how widely separated—how almost opposite— were the developments of the two writers; so widely separated, indeed, that the discovery that as men and artists they had something in common comes almost as oddly as the disclosure of Mr. T. S. Eliot's affinity with Kipling. The first quality, an inestimable arrow in Hope's quiver, was his fine ear for dialogue. (Henry James had a witty turn for social exchanges, but anyone who turns to his plays can see at once how far that talent was from the ability to point and polish actual talk.) The second quality, setting Hope at the opposite pole from James, was his modest concern to be a 'professional' seller of stories, always ready to disclaim the higher reaches of fiction, always ready to stoop to 'tricks of the trade'. Those very passages of social comment that a present-day admirer would most readily quote are often found in the opening paragraphs of his chapters, where they serve as neat exercises in suspense, interrupting and thus sharpening the reader's desire to know 'what happens next'— a trick less characteristic of James than of Dr. P. G. Wodehouse.

A Change of Air concerns an *avant-garde* poet, Dale Bannister, who rents a house at Market Denborough, thus transferring—in the eyes of most of its inhabitants—Bohemia to Arcadia. He quickly becomes involved in local life and politics, scales the county ladder, and when the local Radical quotes one of his own more revolutionary verses in the local press, hastens to disclaim his earlier opinions. There is an oddly distant 'period flavour' about the details of these conflicts between county snobbery and Radicalism, between literary Republicans and the entrenched gentry. But the human situation is both fresh and universal: it is not the prerogative of any one age or political faith to discover that flesh-pots are not over-stuffed with principles. It is all the more distressing when the young author, having set his lively characters in a situation at once entertaining and serious, urbane and symbolic, suddenly remembers the claims of the readers of 'tales' and introduces melodrama: Dale writes an ode to grace the visit of a Royal Duke and the aggrieved Radical, aiming an assassin's pistol at his Lost Leader, hits and kills by mistake the poet's jilted Nellie. Nellie is not the only victim. The novel's poise is shattered, the outmoded mechanics creak like pantomime trapdoors, and at the approach of the larger-than-life, all the carefully observed real life has fled.

A second political novel, *Half a Hero,* was published in the same year, 1893. It has a strong main subject, the rise of the new Labour movement and the shuddering rings caused in the social pond when a great stone, in the shape of a Labour Prime Minister, is plopped into its midst. The scene is New Lindsey, a British colony as remote as Aureataland or Ruritania, but peopled by a recognizable London society; one can hardly stroll in the Park of its capital city without bumping into Cabinet Ministers, the Chief Justice, or the Governor's Lady. Social and political strands are interwoven; the emotional and political temperatures rise together. Quite enough matter, one would have supposed, for a deck-chairnovel designed to catch one's interest without insulting one's intelligence. But no: the demand for melodrama, whether from within Hope's own nature or (more likely) his view of the reader's expectations, will not be denied. The Labour Prime Minister must needs be blackmailed by the husband of his ex-mistress, fall into a squalid public brawl, and be killed in a riot. Amused attendance at Government House and the Chief Justice's ball have hardly prepared us for such drastic goings-on, and once again the accumulated interest is scattered.

However sad it may be to contemplate the damage wrought to Hope's reputation by his over-production (a risk which in his case provoked the full ferocity of Gresham's Law), his early fecundity was certainly impressive. The year of the birth of *Zenda,* 1894, saw the publication of four new novels, and each is a prototype of many later books. Of *The Prisoner of Zenda* itself there is no need to speak—indeed, Hope's own literary reputation has been for too long a prisoner in that crowned and gilded cage. *The Indiscretion of the Duchess* is a piece of tedious triviality cluttered with duels, honour and diamond necklaces—and there were to be several repetitions of this formula. *The Dolly Dialogues* show the master of cynical repartee at his most scintillating—and there is not one of his thirty-odd books without the saving grace of wit. *The God in the Car* proves with what effect Anthony Hope could combine his strongest talents—dialogue and a knowledge of the world of affairs—when he set his mind to it.

The instant popularity of *The Dolly Dialogues* can be attributed to the sharp yet mellow note of their social satire: sharp because the wit has a pointed verve, mellow because the satirist, speaking from within the circle, throws his barbs with a smile of amused toleration and does not hate the objects of his passing ridicule. And so, although the badinage concerns itself mainly with such mild social misdemeanours as philandering, the epigrams scattered through the talk are not so much tart exposures as, in a sense, 'useful' observations delivered with a sly straight face. 'Economy is going without something you do want in case you should, some day, want something which you probably won't want.' No savagery there! Nor is there more than a shrug in the presence of social dishonesty—as when the narrator is surprised that Mrs. Hilary Musgrave should express moral disapproval of Lady Mickelham, because after all 'Mrs. Hilary is quite good-looking herself'. The exact quality of Hope's implicated amusement may be illustrated by the typical theme of one dialogue: a fashionable wife, piqued to hear that her husband has helped a young scapegrace to emigrate after embezzling money in order to live up to the social standard of the lady he was 'cultivating', relents with a pleased smile on learning that the lady was herself. The extent of Hope's participation in the world he exposes is everywhere apparent; his wit played well within the limits of late-Victorian social assumptions:

> 'She has a north-country accent.'
> 'It might have been Scotch,' said I.
> 'She plays the piano a good deal.'
> 'It might have been the fiddle,' said I.
> 'She's very fond of Browning.'
> 'It might have been Ibsen,' said I.

No entrenched order is likely to turn to rend so urbane a critic; among the chorus of praise there was grave commendation from Mr. George Meredith.

The God in the Car, the novel that is said to have caused Cecil Rhodes to exclaim, 'I'm not such a brute as all that', was the book Hope finished a month before he smoked his pipe over the notion of *Zenda.* Here, the political and the social comfortably cohabit: the political actions of the aggressive hero Ruston may flutter social dovecotes, but it is action based upon the world of the doves and is not, this time, a matter of swords and pistols hired from a theatrical costumier. Ruston is like one of the more dashing Elizabethan privateers who cut a poor figure at court, but whose shady frigates were financed by courtiers and by the Queen herself. But the significant quality of this novel is not Hope's ability to set our sympathy veering between the 'bucaneer modernized' and his more squeamish stay-at-home backers, but in the fact that Ruston's Empire-building enterprise is unfolded in outspoken talk among well-informed equals. The plot demands that the standards of society shall be violated by society's licensed Juggernaut, but those standards are taken for granted throughout and were shared by Hope's intended readers. Behind the surface tensions of a serene social group sniffing after glory and riches but, on the whole, daring not to snap, the theme is that of an intelligent woman, accustomed to act through her less gifted menfolk, suddenly confronted with a chance to act for herself—to sail away with the pirate instead of sitting at home with the shareholders. It was, in 1894, a sufficiently daring subject. It demanded a rare degree of 'handling'. It was handling of the kind Hope could best organize. There was no James-like hesitancy as to the nature of the enterprise or the price to be paid for full collaboration. The long struggle between Maggie Dennison's duty to her own personality and her duty to her circle was fought out in the open in passages of fine dialogue only occasionally marred by Hope's distressing 'ays' and 'nays' and 'recking of naught elses'. The climax (and this *is* a James 'situation') comes at a relatively low point, where Ruston confronts Maggie with the intention of 'sending her away' but blurts out that he wants her, while Maggie—whose intention it was to translate love into action by eloping with her pirate—finds her best qualities pulling with rather than against the social magnet, and returns to her husband.

'I am very nervous about it,' Hope wrote in his diary. *The God in the Car* had caused him more labour than any other book to date. It was well received. Personal tributes came from such ill-assorted readers as Field-Marshal Sir Evelyn Wood and H. G. Wells. The former as a man of affairs had known many people like the temptedhostess and her ruthless champion, but 'had never thought to have seen their inward minds so clearly set forth'. The praise is significant; its source is more so. Since Hope's day, there has been a marked decline in the chances of a Field-Marshal being enthralled by the work of a fashionable well-reviewed young novelist. The fault is not wholly with the Field-Marshals. Since 1894 the novel has broken new ground and Hope himself, writing today, would probably have had courage to give his imagination freer rein. But there has been loss, too—the loss of a cultured but not specifically 'literary' body of

readers, who must now search far on the fiction shelves for an intelligent treatment of the sort of problems they, as men and women in society rather than as experts in new modes of expressing niceties of guilt or frustration, know and understand.

By this time Hope had turned his back on the law and was to be for the rest of his life a doggedly 'professional' writer. His constant awareness of the reader was to lead him to squander his gifts on inferior melodramas, but those same gifts also informed his best work. His subtleties were to be subtleties of presentation, and his notable phrases would be valued for their sense rather than their poetry: they were never subtleties of expression rearing up a barrier between writer and reader. He wrote to be read.

III

At the end of 1896 Anthony Hope surveyed a profitable year of writing and then wrote in his diary: 'I have not been very happy. The writing does not, as a life, altogether content me and I grow more and more despondent as to my chance of doing anything really good.' Brought up as a Liberal and Broad Churchman, he had listened to the conversation at his father's dinner-table, had read the *Spectator* and *The Times* from the age of twelve, had followed a steady enjoyable course through Marlborough and Balliol to the Bar, had acquitted himself without disgrace as a Parliamentary candidate, had seemed all set for a public career. At the end of his life Sir Anthony Hope Hawkins, of whom Barrie was soon to write: 'He made more people happy than any other author of our time,' showed no disposition to be faithless to his first love:

> For the political life is in its higher grades a great one, and to be immersed in great affairs makes a man bigger. I have a strong liking and admiration for public men, and I have small patience with people who sneer at them; thinking to be superior, they are merely silly. One sometimes hears a tenth-rate writer, or artist, sneer at Cabinet Ministers, and the least gifted of them had ten times the brains possessed by such critics as these.

The division of loyalty implied by these extracts from Hope's diary in the first flush of literary success and from *Memories and Notes,* the considered summary of his life, is the clue to his status as a novelist. On the one hand, a sense of the dignity of public place and his ability to keep in step, both as man andwriter, with the world of responsible affairs, did preserve him in the long post-*Zenda* period from the temptation to produce nothing but a series of trumpery cloak-and-dagger imitations of that *succès fou.* On the other hand he was content to leave unexplored even in his most ambitious work those compelling below-the-surface areas of human personality which were exerting, throughout his career, an ever-increasing fascination over his fellow-novelists. Nor could he ignore bread-and-butter considerations; to maintain himself and his family in the higher ranks of comfortable officialdom he set himself to earn as much by his pen as he would have earned at the Bar or in public life. To this need, and to his own undoubted enjoyment in spinning an exciting yarn, may be attributed such 'tuppence-coloured' stories as *The Chronicles of Count Antonio* (1895) with its 'damned lot of "Ands" and "Nows" and "Buts"—pseudo-Scriptural' (Hope's own description, when he re-read the novel in 1913); *The Heart of Princess Osra* (1896), compounded of coy homilies and gadzooksery; *Phroso* (1897), chock-full of sieges, secret passages and smothered oaths; *Rupert of Hentzau* (1898), sequel to *Zenda,* in which Rudolph Rassendyll confronts again his engaging adversary against a background of high-souled cavaliers, high-falutin' loyalties and the involuntary charm of a period when an English milord could lightly order a 'special' on a Balkan railway; and *Simon Dale* (1898), an intricate historical romance starring Charles II and Nell Gwyn. Taken at a gulp, these amiable rigmaroles are still readable, once one has grown accustomed to the abominable peppering of 'ays' and 'nays' and 'what befells'; and *Simon Dale,* for all its swagger, comes very near to being a plausible historical novel of real worth. Several of Hope's romances were adapted for the stage (and some, later, for the films). He had always loved the theatre: financially, if in no more lasting manner, the theatre repaid his ardour.

The King's Mirror (1899), considered by Hope himself and by some distinguished contemporaries to be his best novel, owes its distinction to the blending in one volume of the inescapable romance surrounding kings with that mellower more intelligent attitude to life hitherto reserved by the author for his commentaries on the English social scene. For the first time, inhabitants of a Ruritania are allowed as much wit as the frivolous ladies of *The Dolly Dialogues.* The courtiers, still gaudy with Teutonic titles, utter aphorisms no longer restricted entirely to the themes of love and loyalty: much latitude was permissible at the court of a young king who could admit that 'the history of my private life is . . . the record of the reaction of my public capacity on my personal position; the effect of this reaction has been almost uniformly unfortunate'. Real politics and a genuine conflict between love and duty allow King Augustin to speak and write with a sureness of touch unwarranted in the overcharged atmosphere of Strelsau.

IV

Between the publication of *Zenda* and the end of the century Hope had published ten books, was busy with drafts or dramatized versions of several others, had seen his industry rewarded by a growing volume of critical acclaim and was collecting an annual income large enough—even disregarding the change in the value of sterling—to make a modern author pop-eyed with envy. Before 1900, when Hope reached his thirty-seventh year, the diary quoted in Sir Charles Mallet's biography includes such end-of-year entries as 'In money all right: £8500 about (about £3000 from plays, I think)—much

less than last year, but much more than it will be and more than I need.' No wonder he felt able, towards the close of his life, to advise young authors to invest half their earnings! Firmly established with a growing public, well equipped by upbringing and income to cut a respectable figure in social London, he could congratulate himself that neither financially nor professionally had he lost by the sacrifice of his legal career.

Yet he could never have become so skilled in the observation and exposition of the world of affairs had he not still hankered after a more active role. It may be thought that any English Liberal Duke who died, ripe with years and honours, round about the year 1900, must be envied as perhaps the last serene exponent of the art of having one's cake and eating it. Certainly, for a prosperous Radical, 'bliss was it in that dawn to be alive'. Anthony Hope Hawkins had been offered several chances to renew his bid for a seat in Parliament; in 1900 he accepted a Liberal candidacy but had to withdraw, on medical advice. He had come within a hair's breadth of active political experience—and it can be guessed that a man of his gifts would not have languished for long on the back benches, but would have played his part in the great Liberal administrations of the early years of the new century. It was his good fortune that at the time when a political career was finally barred to him, he could feel secure enough in the esteem of the reading public to turn his attention to the mellow 'inside' treatment of the English governing classes in their last autumnal glory.

The germ of *Quisanté* (1900) was a conversation with Lord Chaplin who described how the Bentinck brothers had 'taken up' the young Disraeli. In certain superficialities of manner, gesture and social origins the ambitious Alexander Quisanté bears a resemblance to Benjamin Disraeli, but it needs no Jamesian utterance on the process of artistic creation to lend credence to Hope's statement that his development of the character and career of Quisanté 'was in no way meant to represent or reflect Disraeli's'. There is a wonderful assurance in the writing of *Quisanté,* never previously attained (nor, I think, later surpassed) by Hope. He had begun work on it in 1897—and, for once, it *was* hard work. He took to heart the criticism of his friend the Duchess of Sutherland—'concentrate it!'—and produced the best-constructed of his books. In narrative deployment, literary tact, in the exposition of his major character first through the conversation of the privileged group he was soon to dominate and then in direct presentation of a complex personality—in all these aspects *Quisanté* displays Hope in full mastery over all the resources he had hitherto tried out in widely varying proportions. The opening chapters may be recommended to the attention of any would-be novelist who wishes to learn how to 'place' a character by deft alternation of narrative and dialogue, each paragraph witty in its own right and only slowly revealing a structure more significant than the sum of its parts:

'I think hands and brains are better than manners.'

'I'll agree, but I don't like his hands or his brains either.'

'He'll mount high.'

'As high as Haman. I shouldn't be the least surprised to see it.'

'Well, I'm not going to give him up because he doesn't shake hands at the latest fashionable angle.'

'All right, Dick. And I'm not going to take him up because he's a dab at rhodomontade.'

The general observations, too sensible for epigrams and more genial than biting, are no longer tricks to create suspense but have an organic relation to the book like that of imagery to a poem: 'Most girls are bred in a cage, most girls expect to escape therefrom by marriage, most girls find that they have only walked into another cage'— or again: 'As soon as the ultimate came on the scene, the Dean felt that the game was up; the Crusade depended on an appeal to classes which must be reached, if they could be reached at all, by something far short of ultimates.' In many asides, as when the Dean notes that for many men 'good form' acts as a substitute for conscience, Hope touches that moral-cum-aesthetic nerve already identified by Henry James as so significantly characteristic of the upper reaches of English life at the turn of the century. All in all, Hope now seemed to be in full command of his faculties and less eager to throw sops to Cerberus. His set-piece presentation of minor characters began to show an exuberance of confident enjoyment in the writing:

> It was impossible not to admire the wealth of experience which Mrs. Baxter had gathered from a singularly quiet life; many men have gone half a dozen times round the world for less. Whatever the situation, whatever the actions, she could supply a parallel and thereby forecast the issue. Superficial differences did not hinder her; she pierced to the underlying likeness. When all the world was piteously crying out that never in its life had it heard of such an affair as this of May Gaston's, Mrs. Baxter dived into her treasure-chest and serenely produced the case of the Nonconformist Minister's daughter and the Circus Proprietor. Set this affair side by side with the Quisanté business, and a complete sum in double proportion at once made its appearance. The audacity of the man, the headlong folly of the girl, the hopeless mixing of incompatibles were common to the two cases; the issue of the earlier clearly indicated the fate that must attend the later. LadyRichard could do nothing but gasp out, 'And what happened, Mrs. Baxter?'

> Mrs. Baxter told her, punctuating the story with stitches on a June petticoat.

> 'She ran away from him twice; but he brought her back, and, they said, beat her well. At any rate she ended by settling down to her new life. They had seven children, all brought up to the circus; only the other day one was sent to prison for ill-treating the dancing bear. He's dead, but she still keeps the circus under his name. Of course all her old friends have dropped her; indeed I hear she drinks. Her father still preaches once on Sundays.'

Within five years of the appearance of *Quisanté,* four more novels of society were published, all characterized by a broad-fronted narrative sweep and an exhilarating brilliance of dialogue which in combination are the mark of a more than competent novelist at the height of his powers. Closely related as these novels are to the exact social rules of the period, there is in them a vividness of individual portraiture, a fresh gaiety of commentary preserving the colour of life well beyond the validity of its social setting. All we have to remember, turning to Hope's best novels today, is that high social comedy demands the existence of a class system rigidly endorsed: only thus can spontaneity of revolt be measured, personal freedom be illuminated against social restraints, magnanimous or eccentric behaviour gain its proper effect of surprise. We have only to recognize the pre-1914 distance between Mayfair and Bohemia to enjoy, as Hope and his readers enjoyed, the busy unconcealed traffic between them:

> 'There are believed to be Bohemians still in Kensington, and Chelsea,' observed Tommy Trent. 'They will think anything you please, but they don't dine out without their husbands.'

> 'If that's the criterion, we can manage it nearer than Chelsea,' said Trix. 'This side of Park Lane, I think.'

> 'You've got to have the thinking too, though,' smiled Airey.

The Intrusions of Peggy (1902), from which this quotation is taken, has an extraordinary liveliness: it is as though Oscar Wilde had written the dialogue and Henry James the narrative, and the collaboration had corrected the faults of each partner with the unlikely merits of the other. When Trix Trevella is launched into society, the denizens of the different *quartiers* of Vanity Fair commingle in happy intimacy without losing their separate characteristics—good or bad, high or low, gentle or vulgar. This cross-fertilization, so to say, produces a vitality quite unimpaired by the intervening changes which might otherwise cause a modern reader, accustomed to view his social map in all its post-blitz uncertainty of outline, to ask what all the fuss is about. The early chapters of ***The Intrusions of Peggy*** have a marked(but independent) similarity to the organization and handling of *The Bostonians* and *The Princess Casamassima*—a quality made most explicit in that amused deliberate inflation of language employed by an author who is entertained by the parallel development of private and public lives. When Hope writes 'obligations' for 'unpaid bills' in the sentence:

> The freshness of delicacy is rubbed off, the appeal of shyness silenced, by a hand-to-mouth existence, by a habit of regarding the leavings of the first-floor lodger in the light of windfalls, by constant flittings unmarked by the discharge of obligations incurred in the abandoned locality . . .

—he is akin to James describing with affectionate distaste the milieu of little Hyacinth Robinson in *The Prin-*

cess Casamassima. When Hope, a few pages later, invests squalid violence with a mock-heroic objectivity, he is at precisely the same distance from the subject as James sketching the Tarrant family in *The Bostonians:*

> When her husband was sober, she never referred to what had happened when he was drunk; if he threw a plate at her then, she dodged the plate: she seemed in a sense to have been dodging plates and such-like missiles all her life.

Other parallels, in the lighter air of Hope's Mayfair, suggest themselves. There is something of Merton Densher of *The Wings of the Dove* in the character of Airey Newton; Mrs. Bonfill, considered as a social midwife, is sister to Kate Croy's aunt, Mrs. Lowther, and her brilliant set-piece presentation is worthy of a place beside that of Mrs. Farrinder in *The Bostonians:*

> At the age of forty (a point now passed by some half-dozen years) Mrs. Bonfill had become motherly. The change was sudden, complete and eminently wise. It was accomplished during a summer's retirement; she disappeared a queen regnant, she reappeared a dowager—all by her own act, for none had yet ventured to call her passé. She was a big woman, and she recognized facts. She had her reward. She gained power instead of losing it; she had always loved power, and had the shrewdness to discern that there was more than one form of it. The obvious form she had never, as a young and handsome woman, misused or overused; she had no temptations that way, or, as her friend Lady Blixworth preferred to put it, 'In that respect dearest Sarah was always *bourgeoise* to the core.' The new form she now attained—influence—was more to her taste. She liked to shape people's lives; if they were submissive and obedient she would make their fortunes. She needed some natural capacities in her protégés, of course; but, since she chose cleverly, these were seldom lacking. Mrs. Bonfill did the rest. She could open doors that obeyed no common key; she could smooth difficulties; she had in two or three cases blotted out a past, and once had reformed a gambler. But she liked best to make marriages and Ministers. Her own daughter, of course, she married immediately—that was nothing. She had married Nellie Towler to Sir James Quinby Lee—the betting had been ten to one against it—and Lady Mildred Haughton to Frank Cleveland—flat in the face of both the families . . . It was not small achievement for a woman bred in, born at, and married from an unpretentious villa at Streatham. *La carrière ouverte*—but perhaps that is doing some injustice to Mr. Bonfill. After all, he and the big house in Grosvenor Square had made everything possible. Mrs. Bonfill loved her husband, and she never tried to make him a Minister: it was a well-balanced mind, save for that foible of power. He was very proud of her, though he rather wondered why she took so much trouble about other people's affairs. He owned a brewery, and was Chairman of a railway-company.

If Mrs. Bonfill suggests Mrs. Farrinder, Mr. Bonfill is surely the literary blood-brother of Mr. Farrinder. (It will be remembered how *that* unhappy man was introduced—and dismissed—at the end of a similar paragraph with even shorter shrift: 'She had a husband, and his name was Amariah.')

v

After **Peggy,** three novels varied the social theme by the addition of one new ingredient apiece. **Tristram of Blent** (1901) turns on legitimacy and the prize of an ancient peerage; **Double Harness** (1904) seeks by studying a number of particular marriages, to arrive at a general view of that institution; **A Servant of the Public,** Hope's *Tragic Muse,* draws to the centre of the stage from its usual position in the wings his own abiding interest in all matters concerning the theatre—and especially actresses. Each novel is a solid achievement, but a certain failure of confidence, reflected in a reduced exhilaration of narrative power, allows more of Hope's native melancholy to affect the tone of his writing. **Tristram,** 'set in reality, but tinged with romance', suffers a little from that illogical irritation that afflicts the reader who, identifying himself with a hero, is offended rather than uplifted by that hero's tendency to self-sacrificing altruism. **Double Harness,** brilliantly sustained though it is, appeals to a reader's acquired experience rather than to his untutored instincts, and so gains approval rather than assent. The stoical author comes as near as ever he did to revealing his own nature in passages where fortitude is accepted as substitute for adventure and forbearance for passion. **A Servant of the Public** hovers round the theme of the attraction exerted by an actress, selfish, irresolute and fascinating, over an inhibited young man with twice her decency and half her vitality.

'He is sad without being sour', said *The Times Literary Supplement* of the author of **Double Harness.** The underlying melancholy running through Hope's diary, toning down his triumphs and blunting the edge of disappointments, was leading him—now that he had won the security to write as he himself wished—to dwell more and more on tendencies to withdrawal and renunciation. In **Double Harness,** Grantley Imason's spirited canter on the downs with his Sibyllamounted behind him like a captive princess may give a rare hint of lyrical passion: but it is quickly reduced by both participants to a more manageable level of affectionate independence. 'Between idle praisers and idle blamers, and one's own *inevitable* lack of a balance,' Hope asked himself at about this time, 'where is judgment of one's self?' The writer's life still failed to satisfy him wholly. (A writer who *is* wholly satisfied with his life is unlikely to become a good novelist.) A few years earlier he had noted: 'as I became a young man early from boyhood, so I am becoming middle-aged rather early from youth'. He hated and feared idleness: 'it lets the mind so loose for speculation and review'. Similar instances of an ingrained melancholy may be found in the Mallet biography and in Hope's own autobiographical notes. What distinguishes Hope from some other writers who nurse such temperaments is that he did not consider this attitude to life to be, in itself, sufficient equipment for a novelist.

A below-standard Ruritanian exercise, *Sophy of Kravonia* (1906), and another collection of short stories, *Tales of Two People* (1907), kept the pot boiling before the publication in 1908 of *The Great Miss Driver,* a full-scale study of a *nouveau riche* heiress possessed of great wealth and greater energy who fights to extend her empire over the territories, conventions and hearts of the county gentry. Plot and treatment come very near to the Henry James method; all the apparatus is there even to the detached observer who tells the tale. It is more expository and explanatory than any previous Hope novel, thicker in texture and more sustained in its organization of what Henry James called, so comically for his own immense elaborations, an 'ado'. (Once again one has to rub one's eyes at the knowledge that bouncing Sophy of Kravonia and the minutely observed Jenny Driver sprang from the same pen at much the same time.) In *The Great Miss Driver,* Hope waded in deep. He was not quite out of his depth in all the reiterated subtlety of analysis, but he sometimes gave the appearance of being out of his depth. His characteristic modesty as a writer did extrude, in this new vein, as a real flaw. The failure of confidence shows in such a passage as this:

> Well, they were the joy of her life—it would have needed a dull man not to see that. The real joy, I mean—not what at that moment—nay, nor perhaps at any moment—she would herself have named as her delight. Her joy in the sense in which we creatures—and the wisest of us long ago—come nearest to being able to understand and define the innermost engine or instinct whose working is most truly ourselves—the temptation to live and life itself, which pair nature has so cunningly coupled together.

In other respects the book is well within the Hope compass. Jenny Driver, torn between the attractions of ennobled privilege and the more virile claims of a roughshod man of action, is a typical Hope heroine; Leonard Octon figures as a Ruston or a Quisanté who leaves behind him a more turbulent wake. And the aphorisms, subdued to a thoughtful unbrilliant narrative, hardly stand out at all as clever remarks, but are barely noted with a sad acceptance of their literal truth: 'A mind that thought for itself in wordly matters . . . would very likely think for itself in moral and religious ones too—and such thought was apt to issue in suspending general obligations in a man's own case.'

Mrs. Maxon Protests (1911) returns to the theme of the price paid by those who rebel against the rules of society; once again Hope feels impelled to point out that retribution comes not so much from the world's outraged opposition as from the rapidly declining currency of liberty: 'social liberty might, it seemed, be more exacting than social bondage'. A lighter note had been struck in *Second String* (1910), a reversion to personalities and politics. It is the fable of a tortoise, Andy Hayes, and a hare, Harry Belfield. Andy, devoted to the gilded Harry, eventually wins both his girl and his seat in Parliament. There is a Jamesian mixed foursome; Harry is engaged to Vivien Wellgood but flirts with Isobel, her companion, with whom father Wellgood is secretly in love—a circumstance reinforcing his anxiety to defend his daughter's honour when he catches Harry making love to Isobel. A sub-plot or 'sub-atmosphere' made up rather implausibly of denizens of the London stage throws into relief the county setting—the whole complicated quadrille once again made possible only by considerations, now obsolescent, of marrying 'above' or 'below' one's station: 'The more definite a line, the more graciousness lies in stepping over it.' For all the comings and goings, the elections and excursions, there is a leisurely Edwardian pace about *Second String* allowing clever talk and witty commentary to flower more readily than in the laboured 'placing' of Jenny Driver: 'Harry's feelings passed a retrospective Act by which the love-making and passion became and were deemed always to have been, flirtation and attention.' The hare-tortoise situation is pointed in a phrase echoing the Hope of ten or fifteen years earlier: 'Neither of them is the ideal man, you know. Andy wants an occasional hour of Harry. . . . and Harry ought to have seven years' penal servitude of Andy.'

The Great War of 1914-18 dealt Anthony Hope's world its death blow. The last pre-war novel, *A Young Man's Year,* came out in 1915; by accident but appropriately it harked back to the days of his own first steps on the stage now overshadowed—his young hero, presented by a mellower Hope, fumbles his way to a discovery of the ways of the world and of himself. During the war Hope buried himself in work for the Ministry of Information (for which, rather than for his novels, he received his knighthood). He was growing exhausted, and when he hankered after his non-propagandist pen it was for the old adventure stories and not the more demanding effort to cope with the ways of the battered new world. 'If ever I can write again', he confided to his diary in 1917, 'it shall be a *yarn,* and not why Mrs. Smith proposed to Mr. Brown.' The yarn, when it did arrive (late in 1918), added little to Hope's laurels: it was a re-hash of an earlier 'love and honour' plot, *Captain Dieppe,* which bore no trace of reality or the old knack of dialogue, descended in dispirited fashion from Kings to Counts, and unwisely wore in the new world its 20-year-old tinsel. A final yarn, *Beaumaroy Home From the Wars,* dashed off at speed in 1919, turned sour with a strange disillusion. It has a ghastly scene where a crazed, dying old man gives audience from a shabby make-believe throne while under the delusion that he is the Kaiser. This pitiful mania seemed almost deliberately to figure as anti-masque to Ruritania and perhaps revealed that Hope was not unconscious of the twisted psychological reasons for at least part of the success of *The Prisoner of Zenda* and its companion fantasies.

Two last novels, numbers 31 and 32 in his long output of fiction, were gallant tokens from the man who could write: 'I believe I am so much of a craftsman . . . that, if I were to live again, I would ask only to write better.' *Lucinda* (1920) and *Little Tiger* (1925) are readable reversions to his old interest in women bold enough to defy convention. They would be significant only if he had not done the thing better before. There remained only, before his death, the 'slight and reticent' *Memories and Notes* (1927) to present, not so much a clearer picture of Sir Anthony Hope Hawkins as a confirmation that the temper of his best writing was the temper of the man himself— competent, stoical, never unaware of the profundities underlying life's surface but determined, as a good citizen of the world, not to add insult to injury by facing tragedy in a spirit of resentment or contemplating the common human predicament with undignified fuss. When he *did* complain, it was in rueful professional privacy:

> It is rather hard to keep heart writing when once you know *thoroughly* your own limitations. Through my really productive years from 29 to 43 or thereabouts, the *next one* was always going to be *great*. But now! Oh, Anthony, Anthony!

VI

Anthony Hope's achievement, no less than his limitations, sprang naturally from his consciousness of his own place in a world where private motive and public behaviour were afforded equal attention, where aspects of life could be illuminated not only in terms of blood and glands but also in terms of legal or political imagery. An estimation of that place is only possible after a glance at what, over a 35-year span too recent to be 'history' and too distant to be a memory for most novel-readers, he set himself, as a professional man among professional men, to achieve.

Sir Anthony Hope Hawkins was the most 'clubbable' of men. For years he occupied a two-way embassy between the world of affairs and the world of letters. On many public occasions he was the spokesman for contemporary writers; his whole writing career proclaimed that public life was a fit theme for novelists. Nowadays, for all the lowering of ancient barriers, the two worlds mingle less freely.One rarely sees the young novelist Mr. X. at political parties, and if the Rt. Hon. Sir A. B. should figure in his stories, it will probably be as a none too well observed caricature. There is much to be said, of course, for diving deep below the surface of social life if a novelist has a gift for it (and precious few *have*), and some advantage doubtless accrues to a novelist from moving within strictly literary circles (though what the advantage is, I would not care to guess). In his early twenties, Hope made a character in his first novel throw off an observation that may be relevant to the mingling of his two worlds: 'Wine is better without smoke, and smoke is better without wine, but the combination is better than either separately.'

There is at present no lack of exponents of a type of fiction Hope never attempted—the art of sensitive awareness. Stories now abound in which the reader is invited to share the hero's self-absorption as, scrutinizing with un-governable fascination the black hairs on the back of his hand, he is filled with a sense of significance so overwhelming that only a quiet vomit in some convenient corner, or perhaps the contemplation of the death-throes of a crushed stoat, will serve to reduce the pressure. Such writing can be good or bad. Ruritanian romances can be good or bad. Social comedy, too, can be good or bad— with the added quality of rarity, nowadays, in the publishers' lists. Anthony Hope produced some of the most intelligent social comedies of a period when, in England, a few classical virtues of proportion and high competence were briefly flowering. He had not a poet's equipment, but he did possess, among many more 'civic' qualities, one bright technical skill which flashed, in his hands, with all the delight of imagery: a mastery of the art of dialogue. His interest in behaviour is still shared not only by club diners but by anyone who gossips in a queue, speculates in a bus on the character of his neighbour, or finds pleasure in plucking from experience one or two general observations with an applicability to more than one set of troubled nerves. It would be pleasant to think that a rediscovery of the urbanity and witty fortitude of the author of *Quisanté* or *The Intrusions of Peggy* or *The Dolly Dialogues* might even yet release from ironic bondage the prisoner of *The Prisoner of Zenda*.

FURTHER READING

Biography

Mallet, Sir Charles. *Anthony Hope and His Books: Being the Authorized Life of Sir Anthony Hope Hawkins.* London: Hutchinson, 1935.
> Discusses Hope's life and career as a writer, and presents critical and public response to many of his novels and dramas.

Criticism

Greene, Graham. *The Lost Childhood and Other Essays.* London: Eyre & Spottiswoode, 1951, 191 p.
> In his essay "Isis Idol," Greene considers Hope's talentsas a writer limited, and asserts that Hope knew that the popularity of his work would wane.

Kernohan, R. D. "The Subsequent History of Ruritania: A Narrative Meant to Be Taken Seriously, but Not Too Literally." *Contemporary Review* 261, No. 1520 (September 1992): 142-47.
> Humorously postulates that the fall of the Berlin Wall and the collapse of communist regimes in Eastern Europe will mark the return of Hope's Ruritanian empire.

Wallace, Raymond P. "Cardboard Kingdoms." *San Jose*

Studies 13,No. 2 (Spring 1987): 23-34.
    While acknowledging that George Meredith had
experimented with fictional kingdoms for adventure
romances before Hope, Wallace asserts that Hope was
the first to really define the genre.

For additional information on Hope, see the following sources published by Gale Research: *Dictionary of Literary Biography*, Vols. 153, 156.

Paul Léautaud

1902-1957

(Full name Paul-Firmin Léautaud; also wrote under pseudonym Maurice Boissard) French novelist, memoirist, critic, poet and essayist.

INTRODUCTION

Léautaud is admired for his documentation of France's cultural milieu, which he captured in the autobiographical novels he published early in his literary career, as well as in the extensively maintained journals he kept throughout the first half of the twentieth century. His successive publishing tenures as poet, novelist, and theater critic brought him in contact with members of the various Parisian literary coteries from the fin de siecle to the 1950s; relationships Léautaud recounted in the nineteen-volume *Journal litteraire* (1954-1966; translated and abridged as *Journal of a Man of Letters, 1898-1907*, 1960). Upon its initial publication as well as its posthumous English translation fifty years later, Léautaud's fictionalized narratives of his early years with his womanizing father and brief encounters with the mother who abandoned him to be raised by prostitutes—*Le Petit Ami* (1903), *In Memoriam* (1905), and *Amours* (1906)—sparked a success d'scandal due to its frank handling of extramarital, adulterous, and incestuous sexuality. These short works were translated and published as *The Child of Montmartre* (1959).

Biographical Information

Léautaud's early life is detailed in *Le Petit Ami*, the title deriving from the sobriquet given him by the prostitutes that befriended him as a child. His mother, an actress of minor renown, replaced her older sister as the mistress of Léautaud's father, gave birth to Léautaud, and abandoned her child and his father. Léautaud's abusive father was also an actor who eventually became a prompter in the Comedie-Francaise theater. The family's economic situation required the younger Léautaud to share his father's bed with a succession of lovers, many of whom Léautaud claimed also tried to seduce him. Infrequent childhood visits from his mother enflamed Léautaud's long-standing incestuous infatuation with her. Léautaud held a variety of menial jobs beginning at the age of fifteen, but eventually found modest financial success as a law clerk. His friend Adolphe van Bever introduced Léautaud to contemporary poetry and drama, which served to inspire the young writer to compose the twelve poems he published between 1893 an 1895 in the periodical *Courrier Francais*. The following year *Mercure de France* published two of Léautaud's experimental prose poems—which he described as "essais de sentimentalisme"—that reveal the influence of French Symbolist poets Stephane Mallarme and Maurice Barres. His interest in poetry culminated with the publication of *Poetes d'aujourd'hui* (1900; *Poets of Today*), an anthology he co-edited with van Bever. During the next several years, Léautaud honed his critical skills with essays on his literary idol, Stendhal, and contemporaries Henri de Regnier and Marcel Schwob, as well as published his autobiographical fiction. Shortly thereafter, Léautaud—using the pseudonym Maurice Boissard—took up residency in 1907 as the theater critic for *Mercure de France*, a position he held until 1941. Léautaud returned to the public consciousness with a series of radio broadcasts with Robert Mallett in the early 1950s. These broadcasts were noted for Léautaud's cantankerous and unpredictable behavior, and prompted publication of *Entretiens avec Robert Mallet* (1951), the reissue of his earlier works, and the first several volumes of his *Journal litteraire*.

Major Works

Léautaud earned a Prix Goncourt nomination for *Le Petit Ami*. He followed this success with *In Memoriam*, a narrative concerning the death of his father, with whom Léautaud had a troubled relationship. Léautaud's third autobiographical narrative, *Amours*, details his romantic attachments with different women. Each of these installments were initially serialized in *Mercure de France*. As theater critic for this publication, Léautaud created the flamboyant persona of his alter-ego, Maurice Boissard. While a young, financially troubled Léautaud wrote as Boissard, the critic depicted himself as a middle-aged dandy. This criticism is noted for its extreme examples of subjectivism, which often evidenced itself in scathing commentary and rambling, point-of-view discussions of Boissard's fictional life. Although he lacked financial success for much of his life, Léautaud's tenure as *Mercure de France*'s Maurice Boissard afforded him enough financial freedom to devote the remainder of his literary life to his *Journal litteraire*. The journals are noted for Léautaud's inclusion of many of France's most important writers of the twentieth century, including Andre Gide, Paul Valery, Jean Cocteau, *Mercure de France* editor Alfred Valette, Remy de Gourmont, Guilliame Apollinaire, Jules Romains, and Andre Billy.

PRINCIPAL WORKS

Le Petit Ami (novel) 1903
In Memoriam (novel) 1905

Amours (novel) 1906
Le Theatre de Maurice Boissard (criticism) 1926
Entrietens avec Robert Mallet (conversations) 1951
Journal litteraire [*Journal of a Man of Letters, 1898-1907*] (journal) 1954-1966
*The Child of Montmartre (novel) 1959

*This work is comprised of translations of the formerly published short autobiographical novels *Le Petit Ami*, *In Memoriam*, and *Amours*.

CRITICISM

Henri Peyre (essay date 1955)

SOURCE: "Reviews in Brief," in *The Romantic Review*, Vol. XLVI, No. 3, October, 1955, pp. 237-38.

[*In the following excerpt, Peyre reviews Léautaud's* Journal litteraire, 1893-1906, *praising the work for its personal depictions of writers of the era but faulting the exercise as detracting Léautaud from more literary endeavors.*]

Paul Léautaud was, for generations of readers between 1900 and 1930, the compiler, with Van Bever, of a poetic anthology, *Poètes d'aujourd'hui (1880-1900)* which did more than any other book for the spread and survival of Symbolism. He won some fame as a dramatic critic, under the name of Maurice Boissard: his acrid, lucid judgment was feared by playwrights and producers. He then became well-nigh forgotten until, since 1950 or so, he gave some entertaining and disarmingly candid "entretiens" on the Paris radio. His *Journal,* the first volume of which covers the years 1893-1906, is again attracting attention to an octogenarian who has out-lived Gide, Claudel, Valéry, Colette, Suarès and Matisse, all born around 1870.

Unlike Proust and Gide, Léautaud was no "grand bourgeois." His father was an actor of moderate talent, his mother a woman of less than doubtful virtue who abandoned her infant with little ado. He grew up a child of nature, and also of Paris and of theatres, sharpening an uncanny literary taste, ferociously brutal in words but at bottom a soft-hearted sentimental, athirst for tenderness. The chief interest of his *Journal* lies in the portrayal of the man: contradictory, afflicted with doubts about himself, shy, without illusions, generous and egotistic. His amorous liaisons, related with a rare simplicity, fill a sizable part of his jottings-down, much less disembodied than the diaries of Julien Green or Charles Du Bos, even of Gide.

Léautaud's primary concern was with acquiring the boldness necessary to become fully himself. That boldness did not come naturally to a man who was not endowed with a powerful personality, who had very little imagina-

tion, and who overflowed with sympathy and with kindness for his many literary friends. He had to wrench himself from them and to cultivate a certain "rosserie," at times reminiscent of Jules Renard. The struggle against his own leanings adds much to the interest of a private diary, otherwise encumbered with the usual trivialities of the genre.

Léautaud was an acute and independent observer of his contemporaries. Some of the sketches which he draws of literary circles around 1900 are entertaining. He knew Marcel Schwob intimately; he saw a great deal of Paul Valéry when Valéry toyed with his paradoxes against inspiration and spontaneousness in art, which he was later to take seriously, and his critics even more so. Those were also the days when Valéry was a violent anti-Dreyfus man and shocked his liberal friends by shouting: "Let him [Dreyfus] be shot and heard about no more!" Future thesis writers on Schwob and on Valéry's youth will cull several vivid details from the candid diary of their friend.

Léautaud, who eagerly wished to be no one's imitator and to keep aloof from fashions, fell a prey to one literary vogue—on which a thesis must also someday be written, since theses constitute, after all, our best source of precise knowledge on past literature: he adored Stendhal, identified himself with him, lived over again Stendhal's pathetic, ludicrous loves, disappointments and dreams, wept over the grave of "Arrigo Beyle, Milanese." The Stendhal cult owes much to Léautaud, but it is not so certain that Léautaud, and many of our modern Beylistes, gained equally from their worship of Stendhal. Fascinated by Stendhal's egotism, by his *Journals,* by his ever renewed attempts at autobiography, Léautaud and his friends with whom he associated in the cult became obsessed with introspective analysis and failed to see that Stendhal's supreme achievement lay in three or four novels. A bitter aftertaste spoils the pleasure which Léautaud's discursive and intelligent day-by-day notes first gave the reader. That man, and not a few of his contemporaries, had little to write about and failed to look around them, or in their imagination, for new and raw materials: they were intoxicated by literature and paralyzed by self-awareness. Like many others, they emptied their potential books of much content in order to enrich their intimate Journals. Léautaud is the demonstration through the negative of the courage which Proust, Gide, Valéry had to muster in order to become creators.

W. Somerset Maugham (essay date 1958)

SOURCE: "Three Journals," in *Points of View,* William Heinemann Ltd., 1958, pp. 228-55.

[*In the following excerpt, Maugham presents an admiring overview of Léautaud's life and work.*]

Now I come to the last of my three journalists. Paul Léautaud was the oddest, the most disreputable, the most outrageous, but to my mind the most sympathetic of the three. Though he produced little, two short autobiographical novels, two volumes of theatrical criticism and a number of articles that appeared for the most part in the *Mercure de France,* I am inclined to think that he had a remarkable and individual talent. He had traits that shock one and traits that extort one's admiration. He was an egoist, but devoid of vanity, a lecher without passion, cynical and conscientious, desperately poor, but indifferent to money, harsh in his dealings with his fellows, but to animals compassionate, savagely independent, indifferent to what others thought of him, a brilliant talker with a caustic wit, truthful, honest, but cheerfully tolerant of the dishonesty of others—altogether a very strange man, as will appear when I narrate as best I can something about him. The sources are the two novels I have mentioned, *Le Petit Ami* and *In Memoriam,* the four volumes of his *Journal* dating from 1893 to 1924, and the talks on the radio with Robert Mallet that he gave from November 1950 to July 1951. It is they, by their frankness, their spice, and their revelation of an unusual creature, that brought him at the age of seventy-eight, after the long obscurity of his life, what I would not venture to call fame, but notoriety.

Paul was born in 1872. His father, Firmin Léautaud, the son of a peasant in the Basses Alpes, did not come to Paris till he was twenty, at which age he was apprenticed to an uncle, a working jeweller and watchmaker, who had a shop in Montmartre. On his uncle's death he entered the Conservatoire and eventually became an actor. He was apparently not a good one, for after some years he abandoned the profession to become prompter at the Comédie Française, a job which he held for something like thirty years. Besides acting as prompter, he trained the younger members of the company in elocution and diction. He was a handsome man—so fascinating that he only had to look at a woman with his fine eyes for her to fall. At the time I am now dealing with he had an actress, called Fanny, living with him in Montmartre. One evening Fanny's younger sister, Jeanne, seventeen years old, came to see them. It grew late and they did not like her to go home by herself to Montparnasse, where her parents lived, so Léautaud suggested that she should spend the night with them. As there was only one bed in the apartment the three of them slept together, with Léautaud in the middle. I don't quite know how to put what happened in terms that will not seem coarse: after some amorous dalliance with Fanny, Léautaud transferred his attentions to her sister. Next day her parents turned her out for her misconduct and she went back, having nowhere else to go, to Fanny and Léautaud. A few days later Fanny left the apartment in a huff and Jeanne stayed on. In due course she had a baby. Since father and mother were on the stage, acting separately, it was farmed out. Such were the origins of Paul Léautaud. He did not go back to his father till he was over two, by which time Firmin and Jeanne had separated. Firmin engaged a nurse to look after him. She was called Marie Pezé and he loved her as a mother. He did not sleep in the apartment in the rue des Martyrs, but with his nurse,

partly because he could not be left alone at night and partly because his father seldom came home without a new mistress. When Paul was five, his mother, on her way to Berlin to fill an engagement or to meet a lover, came with her mother, Madame Forestier, to see him in his nurse's attic room. He was lying in bed ill, and very sulky, with his back turned to the two women. Marie Pezé had to force him to say good morning to them. He never forgot the remark his mother made, "My God, how disagreeable that child is!" They stayed five minutes and it was three years before he saw her again. One day she appeared at the apartment in the rue des Martyrs and Paul was brought in. He was shy, hardly daring to look at her, and timidly called her *Madame.* She arranged that next morning he should come to the house where she had taken a room so that they could spend the day together, after which she would leave him at the tavern which his father frequented on getting back from the theatre. He went as planned. He found his mother in bed, sitting up, her hair in some disorder, her arms bare and, her nightdress having slipped, her breast uncovered. She took him in her arms, drew him to her bosom and kissed him. She was very pretty, supple, lively and graceful. She dressed and they went to have luncheon with his father. After that they took a cab and went to the zoo. Paul was allowed to ride a pony. Then they went to the restaurant at the Palais Royal and dined there. After that Jeanne took him to see a play at the Châtelet. They left a little before the end and went on to the Folies Bergère. His mother went straight to the promenade to gossip with old friends. He couldn't get over all the people she knew. They greeted her like a long-lost sister. From time to time she pointed to him and told them who he was. "Oh, it's your son. He's sweet." At closing time they went with a group to have supper at a neighbouring inn. Then Jeanne took him back to the tavern where his father was waiting for him. She kissed him and left. He didn't see her again for two or three years and then only for half an hour. After that he heard nothing of her for twenty years. He was told that she had got married. The day he spent with his mother was his most cherished recollection.

When Paul was eight his father picked up a girl, Louise by name, who lived in the quarter. She was fifteen and he was forty-eight. She spent several nights with him. Marie Pezé, outraged, protested that he was giving the little boy a shocking example, whereupon Firmin lost his temper and, to Paul's bitter grief, discharged her. He took the girl to live with him. Paul was given a tiny room in the apartment. Until then he had been happy enough, but he did not get on with the new mistress, and one day he threw a bottle of ink at her, for which he was severely beaten. His father as ever remained brutal, negligent and dissolute. Every night after dinner Paul was locked up in his room and, notwithstanding his tears, left alone, terrified, in the dark.

A year or two later Firmin Léautaud decided to live out of town and took a house in the neighbouring suburb of Courbevoie. Paul went to school there. At fifteen he went to work in Paris. He earned twenty-five francs, which his father took for his board. I can pass over the next years of Léautaud's life very briefly. He entered the army to do his military service, but was myopic and after seven months was discharged. He got a job at a wholesale glover's and began to write verse. After throwing up this job, he got one as third clerk in an attorney's office. He liked the work and stayed for ten years. Then he entered the office of a certain Lemarquis, who was a trustee in bankruptcy. He was evidently competent, for he was given important assignments. Among others he had to administer the estate of a man who on his death had left two million francs, then eighty thousand pounds, and enormous debts. Lemarquis told him to manage the affair so as to have as much as possible left over for the widow. He did this so satisfactorily (and somewhat unscrupulously) that when the negotiations with creditors came to an end he received a handsome gratuity.

During this long time, after his day's work he was in the habit of going to a *crèmerie,* near the Folies Bergére, where prostitutes had their mid-day and evening meals before dressing and going to the cafés and music halls in the hope of finding customers. He soon became very friendly with them. They would consult him about a new hat or a dress. They would show him their letters and he would write a draft of the answer they should send. Sometimes he accompanied them to a café. They knew he had no money and gave him cigarettes and chocolates. At the evening's end, if one of them hadn't done any business, she would ask him to come back with her, not always to make love, but to go quietly to bed. Sometimes one or other would ask him to come to see her in the afternoon and they would gossip by the hour. They talked of their early years and Léautaud talked to them of his mother. He claimed that these friends of his taught him a great deal. It may be they did.

Owing to a disagreement with Lemarquis, which resulted in his discharge, Paul, in his late twenties by this time, found himself out of a job, with nothing to live on but the gratuity his employer had given him. He shared a room with Van Bever, a minor man of letters with whom he had been at school. Both were miserably poor. Paul's father would give him nothing, but Fanny, his aunt, had never ceased to take an interest in him and did her best to see him once or twice a year. She gave him a few francs now and then and sent him clothes; they were cheap and nasty, but he was grateful for them. He continued to write verses. In the hope of getting them published, he asked Van Bever if he could get Lugné Poë, whose secretary Van Bever was at the time, to give him a letter of introduction to Alfred Vallette, the editor of the *Mercure de France.* When Léautaud went to see him with the letter, Vallette said to him, "One doesn't need an introduction to come here. The only introduction is your verse, good or bad." A few weeks later Léautaud saw himself in print.

He had made a good impression on Vallette. Léautaud was a brilliant talker. Acid, but witty. His repartees were prompt, often cruel, but always amusing. Many years

later he published a very short book, called *Propos d'un Jour,* which was a collection of epigrams, aphorisms and wisecracks. When the critics remarked that there were too many of his own, he retorted that most people were so dull, he seldom came across witticisms as good as his own. Vallette, who enjoyed his conversation, very sensibly advised him to write in prose and during the next three or four years he produced a number of essays which appeared in the magazine. They are stylishly written in a manner presumably well liked at the time, but which Léautaud soon abandoned for one of a more pleasing simplicity. He became a regular contributor to the *Mercure;* he reviewed books and, in collaboration with Van Bever, published an anthology of the poetry of the day which had a considerable success. It is not my intention to describe the two or three more or less serious love affairs, if that is the proper name for them, that Léautaud had. They are uninteresting. He himself said, "Love interests me too little." Van Bever got married and at the beginning of the century we find Léautaud living in a tiny apartment with a young woman called Blanche. Léautaud liked her; she gave him peace and did not interfere with his work. Presently he started on a novel which, at Vallette's suggestion, was to be named *Le Petit Ami.* It was on the whole an accurate account of Léautaud's early life; but when he had finished with his reminiscences of the prostitutes with whom he had consorted, ending up with the charming and pathetic description of the death of one called La Perruche, he found himself at a dead end. Then something happened which, as he said afterwards, was a bit of luck. He received a telegram from his grandmother, Madame Forestier, to tell him that his Aunt Fanny was desperately ill and if he wanted to see her once more he must come at once. The old lady and her daughter had been living for a good many years at Calais, where Fanny, an actress, had been a member of the stock company which played there. Paul supposed that Jeanne, his mother, would have been sent for. He had not seen her for twenty years, but he still remembered the charming, graceful creature with whom so long ago he had spent a day. He wondered how he would find her. He feared he would find a rather battered, serious lady and he was in half a mind not to go. He went. When he got to Calais, his grandmother, whom he had seen but once in his life and then only for five minutes, began at once to talk to him of his mother. Paul knew that she was married, but he learned then that she lived in Geneva with her husband and her two children. Her husband, a man of some importance, had fallen in love with her while she was a member of the company at Geneva, and she became his mistress. She bore him a boy and a girl and then he married her. Madame Forestier told Léautaud that his mother had never once spoken of him. He suggested that it would be embarrassing for her to find him installed there without having been warned. His grandmother told him it was no matter: she wouldn't recognise him.

Paul was thirty. He was a little man, with a heavy brown beard and a moustache. He wore steel-rimmed spectacles. Though his linen was clean, as always, he was so shabby that his grandmother gave him ten francs to go there and then to buy a pair of trousers. His mother arrived at half-past one in the afternoon. Léautaud had just accompanied to the door someone who had come to have news of Fanny when he heard steps on the stairs. He looked over the banister and saw a woman coming up, in a black dress, with a small valise in her hand. He recognised her at once. He told his grandmother she was on the way and shut himself up in his room. Jeanne entered the apartment, kissed her mother and, after taking off her hat and coat, went in to see her sister. Then she asked for luncheon. They were to eat in the kitchen and to get to it the two women, mother and daughter, had to pass through the room in which Léautaud was seated. His mother bowed slightly and said, *"Bonjour, Monsieur."* He answered, *"Bonjour, Madame."* When they got into the kitchen, he heard his mother ask who he was. Since he did not want to hear the answer he made a noise in his room. Later his grandmother told him. "I preferred not to say who you were. It might have been awkward for her. I said you were a friend, someone from the theatre, who had come to help us." Léautaud did not believe a word of it. His mother knew very well who he was, but wanted to act as though she didn't. It was not till she had gone back to Geneva that his grandmother told him the truth. When Jeanne had asked, "Who is that?" she had answered, "It's Paul." "Who is Paul?" "Why, your son."

Anyhow, after a while, Jeanne joined them and the two women began to gossip. She talked of her children with affection. Then his grandmother told Léautaud that, since her daughter would be using his bed, he would have to take a room in a near-by hotel. "I must apologise, *Monsieur,* for making you turn out," his mother said to him then. "Not at all, *Madame,*" he replied. "It's the least I can do."

The ice was broken and, while the old lady went to see about one thing and another, Jeanne asked him to tell her the Paris news, spoke of the Comédie Française and enquired of friends whom she had once known. He told her all he could. As I have said, he was a clever talker and he amused her.

When they had dined, Léautaud sat with his mother in Fanny's room. After some time, she said, "Listen, Paul, I know who you are." She began to talk in undertones of her early youth, her first love affairs when she was fifteen or sixteen, of her husband and children. Then she explained her long silence. She had often asked Fanny and her mother about him, but had learnt nothing. She had read his name two or three years before in connection with something he had written in the *Mercure*. Oh, if she had only known where to write to him! In 1900 she went to Paris for the Exhibition with her husband and children. How she would have hurried to him if she had only known where to find him! Léautaud knew there wasn't a word of truth in anything she said. After all, she only had to write to him at the office of the *Mercure*. He did not speak. When she had done talking he took her to her room. She kissed him. In his eyes she was still young and

desirable. He put his arm round her waist and took her in his arms, and kissed her neck, her eyes, her breast. "You mustn't mind," he said. "What?" "I don't know, but I don't kiss you like a mother." While she was turning down the sheets, he said to her, "I'll go into the sitting-room. I'll come back when you're in bed and sit by you." Though he insisted, she wouldn't let him do that, and he went to his hotel. When he returned next morning he was told that Fanny was dead.

Léautaud had a lot of things to see to, but he and Jeanne were able to pass the afternoon and evening together. They talked. She cross-questioned him about his love life. When they were alone she would put her arm round his neck and say, "Kiss me quick. What would people say if they saw us kissing like this in secret?" And once, "You see, we look like two lovers. What would have happened ten years ago?" He could not but think what he would have felt to kiss her as he would have kissed a mistress—his mother, but, after all, a woman like another. For her he was just a man, and a young man at that. He thought of her slim, graceful body and wondered what her thoughts were when she looked at him. When he left her for the night, as she kissed him again, "You'll never know how much I love you," he said. He asked himself if she had the same passionate feeling for him as he had for her. Who could tell—loose as she had been and as, from the questions she had put to him, still seemed to be?

While Léautaud was undergoing these shattering emotions he did not forget the unfinished book he had left in Paris. From the moment of his mother's arrival, he made notes whenever he had the opportunity. Once she noticed him at it and asked him what he was about. He told her that he was jotting down his expenses. Alone in his hotel room at night, he thought of all that had passed. He told himself that his mother's tenderness did not mean much. But after all, he said to himself, one mustn't ask too much of the poor woman; she did what she could. He took up his note-book and put down all that had happened during the day. He ends the paragraph of *Le Petit Ami* in which he has described this with the words, "Grandeur of the man of letters! One may be a son, one may have found one's mother again after twenty years of separation, the moment one has a book on the stocks, that goes before everything. There are no things that one has felt, heard or seen that one doesn't intend to put in it, however sacred they may be. It may be that these things were not very sacred."

Next day there was a funeral service for Fanny, who was to be buried in Paris. When it was over the two women and Léautaud went home. It had been arranged that he should take the coffin to Paris that evening. Jeanne was to leave next day. Since she would have to wait for three hours in Paris before her train started for Geneva, they agreed that Léautaud should meet her at the station so that he might show her his apartment, after which they could dine together. He arrived in Paris at five in the morning and by ten o'clock everything was finished and Fanny buried. He got Blanche to make herself scarce for a few hours so that his mother should not know that he lived with a woman. The day seemed very long and at five, with an hour still to wait, he was at the station. On the way he had bought a bunch of violets. The train came in. His mother was not on it. He waited till eight, watching one train come in after another. Nobody. Then it occurred to him that she might have changed her mind and had sent a telegram to tell him that she was detained in Calais. He took a cab, a fearful extravagance for him, and went to his apartment. Nothing. He hurried back to the Gare de Lyon and got there at eight-thirty-five. The train for Geneva was to start at eight-fifty. He ran on to the platform and along the train.

Jeanne was sitting in the corner of a carriage, quite quietly, looking at the people who passed. He jumped in. "Well, my boy, what is it?" she said. He burst into tears. She reasoned with him. After all, it was only a date that had gone wrong. "Poor boy," she said. "We'll arrange all that. We'll meet again. We'll make up for it." She kissed him. She was surrounded by parcels and it was obvious that she had never intended to meet him, but had got out of the train at a previous station and gone shopping. It may well be that she did not want to spend two or three hours alone with the unknown son whose demonstrative affection somewhat embarrassed her. The porters were shutting the carriage doors. She offered him a five-franc piece which, bitterly hurt, Paul refused. He put the bunch of violets, somewhat crushed by them, on the seat beside her, said good-bye and left. He cried all night in the arms of Blanche. On arrival at Geneva, Jeanne sent a post-card to Madame Forestier. It ran as follows, "The train got to Paris an hour and a quarter late. I didn't see Paul. Did he get tired of waiting? That grieved me and I don't know what to think."

On the day after these events Paul wrote a ten-page letter to his mother, reproaching her for having treated him so cruelly, but telling her that he loved her with all his heart. On the same day she wrote to him from Geneva. "Only a word in haste," she began, "to assure you of my affection, why had there to be that wretched mishap to deprive me of the sweet hours that I was rejoicing to spend with you, I'd longed to see your room, so that I could follow you in my thoughts, and what a night I passed in that horrid train that was taking me away from you." And she finished, "Good-bye, my dear one, take the tender kisses of your mother who has never forgotten you and to whom your presence has put a ray of sunshine in her heart." Léautaud, when he read this phrase, remarked, "She must read some very poor books."

From then on for a while they wrote to one another almost every day. Jeanne's letters were affectionate, Paul's passionate. In one of hers she wrote, "I must tell you that I am often hurt and worried by the sort of affection that you show me, until now I've ascribed many things to your sentimentality, but your letters, which it was a joy to me to keep, are sometimes so equivocal as to be possibly dangerous, and I think I shall destroy them; what pains me also is to see you interpreting my letters as you do

and however flattered I am by the admiration you show me, I find it excessive and embarrassing." Oddly enough, in one letter she advised Paul to write a novel founded on his early life. It never occurred to her that he had already written a great part of it and was even then busy with the copious notes he had made during the three days they had spent together in Calais. Financial matters arose which further strained their relations. Léautaud's grandmother had taken a fancy to Paul and gave him such stocks as she possessed on the understanding that he should send her the dividends during her lifetime and after her death inherit them. She told the plan to her daughter, who was indignant. "You're not going to give everything you have to this man whom we don't know!" Considering that her husband was well-to-do, whereas her son was penniless, it was not generous on her part.

It would be tedious to describe at length the correspondence between Léautaud and his mother. Her letters grew colder. She complained that he read into them more than she meant. She got it into her head that he was reproachful for her long neglect of him. She was afraid that he might come to Geneva and begged him not to do so without her consent. Finally she asked him to return her letters. He did not send them and she asked for them again; then she wrote, "Until you have sent me back my letters, without leaving out a single one, I shall not write to you." He refused to do so. In a further letter she wrote to him she said, "There's only one thing I regret and that is to have given you in my letters, from a sense of duty, the illusion of an affection that I couldn't feel, as I didn't know you, which all the same I might have had if you had shown yourself worthy of it. I can only congratulate myself on not having brought you up, for I should feel profoundly humiliated. Now whether you come to Geneva or not, doesn't matter to me; we shall be two to receive you; my husband and I . . ." In return he wrote a stinging letter. She answered with one which ended with the words, "I tell you again that I am so indifferent to you, you are so little my son, that I don't feel myself concerned or humiliated by your shameful conduct; it would certainly have been better if I had always ignored you, but what then? You will have passed in my life like a bad dream, which, believe me and notwithstanding everything, will fade quickly from my memory." After that, though he continued to write, she did not reply. She did not even write when he told her in two lines that his father, her old lover, had died.

When *Le Petit Ami* was published it was much talked about, much praised and much abused. Owing to the closeness of the tie that unites mother and son in France, a tie that, though sometimes merely conventional, is for the most part genuine, many readers were frankly horrified. That Paul should have made it clear that he had incestuous desires for his mother, that she should, if not encourage them, at least not discourage them, was shocking. It didn't make it any better that he said they were strangers to one another. She did not repel his passionate embraces; whenever they were alone she kissed him fondly, and it was she who said that they were more like two lovers than mother and son. She even went so far as to hint that if they had met ten years before, when he was twenty, things might have gone differently. One gets the impression that she was far from displeased with his passion and, if she did not yield, it was not for the immorality of the matter, but from her prudence as a respectably married woman. His feelings were unequivocal. Perhaps such feelings are not so rare as is generally believed. An intelligent psychiatrist of my acquaintance, whose work is chiefly with juvenile delinquents, has told me they often tell him, with something like shame, that they would like to go to bed with their mothers. I think he would ascribe it to the promiscuity in which the boys of that class live, the lack of privacy and the fact that the only love they have known is that which their mother gave them when they were children, so that when the sexual instinct became active it was directed towards her. Paul Léautaud was not a juvenile delinquent, but he had been a neglected child, he had longed for his mother's love, he had idolised her and had never forgotten that day when he had found her, half naked, in bed and she had covered his face with kisses; it may be abominable that he should have had the desire to have sexual connection with her when after twenty years he saw her again, so graceful, so charming, so tender, but it was not unnatural. I do not condone, I merely state the facts. You may say he should never have written an account of those three wanton days at Calais: to write was his passion and, devoid of imagination as he was, he could only write about himself and what happened to him.

In 1903 Firmin Léautaud died. After having a son by Louise, the little harlot he had taken to live with him, he married her. Paul detested her, but went to see his father, still living at Courbevoie, every other Sunday. For six years Firmin had been partly paralysed and could only go from one room to another with the help of his wife and his young son. One Sunday, going as usual to Courbevoie, Paul found that his father had grown worse. He spent a couple of days there and returned to Paris. The following morning he received a telegram bidding him come at once. He found his father dying. Four days later he died. Paul Léautaud had always been interested in death and during these four days he stored in his memory every step of his father's disintegration, the conversation of the friends who came to see the dying man, who, after a few minutes during which they expressed their sympathy, began to chatter about their own affairs; the impatience of the man's wife and son, and his own too, because the agony lasted so long. Though they would not admit it, they felt that if he had to die, the sooner the better.

Paul Léautaud wrote a long account of his father's death and published it in the *Mercure*. It was called **In Memoriam**. Some subscribers were so outraged that they refused to renew their subscriptions to the magazine, but in literary circles it was much admired for its ruthless sincerity and its strange mixture of cynicism and emotion. Some members of the *Académie Goncourt* were anxious to give it the yearly prize. Unfortunately it was too short.

It ran to a little over thirty pages. But there was a dearth of candidates for the prize, and members of the academy assured Léautaud that if he could so spin it out as to make something of a book there was no doubt that it would receive the award. Vallette was eager that he should do this, since it would be a good advertisement for the firm. Léautaud was tempted. In theory he did not approve of such prizes, but this one would not only bring him five thousand francs, two hundred pounds, an immense sum for him, but, with the publicity that the choice brought, would ensure a sale of four or five thousand copies. In the *Journal* Léautaud has described at tedious length the discussions that took place. At last it was arranged that he should rewrite two articles that had appeared under the name of *Amours* in the *Mercure*. They dealt with his early love affairs, but it is hard to see how they could possibly have been incorporated in an account of his father's death. Nothing came of it and the prize was given to someone else.

Vallette had for some time been dissatisfied with his dramatic critic and he pressed Léautaud to take his place. The *Mercure* was a fortnightly and he was to be paid seven francs a page, but not more than twenty-eight francs a number. This looks like wretched payment, but the *Mercure* had a circulation of only three thousand and Vallette could not afford to be lavish. After some hesitation Léautaud accepted the offer. For his theatrical criticism he used the pseudonym of Maurice Boissard. This was supposed to be an elderly gentleman of modest means, who was not a man of letters, but who liked the theatre. Léautaud wrote dramatic criticism for seventeen years. At the end of this time he collected his articles and published them in two volumes. Although most of the plays he dealt with have long been forgotten, his articles can still be read with pleasure. They are caustic, lively, humorous and prejudiced. Léautaud had no patience with the plays that sought to instruct, to preach or to moralise. He hated the pompous, the verbose and the artificial. He asked of a play that it should amuse or move. He insisted that people should talk as they talked in real life and was scathing in his condemnation of dialogue that no human being could dream of speaking. He greatly liked the plays of Sacha Guitry. He admitted that he was a light-weight, but in his plays people did speak as they spoke in ordinary life and behaved as it was natural for them to behave. When Léautaud found a play worthless he wrote of anything that occurred to him, and only just mentioned the piece he was supposed to deal with. His victims were incensed, but readers enjoyed his articles and some bought the magazine solely to read them. Eventually it was learnt that Maurice Boissard, the old gentleman living on his savings, was none other than the author of the scandalous **Le Petit Ami** and the hardly less scandalous **In Memoriam**. Rachilde, Vallette's wife, had never liked him. She was in the habit of receiving on Tuesday evenings the literary persons and their wives who cared to come. Some might be authors, or the friends of authors, whom Léautaud, as Maurice Boissard, had made bitter fun of. They did not fail to complain of their ill-treatment. She told her husband, but he answered that

Léautaud was read and the *Mercure* had never been more prosperous. She persisted, others backed her up, and finally Vallette yielded. He took the dramatic criticism in the *Mercure* away from Léautaud. Fortunately for him, however, André Gide offered him, at a much higher rate, the position of dramatic critic on the *Nouvelle Revue Française,* of which he was the mainstay. Léautaud was glad to take it. But that only lasted for two years. It came to an end when he wrote a mocking criticism of a play by Jules Romains and refused to alter a word of it. The editors of the *Nouvelle Revue Française* were in an awkward position. They were publishers as well and they published Jules Romains's novels. Romains was furious at being so cruelly ridiculed in the magazine and they were afraid he would leave them for another publisher. They did not want to lose a valuable property and Léautaud was dismissed. Then he wrote for the *Nouvelles Littéraires,* but, owing to his obstinacy to have every word he had written printed, only for a few months. Thus ended, in 1923, his career as a dramatic critic.

Now I must return briefly to 1907. Léautaud was miserably poor. At one time he was forced to pawn his father's watch and his cuff-links. They brought him thirty-five francs. He was still living with Blanche. The money he had received from Lemarquis was coming to an end and their situation was desperate. In the hope of improving it, she started a boarding-house on funds provided by a former lover. They reckoned that after paying expenses it would give a profit of two hundred francs a month and with this, and the pittance Léautaud earned at the *Mercure,* they could just scrape along. Léautaud had always felt that an author should not live by his pen, but should provide for his board and lodging by some other occupation. It was only thus that he could be certain of retaining his literary independence. He looked about now for a job, but found it impossible to get one that suited him. Then Vallette offered him the post of secretary to the *Mercure de France.* His working hours were to be from nine-thirty till six and he would be paid 125 francs a month. This sum Vallette unwillingly increased to 150 francs, but made it plain that there would be no further rise. Blanche advised him to refuse and keep his liberty. It seemed shocking that at the age of thirty-five, and with the reputation he had acquired, he should accept such a paltry salary; but he was afraid that if he refused the offer Vallette would be angry with him and perhaps no longer want him to write for the magazine. Finally he accepted and on the first of January 1908 entered upon his duties. They were to remind subscribers that their subscriptions were due, see visitors and keep them from disturbing Vallette if he thought fit, receive manuscripts and consider them, correct proofs and in short do any odd jobs that needed doing. He held the post for thirty-three years and on the whole enjoyed it. The life suited him. He met the literary men of the day, and had plenty of time for gossip, which was the great pleasure of his life.

A thousand copies of *Le Petit Ami* had been printed. It took twenty years to sell them. Vallette then wanted to re-issue it. Léautaud refused to let him. He was dissatis-fied with it and wanted to re-write it. There were parts that he thought too literary. Léautaud used the word *littérature* in two ways. When he spoke of *ma littérature* he only meant his writings; when he cried, *"La littérature avant tout,"* it was to affirm his right to write of his mother without respect and of his father without affection. It is true that his mother had no claim to his respect nor his father to his affection. Léautaud took the craft of writing very seriously, and there are numerous passages of the Journal concerned with it. He conceived the notion that he wrote his best when he wrote what had occurred to him on the spur of the moment. I suppose he means by that when he wrote with what we call inspiration. When he laboured to put down on paper what he wanted to say the result, to his own mind, was dull and lifeless. Above all, he aimed at being natural. When he came across in *Le Petit Ami* a grammatical mistake he left it because it had come naturally. He thought that the word that first occurs to one is the best one to use and he would not own a dictionary. In this, oddly enough, Chekhov agreed with him. Léautaud thought that all writers used too many words and that what they wrote would be all the better if they wrote fewer. He had no patience with words put in to balance a phrase; he believed that if one said just what was needed, the phrase *had* balance. He liked poetic prose as little as he liked prosy poetry. He had no use for the flowery and the ornate. He eschewed metaphors and similes. His desire was to be brief, vivid and succinct. All this is reasonable enough and without doubt we should all write better if we bore his principles in mind.

Of course Léautaud had his prejudices. He detested Flaubert for the artificiality and the monotony of his style and claimed, rashly, that anyone could write like him who cared to take the trouble. One of Léautaud's cherished notions was that a writer's style should be so individual that you have only to read a page to name him. That is all very well, but from this Léautaud seems to infer that the style is good. It does not follow. No one who had ever read the novels of George Meredith, and in the later years of the nineteenth century all young men who fancied themselves cultured idolised him, no one who read a page from one of his novels could fail to know who had written it. It is just that fantastic, tortured, acrobatic style that now makes him, notwithstanding his great merits, difficultly readable.

Léautaud had never been out of France. He seldom left Paris. He loved its streets, he loved its shops; he had associations with every corner of Montmartre and the quarter of the left bank which had its centre in St. Sulpice and the Panthéon. In 1911 he left Paris to live in a suburb. This harsh, selfish, bitter man had a passion for animals. The sight of a broken-down nag pulling a heavy cart shattered him so that he could think of nothing else all day. His heart was wrung when he saw in the streets dogs and cats that their owners, going away for a holiday, had left to fend for themselves. When he came upon a lost dog he would go to a shop and buy four sous' worth of cooked meat and give it to him, then try to find someone who would give it a home. Every evening he bought minced meat at the butcher's and took it to the stray cats that wandered about the gardens of the Luxembourg. And remember, he was desperately poor; he had to scrape and save to have enough to eat. On one occasion he came across a dog that was obviously starving. He had only a franc in his pocket for his day's food and that only because he had been thrifty the day before. He went and bought meat for the lost brute. That day, as on many others, he ate only bread and cheese. Léautaud had a cat of his own whom (or which) both he and Blanche doted on. From their constant squabbles it looks as though their passion for Boule, that was the cat's name, was the only thing that kept them together. Boule eventually died and Léautaud found and adopted a strange dog whom he called Amis and to whom he soon grew devoted. The time came when he had to make one of his numerous changes of habitation and for the dog's sake he looked for an apartment on the ground floor so that it could easily be let out. The various *concierges* of the houses he applied at told him that dogs were not allowed, so he decided to live out of town. He found a small house with a garden in the suburb called Fontenay aux Roses and settled there. There he remained for the rest of his life.

It is not clear whether Blanche went with him. From remarks he made in one of his dramatic criticisms, in which, as I have said, he was apt to talk of everything except of the play upon which he was called to deliver judgment, he tells of a woman, presumably Blanche, who lived with him, abandoned him for a rich lover, returned and abandoned him again, and when she once more returned, he would have nothing more to do with her. He said, characteristically enough, that though you no longer love your mistress, when she leaves you for another, you can't help being angry and jealous. He was able now to house all the stray cats and lost dogs that he came across. He often had as many as thirty. It complicated his life. He had to take the train in the morning to be at the offices of the *Mercure* by nine-thirty and when they were closed at six he had to take the train back to Fontenay to feed his animals; then, two or three times a week at least, he had to return to Paris to see a play and did not get home till after midnight. Sometimes he had a woman of mature age to clean up and cook for him, but it was not a success, since sooner or later she made advances to him and, when he rejected them, left in a huff. He was on the whole better off alone. He managed well enough. His tastes were simple. He did not mind what he ate, he never drank spirits, and wine but seldom. His only luxury was tea.

The years went by. The First World War was waged. The Second World War broke out. Most of Léautaud's friends, Van Bever, his oldest friend, died; Remy de Gourmont, with whom he was more intimate than with any other man of letters of his day, died; Alfred Vallette died. Vallette had published his first poems, had encouraged him to write and had printed in the *Mercure* everything he wrote. Though he scolded him sometimes for his unpunctuality in arriving at the office in the morning and for the unconscionable time he stayed away when he went out to lunch, he defended him from the attacks of

his enemies and when he was penniless cheerfully lent him money. He was a curious editor. He never read the contributions to his magazine until they were in print and then only if for some reason he was obliged to. He chose his staff with care and gave them freedom to do what they thought fit. The only thing he asked of them was that they should not bore. He made the *Mercure* an influential magazine with, comparatively, a wide circulation. One day someone asked him if he had read a certain book. "Good God, no," he answered. "Isn't it enough that I published it?" Vallette's successor as head of the firm was a certain Jacques Bernard. One morning when Léautaud arrived at the office, the *concierge* told him that Bernard wished to see him at once. On going to his room Jacques Bernard said to him, "Léautaud, I have decided to part with you for the pleasure of not seeing you any more." He added, "If I have to take money from my own pocket, I'll take it." Léautaud, never at a loss for a repartee, answered, "When one gets such a pleasure, it's worth a certain sacrifice." He took his bits and pieces out of the room he had occupied for three and thirty years, and departed. Thus brutally fired after so long a period, he was destitute. He was sixty-nine. He applied for an old age pension and was granted it. When the war came to an end Jacques Bernard was tried on the charge of collaboration with the enemy. He must have been nervous when he heard that Léautaud was one of the witnesses for the prosecution. The evidence he gave was so temperate that Bernard was acquitted. Some months before this Léautaud had an experience that few of us authors have the luck to enjoy. The Vichy radio announced that he was dead. The news occasioned a great number of articles, and Léautaud was astounded to find that they were laudatory. That was the last thing he expected.

During the German Occupation Léautaud lived quietly at Fontenay aux Roses. He suffered from the cold. Since coal was unobtainable, he cut down the trees in his garden for firewood. Food was scarce and he was reduced to eating four potatoes a day. He cooked them himself. To his sorrow he could no longer provide for the large number of cats and dogs that he had cared for so tenderly. He was forced to get rid of them. The war ended. He made a little money by journalism, but remained desperately poor: it was a stroke of luck for him when someone had the idea, in 1950, of getting him to have a series of conversations on the radio with a writer called Robert Mallet. They were later published and one edition after another was issued. Mine is the sixteenth. Léautaud was seventy-eight. In these talks he proved himself as pigheaded and pugnacious, as vivacious, witty and prejudiced, as scornful of sentimentality, as sensible and unreasonable as he had always been. They delighted listeners. We may hope that the money he received from them enabled him to live in some comfort for the rest of his life. He died in the eighty-fourth year of his age.

I don't know what the reader of these pages will make of the sketch, necessarily inadequate, of the strange man whom I have done my best to describe. He was a card. He cannot be judged by ordinary standards. He was a mixture of heterogeneous traits. He was callous and emotional, ruthlessly independent, passionately interested in literature and indignant with those who made it a business and a source of advancement, irascible and impatient with those who did not think as he did, faithful to those he liked and merciless to those he despised. He prided himself on never having done anyone harm. It is odd that it never occurred to him that a word might be more hurtful than a blow. When people asked him how he could be so kindly to animals and to his fellow creatures so brutal, he answered that animals were defenceless, dependent on people, but human beings could defend themselves. I have said little about his love life. He was interested in women only if he could have with them what the papers nowadays delicately call intimacy. He thought them deceitful, malicious, exacting, mercenary and stupid. From his own accounts he was an unsatisfactory lover—for reasons which the reader, if he thinks it worth the trouble, can find out for himself in the *Journal.* Love, of course, is not the right word in this connection, but the right word is unprintable. He was incapable of love, for he was interested only in himself. He was surely right when he said that love is rooted in sexual attraction and cannot arise without it, but seems not to have seen that it only becomes love when it gives rise to feelings, bitter pains and ecstatic joys, more commendable.

Paul Léautaud looked upon his Journal as his only work of any importance. He attached very little to *Le Petit Ami* and *In Memoriam.* Four volumes of the *Journal* have been published. They deal with his life from 1903 to 1924, but as he went on writing it till the end of it there must be a good many volumes to come. When it is complete it will provide an interesting account of the literary world of his day. It will deal with no such figures as the Goncourts had the advantage of dealing with. Sainte-Beuve, Taine, Renan, Michelet, Flaubert were long since dead. So were the poets Victor Hugo, Baudelaire, Verlaine, Rimbaud, and Mallarmé. These were the great figures that had given distinction to their era and made France the proud centre of culture and civilisation. Even the popular novelists, Alphonse Daudet and Émile Zola, were dead. Who were the authors that Léautaud found to write about? It would be unfair to say that they were trivial. They were gifted, but their gifts were on a smaller scale than those of their predecessors. There was Henri de Régnier, a delicate poet and a graceful novelist; there was Barrés, who intoxicated the young with his *Culte du Moi,* but turned to politics and propaganda; there was the talented and cultivated André Gide. There was Anatole France, much admired in his own day and unjustly despised in ours. There was Moréas, a Greek, whose *Stances* Léautaud admired and whom he liked as a man for his modesty, good nature and bohemian ways; there was Apollinaire, a Pole, who was killed in the First World War; there was Paul Valéry. The writers who held the stage during the first thirty or forty years of this century were talented in their different ways, but they had neither the significance for their contemporaries, nor the authority and influence which their predecessors of the nineteenth century had had for theirs.

The volumes of Léautaud's *Journal* that have so far been published make curious reading. There is a good deal that can be skipped. Léautaud loved a bit of scandal: you cannot at this time of day be interested in the long recital of a sordid love affair between persons you have never heard of. But as a picture of the literary life in Paris during the period of which Léautaud wrote, the book is remarkable. The phrase tells us that dog don't eat dog. That was not the case with these authors. They seldom had a good word to say for one another. There was a certain amount of corruption. An author who had money was not above paying the editor of a newspaper to insert the eulogistic review of his book that he had himself written. Authors were not ashamed to bring all the influence they could bring to bear in order to get favourable notices. Intrigue was general, to get published, to get publicity, to get a decoration; and nowhere was it more rampant than when it was a matter of getting one of the literary prizes, like the *Prix Goncourt,* of which there were already several. It is not a pretty picture and, though Léautaud was an acid observer who preferred to blame rather than to praise, to say a disagreeable thing rather than a pleasant one, you get the impression that it was on the whole a true one. In extenuation it is only fair to add that at the bottom of the corruption, envy, jealousy, backbiting and the rest was the need for money. Writers were wretchedly paid, and if they wanted to make a living, they could not afford to be over scrupulous. Léautaud spent thirty years as an employee, doing work that any clerk could have done, in order to maintain his independence so that he could write, as he claimed every author should, purely for his pleasure. It is greatly to his credit.

I don't know what the reader will think of these three Journalists whom I have to the best of my ability described to him. Not much, I suppose. They had few redeeming traits. Their egoism was ferocious. They were riddled with prejudices. They were monstrously touchy. Though they had little good to say of others, they fiercely resented criticism of themselves. They had no morals. They were indifferent to the arts, with exception of the art of letters, and when, as they sometimes did, they offered an opinion on music, painting or sculpture, it was (at all events to our present judgment) absurd. They were callous to the feelings of others. They were malicious and unkind.

But if they had these traits, we know them only because they have told us of them themselves. If I were asked whether on the whole they were any worse than other men, I should be at a loss for an answer. On one occasion Léautaud was presented to the Abbé Mugnier. The Abbé Mugnier was one of those priests who are now and then produced by the Catholic Church. He was a wit and a scintillating talker. He was a welcome guest at the dinner tables of the Boulevard St. Germain; he would hold the company entranced by his eloquent and amusing conversation. But though (to the scandal of some of his fellow priests) he much frequented the rich and noble, he never forgot his sacred office. The rich and noble too had souls to save. He persuaded the dissolute to mend their ways and won back not a few free-thinkers to the Church. When the party which he had graced with his presence broke up he returned to his very modest dwelling. There he was always to be seen by the poor and humble who came to him in their troubles for advice or aid. He helped them with his money, little though he had, and with his heartfelt sympathy. He was a man of a shining virtue. He knew that Léautaud was an aggressive sceptic—there were few people of his day about whom the Abbé Mugnier didn't know whatever was to be known—and he said to him, "God will forgive you, Monsieur Léautaud, because you have loved animals."

John Coleman (essay date 1959)

SOURCE: "Fin de Siècle," in *The Spectator,* No. 6833, June 12, 1959, p. 863.

[*In the following excerpt, Coleman declares* The Child of Montmartre *an unsuccessful document of the Paris milieu.*]

The Child of Montmartre is a trio of autobiographical sketches first published in the early 1900s and not properly a novel at all, though some sort of mild fictionising has probably gone on and Léautaud's slow unfolding of the characters of his profligate parents is done with the full appearance of a writer calculating, and bringing off, his effects. Léautaud's most accessible charm, of which one well might grow weary over longer stretches, lies in the way he allows his little world the courage of its weaknesses. The bastard son of a *souffleur* at the Comédie-Française and a minor flighty actress, he spent his evenings, and a good part of his days as well, in the company of whores and stage-ladies and no one has better caught the strong pull of the *louche* for those who are capable of feeling keenly enough but distrust emotion: 'I found relaxation in these colourful places; life in them was many-hued, after the inert, monotonous masterpieces.' He comes back to this more than once, commenting in an aside on 'the great books we read later on with either scepticism or envy.' He is careful not to specify the masterpieces he is running away from, but he obviously has a healthy down on them. *Un*healthy, of course, would be the final word on most of his attitudes: 'For is not this very fatigue of love, that glazes and encircles their eyes and hardens their faces a little, the most exciting part of their beauty?' What makes his book such an original and rewarding experience is the scrupulous, slightly ironic honesty with which he sets it all down, the failures if anything more than the conquests. It would be misleading to think of him as a sort of footnote to Lautrec's posters: there is surprisingly little 'period' detail, unless you are prepared to find the reiteration of song-titles and street-names evocative. His tone is modern, deprecatory but utterly self-assured, and the descriptions of his near-affair with his rediscovered mother, of his father's rammish successes and miserable death-bed, and of his own first affair with the sister of a friend (whom he did not like: he did not much like his friends) are delicate and personal

achievements, possible only because you have been early persuaded of his trustworthiness as an observer of the limited range of his own feelings.

V. S. Pritchett (essay date 1959)

SOURCE: "An Egotist of the Half World," in *The New Statesman,* Vol. LVIII, No. 1479, July 18, 1959, pp. 86-87.

[*In the following excerpted review of Léautaud's* The Child of Montmartre, *Pritchett employs Léautaud's autobiographical writings to construct a psychological basis for what Pritchett perceives as Léautaud's misogyny and vitriolic criticism.*]

Léautaud is, in some respects, the Toulouse-Lautrec of French literature and the three fragments of autobiography in this volume are a sweetish liqueur extracted from squalid experience. An essayist who was for many years the distinguished dramatic critic of the *Mercure de France,* he was the son of a prompter at the Comédie Francaise by a minor actress who soon abandoned her child. He was brought up by an old 'aunt', was competed for by his father's innumerable mistresses, and spent his childhood being petted by the tarts of the street in Montmartre where he and his wanton father lived. He skipped school in order to sit in bars with them in the afternoons before they went to 'work'. He was in and out of their boudoirs and bedrooms, gazing at their toilet, listening to their chatter about hats, clothes, rent and men and to their jealousies. Spoiled, gentle, lonely, shy and already an intense little egotist, he grew up in a state of innocence which seems to have lasted longer than it does among the respectable; and when innocence went, he was the 'little friend' who wrote the girls' letters for them and who lived, for all his life, under the spell of their sociability. His parents showed him almost no love and the faculty was in consequence feeble in himself; sex without love—since he belonged to the world where it was always bought—seemed to him gayer, kinder, more various, less exacting and ominous than in respectable life simply because it was perfunctory. It also gave him more time for writing and the stimulus for it, and it agreed well with a cool and inspecting temperament which was a good deal infantile, and the result of injury. Pity is almost Léautaud's only emotion; it is touched with dislike and cruelty and he never lets this or any other feeling get the better of his pessimism or self-love.

Mr Somerset Maugham, a connoisseur of amoralists, has described Léautaud as 'an egoist, but devoid of vanity, a teacher without passion, cynical and conscientious, desperately poor but indifferent to money, harsh in his dealings with his fellows, but to animals compassionate, savagely independent, indifferent to what others thought of him, a brilliant talker, a caustic wit, truthful, honest, but cheerfully tolerant of the dishonesty of others—altogether a strange man'. As a writer he was very much the *belle-lettriste,* with a consciously amateur style and a waylaying mockery.

His first fragment *Le Petit Ami* is as much a piece of introspection about the art of finding the right words for one's memories and nostalgias, as it is of his childhood itself. The book was published in 1903 and caused a small scandal because of one of its episodes. He had grown up and met the mother he only faintly remembered and who did not know him. Halting and embarrassed, he pressed a disturbing flirtation upon her, addressing her as mother and mistress. She was now a reformed and respectable bourgeois with a legitimate family; but he awakened the coquette in her; she was flustered, tempted in imagination. For three days they talked—while his aunt lay dying in the next room—and for months they wrote extravagantly tender letters to each other 'without believing in them overmuch', until the Stendhalian episode ended and the mother sternly reverted to the bourgeois and broke off the correspondence. Léautaud had both feet firmly set in literature and his claws were showing when he played with his mother's sensibility and his own. Literature was his escape and his weapon and he took a cruel pleasure, well-known to artists, in punishing his mother for her heartlessness by heartlessly leading her on, so as to provide himself with one more 'little page' of his book. (In fact, this very heartlessness pleased her.) Léautaud's faults as a writer belong to the period: archness, pretended modesty, the habit of calling things 'little': 'I, my little corner'. 'One acts little plays sometimes sentimental. . . .' One does 'absurd little things'. Why he hated Anatole France, whom he often resembles, it is hard to see; but when Anatole France played, he at least played at passion. There is a hint indeed that onanism rather than lechery was Léautaud's vice.

Under the conscious charm, Léautaud was a rancorous and probably envious critic, as his *Journals* show. His virtue as a writer lies in his power of precise portraiture, his particularity when he is describing the street and shop life of Montmartre, the sociable sight of the Folies Bergère, and also certain macabre scenes like the death of one of his girls in hospital, the death of his aunt and his father; and above all in his emotional honesty. Of course, he had few emotions; but he refused to fake the deprivation. He had a horror of 'literature'. In erotic insinuation he is tactful rather than inciting, never overheated. He was amused by a girl who brought him coffee in the morning and whose breast hung into the sugar bowl when she bent to put the tray down. He could, he frequently notes, supply 'more precise details and livelier scenes' but prefers not. Prudence is part of the titillation. He is describing the mean world in which he has been brought up and is at home, enjoys its garishness, delights in the mercenary nature of his friends, and their hardness as they age. He escapes the depravity of the outsider, and if he is a smug, old sentimental cynic on the surface, he is much more the grim, observant and devastated child underneath. Actually, he was only 35 when *Le Petit Ami* was written and his assumption of the air of premature old age was a literary device. With father bringing home a different actress every night and step-mother carrying on about it, the young Léautaud must have been old at the age of ten. It is natural that he should feel for women as he feels for

animals; a half-contemptuous, half-fascinated charity. Of men, represented by his ruthless father, he was terrified. That, among other things, must account for his rancour as a critic. But he had the talent to etch a small world clearly and without blobbing it with moralistic shadows.

Naomi Bliven (essay date 1959)

SOURCE: A review of *The Child of Montmartre*, in *The New Yorker*, Vol. 35, No. 33, October 3, 1959, pp. 153-55.

[*In the following excerpt, Bliven favorably reviews* The Child of Montmartre, *and finds it supports her notions of the decadence of Paris in the 1890s.*]

Paul Léautaud was a Parisian editor and critic who, around the turn of the century, published three autobiographical novelettes, which have just been translated by Humphrey Hare and collectively printed as *The Child of Montmartre*. The first deals with Léautaud's mother, the second with his father, and the third with his own first love. Léautaud's mother, who was not married to his father, was an unsuccessful actress who eventually found herself a husband and moved to Switzerland, leaving her disreputable past, and her child, behind her. His father, a tireless pursuer of women, failed as an actor and became a prompter at the Comédie-Francaise. Jeanne, Léautaud's first love and first mistress, masqueraded as a nice young girl long enough to seduce him, and then left him for an older, richer man.

Le Petit Ami, the story of Léautaud's mother, begins with a kindly disquisition on some of the Montmartre prostitutes the author knew in his youth. They "formed" him, he says, discussing these unreliable, unhealthy women in the tone of a man of the world recalling what a young hobbledehoy he had been before he was polished in the salons of great ladies. His mother visited him once in his childhood, and he never saw her again until he was grown up; then they met at the deathbed of her sister, his Aunt Fanny. While her sister lay dying, his mother flirted with her son. She asked about his brand-new literary career and spoke of the many mysterious, sorrowful complications that had kept them apart. By the time Aunt Fanny died, Léautaud had been worked into a perfect swivet, a desperate ambition to be loved as a son, confused by an incestuous desire for his mother. She went back to Switzerland, promising never again to lose track of her brilliant boy, but after writing him a couple of letters she dropped him flat; their new relation was, to her, an easy exercise in seduction. The compliment Léautaud pays her at the beginning of *Le Petit Ami,* when he compares her to the unsuccessful streetwalkers he knows—"It really is a great pity my mother was not more ambitious. . . . With her talents, she would be much in vogue today"—is all he thinks she deserves.

In Memoriam, the novelette-memoir about Léautaud's father, informs us that Aunt Fanny, the moribund maiden lady of *Le Petit Ami,* had preceded his mother as his father's mistress and had borne him a child, who died. But the sisters were only two of Léautaud *père's* affairs; he was trying to match Leporello's catalogue of Don Giovanni's conquests, and he came close. Still, for all his victories, he loved nobody and nobody loved him. He married one of his mistresses, who thereby became the author's stepmother, and her notion of marital fidelity was to try to cuckold her husband with her stepson. Léautaud refused her, because of shyness rather than filial loyalty, and she got her husband to throw him out of the house.

When Léautaud met his first mistress, Jeanne Ambert, she was, he tells us in *Amours,* the third book of the trilogy, living in the suburbs with her family, who knew of his wretched home life and sympathetically offered him their hospitality. Léautaud, who was only seventeen, felt that he was betraying their trust by sleeping with Jeanne, but he managed to philosophize away his guilt: "Honest love, pure love, are they not the contrary of love? One does the best one can." And he presently discovered that his guilt was wasted; Jeanne's relatives were no more respectable than his own. They had only been briefly, accidentally posing as a united family, and after their suburban interlude Jeanne, her mother, and her brother returned to Paris, where the father had been living with his mistress, and settled back into a cozy welter of illicit family arrangements.

It is hard to imagine a grimmer youth, but Léautaud was not exhibiting his wounds to arouse the reader's pity; he believed that pity, like love, is either hypocrisy or sentimentality. (He was a victim of the most pathetic illusion of all; he was convinced he had no illusions.) These novelettes were written to shock, and they do shock, because they are steeped in hatred. Léautaud was a good writer, who composed each sentence with exquisite care. Every story has an air of spontaneity, though it is, on the contrary, painstakingly designed, and for maximum destructiveness. *The Child of Montmartre* is a dazzling job of literary articulation that resembles nothing so much as a small, well-balanced knife.

Léautaud did not squander prose on general description, and it may seem at first as if, preoccupied with his own story, he had not told the reader much about the gay, night-blooming Montmartre of the eighteen-nineties. But of course he has told the reader precisely what matters—that its gaiety was a fraud, its glamour was seedy, and its inhabitants most of them, were cold and stupid.

Francis Wyndham (essay date 1959)

SOURCE: A review of *The Child of Montmartre,* in *The London Magazine,* Vol. 6, No. 11, November, 1959, pp. 84-86.

[*In the following excerpt, Wyndham expresses annoyance at Léautaud's repeated contempt for literature, and declares him a minor literary figure.*]

Both *The Square* and *Child of Montmartre* could only have been written by French authors; indeed, they neatly illustrate two extreme manifestations of the national literary character. The cult of compression, the stern elimination of irrelevancies and 'furniture', are developed by Marguerite Duras to a point that is almost ludicrous. One is so conscious of what has been omitted from her tentative dialogue between a lonely nursery maid and a lonely commercial traveller, that one cannot help questioning the necessity of what has been allowed to remain, resenting the deliberate repetitions for taking up valuable space. As a contrast, Paul Léautaud (the Jean Genet of his day) was one of those 'natural' writers who crop up every so often in French literature, break every formal rule, and are extravagantly admired for their lawlessness. All is personal, subjective and defiantly unedited: he put everything he could remember into the three shapeless fragments of autobiography, here translated together, and the many repetitions they contain are less deliberate than obsessional. Yet this method also has a drawback, one strangely similar to that of its opposite: if with Mlle Duras one thinks 'having eliminated so much, she might as well have eliminated a bit more while she was about it', with Léautaud one's reaction is likely to be 'since all his most intimate experiences have gone into this book uncensored, it's rather disappointing that it doesn't add up to more'. The reserved writer, in fact, gives an impression of long-windedness, and the uninhibited writer is finally seen to have revealed very little.

These books share an essentially French quality of seriousness, a preoccupation with finding a way that leads to the truth; their authors happen to have chosen different ways, neither perhaps as direct as they had hoped. With Léautaud it is a truth about his own peculiar temperament; with Mlle Duras it is a more general truth about mankind as a whole. She presents a formal conversation between strangers on a park bench, in which the subject of loneliness is analysed with a hesitant fumbling for accuracy and an elementary lucidity. This is the lucidity found only in simple people who take nothing for granted—a plane of simplicity on which the uneducated and the most austerely intellectual meet. The man in the novel has cultivated means by which he can occasionally and partially reconcile himself to loneliness: small pleasures, interests and distractions, rare moments when he has been moved to a mysterious wonder. The girl, on the other hand, will encourage no compromise; she wants total escape from loneliness or nothing at all; until this expected miracle occurs, she refuses to take steps towards mitigating her condition. The bare design and stark structure of *The Square* urge a symbolic interpretation—indeed, admit of no other; and on this level the honesty of the writing does convey a dignified consideration of the human situation and one of its basic dilemmas. If it lacks the verbal horseplay of *Waiting for Godot* (another symbolic dialogue to which it is possibly related), it is less despairing: communication, Mlle Duras implies, is just possible, though not very probable. But without Beckett's brilliance, triviality is not always avoided; there are times when one suspects that Mlle Duras could have stated her case more successfully if she had chosen a more straightforward and less suggestive manner. She seems to have been in awe of her theme, and to have stressed its magnitude by introducing a note of solemnity into the self-revelations of her speakers. This detracts from their pathos, and also impairs the total effect of concentrated simplicity which should distinguish and justify the bleak medium she has selected (and helped to make fashionable) for the theme's expression.

Paul Léautaud died four years ago at the age of eighty-three. He was the illegitimate son of the prompter at the Comédie Française; brought up by a succession of his father's mistresses, as a child he saw his mother only once—an occasion which left a deep impression on him. As a young man he preferred the company of prostitutes to any other, and led the sort of life that Lautrec painted. At the deathbed of an aunt he met his mother again—now married, but still with all the cocotte's allure that he remembered, and that had established his pattern of sexuality. He fell passionately in love with her, but although she encouraged him to a certain extent, they do not seem to have become lovers. This odd relationship he described in *Le Petit Ami,* first published in 1902; in 1905 and 1906 there followed *In Memoriam,* which was chiefly concerned with his father, and *Amours,* in which he recounted an early love affair with the sister of a friend.

As is often the case with people who take an aggressive pride in their familiarity with, and acceptance by the underworld, Léautaud is on the whole rather a bore. The description of his incestuous passion, and his evocation of *fin de siècle* life on the *grands boulevards* are interesting for a time; but there is something self-conscious about his account of the first (he is more fascinated, and perhaps even more deeply shocked by the situation than any of his readers are likely to be) and his lyrical nostalgia for the bar at the Folies Bergères is highly repetitive and, on examination, not very informative. His nostalgia is too great; it outruns his powers of expression, and finally he can only list names of women, streets, cafés and songs without explaining (as perhaps only a Proust could do) why and how it is that they move him. He also continually expresses a contempt for literature which is always irritating coming from somebody engaged in literary activity—though many people are impressed by this attitude, as it implies a first-hand knowledge of life mysteriously denied to more professional competitors. Léautaud seldom lets one forget his amateur status, but his studied casualness is really a literary trick like any other. Yet he was honest and he took writing seriously: *Child of Montmartre* will endure as a human document but not as a work of art; a work of art demands more than honesty and a serious purpose, more than Léautaud possessed.

Rayner Heppenstall (essay date 1960)

SOURCE: A review of *Journal of a Man of Letters, 1898-1907,* in *The London Magazine,* Vol. 7, No. 7, July, 1960, pp. 92-93.

[*In the following review of Léautaud's* Journal of a Man of Letters, 1898-1907, *Heppenstall faults Geoffrey Sainsbury's translation and editing of Léautaud's original journals.*]

Paul Léautaud died four years ago, aged eighty-four. We may feel that we have always known his name but, for many of us, he materialized only last year with *Child of Montmartre,* the translation of his autobiographical novel, *Petit Ami.* Mr Sainsbury here offers us in abridgement about a quarter of the *Journal Littéraire.* On the jacket, the publishers describe it as a 'first volume' of Mr Sainsbury's English version, but cautiously do not elsewhere show it as Vol. I. There is not much else to translate—a few poems, drama criticism under the name of 'Maurice Boissard', scripts of the radio interviews which made a stir in the early 'fifties. And yet we must feel that our literary acquaintance has been permanently added to by this engaging figure.

His father, an unsuccessful actor, became prompter at the Comédie Française. His mother, some kind of *cocotte,* also loosely connected with the stage, went off and finally settled in Switzerland. In these journals, Paul Léautaud notes down the anniversaries of his father's death and the two letters a year he wrote to his mother. It was a disturbed, harsh childhood, with too little schooling, but with pattings on the head by men of letters. Until he took to writing, and intermittently thereafter, when he was hard up, Léautaud worked in lawyers' offices. Finally, he went on the *Mercure* staff, under that noble editor, Alfred Vallette. Blackbearded, lacking in confidence, 'cynical', he yet preserved a fierce integrity, and in the photograph here his eyes, as Mr Pryce-Jones says, have 'an unassailable air of mocking veracity'. He seems to have been kind to a succession of mistresses, but what he specially loved were stray cats. *'N'est pas fils de putain qui veut,'* said Mme Vallette ('Rachilde'). Gide liked him and, in 1938, finds him still at the *Mercure,* giving vent to 'vast bursts of very sonorous laughter which, as he hinted, do not spring from a very gay heart'.

Gide also found that Léautaud was 'sinking into a sort of most delightful *subjective absolute*' and 'particularly intractable in matters of language, refusing to admit sins against grammar'. This last observation is odd. During the period of the present volume, Léautaud repeatedly says that the only subject which interests him is himself but, linguistically and stylistically, his principal notion was that of 'writing well by writing badly'—a notion he picked up from Stendhal, in whose work he found especially praiseworthy a tendency to begin sentences without knowing how they would end. Stendhal was his chief master, Diderot coming second.

Literary Paris from 1890 to the First World War is fabulously well-documented. Collating the various published journals and reminiscences (Gide, Bloy, Gregh, Charles du Bos and now Léautaud), one could establish what any French writer was doing at pretty-well any moment during the whole quarter of a century. This, I think, bears on

Mr Sainsbury's principles of selection. A specialist in the period has the full text in French. Very minor writers of the day may mean something to the French general reader. The English general reader may think it a pity that Mr Sainsbury so concentrates on visits to the *Mercure* office and on the jockeying for literary prizes. More intimate gossip, more stories about animals, might have widened the appeal of the book, with no loss to the scholar who, as Mr Sainsbury candidly says, could not really use it anyway.

Of one episode, the story of Mme Kaplan and M. Rubenstein, I could not make head or tail, though it seems that the two had been imprisoned on suspicion of being involved in a bomb outrage. The whole business (with which Léautaud was presumably involved as an employee at his lawyer's *étude*) is no less obscure in the full French text. One might have thought that at this point there confronted Mr Sainsbury the choice between doing a piece of original research or omitting the whole thing. The nevertheless vivid Mme Dehaynin also goes quite unexplained, and about her Mr Sainsbury does leave good stuff out. One might further complain of too many translatable words untranslated, far too many misprints uncorrected and a deficient index. But Mr Sainsbury's translation is workmanlike, and there are marvellous portraits of Remy de Gourmont, Huysmans, Marcel Schwob, with a brief and devastating glimpse of the unfortunate Alfred Jarry and the sight of our own Sir Gerald Kelly in an unfamiliar *rôle*. Two mistresses, the evasive Georgette and the indignant Blanche, are so vividly absent we feel we might have lived with them ourselves.

Seymour S. Weiner (essay date 1960)

SOURCE: "Sincerity and Variants: Paul Léautaud's *Petit Ami*," in *Symposium*, Vol. XIV, No. 3, Fall, 1960, pp. 165-87.

[*In the following excerpt, Weiner examines the merits of Léautaud's* Le Petit Ami.]

Paul Léautaud's *Le Petit Ami* first appeared in the *Mercure de France* of 1902,[1] and was published in book form the following year.[2] Since then a small group of enthusiasts have painstakingly followed his sporadic writings through various periodicals. Occasionally some of these pieces were gathered together in a book. But *Le Petit Ami* was personally known only to a few. Ordinary copies have sold for a hundred dollars and more, and those on Holland paper for at least twice that amount.[3] Léautaud opposed its reissue;[4] only since his death has it become generally available.[5]

Léautaud died in his eighty-fourth year on February 22, 1956, but the news was not publicized until three days later. Almost fifteen years earlier (in May, 1941) the same "slightly exaggerated" event had been announced. Léautaud was renowned, since the deathbed description of his own father's demise, as a specialist in physical and

literary necropsy; this misapprehension on his own passing must have seemed like a reprieve. It was indeed a kind of resuscitation, for within the last decade this author, the admiration of a few, became the delight of the general public in France and, to some extent, abroad. A series of radio broadcasts—thirty-eight interviews of Léautaud by Robert Mallet[6] between November, 1950, and July, 1951—though somewhat censored for a mixed audience, made of him a public sensation. The forthrightness of expression, the sonority of voice, the bursts of laughter, the sharpness and individuality of the retorts, the references to the tone and quality of his writings—these revelations elicited an enthusiastic response. Léautaud was envisaged as unique: a "Chamfort du VIᵉ arrondissement," a "voyou de lettres"[7] with a disdain for subterfuge or deceit who cut to the quick with the flick of his wit.

Léautaud prided himself on quasi-complete rejection of dupery: his quirk was to claim truthfulness as his only persuasion. People differed as to the extent of his self-understanding, but partisans and opponents both looked to the revelations of his *Journal littéraire*,[8] which he had been compiling almost daily since 1893. Since his was an admittedly uncharitable and cynical view regarding the degree of altruism and sagacity in man—especially the man of letters!—these commentaries were supposed to contain the data of, along with Léautaud's observations on, his contemporaries. Also, there would be the unvarnished record of his own life!

Le Petit Ami is part of that record, an essential part. It contains the leitmotifs of its author's whole subsequent career; in this work we find the adumbration of the values by which he was to live as well as the psychograph of how they came to be.

This first-person narrative bathes in the chiaroscuro of the fictional [?] autobiography. Twin notes of irony and of heartache echo repeatedly as a series of vignettes portrays certain aspects of Parisian life in the last quarter of the last century. The sometimes sober, sometimes passionate, warmth of nostalgic memory couched in usually simple, suggestive language; the neatness of characterization against selected details of the locale—these fit together to evoke compellingly the world of the story. But the unusual personality of the narrator—sentimentalist, ironist, self-mocker—in search of a direction to his life, and the reasons for wanting that direction, imbues these data with psychological significance. The reader is carried along on the quest. The sudden brusqueness, the sharper tone, with the introduction of a possible incest, make the story dramatic. The reader is impressed by the aptness of the psychologizing, he is absorbed in the labyrinth of the tale: the story, simple in line, is rich in overtones. The reader is persuaded as he is with a Stendhalian revelation, he adduces the passion Baudelaire had for his mother. Nevertheless, *Le Petit Ami* is itself. And, as with any work of stature, the reader wants to reread, to immerse himself in the experiences, the memories, and the feelings of the protagonist. Stirred and intrigued by the author, he knows that this is an extraordinary work.

If the reader is familiar with Léautaud's earlier **"Essais"** and his later **"In Memoriam,"** he can see here the transition between these two manners and conceptions of art. If he knows of the esthetic belief of the author—"Je suis profondément convaincu que le seul antidote qui puisse faire oublier au lecteur les éternels *Je* que l'auteur va écrire, c'est une parfaite sincérité," as Stendhal said in his *Souvenirs d'égotisme*[9]—that in the seeking of style, ideas lose their significance, for the manner supersedes and deforms the content, then alterations may exemplify or negate his ability to implement this creed. Also, the question of whether an author *can* consciously control an unconscious compulsion to project a certain view of himself, when he is the very subject of his artistic efforts, becomes a matter for thought. Jean Selz has claimed, in commenting on Léautaud's *Journal littéraire,* that "Cette étroite liaison entre l'homme et ses écrits nécessitait un usage exclusif de la sincérité. Sans doute était-elle inséparable à la fois de son honnêteté de pensée et de son immoralisme, mais il est évident que tout mensonge eût contesté sa personnalité. Une telle sincérité ne se retrouve dans aucun autre journal d'écrivain. . . ."[10]

There seems, however, to be the inevitability, the *requirement* of a certain artificiality in an art-form. If, on the one hand, literature is not made of good intentions, on the other hand each choice of epithet, each decision to accent this or that aspect involves factors of perspicacity, of design (itself an occult force urging the act of communication), of representation.[11] An examination of variants reveals much regarding the artistic purposes, the changing values, and the degree of specific sincerity a writer may achieve. The data are informative in themselves; to the extent that they achieve or fall short of the author's intentions, they suggest the kinds of problems other artists face.

Since Léautaud made such a cult of sincerity and spontaneous expression, "sans fioritures"; since he felt that the greatest artistry was in the avoidance of artistry (other than what is the authentic, unarranged mode of the writer communicating *his personal* appreciations via words—"la prose d'un homme pour qui le naturel est la valeur suprême," as Henri Rambaud said of Léautaud[12]—the examination of variants in *Le Petit Ami* may be especially pertinent for the general problem of "authenticity" in a work of art. Because of Léautaud's striving for authenticity, does he actually subordinate the use of artistic arrangement and the attention to sophisticated artisanship? Variants may reveal to what extent theory and "good intentions" bow to the conquering dictates of other, more subtle, considerations.

Léautaud did not judge *Le Petit Ami* meritorious enough to reissue without major alterations: he thought that it should be rewritten and compressed into fifty pages. Toward the end of *Le Petit Ami* the narrator states: "je referai peut-être un jour ce livre, en une cinquantaine de pages; je vois si bien ce qu'il faudrait y enlever. . . . Il n'en est pas moins vrai que j'ai senti les choses que j'y raconte de la façon exacte dont je les ai dites. Ma nature est ici en conflit avec mon goût, voilà tout" (pp. 206-207). In 1907 Léautaud again accused himself: "Personne ne sait mieux que moi qu'on écrit toujours plus de mots qu'il en faut. Mais c'est un défaut où l'on tombe, malgré soi, si facilement. Les phrases de catalogue, comme je l'ai dit dans *Le Petit Ami,* il n'y a encore que cela de vrai" (*Journal littéraire,* II, 44; entry of September 23, 1907). The problem of composition versus spontaneity and naturalness remained ever of prime significance to him.[13] In 1924, when asked to permit a new edition of *Le Petit Ami,* he noted in his diary: "J'ai répondu oui à condition de remaniements. J'ai regardé ce soir; des pages décidément ineptes" (idem, IV, 294; entry of April 17, 1924).

But—unless, in the welter of manuscript he has left, there be found a corrected draft—he never got around to accomplishing this except for a partial treatment done for the *Choix de pages* by André Rouveyre.[14]

There does exist, however, an annotated copy of *Le Petit Ami,* glossed by Léautaud at some time when he was tinkering with textual revision. This copy is one of six issued, without stipulation of number, on Holland paper. Through the extraordinary courtesy of Raoul Simonson, a Belgian bookseller and bibliophile who is especially interested in modern writers and who is the fortunate owner of this item, I have been able to collate these emendations and annotations. A microfilm of this unique copy is in the University of Washington Library, as is a copy of the unannotated volume.

The situation is, then, that we have *Le Petit Ami* in four states[15]: the pre-original, the trade edition, the annotated copy of the latter, and the partial revision published by Rouveyre. In addition, we have corollary data in Léautaud's other writings, especially the *Journal littéraire* and the *Entretiens.*

Le Petit Ami first appeared in the *Mercure de France* upon the recommendation of Henri de Régnier, who read the manuscript for the periodical. Léautaud later dedicated the book to him. It was Alfred Vallette who chose the title *Le Petit Ami,* and added the descriptive epithet: *roman.* Léautaud had in mind the title *Souvenirs légers* (a title restored by Rouveyre in the revised version published in his *Choix de pages*). When asked by his editor and publisher to describe his work, Léautaud told him that it concerned "un jeune homme qui est le petit ami de certaines catins" (*Entretiens,* p. 124). But the author himself did not categorize his literature as a novel. Rachilde (Vallette's wife) was convinced—wished to believe—that *Le Petit Ami* was a work of fiction; and Octave Mirbeau, who urged Léautaud to present his book for the Goncourt Prize, must have deemed it eligible for an award limited to novels.

Le Petit Ami is divided into eight chapters, which have each an epigraph.[16] The maxim for the entire work is by Stendhal: "L'extrême des passions est niais à noter." This negative, derogatory, and ironic reflection is borne out by each of the succeeding *boutades,* which reflect the content and the tenor of each chapter: Chap. I, "Il n'y a dans la vie que des commencements" (Mme de Stael); Chap. II, "De toutes les infirmités humaines, la plus triste, c'est le sommeil de l'âme" (Proverbe); Chap. III, "Mon Dieu! que cet enfant est donc désagréable!" (Ma Mère; i.e., of the narrator); Chap. IV, "Rue La Bruyère, quels caractères! Quelles maximes, rue La Rochefoucauld!" (Gavarni); Chap. V, "La plus perdue des journées est celle où l'on n'a pas ri" (Chamfort); Chap. VI, "Mère des souvenirs, maîtresse des maîtresses . . ." (Baudelaire); Chap. VII, "Je t'aimais inconstant, qu'eussé-je fait, fidèle!" (Racine); and finally another quotation from Stendhal for Chap. VIII, "Souvent la fin d'un livre est fort inférieure au reste."

The brief opening chapter establishes the various themes which will be elaborated simultaneously, throughout the book: the personality of the person ("Je"—identified as "Paul" for the first time in Chap. VI, p. 134) who is relating the story; the intention of writing a book of remembrances; the inner vision of his mother, whom he had hardly known. Brought up in an environment of *demimondaines* or lower, he will describe them, the narrator tells us, and his relationship to them. The second chapter describes the routine of these venal persons, promising delights that hardly live up to justifying the importance we accord them; on the other hand, there is the secret delectation of foreseeing their eventual *déchéance.*

The third chapter is twice as long as any other, and is truly the heart of the book. Here we penetrate into the childhood of the teller. Here we are acquainted with the *quartier* bounded by Notre-Dame-de-Lorette and Fontaine streets, Clichy and Rochechouart boulevards, Rochechouart and Lamartine streets. It was at the lodging of the maid Marie that he slept, while his father entertained numerous female transients at his home. All the minutiae of a child's life, stored away in pristine freshness, are a thesaurus from which specimens are unwrapped and fondled. Precise dates, fragments of conversation, specific locales—all have been preserved, along with the sentimental reaction to each incident. Supreme treasure, the precious memory of a visit to his mother, his mother who had abandoned him shortly after his birth in order to follow, as fancy and chance offered, a life of pleasure. His mother, more successful or more fortunate in her career of *volupté* than the women he met regularly in the *quartier.*

The fourth chapter portrays several of these charmers, for "Rien n'est plus pénétrant que la société des femmes; on reçoit d'elles une influence souvent décisive et dont on garde toujours quelque chose" (p. 71). The fifth chapter describes the dancehalls, the balls, the cafés of these ladies, and their interests. The author lingers over a love affair somewhat more lasting than casual *passades*—the momentum of the recital has slowed down almost to inertia. The sixth chapter, second longest in the book, although only half as long as Chapter III, abruptly returns to the mother-son situation. They find one another at the

deathbed of his aunt (i.e., his mother's sister), "dans une ville du nord" (p. 129). To him his mother is as he saw her when he was ten, and he still wants from her the warmth and affection ever associated with her image—and, in addition, the more mature relationship between a male and a female. A sort of equivocal intimacy is nascent when they arrange to meet at Paris. And when that feverishly anticipated rendezvous does occur, it is only a few minutes before his mother's train pulls out for Switzerland where she lives with her legal husband and son by that marriage.

Chapter VII tells of their correspondence, the intensity with which the *sans-mère* awaits confidences and details, only to receive trite, evasive, and cold replies to his passionate missives. And so the author muses on what one may reasonably and unreasonably expect from life. The brief concluding chapter reflects on how this book came to be, with observations on how it should have been written: "Mon bonheur, ç'aurait été d'écrire ce livre comme des *Lettres,* ou comme des *Mémoires,* les seuls écrits qui comptent, avec de petites phrases exactes, courtes et sèches, comme des indications de catalogue, ou à peu près" (p. 206). And he promises that "Du reste, je referai peut-être un jour ce livre, en une cinquantaine de pages; je vois si bien ce qu'il faudrait y enlever" (pp. 206-207).

Well, what did Léautaud remove from the version in the *Mercure de France,* and why? What did he actually accomplish by these alterations? These are questions to be answered by an examination of the textual changes.

The collation of the pre-original (in the *Mercure de France,* text A) with the trade edition (text B)[17] reveals that Léautaud made approximately 160 changes. Their distribution into categories—additions, deletions, substitutions, changes in sense, and altered punctuation— shows clearly that the greatest number of changes consisted of *additions.* Instead of shortening his text, as he had intended, Léautaud made it longer! There are some 72 instances of additions. Some are slight, involving, for example, the addition of a brief epithet:

(A, 694) Ainsi je me distrais auprès de ces créatures

(B, 22) Ainsi je me distrais le plus possible auprès de ces créatures

But others contribute markedly to the *tone* of the whole book, helping to create the atmosphere of mingled diffidence and daring, of superciliousness and yearning:

(A, 687) Je suis bien sûr, en tous cas, que ce livre n'ennuiera pas trop mes amies

(B, 12) En tous cas, s'il assomme le lecteur, j'espère que ce livre n'ennuiera pas trop mes amies qui sont habituées à mon égotisme.

The bareness and directness of the earlier description:

(A, 688) Je songe enfin à ma mère, qui ne m'a guère donné que deux ou trois de ses traits charmants et dont la légèreté et les charmes me marquèrent, vers mes dix ans, d'un souvenir ineffaçable. Ah! ne me dérangez pas. . . .

has become vaguer, more circumspect through the technique of *petites touches* which round out with additional details while softening the direct impact of the presentation:

> (B, 13-14) Je songe enfin à ma mère, à qui je ressemble tant, paraît-il, par le caractère, et que je vis une fois, vers mes dix ans, d'une façon que je n'oublierai jamais. Comme je sais peu d'elle: ce que mon père me dit quelquefois, qu'elle était un peu petite mais très bien faite, mes souvenirs d'enfant, deux ou trois mots d'une parente, et quelques portraits que j'ai. . . . Ah! ne me dérangez pas. . . .

The utilitarian purpose of the time spent with *demi-mondaines* is emphasized in the revision; whereas the earlier text told us that

> (A, 695) Il le fallait bien, si je voulais devenir leur petit ami! Et puis, ça avait si peu d'importance!

the second state interpolates that

> (B, 24) Il le fallait bien, si je voulais me mettre dans leurs bonnes grâces et tirer d'elles, par la suite, des tas de choses pour mon livre. Ça avait si peu d'importance, du reste, qu'elles me roulent plus ou moins.

The documentary nature of **Le Petit Ami,** based on specific events carefully recorded, is further emphasized:

> (A, 185) . . . cahier de notes, pour le mettre au courant

> (B, 154) . . . cahier de notes, dont tout ce chapitre n'est que le développement, pour le mettre au courant

> (A, 189) . . . en retard

> (B, 160) . . . en retard. Sûrement, avec toutes ces histoires, j'allais être au moins un mois sans pouvoir travailler.

> (A, 462) . . . tourné vers moi . . .

> (B, 192) . . . tourné vers moi . . . Ah! c'est donc vrai que lorsqu'on a du chagrin on écrit quelquefois des choses qui ne sont pas mal?

Many of the additions are of a factual nature, adding selected details from the storehouse of memory or from a check of the locale. Thus we learn in the book, as we cannot from the periodical, that a M. Lesur was the director of his kindergarten, and a Leonardo the teacher. The "école communale de la rue Rodier" (A, 699) in B (p. 32) is "l'école communale de l'impasse Rodier, qu'on a dû transférer ailleurs, car je ne l'ai pas retrouvée." The local in A (p. 702) simply identified as being on Rue Notre-

Dame-de-Lorette is in B (p. 36) situated precisely at No. 14, "au premier étage, la première fenêtre à gauche, en regardant la maison." Throughout this section of **Le Petit Ami** there is a multiplication of data describing the *quartier* and its sights. Blended in with these facts are observations of an esthetic nature: we know here (B, 38) that he liked the vignettes on the cover of *La Vie parisienne,* certain paintings of 1860-1880, and was as indifferent then as now to martial pomp ("les musiques militaires, les régiments qui passent, etc., ne me dérangeaient pas plus que maintenant" [B, 41]).

The role of the father is elaborated and, by these additional touches, deepened. The resentment, the emotional and intellectual response to this most cavalier of parents strikes the listener-reader more forcibly as he learns now (the italicized passages are from the book) that

> Je restais très bien assis sans m'ennuyer, *à ce point, même, que plusieurs fois, à cette époque, mon père s'en inquiéta jusqu' à aller chercher des enfants dans la rue pour tâcher de me faire jouer.* (A, 705; B, 41-42)

> . . . autres garçons, *avec qui mon père me forçait d'aller.* (A, 706; B, 42)

> . . . j'y ai vécués! [sic] *bien plus heureux que dans les appartements paternels!* (A, 708; B, 45)

If certain details of a sexual nature are incorporated:

> Encore une mauvaise secousse nerveuse, comme chaque fois, et pour à peine de sensations, tant que je pense toujours à autre chose; sans compter le fidèle remords, aussitôt après . . . (B, 82; cf. A, 137)

(a most revealing, quasi-antithetical observation which implies a moral consideration the rest of the book tries to counter) the reduction of a phrase like "ces jambes agiles, qui enlaçaient si agréablement" (A, 167) to "ces jambes très fréquentées" (B, 127) suggests that physical description in sexuality was not the general purpose of such changes. (We shall return to this point in the subsequent discussion).

Text B contains several additions which are fairly extensive. The writer's encounter with Yvonne and his lack of relations with her are introduced on p. 73, ll. 7-19 and pp. 75-76, ll. 6-26, 1-10. A fuller commentary on Perruche (p. 115, ll. 11-16) affords him the opportunity to quip—while revealing a deep sense of failure and frustration—that "Tu le sais, n'est-ce pas? je ne suis qu'un essayiste. En tout, je vais rarement jusqu'au bout!" The third extensive modification (pp. 189-190, ll. 19-26, 1-6) concerns his mother. Self-exoneration, bitterness, regret: prelude to the finale, the writer wonders at the failure of his relations with his mother: "Après tout, c'est peut-être ma faute? Cœur trop sensible, sentiments trop vifs, yeux trop épris, que j'ai trop écoutés!"—only to mock at himself and his origins: "fils dont on ne parle pas, péché de jeunesse, boulette d'une nuit trop vive!"

Indeed, the last changes (toward the end of the book) stress the author's increasing preoccupation with spontaneity and truthfulness. The earlier version states succinctly: "D'ailleurs, bien finies pour moi, les chinoiseries de l'écriture" (A, 471). B (p. 205) continues: ". . . et les recommencements, comme il y a encore deux ans, quinze fois de la même page." He adds (my italics; in B, 206): "Une phrase ne me plaît pas, *je ne l'arrange pas,* j'en refais une autre, voilà tout."

Preoccupation with esthetics dictated this "aside," where once again our raconteur presents his meditations:

> (A, 471) . . . truquées par l'art!

> (B, 205) . . . truquées par l'art! Mais voilà! Il faut savoir lire, avoir beaucoup lu, et comparé, et pesé la duperie de ce mot: l'art, qu'affectionnent les imbéciles. Alors, on revient de bien des admirations, et tous ces soi-disant grands livres ne tiennent pas une minute.

Let us now turn to the deletions, which should have been more numerous than the additions according to Léautaud's own estimate.

The most striking excision is that of a character, Suzanne, who occupies 25 lines in the *Mercure de France* (septembre, p. 728). The acceptance by the periodical of this portrait, with its bold description:

> Quand nous sommes dans l'intimité, ses camarades et moi, il lui arrive souvent d'embrasser ses seins, qui sont très petits, et de se caresser de mille autres façons, tout comme si elle était seule ou deux. Toutes choses sans importance, naturellement.

would indicate that the possible effect on a timid reader was not the basis for the deletion (the *Mercure de France* prided itself on its independence, although Léautaud was to judge that self-appreciation somewhat blind). Elaboration in the depiction of Yvonne and of Perruche does not duplicate the Suzanne material. There remain two possibilities: either the portrait was removed because it was too faithful to a prototype who wished it not to be retained, or it was pure invention and therefore untrue in terms of the documented, factual basis of **Le Petit Ami.** The tone of the text itself does not suggest that this part is fiction.

Léautaud also cut out a bit about Alice:

> Dire aussi que ma chère Alice, qui me fut d'un bon marché que je n'ai guère retrouvé depuis, est peut-être, comme Loulou, toute défaite et retatinée, si même elle n'est pas morte. (A, 723)

Since this immediately precedes a reference to his mother, now perhaps "une dame un peu abîmée, lente et sérieuse" (B, 67) and follows reminiscences of Loulou, who is "sans doute maintenant une vielle à cabas," there seems an intent not to emphasize the decrepitude of age. This effect of time, platitudinous, may have underlain the

deletion of the italicized phrase (A, 723; not in B, 67): "ce petit garçon, *dont je viens de parler et que rien, non, rien au monde ne peut faire que je le redevienne, ne fût-ce qu'un instant.*" (But this is a note of regret and nostalgia thoroughly appropriate at this place in the story).

Of the approximately eighteen deletions, most have been utilized in the additions: For example, the lines

> (A, 467) . . . une vieillesse un peu tranquille. Et puis, j'avais besoin, ces derniers temps, de me consoler de mes ratages avec ma mère. Au moins, mes amies ne font pas de manières, elles: Un coup d'œil significatif, un court colloque, et l'on va s'aimer. Comme si ça ne valait pas mieux! D'ailleurs, ces quelques soirées . . .

becomes,". . . une vieillesse un peu tranquille. D'ailleurs, ces quelques soirées . . ." in B (p. 199). But we find that "mes ratages avec ma mère" was inserted earlier in "je me suis un peu rattrapé de tous mes ratages avec elle" (B, 195). We find the rest utilized much earlier. Our first version read:

> (A, 694) Tandis qu'avec mes amies, cela alla tout seul. Au bout d'un mois. . . .

Now we find:

> (B, 23) Avec mes amies, cela alla tout seul. Pas besoin, avec elles, de faire des phrases. Un coup d'œil significatif, un court colloque, et l'on va s'aimer. Comme si cela ne valait pas mieux! Ainsi nous fîmes, et je peux le dire, au bout d'un mois. . . .

Thus our deletions are not genuine sacrifices of part of the text, but rather, sometimes, transpositions. A change such as the one just indicated is effective: each part reads smoothly and is tight-knit.

There is some effective tightening up achieved by condensation. The awkward

> (A, 468) . . . si ému après avoir raconté toutes les choses un peu maternelles et beaucoup filiales qui composent ce chapitre . . .

is smoother, even though sacrificing the verbal twist, by saying simply

> (B, 201) . . . si ému, après ce chapitre . . .

Léautaud generally avoided conveying a directness of impression by the use of clichés and vulgarisms. At first he put in the popular "et patati et patata" (A, 457) to indicate that his mother was insistent for the return of her letters, themselves full of clichés. That phrase has been deleted from the book. Her husband, originally identified as "son distingué mari" (A, 449) is referred to later only as "son mari" (B, 173). The edge of irony, of bitterness, was lost with the deletion. Surely Léautaud did not intend to conceal more thoroughly, by less precision, the social situation of his mother's husband, professor and "conseiller administratif," a situation hardly concealed in the text.

The changes in punctuation are almost exclusively the substitution of the exclamation mark for the period. These instances, some seven times, enforce, emphasize the import of each remark for the author. Twice *Ah!* is inserted to start a comment. For greater contrast, the phrase, "Chères créatures, j'allais peut-être les retrouver mères ou en voie de l'être." (A, 189) exchanges the period for a question mark (B, 160); and this remark is immediately followed (in both versions) by "Ah! quelle compensation, alors!" The effect of these alterations is to heighten the tone and underline irony. The same purpose probably suggested the addition of "n'est-ce pas?" after ". . . écrire ces souvenirs si intéressants" (A, 709; B, 47).

Most of the substitutions serve to enhance the general tone of chagrin coupled with a swagger of toughness:

> (A, 688) . . . tout ce dont je vais parler dans ce livre dont le succès méritera peut-être la bienvaillance [*sic*] de ma famille.

> (B, 13) . . . tout ce que je veux fourrer dans ce livre qui me méritera peut-être l'admiration de ma famille.

(The avoidance of a repeated "dont" is evident).

The "chères prostituées" (A, 693) become the "supérieures prostituées" (B, 21). The note of envy, limited by a comparison of an esthetic nature: "Comme je donnerais facilement tout le talent que révèlent ces pages pour revivre toutes ces choses!" (A, 707) broadens when measured by an epithet of general import to the French: "Comme je donnerais facilement l'Alsace et la Lorraine encore une fois pour retourner à ces plaisirs!" (B, 44).

Some substitutions are obviously intended to be more factual. Thus, the "quelques années plus tard" (A, 719) becomes "deux ou trois ans plus tard" (B, 61); the year 1897 (A, 726) is changed to 1896 (B, 72); and "un jeune homme d'environ dix-neuf ans" (A, 729) is approximately seventeen in the revision (B, 78). On the other hand, "ma place chez Maxim's" (A, 723) becomes "ma place quelque part" (B, 67); in view of the additional details we have been furnished on houses and places and streets, this is not a desire to be vague but rather another instance of faithfulness to fact. Our author has searched his memory, he is not sure that that was the place. The avoidance of a mannered style is discernible in the alteration of "douceur recueillie et légère" (A, 697) to "douceur attentive" (B, 28). A phrase which sounds as though it were by Jean de Tinan: " . . . dont les rondeurs intéressaient ma gravité" (A, 165) becomes the somewhat different in meaning, and quite dissimilar in style: "dont les rondeurs, pour un autre que moi, auraient pu avoir leur prix" (B, 125).

A nuance in meaning—and a strikingly intimate observation—is lost in the following change:

> (A, 694) Quand je dis que j'ai horreur du sentiment, ce n'est pas tout à fait exact; mais ce n'est guère qu'après avoir fait l'amour que je puis m'y livrer. Or, avec les femmes, c'est généralement avant qu'il en faut faire. La plupart ont même une telle pudeur, feinte ou réelle, que c'est un tas de manières avant qu'elles consentent à cette chose si simple: aller s'aimer.

> (B, 23) . . . les cinq ou six femmes charmantes auxquelles je songe en ce moment et que j'aurais peut-être eu du plaisir à posséder, il y a quelques années, si elles n'avaient pas eu autant de pudeur! Donner tant d'importance à cette chose si simple et nullement romanesque: faire l'amour!

An author who wishes to set aside conventional morality, which has left its imprint on him, must ever be combatting the insidious. Just as Léautaud had spoken of remorse after sexual intercourse, so at first he expressed himself about one of his *amies* in these terms: "corps pâle et pervers" (A, 146). In the revision, this became "corps pâle et chahuteur" (B, 97). Since both expressions seem rather trite, this change seems to be an attempt to shift from the moral to the physical. But the substitution of "littéraire" (B, 106) for "fatigué" in the expression "mon air fatigué" (A, 152) seems inconsequential. A nicely rhythmic phrase was achieved by transposing "seins charmants, dont on est avide" (A, 461) to "seins charmants, dont on ne peut pas se passer" (B, 190). The effectiveness of the change does not seem to go beyond that. The apparent contradiction in terms used, when "détestable ironie" (A, 472) became "admirable ironie" (B, 206), is the replacement of the indirect by the direct, since the latter adjective conveys the obvious intent.

Since the latter part of *Le Petit Ami* (Chapter VI to the end) relates events which occurred between October 24, 1901, and April 4, 1902, and the book is dated August, 1902, it was terminated just before going to press in the periodical. Henri de Régnier had recommended it in May, probably before the completion of the "final" draft. The "achevé d'imprimer" in book form is dated January 15, 1903. Therefore all of the changes thus far discussed were made toward the end of 1902. On October 7, 1902, Léautaud wrote to Paul Valéry:

> Je viens d'arranger un peu, pour le volume, les deux premiers chapitres, pour enlever un peu le côté marlou, tout à fait faux, et pour mettre des choses plus exactes. En réalité, je suis revenu à ce que j'avais d'abord écrit. Je ne sais quelle fantaisie un peu crispée m'avait ensuite entraîné . . . Tout le reste, à part dix ou quinze lignes, et une femme en moins, sera le même que dans le *Mercure*.[18]

As early as September 4, 1898, Léautaud had counseled himself: "Se surveiller, être conscient, toujours. / Se défier du style de Renan, de tous les styles dits grands styles. / Ne pas faire de phrases faciles, fades. Au contraire, des phrases dures, sèches, même rudes. Une harmonie se dégage aussi de ces phrases. / Simplifier, sans cesse. / Le moins possible d'épithètes. / Une phrase tendre et chantante par ci par là, comme un sourire voilé, atténuera" (*Journal littéraire,* I, 20). Before writing *Le Petit Ami* he had started a novel, "Le Petit Livre des Prostituées," "livre élégiaque, barréssiste" [*sic*] which he had shortly abandoned for *Le Petit Ami* (idem, 21; entry of December 16, 1902).

By May 6 of the following year (1903) Léautaud decided that Chapter VII ought to have a different ending, "plus serrée et moins littéraire" (idem, 72). In August, he thought that he should redo the second half of the exchange of correspondence with his mother, and should end with an examination of his behavior (idem, 82). A half-year later (March 12, 1904), he still thought that

> Ces dernières pages [de la correspondance avec ma mère] sont lamentables. Pourquoi n'ai-je pas eu alors, dans toute l'incertitude même, le courage de couper davantage et terminer plus sèchement . . . Il aurait fallu que j'écrive *The Small Friend* comme cela [le style d'une notice de Régnier]. Cela n'aurait pas empêché l'ironie, la clownerie, qui étaient et sont encore extrêmement *moi* et cela aurait été moins sentimental, moins bête. Je me paierai un jour le plaisir de le refaire pour moi (idem, 117).

As we have seen, Léautaud was quickly dissatisfied with *Le Petit Ami,* even before he wrote freely and rapidly *In Memoriam,* whose trenchant expression and unfilial frankness seemed to him the sincerest form for writing to take.

Let us now consider the annotated copy on Holland paper. From an entry in his *Journal* (III, 171) for May 20, 1914, we know that Léautaud possessed a copy of *Le Petit Ami* on Holland paper, a copy corrected at some unspecified time. Is this the annotated Simonson copy? The latter contains carefully drawn-through lines of text, substitute terms, and marginal comments, all by Léautaud himself. There is some evidence, from the color of the ink, the thickness of the pen lines and a scratchiness in the stroke, and the occasional though infrequent use of heavy pencil, that these changes were not all made at the same time. Their exact dates are not determinable from internal evidence or from the binding, which is not dated.

Certainly this revised text was not yet a wholehearted attempt to redraft the entire work in fifty pages, as Léautaud has early and fairly consistently thought it should be. He actually deleted fifty lines, and struck out some fourteen individual words and twenty phrases. In some fifteen lines he replaced single words or phrases. But he also added a few words, some ten phrases, and a dozen "explanations," that is, marginal glosses such as dates or comments.

The first extensive deletion (p. 14, ll. 7-12) is of a passage expressing Paul's disinterest in civic and political matters. This probably struck Léautaud as an unnecessary interjection, interfering with the free flow of his reminiscences about his mother and the nature of his "amies." This is, then, an artistic rearrangement, sacrificing a facet of Paul's character for the sake of a certain effect.

On page 16 (ll. 13-15), Léautaud substitutes "Mieux vaut tard que jamais" for the last three lines: "Cela me consolerait de n'y avoir pas mis, autrefois, pour leur ingénuité, des détails plus précis et des images plus vives." This change sustains better the sarcastic tone as he envisages himself an eventually appreciated writer. Léautaud changed his appreciation of Jean de Tinan, on whom he had written the *Mercure de France*'s necrological article, appropriately entitled **"L'Ami d' Aimienne."** He struck out the qualifiers "charmant" about *Aimienne* and "de mon cher Jean de Tinan" (p. 37, ll. 17-18). A few pages later (p. 40, ll. 10-11), he deleted the phrases, "tais-toi, mon cœur! . . . si les femmes ne nous ont pas trop fatigués." This has the echo of Tinan's style, a use of language too precious for Léautaud's taste.[19] (We have already seen the deletion from the pre-original text of a phrase that sounded like Tinan's). Further on (pp. 112-113), remarks about Tinan are stringently censured: "Jean de Tinan, plein de grâce et qui m'était si cher" is cut to the name alone; *Aimienne,* "ce livre, qui a plus de valeur qu'il n'en a l'air," loses its adjectival clause; the reference to "mon camarade mort" disappears from the mention of Léautaud's obit on Tinan.

Several of the emendations are passages on style or on artistic intent. Excised no doubt as false is the pretension: "Je n'avais aucune ambition, aucun souci littéraire. J'ignorais le besoin d'écrire et l'ennui de recopier au net" (p. 41, ll. 17-19). Bracketing these lines, Léautaud wrote pithily in the margin: "mauvais." But he has reconsidered the replacement of "mon grand talent littéraire" (A, 707) by Alsace and Lorraine (B, 44; see supra) and restores the original version.

He eliminates as false, "Et moi qui avais toujours cru que la vie n'était pas un roman,—une clownerie, tout au plus!" (p. 178, ll. 12-14). Since he was writing a sort of novel based strictly, he hoped and believed, on life itself, this was a contradiction which should not stand. The urge to quip, to mock himself, had perhaps influenced his sarcastic remark: "J'aurai peut-être acquis d'ici là [quand un peu de temps aura passé] un peu de talent et le goût des jolies phrases, quoique maintenant cela me paraisse difficile" (p. 175, ll. 8-10). He also struck out, on the same page (ll. 14-25), the longest single block of text, which threatens to utilize later his mother's letters and to retaliate thus for her abandonment of him.

A certain "gouailleur" tone is eliminated by removing some brief remarks: "J'ai même acquis tant d'habileté que j'ai l'air d'un miché qui ne veut pas marcher" (p. 106, ll. 19-21). Earlier (p. 127, l. 1), he had crossed out "pas un miché sérieux," indicating that the term itself seemed too slangy or crude.

The greatest number of changes are in the category of the gloss or verification. On the whole, these add to the text. After "Hier encore" (p. 15, l. 12), Léautaud inserts: "le 13 mars 1902." One of his father's mistresses, who shot herself, is identified more precisely: "Elle s'appelait Jeanne Chauffé" (p. 33, l. 10). The details on his *quartier* were to include, after "je crois," "le docteur Berthet, rue de Trévise, chez qui j'allais pour ma santé, avec ma vieille bonne Marie" (p. 39, l. 18)—this sort of added detail obviously satisfies the nostalgic mood of our author, but adds nothing to the tone of the text. We learn (p. 49, l. 6) that Loulou's name was Leroux. Such is the desire for exactness that we learn from a marginal note that "il y a seulement quelques années" (p. 50, l. 20) was June 11, 1899, when Aunt Fanny told him the nature of Loulou's activities in the street. So on p. 61, l. 26, "dernièrement" is defined as "les 5 et 8 mars 1901."

We have a deeper penetration into the arcana of memory through visual recall. When at Véfour's with his mother, he says, "J'étais habillé coquettement, avec un joli chapeau de paille et de belles bottines jaunes que ma mère m'avait achetés exprès" (p. 58, l. 2). (But Léautaud did not notice, or saw no possibly poor pun, in the expression "enfant de cocotte" which would follow shortly with its "coquettement-cocotte" resonance). Memory has deepened, and instead of "J'ai peu de souvenirs de ce spectacle [*Michel Strogoff*]" (p. 58, l. 7), he inserted: "Je revois très bien certaines scènes de cette pièce: le bureau de poste, le fer rouge pour brûler les yeux de Michel Strogoff."

One has the impression, in studying these marginalia, that Léautaud was commenting on his text rather than putting down the alterations themselves. Thus, p. 99, l. 5, about a former mistress, he notes that "Je pourrais donner son portrait ici, telle qu'elle était quand nous étions ensemble. Alors même qu'il lirait ce livre, je suis bien sûr que son mari ne la reconnaîtrait pas." This does not fit with the following sentence, although recourse to a new paragraph would have made the insertion acceptable. The memento, "mauvais—mettre le nom de Batilliat" (p. 113), applies to lines 12-19 as a whole, not to a specific spot. (In his *Journal littéraire,* III, 98-99, Lundi 7 juillet [1913], Léautaud notes of Batilliat: "En voilà un qu'on ne peut accuser d'avoir écrit quoi que ce soit d'un peu osé. On se demande s'il y a jamais écrit quelque chose, tant, écrire à sa façon, équivant à ne rien écrire." On September 16, 1905 [*Journal littéraire,* I, 193], Léautaud had already observed: "ce niais de Batilliat, la prétention et la sottise littéraires faites homme.")

The most interesting details are, perhaps, those which concern his mother. This is the part which had the greatest effect on his readers, and which was the most directly drawn from very recent experiences. There is indeed added poignancy in the revelation, "'Catin! catin!' me disais-je nerveusement tout le long du chemin" (p. 163, l. 12), after his mother has reneged on her rendez-vous with her son. Léautaud thought of emphasizing the bitterness of his mood by inserting after "un si grand garçon" (p. 164, l. 11): "littérateur avec ça, et auteur d'un livre en train"; further down the page (l. 21), he intended to underline "nous rattraperons cela" by adding: "Ah! oui, qu'on le rattra-perait!" But he crossed out both phrases with a dark pencil. He mused over his text, where it could not possibly have been integrated logically or grammatically ("je tâcherai d'être encore ta jolie maman" [p. 169, l. 26]), in this footnote:

> Quand je me demande ce qui pouvait bien se passer
> en elle, en m'écrivant de pareilles choses, je me
> dis: n'était-ce pas (ayant si peu de quoi sentir et
> penser comme mère à mon égard) plaisir de femme
> à s'entendre dire qu'elle est encore jolie?

The public—and friends and critics—had been shocked by the ambivalent, incestuous feelings of Paul for his mother. Readers did not wish to consider this aspect as other than a literary exercise, which *could not* be the very truth. Léautaud had refused to veil his sentiments under the guise of literature. So one may accept as genuine, and in harmony with the sexuality already pervasive in this part of *Le Petit Ami,* the intention of describing the dream about his mother (p. 192, ll. 17-18) more fully. Instead of "je l'embrassais sur ses bras nus," he altered the text to read: "elle était très décolletée et je l'embrassais sur les seins et ses bras nus."

There are two mysterious marginalia. Opposite that part where Paul tells of being tearful in front of his mother, who has not kept her appointment with him and who was trying to comfort him, while talking coolly: "Elle parlait de tout cela posément, comme d'un fait-divers" (p. 164, ll. 14-15), Léautaud has put in the margin and circled: "Histoire de la pièce de cent sous." Is this a specific incident between Paul and his mother, is this a reference to a child being consoled for the loss of a coin which can so easily be replaced? Marie Dormoy, executrice of Léautaud's estate, in the introduction to *Lettres à ma mère* (Paris: Mercure de France, 1956, p. 25), tells us that when her son offered her the bouquet of violets he had so fervently clung to while awaiting her arrival, Paul's mother wished to reciprocate by giving him a five-franc piece. Léautaud, in his *Journal* for May 20, 1914 (*Journal,* III, 172), says that his mother offered him the money because of his obvious poverty.

The other obscure remark concerns the following page (ll. 9-16), where, after her departure, Paul is tempted to seek out "des femmes tendres ou du moins qui savent donner l'illusion de la tendresse." He adds, however: "mais il était si tard"—which suggests that he did not console himself in this way. The margin queries: "Refaire vrai—?" One suspects that such consolation was sought. Mlle Dormoy tells us that after his mother's departure Paul returned to his attic, to spend the night weeping in the arms of his mistress Blanche.

Léautaud assured Valéry that the data on his childhood, the women, all concerning his mother, were true. He felt, however, "ce que j'aurais dû faire, c'est cinquante pages, avec des phrases de catalogue, sèches, exactes, rapides," in order to convey correctly fact and feeling—beauty is the truth. The major part of the last chapter is a reflection on the style—or apparent absence of style—necessary to truthful exposition.

Presumably the changes in the Simonson copy antedate 1925. Were they later, they should have been more numerous, for Léautaud was actively revising in that year. But, as we have seen, the ambition to write succinctly and drily, an ambition expressed as early as 1903, has still to be achieved: Léautaud has deleted and rearranged the bothersome correspondence of the sixth chapter; but the ending of Chapter VII has not been altered in any large measure.

In 1925, two publishers, La Cité des Livres (Castellan) for a deluxe edition and Maurice Decroix for an expensive illustrated edition, proposed to publish *Le Petit Ami*, and the Mercure de France to reprint. Léautaud, once again, promised himself and his publishers to reshape *Le Petit Ami* according to the critical standards he had formulated. In his *Journal littéraire* for April 2, 1925, he wrote:

> Je ne sais ce qu'on pensera du *Petit Ami* dans sa nouvelle version, si je continue comme j'ai écrit jusqu'à présent. Pour moi, c'est mieux, mais les choses drôles ou qui passaient pour telles et qui n'étaient pour moi que bêtises ou fautes de goût, ont disparu, du moins j'ai bien l'intention de les supprimer quand j'en serai aux chapitres dans lesquels elles pullulent. Si je ne me trompe, le livre sera plus vrai, plus sensible, mais non moins amusant, s'il l'a jamais été.[20]

But by the end of the month Léautaud was again dissatisfied with his new rendition. A few months later he confessed (July 12, 1925): ". . . j'ai été influencé, malgré moi, par le premier texte en écrivant le nouveau. Il est vrai que je n'en suis encore qu'au chapitre des souvenirs d'enfance, qui est un peu long et embarrassé. Mais il restera tel quel."[21] He was not even halfway through his revision; no such editions were published. Again, in 1931, he planned to redo *Le Petit Ami*.[22] That latter effort, some fifteen years before Rouveyre's *Choix de pages*, may well have served for the partial revision which he finally did allow to go to press. Rouveyre restored the original title, *Souvenirs légers*.

In the *Entretiens*, pp. 148-152, we have the minutes of the radio debate during which Léautaud and Mallet argued the merits—or lack of value—in *Souvenirs légers* of certain substitutions in vocabulary and in phrasing. There are other notable changes. The new text (for the first two chapters alone of *Le Petit Ami*) has become markedly longer! The intention to remove "le côté marlou" has changed in the other direction: we find many added details (*Souvenirs légers,* pp. 30-32) on the benefits of being *entretenu*: trips, some clothes, occasional sums of money, fine meals. This first chapter also introduces Perruche early (on p. 30), and we have direct references to the verses and the *"Essais [de sentimentalisme]"* published in the *Mercure de France*. Also, a new mistress, Iphigénie—thus baptized by him "pour le sacrifice que lui était devenue de faire l'amour, à cause du mauvais état dans lequel, après le plaisir, elle se trouvait" (p. 31, ll. 28-31)—is introduced.

Similarly, the second chapter of *Souvenirs légers* is longer than the version in *Le Petit Ami*. A whole new section is added on students and the Latin Quarter. Along with this elaboration of the setting we have a much more detailed and extensive *reportage* of conversations with whores and demi-mondaines, accompanied by the formative effect of frequenting such company.

The determination to write this book, with its utilization of these vital experiences, is expressed more directly—not so diffusely as in *Le Petit Ami*. The pleasure of writing, and the growing lack of satisfaction with this pleasure, the insipidity of effusive and mannered fictions, are emphasized too.

A major shift, and another addition, is a series of reflections on the timid type of man who needs encouragement by the woman before he can allow himself to express his desires. Here we have a subtle change: this alters the perspective from that of a short retrospection—i.e., the views of a youngish man—to the comments of a mature man. We feel that the protagonist is quite a bit older than as originally projected in *Le Petit Ami*. This is a loss in immediacy. There is a double purpose in the observation:

> La jeunesse n'a pas de pensée, ni de souvenirs. Elle n'a que de l'instinct, et de l'ignorance. J'aime ce qui a vécu, ce qui a senti, ce qui a aimé, qui en porte la marque et l'expression, en possède le savoir et l'expérience. Non! je ne me vois pas, à la place de ces créatures, entouré d'autant de jeunes filles. Elles seraient pour moi sans le moindre attrait.

This jibes with his preference for the older woman, who has had sexual experience and is on the road towards physical *usure*. It also serves to set the stage for the complex relationship with his mother, at the same time symbol of childhood and affection and the desired mistress. But it is also, especially in the beginning of the quotation, the aphorism of a person who has passed beyond that stage of instinct and of ignorance.

It is apparent that Léautaud never brought himself to the condensation of *Le Petit Ami* he judged suitable. He did achieve a degree of matter-of-factness, of direct expression, through some of his emendations. The harmonizing of tone throughout *Le Petit Ami,* so that the looser, more discursive mood and expression of the first few chapters would take on the abruptness and directness of the last part, remained only a project.

The fact that the chapters about his mother are practically the verbatim use of notes, and that these chapters were written while Léautaud was undergoing a change in esthetic creed, accounts for their lack of marquetry, of embellishments. But should the first part, about his childhood and his entourage, have been presented in the same abrupt fashion? The atmosphere he has rendered is more subtle, more shaded for being as it is. It leads into the other part, and also contrasts with it. Thus it is even more effective than if the tone had been made uniform. By achieving, even though unwillingly, an amorphous blending of diary-confession and fictional recital, Léautaud has given us a more evocative work with which we can establish a more complex empathy.

The perusal of his other autobiographical writings, such as "**In Memoriam**," "**Souvenirs de basoche**," "**Adolphe van Bever**," *Lettres à ma mère,* presents us with a (partial) record of his life, a record that cannot fail to convince us of how terrible his formative years were. Sophistication, experience of life, knowledge in psychology—these help us comprehend (and condone?) his mother-fixation, his love of animals, his cynicism, his animalistic conception of love. His *Journal littéraire* and the *Entretiens* with Robert Mallet leave no doubt that Léautaud's primary purpose was to be honest with himself, and also with his readers. All of these works, plus his other writings (especially his *Théâtre de Maurice Boissard,* his penname for dramatic criticism), convince one thoroughly that Léautaud's subject was Léautaud and, that his essential effort was to see himself.[23]

To see oneself does not signify that one may have no contradictions. Inconsistency may or may not be the mark of great minds, it is surely the mark of humanness.

Léautaud more than suspected this; he confessed (*Journal littéraire,* III, 362; entry of August 29, 1921): "Je pense surtout qu'on ne refait pas ce qu'on a écrit, on n'y est plus, la fraîcheur même, l'entrain de la chose nouvelle, la spontanéité, je dirai même plus, la sincérité." But, while momentarily recognizing this as true, he believed more in the fundamental unity and continuity of his personality,[24] and through the power of art in the power to recapture retrospectively, with the help of exceptional recall and factual data such as diary and other documents, the truth as he had seen it. Léautaud had his share—more than most!—of idiosyncrasies; he refused to admit that he had literary ambitions, he was dogmatic in his denials even when he suspected himself of desiring the contrary. Nevertheless, he was sincere. He faced with some courage an insuperable problem: How to tell the whole truth, when each choice of expression eliminates all the others that are also valid? The ring of authenticity—if not on one level, then on another—that we have in his master's *Vie de Henri Brulard* we find in Léautaud's *Le Petit Ami.* In art, in a sense, even when the man is wrong, the artist is right. Perhaps the world will never see a *journal intime,* and *Le Petit Ami* can be classified as one, which, whether a dry enumeration of facts or a spiritual and intellectual commentary on experiences, will be whole. As Léautaud confessed: "Écrire, c'est mentir. Mentir est peut-être trop fort. Écrire, c'est fausser. Etre exact est bien rare. Toujours on est au-dessus ou au-dessous. Je le sais par moi-même."[25] It seems that the degree of authenticity we discover in a work, whatever its form, is partially in terms of itself and partially in terms of each creator—who himself cannot be the judge for us.[26] Be it Montaigne or Nerval, Stendhal or Gide, Rousseau or Léautaud, clairvoyance and self-dupery argue. Textual changes are a way of penetrating to the arena of the struggle, they expose the beclouded issues. As for the cachet of sincerity . . . well, that will be granted "tel qu'en lui-même enfin le [lecteur] le change."

NOTES

[1] "Le Petit Ami," *Mercure de France,* XLIII, No. 153 (septembre, 1902), 684-731; XLIV, No. 154 (octobre, 1902), 135-193; XLIV, No. 155 (novembre, 1902), 444-473.

[2] The first issue of the first edition bears the address: XV, rue de l'Echaudé-Saint-Germain; the second issue, that of XXVI, rue de Condé, according to Albert Kies, "Les Livres de Paul Léautaud; essai de bibliographie," *La Revue des Amateurs* (octobre-novembre, 1945).

[3] Librairie Jean Loize (Paris), Catalogue No. 16 (1956), item 241, offered *Le Petit Ami,* bound in full morocco and with a slipcase by Huser, for 55,000 French francs. Another copy, bound and cased by P. L. Martin, was offered by Librairie Raoul Simonson (Brussels), Catalogue No. 243 (juin, 1957), item 65, for 9,000 Belgian francs. Léautaud cites 70,000 French francs as the price of a copy on Holland in 1951.

[4] Hector Talvart and Joseph Place, *Bibliographie des auteurs modernes de langue française (1801-19**)* (Paris, 1928-), XII (1954), list: "*Le Petit Ami* [Amsterdam] Edit. de la Béte Noire (Balkema), s.d. (pendant la dernière guerre). . . . Edition clandestine reproduisant l'originale. . . . Elle aurait tiré à 75 ex. seulement sur vergé de Hollande et non mise dans le commerce. . . . Le texte est celui qui a d'abord paru dans les livraisons du *Mercure de France* en 1902." The Librairie Jean Loize Catalogue No. 16, item 245, states that this clandestine edition was published in 1943.

[5] *Œuvres de Paul Léautaud: Le Petit Ami, précédé d'Essais et suivi de In Memoriam et Amours* (Paris: Mercure de France, 1956). The "achevé d'imprimer" is December 5, 1956.

[6] Paul Léautaud, *Entretiens avec Robert Mallet* (Paris: Gallimard, 1951).

[7] Cited by Edmond Dune, "Paul Léautaud ou l'Esprit de Contradiction," *Critique,* XI, No. 92 (janvier 1955), 4.

[8] Seven vols. (Paris: Mercure de France, 1954-59), covering the period 1893-1929, have thus far been published. Additional fragments continue to appear in various periodicals.

[9] *Souvenirs d'égotisme,* nouvelle éd. établ. et comm. par Henri Martineau (Paris: Le Divan, 1941), ch. I, p. 5.

[10] Jean Selz, "Paul Léautaud, ou le paradoxe de l'écrivain," "*Les Lettres Nouvelles,*" IV, No. 37 (avril 1956), 562-563.

[11] Consider, in this respect, the feeling one has from Gide's highly touted *Journal* that Gide is aiming at a view of himself he wishes his reader to have: he tries to manoeuver his beholder into a particular perspective

which will permit only a preordained visualisation. There is an aura of artificiality, of pose, in the very air of candor.

[12] "Aspects de Paul Léautaud," *Le Bulletin des Lettres* (Lyon), XVIII, No. 178 (15 mai 1956), 175.

[13] Léautaud's self-deprecations, stylistically, and reflections on style are too numerous to list; some references and quotations are given further on in this paper. For a comment on his own Nessuscloak in style, see *Journal littéraire*, IV, 52; entry of July 23, 1922. The whole series is also rich in comments on the behavior, in matters of style, of writers like Stendhal, Gide, Proust. See too Ch, 18 in the *Entretiens*.

[14] *Choix de pages de Paul Léautaud, par André Rouveyre* (Paris: Édit. du Bélier, 1946).

[15] The variants in *Le Petit Ami, précédé d'Essais et suivi de In Memoriam et Amours* cannot be taken into account, since there is no evidence that Léautaud made these changes.

Here are some statistics for those who may wish to refer to this edition: *Le Petit Ami* occupies pp. 69-181. This text shows the following variations (italicized by me) from that of the 1903 edition: P. 79, l. 5, "j'ai le plus laissé *de* mon cœur." P. 82, l. 12, "j'aurais *peut-être* cu." P. 82, ll. 21-22, "oh! elles m'ont *monté le coup comme aux autres. Elles m'ont* aussi promis." P. 82, l. 34, "J'aimais *même mieux.*" P. 83, l. 35, "ce qu'on leur donne *et* la tête." P. 107, l. 24, "dans *ce* quartier." P. 112, l. 16, "je ne sais *pas.*" P. 118, l. 2, "*Tu n'*as pas." P. 126, l. 25, "ou trois *de mes* amies." P. 148, l. 17, "réveillait dix *de nos* souvenirs." P. 164, l. 8, "de retrouver *toutes* ces lettres."

A few minor differences—commas, spelling corrections, or "coquilles"—have not been listed.

[16] Henri Albert and Paul Valéry complimented Léautaud on his choice of epigraphs (See *Journal littéraire*, I, 51; entry of December 24, 1902).

[17] Text A compares typographically with version B as follows:

This is the distribution of the 1956 edition: Ch. I, 73-78; Ch. II, 79-84; Ch. III, 85-107; Ch. IV, 108-123; Ch. V, 124-138; Ch. VI, 139-158; Ch. VII, 159-174; Ch. VIII, 175-181.

[18] *Lettres à Paul Valéry, Rachilde, Marcel Schwob . . .* 1902-1918. Paris: Edit. Mornay, 1929 (La Collection Originale, 22), pp. 4 ff; reprinted in *Choix de pages*, p. 261.

This letter is described in Librairie Jean Loize Catalogue No. 16, item No. 242.

[19] R. L. Wagner, in "Le style de Léautaud, ou 'La Leçon d'Anatomie,'" *Mercure de France*, No. 1125 (mai,

1957), 114-126, but especially in the notes on p. 116, points out resemblances between Léautaud's style in *Le Petit Ami* and those of Mallarmé, Marcel Schwob, Gide, and Tinan.

[20] "Journal littéraire," *Mercure de France*, No. 1125 (mai, 1957), 7-8.

[21] *Ibid.*, p. 21.

[22] Librairie Jean Loize Catalogue No. 16, item 244, describes a four-page prospectus by Robert Télin, a bookdealer who used the imprint "Au Lys Rouge," for a new edition of *Le Petit Ami*. This proposed edition, announced in 1931, was to be "complétement remaniée, les parties imaginées ou fantaisistes supprimées, augmentée d'autres parties, rendue plus vraie dans l'expression des sentiments et la peinture des situations." Léautaud withdrew from the arrangement.

[23] Cf. *Passe-temps* (Paris: Mercure de France, 1929), Ch. "Mots, Propos et Anecdotes," p. 255.

[24] Robert Mallet quotes Léautaud as having written in 1925: "Je suis profondément intéressé par l'enfant que j'ai été; j'ai, pour lui, une sorte de tendresse, je pense à lui, je le vois souvent, dans une véritable sorte de dédoublement. Je le rapproche de ce que je suis devenu, de ce que j'ai été et, malgré les années en plus, les occupations différentes, je ne vois pas, dans mes sentiments, mes sensations, les réactions de mon caractére, de grandes différences entre ce que je suis et ce que j'étais, enfant" (*Entretiens*, p. 29).

Surely readers of Léautaud would agree that there is an obvious unity in his work, and continuing motivations and principles in his life. But does this kind of unity assure some degree of freedom from distortion in the revision of a work of art?

[25] *Propos d'un jour* (Paris: Mercure de France, 1952 [c. 1947]), Ch. "Notes retrouvées," p. 53. See also p. 64 and p. 79, for comments on the rapports between style, personality, and truthfulness. Léautaud states that these notes were written between 1927 and 1934.

[26] Léautaud observed at some time: "Ce qui fait le mérite d'un livre, ce ne sont pas ses qualités ou ses défauts. Il tient tout entier en ceci: qu'un autre que son auteur n'aurait pu l'écrire" (*Propos d'un jour*, p. 58).

John A. Green (essay date 1968)

SOURCE: "Marcel Schwob and Paul Léautaud, 1903-1905," in *Modern Language Quarterly*, Vol. XXIX, No. 4, December, 1968, pp. 415-22.

[*In the following excerpt, Green examines the relationship between Léautaud and Marcel Schwob.*]

Marcel Schwob was one of those who encouraged Paul Léautaud at the beginning of the younger man's career.

Five hitherto unpublished letters from Schwob to Léautaud and the latter's recently published nineteen-volume *Journal Littéraire* help to round out that story.[1] The *Journal* records that the friendship began to develop in March, 1903, after the publication of Léautaud's autobiographical novel and first major literary work, *Le Petit Ami,* and that the relationship continued until Schwob's death in February, 1905.[2] The letters, covering approximately this period of intimate association between the two men, date from mid-July, 1903, to the end of November, 1904.

Léautaud was thirty-one when the friendship began, Schwob only five years older. Regularly employed as a secretary in the Paris law firm of Lemarquis, Léautaud was a newcomer to the literary scene, while Schwob, who had begun publishing regularly in 1888, enjoyed the reputation and recognition which his keen mind and impressive list of publications had earned for him. His strength was spent, however, his health was failing, and the two years of life that remained to him confined him, for the most part, to his spacious apartment on the rue Saint Louis-en-l'Ile. To ease his pain, he injected himself frequently with morphine so that he and his wife, the actress Marguerite Moreno, could receive guests every Sunday afternoon into a sort of literary salon. Schwob credited himself with discovering Alfred Jarry, Francis Jammes, Henry Bataille, and Jules Renard,[3] and certainly he had had a hand in furthering the careers of his schoolmate Paul Claudel and the slightly younger Paul Valéry. It was in that same spirit that Schwob, after reading *Le Petit Ami,* invited Léautaud to join him and his guests on Sunday, March 22, 1903, and again two weeks later, just three days before Léautaud resigned from the law firm.[4] On both occasions Léautaud had an opportunity to discuss *Le Petit Ami* with his hosts and with Gide, the comtesse de Noailles, and a number of others. After that he did not often attend the Sunday gatherings (he could not speak English and felt uncomfortable with the number of guests who could[5]) although he became a frequent dinner guest at Schwob's on other days of the week.

When two of Schwob's books appeared on the stands in the early summer of 1903, Léautaud, who had received so much attention from Schwob (and probably complimentary copies of the books), reciprocated and sent him a warm, flattering letter. Schwob responded immediately on July 13, inviting Léautaud to spend the next day at his home:

Paris, lundi
11 rue St. Louis-en-l'Ile

Mon cher ami, comment vous dire à quel point votre lettre m'a touché. Je vous assure que j'aime mieux l'avoir que si on m'annonçait brusquement un tirage formidable (ce que je ne croirais pas).[6] C'est parce que des hommes comme vous ont de l'affection pour mes livres que j'ai gardé la foi qui convient. Il y en a ici et là, tout près et très loin, mais de temps en temps ils se révèlent et c'est une grande joie pour moi—de vous, cette lettre m'est beaucoup plus chère encore. Merci.

Restez-vous ici demain 14 et haïssez-vous cette journée? Si oui, venez la passer avec moi, déjeuner et dîner—je serai seul. Vous lirez tout ce que vous voudrez—et vous ferez ce que vous voudrez. Mais, je vous en prie, ne renoncez à rien pour cela. Ce que je vous offre n'est qu'un pis aller.

Votre ami
Marcel Schwob

Léautaud accepted the invitation, though perhaps he soon wished that he had not. Schwob was in bed, and "d'un moral navrant," probably the first time Léautaud had seen him thus. The discussion centered around Schwob's books, and he no doubt monopolized the conversation. Léautaud had his chance later that night. He noted in his journal: "Mon opinion depuis longtemps sur la littérature de Schwob. . . ." He continued in a paragraph highlighted by the following remarks: "Au fond, très au fond, je n'y trouve aucun intérêt. . . . De vastes lectures . . . puis arrangement . . . une grande délicatesse dans l'art de choisir, un considérable savoir, mais, au fond, tout cela sent les vieux livres. C'est truqué au possible."[7]

It had been an exasperating July 14, but Léautaud, already committed to his *Journal Littéraire,* was too conscientious about that commitment to get even simply by filling his entries with subjective trivia. Over a misunderstanding—and perhaps pushed by the consideration Schwob and others were showing for *Le Petit Ami*—he had resigned from the law office in April, and he took seriously, though not always confidently, his new literary career.[8] He felt great admiration for Schwob, particularly for the man's ability to utter "toujours . . . une parole définitive, juste, exacte," on any subject, but he was beginning to see clearly that Schwob's greatest strength also constituted his greatest weakness.[9] Léautaud sensed that such intimate afternoons as he had just spent with his older friend, quite apart from the Sunday gatherings, provided him with an opportunity to study and understand Schwob in a way that very few others would ever enjoy, and he closed his journal entry for July 14 with: "Il faudra que je développe cela un jour."

A day or two later, apparently still reflecting on the discussion of the fourteenth, and on his own flattering letter which had prompted Schwob's invitation, he confided to his journal:

J'ai beau faire, écrire des lettres flatteuses, soit pour des livres reçus, soit pour des articles sur le *P.A.* [*Petit Ami*], je m'en moque de vous à Elémir Bourges et à lui-mais j'ai peur que nous ne réussissions pas.

A vous de coeur
Marcel Schwob

The vote, though close, went to John Antoine Nau's *Force ennemie,* a decision which the Academy members later regretted. Schwob eventually learned how near

Léautaud had come to winning, and informed him over dinner on Wednesday, February 10, 1904. Later that evening, Léautaud recorded his reaction in his journal:

> Ces jours-ci, [José] Théry [a close friend of Schwob] a vu Hennique, qui lui a dit que j'ai été à deux minutes d'avoir le Prix Goncourt. C'est le sujet du livre qui a fait hésiter. Cela confirme de tous points la lettre de Mirbeau à Schwob, lettre à laquelle je ne croyais pas absolument. Je commence à être vexé. Cinq mille francs de ratés à cause de trois ou quatre sots![15]

The incident rankled, but his situation was far from hopeless. *Le Petit Ami* was bringing in a little money, and the *Mercure de France* had accepted an article he had written on Henri de Régnier. He already had two more articles in mind, and he could take notes for both during his frequent visits to Schwob, since one article was to be on his friend, the other on the Comédie Française, for which Schwob's wife would supply him with the necessary information. Both Schwob and Moreno encouraged him to write another novel for the Goncourt competition that year, and Schwob went so far as to suggest a subject, but Léautaud's reply—again in his journal—was a simple "Non."[16]

For the article on Schwob, Léautaud had begun to reread some of his friend's work—"On ne doit pas se sentir vivre à écrire de telles choses"—and, early in 1904, to take notes on the man himself.[17] At the same time, to ease somewhat Léautaud's financial situation, Schwob had arranged for him to give French lessons to a young Chinese, and on February 16, 1904, Schwob wrote to him about another project:

> Cher ami,
>
> J'ai vu Miss Lonnsberg qui ne vous a pas répondu encore parce que sa pièce n'est pas assez avancée pour que vous y travailliez. 2° acte esquissé-scénario du 1-scénario à modifier du 2. Néanmoins comme elle travaille très vite, cela pourrait bien être pour dans une quinzaine. Ne vous inquiétez donc pas.[18] Vous avez cent fois raison pour le Prix Goncourt. Mais au contraire, que cela vous donne du courage, et pensez un peu au sujet dont je vous parlais.
>
> Venez bientôt,
> Votre ami
> Marcel Schwob

Schwob was unaware that Léautaud had already written a decisive "Non" to any question of trying again for the Goncourt Prize in 1904. Léautaud found it easier at the moment to think of articles for the *Mercure* and other reviews. The one on Schwob dragged on through the spring and then had to be postponed indefinitely when Schwob chose to leave Paris in the hope that his health would improve. He had received an invitation to spend some time with his friend Francis Marion Crawford in Italy. Crawford insisted that the climate and the food would work the same wonders for Schwob that they were doing for himself, and Schwob left Paris on May 15 for what was to be an extended stay. One serious attack after another at Crawford's prolonged it to two months; then a brief respite permitted him to leave Italy, but further attacks delayed his return to Paris until October.

Meanwhile, Léautaud had finished the article on the Comédie Française for the *Mercure*.[19] Schwob, not at all well and needing help with a project of his own, wrote to Léautaud:

> Paris, 29 nov. 1904
> 11 rue St. Louis-en-l'Ile
>
> Mon cher Léautaud, avez-vous un peu de temps libre en ce moment? J'ai un petit service à vous demander relativement d'un index. Pourrez-vous m'aider en ce moment? Et si oui voulez-vous venir causer un jour q[uel]conque entre 6-7?
>
> A vous de coeur
> Marcel Schwob

The index was for the *Parnasse satyrique du XV° siècle: Anthologie de pièces libres,* edited by Schwob.[20] Léautaud agreed to work on the index, and he also showed interest in registering for the brief but brilliant course Schwob began teaching on Villon and his time at the Ecole des Hautes Etudes Sociales on Thursday afternoons, beginning December 8. Léautaud's name does not appear once in the roll book for the course, however.[21] Probably he could not afford the fee, although he told Schwob in mid-February, 1905, that he had been unable to attend because the law firm, for which he had occasionally continued to do some outside work, had kept him busy on a case until the end of January.[22] At this time Schwob recorded in his own unpublished journal:

> Le pauvre Léautaud sort d'ici [February 11, 1905]. Il n'a plus de place chez Lemarquis et demande qu'on lui trouve 50 fr. par mois pour un travail. Ma foi, je l'ai pris à partir de demain pour me servir de secrétaire. Je lui donnerai cela. . . . Il est radieux, et pour deux ou trois mois je pourrai lui donner 50 francs. . . .[23]

Léautaud, who had already resigned from one secretary's job in favor of a literary career, was somewhat less "radieux" than Schwob had thought. "[Pour] faire ses lettres, lui classer ses notes, etc . . . , deux ou trois heures chaque jour. Il ne pourra me donner, pour le moment, que cinquante francs par mois," noted Léautaud in his journal.[24] The article on the Comédie Française had appeared in the *Mercure de France* on February 1, but Léautaud had chosen to publish it under the pseudonym Maurice Boissard. Schwob's pseudonym, Loyson-Bridet, under which he had published *Moeurs des diurnales* in mid-1903, had fooled no one. Léautaud's pseudonym proved more of a puzzle. Ironically, around Paris, and especially at the Comédie itself, people were inclined to attribute the article to Schwob.[25] Perhaps this, certainly Schwob's insistence that Léautaud earn his fifty francs a month, put an end to Léautaud's position as Schwob's secretary after two days of spotty work. Léautaud resigned, and he did not call on his friend again for two weeks. On Monday morning, February 27, he left his apartment to do a little shopping, stopped at a newspaper stand, and was shocked to learn that Schwob had died the previous afternoon, "malade d'une sorte de pneumonie ou grippe infectieuse."[26]

The index for the *Parnasse satyrique* was still unfinished, as was the oft-postponed article on Schwob. Under pressure, however, Léautaud completed both projects in less than two weeks. With the index he simply rendered service to his friend, but through the article it appears that Schwob did him one last favor. Léautaud added essentially nothing new to the thoughts he had first noted in his journal after that exasperating July 14, 1903, but he did take the time to develop them at some length and to soften them somewhat in view of the circumstances of their publication. Schwob's older brother considered it a good article and, more important, so did the staff of the *Mercure*. Remy de Gourmont, in particular, who had felt incapable of writing an acceptable notice himself, was most complimentary.[27] The article brought them together in much the same way that **Le Petit Ami** had first attracted Schwob to Léautaud, and the friendship that subsequently developed resulted in Gourmont using his influence to secure for Léautaud a permanent position with the *Mercure de France*.[28]

NOTES

[1] The originals of the letters are in the Bibliothèque Littéraire Jacques Doucet at Paris, MSS. 7621-16, 17, 18, 19, and 20. I am grateful to the late M. Pierre Bouyou-Moreno and his widow (Schwob's heirs) and to Mme Marie Dormoy (Léautaud's heir) for permission to quote from these letters. Mme Dormoy personally directed the publication of Léautaud's *Journal Littéraire* (1954-1966) by the Mercure de France.

[2] Schwob was only one of many who were impressed by Léautaud and by *Le Petit Ami* during this period. Others include André Gide, Paul Valéry, Remy de Gourmont, Alfred Vallette and his wife Rachilde.

[3] *Journal Littéraire de Paul Léautaud*, I, 118 (March 19, 1904).

[4] *Ibid.*, 66, 67, 69-70 (March 22-April 8, 1903).

[5] *Ibid.*, 79 (August 23, 1903).

[6] The majority of the articles written on Schwob during his career and after his death assert that he was not at all "soucieux de la popularité." The truth seems to be that he experienced the same concern for his publications and popularity that most writers do. Schwob's two books, published by the Mercure de France in 1903, were *Moeurs des diurnales—Traité du journalisme*, published under the pseudonym Loyson-Bridet, and *La Lampe de Psyché*, a gathering under one cover of *Mimes* (1893), *La Croisade des enfants* (1896), *L'Etoile de bois* (1897), and *Le Livre de Monelle* (1894), in that order.

[7] *Journal Littéraire*, I, 74 (July 14, 1903).

[8] Three days before the resignation, Léautaud noted: "si j'écoutais tout ce qu'on me dit, je finirais par me prendre au sérieux et par m'emballer" (*Ibid.*, 67 [April 5, 1903]).

[9] *Ibid.*, 74 (July 14, 1903).

[15] *Ibid.*

[16] *Ibid.*, 111 (February 13, 1904).

[17] *Ibid.*, 91 (November 10, 1903); 97 (January 4, 1904); 117 (March 11, 1904).

[18] I have not, as yet, been able to identify this person or the play in question. This was the kind of work Schwob had been doing, off and on, since his first operation at the close of 1895. It is likely, I think, that she requested Schwob's collaboration, and he in turn-because he was busy with a number of other projects during the spring and summer of 1904-put her in contact with Léautaud.

[19] *Journal Littéraire*, I, 146-47 (October 22-November 8, 1904).

[20] Paris: Welter, 1905.

[21] The original roll book is part of the Marcel Schwob Memorial Collection established at Brigham Young University in 1965. The book contains a number of interesting names, including those of Pierre Champion, François Porché, Henri Longnon, André Salmon, M. Schwab, Max Jacob, Paul Fort, and Picasso.

[22] *Journal Littéraire*, I, 152 (February 12, 1905).

[23] Schwob's journal has probably been lost. Some excerpts can be found among the unpublished Pierre Champion papers at the Bibliothèque de l'Institut in Paris. This one is taken from MS. 5133 (1), p. 147. I am grateful to Michel François, executor of the Pierre Champion estate and General Secretary of the International Committee of Historical Sciences, for permission to publish it here.

[24] *Journal Littéraire*, I, 153 (February 12, 1905).

[25] *Ibid.*, 152, 154 (February 11 and 12, 1905).

[26] *Ibid.*, 158 (February 27, 1905).

[27] *Ibid.*, 176-77 (April 6, 1905).

[28] *Ibid.*, 185-95 (August 18-September 18, 1905); cf. Marie Dormoy, "Histoire du *Journal*," *Journal Littéraire*, XIX, 12.

FURTHER READING

Biography

Harding, James. *Lost Illusions: Paul Léautaud and His World*. London: George Allen & Unwin, 1974, 230 p.

> Traces Léautaud's life, relationships, and work to support Harding's summation that Léautaud was a marginal but admirable literary figure.

Criticism

Connolly, Cyril. *Previous Convictions*. New York: Harper & Row, 1963, 414 p.

> Reprints Connolly's review of Léautaud's *Journal of a Man of Letters*—which he finds competently translated and abridged—and assesses Léautaud as a largely unsuccessful writer whom he nonetheless admires for his critical ingenuousness.

Nishida Kitaro

1870-1945

Japanese philosopher.

INTRODUCTION

Nishida is credited with developing the first modern school of philosophy in Japan, the Kyoto School. Through a career that encompassed three distinct periods of thought, Nishida studied German neo-Kantians as well as the American pragmatism of William James in an attempt to cultivate a philosophical system that allowed Western and Eastern thought to harmonize.

Biographical Information

Nishida was born near Kanazawa, on the coast of western Japan near Kyoto. There he was a childhood friend of D. T. Suzuki, who, like Nishida, became another major force in modern Japanese philosophy. Nishida attended Tokyo University, working as a high school teacher in the Japanese countryside after receiving his degree. At that time Nishida became interested in Zen Buddhism, both studying its theoretical tenets and practicing it in his daily life. Concurrently, Nishida studied Western thought, particularly American pragmatism and German idealism. In 1910 Nishida accepted an appointment at Kyoto University; a year later he published his first work, *Zen no kenkyu* (*A Study of Good*), which outlined his earliest period of philosophical development. He retired from Kyoto University in 1928 and continued publishing books and essays until his death in 1945.

Major Works

Nishida's thought is commonly divided into three distinct periods: early, transitional, and mature. Representing his early period are *A Study of Good* and *Shisaku to taiken* (1915; *Thought and Experience*), both of which focus on the notion of "pure experience"–that is, the belief, strongly supported by the nineteenth-century American philosopher William James, that there exists a single reality that is the basis for all experience and for everything that may be experienced or known. Nishida's middle, or transitional, period is exemplified by the ideas outlined in *Jikaku ni okeru chokkan to hansei* (1917; *Intuition and Reflection in Self-Consciousness*), *Ishiki no mondai* (1920; *Problems of Consciousness*), and *Geijutsu to dotoku* (1923; *Art and Morality*). In these works Nishida was strongly influenced by the German neo-Kantians, and he began the move from believing that pure experience is the basis of all knowing to the idea that self-consciousness or self-awareness is the ultimate activity that serves to unify the reality of self and world. In *Problems of Consciousness* Nishida sought to articu-

late in detail the various forms of consciousness, including sensation (the most basic), feeling, and will, with will being beyond the realm of "intentional consciousness," and free will constituting true individuality that is most clearly communicated through art. *Problems of Consciousness* is generally considered a precursor to the issues explored in *Art and Morality*. In what is known as his mature period of thought, Nishida published *Hataraku mono kara miru mono e* (1927; *From the Acting to the Seeing*), *Ippansha no jikakuteki taikei* (1930; *The System of the Self-Consciousness of the Universal*), *Mu no jikakuteki gentei* (1932; *The Self-Conscious Determination of Nothingness*), the two-volume *Tetsugaku no kompon mondai* (1933-34; *Basic Problems of Philosophy*), and his seven-volume composition *Tetsugaku ronbunshu* (1935-46; *Philosophical Essays*), which contains "Bashoteki ronri to shukyoteki sekaikan" ("The Logic of Place and the Religious World-View"). The mature period itself can be divided into two distinct phases. The first phase consists of *From the Acting to the Seeing, The System of the Self-Consciousness of the Universal,* and *The Self-Conscious Determination of Nothingness,* all of which explore Nishida's concept of *basho*—meaning the place of absolute nothingness–that he first wrote about in *From the Acting to the Seeing.* In this phase Nishida was concerned mostly with the epistemological idea of knowing, or what he called "true seeing." In the second phase, which lasted from 1934 until his death in 1945, Nishida refined his notion of *basho* to mean the beginning point of "social-historical determination." In this final phase of his thinking, Nishida focused on the Buddhist idea of the "true self" and was concerned, especially in his *Basic Problems of Philosophy,* with the more material world of action, especially cultural forms. In "The Logic of Place and the Religious Worldview," Nishida synthesized his ideas into an exploration of the religious consciousness. All of Nishida's work together constitutes the basis for the tenets of the Kyoto school of Japanese philosophy.

PRINCIPAL WORKS

Zen no kenkyu [*A Study of Good*] (philosophy) 1911

Shisaku to taiken [*Thought and Experience*] (philosophy) 1915

Jikaku ni okeru chokkan to hansei [*Intuition and Reflection in Self-Consciousness*] (philosophy) 1917

Ishiki no mondai [*Problems of Consciousness*] (philosophy) 1920

Geijutsu to dotoku [*Art and Morality*] (philosophy) 1923

Hataraku mono kara miru mono e [*From the Acting to the Seeing*] (philosophy) 1927
Ippansha no jikakuteki taikei [*The System of the Self-Consciousness of the Universal*] (philosophy) 1930
Mu no jikakuteki gentei [*The Self-Conscious Determination of Nothingness*] (philosophy) 1932
Tetsugaku no kompon mondai. 2 vols. [*Basic Problems of Philosophy*] (philosophy) 1933-34
Tetsugaku ronbunshu. 7 vols. [*Philosophical Essays*] (philosophy) 1935-46
Nishida Kitaro zenshu. 19 vols. [*The Complete Works of Nishida Kitaro*] (philosophy) 1965

CRITICISM

Valdo Humbert Viglielmo (essay date 1960)

SOURCE: "Nishida Kitaro: The Early Years," in *Tradition and Modernization in Japanese Culture*, edited by Donald H. Shively, Princeton University Press, 1971, pp. 507-62.

[*In the following essay, originally published in 1960, Viglielmo provides an overview of Nishida's early philosophical beliefs.*]

> *Waga kokoro*
> *Fukaki soko ari*
> *Yorokobi mo*
> *Uree no nami mo*
> *Todokaji to omou*
>
> My soul
> Has such depth
> Neither joy
> Nor the waves of sorrow
> Can reach it.[1]

Nishida Kitaro's position as the foremost philosopher of modern Japan is unchallenged. Even his detractors, of whom there are many, particularly among the Marxists and quasi-Marxists, recognize his eminence and do not appear to begrudge him the title of "founder of modern Japanese philosophy." Indeed the very vehemence and frequency of their attacks on him serve only to attest to his significance. It is generally admitted that Nishida departed from the rather crude eclecticism of his predecessors and almost singlehandedly erected an indigenous Japanese philosophy. His first major work, *Zen no kenkyu (A Study of Good)*,[2] first published in complete form in 1911, was truly epoch-making, its impact extending to the present day. From about 1960 there has been a new upsurge of interest in Nishida, with particular reference to *Zen no kenkyu,* after more than a decade of relative inattention, and several full-length books plus numerous articles have been added to the already considerable bibliography. Perhaps the most impressive of these studies is Miyajima Hajime's *Meijiteki shisoka-zo no keisei (The Development of Meiji-type Thinkers).*[3] An-

other unmistakable sign of the new Nishida "boom" is the current publication by the venerable Iwanami Shoten of a new edition of Nishida's complete works.[4]

It is not surprising that many scholars should focus on Nishida's first work and the development of his thought prior to its publication, for, as almost all realize, Nishida's works after *Zen no kenkyu* represent only a broadening and deepening of his basic ideas as expressed in that first work. At no point in the thirty-four years of intense activity which intervened between the publication of *Zen no kenkyu* and his death in 1945 did he make a radical turn in his thought or did he reject any of the fundamental premises of his earlier work. There is only the ever more luxuriant flowering of the buds that emerged in *Zen no kenkyu.* Quite often the terms change, but the substance does not. The seeds of Nishida's thought are to be found in the years before 1911, or, more precisely, before 1906-9, since almost all of *Zen no kenkyu* had already appeared in piecemeal fashion during those years.

What was the process whereby Nishida arrived at the philosophical position he expressed in *Zen no kenkyu* What were the formative influences upon him during his youth and early adulthood that molded him into the type of thinker he subsequently became? It is these questions which have engaged the attention of a growing number of Japanese philosophers and scholars of Japanese intellectual history, and it is to these same questions that I address myself in this paper.

Nishida Kitaro was born on May 19, 1870 (lunar 4th month, 19th day) in the hamlet of Mori in the village of Unoke on the Japan Sea, in Ishikawa Prefecture not far from the city of Kanazawa. (Today a wooden marker indicates his precise birthplace.) When Nishida was three his family moved to another house in the same village even closer to the sea, and it was here, among the pine trees and sand dunes, that he spent his childhood. In his essay of reminiscences **"Aru kyoju no taishoku no ji"** (**"A Certain Professor's Statement Upon Retirement"**) (December 1928) he himself states, rather nostalgically (XII, 168-71): "I was born in a poor village in the North country. In my childhood I attended the village elementary school, and I would play, at my parents' knees, in the pine grove along the sandy shore."

He was the eldest son among five children; he had two older sisters, Masa and Nao, one younger one, Sumi, and one younger brother, Hyojiro. His father, Yasunori,[5] was of an old landholding family, from which, for generations, the village headman had been selected. His mother, Tosa, a devout Buddhist, had a deep attachment to learning, which she inculcated in her eldest son. During Nishida's childhood the family's fortunes declined, ultimately necessitating the family's moving in 1883 to the city of Kanazawa. By then, however, Nishida had already begun the first half of his life, which he rather wryly refers to as "that period when he faced a blackboard" (XII, 169), for he had already completed elementary school with considerable academic distinction, and, encouraged by his second older sister, Nao, in July 1883 he entered the Ishikawa Prefectural Normal School with the intention of becoming an elementary school teacher. he withdrew after a year, in October 1884, having contracted typhoid fever. While out of school, however, he reconsidered his career goals and decided to leave the normal school permanently. Thereafter, for two years, he studied privately under several teachers: literature under Honda Isei, mathematics under Ueyama Shosaburo, Chinese classics under Inkuchi Motoku, and English under Sakuma Yoshisaburo. Ueyama is particularly noteworthy for having been a disciple of Sekiguchi Kai, a pioneer in introducing Western mathematics into Japan. In February 1886 Nishida began the study of mathematics under Hojo Tokiyoshi, the man who undoubtedly exerted the greatest influence upon him in his entire life. In September of the same year he was allowed to enter the Ishikawa Semmongakko, a vacancy having arisen. He studied there until 1890, when he left abruptly shortly before graduation.

His first years at Shiko, or the Fourth Higher School (officially it was the Dai-shi Koto Chugakko, or Fourth Higher Middle School), which the Ishikawa Semmongakko became in September 1887, were full and happy ones. He himself said, in the previously-quoted essay: "My student days at Shiko were the happiest of my life. I was filled with youthful zest and I did everything I wished, heedless of the consequences" (XII, 170).

Hojo, who continued as his mathematics teacher—and as his English teacher also—showed him special kindness. For a time Nishida even lodged at Hojo's home. Indeed Hojo's influence on him was so great that he seriously debated whether to make mathematics or philosophy his career. In the same essay he stated:

> At Shiko the time came for me to decide on my specialization. And I was perplexed about this problem just as many boys are. It was especially difficult for me to decide between mathematics and philosophy. I was advised by a certain teacher whom I respected to take up mathematics. In philosophy not only is skill in logic necessary but also poetic imagination. He told me that he did not know whether I had such ability. This was a thoroughly justifiable comment. I did not have enough self-confidence to deny it. Nevertheless, somehow or other, I could not bring myself to devote my entire life to dry and lifeless mathematics. While still doubting my own abilities, I finally decided upon philosophy (XII, 169-70).

Even though Nishida did not follow Hojo's advice, he continued to have deep respect and affection for him; and despite his preference for philosophy, Nishida's continued interest in mathematics is manifest in the many references to mathematical problems and in his use of mathematical analogies throughout his work. One of his last works, completed in late January 1945, a few months before his death, is actually entitled **"Sugaku** no tetsugakuteki kisozuke" ("The Philosophical Foundation of Mathematics")** (XI, 237-84).

Apart from Hojo, however, there were few teachers at Shiko who exerted a great influence upon him in the selection of his field of specialization. Kosaka states that he does not remember Nishida's ever having spoken of any teacher at Shiko who was especially endowed with philosophical ability.[6] We must then look elsewhere for the major stimuli to Nishida's thought development at that time. We need not look far, however, for among Nishida's schoolmates there was a truly remarkable cluster of keen minds, with a broad range of interests. Nishida quickly attached himself to them, and they became a very close-knit group. Indeed many friendships were formed which were maintained throughout their lives. Even before attending Shiko Nishida had made the acquaintance of Kimura Sakae, later to become world-famous as a seismologist. They had both been students of the aforementioned Ueyama Shosaburo. In a brief essay, **"Kimura Sakae-kun no omoide" ("Memories of Kimura Sakae")** (November 1943) (XII, 252-56), written shortly after Kimura's death, Nishida relates how he and Kimura would study together before going to Ueyama's home for their lessons. Even though their paths separated after they left Shiko they kept up contact and saw each other from time to time. In the essay Nishida expresses admiration for Kimura's work and his pride at having had so many schoolmates like Kimura who became eminent in later life. He also cannot help but voice his sorrow that most of them have already died, and quotes from the English poem: "All, all are gone, the old familiar faces" (XII, 255).

Although Kimura was his first real friend, the boys he first met after transferring to Shiko became his closest ones. Their names read like a partial roster of "Distinguished Men of Modern Japan." We cannot but be amazed at the veritable constellation of luminaries that appeared at this school in a rather remote country town. Yet we must recognize, with Kosaka,[7] that this was merely part of the cultural ferment of early Meiji Japan. However we explain it, it is a fact that the aforementioned Kimura and Matsumoto Bunzaburo, the scholar of Indian philosophy, were one class ahead of him, and, most amazing of all, that Fujioka Sakutaro (Toho was his *go*), Yamamoto Ryokichi (his surname at birth was Kaneda; his *go* was Chosui) and Suzuki Daisetsu (he is better known by his *go;* his given name was Teitaro) were *all* in his class.

Nishida gives a colorful account of the youthful Fujioka in his essay **"Wakakarishi hi no Toho" ("Toho in the Days of His Youth")** (XII, 221-27). He mentions his brilliant record at school (Yamamoto Ryokichi in another article confirms the fact that Fujioka was at the head of the class), his early and deep attachment to literature, especially Japanese literature, and his particular talent in drawing. He comments that, since his desk and Fujioka's adjoined each other, occasionally Fujioka would lean over and even sketch on Nishida's notes. Their friendship was maintained until Fujioka's early death in 1910. In his preface to Fujioka's brilliant pioneer work *Kokubungakushi kowa (Discourses on the History of Japanese Literature)* (1907) (1, 414-20), Nishida gives a moving account of the suffering they both endured at the untimely deaths of their young daughters and how they attempted to console each other. This preface, an eloquent document of the bond that linked the two men, eminent in their respective fields of literary history and philosophy, also tells us a great deal about Nishida the man in contrast to Nishida the philosopher, or perhaps, more accurately, it tells us of Nishida the man as the basis for Nishida the philosopher. From these articles and from other references to Fujioka in Nishida's journal and letters, we can, therefore, learn of the impact Fujioka made on him as a young man, and we are justified in inferring that some measure of Nishida's interest in aesthetics and literature is traceable to this long and close relationship. Fujioka may even be partially responsible for the development of that poetic imagination which Nishida at first doubted he possessed but which, in *Zen no kenkyu* and his later works, he displayed at every turn, despite stylistic shortcomings and the obvious limitations of a technical philosophical vocabulary.

We turn now to Nishida's relations with his two closest friends, Yamamoto and Suzuki. Here we are no longer in doubt about the extent of the influence exerted upon him. Their extensive correspondence and the copious references to them in Nishida's journal show us how deeply they shared their experiences and how unflaggingly they encouraged and helped each other. Of course Suzuki was absent from Japan for long periods during Nishida's life but they nevertheless maintained contact. In fact it should be noted that Nishida's close relationship with Suzuki really began only after they had both completed their education and at the time when Nishida's deepening interest in Zen naturally drew him to Suzuki,[8] whose name both in Japan and in the West is now almost synonymous with Zen. Yet even in his youth Suzuki had already distinguished himself as a student and practitioner of Zen so that Nishida always looked up to him as his mentor in this area.

In another of his essays of reminiscences, **"Yamamoto Chosui-kun no omoide" ("Memories of Yamamoto Chosui")** (December 1942) (XII, 245-51), written shortly after Yamamoto's death, Nishida reviews briefly the more than half century of friendship with him. His sketch of Yamamoto during his Shiko schooldays depicts an intelligent, independent-minded youth, skilled at argument either verbal or written. Nishida recalls that Yamamoto was even asked to write leading articles for the local newspaper and would dash off lengthy ones in a matter of minutes while the messenger boy waited to deliver them to the newspaper office. It is clear that Nishida's mental faculties were sharpened considerably by his close association with Yamamoto, whom he termed in English his "one and only true friend." Nishida, Yamamoto, Matsumoto, Fujioka, and others formed a literary society and brought out a privately circulated

magazine (Nishida even employed a *go,* Yoyoku, at this time), criticizing each other's writings. From Nishida's account of the young Yamamoto it would seem that the latter was not at all hesitant in expressing his views. While unfortunately copies of this magazine have not yet—and may never—come to light (Kosaka states that Nishida once told him that Yamamoto had discovered an old copy and had sent it to him but Nishida could not find it),[9] we do have three letters of Nishida written to Yamamoto during their Shiko days. The first two have no date but are thought to have been written in 1888 or 1889 while the third is clearly dated March 13, 1889 (XVII, 3-9). These three letters are the earliest that have been preserved.

Together they present a vivid picture of the stimulating intellectual relationship between the two teen-age boys. As one might expect, the letters are filled with a youthful ardor and confidence in their mental abilities. And yet their actual content is quite surprising to those who are familiar only with the Nishida of *Zen no kenkyu* and later works. For in the first one Nishida makes a spirited attack, by following strict materialist principles, against Yamamoto's position of the immortality of the spirit. He states bluntly that everything in the universe, including man's heart and mind, is composed of the same elements and that basically there is therefore no difference between animals and plants or even between human beings and minerals. Furthermore, he contends that upon death the most complex mental powers of man dissolve into a simple, elemental energy whereby man's joys and sorrows are broken down and vanish. Towards the end of the letter he relents a bit, however, confessing that he is somehow not entirely satisfied with his theory. He admits moreover that the universe is an overwhelming mystery and that man's powers are too small to comprehend it. Thus, while the whole tone of the letter is immature in the extreme, it nevertheless serves to demonstrate that Nishida was already keenly interested in basic philosophical and religious problems, although his attitude toward them is largely a negative one.

The second letter continues in much the same vein, consisting as it does of an attack upon religion, which Nishida considers as superstition created by man's fear of death and the inadequacy of his intelligence to cope with life's mysteries. He presents the familiar argument that religion begins with man's worshipping awesome forces of nature which he cannot understand. He asserts that if primitive man were to see present-day steam power and electricity, he would probably worship them as gods and that the things we worship as God today will probably be considered by future generations as similar to the totems which African natives now revere. Here again it is fascinating, and even somewhat amusing, to see that Nishida uses precisely the same arguments in this early letter which he refutes so brilliantly twenty-odd years later in *Zen no kenkyu* and which he went on refuting for the remainder of his life. As one might have anticipated, various Marxist critics have gleefully pounced upon these letters and have held them up as evidence that Nishida did indeed start upon his philosophical quest with the proper attitude; needless to say, however, they see his entire philosophical career as a sad decline from this initial state of wisdom. Some of them, such as Takeuchi Yoshitomo, their dean, do attempt to exonerate Nishida of the major responsibility for this "decline" by placing the blame upon the external circumstances of Japan in the 1890's which made it impossible for Nishida to develop further his materialist and anti-religious views. Takeuchi remarks wistfully that "the materialism and anti-religious attitude which contained the buds of a scientific critique of reality withered and died prematurely, and his reliance on man's intellect was lost."[10] It may be possible to consider that the vehemence—or, more appropriately, the ferocity—of the attacks on Nishida by many of the Marxists (a few, such as Yamada Munemutsu, are much more objective) stems in part from their deep regret and chagrin that he should have espoused their views in his youth and then have rejected them so conclusively. Yet even Takeuchi recognizes that these early views of Nishida's are not really the result of any profound and creative thinking (would that not, in any event, be expecting too much of a teen-age boy?) but represent, in large measure, borrowings from Nakae Chomin (1847-1901).[11] Indeed Ueyama Shumpei goes further and makes a detailed comparison of Nishida's statements with passages from Chomin's works to prove that Nishida drew heavily on the latter.[12] The aforementioned Marxist scholar Yamada Munemutsu also comments on this parallel.[13] Yet even if this is true, and Ueyama is quite convincing, we must try to explain why Nishida at that time should have been so attracted to ideas such as Chomin's even as we must try to explain why he discarded them later. Here I cannot but feel that the simplest explanation is the correct one, namely that the teen-age Nishida, as he looked out on the exciting and turbulent mid-Meiji world, with all the extraordinary changes that were then taking place in the political, economic, and social structure of Japan, saw what man could do by exercising his intellect, and came to agree with Chomin that ideas of God, religion, and the immortality of the soul were so much excess intellectual baggage, wholly unnecessary, and even harmful, in the pursuit of tangible goals in what he then considered to be the real world. We must not lose sight of the fact, however, that despite Nishida's materialist and anti-religious views, as expressed in these letters, he did not move so far to the left as to embrace Marxism outright. For Kosaka tells us[14] that Nishida once spoke to him about a boy (Kosaka does not name him) at Shiko with whom he was forever having discussions. This boy, Nishida stated, was such as we would now characterize as a Marxist but Nishida could simply not accept his ideas. Indeed I think that Ueyama's description of Nishida at this time as a Meiji "liberal" is essentially a correct one. Ueyama points out that Nishida was also attracted to the thought of such enlightenment thinkers as Fukuzawa Yukichi and Tokutomi Soho. This would moreover be in keeping with Nishida's anti-Satcho attitude, maintained for many years.

Nishida's confidence in the power of the intellect, as well as his youthful enthusiasm and ambition, are even better demonstrated in the third letter to Yamamoto. Since Yamamoto had impaired his health by studying too hard, and had been absent from a meeting, Nishida wrote him to wish him a speedy recovery and to advise him not to overwork in the future. This very ordinary get-well note is quite revealing, however, for he says that even if Yamamoto has the courage of a Napoleon and the intelligence of a Newton (it is interesting that Nishida should mention two Westerners as examples) this will do him no good if he dies an early death. He goes on to say how sad it would be if Yamamoto, with all his talent, were to die in vain and were to be "lost with the spray of the Japan Sea." He exhorts Yamamoto to take care of himself by asking him rhetorically if he does not wish to see the establishment of the Diet, to plan Japan's future, to preserve the freedom of the world. Here we can see clearly the hopes and ambitions of these two youths and how deeply they were involved in the political and social scene of that day. Nishida reveals in his reminiscences of Yamamoto (XII, 248) that he, Yamamoto, and several other Shiko students went so far as to have a photograph taken of themselves on the day of the promulgation of the Constitution in February 1889 as they held aloft a banner proclaiming their undying devotion to freedom.

This latter incident must also be viewed as an expression, by Nishida, Yamamoto, and the other boys, of protest against the changes that had taken place in their school after it had become Shiko. Nishida writes, in the same essay on Yamamoto (XII, 246-48), of how the friendly, "family" (he actually uses the word *kazokuteki*) atmosphere of the old Semmongakko was replaced by a stiff, bureaucratic, and even "militaristic" *(budanteki)* control. The warm relationship that had existed between teachers and students vanished. Nishida places the blame for this squarely on Mori Arinori, who, as Minister of Education, and as a Satsuma man, was responsible for sending a group of Satsuma administrators, headed by Kashiwada, the newly designated principal, to take charge of the new Shiko. Nishida contends—and, we cannot but feel, correctly so—that their background as Satsuma officials or policemen hardly qualified them as educators. In any event, the closely knit Kanazawa youths and the older teachers were in no mood to accept them. Inevitably tension mounted as the new administrators did not approve of the students' broad academic and literary interests nor of what they considered to be their extremely progressive views. Here it is fascinating to note that these boys from Kanazawa, usually considered to be a redoubt of conservatism, should be cast in the roles of radicals and that the new Meiji leaders should become the reactionaries.[15] In this situation it was natural that Yamamoto, with his aforementioned independent spirit and unwillingness to submit to authority, should have been the first to rebel. Thus he quit the school first and Nishida followed his example shortly thereafter. Here again we have proof of how closely related the two boys were and how deeply influenced Nishida was by Yamamoto. Nishida himself uses the colorful expression: *Watakushi wa toji Yamamoto-kun no kibi ni fu-shite ita.* (At that time I was playing second fiddle to Yamamoto.) (XII, 247)

In the same essay Nishida is careful to refute the charge that he and Yamamoto had been expelled. Kosaka states[16] that when he himself was a student at the same Shiko from 1917 to 1920 there had indeed been a rumor that Nishida and Yamamoto had been expelled because of having started a strike, but Kosaka goes on to say that he had heard from Yamamoto directly that this was definitely not the case. Thus, since the two principals in the episode have issued vigorous denials, we can consider the matter as settled. And yet we do have evidence from another source, namely a letter[17] from Hojo Tokiyoshi to Nishida at about this time, May 18, 1890 (Hojo had already left Shiko in 1888 to take up a position at Ichiko in Tokyo as an instructor of mathematics and physics), to the effect that he is very happy that Nishida has repented of his many absences from class during the previous academic year which had caused his failure, so that we know that Nishida's academic record during the latter part of his stay at Shiko was seriously marred. Kosaka even speculates[18] whether this failure was the cause for Nishida's leaving Shiko, but this seems unlikely since one would hardly think that the school authorities would wait an entire year before dismissing him, nor would they dismiss him at the precise time when, if we are to believe the implication of Hojo's letter, Nishida was actually attending classes regularly and working diligently. And yet of course, despite the assurances Nishida gave his old teacher, he did leave Shiko abruptly shortly before graduation. Miyagawa Toru states[19] that the pretext for Nishida's leaving was illness, but he does not give the source of his information and no other biographer confirms his statement. Here there is a bit of a mystery which needs clarification. Indeed it is rather odd that not one of Nishida's numerous *deshi,* such as Kosaka Masaaki, Shimomura Torataro, or Mutai Risaku, should have clarified it by simply asking Nishida himself.

We do know, from an entry in Hojo's diary, dated August 2, 1889,[20] that Nishida had already appealed to him for help in transferring to Ichiko. Hojo opposed Nishida's plan as unwise so that it came to nought, but it is reasonable to assume that Nishida's dissatisfaction with Shiko continued throughout the 1889-90 academic year until he finally decided to quit school despite his promises to Hojo. Yamamoto's example was certainly a factor, as we have already seen, but Nishida too had definite views on how to further his education by himself, unobstructed by the odious Shiko discipline. He states quite bluntly (XII, 170): "At the time I thought it was not necessarily true that one could not achieve anything by studying alone. In fact I thought it would be better to rid myself of the fetters of school and to read freely. Thus I stayed at home all day and read."

Of course this in no way implies that he had not been reading freely prior to leaving Shiko, for in yet another essay of reminiscences, **"Shiko no omoide" ("Memories of Shiko")** (XII, 164-67), he tells us that he would go up to the school library on the second floor and immerse himself in the books there. Here we have the first mention of his reading Western philosophical works, for he states: "I do not know who bought the book or why but I found Wallace's translation of Hegel's *Logic* and Max Müller's translation of Kant's *Critique of Pure Reason,* the latter of which had been given as a memorial for someone. I borrowed these books and tried to read them, but at the time I could not make head or tail of them" (XII, 166).

Nevertheless Nishida obviously felt that he could read even more freely if he did not have to prepare for specific Shiko courses. And in fact he carried out his plan so thoroughly that he ruined his eyes from too much reading before a year had passed. The doctor actually prohibited his reading at all for a time, forcing him to spend several weeks in a dark room in the Kanazawa Hospital. To add to his problems, his family's financial situation deteriorated, verging on bankruptcy. When Nishida had recovered sufficiently from his illness (he never recovered completely, for he suffered from poor eyesight throughout his life) he reluctantly gave up his plan of studying independently. Somehow or other (this poses another riddle in Nishida's biography) his mother coaxed five hundred yen out of his father to enroll both him and his younger brother in school in Tokyo in September 1891. It would seem that his parents did this with the hope that Nishida and his younger brother could later recoup the family's financial losses in their careers as university graduates.[21] Unfortunately the school he was forced to select was the Special Course of Studies *(senka)* of Tokyo University, which Hojo was quick to point out was the place where only students who had an academic deficiency entered. Hojo thus reprimanded him rather severely and told him to take the regular entrance examination for the university.[22]

Nishida did not follow his teacher's advice, however, and soon suffered the consequences. These were very real and unpleasant, as Nishida himself said: "A Special Studies student at that time was a truly miserable creature. I somehow felt that I was a failure in life" (XII, 170).

It seems that non-regular students were discriminated against severely and that Nishida, extraordinarily sensitive to such things, suffered greatly as a result. Special students were not even allowed to read in the reading room of the library but had to work at desks lined up in the corridor. And since even regular students could not go into the stacks until their third year, naturally Special Studies students were never allowed to do this. Moreover, when he visited the professors he felt that they were very cool and distant in their reception of him. But what seemed to hurt most of all was to see that the former Shiko students, with whom he had associated so closely a short while before and who were now enrolled as regular students, should be treated so utterly differently from him. He says that he "spent his three years there, in a corner, feeling very insignificant." On the other hand he also admits that he had considerable leisure and could pursue his own studies freely. He spent much of his first years, he says, in reading German literature with notes in English, for at Shiko he had barely begun his study of that language. Here we find the beginnings of his turning in on himself, a process of introspection that continued almost without interruption until it bore fruit in the philosophical position which he set forth in *Zen no kenkyu*.

In an essay on Tokyo University life, Nishida indicates that while he learned a great deal as a special student it was not that he was really stimulated by any of the lectures. He tells us that, even though the leading lights of the "first generation" of modern Japanese philosophers, Inoue Tetsujiro, Motora Yojiro, and Nakajima Rikizo, were all teaching there at the time, philosophy was taught primarily by the young German scholar Ludovic Busse, who had been a student of Lotze in Berlin during Lotze's later years. Even though the course Nishida took from him was supposed to be a general introduction to philosophy, it actually amounted to little more than an outline of Lotze's philosophy. At that time even German instructors at Tokyo University lectured in English, and Nishida makes specific reference to Busse's heavy German accent (for example, pronouncing the word "generation" with a hard "g" and a broad "a"), which was especially in evidence when he warmed up to his subject matter. In Nishida's third year he studied under Raphael von Köber, the much-loved moralist and humanist who taught there for more than two decades, from 1893 to 1914. It was von Köber who introduced him to Schopenhauer and who also urged him to study the classical languages of the West so as to be able to read Greek and medieval philosophy in the original. He is reported to have told Nishida in English: "You must read Latin at least."

Nishida in no way lacked for illustrious schoolmates, but because of the obstacles he did not develop any friendships even remotely resembling those he had formed at Shiko. Among the students in the Philosophy Department at that time were the three so-called "Geniuses of '96": Kuwaki Gen'yoku (1874-1946), Anezaki Masaharu (Chofu) (1873-1950), and the famed novelist-essayist, Takayama Rinjiro (Chogyu) (1871-1902), all two years behind Nishida. One year ahead of him, in the English Department, was Natsume Soseki (1867-1916). Nishida gives us the tantalizing bit of information that he and Soseki were actually in the same class in German literature, reading Goethe's *Hermann und Dorothea* under Florenz, the renowned literary historian. Thus, for a brief moment in their youth the eminent philosopher and novelist, perhaps the two most creative minds of modern Japan, were actually classmates. Although unfortunately this association did not develop any further, Nishida makes several favorable references to Soseki's work in his journal, and in a post card to Tanabe Ryuji, dated January 10, 1917, one month after Soseki's death, he says: "I too was filled with sorrow at Natsume's death. Such men as he are truly rare in the modern era and his passing is a tremendous loss to our literary world" (XVII, 190).

Perhaps Nishida was aware that both he and Soseki were really attempting to achieve the same thing by different means: namely, to probe the nature of reality and define man's place in the cosmos.

Although, as I have indicated, during Nishida's stay at Tokyo University he turned inward, spending most of his time by himself reading and thinking, he maintained his interest in political and social developments to a certain degree. This is amply shown in a letter he wrote to Yamamoto dated May 23, 1892, wherein he waxes eloquent and is exultant over what he hoped might be the beginning of the downfall of the Satcho clique: "The spring flowers do not last until summer and the bright moon also wanes. Finally might not the desperate measures of interference really be the beginning of the self-destruction of the all-powerful Satsuma-Choshu forces?" (XVII, 20)

The reference here is to the interference in the second general election of February 1892 on the part of the Satcho-directed government. What really pleased Nishida, however, was the fact that despite this interference the anti-government People's Rights group won an overwhelming majority and that the Minister of Interior of the Matsukata Cabinet, Shinagawa, who had been primarily responsible for the interference, was forced to resign. There can be little doubt that this delight in the government's discomfiture was at least an indirect result of Nishida's earlier bitterness at the government-directed reorganization of Shiko. Be that as it may, Nishida clearly manifested his liberalism at this time, and though his interest in politics lessened during the next two decades it never entirely died. For example, we also find him writing to Tanabe Ryuji on January 22, 1913, expressing the hope that the democratic parties will stand firm and that the bureaucracy and the clan power will be thoroughly destroyed (XVII, 164). Such expressions, and they are numerous, especially after his retirement from Kyoto University in 1928, should go a long way toward proving that Nishida was hardly the apologist for fascism who emerges in the Marxist caricatures of him. And yet these critics appear to have no difficulty in twisting facts and sneering at his philosophy as being that of the petit bourgeois intelligentsia; they consider that whatever good-will (i.e., anti-militarist and anti-nationalist sentiments) he had subjectively, objectively he held views in the same line as fascism and served ideologically to support Japanese imperialism.[23] (Of course there remains the vexed question of some of the writings of Nishida during World War II which might be interpreted as a partial surrender to Japanese nationalism, and yet surely they must be viewed in the over-all context of Nishida's work.)

Nishida's loneliness and unhappiness at Tokyo University seem to have fortified his determination to achieve distinction in scholarship. Miyajima's interpretation[24] that Nishida wished to develop his intellectual powers in order to overcome his feelings of inferiority as a non-regular student is an acceptable one. Indeed, as Miyajima indicates, the truism of depth psychology, that self-depreciation and a feeling of superiority are but two sides of the same coin, is amply borne out by several statements in Nishida's letters to Yamamoto. Be that as it may, however, Nishida did in fact demonstrate unusual intellectual ability in a paper entitled **"Kanto rinrigaku" ("Kant's Ethics")** (XIV, 3-20), believed to have been written as a report for one of his courses with Nakajima Rikizo toward the end of 1891. Although, when Nishida allowed this first philosophical work of his to be published in April 1933, he dismissed it as utterly without significance other than that of indicating the nature of a student's report in the nineties, it shows us nevertheless that Nishida could already at this early age grasp basic philosophical concepts clearly and present them concisely. His style, however, is a rather curious one, for he uses English and some German words (in Roman letters, not *katakana*) for most of the major nouns and even some of the adjectives and verbs. This is probably an indication that many of the terms had not yet been translated into Japanese or at least had not yet been assimilated. Of course it was Nishida who contributed greatly to the translating of Western philosophical terms and the creating of new ones throughout his career, and who thereby provided much of the form as well as the content of modern Japanese philosophy.

In yet another letter to Yamamoto, dated December 18, 1891, Nishida makes his first reference to Suzuki Daisetu's involvement with Zen meditation (XVII, 16). He even says that at the end of November he visited Suzuki at a Zen temple, the Enkakuji, in Kamakura, and his brief comment in *kambun* to the effect that he is envious of those who are detached from the world shows that already he was beginning to be attracted to Zen discipline and meditation.

Nishida makes still another reference to Suzuki's study of Zen, this time under the priest Dokeun, in his letter to Yamamoto written on April 14 of the following year, 1892 (XVII, 19). From this we can infer that he had probably maintained contact with Suzuki throughout the winter of 1891-92 and that his own interest in Zen was deepening. Indeed the editors of Nishida's *zenshu* indicate in the *nempu* (XVIII, 470) that he actually did practice meditation at the Chokonji and Enkakuji in Kamakura at this time, but I have been unable to find any confirmation of this.

Unfortunately we cannot say much about the last two years Nishida spent at Tokyo University, for his major correspondent, Yamamoto, came himself to Tokyo in the fall of 1892 to enter the same Special Studies course that Nishida was taking. (We might well wonder why Yamamoto came after learning of Nishida's many unpleasant experiences, but the riddle is not solved.) Thus there is a hiatus of almost precisely two years between Nishida's last letter from Tokyo to Yamamoto in Kanazawa on September 15, 1892 and his first letter from Kanazawa to Yamamoto in Tokyo on September 19, 1894. Moreover we do not have any other firsthand evidence of his activities at this time other than his reminiscences. We do know, however, that Nishida was graduated from the Tokyo University Special Studies course

in July 1894, at the very time that relations between Japan and Ch'ing China became critical and the Sino-Japanese War began.

Nishida laments in his reminiscences (XII, 244) that, although regular university graduates at that time had no difficulty obtaining positions, non-regular graduates such as he were eyed askance by prospective employers. This fact he learned from bitter personal experience, for despite his having been promised a job at the newly established Kanazawa Middle School by the principal, Tomita, it was finally not given to him but to a holder of a regular university degree. We have a full and moving account of this unpleasant affair in the six letters Nishida wrote from Kanazawa to Yamamoto in Tokyo between September and December of 1894. The first, dated September 19, is a long and detailed account of the complexities relating to the competition for the aforementioned post (XVII, 23-24). Nishida's indignation at Tomita's breaking his promise to him is great, for Nishida reports that Tomita did not have enough courage to stand up to the prefectural officials who proposed that another candidate, Miyai, the holder of a regular university degree in English literature, be considered for the same post. His disappointment at Tomita's weakness is even greater because he had always considered him a man of integrity. As an excellent example of this integrity, Nishida refers to Tomita's having strongly opposed Shinagawa's interference in the general election of February 1892. (From this reference, two and a half years later, we can see what a deep impression the event must have made on his mind.) Thus Nishida suffers doubly from Tomita's action. Indeed his disillusionment is so complete that he wonders whether he would be able to work under such a principal even if he were granted the job. Nishida recognizes, however, that Miyai is certainly better qualified than he to fill a position as an English teacher but he is justifiably angry that both the school and prefectural officials should first have promised the position to him and should then have proceeded to change their minds. At the time he wrote the letter he had already been kept waiting over a month for a decision and his resources were fast giving out. Since he had to support himself and his mother (he oddly does not mention his father, who may have been living apart) he even wondered whether he should go back to Tokyo to find some sort of work, however ill-paying.

The other five letters, dated September 20, October 8, October 20, October 24, and December 1 respectively (XVII, 25-32), continue the melancholy tale. His depression at his unemployment deepens, and in his letter of October 8 he expresses his sadness at discovering, upon first leaving what he refers to in English as the "holy" academic life, that the world is such a corrupt place. By October 24 his situation has become almost desperate and he pleads with Yamamoto to help him find some position at a normal school where he might teach psychology, history, or education. Apparently Yamamoto can do nothing for him, for in the letter dated December 1 Nishida states that he might follow the advice various people have given him, that is, gather private students and give them foreign language instruction, presumably in English or German, or perhaps in both. We do not know whether he actually did this since we do not have any direct evidence of the nature of his activities until May of the following year, 1895.

Several Nishida scholars, especially Miyajima,[25] have been quick to observe that Nishida's struggles to obtain employment in the summer and fall of 1894 coincide precisely with the high point of the Sino-Japanese War and that yet there is not a single reference to the conflict in any of the six letters mentioned or indeed in anything that Nishida wrote at the time. Most of the scholars cannot avoid making a harsh value judgment against him at this point, concluding that his concern for his own well-being at that time was so great as to blot out any consideration of the broader national problems. Even if this conclusion is warranted (which is by no means certain since those six letters hardly represent Nishida's entire intellectual life during that period, and moreover he wrote them for the express purpose of explaining his employment difficulties to his close friend), such unconcern with national political matters can only be considered a moral lapse if one makes it a cardinal principle that everyone should be so concerned. It is interesting that at no point do critics such as Miyajima—and of course the full-fledged Marxists such as Takeuchi, Miyagawa, and Yamada—question their own basic premise that political involvement (on the left, naturally) is an absolute good. They are so quick to condemn any turning inward to a consideration of problems transcending the immediate temporal ones—and this even in a philosopher, whose main task it is to dwell upon the eternal verities and eschew the ephemeral.

And yet, even if we can turn the criticism of the Marxists back upon themselves, it cannot be denied that Nishida did in fact move away from his previous involvement with the national—and even international—political and social scene and embark upon his broader philosophical quest. In this connection we should admit as well that at this time Nishida still retained much of the fierce pride which had been nurtured by the rebuffs at Tokyo University and which now was intensified by the humiliating experience with Tomita. It is only later, as we shall see, that he was gradually able to cleanse himself of the desire for revenge against the world that had not recognized his intellectual eminence and that had treated him so shabbily; it is only later that he was able to engage in his philosophical pursuits without concern for the reaction of the world or without concern as to whether he would achieve fame thereby or not. The fact, however, that his motives at this stage should still have been impure is not too surprising when we realize that he was just in his mid-twenties. Indeed, it would be even more startling if he should have displayed at the age of twenty-five the serenity and devotion to truth he achieved only by dint of great effort at the age of forty.

From the same correspondence with Yamamoto in the fall of 1894 we learn, then, that Nishida was utilizing his time in writing a study of the British Hegelian philosopher Thomas Hill Green (1836-1882). As he says in his letter of October 20, he wants to use his free time to do something "on behalf of the world," and he would like to introduce to his countrymen Green's thought, which he had been investigating for some time. At first he hoped he might bring out a full-length book on the subject but he subsequently lowered his sights and intended to prepare only a brief article. He indicates that he had found Green's thought quite ambiguous and difficult to understand. Nevertheless his determination to present a study of Green, albeit a modest one, may demonstrate that he was attracted to many of Green's ideas on ethics. Moreover, it is clear that Green's basic idea of self-realization exerted a considerable influence on Nishida's system of ethics in *Zen no kenkyu,* where much the same idea of self-realization plays a prominent role. It is interesting to note, however, that by the time Nishida got around to writing this section of *Zen no kenkyu,* some ten years later, he had assimilated Green's ideas so thoroughly that there is not even one direct quotation from Green, or even a reference to him, in the entire volume. In the same letter Nishida asks his friend to help him publish his study, when completed, in the journal, *Kyoiku jiron (Educational Topics),* with which Yamamoto apparently had some connection. We know that Yamamoto was able to comply with this request, for in Nishida's letter to him, dated May 20, 1895, he thanks him for his assistance in this matter.[26] Nishida expresses the concern, at the same time, that his article might be too difficult for the general reader. Unfortunately we cannot assess how justifiable Nishida's fears were, for all copies of that particular issue of the journal have been lost,[27] and thus we cannot make any detailed comments on his first published work at all. It is rather surprising that the editors of the *zenshu,* who were otherwise so painstaking, and who are deserving of every praise for their careful work, should have made no special efforts to locate a copy of this particular article, and even more surprising that Shimomura Torataro, in his Note to Volume XIV (p. 439), where the other early, pre-*Zen no kenkyu,* works are collected, should not have recognized its omission. If this article were extant, it might be fruitful to make a detailed comparison of Nishida's critique of Green's ethics with his own ethical position as set forth in *Zen no kenkyu.* As it is, however, we can make little more than the general statement I have made above.

Nishida's unemployment finally came to an end in April 1895 when he succeeded in obtaining a position as an instructor at the prefectural-run Nanao Middle School annex *(bunko)* on the remote Noto Peninsula. This then was the inauspicious beginning of what Nishida termed the second half of his life, his teaching career when he had "his back to a blackboard" (XII, 169). Despite the obvious inferiority of his position, his spirits rose somewhat at his improved economic status. The meager salary from this teaching position was also undoubtedly responsible for allowing him to marry, and one month later, in May, we find him doing so; his wife was his first cousin, Tokuda Kotomi, the eldest daughter of his mother's younger sister. Kotomi's father, and therefore Nishida's uncle-in-law as well, was a Kanazawa saké-brewer. Nishida's eldest daughter, Ueda Yayoi, describes her mother, in the work of reminiscences,[28] which she produced in collaboration with her younger sister, Nishida Shizuko, as an exemplary wife and mother, who not only did not interfere in any way with her husband's academic pursuits but undertook the management of all of the household duties to enable him to devote himself completely to his studies. Yayoi even feels that this selflessness was responsible for her early death at the age of fifty. She died in 1925, having borne Nishida eight children, six daughters and two sons.

Nishida naturally was quick to realize that, if he wished to make a name for himself in the academic world, he could hardly remain buried in a tiny village of the Hokuriku. In his letter to Yamamoto dated September 8, 1895, he is extremely frank in stating his ambitions and in urging his friend to utilize his talents as well.[29] For a brief moment it almost appears as if his introspective tendencies have been reversed, since he not only advises that Yamamoto advance himself as much as possible but states openly that he has himself recovered from the melancholy which he had indulged in from the previous year. (He undoubtedly refers specifically to his period of unemployment.) Moreover he affirms that his previous retiring and unenterprising attitude (he uses the expressive but not easily translated term *hikkomijian*) had been a great mistake. It is at this point that he makes the statement which, in the light of his previous and subsequent actions, is so startling: "As much as one has obtained [in the way of talents] one should express in the world, and one should [use them to] advance the world. This is our duty." *Onore no etaru dake wa yo ni arawashi yo o susumezaru bekarazu. Kore gojin no gimu nari* (XVII, 35).

A more explicit endorsement of active participation in the world could hardly have been made. He makes his position unmistakable by going on to say, as he had already told Yamamoto earlier during the summer, that he intends to go to Tokyo the following year and study intensively German literature and philosophy, and, casting aside his previous hermit-like attitude, he intends to try to "make his appearance on the stage of the world."

Less than one month later, as shown by his letter of October 2 to Yamamoto, Nishida's mood had changed considerably (XVII, 35-36). He still would like very much to go to Tokyo the following year to pursue his studies, but he now realizes that, with his many dependents, he must find a job to "support" them. (He actually uses the English word.) He laments that he is worrying about this problem day and night. He still is very much involved in his academic work since he indicates that he hopes to complete a history of ethics, treating the major figures of Greek, medieval, and German philosophy, by about summer of the following year. He clearly hopes to use this work to further his chances for obtaining a good position in Tokyo. In his letter of November 18 to Yamamoto, he indicates that he is working diligently on

the history despite the fact that he has few reference works. And yet it would seem that the work was never completed, for it was not published and there are no further references to such a work in Nishida's letters or journal. Of course it is not impossible that he decided to use his material simply as lecture notes for the course in ethics which he later taught. If this is the case, some of his work at this time found its way, in altered form, into the section on ethics of *Zen no kenkyu.*

But to return to the letter of October 2, we find that Nishida concludes with a paragraph indicating that much of the hopefulness and determination of a month earlier had worn off. He asks Yamamoto to recommend him for any positions that might open up in philosophy or German in Kyoto, where Yamamoto was at that time. It is obvious that Nishida is eager to leave where he is, for he finds teaching middle school students a difficult and unrewarding task, and he ends his letter with the gloomy phrase: "I am indeed spending my days unpleasantly." *Jitsu ni omoshirokarazu shoko itashi-ori-soro* (XVII, 36).

The three remaining letters of 1895 reveal a similarly restless, dissatisfied, unsettled state (XVII, 36-40). In that of October 26 he comments on his straitened circumstances, in that of November 18 he inveighs against the entire educational system of Ishikawa Prefecture, and in that of December 19, regarding various problems of school administration, he makes the rather bitter observation that "nothing can be done at a time when fools possess power." As Ueyama points out,[30] the gap between his high hopes and his miserable actual condition causes him intense dissatisfaction.

The events of the next two years, however, brought about a great change in Nishida's external condition and, more gradually, an equally great one in his internal state as well. We do not know precisely how, for no records remain, but it would seem that it was through the good offices of Nishida's inveterate benefactor, Hojo Tokiyoshi, that he obtained a new position as instructor in psychology, ethics, and German at his old school, Shiko, which he had left abruptly before graduation six years earlier. This quite naturally represented a substantial betterment of Nishida's status and automatically meant that he abandoned any plans of studying and teaching in Tokyo or Kyoto. Nevertheless, rather surprisingly, the first letter that refers to this new position, that of March 31, 1896, is in no way a happy one—indeed, quite the contrary (XVII, 41-42). Furthermore, despite the fact that his first child, Yayoi, had been born a scant six days earlier, on March 25, he is not in any way the typical proud father—again, quite the contrary. It would seem that despite this sharp upward turn in his academic career he felt very keenly his greater responsibilities in his home life. This attitude is amply shown by the statements that precede and follow his announcement to his friend of the birth of his daughter. For he clearly states that he now regrets having entered into "family life" and sincerely hopes that his friend will not fall into the same trap (*kikutsu,* literally "devil's lair"). He then laments that he now has many (obviously, too many, as far as he is concerned) links binding him to this "transitory world" *(ukiyo)*, and he fears that day by day his energies will be dissipated. Whether this pessimism is entirely the result of his sensing that his responsibilities are too much for him is open to question. It would certainly seem that some other factors are at work, but we have no way of knowing what they are, for in neither this letter nor the following one, written from Kanazawa on April 8 (XVII, 42), does he go into any detail.

And yet the most significant statement in his letter of March 31, which almost every Nishida scholar quotes, is the one which follows immediately in the letter: "When I go to Kanazawa I intend to visit the Zen priest Setsumon and listen to his religious discourses *(myowa)*." This is the first direct evidence we have that Nishida was moving toward active participation in Zen. It is reasonable to assume that the various religious influences exerted upon him, such as the devoutness of his mother, the example of his revered teacher Hojo, who had long been deeply involved in Zen meditation and had himself studied under the renowned priest Imakita Kosen of the Enkakuji in Kamakura, and of course the stimuli from his friendship with Suzuki, had been working within him for quite some time, and now, with a sense of helplessness brought on by the many pressures of his family situation, that they should have impelled him to seek religious solace and enlightenment.

As I have indicated, however, we cannot say much about the process of this movement toward religion or, more specifically, Zen, during the remainder of 1896, since, with the exception of the brief letter of April 8 to Yamamoto, which is almost entirely taken up with Nishida's reporting that certain criticisms had been made against Yamamoto and with his suggestions for dealing with them, we have nothing written by Nishida himself in the way of evidence. Some scholars have speculated that he already visited Setsumon in the spring or summer of 1896, and this is a most reasonable assumption in the light of his expressed desire in the aforementioned letter of March 31. But of course we cannot be certain of it. Indeed the only documents dating from 1896, other than the letters I have mentioned, are two brief studies which Nishida published in the Shiko journal, *Hokushinkai zasshi,* **"Hyumu izen no tetsugaku no hattatsu" ("The Development of Philosophy Prior to Hume")** (XIV, 21-25) and **"Hyumu no ingaho" ("Hume's Law of Causation")** (XIV, 26-33). We can agree with Miyajima[31] that these essays, which actually are little more than outlines, are probably sections of reports or theses which Nishida wrote while a student at Tokyo University and that even though they are lucid, careful presentations of the subject matter, they hardly represent any original contribution to philosophy or even the history of philosophy. Moreover, they certainly do not give us any indication of the trend of Nishida's thought during this important, and perhaps critical, year of his life, 1896.

One of the main reasons for thinking that this year is so significant is that Nishida began keeping a diary from the beginning of the following year, 1897. Apart from the significance of the content of the diary, which is obviously considerable, the very fact that he started writing one is in itself significant. This fact is, rather oddly, overlooked by almost all Nishida scholars. For the diary surely indicates that the process of introspection, which, as we have seen, began with his leaving Shiko precipitately in 1890, had now reached the stage where he felt compelled to record his interior life and chart its progress in a disciplined way. Thus it is especially unfortunate that we should have no letter or random jottings from the latter part of 1896 to give us some clue as to the events which immediately preceded his starting the diary in early January 1897 and which might have been important factors in his deciding to do so.

Although the first entry in the diary is that of January 3, Nishida wrote a series of undated self-hortatory statements on the inside cover and on the front side of the flyleaf of the diary notebook. We may reasonably assume that he wrote these either before beginning the diary proper or at some point in early 1897. At any rate, these statements certainly indicate his mental state at this time and, as such, are quite valuable in assessing the development of his thought. Even though they are written in a terse, dry, semi-*kambun* style, they reveal the depth of his earnestness and the extent of his determination to order his intellectual and spiritual life. And yet, if we did not know that Nishida went on to write **Zen no kenkyu** and build his own philosophical system, we might be tempted to dismiss these exhortations as rather trite and even pompous, excessively sober and utterly humorless, Confucian-type maxims, high-sounding but devoid of any real content.

I translate the Japanese section of them in their entirety:

Non multa sed multum.

He who desires to become an extraordinary person and perform extraordinary deeds must have a will that does not move, even though heaven and earth crumble, and a courageous and heroic spirit such that even the gods give way.

Neither wealth nor rank can dissipate his heart; neither authority nor force can daunt him; by practicing righteousness he need avoid neither water nor fire.

In everything he establishes his own ideas; he puts them into practice himself and does not rely on others.

To excel others one must have greater self-discipline than others.

The great man must have courage to consider himself ignorant and unwise.

It is of first importance to reflect and think deeply oneself rather than to want to read the works of others. One ought not to read greedily many works; one should read carefully the works of outstanding men of past and present.

The first-rank thinker is a man who does not read widely.

Method of study: read, think, write.

If one has not finished thinking through one matter, one ought not to move on to another; if one has not finished reading one book, one ought not to take up another. (XIII, 3)

On the reverse side of the flyleaf he merely lists the names of major Western philosophers in two groups: "Plato, Aristotle, Spinoza, Kant, Hegel, Schopenhauer, Hartmann, Schleiermacher; Locke, Hume, Leibniz, Fichte, Schelling, Lotze" (XIII, 4).

The first indication we have that he actually began to put into practice this ambitious program of moral, spiritual, and intellectual improvement and that he fulfilled his expressed intention of the previous spring to start Zen discipline comes from the entry for January 14 in this diary for the year 1897 (XIII, 5). At this point it should be mentioned that this diary, from the beginning through the entries of mid-October, is written in German, as are several of the November and December entries as well, doubtless as a kind of intellectual exercise to improve his command of that language which he was then teaching at Shiko. Thus, the entry in question, that of January 14, reads as follows: "Ich besuchte Setsumon-Zenji. Selbst-denken."

Thereafter he paid two more visits to Setsumon in February, on the latter of which Setsumon was ill ("er war krank") and presumably could not see him, and he went to listen to the discourses of another Zen priest, Koshu, in early April and again in early May. Although these five visits to Zen priests over a four-month period surely would not in themselves indicate any very great religious zeal, it is obvious that Nishida was planning much more intensive participation in Zen discipline. He left Kanazawa on June 17 for an extended two-month stay in Kyoto, primarily for the purpose of deepening his spiritual life. He stayed at first with his old friend Fujioka Sakutaro. One week later, on June 24, he had an interview with the Zen priest Kokan at the Myoshinji, one of the most important Zen temples in Kyoto. Doubtless as a result of this meeting, he decided to participate in various Zen practices *(sesshin),* which he did at the Myoshinji from July 1 to July 7 and then again from August 6 to August 12 and also several times at theTaizoin. He returned to Kanazawa on August 20. On August 28 his appointment as professor *(kyoju)* to Yamaguchi Kotogakku was decided upon, for he agreed to follow his benefactor and old *sensei,* Hojo, who had been newly appointed principal there.

But before examining Nishida's activities during his two years (September 1897-July 1899) in Yamaguchi, we must refer to a serious domestic problem that had arisen in the Nishida household during the early part of 1897 and that continued to present difficulties until it was finally resolved in February 1899. Although the terse Ger-

man entries in Nishida's diary do not allow us to view this problem in all its complexity, they do provide us with enough material to state that it was a most vexing one and undoubtedly contributed to a sense of spiritual turmoil which he attempted to overcome in some measure by his involvement in Zen meditation. I cannot, however, agree with Miyajima[32] that this problem was the *primary* reason for his deepening interest in Zen. Surely the fact that his interest in Zen was clearly manifested prior to the occurrence of this domestic difficulty and continued long after it was settled is sufficient proof that the two events are only indirectly related.

In substance this problem centered around Nishida's father's interference in Nishida's marriage, the bad feeling that this stirred up, Nishida's wife Kotomi's suddenly leaving her home with the tiny Yayoi, their returning only to be evicted by Nishida's father, and the separation between the young couple which was agreed upon on May 24. I quote the pertinent entries in the 1897 diary:

> January 22 (Friday) [all the dates are written in Japanese]: Herr Mori kam und sprach von unserem Verhältnis mit Vater.
>
> February 17 (Wednesday): Nachts kam Hr Mori. Wir wurden auf den Vater verdächtig.
>
> April 16 (Friday): Am Abend kam der Vater, mit dem wir den Streit gehabt haben.
>
> April 19 (Monday): Der Vater kam und kehrte ein.
>
> May 1 (Saturday): Der Vater kam.
>
> May 5 (Wednesday): Der Vater kam.
>
> May 9 (Sunday): Kotomi ging aus dem Hause ohne Grunde. Wir alle schlafen nicht.
>
> May 10 (Monday): Diesen Tag keine Nachricht von Kotomi und Töchterchen. Ich ging nicht nicht [sic] nach Schule.
>
> May 11 (Tuesday): Ein Brief kam von Tokuda in Uruschisima anmeldend, dass Kotomi in Uruschisima sei. Ich ging nach Schule.
>
> May 13 (Thursday): Heute kam Kotomi. Der Vater wurde darüber sehr zornig.
>
> May 14 (Friday): Der Vater wies Kotomi aus.
>
> May 16 (Sunday): Heute kam Tokuda und sprach mit Vater.
>
> May 24 (Monday): Heute kam meine Tante. Unsere Ehescheidung.

These exceedingly brief and almost staccato entries, then, present us with a stark account of mid-Meiji family discord in a conservative "castle town" where feudal patterns of social behavior still predominated, where a man could evict his daughter-in-law from his son's home for little or no reason, and where a son had to submit to his

father's wishes even though he, the son, might be economically independent and even though the father might
even be in some degree economically dependent upon
that son, as would seem to have been the case in the
Nishida family. For it does not require very astute reading between the lines to determine that the cause for the
separation (it was not actually a divorce, or
"Ehescheidung") does not lie in any misunderstanding or
quarrel between Nishida and his wife so much as it does
in Nishida's father's interference in their marriage and a
serious quarrel between him on the one hand and
Nishida, Kotomi, and Nishida's mother Tosa (who was,
we must bear in mind, Kotomi's mother's older sister as
well) on the other. The "wir" of the February 17 and
April 16 entries clearly seems to refer to the latter group.
Such an episode as this would certainly be cause for
astonishment if it occurred at a later period in a larger
city such as Tokyo or Osaka but, as Miyajima wisely
points out,[33] similar events take place in Ishikawa Prefecture and other country districts to this very day.

This episode is surely a fascinating one and is fraught
with a veritable network of ironies. For here we see the
young Nishida teaching psychology, ethics, and German
at a newly established *Kotogakku* and delving deep into
Western civilization, or, more specifically, Western philosophy, and yet at the same time he is thoroughly enmeshed in a peculiarly Japanese psychology and Japanese ethic to the extent that he cannot stand up to his
father on a matter of most intimate concern to himself,
his relation with his wife. But perhaps the plight of the
Meiji intellectual caught between two cultures is nowhere
better epitomized than in the fact that Nishida should
write about this feudal or, at any rate, pre-modern, social
situation in a Western language, in this case German, the
language which perhaps more than any other was the
vehicle of modern Western philosophy and indeed of
Wissenschaft in general. One cannot help wondering
whether Nishida himself wasaware of the tremendous
gulf separating the form and content of this section of his
diary.

Although, as I have already indicated, a complete reconciliation between Nishida and Kotomi did not take place
until February 1899 (largely, it would seem, through the
good offices of Nishida's mother, who was, as we have
seen, at once Kotomi's mother-in-law and blood aunt,
and even more important perhaps, Kotomi's father's sis-
ter-in-law, and therefore ideally qualified to effect such a
reconciliation), we learn from the diary entry of August
24, 1897 that "Heute kam Kotomi wieder in mein Haus."
We have no way of knowing the precise nature of the
relationship between Nishida and Kotomi during the year
and a half intervening between August 1897 and February 1899 (in his diary he mentions writing and receiving
letters, but these have been lost), but despite any emotional bonds which may have remained between them,
they were still physically separated almost the entire period, for Nishida left Kanazawa without Kotomi and
Yayoi on September 2, 1897, and after a brief stopover
at the Myoshinji on September 4, proceeded on to

Yamaguchi, arriving there on September 7. Moreover he
lived without his family the entire time he stayed in
Yamaguchi, that is, until his departure on July 8, 1899 to
take up a position again at Shiko, and thus he and Kotomi
were separated, spatially if not emotionally, almost two
entire years, except perhaps for a brief visit on Nishida's
part to Kanazawa—although we have no actual record of
it—in the summer of 1898. Interestingly enough, however, he and Kotomi must have had physical relations
during the nine-day period in 1897 between her return to his
house and his departure for Yamaguchi, for she bore him
their first son, Ken, in June 1898. By a curious coincidence,
Nishida's father, the villain of the piece, died in the same
month at the age of sixty-three. These two events undoubtedly served to hasten the reconciliation between the young
couple. Indeed we may well wonder why another eight
months were required for it to be achieved.

Nishida's two-year stay in Yamaguchi represents the period of his deepest involvement with Zen meditation and
the time during which he demonstrated his greatest religious concern. Perhaps his freedom from family responsibilities enabled him to engage in the religious life more
intensely than had been possible in Kanazawa. (Of course
this freedom could not have been complete since he must
have provided in some way for Kotomi and Yayoi, and
later Ken, in Kanazawa, although we do not know the
extent of that support.) Whatever the reason, however,
the record is clear: his diary for that period and the few
letters that have been preserved show an astonishing zeal
in all matters pertaining to religion and the spiritual life.
Furthermore, this was definitely not simply an academic,
or intellectual, pursuit but one on which he staked his
entire being. His sincerity and wholehearted devotion to
his spiritual quest cannot possibly be doubted.

Already at the end of 1897, in a letter to Yamamoto
dated November 11, Nishida displays a genuine and profound religious mood, quite at variance with his carping
and self-pity of two years earlier (XVII, 43-45). I quote
extensively from this significant document:

> Man's desires are truly deep-rooted, for no sooner
> is one of them satisfied than he wishes for
> something further. When desire rears its head it is
> truly like that of a Hydra. One had better find the
> happiness which comes from cutting it off at its
> base. When man is attached to one thing after
> another, he is forever in a whirl of busyness and
> cannot be calm even for a moment. If man does
> not turn back to the very depths of his soul and
> strike at the root of this delusion, dissatisfaction
> will cause him to suffer at every point. I too, upon
> first coming here, was unhappy wherever I turned,
> but thereafter I pondered the matter carefully and
> now I can say that somehow my spirit is calm.
> When I reflect on the various things about which
> I have been dissatisfied, I am ashamed at my
> meanness of spirit. Have you pondered deeply the
> meaning of the verse from the Sixth Chapter of
> Matthew: "Which of you by taking thought can add
> one cubit unto his stature?" If we abide by this
> teaching I think that no discontent can possibly arise.

This body of ours is important but is there any sense in man's unnecessarily preserving it? Indeed man's life does not reside in his body but in his ideals. When man searches deep within his heart and acts contrary to that which he holds to be the good, i.e., when the self is oppressed by another, then that which is the self is already dead. Tokutomi, even though he exists in the flesh, has surely entered his coffin.[34] When man has probed deeply within his soul, and, attaining his true self, has become one with it, then, even if that moment is a mere instant, his life is eternal. Why do we need to make our spirit suffer and preserve this ugly body? For what reason must one desire the survival of this body? If one plans the eternal existence of the body by betraying the spiritual self in any way, then, even if the body exists, will not the spirit be dead?

If I now think about dying physically, the first things that come to mind are my parents, wife, and child. I certainly have not been free from worry at this time. And yet upon learning recently of the God of the Sixth Chapter of Matthew who cares even for the fowls of the air, which sow not, neither do they reap, nor gather into barns, I have been able to put my soul at rest somewhat. As you doubtless know, the Bible is truly that which soothes our hearts. I cannot but value it above the Analects—how do you feel on this subject?

These quotations from this important letter show us how far Nishida had departed from the materialist views he expressed in that other letter to Yamamoto written some nine years earlier. We are now, at the end of 1897, clearly in a quite different intellectual atmosphere, much closer to that of *Zen no kenkyu* than to anything that preceded it. Indeed several of the basic ideas of his first major work are to be found here in embryonic form: that man must discover his true self buried under the accretions of desire and a frantic busyness, that man's true life resides in his ideals and not in his biological existence, and, perhaps most significant of all, that by attaining his true self and by uniting with it, man touches the eternal and transcends space and time. This latter idea is surely the nucleus out of which grew his basic concept of "pure experience," which he fully developed in his *Zen no kenkyu.*

Ueyama makes several accurate observations with regard to this letter.[35] He comments on the extent of the change in Nishida's basic outlook from the time of his materialist letters to Yamamoto when they were students at Shiko by stating that "this new set of values was one which, in contradistinction to the scientific world-view which considers 'truth' as a gauge of value and which proceeds from *knowledge concerning matter,* constituted a religious world-view which takes 'happiness' as a gauge of value and which proceeds from *intuition of life.*" (Ueyama's italics.) This is essentially a correct interpretation of the process that had taken place in Nishida, one of rejecting, or gradually discarding, a shallow faith in so-called scientific truth in favor of an intuitive, religious approach which sought spiritual enlightenment through attainment of the true self. I also agree with Ueyama in his statement that Nishida's quotation from the New Testament of a portion of Christ's Sermon on the Mount is certainly not to be taken as an indication that Nishida's religious position was a Christian one or even tending in that direction. Rather, his position is one which is neither specifically Christian nor Buddhist (despite his active participation in Zen discipline) but an even more fundamental one, which goes beyond the distinctions between these two major religions, to that point from which all religions spring. Here we have the beginnings of the approach to religion which Nishida maintained throughout his life: he was profoundly respectful of all the great world religions in their highest forms, especially Buddhism, Christianity, and Hinduism, and yet without adhering to any (he cannot be considered an adherent of Zen in the sense that Suzuki Daisetsu is, or in the sense that Kierkegaard is a Christian), he sought to define the nature of the religious spirit itself and grasp that Ultimate Reality of which the conventional terms, such as Buddha, God, and Atman-Brahman, are but pale reflections. Here we are quite clearly in the realm of mysticism, and it must be admitted that Nishida, if not actually a mystic himself, is most certainly a philosopher of mysticism. A recurring pattern throughout his work—especially in evidence in *Zen no kenkyu*—is one wherein his thought ascends in spiral rotations, with a careful logic and a massive and impressive scholarly apparatus, only to end in quotations from the mystics, often Jacob Boehme, Meister Eckhart, or Pseudo-Dionysius, and an admission that he has reached the limits of philosophy. Indeed, his second important work, *Jikaku ni okeru chokkan to hansei (Intuition and Reflection in Self-Consciousness)* (1917),[36] contains the candid statement in the Preface to the revised edition (1941): "I may not be able to escape the criticism that I have broken my lance, exhausted my quiver, and capitulated to the enemy camp of mysticism" (II, 13). Perhaps the only comment we need to add to this is that it is highly doubtful that he actually considered mysticism to be an "enemy" camp.

Religion, and a religious world-view, then, occupy the center of Nishida's thought from this time on, so that even when he is treating certain specific problems within philosophy, he is always doing so within a religious context and he rarely delays in revealing the basis of his thought. For example, in *Zen no kenkyu,* he states quite bluntly that there must be religion at the foundation of learning and morality. And at the very end of his life, in **"Bashoteki ronri to shukyoteki sekaikan" ("The Logic of Place and the Religious World-View."**) (XI, 371-464), published posthumously in 1946, he concludes his life-work on the same note: "The religious consciousness, as the basic fact of our lives, must be the foundation of learning and morality."

But, to return again to 1897, it is interesting to note that the one article which Nishida published in that year, **"Senten chishiki no umu o ronzu" ("A Discussion of the Existence or Non-existence of A Priori Knowledge")** (XIV, 34-45), published in Nos. 14, 15, and 16 of the *Hokushinkai zasshi,* does not in any way reflect this new religious tendency. Instead this brief work can be viewed as the conclusion of the previous period of his career when he showed considerable interest in the more formal aspects of philosophy, such as epistemology and logic, outside of any religious framework. Once again, we can agree with Miyajima[37] that this work adheres quite closely to Kant's theories on the subject and does not display any startling originality. It is fair to assume that Nishida wrote this article, and the four earlier ones, including the one on Green's ethics which has been lost, without any very deep involvement in the subject matter. If this is true, we may also say that it was the growing significance of religion in his life which enabled him to express himself creatively in his subsequent works. For the four brief articles prior to *Zen no kenkyu,* which follow the one in question, are devoid of any dryness (unless it be that of the constricting—and, for the Westerner, or at least for this particular Westerner, quite maddening—*bungo* style in the first three) and amply demonstrate that Nishida has something himself to say other than analyzing or reviewing the work of earlier philosophers.

Throughout 1898 and 1899, even after his return to Shiko in the summer of the latter year, his religious zeal continued unabated. Indeed, he began both years by making week-long retreats at the Myoshinji in Kyoto, and it is not surprising that the fervor of these sessions should have persisted after his return to Yamaguchi, so that we find the references to *daza* (Zen meditation) particularly numerous in the late January, February, and March entres of both years. And yet it would be wrong to think that he concentrated on religion to the exclusion of other things. In these same two years there are many references in his diary to his wide reading, not only in philosophy but in literature in general. For example, Goethe, Shakespeare, and Dante are specifically mentioned. Even lesser figures, such as Lessing, Heine, Goldsmith, Shelley, and George Eliot, received his attention, although naturally it would be most difficult to demonstrate what precise effect, if any, these authors had on the development of his thought. (Goethe is an exception since Nishida later wrote a detailed study of his metaphysical background.) The entries in the diary are so terse that virtually the only thing we can say is that he familiarized himself with many of the important literary figures of the West. Concerning his reading in philosophy we can say much more since he quotes extensively in his later works from those philosophers whose thought appealed to him most or most stimulated him to develop his own ideas on the same subjects they treated.

Nevertheless, despite the breadth of Nishida's intellectual interests at this time, religion, as I have indicated, dominated his mind. The first article he wrote which reflects this new tendency is, appropriately enough, entitled **"Yamamoto Annosuke-kun no 'Shukyo to risei' to iu rombun o yomite shokan o nobu"** (**"A Statement of My Impressions Upon Reading Yamamoto Annosuke's Study Entitled 'Religion and Reason'"**),

which was published in the magazine *Mujinto* (Vol. III, No. 6) in June 1898 (XIV, 46-51). Although it obviously would seem to be primarily a review of another scholar's work, it is actually more a study in which Nishida presents his own views on the subject. Here we can see an amplification of the same views he expressed in the previously quoted letter to his friend Yamamoto. He attacks Yamamoto Annosuke for looking only at the external intellectual aspect of religion and for overlooking its fundamental, internal, emotional aspect. Thus, philosopher though he is, he contends that the definition of religion made by the "cold eye of the philosopher" is not something which has been arrived at by exploring the heart of the actual practitioner of religion, and is therefore false. He further makes the ringing assertion that the essence of religion does not reside in any kind of creed or ceremony but in our departing from the finite world and in our entering the realm of the infinite. He goes on to say: "Shall we call this emotion, or shall we call it intuition? . . . In Buddhism it is termed *gedatsu* (deliverance of one's soul, or the Sanskrit *vimoksa*) and in Christianity it istermed salvation." He contends that the single most important fact in religion is "the entering, by one leap, into the sublime realm *(myokyo)* of infinity and acquiring a standpoint of great peace." Therefore, he naturally believes that the essence of religion cannot be expressed intellectually as are the laws of physics or the principles of philosophy. Nevertheless, after contending in this way that religion cannot really be grasped intellectually, he proceeds to present his own *guken* (humble opinion) regarding a philosophical explanation of religion, which, at first glance, seems to be almost a contradiction of some of his earlier statements in the same article. It is at this point that he presents views which are so close to his position as expressed in *Zen no kenkyu* that I am certain most of the many avid readers of that work would quite easily mistake them for passages from it. For example, he states:

> I cannot think that there is infinity apart from finiteness, or that there is the absolute apart from the relative, or that God, apart from this universe, resides transcendent *(chozai)* outside it. Nay, I think that infinity apart from finiteness is on the contrary finiteness, that the absolute apart from the relative is on the contrary relative, and that God residing transcendent outside the universe is not an omnipotent God. True infinity must be within finiteness; the true absolute must be within the relative. The truly omnipotent God must be within this mutable and fleeting *(ui-tempen)* universe. (XIV, 48-49)

This method of resolving oppositions, such as finiteness and infinity, the absolute and the relative, is basic to *Zen no kenkyu* and all his later work, where he is forever demonstrating that the usual dichotomies of subjectivity-objectivity, activity-passivity, or spirit-matter are more apparent than real and that "true reality" (he particularly favors this redundancy, *makoto no jitsuzai* or *shin-jitsuzai*) is that which includes both terms of the pairs. Thus, this brief review article is significant not only in giving us an outline of some of Nishida's basic ideas but in giving us an indication of his methodology and of the fundamental structure of his thought. He proceeds with his argument:

> However, to enter into the absolute infinity of religion is to enter into true absolute infinity; it is to perceive the reality of the universe *(uchu-jitsuzai)* at the point where it is active in its entirety and it is to attain this in actuality. This cannot be done with the normal powers of understanding. And yet I am not one who believes that we have a kind of special mystical ability apart from the ordinary functions of the intellect, the emotions, and the will *(chi-jo-i.)* I contend that those things which we term the mind, the emotions, and the will are not separate, individual functions but that there must of necessity be one thing which unifies these three aspects. This unity is directly the absoluteand infinity. Must it not be true that at this one point we are able to seize the great source of the universe? (XIV, 49-50)

Here Nishida rejects the view that there is a kind of magical mystical power apart from the ordinary spiritual faculties to unlock the secrets of religion or attain to Ultimate Reality, or that God resides in some far-off nebulous sphere with angels and harps, or with Bodhisattvas and lotus blossoms (choose your imagery). Rather, he maintains, as the great mystics of all faiths have maintained, that God is to be found in the depths of one's soul, that He is there at the very ground of one's being, and that the trinity of the intellect, the emotions, and the will are merely differentiations—and often distortions—of His unity. Surely here we can agree that Nishida is justified in seeing no essential contradiction between Zen and Christianity. For if he arrived at this position through Zen discipline, so too have many Christians arrived at precisely the same position by meditation on and fulfillment of Christ's teaching: "The kingdom of God is within you" (Luke 17:21).

Towards the end of the essay Nishida compares the poet and the philosopher, to the disadvantage of the philosopher, as he quite frequently does in **Zen no kenkyu** and his later works. He rather amusingly states that the poet intuits infinite ideals within finite phenomena and is able to express infinite ideals in finite phenomena but he, Nishida, has not yet heard of anyone becoming a great poet through learning and knowledge. Thus he concludes that the philosopher's manner of looking at the universe is most shallow and incomplete, that the poet's imagination can enter more deeply into the whole than the philosopher's intellectual power, and that the faith of the saint (this is not a precise translation of Nishida's term, *shukyoka,* but closer to his intent than the simple rendering "religious person") is that which is first able to arrive at the very depths of the entirety of the universe. This section of the essay is a sketch of yet another basic pattern in Nishida's thought, that of setting up a hierarchy of value among philosophy, art, and religion. Throughout his work he very often carries discussion of a particular problem up to a certain point and then terminates it with some reference to the worlds of art and religion as the

realms where this problem is fully resolved or where the truth which he is attempting to grasp philosophically is more fully realized. Indeed it may not be an exaggeration to say that Nishida saw his mission in life as one of attempting to discover Reality with his philosophical tools even as do the poet and artist with their pen or brush and as does the saint with his faith and love.

He contends, therefore, further toward the end of the article, that if the philosopher truly wishes to attain his objective of grasping the entirety of reality he must enter into religion, for union *(toitsu-yugo)* with reality is not achieved intellectually *(chishikijo)* but in fact *(jijitsujo).* He thus is not one who agrees that we can erect religion on a philosophical foundation, and he here returns to the assertion he made at the beginning of the article. He goes on to say that if religion needs the assistance of learning it is incomplete. Some may boast that Buddhism is a philosophical religion, but for Nishida this is a defect of Buddhism. "We must not say that Christianity is the more precious because of the medieval Scholastics or that Buddhism is the more precious because it is philosophical. Religion is fact *(jijitsu),* and fact does not exist because there is the explanation of knowledge. The value of fact does not depend on the existence or non-existence of an explanation" (XIV, 50).

Nevertheless, at the very end, he makes yet another turn in his thought, qualifying what he has just stated by asserting that he has not meant to imply that knowledge is utterly unnecessary in religion or that religion and knowledge are mutually incompatible. For he believes that true *(shinsei)* religion must naturally fuse with true knowledge. Quite obviously, Nishida saw his role in philosophy as one of hastening that fusion, or, at any rate, as one of contributing to that true knowledge which, far from being at variance with religion, is the gateway to its very essence.

I have dwelt at considerable length on this early brief study because it has intrinsic importance and also because it clearly demonstrates the tremendous changes that were taking place in Nishida's *Weltanschauung* in the closing years of the century.

As I have already indicated, Nishida maintained his interest in Zen even after his return to Kanazawa in the summer of 1899 to take up his duties once again as *kyoju* at Shiko, teaching psychology, logic, ethics, and German. This return to Shiko is yet further proof, if we needed any, of Nishida's intimacy with Hojo, since Hojo had been appointed principal at Shiko more than a year earlier,[38] and for the third time Nishida changed jobs to follow his revered *sensei.* From yet another letter (XVII, 48) to Yamamoto (without them the Nishida biographer would be in a sorry plight indeed), dated September 15, 1899, we learn how delighted Nishida is at the prospect of being able once again to practice Zen meditation under the priest Setsumon at the Garyuzan, a Zen temple in Kanazawa. He further reveals the extent of his religious zeal by the following statement: "Recently I have come increasingly to feel that nothing, however precious, is more important than the salvation of one's soul. Even if I should spend many years in vain I still wish to [try to] achieve this one thing."

He goes on to urge his friend to take up the same task and practice Zen during the summer of the following year if he has the opportunity.

In another letter, again to Yamamoto of course, towards the end of the same year, that of December 20 (XVII, 49-51), he is very frank in expressing his devotion to Zen techniques in arriving at so-called intellectual unity, although he indicates that he is not really qualified to instruct Yamamoto in Zen and urges him to consult their mutual friend and old classmate Suzuki Daisetsu instead. I quote from that letter: "I cannot really say anything about Zen. You should, however, consult Daisetsu. And yet what method do you think is best to arrive at a so-called unity of thought *(iwayuru shiso no toitsu)?* I think that the Zen method is the most expeditious. . . . Whether I achieve my goal or not I intend to practice it my entire life."

Rather mysteriously we do not have any journal or any letters from the year 1900. Nishida's journal, which breaks off quite abruptly on October 3, 1899, is not resumed until January 1, 1901. And for some unknown reason Yamamoto, who otherwise was so careful in preserving the letters he received from his friend, did not preserve any from that year or else did not receive any from him. The latter possibility is the less likely one, since there was rarely more than a three- or four-month hiatus in their correspondence. Of course it is not impossible that for some reason either the journal or the letters, or both, were suppressed, as was a portion of Soseki's diary. It is interesting that not one of the many Nishida scholars has speculated on the possible reasons for this gap in our records of his life.

We do, however, have one document from the year 1900 which enables us to assert that even if his diary and letters of that year have been suppressed for some personal or family reasons the development of his thought continued along much the same lines as during the previous three or four years. This document is the extremely brief (a mere two and a half pages in the *zenshu* edition) article **"Bi no setsumei"** (**"An Explanation of Beauty"**) (XIV, 52-54), which appeared in the March 1900 (No. 26) issue of the Shiko journal, *Hokushinkai zasshi.* Despite its brevity, however, it reveals quite well the continuity in Nishida's thought. For in it he treats the aesthetic sense as one of a self-effacement, or ecstasy *(muga),* wherein one has transcended ordinary thought and discrimination *(shiryofumbetsu),* and which, at its deepest level, is one with the religious spirit. Beauty, for Nishida, as for Keats, is truth, but an intuitive truth and not a truth attained by the thinking faculty. Here again we have the same hierarchy of value, for he defends this kind of intuitive truth against the criticism that it is merely a poet's fantasy, and asserts that this truth is that wherein we have

departed from the self and fused with things *(onore o hanare yoku mono to itchi-shite)* (quite obviously, Nishida uses the term "self" in two wholly different senses, one pejorative, as here, and the other referring to the true, or enlightened, self); thus it is a truth which we have seen with the eyes of God *(kami nome o motte mitaru shinri)* and, since it represents a profound grasping of the secrets of the universe, is indeed far greater than logical truth attained from without by the processes of the intellect. He concludes this particular paragraph with a rhetorical question which is nothing short of prophetic in the light of the present-day low esteem for the great figures of German idealism: "Even if some day the time should come when the great philosophers Kant and Hegel are not paid the least attention, will not the works of Goethe and Shakespeare, as mirrors of the human heart, be transmitted for hundreds of generations?" (XIV, 54)

Surely Nishida's exalting the poets above Kant and Hegel, whom he also deeply respected and from whose works he quotes frequently, is an indication of one of his basic tenets, namely that logical truth must ever be attuned to poetic truth. And of course it can be seen as further confirmation of his belief that the intellect must ultimately bow before the intuition of the artist and the saint.

He ends the essay by stating that although the aesthetic sense is of the same kind as the religious spirit, they differ in extent. For beauty is ecstasy *(muga* again) of the moment whereas religion is eternal ecstasy. Then, almost as an afterthought, and indicating that his organization is somewhat faulty, he adds that morality, although it originates in the same realm as beauty and religion, still belongs to the sphere of discrimination *(sabetsukai),* for it is built on the idea of duty and that of the differentiation between the self and the other, and good and evil. Thus it does not yet reach the sublime realms of religion and art. The essay, then, begins by attempting to define beauty and ends by comparing the depth and scope of religion, art, and morality.

This brief study can also be seen as a very rough sketch of his mature, detailed work *Geijutsu to dotoku (Art and Morality)* (1923) (III, 237-545), in which he presents a comprehensive treatment of the relationships between the realms of art and morality, covering, among other topics, the three possible pairs within the trinity of truth, goodness, and beauty *(shinzembi).* Inevitably there is also a section of the work entitled "Shinzembi no goitsuten" (The Fusion Point of Truth, Goodness, and Beauty) (III, 350-91), which begins, significantly, with a lengthy quotation from Saint Francis of Assisi's "Hymn to the Sun." Here we have clear proof of the logical course of development from Nishida's ideas in **"Bi no setsumei,"** for once again, almost a quarter of a century later, he sees religion, and the intuition and ecstatic rapture of the saint, as the ultimate state to which both art and morality tend.

Nishida's diary, which, as I have indicated, was resumed on January 1, 1901 after a hiatus of more than a year (that is, if the diary for 1900 has not been either suppressed or lost), further confirms continuation of this religious concern, scarcely diminished from the peak which, by Nishida's own admission,[39] it had attained during his stay in Yamaguchi. A sampling of some of the early entries (XII, 46-57) for the year 1901 tells us quite eloquently (much of the earlier terseness of the diary is gone, together with the German) of the extent to which he was driving himself in his spiritual life and also of his frequent setbacks and periods of aridity:

January 6:[40] The purpose of Zen meditation is salvation. Apart from this there is nothing [of value]. I have much to reflect on within myself.

January 10: I have not meditated for some time; my heart somehow is disturbed.

January 15: When I read I frequently have feelings of impatience. Also I have desire for fame, and my heart is not at peace. I must reflect on this deeply.

February 1: My heart is tarnished and it never seems to have a fixed point; I truly feel that I have achieved nothing for all of my efforts of the past several years.

February 2: A new person arrived, whose specialty is philosophy, and I am concerned and unhappy about the number of my courses being reduced.

February 3: Troubled by yesterday's event I called on Hojo Sensei. He was absent so I could not talk to him, but I meditated and I was deeply ashamed of myself for having so many selfish, petty thoughts. I also realized that this type of problem is not really of any importance.

February 7: One must not forget the source of peace in the pursuit of learning. Fukuzawa Sensei has died. He certainly maintained his independence. A great man must be like that.[41]

February 14: My will to dwell on the Way is slight, and I do not know how many times a day I have forgotten the Way because of trivial desires and fleshly lust. This too is primarily a result of my lacking will power.

February 19: I cannot but be ashamed at the weakness of my religious spirit.

March 17: I received the *go* of Sunshin from Setsumon.[42]

March 25: Beneath the dim lamp the whole family ate their meal with their trays lined up. For some reason I felt this to be sublime. Man's joy does not reside in having mansions and pleasing prospects but simply in the ordinary things and the commonplace.

April 26: These past several days I have been spiritually indolent and have done nothing.

An essay which Nishida wrote later during this year 1901 demonstrates his religious earnestness even more clearly.

It is also a brief one, since he seems not to have wanted to write lengthy articles at this time; he was, by his own admission,[43] conserving his energies for the sustained effort of producing *Zen no kenkyu*. This essay, entitled **"Genkon no shukyo ni tsuite" ("Concerning Present-day Religion"),** was published in the December 1901 issue of *Mujinto* (Vol. VI, No. 12) (XIV, 55-58). In it Nishida addresses the Japanese youth of his day, who were seeking new avenues in religion, which he felt to be in a state of stagnation at that time. He asserts that he desires a reform of both Buddhism and Christianity but goes on to say that he does not mean that *both religions themselves (Butsu-Ya ryokyo sono mono)* (Nishida's italics) should be reformed; rather, he maintains that present-day men of religion (here he uses the word *shukyoka* in its more common sense) should return to the true intent of both the Founders *(ryo-kyoso no shin-i)*. He concludes this particular paragraph with a series of statements that prove conclusively how deeply he respected these two major religions. Rather surprisingly, he here shows even greater respect for Christianity. First he poses the rhetorical question: "How can we disparage Buddhism and Christianity, which were both built by the hands of unexampled saints" (here he uses the familiar term *seijin*) "and which have a history of several thousand years?" Then, while disclaiming any profound knowledge of the sacred scriptures of either religion, he exhorts his readers to look at the four gospels of the New Testament. He declares that the depth of Christ's religious insight is such that today, after several millennia, we are still able to grasp only a small portion of His true spirit and that the more we ponder His every word the more profound this spirit seems. He asserts that never again shall we have a book such as the New Testament. His last sentence is in a sense a summation of some of his statements earlier in the essay to the effect that "religion is life" *(shukyo wa seimei nari)* and not the "fabrication of scholars" *(gakusha no sakui),* for he now declares: "Why then do we need to follow blindly any shallow new religion of scholars?"

The next paragraph consists of a blistering attack on some of the professional purveyors of religion, those who make its propagation an occupation, and who, while having no personal religious experience themselves, cling to dead forms, emphasizing the letter rather than the spirit of the sacred texts. He particularly assails the Christian missionaries who place undue emphasis on the miracles of Christ, using them to prove His divinity. Here Nishida shows his affinity to the most profound Christian thinkers by declaring that Christ's divinity is amply proved in other, deeper senses and that there is nothing baser than appealing to people with this "bribe" *(wairo)* of miracles. He realizes that some may think, by his so arguing, that he opposes Christianity, but he maintains that actually its true significance does not lie in external forms and that Christ Himself, opposing the formalism of the Pharisees, reveals the true spirit of religion.

He ends this brief essay with an appeal to Christian missionaries to develop a pure heart and to merge with the mind of Christ rather than to concentrate on theology, and with an appeal to Buddhist priests to reflect deeply and to give of themselves sacrificially rather than to concentrate on Sanskrit or philosophy.

This essay is a somewhat curious one in that it is the most purely religious, and the least philosophical, of Nishida's entire work. It is, for example, the only one in which he makes detailed references to specific Christian and Buddhist doctrines or criticizes actual religious institutions. Moreover, in several ways this work can even be considered as an attack upon philosophy, or at least as a representation of the view that excessive philosophical speculation can be a hindrance to the attainment of religious insight. And yet of course this essay is, as I have already shown, an excellent indication of the extent of Nishida's earnestness in the spiritual life at that time (late 1901) and of his emphasis upon grasping the essence of religion beneath all of its external forms. Furthermore, we may also view it as the fruition of his religious concern, initiated some five years earlier.

To return to a consideration of his diary, we note that the religious mood, with much self-flagellation and self-exhortation, is maintained throughout 1901 and well into 1902. But from about March or April of the latter year, a very gradual tapering off of religious zeal is perceptible.[44] Perhaps the most reasonable explanation for this change is that Nishida was slowly resolving the basic spiritual problems which had first impelled him toward Zen meditation and discipline. In other words, his zeal was gradually replaced by a calmer, more serene mood, wherein he was able to apply the insights gained by Zen discipline to every area of his life.

I agree with Kosaka,[45] therefore, that from about the end of the following year, 1903, we see this new mood manifesting itself even more clearly. Now that the sense of urgency concerning his own spiritual state has been largely removed, he comes to *reflect* upon religion more than to *participate* in it, and he begins seriously to consider the relationship between religion and philosophy. He extends much further the scope of his reading in Western philosophy in general and the philosophy of religion in particular.

We might perhaps consider that this broader, more comprehensive view of Nishida's manifests itself already with the last of the pre-*Zen no kenkyu* essays, **"Jinshin no giwaku"** (**"The Questions of the Human Heart"**) (XIV, 59-63), begun on May 16, 1903, and published shortly thereafter, in June, in the *Hokushinkai zasshi* (No. 35). Undoubtedly because this brief essay immediately precedes the organizing of his material for **Zen no kenkyu** it is the closest in mood to that work. For, rather than treating exclusively religious problems, in it he discourses freely on science, life, and society in general, dwelling particularly upon man's doubts, fears, and questionings in these areas. (Hence the title.) His style here shifts to the colloquial for the first time. From this change alone we may realize how very close this essay is to *Zen no kenkyu,* also written in the same colloquial style. Nishida maintains in this work that, no matter how happily and unconcernedly man may lead his life, if he in-

tends truly to grasp its essence, he must grapple with the deepest and greatest questions: where life comes from, where death leads to, why he is living, why he is working, and why he is dying. Unless man can cope with these questions which lie in the depths of his heart, he will never be able to obtain true peace. And yet after posing these difficult problems Nishida comes up with a surprisingly simple solution. For he states that neither research, nor great learning, nor talent is needed to solve them but, rather, a pure heart. He asks the reader to look at Peter, a simple Galilean fisherman. He concludes his presentation at this point, obviously referring to religious faith as the answer to the deepest questions of the human heart, although he does not treat religion directly in this essay.

Thus this work can be seen almost as a manifesto proclaiming that Nishida is thereafter going to treat, from a religious viewpoint, these basic philosophical—or, more precisely, metaphysical—problems.

We are now, in 1903, on the very threshold of the world of **Zen no kenkyu.** Nishida's apprenticeship is ended, and he now begins in earnest to fashion the work which will establish him as the "founder of modern Japanese philosophy." Quite obviously the many important events in his life, such as his encounter with the thought of William James, the death of his younger brother Hyojiro in the Russo-Japanese War, and his deep empathy with the brilliant young mystic Tsunashima Ryosen, during the three years before the first section of his famous work was actually published, deserve careful treatment to complete the portrait of the early Nishida, and I hope at some future date to make my own interpretation of them. Nevertheless the major outlines of that portrait are already clear by 1903. For we have seen how he changed from an ambitious, self-confident, extroverted youth at Shiko to a retiring, unhappy, and even bitter young man at Tokyo University, during his period of unemployment, and as a middle school teacher on the Noto Peninsula. Then, with the events of 1896-97 as the turning point, he plunged into Zen meditation and the religious life to effect a complete transformation of his personality and world-view. He changed from a student of philosophy to a philosopher, producing four short essays, in which he adumbrated several of the major themes not only of **Zen no kenkyu** but also of much of his later work. The last of the four, as we have just seen, foreshadows even more startlingly the major works that are to follow. The foundation is laid; he has but to rear the structure.

I hope that in presenting the background to his early years I have also demonstrated that Nishida's thought is not merely of historical interest but has considerable significance for the present day. Indeed I cannot but feel that thinkers of Nishida's stature and type are in extremely short supply, and the world would do well to pay them much greater attention.

NOTES

[1] The *tanka* was written by Nishida in 1923, *Zenshu,* XII, 188. The major primary source for this paper is the

Nishida Kitaro zenshu (The Complete Works of Nishida Kitaro), published by Iwanami Shoten (Tokyo, 1947-53). It contains 18 volumes, 12 in the *Zenshu* proper and 6 in the *bekkan* which includes unpublished material, letters, and the diary. A full index is to be found in XVIII, 501-14. References to the *Zenshu* will be made hereafter by the volume and page number in the text.

[2] I, I-200. My complete English translation of this work, *A Study of Good,* was published by the Japanese National Commission for Unesco (Tokyo, 1960). The volume also contains (pp. 191-217) my translation of Shimomura Torataro's essay, "Nishida Kitaro and Some Aspects of His Philosophical Thought," which has provided some of the basic biographical information for this paper not obtainable from primary sources.

[3] Tokyo, 1960. I am indebted to Miyajima for numerous insights into Nishida's thought, although I frequently differ from him in my interpretation. Perhaps my basic disagreement with him is that his is so often an explanation "by reduction," for he not only explains but is confident that he "explains away." He avoids the bias and invective of the Marxists and the excessive admiration, amounting almost to adulation, of Nishida's *deshi* yet falls into another trap, that of an uncritical faith in the social sciences, particularly social psychology, as capable of providing a complete explanation of any social reality. He rather blithely assumes that once he has given the social and psychological background (with an admirable wealth of detail, to be sure) to the development ofNishida's thought he has fully disposed of it. He rarely comes to grips with the true thrust of Nishida's thought, *qua* thought, and usually looks upon it as merely a kind of emanation from quantifiable, reducible, thoroughly manageable social phenomena. Nevertheless, after saying this, I must admit how useful his work has been to me, especially in enabling me to formulate my own views of Nishida vis-à-vis his.

[4] From the prospectus we learn that it will contain nineteen volumes, in contrast to the previous eighteen. I have been informed, however, that it will contain very little new material relating to Nishida's early years.

[5] Kosaka Masaaki gives the reading "Tokudo" in his *Nishida Kitaro Sensei no shogai no shiso (The Life and Thought of Professor Nishida Kitaro)* (Tokyo, 1947), p. 14. I here follow the more common reading. It is of course not impossible that both are correct. I should mention here that this work by Kosaka also provided me with some further basic biographical information. Indeed, for want of any truly complete Nishida biography, Kosaka's must serve as the best of the secondary sources.

[6] Kosaka, pp. 17-18.

[7] Kosaka, p. 18.

[8] See Mutai Risaku's Introduction to *Nishida Kitaro no tegami—Suzuki Daisetsu e (The Letters of Nishida Kitaro to Suzuki Daisetsu)* (Tokyo, 1950), p. 2.

[9] Kosaka, pp. 18-19.

[10] See Takeuchi Yoshitomo, "Nishida Kitaro," pp. 337-54, in *Nihon no shisoka (Japanese Thinkers)* (Tokyo, 1954).

[11] Takeuchi, p. 338.

[12] Ueyama Shumpei, "Nishida Kitaro," pp. 151-222, included in *Kindai Nihon no shisoka (Thinkers of Modern Japan)* (Tokyo, 1963).

[13] See his *Nihongata shiso no genzo (The Basic Image of Japanese-type Thought)* (Tokyo, 1961), pp. 36-39.

[14] Kosaka, p. 19.

[15] Miyajima, pp. 38-41, gives a detailed account of this confrontation and, surprisingly, even shows that Kashiwada was a more substantial individual than Nishida was willing to admit.

[16] Kosaka, pp. 20-21.

[17] Quoted extensively in Shimomura, *Wakaki Nishida Kitaro Sensei(The Young Nishida Kitaro)* (Tokyo, 1947), pp. 28-29. This work was also useful in providing additional background information on Nishida's youth and early adulthood. I am also indebted to Shimomura personally, for during several visits to his home he spoke to me at considerable length of Nishida, his own revered *sensei,* giving me a better understanding of Nishida's life and work.

[18] Kosaka, p. 21.

[19] See his *Kindai Nihon no tetsugaku, zohohen (Modern Japanese Philosophy)* (Tokyo, rev. ed., 1962), p. 119.

[20] Quoted extensively in Shimomura, p. 27.

[21] See Takeuchi, p. 339.

[22] See yet another of Nishida's reminiscences, "Hojo Sensei ni hajimete oshie o uketa koro" (When I First Was Taught by Hojo Sensei), XII, 257-60.

[23] See Miyagawa Toru, *Kindai Nihon shiso no kozo (The Structure of Modern Japanese Thought)* (Tokyo, 1956), p. 123.

[24] Miyajima, p. 47.

[25] Miyajima, pp. 52-53.

[26] XVII, 33-34. We are not absolutely certain that this letter was written in 1895, for only the month and day appear. And yet all the internal evidence points to its having been written in this year.

[27] See Miyajima, p. 66.

[28] *Waga chichi Nishida Kitaro (Our Father, Nishida Kitaro)* (Tokyo, 1949), p. 58.

[29] XVII, 34-35. Here again the year 1895 is not indicated but, from the contents of the letter, it must have been written in this year since he spent only one September on the Noto Peninsula.

[30] Ueyama, p. 188.

[31] Miyajima, p. 66.

[32] Miyajima, pp. 56-58.

[33] Miyajima, p. 58.

[34] Nishida makes this severe condemnation of Tokutomi Soho becauseof his revulsion at what he considers to be Soho's political betrayal, for Soho at this time moved from an anti- to a pro-government position. As Ueyama, p. 180, points out, this is a clear indication of how highly Nishida had previously revered Soho. This passage, moreover, shows us that Nishida had not utterly lost interest in political matters.

[35] Ueyama, pp. 189-91.

[36] II, 1-350. I have recently finished a complete English translation, and hope to publish it shortly.

[37] Miyajima, pp. 66-67.

[38] See letter to Yamamoto, XVII, 46.

[39] See Kosaka, p. 33.

[40] For brevity I omit reference to the day of the week.

[41] Thus we see that Nishida's respect for Fukuzawa was maintained until the latter's death.

[42] Setsumon selected it from a poem by Tu Fu. See Kosaka, p. 38. Nishida used this *go* in all his literary works for the remainder of his life.

[43] *Waga chichi Nishida Kitaro,* pp. 53-54.

[44] Miyajima, p. 62, is justified in making this observation.

[45] Kosaka, pp. 41-42.

Lothar Knauth (essay date 1965)

SOURCE: "Life is Tragic: The Diary of Nishida Kitaro," in *Monumenta Nipponica: Studies on Japanese Culture,* Vol. XX, Nos. 3-4, 1965, pp. 335-58.

[*In the following essay, Knauth traces Nishida's personal development as recorded in his diary.*]

On June 7, 1965 it was twenty years since the death of the man who has been called "the most demanding thinker Japan ever produced."[1] On this occasion Nishida's publisher is issuing a new edition of his complete works.[2] Though parts of his work have been in the meantime translated into English, German and Spanish,[3] his true significance in world perspective will probably not be fixed till a comprehensive, globe-circling history of modern ideas can bewritten. What is usually known of his work, even in Japan, is ***Zen no kenkyu*** (*A Study of Good*), but one first step on a long journey in quest of philosophical analysis.

The following article, written before a comprehensive estimate of Nishida's work even in the context of modern Japanese intellectual history alone, had been made in a Western language,[4] tries to trace Nishida Kitaro's personal development through the testimony of his diary. This approach does of course beg the question whether his life does "present any singular incident or events worthy of special mention."[5] We believe that no matter how great a man's thoughts, they cannot be separated from the *process* of his personal consolidation. To be sure, the by us imposed necessary selectiveness will let the drama of crisis situations come to the foreground. Easily the most exciting part of this odyssey through the sea of entries, was trying to orient oneself among the plethora of annotations on readings—often abbreviated and not always in the most decipherable *kana* transcriptions. What now, oversimplified perhaps, appears nicely in place, in possibly too well-defined categories, found that context only after reviewing the development of centuries of Western and East Asian thought. As this work progressed, our estimation of Nishida's intellectual achievement grew commensurately; and if some critics attack him for being too rooted in traditional Japanese thought, then his position certainly was no result of an ignorance of the complexities of Western intellectual development. And if other students of his philosophy reproach him for dealing with the problems of the historical world without being a historian, one can easily reply by saying that his knowledge of world intellectual history was as wide and deep as that of many, also Western, historians of considerable reputation.

There has been much talk of a Nishida "System" of philosophy. Positing its presence is perhaps related with the aesthetic, not to say orgiastic, satisfaction some intellectuals, especially Japanese intellectuals, derive from all-encompassing generalizations. Nishida's thought, *Nishida tetsugaku,* goes much deeper, toward complexities of considerable sophistication. The result of his inquiry is not a formula but an insight. It defies being straight-jacketed into plausible schematica and may often be captured only by a literary image. And thus the aging philosopher who had set out to "study life" would write on his last New Year's Day a common place: "Life . . . is tragic."

What follows is but a first attempt to come to grips with the enigmatic personality of the historical Nishida. It is offered as a small token of respect on this anniversary. Hopefully it will show the universally meaningful, human components of the man behind the high-flying ideas . . . even though it be only in fleeting glimpses.

> "Make up your own mind and after doing so, do not
>   depend on others. . . .
> Do not believe indiscriminately in people's
>   words. . . .
> Do not speak of matters that have not matured. . . .
> Do not waste precious time on idle gossip. . . .
> The law of reading matter: To read, to think, to
>   write. . . .
> If you have not finished thinking about one
>   matter, do not shift to another. . . .
> If you have not read one book to its end, do not
> take up another. . . .
> *Non multa sed multum*"
>
> > *Diary,* New Year 1897
> > Dim, cloudy, twenty degrees (C)
> > *Diary,* June 1, 1945

The first and the last entries in Nishida Kitaro's diary mark beginning and end of one of the most extensive diaries written by a Japanese intellectual. Both as personal experience and political history, it provides us with the individual annals and reflections of one of the actors on the Japanese historical stage and leads us in time from Japan recently emerged victoriously from the Sino-Japanese War to a militaristic world power on the verge of certain defeat. We meet its author first as a young instructor in a provincial high school and hear from him last six days before his death, as after a lifetime of personal doubts, the honored ex-professor of philosophy lives ailing in retirement in Kamakura.

Begun at the age of twenty-six, his diary leads us for more than 48 years through the innermost reflections and worries of a developing individual in shifting historical circumstances and a changing world. It portrays the metamorphosis of an extraordinary man who, having to confront his historical situation, tries to define his relationship to this condition, undertaking to reach a meaningful explanation of its reality, and becomes himself a protagonist of an extremely personal drama of cultural and social conflict.

I THE PRE-DIARY OF NISHIDA KITARO

Nishida was born on May 19, 1870[6] in the Mori section of the village of Unoke in Ishikawa prefecture. His father, Yasunori, then 37, was a peasant and his mother, Tosa, 27 at the time, the daughter of a village headman. As the family's oldest son, he was the middlemost of five children.

Ishikawa prefecture was formed, after the Meiji Restoration, of the Kaga and Noto Han. Kaga, because of its riches, had been known, in Tokugawa times, as the Million-Koku-Han. Its *daimyos,* the Maeda family, had been instrumental in the success of the shogunate. It was this economic strength, rather than any privileged political position, which facilitated the rapid introduction of an enterprising Western style school system, especially in the castle-town of this city. And in order to be near the best possible schooling, the Nishida family moved to this city in 1883. When he fell sick of typhus in 1884, Kitaro's schooling was for the first time interrupted. During his recovery he seems to have contacted his mathematics teacher and early mentor, Hojo Tokiyoshi, who was to have considerable influence in his plans for subsequent years.

In July 1886 he was admitted, filling a vacancy, as a second year student in the Middle School attached to the Ishikawa Prefectural College (*Ishikawa ken semmon gakko*), soon, upon his graduation from Middle School, to be renamed the Fourth Higher Middle School (*Daishi Koto chugakko*). After passing the regular preparatory course, Nishida became a first year student of the Fourth Higher School (University Preparatory) in July 1889.

He lived in the home of Hojo Tokiyoshi and at that time came to be interested in Zen Buddhism, of which his mathematics teacher was an adept. Among his classmates were Fujioka Sakutaro, the future writer and critic, and Suzuki Daisetsu, who was to become famous as an interpreter of Zen Buddhism in the West. Kimura Hisashi, a year ahead of Nishida, would be the future world-famous astronomer. With Fujioka and several other friends, Nishida formed a literary society and published a circulating magazine.

The exact political attitude of the young Kitaro is not explicit, but he seems to have been influenced greatly by populist thought of the Tokutomi brothers and the writings of Nakae Chomin.[7]

In 1890 Nishida leaves the Fourth Higher School in midterm. This was the year of the controversy over the "Imperial Rescript on Education" and there is speculation that Nishida was involved in a political incident. A personal chronology in his **Collected Works** limits itself to stating: "Sickness of the eyes."[8] The philosopher's eldest daughter, Yayoi, wrote concerning it:

> Since the family home was on the verge of being lost through my grandfather's blunders, grandmother persuaded him to give her 500 Yen, put them in her purse and went with Kitaro and Hyojiro[9] (Nishida's younger brother) to the Capital, where she entered one in the University and the other in an officer's school.[9]

Nishida was admitted only as a special student to the Philosophy Department of the Faculty of Letters of Tokyo University in September 1891, since he had left the Higher School without graduating. There can be little doubt that he had entered now a decisive period of his academic and philosophical career. He attended lectures by Inoue Tetsujiro, the philosophical synthesizer and founder of modern Japanese philosophy; but it was no doubt the influence of two German-educated visiting professors, Ludwig Busse and his successor, Raphael von Koeber, which, by introducing him to the current of European thought, was to have a long-lasting effect.

The first "literary" contribution of the young Nishida was an obituary on the suicide of his friend Kawagoshi Munetaka in July 1891;[10] his first philosophical manuscript, **"Kanto Rinrigaku"** (**"Kantian Ethics"**).[11] Both date from 1891. The following year he attended Zen Meditations at Kamakura's Enkakuji, where his friend Suzuki had just achieved his *satori* and was to receive the name Daisetsu from Shaku Soen.

On graduating as a special student from Tokyo University, Nishida returned to Kanazawa in July 1894 and took a room in the house of a painter named Tokuda Ko,[12] whose daughter Kotomi[12] he married the following May, after having obtained, in April, a position at the Nanao branch school of the Noto Middle School of the Ishikawa prefecture. The same year he wrote on **"The Ethics of Greene."**

In March 1896, his first daughter, Yayoi, was born and the following month he became a lecturer at his alma mater, the Fourth Higher School in Kanazawa, still making his home with his father-in-law. Also in 1896 two of his essays, **"The Development of Philosophy before Hume"** and **"The Law of Causation in Hume,"**[13] were published in the *Magazine of the North Star Society* of the Fourth Higher School.

II STRUCTURING NISHIDA KITARO'S DIARY

The young instructor of ethics, psychology and German whom we encounter in the first pages of his diary[14] is a perplexed individual in need of personal and social integration. The depth of alienation is intimated by the exclusive use of German, clumsy German at that, for the first ten months of entries, and the lack of his resolution—in spite of a list of high-sounding precepts on the opening page—betrayed by the absence of any entries whatsoever between September 23, 1898 and January 1, 1899.

Besides being a running account of visitors, presents, gifts, letters, expenses and books loaned, lent or read, we may posit that the diary presents Nishida Kitaro in five different roles:

1 A sensitive intellectual worrying about the problem of personal consolidation and intellectual output in an atmosphere of cultural conflict.

2 The head of a household adjusting himself to recurrent family crises.

3 The teacher and adviser on the academic and political scene.

4 The voracious reader of catholic tastes; and

5 The philosopher trying to come to terms with the problematics of individual, universal, social and historical existence and change; attempting to relate the momentaneous to the eternal, under a general system of values and viewpoints.

Of course, these categories are deliberate divisions of the diary content. They overlap frequently and serve only to facilitate analysis. Subject to similar reservations, we can postulate the following rough periodization:

I *Initial Consolidation* (1897-1911)

This epoch is coeval with the last years of Meiji, emphasizes individual and religious experience, and terminates in the publication of his first book, *Zen no kenkyu* (*A Study of Good*) in January 1911, directly under the impressions derived from reading Bergson and James.

II *Problems of Knowledge, Perception, and Value* (1911-1928)

Roughly contemporary with Taisho and Nishida's teaching career at Kyoto University, this period is strongly influenced by Neo-Kantian premises and Husserl's phenomenology.[15]

III *Problems of Viewpoint, Universal Analysis and Historical Validity*

The attempt of a comprehensive definition of the role of individual consciousness and existence in evaluating universal phenomena and the part played by social forms and intellectual formulations in the creation of the historical world.[16]

The two first periods are marked by an interval of family disasters which bring about deep-reaching religious and existential crises immediately preceding the publication of two epoch-making works: *Zen no kenkyu* and *Hataraku mono kara miru mono e.*

III WILL AND INSIGHT: LIFE IS TRAGIC

The perplexed young man who began writing his life's diary on January 1, 1897 started with a list of resolutions calling for intellectual discipline bordering on the ascetic. In his early entries we encounter repeatedly a call for better work habits and admonitions to overcome his idleness. Also there appeared Fukuzawa Yukichi's ideal of fierce personal independence and self-reliance (*dokuritsu dokko*). On hearing of Fukuzawa's death, he wrote on February 7, 1901:

It is certainly worth pondering that the Professor urged self-reliance and independence from others. Really, I should set out into the future the same way.[17]

This emphasis on self-reliance reflected a dissatisfaction with his family situation, on which he commented in a letter to a friend,[18] and possibly also on his dependence on his mentor, Hojo Tokiyoshi. He thought also about the relation between scholarship and life and decided on February 24, 1902 that: "Scholarship exists after all for *life*'s sake, life is most important. If it were not for *life*, scholarship would be useless."[19]

Nishida had partaken in Zen exercises as early as 1891. In 1897, he redoubled his religious activities. Not only did he try to maintain his daily Zen contemplations *(zazeu),* but also contributed to the Pure Land Sect magazine, *Mujinto,* cooperating with Kiyozawa Manshi and Tsunajima Ryosen, and had contact with Japanese Christian preachers as well as Western missionaries. Without doubt, the ascetic ideal in religion intrigued him most, and Zen offered asceticism of a sort. Reflecting on discipline, he observed that Paul Virchow did great things and achieved scholarly accomplishment with only four hours a day set aside for sleep and food intake. But there religious experience held out the possibility of even more dramatic transformation. On New Year's Day 1903 he thought of rebirth through death, as he was spending the holiday in a Zen temple:

> "Men who cannot think of dying, can not think great thoughts," both Kawai and Gordon[20] have said. I tried to think of myself as dying on the thirty-first of December of my thirty-fifth year, but however much I tried, I could not think of it earnestly. . . . No matter how much I thought of death, I could not bring myself to forget the world.[21]

As Nishida moved and labored toward his Zen enlightenment *(satori)* the idea of mystical death and rebirth became increasingly real. At the same time, what Carl Jaspers has called the "paradox of expression," the desire to communicate the heretofore uncommunicable of the mystical experience, appeared: "It would be good if after achieving *satori* in one great truth, one could explain it to others in a modern theory."[22] But as the day of his Zen enlightenment approached, Nishida, influenced by an article he had read in the magazine, *Zenshu,* confessed to doing the right thing for the wrong reason:

> I was mistaken to use Zen for the sake of scholarship. I should have used it for the spirit and the soul. Till I can feel by sight,[23] I will not think of religion nor philosophy. . . .

He even had serious doubt about the total outcome of the Zentraining:

> You, who have come to Kyoto, leaving your home behind and idly wasting your time, shouldn't you return? Going about it this way, you will never achieve anything, not even in years. I had changed the *Koan* again. . . .[23]

But already five days later, on July 28, 1903 he wrote: "The element of danger lies in the width of a hair; the moment of the spirit in one turnabout." *Satori!* In the margin of the diary he wrote that evening two lines by Hakuin, a high priest of the Rinsai sect in Tokugawa times:

> *Winter's menace is not strict*
> *The metamorphosis of Spring, not*
>   *Extraordinary.*[24]

Still, even with Zen enlightenment, Nishida had not found a lasting solution to his personal and creative problem. He was still looking for a key to the secret of human transformation; on pondering Otto Weininger's *Geschlecht und Charakter,* a book very influential among Meiji intellectuals though hardly so in the West, he wondered whether it might not be the denial of sexual desires.

The specter of death, which he had seen as a mystical potential, took on a social reality when his brother Hyojiro, an army officer, was killed at Port Arthur, and Nishida had to care for his wife and child. Still, the mystical bent remained. He began the year 1907 by reading Meister Eckhardt and inserted a poem by Wang Yang Ming:[25]

> *Men have a compass within themselves*
> *The very heart is root and origin of the myriad*
>   *flowers. . . .*
> *I laugh out loud—before my vision was topsy-turvy,*
> *I was looking for outward appearances. . . .*
> *When thinking quietly, free of desires*
> *Then you reach the basis of the myriad universes.*
> *And giving up the unlimited treasures of one's home*
> *Passing from door to door, holding a beggars bowl*
>   *for needy children*
> *All men will find their road to Heaven*

Later in the same January his daughter, Yuko,[26] died of bronchitis, leaving Nishida to reflect upon the mystique of life and death as he wrote: *"Media in vita in morte sumus."* The same June another daughter, born the previous month, died; he himself fell sick.

In the midst of disaster the theme of self-reliance comes again to the foreground. "Try not to have need of people,"*** an entry onMay 31, 1907 read. On July 1, the thought: *The real men of genius were resolute workers, not idle dreamers** called for more discipline in intellectual output. Indeed, this period did lead into a flurry of activity which would result in greater academic and social effectiveness and terminated in the publication of **Zen no kenkyu.**[27]

In the second period from 1911 to 1928, worry about his creative potential had ceased, though he might still be disturbed by the lack of solutions to certain problems. Then, with another family crisis, his wife's paralysis and his son's death, new anxieties began to affect his personal equilibrium, A morbid worry about his smoking habits started to torment him. Repeatedly, beginning in 1921, he wrote *Don't smoke,* in English, on the pages of his diary. He reminded himself that he had to live at least till seventy. This concern with smoking was closely connected with the long-held worry about self-discipline:

> *Don't smoke! Don't speak of yourself! Rely*
> *upon yourself!**
>   *Drei Wablsprueche***[28]

When, in succession, three of his daughters fell ill, his anxiety over smoking mounted to the panic level. "Last night at bedtime, my tongue was bitter and my stomach hurt. It is probably tobacco poisoning. I must definitely forego tobacco," he wrote on May 24, 1922. In addition, apparitions of his dead son pursued him in his dreams. A *waka,* written in February 1924, expresses the nadir of his despondency:

> *My heart has such depth,*
> *neither the waves of happiness*
> *nor sorrow can reach there*[29]

In May 1923 he had implied a mystical experience as he jotted in his diary:

> *From this very day I die to the world. I live only in my philosophy. Everything sacrificed, everything sacrificed. Deep, impressive experience.**[30]*

Nevertheless, this was a productive period and his personal anguish did not diminish his philosophical output. At this juncture he developed the concept of *basho* (topic or locus) and groped toward a new concept of philosophical and historical consciousness. After the death of his wife, in January 1925, he began to write calligraphy, an artistic expression he would cultivate till the end of his life. After he became a member of the Imperial Academy, in June 1927, the diary related another mystical experience:

> In the afternoon I was alone in the house. Quiet thoughts. Quietly, I spent half the day. I did not even smoke one cigarette. . . .

Then, next to a sketch of a big red sun, he wrote:

> *REBIRTH . . . awakened from a bad dream** From a rotten tree somehow a new bud of life can sprout. Today I was most happy.*[31]

Three weeks later he completed the manuscript of ***Hataraku mono kara miru mono e*** (***From Working Things to Seeing Things***) which opened his most productive period: the years after his retirement from active lecturing at Kyoto University.

The personalistic, even autistic, note of the early diary would now completely disappear and his last reflection on the human condition, entered on New Year's Day, 1945, universalized an insight obtained in long years of intense struggle, leading from perplexity to maturity.

> Human life is at all times nothing but worry and trouble: it is *tragic**[32]

IV ENTANGLEMENT AND SIMPLE POIGNANCY

As the head of a household, Nishida faced in his early period a quite chaotic family situation. In May 1897 his wife Kotomi left, taking their daughter along. When she returned several days later, she was expelled by Nishida's (?) father[33] and did not come back to his side till late August. Neither for the birth of his oldest son nor the death of his father do diary entries exist in 1898. Two days after his second son was born, in February 1901, Nishida reflected that, rather than looking for name and

fame, he should conform with the peace of his home. But later the same year he wrote to his old friend Yamamoto:

> Outside the duties of the office and inside the entangling matters of wife and children are getting increasingly bothersome.

Filial and parental responsibility was thrust upon him after he took charge of his late brother's orphaned family; and the first real sign of affection for a member of his family was shown when he nursed his dying daughter, Yuko, in January 1907.

If feelings about his family seemed ambivalent at first, the solidity of his family relations appeared to have a direct correspondence to his creative production and social efficacy. It might also be worth questioning to what extent his fears and anxieties were related to worries and guilt feelings about hissocial and filial responsibilities. His acceptance of an assigned role in the Japanese social system was perhaps symbolized by his returning to his native village, to celebrate memorial services for his Grandfather, Father, Older Sister and Younger Brother, immediately before taking on his life-time teaching position at Kyoto University. It should be noted that throughout the years he maintained good relations with his mother and his younger sister, Sumi.

After he wrote, on May 24, 1911, that "at a certain time he could not stand her, but later he loved her," the reconciliation with his wife seemed to have been complete. Nishida's mother died at the age of 77, in Kanazawa in August 1918. The following June, Yayoi, his oldest daughter who had attended Doshisha University, married Ueda Misao. Disaster struck again when his spouse, Kotomi, suffered a brain hemorrhage, in September 1919, which left her paralyzed for the six remaining years of her life. The following June, Ken, his oldest son, died of peritonitis at the age of 22. While the son's memory pursued him in his dreams and in his poetry, three more of his daughters fell ill with typhus. Then, in January 1925, his wife died after long suffering. The diary entry of her cremation is beautiful for its terseness, as if with that simple poignancy Nishida wanted to capture and relate the story of the transformation of his love for Kotomi:

> 3 p.m.: Cremation, The woman who had been my companion for a lifetime of thirty years became white ashes inside a small urn and I went home.[34]

Two days afterwards he wrote another *waka;*

> *What I planted last fall*
> *at the window*
> *will probably bloom red this spring*
> *but there won't be anybody*
> *to come and look at it.*

As his third period of life began, with the birth of his first grandchild in October 1928, and especially after he married his second wife, Koto, in December 1931, the philosopher's family life reduced itself to one of a doting Grandfather, receiving the visits of children and grandchildren. And he was not to feel again bitterness over the loss of a family member till February 1945, when Yayoi, his favorite daughter, died suddenly.

V FROM HIGH SCHOOL TEACHER TO IMPERIAL LECTURER

The role of teacher found Nishida, at the beginning of the Diary, lecturing in Psychology, Ethics and German at the Fourth Higher School in Kanazawa, where he would return in 1899 now as aprofessor in charge of the same subjects, plus Logic. The intervening two years he had spent as part-time professor at Yamaguchi Higher School, living by himself, having followed there his mentor and protector, Hojo Tokiyoshi. One year after the latter became principal of the Fourth Higher School, he would be again at his side.

He became actively involved in extracurricular student activities and helped form various literary groups, such as the Chikamatsu, Dante, Goethe and Sartor Resartus societies. His most ambitious project, however, resulted in a lasting institution: a student residence and study center called *San San Juku* (The 33 Boarding School) for the year of its founding, Meiji 33 (1900). It was to be a meeting place where students would discuss problems of religion and literature with invited lecturers from various religious sects and denominations. Nishida also participated, both with his students and his colleagues, in the school's sports activities. Observations on political events were scarce during this early period and limited themselves to occasional diary entries on the death of public personages, as Fukuzawa Yukichi; the breakdown of the Russo-Japanese negotiations and public exuberance at the fall of Port Arthur.

In April 1907, Nishida had traveled to the capital in the hope of obtaining a teaching position at Tokyo University, but after interviews with Inoue Tetsujiro and Motora Yujiro, at that time the powers at the Faculty of Letters, he was passed over. By the spring of 1908, Nishida, who recently had twice suffered an attack of pleurisy, had lost interest in his work at Kanazawa and definitely looked for a new position.

In their Kanazawa Higher School student days, Fujioka Sakutaro, Suzuki Daisetsu, and Nishida Kitaro had been intimate friends and had remained in close contact, Fujioka became a professor of Literature at the True Pure Land Sect's Otani University in Kyoto—where Suzuki was to teach later on—and a critic of renown. Suzuki had corresponded with Nishida, and had received money from him when in need, during his stay abroad as editor of Paul Carus' *Open Court* Magazine in Chicago and as lecturer on Buddhism in Great Britain and on the European continent. Finally, in March 1909 he returned to Japan after more than ten years' absence. But soon thereafter, on February 3, 1910, Fujioka Sakutaro died suddenly, and Nishida noted in his diary: "Our parting . . . became a goodbye for eternity. . . ."[35]

Both Nishida and Suzuki became members of the faculty of the *Gakushuin* (Peer's School) in Tokyo in 1909. The same October, Nishida obtained a lectureship at *Nihon Daigaku* and the following August, he was named assistant professor of ethics at the Faculty of Letters of Kyoto Imperial University.

Having made his entry into the power structure of Meiji academic society, Nishida began to devote more of his diary entries to political and social events. He noted the death of Ito Hirobumi, and that he received a gift from the Emperor on the wedding of the Imperial Princess. He also began to be invited to the dinner parties of the Maeda and Iwakura families. During a lecture tour to the Seventh Higher School at Kagoshima, in December 1910, he also reported extensively his visits to the birth and burial places of Saigo Takamori, and Ito and Shimazu. He followed actively the Yanagisawa incident over the administrative control of Kyoto University. During this time appeared for the first time the name of a former *Gakushuin* student, Konoe Fumimaro, and of one of his students at Yamaguchi Higher School, Kawakami Hajime, among his diary entries.

In August 1914, relieved from his chair of ethics in the Faculty of Letters, he was called to the first chair of the History of Philosophy in the Philosophy Department of Kyoto University. For several years the comments on political events were limited to reporting the end of the First World War (its beginning had not been mentioned) and the Rescript announcing an Imperial Regent in November 1921. Most likely because of his great worries in his home, the entries ignored even the Great Earthquake of 1923. Now and then, he mentioned his correspondence with Rickert and Husserl.

Beginning with his third period, the problem of Marxism arose in academic life. Just as he terminated his courses before retirement in 1928, he reported how various students—and Kawakami Hajime—were forced to leave because of Marxist affiliations. In at least one instance, he discussed Marxism with several of his students till late into the night.[36] It should be mentioned that one of his philosophy disciples who had moved in the direction of Marxism, Miki Kiyoshi, died in jail as a political prisoner in 1945. Nishida noted also the Communist incident of January 18, 1933, the 2/26 incident in 1936 and commented on the prohibition of Marxism on January 8, 1937.

Nishida, who had become a member of the Imperial Academy in 1926, became active on the national and international political scene only after 1937. During that year he received various German philosophers.[37] His meetings with Konoe also became more frequent. There appeared repeated entries on his dining with Konoe, Kido and Harada. Also, he began to write on the ideology of the state and *Kokutai* and commented, in August 1940, on Konoe's New Structure Declaration *(Shin taisei seimei)*. On December 14, 1939 he was invited for the first time to lecture to the Emperor on the philosophy of history. However, when he received the news, in November 1940, that he had been awarded the recently created Cultural Medal, he begged off from a State Banquet in his honor alleging sickness.[38] The Imperial Household Secretary Yoshida wasforced to bring the decoration to Nishida's home.

In Japan, Nishida had come under attack from various extremists of the Army and Navy factions controlling the Education and Propaganda offices of the Imperial Government and his writings had repeatedly been censored before publication.[39]

When Japan attacked Pearl Harbor, diary entries were once more missing; Nishida's rheumatism had become so bad that it prevented him from writing at all between October 26, 1941 and May 21, 1942. Of the earlier European conflict he had noted only England's declaration of war and Germany's invasion of Holland. As the reverses of the Berlin-Rome Axis set in, he took renewed interest. He reported the desertion of Italy, opening of the Second Front and the Allied landings in Southern France. He also mentioned the Rundstädt counterattack, but he followed especially the advances of the Red Army under Zhukov from the beginning of the Russian offensive in January 1945 to the fall of Berlin. He commented also with considerable detail the fate of both Mussolini and Hitler, as well as the fight-to-the-last-man editorials of the German radio reports.

Also in the Far Eastern theater, the reverses suffered drew his attention. He reported the landings in the Philippines and on Okinawa; and in considerable detail—to the number and type of aircraft he observed—the large-scale air raids on the Japanese mainland and their devastations. He followed closely the cabinet reshuffles, beginning with Tojo's resignation in July 1944, and mentioned also the rumors of another 2/26 incident in February 1945.

Ironically, it was one of young Nishida's political heroes, Tokutomi Soho, who became the symbol of the ultranationalism which the dying philosopher abhorred. Patiently, Nishida recorded in his diary his daily radio commentaries which grew in never-say-die fervor as the impending catastrophe became increasingly obvious. Finally, on May 10, Tokutomi's comment, after the fall of Nazi Germany, that this time—unlike during the Sino-Japanese and Russo-Japanese Wars—the Japanese nation was spiritless, shocked Nishida out of his equanimity and he commented on the margin: "That is to say they do not want to dance to the tune of leaders of his likes."[40] In this melancholy atmosphere of imminent collapse, the academic and political career of the man who once had said that his biography limited itself to having spent "half of my life facing a blackboard and the other with my back toward it"[41]—but who had come a long way since New Year's Day of 1897 when he had set out trying to be an "uncommon man doing uncommon deeds"[42] came to an end.

VI BROAD READINGS OF CATHOLIC TASTE

It is difficult to assess the bibliography covered by that voracious reader Nishida Kitaro from diary entries alone.

But from the lists and single entries of books he either read or considered worth reading, we may discern lasting predilections, changing periodical emphases and recurrent patterns.

Already the Diary's prologue, which set forth desirable reading habits, had been followed by a list of philosophers and German poets.[43] At the end of 1897, this line-up was enlarged by *The Bible,* Homer, Dante, Shakespeare, among others,[44] and for the first time he included Chinese works and authors: The Four Classics, Lao-tzu/Chuang-tzu and Wang Yang Ming.

In the first period exemplary lives and autobiographies have considerable prominence,[45] and as a peculiar feature—possibly through the deep impression made by Western women during his teaching days—he also included the biographies of Charlotte Cordet, Sonia Kovalevski and Mary Lyon, the foundress of Mount Holyoke College.

Religious biography[46] provided the bridge to an early interest in the history of religion and religious experience. Among the pioneers in the study of comparative religion we find Cornelius Peter Tiele, Pfleiderer and Oldenburg. Representatives of contemporary Buddhist thought were Tsunajima Ryosen, *Byokanroku* and Kiyozawa Manshi, *Shinkozadan.* In this early period of possibility of religious and mystical experience as a means for overcoming the limitations of culture and situation, and to achieve a radical personal transformation, very much intrigued him and let him on one hand to the *Hekiganshu,* a Sung collection of Zen *koan,* long the basic text of the Rinzai sect; the *Rinzairoku* and Hakuin Enkaku's *Orategama:* and on the other, to Origines and Augustin, Thomas a Kempis, Erskine of Linlathen and then to Meister Eckhardt[47] and Jacob Böhme and the mysticism of Rufus Jones, Inge and William James most seminal *Varieties of Religious Experience.*

In the history of philosophy, besides renewing his acquaintance with the Stoics, especially Epictetus, it was mainly post-Reformation thought which commanded his attention.[48] An inquiry into the background of ethics and aesthetics led him to the problems of value and psychological processes.[49] As early as April 1910, he mentioned reading Windelband, who together with the rest of the Neo-Kantian School would play an important role in Nishida's second period.

In the realm of political and social thought, he read Plato's *Republic,* Han Fei-tzu, Liu Hsiang's *Chan kuo t'se,* and *Hakkebun,* a collection of eight T'ang and Sung essayists.[50] Of post-Enlightenment thought he knew Hume's *Utilitarianism,* Rousseau,[51] Proudhon, Bondarev-Tolstoy's *Le Travail,* Kropotkin and Grosse.[52]

Among the Chinese Classics he repeatedly mentioned the *Analects,* the *Tso Chuan* commentary, Wang Yang Ming's *Ch'üan bsi lu,* the novel *Shui bu-chuan* (All men are brothers) and the poems of Li T'ai Po, Tu Fu and Po Chü-i.

Among Western works, classic literature limited itself at that time to Seneca and the Stoics, and generally literary works date from the 19th century or even later[53] and the most extended comments are elicited by the Russian novelists: Turgenev, Tolstoy, Dostoievsky and Gorki. Western literature in translation is represented by Tsubouchi's *Eibungakushi* and Wakematsu Shizuko's *Shokoshi* an adaptation of F. E. Hodgson Burnett's *Little Lord Fauntleroy.*

Traditional Japanese literature calling his attention were the *Kojiki, Makura no soshi,* the *Genji monogatari,* Chikamatsu Monzaemon's plays and the essays of the Tokugawa agrarian thinker, Ninomiya Sontoku. Among recent writings are the literary criticism of Tsubouchi, novels by Mori Ogai, Natsume Soseki, Tobari Chikufu and Tokutomi Roka, and the essays and poetry by Masaoka in the literary review *Hototogisu.* Other periodicals he cites frequently are *Tetsugaku kenkyu, Zenshu, Taiyo, Chuokoron, Mujinto*—to which he contributed—*Kokka,* an art monthly; and Inoue Tetsujiro's *Toa no hikari.*

After the publication of **Zen no kenkyu,** the early literary interest in the religio-mystical experience reappeared only faintly in his reading of Plotin and Zen literature limited itself to the *Jug yuzu.*[54] *(Ten Pictures of the Oxherder).* Among the Church fathers we find Origines and Irenacus, then Ferdinand Baur's book on Christian gnosis. Traditional Christianity is represented again by Kempis and Linlathen, with Cusanus added; and the Reformation, in studies of Luther and Calvin. Of the Buddhist historical canon there were *Shina jodoshi* and *Tan'i shinshu seikyo.*

Though authors defending a religion-centered, metaphysical and idealistic philosophy were still to be found,[55] others, like J. M. Guyau, advocating a vitalistic philosophy, pointed the way toward new concepts of existential and historical development. The primacy of psychological causation was expressed by the still important Henri Bergson[56] and by Lipps,[57] Kramer,[58] Verworn and Paulsen. But two thinkers searching for ever more concrete criteria, Harald Hoeffding in ethics and Georg Simmel *(Die Probleme der Geschichtsphilosophie),* in psychology, began to exert their influence on Nishida.

The interest in neo-Kantian inquiry which made itself felt at the end of the first period, broke through in the second. After 1911,practically all the Neo-Kantians were to be found among the authors read: Windelband,[59] Natorp, Jonas Cohn, Hermann Cohen and Ernst Cassirer. However, in the physical sciences also deep-reaching questions were being asked and this was reflected in the readings. The problem of time, space and mechanics had been raised by Henri Poincaré,[60] Hermann Minkowski,[61] and Melchior Palagyi. B. Riemann and K. F. Gauss were not only challenging inherited concepts of mechanics, but called into question the whole system of Euclidian geometry and traditional physics. These findings had their effect on philosophical speculation, and led to a new openly anti-metaphysical attitude, and from Mach and

Eucken to the phenomenology of Edmund Husserl, whose categories of *noema* and *noesis* Nishida was to use in his philosophy.[62]

At that point, he became deeply interested in the problems of universal historical development, for which he read Vico, A.D. Xenopol, Dilthey, Croce and, again, Cassirer, as well as in the existential philosophy of Soren Kierkegaard *(Entweder-Oder)* and Martin Heidegger.

Attention was also given to socio-political thought as dealt with by P. J. Proudhon and G. Tarde, and to Augustin Rodin's *L'art* and Carl Stumpf's *Tonpsychologie.*

From his Japanese background he took Yasui Sokken's *Rongo shosetsu (Collected Explanations of the Analects)* and among historical works he reread the *Gempei seisuiki.*

The third and most creative period of Nishida's life, which began about 1928, distinguished itself by an increased inquiry into political thought and social analysis. There was also the continued interest in the progress of the natural sciences, an awareness of the growth of neo-orthodox religious thought in the West and a grappling with problems of existential philosophy. Certainly in tune with the times, it saw him also renew his interest in East Asian history and society.

The neo-Kantian Cassirer had acquainted him earlier with the anthropological aspects of universal, historical development. Nishida followed this up by readings of Levy-Bruhl, James Frazer,[63] B. Malinowski.[64] Among sociologists we find Comte, Lorenz V. Stein, Durkheim,[65] F. Toennis, Veblen, Karl Mannheim and Franz Borkenau as well as Max Weber's *Wirtschaft und Gesellschaft* and *Gesammelte Ausätze.* Rousseau,[65] Karl Marx's *Kritik der Politischen Oekonomie* and *Das Kapital* as well as G. Plekhanov, Karl Kautski and Georg Lukacs were included in a review of sociopolitical thought. The problems of law and society came to the foreground in Hegel's *Rechtsphilosophie,* Savigny[66] and Gierke.[67]

The recurring reappraisal in the natural sciences seems to have ledNishida also to a renewed interest in Aristotle and the development of classical science: Heath,[68] Heilberg,[69] Espinas,[70] and Zenthen[71] were all treating the origin and development of science and technology. We also find Karl V. Prantl, the most up-to-date historian of logic, and his contemporary philosopher-scientists: Albert Einstein, Max Planck, Bertrand Russell, Niels Bohr, W. Heisenberg, George Boole, E. Schroedinger and D. Hilbert.

Among the neo-orthodox and existential religious thinkers we notice F. Gogarten,[72] A. Nygren,[73] Karl Barth[74] and Barth's Japanese disciple, Kuwada Shuen, but also Jacques Maritain and Martin Buber. A more mystical mood is represented by H. Scholz and Leon Shestov.[75] One night we find him discussing the *Hekiganshu* and the writing of the Zen sect founder, the priest Dogen.

Many of the items we encounter now among his bibliography, as the Four Classics and the Laotse-Chuang-tzu he had read before, when he set out on his diary. There is also the *I-ching,* and the *P'ei-men yün-fu,* an early Ch'ing phrase dictionary. Again, the *Genji monogatari;* a *Makura no soshi* commentary by Kitayama Kijin, Basho's *Oku no bosomichi* and, among more recent Japanese works, Natsume Soseki's *Kokoro* and the popular Zen poetry of Yamaoka Tesshu.

It is hard to establish which of the Chinese and Japanese works he read for the purpose of relating them to the process of historical evaluation, but the complete works of Kuantzu and the Tso Chuan and Kung Yang commentaries seem to fit this category as does Mori Ogai's *Nishi Amane den* and his *Shibue Chosai* and, also reread, writings by Ninomiya Sontoku. Obviously part of this historical review were the *Kojiki,* a short history of the Yüan and Ming dynasties, but especially the *Gukanshu,* by the Tendai abbot, Jien, and the neo-Confucianist writings by two contributors to the Mito School's *Dai Nibon Nihon Shi:* Asaka Tampaku (1656-1737) and Fujita Toko (1806-1855) as well as the *Sentetsu sodan,* a nineteenth century work on philosophy by Hara Zen Nensai.

In the course of this quest for an adequate historical viewpoint, he continued his readings in Western historiography also: Thucydides, Droyssen, Ranke, Treitschke, Mommsen, Burckhardt, Spengler, Lucian Febvre[76] and N. A. Berdyaev[77] being among the authors read.

The selection in Western fiction as gleaned from the pages of the diary and presented in chronological order were: George Eliot,[78] Schlegel,[79] Cholokhov,[80] Stendhal,[81] D. H. Lawrence's *Lady Chatterley's Lover,* Fyodor Dostoievsky,[82] the poetry of Paul Valery and Baudelaire's *Les Fleurs du mal* as well as Hasanyi's Galileo biography.

VII MATHEMATICAL INTRICACIES AND MYSTICAL UNITY

Nishida Kitaro had been influenced from very early times by Kantian ethics interpreted in rather ascetic terms. The Great Way, or Moral Principle *(daido),* encountered often in the first part of the Diary, in his meditations on moral precepts, seems to approach Kant's categorical imperative, in the sense of being, "the sum of personal maxims of the will which can be at the same time equivalent to the principle of total normative power *(Gesetzgebung)."* That concept of *will,* implying both teleological purpose and internal motive, seems approximate to the meaning of Nishida *kokorozashi:*

> The Great Way *(daido)* does not depend on the place, but on the will *(kokorozashi).* . . . Ask not for small gains and petty accomplishments, give prominence to the will.[83]

He saw the problem of the will as mainly internal and extremely personal; furthermore, his mystical tendency made it hard for him to free his ethics from a psychologistic imprisonment. Only after he had read

Nietzsche and Dostoievsky, who were questioning all accepted ethical premises, and after becoming acquainted with authors like Harald Hoeffding and the Neo-Kantians—who rethought either traditional ethics or Kantian categories from viewpoints which had been tempered by the positivist critique—did he perceive the possibility of a more comprehensive analysis of a complex reality. Just as with the American pragmatists, his early tendency to self-reliance led him to trying to comprehend *life;* at one occasion he said that he would like to emulate William James and study *life.* Among his readings we find many an evolutionist philosopher—he lived, after all, at the high tide of Darwinism—but Nishida would have been hard put to identify himself with the radical conclusions of the Spencerians.[84]

The diary is very meager in glimpses of his philosophical thoughts and speculations during this early period and for a careful analysis of that epoch's philosophical development we would probably refer to his maidenwork, *A Study of Good* (*Zen no kenkyu*) rather than to deduce too much from bibliographical notes and the accounts of doubts concerning his own psychological consolidation.

It is during the second period, that Nishida departed from a highly egocentric stance, bordering on the autistic, and began to perceive structures underlying human relationships. In April 1912, he attempted to analyze the social roles of the principal and various teachers at the Kagoshima Higher School—thus presaging a later sociological concern—but his conclusion still had a highly personalistic tone:

> Men see things as a perfect whole, as they want to see them. It is impossible to see through hypocrisy.[85]

Nishida had still not liberated himself from a pessimistic subjectivism. But a trend from the individual toward the universal expressed itself in the increasing interest in the philosophical problems of history and—under the influence of Windelband and Rickert—their relationship to the natural sciences. In August 1912, he began speaking on this problem. He gave a lecture on **"Natural Science and Historical Science" ("Shizenkagaku to rekishigaku").**[86] published later, both at Kyoto University, in March 1913, and at Tokyo University, the following April.

As Neo-Kantian thought had confronted him with the problems of value and knowledge, his criteria changed increasingly from the internal psychological to the external physical, though always maintaining a postulate of "the whole." New insights led him also from Eucken to Husserl's phenomenology, a certain tendency toward Ostwaldian monism as well as to the existentialists, who, partly under the influence of new concepts of the time reshaped by the natural sciences, revolted against the idea of general teleology and strove toward a new consciousness freed from the exigencies of positivist progressivism and rectilinear historical time. As Heidegger had returned to Duns Scotus in his reevaluation of philosophical premises, so Nishida, like Hegel and Heidegger before him, in October 1918 used Parmenides as a point of departure for his inquiry into the nature of history. Parmenides had referred to *one substance of being* expressing unity, simplicity and permanence:[87]

> In Parmenides the *dialectic discussions of (the) One** takes place because it *lacks content.*** What is called *lack of content** (Inhaltslosigkeit)* can be said to become the *object (Gegenstand)* of the *act itself.*** All *mathematical objects*** have this substance. I wonder whether such things as *group* and *body*** cannot be explained accordingly.[88]

Several days later he followed up these thoughts:

> The *combination of elements** is a *system.** When they are dependent on each other, that is to say, when they form a *group,** they are a *system complete in itself** and this is called a *priori. Act** and *object*** fall under one *system.**[89]

From Parmenides' *one substance of being*, Nishida then moved toward his concept of nothingness *(Nichts)*, which was quite reminiscent, but much anterior, to Sartre's *néant*:

> The so-called *unity*** of the *group** is a function of *nothingness.** Zero** becomes the *unity*** (of everything.)[90]

A good part of his further philosophical production was to have its origin in a consideration of the tension between this "nothingness" and "the whole." A preview of his later concern with "topics" or points of view (Jap.: *basho,* approximating here: *Anschauung*) about which he was to write his first essay in April 1919,[91] was given by this sketchy consideration in October 1918:

> In *analysis**, one has to have *direction.*** Since that *direction presupposes a synthetical whole, point of view*** has to be its basis.[92]

Among these thoughts appeared also the problem of the relation of history to reality and thought:

> As for *history,*** the *whole (static)*** must be transmitted. At the moment when reality is considered *to be determined by the whole,*** it becomes *thought.***[93]

The following January, he wrote:

> In order to make *history*** a *norm*** for action, it has to *be universally valid***.[94]

On New Year's Day 1919, he had thought about a similarity between Duns Scotus and Chinese traditional thought:

> Truth *(shinri)* in sentiment *(joi)*, the *sapientia* of Duns Scotus, is not irrational and must be considered hyperrational. Has not Chinese philosophy made sentiment a basic premise?[95]

In the margin he wrote, in English:

"What is 'concrete'?" . . . If Duns Scotus had posited a primacy of the will, Nishida now related the concept of will *(ishi* instead of *kokorozashi)* to knowledge *(chishiki*[96]):

> Will is specific, knowledge is general. The pragmatists confuse these two.

He also maintained that the object of the will was the historical world and that this will *(Wille)* was its own objective. If a distinction between the moral will *(sittlicher Wille)* and the "avoidance of improper behavior" *(shikarazaru mono)*[97] were to be made, would not the objective of the one be internal and the other, external? That was to say, one would be a matter of autonomy and the other, of heteronomy?[97] This consideration led, of course, right back to his previous psychological interest:

> *Psychologically*** speaking, *freedom (Freiheit)* leads us back to character.** However, this is nothing, but to say that it would have a *cause*** somehow. Isn't *nature*** the essence and the spirit *(Geist)? Causality*** must have begun somewhere. The *world's beginning* takes place [in the interaction] between the *spirit*** and *nature*** of every moment in time.[98]

Nishida was now reaching toward a comprehensive description of reality, under the impact of new findings about time and space brought about by the theory of relativity and quantum mechanics. Still, he could not free himself from assuming a simple correspondence between human and socio-cultural organisms:

> We call having culture, the realization of an epoch's *spiritual unity***. This is the same as an individual having character.[99]

Immediately following the period of these extensive diary entries concerning his stream of thought, he published, in January 1920, the **"Problem of Consciousness" ("Ishiki no mondai".)**[99] Unfortunately, there was to be no other period when he was so explicit in his commentaries and speculations about philosophical problems. From then on, he merely commented on one or the other manuscript he was beginning or terminating; *e.g.* "October 2, 1931: Since today I have been writing on egoism and altruism *(jiai to ta-ai)*[100] and dialectics."[101] In April and May 1937, he had various meetings and conversations with Eduard Spranger, the Dilthey disciple, and later, in November, he received a visit by Karl Löwith, who was also visiting Japan. The following year he discussed his thought with yet another young German philosopher, Robert Schinzinger who was to edit the first book of Nishida's work in a Western language.

His continued interest in the problem of universal historicity became a question of intellectual and political survival as the tenor of the Japanese scene became more and more irrationally chauvinistic. He addressed himself to this development in his lectures on **"The Problem of Japanese Culture" ("Nihon bunka no mondai"),** which on publication, were promptly censored. On the other hand, he was enthused by the possibility of a new order as advocated by Konoe Fumimaro—of whom he said at one time; "He has a good head, but absolutely no power." It also led him to lecture the Showa Emperor on the philosophy of history and to write on *kokutai* and the rationale of the state *(kokka riyu).*

At the end of 1943, he jotted a few fragmentary considerations about nuclear power in the margin of his diary:

> What are, basically, the hypotheses of nuclear
>   power . . .
>   . . . physically? The atom is a solar system
>   . . . creatively? It brings itself into being[102]

It was a pity that he did not elaborate his thoughts on this matter which was to have such decisive influence in the Japanese historical process.

Besides reading the "Jeremiah" chapter of the *Old Testament,* terminating a manuscript on **"Topical Logic and a Religious World View"** and writing calligraphy, he browsed once more, as his life drew to a close, in the writings of Christoph Sigwart, whose aesthetic concerns and *eudaimonic* ethics seemed quite suited for the dying philosopher who could never quite overcome an aesthetic concern with a dynamic whole and a fascination with the intricacies of mathematics first taught him by his early friend and protector, Hojo Tokiyoshi, at Kanazawa Middle School, and a predilection for a mystical unity which, being sensitive to the underlying similarity of all men and all history in their relation to all-permeating nothingness, had promised to help him come to terms with that essence of history which he himself had once called "the constant revolution in the eternal now."

VIII UNIVERSAL VALIDITY CONTROLLED BY THE HISTORICAL MATRIX

Nishida Kitaro had stated in his first work, ***Zen no kenkyu,*** that no matter how much a man born into a certain society were rich in originality, he would always receive the control of its particular social spirit. . . . Though one is deeply impressed by his philosophical scope and universal awareness, it is easy to forget that he was a Japanese intellectual living through a specifically Japanese historical situation. Many of his recent critics, from the Marxist camp or the equally structure-conscious schools of sociological analysis, reject any doubt of his having been tradition-bound by that particular social spirit, consigning him, in one case, to a special category: that of "cringing harmony type" *(jidaiteki chowa kei).*[103]

He can, of course, be censored for not having rebelled outright against the Japanese totalitarian, militaristic system of the war years, and also for cooperating with konoe and writing on *kokutai.* But on the other hand, he repeatedly did break with accepted social precedents. However, there is indeed a very Japanese manner; for example, in his writing *waka*—which are themselves worth separate study and analysis—to express his censure of an Imperial policy, referring at the same time to Kamo no Chomei.[104]

Nishida Kitaro responded totally to an intellectual and historical challenge. He lived through a process of psychological transformation and intellectual development searching for a definition of his individual situations in increasingly universally valid terms. If a complex humanity, achieved in suffering and strife, begins to manifest itself even in this cursory analysis of a small portion of his written record, further study should deepen our understanding of the full role of one of the most unusual thinkers of our century. For Nishida's trying to attain a new awareness and comprehension of the process of historical definition and redefinition of his relation to an ever changing reality is one of the most remarkable chapters of Japanese intellectual history. He tried to do away with the simplistic counterpoising of tradition and modernization which has prevented a good many Japanese thinkers from coming to terms with the subtler and universal meaning of their past and present. He anchored his world view in the not any more changeable matrix of Japanese history and offered a conceptual framework open toward future innovations. He seemed to perceive that only by reflecting honestly upon her past and present actions, could Japan hope to play a significant role in the continuing process of broadening the world-wide knowledge about the individual, the social product of the sum of his experiences, and mankind.

With a feeling for developments that were in store, but which he himself would not live too see, he wrote his friend Suzuki on May 11, 1945:

> Hitler also has attained his wretched last. There is a saying that reason will finally catch up with him who tries to tread the irrational, for after all, there is no way through the irrational.
>
> Today people say that the new direction is toward totalisms trusting in power; however, they rather take [the course] to be toward the anachronisms of ancient thought and the earliest beginnings . . . [but] the new direction lies instead in the opposite, that is toward internationalism. And I wonder whether the world is not going unawares in that direction. . . .[105]

It would be interesting—and profitable—to compare his role with that of the "Generation of 1898" in Spain whom, in trying to define values in the face of a changing world, did also not limit themselves to catching up, but sought to contribute original ideas in the process. Unamuno also read Kierkegaard and Hoeffding, and Ortega y Gasset: Dilthey, Weber; and studied under Hermann Cohen.—Not to speak of the influence of Krause on all of them. They also became again aware of medieval mysticism and the historicity of social organizations and finally turned toward Existentialism and neoorthodox religious thought.

NOTES

[1] Gino K. Piovesana, S. J., *Recent Japanese Philosophical Thought 1862-1962, A Survey,* Tokyo, 1963, p. 91.

[2] Iwanami shoten, is publishing a new edition of *Nishida Kitarozenshu* in 19 volumes—as against the 18 volumes of the first (1947-53) edition. This new edition, besides carrying over two hundred letters, especially to Tanabe Hajime, not heretofore included, will be of special interest to Nishida students since it brings, in volume 16, the whole collection of Nishida's pre-*Zen no kenkyu* manuscripts. This edition is distributed in monthly instalments to subscribers only. The first volume appeared on February 26, 1965. All references cited here are from the first edition.

[3] Translations: Parts of *Nihon bunka no mondai* (The problem of Japanese Culture) in Ryusaku Tsunoda, Th. William de Barry, Donald Keene, comp., *Sources of the Japanese Tradition*, New York, 1958, pp. 857-72; *Intelligibility and the Philosophy of Nothingness*, Three Philosophical Essays, tr. and introduced by R. Schinzinger, Tokyo, 1958—for description see the original German edition below; *A Study of Good*, V. H. Viglielmo, tr. with an essay, "How to read Nishida," by Suzuki Daisetsu, as the prologue and an epilogue by Shimomura Torataro, Tokyo, 1960; German: *Die Intelligible Welt*, Drei Philosophische Abhandlungen, in Gemeinschaft mit Motomori Kimura, Iwao Kovama und Ichiro Nakashima ins Deutsche übertragen und eingeleitet von Robert Schinzinger, Berlin, 1943. It contains: "Die intelligible Welt" *Eichiteki sekai*, cf. *Zenshu* v, 123-185; "Der Metaphysische Hintergrund Goethes" *Goethe no haikei*, cf. *ibid.*, vol. XII: 123-149; and "Die Einheit der Gegensätze" *Zettai mujunteki jiko doitsu*, cf. *ibid.*, IX: 147-222 . . . Spanish: *Ensayo sobre el bien*, Anselmo Mataix, S.J. y José M. de Vera, S.J., tr., Madrid, 1963.

[4] Piovesana's book did not appear till the following fall, and the only adequate outline in English was by the same author: an article "Main Trends of Contemporary Japanese Philosophy," *Monumenta Nipponica*, XI: 2 (1955), 170-184. For a comprehensive bibliography on Nishida, both in Japanese and Western languages see Piovesana's well annotated Nishida chapter, *Recent Japanese . . .* , pp. 85-122.

[5] Piovesana, *Recent Japanese . . .* , p. 86.

[6] The date in the old calendar is 4-19-Meiji 3. This is the correct date, but in order to facilitate his early school entry, the birthdate in the family register is shown as 8-10-Meiji 1, 1868. Cf. *Zenshu*, spec. vol. VI, 467. The family register entry explains also his retirement in 1928.

[7] A recent book treating Nishida's political thought, in a formalistic manner, see: Yamada Munemutsu, *Nihongata shiso no genzo* (The Prototype of Japanese Thought), San-ichi shobo, Tokyo, 1961. Tokutomi: Soho, Roka

[8] *Zenshu*, spec. vol. VI, 463.

[9] Shimomura Torataro *Nishida Kitaro hito to shiso*, Tokyo, 1965, p. 21-22. This is a new, enlarged edition of the same author's *Wakaki Nishida Kitaro sensei*, Tokyo, 1947.

[10] *Kawagoshi Tansai shoden*, spec. vol. II, 118-119.

[11] in *Zenshu*, spec. vol. II, 3 ff.

[12] *Cf. ibid.*, spec. vol. VI, p. 470.

[13] *Cf. ibid.*, spec. vol. II, 21-25 and 26-33

[14] The entire diary was published in *Zenshu*, spec. vol. I, Tokyo, 1951, 710 pp. + epilogue by Nishitani Keiji, pp. 713-728. It will be hereafter referred to simply as *Diary*. The diary manuscript consisted of 48 notebooks of various sizes, the last one, for 1945, being handmade.

[15] Books of this period: *Shisaku to taiken* (Thinking and Experience), 1915, *Fikaku ni okeru chokkan to hansei* (Intuition and Reflection in Self-Consciousness), 1917, *Ishiki no mondai* (The Problem of Consciousness), 1920, *Geijutsu to dotoku* (Art and Morality), 1923, *Hataraku mono kara miru mono e* (From Acting to Seeing), 1927.

[16] Books: *Ippansha no jikakuteki taikei* (The System of Self-Consciousness of the Universal), 1930, *Mu no jikakuteki gentei* (The Self-Conscious Determination of Nothingness), 1932, *Tetsugaku no konpon mondai (Koi no sekai)* (The Basic Problems of Philosophy: The World of Action), 1933, *Tetsugaku no kompon mondai zokuben (Benshoho teki sekai)* (The Basic Problems of Philosophy, Continued: The Dialectical World), 1934, *Zoku shisaku to taiken* (Thinking and Experience, Continuation), 1937, *Nihon bunka no mondai* (The Problem of Japanese Culture), 1940, and *Tetsugaku ronbunshu* (Collection of Philosophical Essays), published in seven volumes from 1932 to 1946.

[17] *Diary*, p. 50 (February 7, 1901).

[18] Furuta Shokin *Shinsei no zenshatachi* Tokyo, 1956, p. 219.

[19] *Diary*, p. 74 (February 24, 1902).

[20] Gen. Charles Gordon Walker, whose biography he had read.

[21] *Diary*, p. 101.

[22] *Ibid.*, p. 113 (June 11, 1903).

[23] *Ibid.*, p. 117 (July 23, 1903). *Kenshu* (see-feeling) expresses the abandoning of distracting ideas and irrelevant thoughts: *monen* and is a premise for attaining *satori*. Cf. the *Dentoroku* a Zen canon collected in Sung China, 1004.

[24] *Diary*, p. 118.

[25] *Ibid.*, p. 170.

[26] *** Quotation marked with asterisks are: *English **German ***French in the Original.

[27] Published in January 1911 by *Kodokan* Tokyo, *cf. Zenshu,* 1, 3-201.

[28] *Diary,* p. 384 (October, 1, 1921).

[29] *Ibid.,* p. 398 (February 20, 1923)

[30] *Ibid.,* p. 400 (May 21, 1923).

[31] *Ibid.,* p. 438 (July 3, 1927).

[32] *Ibid.,* p. 697.

[33] *Ibid.,* p. 15 (May 14, 1897), *"Der Vater wies Kotomi aus."*

[34] *Ibid.,* p. 414 (January 23, 1910), the *waka* on p. 415.

[35] *Ibid.,* p. 236 (February 3, 1910).

[36] *Ibid.,* p. 456 (May 11, 1928).

[37] Spranger, Löwith, Schinzinger

[38] *Diary,* p. 627 (September 22 and November 25, 1940).

[39] *Zenshu,* sp. vol. VI, contains the original versions.

[40] *Diary,* p. 708.

[41] Shimomura, pp. 11-12.

[42] *Dairy,* p. 3. It began: In order to become a prodigious man who attempts to achieve uncommon deeds, one needs a will that even a crumbling universe will not perturb, and a mettle that will ward off even the fiercest and bravest devils. . . .

[43] Plato, Locke, Hume, Leibniz, Kant, Fichte, Hegel, Schopenhauer, Aristotle, Spinoza, Schelling, Schleiermacher, Lotze, Hartmann; Herder, *Cid;* Goethe, Fouqué, *Undine;* Eichendorff, *Aus dem Leben eines Taugenichts* and Chamisso, *Peter Schlemihl.*

[44] Klopstock, Lessing, Schiller, Kleist, Lenau, Heine, Rückert and the Grimm Brothers.

[45] Goethe, *Aus meinem Leben;* George Henry Lewes, *Life of Goethe;* John Bunyan, Ivan the Fourth, Abraham Lincoln, Charles George Gordon, Henry Drummond, Saigo Takamori, Herbert Spenser and Leon Tolstoy.

[46] Young, *The Christ of History;* Stalker, *Life of Jesus, Paul;* Charles Monroe Sheldon, *In His Steps;* Ebina Danjo *Kirisuto-den;* Storz, *Augustin;* Herman Oldenburg, *Buddha* and Inoue's Shakamuni biography.

[47] *Deutsche Theologie.*

[48] Descartes, *Grundlagen der Philosophie;* Spinoza, *Ethics,* and Kant, *Kritik der Urteilskraft.*

[49] Fichte, *Sittenlebre;* Herbart, Sidgwick; Carlyle, *Essay on Heroism, Sartor Resartus;* F.C.S. Schiller, *Humanism,* Emerson, Hartmann, Nietzsche, Hoeffding, Bergson, *Personal Idealism, Les données immediates;* Royce, James and Dewey.

[50] *Pa chia wen* contains essays by Han Yü (762-824), Liu Tsung-yüan (773-819), Ou Yang Hsiu (1007-1072), Su Hsün (1009-1066), Ts'eng Kung (1019-1083), Wang An Shih (1021-1086), Su Shih (1036-1101) and Su Ch'e (1039-1112).

[51] *Contrat Social Emile.*

[52] *Die Formen der Familien und die Formen der Wirtschaft.*

[53] Goethe: *Die Leiden des Jungen Werther, Faust, Wilbelm Meister;* Grillparzer, *Sappho;* Eichendorff. Immermann, Hauff, Hauptmann; Washington Irving, Hawthorne, Shelley, Brontë, *Jane Eyre;* Carlyle, Matthew Arnold, George Eliot; Victor Hugo, *Les Miserables;* Chateaubriand, Dumas, Maupassant; Ibsen; Maeterlink.

[54] These sketches of ten scenes, supposed to be instrumental in inducing *satori* originated in Sung China and were especially popular in the Muromachi period.

[55] F. A. Trendelenburg, Josiah Royce, F. P. Maine de Birau.

[56] *La perception du changement, L'évolution créatrice.*

[57] *Einfüblung bei Mathematik und Ethik.*

[58] *Über logische und aesthetische Allgemeingültigkeit.*

[59] *Gesetz und Norm, Was ist Philosophie? Vom System der Kategorien, Geschichte der Naturwissenschaft.*

[60] *Mechanik, La logique de l'infini, Savants et escrivains.*

[61] *Über Raum und Zeit.*

[62] *Cf.* Piovesana, 1963, p. 109.

[63] *The Golden Bough.*

[64] *Myth in Primitive Psychology.*

[65] *Sociologie et Philosophie; Contrat Social.*

[66] *Recht des Besitzes.*

[67] *Genossenschaftsrecht.*

[68] *The Thirteen Books of Euclyd's Elements.*

[69] *Naturwissenschaft und Mathematik im Klassischen Altertum.*

[70] *Les origines de la technologie en Gréce.*

[71] *Mathematik im Altertum und Mittelalter.*

[72] *Politische Ethik.*

[73] *Agape und Eros.*

[74] *Römerbrief, Weihe.*

[75] *Les révélations de la mort.*

[76] *Geographical Introduction to History.*

[77] *The Meaning of History.*

[78] *The Mill on the Floss.*

[79] *Deutsche Nationalliteratur.*

[80] *Terres desfrichées, Sur le Don paisible.*

[81] *Le rouge et le noir.*

[82] *The Possessed, Brothers Karamazov.*

[83] *Diary,* p. 32.

[84] *Ibid.,* p. 147 (July 3, 1905).

[85] *Ibid.,* p. 290 (April 14, 1912).

[86] *Cf. Zenshu,* vol. I, pp. 268-295.

[87] *One substance of being:* The all-permeating essence speculatively postulated by Parmenides, in which existence and thought are not differentiated.

[88] *Diary,* p. 359 (October 30, 1918).

[89] *Ibid.,* (November 11, 1918).

[90] *Ibid.,* (November 5, 1918).

[91] *Shii jitsugen no basho ni Zenshu* vol. III, 141 ff.

[92] *Dairy,* p. 359 (October 31, 1918).

[93] *Ibid.,* (November 7, 1918).

[94] *Ibid.,* p. 361 (January 10, 1919).

[95] *Ibid.*

[96] *Ibid.,* p. 361 (January 9, 1919).

[97] *Ibid.,* p. 363 (February 6, 1919).

[98] *Ibid.,* (February 15, 1919).

[99] *Ibid.,* p. 370 (November 30, 1919).

[100] *Ibid.,* p. 474.

[101] See note 3.

[102] *Dairy,* p. 677 (End of 1943).

[103] Miyajima Hajime *Meijiteki shisozo no keisei* Tokyo, 1960, pp.376-382.

[104] (1153-1216) refused to live in the strife-torn Kyoto and shunned official recognition, preferring the life of a hermit. cf. *Hojoki* (1212).

[105] *Zenshu,* Sp. vol. VI. p. 426.

Hans Waldenfels (essay date 1966)

SOURCE: "Absolute Nothingness: Preliminary Consideration on a Central Notion in the Philosophy of Nishida Kitaro and the Kyoto School," in *Monumenta Nipponica: Studies on Japanese Culture,* Vol. XXI, Nos. 3-4, 1966, pp. 354-91.

[*In the following essay, Waldenfels discusses the notion of "absolute nothingness" in the Japanese philosophical branch known as the Kyoto School and in the work of Nishida in particular.*]

This paper aims at calling attention to the discussion about "Absolute Nothingness" carried on in Japan. Its contents are restricted to some philosophers of the Kyoto School.

BEING AND NOTHINGNESS

In his article "Buddhism and Existentialism: The Dialogue between Oriental and Occidental Thought," Takeuchi Yoshinori states:

> Whenever discussion arises concerning the problem of encounter between being and non-being, Western philosophers and theologians, with hardly an exception, will be found to align themselves on the side of being. This is no wonder. The idea of 'being' is the Archimedean point of Western thought. Not only philosophy and theology but the whole tradition of Western civilization have turned around this pivot.
>
> All is different in Eastern thought and Buddhism. The central notion from which Oriental religious intuition and belief as well as philosophical thought have been developed is the idea of "nothingness." To avoid serious confusion, however, it must be noted that East and West understand non-being or nothingness in entirely different ways.[1]

Similar questions have been treated in the West, too. For instance, Paul Tillich, to whom the aforementioned article was dedicated, had remarked before:

> Nonbeing is dependent on the being it negates. "Dependent" means two things. It points first of

all to the ontologicalpriority of being over nonbeing. The term nonbeing itself indicates this, and it is logically necessary. There could be no negation if there were no preceding affirmation to be negated. Certainly one can describe being in terms of non-nonbeing; and one can justify such a description by pointing to the astonishing prerational fact that there is something and not nothing. One could say that "being is the negation of the primordial night of nothingness." But in doing so one must realize that such an aboriginal nothing would be neither nothing nor something, that it becomes nothing only in contrast to something; in other words, that the ontological status of nonbeing as nonbeing is dependent on being. Secondly, nonbeing is dependent on the special qualities of being. In itself nonbeing has no quality and no difference of qualities. But it gets them in relation to being. The character of the negation of being is determined by that in being which is negated.[2]

Everything which Tillich says here is true. And yet, answers like this might hardly satisfy the eastern mind for the simple reason that they are given from the western standpoint of understanding being and nothingness and thus do not take fully into consideration the eastern starting point. We might even claim that Japanese scholars hardly began thinking about Heidegger's question, "Why is there any being at all—why not rather nothing?"[3] But then Japanese scholars are equally right when they claim that in the West nothingness did not yet receive proper attention.[4]

Either side has the right to claim that the other makes an effort to consider the issue under dispute not only from his own point of view but also from the opposite side. Here, however, western scholars might complain with good reason that so far they did not get enough help and guidance from their Japanese colleagues.

"NOTHINGNESS" IN NISHIDA'S *A STUDY OF GOOD*

Takeuchi, whom we quoted above, is a disciple of Tanabe Hajime, who himself was successor of Nishida Kitaro in the chair of philosophy of religion at Kyoto University. It was Nishida (1870-1945) who inaugurated what later on became known as Nishida philosophy and the philosophy of the Kyoto School. There are, of course, important differences and distinctions between the philosophical thoughts of Nishida, Tanabe and their disciples and successors. However, in all of them, certain undercurrents are at work. As a central point common to both Nishida and Tanabe, Takeuchi mentions that "the philosophy of Absolute Nothingness is their common concern, i.e., the absolute must be considered first as Absolute Nothingness."[5]

In fact, even a superficial study of Nishida's works[6] proves that nothingness develops more and more into one of the central concepts of his thought. It is a well-known fact that Nishida's basic insights remained to an amazing degree unchanged throughout hislife. He deepens them, he reflects on them from all kinds of different angles, he finds better ways of expressing them and more fitting analogies. He elaborates certain parts of his system and relates them to his central insights, and he does this so well that there is very little which he has to retract later on. No wonder that until now his maiden work *A Study of Good* (1911) has been considered one of the most mature expressions of his thought and one of the classical works of the rather young history of Japanese philosophy.

This point of view is well confirmed by Nishida's own preface to a later edition of his first work in 1936.[7] The starting point of Nishida's philosophy was—what he had called—"pure experience," a term evidently suggested by the philosophy of William James. In his new preface Nishida explains briefly how, under the influence of Fichte's *Tathandlung,* his understanding of "pure experience" had developed into the conception of the "absolute will," and further, under the influence of Greek philosophy, into the idea of "place." "Place" becomes the key word of his logic. As the "dialectical Universal," "place" becomes concrete, and as "action-intuition," the standpoint of the "dialectical universal" becomes direct. The world of historical reality and the world of "action-intuition" or "poiesis" is the world of pure experience. However, after giving this list of rather strange expressions, mostly suggested by the ideas of western philosophers like James and Henri Bergson (experience), Plato and Aristotle (place), Fichte and Hegel (dialectic) and others, Nishida speaks about experiencing things just as they are. Gustav Theodor Fechner wrote somewhere that one fine morning in spring as he looked out at a meadow bathed in sunlight and fragrant with new-blown flowers, where birds were singing and butterflies dancing, it occurred to him that this was the way to see things as they truly are and not the way natural sciences observe things. And then Nishida alludes to a certain personal experience which he made as a high school student in Kanazawa and which might well be considered the real basis for his book. It seems to be typical of Nishida that after a long series of often complicated arguments he usually leads to a place which cannot be expressed any further or to an experience to be undergone rather than to be spoken about.

"We already found his first assertion regarding "nothingness" in his *A Study of Good.* This is in the passage where he treats of God as reality and of the relationship between God and the world. For Nishida, God is the "foundation of the universe."[8] Nishida evidently (as quite a few of his disciples) does not reach an adequate understanding of what Christian thinkers mean when they speak of creation and of God as Creator. For Nishida, creation and transcendence both seem to separate God and the world unduly from each other. There is little doubt that Nishida's concepts of "theism" and "pantheism" have little resemblance to Christianteaching.

> We can think both that God is something transcendent, outside the universe, that He controls the world from without, and even with regard to man operates from without, and we can think also that God resides within, that man is a part of God, that God operates in man from within. The former

is the idea of so-called "theism" and the latter is the idea of so-called "pantheism."[9]

In a way, Nishida rejects both extremes, but he argues much more strongly against the thought of a transcendent God, who, if Nishida were right, would rather be somewhere in the middle between the God of Deism and the demiurgos of Platonic and Gnostic origin. This must be kept in mind, when we come across the frequent reservations Nishida makes regarding the Christian concept of God, even in his later works.

It is reasonable to admit already at this point that the sympathy Nishida shows for the second way is due to his personal interest in Buddhism and mystical experience. Thus he states:

> ... a God who is the creator or superintendent of a universe and who stands outside the universe cannot truly be said to be an absolute, infinite God. I think that the Hindu religion in the remote past and the mystical school which flourished during the 15th and 16th centuries in Europe were seeking God by intuition in the human heart, and this is the most profound knowledge of God.

> In what form does God exist? From one viewpoint, God, as such men as Nicholas Cusa have said, is found by negation, for that which one specifies or must affirm, i.e., that which much be seized, is not God, for if He is that which is specific and must be seized, He is already finite, and is unable to perform the infinite function of unifying the universe (*De docta ignorantia,* Cap. 24). Seen from this point, God is absolute nothingness *(mattaku mu).* However, if one says that God is merely nothingness *(tan ni mu),* this is certainly not so. At the base of the establishment of reality there is a unifying function which clearly cannot be moved. ... God ... is the basis of reality, and only because He is able to be nothingness, is there no place whatsoever where He is not and does not operate.[10]

And a little further Nishida goes on to say:

> Those who desire to know the true God must by all means discipline themselves to that extent and must prepare their eyes to be able to know him. To this kind of man, that which is the power of God in the entire universe is active like the spirit of a painter within a famous painting, and is felt as a fact of direct experience. We call this the event of seeing God.[11]

In part IV, chapter 4: God and the World, Nishida repeats once again what he had said before. He thinks that we can know the characteristics of God and His relationship to the world from the unity of pure experience, i.e., from its characteristics and the relationship to its content.[12]

> ... When the mind encounters black, even though it manifests black, it is not that the mind is black; when the mind encounters white, even though it manifests white, it is not that the mind is white. It goes without saying that in Buddhism it is so, but

even the fact that in medieval philosophy the so-called negative theology of the school of Dionysius employed negatives in discussing God reflects this tendency. Such a man as Nicholas of Cusa stated that God transcends both being and nothingness, and while God is being, He is also nothingness.[13]

Nishida next mentions Jacob Boehme's expressions: God is "quiet without anything," *Ungrund,* "will without object." Describing further the relationship between the absolute and infinite God and the world he says:

> Nothingness separated from being is not true nothingness; the one separated from the all is not the true one; equality separated from distinction is not true equality. In the same way that if there is not God there is no world, if there is no world there is no God.[14]

Considering these passages, a reader unacquainted with the Japanese language and Nishida's cultural background will get any but the right impression that Nishida was deeply influenced in his philosophy by his own religious convictions, that is to say by Zen Buddhism. And this is one instance where—as I mentioned before—western scholars would have reason to ask their Japanese colleagues to throw more light on the concrete data, proving statements as the following one of Suzuki Daisetsu who was a classmate of Nishida during their high school days in Kanazawa:

> Nishida's philosophy of absolute nothingness or his logic of the self-identity of absolute contradictions is difficult to understand, I believe, unless one is passably acquainted with Zen experience. Nishida ... thought it was his mission to make Zen intelligible to the West.[14a]

After statements like these, the western reader might expect that Nishida would deal mainly with Zen, even if he would illustrate his thought with examples chosen from analogous ideas in western philosophy. However, he is greatly mistaken; for the opposite is true. Nishida quotes a great number of western authors and alludes occasionally to Buddhism. Thus it is only after the reader becomes aware of what Nishida does *not* say rather than of what he says that for the first time there is some sort of true understanding insight. And here I agree that some psychological preparation is required for the western reader, some basic knowledge of Buddhism and its understanding of Zen, some knowledge of Nishida's personal background and, finally, some guidance in the study even of the translations of Nishida.[15] For there are, besides the rare cases that Buddhism, the teaching of Shinran etc. are mentioned directly, some quotations, short sayings as they are used by Zen masters in their instructions,—sayings which after some time become dear and familiar to their disciples in the same way as Scripture sayings become dear to the Christian. Often enough these short sayings are not marked as Zen sayings, and since they are not really quotations, they are not indicated as such, and, finally, in translations they are hardly to be recognized as Zen sayings at all.[16]

ON THE EXISTENTIAL COMMITMENT OF NISHIDA

Men in general and Japanese scholars in particular seem to be exceedingly shy in displaying any personal interest in religious questions. In a way this applies also to Nishida. It might be due to this fact that often little attention is paid to the personal background and commitment of a thinker like Nishida. However, after the development of modern hermeneutics, after Heidegger and Gadamer,[17] an attitude like this is hardly justifiable anymore. It is true, data of religious faith (in the strict sense of the word "faith") or religious experience do not become philosophical arguments. However, it is quite possible that by philosophical insight man is invited to realize that human reason is not the last refuge for human existence, and that philosophy does reach its fulfilment only where it ends in "non-philosophical philosophy" (Tanabe).[18] The question might be asked whether the practical refusal to discuss personal commitments does not hinder the true understanding of philosophers like Nishida, and further, whether the same fact is not the main reason why Nishida's philosophy seems to be so utterly difficult to understand.

We can consider Nishida's ontology and logic and try to decide whether his philosophy is more concerned with ontological problems or with problems of logic. One can study (actually, it should be done rather thoroughly) the influence of western philosophical thought, e. g., Kant, Hegel, Husserl on Nishida's philosophy, his understanding of western philosophy and his (justified or unjustified) interpretations of them. One might study him in the light of Hegel's or Heidegger's philosophy. And yet, one might still miss the real scope of his thought in the same way, as Nagarjuna's real intention must remain hidden, unless his religious background is uncovered and fully considered.

It is this dimension of man's personal commitment which should not remain unconsidered. This dimension might not matter much when the field of a scholar is a limited field, rather remote from the central problems of human existence. However, for a philosopher who faces the totality of human existence his personal commitment is of the utmost importance.

In *A Study of Good,* Nishida remarks that "a scholar's acquiring of new ideas . . . , a religious person's acquiring of new awakenings—all are based on the appearance of this kind of unity," and then he adds in brackets: "therefore all are based on mystical intuition."[19] An instance like this proves that Noda Matao is right when he states, "He accepts, from the first, the position of a mystic. His metaphysics has its characteristic motif in his mystic religiosity."[20] He repeatedly stresses the point that in religion man reaches the realm of nothingness which is neither being nor nonbeing. The spirit of nonattachment to both being and nonbeing, which since Nagarjuna was handed on through China to Japan, especially in Zen Buddhism,[21] is quite evident in Nishida's work.

It is doubtful whether Nishida's theoretical knowledge of the history of Zen in particular and Mahayana Buddhism and Buddhism in general was very detailed. Most probably he did not know Sanscrit or Pali. Perhaps his knowledge should rather be compared to the average of the ordinary Buddhist believer of his time. However, some interior development is indicated by the fact that although originally belonging to a Jodo Shinshu family,[22] he was greatly attracted by Zen. As can be gathered from his diary,[23] he practised Zazen meditation for many years. *Hekiganshu* and *Rinzairoku,* two of the most widely used collections of Zen *koan,* are explicitly mentioned in his reading lists.[24]

In 1901 he became "a layman initiate" *(koji)* at his temple and received the Buddhist name Sunshin. On August 3, 1903, while attending a *sesshin* (usually eight days of continuous Zazen) at Kyoto's Daitokuji, he was allowed to practise the *mu-koan* (mu=nothingness); this is one of the favorite *koan* of Zen Buddhism, since it points immediately to the core of Zen Buddhism and its root, Nagarjuna's understanding of the original doctrine of the Buddha.

On July 19, 1905 he writes in his diary:

> I am not a psychologist nor a sociologist; I shall be an investigator of life. Zen is music, Zen is art, Zen is movement; apart from this there is nothing wherein one must seek consolation of the heart . . . . If my heart can become pure and simple like that of a child, I think there probably can be no greater happiness than this. Non multa sed multum.[25]

A year later, on March 25, 1906 we read: "Today I think aboutthe problem of religion, without solving it."

In his diary as also in his letters, Nishida again and again touches religious questions.[26] As professor of philosophy of religion at Kyoto University he has to treat religion. However, when he writes as a philosopher, he rather seldom refers to his personal religious convictions. In the midst of abundant quotations from and allusions to western philosophers like James, Bergson, Kant, Hegel, Fichte, Plato and Aristotle, Cohen, Dilthey, Husserl and even Heidegger,[27] to mystical writers like Dionysius, Eckhart, Boehme as well as Plotinus and Augustine,[28] the comparatively few allusions to Buddhism, be it Zen or Amidism, disappear almost entirely.

It seems that for several reasons, Nishida was convinced that philosophy and personal religious convictions should not be dealt with at the same time, and that philosophical thought should be developed rather independently from one's own personal religion.[29] Religion is an affair of life, not of discussion. Therefore, we should be aware of the fact that for Nishida there is a depth, a "beyond" or a "within" of all things about which man ceases to speak, but which he must experience. This becomes clear from such a paragraph as the following:

> . . . From the standpoint of a religious person, this contradictory self-identity[30] might be considered as God. Religion is not superstition of the past or

opium for ignorant people, but the religious reality is always working at the bottom of history. However, as I mentioned before,[31] I am not discussing philosophy from the standpoint of religious experience. It is the contrary. The standpoint of religious experience consists in the fact that the self dies and the Absolute appears. However, there is no place for words (and) thought. Accordingly, in religion a change of life, what is called 'conversion,' has to take place."[32]

Actually, Nishida had taken a similar view already at the end of his maiden work *A Study of Good:*

> God is not someone who must be known according to analysis and reasoning. If we presume that the essence of reality is a personal thing, God is that which is most personal. Our knowing God is possible only through the intuition of love or faith. Therefore, people who say, 'I do not know God, I only love Him and believe in Him' are the ones who are most able to know God.[33]

In order to discover the hidden undercurrents of his thinking, a more thorough analysis of Nishida's language and vocabulary than has yet been made would be extremely helpful.[34]

"NOTHINGNESS" IN NISHIDA'S LATER STAGES

In an article of high erudition Noda remarks on Nishida:

> Nishida never lost sight of his central problem, namely, the confrontation of Oriental Buddhistic ideas with Western philosophy. . . . This central concern with Buddhism can be detected at every stage of his thought.[35]

In the development of his thought usually four stages are distinguished. The first was marked by the appearance of *A Study of Good.* The second was reached in his work *Intuition and Reflection in Self-Consciousness* (1917).

A Intuition and Reflection in Self-Consciousness[36]

Considering the list of authors quoted by Nishida, it is safe to say that he began to study Bergson, Bolzano, Brentano, Cohen, Fichte, Husserl, Lotze, Rickert—all names frequently quoted for the first time in *Shisaku to taiken* (Thinking and Experience, 1915)—thoroughly, only after he had completed *A Study of Good.* Epistemological questions are treated throughout his life work. And yet, also at the end of this book Nishida states that he was not able to find any new ideas and solutions, and that he might have to surrender himself to the camp of mystery or mysticism.[37]

As in *A Study of Good,* Nishida constantly pushes in the direction of nothingness. In this work he repeatedly states that the Ultimate is not ὄυ but rather something like "ὄυ+μὴ ὄυ", "reason-qua-non-reason," "on-qua-me-on," "experience-qua-thinking," anyway, a pure activity (II, 182; cf. 269f. 283.293.315). We might even say with J. Boehme that where we stand and go, there is God (II, 182).

The final reality is similar to Fichte's "absolute Ego" and "absolute will" (cf. II, 283). It is will "whose cause is totally incomprehensible, and which in itself is a mystery" (II, 272). In a book of Max Stirner, Nishida finds a saying about God, *"Namen nennen Dich nicht"* (names do not express you), which he applies to the "Ego" (II, 272).[38] He searches for other analogies in the West and quotes from J. Boehme ("Ungrund", "the reality is the bottom of an ocean which cannot be reached . . . if it could be reached, it were not reality" (II, 274f)), Dionysius Areopagita ("While God is everything, He is not anything" (II, 275. 283)), Scotus Eriugena, whom he knows most probably only indirectly through J. Huber's book *Scotus Friugena* (II, 278). Nishida repeatedly refers to Eriugena in this work. "If you make God being, it does not fit, if you make Him nothingness, it does not fit; if you call Him motion, it does not fit, if you call Him stillness, it does not fit; He is what is said"—and here Nishida uses a frequently used Zen phrase—"'if you are able to say it,—thirty strokes; if you are not able to say it,—thirty strokes'". (II, 279)[39] God is at the same time—what Eriugena calls—*Natura creans et non creata* and *Natura nec creata nec creans* (II, 279; cf. 287. 301). He is *natura superessentialis,* which means that all categories are denied (II, 277.283). Nishida even refers to Gnostics like Basileides ("ὸ οὐκ ὤν θεᾳς" which Nishida translates "the God who is not (yet?)," *"mizai no kami"*) and Valentinus (βῦθος, depth) (II, 319). One might, therefore, say that Nishida looks in the direction of God in order to clarify his own understanding of the ultimate reality.

On the other hand, he is somewhat attracted by the word "nothingness" and states several times that the "Ego comes from creative nothingness and returns to creative nothingness"; he thinks that this expression is able to reveal the true state of the will (II, 272f; also 275.281; again in later works, cf. especially IV,238f). It is evident that this kind of nothingness does not refer to God (cf. II,281); however, it is also not clearly related to the *creatio exnihilo.* It rather seems that the *"creative* nothingness" is suggested by Bergson's *élan vital.*[40]

Actually, Nishida does also consider the problem of creation, mainly referring to Augustine. Topics like creation from nothing, out of (=from) love (II, 285), the relation of God's knowledge and creation (II, 288), creation and emanation (II, 285.287) appear; for the first time the "eternal now," later on one of the favorite expressions of Nishida,[41] is dealt with here (II, 284).

With regard to western analogies, Nishida's conception remains full of ambiguities. And yet, they disappear if his eastern background is taken into consideration. As Nishida himself states, even a syllogistic way of thinking cannot but admit a final experience behind everything (II, 284). Behind the world of philosophy there is the world of religion, the world of mystery (cf. II,276/7).

When in 1941 the second edition of this work appeared, Nishida confesses that it had marked only a step in his development; it is a document of his interior struggling

(II,13). And he closes with a phrase taken from the Hekiganshu: "Often on account of you I have descended into the 'Green Dragon's Cave'." The expression "green dragon's cave" alludes to an old legend about jewels of many colors hidden in the throat of a dragon. Anyone who wanted to obtain any of these mysterious treasures had to dive into the dragon's mouth, i.e., he had to be prepared to descend into the depth of bitter experience.[42]

B From the Acting to the Seeing

Considering Nishida's thought on nothingness, ***From the Acting to the Seeing*** (1929) is of utmost importance. It is in this work that Nishida not only directs his attention to a place beyond being andnothingness in general,[43] but also aims through to the very nothingness which is the place beyond being and relative nothingness. Most of the authors who were lined up before appear again: Plato, Plotinos, Eriugena, Fichte, Augustine. However, whereas before creative will and action or creative nothingness seemed to describe the final reality, Nishida proceeds now to something which is neither creative nor created but renders creative action possible (cf. IV, 155). For the formed thing is the shade of the formless, and in the space without shadow the infinite form arises *(ibid.).*

After this kind of preparatory explanations, Nishida says:

> We might call it nothingness, but then it is not nothingness which opposes being; it rather includes being. Or we might think of it as the hidden reality, but then it is not the reality which did not yet manifest itself; it must be the reality which, in an infinite manner, transcends whatever is supposed to manifest itself; it must include the infinite hidden reality. (IV, 155)

And then Nishida adds important new analogies. Augustine admired the memory which treasures in itself everything, whether it has form or not, even forgetting itself. Or Fichte knows the great Ego which transcends Ego and Non-Ego. Nishida alludes to Plotinus and Kant. Anyway, what he wants to express must be something beyond self-consciousness and self-awareness in which knowing and acting are united. It must be a place where the One, which unites the personal with the impersonal, the Ego with the non-Ego, the knowing subject with the known object, does no longer become object itself. The true One must transcend any objectivization of the actual experience. It must be something which another Zen expression describes as follows, "After we have gone as far as we possibly could go, we took one more step. (in order to reach it)" (IV, 156).[44]

In this context Nishida rejects also the notion of God as insufficient:

> Or we could think something like the self-consciousness of a transcendent person, that is, God as the unity of infinite self-consciousness. However, also a unity like this is not the apriori of a truly free self-consciousness. Such a God still

does not escape relativity, He is a God who became an object. Therefore, from the idea of a God like this, the freedom of the single person is not preserved, the origin of evil not explained. Something like the self-consciousness of God which develops in world history is nothing but empty time which could be imagined on the grounds of nature. The true God is not the creating God. It must be something like— what the scholars in the field of mysticism call— *Gottheit* (divinity)." (IV, 156/7)[45]

The same work contains the very important treatise on "Place" (Jap. *basho*) (IV, 208-289). This chapter together with the following works ***The System of the Self-conscious Universal*** (1930) and ***The Self-conscious Determination of Nothingness*** (1932) clarifies further Nishida's understanding of absolute nothingness. There is little need to explain in detail how Nishida reaches the place of nothingness. If we would like to decide whether or not—even logically and metaphysically speaking— nothingness is the last valid conclusion of a purely rational argument, then this would be necessary, and the works mentioned should be studied in detail. However, this is not our intention here. Our only purpose here is to demonstrate that the logical argument is at least psychologically influenced by the eastern Weltanschauung. A conclusion like this, of course, is not supposed to create a prejudice against the validity of the philosophical argumentation. But it seems to be a very helpful insight on the way to a true understanding of the arguments.

Here I should like only to refer to the translations of Robert Schinzinger, which gives a sufficient impression of Nishida's way of thinking. The chapter on *The Intelligible World* taken from ***The System of the Self-conscious Universal*** is a superb example of Nishida's way of thinking and arguing.

A certain ambiguity of the concept of "nothingness," however, prevails also here. The concept of "place" or "field" was suggested to Nishida by the concept of "space" in Plato's *Timaios* ("space or receiving place," cf. IV, 209). There are other connections with Lotze (IV, 209 etc.), Lask (IV, 212 etc.), Aristotle (IV, 213 etc.) and others. And yet, these analogies are rather misleading or at least puzzling. For, Plato and Aristotle find "nonbeing" in the realm of "(first) matter," which, as having no form, has no true being. On the other hand, for Nishida the concept of "place" is a positive reality (cf. IV, 26ff). As he had said before, behind the will there is darkness, but this is not pure darkness; it must be the "dazzling obscurity," about which Dionysius speaks (IV, 229).[46]

As we saw before, here too the tendency to identify (if we say it in western terms) or to realize in oneness (if we say it in eastern terms) the two kinds of nothingness is to be found. The question seems to remain unsolved as to how Nishida could identify "eternal nothingness," "the true nothingness," "creative nothingness," and "nothingness" from which God creates matter and time (cf. e.g. IV, 238). An eastern interpretation might solve it by pointing to the true insight of the Zen experience. However, the unenlightened western scholar will find little consolation in this. I personally think that both sides have a point to make. For a reexamination of this question, the analysis of an experience or also the philosophy and theology of the beginning and the end[47] could serve as a possible starting point.

One striking observation cannot pass by unmentioned. As before, Nishida still does little in order to make the unenlightened one understand that it is eastern nothingness which he has in mind. However, why should he? Those who have eyes see, and those who have ears hear:

> If one is really overwhelmed by the consciousness of absolute Nothingness, there is neither "Me" nor "God"; but just because there is absolute Nothingness, the mountain is mountain, and the water is water, and the being is as it is.[48]

People who read Heidegger or who like poetry might find some understanding in this:

> From the cliff,
> Eight times ten thousand feet high,
> Withdrawing your hand,—
> Flames spring from the plough,
> World burns,
> Body becomes ashes and dirt,
> And resurrects.
> The rice-rows
> Are as ever,
> And the rice-ears
> Stand high.

A Zen-Master Kanemitsu Kogun is its author, and Nishida himself explains it:

> The master has given a problem for Zen-meditation, and you are labouring to solve the problems of being, as the farmer over there, on top of the high cliff, is labouring to plough his field. You are hanging onto the usual way to thinking like somebody who is hanging onto an infinitely high cliff, afraid of falling into the abyss. Withdraw your hand! And see: From the farmer's plough spring sparks,—and you, while the experience of Nothingness springs from your labouring thinking, find 'satori,' enlightenment. The Universe has become nothing, and the Ego has become nothing. But in the same spark of Nothingness, you regain the world and yourself in wonderful self-identity. In the experience of Nothingness, everything is as it is: the rice-rows are as ever, and the rice-ears stand high.[49]

It is evident to Nishida that the religious experience surpasses human knowledge completely. "With regard to the landscape of religion, religious experience alone has the last word."[50] And yet, in the same context he stresses that, philosophically speaking, there remains the fact that absolute nothingness, the last and all-embracing Universal, which is beyond all determinations, retains its significance of "mirroring." As Jakob Boehme puts it:

> Since the first will is bottomless, like eternal nothingness, we perceive it as a mirror, in which one sees one's own image, as a life.

About the same time when Nishida wrote the two works we mentioned now, he composed the beautiful little essay on "Goethe's Metaphysical Background," which was also translated by Schinzinger. Articles like this or the excerpts taken from lectures on *The Problem of Japanese Culture*[51] point more directly to the source of Nishida's insight than most of his other works, where most of the time eastern mentality is only the incomprehensible formless background or horizon.

C The Later Stages of Nishida's Philosophy

It is especially in his last works that Nishida states more directly what he has in mind. The place of nothingness is now frequently called "identity of self-contradictories" or "absolute contradictory self-identity"; Schinzinger has summed it up by simply calling it the "unity of opposites."[52]

Maybe the most significant statement of Nishida's position we find in the seventh part of his *Philosophical Essays,* in an essay called **"The Logic of Place and the Religious World View"** (XI, 371-464), which he must have written during the last weeks of his life and which, at all events, is the last essay he was able to complete. Reading this article, we receive the impression that finally he discloses his personal attitude. As the title indicates, he still is working on the full expression of his logic or—we might say—his strictly philosophical approach and its integration with his personal religious commitment or conviction. He quotes from Scripture and Buddhist sources. It is sure that he has settled in favor of the final experience of the Absolute, which, according to him, is beyond any philosophical expression, and, therefore, the "absolute contradictory self-identity" (XI, 398). This expression will not sound strange to us if we keep in mind the *"coincidentia oppositorum"* of Nicholas of Cusa (cf. 138f).[53]

In this last essay, Nishida evidently struggles to find the right expressions. He tries to discard all relativity, all imperfection. The negative sentences which are to exclude misunderstandings are numerous. That is to say, even if he tries to put things positively, he is inclined to deny at least part of it in the next sentence:

> When the relative is confronted with the Absolute, there must be death (Note: Nishida had previously quoted Isaias 6:5). It must become nothingness. We can say that only by death, in a reverse correspondence, our Self is in contact with God, is connected with Him . . . However, what we call death is not pure nothingness. When we say 'absolute,' it goes without saying that it means, 'it cut through the opposing.'[54] But if it only cut through the opposing, it is nothing, it is but pure nothingness. A God who cannot create anything, is a powerless God, He is not God (XI, 396-397).

And he goes on to say that the true Absolute (Japanese *zettai*) is not only determined by the fact that it cuts through anything which constitutes some kind of opposite

(Japanese *tai*) to the *zettai*. On the contrary, in this sense the Absolute has to deny itself in order to be the true Absolute. By being opposite or confronted with the denial or nothingness of the Absolute, the being of the Absolute is,—or we might paraphrase it as follows: By denying anything which hinders the Absolute to be what it is, it is itself. It is the logic of exclusion—in western terms we might call it the *"via negationis"* (way of negation)—by which Nishida tries to state his view regarding the last indescribable reality.

It is only natural that Nishida, in his sincerity, had to reach the conclusion that also that which the West calls God is to be posited in the realm of this final place:

> That which is called the true Absolute, must . . . be self-identical in an absolutely contradictory manner. When we express God in a logical manner, there is no other way to say it than this (XI, 397-398).

Especially comparing statements like this with the frequent quotations of Buddhist expressions, the impression arises that toward the end of his life Nishida must have reached a point where he increasingly felt that Christianity and Buddhism are close to stating the same things. However, in all sympathy for Nishida's thought, it can hardly be denied that Nishida reached the conclusion only a) by prescinding from some fundamental facts of the Christian faith, and b) by interpreting some others according to his own understanding. The fundamental fact and starting point of Christianity is, after all, the free revelation of God in Jesus of Nazareth, which took place in history. It would be an abuse of the term if we would call the denial of this starting point "demythologization." And it would be fatal if a mutual understanding between Christianity and Buddhism would demand from Christianity to weaken itself to the point of utter self-denial. I personally feel that it is one of the weakest points of Nishida's thought that an historical revelation of God in the strict sense, as it is understood throughout the history of Christianity, has evidently no place in his system; we might even say that it is impossible in his system. Compared with this, other points like the confusion of the order of creation (which epistemologically belongs to the realm of philosophy) with the order of redemption (which belongs to the realm of faith proper),[55] his unsatisfying understanding of the doctrine on creation, which can be found even in his last essay (cf. e.g. XI, 400), consequently his interpretation of the relationship of God the creator to the non-creating God, though in themselves important, are nevertheless, secondary.

Yet, notwithstanding these critical remarks, I personally feel that the fundamental insight of Nishida is correct, namely that the final reality—whether we call it "absolute nothingness" or "absolute contradictory self-identification" (= "unity of opposites") or God—is the same, and that every philosophy at the end has to lead into this inexpressible reality. I feel this all the more, since it is meaningless to constitute something beyond the final reality which in the West is, by definition, God. We might disagree about statements made about this final reality which anyway is beyond human comprehension and might not even need comprehension if only we realize ourselves as one and united with it. And yet, the fundamental insight could be agreed upon.

For this reason, western scholars should be more willing to accept for the moment Nishida's intention that his point of view is not meant to be pantheistic, even if it looks like pantheism (XI, 398-399). He personally prefers the expression "panentheism," though I do not know whether he himself was fully aware of the exact meaning of this rather ambiguous term (XI, 399). After all, it depends on its more exact explanation whether or not it is compatible with Christian theology. For, panentheism could, in a way, simply demand from the philosophers as well as from the theologians, a deeper reflection on the relationship between absolute and finite reality, and could remind them to be aware of any unjustifiable conclusions drawn from the teachings on God's transcendence, on His freedom with regard to creation.

It is, of course, always more pleasing to the western mind if it gets a clear-cut term for somebody's philosophy and thus is able to catalogue it. However, this becomes increasingly difficult if we deal with thinkers of other cultural regions. There arises the great danger that we prevent any understanding because of wrong terms. What, therefore, is needed today is much patience and even more listening to each other.

There are other questions which would help Nishida's understanding very much but which cannot be dealt with in this context. It is a well-known fact that in his later years Nishida was thinking very much on problems like the historical world, time and eternity, history and the place of nothingness, human society and the single person, the I-thou-relation.[56] Many of these questions were re-examined and deepened by his disciples. And yet he set the path for all of them, because—whether in agreement or in discord—they are forced to refer to him in one way or another. And therefore, it is safe to say that he is indeed the father of modern Japanese philosophy.

"NOTHINGNESS" IN LATER JAPANESE PHILOSOPHY

In the concluding section, I should like to examine a few reactions to Nishida's philosophy of nothingness. For this reason, I choose his immediate successor at Kyoto University, Tanabe Hajime, who was at the same time one of his most vigorous critics. Then I shall take up Nishitani Keiji and Takeuchi Yoshinori, two philosophers both still living, who followed Nishida and Tanabe in the chair of philosophy of religion in Kyoto. These two philosophers have their own original approach, of course, but it is safe to note that Nishitani thinks more in the line of Nishida, whereas Takeuchi follows Tanabe more closely.

A Tanabe Hajime (1885-1962)

As was mentioned before, absolute nothingness is a common keynote in both Nishida's and Tanabe's philosophy.

However, in their approach and in the development of the idea, they differ considerably. Tanabe's philosophy is most convincingly expressed in his later years, as for instance, in his *Philosophy as Metanoetics* and further on in his various articles on death, or rather on death-resurrection.[57] His basic attitude towards Nishida's philosophy seems to have remained unchanged, although both clarified their personal approach after Tanabe's first criticism. Tanabe himself changed from a more negative criticism of Nishida's philosophical standpoint to a more positive explanation of his own point of view, and in fact, at the end of his life he was much closer to Nishida's conception than he was in the beginning.

Since we do not intend to describe Tanabe's philosophical development, we shall proceed to his last stage after casting a brief glance at his criticism about Nishida. This we find in an article *Looking up to Master Nishida's Thought,*[58] which was written in 1930 after the publication of Nishida's **The System of the Self-Conscious Universal.** Tanabe attacks, first, Nishida's philosophical standpoint as such, and, second, some related topics connected with it. Restricting ourselves to the central question, we might say:

1) There is little doubt for Tanabe that "absolute nothingness" belongs to the realm of eastern religious self-realization. He states about himself that he has a deep sense of admiration for it, especially for the one form which is discussed here and which, according to him, consists in seeing by being nothingness. For him it is a state sublime but difficult to obtain.[59]

2) The main problem for him seems to be that Nishida evidently draws illegitimate conclusions from premises taken from the field of religion and transferred to the field of philosophy thereby transgressing the bounds of philosophy:

> . . . However, is it possible, after all, that philosophy puts such a religious self-realization into a system? A system does not end by just making the final *concretum,* the absolute Totality, something which is to be desired, but it anticipates it as something which is given. Unless one makes the last thing the substratum, a system cannot have an ultimate principle. Of course, the Master makes a clear distinction between the standpoint of religious experience as such and the standpoint of philosophical reflection; accordingly, he makes the self-realization of the final absolute nothingness belong to the former, not the latter, and by the fact that it is the experience of the inner life, which is the noetical determination of the self-realization of absolute nothingness, he makes it the last thing which belongs to philosophy. However, for the Master the experience is persistently supported[60] by the self-realization of absolute nothingness and mirrors it. Accordingly, the place of absolute nothingness is considered as something which determines immediately the place itself. The last Universal does not exist as something which is only desired, but as something which is given.[61]

And again:

> What I doubt is this. Does it not lead to the abandonment of philosophy as such, when philosophy, as philosophy of religion . . . , puts up the last unobtainable Universal, and explains the real being as determination of this Self itself?[62]

The statement that the religious experience of the absolute nothingness cannot become the principle of a philosophical system is evidently the most basic objection which Tanabe has to make.[63] The experience is suprahistorical, philosophical reflection is historical.[64] Against Nishida's logic of place, Tanabe claims that the place of religion is rather the "placeless place" or "place without place."[65] And then, Tanabe argues against Nishida that he emphasizes the irrationality of history;[66] that he needs a principle of darkness in order to explain it.[67] He further doubts whether the combination of eastern religious experience with western philosophical thought, of mystical experience and logical structure was a success; whether, after all, western philosophy of the will, which appeared together with Christianity, was not rather betraying Nishida's philosophy of place.[68]

These and similar questions are, of course, grave problems. And yet, I personally think that they can be thrown back at Tanabe himself. The first question is what is philosophy. As we stated before, there is no reason to object to a philosopher who comes to the conclusion that finally man, in his reasoning, reaches a point where reasoning ends, and that man touches upon a reality which is beyond reason. Moreover, there is no reason to be disturbed if an author sincerely admits that his personal convictions influenced him in his philosophical thinking. That is, in fact, what Nishida concedes when he states in the preface of **From the Acting to the Seeing:**

> For a long time I was wondering whether I might be able to grasp what lies on the ground of my thinking; I made a turn from voluntarism as (e.g., Fichte taught it) to a kind of intuitionism. But I think that what I call intuition differs from what was thought in intuitionism until now and from its appearances. I do not take, as basis, the intuition of the union of subject and object, but I like to think that it consists in seeing all beings and acting things as shades of the things which mirror their *selves* in themselves by denying themselves; as seeing by non-seeing on the ground of all things.[69]

Negative statements like these are seducing indeed. However, I feel that Tsujimura Koichi's observation will prove right, namely that, when Nishida uses expressions like "shades of the things which mirror their *selves* in themselves by denying themselves (=making themselves nothingness)" or when he talks about "infinite depth," he means "absolute nothingness," and this is neither a "dark principle" nor a "negative principle." Tsujimura senses the Zen atmosphere in expressions such as those mentioned above.[70]

Actually during the time when Nishida was working on **From the Acting to the Seeing** an important experience must have taken place. On July 3, 1927, a Sunday, we find the following notice in his diary:

> In the afternoon alone at home. Quiet thinking. I spent half the day in quietude. Miki paid a visit. I did not smoke even one cigarette.

After this he draws in red ink the shining sun, and writes below in German *"Wiedergeburt"* (rebirth) and underlines it. And then he adds, again in German, not quite correctly, *"aus bösem Traum gewacht"* (awakened from a bad dream), and after that in Japanese:

> From whatever dry a tree, a bud of fresh life can spring forth. Today it was extremely joyous.

In fact, nobody who is a nihilist ever composes hymns praising nothingness.[71] "Ungrund," darkness, blindness—images like these might be purely negative images, but they might be positive well; for man is also blinded by too much light. And if non-rationality means nothing more than that rationality is founded in suprarationality, time in eternity, finitude in the infinite—and that seems to be one *possible* valid interpretation of Nishida—then there is no reason to object.

Actually, it seems that in this point Tanabe, in his later years, approaches the point of view of Nishida, especially when he describes his own philosophy as a "non-philosophical philosophy" and terms it "metanoetics."[72] Tanabe himself explains the term. It means that his philosophy transcends any rational intuition. A statement like this retains, on the one hand, the negative decision against any kind of "mystical philosophy" or "intuition philosophy." On the other hand, it now accepts a suprarational, at least psychological basis of his philosophy, namely in opposition to intuition which relies on "self-power," Shinran's (1173-1262) doctrine of faith as it is described in his *Kyo-gyo-shin-sho* (Doctrine-Action-Faith-Evidence).[73] In a way, Tanabe tries to go beyond Nishida. He aims at a philosophy which is centered around one of the most fundamental insights of the Jodo-shinshu sect, namely the way of the Bodhisattva: He "goes" (in order to gain enlightenment), but out of gratitude he returns (in order to help the others finding their way to the land of promise).[74] And since, according to Tanabe's understanding, mysticism stresses only "going," his philosophy takes a step beyond Nishida.

"Metanoetics" means—as indicated by the Greek term "metanoia"—repentance, shame, confession, "change of heart," conversion. It includes the confession of one's own powerlessness; however, the confession leads to the gratifying experience that man's heart is exposed to light in which all our malice becomes powerless. The change of heart is indeed like balsam healing all human pains.[75]

We might summarize "metanoetics" with Takeuchi:

> Metanoetics means (a) the confession (meta-noesis) of reason not being able to hold its own ground in the matter of the ultimate of human existence, and (b) therefore its renunciation of the autonomy ("selfpower") of reason; (c) but at the same time this also means through this self-negation its resurrection from the depth of nothingness to participation with the grace (Other-Power) of Absolute Nothingness, functioning also in its thinking in a reformed manner, which is quite different and away from speculative philosophy; i.e. noetics becomes meta-noetics.[76]

It is worth noting that thus the term "metanoetics" (which, without any explanation, will be very difficult to grasp for western readers, although it has been coined from Greek roots!) has two sides, an ontological and an ethical.[77]

As again Takeuchi points out, Nishida and Tanabe differ in the following way:

> 1) Nishida emphasizes action-intuition, while Tanabe stresses the significance of action-faith in religious existence.
>
> 2) Action-intuition presupposes our existence as a creative element in the creative (historical) world. Tanabe also thinks of the problem of dialectic only in connection with the historical world. But Nishida's creative element in the creative world tries to take the vantage point in the historical world, where, in every moment anew, the perspective of the whole is open to be seen from a different angle. For Tanabe, the road in the historical world is, at every point, like a blind alley, which with decision and courage one must break through in order to find the way out. In a word, against the integral of Nishida, Tanabe stresses the infinitesimal.
>
> 3) For Tanabe, the ethical viewpoint is predominant, and from his ethico-social viewpoint even in his later years he devoted himself to the study of many religions, seeking to unify the truth of the Pure Land Sect and the Zen Sect in Buddhism as well as the truth of Christianity. While for Nishida, from the beginning to the end, the immediate realization of Absolute Nothingness, derived from Zen Buddhism, is the fundamental experience of all his thought.[78]

The third point is the most important because it stresses the different religious standpoints. Tanabe starts from Amidism, although towards the end of his life he also shows considerable interest in Zen.[79] Nishida, although never completely losing his respect for Amidism, dedicates his life to Zen. In a way, for him it was easier than for Tanabe. For, Tanabe wished to reconcile Amidism with Zen, and Buddhism with Christianity. He evidently aimed too high. Today neither the followers of Zen Buddhism and the disciples of Nishida are able to agree with him nor will Christians think that Tanabe really understood them. And this is the tragedy of the great philosopher.

On the other hand, there is today a strong tendency to level down the difference between *jiriki* (= "selfpower") and *tariki* (= "otherpower"). However, I do not think that it is very helpful to deny too hastily the importance of and the differences between these two types of Mahayana-

Buddhism, although I could see that, from a deepened Buddhist point of view, it makes sense to insist that this difference should not be carried too far. Another question is whether the stress on "going and returning" (in the Buddhist sense) is a real antithesis to Nishida's philosophy. However, I should like to leave the discussion of such problems to the specialists in the field.

The question for us would rather be: What is "faith" according to Tanabe? *If* faith is understood as Christians understand it (my expectation right now would be rather that he does not understand it in the same way), then the question between Tanabe and Nishida could be reduced to the objection which we raised before, namely that in Nishida's system there is no place for faith in the full Christian sense, since he disregards the most fundamental facts of Christian belief. Then, in other words, we could say that between Nishida and Tanabe the same questions arise as between Buddhism and Christianity which, after all, belong to two religious structures which cannot be reduced to each other, unless one side shelves its claim of absoluteness.

In the *Heidegger-Festschrift* of 1959 we find the following sentence in which Tanabe distinguishes his own way as well from Zen as from his understanding of Christianity without mentioning the two explicitly:

> Dass einer das Vermögen in sich gewahrt, zum Tode entschlossen zu sein und andere belehrend zu einer gleichen Selbstgewahrnis bringen möchte, oder dass einer eine Belehrung und Zurechtweisung über die Liebe als Weg des Menschen gibt, reicht noch nicht zu, den lebendigen Glauben seines Selbst anderen Menschen mitzuteilen. Weit wichtiger als der Idealismus solcher Verkündigung und Belehrung sind der Entschluss zum Tode und die Handlung der Liebe selbst.[80]

Those who have the Zen experience will never agree with Tanabe who, by his studies on Christianity and Amidism, was led to realize that there are fields left out which, though it might be difficult to express them, will never be covered by mystical experience alone, be it an experience of light or of darkness.

Tanabe describes his own relation to Christianity in the long introduction to the *Dialectic of Christianity*. When he wrote the book in 1948, he could claim that his interest in Christianity began about 40 years before. It was mainly Protestant ethics which added the strong ethical touch to all his thinking. On the other hand, there is little doubt that he received the impression that mysticism is pseudoreligiosity and a kind of "ersatz" for true religious faith.[81]

Tanabe did not become a Christian. He mentions that since he was under the influence of Nishida, he was leaning to Zen intuition, and thus his special interest in Christianity remained naturally superficial (x:8). He studied the conversions of Pascal and Newman, Augustine and Luther. He read Barth's *Credo*. He studied Kierkegaard,

but even now he must confess that he feels it as one of his strongest drawbacks that, as a teacher of philosophy, he was unable to acquire a true understanding of Christian thought (*ibid.*).

He also mentions that he came to realize that Catholicism deserves special attention. The reason he gives is that Protestantism (evidently as he knew it) tends to turn away from the objective world of reality, and that it stresses the interior world and subjective faith alone, whereas Catholicism unites the supernatural spiritual world with the natural world, and through this unity and interpenetration it faces history (x:11). The discussion within Protestant theology that is connected with names such as Schweitzer, Wrede, Hermann, Barth, especially the discussion on the relationship of Paul's image of Christ and the historical Jesus, was obviously difficult for him to grasp (x:11ff). Thus he finally ends up by saying, "I do not believe, please help my unbelief." (x:17)

Besides Tanabe's interior development we should also know how his own interpretation of absolute nothingness is to be understood. It is by action that we realize the absolute nothingness. A sentence taken from the last part of Tanabe's *Todesdialektik*, which was not translated for the *Heidegger-Festschrift*, could serve as a key:

> The Absolute is absolute nothingness, which, only by the practice of death-resurrection, in a moment, we can touch upon and participate in.[82]

All elements are important here:

The Absolute is absolute nothingness: In the last stages of his philosophical development Tanabe no longer considers absolute nothingness as a "negative principle," as he had done most of his life-time.[83] In this simple statement he is very close to Nishida.

by the practice: This points to Shinran's "gyo," exercise, practice, action, something which again has ethical overtones.

only: This shows that even at the end of his life he did not change his basic attitude towards the "Philosophy of self-awareness or self-consciousness" and every kind of mysticism.

death-resurrection: This concept is of utmost importance for Tanabe. It is related to the "great death" in Buddhism and to resurrection in Christianity as well. And yet, also this concept remained ambiguous till the end. For neither death nor life can be considered as a concept which is understood only in one sense and not in another. It has been repeatedly pointed out that the death of his beloved wife played an important role in Tanabe's life.[84] It is a fact that the danger of death in our times was for him a motif to demand a "philosophy of death" rather than a "philosophy of life."[85] And yet, when we read his interpretation of a *koan* taken from the *Hekiganshu*, we realize that Tanabe's existential interpretation of death stems from Buddhism.[86] On the other hand, also here Tanabe claims again that he "learned most about the truth of a 'philosophy of death' from Christianity."[87]

But here immediately the question arises: What is the meaning of the historical moment of man's death? We are dying every day (cf. also 1 Cor. 15:31), and yet, what is the difference between our dying daily and the last moment where our historical being in this world ceases to be? Is it fulfilment or disaster, light or darkness, fate or action, or both? I think that the same antagonism which prevails between the philosophy of being and of nothingness is at work in the antagonism between the philosophy of life and of death. Therefore, it should be asked, first, what does life and death mean in Buddhism and only there, without making any comparisons; secondly, what does it mean in Christianity and in modern western philosophy; thirdly, what does it mean in the ordinary common sense understanding of everybody in the street? Then little by little a common understanding might grow.[88]

The same should be equally true with regard to the understanding of the resurrection. It is a fact that Tanabe uses fundamental terms of Christianity. However, he does it only after denying the central doctrines of Christian faith.

a) According to him God is not a personal God. Instead of that, Tanabe develops his idea of "absolute nothingness-qua-love" and the three-unity of love (God's love; love for God and love among men).[89]

b) He denies the resurrection of Christ as it is understood in Christianity:

"The belief in the resurrection of Christ, in the way as it is determined in the orthodox articles of the faith of the Church so far is only the tradition of a miracle myth which is totally incompatible with natural sciences and history; in order to purify it and to make the mediatory action of reason possible, dialectic becomes necessary."[90]

"Resurrection from death is not an objective incident which occurs directly to the dead person himself, but rather a mutual, mediatory situation which is perceived indirectly by the living person who has been convinced within himself of the fact that he is worked upon by the dead person bound to him by love."[91] Tanabe tries to demythologize Jesus of Nazareth by eliminating all Pauline elements; after all, it was Paul who in chapter 15 of the first Epistle to the Corinthians made the resurrection of Christ the starting point of Christian preaching and faith. Christ's action as saviour is gradually reduced to the action of the Bodhisattva, but since "the humanity of Christ the Son of God . . . gradually became de-emphasized," he seems to become less than that.[92] For, the special characteristics of a Bodhisattva are described as follows:

> . . . while possessing the qualifications for becoming Buddha as the highest existence of man, they forego the fulfilment of this; and in order to

cause the attainment of Buddhahood first among other creatures, they repress their own Buddhahood: finally on this behalf, they push forward directly and unfeelingly on the borderline of good and evil, as a means of grace, even such actions as are said to be evil, which actions become obstacles to their immediate attainment of Buddhahood; and they practice mediatingly, only under conditions of complete self-denial and self-restraint, the absolute-nothingness-qua-love of the resurrection from death.[93] Since a Bodhisattva possesses the Buddha qualities, it of necessity must rise, facing the highest existence of man. However, in order to make the realization of absolute-nothingness-qua-love its main attribute, on the contrary by ascending-qua-descending, it describes a circle and repeats a whirling motion. The realization of life is transformed into death, and the courageous practice of death becomes whirling by causing the breakthrough to a life of resurrection; moreover, usually by life and death aspects being mutually transformed, the whirling motion is everywhere repeated. In order to establish the transforming mediation of life and death, first the fulfilment and fruition of life are necessary.[94]

c) Christian eschatology is rejected. It is worth noting that Tanabe is evidently not aware of the fact that eschatology tries to give the Christian answers to the questions on the fulfilment of man, society and universe. After all, in Christian eschatology Tanabe could have found the true Christian teaching on death and resurrection and on another favorite idea, the *"communio sanctorum* (communion of saints)."[95]

After these critical remarks we might add that, in spite of all this, Tanabe, in all that he affirmed positively came much closer to the true Christian doctrine than he himself probably knew. His understanding of death-resurrection deserves a much more detailed comparison with modern Christian thought on the subject, as for instance Catholic theology on the Paschal Mystery than can be accorded within the scope of the present paper. Even then disagreement will not totally disappear, but it might well be that what he considers Buddhist, is much more Christian than he himself realized.

In a moment, we can touch upon it and participate in it: This sentence indicates again that Tanabe's understanding of absolute nothingness is different from Nishida's point of view. There will be very few that practise the *zazen* meditation who will still agree with expressions like "touching," "participating," "momentarily."

There is another sentence in the same article where Tanabe speaks of the relationship between two people. According to him it is the species by which two human being are at the same time united and yet their difference becomes possible. And then he adds:

> Both must be mutually irreplaceable (German: *unvertretbar,* Japanese *kokan fukano*), and at the same time, by their existential character which is "almost the same" (German *beinahe das Selbe,* Japanese *hotondo doitsu*), interpenetrate each other . . . [96]

Reflecting on this text, Tsujimura comes to the conclusion that, for Tanabe, this statement is not only valid for the relationship of two individuals, but also for "absolute nothingness-qua-love," "the practice of death-resurrection," "the existential community" etc. This, however, leads to the other conclusion that there are still shades of the rejected standpoint of life (alone) or, we might say, of dualism which seems to be incompatible with a truly Buddhist point of view.[97]

In fact, it seems that here also Tanabe is much closer to a Christian understanding of the encounter and final union of God and man than to a Buddhist point of view. However, as we said before, it is the tragedy of Tanabe to remain somewhere between without satisfying either side completely.

In summary:

Tanabe started out with a keen interest in the philosophy of science and mathematics. He studied Kant and like him, insisted on the primacy of practical reason. Throughout his lifetime he never lost his basic distrust of every kind of mysticism[98] (See only his Todesdialektik: Hegel is close to speculative-emanatistic mysticism;[99] a sentence like Leibniz's *praedicatum inest subiecto* could be misinterpreted as a mystical statement,[100] etc.). Against Kant he only remarks that his criticism has to be carried out as *absolute* criticism, i.e. reason itself has to be included: "reason must sink deep into its own ground of nothingness."[101]

The second step in his development is marked by his own criticism of Hegel, which was done after his return from studies in Germany. Besides the influence of Buddhism, it was Hegelian dialectic which led Tanabe to a richer development of his own use of the enigmatic *soku*. In his final stages, *soku* became a kind of key to the solution of many problems.

Soku is usually translated *qua*. However, *qua* is only a partial answer to the question about the meaning of *soku*. *Qua* expresses a certain correspondence between two terms or the respect under which a term is considered. The correspondence could be total so that the two terms express identity and thus become interchangeable. A famous example for this kind is the Buddhist phrase *shiki soku ze ku ku soku ze shiki,* "Form and color, that is emptiness; emptiness, that is form and color." Or the correspondence could be partial, stressing only one respect under which the first term is to be considered; in this case, the terms and the order of the terms do not become interchangeable.

In Tanabe's work we, of course, also find instances of the first kind. However, it seems safe to say that there is in it a strong tendency to the second type. And even if some of the examples we give below could be interchanged, it is still interesting to realize that Tanabe, in fact, does not do it, or only very seldom.

Cf. e.g. the use of the following phrases:

"(absolute) nothingness qua love,"
"the great 'no' qua the great 'compassion,'"
"absolute *tariki* qua *jiriki*"; "absolute 'self-power' qua faith of 'other-power'";
"absolute 'other-power' qua practical faith in 'self-power,'"
"negation qua affirmation" etc.; also the relation of "going and returning."[102]

This again confirms the thought that Tanabe is aiming at a unity which is "almost identity," a union which is primarily reached by action, which is close to, what we might call, moral action. The double aspect of his basic expressions are at the same time his strong point and his weak point. They encourage people, who understand him, to a high form of life which is selfless and dedicated to human society.

However, we realize at the same time that the root of Tanabe's understanding differs from the understanding of Zen Buddhism and the Middle Path ideology. It leads rather to a revival of the habit of *muga* (anatta), i.e., to the denial of the *atman,* the ego, than to Nagarjuna's idea of *sunya.* Consequently, Tanabe shows also far less understanding for and interest in the negative theology of Christianity than Nishida. Nothingness is not another term for the final ineffable, incomprehensible, supra-categorical reality, but on the contrary, something closer to what Takeuchi later on calls "the place of encounter." However, since by his love man in his finitude is unable to add anything to God's infinite essence, he can reach God only indirectly by loving his fellow men; thus, by participating in and cooperating with God's love toward man. And this is, according to Tanabe, the only possible attitude man can take toward God.

We thus reach the conclusion that the attitudes of Nishida and Tanabe are basically different. It must be that for both of them the final answer to man's search for truth and happiness is absolute nothingness, the Beyond of the opposition of being/(relative) nothingness; it is an answer which is undoubtedly meant to be positive. However, the interesting fact is that there two "types" of absolute nothingness seem to appear. For I do not think that the difference between Nishida and Tanabe can be reduced to different methods of reaching absolute nothingness; I rather think that the interpretations of the final reality itself differ.

In a way this is confirmed by the teaching of the most important disciples and successors of both Nishida and Tanabe; I should like to allude briefly to Nishitani and Takeuchi. Like Nishida and Tanabe, Nishitani is a member of the Japanese Academy. Since his retirement from Kyoto University in 1964, he teaches at Otani University in Kyoto, a university which is affiliated with the Jodo Shinshu Sect. Although his family also belonged originally to the Jodo Shinshu Sect, his personal commitment stands with the Rinzai Zen Sect. He is also director of the International Institute for Japan Studies in Nishinomiya, an institute which stresses the interchange of thought with the western world.

In the chair of philosophy of religion, Nishitani was followed by Takeuchi, who, unlike Nishitani, is more committed to Tanabe and, like his teacher, follows personally Amidism rather than to Zen Buddhism. Thus both Nishida and Tanabe have their authentic interpreters today in Kyoto.

B Nishitani Keiji (1900-)

Nishitani described his own philosophical approach recently in an article *My Philosophical Starting Point.*[103] From the very beginning he admits his inclinations toward Buddhism, particularly in the form of Zen.

Before he studied under Nishida, he already felt attracted by Nietzsche[104] and Dostojewski,[105] Emerson and Carlyle, Holy Scripture and Francis of Assisi, Natsume Soseki (1867-1916), and the two famous Zen masters Hakuin (1685-1768) and Takuan (1573-1645). He discovered in himself what Buddhism calls the "great doubt," a doubt which is the only way to enlightenment. He studied nihilism in its various forms, its rejection of ethics and religion, and felt himself impelled to work toward a conquest of nihilism.

The problem of evil has occupied him up to the present time.[106] He studied German idealism and translated Schelling's work on freedom.[107] He paid special attention to the mysticism of the western mystics, in particular of the German mystics, to the women mystics of the Middle Ages, to Eckhart and his disciples, to Böhme. He wrote a short history of mysticism, and an answer to Otto's *Die West-östliche Mystik,* and called it *God and Absolute Nothingness.*[108] In later years he worked on the relationship between the sciences, religion and philosophy and on the relationship of eastern and western cultural influences. His study under Heidegger in Freiburg Br. before World War II is manifest in his work. After his first great work *The Philosophy of Fundamental Subjectivity* (1940), his work *What is Religion?* (1961) is his most important publication, and it is at the same time one of the most brilliant philosophical works Japan has seen for years.[109]

Nishitani is a demanding thinker. He expects much from his readers who are supposed to be acquainted with German philosophy, Buddhist and Zen thought and somewhat with Protestant dialectical theology. Since Nishitani avoids open criticism and reduces the scholarly apparatus to a minimum, it is often difficult to check his sources. However, without going into a detailed study here, some few conclusions can be drawn about his basic point of view, whether we take as background his last work or some of his very comprehensive articles:[110]

1) By calling the final reality mostly "emptiness" and not "absolute nothingness," it is clear that Nishitani distinguishes it a) from any form of nihilism, b) from Tanabe's understanding of absolute nothingness, and c) that he consciously returns to the *sunya* idea of Nagarjuna, i.e., the interpretation which nothingness also receives in the Zen tradition.

2) The famous *soku* is far less important for Nishitani than for Tanabe. Or, to say it more exactly, *soku* is used where it is evidently meaningful, namely in the Zen interpretations of the relationship between the finite and the infinite, phenomenon and reality, time and eternity, personal and impersonal, etc. On the other hand, it is avoided where—maybe—similar things are compared but the relationship is less evident, as e.g. in the relationship of things and explanations eastern and western. In this last point, Nishitani is more reluctant to draw conclusions that might not yet be mature. It is a gratifying experience to see that basic concepts like truth, faith, etc., whose important differences in eastern and western understanding are very difficult to indicate in a western language, are never confused in Japanese and clearly expressed in their proper terms, be they original eastern or Japanese terms or be they translations of western terms.

3) Nishitani never hides his personal commitment in his work. As we repeatedly stated before, we do not see any valid reason against this kind of attitude, since it is very well possible that somebody, though personally committed to a certain *Weltanschauung,* thinks as a philosopher.

4) With regard to Christianity, Nishitani admits certain trends, especially in German mysticism, which go into the direction of the true absolute nothingness. However his understanding of the doctrine of creation as well as his suspicion that Eckhart has to be considered a heretic from an orthodox point of view,[111] prevents him from dealing more closely with the ordinary main-stream theology which, in its best representatives, displayed a profound concern for negative theology throughout the centuries.

A fruitful discussion on the relationship between God and absolute nothingness or emptiness should start from the following premise: Whenever there is something possible which is beyond "God" or which includes "God" (in the sense of the well used Japanese concept *"tsutsumu"*=to wrap up), then that which had been called "God" before, was not God at all. For, whatever detailed explanations we might add, *ex definitione* there cannot be anything which is either more beyond or more within, either in greater distance or in greater nearness and which at the same time is *not* God.

On the other hand, I think that, taking Nishitani's book *What is Religion?* as a starting point for a dialogue, we would be astonished how well many of his basic insights match Christian insights. Moreover, I would expect that the distinctive line would not be drawn between different attitudes towards the relationship of philosophy/religion/sciences (here most probably at least Catholic theology could agree more heartily with Nishitani's arguments than he himself might expect), but between the two fundamental religious attitudes which work at the bottom of Buddhism and Christianity. The final issue against Nishida will probably stand its right also here.

5) Another strong point of Nishitani's philosophy is his affinity to religious practice. Nishitani is connected with

several groups of scholars who try to combine religious, especially Zen practice, with solid study. Unless one is aware of this fact, the danger of underestimating the spiritual impact of Japanese philosophy will be great, especially with foreigners.

In this connection the name of Hisamatsu Shin'ichi (1889-) has to be introduced. He too graduated from Kyoto University and became a disciple of Nishida. However, following Nishida's advice, Hisamatsu not only studied philosophy but also began to practise Zen. Consequently, he dedicated his life to the study and the practise of Zen. Throughout practically the whole time Nishitani taught at Kyoto University (except for a few short interruptions between 1935 and 1964), Hisamatsu taught Buddhism at the same university. Hisamatsu has written repeatedly on Oriental nothingness. A very carefully prepared English translation of an article "The Characteristics of Oriental Nothingness"[112] is extremely helpful in understanding both Nishitani and Nishida.

The astonishing fact is that Hisamatsu determines nothingness not only in a merely negative manner, stating what it is not, but that he goes on and tries to delineate it in a positive way. This done in six steps:

1) "The 'not a single thing' nature of Oriental Nothingness means that as regards that which is generally said 'to be,' there is in and for Oriental Nothingness not one single such thing" (II,76).

"Nothing whatever wherever being Myself and Myself being nothing whatever wherever is Oriental Nothingness" *(ibid.)*.

2) It is "like empty space" (II,80), but "it is not the same as empty-space, which has neither awareness nor life. Oriental Nothingness is the One who is 'always clearly aware.' Therefore it is called 'Mind,' 'Self,' or the 'True Man'" (II,82). It is without obstruction, omnipresent, impartial, broad and great, formless, pure, stable (without beginning and without end), the voiding of being and the voiding of Void, without that which is obtainable (cf. II,80f.83-85).

3) It is Mind-in-Itself: It is "in no sense inanimate like empty space. It is living. Not only is it living, it also possesses mind.

Nor does it merely possess mind; it possesses self-consciousness." (II,86)

"The true Buddha is not without mind, but possesses mind which is 'without mind and without thought,' is not without self-awareness, but possesses an awareness which is 'without awareness'—an egoless ego, is not without life, but possesses life which is ungenerated and unperishing." (II,87)

4) It is Self: "Speaking in terms of 'seeing,' this Mind is the 'active seeing' and not the passive "being seen' . . .

But when I say here that this Mind is 'active,' I mean that this Mind does not obtain as object, but obtains as subject. It does not mean that such a Mind is simply the aspect of 'the active' in separation from 'the passive.' In this Mind there is no duality of active and passive." (II,88)

5) It is the completely free subject (II,91).[113]

6) It is "creative" (II,94ff).

Statements like these are, in fact, all based on Buddhist texts. They are all the more surprising because, in a way, the famous transcendentals of classic western philosophy evidently could be applied to this understanding of Oriental nothingness. And yet, we should be rather hesitant until we know for sure that the translation means what it says.

On the other hand, after this brief indication of the theses of Hisamatsu we feel sure enough to repeat once more that evidently even absolute nothingness admits more (positive) interpretationsthan the first impression might concede. And this, too, explains why the issue of absolute nothingness is not a closed issue not only between East and West, but also among Japanese scholars.

C Takeuchi Yoshinori (1913-)

Finally I should like to indicate the direction of Takeuchi's thought. He is the son of Takeuchi Yoshio, who is a well-known authority on Chinese thought and is also a member of the Japanese Academy. He is a Buddhist priest of the Jodo Shinshu sect. Besides a great number of articles, among them quite a few in English and German,[114] he published a book *The Philosophy of the Kyo-g yo-shin-sho.*[115] In his earlier publications he deals especially with the beginnings of Buddhism, Buddha's search for awakening, etc.[116] His historico-philosophical studies of the fundamental Buddhist insights and concepts thus enable him to broaden the platform from which he develops his ideas about absolute nothingness. In his own development undoubtedly Tanabe played an important role. I presume that his interest in Hegelian philosophy dates back to the days when he studied under Tanabe. For him, of course, Zen is only one possible interpretation of the basic insight of the Buddha. So far he has proposed rather his own positive solution which is found in Amidism. In the future he, too, will have to deal with the question whether Zen is able to integrate Amidism or, vice versa, Amidism is able to integrate Zen, or whether both remain irreducible standpoints in their own right; it is the question which Tanabe left unsolved.

In recent years Takeuchi taught, as visiting professor, at the University of Marburg, Germany and at Columbia University in the USA. In this way he came in contact with leading philosophers and theologians of the West like Jaspers, Tillich, Heiler, Benz, Bultmann and others. Thus the dialogue and the encounter between East and

West, Buddhist and Christian world, became a burning question in his own philosophy. Actually, encounter is one of the keynotes of his philosophy.

Tanabe had stressed the Bodhisattva way. It consisted in absolute-nothingness-qua-love, in dying to oneself in order to resurrect for the others. It is especially the teaching of Jodo Shinshu on compassion (which is not exactly the same as Christian charity) which awakens in man a deep feeling for his neighbor and even for his enemy, (as Takeuchi with Tanabe stresses).[117] And thus again the gratifying side of absolute nothingness appears.

Absolute nothingness is the place of encounter. Actually, Takeuchi goes one great step beyond Tanabe by stating that God is absolute nothingness and being-itself. His idea of absolute nothingness appears clearly in his articles on Nishida and Tanabe, and especially in the article *Buddhism and Existentialism. The Dialoguebetween Oriental and Occidental Thought,* from which we quoted before.[118] He, too, does not stress the affinity between German mysticism and Japanese nothingness; he rather thinks:

> The closest approximation which Western thought offers to our Oriental view is, I believe, the Hegelian notion of "absolute negativity" or "negation of negation." In Hegel, however, due to the primacy of the universal and objective side of his *"Begriff"* (concept), the dialectic of absolute negativity does not express its genuine character as the action of the subject, and so it is bereft of the "passion of inwardness". . . .[119]

Other western authors who could help the understanding of westerners are, besides Tillich, Heidegger and Bergson.[120] They could, therefore, serve as a first initiation to Takeuchi's thought.

And then he puts the question which, in this way, nobody before had asked explicitly:

> How are being-itself and absolute negativity related in God or in the Absolute?[121]

His answer is decided and clear:

> God is at once Being-itself and Absolute Nothingness. It is understandable that I prefer the latter designation, because Absolute Nothingness as Absolute Negativity (that is, the negation of negation) at the same time implies the former, the affirmative.[122]

Two remarks should be added here:

1) In a footnote to the text quoted above, Takeuchi describes his own understanding of the Buddhist roots of absolute nothingness:

> The Absolute Nothingness in early Buddhistic terminology is Non-Self *(anatman).* It is the demand to transcend the God of Brahmatman

mysticism. In Upanishadic mysticism by means of mystical union our finite being participates in Being-itself; in the ultimate fact of our being, our finite self is identical with the Self of Universe. From the Buddhist point of view, this *atman* doctrine is the attachment of our heart, in the subtlest abstraction, to metaphysical theses. When this last barrier is removed by means of 'neither/ nor,' or through thoroughgoing negativity of anxieties—anxiety of non-being, meaninglessness, and sin—non-self (in a negative sense) converts to Non-Self. Therefore, Non-Self is the perfect form of detachment of our heart; so far as it is one's beloved, what belongs to one's self *(atmiya)* should be entirely rejected, even to this last sublime form of Being-itself.It is characteristic of Buddhism that this detachment is regarded as the purest form and the efflorescence of religious love.[123]

2) The answer is given in concordance with Tanabe's philosophy. For, although Tanabe himself never drew the conclusion as explicitly as Takeuchi the latter thinks that Tanabe, in his philosophy of metanoetics, was "successful in bringing into unity, according to his unique way of thinking rooted in his own experience, the innermost cores of Christianity and Buddhism."[124] This last statement is evidence enough for the seriousness with which Takeuchi himself considers the religious attitudes of Buddhism and Christianity.

With regard to Christianity, this can be further demonstrated from his attempts to reserve a place for the fact of an historical revelation in Christianity.[125] The only question is whether the total substance of both sides can be kept intact without sacrificing some fundamental points on the one side or the other. From a Christian point of view, it is e.g., hardly satisfying to call sin "the awareness of the shock of non-self,"[126] or to state about God:

> God as being-itself is the ground of all finite beings, but the *ground of this ground* is His foreground (that is, this real world). Therefore God *must* come to this world every time as an action of *revelation* of His entirety of Being-itself.[127]

Or on the same page:

> If we were to *transcend* the personal God (trinity of God), it would not be toward Being-itself, but rather toward Absolute Nothingness. The concept of Godhead or Being-itself as *standing behind* the trinity of God arises, according to my view, from misunderstanding the personal God as the God of deism. *(italics mine)*

Some other questions which need further clarifications are connected with problems like time/eternity and the three "times" of past/present/future. Takeuchi stated:

> . . . It will not be unreasonable to think that the point of divine-human encounter is located in the *hic et nunc* of religious awakening. Our existence in the world is just a point within the vast ocean of infinite time and space. It does not matter where it is located in the commonly accepted time

reckoning. It may be located in the past or the present or the future. As a happening of the past, it becomes a historical revelation (Christianity); as that of the present, it is the "eternal now" (Christian mysticism and Zen Buddhism); as that of the future, it elicits eschatological expectations (Christianity and Amida Buddhism).[128]

The question here is whether it is really possible to say that human existence "may be located in the past or the present or the future." Moreover, it is extremely interesting to realize that Christianity is connected with all three phases of history, whereas Buddhism is either facing the present (Zen) or the future (Amidism). It could however be that this concept of time differs from the concept of time used in Zen Buddhism. And then it is significant that it is said that questions like the following cannot be answered by man:

> Why is it I and not you? Why is it here and not there? Why now and not tomorrow or yesterday? or the reverse?[129]

It is true, they cannot be answered by man. But the question remains whether it does not have any *positive* importance that it happened to me and not to him, now and not tomorrow.

On the other hand, there are statements which show that Takeuchi, though being a Buddhist himself, comes very close to a true Christian understanding in various points, e.g. where he talks about the "absolute otherness."

> . . . the absolute otherness which comes directly from above to this relative world, in spite of its transcendent character, does not decline to be the *Umgreifendes* that envelops the relative—the correlation of the world and the self—within it.[130]

In fact, we might look forward with great expectation to the publications of Takeuchi. We will then have them at hand for careful study. The same holds true for the publications of Nishitani and those who, like him, follow Nishida and Zen Buddhism.

CONCLUSION

I should like to close the consideration on absolute nothingness by referring to the *Gespräch von der Sprache* ("From a Dialogue on or of the Language"—"between a Japanese and someone who asks questions") which Heidegger published in his book *Untermegs zur Sprache* ("On the Way to the Language"). During the long study behind us we constantly felt how difficult the dialogue on the most central questions of human existence can be.

Often enough words and concepts which are supposed to serve as means of expressions really prevent us from true insights, and this is especially true in the case of translations. Words either fit only partially, or they are used without relation to their original *Sitz im Leben* and are, therefore, used with different emotional connotations; or they are used as attempts to express realities which can-

not be expressed before their context (cultural, religious, psychological, emotional etc.) is explained or even ina certain sense experienced. And yet, we should still like to express what cannot be expressed. And if it is called emptiness, eyes and ears have to be trained in East and West so that they are able to see the invisible, and "to listen to the sound of the one hand,"—which is again nothing but a symbol. Maybe there are already too many words used in the dialogue, and too many which do not fit.

Realizing this we could draw two conclusions, either to become desperately silent (but this would not be creative), or to use words, but slower and with greater care.

And this I learnt from Heidegger's dialogue which I mentioned before. In the dialogue, after all, very few words are used and even fewer are taken from their natural ground. Four (or five) Japanese words are introduced, and they are well chosen: *iki—iro—ku—kotoba (kota).*

Three of them are in a way described.

"Iki," says the Japanese, *ist das Wehen der Stille des leuchtenden Entzückens* ("*Iki* is the blowing of the quietude of shining delight." or "the stir of silence in illuminating ecstasy").[131]

"*Iro* meint mehr als Farbe und das sinnlich Wahrnehmbare jeder Art. *Ku,* das Offene, die Leere des Himmels, meint mehr als das Übersinnliche." (*Iro* means more than color and all things open to our senses. *Ku,* the openness, the emptiness of the sky, means more than 'that beyond the senses.')

And *kotoba,* the Japanese word for "language," means literally "Blütenblätter, die aus *Koto* stammen," "Petals which originate from *Koto.*"

I do not dare to judge whether Heidegger's interpretation of *koto* is acceptable to Japanese scholars. He calls *koto* "das Ereignis der lichtenden Botschaft der hervorbringenden Huld," "the event of the light spending message of creative grace."[132]

Four words, maybe five. They all lead to a depth where human words end, and where the realization of the inexhaustible depth may end in a loud silence. Western people are said to be searching again for the sources of silence and for the inexpressible depth of their own existence in the rich experiences of eastern tradition. On the other hand, it might be that eastern people have to learn again the respect for the single word which is not indifferent to its true meaning. There must be an encounter of silence with the word, and then we both might realize that it is the word which uses us human beings as messengers.

NOTES

[1] See W. Leibrecht ed., *Religion and Culture: Essays in Honor of Paul Tillich,* New York, 1959, p. 292. See also

Takeuchi, "Hegel and Buddhism," *Il Pensiero*, 1962, VII, No. 1-2, pp. 5-46; also Abe Masao, "Buddhism and Christianity as a Problem of Today," *Japanese Religions*, III, No. 2, pp. 11-22; No. 3, pp. 8-31 (here especially p. 13ff) and the discussion in the following issues; Shimomura Torataro, "On the Varieties of Philosophical Thinking," *Philosophical Studies of Japan*, 1963, IV, 1-21; Kishimoto Hideo, "The Immediacy of Zen Experience and its Cultural Background," *Philosophical Studies of Japan*, 1961, III, pp. 25-32.

[2] Paul Tillich, *The Courage to Be*, Yale University Press, New Haven, 1952, p. 40.

[3] See *Was ist Metaphysik?*, Frankfurt M. 5th ed., 1949, p. 38.

[4] See e.g. Ariga Tetsutaro, "A Christian-Buddhist Encounter," *Frontier*, London, 1961, IV, 50-54.

[5] Takeuchi, *Hegel*, p. 45.

[6] For a first survey on the life and works of Nishida, see Gino Piovesana, *Recent Japanese Philosophical Thought 1862-1962*, Enderle, Tokyo, 1963, pp. 85-122. Other introductions in English: Robert Schinzinger, *Nishida Kitaro, 1870-1945, Intelligibility and the Philosophy of Nothingness*, Tokyo, 1958 (evidently an English translation made from the German: *Nishida Kitaro, Die Intelligible Welt*, Berlin, 1943), pp. 1-65; Shimomura, in the English translation of Nishida Kitaro's *Zen no kenkyu, A Study of Good*, tr. by V.H. Viglielmo, Tokyo, 1960, pp. 191-217. This article is also contained in Shimomura's new Japanese book on Nishida: *Nishida Kitaro, hito to shiso*, Tokai daigaku shuppankai, Tokyo, 1965 (a very helpful study on Nishida, which replaces the earlier studies of Shimomura on his teacher); Noda Matao, "East-West Synthesis in Kitaro Nishida," *Philosophy East and West*, Hawaii, 1954-55, pp. 345-359; Takeuchi Yoshinori, "The Philosophy of Nishida," *Japanese Religions*, 1963, III, No. 4, pp. 1-32. Other useful studies by Nishitani Keiji and Mutai Risaku exist so far only in Japanese.

[7] See *Nishida Kitaro zenshu*, Iwanami, Tokyo, 1965, I, 6-7. With regard to our quotations note that we quote the first two volumes of Nishida's works according to the new edition (Iwanami, Tokyo, 1965), the other volumes according to the older edition (Iwanami, 1947-53). Translations are our own unless otherwise specified.

[8] *Zenshu*, 1, 173-174, 178 etc.; in the English translation (abbr.: *E*), pp. 162-163, 167. Our understanding of Nishida's conception of nothingness could be re-examined by comparing it with Nishida's concept of God. However, the latter cannot be fully dealt with inthis article.

[9] *Zenshu*, 1, 175; *E*, pp. 163-164.

[10] *Zenshu*, I, 99-100; *E*, pp. 88-89.

[11] *Ibid.*, p. 100; *E*, p. 89. The author likes to call attention to the fact that, according to Nishida, the encounter with God is basically an act of seeing. However, it is a fact that the Christian concept of divine revelation cannot be fully grasped if it is reduced to *"seeing* God," whereas it is, first of all, encounter with the *Word* of God. The one-sided interpretation of the encounter with the God of Revelation leads to an equally one-sided interpretation of Christian mysticism.

[12] See *Zenshu*, I, 189.

[13] *Ibid.*, pp. 189-190.

[14] *Ibid.*, p. 190; see also Nishitani Keiji, *Shukyo towa nanika*, Sobunsha Tokyo, 1961, pp. 76-78, 112-122.

[14a] *E*, p. III.

[15] For some guidance in reading Nishida, see Shimomura, *Nishida* (note 6), pp. 135-154, also on his Japanese, pp. 216-229. The most important translations are pointed out in Piovesana, *Recent Japanese*, p. 93.

[16] Several examples will be given later on. See also *E*, p. 181 (*Zenshu*, I, 192); "In the above-mentioned situation heaven and earth are merely one finger, and the myriad things are one body with the self . . ." (Nishida spoke before about the place "where we have lost even God" and stated that, according to Eckhart, it is there that we see the true God.) A similar expression "heaven and earth are merely one" appeared before, but there it cannot be recognized in the somewhat misleading translation, " . . . the universe is the only reality" (*E*, p. 28; *Zenshu*, I, 37). Another problem which deserves a detailed inquiry is the question from where Nishida took his philosophical terms. Among the Japanese philosophical terms, a good number has been created during the Meiji period. However, there are others like *jiko* (self), *jiga, ga* (ego), *muga* (non-ego), *genzen, batsugen, jikaku, u* (being) and *mu* (nothing), which have a long history behind them, and quite a few are of Buddhist origin. Recently Tsujimura Koichi applied the Buddhist term *shoki*, a Kegon term, as translation of Heidegger's *Ereignis*. A truly comparative study of terms like these with their western equivalents is highly desirable.

[17] Martin Heidegger, *Sein und Zeit*, 1927; H. G. Gadamer, *Wahrbeit und Methode* (Grundzüge einer philosophischen Hermeneutik), Tübingen, 1960.

[18] See *Tanabe Hajime zenshu*, Nishitani Keiji, Shimomura Torataro, Karaki Junzo, Takeuchi Yoshinori and Oshima Yasumasa ed., Chikuma shobo, Tokyo, 1963, IX, 4 (Preface to "Zangedo toshiteno tetsugaku").

[19] *Zenshu*, I, 42; *E*, p. 33. We should like to discuss the distinction between the moral and the religious sphere, as we find it throughout Nishida's work and, in a way, also in Nishitani's work, some other time. For Nishitani see his article "Shimpishugi no rinri shiso" in *Iwanami koza: Rinrigaku*, Tokyo, 1941, XIV.

[20] See Noda, "East-West Synthesis," p. 347. Note also here that what is called a (psychological) "motif" is not yet a (logical) "proof," and yet, it is correct to admit such a "motif."

[21] For an introduction see Heinrich Dumoulin, *A History of Zen Buddhism*, New York, 1963.

[22] See *Zenshu*, I, 407-409. The short article "Gutoku Shinran" was first published in a Festschrift in 1911, at the 650th anniversary of Shinran's death. Nishida mentions that, though his mother was a devout believer, he was neither a believer nor had he a profound knowledge about the religion of his family.

[23] See *Zenshu, bekkan*, I. All quotations are taken from there. Quite a few interesting texts of the diary and of the letters can be found in Shimomura Torataro, *Nishida Kitaro, hito to shiso*. Nishida's diary is of importance since it portrays vividly his life, his readings and interests, his friends. We find notes in German (actually for about six months he wrote only in German), English, French, which, however, was difficult for him (see p. 236), Latin and Greek. His reading lists include almost all important readings in East and West, Christian, Buddhist and Confucian Texts, philosophy and literature. He is well informed about recent publications, evidently to a great extent through his friends and disciples studying in Europe. Heidegger is mentioned as early as January 3, 1923, and another time on February 22, 1935, when he again orders some books. See *MN*, 1965, XX, 335-358.

[24] *Zenshu, bekkan*, I, 23-25.

[25] See Nishida's description of "pure experience," e.g. *E*, p. 33; *Zenshu*, I, 42.

[26] See also *Bekkan*, II, 55-58: "About My Religion," also Shimomura, *Nishida Kitaro, hito to shiso*, p. 53.

[27] It seems that he studied Heidegger for the first time when he wrote *The Self-Consciousness Determination of Nothingness*. At least here he quotes him. See *Zenshu*, VI, 165-179. However, it is not sure to what extent he understood Heidegger. See his argumentation on Heidegger's *Dasein* on p. 173.

[28] It is a well-known fact that Nishida had a special sympathy for Augustine till the end.

[29] As was mentioned before, in his studies Nishida did not restrict himself to Buddhism, but he studied also Confucian and Christian literature. A similar strong distinction between philosophy and religion seems to be held by Takeuchi Yoshinori; see the article mentioned in note I, p. 364.

[30] This expression is used by Nishida in his later period. Schinzinger, *Nishida*, pp. 49-64, translates it as the "unity of opposites." It stands as another name for "absolute nothingness."

[31] See *Zenshu*, IX, 56-57. "Only by absolute negation, man receives the true life. I say, already I do not live anymore, Christ lives in me (allusion to Gal. 2:20), and I say, after death I shall rise. True culture must be born from there. But I do not intend to speak here of religion. I do not argue from the standpoint of religious experience. I speak from a thorough logical analysis of historical reality."

[32] *Ibid.*, pp. 66-67.

[33] *E*, p. 189; *Zenshu*, I, 200.

[34] See the article of Shimomura, "Nishida Philosophy and the Japanese Language," in: Nishida (see note 6), in which he stresses the basic difference between western and eastern language structures. See also the interesting remarks on the Japanese language in Heidegger's "Aus einem Gespräch von der Sprache-Zwischen einem Japaner und einem Fragenden," published in his work *Unterwegs zur Sprache*, Pfullingen, 1959, pp. 83-155; Watsuji Tetsuro's chapter on the problem of the Japanese language and philosophy, *Watsuji Tetsuro zenshu*, Iwanami, Tokyo, 1962, IV, 506-551.

[35] Noda, "East-West Synthesis," p. 345.

[36] "Jikaku ni okeru chokkan to hansei" *Zenshu*, II, 3-350. *Fikaku* is one of the most difficult and at the same time most central terms of Nishida's philosophy. It is often translated "self-consciousness." Viglielmo uses "self-awareness." In Tanabe's "Todesdialektik" (in *Martin Heidegger zum 70. Geburtstag*, Pfullingen, 1959) the term is translated *Selbstgewahrnis*. The translation is correct if a) it is not taken as a merely psychological concept (for this the Japanese language has at least one other term: *jüshiki*, but also *jikoishiki*); b) if it means a *direct* awareness, excluding or transcending the object-subject relationship. I personally would prefer the translation "self-realization" which has both an ontological and a cognitive component.

[37] *Zenshu*, II, II; Noda translates *shimpi* with "mystery," which the author would prefer (p. 349), Takeuchi with "mysticism" (*Japanese Religion*, III, No. 4, p. 7).

[38] It seems that *watakushi* and *ware* or *ga* are used interchangeably.

[39] After reaching enlightenment, the disciple approaches his master. However, whether he tries to answer his master's question or not, his answer never expresses the experience adequately; it remains insufficient either way, and thus he will be beaten.

[40] See *Zenshu*, II, 271: "Contrary to knowledge, the will is always concrete, therefore, creative, 'elan vital.'"

[41] See Takeuchi, *Japanese Religions*, III, No. 4, pp. 18-23.

[42] See *The Blue Cliff Records (The Hekiganroku)*, translated and edited with commentary by R.D.M. Shaw, Lon-

don, 1961, pp. 31-32. The context reads like this, "'Sun-faced Buddhas, Moon-faced Buddhas,' The Five Sovereigns, The Three Emperors—What are these? For twenty years I have had bitter experiences. Often on account of these old fellows I have descended into the 'Green Dragon's Cave.' I cannot tell the depth of it. You, enlightened, robed monks, do not be careless about this."

[43] For a first description of the (logical) process of Nishida's thought which leads from the physical world through the world of consciousness to the intelligible world, or from being through relative nothingness to absolute nothingness, see *Zenshu*, IV, the chapter on *basho;* Noda, pp. 350-353; Schinzinger's commentary and translation of *The Intelligible World;* "Über Kitaro Nishida's Philosophie," *MN,* 1940, III, 28-39, one of the first articles on Nishida written in a western language and still worth reading.

[44] The Japanese expression *hyakushaku kanto sara ni ippo o susumu* is contained in the collection called *Keitoku dentoroku* which was composed in 1004.

[45] We realize here again that the insufficient notion of creation is one of the real stumbling blocks on the way to some kind of understanding of what people in the West mean when they speak of God. The insufficiency of the notion is partly due to the fact thatthe different ways of using the terms "creation/creative" often escapes attention. Moreover, frequently the study of notions like these is dogmatically restricted to the study of some authors who, for some reason or other, received fame in Japan and, therefore, are considered the legitimate spokesmen for Christian affairs. A more sober study of western *Geistesgeschichte* as *Geschichte* could lead to very important corrections of notions which now are handed on somewhat dogmatically.

[46] This is already one instance which stands against Tanabe's argument which we shall see further below.

[47] See note 9; for a discussion of the terms "beginning" and "end" see the articles "Anfang," "Ende" etc. in *Lexikon für Theologie und Kirche,* Freiburg, 1957, 2nd ed.

[48] Schinzinger (we quote from the English edition), p. 137; *Zenshu*, V, 182.

[49] *Ibid.,* pp. 137-138. The explanation must have been given to Schinzinger privately; it is not contained in V.

[50] *Ibid.,* p. 138; *Zenshu*, V, 182-183. The original is not so strong as the translation could suggest; it says only: "With regard to the landscape of religion, there remains nothing but to leave it to the religious person." At least here Nishida does not make the extremely interesting statement that "religious experience alone has the last word." See about this attitude Joseph Ratzinger, "Der Christliche Glaube und die Weltreligionen," in *Gott in Welt (Rahner-Festschrift),* Joh. Metz *et al.* ed., Freiburg, 1964, II, 287-305.

[51] In *Sources of Japanese Tradition,* compiled by Ryusaku Tsunoda *et al.,* Columbia University Press, New York, 1958, pp. 857-872; also *Zenshu,* V, 429-453.

[52] Schinzinger's third article on the "unity of opposites" belongs to this period; see *Zenshu,* IX, 147-222.

[53] During a recent scholarly convention, Prof. Ariga made the interesting remark that Nagarjuna and the Cusanus stand on the same logical standpoint, namely the Middle Path philosophy.

[54] Unlike the western terms "absolute-relative," the Japanese terms *zettai* (absolute) and *sotai* (relative) imply each other etymologically. Etymologically *zettai* is said with regard to *sotai* and is determined as being free, separated, cut off from *tai* (that which stands opposite). This object *tai* is not expressed in the western term "absolute."

[55] Topics of discussion would be also the relation of faith and experience, the influence of the theological conceptions of Barth, Tillich, Kierkegaard, the meaning of God's "free acts" (see *Zenshu,* XI, 398), the right understanding of Phil. 2 *(kenosis),* etc.

[56] See the first long article in *Zenshu,* VI, 341-427.

[57] *Tanabe Hajime zenshu.* We quote mainly according to the selection prepared by Tsujimura Koichi, *Tanabe Hajime, Gendai Nippon shiso taikei,* Tokyo, 1965, XXIII. The article on death-resurrection can be found there. See also "Memento mori," *Philosophical Studies of Japan,* 1959, I, 1-12, "Todesdialektik," in *Martin Heidegger zum 70. Geburtstag* (note 38), pp. 93-133. For the full text of "Philosophy as Metanoetics" *(Zangedo toshiteno tetsugaku)* see *Zenshu,* IX, 1-269. For a first introduction see Piovesana (note 6), pp. 145-158. Tanabe's philosophy is treated in special issues of *Tetsugaku kenkyu,* No. 489 (articles of Nishitani Keiji, Shimomura Torataro, Noda Matao, Muto Kazuo, Tsujimura Koichi) and *Riso,* No. 357 (1963, n.2). See also the introductions to several volumes of Tanabe's works, especially I, 473-487 (Takeuchi Yoshinori).

[58] "Nishida sensei ni oshie o aogu" in Tsujimura, *Tanabe Hajime,* pp. 341-363.

[59] *Ibid.,* p. 348.

[60] *Urazukeru* is a keyword of the Nishida philosophy. It is well used in connection with the Japanese kimono. In his very useful glossary, Schinzinger explains it as follows, "The Japanese kimono has a precious silk lining which shows at the ends. So the lining envelops, in a way, the kimono. Nishida uses this word 'lining' to indicate the progress from the natural world to the psychological world and finally to the intelligible world. The higher sphere is like an enveloping lining of the lower sphere. The natural world is 'lined' with the intelligible world. The innermost 'lining' is the all-enveloping Nothingness."

[61] Tsujimura, *Tanabe Hajime,* pp. 343-344.

[62] *Ibid.,* p. 345.

[63] *Ibid.,* pp. 348-349, 363.

[64] *Ibid.,* p. 347.

[65] *Ibid.,* p. 349.

[66] *Ibid.,* p. 351.

[67] *Ibid.,* p. 354.

[68] *Ibid.,* pp. 355-356.

[69] *Nishida zenshu,* IV, 5-6. The translation "things" for *mono* is not to be interpreted in the strictest possible sense.

[70] Tsujimura, *Tanabe Hajime,* p. 22.

[71] *Ibid.,* p. 25. The full text of the little poem which Tsujimura mentions can be found in both the German and the English book of Schinzinger. In English it reads, "The bottom of my soul has such depth; Neither joy nor the waves of sorrow can reach it." (see p. 27)

[72] See Zenshu IX. Preface and first chapter of *Zangedo toshite no tetsugaku.*

[73] Tsujimura, *Tanabe Hajime,* p. 266; further, chapters 6-8.

[74] It would be interesting to inquire whether or not the teaching on "egressus-regressus," which is strangely restricted to Hegel, is a true analogy to the doctrine on the Bodhisattva in Mahayana Buddhism. See Takeuchi, *Hegel,* pp. 38-40.

[75] Tsujimura, *Tanabe Hajime,* p. 265.

[76] Takeuchi, *Hegel,* p. 26.

[77] The same two sides can be observed in the use of other terms like "idealism," "nothingness," "truth," etc. In the early times of Japanese philosophy "idealism" was evidently once wrongly connected with the term "ideal." Thus two translations exist: *risshugi* from *riso* (ideal), and *kannenron* from *kannen* (idea). Tanabe uses both, as can be seen in the Japanese text on "Sei no sonzaigaku ka shi no benshoho ka", in Tsujimura, *Tanabe Hajime,* pp. 364-411. However, this difference disappears completely in the German translation of the *Heidegger-Festschrift* where both terms are translated "Idealismus." In the same translation we find the sentence, "Das Wahre muss ewig sein." The Japanese equivalent for "das Wahre" is not *shinri,* but *shinjitsu naru mono* (Tsujimura, p. 366, p. 367). This term, however, is close to the term *makoto* (sincerity), and includes both "truth, reality" and "sincerity."

[78] Takeuchi, *Hegel,* p. 45. Tanabe first studied mathematics and then worked on a philosophy of science and mathematics. Unfortunately he applies a good number of mathematical terms, especially "integral" and "infinitesimal," to his philosophical thought, which, however, obscure rather than clarify his argumentation.

[79] See his article, "Remarks on the Origin of Zen" (*Zengenshikai*), in Yamaguchi Susumu, *Buddhism and Culture* (Suzuki-Festschrift), Kyoto, 1960, pp. 7-24.

[80] *Heidegger-Festschrift,* p. 116. We leave the sentence untranslated because we are not sure which should be taken as the original, the first published German text or the Japanese text which was published after Tanabe's death. Both texts differ considerably, and in fact, naturally the Japanese text is by far more understandable than the German text. The latter is a) shortened (unfortunately even Tanabe's criticism on Heidegger has been cut out almost completely), b) inconsistent in its terminology, c) handicapped by the rather complicated style of Tanabe himself. Nevertheless, both texts have to be considered as original expressions and versions of Tanabe's thought. It is only unfortunate that a rather simple argument (see "Todesdialektik" with *Memento mori*) is obscured by its presentation.

[81] *Tanabe Hajime zenshu,* x, 6.

[82] Tsujimura, *Tanabe Hajime,* p. 409.

[83] See especially his "Shu no ronri" (The Logic of Species), reprinted in Tsujimura, especially pp. 172-173, 190-191, 195, 198.

[84] See Nishitani Keiji, "Tanabe tetsugaku ni tsuite", *Tetsugaku kenkyu,* XLII, 572-573, Tsujimura, p. 53.

[85] *Heidegger-Festschrift,* pp. 93-94, 98, 116, Tsujimura, 364-365, 369, 382.

[86] See *Philosophical Studies of Japan,* 1959, I, 4-10.

[87] *Ibid.,* p. 8.

[88] On the questions about life and death see also *Riso,* November 1963, No. 366.

[89] See "Kirisutokyo no bensho" in *Zenshu,* x, 53; also Muto Kazuo in his article on the Philosophy of Death in Tanabe, *Tetsugaku kenkyu,* No. 489, p. 633. For a correct evaluation of Tanabe's attitude towards Christianity this article is very important, see pp. 627-643.

[90] *Zenshu,* x, 35; see Muto, p. 635.

[91] *Philosophical Studies of Japan,* 1959, I, 7-8.

[92] *Ibid.,* p. 9, also Takeuchi, *Hegel,* p. 39. Actually, Christiantheology can learn much from the questions Tanabe asks.

[93] *Philosophical Studies of Japan*, I, 10. In the *Heidegger-Festschrift* Tanabe speaks about *das Bodhisattva;* the author wonders whether the neuter has been used on purpose (see p. 115).

[94] *Philosophical Studies of Japan*, I, 11.

[95] On the communion of saints see *ibid.*, I, 11-12; See Muto, pp. 635-637. *Heidegger-Festschrift*, pp. 111-122. Tsujimura, *Tanabe Hajime*, pp. 379-386.

[96] *Heidegger-Festschrift*, p. 122; Tsujimura, p. 386; also p. 58.

[97] See Tsujimura, p. 31, 58.

[98] *Ibid.*, p. 367.

[99] *Ibid.*, p. 367.

[100] *Ibid.*, p. 385.

[101] Takeuchi, *Hegel*, p. 26; see also Nishitani, pp. 550-551.

[102] See only the examples given by Tsujimura, pp. 44-46 or the example in the articles in *Philosophical Studies of Japan*, I, and in *Heidegger-Festschrift*, pp. 93-95: x *qua* y. However, as far as I know, Tanabe never says *shisoku-fukkatsu* but always *shifukkatsu*. The author wonders, therefore, whether the translation *Sterben qua Aufersteben* (see *Heidegger-Festschrift*, pp. 106-107, 110, 113, etc.) is legitimate, or why he never used *soku* in connection with death and resurrection.

[103] "Watakushi no tetsugakuteki hossokuten" in *Koza tetsugaku taikei*, Tanaka Michitaro ed., Jimbun shoin Tokyo, 1963, I, 221-230.

[104] See Nishitani Keiji, *Nihirizumu*, Kobundo, Tokyo, 1949.

[105] *Ibid.*, preface; see also *Dostoefuski no tetsugaku* (articles by Watsuji, Kosaka, Nishitani et al.), Kobundo, Tokyo, 1950.

[106] See especially his article "Aku no mondai" in *Shin rinri koza*, Tokyo, 1951, II.

[107] See his *Jiyu ishiron*, Tokyo, 1927, and his *Ningen teki jiyu no honshitsu*, Kyoto, 1948.

[108] See *Shimpi shisoshi*, Iwanami, Tokyo, ca. 1931-33; *Kami tozettaimu*, Kobundo, Tokyo, 1949; also his essay, "Shimpishugi no rinri shiso" in *Iwanami koza: rinri gaku*, Iwanami, Tokyo, 1951, XIV, and "Shukyo tetsugaku," *ibid.*, XV. The introductions of the two works mentioned first are of special importance. Otto's *Die West—östliche Mystik* (English translation *Mysticism East and West*, Meridian Books, New York, 1957) compared Eckhart and Sankara.

[109] *Kongenteki shutaisei no tetsugaku*, Tokyo, 1942, 3rd ed.; *Shukyo towa nani ka*, Sobunsha, Tokyo, 1961 (the first article of the book was translated into English, "What is Religion?" *Philosophical Studies of Japan*, 1960, II, 21-64). Nishitani calls his last work in a subtitle "Shukyo ronshu I," which indicates that further publications on the same subject are to be expected. So far the most important review on the book was written by Abein *Tetsugaku kenkyu*, No.483,pp.83-104. Abe also briefly discusses the relation of Nishitani to his two teachers, *ibid.*, pp. 86-88. Nishitani deals explicitly with Nishida in his work *Kongenteki shutaisei no tetsugaku*, pp. 433-481, where he makes his observations on the criticism of Yamauchi, Takahashi and Tanabe; also in an article "Nishida tetsugaku," in *Tetsugaku koza*, Tokyo, 1950, II, 191-218. On Tanabe see especially his Memorial Address on the occasion of Tanabe's death, "Tanabe tetsugaku ni tsuite," *Tetsugaku kenkyu*, No. 489, pp. 547-577. It is natural that at that time no open criticism was uttered; and yet, it is worth studying which points are stressed by Nishitani and what points remain untouched.

[110] See the important article on the religiosity of the Japanese, "Nipponjin no shukyoshin no mondai", *Kokoro*, 1957, X, No. 8, pp. 2-11; No. 9, pp. 10-24; also "The Problem of Myth," in *Religious Studies in Japan*, ed. by Japanese Association for Religious Studies, Tokyo, 1959, pp. 50-61; "Die Religiöse Existenz im Buddhismus, in *Proceedings of the IX International Congress for the History of Religions*, Tokyo, 1960, pp. 577-583; "Eine buddhistische Stimme zum Thema Entmythologisierung," *Zeitschrift f. Religions-und Geistesgeschichte*, 1961, XIII, 244-262, 345-356, "Shinran ni okeru 'toki' no mondai", in *Shinran zenshu (gendaigo yaku)*, Tokyo, 1958, X, 76-86; "Seio shiso to bukkyo" in *Koza: kindai bukkyo*, Kyoto, 1962, III, 7-32.

[111] Unfortunately so far Nishitani's interpretation of Eckhart and his disciples has received only very little attention from the side of Christian theology in Japan.

[112] See *Philosophical Studies of Japan*, 1960, II, 65-97. For a list of his publications see *ibid.*, p. 148. With regard to our question the most important work is *Toyoteki mu*, Tokyo, 1942, 6th ed.

[113] Hisamatsu's argument loses somewhat by his repeated polemic against Christianity, which shows little enlightenment with regardto this religious attitude. See *Philosophical Studies of Japan*, 1960, II, pp. 69, 88-89, 92-93.

[114] See note 1; also "Das Problem der Eschatologie bei der Jodo-Schule des japanischen Buddhismus und ihre Beziehung zu seiner Heilslehre," *Oriens Extremus*, Hamburg, VIII, 84-94.

[115] *Kyogyo shinsho no tetsugaku*, Tokyo, 1965, 2nd ed.

[116] See "Kyogyo shinsho ni okeru kyo no gainen", *Tetsugaku kenkyu*, No. 330, pp. 23-49; No. 335, pp. 30-52; No. 336, pp. 19-30; "Buddha no shutsudo," *Tetsugaku*

kikan, March 1947, No. 4, pp. 96-124; "Kyudo jidai no Buddha", *Tetsugaku kenkyu,* No. 395, pp. 1-17; No. 432, pp. 1-17; "Zaigo" in *Gendai bukkyo koza,* 1955, I, 69-86; "Engisetsu ni okeru shisaku no kompondoki", in *Yamaguchi hakase kanreki kinen Indogaku bukkyogaku ronso* 1955, pp. 136-144; "Engisetsu ni okeru soisei no mondai", in *Kyoto daigaku bungakubu goju shunen kinen ronshu,* 1956, pp. 153-181. These studies have to be considered as preparation for his later main work. Takeuchi is very interested in reinterpreting certain basic insights of original Buddhism in the light of modern thought and in applying them to our times.

[117] See *Tillich-Festschrift,* p. 315. ssq.

[118] *Ibid.,* pp. 292-295; also *Hegel,* pp. 5, 12-16, 30-32; *Japanese Religions,* III, 8-10.

[119] *Tillich-Festschrift,* pp. 293-294.

[120] See *ibid.,* p. 302.

[121] *Ibid.,* p. 293.

[122] *Ibid.,* p. 302. The statement is even clearer than the occasional statements of Nishida in this direction; see *Zenshu,* VI, 116; XI, 409: "Thus what we call our religiosity, does not spring up from ourself, it is the calling voice of *God or Buddha.*" (Italics mine).

[123] *Tillich-Festschrift,* pp. 364-365.

[124] *Ibid.,* p. 301.

[125] *Ibid.,* p. 315; *Japanese Religions,* III, No. 4, p. 23, 26.

[126] *Tillich-Festschrift,* p. 298.

[127] *Ibid.,* p. 304.

[128] *Ibid.,* p. 315, see also *Japanese Religions,* pp. 18-20.

[129] *Tillich-Festschrift,* p. 315.

[130] *Ibid.,* p. 314.

[131] Heidegger, *Sprache,* p. 141. The discussion on the meaning of *iki,* a difficult term to be translated, is in a way the background of the *Gespräch.* The notion belongs to the realm of aesthetics, but it transcends the subject-object-relationship. There are other expressions used: *das Anmutende* (140), *Anmut, Entzücken als Entziehen, Hinzücken* (for this reason the English "delight" might translate only one aspect of Heidegger's *Entzücken)* *Wink, Botschaft des lichtenden Verbüllens* (141). We might then use the Greek *charis* or the Latin *gratia* and realize that the notion finally leads to what Heidegger himself calls "a mystery."

[132] *Ibid.,* p. 144.

David Dilworth (essay date 1969)

SOURCE: "The Initial Formations of 'Pure Experience'," in *Monumenta Nipponica: Studies on Japanese Culture,* Vol. XXIV, Nos. 1-2, 1969, pp. 93-111.

[*In the following essay, Dilworth examines the idea of "pure experience" as set out in the writings of William James and, later, Nishida.*]

Nishida Kitaro (1870-1945), Japan's foremost modern philosopher, published his first major work, *A Study of Good,* in 1911,[1] the year after he became assistant professor of philosophy at Kyoto University. By all accounts, the leading and generative idea of that work was Nishida's concept of 'pure experience', a term he used throughout *A Study of Good* to develop his central notion of subjectivity which deepened in his later thought into an explicit Zen ontology of the 'self'. This first major work, which won Nishida immediate and lasting acclaim, was actually the fruit of a long spiritual odyssey by the time of its publication in his forty-first year. He had begun to teach philosophy in Kanazawa from about his twenty-fifth year, which was also the approximate time that he took up Zen practice. His Zen practices intensified in his twenty-seventh through twenty-ninth years. For over the next decade his intellectual and religious interests were intertwined in a continuing process of condensation of ideas which finally came into clear focus in *A Study of Good.*[2] The center of this focus was his notion of 'pure experience', which then became the foundation on which Nishida built his philosophical system over the next 35 years.

If we shift our perspective to a date 25 years after the appearance of *A Study of Good,* i.e. to the year 1936, when Nishida, now in his sixties, could look back upon so many years of trail-blazing in modern Japanese philosophy, we can read Nishida's own later evaluation of the leading idea of *A Study of Good.* In the preface to a third edition of that work in 1936 he wrote that *A Study of Good* now seemed like so many ideas of youth, and that, from his present viewpoint, he regarded it as a kind of psychologism. But he says that there was a 'deeper thought implicit in the back of my ideas'. This was 'the standpoint of pure experience' which became the central thread of his philosophy that progressively unwound into his later notions of 'absolute will' in *Intuition and Reflection in Self-Consciousness* (1917) and of 'the place/ field of Nothingness' in his key work, *From the Acting to the Seeing* (1927). His notion of 'place/field' in turn became the idea around which he wove his later concepts of the 'dialectical universal' and 'active intuition' from 1930 through 1936. He finally affirmed: 'The notion of a world of immediate or pure experience in this work [*A Study of Good*] became what I now consider as the world of historical reality. Indeed, the world of active intuition, the world of *poesis,* is truly the world of pure experience' (*A Study of Good,* p. 7; Preface to 3rd ed., 1936).

Therefore, in retrospect, Nishida himself linked the concept of 'pure experience' to every important turning point in his career. He even alludes in the 1936 preface to his youthful experience when, walking along the street in his Kanazawa high school days, he had a kind of dreamlike experience of considering all things as one 'pure experience' (p. 7). This statement was the echo of his remark in the preface of 1911 wherein he wrote that 'for a long time before that' he had the idea of 'explaining everything by taking pure experience as the only reality' (p. 4). In sum, the original contribution of *A Study of Good* lay in his presentation of the notion of 'pure experience'. Nishida actually wrote Section One of that work, entitled 'Pure Experience', after he had written Section Two ('Reality') and Section Three ('The Good'); but it was Section One which gave the whole work its leading idea.

Indeed, the philosophical ideas of *A Study of Good* were so integrally grounded in the concept of 'pure experience' that the contribution of the whole work would by and large vanish if we were to imagine the text without this concept elaborated in Section One. Apart from the notion of 'the standpoint of pure experience', *A Study of Good* would be a rather commonplace restatement of ideas of such authors as Berkeley, Spinoza, and especially of the German transcendentalism which was becoming the intellectual climate of philosophical circles in Japan at that time. The value of SectionOne, 'Pure Experience', was that it transfused these categories with a new life by the mediation of the newer empiricism and vitalism of James and Bergson, and by his own Zen-colored ideas. Nishida had been drawn to the more experiential emphases of James and Bergson in the five or so years before the final emergence of *A Study of Good* as a formal publication in 1911.

Therefore, it would also appear that whatever his personal experiences—his youthful intuition of a unifying pure experience, his active Zen practice, his concern for religious and aesthetic questions from his thirties, etc.—it was the fresh phenomenologies of experience found in the contemporary writings of James and Bergson which provided the key that unlocked the notion of 'pure experience' as a philosophical category for Nishida. The notion of pure experience, in turn, released in Nishida's thought the deeper streams of Japanese tradition, especially Buddhist, which were already being synthesized with the German transcendentalism fashionable in the philosophical world of Nishida's twenties and thirties. Thus the notion of 'pure experience' gave a richer phenomenological grounding to German idealism, but it did so by returning to the Buddhist heritage within Japanese tradition.[3] This new synthesis of contemporary and traditional thought was one reason for the impact which *A Study of Good* made on Nishida's times.

THE MEANING OF NISHIDA'S CONCEPT OF PURE EXPERIENCE

In view of the importance of the concept of pure experience in *A Study of Good* and for his whole career, the present study will present Nishida's formulation of this central idea as it was first expressed in Section One, 'Pure Experience', of that work. It will then compare the notion of 'pure experience' in James' *Essays in Radical Empiricism* in order to discover how Nishida used this important source of his own ideas for his own purposes.

Let us start with the first paragraph of Section One of *A Study of Good*. I have translated this text in full, and have included the original phrases which I feel are most worthy of note at this point. Nishida's text gives evidence of starting with a full position concerning the nature of experience:

> Experience means to know reality exactly as it is. It is to know by entirely abandoning the artifices of the self and by following reality. Since usually those who discuss experience actually conjoin thought of some sort to the idea, 'pure' means precisely the condition of experience in itself, without the admixture of any thinking or discrimination. For example, it means, at the instant of seeing color or hearing sound, the experience prior not only to thinking that it is the function of an externalthing or that it is my feeling, but before even the judgement of what this color or sound is, has been added. Therefore pure experience is identical with immediate experience. When one immediately experiences a conscious state of the self, there is still neither subject nor object; knowledge and its object are entirely one. This is the purest form of experience. Of course, the meaning of the word 'experience' is usually not clearly defined. Authors like Wundt even call knowledge which has been deduced on the basis of experience an indirect experience, and call physics, chemistry, etc. learning of indirect experience. However, not only can we say that these kinds of knowledge are not experience in the true sense. Even in respect to phenomena of consciousness, the consciousness of another person cannot be experience for the self; also in the consciousness of the self, even when a recollection of the past is present, once we judge it, it is no longer pure experience. True pure experience is not meaning in any sense. It is only present consciousness of reality in itself. (pp. 9-10)

This opening paragraph of *A Study of Good* has probably been the most often read paragraph of modern Japanese philosophy in the past half century.

The point of this initial statement is that experience must be defined as knowing events exactly as they are, without the addition of any thought or reflection. It is experience prior to conceptualization and verbalization. It should be noted that this apparently faultless statement has already begun to part company with James' idea of 'pure experience' in a fundamental way. For Nishida's main point is to empty experience of all content—i.e. intellectual content, meaning content—by a reductionism of all mental phenomena to present experiential immediacy, which is its 'purest' form. Or again, it is to find such experience already 'empty', prior to the superimposition of intellectual meanings. Although no explicit Zen overtones are evident in this text, the reader may well keep this nuance in the back of his mind in the ensuing analysis. For the

Japanese phrases which I have cited above may perhaps already suggest such a Zen nuance, as well as illustrating the particular power of the text.[4]

Nishida goes on to say that all mental phenomena are experiences of the present. Past memories and abstract thoughts are also thus reducible to facts of direct, i.e. pure experience. He quotes James' *Principles of Psychology* to the effect that even elements of conceptual representation are kinds of feelings in the present. He then refers to James' concept of the 'fringe of consciousness' as a further illustration of the inclusive immediacy of present consciousness. And alluding to, but not fully understanding, James' idea of 'the consciousness of various kinds of relations' (of *Essays in Radical Empiricism*), he argues that such consciousness, similar to sensation and perception, is to be included withinexperience itself (p. 10). Nishida's point remains the simple reduction of all kinds of mental phenomena to experiential immediacy itself. He does not here attempt to state that mental phenomena are conjunctive (and disjunctive) relations which constitute experience in a processive sense, so that meaning too is a kind of relation within the flow of experience, as James had implied.

Leaving this latter point for now, we may further note that Nishida goes on to factor experience in the following way. First, pure experience is simple, in the sense that 'no matter how complex it is, it is always one simple reality at that instant' (p. 10). Secondly, it is always original, or creative. Thirdly, it is identifiable with, but not limited to, the sphere of attention. For we can turn attention to 'a condition prior to the subject-object distinction' (p. 11). This latter point then becomes the burden of the longer ensuing argument. Indeed, 'the unity of subject and object' becomes the central idea of Nishida's whole career, which reached its culmination in an explicit Zen ontology of the 'field of nothingness' beyond subject-object distinctions. Nishida here states that the 'purity' of experience does not lie in the fact that it is simple and unanalyzable, but rather in the point of 'the strict unity of concrete consciousness' (p. 12). He gives certain examples of this point. The first is that of the 'consciousness of a newborn child', to illustrate the idea that consciousness is essentially one system, which develops and differentiates of itself, but never loses its primordial form of unified immediacy. The next three examples all refer to the state 'in dreams' further to define the same idea of consciousness as 'systematic development' which never loses its primordial oneness. Thus Goethe is said to have intuitively composed poetry in dreams. The case of dreams seems to exemplify 'self-development' in which the confused totality remains pure, and internal, perceptual experience.

Therefore, to Nishida, the concrete immediacy of experience did not preclude systematic development. On the contrary, a 'system of consciousness', like an organism (or a dream), 'differentiates and develops'. He cites James' doctrine of 'feelings of tendency', and the teaching of voluntaristic psychology that consciousness is 'the

form of the development of the will in the broad sense'. The latter especially bears witness to the unity of subject-object in the concrete immediacy of action (pp. 14-15). But throughout this elaboration of his train of thought, the former examples of the consciousness of the newborn child and of dreams, with emphasis on the 'condition of the chaos and non-distinction' of pure experience, continue to color the nuance of the text. These examples, as also that of the will (Nishida quotes Schopenhauer), are meant to reduce experience to a state prior to conceptualization. He even says that 'pure experience can be said to be the intuition of reality in itself, and not to be meaning'(p. 15). Meanings and judgements not only 'do not add any richness to the content of this experience in itself', but are the parts which are 'abstracted from original experience and poorer than it'. Thus 'dreams' but not 'meanings' have been chosen to exemplify the doctrine of pure experience at this juncture.

MEANING AND PURE EXPERIENCE

What, then, is the precise relation between meaning and pure experience? It was inevitable that this question should arise here. In one sense, Nishida's position up to this point is a mere phenomenalism of the present instant which, as Hume's analyses of perceptual immediacy suggest, 'tells no tales' about the rest of the universe. For an immediate instant of perceptual experience simply is what it is. But in another sense, Nishida's position may again suggest a kind of Zen phenomenalism which finds experience richest in its own subjective immediacy, after it has been 'emptied' of the noise of meanings or the illusions of words and ideas. The examples of the consciousness of the newborn child and of dreams well serve the purpose of 'telling no tales' about the world of conscious discrimination. Thus, while there is no explicit Zen references throughout the whole of *A Study of Good*—Nishida seems to have avoided them by conscious choice—the reader may well be motivated to ponder this nuance, and the issues involved, from this point on.[5]

To answer the above question of the relation between intellectual contents and pure experience, Nishida first makes the point that 'we cannot go outside the sphere of pure experience.' Therefore, meanings and judgements are born 'by the combining of present consciousness with past consciousness' (p. 16). In other words, they are 'included within the unity of a larger system of consciousness'. On the other hand, meanings and judgements imply the 'destruction' of the condition of pure experience. For they imply 'relations with others' or external relations in the sense of the relation between present and past consciousness. Such a 'relation' clearly threatens the phenomenalism of present immediacy developed to this point, by raising for the first time the question of externality.

We may recall that Hume, among other traditional empiricists, pointed out that the problem of relation could not be legitimately solved by superimposing any rational agents of unification. But having no psychology of the inner 'stream of consciousness' to work with, Hume was content to leave the problem of externality where it was, i.e. with his 'empirical' doctrine of the association of ideas. However, Kantian philosophy and post-Kantian idealism then joined together what Hume had torn asunder by transcendental *a priori* agents of unification. The result of this 'rationalistic' reaction to Hume's position was to de-realize (i.e. 'subsume')relations into a larger 'ideal immediacy'. Nishida has inevitably run into these same questions in his phenomenalism of present immediacy, as stated above. There is the impression that his doctrine also leans toward the nuance of emptying, i.e. de-realizing relations in an idealistic way, by way of reducing them back to the 'richness' of pure experience in its immediacy. To Nishida, 'meanings' and 'judgements' somehow destroy this primordial oneness of non-externality. In this sense, with possible Zen overtones, Nishida may already have been walking the idealistic path to solve the problem of discriminatory consciousness, i.e. the problem of 'relations' in epistemological form. Witness his statement that 'in the background of the consciousness of relations such as meaning or judgement there must be a unified consciousness *which causes these relations to be established*' (p. 16, stress added). This concept of 'in the background' or 'behind' is repeated throughout this section to serve the function of reducing one act of consciousness (infected with externality) to another consciousness (which is not), as the above text already illustrates. The former kind of consciousness is treated as an 'abstraction' from the latter; the latter causes the former to be established.

The concept of 'in the background' in fact became one of the key ideas running across Nishida's writings. To a philosopher committed to the idea of hierarchies of experiential concreteness—or of an absolute in terms of which 'richer' and 'richest' conditions of subjectivity can be formulated—such a concept may be a useful, even necessary, way of talking about experience. But the categories of 'abstract' and 'concrete' are precisely the problematic ones, as we shall see in the ensuing analysis.

To anticipate a later comment, it may be said that although Nishida here takes pains to say that there are only 'differences of degree' between intellectual contents and pure experience, or that 'they are two sides of the same consciousness' (pp. 16, 17), he lacks James' empirical sense of the *flow* of experience to state that intellectual contents are one kind of conjunctive, transitive relation constitutive of experience itself. Even intellectual contents, in James' position, are *irreducible* kinds of relational experience. They are accordingly not poorer, thinner, or more abstract editions of a richer immediacy behind them. Nishida's ambivalent attitude toward 'relations' seems to indicate that he had not fully grasped James' notion of consciousness defined in functional terms which he cited at the very beginning of *A Study of Good.* He does quote James in his second chapter, entitled 'Thought', of Section One, 'Pure Experience', on the point that thought too is a kind of experience. But his subsequent analysis remained that of describing pure experience 'in the background' or 'at the foundation' of

intellectual content. In Nishida's position, the background or foundation is always richer than the abstractions of discriminating consciousness.

Therefore, the main thrust of Nishida's argument retained the reductionistic nuance of the language of a 'larger system of consciousness' which overcomes the externality of relations. Nishida thus went on to define 'truth' functionally, i.e. in pragmatic terms, and declared that the ultimate goal of knowledge is practice (p. 23). But consciousness is always said to be 'essentially one system', whose natural condition is to 'develop and complete itself' (p. 24). Along this road to self-completion, 'contradiction and conflict' arise by the activity of 'reflection', so that the process of thought issuing in action means that it '*must attain to* the unity of pure experience' (p. 25, stress added). Thought is 'the state of incompletion' of pure experience; or again, the latter 'has the universal aspect, i.e. it *contains thought*'. From this juncture Nishida's description never departs from the Hegelian language of the 'concrete universal' (pp. 25-8), a point to which we shall again allude after comparing Nishida's position with that of William James. He concludes the chapter on 'Thought' by saying that pure experience and thought differ *relatively,* but not *absolutely* (p. 28).

Even in the next chapter, which takes up the question of the 'will' in relation to pure experience, Nishida follows the course of arguing that consciousness is a system of self-development in which thought and the will are relative functions of the Hegelian 'concrete universal' (pp. 28-36). Pure experience is always the absolute ground of this relativity of thought and the will. But the distinction between thought and the will is born in the instance in which subjectivity and objectivity are separated and which *has lost the condition* which is the unity of pure experience (p. 36, stress added). In this frame of reference, the will takes on a certain primacy over thought in that its actualization is always a concrete process of unification of actual and ideal, subject and object. Therefore, as he would develop in his next major work, ***Intuition and Reflection in Self-Consciousness*** (1917), the will is an 'even more fundamental conscious system than that of universal knowledge' (p. 39). For it overcomes the subject-object dualism in the immediacy of action. But an idealistic reductionism again appears in this implied hierarchy of values just cited. Instead of saying that both thought and will experiences are functional activities constitutive of experience, so that each kind of experience stands on its own base, Nishida's position has rather concluded to a doctrine of relative gradations of experience reducible to an absolute kind of immediacy, i.e. 'pure' experience. That the entire first section of 'Pure Experience' of *A Study of Good* ended with a chapter on religious intuition (under the title 'Intellectual Intuition' pp. 40-5), which culminated in the idea of the *primacy* of religious intuition *over* thought and the will, is another proof of this point.

In the final chapter of Section One of *A Study of Good,* Nishida returned to the point of the ultimate *Identität* (he cites Schelling) of pure experience. He returned also to the illustration of childlike immediacy which he says is operative at the basis of morality, art, and religion. This ultimate kind of 'intuition' is 'far richer and deeper' than perception in the usual sense (p. 40). Although we might note that, in terms of pure experience, there is no logical reason why 'intuition' should be richer and deeper than 'perception' the notion of pure experience has evidently been enlisted on the side of a hierarchy of values culminating in a kind of aesthetic religiosity which again suggests Zen overtones. Nishida indeed declares here that this religious intuition is connected with the 'true self', which is 'rest within motion', 'action and non-action'. We also find the unity of knowledge and of the will in such intuition, which 'transcends and is the foundation of both of them' (p. 45). If we recall that this Section One, 'Pure Experience', was actually written in sequence with Section Four, 'Religion', of *A Study of Good,* the coloration of Nishida's concept of 'pure experience' will be further suggested.

To summarize Nishida's initial formulation of the notion of pure experience, we see that his thought moved from a phenomenalism of present immediacy beyond subject-object distinctions to an articulation of the concrete universal of experiential systems. The values of wholeness and of immediacy dominate his analysis, which tends to see hierarchies of abstract and concrete functions within pure experience. Pure experience is the absolute ground of all relative systems, and the criterion of concreteness as well. This criterion became the leading concept throughout the whole of *A Study of Good,* which went on to develop a system around the three main headings of 'Reality' (Section Two), 'The Self' (Section Three), and 'Religion' (Section Four).

PURE EXPERIENCE IN WILLIAM JAMES

In September 1904, William James published an essay entitled 'A World of Pure Experience'. Feeling that philosophy 'was on the eve of a considerable rearrangement', James submitted in this essay a set of ideas in which he said 'for many years past my mind has been growing,' because of which 'rightly or wrongly, I have got to the point where I can hardly see things in any other pattern' (p. 40).[6] He called his own contribution 'radical empiricism', and offered it to the world 'as a possible ferment of new growths or a nucleus of new crystallization'. His doctrine was tentatively put forward at this time, but it grew into a series of articles later collected into the volume *Essays in Radical Empiricism,*[7] which was to be a distinct contribution to the history of philosophy. It became the point of departure for new growth and vigorous debate among such diverse figures in the world of modern philosophy as John Dewey, F. H. Bradley, A. N. Whitehead, and Nishida Kitaro.[8]

I have suggested above that the concept of 'pure experience' taken from James' 'radical empiricism' was the generative idea which—under Nishida's own pen, of course—gave the whole of *A Study of Good* its real interest. James' essays of 1904-5 seem to have been intro-

duced to Nishida by D. T. Suzuki between that time and the publication of *A Study of Good* in 1911. Nishida's personal library now preserved at Kyoto University contains one bound collection of offprints of most of James' essays written in 1904-5.[9] Although it is not known for certain when these offprints were collected, Nishida must have had them in his possession almost immediately after their appearance for him to have incorporated some of James' ideas into *A Study of Good.* He also possessed James' monumental *Principles of Psychology* (in two volumes, 1890); his personal copy contains underlining and marginal comments on passages which he incorporated into *A Study of Good.*

Thus with his careful reading of *Principles of Psychology* (it is still James' masterpiece), and his subsequent reading of the essays on 'radical empiricism', Nishida was able to submit his own contribution to the new growth and debate initiated by James. This point alone tells us something about Nishida Kitaro and the 'modernization' of Japan. Although separated by global distances from Boston, Nishida was writing in the relatively remote area of Kanazawa, in the late years of the Meiji period, a philosophical work which was an original assimilation of these contemporary American ideas.[10]

We have studied above the initial wording of Nishida's concept of 'pure experience' articulated in Part One of *A Study of Good.* Here I should like to present a similar analysis of the exact wording of James own notion of pure experience as he developed it in his essays of 1904-5. Since Nishida himself read and incorporated this concept into his own text, a comparative study of Nishida's and James' formulations should shed light on the directions in which each philosopher was moving. Such a comparative analysis may serve to clarify the content of the thought of both concerning 'pure experience', and at the same time illustrate that the basic tendencies of their thought were significantly different.

Immediately before his essay 'A World of Pure Experience', James published another tentative essay entitled 'Does Consciousness Exist?' (1904), which set the stage for the former essay. Since the two form one piece, I will begin my analysis with the former article. In that essay, James stated his thesis that the notion of 'consciousness'—variations on which idea have occurred throughout the history of philosophy in the dualisms between 'thoughts and things', 'spirit and matter', 'soul and body', and more recently in the 'transcendental ego' of modern German philosophy—was on the point of disappearing altogether. He wrote that it is 'the name of a nonentity, and has no right to a place among first principles'. Having for years taught its non-existence to his students, he has endeavored to give them 'its pragmatic equivalent in realities of experience' (pp. 2-3). He then elucidated this point by adding that, while denying that the word 'consciousness' stands for an *entity,* he insists 'most emphatically that it stands for a *function',* and that 'there is a function in experience which thoughts perform,' i.e. the function of knowing (p. 4).

No less a thinker than Whitehead has evaluated this key distinction in James' mind as a turning point in modern philosophy.[11] What James was accomplishing here was a crucial, and final, break with traditional 'substance' language in favor of 'functional' language in the description of experience, which he, as Whitehead after him, developed into an ontology of processive relations. James' thesis in this essay was that a primordial stuff of 'pure experience' can be conceived, in terms of which

> knowing can easily be explained *as a particular sort of relation* towards one another *into which portions of pure experience may enter. The relation itself is a part of pure experience.* (p. 4; stress added)

In the last analysis, James' radical empiricism was grounded in this notion of relation as a part of pure experience. It was an empiricism of transitive relations which, drawing upon the brilliant phenomenology of the 'Stream of Thought' of his *Principles of Psychology* (ch. 9), drove a decisive wedge into the classical empiricism of Hume and the subsequent transcendental rationalisms articulated to defend against Hume's critique of relations.

There are two sides to James' radical empiricism. The first side is the simpler, and actually the less important aspect of James' position, although it seems to have been the point which most attracted Nishida's attention. This was James' many incisive analyses and metaphors which described a condition of experience prior to subject-object distinctions in rational analysis, and which therefore precluded, on empirical grounds, the possibility of reifying 'thought' and 'things'. This was particularly the burden of the argument in 'Does Consciousness Exist?' He wrote:

> Experience, I believe, has no such inner duplicity; and separation of it into consciousness and content comes, not by way of subtraction, but by way of addition—the addition, to a given concrete piece of it, of other sets of experiences . . . (p. 9)

But this text already illustrates the second, and more important, side of James' doctrine. The 'addition, to a given concrete piece of it, of other sets of experiences' meant preciselythe inclusion of the functional or transitive relation of knowing within the flow of experience itself. While this too sounds like Nishida's own account, there was actually a significant difference, as we shall see.

A MULTIVARIATE FIELD OF EXPERIENCE

Let us first briefly establish the first aspect of the 'immediacy' of pure experience prior to subject-object distinctions. In 'Does Consciousness Exist?' James pointed to 'double-barrelled terms' such as *experience, phenomenon, datum, Vorfindung,* whose simultaneous subjective and objective nuances tend to replace the 'single-barrelled terms' of *thought* and *thing* in modern philosophy (p. 10). Locke and Berkeley contributed the entering wedge for this more concrete way of understanding the

dualism, but they did not take their analyses to a radical level. James gives examples of how the same room or the same spatial context gets counted twice over as a 'field of consciousness', i.e. of how pure experience in its immediacy functions multivariately according to change of perspective or context (pp. 13, 21). Thus the same perceptual context 'tends to get counted twice over', for pure experience is perfectly malleable and amenable to a multivariate functional analysis. It has no pregiven ontological structure. Its subjectivity and objectivity are 'functional attributes only, realized only when the experience is "taken", i.e. talked-of, twice, considered along with its two differing contexts respectively, by a new retrospective experience, of which that whole past complication now forms the fresh content' (p. 23). He concluded this essay with a phenomenology of the actual homogeneity of thoughts and things, showing the interchangeability of adjectival descriptions of 'thoughts' and 'things', and the especially ambiguous sphere of appreciations and value judgements, in which 'sometimes the adjective wanders as if uncertain where to fix itself' (pp. 28-35).

In a later essay, 'The Place of Affectional Facts in a World of Pure Experience' (May 1905), James continued this line of analysis of the homogeneity of thoughts and things in pure experience. Affectional experiences 'float ambiguously' between subject and object; their ambiguity 'illustrates beautifully my central thesis that subjectivity and objectivity are affairs not of what an experience is aboriginally made of, but of its classification' (p. 14). He continues his phenomenology of the wandering nature of adjectival qualities in the field of pure experience (pp. 141-5). Moreover, the shifting place of 'secondary qualities' in the history of philosophy 'is another excellent proof of the fact that "inner" and "outer" are not coefficients with which experience comes to us aboriginally stamped, but are rather results of a later classification performed by us for particular needs' (p. 146). The 'persistent ambiguity of relations' (p. 148), and the example of 'our body itself', which is 'the palmary instance of the ambiguous' (p. 153), also blur the lines traditionally drawn between subject and object, and suggest an immediacy of 'pure experience' itself.

We note in these texts a certain consistency of emphasis on the non-dualistic condition of experience which James shared with Nishida. But it should be further noted that differences are emerging as well. James' orientation lay more in the direction of describing a multivariate field of experience than of arguing to the conclusion of 'immediacy' for its own sake. In no text cited does James use the comparative or superlative cases of 'purer', 'purest', to describe 'pure experience', as Nishida frequently does. At no point did James employ the idea of a pure experience 'behind' or 'in the background of' thought or perception. While he spoke of immediacy of experience throughout, James did not endeavor to find that immediacy by emptying experience of its content. In fact, all his examples refer to content—'meaning' content—which is no less immediate for being intellectual content. Such content is not referred to as an 'admixture' of 'experience in itself' (Nishida's *keiken sono mama*), or as the 'artifices of the self' or as 'the state of incompletion' of pure experience. James makes no attempt to describe thought content arising in the instance 'which has lost the unity of pure experience'. A hierarchy of values culminating in the primacy of religious intuition over thought (learning) and the will (morality) was far from James' mind, while Nishida used just this variation of his own theme of pure experience as a jumping off point for a reading of 'reality' in idealistic terms (*A Study of Good,* Section Two), and for a theology of the relation between the 'true self' and an 'absolute Self' (*A Study of Good,* Section Four; continued in *Intuition and Reflection in Self-Consciousness,* esp. Sections 40-4).[12]

Finally, while Nishida, with Zen overtones, 'emptied' experience of all content to find a richer experience which he found no trouble articulating in the language of Western idealism, James had actually pursued his own analysis of 'A World of Pure Experience', 'The Thing and Its Relations', etc. as a critique of transcendental idealism, particularly that of F. H. Bradley, Royce, and Hegel.

MEANING AS TRANSITIVE RELATION

Let us turn now to the second, and more important, feature of James' radical empiricism. This was his doctrine of transitive relations which involved the knowing relation itself within the flow of pure experience. Not only was this an ontological position which grounded James' *Pragmatism* and *Meaning of Truth;* it was James' basic argument against the language of Western idealism to which Nishida was drawn. While Nishida's reductionism of perceptual and intellectual contents to 'experience just as it is' ran into difficulty precisely with the 'relation with others' which 'meaning' and 'judgement' implied, the same knowing relation became the very heart of James' radical empiricism.

We have seen above that James, in denying that consciousness stands for an entity, most emphatically affirmed that it stands for a *function.* The knowing relation was described as 'one particular sort of relation towards another into which portions of pure experience may enter' (p. 4). Since relations are constitutive of the functional field of pure experience, or, in other terms, contrary to traditional empiricism, relations are *experienced,* knowing was described in functional terms without having recourse to the *a priori* agents of unification of transcendental idealism. In 'Does Consciousness Exist?' James therefore concluded:

> The peculiarity of our experiences, that they not only are, but are known, which their 'conscious' quality is invoked to explain, is better explained by their relations—these relations themselves being experiences—to one another. (p. 25)

In his next essay, 'A World of Pure Experience', James spelled out some of the consequences of this view.

In this latter expression of his position James stated that 'radical empiricism' signified an empiricism which nei-

ther includes elements not directly experienced nor excludes any element so experienced. For such a position,

> The relations that connect experiences must themselves be experienced relations, and any kind of relation experienced *must be accounted as 'real' as anything else in the system.* (p. 42, stress added)

I have underlined the phrase which suggests the different direction in which James' thought was moving, if my above reading of the Zen coloration of Nishida's reductionism is allowed. Ordinary empiricism went astray, according to James, in stressing disjunctive relations exclusively, even though both conjunctive and disjunctive relations are 'fully co-ordinate parts of experience'. Rationalism then attempted to correct ordinary empiricism's atomistic perceptual world 'by the addition of trans-experiential agents of unification, substances, intellectual categories and powers, or Selves'. Radical empiricism, on the contrary, endeavors to do 'full justice to conjunctive relations' (pp. 42-4).

From this beginning, James went on to tackle the question of conjunctive transition head on. The conjunctive relation 'which has given the most trouble to philosophy', he declared, 'is the co-conscious transition, so to call it, by which one experience passes into another when both belong to the same self' (p. 47). This was precisely the relation which gave trouble to Nishida's initial statement of pure experience, as noted above. Personal histories are processes of changes in time, as James stated, and 'the change itself is one of the things immediately experienced.' Change means in this instance experience of continuous transition in contradistinction to discontinuous transition. But such continuous transition—such as the relation exemplified in the knowing process—is one sort of conjunctive relation, i.e. a definite sort of experience directly lived. Therefore, 'there is no other *nature,* no other whatness than this absence of break and this sense of continuity in that most intimate of all conjunctive relations' (p. 50). These originally given continuities 'stand on their own bottom' without the need of introducing the 'artificial conception of the relations between knower and known' (p. 52). And thus, contrary to transcendentalist theories, the knowing relation takes place 'in the very bosom of finite experience'. For conjunctive relations are constitutive of pure experience.

We can note here the same stress in James on the notion of multivariate contexts of experience, rather than Nishida's prime focus on im-mediacy. If we recall James' famous chapter, 'The Stream of Thought', in *Principles of Psychology* (vol. I, ch. 9), we can see further how this doctrine of 'A World of Pure Experience' continued to be a brilliant phenomenology of 'felt transitions' under James' pen. 'Flow' metaphors pervade James' analyses in a manner hardly matched by even Bergson or Whitehead. Indeed, this discovery of process and novelty (in James' 'open universe') was central to the larger contribution of American philosophy represented by James, C. S. Peirce, Dewey, G. H. Mead, and Whitehead. It is a doctrine whose pervasive tone is quite another thing from the introverted subjectivity of Nishida's analysis of experience, to say nothing of his affinity with rationalistic and idealistic doctrines from *A Study of Good* on. James could write: 'Knowledge of sensible realities thus comes to life inside the tissue of experience. It is *made;* and made by relations that unroll themselves in time' (p. 57). To be experienced as continuous 'is to be really continuous, in a world where experience and reality come to the same thing' (p. 59). In such a world,

> Transitions and arrivals (or terminations) are the only events that happen, though they happen by so many sorts of path. The only function that one experience can perform is to lead to another experience; and the only fulfilment we can speak of is the reaching of a certain experienced end. (p. 63)

Contrary to Nishida's Zen-colored approach, thoughts are nothing illusory as 'artifices of the self' or 'admixtures' of pure experience. Still less do they 'destroy' the unity of pure experience or constitute a thinner and more abstract version of it. James could also affirm: 'Wonderful are the new paths and the short-circuits which the thought-paths make' (p. 64). He then elaborated this key idea of *thought-paths as experience-paths* at some length (pp. 62-6).

James' genius for felt transition, then, seems to imply a non-dualistic outlook quite different in tone and direction from Nishida's concept of pure experience. I will briefly cite a few more of James' 'flow' metaphors further to highlight this contrast. For James, knowing, as later Dewey was to emphasize, involves the uncertainty of an unfinished universe, and implies a dramatic universe which is still pursuing its adventures. It is a series of 'flightings and perchings' in a continuously unfolding landscape. Or, to change the simile, when one particular thought-path is momentarily unchallenged, 'we commit ourselves to the current as if the port were sure. We live, as it were, upon the front edge of an advancing wave-crest, and our sense of a determinate direction in falling forward is all we cover of the future of our path.' Our experience 'is of variations of rate and of direction, and lives in these transitions more than in the journey's end' (p. 69). Therefore, 'experience of tendency' is the very stuff of so-called objective reference. It is an incident of the fact that so much of experience 'comes as an insufficient and consists of process and transition'. Thus our fields of experience 'have no more definite boundaries than have our fields of view. Both are fringed forever by a *more* that continuously develops, and that continuously supercedes them as life proceeds' (p. 71). The notion of 'knowledge still *in transitu*' therefore implies a pragmatic process of 'making itself valid like everything else' (p. 76). Or again, thought-paths are one kind of experience-paths in this processive universe.

'With transition and prospect thus enthroned in pure experience', James declared that it was impossible for him to subscribe to Berkeley's idealism—just what Nishida went on to do after reading James' essay 'A World of Pure Experience and after writing his own Section One

on 'Pure Experience' in *A Study of Good.* James concluded that radical empiricism was a 'mosaic philosophy' in which 'the pieces are held together by their own bedding,' instead of connections being guaranteed by Substances, transcendental Egos, or Absolutes. In radical empiricism there is no such transcendental bedding. Like the flightings and perchings of a bird, 'the more substantive and the more transitive parts run into each other continuously.' Thus 'experience itself, taken at large, can grow by its edges.' It is precisely these relations of continuous transition experienced which 'make our experiences cognitive' (p. 86). James concluded that 'The universe continuously grows in quantity by new experiences that graft themselves upon the older mass,' and that this kind of outlook 'harmonizes best with a radical pluralism, with novelty and indeterminism, moralism and theism . . .' (p. 90).

As a final look at James' position, we can notice that in his article 'The Thing and Its Relations', published in January of 1905, James further articulated a point that runs contrary to Nishida's formulations, although Nishida seems to have read this very article before developing his own notion of 'pure experience'. James declared that 'experience in its immediacy seems perfectly fluent' (p. 92). 'Pure experience' is the name which he here gives to 'the immediate flux of life which furnishes the material to our later reflection with its conceptual categories' (p. 93). This is the very crux of the difference between Nishida's and James' notions of pure experience. To Nishida, the point is the 'im-mediacy' of experience in the sense of a richer unity beyond subject-object distinctions. To James, pure experience meant immediate flux or transition of which thought is one particular kind of constitutive element. Directly after the above text James went on to say that only new-born babies, or men in semi-coma from sleep, drugs, illnesses, or blows, may be assumed to have a 'pure' experience 'in the literal sense of a *that* which is not yet any definite *what*' (p. 93). We recall that analogies taken from the experience of a newborn child or 'dreams' were employed by Nishida more readily than 'meanings and judgements' which break the unity of pure experience and were 'poorer than it'. James' own comment was that:

> Pure experience in this state is but another name for feeling or sensation. But the flux of it no sooner comes than it tends to fill itself with emphases, and these salient parts become identified and abstracted; so that experience now flows as if shot through with adjectives and nouns and prepositions and conjunctions. Its purity is only a relative term, meaning the proportional amount of unverbalized sensation which it still embodies. (p. 94)

Presumably James, if he had been made aware of Nishida's position as stated in the beginning of *A Study of Good,* might have stated the difference of his own concept by pointing to just this sort of passage.[13]

CONCLUSION

Having completed this brief survey of the notions of 'pure experience' in Nishida Kitaro and William James,

I would like to set forth a few conclusions which, although preliminary and tentative, may contribute to the clarification of the thought of each. James' world of pure experience was indeed, as his phrase puts it, 'a philosophy of plural facts'. The notion of pure experience was employed, not to suggest a richer unity behind the thinner and more abstract editions of perception and thought, but to guarantee the reality of concrete perceptual and intellectual contents themselves. His radical empiricism may even be said to have been a kind of belief in the democratic value of facts in theplural, including knowing relations which are usually felt to carry so much of the intrinsic reaping of value in our daily activities. Therefore James, who with C. S. Peirce was the founder of American Pragmatism, stressed the creativity of intelligence in the making of fact and society. 'Facts' were read in terms of pure experience as conjunctive and disjunctive transitions constitutive of the universe (and pluriverse). As relations experienced, i.e. as experiences of transition, they constitute a world 'perfectly fluent'. The rather large amount of space which James gave to his critique of idealism bears witness to the fact that James himself felt that there was a fundamental point at stake, namely that the notion of any transcendental agency of unification 'derealized' the reality of felt transitions of experience.

In this frame of reference, James conceived the knowing relation as one particular sort of conjunctive transition constitutive of experience. Thought-paths are precisely experience-paths, i.e. one sort of way we turn corners and get things done. While James' position was a repudiation of a dualism based on the false presupposition of the disjunction between subject and object, the knowing relationship was not regarded as 'purer' or 'impurer' than any other kind of conjunctive or disjunctive transition constitutive of experience. All experiences have intrinsic value as functions of a larger field of experience. In James' view, even the attempt to 'empty' experience of intellectual content would simply be another kind of content, i.e. another kind of conjunctive transition grafted upon past experiences to meet a particular need. In sum, James' position was that all experiences, including intellectual ones, are transitive relations in a multivariate context of pure experience.

Nishida's position began from a similar phenomenalism of the immediacy of experience. But his interest seems to have been more on the fact of im-mediacy itself, i.e. the 'state' or 'condition' of non-discriminatory unity, than on James' concern for felt transition. Throughout the whole of *A Study of Good* (1911) there is no attention given to the question of what James called 'novelties forever leaking in' upon experience. On the contrary, the concluding religious idealism of Section Four, 'Religion', of that work suggests that Nishida's basic orientation was hardly a 'radical empiricism' or 'radical pluralism'. Even in Section One, 'Pure Experience', Nishida exhibited a tendency which I have called 'idealistic' for want of a better word to describe a notion which uses the language of Western idealism, especially of Hegel's 'concrete universal', but which suggests Nishida's Zen background as

well. In the elaboration of his own notion of pure experience, the idea of a 'purest' experience is never lost sight of. The language of 'to know reality exactly as it is'; of the 'admixture/adulteration of thought or discrimination'; of a 'condition prior to subject-object distinctions'; of meanings andjudgements which 'do not add any richness to the content of experience', and which are 'abstracted from original experience and poorer than it'; of the 'destruction' of pure experience by 'relations'; of pure experience 'in the background' which causes these relations to be established; of thought as 'the state of incompletion' of pure experience; of thought and the will 'having lost the condition which is the unity of experience'—such phrases add up to depict the concept of a 'richest' experience in Nishida's mind which might best be understood in terms of the Zen notions of 'emptiness' or 'nothingness'. That Nishida himself so interpreted the link between his early notion of pure experience and his later Zen ontology of the '*topos* of nothingness' developed from *From the Acting to the Seeing* (1927) has already been pointed out.

Thus I am suggesting that a comparative analysis with James' radical empiricism does bring out by contrast the nuances of Nishida's thought which he never explicitly stated until his later writings. An interesting question, which I can only pose here, is whether Nishida's later ideas of the 'field of nothingness', 'transition from the formed to the forming', 'action-intuition', '*poesis,*' etc. were merely a deepening of his initial concept of pure experience, or whether these later ideas may have brought him to a ground closer to James' radical empiricism.

NOTES

[1] All references are to *Zen no kenkyu* (A Study of Good), I, *Nishida Kitaro zenshu* (The Complete Works of Nishida Kitaro), 19 vols., Iwanami Shoten, 1965, 2nd ed. For brief introductions to Nishida's thought in English see Yoshinori Takeuchi, 'Nishida's Philosophy as Representative of Japanese Philosophy', in *Ency. Brit.*, v. 12, 1966, pp. 958J-62; Y. Takeuchi, 'The Philosophy of Nishida Kitaro', *Japanese Religions*, 1963, III-IV, pp. I-32; Hans Waldenfels, 'Absolute Nothingness: Preliminary Considerations on a Central Notion in the Philosophy of Nishida Kitaro and the Kyoto School', *Monumenta Nipponica*, XXI, 3-4, 1966, pp. 354-91; G. K. Piovesana, *Recent Japanese Philosophical Thought*, 1862-1962, Tokyo, 1963, pp. 85-122; Matao Noda, 'East-West Synthesis in Nishida Kitaro', *Philosophy East and West*, 1954-5, pp. 345-59; Torataro Shimomura, 'Nishida Kitaro and Some Aspects of His Philosophical Thought', in *A Study of Good*, V. H. Viglielmo trans., Tokyo, 1960; R. Schinzinger, introduction and translation of *Nishida Kitaro: Intelligibility and the Philosophy of Nothingness*, Tokyo, 1958.

[2] A forthcoming study by V. H. Viglielmo, 'Nishida Kitaro: The Early Years', in a larger collection of monographs to be published by Princeton University Press, will be the most comprehensive study in English of

Nishida's early religious life up to *A Study of Good* (1911). I have had the advantage of reading this monograph inmanuscript. For the life of Nishida, see Piovesana, *op. cit.* and L. Knauth, 'Life is Tragic: The Diary of Nishida Kitaro', *Monumenta Nipponica,* XX, 3-4, pp. 335-58.

[3] Miyagawa Toru, *Nishida, Miki, Tosaka no tetsugaku* (The Philosophies of Nishida, Miki, and Tosaka), Tokyo, 1967, pp. 22-3.

[4] I am referring, of course, to the Buddhist doctrine of emptiness, or *sunyata,* which became central to the Zen approach.

[5] Nishida's concept of Nothingness explicitly emerged only with his work *From the Acting to the Seeing* (1927). It was then developed in his next several works, i.e. *The Self-Conscious System of the Universal* (1930), *The Self-Conscious Determination of Nothingness* (1932), *Basic Problems of Philosophy,* 2 vols. (1933-4), and in his later essays. Cf. Takeuchi, *op. cit.* and especially Waldenfels, *op. cit.*

[6] William James, *Essays in Radical Empiricism,* New York, 1912, pp. 40-1.

[7] These essays included 'Does Consciousness Exist?' (September 1904), 'A World of Pure Experience' (September 1904), 'The Thing and Its Relations' (January 1905), 'How Two Minds Can Know One Thing' (March 1905), 'The Place of Affectional Facts in a World of Pure Experience' (May 1905), 'The Experience of Activity' (January 1905), 'The Essence of Humanism' (March 1905). All references will be to the volume, *Essays in Radical Empiricism,* 1912.

[8] Besides the considerable correspondence between James and Bradley, James' position was one of the main themes of Bradley's *Essays on Truth and Reality,* Oxford Press, 1914. The influence of James on the thought of John Dewey, Henri Bergson, etc. needs no elaboration here. But see also James' influence on Samuel Alexander's *Space, Time, and Deity,* London, 1927, which in turn influenced Whitehead. Whitehead's debt to William James is attested to in many parts of Whitehead's writings. See n. II below.

[9] According to the catalogue of Nishida's personal library, *Nishida bunko mokuroku,* published by the Kyoto University Bungakubu Library, January 1954, Nishida possessed all the above-cited articles of James in offprint form. He also possessed copies of James' *Pragmatism, Principles of Psychology,* 2 vols., *The Meaning of Truth,* and *Varieties of Religious Experience.* It does not mention James' *A Pluralistic Universe,* which differed greatly in ideas from Nishida's early religious thought.

[10] We should recall that this was about the time of the Russo-Japanese War (1904-5), or immediately after— less than five decades since Fukuzawa Yukichi's *Seiyo jijo* written in the last years of Japan's feudal period.

[11] Whitehead, *Science and the Modern World,* New York, 1925, p. 130:

> The history of philosophy runs curiously parallel to that of science. In the case of both, the 17th century set the stage for its two successors. But with the 20th century a new act commences . . . In attributing to William James the inauguration of a new stage in philosophy, we should be neglecting other influences of his time. But, admitting this, there still remains a certain fitness in contrasting his essay, *Does Consciousness Exist?,* published in 1904, with Descartes' *Discourse on Method,* published in 1637. James clears the stage of the old paraphernalia; or rather he entirely alters its lighting . . . The discrimination between an entity and a function is therefore vital to the understanding of the challenge which James is advancing against the older modes of thought . . . I shall for my own purpose construe James as denying exactly what Descartes asserts in his *Discourse* and his *Meditations.*

[12] The *Nishida bunko mokuroku* does not mention *A Pluralistic Universe* among James' works possessed by Nishida. If Nishida did not own, or read, such chapters as 'Monistic Idealism' (ch. 2), and 'Hegel and His Method' (ch. 3) in *A Pluralistic Universe,* he still possessed, and had read, in addition to the above-cited essays, further offprints such as 'How Two Minds Can Know One Thing', 'The Experience of Activity', and 'The Essence of Humanism', which were clear attacks on idealism, especially that of F. H. Bradley.

[13] James died in 1911, the year of the publication of *A Study of Good,* which was then not translated into English until V. H. Viglielmo's complete translation in 1960. The best introduction to James' philosophy and the wider literature connected with it is that of John McDermott, 'Person, Process, and the Risk of Belief', pp. xiii-xliv, in John McDermott, ed., *William James,* Random House, 1967.

David Dilworth (essay date 1969)

SOURCE: "The Range of Nishida's Early Religious Thought: *Zen no kenkyu,*" in *Philosophy East and West,* Vol. XIX, No. 4, October, 1969, pp. 409-21.

[In the following essay, Dilworth examines Nishida's contributions to modern religious philosophy in Japan, which eventually led to the founding of the Kyoto School.]

The intellectual career of Nishida Kitaro, generally regarded as Japan's foremost modern philosopher,[1] grew out of his early Zen experience and his philosophical interest in the question of religious experience. The efforts of many Japanese thinkers who, indebted to Nishida, have contributed to the movement of "philosophy of religion" in modern Japan are illustrative of this central orientation in his own thought. This movement has its roots in the wider spiritual, particularly Buddhist, heritage of Japanese tradition, and even in modern times can be thought to antedate Nishida.[2] Nevertheless, probably the first philosophically original assimilation of Eastern and Western religious ideas in modern Japan is attributable to Nishida Kitaro, whose range of epistemological and metaphysical ideas introduced a broad conceptual framework which became, and remained, the point of departure for the "Kyoto school" of modern Japanese religious philosophy.[3]

Nishida's overall contribution was hardly limited to religious philosophy. Nevertheless, his whole career was a developing process of articulation of fundamental religious attitudes which permeated his early Zen training prior to the publication of his first major work, **Zen no kenkyu** [*A Study of Good*].[4] To express these deepening attitudes he continued on his intellectual journey from the publication of that work in 1911 until his death in a Zen monastery at Kamakura in 1945. His religious philosophy was thus coextensive with his whole literary career, which itself was grounded in his own personal reactions as an intellectual of the late Meiji, Taisho, and Showa periods.[5] We must note his participation in this wider social experience which, subject to cultural and intellectual influences from both East and West, formed the concrete tissue of feelings and ideas available to him as a person living through a time almost coextensive with modern Japanese history up to the end of World War II. Nishida's writings have particular interest, as they are representative of the sophistication of philosophical ideas which the modern Japanese intellectual world attained in a relatively short period of time. Scholars interested in the theme of "modernization" in the late Meiji and early Taisho periods can find in Nishida's case an important example of a continuous assimilation of Western categories which contributed in part to the development of Japanese philosophy to its present high level.

Judging from the subsequent orientation of the "philosophy of religion" movement in Japan, the synthesis of Eastern and Western ideas achieved in Nishida's thought has indeed had its main impact in the area of religious philosophy, as noted above. While to some, including the present writer, such a development may seem to be an unnecessary restriction of the possibilities which his thought suggests, it can hardly be denied that Nishida's own focus of attention stimulated that direction.[6] From his key transitional work of 1927, **Hataraku mono kara miru mono e** [*From the Acting to the Seeing*], which began an explicit articulation of a generalizedZen "logic of the East" centering upon the concept of the "*topos of nothingness*" *(mu no basho*[a]*)*, Nishida's ideas were a deepening quest intellectually to repossess certain fundamental "Oriental" religious experiences. He thus began a dialogue with Western religious ideas which, particularly from a Buddhist position, has continued down to today.[7]

The present article can do no more than mention the full career of Nishida Kitaro, and those of his followers and critics. It is primarily intended to be a summary of and commentary on the religious ideas which Nishida presented to the world in his first major work, *A Study of Good*. Because of this restriction, it will be impossible to trace here the gradual transition in Nishida's position from 1911 to his later "logic of the East," which has become his chief claim to originality as a world thinker. A few excellent introductions to this total development of Nishida's career already exist in English.[8] My aim will rather be to focus upon this limited area of Nishida's first work as one illustration of the kind of assimilation of Western philosophical ideas which occurred in Japan during the late Meiji (1868-1912) and Taisho (1912-1926) periods. It will also be to study these ideas as philosophical categories that are intrinsically interesting as philosophical categories.

THE STRUCTURE OF A STUDY OF GOOD

Nishida's career was launched with the publication of *A Study of Good* in 1911, the year after he became assistant professor of philosophy at Kyoto University. This work, which won Nishida instant respect and which has been the most widely read of his works, was the product of a long period of maturation during his years as an instructor in the Kanazawa school system in the last decade of the Meiji period.[9] But in a certain sense his intellectual preparation for the writing of this book took an even longer time. When the work was published in his forty-first year, it was already the culmination of at least twenty years of thought and experience; that is, the last two decades of the Meiji period.

In retrospect, this process of intellectual maturation in an individual growing up in the relatively remote area of Kanazawa during the turbulent 1890s and 1900s is a fascinating example of how intellectual currents pulsate like electronic waves across a land to come to focus in an individual localized form. His first steps as a student of philosophy; the stimulation of several brilliant classmates and friends, including D. T. Suzuki; his youthful "Meiji liberalism"; his three introspective years at Tokyo University, where he came into contact with the new German philosophy that has dominated Japanese philosophical circles ever since; a deepening interest in Zen practice from his early twenties; his writing, at the age of twenty-three or twenty-four,a study of the British Hegelian philosopher T. H. Green; his first teaching assignment at the age of twenty-five, followed by busy years teaching psychology, ethics, and history of philosophy; actual Zen practice from about this same time which reached its greatest intensity during his twenty-seventh through twenty-ninth years—these experiences formed traces on Nishida's subconscious spiritual life, which, by a constant process of condensation and recondensation in the light of new experiences for another decade, were to issue forth in *A Study of Good*. The question of religion seems to have dominated his attention from before his thirtieth year, when he also began to show a more critical philosophical mind and to write brief philosophical pieces.[10] From around 1903 he began to turn his attention to the task of transforming his lecture materials and new insights into *A Study of Good.* Years of further study and reflection produced the work which, in retrospect, was probably the single most influential contribution to Japanese philosophy in modern times.

A careful analysis of the content of *A Study of Good* also suggests that it reflects a gradual transformation of earlier materials into book form. While Nishida had integrated its contents into a coherent system by the time of its publication in 1911, it was still a rather loosely joined entity comprised of four main section: (1) "Pure Experience"; (2) "Reality"; (3) "The Good" and (4) "Religion." Nishida confirms this structural impression by his statement in the Preface that he wrote the second and third sections first. He actually planned to publish the ontology of Section Two immediately, but was prevented by illness from doing so. Section Three was ostensibly a reformulation of his early essay on Green's ethics in the light of his later lectures and reflection. The first and fourth sections were then written, presumably in that sequence, as internal evidence suggests. Perhaps out of a consideration of this history of the manuscript, Nishida invited his readers, in the Preface of 1911, to skip over the initial portion (four chapters) of the first section, "Pure Experience," and begin the sequence of ideas from Part Two, which he called the "core" of his philosophical thought at that time. But he named the work *Zen no kenkyu* [*A Study of Good*] after the content of Sections Three and Four to indicate that his ontological ideas were meant to lead up to the central questions of moral and religious, i.e., human, life itself (pp. 2-3).

What the history of the manuscript indeed reveals is that the last section on "Religion" was the final form of Nishida's thought to that juncture. In that sense it rounded out the system of ideas with which he launched his philosophical career. We can only touch upon the contents of that system here. Section One, "Pure Experience," took off from William James's notion of the same name. It was a rejection of both the atomistic psychology of classical British empiricism, and the sensationalism of the laterpositivistic epistemologies which had been vaguely, and illogically, allied with the classical material atomism of post-Newtonian cosmology. Nishida aligned himself with this modern endeavor to read the immediacy of experience in terms of a functional analysis of organically relating tissues of relations in which the classical dualisms of subject-object, mind-matter, etc., were regarded as abstractions superimposed upon the immediacy of experience itself. At the end of Section One Nishida exhibited a clear intention of reading the notion of "pure experience" as a primary "religious intuition" of the experient subject.

In Section Two, "Reality," Nishida went on to part company with James's radical empiricism in favor of a kind of idealistic rendering of reality in terms of "spirit" in language which was predominantly that of Berkeley and Hegel.[11] For example, citing Berkeley, Nishida proceeded to shift the center of metaphysical gravity away from the "independent thing" categories of traditional philosophical description to the "experient subject" categories of the *esse est percipi* point of view. He thus began to ontologize the notion of experience in a way somewhat foreign to William James, but consistent with his Zen insights. Particularly in his brief treatment of God in Section Two, chapter ten, entitled "God as Reality," he showed signs of a larger spiritual ken which we know to have included Buddhist insights. However, he formulated his ideas here in language drawn directly from Western idealistic categories, which were in turn subsumed and developed into the fuller treatment of the notion of "Religion" in the fourth part of the text. Even the third part, as previously noted, was an elaboration of a notion of moral "self-realization" which came from the ethics of the British Hegelian philosopher, T. H. Green.

With this brief sketch of the background to Section Four, "Religion," of *A Study of Good,* let us turn directly to the first formulation of explicit religious categories in Nishida's career. For purposes of analysis I will follow the categoreal development of its four main chapters as they occur in the text, paying particular attention to the philosophical language and logic of Nishida's argument.

THE CONCEPT OF RELIGION AND PANTHEISTIC TENDENCIES

1. The opening chapter of Section Four, entitled "The Religious Demand," serves as a point of departure for Nishida's formal remarks concerning the nature of religion, which incidentally shed light on his own understanding of the notion of pure experience. This is evident from the opening sentence of the chapter, where it is said that "the religious demand is the demand with regard to the self, a demand concerning the life of the self" (p. 169). The whole work to this juncture is a metaphysical discourse on the life of the self, that is, a rational articulation of the variousimplications of the notion of subjectivity itself. In this present context Nishida turns attention to felt moral and religious exigencies in the life of the person as the basis for further philosophical analysis: "It is the demand wherein the self perceives its relativity and finitude, and at the same time joins with the absolute and infinite power, thereby desiring to acquire the true life of eternity." Nishida thus makes a start on the basis of the philosophical datum of the religious exigency itself. If we recall his formal Zen training and personal religious interests, this point becomes more plausible. The religious demand, he insists, is identical with the life demand. It is "the deepest demand of man's heart," since it seeks an all-embracing unity which transcends even the unities of knowledge and the will (p. 172). Therefore, the question of the religious demand is made central to the notion of pure experience in *A Study of Good.*

Now, what is the religious demand in concrete terms? Nishida first affirms, contrary to much vulgar superstition which has traditionally passed under the name of morality and religion, that the true religious attitude cannot be based on thoughts of selfish merit or fear. Nor is it a demand for "self-peace," which mistakenly finds the significance of religion in "extinguishing the temperament of enterprise and activity by taking up a negative life of small pleasure and no distress" (p. 170).[12] He states that "peace" is rather the result of true religious experience, the demand for which, positively taken, is "the great demand of life which one is unable to end even if one wishes to do so." It is the demand of the appetitive center of the personality, the most powerful desire of which is to center the self in the universe of its experiences. Moreover, it is the demand for the largest experience of the self as unifying center. In the process of discovering this true center the self perceives the fact of its relative perspective in the world of pure experience. Accordingly, religious experience is precisely that pursuit of "absolute unity" by wholly casting aside one's own finite relativity. This phenomenology of the religious attitude clearly suggests Nishida's Zen background. But in the precise formulation of it Nishida returns to his idealistic position of the unity of consciousness, which is the source and center of the original state of the subjectivity of the self. He writes that the religious exigency is identical with "the demand for the unity of consciousness, and at the same time for union with the universe" (p. 172). Thus the question "why is religion necessary" is synonymous with "why is it necessary to live," for the demands of religion are those of life itself (pp. 172-173).

In sum, we note that Nishida launched his explicit religious ideas with a kind of phenomenological analysis of the experiential exigency of the religious attitude itself. While the larger premises for this chapter are already contained in the precedingsections of the book, the present chapter is also a fresh confrontation of experiential content relating to the religious exigency itself. A certain generalized Zen religiosity may well have been the deeper motivation for Nishida here. The chapter is an implicit statement of precisely the kind of personal religiosity which Nishida developed in his later writings in which a Zen ontology predominates.

2. In Chapter Two, entitled the "Essence of Religion," the structure of the religious experience is more deeply analyzed. Generically, religion is defined as the relation between God and man. Here God is intended to mean "the foundation of the universe," and man is said to mean "our individual consciousness." Nishida then affirms that the mutual relation of things differing in essence cannot be established outside of self-interest. Therefore he positively defines the religious relation to be the "relation of a God and man of the same nature," i.e., "there must be the relation of father and son" (pp. 173-174). Why Nishida uses the analogy of father and son[b] at this juncture is not perfectly clear. Nor does it seem perfectly apposite in the light of the general orientation of his thought, which, using his own terms, is more pantheistic[c] than theistic[d]. But apart from the merits of his use of the anthropomorphism of father and son, Nishida's account consistently endeavors to enunciate a doctrine of internal relation between God and man, where the "basic thought of all religion" is defined in terms of a twofold requirement: (1) that "God and man have the same nature," and (2) that "man returns to his origin in God." The text

continues: "But merely for God and man to have the same interests and for God to help us and protect us is not yet true religion. God must be the foundation of the universe, and at the same time our foundation, for our returning to God is returning to that source. Moreover, God must be the object of all things, i.e. God must also be the object of man, and every man must find his true object in God" (p. 174).

Precisely because of this experience of God as immanent ground and source do we "feel infinite warmth in God and are able to attain to the essence of religion, which is to live in God" (p. 176). As both Augustinian and Buddhist traditions have maintained, each in its own way, we lose our self to find our true Self.

Another way Nishida articulates the relation of immanent ground, which is the essence of the religious relation, is that "our spirit is the partial consciousness of God." Even though God and man do "possess the foundation of an identical spirit," it might still seem possible to conceive of God and man as mutually independent. But he cautions that this is "viewing from the flesh and distinguishing spirit temporally and spatially," for "those who possess the same foundation in spirit are the same spirit." He even affirms that our spirit[e] *(seishin)* must be the "same substance asGod"[f] and that "God and man are the same substance"[g] (p. 177). Citing Boehme's mystical idea of *die innerste Geburt,* he declares that we reach God through the deepest internal life.

Further clarification of the basic thought of this chapter seems unnecessary at this point, since the theme of the relation between God and man is given even more explicit philosophical structuring in the next two chapters, which deal with "God" and with "God and the World," respectively. Here we may note that Nishida's position has quickly moved far beyond the phenomenology of the religious exigency of the previous chapter. In addition to analogies with types of Buddhist thought, it shows awareness of the main line of mystical and pantheistic thought in the Western tradition, to which Nishida frequently alludes in this final section of *A Study of Good.* The key point of this *itinerarium mentis in Deum* tradition is the concept of internal and immanent relation, based on identity of substance, between God and man. Nishida has taken this central point and generalized it into the essential definition of the religious relation itself. In a certain sense his thought here exhibits a degree of eclecticism and use of Western philosophical categories which probably cannot be said to be truly Zen in connotation. For the Zen concept of the experience of "self-mind"[h] and the Western concept of *itinerarium mentis in Deum* part company over the question of duality, which Western religious thought retains to some extent. Nishida avoids all reference to this problem in the present context.

3. The subsequent chapter, entitled "God," may be said to be the most important chapter of this series, in that Nishida's conception of God is developed in a philosophical language that is precise and systematic. It there-

fore serves to clarify some of the ideas previously entertained. At the very start, for example, Nishida reiterates his contention that God is not to be conceived "as a transcendent creator outside the universe," but as "directly the ground of this reality." He elucidates this point by adding: "The relation between God and the universe is not such as that between an artist and his work, but is the relation between essence and phenomenon, and the universe is not a thing created by God, but is a 'manifestation' of God" (p. 178). In this context Nishida seems definitely to be employing a "substance" language in the description of God. "Essence and phenomenon,"[i] "manifestation of God"[j] and the like are all expressions of this "substance" language and the "logic of identity" consistently witnessed throughout this important chapter. At no time does Nishida really depart from the Spinozistic or Hegelian frame of reference previously noted, although Nishida's rendering of this line of thought may well be original. However, we may be permitted to inquire whether "substance" language, even in a Spinozistic or Hegelian (i.e., non-Aristotelian or non-Cartesian) sense, is the most adequate kind of language in a philosophical description of God and of therelation between God and the universe. Nishida himself does not seem to entertain this question in *A Study of Good,* even though his previous discussion of pure experience may have prepared us for the possibility of alternative kinds of philosophical categories in articulating these metaphysical concepts.

I will leave this question of philosophical language pending for the time being in order to follow Nishida's own argument. Having begun with the repudiation of God as external creator in favor of his own notion of the internal manifestation of God in the universe, Nishida somewhat inconsistently goes on to offer an argument which is almost literally a page from Newton (he also mentions Kepler), when he argues from the order of natural phenomena to "the one unifying power behind them in control." This notion is even applied to the human soul as well, when it is said that ". . . throughout the East and West, a tremendous unifying force is in control" (pp. 178-180). Nishida himself had rejected the "causal" argument for God's existence in a previous passage (pp. 98-100). The present line of reasoning seems inconsistent with several previous premises, and is in fact not pursued too far. Returning to his *esse est percipi* position that "we cannot know matter separately as an independent reality apart from our phenomena of consciousness, Nishida reiterates the point that "the facts of direct experience . . . are only these phenomena of consciousness." He therefore postulates that we must return to the self, for "the secret key to explaining the universe lies in the self." Even what Newton and Kepler observed as the order of natural phenomena is actually nothing more than the order of our phenomena of consciousness (pp. 181-182). But God, it has been argued, is the foundation of reality; therefore God, as the unifier of consciousness, is the unifier of the universe. In a fuller text: "God is the unifier of the universe, and the universe is the expression of God. This comparison is not merely metaphoric, it is fact. God is the greatest and ultimate unifier of our conscious-

ness. Indeed, our consciousness is a part of the consciousness of God, and its unity comes from the unity of God" (p. 182). What we are seeing, then, is that despite his basic Zen religiosity Nishida tended to philosophize in *A Study of Good* in language which was heavily indebted to Western idealism.

To summarize the remaining arguments of the present chapter, I will endeavor to reduce a longer text to three fundamental premises and three conclusions. The first premise is that "that which controls spirit must be the laws of spirit." Second, "spirit is not merely the combination of these functions, but behind spirit there is one unifying force, and these phenomena are its expression." The third premise (itself a conclusion) is that this unifying force connotes a spiritual personality, and God "is the one great personality who is the ground of the universe," or conversely, the universe is "the personal expression of God" (p. 182). The first conclusion is that"reality must be directly the thought and will of God" (quoting Spinoza, *Ethics* I. 16). Second, because of God's universal consciousness, "in God everything is actuality, and God is always active. . . . In God there is neither past nor future. . . . God resides in the eternal now. . . . In God there is no hope, reflection, or memory, and consequently there is no consciousness of a special self. . . . God is absolute freedom. . . . In this kind of God there is no variable will" (pp. 183-184). God is "infinite love" (p. 185). Third, God's personality must be transpersonal, by virtue of being "the one great intellectual intuition at the base of the universe," and "the unifier of pure experience which embraces the universe" (p. 186). These citations represent the substance of Nishida's argument concerning the attributes of God, as the scholastic philosophers might call them. To a student of Western theism they are familiar ideas. Nishida himself offers a generous sprinkling of allusions to Augustine and the Renaissance mystics throughout this chapter.

4. The fourth chapter, entitled "God and the World," does not introduce radically new material. It is a continuation of the main threads of the preceding chapter, with further emphasis on the relation which obtains between God and the world. Nishida's argument is that this relation can be inferred from the relation of the unity of consciousness to its content. On this premise, he concludes to the pure subjectivity of the Divine. This is the concept of the Divine inscrutability, which is common to Buddhism and the *via negativa* of Western theology. Here we may expect to find Nishida developing the idea of *via negativa* along Buddhistic lines, as he does in later writings. However, no such attempt is made. Nishida pursues his idealistic position in a most thorough-going manner. He writes: "such things as God's eternity, omnipresence, omniscience, and omnipotence, must all be interpreted from the characteristics of the unity of consciousness" (p. 190). Citing Hegel, he concludes:

> Nothingness separated from being is not true
> nothingness; the one separated from the all is not
> the true one; equality separated from distinction is

not true equality. In the same way that if there is no God there is no world, if there is no world there is no God. Of course, when I here say the world, I do not mean only this world of ours. Since, as Spinoza has said, the 'attributes' of God are infinite, God must include infinite worlds. However, the universal expression must belong to the essence of God and is certainly not an accidental function. It is not that God previously created the world but that He is its eternal creator. (p. 190)

From here Nishida goes on to speak of God's "necessary" or "essential" manifestation in the phenomenal world. Thus "God reflects on Himself, i.e. makes a mirror of Himself prior to therevelation . . . and from this, God and the world develop." In another expression of the Hegelian logic, "God in expressing His deepest unity must first be greatly disintegrated" (p. 192). While Buddhist overtones may perhaps be read into these statements, Nishida himself chooses to take an analogy from Christian sources: "Man, if seen from one side, is directly the self-awareness of God. If we employ the legends of Christianity, precisely because there was the fall of Adam is there the salvation of Christ, and consequently the infinite love of God has become manifest" (p. 193).

From the foregoing material we can conclude that Nishida's first formulation of ontological and religious categories was an interesting assimilation of Western idealistic language which had a certain originality in that its pantheistic direction was further grounded in his own notion of pure experience. On the whole, it reflects a comprehensive grasp of the literature and thought structure of Western mysticism and transcendentalism. Nishida was evidently drawn to Western pantheism at this early stage in his career.

CONCLUSION

In this survey of the religious categories of Nishida's first major work, *A Study of Good,* we have noted a definite trend in Nishida's thought to ontologize the notion of pure experience in a way somewhat foreign to William James. Certainly his pantheistic conclusions differed from the theistic ideas of James's *A Pluralistic Universe.* Since James and other authors suggest alternative ways of developing this initial notion, we may conclude that Nishida's basic affinities lay elsewhere. He had been introduced to the writings of William James by D. T. Suzuki, and had read James and Bergson in the years immediately prior to the publication of *A Study of Good.* Their writings seem to have mediated his own earlier ideas concerning a "condition of pure experience" prior to subject-object distinctions in the immediacy of experience. But he found similar ideas in Berkeley, Spinoza, Hegel, and the tradition of Christian mystical writers. In the last analysis, his greater affinities were with the latter stream of idealistic and pantheistic tradition in the West. When he proceeded to formulate his own religious categories in *A Study of Good* he took pains to identify his own position with this mystical element of Western tradition. He subordinated Buddhistic insights to this thought

structure, presumably because he was still in the process of finding his way among these ideas to his own position. In this first work we see the beginning of Nishida's life-long process of drawing upon the rich background of Eastern and Western tradition and attempting to assimilate it into a larger position. This catholicity of interest should be evident from even the foregoing brief survey. Nishida's mild eclecticism at this early point in hiscareer gave evidence of his desire to participate intellectually in the widest structure of theistic ideas.

In his next three major works, *Intuition and Reflection in Self-Consciousness* (1917), *Problems of Consciousness* (1920), and *Art and Morality* (1923), Nishida continued to feel his way among Western religious ideas. But a polarity between the language of God and of the "self" began to emerge with increasing emphasis on the "self" itself. Thus Nishida's early interest in Western pantheism, evidenced especially in *A Study of Good* and *Intuition and Reflection in Self-Consciousness,* gave way to a deeper philosophical anthropology in which the interchange of "God" and "self" suggested a deeper ground. He explored this deeper ground beginning with his epochal *From the Acting to the Seeing* (1927), where he explicitly moved his position to a generalized Zen ontology of the "*topos* of nothingness" by pursuing a demand to "give the philosophical basis" of the experience of "seeing the form of the formless" and "hearing the voice of the voiceless" which lies "at the root of Eastern culture transmitted by our ancestors for thousands of years" (*From the Acting to the Seeing,* p. 6). By this time, however, he had already gone through a long process of assimilation of Western categories, so that his interest in articulating the "logic of the East" was in a sense mediated, and enriched, by his knowledge of Western ontology. This philosophical *itinerarium* gave Nishida greater insight into his own tradition, and added to his appreciation of the contrast between Eastern and Western spiritual disciplines. He became the spokesman of the logic of the East only after immersing himself in the logic of the West.

A Study of Good was only the first step for Nishida Kitaro. As philosophy in the sense of pure *tetsugaku*ᵏ it may well be judged to be the work of youth. One is prompted to make this criticism in the light of Nishida's later sophistication as an original thinker. Yet even in his own times *A Study of Good* represented original philosophical talent and fresh insight that won the acclaim of contemporary readers. This fact also suggests that Nishida's early assimilation of Western ideas was more than eclectic. It was the beginning of a new synthesis of East and West. Its creativity contributed to the "modernization" of the intellectual life of modern Japan by setting a new standard for Japanese philosophy. His early religious ideas especially heralded a new direction which was to become the "philosophy of religion" movement of the "Kyoto school."

NOTES

[1] See Takeuchi Yoshinori, "Nishida's Philosophy as Representative of Japanese Philosophy," under "Japanese Philosophy," *Encyclopedia Brittanica,* 1966 ed.

[2] Takeuchi, *op. cit.,* p. 959. Cf. Watsuji Tetsuro, *Nihon no rinri shisoshi* [A History of Japanese Ethical Thought], 2 vols. (Tokyo: Iwanami Shoten, 1952), II, 781, 792. In his early works, Hatano Seiichi (1877-1950) stimulated a study of Western thought by such works as *An Outline of the History of Western Philosophy* (1897), *The Origins of Christianity* (1909), and especially *A Study of Spinoza* (1904, in German; translated into Japanese in 1910).

[3] Hans Waldenfels, "Absolute Nothingness: Preliminary Considerations on a Central Notion in the Philosophy of Nishida Kitaro and the Kyoto School," *Monumenta Nipponica* XXI, no. 3-4 (1966), 354-391. This article treats of Nishida Kitaro, Tanabe Hajime (1885-1962), Nishitani Keiji (1900-), and Takeuchi Yoshinori (1913-), and gives copious references to a wider literature of the "Kyoto school."

[4] *Zen no kenkyu* [A Study of Good], trans. V. H. Viglielmo (Tokyo: Japanese Government Printing Office, 1960). Professor Viglielmo's forthcoming study, *Nishida Kitaro: The Early Years,* to be published by Princeton University Press, will be the most comprehensive coverage of Nishida's early religious life up to the publication of *Zen no kenkyu* that is available in English. Further information on the life and thought of Nishida in English is in G. K. Piovesana, *Recent Japanese Philosophical Thought, 1862-1962* (Tokyo: Enderle, 1963), pp. 85-122; and in L. Knauth, "Life is Tragic: The Diary of Nishida Kitaro," *Monumenta Nipponica* XX, no. 3-4 (1965), pp. 335-358. Waldenfels, Piovesana, and Knauth furnish further information on translations of Nishida's works.

[5] *Nishida Kitaro zenshu* [The Complete Works of Nishida Kitaro], 19 vols. (2d ed.; Tokyo: Iwanami Shoten, 1965). A partial listing of Nishida's major philosophical works must include: *Zen no kenkyu* [A Study of Good], 1911; *Jikaku ni okeru chokkan to hansei* [Intuition and Reflection in Self-Consciousness], 1917; *Ishiki no mondai* [Problems of Consciousness], 1920; *Geijutsu to dotoku* [Art and Morality], 1923; *Hataraku mono kara miru mono e* [From the Acting to the Seeing], 1927; *Ippansha no jikakuteki taikei* [The Self-Conscious System of the Universal], 1930; *Mu no jikakuteki gentei* [The Self-Conscious Determination of Nothingness], 1932; *Tetsugaku no kompon mondai* [Basic Problems of Philosophy], 2 vols., 1933-34; and six volumes of philosophical essays.

[6] Watsuji Tetsuro (1889-1960), while indebted to Nishida's thought, is one example of a modern Japanese philosopher working outside of the "philosophy of religion" movement. Watsuji's *Fudo* [Climate: A Philosophical Study], trans. G. Bownas (Tokyo: Japanese Government Printing Office, 1961), is available in English. Its introductory essay is particularly suggestive of the possibilities of philosophical thought outside of the specific context of religious philosophy. Watsuji's major writings were in the field of ethics, e.g., *Ethics as a Philosophy of Man* (1934), *Ethics* (3 vols., 1937-49), *A History of Japanese Ethical Thought* (2 vols., 1952). Cf.

Takeuchi Yoshinori, "Watsuji Tetsuro," *Encyclopedia Brittanica,* 1967 ed.

[7] For example, Takeuchi Yoshinori, "Buddhism and Existentialism: the Dialogue between Oriental and Occidental Thought," in *Religion and Culture: Essays in Honor of Paul Tillich,* ed. W. Leibrecht (New York: Harper & Row, 1959); Takeuchi, "Hegel and Buddhism," *Il Pensiero* VII, no. 1-2 (1962), 5-46; Abe Masao, "Buddhism and Christianity as a Problem of Today," *Japanese Religions* III, no. 2 (1963), 11-22; no. 3, 8-31; "A Symposium on Christianity and Buddhism," IV, no. 1-2 (1964), 5-52 and 26-57; "Christianity and Buddhism: Centering Around Nihilism and Science," V, no. 3 (July 1968), 36-62. For further references to relevant literature see Waldenfels, *op. cit.,* p. 354 and *passim.*

[8] Introductions in English to Nishida's thought are found in Takeuchi, *op. cit.,* and "The Philosophy of Nishida Kitaro," *Japanese Religions* III, no. 4 (1963), 1-32; Matao Noda, "East-West Synthesis in Kitaro Nishida," *Philosophy East and West* IV, no. 4 (1954-55), 345-359; Shimomura Torataro, "Nishida Kitaro and Some Aspects of His Philosophical Thought," trans. V. H. Viglielmo in his *A Study of Good,* pp. 191-217; *Nishida Kitaro: Intelligibility and the Philosophy of Nothingness,* trans. with an introduction by Robert Schinzinger (Tokyo: Maruzen, 1958); Nishida Kitaro, "The Problem of Japanese Culture," trans. Masao Abe, in *Sources of Japanese Tradition,* ed. Ryusaku Tsunoda, William T. de Bary, and Donald Keene (New York: Columbia University Press, 1958), pp. 857-872.

[9] *A Study of Good,* p. 3. All references are to vol. 1 of *The Complete Works of Nishida Kitaro* (see above, n.5). While I am quoting the Japanese text, I have made full use of V. H. Viglielmo's translation of *A Study of Good.* My translations in some instances differ slightly from his. I have had the advantage of invaluable conversations with Prof. Viglielmo on Nishida during his stay in Kyoto during the spring of 1968.

[10] Viglielmo, "Nishida Kitaro: The Early Years" (manuscript), pp. 47-54, 60-63.

[11] The chapter headings of Section Two themselves bear witness to his point: "Phenomena of Consciousness are the Only Reality" (chap. 2), "True Reality Always has the Identical Form" (chap. 4), "The Basic Form of True Reality" (chap. 5), "The Only Reality" (chap.6), "The Differentiation and Development of Reality" (chap. 7).

[12] This fine rendering, as well as several others in this section, is that of V. H. Viglielmo's translation of *A Study of Good,* p. 158.

Shibata Masumi (essay date 1981)

SOURCE: "Views and Reviews: The Diary of a Zen Layman, The Philosopher Nishida Kitaro," in *The Eastern Buddhist,* Vol. XIV, No. 2, Autumn, 1981, pp. 121-31.

[In the following essay, Masumi discusses elements of Zen practice as evidenced in Nishida's early diaries.]

Nishida Kitaro was born in 1870 in a village in the region of Kanazawa on the Japan Sea. He was to become the most important philosopher of modern Japan. Whether one agrees or not with his philosophical principles, the future of Japanese philosophy must take account of Nishida's world of thought as its starting point.

Before he wrote his first work, *A Study of Good* (1911), he had practiced Zen for decades. Obviously this zazen discipline greatly influenced the formation of both his personality and his thought. He began Zen practice at Kencho-ji and Enkaku-ji in Kamakura when he was twenty-three and a student at Tokyo University. Suzuki Daisetz had been his classmate in Kanazawa. Most probably Suzuki had an early influence on him, although Nishida at the time was not yet particularly interested in zazen practice. He writes about this period of his life: "I did not try to befriend my teachers. I did not have any friends at all. I went every day to the library without talking to anybody, read a great deal, and thought about what I had read in solitude."

When at last he devoted himself wholeheartedly to zazen, he was twenty-eight years old. In the detailed account of his inner struggles which he laid down in the journal he kept, and in letters to his friends, we find an interesting example of a layman's Zen practice, and at the same time we may trace his own particular development.

Nishida had the habit in his younger days of keeping a diary and of writing on the second page of the cover of each year's journal, in calligraphy, what he resolved to do in the year to come as well as the books he promised himself to read and the thinkers he planned to study. For 1897 he wrote: "A real man should have the courage to look upon himself as an ignoramus and an illiterate person." This betrays his will to attain fundamental insight by religious practice. From July 1 to 7 of that year and again from August 6 to 12 he took part in a sesshin at Myoshin-ji under the Zen master Kokan. From 1898 onward his notes on zazen became quite frequent. On page two of that year's journal he copied these stories to serve as exemplars:

> "Long ago, T'zu-ming practiced zazen with six or seven of his friends. It was very cold and his companions got discouraged. T'zu-ming, however, stayed awake all night and gave himself courage by recalling that for the ancients the greater the pains taken, the greater the light attained. What was he, after all? he thought. Although alive, what good was he to others? If he were to die, who would miss him? When all was said and done, of what use was he? In order not to fall asleep, he pricked his thighs with a gimlet."

> "If others reached their goal by trying ten times; I'll try a hundred times, if it took them a hundred times, I'll give it a thousand tries."

> "Yi-an Chiun pursued Zen with particular fervor. Every night he complained, 'Today was a lost day again. I have no idea yet how to direct my spirit tomorrow.' He never exchanged a word with the other members in his community. . . ."

> "When Kosen decided to study Zen, he swore: 'From now on I am going to seek the Great Way. If in five or ten years I have not reached enlightenment, it will mean that I am just a rotten stick, or a fence smeared with excrement. Then surely I would have been useless for anything in this world and I will hide myself in the mountains and never show my face again.' After this resolution and without caring any more about his bodily well-being, he set out on his search for the Way."

The first week of January, 1898, he was then twenty-eight, Nishida went to Myoshinji to devote himself totally to zazen and sanzen. A monk told him that he had known someone who even after sixteen years had not reached awakening. Nishida wrote in his journal:

"When I heard that, my hair stood on end. Would I be someone of that ilk? But then, thinking further, I felt: All right then, let us suppose I couldn't reach it all my life, so what! If I am incapable or too slow-witted, what would it help me to devote myself to something else! I have heard it said that it took Master Reiun more than twenty years to attain enlightenment." Every day from then on Nishida made a note of the number of hours of zazen he had done. In his diary he wrote: "Master Torei said: 'When you sit, seek while sitting; when you walk, seek while walking; when lying down, seek while lying down; when you eat, seek while eating and when you talk, go on seeking. When you work, in whatever you do, seek while working.'"

In 1899 he wrote: "I received a rude letter from Mr. X. It made me boiling mad. It upset me all through my zazen and I felt very ashamed. I got up and started to answer him. I was particularly ashamed because of my lack of willpower. That night I could not concentrate on my zazen either." It was not until the next afternoon that he quieted down, but his heart only recovered its serenity in the evening when he read Bassui's "Sermon on Zen." His entry for February 23 is: "Zazen at dawn. Have been very disturbed. I could not help thinking that I have to get on with my studies. I must take Te-shan as my example." And the next day: "Zazen at dawn—I can't get rid of the idea that I should not just read ancient texts and other people's thoughts." He became more and more torn between zazen study and his thirst for learning and knowledge.

On March 14 he wrote: "I have made a new decision: from tomorrow on I'll practice zazen for an hour in the morning and without excuse from eight to eleven p.m." A few weeks later he noted: "Never for a moment even must you lose sight of the koan *mu*." But a month after that he complained: "My morning zazen has already been spoilt by sleepiness. I am too troubled by the thought that I definitely must read Dante." Replying to a letter of a childhood friend Yamamoto Ryokichi he wrote: "What do you do to focus your thought? As far as I am concerned, I believe that Zen is the shortest way to such a unification, and if I am unable to do it by this shortest method, it would probably be vain to try some other way. So whether I get somewhere or not, I'll go on practicing zazen all my life."

In 1900, when he was thirty, there are no diary notes, no letters to be found. Did he stop writing in order to concentrate even more on his zazen? He started the year 1901 again by doing zazen practice in the hermitage of Master Setsumon during the first week in January. At the end of the week the Master invited him to his room for a talk, about which Nishida jots down: "The essence of sanzen lies in a profound, clean, and single-minded effort. People tend to use Zen for all kinds of purposes. That is a great mistake. The essential purpose of sanzen is to be freed from life-and-death. There is no other purpose. I reexamined myself from the very ground of myself." Maybe this was the time he had started to think that he might utilize the insights he had grasped in zazen as the basis on which to build a philosophy. A few days later Setsumon taught him a method of "inward meditation" which he firmly resolved to use from then on.

On February 14, he received a letter from Suzuki Daisetz which caused him to reflect: "Suzuki writes, 'I find my peace of mind in the precept: "However many sentient beings there are, I vow to save them all." 'Suzuki has a serene and noble heart! How I envy him. As far as I am concerned, I exhaust my body and soul every day with all kinds of selfish desires. Shame! Shame! My will for the Way is weak. Many times every single day I forget all about the Way. My will and my flesh are weak. Today especially I committed a great mistake and it is all because I lack the will-power to remain stoical."

His inward struggles were violent. While reading a biography of Saint Paul that April he wrote: "I really admire that strength of character. What Christianity is now, is due to personalities like that." Nishida's interest was not limited to Zen, and he wrote in a letter to his friend Yamamoto: "The Bible is a real consolation to me. I find it superior to Confucius' *Analects.*"

In May the journal records: "Several years have now elapsed since I started Zen. Sometimes I advance, sometimes I retreat, I reach nothing. I am really shamefaced." Beginning July he heard about Yamaoka Tesshu and wrote down: "What I admire in him is the perseverance of his day-long concentration without relaxation. That is the way one should be, for it is easy enough to have spurts of momentary courage, but it is permanence that is really difficult." And soon after he wrote to Yamamoto: "Besides knowledge and ordinary ethics there must be the unwavering spiritual fact in confrontation with whatever questioning which may come up. Without that, I believe, life has no meaning whatever."

In 1902, at age thirty-three, the first lines he wrote on New Year's day were: "Five years already gone, flabbily

and without results." And late February he wrote himself a code of conduct: "After all, our studies enrich our lives, even if we can't make use of them. Life is what is most important and without life study is totally useless. One should not read too quickly and skip over things." It was at that time that Nishida taught ethics at Kanazawa and was constantly aware of not wanting to get stuck in sheer theory, but to remain in constant touch with the deep experience of the human soul. Until then he had concentrated completely on the *mu* koan, but in August Master Setsumon advised him to replace it by the "Sound of One Hand" which he felt was more suitable for Nishida.

Generally speaking, philosophers, discursive thinkers like Nishida, are not particularly adaptable to zazen. In a letter to Suzuki in October of that year Nishida questions himself:

> I believe that sanzen does not help me at all. It would be sufficient to concentrate completely on one's koan and to try during everyday life to keep concentrating on it in order to reach awakening by oneself. Even if the Master tells you that you solved your koan, if you don't feel satisfied with yourself, what is the use? When I think of some of the Zen adepts of our time, people who would not even want to have anything to do with a man of inferior capacities like myself, who pass koans easily and therefore think that they are profound and superior beings, and when I look at these people in their daily life and listen to what they talk about, I am not particularly impressed. How do you see this? Your letters stimulate me very much and I would be so happy if sometimes you'd give me your views on religion. Although from time to time I am in the profane world and once in a while come out of it, though without really reaching 'That' absolutely, I'll never find peace, even in death. I just wish that you would understand what I so sincerely search for.

This is the attitude of a real Zen man, for it is important not to become dependent on a master: the criterion is within oneself.

On the last page for that year the journal says: "Zazen every evening from 9-11, reading from 6-9. Sunday afternoon zazen. Sunday evening reading." In 1903 (he was then thirty-four), he once again stayed with Setsumon from New Year's Eve for a week or more, but on New Year's day his journal is full of complaints: "I practiced zazen all day long, but sit as I may, I am not able to attend to things seriously. I think of everything at the same time. I long for a trip to Europe, I dream of becoming a university professor. I have all kinds of pains from sitting, and they distract me. Somebody said that one can't do anything worthwhile, without considering oneself already dead. So I tried to persuade myself that I died on December 31st, 1902. But I don't really believe it. The ancients say that one must abandon all things. I must absolutely abandon everything and believe I am dead, otherwise my practice will never be pure."

From then on one finds in his journal various notes about his readings from Dante and Goethe's *Faust,* but nothing about zazen until January 31st when he spent an afternoon at Master Setsumon's hermitage; and then nothing but a note: "Evening, zazen, all kinds of ideas turning in my mind as in a beehive, I am surely not serious." That June he writes: "Just finished reading the *Awakening of Faith in Mahayana* by Ashvaghosha. Often I feel like doing historical research on Buddhism, but there are too many things I want to do at the same time, and I am too keen on a reputation. If I wake up to a great truth and succeed in explaining it in today's words, it will suffice. No other useless desires should be born in me. People who want to do thirty-six things at the same time, end up without finishing a single one." His heart seems constantly to be involved in a tug of war between the immobility of zazen and demonic impulses in constant motion!

Between July 19 and August 6 he stayed with Master Koshu at the Koho-an of Daitoku-ji for sanzen. During this short period the highs and lows of his moods are described in his journal. On the 19th, for instance, he was received by Koshu and found the master simple and informal. After this visit he resolved again: "This timeI'll practice firmly," but four days later he wrote: "It is wrong of me to wish to practice Zen in order to use it as part of my total knowledge. I should practice it simply for my spirit and my life until I can see into my Essence. I should not even think of either religion or philosophy! You, Nishida, left your family far away, and came to Kyoto. Would you dare to go back home without having reached a single one of your objectives, and that because of sheer laziness? If that is the way you spend your years, where will it lead you? The Master has changed my koan again. He gave me the 'Phoo Phoo' koan."

And on the 25th he wrote: "Today and yesterday sheer laziness. My koan has been changed and it had just done me in." The next day: "Today's monks are meaningless, valueless, worthless. What does all the practice really lead up to?" All during his life Nishida went on proclaiming: "Today's Zen bonzes know very little and that is terrible." Until the end of his life he kept a critical attitude toward traditional Zen.

On the 27th he wrote: "Oh how evil, how demonic! One thinks of Jesus' suffering in the desert." As he went through that internal struggle during his sanzen on the 3rd of August, the master approved Nishida's understanding of the *mu* koan. Nishida writes in his notes: "Nevertheless I am not in the least satisfied." Apparently philosophers, whose life consists of "doubts," never succeed in the great sudden Awakening so often mentioned in Chinese Zen stories. Probably a philosopher can never completely abstain from reasoning.

When he was thirty-five, in 1904, he did not follow his habit of starting the year with another stay at Setsumon's hermitage. He stayed at home, more and more concerned with a personal deepening out of his philosophical thought, grounded in his own experience, than in Zen practice. On January 2 we find: "I have often wanted to learn French. I have the impression that of the philosophi-cal works of the Middle Ages the best ones are in French"; and on January 3rd: "I'd really like to read Saint Augustine." A few days later, however, he started to read William James' *Varieties of Religious Experience.*

In February the Russo-Japanese War started and that same year his younger brother Hyojiro was killed on the battlefield, at Port Arthur. Nishida wrote about it to his friend Yamamoto: "However I may try, I just can't forget the ties that have united us since childhood. Each time I think of it, I find it unbearable. He who left us recently in the bloom of youth, has become part of a foreign earth. One can't even bring his body home. I have just put a flower on the little memorial for him in the midst of a pine forest, the winds were moaning, and I could only cry. Is life not utterly sad?"

In contrast to Aristotle, for instance, Nishida's thought is anchored in the pains of living. He felt sympathetic to the intuitive philosophy of Pascal and Maine de Biran. His readings of that year are reflected in many notes in his journal: Spencer, Schiller, Schopenhauer, Dante, Hegel, Gorky, Spinoza, the Bible, *Kojiki.* . . .

In 1905, at age thirty-six, he began the year again with an intense session of zazen and sanzen at Master Setsumon's. On January 5th the city of Kanazawa organized a lantern parade to celebrate the taking of Port Arthur. In his journal he cries out his indignation and disgust about such manifestations, expressive of the unawareness of people, of their ignorance of the sacrifices that victories of this kind demand, their incapacity of seeing into the future. That day he wrote: "Since last night my spirit has been very troubled. I have too much ambition left, without any self-knowledge, but there is nothing to be done now than to continue doggedly on the way I have chosen. I am too old to change my ways."

During the school recess in April, he spent another week at Setsumon's, without having much zeal for his zazen, received some friends and went to visit others. Then, on July 3, the diary confesses: "Reading a biography of Spencer, it struck me that even I could probably become some kind of scholar. I am told that James' research is now veering toward philosophy. That will be very interesting." Obviously Nishida's own efforts were already directed to philosophy rather than Zen, but according to the journal he spent another period at the hermitage in July and also five days in Kokutai-ji in the neighboring prefecture.

In 1906, at age thirty-seven, he started the year once more with zazen, but in March he wrote to his friend Hori quite bitterly: "For a long time now I have felt like a country bumpkin. There is no strong personality around, who can guide me and hence my field of research is becoming more and more arid. In three years I'll be forty, I'd better begin to prepare for it now. Ordinary reading one can of course do anywhere, but to undertake some project systematically can't be done easily when you live as a country bumpkin. And so if the opportunity would present itself, I'd be off to Tokyo to live."

In July he wrote to D. T. Suzuki, who was then in the United States: "I intend to continue my religious disciplines till the end of my life. Nevertheless my real field is rather that of scholarship. What do you think? If possible I would like to gather my thoughts in a book. Up till now philosophy has to a great extent based itself on logic. I would like to attempt to base it on psychology."

After 1907, when he was thirty-eight, the diaries only rarely contained passages on zazen, but during those years his *A Study of Good* was progressing chapter after chapter, until finally in his forty-second year the book was published. Yet it was very much earlier, when he was still a student, that Nishida had planted the seeds for this work. At the end of his life he spoke of it retrospectively in a magazine article:

> "When I was studying in the Fourth Higher School in Kanazawa, I often exchanged ideas with one of my schoolmates about Marxism and Materialism. He had a tendency to explain everything by 'matter.' I didn't mind admitting the truth of part of his theories, but I could never believe that 'matter' was the fundamental reality. He was not wrong, just all too abstract, missing the essential problem. One day, walking through the streets of Kanazawa at sunset, among people going about their business, the sounds of the evening in my ears, this revelation came to me: 'Just as it is, all this is reality. What they call "matter" on the contrary, is an abstraction of this reality.' This was the first little twig that grew into my first book, *A Study of Good.*"

And on another occasion also, Nishida alluded to this experience: "I have tried to disentangle things and at last I have felt the *immediate* in which I ground myself and that I had felt much earlier. The first time was when I was still a student at the Higher School in Kanazawa. I was walking down the street one day and suddenly I somehow had this feeling about it. It is still very clear in my memory even though it happened so very long ago."

Those ten years of polishing, as it were, this first intuition by zazen, and by reading and thinking, made it possible for him to bring *A Study of Good* to its conclusion. But it does not say a word about Zen. Scrupulous as he was, he did not really consider himself knowledgeable about Zen. If one reads his book without knowing certain passages from his journal, one would not suspect that for ten years he practiced zazen. In *A Study of Good* his starting point is pure experience, prior to the opposition between subject and subject and without any separation between intellect, sentiment, and will: "When we are absorbed in listening to beautiful music, forgetting our own existence and that of all that surrounds us, the sound of music alone exists in the world. That is true reality." Let us take a simple example from everyday life: when it is hot and we feel the heat, the "hotness" and we are inseparable. That this heat is the quality of fire, and that our skin has felt the heat, is actually a second phase after our analysis of the sensation. The fundamental reality consists of a single factum: heat, before all other consideration

about "us" and "it." Starting from that immediate reality, *A Study of Good* encompasses systematically the distinction between subject and object, reasoning, will, intellectual intuition, nature, acts, the good, religion, etc.

In this manner Nishida deals with the problems belonging to philosophy, but he always believed that the essential problem of philosophy was life itself. Hence he chose as the title for his first work "A Study of Good." At that time Western philosophy moved in two directions: neo-Kantianism (Rickert and others) and empiricism (James, Bergson, etc.). Nishida found affinities with the latter, yet delved in the former for subjects of reflection. All during his life he sought to solve the problems of Western philosophy while taking as his basis the Nothingness of Mahayana Buddhism. He said: "Modern scientific philosophy must advance according to the logic of western thinking. Confucianism, the philosophy of the *I Ching* (the Book of Changes) and Buddhism are nowadays caught in a blind alley."

Miki Kiyoshi, one of his foremost disciples, believed that what is Japanese or Oriental in Nishida's thought is not exclusively the result of his interest in Zen. Nishida often speaks of the priest Shinran of the Pure Land school, and finds an echo of his thoughts in the historical conceptions of the great scholar of Japanese literature, Motoori Norinaga. Miki also asserts that what is Oriental in Nishida comes out of his own self. *A Study of Good* contains passages that are Western in expression, but Oriental in content. For instance:

> God is not transcendent outside of Reality. The Ground of Reality is God. He who has annihilated the split between subject and object and who has unified nature and spirit, is God.

Or else:

> The way of knowing the True Self and of being one with God consists only in acquiring the capacity of unifying subject and object.

In such utterances we find something which is Oriental, which never enters into Christian conceptions. And where he says: "The True Self is the substance of the universe," he quite naturally makes us recall Atman = Brahman. For Nishida, the universe is not God's creation, but God's manifestation. Hence, man finds in God his True Self.

Also, for Nishida there is no radical evil. All realities are fundamentally good at their origin. Evil is caused by the contradictions and the disharmonies of the system of realities and these contradictions and disharmonies follow from the decomposition of these realities. They are therefore elements in the evolution of these realities which develop by means of contradictions and disharmonies. One might say therefore that evil is a constructive constituent of the universe. In order to express the deepest unification, God must first to a high degree divide himself. The disharmonies are to a great extent indispensable elements of the unification. Of course evil is not the unification and progress of the universe and evil must therefore not be taken as an aim. The world does not become worse because of the existence of sin, evil, and suffering, but on the contrary becomes deeper and richer through it. As we have seen in his journals, Nishida was strongly attracted by religion. For him religion is the very aim of philosophy; and on it, ethics and profound knowledge are founded.

Two years after the publication of *A Study of Good,* when he was forty-four, Nishida was appointed to the chair of Religious Philosophy at Kyoto University for the year starting in August 1918. Fortunately, one of his students, Hisamatsu Shin'ichi, made careful notes of these lectures. They became part of the fifteenth volume of Nishida's collected works. From these lectures, in which he presented a critical review of the theories of religion as they had been formulated in Germany, France, England, and America, one discovers that Nishida had widened the field of his reading considerably and that his erudition had become far greater than at the time he wrote his first book.

We shall limit ourselves to his reflections on theodicy. He distinguishes four categories of conceptions relative to this question, as they appear in diverse Western philosophies:

1. Originally evil did not exist, hence the existence of evil is merely the result of our subjective view. Hence evil is a privation (something lacking). This idea can be found in Spinoza as well as Saint Augustine.

2. Evil opposes itself to the divine perfection. Hence the origin of evil is outside of God. For the neo-Platonists matter is at the origin of all evil. Matter stands opposed to God and has according to them not been created by God. They are radically dualistic. The human body, concretely speaking, is for them the root of all evil. Plotinus was more moderate: for him matter is the lowest degree of the emanations of the One, hence it is bad. Such thoughts, tinged with Manichaeism, influenced Saint Augustine.

3. The current of thought which seeks to find the origin of evil in God himself may be found in several generations of Western mysticism. Eckhart coined the formula: "Nature in God." Boehme, Schelling, and Hegel show the same general tendency. Leibnitz, although his thought differs greatly from that of the mystics, agrees with them in the sense of not seeking the origin of evil outside of God.

4. In Kantian thinking, evil is an indispensible means for man to advance in religion. It abandons completely all theoretical proofs of the raison d'être of evil and considers it from a practical point of view.

As we said earlier, Nishida in his *A Study of Good* agrees with the third point of view: evil is a necessary aspect of Reality. The contradiction is the essence of Reality. The appearance of the contradiction in Reality is indispensible to its development. One may say then that from the point of view of the Whole, evil as such does not exist—a conception close to that of Spinoza.

In the beginning Nishida was inclined to identify Zen with Western mysticism. Later he came to the conclusion that they pointed in opposite directions. His disciple Hisamatsu Shin'ichi remarks, in an article on Plotinus, on the similarities he found between Plotinus and the Zen experience.

In 1928, when he was fifty-nine, this was Nishida's response: "The article is good from the point of view of those for whom only their personal experience is basic. Maybe Plotinus was such a man and then what you say is valid as an interpretation of Plotinus. But from a philosopher's standpoint I believe it to be preferable to find the Principle in the fact, instead of the other way around. From this point of view Plotinus' thought does not satisfy me."

In 1936, at sixty-seven, he developed these ideas in a conversation with Miki Kiyoshi: "Some people identify Zen with Western mysticism, but I believe Zen to be more realistic, perhaps even too realistic, and rather different from what outsiders may say about it. Zen has a rather strange way of thinking. Occasionally it may become quite materialistic."

In 1943 Nishida wrote to his disciple Nishitani Keiji: "For sure, I am not a Zen specialist. But people in general have the wrong ideas about Zen. I believe that the life of Zen consists in grasping Reality. I would like by all means to see it included in philosophy, but that may be impossible; it has been my fondest wish ever since I was thirty. What you assert I agree with, but if ignoramuses pigeonhole me in the Zen category, I must protest energetically. Such people only see $x = y$ without knowing either Zen or my philosophy. And they are mistaken about both."

His last article, written a few months before his death in 1945, deals with religion. It sums up his entire religious thinking at its full maturity. His conclusion is indeed that Zen and Western mysticism, although very close, go off in different directions. Zen has up till now developed by assimilating all of Oriental thought, but in the future, thanks in large measure to Nishida's thought, I think it is bound to make another leap forward.

After his death, part of Nishida's ashes were buried in the garden of Reiun-in at Myoshin-ji. His disciples in Kyoto placed an unhewn rock on it which they felt represented Nishida's character most truly.

Takeuchi Yoshinori (essay date 1982)

SOURCE: "The Philosophy of Nishida," in *The Buddha Eye: An Anthology of the Kyoto School,* edited by Frederick Franck, Crossroad, 1982, pp. 179-202.

[*In the following essay, Yoshinori presents an overview of Nishida's philosophy and places it within the Japanese Buddhist tradition.*]

I

At the present juncture of history, our world, hitherto divided into East and West, is in a rapid process of integration. Our great problem in this connection is the failure of spiritual progress to keep up with progress in science and technology. There is still not a little misunderstanding between cultures and ideologies. But I suspect that where there is misunderstanding there is also the possibility of understanding. Fortunately there is today, both in the West and in the East, a growing interest in the problem of the East-West synthesis. And perhaps it is not unwarranted to seek in the spiritual traditions of the East for something that will contribute to the development of thought in our contemporary world, a world menaced with dehumanization as a result of technological progress.

Having assimilated various cultural traditions of the East, Japan has developed her own culture. And in our philosophy, attempts have been made to interpret the spirit of the East in terms of modern Western thought. Up to the present, philosophical thinking in Japan has shown more creativity in the field of religious philosophy than in other fields. But it is likely that it will extend the scope of its thinking into all the domains of human culture and try to meet the challenge of cultural problems arising from our contemporary situation. In the West too, there are persons who are seriously concerned with the meaning of Oriental culture. American pioneers in Chinese studies, such as Ezra Pound and Irving Babbit, are men of broad vision who have approached Chinese literature and philosophy not merely with a historical interest, but also with the expectation of finding there something that appeals to the mind of contemporary man, something which can be revivified and reconstructed for the new, wider horizon of the coming age. Here in Japan I have met many a scholarly visitor whose loftiness of spirit has likewise impressed me. On my recent visits to universities inGermany and the United States I could sense that there prevailed everywhere an open-mindedness, which is indeed absolutely necessary for the study of philosophy and culture. I have therefore ventured to attempt here an interpretation of Nishida's philosophy, mainly for the sake of Western readers. It is my hope that it may provide them with an aid to penetrate into the spirit of Oriental-Japanese culture.

Preliminary Remarks

1. The history of Japanese philosophy during the last half century or so may be divided into three periods, each of which is represented by a group of thinkers. First, we have those philosophers who had accomplished their work by the middle of the century. Dr. Suzuki Daisetz belongs to this group though he was still active after that. However, his case is an exception. Generally speaking, the works of the philosophers of this group already belong to history so that a fairly clear-cut outline of their thought may be drawn for appraisal from our present situation. By well-nigh unanimous consensus, the first

place of distinction among these philosophers has been assigned to Nishida Kitaro (1870-1945).

Then, there came those who built their structures on the foundations laid by the first group. It is noteworthy that many of them were inspired by the thought of Nishida. They studied it carefully, commented on it—a task difficult even for a Japanese[1]—and applied his philosophical principles to many special problems untouched by Nishida himself. "As Nishida restricted himself rather to the pursuit of basic principles, so the development of the special areas became their work. They developed logic, ethics, aesthetics, and philosophies of religion, history, and science based on his thought," as Professor Shimomura Torataro says.[2]

It is rather difficult to form a judgement as to the value and merit of their work, because they stand too near to us; proper distance will be required for an objective estimation.

In the third place, there are philosophers of a still younger generation. Some of them came under the influence of Tanabe Hajime (1885-1962), while others are much inspired by Hatano Seiichi (1877-1950). Other philosophical influences, including those of more recent philosophies in Europe and America, are also felt by them. And their thought is still in the process of formation.

2. In the historical context mentioned above, the role and significance of Nishida Kitaro are especially great. It is no exaggeration to say that in him Japan has had the first philosophical genius who knew how to build a system permeated withthe spirit of Buddhist meditation, by fully employing the Western method of thinking.

Nishida began his philosophical activity around the turn of the century and was for decades a leading figure in his field. It is hardly possible to talk about Japanese philosophy apart from Nishida's influence. Tanabe was also at first a disciple of Nishida, though he later criticized Nishida's philosophy and through this criticism established his own philosophy. After the death of Nishida, Tanabe became the most notable philosopher not only among those who had learned from Nishida but in the entire philosophical circle in Japan. It may indeed be said that the path of philosophical thinking in Japan was beaten mainly by these two men, who criticized each other through lectures and seminars and through writing. Thus they stimulated each other so that each developed his own philosophy further and more profoundly. Not only did they learn from each other, but they constantly kept abreast with the philosophical trends of the West, thus receiving much incentive to delve further down.

Nishida's Philosophical Pilgrimage

1. Nishida derived his basic insights from his long, concentrated practice of Zen. But he was also much inspired by the philosophy of William James and tried to interpret

his own basic insights philosophically with the use of psychological concepts borrowed from James. The opening page of Nishida's **Zen no Kenkyu**[3] (*A Study of Good*), 1911, indicates the general direction of his thought:

> To experience is to know events as they are. It means to cast away completely one's own inner workings, and to know in accordance with the events. Since people usually include some thought when speaking of experience, the word "pure" is here used to signify a condition of true experience itself without the addition of the least thought or reflection. For example, it refers to that moment of seeing a color or hearing a sound which occurs not only before one has added the judgment that this seeing or hearing is related to something external or that one is feeling this sensation, but even before one has judged what color or what sound it is. Thus, pure experience is synonymous with direct experience. When one experiences directly one's conscious state there is as yet neither subject nor object, and knowledge and its object are completely united. This is the purest form of experience.[4]

The concept of pure experience, here expounded, is the Western philosophical mold into which Nishida poured his own religious experience cultivated by his Zen training. As it is beyond the dichotomy of subject and object, so it is far removed from the difference of whole and part. The whole universe is, as it were, crystallized into one's own being. In the *total activity* of one's own pure and alert *life* one's entire being becomes transparent, so that it reflects, as in a mirror, all things as they become and also participates in them. This is "to know in accordance with the events." The profoundness of reality, the directness of one's experience of reality, a dynamic system developing itself in the creative stream of consciousness—these are indeed motifs characteristic of Nishida's philosophy, all suggesting where his thinking was ultimately rooted.

But James was not the only philosopher who influenced Nishida in his initial stage. The impact of Hegel's philosophy was likewise conspicuous, as pointed out by Professor Noda Matao:

> Thus, pure experience comes to cover actually the whole range of knowledge, physical, mathematical, and metaphysical. The "pureness" of it, in part, means ultimately to be free from egocentricity.
>
> Here Nishida's thought is akin to the dialectic of Hegel. Nishida's pure experience proves to be a spontaneously developing totality which includes even reflective thinking as its negative phase, and in the end pure experience is identified with ultimate reality. The title of one of the chapters in his "Study of the Good" characterizes Nishida's position somewhat crudely as "Consciousness Is the Unique Reality."[5]

According to Nishida, judgement is formed by analysis of the intuitive whole. For instance, the judgement that a horse runs is derived from the direct experience of a running horse. The truth of a judgement is grounded on the truth of the original intuitive whole from which the judgement is formed through the dichotomy of subject and predicate or that of subject and object. For the establishment of its truth a judgement is, through its dichotomy itself, referred back to intuition as its source, because intuition is here considered a self-developing whole, similar to Hegel's Notion *(Begriff)*. As Hegel says, "All is Notion," or "All is judgement," so could Nishida say, "All (reality) is intuition," or "All reality is immediate consciousness." For this is practically the import of his dictum, "Consciousness Is the Unique Reality."

2. Next came to Nishida the influence of Bergson's philosophy. But he tried to synthesize it with Neo-Kantian philosophy, which was at that time quite prevalent in philosophical circles in Japan. He thus entered the second stage of his thinking, the result of which was incorporated into a book entitled *Jikaku ni okeru chokkan to hansei (Intuition and Reflection in Self-Consciousness)*, 1917. His basic notion did not undergo any change, but he tried to express what he once called pure experience in a different way.[6] Neo-Kantian influence led him to eliminate from his thought all psychological terms and to follow strictly the path of logical thinking to the end. Actually, however, he found himself standing at the end of a blind alley, where he was met by something impenetrable to his logic. "After a long struggle with the Unknowable my logic itself bade me surrender to the camp of mysticism," so he himself says in effect. Thus the self as the unity of thought and intuition now requires a mystical background. According to Nishida, the self as the unity of thought and intuition is pure activity, similar to Fichte's "pure ego." But the self ultimately finds itself in the abyss of darkness (corresponding to the *Ungrund* or *Urgrund* of Jakob Böhme) enveloping within itself every light of self-consciousness. This darkness, however, is "dazzling obscurity" (cf. Dionysius the Areopagite) giving the self an unfathomable depth of meaning and being. The self is thus haloed with a luminous darkness.

3. The third stage of Nishida's philosophy was marked by a reversal of his whole procedure, as is shown in his *Hataraku mono kara miru mono e (From the Acting to the Seeing Self)*, 1927. Whereas he had always made the self the starting point for his philosophical thinking, he now parted definitely with transcendental idealism, or rather, broke through it, to find behind it a realm of reality corresponding to his own mystical experience. This may be called the realm of non-self, which should not be confused with Fichte's non-ego as the realm of the objective over against that of the subjective. The "non-self" of Nishida is the ultimate reality where all subject-object cleavage is overcome. In accordance with Buddhist tradition he called it "nothingness" *(mu)*,[7] and sought to derive the individual reality of everything in the world, whether it be a thing or a self, from the supreme identity of Nothingness.

The "pure ego" of Fichte, as the universal consciousness or consciousness in general, is still abstract, while the "non-self" of Nishida establishes itself as individuality in the Absolute Nothingness, which includes, not excludes, the individual reality of the thing-in-itself. Indeed, the problem of the individual now became Nishida's chief concern. In his quest for a solution, he made an intensive study of Greek philosophy, especially Plato and Aristotle. He found the thinking of these philosophers to be relatively free from the cleavage of subject and object, in comparison with modern Western philosophy which always presupposes, consciously or unconsciously, the *cogito* as the starting point of thinking. The ontology of Plato and Aristotle rather makes a *logic of reality* reveal itself, a logic which explains the world of reality as seen from within. Whether one calls it "explaining" or "seeing," it is to be understood here as an act taking place in the world of reality itself.

In the judgement *S is P,* the subject denoting an individual or singular substance and the predicate representing a universalconcept are joined in unity. But here there is a paradox in that the individual and the universal are, on the one hand, independent of each other, and yet, on the other hand, include each other.[8] How is it possible to reconcile Plato and Aristotle with their different views of the universal and the individual? As a matter of fact, this is precisely the problem taken up by Hegel with regard to dialectics and developed in his *Science of Logic.* According to Hegel, "being" is the truth which makes a judgement possible by joining within itself both the subject and the predicate. "Being," however, is the Notion, which is the universal concept represented by the predicate. In spite of his emphasis on the subject as individual, the whole truth of the judgement is, in the last analysis, absorbed into the act of the universal concept subsuming the individual to itself. In contradistinction to this universalism of the Notion, Nishida seeks to clarify the meaning of the individual from a different viewpoint, viz., from that of Absolute Nothingness. Thus he propounds that Nothingness or *mu* is the universal which is to be sought behind the predicate as a universal concept. He then developed the idea of the "locus of Nothingness" (*mu no basho*), adopting the concept of *topos* from Plato (cf. *Timaeus*) and that of *hypokeimenon* from Aristotle (cf. *Metaphysica*). From this time on Nothingness is explained as the uniqueness of the *locus.*

4. In the fourth stage of the development of his thought, Nishida applied the idea of the locus of Nothingness to the explanation of the historical world. The following account is an attempt to interpret the thought of Nishida as it matured in his later stages.

II

It is clear that the idea of Nothingness is derived from the "intuition" of Zen-Buddhism, called "pure experience" by Nishida. In his third stage he suggested a different attitude to be taken toward the real nature of things in contradistinction to that taken by Westerners. It is the attitude of seeing the form of the formless and hearing the voice of the voiceless. This is, according to Nishida, what has been cultivated in the tradition of the East. The following words may be quoted in this connection: "By intuition (or seeing) I mean our way of seeing the being of things in the world, through which we see a being and also our own act of seeing, as a shadow of the Self-reflection of Nothingness—I mean the shadow of the Self-reflection of Nothingness which performs its function by projecting itself on one point within its *locus.*" This may be a thought rather difficult for the Western mind to follow, so I give here some illustrations.

(1) Let us consider the *haiku* of Matuso Basho, because the relationship between his *haiku* and Zen-Buddhism is particularly noteworthy.

> *Furu-ike ya*
> *kawazu tobikomu*
> *mizu no oto.*

> The old pond—
> a frog jumps in;
> the water sounds.

For the appreciation of this *haiku,* if you imagined yourself to be a frog jumping into the old pond, and making a splashing sound, you would have missed the point. The purport of this short poem is rather to describe the silence that prevails. Basho always pictures his theme with a touch of vivid action, but only in order to emphasize stillness by contrast—to form a synthesis of both, so to speak. Although the sound made by the frog suddenly, and only for an instant, breaks the tranquility of the place, the latter is all the more heightened thereby.

Of similar import is an old Chinese poem, which may be translated as follows:

> A bird gives a cry—the mountains quiet all the
> more.

A psychological analysis of this experience will show that for the one who has, through the voice of a bird, realized the stillness in the mountains, the voice is felt first as disturbing; then by contrast the first stillness is recollected, and this deepened feeling of stillness prevails in his mind by integrating all the three moments of stillness, voice, and Stillness into one single impression. The voice of the bird here becomes the voice of the stillness itself.

In the light of Nishida's *pure experience* as the truth of experience, from the outset the voice of the bird expresses the feeling of stillness. For the voice of the bird is as a voice, a "shadow of stillness," or rather, a mirror which reflects the quiet mountains. Here the audible thing acquires its existential, i.e., *ex-sistential,* background, from which it appears in a transparent and transfigured form.

> *Shizukesa-ya*
> *iwa ni shimi-iru*
> *semi no koe.*

>   Oh! the stillness—
>   the voices of the cicadas
>   penetrating the rocks.

Here the cicadas, noisy in one sense, are with their voices revealing the voicelessness of the silent whole of the landscape. As the cicadas' chorus, like showers, penetrate the rocks, so the stillness of the place where he stands sinks deep into the heart of Basho. There he stands still and does not move an inch. Even the slightest movement on his part would be enough to make the cicadas stop at once.

Thus the hearer himself participates in the stillness. One's hearing a bird or a cicada, and one's *existing* there as a bird or a cicada, are one and the same thing, since in the pure experience the reality of a thing includes one's realization of it.

One might think the bird remains the same, both before and after the hearer's presence at the place, thus reducing the feeling of stillness to his private emotion. But this is no way of meeting the bird as an individuum communicating to you the mountain-stillness, nor of meeting anyone whom you may address, "thou." For the compassionate relationship of "I and thou" always implies mutual participation in being. The bird participates in the stillness of the mountains; and the hearer participates in the meeting between the bird's cry and the mountains' silence. This relation of the three, the bird, the hearer, and the mountains, may find an analogy in a national flag which communicates the dignity of the nation represented by it to the person who shares the life and being of it—unless one thinks of a flag merely in terms of its material.

The "objective" way of seeing and hearing does not reveal the true nature of a thing seen or heard. It is rather by self-negation on both the side of the subject and the object that true communication between them is established. On the one hand, the hearing of a voice as an isolated sound is to be negated and, on the other hand, the apparent objective being of a bird is also to be negated. Only in this way, the voice of stillness will be realized on both the side of the subject and the object. Thus a poet opens his eyes in the "place" where the bird he hears is transfigured, and the bird on its part gets its living environment wherein to fly and sing as a true individuum. The poet and the bird, as "I and thou," are joined on the same spot, to exchange words of silence, whereby the stillness of the whole atmosphere is enhanced the more. And now the stillness widens its expanse more and more—into the locus of Nothingness.

Therefore, the appreciation of the above-quoted poems may be made easier by repeating the first lines after the last. Thus:

>   Oh! the stillness—
>   the voices of the cicadas
>   penetrating the rock;
>   Oh! the stillness!

>   The old pond—
>   a frog jumps in;
>   the water sounds—
>   The old pond!

In this case the description of the scene is itself part of the reality; furthermore, the poet himself belongs to the activity of the locus of Nothingness. The truly dynamic character of Basho's poems is thus clear. We have already spoken of his synthesis of action and stillness. Its ground may be shown in the following way: (a) On the one hand, the poet who sees and describes the scene belongs to the scene in its entirety: the whole act of description is done from within the scene itself. He himself is the point of self-reflection of the world from within itself, in the Stillness in which he whole-heartedly participates. This Stillness of *sabi,* as Basho calls it, is the spirit of his *haiku.* (b) On the other hand, stillness is there in contrast with an action in which the poet himself participates. Thus the stillness of the old pond is contrasted with the motion of the frog jumping in. But, at the same time, the stillness and the action work on each other and out of their interaction and interrelation in the deepest dimensions comes the "sound of stillness," the sound of the still water prevailing ripple by ripple over the whole length and breadth of the pond as a wave of voiceless voice. Therefore in the result, the description of a motion may thus be considered as a part of the Stillness itself, and this suggests the idea of *shiori,* another favorite idea of Basho.[9]

(2) Another example may be taken from Japanese archery. A German philosopher, Herrigel, has written a very telling book on the subject, entitled *Zen in the Art of Archery.* From olden times the discipline of archery has cultivated an attitude of mind which approaches the serene mind of a sage. If one's arrow doesn't hit the mark, the first thing one should do is to reflect on oneself and to reform one's own attitude instead of looking for the cause of the failure in externals.

In Japan, the beginner in archery learns the use of bow and arrow in front of a simple bundle of straw as target, set three or four feet from him. He must be trained to get his posture right and to keep his mind in good order. After a long preliminary training of this sort, he is then permitted to confront a real target, not yet to aim at it, but simply to acquire the knack of meeting the bull's-eye by intuition. If an archer simply aims at the bull's-eye, there is a chance of his hitting it, but he may also miss it. But if the bull's-eye and the bowman become one so that the arrow by itself arrives at the bull's-eye, he will never miss it. Psychologically this implies a kind of incubation in the subconscious. At any rate, the bowman must forget the fact that he is standing in front of the bull's-eye, to let the arrow leave the bowstring by itself without any effort on his part. This absorption in archery is similar to the self-concentration practiced in Zen. Having mastered the art of archery, Herrigel himself could very well appreciate the quintessence of Zen meditation. As a matter of fact he was the first man who introduced Zen philosophy to the German-speaking world.

Now, according to Rinzai (Chin.: Lin-chi, died 867), the famous Chinese Zen master, a fourfold consideration is needed for enlightenment:

(a) to let the subject (man) go and the object (environment) remain;

(b) to let the object go and the subject remain;

(c) to let both subject and object go;

(d) to let both subject and object remain.

The meaning of this "fourfold consideration" may be clarified by means of the poems already quoted: (a) In order to hear a bird or cicada as a voiceless voice of the mountain, the ordinary way of hearing and seeing is first to be negated, so that one may participate in the Stillness of the mountain by returning to the depth of one's own being. (b) But, even if one could apprehend the voiceless voice of the bird, thus to be overwhelmed by it—even so, if one could not make a poem to describe it, one's understanding of the Stillness would not be complete. (c) Therefore, the distinction of subject and object should be negated to enable one to return to the common ground of absolute negativity (the locus of Nothingness). And then (d) from there, from the profundity of negation, one will be able to let the thing reappear in absolute Stillness, in which both subject and object stand as they really and truly are.

Or, to take again the example of archery, the man who practices it must (a) reform his own self, (b) then face the target; but (c) in the consummate skill of his art one will have learned to forget both himself and the target. Between the shooter and the bull's-eye something like a magnetic field will thus be prepared, (d) so that the arrow now flies to the bull's-eye as a piece of iron is attracted by a magnet.

This fourfold consideration of Rinzai suggests stages of spiritual development similar to the Hegelian dialectic of *An-sich-sein, Für-sich-sein,* and *An-und-für-sich-sein.* In Hegel too, the absolute negativity, which performs its function of negation with respect to both subject and object, has the two aspects of a simple negation *(Vernichtung)* and preservation *(Aufbewahrung).* So it might seem to correspond exactly to the third and fourth stages of Rinzai's dialectic. But the latter should rather be considered a dialectic in locus. It is to be noted here that Hegel also, in his "dialectic in process," presupposes the whole process in its perfection, as it has recently been discussed by Heidegger.[10]

Therefore, the dialectic in locus includes within itself the dialectic in process. But the former surpasses the gradual process, and can reach any stage at any time according as the occasion demands. The difference between them may be compared to that between a teacher and his disciple. The teacher is he who has already attained his goal and retraces his steps for the benefit of his disciples who are on their way to the goal. For them it is obligatory stage by stage to follow the dialectical process, while the teacher himself is able to

attain any point at any time regardless of dialectical sequence. Rinzai's four categories are the master's way of meeting his disciples. "Sometimes I let the subject go and the object remain, sometimes I let the object go . . . , sometimes I let both subject and object go, and sometimes I let both subject and object remain." These words may well indicate that Rinzai had in mind, in contrast to Hegel, a dialectic taking place within the locus of Nothingness, comprehending everything in the world as the topological self-determination of Absolute Nothingness.

With regard to the awakening of the religious consciousness, Kierkegaard, in contrast to Hegel's idea of the continual development of the spirit from immediate sense perception to absolute knowledge, advocated "stages" of life maintaining that from stage to stage a leap intersects the gradual development. It seems, however, that Kierkegaard was all too eager to criticize the immanental dialectic of Hegel, to stop to think what difficulties his own so-called qualitative dialectic might have.

The same problem also emerged in Chinese and Japanese Buddhism in the form of the relation of *ton* (sudden awakening) and *zen* (gradual awakening). Thus, Nishida's dialectic in the locus of Nothingness is to be understood in relation to the essential problem of dialectic in religious awakening.

III

In the fourth stage of his development, the idea of the locus of Nothingness is applied to the explanation of the historical world. Although the basic character of the locus does not undergo any change in this development, yet his method of treatment shows much progress in precision and refinement of expression. About this time, senior philosophers in Japan were being attacked by their younger contemporaries who advocated leftist philosophy. Facing this abrupt change of philosophical climate, Nishida as well as Tanabe found it necessary to restudy Hegel in order to thinkthrough the problem of dialectic and to meet the challenge of Marx squarely. Another current of thought, which obliged them to reexamine Hegel, was the dialectical theology of Karl Barth.

Dilthey's philosophy of history, with its hermeneutic method, also influenced them. Thus their philosophical interest now shifted from epistemological and metaphysical problems to those of history and society. How was Nishida to proceed in this new field with his "topology" of Nothingness?

For an explanation of Nishida's mature thought, it is necessary to direct attention to the three key ideas developed in succession during this stage of his thought (1930-1945): (a) the Eternal Now, (b) action-intuition, (c) the historical world as an identity of contradictories.

(A) The Eternal Now

The "topos" character of Nothingness becomes clear, when we consider the concept of the Eternal Now. The being of every thing in the world has its presence in time. Presence in time means being in the present, in contrast to the past and the future. In the present, one is aware of one's self as an *individuum.* This way of being present in time, where one's entire being, both self-consciousness and freedom included, and the being of other things in the world are involved, is a fact of immediacy, from which one starts one's search for truth. (a) But this kind of presence is momentary and therefore transitory: "It appears to be, only to disappear, and disappears, only to let a new present appear." Being and non-being are mixed in their very structure. The present, therefore, is a unity of contradictory moments. Further, (b) although it is momentary, the present envelops the whole succession of the temporal order, because past, present, and future, all belong to the present. As St. Augustine said in his *Confessions,* "The past is the present of the past, the present is the present of the present, and the future is the present of the future." All of them are measured from the standard of the present, without which we could never understand their meaning. So the infinite series of moments in the temporal order from the incalculable past to the incalculable future, depends on the momentary present of "here and now." The present is the monad of time which represents in itself the infinite span of past-present-future, although itself belongs to this series as an infinitesimal part of the whole. (c) It follows that the present determines itself. It is the present of the present. From this center of "self-determination of the present," time flows—it flows, as it were, from the present to the present. This is an evidence of the immediate self-consciousness. It is a fact of man's being and sense of freedom. But man's consciousness of being and freedom is closely bound up with the sense of his transiency—we are those"whose names are written in the water." (d) On the other hand, the infinite time series, though not to be identified with Eternity itself, must nevertheless be regarded as representing one of its essential qualities. How is it then possible that the transient moment, the infinitesimal atom of time, should include in itself a property of Eternity?

According to Nishida, it is because the present is rooted in the Eternal, insofar as the Eternal is another name for the locus of Nothingness. It reflects itself, and the focus of its self-reflection is the present of the present. The rectilineal reckoning of time may be compared to the rutted road as the wheel of the "topological" world-whole turns around, i.e., as the locus determines itself. Thus into the present itself, as well as into the past-present-future series, the Eternal projects itself. The clarification in this way of the character of the present, as the center of the "topological" self-determination, is a most important contribution made by Nishida to our understanding of time. That the present is Eternity is not to be understood in the mystical sense, in which time is, as it were, a running horse, while the present is its saddle, so that only by sitting in the saddle of *nunc stans,* can one realize the eternity of the present. Nishida's conception of time is more dialectical. To him, the present and Eternity are in contradictory opposition to each other, on the one

hand; while, on the other hand, the one may be regarded as the same as the other, seeing that they are related to each other through their ultimate self-identity. These two points need further explanation:

(a) The relation of the present and Eternity is not simple identity; from the present there is no road leading to the Absolute (Eternity). On the contrary, the whole series of time, to say nothing of the transient present instant, is a mere nothing in the face of Eternity. (b) But Eternity, as the locus of Nothingness, envelops within itself every individual instant, giving life to it. Eternity establishes the instant as a true (independent and self-determining) *individuum,* i.e., as the present. Therefore, Eternity and the present are related to each other in a relation of disjunctional conjunction (or conjunctional disjunction).

This means that Eternity is reflected in the present, while at the same time, the present itself is reflected in the mirror of Eternity. If the meaning of Eternity is sought objectively, not a trace of it will be found. There will be nothing but a stream of time. For time and Eternity are as far apart from each other as the sky in the clearest moonlight is from the stream below. But to the one who rows along the stream, every ripple reflects the moon, every moment reflecting the light of Eternity. But Eternity, in its turn, reflects in its mirror every instant of time. All the monads are included in the world (Leibniz); as Nishida interprets it, this means that the world reflects in itself all the monads within it.All things in the world do not pass into the past (non-existence) in vain. They are all recollected by Eternity. Thus the being "whose name is written in the water" is at the same time the one "who is registered in the presence of Eternity."

Bergson and more recently an American philosopher, Professor Charles Harthshorne, also think that all the events of the past are restored in a metaphysical remembrance.[11] It seems that Nishida thought through the problem more radically: not only the events of the past, but also those which will happen in the future, are all reflected in the mirror of Eternity. They are all present in the Eternal Now.

As the independent, self-determining *individua* relate to each other in the self-determination of the locus of Nothingness, so one self-determining present relates to another in the self-determination of Eternity, which is the locus. Every present moment is an independent monad of time. But all the moments of time put together form the continual time series of past-present-future. The linear time is made up of the instants in their "disjunctional conjunction." Time is thus a "continuity in discontinuity." Each instant leaping into the next is thereby interwoven into the creative synthesis of the Eternal Now, and the past-present-future time is now a trace left by the Creative Now.

Furthermore, time, as a linear trace of Eternity, has two contrary directions. In the direction from the past through the present to the future, there develops a world of cause and effect. It is the physical world, where the past determines with necessity the future. In the biological world, where the individual living being obtains significance, time moves in the reverse direction: from the future through the present into the past. This is the teleological mode of time in contrast to the causal one. The Eternal Now itself, however, as the synthesis of those opposite directions, runs from the present. There the time-stream from the past and the timestream from the future meet with each other so as to make an infinite circle. Of course this is only another shadow of the Creative Now, just as linear time is only a trace of it.

The Creative Now is a synthesis not only in time but also in *space*. So let us now consider its temporal synthesis in space. As we have seen, every present moment is the present of an individual life. But the present in its proper sense must be considered as the present of world-history. So the present of the world, refracting itself into the myriads of individual lifetimes (present moments), gathers these, at the same time, into the original unity of time, the present of world-history.

For according to Nishida, the world is in itself the self-reflecting living being in which all the individuals arecomprehended. The world is the body of the Eternal Self, or rather, Non-Self, as the individual existence in the body is the manifestation or embodiment of the individual self.

Now, every present moment is a monad of time. It recollects (reassembles) as the present instant all the instants of "past-present-future" into the "topological" field. And every instant, as a reflection of Eternity, is unique and independent. So apart from the linear time order, there must also be a temporal synthesis in *space* at every present moment. Joining the ends of the past and the future, time forms an infinite circle in the locus of Nothingness, where all the instants are situated in the center, because the circle is infinitely large. Therefore, every present has the character of a temporal synthesis in space. And the present of world history, refracting itself into the myriads of present moments of individual lives in the world, shows exactly the same structure, whether as the present of the whole or as that of the individual. The world and the individual, the present of world history and the present correspond to each other as macrocosm to microcosm.

Thus time is determined in two ways, linear and circular (spatial). These two different dimensions of time are interwoven at every moment, whether of individual life or of the world.

Nishida's consideration of this problem is many-sided but his central idea in this regard is the "disjunctional conjunction" between Eternity and the present. He often quotes the verse by Daito Kokushi (1282-1337), a famous Zen master in Japan:

> From eternity to eternity Buddha (the Absolute) and I (the relative) are separated from each other, yet, at the same time he and I do not fall apart even for a single moment.

> All day long Buddha and I live facing each other, yet he and I have never a chance to meet each other.

To Nishida God is *deus absconditus* and *deus revelatus* at the same time. Here is the same dialectical relation as obtaining between Eternity and the present. The present, while representing in its essence the character of Eternity, yet is, as momentary moment, set free from the Eternal. In its momentariness it acts creatively at every instant, and in the creative act of every independent instant is the revelation of Eternity itself.

(B) Action-intuition

According to Nishida, not only the memory of the whole past but also of the whole future is stored in the Eternal Now. Does this not, even against his will, mean fatalism?

By asking this question one is duly introduced to the idea of "action-intuition." The past-present-future line of time is found in the world of cause and effect. The cause is that which determines the result unconditionally, and the law of causality prevails in the whole physical world. Strictly speaking, modern physics has begun to reveal another aspect of this problem which comes near to Nishida's consideration of the historical world.[12] But here only the classical theory of physics is to be considered. The universal validity of the law of causality is established by reason. It is the rational belief of man that nothing in the world occurs without sufficient causal ground. A teleological worldview will not change the matter completely. Teleologically, time runs from the future through the present into the past. It is also through reason that this scheme of time-order is established in the world. Praising the work of human reason, Hegel spoke to the following effect: By reason it is known that in nature the law of gravity prevails. Things are forced to go down. But by this force also, a heavy stone can be raised. For instance, the pillars of a gate sustain a stone-beam aloft against the force of gravity. Thus reason can convert the force of nature by obeying nature's own law.

The teleological world with its future-present-past scheme of time reverses the order of the physical world with its past-present-future scheme of time. Nevertheless, the causal and teleological points of view have this in common, that they consider the world objectively, i.e., from outside the world and time, as if the observer himself did not belong to it. This is natural, because reason itself does not belong in the world of time, contemplating its objects *sub specie aeternitatis*. It undergoes neither birth nor death. From eternity to eternity, reason remains the same, while human beings are transient always existing under the contradiction between Eternity and the present.

In the inanimate world, understood in the above sense, freedom and necessity are combined in such a way that the *telos* presides over the physical nature only in a formal way. The future-present-past scheme of time does not yet truly meet with the past-present-future scheme. But in the biological world teleology in the proper sense of the term may be more fully recognized. There teleological time becomes the living principle working from within the biological process. There, according to Nishida, time breaks through physical space at many points, forming, so to speak, curvature in various ways, and thus producing multifarious species. As Rilke reported in a letter to a friend of his that bulbs in his garden had pierced the surface of the globe on that day, so for Nishida the shooting of buds is a symbol of teleological time crossing the physical world perpendicularly and forming itself into species. By the resistance of space, time is obliged to take various winding roads so as to make special visible forms *(species)* appear. The curvature of time into species may be compared to swellings in a body of water contingent on disturbances on the water's surface.

Thus in the biological world time is encased in space and refracts itself into a myriad of individual life-forms. There individuals are the ultimate; they do not come to be from species or genus or universal concepts. As Aristotle said, "a man from a man"—an individual comes to be only from another individual of the same species. In this creative relation of "from individual to individual," one may presage Nishida's existential category of the historical world: "from the created to the creative." But in the biological world the Creative Now is still treading the ground without marching. Only in a truly creative Synthesis will it be able to go forward.

Nishida insists that the world, whether biological or historical, should be seen from within itself, so that the very act of seeing may be a happening in the world. Thus a historical consideration *belongs in* history; it must be a consideration undertaken from within history. What a historian can do for his part, in this consideration, is to contribute a bucket of water into the tide of time (Toynbee). Here a view-point is taken which is qualitatively different from both the causal and the teleological. In the historical world necessity also prevails, but it is neither the necessity of causality nor that of teleology but the necessity of destiny and death. And here the self-consciousness of destiny, death, sin, fundamental ignorance *(avidya).* etc. has a dialectic character, so that the present, afflicted with its fragile transiency and with the consciousness of man's bottomless nothingness, is converted into the blessing of participation in the Absolute (Nothingness), or into the Absolute in disjunctional conjunction.

A fact in the world is, according to Nishida, always an event in the sense of *Tat-sache.* It is at once an act and a happening in the world. "We are creative elements in the creative world," says Nishida. Notwithstanding destiny, death, sin, and ignorance; notwithstanding human struggles, social evils, injustices, wars, and catastrophes; with all its darkness, the world is still, in its true reality, the creative Synthesis and also the sacred result of this Synthesis. Time runs infinitely from eternity to eternity.

But at every moment (instant) time is confronted with its beginning and with its end. It would be justifiable to say that time is redeemed by the incarnation of the Eternity in the instant, which is a point of time and yet, in its true nature, stands outside of time. All events, present, past, and future, are results of the creative Synthesis of the Eternal Now. As such they are recorded in the memory of it.

Now we have virtually treated the problem of action-intuition according to the pattern which we discussed in connection with archery and *haiku.* As the bull's-eye and the archer, or rather, his act of shooting and his seeing the bull's-eye, become one, the event of arrow-shooting takes place as a self-determination of the animated field of intense "magnetic" direction (i.e., the self-determination of the distance). Therefore, the event itself may be said to be the self-concentrated expression of this field—the shooter, himself a part of the event, being nothing but a self-conscious focus of it. The event as a self-reflection of the world attains self-consciousness in the disciplined mind of the archer. Basho's *haiku,* his making the poem and being moved to it by the scene itself, will perhaps provide a better example of seeing and acting in dialectical unity (action-intuition). Here, the frog becomes one with the poet, and in this frog-poet event the Stillness of the whole scene expresses itself. So pregnant and suggestive is his *haiku:* it not only communicates to others the innermost heart of the poet; it also communicates the heart of the author to the author himself. And the Stillness here expressed acquires its depth as the poem resonates within itself. For it includes both the act of seeing and that of composing in their reciprocity so that their meaning is more and more deepened. Through this reciprocal process of seeing/acting (composing), the heart of the author becomes transparent and lets a poem crystallize itself. To the one who with concentration examines a sapphire, a moment suddenly comes when the inner world of the small gem reveals itself. The admirer's sight now penetrates deep through its surface, therein to find the blue sky in its infinite depth and breadth. In the same way, the very compact expression of a *haiku,* will introduce one to the depth of the poet's heart. The poet is the focus of the field wherein the whole Stillness of a landscape is completely concentrated. Therefore he may be called "a creative element of the creative world."

According to Nishida, action-intuition is the structure and dynamics of all creative activity. When a sculptor carves a statue, he sees its form anew at each attack of his chisel. The seeing of the form thus induces him to further chiselling. This reciprocal process of acting/seeing, in the dynamic unity of action-intuition, is repeated to the end of his work. Further, when it is completed, it may inspire him and even urge him to undertake another piece. A work of art, especially a master-piece, acquires existence and dignity of its own so that it may be admired even by the artist himself. As soon as it leaves his hand, its own career in the world is started. Thus it is from his seeing that the artist receives his urge to creation. It determines his work and thereby in a new way carves out his career as well. Here again the same reciprocal relation of seeing/making may be noted. Nishida in his later years often used the phrase "from the created to the creative," to express the character of the creative function of intuition-action. This reverses the ordinary conception of artistic work, which moves from the creative to the created, but Nishida's formula seems toexplain creative activity in a far more adequate way. For any creation through human action becomes possible only if the self-reflecting world expresses itself in a human being, and he on his part expresses himself as he sees his own reflection in the mirror of the world, both of them together performing their creative Synthesis in the historical world. Nishida thinks that his formula is near to T. S. Eliot's conception of "tradition" as the historical force transmitting and creating civilization for the coming age.

A way of thinking akin to Nishida's is found in the recent development of Heidegger's philosophy, although there was no direct influence either way. In his essays on "Things" *(Das Ding)* and "Building, Dwelling, and Thinking" *(Bauen, Wohnen, Denken),* Heidegger uses the pregnant symbol of the "four-together." This is a square in which *earth, heaven, divinities,* and *mortals* are gathered together. The present age has forgotten this original unity of the four and has, accordingly, become "materialized." The present age is called "atomic," but this name is ominous, because it is for the first time in history that an age has been named by those who belong to it after a phenomenon of physical nature. Due to the remarkable progress of science, the present world has practically overcome distance in time and space. Far-away occurrences may be seen and heard as if they were taking place here. Things in the remote past and in the remote future may be controlled by the human brain and action; and, of course, the stars and their orbits are being exactly observed and measured. But do the things really become so much nearer to us? Removal of physical distance does not necessarily result in the nearness of things. On the contrary, things are becoming more and more remote through their very proximity to man of the present age.

How does this uncanny problem arise? Solely by forgetting the Truth of beings and by treating beings merely as objects. Here Heidegger's philosophy of Being meets with a philosophy of Nothingness—because Being and Nothingness are identical in their contradiction.

A bridge across a river joins the parts of land on both sides of the river. But their respective landscapes may still retain their characteristics in spite of their union by means of the bridge. Thus the two landscapes (the earth) as well as the people (the mortals) who dwell there are joined together at the bridge, as a point of their concentration. But, not only the earth and people come together in the building of the bridge. The heavens also participate in the work. For the climate and weather of the locality have much to do with the construction. If due consideration is not given to these factors, the bridge might be washed away by the swelling waters. In fact, the bridge lets flow not only the stream of water under it, but also the meteorological streams across it. Thus earth, people,

and heaven come together in concentration for the building of the bridge. Further, the grace of divinities is also at work there, and this to the extent that the enterprise is a human undertaking. From ancient times a bridge has been a sacred thing, symbolizing in its structure the being of man as a bridge from this side over to the Other-side, to be fulfilled through the grace of the Beyond.

Therefore, a bridge is a "thing" in which the four parties of heaven, earth, mortals, and divinities join together. As to the location of the bridge, of course, one particular point of the river is chosen, out of the many possibilities, for the concentration of the four factors. It is through human decision that the choice is to be made, with due consideration of the advantages and disadvantages of the place. Only then is the task of construction to be accomplished. Seeing and acting are thus a matter of human responsibility. And a bridge actually built in this way is a "thing" in its proper sense. As in the cases of the "poet-frog," or the "bull's-eye-archer," the "thing" here is an event, or a ring into which the whole world is concentrated and reflected. The "thing" is, according to Heidegger, the interplay of these four factors mirroring each other, and the unity of this interplay is the world as it turns around historically. The "thing" can exist only through human participation in it. And this human participation is man's "dwelling" in so far as he actually realizes and builds it. *Bauen* ("to build") is in its original meaning (Old High German, *buan*) the same as *wohnen* ("to dwell") and, furthermore, *bauen (buan)* comes from the root common to *buan, bhu, beo,* which means "to be," as it is still clear in the forms of *ich bin, du bist.*

This suggests that originally man's being is his dwelling, and his dwelling is his building a "thing" in his nearness to the truth of the thing, insofar as man is a mortal living on earth, under heaven, and by the grace of divinities. But man has lost his dwelling, and is estranged from divine grace. He now finds himself in the night of the world. The Truth of beings is now concealed from him, and it is for this very reason that beings in their sheer objectivity alone are so clear and self-evident to his consciousness. Seeing is now seeing an object in its objectivity, and even one's own self is thought of in an objective way.

Heidegger says that it was through intuition accomplishing a work of art that Plato realized the pure essence *(eidos)* of a thing. Here the subject and object are still yoked together, in contrast to the modern objectivization of thinking and seeing. Nonetheless Plato's *eidos* is objective in the sense that it is conceived after the pattern of making a thing by technical means.[13] Therefore, in order to recollect the nearness of the "thing," one must search further back in earlier Greek philosophy.

Now it is necessary to define carefully the terms "seeing" and "intuition." (a) To "see" a thing means usually to see a thing in a particular space-time locus: one sees a thing somewhere and sometime. Seeing in this sense is the first stage of discerning an object. (b) "Intuition" is immediate perception of an object. It is neither *cognition* nor *recognition,* and is reached neither by inference nor by recollection. In this sense, it may not be very different from "seeing." (c) But more technically, "intuition" is direct knowledge of the truth, or of the whole of the thing in question. For the sake of clarity, let us use the term "intuition" here in the latter sense only. Thus, it is not through seeing these roses in the garden, but by judging that they are white that one is concerned with the problem of truth. On the other hand, intuition belongs to the realm of truth from the very start, although it is also a direct perception.

However, Nishida uses the word "seeing" in the sense of "intuition" as defined under (c). According to him, it is related to "acting" and "making." Although it is immediate, "seeing" presupposes training and comes to perfection only after adequate training. The beginner sees the bull's-eye in a way qualitatively different from that of the master. Likewise, the same roses in a garden may be seen quite differently by various people. If an artist sees them, his "seeing" will soon develop into a painting. In making the painting he is so absorbed in seeing and acting that he forgets himself completely. He sees and acts as if it were not himself, but the roses themselves manifesting their true being. In his essays Nishida often speaks about "seeing without an observer," "acting without an agent," or "seeing and acting on a thing by losing oneself in its being." Referring to Dogen (1200-1253), a Japanese Zen master, Nishida explains the quintessence of action-intuition as follows:

> To learn the way to Buddha is to learn the true Self. To learn the true Self is to forget it. To forget the Self is to bear witness to the Truth of all things in the world insofar as they reveal themselves. To do so, we must learn to loose the fetters of "mind-body" of ourselves as well as of others. It is illusion to think that we can learn and confirm the Truth through our effort of transporting our selves to things. In the Buddhist Enlightenment, all things of their own accord testify as self-evident (in the mirror of the Non-Self) that they themselves are the way and the truth of Buddha.

Here assuredly, is the whole of the situation,—seeing-acting, object, and its environment—subsisting all at once. To see a "thing" is to participate in the ring of these elements in the locus of Nothingness. Seeing is within the interplay of these elements' mirroring of each other. Therefore, seeing, at every stage of making, is in itself an intuition of the whole.[14]

NOTES

[1] In preparing this article I myself owe much to those interpreters of Nishida's philosophy.

[2] Shimomura Torataro, *Nishida Kitaro and Some Aspects of His Philosophical Thought,* as quoted by V. H. Viglielmo in his translation of Nishida's *A Study of Good,* Tokyo, 1960, p. 199.

[3] There is no relation between the following words, pronounced the same way but written with different characters: *zen,* the good; *zen* of Zen Buddhism; and *zen* meaning gradual.

[4] Nishida, *A Study of Good,* p. 1.

[5] Noda, "East-West Synthesis in Kitaro Nishida," in *Philosophy East and West* IV/4 (1955): 347.

[6] Nishida himself, even in his old age, maintained that the concept of pure experience remained basic throughout his works, although the expression of it had undergone revision and remolding.

[7] Personally I would prefer "non-being" as an equivalent for *mu.* But "nothingness" is more commonly used in this sense. Wherever I use the latter term, I do so simply following current usage in English.

[8] With Aristotle, Nishida defines the individual as the substance which is ways the logical subject and can never be reduced to the predicate. He maintains that if we try to determine the individual substance by a universal concept, we shall never arrive at the goal even by an *ad infinitum* repetition of specifying the universal by successive delimitations of the general concept. Therefore, the individual is rather to be defined as something which determines itself by itself. In the very concept of "Caesar" his crossing the Rubicon may be said to be predestined (cf. Leibnitz, *Discourse on Metaphysics*). Thus in the concept of the individual all of its predicates, i.e., all of the universal concepts that can be predicated of it, are to be considered as included. In this sense, then, *the individual determines the universal.* On the other hand, however, the universal must be considered independent from the singular or the individual (Plato). There is indeed a qualitative difference between the universal and the individual. From this angle, it may be said that the truth of a judgment depends upon the predicated universal. The universal cannot be determined by anything else, therefore it should be considered as determining itself by itself. The individual is, in this sense, a specimen of the general concept. In other words, *the individual is subsumed to the universal.*

[9] Cf. Komiya, *A Study of Basho;* chap. II, "On *Sabi* and *Shiori.*"

[10] Cf. *Identität und Differenz,* p. 38.

[11] Otherwise, it would be impossible to explain our daily experience of recollection, according to Nishida.

[12] Nishida interprets the operationism of Bridgman in the following way: "Bridgman says that the basic concepts of physics have hitherto been defined, apart from the physical operation, as some qualities of things, as in the case of Newtonian absolute time. In line with Bridgman, I (Nishida) think that philosophy has hitherto conceived the structure of the objective world in an abstract manner,

apart from our formative activity *(poesis)* in the historical world. . . . The content of the philosophical principle that is truly concrete should be given from the operational standpoint. In respect to all abstraction and analysis it should be specified from what standpoint and in what way they are performed," translated by Prof. Noda in his "East-West Synthesis in Kitaro Nishida," p. 356.

[13] Heidegger, *Vorträge und Aufsätze*, pp. 11ff.

[14] The article breaks off here rather abruptly, without developing the third theme of the historical world as an identity of contradictories which had been announced at the outset of section III. Professor Takeuchi had intended to write a sequel to this essay, but his plans were never realized. [Ed.]

Shukei Takabayashi (essay date 1986)

SOURCE: "Japanese Philosophy and General Semantics," in *ETC: A Review of General Semantics*, Vol. 43, No. 2, Summer, 1986, pp. 181-90.

[*In the following essay, Takabayashi contends that Nishida's philosophy includes a system of general semantics.*]

INTRODUCTION

Let us start with words that have a familiar ring: "When we view the same stone, we believe that each person has the same idea. But actually it differs according to each person's characteristics and experience."[(1)]

It would certainly not be difficult to imagine S. I. Hayakawa speaking about viewing the world through the prism of our past experience, insisting that each person perceives an outward world through an inward world of his own. But in fact the words quotedare those of Kitaro Nishida, written in 1901 in his *A Study of Good.* In Hayakawa's words, the same thesis is developed as follows:

> When we consider further that each of us has different experiences, different memories, different likes and dislikes, it is clear that all words evoke different responses in all of us. We may agree as to what the term "Mississippi River" stands for, but you and I recall different parts of the river; you and I have had different experiences with it; one of us has read more about it than the other; one of us may have happy memories of it, while the other may recall chiefly tragic events connected with it. Hence your "Mississippi River" can never be identical with my "Mississippi River."[(2)]

In their attitude toward language, the general semanticist Hayakawa and the Zen Buddhist and philosopher Nishida have indeed much in common. Both stress that people are actually living in personal worlds that have very little in common; both are aware of the inadequacies and pitfalls of linguistic conceptualization; both em-phasize the important role that language plays in thinking and perceiving.

The thesis of this paper is that Nishida's philosophy contains a system of general semantics. I would like to suggest that general semantics and Nishida's philosophy have made similar analyses regarding the relationship between language and thinking.

NISHIDA AND WHORF

Kitaro Nishida, generally regarded in Japan as the foremost modern philosopher, was born in 1870 in a small village in Ishikawa Prefecture. He received his early education in local schools. While in high school, he got acquainted with D. T. Suzuki and they remained close friends until his death. Upon graduation as a special student from Tokyo University, he taught for ten years in his hometown. During this period he was deeply interested in Zen Buddhism, visiting temples for meditation. He attained enlightenment at the age of thirty-three. He was appointed professor of philosophy at Kyoto University in 1910 and taught there for twenty years. After his retirement his philosophical activity was so vigorous that he deepened his views until his death in 1945. It is believed that his philosophy is based upon his Zen experiences and he gave Zen Buddhism its own place in the philosophical world-view.

A series of textual comparisons of Nishida's writing and the writing of Whorf will give us a general picture of Nishida's thought.

LINGUISTIC FIELD

The meaning of a word is determined by the position it occupies in the semantic field. Whorf talks about this principle known as the theory of the linguistic field as follows:

> . . . if a race of people had the physiological defect of being able to see only the color blue, they would hardly be able to formulate the rule that they saw only blue. The term blue would convey no meaning to them, their language would lack color terms, and their words denoting their various sensations of blue would answer to, and translate, our words "light, dark, white, black," and so on, not our word "blue." In order to formulate the rule or norm of seeing only blue, they would need exceptional moments in which they saw other colors.[(3)]

Whorf's idea would be entirely acceptable to Nishida:

> . . . when one looks at a color and determines that it is blue, the original color perception is in no way clarified by this; one has merely established a relationship between this and a similar earlier perception.[(4)]

> The contrast is a necessary condition of the establishment of consciousness.[(5)]

> . . . concerning characteristics, one being established

means necessarily that it is established in opposition to another. For example, if red were the only color, there would be no way for it to appear; in the appearance of red there must be colors which are not red; and in one characteristic being compared with and distinguished from another, both characteristics must basically be the same, for things which are wholly different in kind and do not have any point in common between them cannot be compared and distinguished.[6]

Both Whorf and Nishida agree that a certain color is defined according to its position in the total color field.

TIME CONCEPT

In his contrastive studies of English and Hopi, Whorf concludes that conceptualization of time varies from language to language. In English presented as a continuum, time is treated like a commodity. As E. T. Hall points out, it can be sold and bought. Whorf observes that Hopi handles time like duration; it gives less importance to the distinction of past, present, and future as in English.

Whorf presents his concept of time as follows:

> . . . if we inspect consciousness we find no past, present, future, but a unity embracing complexity. Everything is inconsciousness, and everything in consciousness is, and is together. There is in it a sensuous and a nonsensuous. We may call the sensuous—what we are seeing, hearing, touching—the "present" while in the nonsensuous the vast image-world of memory is being labeled "the past" and another realm of belief, intuition, and uncertainty "the future"; yet sensation, memory, foresight, all are in consciousness together—one is not "yet to be" nor another "once but no more."[7]

It is interesting to note that Nishida builds a similar view. He says:

> . . . there are people who think that yesterday's consciousness and today's consciousness are perfectly independent and no longer are considered as one consciousness. When we try to think from the standpoint of direct experience, however, we find that such a distinction is merely a relative one and not an absolute one. . . . there will be no case when we do not consider yesterday's consciousness and today's consciousness as one activity of consciousness; in the event that we think about a certain single problem over several days, or plan one enterprise, clearly we are able to view them as the same consciousness operating continuously but merely differing in length of time.[8]

> In the case of memory, consciousness of the past is not a thing which emerges suddenly, and consequently one does not directly perceive the past. Even the feeling of the past is present consciousness.[9]

Whorf believes that time is man-made through his objectification, and therefore it is arbitrary. In the words of Whorf:

> We can of course construct and contemplate in thought a system of past, present, future, in the objectified configuration of points on a line. This is what our general objectification tendency leads us to do and our tense system confirms.[10]

Nishida has in mind a notion similar to Whorf. He points out:

> Phenomena of consciousness are things which change from time to time and from moment to moment, and the same consciousness does not arise twice. Even if yesterday's and today's consciousness are the same in their content, the thought that they are completely different consciousnesses is not one derived from the standpoint of direct experience but on the contrary is a result of having hypothesized a thing called time and of having deduced the phenomena of consciousness as things which appear therein. . . . Since that which we call time is nothing more than a form which orders the content of our experience, for the idea of time toarise, the content of consciousness must first be able to be fused, to be unified, and to become one.[11]

LANGUAGE AND THOUGHT

Whorf believes that language plays an important role in thinking and perceiving. Language is not merely a reporter of extra-linguistic events. Rather it is a shaper of experience. In Whorf's words:

> . . . the background and linguistic system (in other words, the grammar) of each language is not merely a reproducing instrument for voicing ideas but rather is itself the shaper of ideas, the program and guide for the individual's mental activity, for his analysis of impressions, for his synthesis of his mental stock in trade.[12]

Concerning the relationship among language, thinking, and consciousness, Nishida asserts as follows:

> We cannot think without language.[13]

> Language makes it possible to form ideas. The linguistic category red creates the concept of "redness."[14]

> We regard the world of consciousness simply as the inner world. But the fact is that the world of consciousness is built upon the linguistic expression.[15]

> Our mind is an infinite flow of consciousness. It infinitely appears and disappears, and it cannot be perceived as a form. Development of language gives new meaning to our consciousness. Language is not expression of reality, but a form of reality.[16]

NISHIDA'S THOUGHT AND GENERAL SEMANTICS

1. Language and Culture

What the general semanticist calls the subject-predicate structure of language is the grammatical construction which speaks in terms of action upon object. This structure assumes that an actor is the cause of action. In the words of Dr. Marsh:

> English is one of the Indo-European languages. It is a superb language, but like every language, it has its built-in strengths and limitations. One of the characteristic features of the Indo-European languages is that they rely heavily on the subject-predicate structure. . . . We say "The dancer danced." But this ignores the fact that the dancing is the dancer and the dancer is the dancing. If there's no dancing, there's no dancer.[17]

A major implication of his claim is that subject-predicate structure of English, which puts emphasis on agentivity, makes us think that actor exists apart from action, but in reality there is no such distinction; actor is action and action is actor.

We could find a similar argument in Nishida:

> Usually we think that there is some lord of activity and that from this there has emerged activity. Seen from direct experience, however, activity itself is reality. What we call this lordly thing is an abstract concept. Since we think that the opposition of unity and its content presents mutually independent realities, this kind of idea arises.[18]

> At the point where one thoroughly exhausts the entire force of the self, one almost loses consciousness of the self, and only where the self is not conscious of the self does one first see the true activity of the personality. Let us try to look at works of art. The true personality, i.e., originality, of the painter appears in what kind of circumstances? We are not as yet truly able to see the personality of the painter while he consciously is making various plans. We are able to see it first when, as a result of many years of labor, he is matured in technique and arrives at the point that wherever his will tends his brush automatically follows.[19]

Here Nishida discusses the philosophy of "suppressing" oneself in art. It seems that this idea of the lack of agentivity toward an object is mirrored in the grammatical structure of Japanese. To illustrate this point, let us start with the typological analyses of both English and Japanese.

The English sentence must have a subject and a predicate. This grammatical construction leads to the concept of the law of identity. As Wendell Johnson says:

> . . . Our common subject-predicate language implies a relatively static world of absolutes, generally two-valued, and it is more or less conductive to identification.[20]

Glen Fisher, an eminent expert on communication studies, develops the same thesis as follows:

> The English language is a subject-predicate "model," as are most of the Indo-European languages. The subject-predicate quality leads one to look for a fixed descriptive relationship between subjects or things and their qualities or attributes (e.g., the lake *is* blue; the stove *is* hot). Thus English tends to suggest, as Aristotelian logic does, that something *is* or *is not;* it is good or bad, black or white. It takes much more effort to describe conditions which are not exactly one way or another—a problem which modern scientists face when they use English to discuss molecular motion or relativity.[21]

In the subject-predicate structure of English, emphasis is placed on agentivity. To quote Fisher again:

> In its conception of action and events, English is an actor-action-model, and tends to suggest this perception of the universe and what happens in it. The actor-action-result pattern is very useful for conceptualizing mechanics, business, and much of science. It suggests the question "What *caused* that?" or "What effect will this have on the end result?" This pattern is consistent with the American personality pattern, and with the optimistic and activistic outlook which seems to underlie the success achieved by English-speaking societies in their highly productive, scientific economic system.[22]

Edward C. Stewart expresses the same view:

> . . . The language itself provides a precedent for it in its clear differentiation of subject and predicate. When there is a predicate in the language but no subject, then one is assumed. The word "it" often suffices for the missing subject, as in the sentence: "It rained." At the level of gross behavior, events or actions also require a "cause" or an agent who may be held responsible. The idea of a natural "happening" or "occurrence" is not a familiar or acceptable one for Americans, as it is for instance for the Chinese. Americans are not satisfied with statements of fact until they have determined who is responsible, who did it or who caused it to be done. "Where there's smoke, there's fire" means that each effect or event has a causative agent.[23]

The subject-predicate structure gives rise to the philosophical concepts of substance and attribute. Consider carefully the following analyses made by Johnson and Whorf:

> To say that *John* is a noun is to say, according to the traditional rules of language usage, that John is a thing of some sort. To say that John is smart, and to say that *smart* is an adjective, is to say that smartness is a quality of John. This leaves us implying a relationship of inclusion, or possession: the smartness is possessed by John, or is included in him. This sort of language structure implies that reality is made up of things that possess qualities. In other words, the qualities, the colors, shapes, odors, etc.—*belong to the things.*[24]

Whorf says:

> The Indo-European languages and many others give great prominence to a type of sentence having two parts, each part built around a class of word—

substantives and verbs—which those languages treat differently in grammar. . . . The Greeks, especially Aristotle, built up this contrast and made it a law of reason. Since then, the contrast has been stated in many different ways: subject and predicate, actor and action, things and relations between things, objects and their attributes, quantities and operations. And, pursuant again to grammar, the notion became ingrained that one of these classes of entities can exist in its own right but that the verb class cannot exist without an entity of the other class, the "thing" class, as a peg to hang on.[25]

Let us take a look at Japanese language. A Japanese sentence need not have a subject. On many occasions, when the subject is clear in context, it is omitted. Dispensability of the subject in Japanese makes it easy to organize extralinguistic events without postulating an external agent to control the process in which action is involved. Because of this linguistic character, a Japanese sentence, contrary to an English one, does not always speak in terms of actor acting upon an object. This characteristic is explained in terms of the contrast between the AGENT+ACT type (English) and the EVENT type (Japanese). Listen to Dr. Ikegami:

> . . . the former (AGENT+ACT) is a type of language which says, "Spring comes" and the latter is of a type which says "(It) springs."[26]

It may be asked, "What is the basic structure of Japanese?" if it does not necessarily have a subject. As pointed out by Dr. Ikegami and others, a common sentence pattern in Japanese consists of a topic followed by a comment, and the topic need not be the agent of the action. The speaker gives a topic he is going to talk about and then says something about it.

An example is: "Elephant-wa, trunk-ga long." It would not be accurate to translate this sentence as "The elephant has a long trunk." A better translation would be, "Speaking of the elephant, its trunk is long."

It can be said that English is a subject-centered language while Japanese is a predicate-centered language. In English subject is either actor or substance. Actor controls the object to which his action is directed, and substance has a quality. As Paul Henle points out, in either case, "subject is an enduring object."[27]

Predicate-centeredness of Japanese means two things. First, as we already saw, a subject is not always obligatory in a sentence. Second, in the topic-comment structure, topic is broader and more inclusive than the comment. This characteristic seems to be congenial with the idea that reality is complex and what we say about it amounts to be bits of comments, being a blurred and jerky picture of it.

2. Process Orientation

Referring to Heraclitus, Johnson points out:

> . . . Upon the foundation of the process character view of reality the whole structure of general semantics has been erected.[28]

Johnson implies that we live in a dynamic world where everything is constantly changing. Such a thought leads inevitably to Nishida. Note that he owes much of his thought to Heraclitus:

> Usually one thinks that a thing which is a fixed object exists as a fact. But a fact in actuality is always an event. As the Greek philosopher Heraclitus has said, all things move and nothing stands still *(Alles Hiest und nichts hat Bastand):* reality is moving and is a continuation of events which do not stand still even for a second.[29]

3. Levels of Abstraction

Levels of abstraction is the fundamental concept in general semantics. The premise is that man does not experience reality directly. Concerning a hierarchy of abstraction levels, Bois discusses four levels; WIGO, Experience, Description, and Generalization.[30] The first two levels deal with the nonverbal world while the third and the fourth level respectively are concerned with the verbal world.

We could find that Nishida does a similar analysis of the abstraction process. Starting with sensory organs as the filter which limits our input, he writes as follows:

> The independent existence of matter and spirit is thought of somewhat as an intuitive fact, but when one reflects a bit, it immediately becomes clear that this is not so. What is this desk now before my eyes? Its color and its form are the sensation of the eye; my feeling of resistance when I touch it is the sensation of the hand. Even such things as the form and condition, size, position, and movement of matter—all that which we directly perceive—are not the objective states of the matter itself. To perceive matter itself apart from our consciousness is fundamentally impossible.[31]

> To experience means to know events precisely as they are. It means to cast away completely one's own inner workings, and to know in accordance with the events. Since people usually include somethought when speaking of experience, the word "pure" is here used to signify a condition of true experience itself without the addition of the least thought or reflection.[32]

It is important to note that there is a profound difference between general semantics and Nishida's thought regarding the verbal world. General semantics aims at handling it with more precision. In Nishida's pure experience approach, on the other hand, little emphasis is placed on the verbal expression of true reality. Rather it is regarded as only a hindrance. In his own words:

> . . . the conscious state of unity of intelligence, emotion, and will, wherein both subject and object

are submerged, is true reality. If we conceive of an independent, self-contained, truth it spontaneously comes to appear in this form. The true state of this kind of reality is something which we must only apprehend and not something we must reflect upon, analyze, or must be able to express in words.

True reality, like the true meaning of art, is a thing which cannot be transmitted from one to another. What is able to be transmitted is simply an abstract shell. We think that we are understanding the same thing by the same words, but its content necessarily differs somewhat.[33]

He does not give any place for logic and reasoning in the explanation of reality. To quote him again:

If, based on direct knowledge which does not contain the slightest hypothesis, we view things, we see that reality lies only in our conscious phenomena, namely in the events of direct experience. To call the rest reality is nothing more than an assumption emerging from the demands of thought. It is obvious that in the activity of thought, which already does not go beyond the scope of conscious phenomena, there is no mystical faculty to intuit à reality beyond experience, and these hypotheses are only abstract concepts which have emerged in order that thought may organize systematically the events of direct experience.[34]

4. Extensional Orientation

Since we have a tendency to view reality through the lenses of linguistic categories, we select similar characteristics out of the world and neglect others. One of the extensional devices in general semantics to deal with this tendency is indexing. The knowledge that student 1 is not student 2 helps us pay attention to individual differences of students.

Nishida develops a similar thesis in humanistic terms. He says:

That which gives absolute satisfaction in an individual is the realization of the individuality of the self. That is, it is expressed in the practice of one's own special characteristics which cannot be imitated by others. The manifestation of individuality is possible for everyone without reference to the talents or circumstances of that person. Just as every person has a different face, so too does he possess unique characteristics which cannot be imitated by another. Moreover, the realization of them gives each person supreme satisfaction and makes him a necessary component in the evolution of the universe.[35]

CONCLUSION

Nishida's philosophy and general semantics furnish us with a meeting point for East and West in two respects. First, both systems hold the view that reality has a process nature. It is interesting that they refer to Heraclitus, the founder of the process philosophy.

Second, both Nishida's philosophy and general semantics have probed into nonverbal awareness of immediate experience.

However, Nishida's analysis of the verbal world is not as developed as general semantics. For Nishida, with his enlightenment experience in Zen, the goal is to acquire a complete departure from the verbal world and to be on the level of pure experience.

NOTES

[1] Kitaro Nishida, *A Study of Good,* V.H. Viglielmo, trans. (Tokyo: Printing Bureau, Japanese Government Ministry of Education, 1960), p. 78.

[2] Samuel I. Hayakawa, *Symbol, Status, and Personality* (New York: Harcourt Brace Jovanovich, 1958), p. 8.

[3] Benjamin L. Whorf, *Language, Thought, and Reality* (Cambridge, MA: The MIT Press, 1956), p. 209.

[4] Nishida, *op. cit.,* p. 7.

[5] *Ibid.,* p. 50.

[6] *Ibid.,* p. 58.

[7] Whorf, *op. cit.,* pp. 143-144.

[8] Nishida, *op. cit.,* pp. 62-63.

[9] *Ibid.,* p. 2.

[10] Whorf, *op. cit.,* p. 144.

[11] Nishida, *op. cit.,* pp. 63-64.

[12] Whorf, *op. cit.,* p. 212.

[13] Kitaro Nishida, *Complete Works of Kitaro Nishida,* Vol. 13 (Tokyo: Twanami-shoten, 1966), p. 143, my translation.

[14] Kitaro Nishida, *Complete Works of Kitaro Nishida,* Vol. 4 (Tokyo: Twanami-shoten, 1965), p. 160-161, my translation.

[15] Kitaro Nishida, *Complete Works of Kitaro Nishida,* Vol. 10 (Tokyo: Twanami-shoten, 1965), p. 430, my translation.

[16] *Ibid.,* p. 180, my translation.

[17] Richard P. March, "Limiting Structures of Language and Culture," in *Teaching General Semantics,* Mary Morain, ed. (San Francisco: International Society for General Semantics, 1969), pp. 106-109.

[18] Nishida, *A Study of Good, op. cit.,* pp. 61-62.

[19] *Ibid.,* p. 143.

[20] Wendell Johnson, *People in Quandaries* (San Francisco: International Society for General Semantics, 1946), p. 276.

[21] Glen H. Fisher, *Public Diplomacy and the Behavioral Sciences* (Bloomington: Indiana University Press, 1972), pp. 119-120.

[22] *Ibid.,* p. 120.

[23] Edward C. Stewart, *American Cultural Patterns* (Chicago: Intercultural Press, 1972), p. 28.

[24] Johnson, *op. cit.,* p. 121.

[25] Whorf, *op. cit.,* p. 241.

[26] Yoshihiko Ikegami, "How Universal is a Localist Hypothesis? A Linguistic Contribution to the Study of 'Semantic Styles' of Language" (Trier: Linguistic Agency, University of Trier, 1978), p. 13.

[27] Paul Henle, "Language, Thought, and Culture," in *Language, Thought, and Culture,* Paul Henle, ed. (Michigan: The University of Michigan Press, 1965), p. 10.

[28] Johnson, *op. cit.,* p. 23.

[29] Nishida, *A Study of Good, op. cit.,* p. 57.

[30] J. Samuel Bois, *The Art of Awareness* (Iowa: Wm. C. Brown Company Publishers, 1978), pp. 84-85.

[31] Nishida, *op. cit.,* p. 39.

[32] *Ibid.,* p. 1.

[33] *Ibid.,* pp. 53-54.

[34] *Ibid.,* pp. 42-43.

[35] *Ibid.,* pp. 146-147.

Andrew Feenberg and Yoko Arisaka (essay date 1990)

SOURCE: "Experiential Ontology: The Origins of the Nishida Philosophy in the Doctrine of Pure Experience," in *International Philosophical Quarterly,* Vol. XXX, No. 2, June, 1990, pp. 173-205.

[*In the following essay, Feenberg and Arisaka examine Nishida's doctrine of pure experience as influenced by William James.*]

I. INTRODUCTION: THE DISCOVERY OF EXPERIENCE

The early twentieth century was a time of gathering crisis in the European intellectual world. In the previous generation only isolated thinkers challenged the dominant naturalistic and neo-Kantian paradigms. Nietzsche, for example, argued that Western philosophy was still a tributary of decaying Christian theology and the old Aristotelian metaphysics of substance. But signs of general breakdown multiplied as the turn of the century neared. A rising generation of philosophers challenged the prevailing consensus in the name of new doctrines of life and experience.

These new doctrines were as opposed to empiricism, with its emphasis on the epistemological function of experience, as they were to Kantian transcendentalism and naturalism, accused of substituting abstract theoretical models for the concrete reality at the foundation of existence. The new philosophers claimed that philosophy must begin with "human life," the "things themselves," the raw material of experience. They objected to contemporary thought on the grounds that despite all its efforts to escape from the speculative tradition, it was still under the influence of Aristotelian-Cartesian categories and assumptions. This was an international trend preparing a resurgence of speculation on anentirely new basis in phenomenology and existentialism.

Although these new philosophers shared the basic claim of the primacy of experience, they formulated it very differently and contributed to very different theoretical developments. For example, Mach's positivistic phenomenalism influenced Einstein's analysis of motion in terms of the experience of observing subjects in the world. Dilthey's *Lebensphilosophie,* with its emphasis on understanding forms of life from within, influenced many trends in German culture, including the early development of sociology and phenomenology. The American pragmatists reconstructed the notion of truth from the standpoint of experience and action. Their work opened the way to the development of operationalism and process philosophy.

In sum, the new doctrine of experience was an important international crossroads in the world of early twentieth-century philosophy. This article concerns the decisive consequences for Japan of a remarkable encounter at that crossroads between one of America's leading philosophers and the man through whom Japanese philosophy emerged as a distinctive tradition of modern thought.

William James (1842-1910) in the United States and Kitaro Nishida (1870-1945) in Japan were the chief exponents of the new concept of experience in their respective countries. In addition to his better known works on psychology and pragmatism, James held a metaphysical doctrine of "pure experience" developed in *Essays in Radical Empiricism.*[2] Nishida's first philosophical work, *A Study of Good* [*Zen no kenkyu*], also develops the notion of "pure experience *(junsuikeiken)* under the influence of James.[3]

A further preliminary word regarding Nishida is in order at this point since he is not well known outside the field of Asian studies, and his few translated works do not make easy reading. The major figure in modern Japanese philosophy, he was the first Japanese not only able to understand the advanced trends of Western thought, but also to employ the Western heritage to elaborate an original philosophy of his own. But Nishida never became "Westernized," nor did he attempt to use his knowledge of Western thought to explain East to West. His philosophy represents the originality of his own culture in much the same way as the work of a Western philosopher, e.g., Kant or Bergson, might show the influence of our Greek or Christian heritage.[4] Interest in his thought lives on in the "Kyoto School," which continues to study what is known in Japan as "The Nishida Philosophy," and among a growing number of independent thinkers who have found anticipations of an alternative or "post" modernity in Nishida.[5]

For James "radical empiricism" meant the reconstruction of metaphysics on an experiential basis. This paradigm shift required the overthrow of traditional substantialist notions of subject and object, according to which meaning is imposed by the subject on the chaos of experience. Along these lines, James argued that pure experience must be a domain of meaning prior to any subjective order. Nishida adopted this position and went still further to locate the subject within this domain as a phenomenon among others, something James had also attempted to do but with less consistency and conviction.

In some respects clumsy and unconvincing, these innovative theories offer a remarkable anticipation of concepts developed by Husserl, Heidegger, and the existentialists.[6] The comparison of James and Nishida with these later thinkers therefore brings out the continuing relevance of the early attempts to construct a doctrine of experience.[7] The most basic similarity lies in the fact that experience, which was traditionally treated as an epistemological category, begins to play a central ontological role as well.

Although they lacked the rigorous theoretical underpinnings Husserl and Heidegger later gave to the study of the concept of experience, James and Nishida were among the first to attempt to construct a theory of immediate participation in being in opposition to the dominant naturalistic and Kantian theories. They argued that experience is not a result of perception but its presupposition. Experience is thus not something we could hope to explain causally, e.g., by neurophysiological studies of the sense organs. The concepts of subjectivity and perception are abstractions constructed on the basis of a more fundamental experiential field that cannot be objectified.

The remainder of this article examines Nishida's doctrine of "pure experience," shows how, following James, he attempts to reconstruct the notion of experience as an ontological category, and explains the subsequent transformation of this new doctrine of experience into the "field theory" of the later Nishida Philosophy. This is a full agenda, particularly since there is considerable controversy surrounding the relations between James and Nishida, some scholars arguing that the latter's philosophy is basically a Buddhistic form of pantheism quite different from James's despite their use of a similar terminology.

To us this dispute is more than a matter of textual interpretation: the question of Nishida's relation to James really concerns whether or not his doctrine of experience is relevant to twentieth-century philosophical debates at all or whether it merely recapitulates a certain traditional view of Eastern religion. And that dilemma is in turn related to fundamental methodological questions in the understanding of Nishida's thought.

Nishida's foreignness and his very difficult style pose problems Western interpreters often solve by emphasizing his Buddhist roots; this approach finds support in the tradition of the Kyoto School, which took on an explicitly religious aspect after World War II. But the Buddhist reference, while illuminating many aspects of his thought, has unfortunately limited Nishida's philosophical audience in the West. It also shifts the emphasis of his thought, which is not so much bent on recapturing the past as it is focused on constructing the future. Nishida, we will argue, was a resolutely modern thinker attempting to articulate a specifically Japanese form of modernity which would descend from the Japanese tradition in much the same sense in which Western modernity descends from our own feudal and ancient past.[8]

By "modern" we mean a form of civilization which enjoys the cognitive and material fruits of science and technology, while suffering the foundationlessness consequent upon the decline of religiously inspired metaphysical certainties. In the West, "modernity" begins in the seventeenth and eighteenth centuries with the attempt to substitute man for God in charge of the world, but that project is in deep crisis in the period that interests us here. From Nietzsche on, more and more thinkers join the attempt to find a radically different kind of modern worldview that is not just secularized Christianity. This new position is based on the concept of finitude and entirely freed from the theological preoccupations of the past.

Perhaps no other non-Western culture has ever had a better opportunity to achieve such an alternative modernity than Japan, given its historical independence, and the high level of indigenous literary, technical, and organizational culture it brought to the modernization process. In this context Buddhism is indeed relevant to the development of Japanese philosophy insofar as it is a religion without a transcendent deity. The absence in Japan of both Christianity and anything like its Cartesian and Enlightenment secularizations thus opened the way to a thought of finitude unshadowed by the dead weight of past infinities.

We have approached Nishida's work with these assumptions about his modernity in the background. In the next sections we try to resolve the controversy around his relation to James in a way which explains the central role of the new doctrine of experience in both Nishida's early and later views, distinguishing his basic position clearly from the pantheistic tendencies which, admittedly, mar his early work. We argue that Nishida uncovers fundamental problems in the doctrine of pure experience he shares with James which are resolved only in his later work.

That work constitutes a series of attempts to understand being under a finite horizon, that is to say, without assuming an absolute spectator on or creator of reality. We discuss severaldifferent formulations of Nishida's position as a theory of finitude, and compare it with existential ontology and with what we call "field theories" of society. These latter reduce social facts to human interactions in a variety of different ways in order to dereify the concept of society. In his middle works, Nishida proposed such a social ontology himself, and went on in his last period to reconstruct his own concept of experience in social terms. The result is *an attempt to interpret being as such in the forms of a social ontology.* The concluding section of this paper ranges widely beyond philosophy, to computer science and art, for models with which to compare Nishida's theory.

II. THE "PURE EXPERIENCE" CONTROVERSY

In *Essays in Radical Empiricism,* James states that "the instant field of the present is always experience in its 'pure' state, plain unqualified actuality, a simple *that,* as yet undifferentiated into thing and thought. . . ."[9] By "pure experience" James means direct or "lived" experience of the world prior to reflection and conceptual categorization.[10] Pure experience is thus "the immediate flux of life which furnishes the material to our later reflection with its conceptual categories."[11]

Traditionally, such experience has been treated as an unformed sensory flow. James sometimes says as much; for example, he states that "Only new-born babes, or men in semi-coma from sleep, drugs, illnesses, or blows, may be assumed to have an experience pure in the literal sense. . . ."[12] This position, however, appears to be inconsistent with his principal accounts of pure experience which do not treat it as an unusual subjective condition; instead he generally maintains that pure experience is always and everywhere available, prior to the distinction between subject and object, spirit and matter.[13]

> As "subjective" we say that the experience represents; as "objective" it is represented. What represents and what is represented is here numerically the same; but we must remember that no dualism of being represented and representing resides in the experience *per se.* In its pure state, or when isolated, there is no self-splitting of it into consciousness and what the consciousness is "of." Its subjectivity and objectivity are functional attributes solely, realized only when the experience is "taken," i.e., talked-of, twice, considered along with its two differing contexts respectively, by a new retrospective experience. . . .[14]

James's view is further clarified in his doctrine of "radical empiricism," which rejects the traditional empiricist construction of experience as a collection of atomistic sense data connected by subjective associations. In contrast, he argues that "To be radical, an empiricism must neither admit into its constructionsany element that is not directly experienced, nor exclude from them any element

that is directly experienced."[15] The chief claim of this new doctrine is that, insofar as the relations which connect experiences, such as "by," "after," "from . . . to," are themselves experienced, they must be counted as just as "real" as the terms related.[16]

Although this position appears to be a retreat from the general constructivist assumptions of nearly all post-Kantian philosophy, it is not just a return to naive realism. Radical empiricism is also a rather crude anticipation of the phenomenological concept of the "noema" as the meaningful object in the stream of consciousness. This object is not mere sense data, but has its own intrinsic order, which can be explicated by phenomenological description. The introduction of the noema eliminates the psychologistic construction of experience by a soul-thing which would itself be *in* experience and causally related to its objects. James's intent is similar: if relations and meanings are already parts of pure experience, he does not need external meaning-positing entities such as the "Substances, Transcendental Egos, or Absolutes of other philosophies."[17] Instead, experience has its own coherence; it is like a "mosaic" in which the pieces blend smoothly into one another.[18]

Nishida's frequent reference to these ideas indicates a Jamesian source for his own concept of pure experience, as Ryosuke Ohashi, among others, points out.[19] For example, Nishida begins *A Study of Good* by stating that:

> To experience means to know events just as they are. It is to know things without the self's operations interfering. What we normally consider experience is filled with thoughts. "Pure" means, however, the state prior to thought. For example, when we see a color or hear a sound, pure experience is prior to thoughts such as "this is an external event," or "I am feeling such and such," or even prior to judgments of the color or the sound. Pure experience is thus identical to direct experience.[20]

As with James, pure experience for Nishida is immediate or prereflective experience prior to conceptual categorization.

Like James, Nishida argues that experience is "as yet neither subject nor object," and that "knowledge and its object are one."[21] The distinction between subject and object, according to Nishida, "occurs as an opposition when the unity of experience is lost."[22] The subject does not "have" the pure experience "of" the object, but rather pure experience is a unified totality, and subject and object come to be differentiated within that totality through reflection.

Nishida also agrees with James that once the primacy of the subject-object split is rejected, the mental and the physical cannot be clearly distinguished. The external world is not an independent existence standing in a certain relation to consciousness; rather, the external world and consciousness are two aspects of pure experience which, as a single reality, is itself neither psychical nor material. Moreover, relational prepositions such as "from . . . to" are experienced as just as real as the terms involved. As Masaaki Kosaka points out, this line of argument is clearly borrowed from James.[23]

Despite such similarities, Tadashi Ogawa and Torataro Shimomura believe that James and Nishida hold fundamentally different notions of pure experience.[24] And Keiji Nishitani writes that "standpoints such as Mach's and James's are still not exactly that of 'true' pure experience."[25] These views are largely due to Nishida himself who misrepresented James's position in several remarks in texts other than *A Study of Good.* For example, in a small essay entitled **"Relations and Connectives in Pure Experience,"** Nishida writes:

> James says that various experiences are independent of one another, and that these experiences are externally connected by [another external set of] experiences of relations. Does he not think that relations are like external "hinges" which connect experiences?

> From my point of view, relations as described by James are still external. James himself states that his philosophy is like a "mosaic" philosophy, and I think it is indeed the case.[26]

Here Nishida overlooks the fact that later in the very essay which he criticizes ("The World of Pure Experience"), James explicitly rejects such an interpretation of his position, writing:

> At the outset of my essay, I called it a mosaic philosophy. In actual mosaics the pieces are held together by their bedding, . . . In radical empiricism, (however) there is no bedding; it is as if the pieces clung together by their edges, the transitions experienced between them forming their cement. Of course, such a metaphor is misleading, for in actual experience the more substantive and the more transitive parts run into each other continuously, there is in general no separateness needing to be overcome by an external cement; . . . .[27]

David Dilworth proposes another way of distinguishing James's position from Nishida's, arguing that for Nishida pure experience has no "intellectual content," i.e., pure experience, is "empty" or "void of meaning," whereas James finds meanings in pure experience.[28] This interpretation, however, relies too exclusively on a few remarks in which Nishida, like James, waffles on the implications of his concept of prereflective immediacy, sometimes speaking of pure experience as though it were antithetic to meaning.[29]

More frequently, he rejects this formulation because of its inconsistency with the notion that pure experience is prior to subjectivity and objectivity. Given that assumption, he has no place for a Kantian or an empiricist view of meaning as created by a subject, but must hold, on the contrary, that "even the various relations among experiences, as well as sensation and perception, must be in-

cluded" in the events of direct experience.[30] Nishida thus recognizes that his position requires meaning to be "desubjectified," precisely as James argued, and included in pure experience, and he therefore states explicitly that "such a thing as pure sensation does not exist."[31] He concludes, with specific reference to James:

> Traditionally, thinking and pure experience are considered to be entirely different types of psychical activities. . . . But, as James says in a little essay titled "The World of Pure Experience," if relations were included in experience, thinking could be considered pure experience as well.[32]

Here we are squarely within the framework of radical empiricism.

III. INDIVIDUALITY AND SELF-DEVELOPMENT

Despite these very considerable similarities between James and Nishida, the latter did produce an original account of pure experience. This account falls short of James's radical experiential standpoint in some respects while in others it anticipates a still more radical phenomenological position. Nishida's contribution was to work out the consequences of relativizing the subject/object relation for the concept of individuality and the process character of experience, consequences which at least partially escaped James's view.

1.

James's non-subjectivistic notion of experience rests on the claim that consciousness is not a thing but a *function.* For example, in "Does Consciousness Exist?" he states: "There is no aboriginal stuff or quality of being out of which thoughts are made, but there is a function in experience which thoughts perform, and for the performance of which this quality of being is invoked. That function is *knowing.*"[33] Consciousness is thus not an entity which *represents* the object; rather, it is an intentional flow which *includes* the object.

The rejection of the primacy of consciousness alters the ontological status of individuality. Since James begins from immediacy rather than from the subject, pure experience cannot be "placed" in individual consciousness. The individual does not "have" pure experience, but rather must be viewed as one of the "parts" of that primordial experiential flow. James writes that pure experience "does not belong merely to an individual, but should be understood more as a primal stuff of which everything is composed."[34]

But this dereification of individuality appears to be inconsistent with James's individualistic psychology and his theory of intentionality.[35] Thus it is not surprising that he frequently ignores his own most radical conclusions and argues for a theory of individuality based on the continuity of personal flows of experience. These ambiguities show that implicitly James continues to view pure experience as the immediate flow of *one* consciousness, despite the fact that his theory of consciousness as function no longer really supports such a view. Thus even though he overcomes subject-object dualism within each consciousness, the distinctness of different minds is presupposed.

This approach presents a twofold problem for James's theory of pure experience. First, his definition of individuality depends on the continuity of the flow of consciousness, but there are in fact many occasions, such as sleep, when the continuity is broken. Moreover, in highly coordinated group actions such as music and sports, players claim that various perfectly coordinated movements emerge from the situation without conscious effort. In such cases, one might argue from the theory of pure experience that different minds share in an identical, transindividual experience in some way distinct from the merely additive effect of the conscious coordination and comparing of separate experiences. These considerations suggest that, in the absence of substantialist assumptions about the self, individuality might be understood as a relative, locally valid mode of organization of experience.

Second, once pure experience is defined as the presubjective, prereflective "simple *that*," then it cannot be understood as primordially divided into "different sequences." Different sequences of experience arise as such only after various self-consciousnesses are established in reflection. In the prereflective state there is only one flow of "simple *that*" which is potentially many subjects and objects. The difference between my flow and your flow is not a fundamental fact, but is a result of the different ways in which the same pure experience is abstracted in reflection. This objection to James's formulation raises problems of its own, such as the basis of such reflective processes, but it is at least consistent with the notion that pure experience is ontologically primary, and is not a merepsychological state of the individual subject.

The underlying problem James failed to confront might be called the *antinomy of indexicality and immediacy*. Either indexical reference points, such as "my" and "your," through which experience supposedly "flows" are secondary qualities of some more fundamental immediacy, or immediacy is itself merely a state of an individual consciousness defined by its fundamental indexicality. Thus, one can have indexicality or immediacy, but not both without a radical theoretical departure James hinted at but did not undertake.

Contrary to James, who waffles on the consequences of his own assertion that individuality is a mere function of experience, Nishida enthusiastically embraces the notion that "Individual experience is no more than a particular, limited area within experience."[36] Subjectivity, Nishida argues, is an abstraction derived from a more fundamental pure experience in which the "I" is not yet distinguished. Nishida writes: "It is not that there is the individual and thus the experience, but rather, there is the experience and thus the individual."[37] Following the logic of immediacy to its conclusion, Nishida claims that in the state of pre-subjective pure experience "one is unable to make absolute distinctions between oneself and another."

Although yesterday's and today's consciousnesses seem independent of one another, they may be thought of as one consciousness because they belong to the same individual system. Perhaps a similar relation may be found between different individual consciousnesses.[38]

This passage shows that Nishida was willing to accept even the most paradoxical consequences of his reversal of the traditional relationship of experience and individuality. James too had noticed the paradox but tried to avoid it. While the cultural differences between America in the age of rugged individualism and restoration Japan cannot explain their philosophical differences, it is tempting to argue that Nishida was less troubled by these consequences of the theory of pure experience than was James because Japanese culture de-emphasized the autonomy and separateness of individuality and emphasized its integrated position within a larger network or relations such as society and nature.[39]

2.

These remarks lead to a consideration of the problem of temporal succession in pure experience. Once James disposes of the meaning-positing subject, the flux of pure experience can no longer be accounted for as a mere accident of that subject's movements but must have some source in experience itself. Experience must beessentially a process with its own internal motivations, and not a stationary thing observed by a moving subject. Toward the end of "A World of Pure Experience" James sheds light on this problem, anticipating the phenomenological concept of "horizon." He states that "Experience . . . can grow by its edges," because one moment proliferates into another by transitions which, whether conjunctive or disjunctive, "continue the experiential tissue."[40] But James failed to develop the implications of this suggestive insight.

Nishida went much further in this direction, but unfortunately missed the phenomenological turn at which James had hinted. Instead of pursuing the notion that the stream of consciousness is structured as an immanent process of growth, Nishida objectified that growth, arguing that pure experience is "self-creative" and "systematic," an ontological reality that functions according to its own autonomous laws. In his explanations of this concept, experience no longer seems to be presented to a subject which is uniquely located with respect to it in the "here and now." And it may be asked whether there can be a concept of experience without some sort of reference to what Joseph Flay calls "a privileged center of indexicality."[41] Thus Nishida's doctrine is fraught with ambiguity and appears to regress from a philosophy of experience to some kind of naive pantheistic metaphysics.

Nishida argues, for example, that "Immediate reality is not a passive thing. It is an independent, self-contained activity. It would be better to say, 'to be = activity'" instead of the "'*esse* is *percipi*' of Bishop Berkeley."[42] Nishida extends this notion of activity to thought, arguing that thought too "moves" itself autonomously: "It is not our voluntary operation which advances thought. Thought develops by itself. . . . Thought has its own laws of operation, and it operates by itself."[43] He derives the law of this self-movement from Hegel, claiming that universality is not an abstraction from similarities but an implicit force of development within the particular. Indeed, he argues, "An event of pure experience is the universal realizing itself."[44]

Nishida has not far to go from here to arrive at a theology of experience. Since reality is prior to the subject/object split, our true selves in that prereflective state are not merely individual but are at one with the unifying activity of reality itself.[45] All knowledge is thus self-knowledge of a higher Self:

> The universe is founded on the unifying activity of the Self, and our individual selves are particular subsystems within that reality. As Buddhists say, the universe and the self have an identical basis in being, or rather, they are actually identical.[46]

Nishida concludes in unabashed pantheism, writing that "the universe is a manifestation of God," and that "God is one greatpersonality founding the universe."[47] He borrows Boehme's expression according to which God, as objectless will, generates the world out of Himself by reflecting onto Himself, as both mirror and reflection.[48]

3.

Nishida's position on individuality and succession in experience is summed up in the following programmatic proposition: "The notion that consciousness must belong to someone merely means that consciousness must be unified in some way. It does not mean that there must be an owner; such a thought is plainly dogma."[49] The "unity" of consciousness, i.e., the fact that the succession of experience is not merely a chaos of events but forms a meaningful totality, must be functionally explained in terms of the characteristics of pure experience itself and not reduced to "ownership" by a subject. Nishida's task, then, is to find a structural order in the world of experience itself which would refer us indirectly to a relatively unified subject of that world.

What are these characteristics, this structural order? And what kind of a subject do they allow us to infer? It is in answering these questions that Nishida falls short of our expectations and regresses from suggestive prephenomenological insights to a naive form of objective idealism. But it is also important to note the missed phenomenological turn, for there is an alternative way of pursuing Nishida's line of inquiry which reveals it to be a fruitful starting point despite his own initial failure.

One might begin exactly as does Nishida by rejecting a substantialist theory of consciousness, and re-establish a workable notion of individuality and experiential process without making any metaphysical assumptions. What is required is an analytic of the way in which experience is inherently referred to finite subjects in the world much as

the inside of a glove "refers" to the hand that it is designed to fit. This analytic can be constructed by treating indexical properties of immediate experience "noematically," as dimensions of experience itself rather than as consequences of the physical position of the subject in objective time and space. Heidegger's concept of *"Weltlichkeit"* offers just such a solution to the problem.[50] But at this early point in his career, Nishida has only identified the place in which such concepts would serve in a theory he cannot yet develop. As a result, he ends up treating individual consciousnesses as branches of some universal consciousness which would be the subject implied in the sum of all experience.

Kosaka argues persuasively on this basis that the teleological elements in Nishida's theory of pure experience distinguish it from James's.[51] From our standpoint Nishida's early metaphysics appearsas a throwback to a speculative tradition James had already transcended, but there is more to it than that. Like Japan itself in this period, Nishida's thought telescopes in a few short years stages of development that took generations in the West. The law of "uneven and combined development" is at work in philosophy too. At the very moment that he appears hopelessly lost in the mists of emanationist metaphysics, he is studying modern physics, engaging in one-sided debates with German philosophers on the foundations of arithmetic, and introducing Husserl's phenomenology to his Japanese colleagues.[52] The astonishing outcome of the synthesis of these apparently immiscible elements was a new system, the Nishida Philosophy.

IV. THE CONCEPT OF "PLACE"

A modern reader of *A Study of Good* finds Nishida shipwrecked on both the Scylla of psychologism and the Charybdis of dogmatic metaphysics despite intriguing gestures toward an original position. To the extent that he wants to build a theory of experience, it is difficult to see how he can avoid a reference to the subject, but he still has no rigorous account of the nature of subjectivity. He himself recognized the problem, and in the third Preface to *A Study of Good* he wrote, "Looking back, I am not surprised that the standpoint of the book can be criticized as psychologistic; after all, it describes consciousness."[53] Nishida's mature doctrine begins with his discovery of an escape from this dilemma of psychologism and pantheism.

Nishida's way forward leads him, and with him the tradition of Japanese philosophy as a whole, deep into the heart of modern continental philosophy, especially neo-Kantianism, phenomenology, and Hegel. The philosophical dependence of Japan on Germany, which continues to this day, is less surprising than it may seem at first. During the Meiji era, Japanese society was modernized through direct imitation of European ideas and methods. A large part of the intellectual elite went to Europe to be educated. In philosophy in particular, several centuries of isolation ended in two phases: first, a rationalistic phase much influenced by Herbert Spencer; and second, a truly formative reaction stemming from the encounter with German idealism and phenomenology.

Naturally, the Japanese appropriation of continental philosophy transformed it significantly. The difference in language and culture is quite considerable. As noted above, one need not accept a linguistic or cultural determinism of some sort to see that many assumptions of Western philosophy would appear arbitrary in that context. By the same token, the Western "destruction" of the dominant metaphysical tradition, which can only be expressed with difficulty in Western languages, sometimes appears self-evident against the Japanese background.

This is the case, for example, with Nishida's most important innovation, his "logic of *'basho,'*" usually translated as "Place," or *"Topos,"* by which he means, very roughly, a variety of relational ontology. Contextuality becomes an essential category of being in this theory. As Nishida put it, no being can exist by itself, but all being is an "In-being." This view has obvious sources in Hegel and Heidegger, but it is also congruent with deep features of Japanese, a context-dependent language that tends to blur the distinction between inner states of the subject and the objective world.[54]

Although Nishida might have reached his intellectual destination by following the path from phenomenology to ontology taken by Heidegger and others in the existentialist movement in Europe, he did not do so. Instead, a solution was suggested to him by Fichte, a philosopher completely neglected in Europe in this period. Yet this neglect was no doubt unjust, as Nishida's recovery of Fichte shows. Fichte should interest us too because he stands in a relation to Kant somewhat similar to the relation of Heidegger to Husserl: both disciples ontologized the thought of the master, opening the way from a doctrine of consciousness to a doctrine of being.

Kant's "critical" method marked a sharp break with all kinds of traditional metaphysics, including the pantheistic doctrine with which Nishida flirts in *A Study of Good*. Criticism is not knowledge of Being, but rather involves a reflective withdrawal from the immediacy of knowing to a meta-position with respect to every exercise of the faculty of reason. This critique nevertheless issues in a rarefied post-metaphysical Being of sorts, a "transcendental ego" which encompasses both the empirical self and its Other, experience.

It was Fichte who found the way back to speculative philosophy through radicalizing this outcome. Whatever Kant's own intention, Fichte argued, he had reconceptualized the entire process of knowing as a self-relation in reflectively unifying subject and object on the transcendental field. Fichte interprets this self-relation ontologically as an active process in a way which brings out clearly the specific non-psychologistic self-referentiality of Kant's notion of experience as construction. It was self-reference, thus conceived as an active process, that became the basis for Nishida's position.

Fichte's attempt to reduce all relation to the Other to a special kind of self-relation resonated with Nishida's

studies of mathematics and the foundations of arithmetic. He was interested in mathematical series and the concept of recursive operations, both of which appear frequently in his works as metaphors for knowledge. Nishida uses these mathematical metaphors to overcome the constant temptation to regress to an objectivistic logic in which the existence of the world precedes its presence to finite individuals. For this view, with its typical notion of knowledge as representation, Nishida substitutes another in which the subject's relation to the world is ultimately a self-relation. He writes, for example, that:

> Knowledge is in the first place an "enfolding." But where the "enfolded" is external to the "enfolder," it is a mere being comparable with an object in space. But when the enfolder and the enfolded are one and the same, when they give rise to an "infinite series" which endlessly works over the material in which it itself consists, then we have an "infinite function" or "pure act."[55]

Under the influence of Fichte, and with this mathematical confirmation, albeit metaphoric, Nishida asserts that self-consciousness is not just a psychological phenomenon arising by abstraction out of pure experience, but that at a deeper level it is confounded with the original presence of experience itself. That presence, the "givenness" of experience, must somehow be conceived in relation to some sort of subjectivity, or else it would be difficult to understand in what sense it would be the presence of anything we would want to call "experience." But to whom or what is this presence presented? By reducing individuality to a mere function, Nishida's doctrine of pure experience appears to block all the usual answers to this question, such as a psychological or transcendental conception of consciousness.

This very difficulty may have been at the origin of Nishida's remarkable advance. He argues that we must not attempt to conceive of consciousness as an entity functioning under the objectifying glance of a theoretical observer. In this customary view, we take the subject and object of knowledge as forming together an object for a higher self-consciousness which perceives them as mutually determining. This critical perception, in turn, can become an object of reflection for a still broader self-consciousness which can itself be considered as a candidate for further reduction to an element in a higher unity, *ad infinitum*. At no point do subject and object escape the antinomial regress.

To avoid this, Nishida argues, the regress of self-consciousness, which constitutes an infinite series, must be reconceptualized as an oscillation between a *thematized* consciousness-as-object and an *operative* consciousness-as-field. All objectified consciousness-as-object implies the field of preobjective consciousness in which awareness is actually exercised rather than known. There is a certain resemblance between this idea and Sartre's notion of "non-positional" self-consciousness as a dimension of all consciousness of objects, including the self, by which awareness is intrinsically and implicitly associated with an individual subject. But Nishida's notion of self-consciousness is far more radically non-objectifiable than is Sartre's, and is not even attached to a specific individual. Nishida identifies this consciousness with the "inner self" of the subject in a totally impersonal sense which will be further discussed in the next section.[56]

With this insight, Nishida recovers the core of Fichte's doctrine of the ego from generations of crude metaphysical misinterpretation. As Dieter Henrich has recently shown, Fichte was well aware of the problem of infinite reflective regress described by Nishida. It was to avoid just such a regress that Fichte introduced his notoriously obscure language of "self-positing": The transcendental self is non-objectifiable and immediately self-conscious, existing through its very self-consciousness.[57] But Fichte's position is haunted by a continuing ambiguity that Nishida attempts to resolve. As Robert Pippin describes the problem,

> Fichte's fundamental or first principle still implies a distinction between the self as positing, and, as a result of that positing, as posited. . . . Fichte is still wedded to the bipolarity of the reflective model. Even though that relation is now one of activity and result, rather than of subject and object, there is still such a relation. Fichte tried to deny this result by claiming that the I does not exist prior to or as a result of this positing, that it just *is* such self-positing, but he gave us no clear way to see how that could be described.[58]

By contrast, Nishida argues that givenness is not a relation to a subject, but is a functional aspect of pure experience itself. He writes, "The true epistemological subject is not the self known in introspection, but the unifying activity which constructs a certain objective world. This self cannot become an object of reflection."[59]

In his later works, Nishida expands this insight into an account of prereflective givenness as a transcendental "Place" or "field" on which pure experience unfolds. As a self-determining totality, the *Topos* is the "medium" in which the apparently independent subject and object are united in a contradictory self-relation. The methodological principle which underlies this insight is summed up in the assertion that, "The mutual determination of two things can be seen as the self-determination of one thing."[60] This position requires reconstruction of the concept of subjectivity in a sharp break with the surviving Cartesian heritage of Western thought. Here we can see Nishida attempting to incorporate his earlier theory of the self-development of experience into his theory of consciousness, so that the former will no longer compete with the latter as an objectivistic, pantheistic alternative.

Nishida developed several discourses of his own in which to articulate his insight. Unfortunately, none of these discourses can be considered entirely successful at communicating what is new in Nishida's thought, as he himself recognized at the end of his life.[61] It is beyond the scope of this article to review all of these often complex and obscure formulations. We prefer to stick closely to our theme, which we take to be central, the transformation of the idea of pure experience in the concept of *Topos*. This approach is necessarily partial, but has the advantage of enlarging the context of interpretation to take into account suggestive links between Nishida, existentialism, critical social theory, and recent work in systems theory.

V. FROM BEING TO NOTHINGNESS

Nishida's attempt to resolve the contradictions in *A Study of Good* led him to the discovery of a new basis for his philosophy, the concept of "Place" or *Topos*. Nishida first presents this concept in *From Activity to Vision* (*Hataraku mono kara miru mono e,* more nearly literally, *From The Acting to the Seeing,* 1927). There he elaborates a critique of the limits of Kant and Fichte's constructivist conception of knowledge, and proposes a Hegelian alternative that culminates in a theory of consciousness which in some respects resembles the concept of transcendence in Heidegger and Sartre.[62]

Nishida's new theory is an ultimate attempt to overcome the psychologism implicit in the notion of experience. Psychologism, he argues, stems from the tendency to think knowledge from the standpoint of knowledge, a view which objectifies the subject as a thing. Nishida poses the problem differently and seeks to identify a standpoint beyond knowledge from which to think the concept of knowledge. For reasons that will be explained below, Nishida hopes to accomplish this through reposing the problem of consciousness "objectively," in terms of the nature of the judging activity in which knowing largely consists.

Nishida believes that if he can find a solution to the age-old "problem of universals," he will have also discovered a solution to the relation of consciousness and being. He follows Hegel in developing his argument through a hierarchy of types of judgment, each of which encompasses the levels below it in the system by supplying a more "concrete" context for the operations it makes possible. In each case, the passage toward the concrete involves a recognition of more complex dimensions of the living human subject and especially its active nature. Thus in Nishida's system, one moves from the relatively abstract notion of objective judgments about things to the practical encounter of the human being with meaningful objects of action.[63]

This account of knowing is unified by Nishida's application of his concept of "Place." Knowing, he argues, requires an empty field on which the object is "projected." This field stands opposed to objects as their *Topos* in knowledge much as a movie screen is required in order to see a movie. In Sartrean terms, we could say that the subject "transcends" being by withdrawing into an abstract "distance" of nothingness in order to construct a world. Nishida qualifies this as a "relative nothingness" because it exists in relation to objects as the specific absence through which they appear.[64] Just so, a movie screen must be blank, a visual "nothingness" relative to the luminous images cast upon it.

At the lowest level, this process of projection is interpreted in quasi-Platonic terms as the "embrace" of particulars by the universal under which they are placed in the formulation of judgments about them. The "red book," in Nishida's terminology, is "enfolded" by universal redness in the judgment that connects object and concept. The particular, as substance, is projected upon the universal in which it finds its predicative determination. A similar relation of the relatively less to the relatively more universal applies in the domain of concepts, each concept repeating the enfolding process at ever higher levels of abstraction, ever more attenuated levels of being, until empty nothingness is attained.

At a higher level of knowing, Nishida substitutes a Hegelian notion of the "concrete universal" for formal universality, but in the end he rejects Hegel's attempt to unite subject and object in the "Idea." Hegel had hoped to show that the individual object contains no immediate content inherently alien to reason. But Nishida accepts the neo-Kantian consensus according to which the gap between conceptual knowledge and reality can never be bridged; the substratum of judgment, the lowest level of the hierarchy of projection, is an infinitely complex experiential totality which ultimately escapes knowledge.[65] With this, Nishida makes a devious return to the Aristotelian notion of "substance" as the subject that can never become a predicate and is thus in a certain sense unknowable.

At the highest level, Nishida interprets knowing as a kind of activity and as a dimension of human action generally. At this level we are referred back from the universal to the concrete conscious subject which is its *Topos.* That subject is not a mere spectator on the universe but is an active being. Nishida's very difficult problem is to develop the standpoint of that acting subject as fundamental, more fundamental than the standpoint of the subject of judgment. Koyama explains:

> In intellectualism, the original *Tatsache* is seen only as presented in consciousness. In other words, the viewer himself isnot an actor; the viewer merely observes what the actor does. This standpoint mistakenly claims the activity on the screen to be the [real] *Tatsache,* or the presented *Tatsache* to be the real one. The "viewer" in this standpoint can "see the world," and this standpoint presupposes that whatever is not in consciousness cannot be known. But in the original *Tatsache* itself, such intellectualism is excluded. The actual, existing *Tatsache* consists simply in the acting of the actors on the stage. We cannot ever really escape that [on-going] world to a standpoint from which to view it.[66]

At this point the argument takes a surprising turn without precedent in Western philosophy. Nishida appears to be heading toward a theory like Sartre's, in which some sort of non-positional self-consciousness inherently attached

to action is analyzed as a further object of knowledge. But in fact he moves in quite a different direction and attempts to *bring into philosophy this self-consciousness in all its immediacy and particularity.* It is as though Nishida wants us to turn inward and take the revelation of our own unsurpassable subjectivity as a kind of placeholder for a literally unthinkable category in his philosophical system. This category, represented by our actual operative consciousness, is the ultimate *Topos* of being which he also calls "absolute nothingness."[67]

Nishida interprets *this consciousness qua "Topos"* as a kind of absolute predicate which can never become a subject, correlated with the concreteness of the true individual, the Aristotelian substance, the subject which can never become a predicate. This non-objectifiable consciousness, or *Topos,* can alone "receive" being in its true individuality, without substituting a conceptual universal of some sort for what is absolutely and obdurately particular in reality itself. Instead of bringing the individual under the sway of universals, it is grasped in its immediacy. Masao Abe explains: "Only 'place' or Absolute Nothingness can subsume the individual without marring its uniqueness and trans-rationality and thereby allow it to be known precisely as an individual."[68]

According to Nishida the *Topos* of "absolute nothingness" is no immediate return from knowledge to immediacy but is rather the result of a dialectical development. It embraces both immediate consciousness and its objects in a double negation by negating even the relative nothingness that separates them in knowledge.[69] "From the standpoint of absolute nothingness, the notion of nothingness itself disappears, and all beings appear 'as they are.'"[70] Knowing is shown to presuppose a basis in a consciousness purified of any trace of objective reality, a consciousness which cannot itself be known but only lived as the very consciousness *in* which awareness *is.*

Here we are no longer *in* knowledge, in the usual sense of the term,with its correlated structure of nothing and something, consciousness and object, but have rather passed beyond these oppositions to pure experience. Knowing is encompassed by a larger system in which cognitive acts and their objects are grasped existentially in pure unobjectifiable "vision" *(miru mono).* In vision immediate appearances are no longer negated by the activity of knowing but are revealed as the very stuff of reality. The contrast between seeming and being breaks down very much as in the phenomenological concept of pure consciousness. It is this notion of vision that stands in for pure experience at the moment of Nishida's discovery of absolute nothingness.[71] As Abe writes, this is "the standpoint in which the knower and the known become one, the standpoint of knowing without a knower and seeing without a seer—in other words, the standpoint of consciousness that is truly the subject, not the object, of consciousness."[72]

In the remainder of this paper, we will explore this central concept of Nishida's philosophy in three stages. In the next section, we will discuss the relation between the *Topos* and the Heideggerian concept of the "clearing" as a preobjective participation in being. Like Heidegger, who also appears at first sight to confuse anthropology with ontology, Nishida treats subjectivity as the *essential* standpoint on being. The following section considers Nishida's social theory, which is an attempt to construct a social ontology similar to that of the early Marxist Lukacs and, like it, is based on the primacy of action. In addition, by recognizing the social nature of subjectivity, Nishida's social theory opens the way to the attempt in his last writings to create an ontology based on the multiplicity of interacting subjects. This ontology is treated in our conclusion. Let us turn now to the comparison of Nishida and Heidegger.

VI. NISHIDA AND EXISTENTIAL ONTOLOGY

Nishida's passage **From Activity to Vision** is explicitly related to certain Buddhist metaphysical conceptions, e.g., "absolute nothingness," which return even more forcefully in his last essay.[73] But, as we will show in our conclusion, it would be a mistake to read him as an advocate of religion in any ordinary sense of the term. In fact, he attempts to square the metaphysical circle at the intersection of Buddhism and twentieth-century ontology by conceiving pure experience as the essential foundation of existence.

As Dilworth notes, Nishida identifies the common thread that links the existentialist discovery of concrete experience as an unsurpassable absolute and "a long tradition of Eastern metaphysics which expounds that true reality can be affirmed and lived only through an experiential dialectic of negation."[74] The Buddhist idea of an impersonal field of pure experience, prior to the differentiation of subject and object, is in some sense beyond subjectivity without leaving the ground of finite consciousness. This conception, which earlier Western philosophers treated as a mere phantasm, begins now to make sense on Western terms. Nishida sees his task as introducing into philosophy those aspects of such a conception which are philosophically relevant and which advance the argument as he finds it in Western thought.[75]

It can now be seen, for example, that many of the peculiarities of the Eastern conception of consciousness are related to the difficulty of articulating the finitude of the subject without psychologism, that is to say, without a framework that presupposes the objectivity of being as encompassed by the thought of an infinite knower. In the West, where from the foundation of metaphysics to Nietzsche, God reigns unchallenged as a real or hypothetical absolute spectator on objective being, this problem cannot even appear without a double revolution, first against religion and second against scientism.

It was the new doctrine of experience, and especially phenomenology, that accomplished this double revolution. Husserl introduced a new way of understanding subjectivity as "pure consciousness," conceived not as a thing in the world but as the scene on which the world is subjectively enacted. It is the "prereflective givenness" of experience to which we always have an intuitive access but which we can never adequately thematize as an object of consciousness.

Representing this field is extraordinarily difficult because of our natural tendency to treat whatever we think about as though it were a thing even when that is precisely what it is *not*. Thus we have trouble conceiving of our own body-in-use, as opposed to seeing it as others see it, although there is nothing of which we have a more constant and intimate experience. This hand which types, insofar as it serves me at the keyboard, seems to escape full awareness until I look at it directly as though it were someone else's hand, anyone's hand, and not my own. Experience generally, prior to reflection, poses for us a similar problem of omnipresent invisibility.

Husserl's main innovation was to make it possible to talk about this invisible domain without falling back into objectivism. In his influential early works, he constructed a peculiar language of his own designed to avoid any reference to a reality independent of consciousness, and therefore any relation between these two separate and coextensive realms of being. *"Erlebnissen,"* as the contents of pure consciousness, he called *"reell"* in contrast to "real" *(wirklich)* things in the world. Pure consciousness is an "immanent domain of being," an impersonal "field" in which being is "lived" prior to the empirical subject/object split. It is not to be confused with the "ego" that lies under its horizon, and it is "out of connection" with empirical reality and strictly speaking incommensurate with it. But Husserl stopped short, at least in his published works, of offering an explicit ontological account of pure consciousness.

The ontological implications of phenomenology were finally made clear by Heidegger, who broke the last link between the traditional concept of consciousness and the emerging concept of being as an experiential field. Thus new speculative philosophies were born out of the doctrine of experience and came to dominate a whole period in the history of twentieth-century thought through the work not only of Heidegger, but following him of Sartre, Merleau-Ponty, and the other existentialists.

According to these philosophies, any account of being must explain its "presence" as in some sense an essential rather than as a merely accidental feature of the real. Furthermore, that presence is by definition only "to" finite subjects, themselves in the world. If presence is an ontologically general feature of being, rather than an accident of the encounter of two ontically determined beings (a subject and an object), then it precedes and founds specific perceptual acts.

To perceive, it is not enough to be "in" the world as an object, involved in causal interactions with other things like a rock or a tree. Out of such interactions no perceived "world" can arise. Rather, we must be "in" the world in a perceptually salient manner from the beginning, that is to say, not as a thing, even a very special type of thing with elaborate senses and a brain, but as a locus of experience irreducible to merely objective determinants. With Heidegger, we might say that perception must be founded on the possibility of being "disclosing" itself.

This shift in emphasis transforms the function of basic phenomenological concepts in a direction similar to Nishida's theory. The most important such shift concerns phenomenological intentionality, the givenness of experience to the active focus of awareness. This concept supplied the initial means of avoiding psychologism. With the concept of intentionality, the subject could be referred to exclusively through its acts rather than as a Cartesian "thinking thing" located somehow among the world of objects. In later existential ontologies, following Heidegger, the remaining subjectivistic implications of the notion of intentional consciousness are overcome as its functions are transferred to Being, which "gives" itself, with the paradoxical result that presence acquires in some sense the active powers of awareness.[76]

This conception of existence as an act of "presencing" rather than as a mere passive enduring in being, is the inner link betweentraditional and modern ontology, including the ontology of Nishida. It appears in a number of different metaphysical systems. Heidegger finds it in the Pre-Socratic notion of *physis,* and something very much like it is explicit in Thomas Aquinas's attempt to think existence as an act, on the metaphor of divine creation. Because this conception came down to modern times through theological systems like that of Aquinas, the secularization of Western thought led to its eventual eclipse, but with Heidegger existence is interpreted once again as a dynamic process.

It would be a mistake, however, to see in Heidegger a simple regression to traditional metaphysics. The "act" of existing in his thought has a distinctly post-Kantian cast. The complex of concepts that describe it, such as "disclosure," "Open," "clearing," "transcendence," and "nothingness," are all descended by one route or another from the transmutation that consciousness undergoes in his thought.[77] Thus this act, the "standing forth" of Being from nothingness, can no longer be ascribed to things *per se* or to a God but must be understood under a finite horizon of being.

In Nishida's later theory too there are *only* finite beings; no absolute spectator founds the existence of things by its creative glance. Thus to the extent that existence is conceived as a sustained act of being, it must depend on the experience of finite subjects, the only subjects that are possible on the terms of the theory. But in Nishida these subjects too lose their "substance" in the realization that their being is no more sustained by divine intuition than that of any other thing. This "emptying" of the subject completes the general dissolution of substantiality which begins with Nishida's critique of the objectivistic conception of consciousness.[78]

How can one *think* such a paradoxical refusal of objectivity, even the objectivity of the subject? The Buddhist tradition contains an answer which resonates with phenomenological themes in the West: the return to "the things themselves," to the raw material of pure experience prior to all positings of being. But Nishida regards phenomenology and existentialism as insufficiently radical: their turn toward the immediate still involves treating pure experience as an instance, an example of something known, whereas, as we have seen, Nishida moves away from phenomenology in identifying the original disclosure of being with *this* consciousness and its objects as such, precisely in their insuperable immediacy and particularity.[79] Here the experienced would is met on the side of the subject by a function as void of substantiality as itself, and the correlation between the two takes the form not of knowledge but of an always available encounter with the immediate presence of being. Existence as pure experience is an impersonal awareness in and by which things *are* as a world on the *Topos* of nothingness. As Nishida writes,

> If one is really overwhelmed by the consciousness of absolute Nothingness, there is neither "Me" nor "God"; but just because there is absolute Nothingness, the mountain is mountain, and the water is water, and being is as it is.[80]

> Insofar as they are "as they are," [things] are themselves nothingness. To see things in this way is to see them from within, to see reality as psyche. This is the unique *Topos* of nothingness, in which each thing projects itself onto itself, that is to say, as self-awareness.[81]

VII. THE SOCIAL FIELD THEORY

In Nishida's middle period, this very abstract conception of existence was concretized through a radical reflection on the nature of history. That reflection in turn allowed Nishida to leave behind any lingering idealist reliance on the centrality of individual consciousness and to recast his theory in his last writings as a kind of universal social ontology.[82] In this section, we will sketch a brief account of Nishida's social theory as an application of his concept of the *Topos,* which must therefore be discussed here at the outset.

Nishida initially explained his concept of *Topos* by analogy with Plato's "receptacle" of the Ideas. He began, therefore, by comparing the *Topos* to a "space" within which things are. This analogy refers to the essential "enfolding" in which all of being is involved: no thing stands alone, but all things stand "in" something else.[83] Thus all physical objects have a place in the cosmos: numbers are part of the number system, organisms belong to their environments, human beings to society, and so on. Although these relations of belonging are general and specify no particular connection, *some* sort of contextual dependency is essential to the very being of things. Nishida invents a new ontological category, *oite aru,* which can be translated literally as "In-being," to describe this essential attribute of being.[84]

The Platonic analogy, however, breaks down quickly, for its spatial character presupposes the complete externality of the *Topos* with respect to that which abides within it. Things exist "in" space, but they are indifferent to space just as space is indifferent to them. This is not the relationship of being to its In-being which Nishida wants to describe. He is searching rather for something more like the dialectical concept of the concrete totality which *is* its contents even as it embraces them.

In fact, Nishida was able to find support for such a notion in modern physics. He writes, "Physicists at first considered space to be the field in which forces operate; and then, based on Maxwell's idea of electromagnetism, space became thought of as the field of forces. Whatever is universal is active and in motion."[85] The *Topos* considered as a field of forces has a distinctly dereifying significance. It contributes to Nishida's attack on the traditional substantialist conception of being, according to which things and their essences are ultimate ontological units. In this regard Nishida is unhesitatingly modern, and even writes sympathetically about operationalism, which he sees as an ally in the struggle against substantialist metaphysics because it reduces all beings to actions.[86]

Nishida's field theory is dialectical and rests on the idea of essential relations, which underlie and in some sense constitute their terms as such. Pure experience now appears as a heuristic concept which desubstantializes objects and brings them all into connection on a field of givenness beyond objectivity. This dialectical conception begs to be applied to society, and in fact in Nishida's middle period he employs it as the framework for understanding the constitutive role of interaction in the social world. It should be said that here Nishida follows in a long line of social thinkers who preceded him on this path.

The theory of the mutual interdependence of master and slave in Hegel's *Phenomenology* appears to be the original source of the many dereifying field theories of the social, although it has been argued that novelistic psychology was based on precisely such a perspective as early as Cervantes.[87] Hegel's approach reached sociology indirectly, primarily via Marx.[88] In fact Marx influenced Nishida's formulations which in turn influenced Japanese Marxism through his student Kiyoshi Miki.[89]

Social field theories appear increasingly in modern sociology, beginning with George Herbert Mead and continuing to our day with such theorists as Harold Garfinkel, Irving Goffman, Pierre Bourdieu, and, with a biological reference, Humberto Maturana and Francisco Varela. These theorists substitute the circularity of a system of practice for the supposed substantiality of social "things."[90] They identify reciprocal, mutually supporting interactions as the ontological foundation of apparently independent social objects such as persons and institutions, and reject the implicit substance metaphysics that underlies most attempts to think the social.[91]

Performativity is a particularly clear example of a field effect, as in the familiar textbook example of a child labeled by his teachers as unintelligent or smart, and acting accordingly. As Bourdieu writes, "The mind is a metaphor of the world of objects which is itself but an endless circle of mutually reflecting metaphors."[92] Maturana and Varela's formulation identifies what they call "structural coupling" as the basis of "consensual domains" such as mating behavior in animals, or language and culture in human society. These are social regularities that arise from mutually triggered and mutually reinforcing behavioral sequences.[93]

Nishida too wants to argue that individuality and the social world it produces stand in such a reciprocal relationship. This is a difficult point to make, since it denies both the priority of the social—a position that Nishida identifies with Hegel and Marx—and that of the individual. Society is not a reified fact or thing, but neither can it be explained as a simple product of individual activities, as in methodological individualism. Nishida argues rather that society is the result of the "mutual determination" of acting persons who are themselves social products. Neither society nor the individual self is a "substance," but both exist only in the circuit of interaction.[94] He interprets this conclusion in terms of his concept of the *Topos*.

> Individuals are mutually determined, and this mutual determination presupposes the 'place' of their mutual determination. Mutual determination in such a 'place' must also imply mutual negation. In such terms, the mutual determination of individuals is the self-determination of their medium, i.e., the determination of 'place'.[95]

Nishida's position might be represented in an argument in three stages. First, individuals, he holds, are real; if they were not, if their individuality were illusory, then action would be impossible and only change or movement would exist.[96] But, secondly, the mode of existence of the individual is action and action is always and necessarily interaction in a pre-existing environment. Hence there is a sense in which individuals are not real but exist only as parts of a system. In the third place, however, it can be shown that the environment itself exists as such only through a selection which establishes the pertinence of its various parameters to those individuals. Thus "The self-determination of the individual is in one respect the self-determination of the environment."[97] Nishida does not attempt to decide between these poles of his dilemma, but instead regards it as a totality of moments held together in the social *Topos*. As such, it yields a conception of the action system as "self-determining" in and through its individual moments.

Nishida believed that the application of the *Topos* concept to society enabled him to transcend Marxist determinism and to grant action its full significance as the ontological foundation of social development.[98] Despite their very different political views, this theory has a remarkable similarity to certain aspects of Lukacs's early "philosophy of praxis." For example, both attempt to overcome determinism through an attack on the objectivistic view of historical time as a linear progression in which the present is a mere accident. As Lukacs writes,

> When the concrete here and now dissolves into a process it is no longer a continuous, intangible moment, immediacy slipping away; it is the focus of the deepest and most widely ramified mediation, the focus of decision and of the birth of the new.[99]

Like Lukacs, Nishida attempts to construct a new view of history based on the "standpoint of the present." The present is the locus of social production as the moment of action and the "'place' of contradiction."[100]

The dynamic process in which society and the historical subjects interact is a continuous creation, a "poiesis," or "praxis" which sustains them from moment to moment and in which they have their whole being. Individuals act *out* of the past *toward* the future *in* the present, creating a new present. Past and future are only real in this relation they sustain with action. History, Nishida argues, is the passage from "present to present" through the concrete synthesis of past and future.

Understood in this way, history transcends both causal and teleological categories and represents a new type of reality *sui generis.*

> In the historical-social world . . . past and future are in general confrontation, and formed and forming confront each other as well; the formed forms even the forming, and the creature forms the creator. The individual not only passes away into the past; it also produces a producing, and this is true productivity.[101]

Society thus cannot be characterized fundamentally either by its economic or cultural dimensions (its past), nor by its ideals (its future), but is rather in essence a certain "style of productivity."[102] As such it requires interpretation as a "work" almost as though it were an aesthetic achievement. With this notion of historical "style" Nishida attempts to reconstruct the Hegelian understanding of society as "objective spirit" in the framework of an ontology of action.

VIII. THE PARADOX OF FINITUDE

In this concluding section, we will offer an interpretation of Nishida's last essay on **"The Logic of the Place of Nothingness and the Religious Worldview"** (**"Bashoteki ronri to shukyoteki sekaikan,"** 1945). This essay can be seen as an attempt to think through the most puzzling implications of the concept of pure experience in a world of multiple subjects. This interpretation will bring us face to face with the inner paradox of Nishida's philosophy: self-reference as the meaning of existence on the field of finite subjects. Because, for the most part, contemporary philosophy engages the theme of paradoxical self-reference only to dissolve itinto acceptable propositions purged of inner contradiction, it is difficult to find an illuminating philosophical background against which to discuss Nishida's paradoxical logic. Instead, we must look for interesting comparisons with Nishida primarily to movements of thought outside philosophy. From this standpoint, his work reveals a surprising relevance to recent discussion of self-reference in biology, systems theory, and computer science.

Let us begin with Nishida's understanding of God in this final essay. Nishida argues that the "true absolute" (God) is absolute precisely in standing unopposed to any other being. Insofar as it is beyond all opposition, it is not even relative to the relative and cannot be conceived as transcendent. He concludes that the true absolute "must possess itself through self-negation. The true absolute exists in that it returns to itself in the form of the relative. The true absolute One expresses itself in the form of the infinite many. God exists in this world through self-negation."[103]

On first glance, this would appear to be a pantheistic position since Nishida seems to be saying that God *is* "in" everything. But Nishida rejects this interpretation because, he argues, pantheism is objectivistic and treats being as unproblematic. His own doctrine, he claims, follows the "negative theology" of Nagarjuna which calls into question all positings of being.[104] In precisely what sense Nishida is really a follower of this eminent predecessor, we must leave to scholars of Buddhist metaphysics.[105] The important point for the argument here is that Nishida offers an original way of thinking his paradoxical dialectic in which the passage from the one to the many takes place not through a positing of being but through an absolute negation: the affirmation of things is the denial of God.

In philosophical terms, the concept of God enables us to think the universe as a whole under a single transcendent glance. The secularization of this conception has veiled its theological origins. These are still visible to some extent in Kant, who postulates a God-like "divine intuition" as the subject corresponding to the thing-in-itself. This concept reveals the underlying truth of the scientific *cogito* as a hypothetically disincarnated glance. It is precisely such easy solutions that Nishida rejects: he includes God in his dialectic, not as a logical *deus ex machina,* but rather to disperse His function as absolute spectator into the world.

If we cannot legitimately refer to being as a whole as an object that exists passively in the eye of God, or to some sort of epistemological equivalent, then this unity must emerge from a process of interaction among the many finite existences. But to make matters still more complicated, these finite existences no longer fall under the glance of the deity either. They must beconceived not as objects, or "souls" *à la* Bishop Berkeley, but rather as centers of pure experience, without objective content or substantiality prior to the experiential act in which they have their entire being. The whole thus rests on the conscious individuals who themselves rest on the whole they constitute in their experience of it. The world process is confounded with that "vision" in which the act of being is realized and which Nishida now analyzes as a dynamic field of forces, a "self-transforming matrix."[106]

This matrix Nishida theorizes through the concept of "mutual expression" of self and world by which he attempts to avoid objectivistic representationalism. He explains the individual as a self-determining system in which the world is "expressed," and which thereby expresses itself in a world. "I am," he writes, "an expressive monad of the world."[107] The reference to Leibniz suggests both Nietzschean perspectivism and the Heideggerian concept of transcendence. It is interesting that like Nishida, Heidegger should have found the "monad" an illuminating metaphor to his own conception of the self. Heidegger writes, in a passage which helps to understand Nishida's intent:

> As a monad, the Dasein needs no window in order first of all to look out toward something outside itself, not because, as Leibniz thinks, all beings are already accessible within its capsule, so that the monad can quite well be closed off and encapsulated within itself, but because the monad, the Dasein, in its own being (transcendence) is already outside, among other beings, and this implies always with its own self.[108]

Or, in Nishida's language:

> The world that, in its objectivity, opposes me is transformed and grasped symbolically in the forms of my own subjectivity. But this transactional logic of contradictory identity signifies as well that it is the world that is expressing itself in me. The world creates its own space-time character by taking each monadic act of consciousness as a unique position in the calculus of its own existential transformation.[109]

According to Nishida's neo-Leibnizian conception, the world is a society of such monads, a view that converges surprisingly with the concept of biological autonomy as it has been developed by Maturana and Varela. According to their theory, organisms are inherently self-referential beings, "autopoietic" processes of continual self-production, capable of maintaining their structure in a dynamic relation to the world around them. When extended to the consideration of language and culture, where the medium in which the organisms act is produced as a "consensual domain" by their own interactions, this autopoietic conception approximates in structure to Nishida's theory.

Being for Nishida is exhaustively describable as a "consensual domain": the individuals do not mentally represent a pre-existing world but rather organize their own identity through the transactions in which the world "expresses" itself within them. A world is in fact nothing more than the mutual identity-shaping interactions of the individuals in the cultural and historical universe they generate. The world is thus not a pre-existing thing but a *Topos* of "structurally coupled" interactions resonating together in the construction of a dynamic unity that holds the place of "objectivity" in the usual substantialist conception.

Each existential monad originates itself by expressing itself; and yet it expresses itself by negating itself and expressing the world. The monads are thus co-originating, and form the world through their mutual negation. The monads are the world's own perspectives; they form the world interexpressively through their own mutual negation and affirmation. Conversely, the concrete matrix of historical actuality that exists and moves through itself enfolds these monadic perspectives within itself. . . .

> A conscious act is a dynamic expression. It is a self-determination of a concrete transpositional matrix, a structure of mutual revealment of self and world. Our selves, the expressive monads of the world, constitute points of the world's own expression in and through our self-expression.[110]

Nishida substitutes this concept of mutual expression for the objectivistic dualism of knowledge and being; expression is "a contradictory identity, the dynamic equivalence of knowing and acting."[111] To know the world is not to escape beyond objectivity to the *cogito* but is rather a world-constituting intervention just insofar as it is a modification of the subject. The subject is thus an autonomous self-referential being, but, conversely, the very process of its self-reference, along with that of other subjects, is precisely what we mean by a world in the first place.

Nishida's conception of being thus resembles Escher's print of the self-drawing hands which exist only through producing each other, and which produce each other as their only activity. (See Appendix.) For Nishida, this structure is, strictly speaking, all there *is:* reality is a self-referential process, a kind of infinite recursive self-production.

Escher's self-drawing hands are also emblematic of the concept of the "strange loop" or "entangled hierarchy" introduced by Douglas Hofstadter in his book *Gödel, Escher, Bach.* The strange loop arises when moving up or down in a logical hierarchy at some point leads paradoxically back to the starting point. In the Escher print, the hierarchy of "drawing subject" and "drawn object" is "entangled" by the fact that each hand plays both functions with respect to the other.[112] As Heraclitus wrote at the origins of philosophy, "The way up and the way down are one and the same."[113]

On Hofstadter's terms, Nishida's ontology is an entangled hierarchy. This ontological strange loop is already implied in the notion of pure experience. We can represent the loop in two movements. First, "the way down": in purely logical terms, the concept of experience implies a hierarchy of observer and observed, meta-position and object-position. Second, "the way up": experience, as a totality, is situated hierarchically with respect to things which appear "in" experience as mere parts, including the subject of experience itself.

Experience thus refers us to a subject, which would be situated hierarchically in the position of observer, but the subject refers us back to experience within which it itself appears as an observable object. Experience is both that which is "drawn" by the subject and that which "draws" the subject. The subject "has" experience but is also "in" experience, and both propositions are equally true. Merleau-Ponty calls this paradoxical form a "chiasm"— a totality which unites two inverse structural orders of the parts.[114]

Nishida's later theory enriches this early conception by reinterpreting the subject of experience in more complex ways as an active historical being, but it does not fundamentally change the structure. The individuals both are acted on by the world, which expresses itself in them, and are producers of the world, expressing themselves in it, in the inextricably entangled relationship of the "self-transforming matrix."

We have come a long way from Nishida's reflections on the concept of God, with which we began this section, and yet we have also returned by a circuitous route to the heart of his religious conception. The fact that he interprets this matrix as the totality of being requires him to confront the full force of its paradoxical structure in a way that the contemporary Western thinkers to whom we have been comparing him do not.

Hofstadter's strange loop, for example, is never more than a partial subsystem in a consistent, objectively conceived universe. He evades ultimate paradox by positing an "inviolate level" of strictly hierarchical relations above the strange loop and making it possible. He calls this level "inviolate" because it is not logically entangled with the entangled hierarchy it creates. In the case of the Escher drawing, the paradox exists only because of the perfectly unparadoxical activity of the actual printmaker Escher who drew it in the ordinary way without himself being drawn byanyone.

When the self-referential model is extended to biological organisms, the puzzle deepens. Living things produce themselves in a process which presupposes their prior existence. This prior existence we are now accustomed to identifying with the "genetic program," but it too at its own level is caught in the same dilemma. One cannot ascribe the production of these paradoxical organic structures to an external agent since, in the language of computer science, they are "self-programming," an apparent contradiction in terms.

It is still possible, however, to evade the full force of the paradox through a Kantian strategy. Jean-Pierre Dupuy, for example, ascribes the paradox of biological autonomy to the structure of our knowledge of nature.[115] Science, he argues, like Escher drawing the intertwined hands, operates from an "inviolate level" in conceptualizing organisms in the paradoxical form of self-referring beings. But Dupuy notes that this condition of knowledge is also its inherent limit. As in Kant, objectivism returns by the backdoor of a thing in itself situated on a hypothetical field of "divine intuition" beyond the paradoxical structure of the world as we know it.

Dupuy's argument invites a response from the standpoint of Nishida's theory. As we rise in the hierarchy of abstraction from experience to scientific knowledge of reality to critical self-knowledge, we discover that the correlation of the non-paradoxical and the paradoxical is unsurpassable. This correlation is the mark of the limits of knowledge, which in knowing its own limits falls into a typical self-referential paradox. On what "field" are we able to think the ultimate paradox of a knowledge which, like Socrates, knows itself not to know? The consciousness of the limits of knowledge returns us to pure experience, which acquires new validity exactly "as it is" through the relativization of the system of abstractions in which it was displaced.[116]

The elimination of the last theological ghosts is the chief work of philosophy since Nietzsche. The aim is to overcome deep assumptions about the world which arose originally in a religious context, where the existence of God was taken for granted, but which continue to have force today in the guise of an objectivistic world view. Nishida participates fully in this new form of *epistemological atheism,* which is not incompatible with a certain religious vision.[117]

Nishida discusses religion in a peculiarly disinterested way that systematically evacuates it of all its usual claims, such as the existence of God, immortality of the soul, mystical enlightenment,belief in doctrine, even the promise of peace of mind, which Nishida suggests has nothing to do with religion. His religiosity cannot be confused with faith in any ordinary sense of the term. In this respect too, his philosophy is self-consciously modern, with a concept of religious truth that is not incompatible with the scientific demands of modern culture.[118]

What is that concept? Paradox is the final form in which the sacred manifests itself in a disenchanted world. Insofar as the self participates in the dynamic process of world-making through its transcendence as absolute nothingness, its deepest self-awareness is identified with that process. Yet the self is also lost in the world as an object and indeed only exists as a self in that loss. This contradiction is not overcome in special observances or mystical states, but must be assumed in the midst of everyday experience. Here is the ultimate strange loop in Nishida's theory: the pursuit of the sacred leads us not to an otherworldly domain, above existence, but back to the heart of the everyday. Insofar as the self is or belongs to the absolute, "ordinary human experience is eschatological in character."[119] In the words of a Chinese sage, therefore, "Even to set upon the quest for awakening is to go astray."[120]

Because the Japanese religious vision is in harmony with such a conception, Nishida concludes his essay with the hope that chastened and deepened by historical experience, the Japanese spirit "can become a point of departure for a new global culture."[121] This wish is expressed in 1945 in the context of impending defeat, transparently coded in the fate of the ancient Jews. They did not lose their spirit even in Babylon, Nishida writes, and, anticipating a ruder contact of cultures than his own early encounter with the thought of William James, he notes that the patriot Jeremiah "warned his people by calling Nebuchadnezzar the servant of Yahweh."[122] Let us conclude with these words, the eternal promise of high destiny even to the vanquished.

NOTES

[1] We would like to thank Ryosuke Ohashi for suggesting the research project on pure experience with which this study began. We would also like to thank David Dilworth, Deborah Chaffin, Robert Pippin, Frederick Olafson, and Alastair Hannay for helping us think more clearly about many issues in this paper.

[2] William James, *Essays in Radical Empiricism and A Pluralistic Universe* (New York: Peter Smith, 1967).

[3] Kitaro Nishida, *A Study of Good,* trans. V. H. Viglielmo (Tokyo: Japanese Government Printing Bureau, 1960). This work, originally published in 1911 as *Zen no kenkyu,* is reprinted in *Nishida KitaroZenshu,* Vol. 1 (Tokyo: Iwanami, 1965).

[4] Thomas Kasulis, "The Kyoto School and the West," *Eastern Buddhist* 15 (1982), 133.

[5] See Keiji Nishitani, *Religion and Nothingness,* trans. J. V. Van Bragt (Berkeley: Univ. of California Press, 1982); Yujiro Nakamura, "Nishida: Le Premier Philosophe Original au Japon," *Critique* 39, Nos. 428-29 (1983).

[6] James Edie, *William James and Phenomenology* (Bloomington: Indiana Univ. Press, 1987).

[7] There is no secret about the link between James and Husserl, who learned from the American psychologist that all of experience can be represented in the "stream" of consciousness. James's concept of "fringes" also anticipates the Husserlian concept of "horizon." But are these anticipations significant enough to justify treating a philosopher like James as a precursor? David Dilworth has persuaded us that such an approach to James and Nishida, in the light of their anticipations of phenomenology and existentialism, may violate the unity of their own work. This objection raises methodological questions concerning the study of the history of philosophy which we cannot address here. We do believe, though, that despite its limitations a teleological approach such as ours is not arbitrary but is in some sense constitutive of the historicity of philosophy, of its way of accumulating a past and transcending it in the activity of tradition.

[8] Thomas Kasulis, "Foreword" in Robert Carter, *The Nothingness Beyond God* (New York: Paragon House, 1989), p. xii. For an analysis of the context in which the problem of modernity was posed in Japan during World War II (the "Overcoming modernity" movement—*Kindai*

no chokoku), see H. D. Harootunian, "Visible Discourses/Invisible Ideologies" in *Postmodernism and Japan,* edd. Masao Miyoshi and H. D. Harootunian (Durham: Duke Univ. Press, 1989).

[9] James, p. 74.

[10] Bernard Brennan, *William James* (New York: Twayne Publishers, 1968), p. 61.

[11] James, p. 93.

[12] *Ibid.*

[13] *Ibid.,* p. 10.

[14] *Ibid.,* p. 23.

[15] *Ibid.,* p. 42.

[16] *Ibid.*

[17] *Ibid.,* p. 86.

[18] *Ibid.* Bertrand Russell once called James's theory of pure experience "neutral monism" because he thought pure experience was a "neutral stuff," neither subject nor object, physical nor psychical (Marcus Ford, *William James's Philosophy: A New Perspective* [Amherst: Univ. of Mass. Press, 1982], p. 76). John Wild also criticizes James on the basis that such a notion of "neutral stuff" is a regression into "abstract atomism or 'mind-stuff' theory" which violates James's earlier conceptions of the intentional structure of consciousness (John Wild, *The Radical Empiricism of William James* [New York: Doubleday, 1969], p. 367).

James, however, explicitly rejects such a notion of "stuff" by stating that "there is no *general* stuff of which experience at large is made. There are as many stuffs as there are 'natures' in the things experienced" (James, p. 26). Thus, although James does use the expression "stuff," "portion," or "units" of pure experience and say that mental and physical entities are "made of" pure experience, he does not mean that experience is a metaphysical substance as in monism.

[19] Ryosuke Ohashi, "Zur Philosophie der Kyoto-Schule," *Zeitschrift für philosophische Forschung* 40, no. 1 (1986).

[20] Nishida, p. 9. This and other translations from *A Study of Good, From Activity to Vision,* and from Japanese secondary sources by Yoko Arisaka. Some other translations from Nishida have been slightly modified. References are to Japanese editions unless otherwise indicated.

[21] Nishida, p. 9.

[22] *Ibid.,* p. 42.

[23] Masaaki Kosaka, *Nishida Kitaro Sensei no Shogai to Shiso* [The Life and Ideas of Professor Nishida] (Tokyo: Sobunsha, 1947), p. 66.

[24] Tadashi Ogawa, "The Kyoto School of Philosophy and Phenomenology," *Annalecta Husserliana* 8 (1978), 209; Torataro Shimomura, "Nishida Kitaro and Some Aspects of His Philosophical Thought" in Nishida, p. 201.

[25] Keiji Nishitani, *Nishida Kitaro: Sono Hito to Shiso* [NishidaKitaro: The Person and The Ideas] (Tokyo: Chikuma Shobo, 1985), p. 117.

[26] Kitaro Nishida, *Shohen* [Shorter Works] in *Nishida Kitaro Zenshu,* Vol. 13, p. 97.

[27] James, p. 86.

[28] David Dilworth, "The Initial Formations of 'Pure Experience' in Nishida Kitaro and William James," *Monumenta Nipponica* 24, nos. 1-2 (1969), 96-97.

[29] *Zen no kenkyu,* pp. 13, 16.

[30] *Ibid.,* p. 10.

[31] *Ibid.,* p. 58.

[32] *Ibid.,* p. 19.

[33] James, pp. 3-4.

[34] *Ibid.,* p. 4.

[35] Wild, p. 367.

[36] *Zen no kenkyu,* p. 28.

[37] *Ibid.*

[38] *Ibid.,* p. 55.

[39] This reading leads us into the controversial terrain of the so-called *"Nihonjinron,"* theories of Japanese exceptionalism. Relevant discussions are found in Hajime Nakamura, "Consciousness of the Individual and the Universal Among the Japanese" in *The Japanese Mind: Essentials of Japanese Philosophy and Culture,* ed. Charles Moore (Honolulu: Univ. of Hawaii Press, 1967), p. 182; and Augustin Berque, *Vivre l'espace au japon* (Paris: Presses Univ. de France, 1982), sections 11, 35, 37. For a general critique of this approach, however, cf. Peter Dale, *The Myth of Japanese Uniqueness* (London and Oxford: Croom Helm and Nissan Institute for Japanese Studies, 1986).

[40] James, p. 87.

[41] Joseph Flay, "Experience, Nature and Place," *The Monist* 68 (1985), 473.

[42] *Zen no kenkyu,* p. 54.

[43] *Ibid.,* p. 20.

[44] *Ibid.,* p. 25.

[45] *Ibid.,* p. 33.

[46] *Ibid.,* p. 154.

[47] *Ibid.,* p. 182.

[48] *Ibid.,* p. 191.

[49] *Ibid.,* p. 55.

[50] Frederick Olafson, *Heidegger and the Philosophy of Mind* (New Haven: Yale Univ. Press, 1984), pp. 39-40, 44-45. Joseph Flay's theory of "primordial place" suggests another way of working out these problems that has a certain resemblance to Nishida's later theory of "Place." (Cf. Flay.)

[51] Kosaka, pp. 75-76.

[52] Yoshihiro Nitta, Horitaka Tatematsu, Eiichi Shimomisse, "Phenomenology and Philosophy in Japan," *Analecta Husserliana* 8 (1978), 8.

[53] *Zen no kenkyu,* p. 6.

[54] See, for example, Berque's comment: "In French, even when the [subject] is impersonal, the morphology of the language expresses it clearly: 'It is cold' is not the same thing as 'I am cold'. Japanese will say *'Samui'* in both cases. In such an utterance one cannot determine who is the subject of the impression of coldness: that impression is at once in the air and in the person who feels it. Cold impregnates the scene of the utterance. . . . Similarly, the child who says *'Kowai'* ('I'm scared') speaks both of the feeling he experiences and of that which inspires it as its object" (p. 39). Compare these everyday expressions with Heidegger's discussion of *"Befindlichkeit,"* mistranslated as "state-of-mind" in English: "The mood has already disclosed, in every case, Being-in-the-world as a whole, and makes it possible first of all to direct oneself towards something. Having a mood is not related to the psychical in the first instance, and is not itself an inner condition which then reaches forth in an enigmatical way and puts its mark on Things and persons" *(Being and Time,* trans. J. Macquarrie and E. Robinson, [New York: Harper and Row, 1962], p. 176). Hence, "Fearing, as a slumbering possibility of Being-in-the-world in a state-of-mind . . . has already disclosedthe world, in that out of it something like the fearsome may come close" (p. 180). Cf. Olafson, p. 106.

[55] Kitaro Nishida, *Hataraku mono kara miru mono e,* in *Nishida Kitaro Zenshu,* Vol. 4, p. 216.

[56] Ohashi, p. 128.

[57] Dieter Henrich, "Fichte's ursprungliche Einsicht," *Subjektivitat und Metaphysik* (Frankfurt: Klostermann, 1966). Cf. J. G. Fichte, *The Science of Knowledge,* trans. P. Heath and J. Lachs (Cambridge: Cambridge Univ. Press, 1982), p. 129. (We are grateful to Robert Pippin for pointing out this connection.)

58 Robert Pippin, *Hegel's Idealism: the Satisfactions of Self-Consciousness* (Cambridge: Cambridge Univ. Press, 1989), p. 49.

59 Kitaro Nishida, *Intuition and Reflection in Self-Consciousness,* trans. V. Viglielmo, T. Takeuchi, and J. O'Leary (Stonybrook: State Univ. of New York Press, 1987), p. 165.

60 Kitaro Nishida, *Fundamental Problems of Philosophy,* trans. D. Dilworth (Tokyo: Sophia Univ. Press, 1970), p. 57.

61 Kitaro Nishida, *Last Writings: Nothingness and the Religious Worldview,* trans. D. Dilworth (Honolulu: Univ. of Hawaii Press, 1987), p. 125. For the original text, see *Nishida Kitaro Zenshu,* Vol. 11.

62 David Dilworth, "Nishida Kitaro: Nothingness as the Negative Space of Experiential Immediacy," *International Philosophical Quarterly* 13 (1973), 478. Cf. Ryosuke Ohashi, "Nishida tetsugaku no 'tetsugakushi teki' igi" [The Philosophical-Historical Significance of Nishida Philosophy] in *Nishida Tetsugaku,* edd. R. Ohashi and Y. Kayano (Tokyo: Minerva Shobo, 1987), pp. 103-104.

63 In this aspect of his work, Nishida is undoubtedly at his most obscure, but fortunately a recent article by Masao Abe guides us through these complexities toward the point that interests us here, Nishida's theory of experience. See Masao Abe, "Nishida's Philosophy of 'Place,'" *International Philosophical Quarterly* 28, no. 4 (1988). Cf. the classic treatment of these problems in Iwao Koyama, *Nishida Tetsugaku* (Tokyo: Iwanami Shoten, 1935.)

64 *Hataraku mono kara miru mono e,* p. 220.

65 Abe, p. 366.

66 Koyama, p. 127.

67 Ohashi, "Nishida tetsugaku no 'tetsugakushi teki' igi," pp. 103-104.

68 Abe, p. 368.

69 Robert Nozick has attempted to give a purely logical account of this dialectic, which is found not only in Eastern philosophy but also in certain forms of neo-Platonic mysticism in the West. He writes, "I suggest we understand the beginning of the Hymn of Creation, 'nonbeing then existed not nor being,' as saying that the pairs being and nonbeing, existent and nonexistent, and is and isn't have presuppositions, that the terms within these pairs apply and exhaust the possibilities only within a certain domain, while outside this domain a thing may be neither." Absolute nothingness would refer to that which is "neither" in this sense. (Robert Nozick, *Philosophical Explanation* [Cambridge: Harvard Univ. Press, 1981], p. 152.)

70 *Hataraku mono kara miru mono e,* p. 248.

71 Abe, p. 371; Carter, p. 60.

72 Abe, p. 370.

73 *Last Writings.*

74 "Nishida Kitaro: Nothingness as the Negative Space of Experiential Immediacy," p. 482.

75 For a remarkable contemporary exploration of the relevance of the Buddhist conception of consciousness to existential ontology and cognitive science, see the forthcoming book of Francisco Varela and Evan Thompson, *Worlds Without Ground: Cognitive Science and Human Experience.*

76 For a persuasive account of this central problem, see Olafson, *Heidegger and the Philosophy of Mind.*

77 For an explanation of this conception by a man who studied with both Nishida and Heidegger, see Nishitani, *Religion and Nothingness,* chapters 3 and 4. Martin Heidegger, *On the Way to Language,* trans. P. Hertz (New York: Harper and Row, 1982) contains a relevant dialogue on the relation of Western to Japanese thought.

78 Kitaro Nishida, *Intelligibility and the Philosophy of Nothingness,* trans. R. Schinzinger (Honolulu: East-West Center Press, 1958), pp. 136-37; Nishitani, *Religion and Nothingness,* pp. 96-97.

79 *Intelligibility and the Philosophy of Nothingness,* pp. 97-98.

80 *Ibid.,* p. 137.

81 *Hatarku mono kara miru mono e,* p. 248.

82 Ohashi sees a *"Kehre"* here similar to Heidegger's. "Nishida tetsugaku no 'tetsugakushi teki' igi," p. 104.

83 *Hatarku mono kara miru mono e,* p. 209. Cf. Martin Heidegger, *An Introduction to Metaphysics,* trans. R. Mannheim (New York: Doubleday, 1961), pp. 54-55.

84 *Hataraku mono kara miru mono e,* p. 209. Kosaka writes: "In the early summer of *Taisho* 15, Nishida *sensei* asked me to proofread and prepare a manuscript of an article which he wrote for *Tetsugaku Kenkyu.* It was the article *'Basho.'* I proofread and copied it with great care, but every time I came across the expression *'oite aru,'* which he used frequently, I felt uneasy about it. I should not have been concerned for Nishida *sensei* used it over and over in the original. But I was hesitant to take the manuscript to the printer, for the expression did not seem [grammatically] correct. So I took the manuscript and the original together and visited Nishida *sensei.* Boldly [without *enryo*] I said to him that I could not 'swallow' the expression *oite aru,* and asked him whether the ex-

pression was supposed to be that way. *Sensei* flipped the pages of the manuscript and finally said, 'Yes, that's all right.' This expression! The one which founds his *basho* concept, which introduced many similar notions later in Japanese philosophical circles, which must have been born through such painstaking philosophical reflection! . . ." (Kosaka, p. 131).

[85] Kitaro Nishida, *Art and Morality,* trans D. Dilworth and V. Viglielmo (Honolulu: Univ. of Hawaii Press, 1973), pp. 134-35.

[86] Matao Noda, "East-West Synthesis in Kitaro Nishida," *Philosophy East and West* 4 (1955), 356.

[87] René Girard, *Mensonge Romantique et Vérité Romanesque* (Paris: Grasset, 1961).

[88] Walter Buckley, *Sociology and Modern Systems Theory* (Englewood Cliffs, NJ: Prentice-Hall, 1967), p. 18.

[89] Hitoshi Imamura, "Marxisme japonais et marxisme occidental" in *Le Marxisme au Japon, Actuel Marx,* no. 2 (1987), pp. 46-47. The question of influences deserves investigation. Did Miki return to Japan from Germany with Lukacs's *History and Class Consciousness* in his suitcase? If so, would it be Miki who influenced Nishida rather than the reverse? Or was Nishida's social theory a direct product of his reflections on Marx and Hegel?

[90] Andrew Feenberg, *Lukacs, Marx and the Sources of Critical Theory* (New York: Oxford Univ. Press, 1986), p. 197.

[91] Norbert Elias, *What is Sociology?,* trans. S. Mennell and G. Morrissey (New York: Columbia Univ. Press, 1978), pp. 111-13.

[92] Pierre Bourdieu, *Outline of a Theory of Practice,* trans. R. Nice. (Cambridge: Cambridge Univ. Press, 1977), p. 9.

[93] Humberto Maturana and Francisco Varela, *The Tree of Knowledge* (Berkeley: Shambhala, 1987), chapter 8.

[94] David Dilworth, "The Concrete World of Action in Nishida's Later Thought," *Analecta Husserliana* 8 (1978).

[95] *Fundamental Problems of Philosophy,* p. 134.

[96] *Ibid.,* pp. 46-47.

[97] Nishida, *Fundamental Problems of Philosophy,* p. 72. This conception is elucidated by the modern concept of the environment as in some sense preconstructed by the organism. Cf. Maurice Merleau-Ponty: "The form of the excitor is created by the organism itself, by its own way of offering itself up to action from without" (*La structure du comportement* [Paris: Presses Univ. de France, 1942], p. 11).

[98] Noboru Shirotsuka, "Nishida Tetsugaku to no Saikai" [Re-encountering Nishida Philosophy] in *Nishida Kitaro Zenshu,* Vol. 4, volume insert, pp. 6-7.

[99] Georg Lukacs, *History and Class Consciousness,* trans. R. Livingstone (Cambridge: MIT Press, 1967), pp. 204-205.

[100] *Intelligibility and the Philosophy of Nothingness,* p. 177.

[101] *Ibid.,* p. 179.

[102] *Ibid.,* p. 178.

[103] *Last Writings,* p. 69.

[104] *Ibid.,* pp. 70-71.

[105] Carter, *The Nothingness Beyond God,* pp. 63-68.

[106] *Last Writings,* p. 50. This is a free but illuminating rendering of a phrase which, in its context, reads: ". . . jiko no uchi ni jiko o utsusu koto ni yotte uchi to soto to no seigoteki ni . . .ugoki iku sekai," or, roughly, ". . . by reflecting itself within itself it achieves a simultaneous, systematic adjustment of internal and external worlds."

[107] *Last Writings,* p. 52.

[108] Martin Heidegger, *The Basic Problems of Phenomenology,* trans. A. Hofstadter (Bloomington: Indiana Univ. Press, 1982), p. 301.

[109] *Last Writings,* p. 52.

[110] *Ibid.,* pp. 58-59. For Nishitani's explanation of a similar conception, see *Religion and Nothingness,* pp. 146-50.

[111] *Last Writings,* p. 84.

[112] Douglas Hofstadter, *Gödel, Escher, Bach* (New York: Basic Books, 1979), pp. 689-90.

[113] Philip Wheelwright, *Heraclitus* (New York: Atheneum, 1964), p. 90.

[114] Maurice Merleau-Ponty, *The Visible and the Invisible,* trans. A. Lingis (Evanston, IL: Northwestern Univ. Press, 1968), p. 138.

[115] Jean-Pierre Dupuy, *Orders et Désordres* (Paris: Seuil, 1982), p. 244.

[116] A related argument is made with reference to the "problem of completion" in Wittgenstein and Russell by Robert Wargo in The Logic of Basho and the Concept of Nothingness in the Philosophy of Nishida Kitaro (Univ. of Michigan, diss., 1972, chapter 4, pp. 342-43, 356-58).

[117] Feenberg, pp. 228-32.

[118] *Last Writings,* p. 122. David Dilworth, "Nishida's Critique of the Religious Consciousness" in Nishida, *Last Writings,* pp. 28-29.

[119] *Ibid.,* p. 109.

[120] *Ibid.,* p. 115. The Western philosopher whose religious sensibility seems closest to that of Nishida is Henry Bugbee. See his philosophical journal, *The Inward Morning* (New York: Harper and Row, 1976). Cf., for example, pp. 174-76.

[121] *Last Writings,* p. 112.

[122] *Ibid.,* p. 116.

Woo-Sung Huh (essay date 1990)

SOURCE: "The Philosophy of History in the 'Later' Nishida: A Philosophic Turn," in *Philosophy East & West,* Vol. 40, No. 3, July, 1990, pp. 343-74.

[*In the following essay, Huh discusses Nishida's two primary philosophical preoccupations: the philosophy of self-consciousness in his early writings and the philosophy of history later in his career.*]

I. INTRODUCTION

This essay on the philosophy of history of Nishida Kitaro (1870-1945) begins from my conviction that Nishida in his writings pursued two main lines of thought, almost equally pervasive and persistent. These lines are the development of a philosophy of self-consciousness in his pre-1931 corpus and the philosophy of history-politics in his later writings. Both philosophies are essentially ontologies, by virtue of what Nishida calls the application of forms of self-consciousness (*jikaku no keishiki*).[1] These forms function in almost every phase of Nishida's philosophy, with the notable exception of his discussion of the sciences, and in the main include activity, self-determination, actuality, one-qua-many logic, and immanent-qua-transcendent logic. Of course, Nishida did not begin his philosophic enterprise with a clear awareness of these forms of self-consciousness and with an intent to apply them variously. Rather, his understanding of the forms was the result of an enormous struggle to give full reality to the phenomena of consciousness. Nishida finally arrived at a full grasp of these forms only in his mature theory of self-consciousness, around 1929 or 1930. Then, in what I call the turn in Nishida's philosophy, he extended their application to nonconscious phenomena, such as the historical epoch and the state.

Whatever Nishida applied the forms of self-consciousness to was ascribed, in virtue of this application, full reality in Nishida's texts. In general, these forms are applied in turn to pure experience, to artistic creation, to

acts of self-consciousness, to the historical epoch, to the state, and to the emperor. The extension of his forms from acts of self-consciousness to the historical epoch occurred about 1931 and is the most decisive shift in Nishida's philosophy, because it paved the way for his return to a world which he had once rejected and called transitory. This turn signifies not only that the applications of these forms are turned from conscious phenomena to nonconscious phenomena, it also reflects Nishida's own critical stance toward his earlier religious-soteriological philosophy.

The first formulation of the philosophy of self-consciousness can be traced back as far as 1904, with its culmination occurring in volume 5 of *Nishida Kitaro zenshu* (*Nishida's Complete Works*). The philosophy of history consequently begins with a few essays written in 1931 and 1932 and evolves into a systematic philosophy of history, which eventually coalesces with his political conceptions. During the period of the formulation of the philosophy of self-consciousness, we find Nishida arguing for the supremacy of the soteriological or religious world of inner man (*homo interior*), against what he calls the world of external man (*homo exterior*). This approach thus gives less reality to the historical world and remains fundamentally an internalism, centering on acts of self-consciousness. However, Nishida changes this position when he grants similar reality to the historical epoch. He thereby abolishes the once sharply held dichotomy between *homo interior* and *homo exterior*. This turn enables Nishida to pronounce the absoluteness of each epoch instead of the absoluteness of each act of self-consciousness, and the self-determination of an epoch instead of the self-determination of self-consciousness ("History" 12: 62). As an extension or exemplification of his philosophy of history, he then discusses various political notions such as national polity and the state.

In one of the most important essays showing this turn, **"Concerning Self-consciousness,"** Nishida clearly indicates that in that essay and in previous essays which deal with the historical world, he is "directly unifying self-consciousness and the historical world" (10: 515). This short passage reveals not only Nishida's intent, but also his assumption that the forms of self-consciousness, primarily distilled from his discussion of artistic creation and conscious phenomena, are applicable to nonconscious phenomena. A key question for evaluating Nishida's entire texts, then, is whether an act of self-consciousness and a historical epoch are indeed similar enough that this "direct union" is possible, as Nishida clearly assumed.

Unfortunately, this question has not been squarely faced, either by Nishida or in the secondary literature. To begin with, Nishida's discourse of history-politics has often been neglected or treated inadequately by scholars. As if Nishida foresaw the reception of his philosophy of history in the academic community, he wrote, in 1945, immediately prior to his death, the essay **"Watakushi no ronri ni tsuite"** (**"Concerning My Logic"**), often called his *zeppitsu,* or "final words." It starts with this remark: "As a result of many years of study, I believe I have clarified the form of thought seen from the perspective of the historically active self (*rekishiteki koiteki jiko*), or the logic of the historically formative act (*rekishiteki keisei sayo no ronri*)" (12: 265). Nishida also laments that his previous logic was established from the perspective of the abstract and conscious self (*ishikiteki jiko*) and that people had taken his logic as religious experience, but not as a logic (12: 265-266). This additional remark suggests Nishida's own accusation against contemporary scholarship for misunderstanding his logic as being limited to religious experience. To repudiate this common misconception, he started his final words with the pronouncement of his logic as historically formative. Moreover, it appears here that the form of thought or logic refers to "forms of self-consciousness," and that the rejected perspective of the conscious self may include his own earlier philosophy of self-consciousness.

With this preliminary understanding of the general movement of Nishida's philosophy, in this article I shall examine how Nishida's philosophy of self-consciousness turns to philosophy of history, by contrasting the different meanings given to "forms of self-consciousness" in both philosophies. First, I shall explore the nature of the philosophy of self-consciousness, and then I shall analyze a few essays written in 1931 and 1932 in which many key aspects of the philosophy of history are laid out. Third, I shall elucidate these aspects in their position in Nishida's fully established philosophy of history. Finally, I shall examine the legitimacy of Nishida's enterprise of uniting the forms of self-consciousness and historical reality.

II. MATURE THEORY OF SELF-CONSCIOUSNESS

According to Nishida's mature, or most radical theory, self-consciousness is not only a particular state of consciousness (5: 425), it is its "fundamental form" (5: 433).[2] The complete form of self-consciousness is "self's seeing itself in itself," which involves three moments: "seeing," "itself," and "in itself" (5: 433).[3] "Seeing itself in itself" is deemed religious salvation, as Nishida once employed the Buddhist term *gedatsu* to signify this salvation (5: 179). Self-consciousness, according to Nishida's characterization, is active or self-determinative, self-cognitive, self-intentional, instantaneous, unique and complete, joyful, and religious.

Active and Self-determinative

The foremost character of self-consciousness is its activity. The claim that self-consciousness is not passive but active, is almost omnipresent in all of Nishida's texts belonging to the philosophy of self-consciousness. This active nature is emphasized by the numerous active forms of verbs: seeing, acting, moving, determining, illuminating, reflecting, "conscious-ing" (*ishiki-suru*). All these active forms of verbs are carefully and constantly opposed to their passive forms: seen, acted, determined, illuminated, reflected, "conscioused" (*ishiki-sareta*).

Nishida associates the terms "noesis" and "noema," independently of Husserlian understanding, with the "seeing" and "seen" aspects of consciousness.[4]

One of the most important characteristics of the activity of self-consciousness for Nishida's logic of place (*basho*) is that it is "self-determining (*jiko-gentei*) or self-forming (*jiko-keisei*) or *causa sui.*" "*Gentei-suru*" and "*keisei-suru*" literally mean "to determine" or "to limit," and "to form" or "to shape," respectively. Nishida argues: "The true self must be self-determination. The deeper the sense of self-determination becomes, the deeper the consciousness of self-consciousness (*jikaku no ishiki*) becomes" (5: 355).

The notion of place is concomitant with self-determination or activity. Self-determination entails the rejection of determination by others, whether it is a Platonic universal, theistic God, or Hegelian Spirit. A self-determining entity cannot be located in something other than itself. Nishida thus often called place "the place of nothingness" ("Basho," 4: 243, 244) and thus the only possibility for a self-determinative act of self-consciousness is to locate itself in itself. In other words, "self's seeing itself in itself" means that each act of self-consciousness is located in itself. The third "in itself" element is expressed by the notion of *basho* (place). Therefore, the logic of *basho* is the logic which safeguards the full reality of each act of self-consciousness. Thus, Nishida argued, "True place (*basho*) is like a mirror in which self illuminates its own image or shines itself" (4: 226). This notion of place, after the turn, shifts to include a new meaning, that is, a historical place, or a public place which is historical reality.

The forms of self-determination also include the concept of free will. For instance, Nishida defines free will as "self-determination which sees absolute nothingness" (5: 379). Hence, insofar as our selves are in any sense objectified, free will is inconceivable. This free will is directly connected to the notion of creativity, or creation *ex nihilo*. In the philosophy of self-consciousness, contrary to the position in his philosophy of history, Nishida maintains a firm belief in the existence of creation *ex nihilo* (*mu yori u*). Its most important examples are the changes of consciousness (16: 442). Creativity and freedom are also understood as liberation from environmental determination and the necessary determination of the past (6: 369). This radical understanding of creativity and freedom will be changed in the philosophy of history, as the latter emphasizes the givenness of a specific historical world and the existence of the surrounding world.

Self-knowing

Self-consciousness is cognitive, indeed, self-knowing (*jichi*) (4: 300). In the theory of self-consciousness, "all knowing is the [self's] illuminating itself in itself, or the self sees self [in itself]. This is the most complete form of knowing" (4: 132).[5] The frequent formulas of seeing-qua-acting and acting-qua-seeing refer to this self-knowing. On the basis of this ultimate form of knowing, Nishida sharply criticizes knowledge, which presupposes a subject-object dichotomy. For instance, Nishida argues: "We must distinguish at least two fundamentally different directions: one is that of knowing objects, another that of self-consciousness" (4: 293). Moreover, the qualitative difference between these two levels is too wide to move from one to another (6: 144).

Self-intentional or Self-content

In Nishida's mature theory, self-consciousness is object-less. It is not intentional or other-directed, but self-directed. Nishida defines "intending" as the "constitution (*kosei*) of self-content in itself" (5: 149). That consciousness which becomes conscious of itself is that which takes as its essential feature not "simple intending" but "self-consciousness" (5: 149-150). Nishida repeats, "What is intended must be self-content (*jiko naiyo*) which is illuminating in itself" (5: 431). Intellectual self, another name for objectified self, is treated most harshly by Nishida, on the ground that it requires something transcendent (*choetsuteki*), not given by consciousness itself, and hence is intentional (5: 127). Nishida here seems to argue that only when self-consciousness loses its own content and degenerates into the intellectual self whose main function is simply "mirroring" or "representing," does it then takes the nature of intentionality, which needs a transcendent object.

Temporal

As far as the temporal aspect of self-consciousness is concerned, time is an instant, and an act of consciousness is instantaneous being. An act of self-consciousness is not only simply eternal but also temporal: eternal in the sense that each moment of time touches the absolute, temporal in the sense that it is momentarily acting. This understanding of the temporal character of self-consciousness is variously expressed by Nishida: the discontinuity of continuity, the self-determination of eternal now, and the present's determination of present itself. All these expressions of and arguments for temporal existence are meant to establish the fact that *lived time,* better expressed as *living time,* consists of each moment, absolutely independent from both preceding and following moments. The uniquely acting and truly present self-consciousness will not allow anything substantial or potential to dictate itself. Nishida forcefully commands us "not to think that there is in any sense a potential which is underlyingthe self" because "there is self-consciousness only when present determines itself" (12: 77-78). Another characteristic of Nishida's discussion of time is his connection of "discontinuous continuity" to the notion of spatial or circular.[6] These two metaphors, space and circle, may have helped him visualize the fullness and completeness of each moment. The spatial element seems to be employed to signify that each moment is a complete and absolute world, independent from other moments. On the basis of this spatial characteristic of temporal fullness, Nishida repudiates the pure duration of Bergson.

The indivisibility of pure duration is not sufficient to express the "discontinuous aspect" of each act of self-consciousness, or moment of true life. Thus, Nishida argues that pure duration does not show a discontinuous aspect, or absolute negation (7: 82), nor does it show true death (6: 356) or true concrete life (7: 131).[7]

One-qua-Many

Each act of self-consciousness is both individualistic and universal. The fact that each act of self-consciousness is individualistic and unique is the basis on which Nishida distinguishes mental phenomena from natural phenomena, for only the former "possesses a direction to individualization" (3: 403). Contrary to this, "that which is common to everyone and can be repeated any number of times, is not reality" (3: 444-445). This notion of individuality is related to both "reality" and "creativity": "The reason individual (*kojinteki*) consciousness, compared to communal consciousness (*kyodo ishiki*), which is a kind of simultaneous existence, possesses true reality as a continuous unity is that it is creative" (3: 407).[8]

The uniqueness of acts of self-consciousness becomes the characteristic mark of human existence, distinguishing it from animal life, because "within the consciousness of an animal, which acts by instinct, there functions only a kind of racial self (*shuzokuga*), which cannot yet be called an individual self (*koseiga*)" (3: 403-404).

Nishida also believed that he needed the notion of universality for individuality. One often sees passages similar to the following in Nishida's text: "In self-consciousness there will be a unity . . . of the universal and the particular. What we call self refers to this point" (4: 83). This relation between "individual" and "universal" may be put into the most important logical apparatus in Nishida's philosophy: one-qua-many and many-qua-one logic. As a matter of fact, this logic is applied in every dissolution of the many dichotomies embedded in either subject-logic or object-logic, which in turn are based upon the Platonic and Aristotelian logic of "One over Many."

Emotional Aspect of Self-consciousness

At one place Nishida names "self's seeing its own content" as "feeling self-consciousness" (*kanjoteki jikaku*) (5: 138), or "emotional consciousness" (*joiteki ishiki*) (5: 274). He further argues, "seeing the self is joy and losing it is sadness" (5: 275). Almost paraphrasing a passage from *On the Trinity* of Augustine, Nishida argued for the trinity of man. "In self-consciousness, 'I,' 'self-knowledge,' and 'self-love' are identical" (12: 116).[9] One has to emphasize that his arguments for the trinity of human existence all are concerned with *homo interior.* "The human sciences of *homo interior* are based upon the emotional self-consciousness" (12: 23). We thus see one of the fundamental characteristics of Nishida's philosophy of self-consciousness: its personal content, its emphasis upon human interiority (*naka*) and *homo interior.*

All these phrases represent or signify the fundamentally soteriological character of Nishida's philosophy of self-consciousness.

Religiosity

"Self's seeing itself in itself" is seen as awakening or salvation. One of Nishida's earliest usages of religious-soteriological meaning is found in part 4, "Religion," in *A Study of Good.* In this context, "religious demand is the demand with regard to the self; it is demand concerning the life of the self." In the same section, arguing for the ultimacy of the religious concern, Nishida identifies the religious demand as the demand for the unity of consciousness (1: 172).

Here Nishida also believes that the communal consciousness is an expression or part of the demand for the unity of consciousness. But this communal consciousness loses its primacy to the religious demand, because the religious demand for the unity of consciousness is "the ultimate point" of the demand for the unity of consciousness (1: 171). The usage of "religious," understood as the unity of the individual consciousness rather than communal consciousness, developed into one of the most distinctive features of the philosophy of self-consciousness. However, the concept of communal consciousness reappears in the philosophy of history in the form of "the spirit of an epoch," "species mediation," and especially in the notions of the state and people.

III. THE TURN

To examine the emergence of Nishida's philosophy of history, it is necessary to understand precisely how the notion of history was previously treated in the philosophy of self-consciousness.

In part 4 of the essay **"Ippansha no jiko gentei" ("The Self-determination of the Universal")** (written in 1929), in volume 5, which I think is one of the earlier discussions of historical reality in the context of the mature theory of self-consciousness,[10] Nishida discusses the historical self, historical determination, and historical content, as well as their individuality and non-rationality. A careful reading reveals, however, that Nishida always places "religious experience" or the "seeing" aspect of self-consciousness at the foundation of historical self or reality.

In this pre-turn essay, based upon a sharp distinction between the two levels of self-consciousness and historical self, Nishida argues: "Historical content can be seen as the noematic or expressive content of noetic determination of the self which sees its own nothingness" (5: 400-401). This is one of the first places where Nishida identifies "historical content" as the noematic content of noetic determination of the self.

In reminding us of the forms of self-consciousness, Nishida argues: "Historical reality is established by the self-conscious forms *(jikakuteki keishiki).* In other words, it must be self-conscious reality" (5: 398). He argues: "Historical self-consciousness *(rekishiteki jikaku)* is grounded in noetic determination which sees nothingness, hence it cannot see itself and its concrete noema. This is why history is understood as irrational" (5: 398). Despite his positive understanding of historical reality as self-conscious reality, he grounds historical self-consciousness in noetic determination, which is nothingness, non-substantial, and also the basis of the irrationality of history.

In this essay, Nishida is firmly convinced that religious or existential self-consciousness underlies the historical aspect of human existence. Hence, at this stage Nishida is still emphatic:

> Historical self *(rekishiteki jiko)* is merely seen in the realm of expression. . . . As far as the self which was born at a specific epoch *(jidai)* is determined noematically, it is ruled by the spirit of epoch. . . . [But] there is, at the bottom of the self, something which transcends history. At the bottom of our activity, there is absolutely deeper self in the direction of noesis. . . . It is self-determination of self which sees nothingness. Instinct, society, or history are merely images of this self in the noematic plane, they are merely seen self. (5: 401-402)

In all these quotations, the historical world, as well as the expressive world, is merely seen. It is certainly deemed less ontologically real, since "at the foundation of historical determination, there is already noematic determination in the self-consciousness of absolute nothingness" (5: 409). That something deeper than history, historical activity, is called "inner life" *(naiteki seimei)* (5: 413) or "religious life" (5:414).[11] For Nishida the inner self, noetic determination, and noetic meaning of the self-consciousness of absolute nothingness are identical (5: 462). As a consequence, the world of personality, the locus of personal freedom, is outside *(soto)* the historical world (5: 336). Quite differently from the later position of the philosophy of history, Nishida here attacks the notion of the spirit of the epoch *(jidai seishin),* because it is merely an abstract and noematic content and a general form [*Gestalt*] common to various idealistic contents in an epoch (5: 399).

Thus understood, before the turn, the self-consciousness of absolute nothingness always has ontological priority over historical reality, which can have any reality only to the extent that it is grounded in the noetic aspect of self-consciousness. The philosophy of self-consciousness and its emphasis on temporal existence, together with its negation or disparagement of historical existence, are strongly reaffirmed in the very important essay **"Ningengaku" ("Human Studies")** (12: 18-30), which was published in August 1930.

In **"Human Studies,"** for example, Nishida argues for internal human existence beyond historical existence, because "if we are seen as simply historical existence, then the significance of a truly free human being would be lost. A merely historical human study is not a true human study. True human studies are not the human studies of the external human being *(homo exterior)* but of the inner human being *(homo interior)*" (12: 20). Believing that historical existence generally is understood as belonging to *homo exterior,*[12] Nishida emphasizes, "What is truly being in its deepest sense must be internal human being" *(naiteki ningen)* (12: 20). Moreover, the foundation of the external human being should be sought in the internal human being. The historical self *(rekishiteki jiko)* is transcended by the individualistic self *(kojinteki ningen)* (12: 27). Philosophy is "the science of self-reflection of the internal human being" (12: 30). He further emphasizes that the most immediate *(chokusetsu ni shite)* and concrete reality *(gutaiteki naru jijitsu)* is individualistic or personalistic *(jinkakuteki)* (12: 29). What is that which is personalistic? It is "self-conscious determination in which self, as nothingness, sees itself" (12: 29). In short, in the philosophy of self-consciousness, Nishida made a sharp distinction between *homo exterior* and *homo interior,* assigning authentic human existence only to the latter.

However, the main idea of this essay will be recanted by Nishida later, when the sole supremacy of the existential or religious thinking is challenged by the firm establishment of the philosophy of history. In 1937, when the philosophy of history was well under way, Nishida collected, in a single volume entitled *Zoku keiken toshisaku* (**"Sequel to Experience and Thought"**) (12: 5-195), some of his essays previously published in 1930-1931, and in so doing, he added a short but valuable assessment at the end of each essay:

> In this essay ["**Human Studies**"], the world of history was considered as external, in contradiction to the internal human being. I thought the internal human being was concrete *(gutaiteki).* The historical world was understood only in the ordinary sense. But I do not think in this way any longer. The internal human being exists in the historical world. If I hereafter wrote **"Human Studies,"** then it would be very much different from this essay. Human being is historical human being; it must be the creative element of a creative world. The thought of a human being represented in the *Trinity* of Augustine is the human study which sees human beings from the perspective of the transcendent God. This must be reexamined rather as the human study of historical human being. I think that when I wrote this essay my focal point was *homo interior.* (12: 30)

In this passage, Nishida holds that human studies should be based not upon *homo interior* but upon the historical human being. Moreover, the locus of concreteness and creativity are neither the internal human being nor artistic creation, but the historical human being. The ordinary manner in which the historical world has been dealt with should be reoriented. He also rejects the Trinity of Augustine from the new perspective of the immanent-quasitranscendent logic. This passage also implies that Nishida

would criticize his own earlier trinity of "I," self-knowledge, and self-love, all of which are identical in self-consciousness. Consequently, in many respects, this short note convinces me that Nishida became sharply critical of the internalism of his earlier position giving primacy to self-consciousness over historical existence.

Expression (Hyogen) and Body Before the Turn

The change clearly expressed in **"Human Studies"** and elsewhere does not occur abruptly. Rather, it results from careful preparation, part of which is to expand and give a higher ontological status to the realm of expression. One principal development involves Nishida's understanding of the locus of expression: the main locus of expression in his earlier philosophy is in artistic creation, whereas its proper locus in the philosophy of history is primarily the historical world. Finally, even the political world is included as an expressive world.[13]

Philosophically, this reflects the movement from a sharply dichotomous position between the "seeing" (noetic) world and "seen" (noematic) world, with which the expressive world is identified, to a position which grants equal reality to expressive or noematic worlds. This movement finally reaches the position that all human existence occurs in the expressive, that is, historical-political, world. Consider this passage revealing how the world of expression took shape in the philosophy of self-consciousness:

> Active self can be found in its [self-consciousness of the absolute nothingness] noetic direction and "expression" in its noematic direction. But the active self cannot noematically determine its own content because it, as nothingness, has the sense of its own noetic determination. Therefore the active self in its broader sense must be divided into two parts: the part facing noematic aspect and the part facing noetic aspect. (5: 451-452)

In this passage, Nishida initially seems to confirm the position of the mature theory of self-consciousness that the active self cannot noematically determine its own content, but can only be found in the noetic direction. However, in order to make room for the expressive world, Nishida here divides "active self" into two aspects: noetic and noematic. This division gives some reality to the noematic aspect. Considering that immediately after his most mature and radical formulation of self-consciousness Nishida shows a concern for the noematic world, it appears that the true motive of this passage is to introduce an "intermediary world" which provides a possibility for mitigating his radical internalism or emphasis on *homo interior* and his strong focus on consciousness. He gives more reality to external nonconscious phenomena. Because of this mediating function, I consider the development of the notion of expression to be one of the most important preparations for Nishida's later turn to the philosophy of history.

Another significant aspect of Nishida's theory of expression is his view of the inseparability of expression and body, which is the theoretical basis for giving a positive value to the idea of body in Nishida's text. This line of thinking, developing through the notion of the bodily determination of self-consciousness, eventually culminates in the notion of historical body.

Prior to this positive view, however, Nishida's earlier texts contain many passages giving a rather negative value to the body. For example, in 5: 336 Nishida contrasts noetic determination with bodily determination, which is here identified with noematic determination. One of the favorite examples of bodily determination of self-consciousness, in the philosophy of self-consciousness, is artistic creation.[14] The link made between expression and body is inherited by the notion of historical body, whose locus is historical space and the state. As the notion of expression fully matures in the philosophy of history, so too does the notion of body culminate in the notion of historical body.

Traditionally it has been understood that Nishida turned from the social world to the inner world for the solace arising from the practice of Zen meditation, and on the basis of that experience developed his philosophy.[15] I agree with many other scholars that his earlier philosophy is intimately related to his biography. In a letter (no. 26, 18: 41-42) which was written in 1896, Nishida employed the term "transitory world" (*ukiyo*) for the surrounding world, including family life (18: 41). In response to this experience of *ukiyo,* Nishida removed himself from the sociopolitical world, and moved into the world of certain, indubitable self's seeing itself in itself, an absolutely self-sufficient or self-determinative world.

By virtue of his philosophy of history, Nishida is going to return to the world he once deserted and called transitory. But this time, the transitory world does not remain transitory. It takes on full reality and becomes as divine-like as an individual act of self-consciousness. His returning to *ukiyo* is possible only after this world is secured as an ontologically real world or religious world by the application of the forms of self-consciousness. In that newly born world, there is an almost perfect harmony or unity between individuals and state, in a way similar to Hegel's argument in *Reason in History*. Hence, the state becomes the divine Idea as it exists on earth.[16]

The Significance of "History" (12: 31-63)

It was in 1931 that Nishida made the most important turn in the overall developing of his philosophy. This turn actually was expressed in a few essays, including **"Rekishi"** (**"History"**) (published in August 1931). Together with this essay, five others published in the same year reveal how keenly Nishida was aware of the problem of time and history.[17] **"History"** is the earliest essay in which we can notice all the essential features of what I call the turn in Nishida's philosophy: the integration of the notion of expression and the historical world and its inseparability from the notion of body, the applications of some key forms of self-consciousness to a historical

epoch, seminal ideas of acting intuition, and even his fondness for the phrase "each epoch is immediate to God" of Leopold von Ranke (1795-1886).[18]

As to the almost total integration of the notion of expression and the historical world, Nishida's definition of history here eloquently confirms this: "But history is not so-called inner sensation, such as what we think or feel in our minds. It must be externalized conscious contents through action. It must be the contents of expression in its broader sense" (12: 35). "Therefore, we are born and die in history. No hero would escape being the historical product" (12: 36). The marriage between the notion of expression and history is reemphasized in this essay: "History maybe called the self-conscious process of that which expresses itself. . . . One may argue that our true self exists in history, and we have a true self-consciousness in history" (12: 47).

In this essay, Nishida's analysis is still based upon his distinction between noetic and noematic directions, calling the first the "self-determination of love" and the latter the "self-determination of time" (12: 42). The important point, however, is that even though the self-determination of time is grounded in the self-determination of love, it has its own positive reality. Also Nishida here relates the notion of action to the "externalization" of our thoughts and feelings. "The acting self reveals itself by self-expression" (12: 43). This usage of "action" here leads Nishida to coin the term "acting intuition," one of the key concepts for his self-criticism of his own earlier "conscious-ism" or "internalism."

Unlike the ordinary sense of history mentioned above, true history for Nishida must be one which has "the meaning in which present determines present" (12: 47).

> If history is taken to mean "the determination of eternal now," as I have argued above, then our self-consciousness as the determination of nothingness . . . must be deemed the idealistic content which unifies each epoch in historical determination (*rekishiteki gentei*), or the spirit of the epoch. As the temporal determination is seen from the perspective of the present's determination of present, so each and every epoch is the absolute, from which our entire life is seen and determined. (12: 50)

In this passage, one of the forms of self-consciousness, the determination of the eternal now, is employed to explain "history" and "epoch." The "spirit of the epoch," previously rejected, is raised to full ontological status by the form of determination of the eternal now.

Then Nishida relates true history to society and to "all of humanity." "True history, as the determination of nothingness which includes time, proceeds through the self-consciousness of society. Therein there must be something called all of humanity" (12: 51-52). Here in this passage, Nishida relates self-consciousness, true history, society, and all of humanity. Perhaps it is at this juncture that the philosophical link between history and politics is made in Nishida's texts, culminating in historical-political thinking. Thus it is easy for Nishida to quote the following passage, which may be called the motto of his philosophy of history, from "On the Epochs of Modern History," by Leopold von Ranke, whom Nishida called the great historian: "Every epoch is immediate to God, and its worth is not at all based on what derives from it but rests in its own existence, in its own self" (12: 61).[19]

His "turn" enabled Nishida to pronounce "the absoluteness of each epoch" and the "self-determination of epoch" (12: 62). Anyone can become a "historical man" (*rekishijin*) (12: 47) or "historian" (*rekishika*) (12: 55) upon taking the position of the present's self-determination.

The essay **"Self-Love, Other-Love, and Dialectic"** (published in February and March 1932; 6: 260-299) clearly argues that the immediate and most direct world for us, wherein we are living, is not the so-called material world or conscious world: "We are living in the world of activity (*koi*) in its broader sense and in the expressive world. We are concretely historical man" (6: 266). According to this passage, the world of activity, or expressive world, and the historical world seem to signify one and the same world, which is neither the material world nor the conscious world. Along the same line, Nishida argues, "What is immediate as determination of nothingness, must both determine itself and have the meaning of expression" (6: 266). Moreover, this passage also recants his earlier position as to the locus of immediacy, by holding that the "immediate" or most direct world must have the meaning of expression. In this manner, Nishida rejected his previous understanding of "conscious world" and expanded it to include historical world. Hence, "we are historical man."

Another important point made in this essay is its emphasis on the notion of body in relation to the notion of expression (6: 262-263). "True self lies neither in the cortex of the brain, as a physiologist says, nor in the consciousness, as a psychologist argues. It, as the bodily self (*shintaiteki jiko*) which actively determines itself, resides in the broader sense of history" (6: 266). More significantly, the notions of personality and sublimated body are employed in order to refer to the same notion (6: 268). Finally in this essay the notion of bodily self in history culminates in the concept of historical body: "We can be free only as historical reality. There is a free man underneath the present's self-determination of itself. The free man must have historical body (*rekishiteki shintai*)" (6: 293).[20]

Although it is unclear whether the consciousness rejected in 6: 266 refers to his mature philosophy of self-consciousness, it is not only quite possible but also consistent that all these new emphases on active determination and "bodily self in history" or historical body are rejections of the internalism or "consciousness-ism" embodied in his mature theory of self-consciousness.

Later, in the essay entitled **"Inochi no tetsugaku ni tsuite"** (**"Concerning the Philosophy of Life"**) (published in 1932, 6: 428-451), history is itself called "Thou" (6: 444), and, in a very Rankean passage, Nishida argues in favor of the historical world:

> There must be the meaning of creation of value when we face God through history. We are determined both in and through history. The God, apart from historical determination, who faces abstractly individual selves, is simply transcendent God and is not true God. . . . I and You, residing in history, determined by history, are the creation of God. (6: 427)

Here again, as in his pre-turn philosophy, a transcendent God is rejected as the true God, but on different grounds. In the philosophy of self-consciousness a transcendent God was rejected on the basis that each act of self-consciousness is itself the locus of divinity in humanity. Here the true God is realized in historical determination, that is, in and through history. This clearly portends the later divine character given to a historical epoch, and thus leads Nishida to give a new interpretation to the notion of "self-determination of the eternal now." Both his rejection of any transcendent God and his notion of "historical determination" are important because they are the grounds by which Nishida repudiates any sharp dichotomy between the Kingdom of God and the kingdoms of this historical world, and by which he argues for fuller ontological status for history. The God who is separated from the historical world is seen as not a true God. In section 2 of *The Logic of Place and the Religious Worldview* (1945), Nishida will call this transcendent God objectified God, and will thereby reject Karl Barth's notion of the transcendent God.

In this manner, in several essays written in 1931 and 1932, beginning with **"History,"** we can see a full integration of the expressive world and historical reality. Nishida shifts from a primacy of consciousness to give similar primacy to history, which was previously held as a less ontologically real world but which now is given full ontological status.[21] The significance of these essays does not stop here, since his emphasis upon history strongly implies a criticism of the internalism of his own mature theory of self-consciousness.

The essay **"History,"** marking Nishida's most significant turn, did not present the full implications of the philosophy of history, as all of Nishida's philosophical developments evolved slowly. The best example of its gradual establishment can be seen later in Nishida's complete rejection of the notion of noetic aspect. For instance, in its republication, Nishida gives us this following reflection at the end of **"History,"** six years after its first appearance in *Shiso:*

> In this essay, I have already maintained that we exist in the historical world. But I also argued in those days that the foundation of the historical world is always self-consciousness, love, or something noetic.

I could not but hold this kind of view. Although I do not say that this view is erroneous, it cannot avoidbeing abstract (*chushoteki*). (12: 63)

This passage confirms that in the essay **"History,"** Nishida already held a philosophy of historical existence. But he later became dissatisfied with the fact that he had not been radical enough, in still grounding the historical world in "self-consciousness, love, or something noetic." This link is rejected as "abstract," a criticism particularly directed to a passage in which Nishida distinguished noematic self-determination of time from neotic self-determination of love (12: 42). Nishida felt that this kind of language was still a relic of the philosophy of self-consciousness. At least since that moment, any deep-rooted hierarchy between noetic and noematic aspects is banished forever from Nishida's texts.

IV. MATURE PHILOSOPHY OF HISTORY

In order to understand Nishida's philosophy of history and its criticism of the philosophy of self-consciousness, it is important to consider Ranke, because it was with Ranke that Nishida felt the most intimate tie in his thinking on the historical epoch and the state. He may be the only Western thinker who was never outgrown or deserted by Nishida. Since 1919, when Nishida quoted for the first time Ranke's celebrated phrase "Every epoch is immediate to God" *(Jede Epoche ist unmittelbar zur Gott),*[22] he never changed his fondness for this phrase and for Ranke's general view of a historical epoch and the state. Even in a few places in his letters, Nishida revealed a great enthusiasm for Ranke.[23] Nishida's thinking on history and politics was permeated by the phrase "every epoch is immediate to God," for at least his last ten years (1935-1945), which roughly corresponds to the period when the essays of volumes 8-11 were published. Hence, this phrase is to be taken as the main theme of the philosophy of history, in contrast to "self's seeing itself in itself," the leitmotif of the philosophy of self-consciousness.

Nishida's turn to philosophy of history in essence means that all the earlier key terms are historicized and at the same time given full reality by application of the forms of self-consciousness. Self-consciousness is changed into historical self-consciousness, individual becomes historical individual, activity becomes historical activity, and place becomes historical or public place. In this manner, history itself becomes divine, reaching the status enjoyed previously only by each act of self-consciousness, or by the "internal human being." For example, the notion of epoch is upgraded. It becomes the foundation of such political conceptions as nation (*minzoku*), state, and the emperor. At that point we may call Nishida's thought historical-political philosophy.[24]

In the philosophy of self-consciousness, the notion of individualrefers to each act of self-consciousness, whereas in the philosophy of history, the concept is applied to several entities, giving them full ontological status: to begin with, an epoch, state (*kokka*), society, species (*shu*), and individual carrying the task of the epoch. Among these, "epoch" appears to be the most important notion, considering its frequent occurrence in his writings on the philosophy of history.

Self-determinative and Active

In the first essay of volume 8, **"Sekai no jiko doitsu to renzoku"** (**"Self-identity and Continuity of the World"**), Nishida grants the same self-determinative character to "epochs" as he did to acts of self-consciousness.[25] He argues in effect that a previous epoch cannot be the cause of a following one in the self-determination of eternal now, nor can a following epoch act as the purpose *(telos)* of a previous one, because what resides in the historical present is considered particularistic self-determination. The duration of each epoch does not seem to matter to Nishida, insofar as each and every epoch is conceived as an ontological event or unit. No matter how long it is, each epoch has the same ontological value. In particular, Nishida evidently deemed his own time an ontologically real unit, or an epoch.

The notion of acting intuition, together with its criticism of the internalism of the mature of self-consciousness, is thematically dealt with in the 1937 essay **"Koiteki chokkan"** (**"Acting Intuition"**) (8: 541-571) and other essays in volume 8. According to Nishida, historical life requires both activity and intuition as well. He fears a passive interpretation of the concept of intuition: "Intuition is [erroneously] seen as self's absorption (*botsunyo*) into things, and hence therein activity will disappear" (8: 542).[26] Furthermore, he insists that as long as our activity is historical, then our activity is itself intuitive as well. Hence intuition is not necessarily passive, although self's absorption into things or the status of ecstasy (*kokotsu*) is a certain sort of passivity, losing historical activity (8: 541-542). This essay shows that Nishida attempted to return to the historical world by his new emphasis on the active aspect of acting intuition.

Although there are familiar phrases from the philosophy of self-consciousness, such as "acting-qua-seeing" and "seeing-qua-acting" (8: 318, 8: 407), they "must be deemed in the world of historical reality" (8: 407). This understanding of "acting" did not exist in the acting-qua-seeing of self-consciousness.[27] The notion of action is newly employed to mitigate the passivity embedded in those notions which primarily relate to consciousness. Seeing-qua-acting as understood here should not only be distinguished from the seeing-qua-acting of the philosophy of self-consciousness, but also be taken as a criticismof the internalism of that earlier seeing-qua-acting.

Another aspect of acting intuition is its essential relationship to the concept of body, or historical body. In this way, "bodily acting" is not a subjective fact, but "subjective and objective historical fact" (8: 344). Moreover, the concept of body is deeply related to the concreteness of a specific time and place (*basho*). Nishida explains that preserving the body is identical to remaining in a specific place and time of the historical world (8: 346).

In volume 11, Nishida calls body "the tool of world spirit" and "the bodily organ of historical life" (11: 334).[28] By such passages describing body as the necessary medium of historical life, he may mean that one is supposed to follow historical duty with body and mind, because our true self resides in the historical and practical self. Nishida argues that there is no practice except for historical activity (11: 168). Then, interestingly enough, he cites Dogen in order to support the fact that we grasp true self in the negation of the abstract and conscious self, that is, in *"shinjin ichinyo"* (the unity of body-mind) (11: 168). It is important to note that Nishida's citation of Dogen and the unity of body-mind must be placed in the context of the philosophy of history.[29]

Unknowability of an Epoch

After the turn, acting occurs in the historical place, and is related to the uniqueness and unknowability of the historical epoch. If there is no universal law underlying each historical epoch, then there is no way to have a cognition of it. Nishida cannot help but agree with Ranke that the law of development of historical nature must go beyond human thought (8: 89). In volume 8, Nishida repeats again and again Ranke's dictum: "Every epoch is immediate to God, and its worth is not at all based on what derives from it but rests in its own existence, in its own self."[30] In this sense, the history of philosophy as a search for any underlying principles cannot be a legitimate subject in Nishida's philosophy of history.

Nishida opposes Wilhelm Dilthey's (1833-1911) conception of the historical world as an object of understanding, rather than that which determines personal action (7: 179). In contrast to Nishida, Dilthey takes the notion of understanding as the core of human sciences and requires general knowledge at every stage of operation—even when focusing upon individual persons. Dilthey argues:

> Beyond all reproduction and stylization of the factual and singular, thought *(Denken)* strives to arrive at knowledge of the essential and necessary: it strives to understand *(verstehen)* the structural coherence of the individual life and social life. We only gain control over social life to the extent that we grasp and employ regularity and coherence *(Regelmässigkeit und Zusammenhang)*. The logical form in which such regularities are expressed are propositions whose subjects are general, just as their predicates.[31]

According to this passage, human thought essentially strives to find structural coherence and regularity both in individual life and social life, and it needs an appropriate logical form, which may be expressed as "one-over-many," the antithesis to Nishida's logic of one-qua-many. Together with this logic, Nishida's emphasis upon the present's determination of present epoch disallows any possibility of understanding structural coherence and regularity. Indeed, because of his radical notion of discontinuous continuity, a historical epoch will have no such coherence and regularity to begin with. The logical character of "universal" in Nishida's one-qua-many logic has nothing to do with the concept of understanding or historical knowledge, but is required to emphasize the individuality of a historical epoch. Consequently, Nishida does not deal with the question of "universals" embedded in the structure of historical thought and knowledge.

Historical Mediation and Historical Constitution

In the philosophy of history, in contrast to self-constitution and self-content, he employed the term "historical constitution" *(rekishiteki koseisayo)* (8: 550), and introduced the concepts "historical mediation" (10: 123) and "external mediation." For instance, the philosophy of history takes "historical world" as both "external and internal" (8: 534). The historical world, including its best examples, the state and the emperor, being also internal, is not something which stands over against the self, and thus it transcends merely being an object of cognition.

As to the meaning of external mediation, let us examine another passage: "Facing the aspect of the past of the world, we can always think of the environmental world. What appears in reality is already what has existed. What exists must be deemed to be externally mediated. . . . The species life . . . must be the one which is environmentally managed" (8: 536). "The past," "the environment," "what has existed," or "what is given"—these are the main images of externality, and they are all very close to the description of historical reality or historical determination. Elsewhere, we find a ground for this interpretation:

> But the fact that history moved from what is individualistic to what is individualistic does not mean that it is the movement from something spiritual *(seishinteki)* to another spiritual. Nor does it mean that the foundation of the world is spiritual. In it [history] there always exists the world of what has been formed. It is deemed the world of absolutely external mediation, or what has been absolutely determined and changes itself self-contradictorily, including its self-negation. (8: 561)

According to this passage, the world includes what has been formed and is seen as the world of external mediation. "What has been formed" is also seen as "the historical reality which has been given" *(tsutaerareta rekishiteki genjitsu)* (8: 562). Moreover, one has to note that this external mediation is placed against a sort of spiritualism, according to which every movement and the foundation of the world itself are considered to be spiritual.

Perhaps both the transformation of self-content into historical mediation and the introduction of external mediation enabled Nishida to distinguish historical constitution or historical making from intuitive equanimity, by which he may refer to the same phenomena as internal salvation.

> Those who consider historical constitution, taking acting intuition as its foundation, do not claim that the aim of life resides in "intuitive equanimity" *(chokkanteki seishi)*. Our aim absolutely resides in

historical constitution. In other words, human existence resides in historical making (*rekishiteki seisaku*). (8: 550)

It is not clear what is meant by intuitive equanimity. But it is arguable that this comes very close to the aforementioned "separation from the world" and "self's absorption into things." Intuitive equanimity, absorption, and ecstasy are all very near what he called *gedatsu* in the philosophy of self-consciousness.

In adjusting the concept of place (*basho*) after the turn, Nishida employs the notion "historical space" (*rekishiteki kukan*), which is called public place (*oyake no basho*) (10: 98) and which has social-historical determination. Nishida also argues that the self-determination of place has a creative significance, and "must have the meaning of social and historical determination" (7: 170-171).[32]

Being of the Place

The emphasis upon "what has been given as historical reality" and historical space allows the concept of "being of the place" (*bashoteki u*), to express all the new developments that follow Nishida's turn: the ideas that each individual is historically mediated and that historical reality is given as "something" (*atta mono*) (8: 576), not as "nothing." In this sense, consider the following passage: "Therefore, the self-identity of place, that is, what I call "being of the place" (*bashoteki u*) must mean that place determines place itself in the manner in which the immanent is transcendent and the transcendent is immanent. . . . Therefore, I call it the self-determination of nothingness" (10: 480). Historical place as public place cannot be called the place of absolute nothingness, but being of the place, referring to absolute being. Although Nishida employs the same term, "the self-determination of nothingness," one cannot take it to mean what it did in the explication of acts of self-consciousness. Perhaps this "nothingness" here is nothingness in the sense that it guarantees the absoluteness of historical reality, through the application of such forms of self-consciousness as self-determination and immanent-qua-transcendent logic.

Moreover, "being of the place" also forces Nishida to change his view on the notion of creation *ex nihilo,* which becomes impossible in the philosophy of history, because "what has been given" is "something," not "nothing." "Creation is not creation *ex nihilo*. What happens must be what has existed (*atta mono*)" (8: 576).[33] Even in this new philosophy Nishida still does not negate the "determining aspect" or "creative aspect" of the historical world,[34] but his new emphasis seems to fall upon the givenness of a historical environment.

In sum, external mediation and *bashoteki u* are associated here with "the historical reality which has been given," as the material stuff on which we must exert our formative activity. This anti-internalism argues against the earlier position in the philosophy of self-consciousness described by the doctrine of self-content or self-mediation.

Thus in part Nishida's introduction of and emphasis upon something external, externality, or historical mediation may be his own intentional objection to the self-content theory of his earlier internalism.[35]

In view of Nishida's logic of the absolute-qua-relative and his rejection of Barth's notion of a transcendent God, one has to recognize that Nishida's later characterization of the logic of *basho* as "historical" is greatly different from the logic of *basho* of self-consciousness: "My theology of the logic of place (*bashoteki ronriteki shingaku*) is neither theistic nor deistic, neither spiritual nor natural. It is historical (*rekishiteki*)" (11: 406). This passage clearly leads us again to Nishida's own awareness of "the direct union of self-consciousness and the historical world," and to his religious-historical thinking, uniting earlier self-consciousness logic and his later philosophy of history.[36] And the logic of place here cannot be taken to mean that of the philosophy of self-consciousness.

Temporality

The transformation of temporality between philosophies of self-consciousness and history is quite simple and clear: "An epoch determines itself" is equivalent to "present determines itself" (8:452). With this simple equation, the discontinuity of continuity is applied to historical epochs, causing an epoch to share the same ontological features of each temporal act of self-consciousness. In this connection, Nishida explains:

> In the depth of the historical world, it is impossible to think of something substantial. The world of fact which determines itself without any determinant, determines itself individually. That is, it forms itself individually. . . . Hence, history does not have its substance in the past, nor any purpose in the future. . . . The historical world, as the self-determination of absolute present, always takes its task in the present. What unifies history must be this task (Ranke's *Tendenz*). (10: 380)[37]

In this passage, as with the self-determination of the absolute present in each act of self-consciousness, the independence of each epoch from both the previous and following epochs is emphasized. Thus, Nishida completely rejects the possibility of any sort of underlying law or principle, or anything substantial in the depths of the historical world which may decide its course by the subsumption of the epoch. At this point, Nishida cites Ranke to confirm this equation: "The historical epoch, as Ranke has already told us, cannot be seen as the simple result of the previous epoch nor as the preparation for the following epoch. It has its own independent meaning" (10: 380).

Following this line of thought, in another essay, Nishida argues for a close affinity between Mahayana Buddhism and Rankean thought. In **"Yotei chowa o tebiki to shite shukyo tetsugaku e"** (**"Towards the Religious Philosophy through Pre-established Harmony"**),[38] he states: "From this standpoint of present's determining present itself, each moment is the beginning and end of the world.

Even historians think each point in the historical world is a beginning (Ranke)" (11: 132). But Nishida laments, "Unfortunately, today's Buddhists forget this kind of authentic meaning of Mahayana." Therefore, "Eastern culture must revive itself on this standpoint and give new light to the world culture" (11: 132). He then immediately argues in religious-political language: "Our national polity (kokutai) as the self-determination of absolute present is the standard of historical activity *(rekishiteki koi)* in this respect. This sort of true spirit of the Mahayana is kept alive only in Japan in the East" (11: 132-133).

The most astonishing move made by Nishida here seems the way in which he directly links Ranke and what he calls the authentic meaning of Mahayana Buddhism. His religious-political language finally reached out to include even the Mahayana tradition.

In the philosophy of self-consciousness, the "spatial" is a metaphor which does not imply spatial extension. In philosophy of history, however, it refers not only to a logical character of absoluteness, but to extensive spatiality. It refers to a specific place, for example, Japan. Although the first sense of space has nothing to do with the second one, the metaphor of spatiality helps Nishida bring together the previous absoluteness and a specific regional place. Moreover, from this new understanding of the spatiality of time, Nishida revisits the *élan vital* of Bergson and repeats his criticism of its lack of a spatial aspect. But this time the ground of his criticism is an actual geographical sense of space, not the logical character of self-consciousness.[39]

One-qua-Many Logic

As was the case with the philosophy of self-consciousness, so one individual cannot be called a genuine individual in the philosophy of history: "'A' exists by facing, 'B'; 'B' exists by facing 'A.' This is what is meant by saying that an individual can become individual by facing other individuals" (8: 88). This logic is applicable both to the epoch and to the state. For example, Nishida argues, "What is social and historical is not simply general but is both individualistic and universal. It must exist as the self-determination of the dialectical universal" (7: 232-233, trans. Dilworth, p. 121). In **"National Polity"** (kokutai), Nishida argues for the necessity of individual-qua-universal logic and rejects the standpoint of abstract logic in which the whole and individuals oppose each other, asserting that from the standpoint of the historical creation, both directions must become one (12: 398).

When the notion of a plurality of individuals is applied to nations, however, it seems that Nishida bends this logic, because Japan does not remain an individual but becomes the center of Asian countries. This is exemplified by his support of the campaign for the Co-Prosperity Sphere of Greater East Asia (Dai-Toa kyoeiken).[40]

Furthermore, in order to be individualistic (koseiteki) one's existence is supposed to assume the task of one's own epoch, or the task of the people. A people (minzoku) or an individual *(kojin)* cannot become individualistic unless they assume the epoch, because "assuming the epoch' *(jidai o ninau mono)* is considered to be individualistic" (8: 574). Note that the notion "individualistic" is newly employed in the philosophy of history to emphasize the fact that any individual (ko) which is separated from the species formation (shuteki keisei) is not a living thing (8: 528).

Previously in the philosophy of self-consciousness, a sharp distinction between racial self and individual self was made on the ground that each unique act of self-consciousness has individuality. But Nishida here emphasizes "species formation," even though the species of species formation is quite differentfrom the earlier racial self, which was refuted as animalistic and lacking in individuality. The species, the state, and the epoch do not subsume the historical individual, who is supposed to assume or carry the epoch. Rather, applying the one-to-many logical form of self-consciousness, the unity of a historical individual and a historical epoch is emphasized.

Nishida's turn thus affected his understanding of the relationship between individual and epoch. In most cases, his earlier position on the irreducibility of individual to racial self is transformed into a new position in which an intimate relationship, or a sort of unity, obtains between, on the one hand, the historical individual and, on the other hand, the species or the state. However, this explanation does not mean that there has in fact ever been such a unity between Japanese citizen and state. Rather this sort of metaphysical explanation of the unity of a citizen and nation has been understood by many scholars as a tool of fascism.[41]

Politics

One of the important consequences of the neglect of Nishida's philosophy of history is the neglect of his political thinking, or the taking of it as extraneous to Nishida's philosophy. Unlike in the philosophy of self-consciousness, in the philosophy of history, Nishida showed a firm conviction regarding the close relationship between philosophy and politics. "Philosophy cannot leave politics and politics cannot leave philosophy" (12: 393).[42] One has to note that in his concept of politics the notions of whole and harmony have primary importance. For instance, "politics is the art by which the society as a whole maintains itself" (12: 329). In another key passage, he argues: "Politics is essentially . . . the art of the whole as historical species. It is not a simple morality. . . . Aiming to achieve the human formation as historical species, politics must be absolutely moral" (12: 330).

As a result of the emphasis on harmony, unity, and the whole, he does not discuss conflict or tension among different groups in a polity, or politics as the art of solving that conflict or tension. He rarely confronts the possibility of conflicts or tension in national politics. His absolute notions of state and emperor lead him to define politics as "the art of the whole as historical species." Thus, in light of this understanding of the unity of religion and politics, one has to be extremely careful not to be blinded by Nishida's usage of familiar religious-soteriological language and thereby miss his discourse on history and politics. We must note that this sort of discourse represents a religious-historical line of thought in the "later" Nishida, and that this religious language, greatly different from its usage in the philosophy of self-consciousness, is political and cannot be internalistic.

In the fifth and last section of *Last Writings,* for example, one finds an explicit account of the full integration between religion, history, and the state. At the outset of this section, Nishida argues that religion is not a special psychological condition of special people; rather the term religion must be employed to reveal the religiosity of the historical world.

> Insofar as the self is a historical reality born from the historical world, acting in the historical world, and dying to the historical world, it must be religious. We should speak in this way in respect of the ground of the self. (11: 447, trans. 109; with change)[43]

Nishida similarly discusses immanently transcendent logic.

> That each of our actions is *eschatologisch* as the self-determination of the absolute present is what, in my judgment, Lin-chi refers to variously as "the total act," "The Buddha-dharma has no special place to apply effort," and "The way of enlightenment is the ordinary and the everyday." The interpretation of the eschatological here is different from that of Christianity. It is discovered in the direction, not of the objectively transcendent, but of what I called the immanently transcendent." (11: 448, trans. 110)

The full integration of Buddhism and the logic of immanent and transcendent in the context of historical world is revealed here again. The fact that discourses of religion and history are inseparably coalesced in this part of Nishida's text may contribute to much of the misreading and overlooking of the philosophy of history. As to the essence of religion, against his earlier definition of religion in the first section as "the event of the soul" (*shinrei*), Nishida argues: "Religion, therefore, is not simply an event within the individual consciousness. It must be the self-consciousness of historical life" (11: 455, trans. 115-116; with change).[44]

Furthermore, he affirms the historicity and religiosity of a nation: "Every nation (*minzoku*), as a formation of the historical world, is its own expression of God" (11: 456, trans. 116). Indeed, the last two pages of *Last Writings,* containing explicit mention of the unity of nation and religion, start with Nishida's own retrospective observation. "I have touched upon the relation between nations and religion from the fourth volume of my *Philosophical Essays* [volume 10]." Then Nishida promptly proceeds to

argue, Each nation is a world that contains the self-expression of the absolute within itself. . . . The nation is religious" (11: 463, trans. 122). Nishida even seemed to lament that a fusion between Christianity, with God as Lord, and the nation may easily be conceived; but this is less easily conceived with respect toBuddhism, which in the past has even been regarded as nonnational (*hikokkateki*) (11: 464).[45]

After quoting a passage of the *Sukhavatavyaha Sutra,* Nishida ends his *Last Writings* with Suzuki's comments on this passage and his final world on the fusion of Pure Land Buddhism and the nation:

> This corrupt world (*shaba*) reflects the Pure Land (*jodo*), and the Pure Land reflects this corrupt world. They are mutually reflecting mirrors. This points to the interconnectedness, or oneness (*ichinyosei*), of the Pure Land and this corrupt world. I think I am able to conceive of the nation in these terms. The nation (*kokka*) must reflect (*utsusu*) the Pure Land in this world. (11: 464, trans. 123; with change)

In sum, many of Nishida's later writings on the surface level contain remarks and passages which look like religious-soteriological thinking. However, each and every section on its deeper level contains an essential aspect of the philosophy of history, and finally emphasizes the inseparable relationship among religion, history, and politics. This line of thinking seems to culminate in section 5, where the Pure Land and the *shaba* (thus, the state) absolutely coalesce into a unity.[46]

However, there are some cases in which religiosity is not totally reducible to history or the state. In other words, Nishida seems to argue that the historical world is always religious but that the converse is not true. Religion taken as the event of the soul (*shinrei*) is not always compatible with the "religious" in the claim that the state is religious. Elsewhere, Nishida once negated the identity of religion and state by maintaining, "the nation is not the savior of our souls" (11: 463). This line of thinking made Nishida argue that a religious person and a citizen must be distinct from each other. "If they are not, the pure development of each will be obstructed, regressing into the medieval identity of the two" (11: 463-464). Nishida may have felt a Kierkegaardian contradiction between the knight of morality· and the knight of faith, or perhaps between his two philosophies of self-consciousness and history. It is difficult to determine how strongly the "later" Nishida meant to separate soteriological concern from the historical reality, or religious truth from the state's morality, because the discussion here is so short. However, seen under the weight of the texts cited here and other works written from 1931 to 1945 and contained in volumes 6-12, this separation of religion from the state seems very weak in light of his overriding concern with historical-political thinking.[47]

One of the interesting consequences of the turn from the philosophy of self-consciousness to the philosophy of history is the contrasting of equanimity or serenity of individual mind with the loyalty and filial piety discussed in the philosophy of history. Satisfaction and joy were understood as the emotional reward of "self's seeing itself in itself," but serenity of mind is rejected in the historical-political line of thinking. In **"Towards the Religious Philosophy through Pre-established Harmony,"** convinced that there is a unity between religion and the state, Nishida rejects a traditional understanding of religion as "the serenity of the individual" (*kojin no anshin*), for that would be nonnational (11: 144). For him, "simply seeking self's serenity" is selfish desire. It stands exactly opposite to what is truly religion. Contrary to this misunderstanding of religion, Nishida argues, "the world of absolute present" is absolutely "historical-formative" (11: 145). He further emphasizes:

> Thus it [religion] must be "national" (*kokkateki*). The state is simply the form of self-forming (*jiko keisei*) of the historical world . . . We ourselves . . . must be national. True submission to the state (*kokka zuijun*) comes from true religious self-consciousness. (11: 145)

It is not clear that the rejected serenity of mind refers to the earlier satisfaction and joy, but Nishida's historical-political thinking and the true submission to the state (loyalty) have a definite tendency to belittle or replace this sort of satisfaction. Also Nishida's rejection of his earlier Augustinian Trinity suggests that we can indeed take this as a rejection of such individual satisfaction (12: 30).

Perhaps it is safe to argue that in the philosophy of history the conceptions of self-love and self-satisfaction become the conceptions of "loyalty and filial piety," which may be deemed the emotional aspects of the philosophy of history and politics. For instance, the notion of loyalty is understood as "the expression of pure feeling" and "the loftiest moral ideal of Japan" (7: 443).[48]

V. CONCLUSION

Based on his conviction about the direct union of self-consciousness and the historical world, Nishida gives different meanings in his historical-political philosophy to many of the forms of self-consciousness taken from the philosophy of self-consciousness, primarily in order to revise and criticize his earlier internalism. The "later" Nishida's effort to effect direct union suggests a few conclusions.

First, if one misses the real significance and the wide scope of the direct union of self-consciousness and the historical world, by overlooking Nishida's discourse on history and politics, then one will see only the forms of self-consciousness. As a result, when discussing the concepts most prevalent in Nishida's later writings, such as the notions of historical self-consciousness, historical self, historical determination, and historical body, one will miss the far-reaching import of the adjective "historical." The familiar characterization of pure experience or Zen intuition as the motif or essence of Nishida's

entire philosophy must be amended; this reading misses both the philosophy of history and its internal criticism and rejection of some key aspects of the philosophy of self-consciousness.[49]

Second, Nishida's later philosophy may be seen as his effort to overcome his earlier sharp distinction between *homo interior* and *homo exterior,* by giving fuller reality to the latter. But the manner in which Nishida puts away his internalism remains basically internal, since the forms of self-consciousness themselves which he uses to overcome that internalism are internally originated. Nishida's extension of the forms of self-consciousness to his historical-political thinking, or his assertion of a direct union of self-consciousness and the historical world, is problematic. His extension of the forms of self-consciousness in order to grant true individuality, or true reality, to an epoch, state, and society, is done in a somewhat arbitrary manner. He never establishes why he gives primacy to, for example, an epoch, or to the state, or to Japan over other East Asian states.

Third, the deeper problem is whether it is possible to apply forms of self-consciousness, which originate in the discussion of acts of self-consciousness, to nonconscious phenomena. If one believes that these are categorically different entities, then Nishida clearly makes a category mistake. Nishida's direct union of self-consciousness and the historical world fails to appreciate the possible incompleteness of a historical epoch and the culpability of the state. I would call this union a category mistake, since acts of self-consciousness and a historical epoch are not similar enough to be treated by similar forms of self-consciousness. Hence, Nishida's turn to the philosophy of history is a wrong turn.

NOTES

[1] In the last essay of volume 10, "Jikaku ni tsuite" (Concerning self-consciousness) (published in 1943), Nishida refers to the forms of self-consciousness (*jikakuteki no keishiki*) (10: 479), or the forms of self-conscious being (*jikakuteki u no keishiki*) (10: 485). However, a much earlier passage may indicate a long history for this notion: "Historical reality is established by means of the forms of self-consciousness (*jikakuteki keishiki*)" (5: 398).

In the first citation, 10 refers to the volume number of *Nishida Kitaro zenshu* (Tokyo: Iwanami Shoten, 1965-1966) and 479 to the page number in this volume. All subsequent citations of Nishida's works will follow this manner of citation. All translations are mine except when the translators are mentioned.

[2] "Self-consciousness is fundamentally the function of consciousness" (6: 94).

[3] For a similar argument, see 7: 100: "That 'self's seeing itself in itself' is the fundamental form of all mental acts."

[4] It is important to remember that the origin of Nishida's employment of 'noesis' and 'noema' was not exclusively his encountering Husserl, but also the *noesis* of Greek philosophy.

[5] It appears that there was a period when Nishida searched for the possibility of self-knowing. For example, "Consciousness at every moment includes the possibility of reflection and opens onto the world of knowledge" (2: 308).

[6] In Nishida's text, the two abstract notions of spatiality and circularity are usually expressed in the adjective forms, *kokanteki* and *enkanteki*.

[7] For similar arguments, see also 6: 433, 8: 179, 8: 380, and 9: 158-159. The conception of life in Bergson is thus neither the truly acting self nor truly objective. Nishitani Keiji, while recognizing the difference between pure experience and pure duration, did not pinpoint just how Nishida saw that distinction. He simply says: there is a great difference between pure experience and pure duration; the former is very volitional and subjectivistic, but the latter is very full of life *(seimeiteki)* (Nishitani Keiji, *Nishida Kitaro* (Tokyo: Keiso Shobo, 1985), p. 119).

[8] *Art and Morality,* trans. David D. Dilworth and Valdo H. Viglielmo (Honolulu: The University Press of Hawaii, 1973), p. 115.

[9] See, for example, *De Trinitate,* book 9, *Basic Writings of Saint Augustine,* ed. W. J. Oates, vol. 2 (New York: Random House, 1948), p. 789.

[10] It is not the case, however, that Nishida's first mention of history occurred in the context of the philosophy of self-consciousness. Even before Nishida fully developed this context, he showed a keen interest in history. It was the individuality or uniqueness of mental phenomena that was primarily responsible for this interest. However, in spite of a number of similar references to history in volumes 1 through 3, there was neither a serious attempt to deal with historical reality thematically, nor an effort to place it within the context of the philosophy of self-consciousness.

[11] We can find similar arguments for this hierarchy: "Only when one stands on the position of absolute nothingness, does one see religious life behind history . . ." (5: 416). "In religious experience there is no perceived self in any sense. And being truly no-self, we are living in the deep inner life" (5: 444).

[12] For details, see 12: 19-20.

[13] For details, see 7: 329 and 8: 210.

[14] For details, see 3: 268, 307-308, and 543-545.

[15] According to Suzuki Toru, for example, the main motif of Nishida's thought was sadness. See *Nishida Kitaro no sekai* (the world of Nishida) (Tokyo: Keiso Shobo, 1977), p. 15. For similar arguments, see also Nishitani Keiji, "Nishida's Philosophy: Its Position in the History of Philosophy," in Nishitani, *Nishida Kitaro;* and Nakamura Yujiro, *Nishida Kitaro* (Tokyo: Iwanami Shoten, 1983), pp. 42-45.

[16] One may pose an important question: Why did this turn occur? Or, why did he move from the philosophy of self-consciousness to the philosophy of history? Unfortunately, Nishida did not point to any reason for this turn. I suspect that, together with the philosophical preparations for this turn, various not strictly philosophical pressures may have contributed to Nishida's rethinking of his historical-political notions. His disciples and colleagues may have pushed Nishida to reconsider the problem of history. (For Tanable Hajime's possible influence, see 7: 179.)

Second, the historical situation, the political absolutism of the 1930s, centering on the state, national polity, and the emperor, may have exerted a powerful influence on Nishida, pushing him to reexamine his previous view of the transitory world and history and finally give a new meaning to it. One has to admit that it is a matter of speculation as to what extent all these factors, including the philosophical preparations, played their respective roles in the development of his historical-political thinking, but one may reasonably argue that the radical change in the national and international scene may have had the greatest role in the emergence of his philosophy of history.

In light of the fact that the rapidly changing political situation is one of the several grounds of his turn, the philosophy of history may have played a similar personal role as did the philosophy of self-consciousness and pure experience, giving solace or psychological salvation to Nishida, saddened or horrified as he may have been by the transitory world. His first philosophy of acts of self-consciousness directed him to a realm which transcends the transitory world, whereas his second philosophy transforms it into a real, indubitable, and certain world. In the face of great uncertainty, his ontological assertions may have been needed in order to defend his own psychology against uncertain, radically changing situations. In this sense, his entire philosophy may be seen as a personal soteriology designed to save the troubled soul of the philosopher Nishida. Perhaps the difference lies in that his philosophy of self-consciousness may be said to give solace in a negative, transcending manner, whereas the second philosophy does so in a positive, transforming manner.

[17] The five are as follows: "Watashi no zettai mu no jikakuteki gentei to iu mono" (What I call self-conscious determination of absolute nothingness) (published in February and March 1931), 6: 117-180; "Watashi no tachiba kara mita Hegeru no benshoho" (Hegel's dialectic from my perspective) (published in February 1931), 12: 64-84; "Eien no ima no jiko gentei" (Self-determination of eternal now) (published in July 1931), 6: 181-232; "Jikanteki naru mono oyobi hijikanteki naru mono" (The temporal and the atemporal) (published in September 1931), 6: 233-259; and "Gete no Heikei" (Goethe's back-

ground) (published in December 1931), 12: 138-149. Among these essays, "History," "Hegel's Dialectic from My Perspective," and "Goethe's Background" are included in volume 12, which was edited and published posthumously by the editors in 1948.

[18] Even in 1931, prior to the publication of those transitional essays, the ontological disparity between the historical world and the self-conscious world was maintained. One thing, however, must be noted concerning these essays. The notion of primordial history *(Ur-geschichte; genshi rekishi)* is employed as identical to the determination of eternal now (12: 83). Nishida used this term to refer to the self-determination of absolute eternity and says, "Our personality *(jinkaku)* is established by it" (6: 150-151). The conception of *"Ur-geschichte"* is again used to refer to the eternal now, to distinguish it from the normal sense of history (6: 215). The notion of *Ur-geschichte* occurs in all the 1931 essays and seems to portend that a philosophy of history is slowly but finally emerging.

[19] The English translation is quoted from Leopold von Ranke, *The Theory and Practice of History,* ed. and trans. G. G. Iggers and Konrad von Moltke (New York: Irvington Publishers, Inc., 1983), p. 53.

[20] Several pages later, Nishida seems to open up a new historical world by destroying the old notion of "individual" in order to accept a larger and broader world:

> Thus being historically means active self-determination, that is, acting-qua-being. And it also means that it has both the meaning of expression in the sense of the destruction of theindividual and the meaning of "ought" in the sense of movement to the other by means of the negation of the self. (6: 297)

For a similar argument, see 6: 299. In "Jiyu ishi" (Free will) (6: 300-340), Nishida also argues, "Our individual self as historical being is living and dying in this sort of [immediate and historical] world" (6: 331). "True body is historical fact" (6: 330). And "true time is historical time" (6: 342).

[21] The same change may be found in "Goethe's Background": it [history] is eternal rotation in the "now" (12: 149). Time and history are here easily put together.

[22] See, for example, 3: 189, 7: 325, and 10: 254. Notice that references to this phrase occur in early, transitional, and late Nishida, respectively.

[23] For details, see Letters 1065 and 1071 (18: 583, 586, written in 1937). These were sent to his disciple Kosaka Masaaki.

[24] As an example of how the discussion of history is inseparably related to that of politics, one has only to remember that Ranke presents one of the most characteristic examples of the way in which Prussia, from the beginning of the nineteenth century, was able to win over adherents to its policy. For details, see A. Guilland, *Modern Germany and Her Historians* (Westport: Greenwood Press, 1970), p. 70.

[25] Among other conceptions which are similarly self-determined, Nishida includes the notion of a generation *(sedai)*. "A generation in history refers to history's naturalization of itself. It [*sedai*] is established at the point of history-qua-nature which is self-determination of the eternal now. Here the world of expression may be said to determine itself" (8: 196).

[26] Nishida further argues: "People claim that we are intuiting by virtue of activity and that activity cannot be originated from intuition. This sort of claim is possible because one considers neither the fact that our activity is absolutely historical nor that we, being individuals of the historical world, are active. It is because they abstractly see the self" (8: 542-543).

[27] Based upon the unity of act and intuition as historical life, Nishida rejects the idea that intuition involves only consciousness: "Consciousness *(ishiki)* is intuition devoid of formation, that is, non-creative acting intuition" (8: 330). "True self-consciousness *(jikaku)* is not of consciousness *(ishiteki)*. It lies in true creativity" (8: 332).

[28] As Nishida distinguishes the historical world from the physicaland animalistic world (9: 172), so also does he distinguish historical body from biological body. See also 9: 177-178 and 14: 265 ff.

[29] In *Religion and Nothingness,* Nishitani makes a short remark, mainly in terms of *samadhi,* on Nishida's notion of historical body. However, in the light of the intimacy between Nishida's notion of historical body and his philosophy of history, Nishitani seems to have misidentified the background of this notion. See Keiji Nishitani, *Religion and Nothingness,* trans. Jan Van Bragt (Berkeley: University of California Press, 1982), pp. 190-191.

[30] Ranke, *Theory and Practice of History,* p. 53.

[31] Dilthey, *Gesammelte Schriften,* vol. 5, p. 342. Quoted in Michael Ermarth, *Wilhelm Dilthey: The Critique of Historical Reason* (Chicago: The University of Chicago Press, 1978), p. 264.

[32] For a similar argument, see also: "The determination of place must always have the sense of social and historical determination" (7: 164).

[33] For a similar assertion, see 8: 456.

[34] There are also some passages in which Nishida retains some of his earlier emphasis on creation *ex nihilo.* For example, in the essay "Concerning Self-Consciousness," Nishida argues, "The creation of things is established through absolute negation. And it must include self-negation, and the movement toward new creation" (10: 526).

[35] The change in the meaning of *bashoteki u* in the philosophy of history has often been disregarded or resisted. One example may be found in David Dilworth, trans., *Last Writings: Nothingness and the Religious Worldview* (Honolulu: University of Hawaii Press, 1987). Consider his translation of the following passage:

> Therefore the term "world" does not signify for me that which stands over against the self, as it is commonly understood. *It signifies the concrete world that has the logical form of a self-transforming matrix.* (11: 403, trans. p. 73; my emphasis)

The literal translation of the italicized part would be:

> It signifies the absolute being of the place *(zettai no bashoteki u)*.

The meaning of the first part of this passage is clear. In general in Nishida's philosophy, the subject-object dichotomy between self and world is always negated. In this context of thephilosophy of history, however, the world is identified with *bashoteki u*. I see no difficulty in taking the phrase *zettai no bashoteki u* as emphasizing "what has been absolutely given to us." For a similar passage, consider also: "The true absolute being *(u)* must be infinitely creative and must be historical reality itself" (11: 400).

[36] Dilworth translates: "Hence my theology of the absolute present is neither theistic nor deistic—a theology neither of mere spirit nor of mere nature. *It is the theology of the existential matrix of history itself*" (11: 406, trans. p. 76). The unnecessary addition of "existential matrix" seems to reveal a general tendency of his reading of the text in the direction of a religious-soteriological understanding of the "later" Nishida, rather than of a religious-historical philosophy.

In another passage, Dilworth added "human" to the term "historical" *(rekishiteki)*. Compare 11: 384 to his translation (p. 57). In his translation of a passage from 11: 388, Dilworth renders the phrase *"wareware no jiko sono mono ni chokusetsu naru jikojishin o keiseisuru rekishiteki sekai"* as "the self-forming historical world that is immediately expressed *in the self*" (p. 61; my emphasis). This interpretive translation, which takes the historical world as the world which is "immediately expressed *in the self*" implies an internalization of the historical world, which Nishida directly opposed. To introduce and establish the externality of the historical world, or its givenness to us, Nishida expressed here the idea that the historical world is immediate *(chokusetsu naru)* to the self. It cannot be in the self, but rather we ourselves reside in or face it. In the final sentence of this passage, the logic of place *(bashoteki ronri)* is translated by Dilworth as "the logic of the human-historical world." Since no reason is given for this translation, I do not know why he made that change. Like the term "existential," the change smacks of a sort of psychological resistance to the philosophy of the historical world and its

logic and of an unproven assumption in favor of the religious-soteriological understanding of the "later" Nishida.

[37] For the same idea, see 7: 410.

[38] This was originally published in *Shiso* in 1944, a year before Nishida died.

[39] For details, see 8: 189. A similar argument is also found in 7: 15.

[40] In many of his political writings, especially in "The Principle of the New World Order" (12: 426-434), Nishida embraces and gives ontological primacy to the principles of the New World Order and the East Asia Co-Prosperity Sphere *(Toa kyoeiken)*.

[41] Such scholars include Arima Tatsuo and Tsurumi Shunsuke. For details, see Arima's *The Failure of Freedom: A Portrait of Modern Japanese Intellectuals* (Cambridge, Massachusetts: Harvard University Press, 1969) and Tsurumi's *An Intellectual History of Wartime Japan 1931-1945* (London: Kegan Paul Inter., 1986).

[42] "Gakumonteki hoho" (The method of science), including this passage, was originally a public lecture given in 1937, in which Nishida sided with the rational spirit, excoriating the contemporary attitude which exclusively emphasized the emotional aspect of human spirit.

[43] Dilworth renders *"kontei"* as "existential ground," which contains the unnecessary adjective "existential."

[44] In view of Nishida's insistence that religion must be the self-consciousness of historical life, I have used the phrase "religious-historical" to describe his later writings. This is in contrast to his earlier philosophy of self-consciousness, which may be called religious-soteriological. One of the easiest ways to identify the fallacy of soteriolization in Nishida scholarship is to distinguish two different meanings of "religion" and "religious" in Nishida's text: one is religious-soteriological, the other is religious-historical. When I speak about the turn in Nishida's philosophy, that includes the shift from the first sense of religion to the second. What I call the fallacy of soteriolization usually occurs when one overlooks the second meaning of "religion" and "religious."

[45] Dilworth renders it into "apolitical."

[46] One of the most noticeable consequences of Dilworth's tendency toward soteriological reading is his separating the final two pages of section 5 from the rest of it. He inserted a short line, lacking correspondence in the text (11: 463, trans. p. 122). The separation made by Dilworth seems to indicate that the philosophy of history and even the philosophy of politics are not intrinsic to Nishida's thinking.

[47] There is a sense in which the later philosophy may be called religious-existential-historical without a contradic-

tion: religious in the sense that forms of self-consciousness make all historical realities ontologically primary; existential in that they are not simply given as absolute principles, but as something facing individuals; and historical in that these realities are basically historical. At the same time, there seems an unavoidable tension inherent in the "later" Nishida, which did not occur in Nishida's early philosophy, that is, between the religious-existential (soteriological) and the religious-historical, or between arguments for state-qua-morality and for the separation of religion from it.

Thus, a reader of the "later" Nishida has to face the question of how to perceive him within this tension. Although this article may overemphasize the historical side, one must at least recognize and tackle the problematic character of the "later" Nishida, which becomes possible only after the philosophy of history-politics is dealt with thematically.

[48] Nishida seems to reveal his own resolution for the Emperor in 7: 443, by citing an ancient poem as he discusses different cultural forms: "Though if I go by sea, my corpse may be tossed by the waves, though if I go over the mountains, my corpse may be covered over with the grass, I shall have no regrets to die for the cause of the Emperor" (in *Nishida Kitaro's Fundamental Problems of Philosophy,* trans. Dilworth (Tokyo: Sophia University, 1970), p. 248). This also reminds us of Nishida's own lecture to Emperor Hirohito, given in January 1943. For details, see "Draft of a Lecture to the Emperor: Concerning Philosophy of History" (12: 267-272).

[49] For this misreading, see Dilworth's two essays on Nishida's *Last Writings,* which he calls the *fons et origo* of the Kyoto school, "Nishida's final essay: The Logic of Place and a Religious World-view," *Philosophy East and West* 20 no. 4 (October 1970), and "Introduction: Nishida's Critique of the Religious Consciousness," which Dilworth attached as the introduction to his English translation of *Last Writings* (1987). Both essays suffer from the same neglect of Nishida's discourse of history-politics and its intimate tie with Ranke's thinking. In the first essay, for example, Dilworth treats *Last Writings* as containing "all of these threads of thought in one synthesis articulated from the point of view of the meaning of the religious consciousness" (p. 357). In the latter essay, Dilworth presented a similar characterization by arguing that Nishida's four decades of work culminated in "final form in a philosophy of religion" (p. 6). He also maintained that Nishida's chief contribution to twentieth-century philosophy is in "the philosophy of religion" (p. 2). Dilworth's employment of the term religion, however, does not seem to include religious-historical thinking, as is indicated by his claim that for Nishida religious consciousness is fundamentally self-awareness (p. 16).

Moreover, in "Postscript: Nishida's Logic of the East," preceded by his translation of "Concerning My Logic," Dilworth nowhere mentions the key terms, "the logic of the historically formative act" and "the historically active

self." Taking this logic as the logic of the East and "Asian Nothingness," Dilworth critically places Nishida's confrontational attitude between East and West in the context of how one has to proceed in hermeneutical discourse, which was not Nishida's concern.

However, Dilworth does not completely disregard Nishida's social-historical philosophy. In his commentary essay on volume 7, "The Concrete World of Action in Nishida's Later Thought," in *Analecta Husserliana,* vol. 8, ed. Nitta and Tatematsu (Dordrecht: D. Reidel, 1978), he often discusses the social-historical world. Dilworth correctly argues both that the social-historical world is self-determining and that this new development may be a modern form of the Mahayana Buddhist tradition. But it seems to me that in explaining the "radical social-historical field" where "the personal actions of active selves take place" (p. 253), he does not consider the historical epoch and the state as key social-historical fields.

Another interpretation of Nishida's social-historical thinking is found in Dilworth and Silverman, "A Cross-Cultural Approach to the De-Ontological Self Paradigm," *Monist* 61, no. 1 (January 1978): 92. Nishida certainly discussed social-historical determination and praxis, but the de-ontological perspective spoken of in this essay does not reflect the fact that Nishida's later philosophy of history is the result of the application and transformation of many forms of self-consciousness. In addition, Dilworth improperly claimed similarities between Sartre and Nishida. Nishida's notions of "praxis" and "social and historical" are essentially those of his philosophy of history, and are very different from those of Sartre.

Dilworth of course is not the only commentator to "oversoteriolize" Nishida. Much of the secondary literature commits a similar error. Here suffice it to mention one or two examples. For instance, G. K. Piovesana, one of the rare people who perceived the significance of the philosophy of history, unfortunately could not avoid soteriolizing Nishida's later philosophy, when he focused solely upon the religious aspect of Nishida's *Last Writings,* which Piovesana called "a real statement in which the great philosopher wanted to give a final view of his thought." For details, see G. K. Piovesana, *Contemporary Japanese Philosophical Thought* (New York: St. John's University Press), pp. 115-116. On Piovesana's reading, Nishida's essay opens with an exhortation to become more religious minded (p. 116). Of course, his term "religious minded" does not seem to include the religious-historical connotation, as there is no mention of the historical world, the historical individual, or the state.

Nakamura Yujiro also dealt with Nishida's philosophy of history. However, there are two main points about his treatment: first, he discussed the philosophy of history as the subsection of a larger chapter. "The Expressive World" (*Nishida Kitaro,* pp. 114-118). Second, it was seen as a simple development from Nishida's thinking on pure experience or the logic of nothingness (ibid., p. 117). His point about the relationship between the conception of thehistorical world and the expressive world is insightful, but neglects the fact that the philosophy of history is a more deeply penetrating theme than the notion of expression itself, and he made no attempt to relate the philosophy of history to the political thinking of Nishida. He correctly pointed out that Nishida's understanding of historical body is concerned with the absolute notion of the circular, or the vertical, mythic notion of time, and is distanced from "relative history" (ibid., p. 172). However, he missed the importance of the notion of the historical epoch, and thus showed a general indifference to Nishida's philosophy of history, as he characterized Nishida's philosophy as a philosophy of inner life *(naibu seimei),* an essential concept of the religious-soteriological philosophy (ibid., p. 43). Thus, he could not raise the question of the appropriateness of Nishida's expansion from the inner world to the historical world.

G. S. Axtell (essay date 1991)

SOURCE: "Comparative Dialectics: Nishida Kitaro's Logic of Place and Western Dialectical Thought," in *Philosophy East & West,* Vol. 41, No. 2, April, 1991, pp. 163-84.

[In the following essay, Axtell explains Nishida's theory of the "unity of opposites," using the notion as grounds for a comparative analysis of Eastern and Western thought.]

I. INTRODUCTION: CONTRARIETY AND COMPARATIVE PHILOSOPHY

An emerging theme of Nishida Kitaro's later works was expressed in the complex phrase *"zettai mujunteki jikodoitsu,"* variously translated by Schinzinger as "absolute contradictory self-identity," "the self-identity of absolute contradictories," or more simply as "oneness" or "unity" of opposites. The theory of contrariety or opposition that Nishida (1870-1945) worked out between 1927 and 1945 can be taken as a stimulus for East/West comparative thought. This is so because of the special significance of Nishida's thought, but also more generally because contrariety is itself a prime subject for comparative philosophy.

The eminent philosophical anthropologist Mircea Eliade once said that "the union of opposites" is a basic category of archaic ontology and comparative world religions. Eliade's claim is contentious only in that the reference to "union" subtly provides a characterization and suggestion of a particular way of conceptualizing felt oppositions and polarities. The initial fact is that of felt opposition itself; the ensuing demand or problematic is that of a conceptual understanding of contrariety. The thesis of "union" that Eliade refers to is a conceptual response to this problematic. It is a theoretical means ofunderstanding both opposition itself and the character of the real.

It has been a common temptation in modern anthropology to judge as somewhat archaic and mystical the ancients'

dependence on opposites as principles, and their cosmogenies and cosmologies, which reflect traditional myths of polarity. This judgment is not unfounded, for it has been a common tendency of humans to begin reflection with the simplest scheme of categories and distinctions. Schemes such as those found in ancient tables of opposites may indeed be judged to reflect a primitive state in the conceptual organization of experience. But the problem which such judgments address is only that of comparative levels of development or sophistication in how a thinker deals with the need for organizing experience; they do not and cannot resolve the questions of the very presence and role of opposites in human thought. The demand for conceptual response to these latter questions is one of the initial demands laid upon a thinker, and one which was of great concern to the learned from an early point in history. Answers to this demand are found in Taoist, Hindu, and Buddhist traditions; they are also deeply ingrained in the Greek roots of Western traditions, as is illustrated by the depth of Greek thought on contrariety found in Aristotle and his predecessors.[1]

Misunderstandings of the relation of logic both to metaphysics on the one hand, and to epistemology on the other, have led many logicians to expect that the foundations of the laws of logic would be independent of an account of contrariety. My point here reiterates one that Bradley found important, that the principles of logic presuppose rather than explain the presence of opposites in human thought. They organize our understanding of affirmation and negation, identity and difference, hopefully keeping us from falling prey to conceptual fallacies, but are wrongly understood when taken to explain the origin and prevalence of opposites generally to the human mind. It is little wonder, then, that during the Modernist era in Western philosophy, the principles of identity, non-contradiction and excluded-middle were often characterized as actual 'laws of thought' which reflect natural limits of discursive thought.

The "deep problem about opposites" which Plato recognized and addressed has not left us; but particularly in Western thought it has often been pushed to the side as a concern only for those studying "deviant" logic and "archaic" thought. A common reason given for pushing the issues of contrariety to the background as unhelpful in conceptualizing the relation between language and reality is the work of Aristotle on logic. Aristotle was first among the Greeks to call into question the license of his predecessors to "adopt opposites as principles."

> For they all identify the elements, and what they call theprinciples, with the *contraries,* although they give no reasons for doing so, but are, as it were, compelled by the truth itself.[2]

Here Aristotle both makes explicit a central role for his own metaphysical uses of opposition or contrariety *(enantion),* and grounds his predecessors' uses of such principles in a seemingly mystic insight into truth. For all his foundational work on the principles of identity, contradiction, and excluded middle, and for all his revision of earlier abuses of language and logic, Aristotle's theory of enantion remains in many ways at least as wrapped up in metaphysics as those of his predecessors. His own metaphysics is found in the suggestion that discursive thought is a reflection of reality, and that the dependence of intelligible discourse upon basic rules of consistency is a reflection of the essential and self-identical character of the real. In Aristotle's thought, contrariety was far more than the idea of the relation between logical posits; it was a cosmic force underlying real change, and informing both the basic human categories of thought and the conditions for intelligible discourse.[3]

Current interest in naturalizing epistemology, however, indicates both a difference between (deductive) logical proof and epistemological justification, and the ultimate dependence of modes of justification upon the actual character and limitations of human thought processes. For those who take this turn, a rethinking of the supposed independence of the principles of logic from the problem of contrariety is one of the ensuing demands. The significance of the early emergence of tables of opposites and correlative reasoning in man's development cannot be missed on a philosophical anthropologist. Indeed in recent years, philosophical anthropologists have brought renewed interest to bear on the problem of a philosophically adequate account of contrariety. G. E. R. Lloyd's *Polarity and Analogy: Two Types of Argumentation in Early Greek Thought,*[4] studies the polar and the analogical as two types of reasoning that have typically emerged earliest in primitive and archaic cultures. Such cross-cultural study of the phenomena of classificatory and explanatory principles underlines alternative ways of conceptualizing the world and, from a philosophical perspective, bears strongly on questions of the relation of language to reality. In Eliade and others interested in myth and metaphor, one finds sound reason for suspicion of the tendency, so prevalent in the archaic mind, to reify the products of mental abstraction into cosmic forces and philosophical first principles.

This introduction to the problem of contrariety should serve as background for my development of Nishida's theme of *zettai mujunteki jikodoitsu.* O'Leary's commentary on Nishida's later work chastises him for obscuring his own themes in "complex dialectical language" and bids the comparative philosopher to approach Nishida through 'a more strictly phenomenological approach',—this despite Nishida's own acknowledged protest against nondialectical 'interpretive phenomenology'.[5] While the influence on Nishida of existentialism and phenomenology is unmistakable, the present essay will depart from the now-standard comparative methodology that O'Leary recommends. Nishida was himself actively engaged in comparing Aristotelian, Hegelian, and Marxist logics, or *ronri.* Such comparisons served Nishida both in clarifying important differences and in clearing conceptual ground for the introduction of his original *benshoho* or dialectic. In this essay I will attempt to further these pursuits by moving the context of discussion beyond such historical figures of the Modernist era to the

arena of contemporary currents in both nonmaterialist and materialist dialectics. I take Nishida's own studies of contrasting logics as a prime example of the approach I am here calling "comparative dialectics." This is an approach which also has a number of notable forerunners in T. R. V. Murti's and E. H. Johnston's comparisons of Nagarjuna with Western dialecticians, in A. Verdu's *Dialectical Aspects In Buddhist Thought,* and, from the Chinese side, in Wee Chang-Tan's *Dialectica Reconciliae* and A. C. Graham's *Yin-Yang and the Nature of Correlative Thinking.*

Of course, "dialectical" philosophy is far from a homogenous grouping. But it is both the similarities and the differences among those who explicitly claim to espouse a dialectical ontology or meta-methodology which will fuel the discussion. Indeed the first point of this essay is in the comparative methodology developed. While the basic conceptual antitheses that predominated in the East differ from those of the West, I hope to demonstrate in the sections below Nishida's awareness of certain meta-methodological issues germane to any dialectical philosophy, East or West. Identifying such a group of common issues, I believe, can help the inquirer understand Nishida's notion of concrete dialectical logic, and further one's ability to assess critically the philosophical adequacy of Nishida's *benshoho* or dialectical conception of the world as a synthesis of Eastern and Western philosophy.

II. METHODOLOGICAL AND ONTOLOGICAL MATERIALISM

Nishida cites indebtedness to Hegel for the notion of a "concrete logic" which tries to grasp reality in its historical unfolding. For both men, in a sense, history is an ascending self-realization of the absolute. For both as well, the concept or idea is an act of dialectical formation by self-consciousness. In this movement, for Hegel, knowledge becomes the grasping of *"der Konkrete Begriff"*—the Concrete Concept. Despite Hegel's emphasis on the historical context of self-conscious beings, Marx is commonly credited with 'turning Hegel's logic on its head' by (1) replacing its conceptually oriented basis with a praxis-oriented one, and (2) replacing its ontologically idealist basis with a materialist one. As I interpret Nishida, he follows Marx in the first of these shifts, but resists the polarity of ontological materialism and idealism.

Nishida has drawn the fire of numerous dialectical materialists for statements such as this from "The World of Action" (1933-1934): ". . . to define dialectics materialistically, as do present-day Marxists, is ultimately to negate dialectics and to revert to physical science."[6] But Nishida's point can be illuminated if we consider a distinction Joachim Israel draws in *The Language of Dialectics and the Dialectics of Language*[7]: the distinction between "methodological" and "ontological" materialism. Israel's distinction and outlook is illuminating of Nishida's own view. A methodological materialism in Israel's sense begins not from transcendental reflection, but from thought in its action-orientation in the social-historical world. Though 'methodological materialist' may not capture Nishida's position, this notion does help explain the centrality of action-orientation in Nishida's account. For Nishida the starting place for reflection is social consciousness; the life-world is a historical world and provides the starting point for philosophical reflection. The unity of acting and sensuous intuition means for Nishida that the world of actuality in which we all live and die is a world of action. *Koiteki chokkan* or "action-intuition" is emphasized to indicate that there is no action without intuition and no intuition without action. "We act through seeing, and we see through acting."[8]

To a great extent, then, as testified by his own discussions of Hegel and Marx, Nishida follows Marx to a dialectical logic which is also a dialectic of theory and praxis—to a "concrete" dialectical logic which relates the "concept" to a metaphysics of the "Acting-Self" (*Hataraku jiko*).[9] Hegel of course already thought his logic to be "concrete" in contrast to that of the schoolmen of his age. Indeed Hegel objected also to Kant's understanding of the "antinomies of pure reason," on the grounds that it implied "that Thought or Reason, and not the World, is the seat of contradiction": "It is no escape to turn around and explain that Reason falls into contradictions only by applying the (Kantian) categories. For this application of the categories is maintained to be necessary."[10]

But taking note of Hegel's idealist construal of the "World," we must see that this statement is a criticism of Kant's ahistorical or pure a priori reason, rather than an affirmation of materialist views of contradiction; it is a criticism of the "abstract understanding's" framework for understanding contrariety, and rightly places Kant within a broadly Aristotelian tradition. Yet Hegel's historicism was not enough for Marx, who saw Hegel's analysis as essentially still one of conceptual definition. In shifting this basis to the concept in its action-orientation, Marx more closely affirms Nishida's contention that "The unity of our consciousness is essentially grounded on action. Our action is not merely movement. Action must have the significance that we see something through it."[11] Israel's recent distinction thus helps make sense of Nishida's praxis orientation, as well as of his insistence that we disentangle what is true in Marxian dialectic from its materialist base. But Nishida would side with neither Hegel nor Marx on the metaphysical issue, and approaches a more adequately dialectical ontology to the extent that he is able consistently to extricate himself from the debate and demonstrate the shared assumptions at its base.[12]

III. THE TELEOLOGICAL AND THE MECHANICAL

The Kantian background of the antinomies and Fichte's 'Kantian' philosophy of antinomical materialist and idealist systems is deeply reflected in Nishida's later writings. Many of the theoretical oppositions Nishida develops, such as the "Teleological" and the "Mechanical,"

and "Subjectivity" and "Objectivity," reflect a period of formulating his *benshoho* in the terms of the Fichtean opposition between the systems of the Ego and the Non-Ego, or "Idealism and Dogmatism."

At the same time, however, Nishida is keenly aware of the ways in which Fichte's views militate against dialectical philosophy. Fichte had changed the epistemological focus from the opposition of consciousness and things to an opposition within the "I" itself. The unavoidable contradiction of materialist and immaterialist ways of conceptualizing the world meant for Fichte that a nonlogical choice had to be made between these two monistic systems, regarded as exclusive and exhaustive. As Ilyenkov commented in *Dialectical Logic* concerning Fichte's demand for a "personal" choice between the two systems,

> From two different, dualistically isolated halves, having no connection at all with each other, you could not create a single, integral system. What was needed was not dualism, but monism, not two initial principles but one only.[13]

But for Nishida, Fichte's apparent antinomy arises from an acceptance of an abstract logic which makes the ego and the non-ego, and hence the contrary systems inspired by the privileging of each, appear unconnected and independent. Nishida reaffirms Fichte's central thesis that reflection upon self-consciousness can proceed in either of two radically different directions; it can proceed in the direction of the determination of the physical world by the self, or of the self by the physical world. The one direction is portrayed by Nishida as leading to a monistic and teleologically dependent world view, and the other as leading to an atomistic, mechanical world view. But Nishida views both systems as abstractions out of a single world of actuality; taken singly they each reflect only an "aspect" of the concrete life-world.[14]

Hence Nishida answers 'Neither/Nor' to Fichte's demand for an Either/Or choice between the metaphors of the teleological and the mechanical. The move reveals a significant part of what Nishida has taken over from phenomenology and Lebensphilosophe. In Nishida's words,

> Many people first presuppose opposing worlds of subjectivity and objectivity or immanent and transcendent worlds, and then consider the actual world as the mutual determination of such worlds. But it is not that such opposing worlds exist independently, for such worlds are always to be conceived from this actual world as two directions of this actual world.[15]

Or again,

> . . . It is not that subjectivity and objectivity unite, and are then actual. Both can be conceived from a dialectical reality, i.e. from a dynamic reality which is self-determining. Self-determining reality, i.e. dynamic reality, must be self-contradictory. Subjectivity and objectivity may be regarded as different directions of that self-contradiction.[16]

Like Heidegger and Merleau-Ponty, Nishida is calling us out of the different directions in which self-reflection naturally leads, to the prereflective or concrete life-world from which these reflections originate. Meta-methodologically, Fichte's pseudoantinomy is avoidable because the plurality of available reflective approaches should lead us to acknowledge alternative meta-logics of inquiry, which, while individually limited, can yet be seen as developments of mutually complimentary systems of thought.

A dialectical theory of knowledge is of an inherently *normative* character; but conflict within a normative system cannot without distortion be modeled like contradiction within a system of purely descriptive claims. Fichte's demand is premised on just such a confusion, and is another reflection of what Richard Bernstein calls the 'Cartesian Anxiety' in Modern thought. That "logic" abstractly construed cannot decide the issue only means that the prospects for reconciliation depend upon shifting the issue to a 'higher court' of values and meanings.

Israel makes a point that is related to the attempt of dialectical thinkers to reconcile and move beyond the "isms" of Western philosophy. For he insists, as might Nishida himself, that though dialectical philosophy is neither of the reductionistic alternatives of materialism or idealism, it is also strictlyspeaking neither a form of dualism nor of "neutral monism." Israel argues that "neutral monism" is a mischaracterization in that it fails to exhibit the essential uniqueness of a dialectical understanding of interrelation within a system. For Nishida, too, it seems, the one who understands the self's "absolutely contradictory self-identity" understands also the dialectic of the One and the Many, and is posing a radical alternative to all monistic/dualistic metaphysical stances.

In chapter 3 of *The Dialectical World,* Nishida represents Western metaphysics as having taken the direction of "reality as form," in contrast to Eastern approaches, which have treated it as "formless." The Aristotelian identification of individual substance with "Being"—with form and self-identical existence—expresses the assumption of grounding metaphysics in the substantial union of matter and form. Hegel's metaphysics, too, reflect this affirmation of Being. Nishida sees Hegel as still following Aristotle in the notion of hypokeimenon, that is, a "substance that becomes subject," and which leads to a "logic of the subject." For Nishida the concrete universal is developed as the universal of *"mu"* or "nothingness." His logic is characterized as a "logic of the predicate" that must not become subject.[17] Yet to Nishida the "form" and "formless" characterizations of reality have an intriguing degree of parity. Each mode of conceptualization seeks transcendence of the historical life-world, but achieves it only through a kind of reduction, carried through on the shoulders of contrasting metaphors of the spatial and the temporal.

> To conceive of the ground of the world in the direction of its spatial determination from the actual spatial-temporal world is the idea of being. To conceive of it in the direction of its temporal determination can be said to be the idea of nothingness. The former conceives of the world in an objective direction, the latter in a subjective one . . . the one sought the eternal and changeless by transcending the actual temporal-spatial world in the direction of objectivity, of spatial determination; the other sought it in the direction of subjective determination, of temporal determination.[18]

Like Bergson, Nishida's own philosophy and logic are often laid out in terms derived from the metaphor of the temporal, and most of his criticisms are addressed to Western thought as dominated by the metaphors of the spatial and the mechanical. Yet on my reading there is a striking sense in which Nishida indicates the need for a deeper pluralistic or perspectivalist account of self-reflection as a basis for mutual East/West understanding. Each of the two directions of self-reflection taken separately may be inadequate to the whole. In the development of this notion, Nishida's *benshoho* begins to pull him beyond even his deep commitments to the Buddhist framework. For there is no explicitsuggestion that either the idea of being or the idea of nothingness is cognitively privileged. Indeed, ". . . The dialectical world cannot be conceived only in the aspect of negation. For the world (also) determines itself in the form of self-identity."[19]

IV. VIA NEGATIVA AND RELIGIOUS CONSCIOUSNESS

Nishida's pluralistic ontology, which admits of both a via negativa and a via affirmativa, is more fully developed by Nishida in the context of religious consciousness. The problem of finding common ground for understanding religious consciousness has been of major concern to the Kyoto School and a major subject of debate within that school. Nishida has been widely interpreted as synthesizing the Buddhist *"sunyata"* with the Christian *kenotic* tradition of self-emptying into *agape.* In *The Logic of the Place of Nothingness and the Religious Worldview* (1945), he developed an understanding of the religious consciousness based on a new conception of his logic of the place of nothingness, or *"mu no basho ronri."* The great importance Nishida laid on understanding his logic involves this claim that *mu no basho ronri* is a vehicle to the deepest levels of the existential self and conciliates the *sunyata* and *kenotic* traditions as variants.

David Dilworth's recent translation and commentary on Nishida's *Nothingness and the Religious Worldview*[20] is an important effort in this direction. He emphasizes that Nishida's incentive to the negative theology as the character of this religious world view is to be found in the nature of relationality itself.[21] The self and the absolute stand in a paradoxically nondual relationship, from whence man derives his own essentially self-contradictory identity. But this means also that a transcendent and unchanging God cannot be the real absolute, since it would stand over against, rather than contain, the immanent.[22]

The true absolute does not merely transcend the relative. If it did, it could not avoid being a mere negation of it and, on the contrary, would become relative, too. Hence I have argued that the true absolute must face its own absolute negation within itself.[23]

Seen from the side of the self rather than from the logic, Nishida says that the self, reaching out, confronts the absolute; but this is experienced only as a reaching into one's own inner depths.[24] By 'transcending immanently' (*naizaiteki choetsu*), the paradoxical nonduality of the immanent and the transcendent, or of self and absolute, may be experienced.

The universal of *mu* is the universal of the true existential and religious self. *Mu no basho Nishida* sometimes depicts as the most enveloping of all universals, that which defines the intelligible world. ". . . It may be called the place of absolute nothingness."Here reality is grasped in the way of unity of opposites. The conception bears similarity with some Neo-Platonic notions of the absolute which were influential also for Hegel.[25] But here also one finds the creative act in the determination of the present moment. Nishida uses "action-intuition" in this context as well to remind us that "truth arises from that standpoint where the point of departure of cognition is not lost at any point; truth always returns to its point of departure in the immediately given."[26] The intelligible world is thus also representative of the fullness of the existential moment, for ". . . the world which moves itself through contradictions, as unity of the many and the one, always contradicts itself in the present; the present is the place of contradiction."[27]

There is always a sublimation and a retention (*Aufgehoben*) of the past in the present. But although the present is an ever renewed synthesis, the conflict is never fully resolved. Nishida sometimes characterizes his dialectical logic as "negative" (and his account of religious consciousness as a *"via negativa"*), to emphasize that he is not attempting to construct a synthesis that resolves opposition. The favoring of what Dilworth calls the "agonistic," "paradoxical," or Kierkegaardian formulations of the religious self toward which Nishida leans is illustrative of much of the character of Nishida's *benshoho* in this particular sphere.[28] It is meant to illustrate to the reader that the contradictory identity of self and absolute refers us to a relation that is unmediated by concept.

> In this paradox of God—that is, our face-to-face relation with the absolute in a dialectic of presence and absence—there is the Zen celebration of ordinary human experience. It is the dimension of absolute freedom, as the self-determination of the absolute present itself.[29]

V. LOGICAL AND DIALECTICAL CONTRADICTION

The central term of negation in Zen accounts of contrariety, *"mu,"* cuts radically across the divide between linguistic and real opposition. As was the case with Hegel, most of the examples of "contradiction" presented by Nishida are not primarily propositional but indicate something more general and experiential, like felt "tension," "opposition," "contrast," or "polarity." One prime example is the conflict of life and death, which is made representative of the character of contradictions at the base of the self. The concrete character of the oppositions that Nishida says make up our contradictory self-identity are amply illustrated in his insistence that self-reflection begins when the self comes face-to-face with death and realizes its own finitude.

This quite general use of *"mu"* makes it difficult, as was noted above, to be clear when Nishida intends to indicate linguisticutterances or the character of experience. These difficulties aside, the concrete character of "contradictions" in Nishida philosophy indicates the relationship that logic has to experience. Our understanding of his *benshoho,* and of the seriousness of his claim of the logic of place (*bashoteki ronri*) *as* a logic, may be aided immeasurably by close attention to a distinction Hegel understood as that between "dialectical" and "logical" contradiction.

It is often thought that Hegel viewed the formal-logical laws of non-contradiction and excluded middle as eliminable because they held metaphysical views forbidding change and development, and thereby denatured the ontological principle of the universal contradictoriness of things and phenomena. But while Hegel did oppose such metaphysics, he did not ontologize the formal-logical principles in this way. Hegel's critique of the laws of thought, as found in his *Science of Logic* (1812), is not a criticism of the validity of rules per se, but of the *status* accorded to them by the "abstract understanding."[30] By critiquing the understanding of 'laws of thought' held by the "schoolmen" of his time, he rather considered himself to be avoiding a confusion of the discursive laws with the nature of the real. The distinction between logical and dialectical contradictions was one which Hegel developed in order to extricate himself from the schoolmen's confusions.

Hegel describes himself as critiquing and "reinterpreting dialectically" the prevalent understanding of contradiction. *Dialectical contradiction* can be broadly construed as the experienced quality of opposition or conflict. *Dialectical contradictions* are different from both the abstract and the concrete understandings of logical contradiction.[31] As Lawler summarized, in "Hegel on Contradictions-Misinterpretations,"

> Hegel distinguished between logical contradiction, including logical contradiction understood dialectically, and dialectical contradiction properly speaking. It is only by understanding the more fundamental concept of dialectical contradiction that it is possible to comprehend the "place" or relative importance of (formal) logical contradiction (or the law of noncontradiction) in scientific thought.[32]

Nishida's development of a "concrete" logic depends, like Hegel's earlier effort, on a new conception of the relation between logical and dialectical contradiction.[33] Thus Nishida writes,

> From the standpoint of abstract logic, it is impossible to say that things which contradict each other are connected; they contradict each other just because they cannot be connected. But there would be no contradiction if they did not touch each other somewhere. Facing each other is already a synthesis. Here is thedominion of dialectical logic.[34]

In an illuminating volume of articles concerned with Hegelian and Marxist views of these issues, *Dialectical Contradictions* (1983), Mussachia denies that the principles of logic have any necessary ontological implications for the manner in which object-hood or self-identity must be understood. He argues instead that they have only a delimiting implication, a "minimal empirical or ontological 'import,'" which can be summed up in the assertion that reality is whatever it is—that it is 'consistent,' whether we regard it as essentially static or as changing or whatever."[35] Nor, he believes, should the ontological principle of the contradictory development of knowledge be taken to imply any 'failure' of the logical principles, rightly understood. As Narski, too, insists,

> . . . the formal-logical law of contradiction forbids precisely formal-logical, but not dialectical, contradictions, and therefore should not and cannot conflict with the law of universal dialectical contradictoriness.[36]

The ontological status of dialectical contradictions has recently resurfaced as a point of debate between Hegelians and dialectical materialists. H. Horz characterizes the materialist position thusly:

> Dialectical contradictions are the objectively existing unity of interacting opposites. The recognition of the objective existence of opposites distinguishes materialist dialectics from all other forms of dialectics. . . .[37]

The uniqueness of Nishida's account I see as centering on an understanding of the "objectivity" of experienced contradiction quite different from both Hegel and Marx. In the final two sections I will develop my reading of Nishida's account of contrariety, focusing firstly on the role of opposites in human thought processes, and secondly on aspects of their philosophical status.

VI. APPOSITE OPPOSITES AND DIMENSIONS OF EXPERIENCE

In the philosophical anthropology that G. E. R. Lloyd develops in *Polarity and Analogy,* three reasons are considered for the ancients' common uses of opposites as "causes at work" and as "principles of explanation."[38] One of these is the simplicity and conceptual clarity which opposites afford. A second reason is the apparent comprehensiveness of bipolar arguments and classificatory schemes. Of course, discerning philosophers such as Lloyd would not take either of these first two reasons as cogent or as an epistemically sound basis for selection of theoretical nomenclature. Indeed it is important to see that they are both philosophically *suspicious* reasons for adopting opposites asprinciples. "Simple" classifications may be ill-suited to the complexity of phenomena and lead to gross hypostatization. The "apparent comprehensiveness" of pairs of opposites for classificatory purposes is likely to mask the implicit adoption of a dualistic metaphysics by the classifier, and to invoke a confusion of linguistically conventional boundaries with the limits of thought and possibility.

But the third reason Lloyd gives is *quite* philosophically intriguing: conceptualization in terms of pairs of opposites, he argues, helped the Greeks *define "regions" or "dimensions" of experience.* "Any pair of opposites . . . defines a dimension." This presents a more fruitful way also to approach Nishida's account of contrariety. A central theme of Nishida's *benshoho* is that "there is always identity at the root of mutual contradictories."[39] "Self-identity" is not static as in abstract logic, but is the identity-in-difference of the permanent flow—or of the infinite whole of the process. Nishida uses "absolute" to mark the ontological implications of the aspects opposed or identified. Identity-in-difference is explored by Nishida through his contention that what he calls "absolute contradictories" have a relation *like "species" within the same "genus."* As he put this in ***The World of Action,***

> Mutual contradictories must be absolutely different, on the one hand, yet very similar, on the other. They must exist in the same genus. Colors and sounds are not contradictories.[40]

The concept of dimensions of experience is important since it forces us to return our focus from reified "aspects" or determinations of a dimension of experience, to the primary phenomena of the dimension itself. For example, it may shift focus from judgments of objective "goodness" or "evilness" to the ethical dimension of experience or action itself.[41] Ogden makes a similar point in logic when he notes that mere difference does not create opposition; and according to U. C. Ewing, "There are no opposites that are completely isolated as separate and unrelated entities." Israel explains this by arguing that to state that two things are contradictory is arbitrary: one ought to say rather that two things are contradictory "within a specified totality." According to Nishida, too,

> Things that resist or conflict with one another presuppose the same underlying generic concept. For they oppose one another in the determination of the same universal concept.[42]

The meaning of Nishida is captured in part by a distinction Archie Bahm discusses between "inapposites" or merely different "posits," and *"apposite opposites,"* which are thematic pairs such as hot/cold, or wet/dry. Why exactly do we count certain terms asnatural contraries? The "good reasons" we have for assimilating two terms as a natural pair of opposites is again that they are opposing determinations or aspects of a self-identical dimension of experience. According to Bahm this notion of natural "apposition" cannot be reduced to a contrast between conceptual definitions:

> Appositeness pertains to a closeness of relationship between two opposites which, in spite of their negation of each other, share something in common which is essential to the nature of each as a posit. . . . It is this commonness which constitutes them a pair. . . . This something, which apposite opposites share in common, is to be found wholly in neither of them. . . .[43]

This problem is treated by both Bahm and Errol Harris as deeply involving the relation of particulars and universals. In Errol Harris' recent work *Formal, Transcendental and Dialectical Reasoning* (1987),[44] a systems-theoretical explication of dialectical reasoning is developed. On this account the ground of both identity and difference is understood as the structure of the relational system to which both belong. "As every phase in the scale is a provisional whole premonitory of the ultimate totality, it must be evident that both forms are really but two aspects of one relationship: that between the universal and its particulars."

For Nishida, an Aristotelian "logic of the subject that cannot become predicate" would be a reflection of a world of essential kinds. But in a world characterized by *engi,* mutual interdependence and codependent arising, such Aristotelian logic is a vehicle to partial understanding at best. Nishida's predicate logic is based upon the transcendental predicate as a kind of universal that alone can give knowledge of things. In Nishida's thought the starting point for philosophical reflection and for logic is the "dialectical universal," "that which, contradicting itself, is yet identical with itself."[45] This special predicate is the presupposition of the intelligible world, and is considered necessary for grasping the individuality of things. As such it is identified with *basho* as the field of the mutual determination of the particular and the universal.

This problem has had most discussion in Western circles where it involves debate between logics based on "extrinsic" and on "intrinsic" relations. In substance metaphysics, the starting point is the discretely existing particular or primary substance. If there is a comparison between relata to be made, both relata are viewed as independent, definable without reference to one another. The problem with the thesis of extrinsicality is that it conflates logical and ontological questions. This is seen in the understanding of "truth conditions" in Aristotelian logic. That "A is true just if not-A is false" and "A is false just if not-A is true," the Aristotelian asserts, is necessarily true. But becausethe notion of analyticity and an understanding of conventionality in definition are lacking, the necessity that Aristotle asserts for principles of identity and noncontradiction is considerably overstated. It is important to recognize that these "truth conditions" are conventions for definitions of A and not-A as linguistic subjects and predicates. Such truth conditions are a matter of analytic rather than synthetic a priori reasoning, and their tautologous character is recognizable only within a system of two-value logic.[46]

Israel argues that all dialectical logic is a logic of intrinsic relations, and contrasts dialectical logic with the extrinsic relations characteristically recognized in Aristotelian substance metaphysics. In Israel's systems theory, intrinsicality of relations is a reflection of systematicity and of inter-relatedness of definition within a system. Relata are what they are only in relation to one another and in the context set by the system in which they arise. The starting point is the system itself—the totality or dialectical whole which is the ground for both the identity and difference of its own aspects.

I emphasize the comparison of systems theory with Buddhist logic, because this redresses a common misconception about Buddhist logic. The claim that Buddhist logic is not a logic at all is grounded on the contention that it rests upon claims of mystical insight into a Buddhist "higher truth" beyond discursive thought, or upon objectivistic (unmediated) grasping of the "absolute present" (*zettai genzai*). I do not of course deny that mysticism and direct perception of *zettai genzai* by the enlightened mind are cherished aspects of Kyoto school teaching. Many schools of Buddhism seem to me to conflate logic and ontology by bringing tenets of mysticism into the discussion of contradiction. My argument is rather that Nishida's critique of two-value logic and of contradiction 'abstractly' understood is logically independent of such claims. Indeed I think his critique fits quite well with the thesis of the *pragmatic* character of logical axioms as explicated by some mainstream American pragmatists. As C. I. Lewis once commented, the laws of thought can avoid a pragmatic status only if they are considered a priori synthetic judgments. Pragmatism makes a break with this tradition that runs past Kant and at least as far back as Aristotle. In developing the implications of his "pragmatic conception of the a priori," Lewis argued that the laws of thought "make explicit our general modes of classification. And they impose upon experience no real limitation."[47]

> The laws of logic are purely formal; they forbid nothing but what concerns the use of terms and the corresponding modes of classification and analysis. The law of contradiction tells us that nothing can both be white and not-white, but it does not and can not tell us whether black is not-white, or soft or square isnot-white. To discover what contradicts what we must always consult the character of experience. Similarly the law of the excluded middle formulates our decision that whatever is not designated by a certain term shall be designated by its negative. It declares our purpose to make, for every term, a complete dichotomy of experience, instead—as we might choose—of classifying on the basis of a tripartite division into opposites (as black and white) and the middle ground between the two. Our rejection of such tripartite division represents only our penchant for simplicity.[48]

VII. APPOSITION, NEGATION, AND MEDIATION

Some of the questions I have raised touch upon the familiar debate between realism and nominalism on the relation of language to the real. Does language, including and especially those terms of opposition which so often find their way into the most basic levels of classification, 'cut reality at the joints', or do they cut it at best in conventional ways reflecting only the user's cognitive abilities and interests? Lloyd uses his studies of primitive and archaic classification to defend a nominalistic response. C. R. Hallpike similarly considers the cross-cultural prevalence of binary and dualistic classification at early stages of social development in *Foundations of Primitive Thought,* yet argues quite oppositely and quite brazenly for realism:

> . . . the prevalence of dualistic classification is not principally a manifestation of a binary property of the human mind, imposing itself on a neutral range of phenomena, but rather an accommodation to a dualistic reality.[49]

Nishida can be interpreted as intending to take the middle path between these alternatives, as he does with materialism and idealism. Both the "in the mind" and "in reality" options are extreme positions, to be avoided via Nishida's recourse to the primacy of experience. Such an interpretation might place him closer to the view Levi-Strauss advocated:

> . . . Perhaps it must be acknowledged that duality, alternation, opposition and symmetry, whether presented in definite forms or in imprecise forms, are not so much matters to be explained, as basic and immediate data of mental and social reality which should be the starting point of any attempt at explanation.[50]

We can take Nishida's account of the fundamental opposition between the One and the Many as representative of his notion of the self-identity of absolute contradictories. Here as before, neither the whole nor the parts can be said to be real except in relation to one another. All conceptualization in terms of opposites proceeds as abstraction of aspects out of dialectical wholes. "At the base of the world there are neither the many nor the one." What is real is rather a unity or dialectical whole which contains in itself the conditions for its own diffusion. In the dialectical whole, the particular and the universal are fully interfused. The contradictory self-identity of a dialectical whole represents a mode of being that is at once already a unity of the actual and the possible, the particular and the universal. The logic of *soku hi* or "is and is not" represents a balanced logic of symbolization reflecting sensitivity to the mutual determination of universality and particularity in nature, and a corresponding emphasis on nonattachment to linguistic predicates and subjects as representations of the real.

> At the base of the world, there are neither the many nor the one; it is a world of absolute unity of opposites, where the many and the one deny each other . . . in the depth of the world there are neither one nor many, and . . . through mutual negation of the one and the many the world is from the formed to the forming.[51]

My central concern in this essay, contrariety as a problem shared across East/West boundaries, thus returns to the focus. Nishida's unique approach to contrariety involves a novel conception of the role that opposites play in human thought: they are *forms of mediation* between self and the environment. The generation, maintenance, and criticism of opposites in conceptual thought is necessary as a form of mediation with the world. "Productivity through action-intuition means: the individual confronts transcendence, confronts the absolute, *has as mediation the unity of opposites.*"[52]

Nishida says both that the individual confronts the absolute unity of opposites (that is, *confronts the absolute*) and that he has the unity of opposites as *his form of mediation with the absolute.*[53] But this ambiguity concerning the status of apposites must be seen within the context of logic concretely understood. It does not cast Nishida into the camp of either nominalism or realism. Rather, Nishida is insisting that the experienced world is *not a world already fully formed for us.* Identity cannot be understood apart from negation; negation is an initial creative act of self-reflection that makes possible both identity and difference. The self must become active and creative in the process of the formation of his world. "Seeing the world through action-intuition implies forming the world through action-intuition." Only in this creative act do we as forming factors become true individuals in and over against a world. Here again the cognitive method of active intuition is concrete logical, for "Concrete logic is just where we as historical-productive Self progressively grasp reality."[54]

VIII. CONCLUSION

On the view I have developed, the concern to articulate and disambiguate the relationships between language and reality, or logic and experience, is strongly shared across the divisions between Eastern and Western traditions. What I have objected to in characteristically Western approaches to the subject after Aristotle is its detachment from the problem of contrariety. The disregard for the problem of contrariety is correctable by a closer examination of such sources as the dependence of Aristotelian logic on a metaphysics of contrariety, Nishida's syncretic philosophy, and the work of a wide range of contemporary thinkers in the West who hold affinity for dialectical ontology. This, I have argued, shows the need for a philosophical anthropology of contrariety and for what I have called "comparative dialectics" as a meta-methodology for comparative and syncretic philosophy.

In an afterword to Nishida's final work, **The Logic of the Place of Nothingness and the Religious Worldview,** Nishida reflects upon his *benshoho* logic as a form of thinking intended to "clarify . . . the historically formative act from the standpoint of the historically active self itself."[55] He emphasizes the central importance of this logic to the understanding of his thought, and says that those academics who brush aside a logic of contradictory identity as 'not a logic at all', have only proliferated misunderstandings rather than clarified issues. In this I would agree with Nishida, for "logic" is a term that has too often connoted a strictly deductive way of thinking to the exclusion of ampliative or non-deductive thought processes. Discursive thought is far too complex and inventive to be contained within deductive models. Our epistemology therefore must attend to the actual form(s) of human thought, and "The standpoint of theory of knowledge, where subject and object confront each other, must be examined critically. Knowledge, too, is a happening in the historical-social world."[56]

I end therefore in agreement with Nishida that logic(s) must be understood in the broadest sense as the discursive form(s) of our own uniquely human thought processes. "Logic is the discursive form of our thinking. And we will only be able to clarify what logic is by reflecting on the form of our own thinking."[57] Confusion rather than clarification, Nishida has shown, has been the result of attempts to settle this matter by allegiance to the abstract understanding and a priori synthetic conceptions of logical principles. A more pluralistic conception of logic would seem to be one outcome of the undercutting of these foundations in Classical and Modern epistemology. Our analysis of pragmatic and systems-theoretic conceptions of logical principles has underlined this implication. Yet Nishida's comparisons of different logics in the development of his *benshoho* serves also the more synoptic goals embraced in the search for a common basis for intercultural dialogue. *A philosophically and cross-culturally adequate understanding of contrariety is a precondition for working out such a common basis.* Like Nishida I remain optimistic that logic andepistemology on a concrete footing may yet succeed where the abstract understanding has failed, and thereby achieve a goal which has long inspired dialectical thinkers both East and West.

NOTES

[1] Cf. J. P. Anton's *Aristotle's Theory of Contrariety* (New York: Humanities Press, 1957).

[2] Aristotle, *Metaphysica* 1004b.

[3] Anton, *Aristotle's Theory;* see especially chap. 2, "The Ontological Foundations of Contrariety and Its Relation to Substance as Nature," and chap. 4, "Contrariety in the Locus of Process and in the Categories."

[4] G. E. R. Lloyd, *Polarity and Analogy* (London: Cambridge University Press, 1966).

[5] Nishida Kitaro, *Intuition and Reflection in Self-Consciousness,* trans. by V. H. Viglielmo with T. Toshinori and J. S. O'Leary (New York: State University of New York Press, 1987), Introduction, p. ix.

[6] *Fundamental Problems of Philosophy,* trans. by David A. Dilworth (Tokyo: Sophia University, 1970), p. 94.

[7] Joachim Israel, *The Language of Dialectics and the Dialectics of Language* (Atlantic Highlands, New Jersey: Humanities Press, 1979).

[8] *Intelligibility and the Philosophy of Nothingness,* trans. by Robert Schinzinger (Honolulu: East-West Center, 1958), p. 174. Action-intuition is the ground for the subject/object distinction, which Western epistemology so often takes as primary. "[S]uch dichotomies are always the negation of the unity of subject and object" (*Fundamental Problems of Philosophy,* pp. 138-139; cf. p. 32).

[9] *Intelligibility and the Philosophy of Nothingness,* p. 211.

[10] G. W. F. Hegel, *Lesser Logic* (1830), sec. 48 (London: Oxford University Press, 1975), pp. 76-77.

[11] *Fundamental Problems of Philosophy,* p. 181.

[12] I interpret such issues of orientation as meta-methodological ones and regard them as being informed by ontology. In my view, Nishida has an ontology, albeit a specifically dialectical one, that is committed to neither Materialism nor Idealism. But the shift to reinterpreting many ontological questions asmeta-methodological ones is appealing to me, as it brings with it a normative conception of meta-level discourse.

[13] E. V. Ilyenkov, *Dialectical Logic* (Moscow: Progress Publishers, 1977), p. 120.

[14] Only by seeing it thus, Nishida insists, will the development of the world have definite form or preserve the creative act "from the formed to the forming." By seeing the world only from the many, or only from the one, and by thinking the world only as mechanism, or only teleologically, there is no "from the formed towards the forming" (*Last Writings: Nothingness and the Religious Worldview,* trans. by David Dilworth (Honolulu: University of Hawaii Press, 1987), p. 62).

[15] "The Dialectical World," in *Fundamental Problems of Philosophy,* p. 170.

[16] *Fundamental Problems of Philosophy,* p. 247.

[17] Nishida says that the ground of identity is found neither in the direction of the subject as subsumed under the predicate, nor of the predicate as unified by the subject. Nishida identifies these alternatives as realistic and idealistic, respectively, and argues instead for the basis of identity "in an underlying pre-cognitive ground" (*Intuition and Reflection,* p. 140; cf. *Fundamental Problems of Philosophy,* p. 22).

[18] *Intuition and Reflection,* p. 171.

[19] Ibid., p. 211.

[20] Cf. *Last Writings.* For Nishida, "this logic of the contradictory identity of the absolute is a 'negative theology' in an entirely different framework." See, especially, pp. 69-70.

[21] Cf. *Last Writings* 110 and 118: "I think however that a God who does not empty himself, a God who does not

express himself through his own self negation, is not the true absolute."

22 *Last Writings;* cf. pp. 75, 87.

23 Ibid., p. 87.

24 Ibid.; cf. p. 110.

25 "The thought of totality, the intelligible world, is the concrete Idea as we have seen it with the Neo-Platonists" (*Lectures on the History of Philosophy* (1895), p. 548). This point is made by Graham Priest, "Dialectic and Dialetheic," *Science and Society* 53, no. 4(Winter 1989): 398.

26 *Last Writings,* p. 115.

27 *Intelligibility and the Philosophy of Nothingness,* p. 177.

28 I have interpreted *"benshoho"* as "dialectic" broadly, in a sense encompassing both what Dilworth calls "dialectic" (sublational logic) and what he calls "agonistic" (paradoxical logical). Nishida's leaning toward the agonistic side of Dilworth's distinction is important in understanding his differences with Hegel or with more traditional forms of Buddhism. Yet I see little justification in defining dialectic in Dilworth's quite narrow fashion, or in the license he takes in the *Last Writings* to vary the translation given to *"benshoho"* and other of Nishida's terms in order to help carry the meta-philosophical categories he favors in his commentary.

29 *Last Writings,* p. 111.

30 See James Lawler's "Hegel on Contradictions-Misinterpretations," in E. Marquit, P. Moran, and W. Truitt, eds., *Dialectical Contradictions* (Minneapolis: Marxist Educational Press, 1985), pp. 16-17:

> . . . Hegel is concerned not with the elimination of the principles of formal-logical principles per se, but with an examination of their place in the overall movement of thought, and a rejection of a philosophy of logic that presents such principles as self-evident absolutes that are intuitively 'given.'

31 Hegel, *The Science of Logic* (1812).

32 Lawler, in Marquit et al., *Dialectical Contradictions,* p. 14. See also R. Norman and S. Sayers, *Hegel, Marx and Dialectic: Debate* (Harvester's Press, 1980); S. Sayers, *Reality and Reason: Dialectic and the Theory of Knowledge* (Blackwell, 1985).

33 Lawler, in Marquit et al., *Dialectical Contradictions,* p. 14: "Hegel distinguished between the concept of logical contradiction (i.e., formal logical contradiction) understood within this framework (that of "abstract understanding") and logical contradiction understood within the framework of dialectical theory. . . ."

34 *Intelligibility and the Philosophy of Nothingness,* p. 177.

35 Lawler, in Marquit et al., *Dialectical Contradictions,* p. 13.

36 Narski, "Hegel's Interpretation of Contradiction," in Marquit etal., *Dialectical Contradictions,* pp. 46-47. This point is a basis for preference for certain self-contradictory uses of language by those using Marxist methods in science. Social and physical tensions are among the most empirical of posits, and hence methodological expression of hypotheses in terms of dynamic oppositions is taken to reflect both the nature of the real and the "contradictory development of thought."

37 H. Horz, "Dialectical Contradictions in Physics," in Marquit et al., *Dialectical Contradictions,* p. 205.

38 Lloyd examines especially the sophistication in the shift away from "tables" of opposites and from treatment of opposites as metaphysical "forces at work," to treatment of them as principles of classification, etc. Cf. Pythagoras' table of opposites in Lloyd's "Theories Based on Opposites in Early Greek Thought," chap. 7 of *Polarity and Analogy.*

39 Lloyd, *Polarity and Analogy,* p. 23.

40 *Fundamental Problems of Philosophy,* p. 14.

41 For a thoughtful development of a dialectical view of ethical reflection, see Michael Kelly's recent "The Dialectical/Dialogical Structure of Ethical Reflection," *Philosophy and Rhetoric* 22, no. 3 (1989): 174-193.

42 *Fundamental Problems of Philosophy,* p. 3.

43 Archie Bahm, *Polarity, Dialectic and Organicity* (Albuquerque: World Books, 1977), p. 8; see also p. 73.

44 Errol Harris, *Formal, Transcendental and Dialectical Thinking: Logic and Reality* (Albany: State University of New York Press, 1987), p. 160.

45 *Intelligibility and the Philosophy of Nothingness,* p. 55.

46 Graham Priest, (1989): 388-415.

47 C. I. Lewis, "A Pragmatic Conception of the A Priori," in A. Rorty, ed., *Pragmatic Philosophy* (New York: Doubleday Anchor, 1966), p. 353.

> The traditional example of the a priori par excellence is the laws of logic. These can not be derived from experience since they must first be taken for granted in order to prove them. They make explicit our general modes of classification. And they impose upon experience no real limitation. Sometimes we are asked to tremble before the specter of the "alogical," in order that

we may thereafter rejoice that we are saved from this by the dependence of reality upon mind. But the 'alogical' is pure bogey, a word without meaning. What kind of experience could defy the principle that everything must either be or not be, that nothing can both be and not be, or that if x is y and y is z, then x is z? If anything imaginable or unimaginable could violate such laws, then the everpresent fact of change would do it every day.

[48] Ibid.

[49] C. Hallpike, *Foundations of Primitive Thought* (Oxford: Oxford University Press, 1979), p. 224.

[50] In Hallpike, ibid.

[51] *Intelligibility and the Philosophy of Nothingness,* pp. 168-169.

[52] Ibid., p. 209.

[53] Ibid., p. 208. Cf. *Fundamental Problems of Philosophy,* p. 4: "The true individual can be regarded as the ultimate determination of the universal, but at the same time, it determines the universal. The true individual must be an acting individual."

[54] *Intelligibility and the Philosophy of Nothingness,* pp. 240 and 224; cf. 204 and 207.

[55] *Last Writings,* p. 125.

[56] *Intelligibility and the Philosophy of Nothingness,* p. 171.

[57] Ibid., p. 126; see also Fundamental Problems of Philosophy, p. 113: "Logic does not mean the science of abstract thinking, as is usually thought. True logic must be a science of concrete thinking. True dialectic must be a path by which reality explains itself."

Masao Abe (essay date 1992)

SOURCE: "'Inverse Correspondence' in the Philosophy of Nishida: The Emergence of the Notion," in *International Philosophical Quarterly,* Vol. XXXII, No. 3, September, 1992, pp. 325-44.

[*In the following essay, Abe discusses the major tenets of Nishida's philosophy, particularly that of "inverse correspondence."*]

TRANSLATOR'S INTRODUCTION

Some commentators on Japanese culture find it useful to restrict the term "philosophy" to the work of those Japanese thinkers whose work has been influenced directly by western systems and categories of thought. Philosophy in this sense is less that 150 years old in Japan. The work of Kitaro Nishida (1870-1945) marks the first sustained attempt at a critical synthesis of western and eastern thought. The article by Masao Abe that follows here in translation addresses the origins of the term "inverse correspondence" *(gyakutaio)* and its relationship with some of the key elements of Nishida's philosophical system. For those unfamiliar with the work of Nishida, this introduction to the article offers a brief treatment of (1) the "place of absolute nothingness," (2) the related concepts of "contradictory self-identity" and "inverse correspondence," (3) the influence of Zen and Pure Land Buddhist thought on Nishida, and (4) the criticism leveled against Nishida's philosophical system by his younger colleague Hajime Tanabe.

After his initial experiments with the thought of William James and the neo-Kantians, Nishida's philosophical standpoint as such became visible in 1927 with his notion of the "place of absolute nothingness." Nishida had become dissatisfied with the psychologism and mysticism of his early work. To counter this psychologism, he began what would become a life-long investigation into the realm of the "non-self," what Buddhism calls "nothingness" *(mu)*. To avoid the attendant problem of mysticism, he began to work out a "logic" *(ronri)* of nothingness rooted in the cultural experience of Japan. In this regard, Nishida presented his idea of "absolute nothingness" in terms of the metaphor "place."

In search of the realm of the non-self and its logical structure, Nishida began to think about the concrete "place" *(basho)* out of which the dualism of subject and object arise mutually. The most abstract "place" is the world of physical objects (the *basho* of relative being). Less abstract is the "place" of self-consciousness (the *basho* of relative nothingness in contrast to the relative beings which appear within consciousness). At this point, Nishida asked if the "place" of relative nothingness is self-contained or nested within a yet more concrete realm of reality. Guided by his Buddhist heritage and its rejection of a substantial self, Nishida argued that the most concrete "apriority" is the "place of absolute nothingness" which is prior even to the duality of being and non-being.

In his final essay, **"The Logic of Place and the Religious Worldview,"** Nishida used his notion of absolute nothingness to clarify his philosophy of religion. To the extent that absolute nothingness is a philosophical approximation of Zen Buddhism's *mu*, Nishida's thought is largely shaped by the aesthetic religiosity and intuitionism of Zen. In his final essay, however, Nishida directed his attention to the problem of God and religious faith inChristianity and Pure Land Buddhism.

The Kamakura period (1186-1333) was a time of cultural upheaval and social anomie in Japan. Not surprisingly, it was also a time of great religious innovation. New schools of Buddhism arose, no longer based on the doctrinalism and ritualism of the early sects. The Zen movement emphasized meditation techniques and religious intuitionism. The Pure Land movement sought salvation through existential faith in the benevolence of Amida Buddha. Honen, the founder of the Pure Land Sect, preached a doctrine of total faith in the Amida Buddha's vow to save all who call on him through the recitation of the Name of Buddha *(nembutsu)*. His disciple, Shinran, the founder of the True Pure Land Sect, contrasted the way of the saint (the "self-power" path to salvation through contemplation) with the way of the ordinary sinner (the "other-power" path to salvation through faith in the grace of Amida). As a religion of faith, Pure Land Buddhism raises the problem of the dualism of the believer and Amida. In his last essay, Nishida addressed this problem in Buddhism (and in Christianity) by means of the concepts of "absolute contradictory self-identity" and "inverse correspondence."

Logically, the structure of absolute nothingness is double negation. Being is negated by non-being. This is relative nothingness. In absolute nothingness, the negation of being by non-being is itself negated. This negation of negation leads to the absolute affirmation of being in which things finally appear most concretely in their "suchness." Since absolute nothingness is not opposable to anything, it can be realized only paradoxically as a self-identity of absolute contradictories. Perhaps this will be easier to understand if we compare Nishida's Buddhist view of nothingness with Hegel's *Begriff*. Hegel declares, in his famous aphorism, "the rational is the real." Contradiction is overcome through the sublation of opposites until history reaches its end in the final synthesis (the absolute *Begriff*). Nishida, in contrast, saw contradiction as constitutive of reality itself. Instead of being overcome sublationally by means of *Begriff*, absolute nothingness realizes contradictions in their "suchness." Therefore Nishida's notion of ultimate reality as absolute nothingness requires a paradoxical logic of the contradictory self-identity of opposites.

Nishida's understanding of absolute nothingness as "place" and "contradictory self-identity" came under severe criticism by his colleague Hajime Tanabe. The *locus classicus* of Tanabe's critique of Nishida is his *Philosophy as Metanoetics* where three points of difference are outstanding. (1) Nishida thought of absolute nothingness in terms of an intuition into the immediacy of experience prior to the dualism of subject and object. His use of "place" as a basic metaphor for nothingness is consistent with thisintuitionism. Tanabe argued that absolute nothingness cannot be known intuitively as *gnosis* but only "metanoetically" through the death and resurrection of the self. Thus Tanabe claimed that Nishida's "place" is a variety of the emanationism of Plotinus. (2) The roots of Nishida's intuitionism lie in his affinities with the aesthetic religiosity of Zen Buddhism. Tanabe, during the war period and after, was influenced by Pure Land Buddhism's emphasis on faith, conversion and grace (other-power). (3) For Tanabe, truth is fragmented and intensive, touching the individual historically and ethically through conversion. Thus he criticizes Nishida's intuitionism for its emphasis on logical structure and aesthetics at the expense of the ethical. Absolute nothing-

ness, understood as "place," is no more than a mystical contemplation incapable of engaging history ethically.

How do the concepts of absolute nothingness and contradictory self-identity philosophically clarify the relationship between Amida (God) and the world? It is in this regard that Nishida introduced his notion of "inverse correspondence" *(gyakutaio)*. In his earlier work, Nishida thought of God as *Gottheit,* the ground of the world and the self. In his final essay, he speaks of God in the context of absolute nothingness as the absolutely contradictory self-identity which contains its own self-negation within itself. God is the "place" where paradoxically the duality of God and the self disappears without annulling their difference. Therefore faith reveals the paradox of religious truth, viz., that at their root, God and self form a self-identity of absolute contradiction. To express this relationship with more precision, Nishida introduced the phrase "inverse correspondence."

The following article, "'Inverse Correspondence' in the Philosophy of Nishida," is part of a series of three essays by Masao Abe on this topic. As the subtitle "The Emergence of the Notion" indicates, this first part discusses how Nishida came to the idea of "inverse correspondence" partly in response to the criticisms of Hajime Tanabe. In the second and third installments, . . . the author tries to reach a critical understanding of Nishida's pivotal term. (Note: Translator's footnotes will be designated by alphabetical superscripts. Translator's addenda to Abe's footnotes will be indicated by TN.)

"INVERSE CORRESPONDENCE" IN THE PHILOSOPHY OF NISHIDA: THE EMERGENCE OF THE NOTION

I

Religion constitutes both the point of departure as well as the ultimate destination of the philosophy of Kitaro Nishida. The preface of Nishida's maiden work, *An Inquiry into the Good,* contains a clear statement of his views: "From my perspective,religion constitutes the consummation of philosophy." Similarly, the fourth and final chapter of this work is allocated to religion. It is well known that the theme of religion is also prominent in his last completed work, **"The Logic of Place and the Religious Worldview."** In the opening paragraph of the fourth chapter of *An Inquiry into the Good,* which bears the title "Religion," he wrote: "The religious demand concerns the self as a whole, the life of the self."[1] This was Nishida's consistent, unchanging view of religion to his final essay. Be that as it may, this does not mean that he thought of religion simply in terms of the problem of the interior tranquility of the individual. Instead, Nishida grasped religion in terms of the problem of the ground of the world's existence. Although this insight appears previously in *An Inquiry into the Good,* we see it steadily deepened and clarified in the later philosophy of Nishida. Without a doubt, as the title of the final essay indicates, the problem of religion is presented in terms of the problem of a religious worldview. This is quite natural for

Nishida who insists that the world begins where the self begins; that the ground of the self's existence is simultaneously the ground of the existence of the world. In fine, religion provides the common foundation of both the self and the world. Consequently, religion concerns the problem of the ground of the existence of all things. Furthermore, Nishida consistently tried to grasp the truth of religion logically. The "logic" required for this project is the "logic of place" [*bashoteki ronri*] which, for Nishida, is the most concrete logic.[a] For this reason, here and there in the final essay we find the view that "only by means of the logic of place can the religious world be thought" (NKZ 19, 425). Not surprisingly, it is as a result of this position that the title of the essay itself became **"The Logic of Place and the Religious Worldview."**

Therefore, although this last essay certainly represents Nishida's doctrine of religion, this by no means implies that his view of religion is separate from the problem of philosophy and logic, or for that matter a standpoint isolated from a grasp of the historical world. By being linked to a thoroughly philosophical logic, the logic of place, the final essay offers a doctrine of religion which tries to grasp the existence of the self and the historical world out of the deepest foundation of both. In fine, it is a doctrine of religion which seeks to grasp the whole of historical actuality logically. Accordingly, **"The Logic of Place and the Religious Worldview"** (a piece in which the whole body of Nishida's philosophy is condensed and crystallized) may be regarded as dealing in almost full scale with religion as "the consummation of philosophy," as Nishida wrote in the preface to *An Inquiry into the Good*. On the one hand, the philosophy of Nishida is a philosophy of the logic of place throughout, while on the other hand, it is also a philosophy of the worldview of religion. Since the logical and religious elements are not only inseparable butmutually interpenetrating and determining, Nishida's thought offers itself to us as one living philosophy.

In order to explore Nishida's philosophy along these lines, we need to take up the above mentioned end point of Nishida's philosophy as it is presented in **"The Logic of Place and the Religious Worldview."** Specifically, I would like to address myself to the notion of "inverse correspondence" [*gyakutaio*] as it is found therein.

Two issues regarding the notion of "inverse correspondence," as discussed in the final essay, are outstanding. In the first place, "inverse correspondence" is a peculiar notion unique to Nishida's thought. This is the case because "inverse correspondence" precisely captures the essence of religion common to the various religious traditions even though it must always be understood as a logical and philosophical concept. In the second place, the notion of "inverse correspondence," which made its appearance in Nishida's later years, brings with it the problem of its similarity and dissimilarity to Nishida's hitherto foundational notion of "absolute contradictory self identity" [*zettai mujunteki jikodoitsu*], and the problem as to whether or not the relationship between these

two notions underwent development and change. To be specific, if "inverse correspondence" were simply another term for "absolute contradictory self identity," would this indicate that the two terms are identical in meaning? Do their points of emphasis differ significantly, even though they refer to exactly the same issue? Does "inverse correspondence" indicate a deepening and concretization of the notion of "absolute contradictory self identity" or do these two notions indicate two different standpoints? All these problems attend Nishida's use of the term. Tanabe's ambivalence regarding these questions is illustrative.[b] When it came to the notion of "absolute contradictory self identity," Tanabe was capable of marshaling severe criticisms. Even in his later lectures, collected and published in his *Introduction to Philosophy,* Tanabe continued to express disagreement with the notion of an "absolute contradictory self identity." Yet regarding the notion of "inverse correspondence," his expression of approval is simply stated: "Truly, this is an appropriate notion."[2] In the light of all this, a discussion of "inverse correspondence" would not only be important for clarifying the core of Nishida's thought, but also useful in elucidating the problems which lie hidden within the inconcealable philosophical opposition between Nishida and Tanabe.

And so, what sort of idea is this "inverse correspondence" and what meaning did this come to have for the later Nishida? How is it related to the proceeding notion of "absolute contradictory self identity," the fundamental notion of Nishida's thought?

II

Any consideration of "inverse correspondence" will immediately recall statements that appear in **"The Logic of Place and the Religious Worldview,"** statements such as:

> Only by dying does the self encounter God in terms of an inverse correspondence. (NKZ 11, 396)

> We are always encountering the Absolute One in terms of an inverse correspondence through self negation. (NKZ 11, 426)

Therefore, it seems at first that the phrase "inverse correspondence" is used exclusively to express the relationship between a human being and God, or between the Absolute One and the self. In this respect it might be thought that the term is used by Nishida only within the purview of religion.

Yet the notion of "inverse correspondence" does not appear for the first time in **"The Logic of Place and the Religious Worldview,"** nor is it terminology used solely to express the relationship between God and a human being. As pointed out earlier,[3] in Nishida's **"The Philosophical Foundations of Mathematics,"** (written immediately before the final essay,[4] the expression is used frequently in regard to the problem of philosophy and mathematics. In set theory, when the respective elements of two numerical quantities, considered together, correspond to one another, the relationship obtaining between the quantities is said to be one of "equivalence" *(Äquivalenz)*. Nishida expresses this equivalence in the phrase "mutual correspondence" (NKZ 11, 24). Moreover, he states in the opening paragraph of **"The Philosophical Foundations of Mathematics"**: "Instead of thinking logically about numbers through natural numbers, conversely we should try to think of numbers from the standpoint of logic" (NKZ 11, 237). This demonstrates his intention to grasp set theory from the perspective of the logic of place and the principle of contradictory self identity. In order to be able to say that the two numerical quantities correspond or do not correspond to one another mutually, there must be a standpoint at their foundation which contains both and reflects both in itself. Only from the standpoint where both quantities thoroughly negate each other and imply an inverse determination at their ground does there arise a mutual correspondence. Speaking from the standpoint of the logic of place, each individual thing stands in inverse correspondence to itself and at the same time, individual thing and individual thing oppose one another infinitely in inverse correspondence. Mathematicians deal with the existence of the mutual correspondence of numerical quantities as *Äquivalenz* but this mutual correspondence is possible only in terms of an inverse correspondence and an inverse determination from within thestandpoint which embraces and reflects the mutual correspondence within itself.

In my understanding, this is the basic import of the philosophical foundation of mathematics seen from the standpoint of the logic of place. From this basic perspective, Nishida pursues a detailed discussion of set theory. I will only briefly summarize my understanding. The mutual correspondence which mathematicians call *Äquivalenz* should not be understood as a parallel relationship on one and the same plane. Rather, mutual correspondence is fundamentally a relationship of inverse correspondence. It seems to me that Nishida's point is that true *Äquivalenz* is possible only in and through correspondence which is profoundly an inverse correspondence. Thus here we see an example in which the term "inverse correspondence" is used in reference to mathematical problems prior to **"The Logic of Place and the Religious Worldview."**

There are also examples of the usage of the term "inverse correspondence" even prior to **"The Philosophical Foundations of Mathematics."** Sometime prior to this work, Nishida apparently hit upon the idea of "inverse correspondence" which he used in his doctrine of religion. Probably, the idea came to Nishida through his discussions and correspondence with Dr. Risaku Mudai[c] concerning Mudai's book, *The Logic of Place.* Specifically, I would like to examine Nishida's letter of 2 December, 1944 addressed to Mudai. Mudai had presented his recently published *The Logic of Place* to Nishida on the previous day (1 December). The rather lengthy letter of 2 December was a note of thanks. In this letter, Nishida wrote: "Correspondence understood in terms of

'place' [*basho-teki taio*] fascinates me. It seems that we must clarify the meaning of a logic [of] place in this aspect." (NKZ 19, 354; letter 2052) Since Mudai had used the phrase "correspondence in the place [of absolute nothingness]" in his above mentioned book, I suppose that the phrase may have been his own neologism. According to Mudai, correspondence indicates ". . . the standpoint of *jinen honi*[d] or that of *mugi no gi*[e] in which the individual, by abandoning himself or herself and by living with steadfast faith, becomes, in effect, the arising of the world beyond the individual."[5] Mudai calls this type of correspondence, *correspondence in the place* [of absolute nothingness] as distinguished from an objective correspondence which consists of a parallel correspondence between X and Y. In this standpoint of "place" (which is comparable to *mugi no gi*) not only does correspondence between X and Y arise in the place [of absolute nothingness], but what is more, "[t]he fact that there is a correspondence in the place between X and Y, indicates that there is a yet more fundamental correspondence in the place between X and this place itself and Y and this place itself."[6] Nishida found Mudai's idea of correspondence in the place [of absolute nothingness] "fascinating."

Twenty days after this (the 21st of December) in a note addressed to this same colleague, Nishida observed that "[t]he self and the world do not merely oppose one another as 'coordinates' but correspond to one another in terms of a contradictory self identity" (NKZ 19, 366; letter 2077). On the following day, 22 December 1944 (about one month and a half before beginning to write **"The Logic of Place and the Religious Worldview"**), in a note once again addressed to Mudai, the term "inverse correspondence" [*gyakutaio*] appears as Nishida's own neologism. Moreover, it is clearly defined.

> Correspondence [*taio*] understood in terms of the logic of place must always be a matter of inverse correspondence [*gyakutaio*]. In looking at the correspondence of the world and the self, the totality and the individual from the perspective of the logic of place, [one cannot say] that the individual thing becomes the totality and the totality becomes the individual. Instead, since the world and the self are thoroughly opposed to each other, they are related in terms of a contradictory self identity. Correspondence in the logic of place is fundamentally an inverse correspondence. We must consider the problem of correspondence from this standpoint. . . . I would suggest that you consider your notion of correspondence within the logic of place more radically from the standpoint of an inverse determination. Does this not then lead us to a clear realization of a contradictory self identity? (NKZ 19, 368; letter 2079)[7]

From the contents of this letter, it is clear that Nishida was stimulated by Mudai's notion of "correspondence in the place [of absolute nothingness]." My guess is that Nishida came up with the term "inverse correspondence" from this source. That is to say, Mudai spoke of correspondence (i.e., correspondence within the place of nothingness) and Nishida responded by saying that the true correspondence must be "inverse correspondence." In fact, after this time, the term "inverse correspondence" appears frequently in Nishida's letters to Mudai and elsewhere.[8]

III

Now there are three points which merit our attention. In the first place, correspondence, i.e., true correspondence seen as an inverse correspondence as we saw above as a problem for a logic of place, pertains to individual things (such as an X and a Y). It is not simply limited to the religious problem of God and the self. This point can be understood from the fact that the notion of correspondence in the place [of absolute nothingness], as presented by Mudai, arises from the philosophical objective of constructing a logic of place in contrast to an objective logic, a transcendental logic, a dialectical logic and so forth.

Regarding the second point about which we must be aware, for Mudai, the philosophical notion of correspondence in the place [of absolute nothingness] is molded by the True Pure Land Buddhist doctrines *jinen honi* and *mugi no gi.*[f] Responding to Mudai, Nishida also had True Pure Land Buddhism in mind in thinking of the logic of place and its notions of correspondence and inverse correspondence. This point is reflected in his letters.

> Certainly, I think you are getting at the logic of place from the point of view of True Pure Land experience. To be sure, I too am aware that faith, as understood in True Pure Land Buddhism, can give logical expression to the logic of place. Moreover, I think this course must be pursued. (NKZ 19, 354; letter 2052)

> As the self determination of the place [of absolute nothingness], we will be grasped by the light *(Gottheit)* of Amida, nay we are already grasped by it. It is precisely at this point that the logic of place itself, in truth, forms the basis of the worldview of True Pure Land Buddhism. (NKZ 19, 369; letter 2079)

The third point which merits our attention is the fact that the letters addressed to Mudai during this period concerning the logic of place as the foundational standpoint of True Pure Land Buddhism include Nishida's severe criticism of Tanabe. For instance, in the above mentioned letters of 21 and 22 December, the key passages cited regarding inverse correspondence were set down in the context of Nishida's vehement criticism of Tanabe. (This point will be taken up below.)

Confining our attention to these letters, we see that Nishida came to the notion of *inverse correspondence* prior to the writing of his final essay, **"The Logic of Place and the Religious Worldview,"** and prior even to **"The Philosophical Foundations of Mathematics"** which preceded it. What occasioned Nishida to develop this terminology were his conversations with Mudai,

whose own phrase was *correspondence in the place* [of absolute nothingness]. We should not think of this, however, as a sudden change in Nishida's views or as the introduction of a novel intellectual factor into his thought. Instead, we should think of Mudai's neologism, "correspondence in the place [of absolute nothingness]" as instrumental in teasing out meanings which had existed previous to this period in the foundations of Nishida's philosophy by acting on them as a kind of catalyst, crystallizing them into the term "inverse correspondence." I believe that the idea which would eventually lead to the term "inverse correspondence" was not fully conscious in the thought of Mudai himself up until this point, for was it not Nishida who pointed this out to Mudai and urged him to inquire more deeply into this issue? The following quotations, taken from a previously cited letter (#2079), plainly indicate the circumstances of this period as discussed above.

> Correspondence in the logic of place is fundamentally an inverse correspondence. We must consider the problem of correspondence from this standpoint. . . .

> . . . I would suggest that you consider your [notion of] correspondence within the logic of place more radically from the standpoint of an inverse determination. And does this not then lead us to a clear realization of a contradictory self identity? (NKZ 19, 368; letter 2079)

IV

And so, what notions did Nishida have previous to being prompted by Mudai's term, "correspondence in the place [of absolute nothingness]," which lie behind Nishida's claim that "correspondence, fundamentally, is inverse correspondence"? Notice that when we read the texts that come after his article entitled "Basho,"[g] the verb *taisuru,*[h] as in the expression "something is opposed [*taisuru*] to something else" appears with frequency. The most typical pattern is found in the expression, "The individual, by being opposed [*taisuru*] to another individual, is an individual" (NKZ 11, 426). I think that this statement is extremely typical not only for Nishida's use of *taisuru* but also in the sense that it encompasses Nishida's philosophy as a whole. In Nishida's case, to claim that "the individual opposes the individual" never simply means that the individual and the other statically face each other in one and the same dimension. It means, instead, that they dynamically oppose each other and that this dynamic opposition works mutually in the creation of something new. This mutual working of dynamic opposition means that the one tries to appropriate the other by means of a thorough negation of the other. It means that the other is negated and the self is affirmed and, at the same time, it means that the self negates itself and stands in the place of the universal beyond the self and the other. Finally, it means that the self is affirmed by means of an inverse determination arising out of this universal place. The creation of novelty arises out of this mutual working since the ground of creativity is the self determination of the universal beyond the self and the other.

And so, when Nishida says that, "the individual, by being opposed to another individual, is an individual," then:

1) The individual, by opposing another individual, does not oppose the other directly as an object in the same plane, but opposes the other in terms of a mutual nega-tion-*sive*-mutual affirmation.

2) No individual is closed in on itself as a simple self identity. Instead, by breaking through this simple self identity, each individual confronts itself in terms of a self negation-*sive*-selfaffirmation.

3) In order for points (1) and (2) to be the case simultaneously, the universal must unfold itself at its foundation beyond the self and the other; the "place" of this universal must be self determining. Furthermore, the self determination of this place is not a simple, direct, self determination. This place determines itself by means of a self negation-*sive*-self affirmation. Accordingly, the self determination of place is not the self determination of an abstract immediacy devoid of any content.

4) Instead, the self determination of place jointly enables and gives a foundation to the following two realities: first, the opposition or encounter [*taisuru*] of the individual and the other by means of a mutual negation-*sive*-mutual affirmation, and second, the correspondence [*taisuru*] of each individual to itself by means of a self negation-*sive*-self affirmation. If this is in fact the case, it means that the self determination of each and every individual as well as the mutual determination that takes place between individuals is determined by means of the negation-*sive*-affirmation arising from the universal place.

The above mentioned four points are all implied whenever the term *taisuru* is used in the philosophy of Nishida. Each point is conceptually distinguishable from the other and simultaneously implied in this single term because *taisuru* never means simply to correspond directly. It always means to correspond by means of nega-tion-*sive*-affirmation. In other words, *taisuru* implies that not being directly in correspondence is paradoxically correspondence in its *true* sense. Furthermore, precisely because this opposition by means of negation-*sive*-affirmation can be applied to each of these conceptually distinguishable four points, in reality all four are dynamically one. It is well known that Nishida called this correspondence in terms of negation-*sive*-affirmation *inverse determination* by distinguishing it from simple determination. At any rate, this is the meaning of the term *taisuru* as it is used by Nishida.

Since the term *taisuru* increasingly takes on the sense of *enfolding while being enfolded, reflecting while being reflected, creating while being created,* I believe that it is a term that has an extremely deep and important meaning in Nishida's philosophy. For this reason, it is quite natural for Nishida immediately to have hailed Mudai's notion as a "good idea" when, in using the term "correspon-

dence" [*taio*], Mudai was insisting that true correspondence is not a matter of the individual and the other confronting each other in terms of a simple parallel correspondence in an objective way, but a correspondence in the place [of absolute nothingness] in which the individual can establish the universalwhile maintaining itself in its uniqueness. Along with this, Nishida discerned that Mudai's notion of "correspondence in the place [of absolute nothingness]" does not include a clear realization of the above mentioned four points which are simultaneously implied in Nishida's notion of *taisuru*. This is the reason he says: "I would suggest that you consider your [notion of] correspondence within the logic of place more radically from the standpoint of an inverse determination. And does this not then lead us to a clear realization of a contradictory self identity?" (NKZ 19, 368; letter 2079) Once again, this is why Nishida urged Mudai to investigate these problems more thoroughly from the standpoint of an inverse determination and suggests that if we think along these lines, the contradictory self identity of all in the place [of absolute nothingness] will be grasped more clearly. At the same time, Nishida affirmed his own point of view when he stated: "Correspondence understood in terms of the logic of place is basically an inverse correspondence. It is from this standpoint that we must think of correspondence." (Ibid.)

v

Let me summarize the above. First, the inspiration behind the coining of the *term* "inverse correspondence" was supplied by Mudai's phrase, "correspondence in the place [of absolute nothingness]." This took place before the composition of **"The Logic of Place and the Religious Worldview"** (to be exact, two months before its composition), through Nishida's conversations with Mudai and less directly through their letter writing.

Second, the *thought itself* invoked by the term "inverse correspondence" did not spring from Mudai's thinking. Rather, it roots lie in the foundations of Nishida's philosophy, antecedent to his conversations with Mudai. The idea is implicit, for instance, in a term such as *taisuru* (to oppose, confront, correspond).

Third, "inverse correspondence" and the earlier *taisuru* are not terminology whose usage is restricted solely to the religious problem of the relationship between God and the individual. Instead, the term can be applied to all sorts of beings. This is indicated typically by the statement, "The individual, by being opposed to another individual, is an individual." And what is more, the term "inverse correspondence" applies with equal force to all of the above mentioned four points pertaining in the earlier term *taisuru*.

There is a fourth point which needs to be elucidated. While the claim made in the third point remains fundamentally and essentially true as stated, Nishida in fact came up with the neologism "inverse correspondence" through his conversations with Mudai in the context of

True Pure Land Buddhism or at least a context deeply related toTrue Pure Land thought. As set down above, Mudai's own notion of "correspondence in the place [of absolute nothingness]" was rooted in his True Pure Land Buddhist experience. Nishida demonstrated his own deep interest in the True Pure Land perspective by immediately embarking on a thorough investigation of Mudai's idea of "correspondence in the place [of absolute nothingness]" even though he ended up conversely with the notion of "inverse correspondence" within his own unique perspective.

In the above I wanted to clarify somewhat these four points regarding the emergence of the notion of "inverse correspondence." Among them all, the fourth point is exceedingly important for an understanding of **"The Logic of Place and the Religious Worldview"** in which Nishida's theory of religion should be understood as the ultimate shape of Nishida's philosophy. Accordingly, I would like to add a further reflection on this fourth point and especially on Nishida's profound interest in True Pure Land Buddhist thought during this period.

In the letter cited earlier which was addressed to Mudai and dated 20 December of the year previous to the writing of the final essay, we find the following statement: "We, as the self determination of the place [of absolute nothingness], will be grasped by the light *(Gottheit)* of Amida, nay we are already grasped by it. To be sure, it is precisely at this point that the logic of place itself forms the basis of the worldview of True Pure Land Buddhism." (NKZ 19, 369; letter 2081) After this, in a letter dated 6 January also addressed to Mudai, the following passage appears:

> Daisetz [Suzuki]'s "logic of *myogo*"[i] is a fine idea. True Pure Land Buddhism is of necessity built on this logic. It ought to be thought of from the standpoint of my notion of the contradictory self identity of the expressing and the expressed. That is the ground of heaven and of earth and also the ground of religiosity. From the depths of the self determination of the absolute present, we hear the name of Amida Buddha. Henceforth, we must think deeply about the idea of inverse correspondence in terms of the logic of place based on contradictory self identity. Mutual communication between the I and Thou is also a matter of inverse correspondence. (NKZ 19, 375; letter 2092)

In a card addressed to Keiji Nishitani, also dated 6 January, the connection between True Pure Land Buddhist thought and inverse correspondence takes on a more determinate form.

> It seems that some may say the logic of place is a logic of contemplation representing the path of the sage [*shodomon*]. But I believe that the logic of the contradictory self identity of the expressing and the expressed is precisely the logic of True Pure Land Buddhism out of which the voice of Amida calls us and whichtakes the name of Amida as its foundation. In the logic of place, we can

think of the principle of inverse correspondence because we do not encounter Amida Buddha as an object. (NKZ 19, 375-76; letter 2094)

It was precisely at this time, January of 1944, that Nishida was writing **"The Philosophical Foundations of Mathematics"**[9] after which he was planning to write on the philosophy of religion. This is clearly indicated in his card to Mudai of 6 January: "I am finished writing about 'life' [a reference to an article soon to appear in the journal *Shiso*] and have turned to the foundations of mathematics. But when I have finished with this, I think I will try to write on the True Pure Land Buddhist worldview." (NKZ 19, 375; letter 2091) This is the first reference to the doctrine of religion in all his diary and letters. The reference, "I will try to write on the True Pure Land worldview," shows that at this point in time Nishida was formulating in his mind the doctrine of religion which he began to write about one month later under the title, **"The Logic of Place and the Religious Worldview."** Actually, however, his completed doctrine of religion (notice that the brief statement "a doctrine of religion has almost been finished" appears in his diary entry of 24 April; see NKZ 17, 705) elucidated the essence of religion at the foundation of the various religions including True Pure Land and Zen, Buddhism and Christianity. If I might borrow Nishida's own words, it elucidated "the reality of spirit" (NKZ 11, 371) and the "foundational reality of our lives" (NKZ 11, 418). Moreover, this elucidation approaches its theme in terms of the logic of place. It is not simply a True Pure Land Buddhist worldview. The intention of Nishida's doctrine of religion, in its completed form, is readily apparent in a letter, dated 11 March of the same year and addressed to Daisetz Suzuki, which was written probably when the final essay was not but half completed:

> Currently I am writing about religion. I want to clarify the fact that religion cannot be understood with the usual objective logic, but requires my logic of contradictory self identity, i.e. a logic of *sokuhi*.[j] I want to bring to light the person, that is to say individuality, from the standpoint of the *Prajña-paramita Sutra* with its logic of *soku-hi* and to tie this together with the actuality of the historical world. (NKZ 19, 399; letter 2144)

In other words, Nishida was trying, (1) to capture religion with the logic of contradictory self identity; (2) to bring individuality to light from the standpoint of the *Prajña-paramita Sutra* with its logic of *soku-hi;* and (3) to tie these together in the actuality of the historical world.

These three factors should be interpreted as the fundamental aims lying behind Nishida's completed doctrine of religion. Even thoughthis is the case, the following fact, I believe, cannot be denied. As can be seen from letters written to Mudai and others during this period prior to the writing and conceiving of the doctrine of religion, Nishida retained a deep interest in True Pure Land Buddhism and was intending to write about the

"True Pure Land Buddhist worldview." He was thinking out the notion of inverse correspondence in the logic of place in terms of a logic of the True Pure Land doctrine of *myogo*.

VI

Thus, as was mentioned earlier, Nishida was interested in True Pure Land Buddhism and especially interested in discovering, within the foundations of *myogo*, a model for the logic of place in which the self and God (the Absolute One) correspond to one another in terms of a contradictory self identity. In both of these interests and especially the latter, there was a deep resonance with Mudai's philosophical attempts to construct a logic of place based on this same True Pure Land Buddhist experience. As noted above in regard to the mutual resonance of these two philosophers, Nishida's phrase "inverse correspondence" was brought to light by Mudai's "correspondence in the place [of absolute nothingness]." But as also was mentioned, we must also not overlook the fact that the philosophical exchange of ideas between these two thinkers, which led to the birth of "inverse correspondence," was taking place inseparably from Nishida's harsh criticism of Tanabe's philosophy.

As is well known, for a long time previous to this Tanabe had been criticizing Nishida's views on "place," "absolute contradictory self identity" and "action-intuition" for ultimately degenerating into an aesthetic or mystical intuition which fails to sustain "absolute mediation" through "action."[k] During 1944-1945, in the midst of his deadlock with rationalistic "self-power" philosophy, Tanabe began to advocate his "philosophy as metanoetics": "I entrust my life to the promptings of 'other-power' and practice repentance [*zange*]. Trusting in other-power, I witness to my personal conversion-resurrection. In this fashion, the action-faith-witness of *metanoia* [*zange*] becomes my philosophy in which I am resurrected."[10] Clearly implied in Tanabe's advocacy of "philosophy as metanoetics" is a rejection of Nishida's philosophy as a contemplative philosophy which takes the path of the sage without sustaining an absolute conversion through repentance.[11]

In the same period that Tanabe's criticism of Nishida's philosophy was maturing, Nishida and Mudai were exchanging the letters which we have been citing. In these letters, as noted earlier, Nishida wrote: "Without a doubt, you [Mudai] have grasped the logic of place through True Pure Land Buddhist experience. I as well am confident that True Pure Land Buddhist faith can be given logical expression by means of the logic of place. Furthermore, I thinkthat this must be done so." (NKZ 19, 354; letter 2052) Thus, Nishida gave voice to his strong sympathy for Mudai's position and clearly indicated the aims of his own philosophy. Writing to Mudai, Nishida stated:

> Since you grasp things in the True Pure Land way and since you have been successful in entering into the True Pure Land perspective, you must

continue on this course. You understand quite well the relationship between the enfolding and the enfolded, but in order to link this principle more profoundly with actuality, we must also delve deeply in the direction of opposition and contradiction. "Correspondence in the place [of absolute nothingness]" is a good insight. The logic of place must be more clearly articulated in this respect. We must continue to think deeply along these lines. (Ibid.)

And as we noted earlier, parallel to these discussions with Mudai, everywhere in the correspondence of this period we find severe criticisms directed toward Tanabe.

For instance, the previously cited letter of 22 December addressed to Mudai begins in the following manner:

> Salvation through faith is inconceivable in Tanabe's way of thinking. In short, conversion [*eshin*] is essential. Does Tanabe's view represent the religious world? In the religious world, the unenlightened, sinful human being hears the call of Amida Buddha and enters into faith. It is this standpoint of transformation [*tenkan*] that is required. The sinner was alone and in anguish up to this point but the truth is that he has been carried in the bosom of the Buddha all along. He has entered into the light of the Buddha and has been led by the hands of the Buddha. What is absolutely required is this "being embraced." (NKZ 19, 356; letter 2079)

In a similar vein, the following comments are found in the same letter:

> Tanabe sees the Buddha in a distant heaven and goes up to that place by approaching it any way he can. This man's notion of *metanoia* [*zange*] is not *metanoia* at all. It is merely *remorse* [*kokai*]. He makes his advance by sheer self power. *Metanoia* is a soul-searching which rises out of the ground of the life of the self. There it is reborn and comes to fruition. This man Tanabe is stuck on a fixed concept without a deep analysis of actuality and experience. Has this man, who has decided that my philosophy is merely about mystical intuition, even read my work? (Ibid.)

Proceeding in this fashion, the same kind of criticism of Tanabe is raised in a letter dated 21 December to Mudai.

The gist of Nishida's complaints against Tanabe, which can be seen in the letters of this period, can be summarized in two points:

1) Tanabe sees Buddha as being in a distant heaven and tries to reach this distant heaven by means of self-power. His position is lacking in a sense of transformation and conversion which are essential to the standpoint of religion. Therefore, Tanabe's so-called *metanoia* never amounts to anything more than remorse in the moral sense. It is not a religious transformation arising through a self examination at the ground of the soul: "If we approach the Buddha by means of volition and effort, the

religion which results is merely the path of the sage which is based on our own activities. Is this not merely the ethical?" (NKZ 19, 369; letter 2081)

2) Tanabe, by looking on the logic of place simply as a logic of contemplation, sees it as the path of the sage, to which Nishida responds:

> "Place" is not contemplated objectively. Rather, is it not the "wherein" of the self? The self and the world do not merely oppose one another as coordinates, rather they correspond to one another in a contradictory self identity. (NKZ 19, 366; letter 2077)

> The Buddha is not that which is known in contemplation. Since the Buddha cannot be contemplated, we simply call his Name [*myogo*]. (NKZ 19, 367; letter 2077)

> Can the Buddha's call and salvation ever arise from a standpoint like Tanabe's? (NKZ 19, 376; letter 2093)

VII

Confining our attention to these letters, we have been able to see that Nishida's intention of articulating a logic of place (in sympathy both with Mudai and with True Pure Land Buddhist experience) and also Nishida's critique of Tanabe (who misunderstood True Pure Land faith as merely a form of ethical remorse [*zange*] and misunderstood the logic of place as contemplation) are but two sides of the same coin. Yet what is it that forms the basis of this two-sided coin? I believe it is Nishida's belief that the logic of place can be discerned in True Pure Land Buddhist faith. In other words, it was Nishida's conviction that the worldview of True Pure Land Buddhism could be established precisely by recourse to the logic of place.

This can be clarified by means of the following two-fold inquiry based on citations from the letters of this period:

1) According to True Pure Land Buddhism, sentient beings do not contemplate Buddha. It is impossible for them because of serious sin. For this very reason, Amida calls out to sentient beings and transfers the merit of *myogo* [the Name]. Sentient beings are thus saved by entrusting themselves to the Buddha and by chanting the *myogo*. Here we are able to see a model for correspondence in the place [of absolute nothingness], i.e., correspondence understood in terms of the logic of place.

> A True Pure Land worldview, in which one does not hear the voice of Amida, is not a True Pure Land worldview at all. From where, in such a world, does the salvation of the Buddha arise? This fellow [Tanabe] thinks about religion with his head only, without becoming engrossed in experience, and does not realize religion as it actually is. The realm of repentance [*zange*] by itself is the realm of ethics and not the realm of religion. The religious

mind itself does not arise from within the self; it must come from that which is "other." [Tanabe] seems to be thinking even now that "place" is something to be contemplated. (NKZ 19, 366; letter 2077)

> The self determination of "place" is the manifestation of the Buddha in glory over-against our individuality and the voice of radical salvation (NKZ 19, 367; letter 2077)

These citations indicate Nishida's intention to uncover the real meaning of correspondence in "place" as it is implied in the teaching that sinful sentient beings are taken up into the compassion of Amida Buddha and enter into salvation merely by reciting the Name [*myogo*]. The Name, as the self determination of "place," can be adequately grasped from the standpoint of the contradictory self identity of the expressing and the expressed.

2) Nishida's claim does not mean that sentient beings are simply enfolded within Amida. Yet neither does it mean that the place [of absolute nothingness] enfolds the individual without any opposition. In such a "place," there can be heard no earnest calling of the Amida. Nor does the Original Vow of the Amida passing down through the Five *Kalpas** arise therein. Sentient beings are endlessly transmigrating through *samsara* because they do not persist in their faith in the Vow of Amida Buddha. There is opposition between the Buddha and sentient beings. Yet the Buddha, who overcomes this opposition, thoroughly enfolds sentient beings.

> According to the logic of place, the individual and the universal oppose each other completely in terms of a mutual negation, that is to say, the Buddha (*noema*) and the self (*noesis*) oppose one another completely. Yet we, as the self determination of "place," will be grasped—nay are already grasped by the light of Amida. It is precisely at this point that the logic of place itself truly forms the basis of the True Pure Land Buddhist worldview. (NKZ 19, 369; letter 2081)

> In the self negation of "place," individual thoroughly opposes individual in a mutual negation. But conversely, this means that through a self affirmation, individual and individual are linked together in an inverse correspondence and that "place" forms itself from the created to the creating. On the one hand, this world is the world of unquenchable desire and yet it is the world of the Buddha's compassion. Daisetz [T. Suzuki] says that paradise is reflecting itself in this world of corruption and that this world of corruption is reflecting itself in paradise. I have yet to get into this issue of correspondence, but the opportunity to do so would be most welcome. (NKZ 19, 379; letter 2102)

The Buddha enfolds sentient beings in overcoming opposition. The "place" [of absolute nothingness], by overcoming the opposition between individual and individual as well as the opposition between the individual and the totality, enfolds them by means of a contradictory self identity. And so, when the notion of "correspondence" is addressed in the logic of place, "correspondence" must of necessity become an "inverse correspondence." Here, "inverse correspondence" as such is the key to understanding that the logic of place provides a foundation for the True Pure Land Buddhist worldview.

In regard to these two points, Nishida's idea was that the structure of *correspondence* in accordance with the logic of place is manifest within True Pure Land faith.

Did not Nishida arrive at the notion of "inverse correspondence" by following this line of thought and being influenced by Mudai's phrase "correspondence in the place" [of absolute nothingness]? Mudai raised this issue as a question for Nishida while he was trying to grasp deeply and experientially the faith of True Pure Land Buddhism. Here it cannot be denied that Nishida's counter-attack against Tanabe's criticism of his philosophy became an important turning point for him: "Correspondence, seen in the light of the logic of place, is fundamentally an inverse correspondence. We must consider the problem of correspondence from this standpoint." (NKZ 19, 368; letter 2079) This statement should be taken with all the problems such as those we have seen above as a background.

All the same, this does not mean that Nishida's reaction against Tanabe's criticism of his philosophy became the motivating force behind Nishida's discovery of the principle of inverse correspondence within True Pure Land Buddhist faith. Clearly Mudai's phrase, "correspondence in the place [of absolute nothingness]" acted as a stimulus to Nishida and led to theneologism "inverse correspondence." Yet, the idea itself, which is so well captured by the phrase, can be found within Nishida's previous work. In a similar way, Tanabe's criticism of Nishida's philosophy also acted as a stimulus to Nishida. Thus it is while referring to the idea of *myogo* in True Pure Land Buddhism that Nishida made the claim, "correspondence, within the logic of place, must always be an inverse correspondence" (ibid). This approach was made by reflecting on the True Pure Land faith already experienced by Nishida and by transforming it into the logic of place. It is not the addition of new thought into the philosophy of Nishida. In other words, I think that Tanabe's criticism of Nishida's philosophy was only one of the catalysts behind the birth of the phrase "inverse correspondence."

This is because Nishida's basic perspective, i.e., the logic of place, is fundamentally not the standpoint of contemplation and the path of the sage as criticized by Tanabe. Instead it indicates the standpoint of absolute contradictory self identity in which the dynamic relationship of negation-*sive*-affirmation is realized simultaneously in terms of all of the previously mentioned four points, that is the individual per se, individuals in their mutuality and finally each individual in relation to the place [of absolute nothingness] itself. Thus from the beginning, Nishida's basic perspective had the structure of inverse

correspondence. Consequently, based on the letters we have reviewed up to this point, we have seen that Nishida was deeply interested in True Pure Land Buddhism at this time in his career. Although it can be said that he took advantage of the various opportunities Mudai's ideas and Tanabe's criticisms afforded him, he clearly and consciously realized the idea of *taisuru* implied in his own standpoint of the place [of absolute nothingness] in terms of the problem of correspondence or inverse correspondence. Similarly it cannot be denied that Nishida thought he would try to write about a "True Pure Land Buddhist Worldview" as a doctrine of religion. Yet in fact, his completed doctrine on religion is not simply exhausted by the True Pure Land Buddhist worldview. By relying on the standpoint of the logic of place, it grasps the essence of religion itself, including True Pure Land and Zen, Christianity and Buddhism, in a doctrine of religion broader than merely that of a True Pure Land perspective. In fact in his final essay, Nishida uses the term "inverse correspondence" to open up the essence of religion in general. In support of this claim, Nishida wrote:

> The self encounters God in an inverse correspondence only by dying. (NKZ 19, 396)

> We are always encountering the absolute one in terms of an inverse correspondence through self negation. (NKZ 19, 426)

Regarding this point, it seems clear that, in constructinghis doctrine of religion, Nishida was approaching religion by reflecting deeply on True Pure Land Buddhist faith. Yet by the time that this inquiry was completed, he had not stopped at articulating merely a "True Pure Land Buddhist worldview." He sought instead to discern religion's essence taking the logic of place as a basis which he had been constructing up to that point. This is clearly discernable from the emphasis he places in **"The Logic of Place and the Religious Worldview"**: "Religion, from the standpoint of philosophy at least, can be grasped only by means of the logic of place" (NKZ 19, 425).

In the above, we have considered the question of how the notion of "inverse correspondence" emerged in Nishida's thinking. Presuming that these considerations are not seriously in error, I hope that they will contribute something toward an understanding of Nishida's doctrine of religion as reflected in **"The Logic of Place and the Religious Worldview."**[12]

NOTES

[1] *Nishida Kitaro Zenshu* [The Collected Works of Kitaro Nishida] (Toyko: Iwanami, 1965-66), 1, 169 (hereafter NKZ, volume followed by page number, as here). [TN: See also *An Inquiry into the Good,* trans. Masao Abe and Christopher Ives (New Haven: Yale Univ. Press, 1990), p. 149.]

[a]Nishida's use of the term "place" *(basho)* is in need of some explanation. Three points are outstanding. First,

basho is related to the term *topos* in the *Timeaus* as "the matrix of all becoming." David Dilworth speaks of *basho* as a "latticing of *a priori* frameworks" into increasing levels of presuppositionlessness (see *Last Writings* [Honolulu: Univ. of Hawaii Press, 1987], p. 16). In this way, the most abstract level of reality is the "world" of physics. More concrete fields of reality are the biological and historical worlds. The most concrete universal, the logical space within which all reality is encompassed, is the "place of absolute nothingness."

Second, Nishida's concrete universal should not be confused with the "nothingness" which lies in contrast to beings as their negation (relative nothingness). The most concrete level of apriority cannot be placed over/against anything. The nothingness of the concrete universal is absolute in that after the relative being of all things is negated in the quest for the ground of reality itself, relative nothingness itself is negated to realize the most concrete universal experienced in the absolute affirmation of all things in their suchness. Thus the "place of absolute nothingness" constitutes the "where-in" of all reality, in which the individual thing shows itself in its concrete immediacy prior to the imposition of conceptualization and judgment.

Third, the "place of absolute nothingness" constitutes a "logic" not in the manner of an "objective" logic based on the principles of simple self-identity and non-contradiction, but rather in the Buddhist sense of the concrete structure of reality out of which arises the possibility of judgment based on these principles.

[b] Hajime Tanabe was Nishida's younger colleague in the philosophy department of Kyoto Imperial University. Despite their earlier collaboration, Tanabe gradually broke away from the course being charted by Nishida. Thus, in contrast to Nishida's use of the "logic of place," Tanabe throughout the 1930's was developing his "logic of species."

[2] *Tanabe Hajime Zenshu* [The Complete Works of Hajime Tanabe] (Tokyo: Chikuma Shobo, 1964), vol. 11, p. 492.

[3] See also Shizuteru Ueda, "Gyakutaio to byojotei" [Inverse Correspondence and the Ordinary Life] in *Riso* [Ideal] 537 (1978), 39.

[4] "The Logic of Place and the Religious Worldview" was drafted on February 4, 1945 and completed on February 14 of that same year. "The Philosophical Foundations of Mathematics" was drafted on December 23, 1944 and completed on January 25, 1945.

[c] Risaku Mudai (1890-1974), one of Nishida's early students, developed Nishida's philosophy through the study of phenomenology under Edmund Husserl. He was also interested in Pure Land Buddhism and created a unique philosophy under the influence of Shinran. Eventually he taught philosophy at Tokyo Bunri University.

[d] *Jinen honi*, a technical term taken from the Japanese Buddhist tradition and especially associated with the True Pure Land Buddhist thought of Shinran (1173-1262), denotes the ultimate "naturalness" of things, prior to the distortions of discriminating consciousness. Abe elsewhere has spoken of *jinen honi* as the "original naturalness underlying both man and nature" and as the "spontaneity" of things in themselves which arises in the overcoming of the cognitive dualism of subject and object. See Masao Abe, "Buddhism and Christianity as a Problem for Today," *Japanese Religions* 3 (1963), 28; *Zen and Western Thought* (Honolulu: Univ. of Hawaii Press, 1985), p. 150; and *The Emptying God,* eds. John Cobb and Christopher Ives (Maryknoll, NY: Orbis Press, 1990), p. 31.

[e] The expression *mugi no gi* is likewise taken from the Japanese Buddhist tradition and especially from the work of Shinran. It might be translated "no-self acting is true acting," suggesting that Amida's "other-power" is working in our own selfless faith in Amida. See Shinran's *Tanisho: A Shin Buddhist Classic,* trans. Taitetsu Unno (Honolulu: Buddhist Study Center Press, 1984), p. 16.

[5] Risaku Mudai, *Basho no ronrigaku* [The Logic of Place], p. 7. [TN: full bibliographic information unavailable.]

[6] Ibid., p. 9.

[7] What is more, according to Nishida's diary, after the writing of these letters, the writing of the above mentioned "Philosophical Foundations of Mathematics" was begun on December 23.

[8] For example, the letters addressed to Mudai and dated 6 January, Showa 21 (letter 2092), and 25 January (letter 2102). Besides these, there is the letter addressed to Keiji Nishitani (letter 2093).

[f] Honen (1133-1212), founder of the Pure Land School *(Jodoshu)* of Buddhism in Japan, should be distinguished from Shinran (1173-1262), founder of the True Pure Land School *(Jodoshinshu).* Although in his letters especially Nishida does not always take sufficient pains to distinguish these two movements, his treatment of the Buddhist notions of *jinen honi* and *mugi no gi* is from the perspective of Shinran and the True Pure Land School.

[g] The article *"Basho"* [Place], in which Nishida established his unique notion of "place," was written in 1926 and has been included in NKZ 4, 208-89.

[h] This verb and the compounds formed using this Chinese character can be rendered in English in a multitude of ways depending on context. Alternatively, it means "to face," "to confront," "to be in opposition to," or "to correspond to," etc.

[i] *Myogo* refers to the "Name of Amida," the principal Buddha in the True Pure Land Buddhist tradition. By

reciting the *nembutsu (namu-amida-butsu),* one is called by Amida in the very act of calling out the name of Amida.

[9] See note 4 above.

[j] Nishida's use of the phrase *soku-hi* [*sive-non*] raises the issue of the specifically Mahayana Buddhist character of Nishida's dialectics. Often the phrase is shortened to simply *soku,* as in the formula "affirmation-*soku*-negation." For this translation, the *soku* has generally been rendered with the Latin conjunction *sive,* following Jan Van Bragt's translation of Keiji Nishitani's *Religion and Nothingness* (Berkeley: Univ. of California Press, 1982). When placed between two contradictory concepts, as in Abe's formula"affirmation-*sive*-negation," the intention is to overcome the logical impertinence of the contradiction by returning to the "place" out of which the opposing concepts are realized as such in disclosing their true reality.

[k] The differences between Tanabe and Nishida, whose philosophies together form the logical foundation of the Kyoto school, are too subtle and complex by far to summarize here. Tanabe held that Nishida's notion of an intuition into the "place" of absolute nothingness inevitably decays into a philosophy of contemplation based on the innate intuitive powers of the subject ("self-power"). Instead of "place," Tanabe offered his logic of "absolute mediation" *(zettai baikai)* which arises only through the death and resurrection of the subject in the experience of existential transformation by "other-power."

[10] Tanabe Hajime, *Zangedo toshite no tetsugaku* (Tokyo: Iwanami, 1946), p. 3. [TN: For a translation of this work, *see Philosophy as Metanoetics,* trans. Takeuchi Yoshinori, foreword by James Heisig (Berkeley: Univ. of California Press, 1986).]

[11] For example, in this same work *(Zangedo toshite no tetsugaku),* there are the following passages: "The nothingness of self-identity exists already beyond mediation and approaches being. This is not the self-awakening of action. It is nothing but the content of contemplation. From such a standpoint, there is no metanoia. This standpoint is filled with an identity beyond the opposition of self and other. This is not the limit from which we speak of transformation" (p. 10); "To determine the direction of absolute transformation and to establish a cyclic development is simply not the dialectical expression of the absolute contradiction of self-identity. What is more, since this is the standpoint of contemplation, it cannot rise above mere equivalence and does not attain absolute mediation" (p. 11); and "Also, in regard to 'action-intuition,' this 'action' is simply an aesthetic expression-formation devoid of the axis of transformation through Other-power and does not ever get beyond the extension of intuition" (p. 12).

* In Indian thought (Hindu as well as Buddhist) a *kalpa* is an immensely long period of time. According to the

Sukhavativyuha Sutra, the Bodhisattva Dharmakara became the Amida Buddha after meditating for five kalpas.

[12]This essay is a revised and enlarged version of the introduction to the author's lecture, "The Problem of 'Inverse Correspondence' in Nishida's Philosophy," delivered on November 17, 1979 at the Kitaro Nishida Memorial Lecture in Kyoto. The author expresses his gratitude to Professor James Fredericks for his careful translation.

William Haver (essay date 1993)

SOURCE: "Thinking the Thought of That Which Is Strictly Speaking Unthinkable: On the Thematization of Alterity in Nishida-Philosophy," in *Human Studies,* Vol. 16, 1993, pp. 177-92.

[*In the following essay, Haver examines the notion of alterity, or otherness, in Nishida's works from the 1930s.*]

Any theoretical practice which would aspire both to identify itself as a practice and to be *in fact* a practice, a determinate historical and political intervention, must undertake rigorously to acknowledge its own non-transcendence, to theorize the limits of its enabling rationality. If it does not undertake that acknowledgment, any theoretical labor (or "philosophy") must resign itself to an ineffective and inconsequential transcendental subjectivity putatively situated outside of history. In order to acknowledge its non-transcendence and the limits of its enabling rationality, it must have some sense of that non-sense which exceeds or is situated "beyond" its own proper limits; it must, that is to say, produce the concept of otherness or alterity. And we know that a very large literature testifies, in one way or another, to the dangers which wait upon any attempt to conceive alterity: either the difference of that alterity will be construed as an inchoate rationality (as the "pre-modern," for example, which is destined to be rationalized or modernized) or that alterity will be construed as the negative image or mask of an essential similitude. In any case, the radical alterity of the other, that difference which makes the other in fact other to any rationality's proper identity, is reduced to the negative and therefore subsidiary term of a binary opposition. If otherness is to be in fact other, then that otherness can only be said to be neither the same nor different and both the same and different, for nothing authorizes one to exclude similitude from the possibilities of the unknown otherness of the other. "Alterity," therefore, cannot merely be thematized as the negative term of a binary opposition, defined only by its exclusion from the proper identity of what counts as rationality; it must, like the zero, "infinity" or "contradiction," figure in thinking as the *thought of* a specific resistance to rationality, as that which for a determinate rationality resists appropriation or rationalization absolutely.

For any theoretical practice or philosophy, alterity or otherness can therefore never be merely a "category" or a "concept" in the usual acceptances of those terms, because categories and concepts are, precisely, categories and concepts which *belong to* the properly rational understanding. Alterity can only be thought then as the limit (or indeed, an impossibility) of categorization and conceptualization, but also as the sole condition of possibilityfor categorization and conceptualization: no logic of non-contradiction is possible without the enabling thought of contradiction. It is not merely as the "outside" of thought that alterity imposes a limit, but as the innermost possibility for coherence that alterity (the thought of the unthinkable) operates. But how then is it possible to think at all if one thinks that thought, how is it possible to "do" philosophy (or theory) in the wake of that thought which entirely disrupts any thought of philosophy as the aspiration to a possible universal coherence?

The entire textual production of Nishida Kitaro (1870-1945), widely regarded as the major philosophical figure on the Japanese intellectual scene in the twentieth century, can be read to be centrally concerned with this and related questions in their manifold dimensions. Among these questions, which are at once theoretical and practical (and in that conjunction, political), is the question of what a "properly philosophical" text should be. Which enjoins upon Nishida's readers the consequent question of what an appropriate reading, which would respect the specific discursive strategies of a textual practice, might be. In this paper, I undertake a reading of the thematization of alterity in certain of Nishida's texts from the early thirties; because this reading is no more than a necessary first gesture, I follow in large part the usual common sense procedures of paraphrasis, synopsis and therefore synthesis. Because such procedures assume texts to be at least ideally entirely coherent, non-contradictory expressions of a putative totality denominated the thought ("Nishida-philosophy"), they enforce certain exclusions, possibilities and necessities. But because Nishida-philosophy, as theoretical *practice,* situates philosophy "itself" in critical jeopardy, and because such a practice, although it is possessed of a certain systematicity, does not constitute a philosophical system construed as a fully rational, entirely coherent closure—because it thematizes the resistance to categorization and conceptualization of "alterity"—and because it operates, rather, as a disjunct (that is to say non-linear, non-narrative) series of discontinuities organized around an equally discontinuous series of contradictions, it follows, then, that any representation of such a practice which would obscure those discontinuities and aporiae through paraphrasis, synopsis, synthesis and the judgment of the understanding, essentially rejects the critical possibility of the *practice* of Nishida-philosophy: the text fights back. But this acknowledgment is one, perhaps the sole, possibility for the thematization of alterity in our own practices.

The preface which Nishida provided in 1932 for the essays which comprise *Mu no jikakuteki gentei* [*The Self-Aware Determination of Radical Negativity*] opens with the insistence that

> At the base of what is thought as actuality [*jitsuzai*],there must be that which is thought to be utterly irrational [*higoriteki*]. What is merely rational is not actuality. But how the irrational, even though it is irrational, can be thought must be clarified. In the structure itself of our logical intellection there must be a reason which is the condition of possibility for one to say that the irrational can be thought. [Or], if one says that the irrational cannot be thought, the reason which makes it possible to say that must be clarified. To speak of that which cannot be thought is already a thinking: that fact itself must be a contradiction (1932a:6).

Actuality as such and in itself—as the Real—is literally unthinkable from any rationalist perspective, yet we are capable of positing actuality or the Real precisely *as* that which is unthinkable, precisely *as* the irrational. The contradiction lies in the fact that rationality is capable of positing an "outside" of rationality, its Other; if we cannot think the unthinkable, we can posit the limit of the thinkable, we can think the unthinkability of what is strictly speaking unthinkable. We cannot therefore either merely "bracket" actuality or the Real as Kantian noumenon or merely posit actuality as the self-alienation of Reason, the phenomenal alterity which constitutes the phenomenality of the Real as Reason's Other, an actuality assured of its restoration or salvation in the *Aufhebung* of the Hegelian dialectic. In other words, we must read Nishida to say, "contradiction" (presumptively, the unthinkable) is not merely the limit of rationality, that which divides the rational from the irrational, but is moreover, *as* the limit of rationality, the condition of possibility *for* rationality.

Nishida recognized that Hegel must be acknowledged to have accounted himself a "materialist," as it were, in contradistinction to Kantian idealism; Hegelian logic would thereby acknowledge contradiction not only as limit, but also as logic's condition of possibility. Yet Hegel, of course, acknowledged the materiality of phenomenal actuality only to negate that actuality in the *Aufhebung* and thereby to preserve that actuality—as negated actuality—in ideality. Concomitantly, contradiction in the Hegelian dialectic is merely a contradiction destined to be resolved in the encompassing rationality engendered in and by the *Aufhebung.* Thus, Hegelian logic remains, in spite of various claims made on its behalf, a logic of the positivity of the ob-ject (*taisho: Gegen-stand,* that which is taken to be presented or given to consciousness and therefore presumptively "is," *as* object, present *to* consciousness), a logic of the ultimately ontological positivity of the subject of predication (*shugo*), a logic of the positivity of the noema. It therefore remains a logic which cannot take account of that which refuses ob-jectification, that which is pre-predicative or radically apredicative, or of the act of noesis. Hegelian logic therefore can only conceive being, or indeed the Being of beings, as continuity, contradiction as alienation or error, materiality as the (inverse) positivity of (self-alienated) ideality (1931a). The Hegelian dialectic cannot, that is to say, conceive negation as other than in *symmetrical* opposition to positivity; it cannot conceive negation as a primordially *asymmetrical* radical negativity *(mu)* or alterity, as Other. At issue for Nishida are questions concerning radical negativity (historicity and death), the status of contradiction, the status of the "individual thing" *(kobutsu)* in relation to predication (as the particular vis-à-vis the universal, or as Aristotelian *hypokumeinon,* but also as a singularity which resists absolutely subsumption within universals), time and temporality, limits and determinations *(gentei)* and desire.

One of the fundamental points of departure for inquiry, then, will be the putative mutual exclusivity of life, as the continuity of being, to death, as that absolute loss which is historicity, the guarantee that all continuity must be thought as the continuity of discontinuities. This relation, which is also the very impossibility of relationality, is marked throughout the later essays of *Mu no jikakuteki gentei* (particularly in **"Watakushi to nanji"** [**"I and thou"**] [1932d]) with the term *soku*. The term *soku* is used throughout in the formulation *"sei soku shi"*: "life *soku* death" and also, perhaps more fundamentally, as "being born *soku* dying." Among the many connotations which this usage evokes is the possibility that it does indeed mark a necessary co-incidence of oppositions. But this reading of itself specifies neither the nature of that coincidence nor the necessity for that coincidence; it does not yet specify that coincidence as *contradiction,* both relation and non-relation. If we read the *soku* as *"qua,"* according to another possibility, then we are confronted with the implied copula of the *qua.* Certainly, were it possible to posit an exclusively predicative copula, we might read "death" as the predicate of "life" when "life" is equated with being. But it is only as a conditioned being, as what Lacan called a subject, that "I" can make death *my* project, a projected (and therefore for the "I" an entirely unknowable) predicate of my subjectivity. But in that case the "I" is entirely enveloped in the orders which constitute "my" subjectivity as, in fact, "mine." Furthermore, even if the "I" conceives of death as implacable fatality, *for the "I"* that *eventual* encounter can only be structured within delay or deferral, as a perpetually postponed absence. As Bakhtin pointed out, my ownmost death is precisely that which can never belong to anyone at all. In any case, as Nishida had argued long before, the predicative copula cannot be divorced from the existential copula (1926:229ff.); and if it is the existential copula which expresses the relation of life to death, then the *soku* is no more than a *consolation,* for it would maintain that there is no difference between life and death. A further possibility is that the *soku* expresses a parallel relation of two entities to a third, accordingto the scheme "as A is to C, so B is to C." Thus: as living or being born *(sei)* is to Life *(seimei),* so death or dying *(shi)* is to Life. This of course does not "solve" our problem, but it does complicate it in a particularly fruitful way, for we now know that we are dealing with three rather than two "unknowns," *and that therefore the relation of A to B, living to dying, is not a direct relation but one of parallel disjunction.* And this disjunction is in the first instance a "temporal relation." Tentatively, there-

fore, we shall read *sei soku shi* as "the disjunct simultaneity of living and dying, of being born and dying," of presence and absence. Can this reading be supported?

> It is usually thought that we are born into and go towards death within something like an "absolute time" which flows from an infinite past to an infinite future. However . . . "true time" cannot be thought on the basis of such a way of thinking. Time must begin from the fact that the immediate present sets a limit to or determines the immediate present because the self *[jiko]* sets a limit to or determines the self; where there is the self of each person, there must be a time particular to each self. The ego *[ware]* is not within time, but time which is within the ego: "absolute time" is no more than that which has been thought (1931b:187).

What is at stake for Nishida in this critique of "absolute time" is the notion of time as a *given* consecutive linearity. In *Hataraku mono kara miru mono e* [*From the Acting to the Seeing*], Nishida had argued that such a conception of time was not only misleading, but that it allowed no space for freedom; thus he argued that a more nearly appropriate image for the representation of time than a straight line (upon which all points are determined) would be a curved line upon which every point is *determinative* (1924:79-96). In order to sustain his critique, Nishida repeatedly turned to the celebrated passage in Augustine's *Confessions* which is animated by the observation that we know what time is until such time as we attempt to say or think what time is; until we attempt to define and thus delimit time for the purposes of thinking. Following Augustine, Nishida noted that we can only *know* "past," "present" and "future" from within the immediate present, as *centered (chushin to shite)* within the immediate present. Past and future in themselves and as such are always necessarily *absent,* inaccessible. Past and future are always extinguished *(kesareta)* within the immediate present. It is only *memory* within the immediate present which constitutes the "past" as (ideal) ob-ject; it is only *anticipation* within the immediate present, the adumbration of what has not yet come, which constitutes the "future" as an equally ideal ob-ject (1931b:182). And if past and future can themselves only be thought within the immediate present, they can offer no perspective from which to set a limit to or todetermine the immediate present. Furthermore, it is by virtue of its very immediacy that the immediate present can never be susceptible to capture *(tsukami):* "When the immediate present as such is captured, it is already not the immediate present" (1931b:185). Because we can never alienate ourselves from the immediate present, the immediate present can never become an ob-ject other to ourselves, and is therefore not that which can be "captured" within the protocols of rationality which determine our thinking. The immediate present is in this sense always recessive, essentially *absent*. This elusiveness of the "immediate present" thereby becomes unthinkable, a contradiction. And by the same token, this elusiveness cannot be merely a predicated *characteristic* of the "immediate present" construed as an object of knowledge. That is to say, the immediate present is that which knowledge is always fated to miss, the site of an inevitable *méconnaissance:*

> Where the immediate present sets a limit to or determines the immediate present itself, there is the self; where the self sets a limit to or determines the self itself, there is the immediate present; that which comes from an infinite past comes to here; that which goes forth to an infinite future goes forth from here; it is possible to think that it is here that an infinite past is extinguished, that it is here that an infinite future begins. In the sense that it extinguishes and envelops the past, it may be considered reason; in the sense that it inaugurates the future it may be considered free will—but in the sense of setting a limit to or determining the self itself without there being that which sets a limit or determines, it can be thought to be absolutely irrational (1931b:190-191).

This irrationality, which denies only the adequacy of rationality to the representation of the whole, marks, rather, the fundamental incoherence of our experience of the materiality of the concrete, which can after all only be posited as a materiality which obtains in an immediate present (and which is thereby no longer an "experience" in the traditional philosophical sense of the term): one cannot speak of the materiality of the past *as such,* least of all of the materiality of the future *as such.* We are only able to *posit* a concrete existing in a hypothetically previous or future immediate present. It is precisely this act of the *hypothesis* of a previous or future immediate present which calls forth the notion of historicity, as *essential* and therefore *undetermined* difference over "time." It is the body—the living, dying body—which is the guarantee of our confrontation with the materiality of the concrete. Both mindful (*seishinteki*) and physical, the body, because it can exist no where but in the immediate present, is inalienable from the unmediated presence of its experience; even the body which is said to be "unconscious" is subject to its own materiality. But, *at the same time,* because the immediate present cannot be "captured" within the orders of rationality, the body is always *absent, recessive.* The body, therefore, is the *site* of the contradiction of the immediate present. And because the body is the site of contradiction, it is a historical body; it is this very historicity of the body which belies the concept of "time" as a unilinear progression (1931b:194-196, 201-202; cf. 1932b:262-268). So it is not for nothing that the above quotation is couched in the metaphor of a topography, for the fact that the immediate present sets a limit to the immediate present itself is the fact that the immediate present, the locus of a rupture in "time," is the *chora* or *topos* of radical negativity (*mu no basho*) (1931b:186, 234). It is what the later Nishida would term "historical space" (*rekishiteki kukan*), that which is *both* the ground of any possible conception or awareness of history (because it is the site of materiality, difference and the effective event—discontinuity) and *also* that which gives the lie to any common sense conception of historical consciousness as the unproblematic recuperation of a temporal totality into the rationality of the understanding. In other words, it is both the enabling condition of possibility for "historical consciousness" *and* that alterity (difference, spacing, syncope) which guarantees that "historical consciousness" does not itself transcend the depredations of historicity.

In using the term "incoherence" to reproduce certain aspects of the notion of the *topos* of radical negativity and of the "immediate present," which is to say of the Real, we mean to denominate not only the lack specific to knowledge ("truth") but also, and even more central to the concerns of this essay, the fact that the totality (according to whatever reading of the term) *does not cohere:* the totality is always an untotalizable totality; the totality is *virtual,* history is present only in its effects. Or, as Nishida quoted Pascal, the "totality" (God in Pascal) is "une sphère infinie dont le centre est partout, la circonférence nulle part" (1931b:187; French in Nishida's text). This metaphor of decentering denominates a contradiction, and it is *as* a contradiction that it prefigures the discursive field of Nishida's articulation of the personal (*jinkaku*) as well as of the social. (In fact, it is that very decentering which defines the "personal" which *is* the social; thus it will be the case that the non-relating relation of temporality will be at the same time the non-relating relation of the social. The historico-social relation is inseparable.) What is important for us here is that it is his conception of the "immediate present" which *enables* this decentering.

Has then the *soku,* as the sign of that decentering which is the extinction of "time" in the rupture of the immediate present, become the name for a radical dispersion; has it become only the emblem of an entropy—which would thereby signal an utterly *ineffective* historical quiescence? Is this decentering the mere repetition of an infinite process devoid of all effectivity rather than the historicity of production, which would imply at least the possibility of effectivity (as an acting upon the "world")? It would hardly seem so. For it is only *because* of this decentering engendered in the rupture of the instant (*shunkan*) that historical effectivity might be at all *possible,* that our mere activity might come to bear the name of action: "It is only when we truly wager ourselves (*isshin*), it is only when we truly commit ourselves, that we touch upon the true instant" (1932b:290). In a sense, of course, this wager is no wager at all; to wager one's very being, one's *isshin,* to raise the stakes to the level of life and death, is to wager beyond all "economic" rationality: it is a wager which can only be lost. This is "being-absolute-for." Here, "being-absolute-for," as "being-absolute-for-death," is not only essentially different from a "desire for death," it is antithetical to the desire for death because the desire for death is essentially a desire for the closure of identity. "Being-absolute-for" is the enactment of a rupture, a refusal of closure and of identity—in the interest of sustaining the possibility for action, a possibility which Nishida called freedom. And this being-absolute-for can only transpire in the instant because it is only in the instant that the self as constituted in memory (the past) and in aspiration (the future) is lost. It would be quite possible to read into Nishida at this point the vitalism of an anarchism or, indeed, the violence of a religious terrorism. Save that the "instant" specifies a *mutuality* of life and death, memory and forgetting, self and other, a mutuality which Nishida called the "dialectic." (It must nevertheless be emphasized that this conception of a dialectical relation is at all times a refusal of *closure.*) For although the relation among various instants is in some sense aleatoric—a "leaping" *(hiyaku),* a "discontinuity" *(hirenzoku),* a disjunction *(bunri)* (1931c:265)—and therefore is not a "relation" at all, it is nevertheless the case that the self is not merely a "concrete universal," but a "leaping unity" *(hiyakuteki toitsu),* a "continuity of discontinuity" *(hirenzoku no renzoku)* (1931c:283).

And it is so insofar as it is compounded of *both* memory and forgetting. Reading Augustine, Nishida wrote that "it is not only that we remember that we remember, that memory too is within memory, but it can be said that forgetting also is within memory" (1931b:229). The insight that forgetting is within memory, that both memory and forgetting are situated in that immediate present which is irretrievably absent to consciousness and which is therefore the presence of absence, and that the relation between memory and forgetting is therefore one of disjunct simultaneity, is a fundamentally important insight. For, although it is readily apparent that memory is the condition of possibility for forgetting, it is perhaps less apparent that forgetting isconversely the condition of possibility for memory. For what this formulation suggests is that the questions of "disjunct simultaneity," of the "immediate present," and of "repetition" are in fact questions concerning the status of predication and the status of the subject of predication, the individual thing as the Aristotelian *hypokumeinon* (that which can be the subject of predication, but which can never be the predicate of anything else). Much is implied here.

An investigation of the status of the individual thing, Nishida was to write in a 1939 preface to the third volume of his philosophical essays, had been one of the constant occupations of his philosophical practice (1939:3-7). So much is this the case that any investigation which would be even provisionally adequate to Nishida's mediations on the individual thing would be a major study in itself. Here we can only suggest one or two aspects of the topic necessary to the present discussion, a stricture which will apply with equal stringency to our reading of Nishida's reflections on predication. The individual thing in its materiality, in itself and as such, can only be located in the present absence of the immediate present; its being is therefore contradictory. It is this ontic being of the individual thing which subverts the putative transparency of the copula and demands that Being "itself" always be written *sous rature.* But there is another sense in which the individual thing is possessed of "absolute contradictory self-identity" *(zettai mujunteki jiko doitsu).* For, as Nishida was to write in an essay of 1941,

> The individual thing must be absolutely that which

determines or sets a limit to the self itself from within the self. The monad has no windows. But one individual thing alone is no individual thing. An individual thing is an individual thing because it opposes [other] individual things. An individual thing is an individual thing because it mediates the world, that is, it is as an individual thing of the world that the individual thing is an individual thing. The individual thing must therefore be absolutely contradictory being (1941:281).

That separation which is the very individuality or singularity of the individual thing is the absolute determination of the individual thing; those limits which circumscribe the being of the individual thing and mark its utter irreplaceability must be immanent within the interiority of the individual thing: "my death," for example. Yet, *at the same time,* the individual thing can only be determined or defined in terms of that which it is not, in its absolute separation *from* everything else, from everything which is exterior to it. In this respect, it cannot possibly be self-determinative, it can only be posited in a relationality to its outside; thus its absolute difference is erased. The contradiction which is the individual thing thus subverts thestraightforward opposition of inside to outside, interiority to exteriority.

As such and in itself, the individual thing in its singularity therefore refuses absolutely all predication, above all that of ontological Being, and all denomination in any referential signifying system or practice: as such and in itself, the individual thing bears no name, least of all that of "individual thing." A short fiction by Jorge Luis Borges, "Funes the Memorious," will perhaps make explicit the conundrum of the "individual thing" in relation to the question of memory and forgetting:

> Locke, in the seventeenth century, postulated (and rejected) an impossible language in which each individual thing, each stone, each bird and each branch, would have its own name; Funes once projected an analogous language, but discarded it because it seemed too general to him, too ambiguous. In fact, Funes remembered not only every leaf of every tree of every wood, but also every one of the times he had perceived or imagined it . . .

> With no effort, he had learned English, French, Portuguese and Latin. I suspect, however, that he was not very capable of thought. To think is to forget differences, generalize, make abstractions. In the teeming world of Funes, there were only details, almost immediate in their presence . . .

> Ireneo Funes died in 1889, of congestion of the lungs (Borges 1964:65-66).

But of course, if the logic of that fabulous world which could be signified only by an infinity of proper names (the "proper" of each individual thing), a world without forgetting, without loss, without death, which was the world of Ireneo Funes, were forced to its limit, the fable would become a teratology because not only thought but the referential signifying systems or practices which sustain thought would be impossible. What Borges would have envisioned in that case would have been the teratology of psychosis, the name become proper only to the monstrous. It is precisely in forgetting the luminosity of the Real that memory becomes possible; memory, so-called, cannot be therefore an unproblematic continuity. Rather, it can only be a continuity of discontinuities. Therein lies the alterity which haunts all signification, all discourse, all thought. The individual thing, then, is the site where signification exhausts itself in an infinite congestion of the proper, the site where *this* thing, in itself and as such, drives referential signification to the absolute limit of its possibility. In this sense naming, predication, thetic articulation, and indeed memory, would erase alterity and difference, and would represent the resolution of thatcontradiction which "is" being. Referential signification therefore is unavoidably error and *méconnaissance,* but error and *méconnaissance* as the condition of possibility for all communication; indeed, for signification itself.

But if referential signification *occludes* the incommensurability of the *ipse,* at the same time it marks the *passages* of difference, alterity and contradiction. (Difference, alterity and contradiction can of course only be marked as passages—albeit passages to no where because they are not ontological states but the very rupture between the ontic and the ontological; it is this rupture which implies both difference and passage which is marked, we think, in Derrida's deployment of the term *différance* (Derrida 1982:1-27). Now this marking is neither a naming nor denotation, nor can it be either sign or representation, for what is marked is precisely an absence. That which both occludes the contradiction of the being of the individual thing and yet marks the passage of the incommensurability of difference, alterity and contradiction we shall follow (and Levinas, among others) in calling the trace *(konseki):* the trace always already will have been the "trace of the Other" according to the vocabulary of Levinas. The trace of the incommensurable Other, in its very marking of the "individual thing" in memory, thereby marks the passage of desire and of passion. It is banal, but none the less indicative, to remark that remembered passions and recollected desires are at best "pale reflections" or "faded remembrances" of desire, mementos of the death of that passionate action which enacts the separation of the individual thing; were they not such unsatisfactory souvenirs of passion we might legitimately speak of the satisfaction of desire. Moreover, if memory were somehow adequate to the passion which it remembers, if there were no loss in memory, we would soon be surfeited in *jouissance:* repetition itself would be impossible. Can memory represent and thereby represent passion? Perhaps. But in any case, memory can never "re-presence" the past: "History does not re-presence [*saigen*] the past; it is the *Gleichnis* of all that has been" (1940:145). We note, therefore, that memory marks—with traces—the death of the passionate action of the desiring self, a death which we have forgotten.

Thus, memory brings together heterogeneous "instants" into a "unity of disunity," a "disjunct unity," of the ego of one instant and the ego of another instant. But these disparate egos can *only* be seen as disparate if they are seen (remembered) as ob-jects other to the ego which in fact brings them together; and they can only be seen as other on the basis of that negation of the self which is called forgetting. Memory not only includes forgetting, but depends upon it: the self must be dismembered if it is to be remembered (1940:211-19). This would seem to suggest, then, that remembering establishes the self as the *seen* self (that is, as the noematic self) in what Lacan called the Imaginary; this ob-jectified selfthus belongs to the realm of being *(yu).* It is seen there by the seeing self (that is, by the noetic self), the acting desiring self which belongs to the transitivity of radical negativity *(mu)* (1940:195). But insofar as the only seen self which can possibly be seen to be absolutely self-identical, absolutely coherent, is the *dead* self, the completely ob-jectified self of being is, in fact, dead. It is therefore only an apparent paradox that the self of radical negativity, in the nugatory act of forgetting, affirms life, and that the seen ob-jectified self is the "negation" of that affirmation. It is for this reason that only man can know death, that only man can commit suicide (1936:287, 277). It is in the split between the noematic self and the noetic self that it is entirely logical to speak of the affirmation of negation and the negation of affirmation. The disjunct simultaneity marked by the *soku* is a fundamental split in the self, a rupture which enables the self to re-produce its self within memory. But it is not only the self which sees the self, of course, for the self is at all times seen by the other (most especially, of course, when it sees itself): the *soku* thereby discloses the sociality which constitutes the "I" and the "Thou."

Desire *(yokkyu, yokubo, nozomi),* Nishida argued, is never to be conflated with the fulfillment of the demands imposed by biological necessity. The desire for water is never to be conflated with the body's need for H2O; sexual desire is not a response to the necessity of perpetuating the species. Thus, we may legitimately speak not only of sexual desire, but also of the desire for knowledge, the desire for fame, the desire to produce an *oeuvre.* But in all cases, desire is always a desire *for* an ob-ject, an ob-ject which is hypostatized as a *thing.* Furthermore, because the ob-ject-things of desire are fundamentally the ob-ject-things of our concern or care *(kanshin),* all ob-jects of knowledge (ob-jects which in fact constitute that knowledge as such) are also ob-jects of desire. In Nishida, desire is always in excess of biological necessity, which means that no thing is itself ever sufficient to satisfy desire permanently. Desire is essentially insatiable, aroused ever anew from the ashes of its satisfaction: "Desire is extinguished on the basis of its satisfaction; satisfaction again gives birth to desire: desire must be dialectical being" (1932b:270; cf. 260-261). Because desire is never finally satisfied by the ob-ject-thing which is desired, desire itself cannot be an effect of the existence of desirable things, but must rather be that which calls things, in their specification *as things,* into being. Thus, desire does not merely express the self, but actualizes the self as such (that is, affirms the self to be the self of desire, both desiring and desired self). Desire actualizes the self because desire underlies the acting, noetic self which constitutes as noematic ob-jects those ob-jects which are desired. Thus the acting (desiring, noetic) self, the self of discontinuity, seeks, through the act of constituting the noematic self, toestablish that noematic self as continuity: "desire seeks to sustain the continuity of the self," discontinuity seeks continuity (1932b:279; cf. 269). What is desired in the desire for the self is that self which is, precisely, a self-identity which transcends discontinuity. Insofar as the only possible condition of absolute self-identity (when the self, that is, is entirely identical to its ob-jectivity) is death, one of the two aspects which constitute the "contradiction of the *being* of the self" is a desire for that aspect which is absolute death. The other aspect of the self is that which is absolute life. The relation is one of disjunct simultaneity, thus dialectical (1931b:200; cf. 1932c:342). Desire, then, is desire for an ob-ject-thing, most fundamentally desire for the ob-jectification of the (noematic) self *as* thing; it is a desire for death. Thus it would seem that for Nishida desire, even though it is essentially insatiable, never recognizes its own insatiability; paradoxically, it always seeks satiety ever anew; it seeks stasis, identity, continuity and the closure which is the "economic" adequacy characteristic of what Freud called the "pleasure principle."

Love (*ai,* a term which Nishida later rejected, on the basis of its susceptibility to a certain "sentimentalism" in favor of *agape*) is essentially different from desire. Whereas the ob-ject towards which desire is directed is always a *thing* (and can include other human beings among its ob-jects when they are reduced to the status of mere things), the ob-ject towards which love is directed, is always another *person.* Love can obtain only between one person and an other and thus differs from desire as *eros* differs from *agape.* Because love is not directed towards a thing, or towards another person *as* thing, it does not seek the satiety which the thing is thought to provide desire. Love, therefore, is in no way bound by the economic rationality of the "pleasure principle," and is, in fact, a transgression of that presumptive adequacy. It would seem to follow that love is at all times a refusal of stasis, continuity and the closure imposed by *identity,* most particularly by the identity imposed by the unquestioned acceptance of the mortuary self of the neoma. Thus, too, "love" becomes the mark of a non-relating relation, the mark of the aporiae of intersubjectivity. It is in this sense that loving is a negation of the "self." At the same time, love is respect *(kei)* for the alterity of the other, an alterity which guarantees that the other also is not the merely mortuary identity of a "self." This respect is therefore directed towards the other's constituting alterity, a constituting alterity which Nishida termed the personal *(jinkaku).* Love, then, is established in difference, the ruptures and discontinuities of alterity, *not* in the *fusion* of "self" and "other": not only is the I always other to its "self," but the Thou is always other to the

"self" of the Thou (1932b:272-278). Because one loves on behalf of no value *(kachi)* whatsoever (1932c:319), "love" is the name for an *absolute* commitment to a decentering, toreproduction, to that alterity which constitutes the personal of the other; an absolute commitment to that *negation* of the "self" which Nishida termed the social—and which can only be based upon the *recognition* of the personal of the other.

Drawing his metaphor from chemistry, Nishida wrote that the personal is the "sublimated body" *(shoka serareta shintai)* (1932b:268). Certainly, this can be read to suggest that the personal is in some sense a "spiritual aura" as a "higher level" which the human being attains. But it is *also* a metaphor of decentering; for whatever "sublimation" means in a technical sense to the chemist, the image of the process of change from solid to liquid to gas is one of dispersion, of a loss of center. And indeed, Nishida took pains to refuse any "spiritual" reading of his notion of the person:

> It is thought that the personal self is our spiritual self which throws off the shackles of the body. But what we are thinking as the personal must be utterly like an individual thing; there must be an unreachable irrational something at the heart of the personal: without the body, there is no "personal." That which is thought as irrational in the depths of our bodies must, to the furthest extent, possess both the sense of killing us, of negating us, and of affirming us, of giving birth to us (1932d:375).

For Nishida, the body, because it is the guarantee of our confrontation with temporal incoherence (insofar as it is the locus of that continuity of discontinuity which belies any notion of the self as a unilinear continuity of consciousness) is thereby the guarantee that notions of self and other (or interiority and exteriority) are essentially confounded: "The self-awareness of our personal selves is established on the basis of seeing the absolute other within the self, on the basis of seeing the self in the absolute other" (1932a:9). Moreover, to say that one *sees* the absolute other in the self is to say that the absolute other *is* the self. More precisely, to *see* the absolute other within the self is the act of noetic determination; to say that the absolute other *is* the self is the noematic act of determination (1932d:387). In what sense can the absolute other *be* the self and still be absolutely other? The personal I *(watakushi)* of yesterday and the I of today constitute an alterity; for the I of today the I of yesterday is the Thou *(nanji);* for the I of yesterday the I of today is the Thou; the relation between the I and the I which is the Thou is a relation of discontinuity, a dialectic in which each sets limits to and determines the other, constitutes the other as an exteriority, as different, as in fact Other (1932d:415). It is here that Nishida recognizes that the I comes into being through the word of the other. It is here that what Nishida called a dialectic becomes what readers of Bakhtin will recognize as the *dialogic.* And this dialectical or dialogical relation is not a relation of a self and an other who subsequently enter into an "intersubjective" relation; rather, it is within, *and as an effect of,* the dialectic that the alterity of self and other is constituted. This is to insist on the absolute primacy of the social in the determination or the setting of limits to, both the I and the Thou. The social is therefore the space of conflict and contestation which establishes an inevitable and necessary possibility for *méconnaissance* between the I and the Thou; without that possibility of *méconnaissance,* the I and the Thou could never be articulated as other to themselves:

> What we call a true self-awareness which is thought to see the absolute other within the self itself must be social. It must be founded upon the spatial relation of person and person . . . The I and the Thou stand in a mutually dialectical relation. Therefore the I knows the Thou according to the echo of the personal action of the I, the Thou knows the I according to the echo of the personal action of the Thou . . . [I]t is on the basis of the response of action and action that the I and the Thou know each other . . . The I knows the Thou because the Thou responds to the I; the Thou knows the I because the I responds to the Thou . . . The I does not know the Thou on the basis of entering into the Thou's feelings; the I knows the Thou according to the fact that the personal of the I responds directly to the personal of the Thou. *The I knows the Thou more on the basis of mutual conflict with the Thou than through sympathy.* One can say, then, that it is on the basis of such responses that the I knows the Thou, the Thou knows the I; and, *that the I cannot know the I without the responses of the Thou; the Thou cannot know the Thou without the responses of the I* . . . The relation between person and person must be one of dialogue *(hanashi-au),* one of mutual response (1932d:391-93; emphases added).

Some few pages later Nishida specified the dialogic relation as one of *interpellation,* of hailing *(yobikake, yobigoe)* (1932d:397-399). The I comes to know the I because it is hailed not only by the Thou, but by the *thing* as well: the I is literally *called to* "subjectivity," and that call can come only in languages, both verbal and nonverbal (including social customs and mores) (1930:13-14; cf. 1932d:341). We know who we think we are "in our being" because we have been hailed as such; we therefore differentiate our "selves" from the other in an enunciative act of interpellation which is the process by which we variously give coherence or "*make* sense" of the radical incoherence of the totality. And if it is the case that the differentiation of self and other is an effect of interpellation, which is a kind of *naming,* but is also an *acting,* then the alterity of those who will become master and slave according to some readings of the Hegelian text is a *precondition* necessary to begin the struggle of life and death: "the pact," as Lacan wrote, "is everywhere anterior to the violence before perpetuating it" (Lacan 1977:308). But the personalI is an I who recognizes its own founding alterity, an I who realizes its fundamental dependence upon being hailed by the other *in order to* posit the I in opposition to the Thou, *in order to* posit the mutual exclusivity of life and death. The I

therefore recognizes that the terms which *enable* the instauration of the struggle for pure prestige are not, in fact, mutually exclusive; and this is a recognition which will have come only within a certain delay for those who will be master and slave. It is in *this* sense that the relation between the I and the Thou is one of conflict and contestation, certainly; but, or perhaps *thereby,* it is a relation of love or *agape*—a non-relating relation which is other to the usual courses of intersubjectivity—rather than one of power. For, finally, this is a recognition that the historico-social is a plurivocity, and as such is the site of an unsurpassable heterogeneity.

The years between Nishida's retirement from Kyoto Imperial University in the early thirties until his death in 1945 were the most fecund in terms of his textual production. The thematization of alterity in that body of work moves in a number of quite different, contradictory directions. The work of the period, for example, encompassed at once a sustained and powerful reading of Marx and Lenin (one which was highly critical of Lukàcs and "Western Marxism," as well as a defense of the statist ideology of the Emperor-system. The questions raised by these texts demand an attention which they are just beginning to receive. Yet early and late, one thing seems to remain constant: the attempt to thematize alterity and thereby to begin to think the theoretical, philosophical enterprise as a *practice* such as would "wager life and death" (1944:147), an intervention in the conjuncture of the historico-social world. Then, as in the most recent work in critical theory, what has been at issue is the attempt to open a space for critique which might open upon the possibility for politicality as such—a possibility which, needless to say, has yet to be brought into being. For we do not yet know what the political might be: Nishida's texts, as do our own, belong to the prehistory of the political.

WORKS CITED

Borges, J. L. (1964). Funes the memorious. Trans. J. E. Irby. In D. A. Yates and J. E. Irby (Eds.), *Selected stories and other writings.* New York: New Directions.

Derrida, J. (1982). *Margins of philosophy.* Trans. A. Bass. Chicago: University of Chicago Press.

Lacan, J. (1977). *Ecrits: A selection.* Trans. A. Sheridan. New York: Norton. Nishida Kitaro.

All citations are to the *Nishida Kitaro zenshu.* Ed. Abe Yoshishige et al. 2nd ed. 19 vols. Tokyo: Iwanami, 1965-1966.

(1924). *Naibu chikaku ni tsuite. NKz* 4:76-134.

(1926). *Basho. NKz* 4:208-289.

(1929). *Ippansha no jikakuteki taikei. NKz* 5.

(1930). *Hyogenteki jiko no jiko gentei. NKz* 6:13-85.

(1931a). *Watakushi no tachiba kara mita Heegeru no benshoho. NKz* 12:64-84.

(1931b). *Ei-en no ima no jiko gentei. NKz* 6:181-232.

(1931c). *Jikanteki naru mono ovobi hijikanteki naru mono. NKz* 6:233-259.

(1932a). Preface to *Mu no jikakuteki gentei. NKz* 6:3-11.

(1932b). *Ji-ai to ta-ai oyobi benshoho. NKz* 6:260-299.

(1932c). *Jiyo ishi. NKz* 6:300-340.

(1932d). *Watakushi to nanji. NKz* 6:341-427.

(1936). *Ronri to seimei. NKz* 8:273-394.

(1938). *Rekishiteki sekai ni oite no kobutsu no tachiba. NKz* 9:69-146.

(1939). Preface to *Tetsugaku ronbunshu,* v. 3. *NKz* 9:3-7.

(1940). *Poieshisu to purakushisu. NKz* 10:124-176.

(1941). *Kokka riyu no mondai. NKz* 10:265-337.

(1944). *Dekaruto tetsugaku ni tsuite. NKz* 11:147-188.

Brian D. Elwood (essay date 1994)

SOURCE: "The Problem of the Self in the Later Nishida and in Sartre," in *Philosophy East & West,* Vol. 44, No. 2, April, 1994, pp. 303-16.

[*In the following essay, Elwood discusses similarities between Nishida and Jean-Paul Sartre in their respective theories of theself.*]

I. INTRODUCTION

A curious little monograph titled *Shuzo Kuki and Jean-Paul Sartre: Influence and Counter-Influence in the Early History of Existential Phenomenology* was published, in 1987, for the *Journal of the History of Philosophy.*[1] In this monograph, Stephen Light reveals that in 1928 the French existentialist Jean-Paul Sartre (1905-1980) had weekly discussions with the Japanese philosopher Kuki Shuzo (1888-1941). It seems that in 1976, a certain Professor Akio Sato discovered a notebook marked "Monsieur Sartre" while cataloging Kuki's papers. Apparently Kuki and the young Sartre engaged in conversations on the topic of modern French philosophy. Although it is not clear that Sartre exerted any special influence on Kuki, it is now evident that it was Kuki who played the crucial role of introducing Sartre to the thought of both Husserl and Heidegger, rather than Raymond Aron, as claimed by Simone de Beauvoir in *La Force de l'age.*

Not only is Light's shrewd detective work significant for the history of philosophy, it also draws attention to the unusual life and thought of the Japanese philosopher Kuki. Light's monograph provides a translation of Kuki's Parisian writings, twelve of which are a comparative analysis of Japanese and Western philosophy. The subtitle of the monograph, however, appears somewhat misleading when we consider that there is no mention of Sartre in Kuki's Parisian writings. This is not surprising, of course, since Sartre was still unknown as a philosopher at the time Kuki composed these various essays. In any case, it might be suggested that Sartre's absence in these writings serves to highlight a largely uncharted territory in the history of East-West comparative philosophy. Although some, like William Bossart, have labored to compare Sartre's theory of consciousness with the Zen doctrine of no-mind, little effort has been made to analyze Sartre's philosophy in comparison with Japanese philosophy—for example, with the Kyoto-ha or Kyoto School of philosophy.[2]

One might expect this to be the case, considering the meager interest in Sartre among the Japanese intelligentsia. In 1955, Gino Piovesana observed that Husserlian phenomenology became familiar in Japan after 1921. Later there emerged a special interest in Heidegger and Jaspers. He suggests that this was due to there being something about these thinkers that particularly suited the Japanese ethos. Piovesana observes that the publications of the Kyoto School of philosophy give the impression that the school, which had earlier been associated with idealism, became a center of existentialism after the war. However that may be, it is apropos to note with Piovesana that the esteem which Western existentialists enjoyed among adherents of the Kyoto School did not extend toeither Sartre or Camus.

In 1921, Kuki went to Europe for more than eight years of study at the universities of Heidelberg, Freiburg, and Marburg with Rickert, Husserl, and Heidegger, respectively. Later he moved to Paris to study under Bergson. After his return to Japan he received a professorial position at Kyoto Imperial University where he taught alongside Nishida Kitaro (1870-1945), the central figure of the "Kyoto School" of philosophy and generally considered the foremost philosopher of Japan. Loosely associated with the "Kyoto School" himself, Kuki held Nishida in the highest esteem.

In Europe, Kuki had the opportunity to study with many of the European philosophers who most absorbed Nishida's attention. Both Kuki and Nishida eagerly assimilated Husserlian phenomenology. As Stephen Light has noted, however, Kuki "remained distant from Hegelian phenomenology."[3] Light also cites Professor Omodaka Hisayuki's observation that Kuki is set apart from Nishida's intellectualism by virtue of Kuki's emphasis on affectivity.[4] Given the apparent disparities, the common influence of Husserl and Heidegger on both Kuki and Nishida, coupled with what we have noted above about Kuki's remarkable bequest to Sartre, form a fascinating montage which is all the more compelling when we recognize the paucity of attempts made at a comparative analysis of Sartre and Nishida.

Considered against this intriguing tapestry, the influence of French vitalism and German existential phenomenology on both Nishida and Sartre make the comparative analysis of these philosophers an imperative concern for East-West comparative philosophy. If Kuki was a leading exponent of existential phenomenology in Japan, certainly Nishida's importance in its transmission to Japan was no less pronounced. It was Nishida who first initiated discussion of Husserl in an article of 1911, shortly after the first French article on Husserl.[5] It is, of course, common knowledge that Sartre was the leading existential phenomenologist in France. Despite their mutual involvement with existential phenomenology, however, concern with the comparative analysis of these philosophers is relatively unprecedented.

It is, of course, not difficult to see that although there is no record of influence between Nishida and Sartre, there is a certain affinity between the Nishidan and the Sartrean theory of the self. Nishida's definition of the self as the "self-consciousness of nothingness" is reminiscent of the Sartrean "self," which is the nonsubstantial and "nihilating" cogito. This cogito is nonthetic with respect to itself. As the "self-consciousness of nothingness," the ontological foundation of the self is deontological, as it were, like Sartre's "being-for-itself."[6] This analogy has been noted by David Dilworth and Hugh Silverman in their article, "ACross-Cultural Approach to the De-Ontological Self Paradigm." In this article, they indicate that the notion of the "self-consciousness of nothingness" is parallel to the Sartrean nonthetic or "nonpositional" self-consciousness.

Asserting that Sartre's "nihilating" consciousness, which always remains nonthetic with respect to itself, typifies the deontological position, they propose that

> An analogous conception of non-thetic self-determination appears in Nishida Kitaro, whose central notion of *mu no basho,* 'the topos of nothingness,' is a modern Buddhist counterpart to Sartre's existential phenomenology. Like Sartre's pre-reflective *cogito,* Nishida demonstrates a conception of consciousness after the analogy of the 'eye that cannot see itself.'[7]

Dilworth and Silverman go so far as to contend that Nishida's notion of *mu no basho* can be translated, "without the least departure from Nishida's meaning," in terms of nonthetic self-consciousness. For both Nishida and Sartre, the self establishes its identity only in situation.

As startling as the resemblance is, however, it is important to recognize that, in certain respects, Nishida's views on the self are radically dissimilar from those of Sartre. It might be said that they have different theories of self-negation. Whereas for Sartre, death is "that which on principle removes all meaning from life," for Nishida,

only by confronting the "eternal death" of the self can one become an authentically self-conscious individual. By the self-consciousness of the "eternal death" or nothingness of the self, one truly realizes the singularity of one's existence.

Although Nishida and Sartre both highlight the absolute nothingness of the self and the existential anguish experienced in the encounter with this absolute nothingness and freedom, Sartre tends to depreciate the significance of death in a fashion unlike Nishida. In this article, we hope to show that Nishida's notion of the self-consciousness of the "eternal death" of the self has an ontological and religious significance not discernible in Sartre's theory of nonthetic self-consciousness. In the process, we intend to elucidate aspects of both affinity and dissimilarity with respect to the problem of the self in the later Nishida and in Sartre.

II. THE RELIGIOUS EXIGENCY

Published in 1911, only one year after he became assistant professor at Kyoto University, *A Study of Good* or *An Inquiry into the Good* (*Zen no kenkyu*) won immediate acclaim and was the launching of Nishida's career.[8] In the chapter titled "TheReligious Demand," he established the tone for the concluding section, "Religion," which served as the culmination of his first treatment of his pivotal theme of "pure experience" and was the inception of a very long philosophical inquiry into the problem of the self. Over thirty years later, in his final essay, **"The Logic of Place and a Religious World View,"** we encounter the same concern expressed in his work of 1911, to break through the ubiquitous subject-object dichotomy in favor of "seeing" or "intuition" in a deeper, and clearly religious, sense. He begins this essay asserting that philosophers cannot fabricate religion from their philosophical systems; their task is to "explain this event of the soul." He rejects the notion that religion is hopelessly illogical and "mystical," implying that his intention is to provide a logic whereby religious experience can be elucidated and drawn into a broader community of intelligent discourse.

Although Sartre adopts an atheistic standpoint, one can say that the religious exigency is of paramount importance to his view of the human condition. For Sartre, the basic human drive is not the Freudian libido or the Adlerian will to power; it is a certain sort of religious urge. Sartre's interpretation of religiosity is somewhat singular. He asserts that "To be man means to reach toward being God. Or if you prefer, man fundamentally is the desire to be God."[9] For Sartre, however, God is the impossible but ideal synthesis of the "in-itself-for-itself" (*en-soi-pour-soi*). The drive to *be* this impossible synthesis is the "fundamental project" of humankind, one which is tragically doomed to fail. Humankind suffers, then, from a perennial religious "complex" characterized by an ultimate frustration. Although God is impossible, the religious ideal is basic to being human; hence human beings have abundant religious experiences. We can say, then, that Nishida and Sartre would concur that we experience a religious exigency, but differ in their respective interpretations of such.

In his essay titled **"Towards a Philosophy of Religion with the Concept of Pre-established Harmony as Guide"** (1944), Nishida asserts that we can only enter into the "religious dimension" insofar as, along the "road of life," we confront self-contradiction in "the very depths of the self-awareness of the self. . . ."[10] Hence, he states that "Religion is the problem of the self."[11] Sartre, on the other hand, would doubtless eschew such an assertion lest it imply a "religious" interpretation of the self. As we have seen, however, he is very much concerned with the "problem of the self." The problem of the self, for Sartre, is tragically religious in character. In a sense, both Nishida and Sartre equate the religious question and the problem of the self. They also tend to characterize the self as a nothingness. Despite these affinities, however, not only do Nishida and Sartre develop radically divergent ontologies, but they express distinct orientations toward self-negation, death, and religiousconsciousness.

Sartre, for his part, does not allow for the possibility of an autonomous religious mode of consciousness. The phenomenon of so-called "religious consciousness" merely reflects the structure of consciousness as conceived by his ontology. Nishida, on the other hand, introduces his essay of 1945 by asserting his notion of an autonomous religious dimension. He proposes that Kant was able to view religion only from the standpoint of moral consciousness. He comments on Kant:

> For Kant, religion was meaningful only as a supplement to morality. I do not find any uniqueness accorded to religious consciousness in his thought, and I wonder if he was aware of any such uniqueness.[12]

Never wavering from his recognition of Kant's eminent stature and significance, Nishida sought to break through and expand the Kantian framework so as to develop a structure permitting multifarious fields of experience wherein religious consciousness is granted apriority.

The task of contrasting Nishida's orientation with Sartre's, however, is not simply a matter of relating Sartre to a post-Kantian version of idealism. In breaking through the Kantian framework, Nishida does not here exhibit his earlier inclination to pursue a neo-Kantian direction. Neither can a contrast be developed in terms of Sartre's critique of mysticism. No longer does Nishida concede to any view of religious consciousness as "mystical." In the course of his last writings, "moral" and "mystical" interpretations of religious experience give way to a pervasive Zen coloration wherein the religious is seen in the "ordinary and everyday." Concomitant with this is Nishida's insistence that the absolute is not to be found in the direction of an objective transcendence wherein God possesses a separate personality; rather, it is to be found in a Buddhistic direction of "immanent transcendence" wherein we discover that we are in the embrace of absolute compassion.

In Nishida's last writings, not only do we begin to see a distinctive religious emphasis on the "ordinary, and everyday" world, but we see a correlative emphasis on the historical world. Critical of the "otherworldliness" which he discerns in traditional Indian Buddhism, Nishida expresses a religious form of worldliness wherein he seeks a "true absolute dynamism" beyond mere passivity. When we consider this in terms of Sartre's critique of religious "quietism" and mystical otherworldliness, it becomes apparent that Sartre's criticisms cannot be applied to Nishida's views as expressed in his last writings, but in some ways even concur with Nishida's own criticisms. Rather than pursue a comparative analysisof Nishida's and Sartre's respective orientations toward religious experience per se, however, we turn first to consider some aspects of the problem of the self, which, as we have noted above, is regarded by both Nishida and Sartre as intimately related to religious questions.

III. EXISTENTIAL ANGUISH AND THE PROBLEM OF THE SELF

In his last writings, Nishida returns to his early critique of notions of rational and moral apriorities of the self. He expresses the conviction that the entire question of the self-autonomy of the moral and the rational is basically irrelevant to the fundamental religious question of the very existence of the self. As mentioned above, the very existence of the self becomes problematic when we are self-conscious of the self-contradictions of the self. He observes that

> The sorrows of human life and its self-contradictions have been constant themes since ancient times. But many people do not face this fact deeply. When this fact of the sorrow of life is faced, the problem of religion arises for us. (Indeed, the problem of philosophy also arises from this point.)[13]

Through a deep confrontation with the sorrows and self-contradictions of life we can reach the "standpoint of total freedom and self-authenticity."

The confrontation with the sorrows and self-contradictions of life is a standard characteristic of existentialist philosophy. In an essay titled "The Humanism of Existentialism" (found in *Essays in Existentialism* [1965]), Sartre endeavors to defend existentialism against certain popularly held criticisms.[14] It is generally known, he says, that the basic charge against existentialism is its apparent emphasis on the tragic side of life. He wonders, however, if those who accuse existentialism of being too gloomy are reacting not so much to its apparent pessimism as to its optimism. He inquires if what really scares such reactionaries is not the sense in which existentialism "leaves to man a possibility of choice?[15] Existential choice is self-conscious choice which we actively determine. We can, of course, remain passive. In which case we have still *chosen* passivity.

Freedom, for Sartre, is not merely a description of external conditions wherein humanity confronts alternative possibilities. Freedom is the state of being to which "being-for-itself" is condemned. We make choices, but "we are not free to cease being free."[16] If freedom is the very being of consciousness, what form does the consciousness of freedom assume? According to Sartre,

> ... it is in anguish that man gets the consciousness ofhis freedom, or if you prefer, anguish is the mode of being of freedom as consciousness of being; it is in anguish that freedom is, in its being, in question for itself.[17]

For Sartre, freedom (the very "being of consciousness") becomes problematic to itself in its self-consciousness. In freedom, the human being *is* both his or her past and future, but only in the form of "nihilation." Humans become self-conscious of "being both this past and future and as not being them."[18]

We see here a Sartrean expression of that problematicity of the very existence of the self which Nishida has identified with the religious question. Much in the same way as Nishida had asserted, Sartre finds that the very being of consciousness becomes problematic when we are self-conscious of the self-contradictions of the self. The self-contradiction cited above consists in the self both being and *not* being its past and future. This self-contradiction emerges for Sartre because it is in freedom that human reality separates its present from its past and future by "secreting" its own "nothingness." Thus, we are also speaking here of the self-consciousness of freedom. With respect to Nishida, it is apropos to observe that in the voluntaristic stage of his thinking (1917) he describes the self-consciousness of the "absolute free will" as the basic form of consciousness. This might be thought to have some proximity to Sartre's assertion that freedom is the being of consciousness, although, strictly speaking. Sartrean freedom cannot be equated with so-called "free will." In any case, we need to consider Nishida's view of self-determination. Let us first consider, however, the character of Sartrean anguish.

We have seen that Sartre asserts that it is in anguish that man gets his consciousness of freedom. In *Being and Nothingness,* he cites Kierkegaard as characterizing anguish in the face of what one lacks as anguish in the face of freedom. He also notes that Heidegger, who was greatly influenced by Kierkegaard, considers anguish as the apprehension of nothingness. In Sartre's view, these two descriptions of anguish are not contradictory. In anguish we confront our utter freedom as a consciousness which is intrinsically obliged "to be its own nothingness" or which incessantly experiences itself as the "nihilation" of its past being. Thus Sartre posits that "Consciousness is a being, the nature of which is to be conscious of the nothingness of its being."[19] This notion of the nothingness of consciousness is an intrinsic aspect of both Sartrean and Nishidan philosophy. Our concern at this point, however, pertains to Nishida's mature thought. In the discussion that follows, we shall observe some significant disparities between Sartre's and Nishida's respective points of view with respect to the problem of the self.

According to Sartre, the first principle of existentialism is that"Man is nothing else but what he makes of himself."[20] For Sartre, this means not only that "man defines himself," but that prior to doing so he is indefinable "because at first he is nothing." No explanations can be made by reference to any fixed and given human nature. Not only is there no a priori meaning or value, but there is no universal or ready-made human nature or essence that can be revealed by any a priori theory of humanity or any religious interpretation that purports to speak of humanity prior to and apart from its actual existence. Hence, by existentialism Sartre means the doctrine "that existence precedes essence, or, if you prefer, that subjectivity must be the starting point."[21] Subjectivity must be the point of departure because human beings are self-consciously problematic to themselves, because they are responsible for what they are, and because "it is impossible for man to transcend human subjectivity."[22]

In asserting that existence precedes essence, the existentialist views himself as turning the tables on nearly all classical philosophy, from Plato to Hegel, wherein existence always derives from essence. Plato, of course, emphasized the search for essence by virtue of its inherent immutability. In Sartre's view, the notion is carried down through the ages that each individual human being is a particular example of a universal concept of "man." Thus it is widely assumed that the essence of human being "precedes the historical existence that we find in nature."[23] Existentialism, on the other hand, expresses a distinctive concern for the concrete existence of the individual. Therefore, the existentialist critique of essentialist accounts of humanity goes hand in hand with its critique of determinism. If there is no fixed human nature, then humanity must be wholly free. This means that human beings must be wholly accountable for their behavior, and it is only in cowardice that they turn to "deterministic excuses," seeking to hide from the "complete arbitrariness" of their existence.

Nishida, for his part, shares the existentialist concern with the concrete existence of the individual. In his last writings, however, he asserts that "what exists must have some nature."[24] Nishida reasons that if we consider the autonomous action of the self to be freedom, we are already presupposing that the self is endowed with some sort of determinate nature, "for if the self were merely amorphous, there would be no autonomy."[25] It is often said that to act out one's essence or to follow one's essence is freedom. Hence, Nishida says that "mere arbitrariness is not freedom."[26] But wherein can we locate this essence of the self? Nishida denies that it is adequate to associate the nature of the self with rationality. The rational self can be anyone's self. It is not yet the unique, concrete individual and personal self which *"determines itself"* as one "focal point of the world." This personal, individual self exists in the self-consciousness of its own eternal nothingness. Although the Nishidan notion of theessential nature of the self is notoriously recondite, it is clear that its focal concern is with the "absolute contradiction" which he finds manifest in this *self*-consciousness of the nothingness of the self.

From a Sartrean perspective, the nothingness of the self is precisely the existential condition which negates essentialist notions of the self. Let us be clear, however, that Sartre does not deny that there is something we can call a human essence. Sartrean "essence," however, is only a consequence of the "for-itself's" activity or self-definition. There is no preestablished or inescapable pattern for "human nature." Each human being makes his or her essence as he or she lives. We should also bear in mind that although Sartre denies that it is possible to find a universal essence in each human being that would be our shared human essence, Sartre still affirms that "there does exist a universal human condition."[27] Sartre does not deny that there are certain a priori boundaries which define the human situation in general. Although historical situations vary, there is no variance in the obligation to exist in the world, to work in the world, to live among others, and to be mortal. These limits are "neither subjective nor objective, or, rather, they have an objective and a subjective side."[28] In that they are ubiquitously discernible, they are objective. In that they are *lived* and because *human beings freely determine their existence with respect to them,* they are subjective.

Although it may be tempting, for good reason, to characterize Nishida's view as simply another version of the essentialism that Sartre is opposed to, it is appropriate to consider whether what Nishida seems to regard as the essential nature of the self strays in any drastic sense from what Sartre deems to be the a priori limits which define the "universal human condition." In other words, when Nishida takes freedom to consist in acting out one's essence, is he expressing a view which departs radically from Sartre's view of the subjective side of the a priori limits wherein humanity freely determines its existence in reference to such limits? We shall have to bear this question in mind. At this point we can only make some observations. Although Nishida allows for some sort of rudimentary "essence" of the self, he does not view such assertions as invalidating his principal tenet that the self is ultimately "absolute nothingness. "The Nishidan notion of the essential human nature seems to refer to the a priori limits which define the universal human condition and in terms of which human beings freely determine themselves to be a "focal point of the world."

In *Being and Nothingness,* Sartre describes the basis of the psychobiological condition of "man" and his unavoidable connection with the world and with the past under the category of "facticity."Facticity is the universal human condition. It is the "for-itself's" necessary connection with the "in-itself." By virtue of facticity we can say that the "for-itself" exists. If we were to suggest that Nishidan essence refers to facticity, however, we would depart from Sartre's perspective. For Sartre, facticity is *not* an essence of humanity since its meaning depends on the "for itself" for its interpretation. Nishida, for his part, is no less emphatic as to the input of consciousness with respect to the meaning of facticity. That we act consciously, he says, means that each of us is an "expressive point of the world" and that the world is "subjectively appropriated by our self."[29] Nishida explains that

> . . . the world which stands over against us as something thoroughly objective is transformed into a world of signs within us, is grasped by us as a significative world.[30]

IV. THE SELF-CONSCIOUSNESS OF DEATH

The essential human nature for Nishida lies in the fundamental self-contradiction of self-existence as manifest in our self-consciousness of our absolute nothingness. This self-contradiction is especially exemplified in the self-consciousness of that supreme a priori limit, death. All living things die. Being a living thing, I know that I, too, will die. This is not, however, what Nishida has in mind. In the case of this sort of knowledge of *my* death, he says, "I am objectifying myself and regard myself as a thing."[31] Some say that when the flesh dies, the spirit lives on. For Nishida, the notion of "living in the spirit" suggests rationality and morality. It pertains to our access to the rational and the universal. The rational and the universal, however, are not living things. Hence Nishida says that "For reason to be self-conscious of death has no meaning."[32] Self-consciousness of the "eternal death of the self" arises when the self confronts its own absolute negation. This can only happen to an individual since only such a being can truly know that it is an individual. Only such a being is a "true individual, a true person."

Sartre, for his part, asserts that it is not possible for the "for-itself" to be aware of its own possibility of dying. "*My* death" always remains exterior to my awareness. Sartre explains that

> Death is not *my* possibility of no longer realizing a presence in the world, but *an always possible nihilation of my possibles, which is outside of my possibility.*[33]

Although I can imagine someone's death, *my* death is incomprehensible to me. Hence, Sartre asserts that the fact of death indicates the ultimate "triumph of the point of view of theOther over the point of view *which I am* toward myself."[34] Sartre is critical of what he calls "the idealist attempt to *recover* death." In this attempt, he says, death as the end of life is interiorized and humanized. Death becomes the meaning of life "as the resolved chord at the end of a melody." Recovering death in this way means making it *mine.* By thus interiorizing death, it is individualized. No longer the great unknowable, it becomes "the phenomenon of *my* personal life which makes of this life a unique life."[35]

Certainly this notion of the recovery of death whereby my life is individualized seems suggestive of Nishida's views already noted above. Although Sartre recognizes the advantage of such views and the "undeniable portion of truth" involved, he finds it necessary to review the entire question, unwilling to concede that there is any "personalizing virtue" to be associated with *my* death. Sartre's critique focuses largely on Heidegger's view of *Dasein* as *Sein zum Tode.* In Sartre's reading, the most positive content of Heidegger's *Entschlossenheit* ("resolute decision") pertains to the notion of the attempt to "recover" death by transforming it into an *expected death.* In Sartre's view, the counsel is easier to give than to follow. Death is one thing which I cannot appropriate or "recover" as *mine.* Although Sartre deems it suitable to insist that we must live each moment as if we might die, he insists that this does not indicate that we should make death into an object of contemplation as if it could disclose the meaning of our acts. Death does not give meaning to life; it is "that which on principle removes all meaning from life."[36]

This is not the place to consider Sartre's views on death in any detail. It is, however, opportune to consider in what sense the general thrust of his evaluation may be said to apply to Nishida. Unlike Sartre, Nishida emphatically asserts that it is possible to be self-aware of one's "own eternal death." Nishida is not trying to say that one can imagine or expect one's own death, or that one can reflect on it. He means *that one can become genuinely aware of one's own death.* As noted above, Nishida is not speaking of the mere reflective observation that, being a living thing, I must die since living things always die. This sort of knowledge of one's death is still founded on the objectification of one's self as a thing and cannot be a genuine awareness of one's death. Sartre's view, as we have already seen, is that we are confined to this sort of knowledge. There can be no genuine awareness of one's own death because one's own death always remains totally exterior to one's awareness. I cannot prepare for death or recover it as *mine* since it is always beyond me. Once I die, *my* death is available only as the point of view of others.

It is clear that Nishida's intention is not to counsel us to contemplate death as an object in an endeavor to appropriate one's death by transforming it into an *expected death,* in the manner towhich Sartre refers. Nishida is saying something even stronger than any assertion suggesting that we can extract the meaning of our lives from our death. He is reminding us that living *is* dying. He maintains, therefore, that we cannot even have lives as self-conscious individuals without death. A plant or animal may have no knowledge whatsoever of its own death. Nishida says that, "Something which does not know of its own death does not possess a self."[37] We might even say that it has no death. The more aware one is of the "eternal death of the self" the closer one approaches authentic individuality or personhood.

Nishida goes so far as to say that the awareness of the eternal death or "eternal nothingness" of the self is the "fundamental reason for the very existence of the self."[38] That we know the self in self-negation is the "absolute self-contradiction" of the self's existence. This absolute self-contradiction is the raison d'être of the self. The self, in other words, cannot *be* otherwise. That "we know the self in self-negation," does not imply the mere judgment that the self dies or that the self is nothingness. The self is not self-conscious through mere self-reflection. Only when we are genuinely aware of the eternal death of the self or "its own eternal nothingness" can we become truly self-conscious. By facing this "eternal nothingness" we can truly realize the singularity of our existence. In ratio to the degree of self-consciousness, the religious exigency emerges and we experience religious and existential anguish. This is because the self leads this absolutely contradictory existence.

Although Sartre highlights the nothingness of the self and the encounter with absolute freedom in anguish, he tends to depreciate the significance of death. For Nishida, on the other hand, the nothingness of the self *is* the "eternal death" of the self without which there would be no self. For Nishida, then, *death has an ontological significance* with respect to the existence of the self which does not appear in Sartre. This discrepancy is all the more notable when we consider that, like Nishida's self, the Sartrean self is absolutely self-contradictory; that is, the prereflective cogito is a self only as lacking a self. Sartre's view of the self as lacking a self correlates with his rejection of any notion of an essence of the self. Similarly, Sartre rejects any notion of a "transcendental self." Nishida, on the other hand, utilizes the notion generously up until his last essays.

NOTES

[1] Stephen Light, *Shuzo Kuki and Jean-Paul Sartre: Influence and Counter-Influence in the Early History of Existential Phenomenology* (Carbondale and Edwardsville: Southern Illinois University Press, 1987). Also see the review of this book by Steve Odin, *Philosophy East and West* 41 (1991): 577-583.

[2] William Bossart, "Sartre's Theory of Consciousness and the Zen Doctrine of No-Mind," in *The Life of the Transcendental Ego,* eds. Edward S. Casey and Donald V. Morano (Albany: State University of New York Press, 1986).

[3] Stephen Light, *Shuzo Kuki and Jean-Paul Sartre,* p. 11.

[4] For a discussion of Nishida's so-called "intellectualism," see my dissertation, "A Comparative Analysis of Nishida and Sartre with Special Reference to their Respective Ontologies" (University of Tennessee), pp. 23-27.

[5] See Light's comments in *Shuzo Kuki and Jean-Paul Sartre,* p. 26 n. 2.

[6] "Being-for-itself" (*être-pour-soi*) is the being of consciousness conceived as a lack of being, a relation to being or a desire for being. "Being-in-itself" (*être-en-soi*) is the being of the phenomenon conceived as the nonconscious being which always overflows the knowledge we have of it.

[7] David A. Dilworth and Hugh J. Silverman, "A Cross-Cultural Approach to the De-Ontological Self Paradigm," *The Monist* 16, no. 1 (January 1978): 91.

[8] Nishida Kitaro, *An Inquiry into the Good (Zen no kenkyu)*, trans. Masao Abe and Christopher Ives (New Haven: Yale University Press, 1990). Earlier edition: *A Study of Good (Zen no kenkyu)*, trans. Valdo H. Viglielmo (Japan: Ministry of Education, 1960).

[9] Jean-Paul Sartre, *Being and Nothingness (L'Etre et le Néant)*, trans. with introd. by Hazel E. Barnes (New York: Washington Square Press, 1956).

[10] Nishida Kitaro, "Towards a Philosophy of Religion with the Concept of Pre-established Harmony as Guide," trans. David A. Dilworth, *The Eastern Buddhist* 2, no. 1 (June): 19-46.

[11] Ibid.

[12] Nishida Kitaro, "The Logic of *Topos* and the Religious World-view," part 1, trans. Yusa Michiko, *The Eastern Buddhist*, N.S., 19, no. 2 (Autumn 1986): 1-29.

[13] Nishida Kitaro, "'Religious Consciousness and the Logic of the *Prajñaparamita Sutra*,' Section II of 'The Logic of Place and a Religious World-view'" (1945), trans. David A. Dilworth, *Monumenta Nipponica* 25, nos. 1-2 (1965): 210-216.

[14] Jean-Paul Sartre, *Essays in Existentialism* (New York: CitadelPress, 1974).

[15] Ibid., p. 33.

[16] Jean-Paul Sartre, *Being and Nothingness*, p. 567.

[17] Ibid., p. 65.

[18] Ibid.

[19] Ibid., p. 86.

[20] Jean-Paul Sartre, *Essays in Existentialism*, p. 36.

[21] Ibid., p. 34.

[22] Ibid., p. 37.

[23] Ibid., p. 35.

[24] Nishida Kitaro, "The Logic of *Topos*," p. 22.

[25] Ibid., p. 21.

[26] Ibid., p. 22.

[27] Jean-Paul Sartre, *Essays in Existentialism*, p. 52.

[28] Ibid.

[29] Nishida Kitaro, "The Logic of *Topos*," p. 5.

[30] Ibid.

[31] Nishida Kitaro, "Religious Consciousness," p. 204.

[32] Ibid.

[33] Jean-Paul Sartre, *Being and Nothingness*, p. 687.

[34] Ibid., p. 691.

[35] Ibid., p. 682.

[36] Ibid., p. 690.

[37] Nishida Kitaro, "Religious Consciousness," p. 213.

[38] Ibid., p. 205.

Thomas P. Kasulis (essay date 1995)

SOURCE: "Sushi, Science, and Spirituality: Modern Japanese Philosophy and Its Views of Western Science," in *Philosophy East & West*, Vol. 45, No. 2, April, 1995, pp. 227-48.

[*In the following essay, Kasulis presents a contrasting picture of Japanese and Western scientific theory and practice and examines the ideas of Nishida and other Japanese philosophers regarding this difference.*]

Japan seems to present two profiles to the West. One is that of a Westernized nation that is a major economic power in the world. Seeing the skyscrapers of Tokyo's downtown districts, hearing Western rock or classical music even in village coffee shops, or tasting the French cuisine of its fine restaurants, it is easy for one to think of Japan as part of the Western-based family of cultures. This face of Japan seems to confirm the interpretation of Habermas and others that European rationality is dominating the world. We might be led to expect that with the passage of time, Japan will become, if anything, even more like the West.

Yet, there is also the other, non-Western, profile as well. It appears to the consternation of foreign business people trying to establish Western-like contractual relations with Japanese corporations. It appears to the frustration of social scientists in their attempts to apply to the Japanese context Western models of social, political, or economic analysis. It appears even to philosophers who have tried to study Japanese thought. Charles Moore, the founder of the East-West Philosophers' Conferences half a century ago, felt able to write authoritatively about the "Chinese mind" and the "Indian mind." When he tried to write about the "Japanese mind," however, he could do no better than call it "enigmatic."[1] These reactions raise serious questions about how really "Western" Japanese rationality has become.

In short, Japan is a striking example of an Asian nation that has been successful at Western-style industrialization, technological development, and capitalistic expansion. Still, it has somehow also kept much of its own values and modes of behavior. How can this Western thinking and Japanese thinking exist in the same culture? Part of the answer is undoubtedly social or historical and best left to the analyses of specialists in those fields. Part of it is also philosophical, however. Since the major influx of Western ideas and technology into Japan in the latter half of the nineteenth century, Japanese philosophers have often addressed these very issues. In particular, they have asked (1) what the Western form of scientific and technological thinking is and (2) how it might function in Japan without eroding spiritual and moral values traditional to East Asia.

In this essay we will briefly examine two philosophical strategies representative of trends in modern Japanese philosophy. First, we will examine the early twentieth-century thought of Nishida Kitaro and his attempt to put Western science into its place, a logical realm subordinate to that of ethics, spirituality, and aesthetics. Second, we will explore how a contemporary Japanese philosopher, Yuasa Yasuo, has seen a possible complementarity between modern Western science, especially medicine, and traditional Asian thought about the mind-body complex. Before discussing either philosophical approach, however, we need a sketch of the historical and cultural context of the Japanese encounter with Western thought. Only against that background can we clearly frame the problematics of modern Japanese philosophy.

To frame the specifics of the historical circumstances under which Western thought entered modern Japan, it is first useful to consider generally how ideas move from one culture to the next. Often, of course, they are imposed on a culture by a foreign military occupation. Until 1945, Japan was not in such a situation, however, and by then its internal processes of modernization (or Westernization) were already well under way. For that reason, there has been no prominent modern Japanese philosophy of "decolonization" as there has been in twentieth-century Indian, African, Islamic, and (to a lesser extent) Chinese thought. Even among Japanese critics of Westernization, the rhetoric has usually not been what "they" (Westerners) have done to "us" (Japanese), but what "we" have done to "ourselves."[2]

In short, Westernization was somewhat like an import item for Japan in the free marketplace of ideas. The issue may have been conditioned by external circumstances (most notably, the expansion of Western imperialist powers into Asia and the Pacific), but to some extent, at least, the Japanese welcomed the imported product. The question is: under what circumstances does a culture freely accept foreign ideas? This is too complex an issue to address fully here. It is easy to let such a question drift off into abstract dialectics concerning the logic of intercultural (mis-)understanding, however. So, for our background purposes, let us simply pursue for a bit the marketplace analogy. How does a product penetrate a foreign market? First, there must be a system of distribution: the product must be made available to the foreign market.

Second, the product must develop an attractive image in the new culture. Third, the product must meet some need, or generate some need, in the perception of the potential consumers. Last, the product must suit the tastes of its new cultural home.[3]

To explain these basic categories further, let us consider an extended analogy: the rapidly growing number of sushi restaurants in U.S. urban areas. How can we understand this phenomenon in terms of the marketplace principles just outlined?

It is not simply the inherent taste of sushi that has given it its market niche in the American restaurant industry. Since the 1950s it has been common knowledge in the United States that the Japanese eat raw fish, yet few Americans wanted to try it. The issue, therefore, is what motivated Americans to want to try it. What changed between the 1950s and the 1980s such that a broadening spiral of supply and demand could develop?

The most obvious difference, of course, was the emergence of Japan as a powerful economic presence in the world generally and in the U.S. specifically. This economic change caused more Japanese business executives to reside temporarily in the United States, thereby establishing the demographic base in large cities for economically supporting a small number of local sushi restaurants. At the same time, more Americans visited Japan for business reasons, often sampling the local fare as part of the hospitality extended by Japanese business associates. Hence, availability increased. Furthermore, as Japan became one of the richest countries in the world, Americans came to admire its power. Americans began to think it worthwhile to emulate the Japanese, not merely observe them from afar as a land of exotica. Hence, we find the principles of availability/distribution and positive image.

One Japanese quality Americans admired was their health. The average Japanese male's life expectancy was almost a decade longer than the average American's. One factor in maintaining that health might be the Japanese low-fat, low-cholesterol diet. As the young American professionals of the baby boom years approached middle age and began to worry about heart disease, the "power lunch" of raw beef and egg so fashionable on Wall Street in the early 1980s was increasingly replaced by foods like sushi. This data shows that sushi was perceived as fitting a societal need to shift dietary habits. The third criterion of the marketplace was met.

The first three factors combined to create a context in which a significant number of Americans would try eating sushi. Then, the fourth condition could be met. If the Americans would acquire a taste for the new food—if they found sushi to be a desirable dietary option—it would become possible for sushi bars to establish a market niche in the American restaurant business. That is what seems to have happened.

Similar conditions had to be met for Japan to assimilate Western ideas, science, and technology. There were two major periods of influx from the West: the sixteenth century and the modern period starting in the mid- to late nineteenth century. In the first case, Westernization was eventually rejected, whereas in the modern period, it has been accepted. Let us briefly examine each case in terms of the four conditions just outlined.

The first factor is availability. In the sixteenth century, Westernization was offered to Japan primarily via Spanish and Portuguese Jesuits and Franciscans. Following the arrival of the missionaries, there was a moderate amount of trade between those European countries (including the Dutch shortly later) and Japan.

The second factor is the positive image of the host culture. The power trappings of Europeanization and Christianity were dual. First, they brought knowledge of the outside world. Maps helped explain the geopolitical constitution of the lands beyond Asia. These were relevant to assessing the opportunities and dangers of future contact with Europe. The Japanese also found the foreigners fascinating: the aristocrats and samurai experimented with things European, including Portuguese dress. The Japanese admired the European worldliness, including the news, ideas, and goods they brought from afar. It might be noted, however, that the Japanese did find the Europeans rather crude culturally. There was some interest in Western foods (sukiyaki, for example, apparently developed as an attempt to make a Portuguese stew with native ingredients) and some exposure to Western art, but in general the Japanese felt more consternation than admiration for the unbathed, bearded barbarians. Most importantly, however, the Europeans brought new technology: some medical and scientific knowledge, but also the military technology of rifles and cannon. This brings us to the third condition—internal need.

For centuries preceding the arrival of the Westerners, Japan had been in a state of civil war, in which various barons were jockeying for territory and political power. There was the need for unification under a new military-political order. The strife ended with the rise to power of three successive military dictators: Oda Nobunaga (1534-1582), Toyotomi Hideyoshi (1536-1598), and Tokugawa Ieyasu (1542-1616). His mastery of Western firearms helped Nobunaga dominate the country militarily, for example. The new leaders initially respected and encouraged Christianity as an aid to unification. They feared the political and military power of the Buddhist sects, many of them having their own militia of armed monks, often numbering in the thousands. Therefore, conversion of the populace to Christianity was not only tolerated, but to some extent encouraged. In short, the introduction of both Western weaponry and Western religious ideas together served the need of unifying the country under the hegemony of the respective military dictators.

The support for these Western influences soon eroded, however. Ironically, this happened because Christianity and weapons technology no longer served the purposes of protecting the sovereignty of the military elite. Hideyoshi learned that the history of the world outside Japan showed that where European missionaries went, European navies and armies soon followed. That hundreds of thousands of Japanese might have a spiritual bond with priests connected to the imperialist courts of Europe was not an idea that Hideyoshi and Ieyasu relished. Christianity was, therefore, first persecuted and then proscribed.

The Tokugawa shoguns also realized that guns did not serve the purpose of a unified state under an iron-fisted rule. A peasant can be taught to fire a rifle in a few hours and kill a samurai swordsman who has spent decades perfecting his skill. Furthermore, ten men with rifles and cannon could kill a hundred archers and swordsmen. Hence, by the 1630s guns were, in effect, banned.[4] If the Tokugawas could ensure that only the samurai had power and that this power was strictly controlled by regulating the numbers and locations of the samurai, they could effectively rule the country through a central bureaucracy. They did so for over 250 years. During most of that time, with the exception of a few Dutch traders who visited an outlying island under scrupulous supervision, Japan closed itself off from European contact. Hence, the Europeanization process lasted for less than a century, and its effects were intentionally restricted severely.[5]

The influx of Western scientific ideas nurtured a burgeoning Japanese interest in studying the material world. It might be thought that Japanese intellectuals would be hesitant to relinquish that interest. It is significant, however, that Neo-Confucianism, especially that of Zhu Xi, also entered Japan in the fifteenth and sixteenth centuries, primarily via Zen Buddhist monks who brought back to Japan texts acquired during their pilgrimages to China. In that Neo-Confucian tradition there was also the notion of investigating natural things to understand their laws or principles. So, although there was not the mathematical dimension emergent in the contemporary Western science, Neo-Confucianism did offer an empirical interest in the ways of nature.[6] The Tokugawa shoguns opted to support that East Asian empiricism over its Western counterpart. Why? Partly because Neo-Confucianism framed its naturalism within a social ethic, a dimension of its system that the shogunate could use as part of its state ideology. In short, although Western science and technology were available in the sixteenth century and although they often had the right image, their practical need was limited and temporary. They also lacked the ethical orientation to fit the image of the state that the Tokugawa shoguns had wanted to foster. So, it was marginalized.

The second Europeanizing phase in Japan is more pertinent to our philosophical purposes. When Commodore Perry forced Japan to open its ports to trade with the West in 1853, Japan once again encountered Westernization in a dynamic and disturbing way. Accessibility to the West had suddenly become a given. The West was at Japan's doorstep, and unlike the early seventeenth century, Japan was no longer in a position to tell it to go away. Japan felt squeezed and threatened. The United

States had expanded across North America and into the Pacific; Britain and France were sweeping across the Asian and African continents; and Japan's nearest mainland neighbors, China and Russia, were countries of continental dimension.

The second condition for developing a taste for the foreign was also clearly present—a respect for the foreign culture. Western technology, including the technology of warfare, had developed enormously since Japan's last direct contact. The Tokugawa shoguns had kept Japan in a basically feudal mode for about 250 years. Japan envisioned two possible destinies: either be a pawn in the imperialist power plays of European and North American expansion or be an imperialist power in its own right through extensive economic, political, social, and technological reconstruction. It chose the latter course. It undertook an extensive program to modernize all sectors of the society: the government, education, industry, and the economy. Much of this movement was obviously a response to the outside threat of imperialist encroachment. At the same time, however, it was a response to an internally generated need—our third condition for accepting the foreign.

The Western intrusion came toward the end of a process of national change. The power of the shoguns had waned over the decades, and thoughts of revolutionary change had been brewing for some time. Through information leaking into the country via the heavily restricted trade with the Dutch, intellectuals were at least peripherally aware of the scientific, medical, and technological revolution occurring in the West. Hence, the internal desire for political and social reform dovetailed with the fear of foreign encroachment. Together, they supported the modernization movement.

By the early twentieth century, Japan had achieved a marked success. It had defeated both China and Russia in wars and had signed a major pact with Great Britain that treated the two countries more as equals. The development of science and technology had become a high priority in education, politics, and the economy.[7] There could be no turning back. The new Japanese industrial society had an enormous appetite for natural resources not available within its own archipelago. Modeling itself on its Western imperialist mentors, Japan looked to secure its supply of resources overseas on the Asian mainland and throughout the Pacific Basin. Japan had become an imperialist power and had set into motion a sequence of events that would result in the Pacific theater of World War II.

It is clear, therefore, that the first three conditions—accessibility, respect for the foreign culture, and internal need—were met. Japan had had a profound taste of Westernization. The issue was now whether that taste was palatableand desirable. In the early part of the Meiji period (1868-1912), intellectuals had expressed the hope that Japan could modernize without changing its underlying cultural value system. This ideal had been expressed in the slogan "Eastern morality and Western techniques" *(toyodotoku to seiyogeijutsu)* popularized by Sakuma Shozan (1811-1864), for example. The more the Japanese intellectuals studied Western culture, however, the more skeptical they grew about the possibility of changing their country's social, economic, and political system without also changing its religious and moral values. Toward the end of the nineteenth century, for example, there was even an idea that science and Christianity had developed together so intimately in the West that it might be advisable for the Japanese emperor to convert to Christianity. The pro-Christian contingent did not win out in the end, and the emperor remained the chief priest of Shinto. Still, many prominent families in the modernization movement did convert. Even today, although Japan is only one percent Christian, Christianity's influence among higher social and economic classes is inordinately strong.

The examples of Sakuma's slogan and the plan to baptize the emperor are revealing. Obviously, even early on, the Japanese were acutely aware of two philosophically significant points. First, Western science and technology seemed to be packaged with a value system, one that at least appeared inimical to traditional Japanese values. Second, many intellectuals sensed that the historical development of the Western economy and the technological world it governed were somehow related to Christianity. Yet, they also sensed, much to their credit, that the connection between Western science and Western values and the connection between Western economics or politics and Western religion were contingent historical facts, not logical necessities. That is, they did not make the common mistake of assuming that what had happened had to have happened. They would, almost from the start, hope that they could have Western economic and technological development without adopting Western values in religion, ethics, and aesthetics. Was this hope justified? This has been a major issue in modern Japanese philosophy.

In exploring this issue, we must be wary of Western cultural assumptions about science. In the West, one often thinks of scientific thinking as acultural, a universal form of theory and practice transcending national boundaries. Unlike art, religion, society, and even morals, we do not tend to speak of, say, French physics as opposed to Indian physics, or German biology as opposed to Chinese biology. Certainly, there may have been indigenous Asian ideas about physical things or life, but they were not "scientific" in the modern Western sense of a science involving empirical observation, controlled experiment, and mathematical modeling.[8]

Certainly, there is much truth in that view of science. (Only in the past couple of decades has the West undertaken a postmodern critique of science, increasingly treating it as a social and cultural construction.) Yet, it is also true that the view of modern technology in Japan is quite different from the one dominant in the West. We must remember that it is the West that invented the modern scientific method of discovery and the technological principles for applying what was learned. Japan, as it has with so many other things that have become important to itself, imported the very idea of modern Western science. For the West, scientific thinking was a natural culmination of a sequence of ideas and trends in its history. It developed science originally as a way of discovering the laws, at first assumed to be the divine laws, of the universe. Assuming God gave humans the rationality to find the divine pattern, early modern Western scientists reasoned that it was their destiny to use that knowledge to complete the act of creation, to modify the world, to make it a better place.

For the Japanese, however, the modern scientific and technological mode of thinking came from outside only about 150 years ago. With their traditional Buddhist and *yin-yang* notions that the world is always in a process of change, technological alteration was accepted as part of the natural order. Nature is changing, so we must adapt to it. Indeed, we are part of the natural change itself. From the traditional Japanese perspective, human technology is as natural as, say, the technology of a beaver. It is not part of a divine plan.[9]

This raises doubts about the common Western presupposition that science and technology must destroy traditional, non-modern, non-Western forms of human rationality, values, and spirituality. We often forget what modern science's own ideology is supposed to maintain: science is essentially value-free. The problem is that the Western tradition has intimately connected science with scientism, that is, with the belief that the scientific way of knowing is somehow primary, foundational, or privileged. We should also note that in our scientism, we tend to collapse science into the realm of physics, that is, the discipline which gives a mathematical model for the forces of the universe. The Galileos, Keplers, and Newtons were interested in finding the key to explaining the universe. Mathematics became that key. To go from the idea that mathematics is the key for all scientific knowledge to the idea that scientific knowledge is the key for all knowledge in general was obviously a great leap, but one that enthusiasm could span. Westerners were seeking a replacement for the medieval science of theology; they wanted a single, holistic theory that would yield the one great, uppercase Truth.[10]

The Japanese, on the other hand, were not traditionally looking for that. They were often interested in having a set of lowercase truths, each getting the job done for the task at hand. For them, truths were not monolithic but plural, not holistic but partial. The truth varies with the context. Without context, there is no truth.[11] As Zen Master Dogen (1200-1253) argued in the "Genjokoan" chapter of his *Shobogenzo,* the fish is correct to see the ocean as a translucent emerald palace. The human being far out at sea is correct to see the ocean as a great circle. The celestial deities are correct to see the ocean as shining like a string of jewels in the sunlight. They are incorrect only if they claim that their view is the only correct view.[12] Therefore, the Japanese had the tendency to ac-

cept science without its being a scientism. Science is true within its own context; traditional Japanese values in religion, ethics, and aesthetics are also true within their own contexts. This interpretation of science as no more than one example of multiple, equally valid contextual systems was sometimes found in turn-of-the-century Japanese philosophy.[13]

As students of Western philosophy, however, Japanese thinkers began to see difficulties in a theory of contextual truth that did not articulate any hierarchy or criterion of appropriateness for the different contexts. In such a philosophy, there could be no overall consistency, nor any dialectic progress toward an ever more inclusive system. Surely, it was thought, some forms of rationality necessarily evolve out of others; some forms of thinking are simply of a higher order than others. Once a culture develops science, it does not go back to animism. At least such was the argument of Western thinkers like Comte and Hegel, and the early twentieth-century Japanese philosophers were acutely aware of their theories. Is scientific knowledge somehow higher than, say, religious ways of explaining and assimilating reality? Is scientism—a possible byproduct of Westernization—philosophically justified? If so, Western technique could not logically exist alongside Asian morality.

These concerns were anticipated by Japanese philosophers early in this century. Nishida Kitaro (1870-1945), the founder of the Kyoto School, ruminated about this problem throughout his career. We will consider two major phases of his thought. The first phase was developed mainly in his first book, *An Inquiry into the Good* (*Zen no kenkyu*), written in 1911.[14] *Inquiry into the Good* was written at the very end of the Meiji period, a time when Japanese national confidence was on the upswing and the country had the opportunity to reflect seriously on the full implication of Westernization. In that pioneering work, indeed in all his works to follow, Nishida struggled with the great philosophical issue of his time—the juxtaposition of Western science and technology with traditional Japanese values. If Japanese values were to coexist alongside Western empiricism, there would have to be a common philosophical structure embracing and grounding the two. Otherwise, Japan would, intellectually, at least, suffer a cultural schizophrenia.

As a philosopher, Nishida was able to take the issue out of its culture-bound form (such as the question of whether the emperor should become Christian in order to help modernization) and universalize it into the classic Western problem of the relation between fact *(is)* and value *(ought)*. In this way, Nishida saw himself addressing a fundamental philosophical question, not just a cultural problem. One option open to Nishida was to follow the route of Hume and Kant, bifurcating fact and value into two separate domains and (for Kant) two different kinds of reasoning. This approach would, of course, affirm the possibility of separating Western science from Japanese values. But at what cost? Nishida knew that such a separation of *is* and *ought* was itself a divergence from the Eastern tradition. It was, in the final analysis, a Western approach to the problem, and it would indeed seem strange that only a foreign way of thinking could justify preserving Japanese values.

So Nishida tried to bring fact and value, empiricism and morality for religion or art), back together in a way consonant with the Asian tradition. At the same time, he thought his theory should be Western enough in form to serve the needs of an increasingly Westernized society. Here Nishida, like his childhood and lifelong friend D. T. Suzuki, found the writing of William James particularly provocative.[15] Rather than analyze science and value as two unrelated systems of reason, Nishida used James' notion of "pure experience" to articulate the common experiential flow toward unity underlying both the scientific and valuational enterprises. The surface differences notwithstanding, on a deeper level, science, morality, art, and religion share a single preconceptual drive (or "will") to unity. On the intellectual level, Nishida called this process "the intellectual intuition." Such was the basic thrust of his maiden philosophical work.

This solution to the fact/value, or is/ought, dilemma also satisfied Nishida as a practicing Zen Buddhist. Zen's ideal is the achievement of a preconceptual state of experiential purity ("no-mind") that becomes enacted pragmatically in various concrete ways, including thought.[16] For both James and Zen, thought is the temporary response to a break in the original unity of experience, a response which is itself intended to bring back the original unity of the experience. As Nishida put it, "pure experience is the alpha and omega of thought."

Inquiry into the Good became immediately popular among Japanese intellectuals and is probably today still the best-known work in modern philosophy among the Japanese. It is questionable how many of those intellectuals actually fathomed the nuances of Nishida's theory, but the major point for them was that Nishida had made Western-style philosophizing into something Japanese. His writing style had a Western ring to it, yet its fundamental insights wereconsistent with Japanese tradition. With *Inquiry into the Good,* modern Japanese philosophy—the so-called Kyoto or Nishida School—was born.

As Nishida's philosophical thinking further matured, however, he grew dissatisfied with *Inquiry into the Good*—not with its purpose, but with its philosophical form, its structural presuppositions. In particular, he criticized its psychologism (or "mysticism," as he sometimes called it). At the heart of his uneasiness was that *Inquiry into the Good* had attempted to solve the problem of the science/value split by appealing to a kind of experience, asserting it to be the ground of both the *is* and the *ought.* Nishida's readings in the Neo-Kantians during the period shortly after the publication of *Inquiry into the Good* made him sensitive to the problem of how forms of judgment, rather than strata of experience, interrelate.[17] That is, his concerns shifted from philosophical psychology to epistemology.

Throughout his life, Nishida constructed and subsequently razed his own attempts at systematic philosophy. He was an adamant critic of his own work and never seemed satisfied with the mode of explanations he had developed thus far. So the second phase of his thought rejected the idea that *Inquiry into the Good* had explained anything at all; it had simply described the drive of consciousness toward unification. One problem was that the psychologistic standpoint could only trace the evolution of thought in the individual's experiential process. It could, for example, describe how the desire for unity would lead to the emergence of scientific, moral, and religious thinking. But what about the fields of science, morality, and religion themselves? How can we analyze the interrelation of their claims without limiting them to modes in the biography of a particular person's own experience? It is, after all, one matter to say that my empirical, moral, aesthetic, and religious experiences relate to each other, and quite another matter to say that science, morality, art, and religion are related. The first is to connect experiences within myself, the latter to connect kinds of judgments about what is right. Nishida was impressed with the Neo-Kantian attempts to articulate and explain the rationale of judgments and came to believe his earlier, Jamesian view to be overly subjectivistic.

This new interest led Nishida to examine more closely the structure of judgmental form, what he called its "logic" (*ronri*). The fundamental insight he explored was that any judgment necessarily arises out of a particular contextual field, place, or *topos.* The Japanese word for this contextual field is *basho.* There may be a plurality of truths and contexts, but how do those contexts interrelate? In effect, Nishida wanted to argue for the priority of the religious over both the idealist and empiricist, over both thepsychologistic and the scientific. Although his argument was complex and refined or revised over many years, we can briefly summarize his point here in order at least to suggest how his line of thought developed.

Nishida analyzed closely the logical structure of judgmental form. Because he believed that any judgment necessarily arises out of a particular contextual field or place, his task in his later years was to explain the logic of those fields (*basho no ronri*). One way this system came to be formulated was in terms of the three *basho* of being, relative nothingness, and absolute nothingness. Roughly speaking, these corresponded to the judgmental fields of empiricism, idealism, and what he called the field of the "acting intuition" (*koiteki chokkan*).[18]

Nishida's "logic of *basho*" is a complex system always in flux and under revision. Still, it represents Nishida's most integrated and systematic attempt to deal with the issues of fact and value. To see the overall structure of Nishida's logic of *basho,* we can consider a simple empirical judgment—for example, "this table is brown." Scientific statements are generally of this form. They seem to express pure objectivity; the observer is so neutralized that he or she does not even enter into the judgment per se. They are statements about what is, statements about being (hence, the nomenclature "*basho* of being").

Yet, Nishida asked in what contextual field *(basho)* is such an objective judgment made? Where does one stand in making such a judgment about being? Nishida argued that such a judgment actually also makes judgments about our own consciousness. To neutralize the role of the observer as ordinary empirical judgments do is to say something about the observer—its role can be neutralized and ignored. This is an odd thing to say, however, since the larger contextual field of the judgment "the table is brown" is something more like "I see a brown table, and because what I see is real and external to my self, I can delete any reference to the self." So, Nishida maintains, the field or place of empirical judgments is really within the encompassing field of judgments about self-consciousness. Empiricism is actually dependent on, stands within, a field of judgments about self and its relation to the objects of experience. Since empirical judgments, as empirical judgments, ignore the being of the self, treating it as a nothing, this encompassing field can be called the "*basho* of relative nothingness." The self is, relative to empirical judgments, treated as a nothing. Of course, from the standpoint of the *basho* of relative nothingness, the self is very much a something, the very thing empiricism assumes, yet ignores. This insight, when taken literally, becomes the basis for idealism, theories that maintain that all knowledge is based in the mind.

Yet, Nishida was no idealist either. He criticized idealists (including Kant, Hegel, and Husserl) for not recognizing the true character of the *basho* within which their theories were formulated. The mistake of the idealists, according to Nishida, is that they think of the self as a thing, either a substance or a transcendental ego. Nishida claimed that the "I" in the previously stated judgment "I see a brown table and. . . ." is not an agent, but an action, what he called the "acting intuition." So the *basho* of idealism that sees the self as both subject and object is itself encompassed by a third *basho,* the contextual field of "absolute nothingness." The acting intuition is both an active involvement in the world and an intuitive reception of information about that world. It is a process, not a thing, so it can never be either the subject or the object of itself. It can never be the gist of judgment—it is absolutely a nothing when it comes to any judgment. Hence, it is called "absolute nothingness."

The acting-intuiting process (the absolute nothingness) is, therefore, the true basis of judgments about both fact and value. On the surface level, fact is, as it were, the intuiting side, whereas value is the acting side. Yet, one never exists without the other. The two are moments or profiles of a single process. The facts we discover are influenced by what we value, and what we value is influenced by what we discover. Thus, as Yuasa Yasuo has explained in his analysis of Nishida,[19] the intuition is also active (informed by value) and the acting is also passive (as response to data received). The two poles of the process are totally inseparable.

For Nishida, therefore, science cannot replace spirituality, nor can it be separated from questions of value. Within its own terms, in its own *basho,* science can advocate an impersonal, value-free objectivity. But what makes science possible is the scientist—a person with interests, values, and creativity. It is human intention that cordons off a place within which science can function.

Furthermore, human intentionality can be explained within its own mentalistic or idealistic terms, as we do in phenomenology, psychoanalysis, and some forms of psychology. In taking the self as their starting point, these disciplines have a clearly demarcated field within which to function. Yet, Nishida asks, what makes that field possible? Even "self" is a construction. It is not a given, but a product. As the idealists recognize, the self creates values that direct human activities like science. Nishida noted, however, that focusing an analysis on the self, indeed the very idea that there is a self, is itself a value. Nishida maintains that there is something more basic than self that constitutes the self—a responsive and creative process. That there is something more basic than self is a fundamental insight related to religious, ethical, and (sometimes) aesthetic values. It is this ineffable ground that is the basis for both self and the empirical world as known through science. At least such was Nishida's argument.

To sum up, in Japan, science did not have to break free of religious roots. It did not have to establish its hegemony. Rather, science and technology were foreign imports used to meet a set of practical needs related to political, military, and economic necessity. The traditional Japanese understanding of religion in terms of responsiveness and creativity was not displaced or successfully challenged by a new way of knowing. It did not have to be. The spiritual could continue to be a cornerstone of Japanese values, and, as Nishida tried to show, science could be seen as a special contextual extension of it, rather than a challenger to it.

Of course, not every Japanese philosopher agreed with Nishida. Yet, his impact has continued to be significant in Japan. In preparation for the college entrance examinations, only one book of Japanese philosophy is required reading: Nishida's *Inquiry into the Good.* Nishida's philosophical system is significant as an early, prewar philosophical struggle to articulate how it was possible to maintain "Asian values" and still develop "Western technique." His theory, in effect, justified what was already the social practice of giving science its "place" alongside the "places" of traditional religious and moral values. His philosophical theory showed, if nothing else, a distinctively Japanese way of accepting science without paying homage to the totem of scientism.

Has this tradition continued into more recent Japanese philosophy? The Kyoto School of philosophy founded by Nishida remains one of the most vigorous traditions in Japanese thought today.[20] Even philosophers who are not directly connected with the school still appreciate Nishida's pioneering work. We may wonder, therefore, whether there can be some fruitful interaction between Japanese and Western thought in the future. Yuasa Yasuo (1925-) is a Japanese philosopher who has been giving this issue some extensive thought over the past two decades, especially in terms of philosophical and medical views of the body. Since his works are beginning to be available in English translation,[21] let us briefly discuss his theory and its implications for our present theme.

Yuasa notes that, like science in general, Western and Asian medical traditions arose out of a radically different set of assumptions. He especially focuses on contrasting models of the body. With the birth of modern science in the West, the metaphor of the body as mechanism has become highly influential. Against this background, the West has tended to understand the living body's relation to the dead body as analogous to a machine that is either operative or turned off. Hence, modern Western medicine derives to a great extent from the anatomical information learned through thedissection of corpses or vivisection of animals, neither of which allows access to the functions of the conscious human body. More recently, the model was enhanced by the study of physiology in terms of organs and their biochemical functions. For Yuasa, what is significant is that most of this information was amassed under the assumption that the body can be understood independently of the mind, the physical mechanism independently of consciousness.

Asian forms of medicine such as Chinese acupuncture, on the other hand, developed out of the study of living, conscious human beings. The operative assumption is that the mind-body forms a single energy system responsive to the field in which it functions. To a traditional Asian medical theorist, it would be counterintuitive to study a dead or unconscious human body. It would be like trying to study electromagnetism with the electric current turned off.

Because of this difference in philosophical assumptions, Asian and Western medical traditions developed expertise in radically different aspects of human health and disease. Acupuncture developed highly sophisticated procedures for controlling pain, for example. (It is hard to study pain by dissecting a corpse.) On the other hand, Western medicine became expert at the physical manipulation of the body through surgery, for instance. (Surgery would not develop very far in a culture where patients were conscious and unanesthetized.)

In recent decades, Western medicine has developed increasingly sophisticated instruments for studying the living, conscious human being. There has been, therefore, a concurrent interest in psychosomatic and holistic approaches to medicine. Conversely, Asians have been learning Western medical techniques and have shown an interest in Western surgical, pharmaceutical, and diagnostic approaches. So, we are finding a situation in which two different conceptual schemes—and their correspondingly different claims about the body—are being brought into conjunction. Can the two systems influence and enrich each other? Yuasa claims they can, but only if each side is willing to call into question some of its most treasured assumptions. Since the Western tradition is more familiar to most of us, let us list just two major assumptions that Yuasa believes must be rethought in the Western view of the body.

According to Yuasa, the modern West has generally tended to assume that the relationship between the mind and the body is fixed and universal. That is, Western theorists tend to ask, "What is *the* relationship between the mind and the body?" Yuasa points out that, in contrast, most Asian traditions assume there is a range of interaction and integration between mind and body. For example, as I learned to type or play the piano, the relationship between my mind and my fingers changed. Originally, my mind had to "tell" my fingers what to do in a separate, self-conscious act. The fingersresponded slowly, awkwardly, and imprecisely. Now my fingers are more the extension of my mind when I type or play the piano. This suggests modification in the mind-body system.

Yuasa also points out that traditional Asian medicine retained its intimate relation with Asian spiritual disciplines. The Indian yogin is a good example of how the integration of mind and body is considered to be both a spiritually and medically healthy goal. As we noted already, modern Western science had to separate itself from religion in order to develop. Fasting, contemplation, prayer, chanting, and repetitive ritual exercises can all shed light on aspects of our bodies as well as our souls, but these activities have fallen outside the concerns of the Western scientific study of the body. Modern Western medicine has only recently begun to explore the therapeutic benefits of biofeedback, relaxation exercises, visualization techniques, and so forth. In effect, these originally spiritual exercises are beginning to find their way back into our Western understanding of the body.

The second assumption that Yuasa believes Western mind-body theories should reexamine concerns what he sometimes calls the "third entity" that is neither mental nor somatic, but the basis of both. Taking physics for its paradigm, modern Western science has drawn too strong a bifurcation between matter and energy. If we were to take biology, not physics, to be the ground of science (as Asian cultures did, in many respects), then we would see the need for this third term. In fact, we would be asking not about matter and energy's applicability to biology, but rather about this third term's relation to nonhuman phenomena. Yuasa believes that in East Asia, the Chinese concept of *qi (ki* in Japanese) is just such a third term. It is interesting that it is foundational to East Asian theories of acupuncture, artistry, electricity, and cosmology alike. What Yuasa calls for is a more Western physical study of this phenomenon that is not even as yet recognized as a category in the West. Such research is, in fact, under way in both China and Japan.

From the examples of Nishida and Yuasa, what summary statements can we make about the modern Japanese philosophical views of science and technology?

1. A non-European culture can accept Western science and technology without necessarily destroying the roots of its traditional value systems. The opposition of science and spirituality, the bifurcation of *is* and *ought,* is a consequence of historical developments in the West and need not apply to other cultural traditions with different histories. For these oppositions not to occur, however, science must not degenerate into a scientism, the belief that only the scientific form of knowledge is valid or that scientific knowledge is the ground of all legitimate forms ofknowing. The evidence suggests that the Japanese have been able to accept science without falling prey to scientism. Nishida's and Yuasa's philosophies give two prominent rationales for keeping science distinct from the assumptions of scientism.

2. The Japanese philosophical tradition for centuries has resisted the idea of developing a single monolithic ontology implying the existence of a single, all-embracing Truth. Rather, the Japanese have traditionally emphasized a world of multiple truths, each dependent on its context. This is not, it should be noted, a relativism, but a pluralism. Relativism would maintain that there is no standpoint by which to judge truth. Pluralism maintains that truth can only be judged from one standpoint at a time, and the standpoints themselves can be judged as appropriate to the questions asked. Within a given context, things are absolutely true or false, not just relatively so.

The Japanese view lends itself to seeing Western logic and scientific thinking as a pragmatic tool for addressing certain problems, rather than as an attempt to explain all things within one supersystem. The god of Western logic and empiricism can only be a henotheistic god, not the monotheistic god that scientism tries to make of it.

3. Following on the previous point, we can wonder about the relation between pluralism and philosophy or religion. Today there seems a need to express our philosophical and religious commitments within a pluralistically open context. Does the Japanese view of truth better lend itself to that enterprise than do the more monolithic, system-building approaches inherited from our Christian and modern Western philosophical traditions? Is part of the success of the Japanese economy related to the culture's capacity to recognize the dependence of truth on context and to move freely and flexibly among different contexts and seemingly different truths? As the world becomes economically, politically, and even philosophically and scientifically more interdependent, the alternatives seem to be either the enforcement of a hegemonic uniformity or the development of the capacity to live within an increasingly pluralistic context. If the latter alternative is preferred—and I would argue it is—might the West learn something from the Japanese experience and the philosophies developing out of it?

NOTES

Japanese personal names that appear in both the text and the notes may be in either traditional Japanese order (family name first) or in Western order (family name last). Also, conventional usage sometimes requires that historical personages be referred to by their *given* rather than their family names. Here are the names as they appear with *given* name for each in italics: *Masao* Abe, *Setsuko* Aihara, Inou *Enryo,* Inoue *Tetsujiro,* Kuki *Shozo,* Nagatomo *Shigenori,* Nakayama *Shigeru,* Nishida *Kitaro,* Nishitani *Keiji,* Oda *Nobunaga,* Sakuma *Shozan,* *Masayoshi* Sugimoto, Takeuchi *Yoshinori,* Tanabe Hajime, *Kazuaki* Tanahashi, Tanizaki *Jun'ichiro,* Tokugawa *Ieyasu,* Toyotomi *Hideyoshi,* Yamamoto *Seisaku,* Yuasa *Yasuo.*

[1] See Charles A. Moore, ed., *The Indian Mind: Essentials of Indian Philosophy and Culture, The Chinese Mind: Essentials of Chinese Philosophy and Culture,* and *The Japanese Mind: Essentials of Japanese Philosophy* (all Honolulu: East-West Center Press, University of Hawaii Press, 1967). Moore's "Introductions" to each volume are titled, respectively: "The Comprehensive Indian Mind," "The Humanistic Chinese Mind," and simply "Introduction." The first sentence of the Japanese volume starts: "The Japanese thought-and-culture is probably the most enigmatic and paradoxical of all major traditions . . ." (p. 1). The length of the introductions are perhaps also revealing. The Indian volume is sixteen pages of text, the Chinese ten, and the Japanese three.

[2] A good example of this ambivalence among Japanese intellectuals about the process of modernization is Tanizaki Jun'ichiro's essay, *"In'ei raisan,"* written in 1933. A fine translation is the short book by Tanizaki, *In Praise of Shadows,* trans. Thomas J. Harper and Edward G. Seidensticker (New Haven, Connecticut: Leete's Island Books, 1977).

[3] As Tanizaki's *In Praise of Shadows* suggests, there is an aesthetic dimension to the acceptance of foreign ways. Similarly, in his *lki no kozo* (The structure of *iki*) (Tokyo: Iwanami Shoten, 1930), Kuki Shuzo typically characterized cultural influences in terms of "hue" and "tint." These examples suggest that Japanese thinkers often thought of the impact of culture in terms of aesthetic rather than logical categories.

[4] For a general account of the initial acceptance and later prohibition of firearms in Japan, see Noel Perrin, *Giving Up the Gun: Japan's Reversion to the Sword, 1543-1879* (Boulder, Colorado: Shambala Publications, Inc., 1979).

[5] The shoguns did allow and even endorsed a very limited influx of Western scientific works, so-called *rangaku* or "Dutch Learning." These were primarily limited to anatomy, medicine, astronomy (for calendar-making), and gunnery.

[6] It is noteworthy that the first translated work of Dutch Learning related to mathematics did not appear until 1857, after the period of seclusion was over. See the table in Masayoshi Sugimoto and David L. Swain, *Science and Culture in Traditional Japan* (Cambridge: MIT

Press, 1978; Rutland, Vermont: Charles E. Tuttle Company, 1989), p. 331. The book discusses the influx of Chinese science to Japan in two "waves:" 600-894 and 1401-1639. The two premodern Western "waves" were 1543-1639 and 1720-1854. This detailed study adds important nuance to many of the necessarily generalized historical statements in this essay.

[7] For an excellent institutional history of the development of modern Western science in Japan, see James R. Bartholomew, *The Formation of Science in Japan* (New Haven, Connecticut: Yale University Press, 1989).

[8] Of course, cultural historians of science have generally pointed out the qualifications that must be made about this view of science as Western. In the case of Chinese science, for example, there has been extensive research by such scholars as Joseph Needham and Nathan Sivin. See, for example, Needham's multivolume *Science and Civilisation in China* (Cambridge: Cambridge University Press, 1954-) and Sivin's *Chinese Alchemy: Preliminary Studies* (Cambridge: Harvard University Press, 1968). Also, see Nakayama Shigeru and Nathan Sivin, eds., *Chinese Science: Explorations of an Ancient Tradition* (Cambridge: The M.I.T. Press, 1973).

[9] A contemporary example illustrates this poignantly. At some major intersections in many large Japanese cities, there are electronic billboards giving readings of the time of day, the temperature, and the levels of noise and carbon monoxide. As the traffic light changes and the vehicles move, one can see the noise and carbon monoxide numbers zoom upward. If such a sign were to appear on most American or European street corners, it would be a political statement about the danger of pollution. In Japan, however, it seems to be taken often as simply an indicator of what is the case. There is the temperature and there is the carbon monoxide level—two givens. This, I think, is one reason the Japanese, despite their love of nature, were slow to address environmental pollution. Technology was seen as natural, not the human intervention into the natural. Of course, Japan did eventually respond to the environmental crisis and has made tremendous strides, in some cases outstripping the West. But even the cleanup campaign was never posed in the humanity-nature dichotomy. It was simply humans taking part in the natural process of purification. Humanity acted out of the need for self-preservation and health, not out of any sense of moral responsibility to the environment.

[10] That the enterprise of technological development can differ in Japan from the West is illustrated by the following anecdote, related to me by a research and development officer of a major U.S. electronics company. Japanese corporations hold all the major patents on the technology for the home videocassette recorder. How did this technological advantage occur? In the 1970s the majorAmerican electronics companies held a joint meeting concerning the future of home video equipment. At that time, two possible formats had been developed.

First, there was the videotape format: it had the advantage of being able to record as well as to play back prerecorded materials. The second was the videodisk format, which was somewhat better in reproductive quality but lacked the capacity to record. Obviously, the videotape system would be more marketable. The problem, however, was the complexity of the videotape mechanism. In a video recorder, unlike an audio recorder, both the tape heads and the tape surface must be in constant movement. Hence, the mechanism was very fragile and the tape tended to get wound around the tape heads causing a breakdown. Although rugged machines had been developed for professional use, the engineers were skeptical about the prospect of an affordable machine that would stand up to the rough use found in the typical American home. They exchanged data about the physics of the mechanical problem and decided that there could be no practical solution.

Meanwhile, the Sony Corporation engineers were tackling the same problem. Instead of swapping formulas, however, they assigned a team of engineers to study the situation. Their approach was to examine the prototype machine for hours, days, and weeks on end, watching how the tape continually got entangled. Then one of the engineers bent a little piece of wire into an odd shape and inserted it into a crucial point in the tape path. The problem was resolved. The production cost of the piece of wire that made the VCR possible, I was told, is about nineteen cents. The interesting part of the story for our purposes is how the Japanese engineer explained to my informant how they came to their sophisticated, technical solution of the problem. He said that they just watched the tape get entangled over and over again until they saw the way to "help the tape go where it wanted to go." The home VCR was the offspring of a marriage between technology and animism.

Another way of posing this is that the Japanese engineers took the attitude of invention rather than pure science. They "tinkered" with the physical object instead of first placing it under the universal categories of mathematical physics. Ironically, this used to be called "Yankee ingenuity."

[11] There were exceptions to this general tendency to seek contextual truths over a single, comprehensive, systematic Truth. In the early Heian period, for example, Kukai's esoteric Buddhism tried to develop a comprehensive philosophical system including metaphysics, epistemology, a theory of language, and aesthetics. It did not develop much after him as a continuing tradition, however. In the Tokugawa period, Zhu Xi's Neo-Confucian philosophy also had some tendencies toward developing a single, comprehensive system of truth. It was undermined almost immediately, though, by the moreantirationalistic, indigenous development of *kogaku* and *kokugaku*.

[12] This work has appeared in various translations. See, for example, Kazuaki Tanahashi, ed., *Moon in a Dewdrop:*

Writings of Zen Master Dogen (San Francisco: North Point Press, 1985). The fascicle *"Genjokoan"* is translated as "Actualizing the Fundamental Point," and the passage cited is found on page 71.

We may also note in passing that Dogen's position on this point is akin to the pragmatism of Hilary Putnam's "internal realism," for example. For Putnam, truth or meaning is relative to the concepts in which it is framed. As the conceptual systems change, different propositions or theories will be true, even propositions that, if they had shared the same conceptual system, would be incompatible. Putnam develops this view in, for example, his book *The Many Faces of Realism: The Paul Carus Lectures* (LaSalle, Illinois: Open Court Publishing, 1987). This parallel exemplifies the extent to which Dogen's type of philosophical stance cannot be discounted as merely "premodern" in the Western sense.

[13] On trying to set the contextual domains for realism vs. idealism or science vs. spirituality, see the discussion of Inoue Enryo and Inoue Tetsujiro, in chapter 1 of the dissertation by Robert J. J. Wargo, "The Logic of Basho and the Concept of Nothingness in the Philosophy of Nishida Kitaro" (Ann Arbor: University of Michigan, 1972).

[14] Nishida Kitaro, *An Inquiry into the Good,* trans. Masao Abe and Christopher Ives (New Haven, Connecticut: Yale University Press, 1990).

[15] Suzuki tended to focus on James' *Varieties of Religious Experience,* whereas Nishida was more interested in the *Psychology* and *Essays on Radical Empiricism.* This suggests the fundamental difference in their orientations: Suzuki was more religious and mystical, Nishida more psychological and epistemological.

[16] For an account of Zen Buddhism that emphasizes this aspect, see my *Zen Action/Zen Person* (Honolulu: University of Hawaii Press, 1981).

[17] For a highly edited translation of Nishida's journals on his reading of the Neo-Kantians, see his *Intuition and Reflection in Self-consciousness,* trans. Valdo H. Viglielmo with Takeuchi Yoshinori and Joseph S. O'Leary. (Albany, New York: State University of New York Press, 1987).

[18] The best treatment of this aspect of Nishida's thought is the dissertation by Robert J. J. Wargo, cited in note 13 above. The dissertation's Appendix includes a translation of Nishida's "General Summary" in his *The System of Self Consciousness of the Universal,* a crucial formulation of Nishida's position at this stage of his thought.

[19] Yuasa Yasuo, *The Body: Toward an Eastern Mind-Body Theory,* ed. T. P. Kasulis, trans. Nagatomo Shigenori and T. P. Kasulis (Albany, New York: State University of New York Press, 1987), chap. 2.

[20] Two other prominent members of the Kyoto School interested in the place of science were Tanabe Hajime (1885-1962) and Nishitani Keiji (1900-1990). Some of their works have become available in English: Tanabe Hajime, *Philosophy as Metanoetics,* trans. Takeuchi Yoshinori (Berkeley: University of California Press, 1986); Nishitani Keiji, *Religion and Nothingness,* trans. Jan Van Bragt (Berkeley: University of California Press, 1982); Nishitani Keiji, *The Self-Overcoming of Nihilism,* trans. Graham Parkes and Setsuko Aihara (Albany, New York: State University of New York Press, 1990); and Nishitani Keiji, *Nishida Kitaro,* trans. Yamamoto Seisaku and James W. Heisig (Berkeley: University of California Press, 1991).

[21] So far, three book-length works have appeared: Yuasa Yasuo, *The Body* (see note 19 above); David Edward Shaner, Shigenori Nagatomo, and Yuasa Yasuo, *Science and Comparative Philosophy: Introducing Yuasa Yasuo* (Leiden: E. J. Brill, 1989); and Yuasa Yasuo, *The Body, Self-cultivation, and Ki-energy,* trans. Shigenori Nagatomo and Monte S. Hull (Albany, New York: State University of New York Press, 1993).

Steven Heine (essay date 1996)

SOURCE: "Is the Place of Nothingness Not a Place?: Worldmaking and Criticism in Modern Japanese Philosophy," in *Worldmaking,* edited by William Pencak, Peter Lang, 1996, pp. 99-120.

[*In the following essay, Heine analyzes Nishida's concept of time and space, contending that the philosopher sought to "reconcile conceptual polarities and dichotomies based on traditional Zen Buddhist doctrines."*]

I

JAPANESE CONCEPTIONS OF TIME AND SPACE

Philosophical worldmaking can be said to consist of the constructing, or the reconstructing, of the fundamental elements of time and space. Typically, traditional and modern Japanese thinkers argue for a synthetic, nondualistic outlook which emphasizes the inseparability and ultimate identity of these two elements, for '(t)he 'now' of immediacy is always a 'here' as well.'[1] That is, the categories of time and space are equalizable and interchangeable. A prime example of a view of the unity of time and space is Nishida Kitaro's (1870-1945) notion of the 'logic of place' *(basho no ronri)* based on a 'contradictory self-identity' *(mujunteki jiko dôitsu)* that characterizes 'absolute nothingness' *(zettai mu),* which refers to the interdependence, ultimate insubstantiality, and thus the absolute mediation of nonobjectifiable opposites. Nishida, the founder of the Kyoto School of modern Japanese philosophy, seeks to reconcile conceptual polarities and dichotomies based on traditional Zen Buddhist doctrines that situate enlightenment in terms of the nonduality of ultimate *(nirvana)* and mundane *(samsara)* reality, and in a way that recalls the Western monistic tradition expressed in Gnostic and Neo-Platonic sources.

'In my view,' he writes, 'the phenomenal world is spatial in the form 'from many to one' . . . and yet is temporal in the form 'from one to many'. . . . This is the self-contradictory structure of the conscious act.'[2] For Nishida and the Kyoto School, oppositions and contradictions involving temporality and spatiality are illusory ideations which can and must be overcome through contemplative philosophical insight, often supported by meditation experience.

Nishida's notion of place represents the culmination of his lifelong philosophical quest to discern the ground of pure experience by drawing on East Asian sources, especially Zen thought, from which basis he engages in dialogue with a variety of Western philosophical standpoints, including classical Greek philosophy and medieval mysticism as well as modern American pragmatism, German idealism, and continental phenomenology. For Nishida, place does not refer to an idea of utopia or heterotopia, but functions as a metaphor for the transformative matrix that lies at the basis of all perceptions of consciousness and acts of judgment. Nishida's position has long had its critics, including Buddhists, who feel that place reifies and objectifies nonsubstantive, impermanent reality, and non-Buddhists, who maintain that Nishida has failed to address concrete social and ethical issues. In particular, the social critics suggest that Nishida, at least in part, may have developed the notion of place, which he tends to associate in some passages with imperial hegemony, in support of Japanese nationalist ideology before World War II.

My aim in this paper is to review critically Nishida's philosophical writings that express the notion of place as well as the various criticisms that have emerged both prior to and since the war. I will argue, however, that the problematics in Nishida's philosophical worldmaking do not stem so much from the kinds of metaphysical or socio-ethical limitations suggested by most critics, but rather from the fact that his modern logical style of thought and writing fails to capture the traditional Zen form of expression that uses irony and paradox to undermine its own assertions. In other words, the reification of place which critics point to in Nishida derives from the absence in his writings of the kinds of rhetorical devices that are found in the medieval Sino-Japanese Zen records that he seeks to convey to a twentieth-century audience which try to insure that all conceptualizations are seen as provisional pedagogical tools rather than objectified, hypostatized entities.

I will begin with a brief overview of traditional Japanese thought concerning time and space and of Nishida's role as its primary modern interpreter.

The modern Japanese sense of worldmaking based on establishing an identity of time and space is the result of the historical interplay and theoretical resolution of two conceptual currents: the Buddhist view of impermanence (*mujô*) as the key manifestation and symbol of the insubstantiality of reality experienced during times of loss, uncertainty, instability, death, and dissolution; and the indigenous Shinto emphasis on the sacrality of spaces understood in terms of the 'betweenness,' gaps, or intervals (*ma*) lurking betwixt and between conventional sites, such as shadows, openings, hollows, crevices, etc. An interesting poetic expression of the unity of impermanence and spatial gaps evoking the aesthetic ideal of 'profound mystery' (*yûgen*) is the following 5-line, 31-syllable verse (*waka*) by the medieval Buddhist poet, Saigyô:

> A heart subdued (*kokoro naki*)
> Yet poignant sadness (*aware*)
> Is so deeply felt;
> A crane flying over the marsh
> As autumn dusk descends.

Here, Saigyô depicts the experience of a transcendental emotion, deeper than and enriching the usual sense of Buddhist detachment suggested in the opening line, based on the contemplation of a deceptively simple natural scene: the bird flying off at the time of transition in the daily and seasonal cycles symbolized by the twilight sky. In the image of the 'autumn dusk,' an example of *yugen* frequently used in medieval literature, temporal and spatial qualities converge to suggest movement, ephemerality, and distance in a physical as well as a spiritual sense.

Nevertheless, despite persistent claims of nonduality, there is a tendency for Japanese thinkers to give a preference or priority to one side of the identity, either to the side of temporality or to the side of spatiality, while subsuming the other side within the dominant one. For example, the thirteenth century Zen thinker Dôgen formulates a cluster of doctrines stressing the unity of time and space, including 'being-time' (*uji*, or all beings are time and all times are being), 'here-and-now enlightenment' (*genjokoan*), and 'impermanence-Buddha-nature' (*mujobussho*, or the equality of transiency and ultimate reality). In an effort to restore the significance of the basic Buddhist doctrine of impermanence, which he felt was distorted by disguised assumptions of eternalism among his contemporary philosophers, Dôgen tends to give priority to temporality and to view spatiality as an extension of it. He argues, 'The mountain is time and the sea is time. If they were not time, there would be no mountain or sea. You must realize that the time of the mountain and sea occurs right now. If time should deteriorate, the mountain and sea will deteriorate as well; and if time does not deteriorate, neither will the mountain or sea.'[3] In this case, the identity of time and space (or beings) is argued from the standpoint of the former rather than the latter, as mountains and seas are defined by their innate link to temporality.

On the other hand, some Japanese thinkers exhibit the reverse tendency of emphasizing the identity of time and space from the standpoint of spatiality, thereby subsuming temporality within it. For example, traditional Pure Land Buddhist thinkers such as Genshin portray enlightenment as a spiritual rebirth (*ojo*) in the 'western Paradise' that is described in exquisitely vivid language as a realm filled with timelessly precious and beautiful objects. Also, both esoteric Buddhist and Shinto priests have built temples and shrines following the occult law of geomancy, according to which there are sacred spiritual-physical energies or force-fields linking sacred mountains and other natural locations. An interesting modern example of giving priority to space is found in the critique of Martin Heidegger by Watsuji Tetsuro. Watsuji, a Kyoto School intellectual historian and anthropologist known for initiating cross-cultural philosophical interpretations of Dôgen's view of time in comparison with Hegel, Bergson, and others, also was critical of Heidegger for overemphasizing temporality at the expense of a clear focus on spatiality. In his work *Climate and Culture,* written in the late 1920s when Heidegger was first being translated and interpreted in Japan, Watsuji begins by arguing that Heidegger's analysis in *Being and Time* of Dasein (or Being-there) as Being-in-the-world tends to neglect the side of 'worldhood' or 'there-ness.' These notions are introduced and discussed by Heidegger, but they are given relatively little attention when compared to the way he highlights the existential issues of anxiety, guilt, and death that are crucial to the formation of temporality. Watsuji goes on to examine the climatic roots of various cultural ideologies and religious traditions, including the monsoon, temperate, and desert climate mentalities.

Nishida Kitaro also seems to give priority to space in formulating his primary metaphysical principle of 'place' *(basho),* or the place of absolute nothingness *(zettai mu).* The notion of place, which can also be translated as field, context, locus, or topos (Nishida was influenced by Plato's notion of *topos),* refers not to a specific location or site but to the 'where' of ultimate reality ruled by the principle of contradictory self-identity, 'an undifferenti-ated . . . arena where all things arise, except that it is not a place or arena, but an aperture or opening.'[4] Place remains beyond yet functions through particular locations in space. Therefore, Nishida frequently stresses that place 'has a spatial character in respect of the one negating the many in the order of coexistence, and is temporal in respect of the many negating the one in the order of occurrence. Time and space are not independent forms, but only dimensions of the self-transforming matrix of space-time.'[5] Nishida also extensively examines temporality in developing the notion of the 'continuity of discontinuity' *(hirenzoku no renzoku),* which clarifies the significance of the eternal now in relation to the passage of time. Yet, in the culminating stage of the development of 'Nishida philosophy' (or 'Nishida *tetsugaku'*) he chooses a spatial rather than a temporal metaphor, in large part to demonstrate that absolute nothingness is not an abstract, ethereal realm, but is invariably manifested in concrete reality. Nevertheless, '(t)he Platonic analogy . . . breaks down quickly, for its spatial character presupposes the complete externality of the *Topos* with respect to that which abides within it.'[6]

The title of Jonathan Z. Smith's book, *Map is Not Territory,*[7] which deals largely with the encounter between universal and local religious traditions, suggests that spaces and places are not to be understood only as literal sites but as conceptual lattices shaped in large part by ideological assumptions and bids for power. While this is partly the case for Nishida, he also emphasizes the contrary view, that is, that place is not only conceptual but occurs right here-and-now in the concrete world. Yet, Nishida's view is different than Gaston Bachelard's topo-analysis in *The Poetics of Space,*[8] which analyzes quaint microcosmic locations, especially in the home environment. Nishida focuses on the macrocosmic, or, rather, on the 'where' that is beyond the distinction of macrocosm and microcosm, or universal and particular. Nishida, who was very much influenced by Husserlian phenomenology, may not have been familiar with Heidegger's work, especially the post-*Being and Time* writings. But his use of the image of place recalls the later Heidegger's turn to spatial metaphors, such as 'clearing,' 'region,' and 'four-fold,' though Heidegger also frequently writes of Being in a temporal sense as an 'event' *(Eriegnis)* or 'event of appropriation.'

It is important to recognize that, although almost always translated as the 'logic of place' (or field, context, locus, topos, etc.), Nishida's approach is actually a 'topo-logical or contextual logic,' based on his use of the adjectival form in Japanese *(bashoteki ronri)* rather than the prepositional *(basho no ronri,* or 'logic *of* place').[9] Thus, Nishida's topological logic (sometimes referred to as predicative logic), in contrast to objective, subjective, or even dialectical logic, neither proposes a formal logical analysis of place in contrast to other categories such as the void nor intends either a reification of place as an other-worldly absolute or a hypostatization of it as a particular locale. Nishida's view is not a utopia in the sense of a perfect place (literally 'no place,' *u-topos*) or a heterotopia as a collection of multiple individuated locations. Although influenced by traditional Japanese notions of sacrality, he does not wish to identify place with holy mountains, geomantic forces, or ritual symbols such as mandalas (circular symbols used in meditation) or stupas (shrines commemorating burial or other sacred sites). Nor does he resurrect the traditional Buddhist notion of pure space *(akasa)* as a symbol of *nirvana* that resolves the problematics of the world of *samsara* characterized by the incessant flux of time.

Yet, the question naturally arises: Where is this place, and why does Nishida refer to its process of 'self-determination'? If the place of nothingness is not a place, why use spatial imagery? And if it is potentially any and every place, how can the appropriate sites be located and distinguished from those that do not disclose the absolute? Nishida's philosophy has received persistent criticism from a variety of sources raising such questions, from Zen and Pure Land Buddhists as well as from Marxists and other non-Buddhists, and for philosophical, religious, and, very frequently, political reasons. Nishida's two foremost disciples, Tanabe Hajime (influenced by Pure Land theology) and Nishitani Keiji (deriving from Zen mediation), are among his sharpest critics who argue for understanding place in a more metaphorical, existential sense as an interior capacity for fulfilled subjectivity. At the same time, both before and after the second world war, Marxists and leftists, who apparently originally coined the moniker 'Kyoto School' in the 1930s as a negative term, have taken Nishida to task for the nationalist implications they find in his wartime writings—a Hegelian-Heideggerian tendency to identify the place of the absolute with the state, in this case, imperial Japan.

Nishida's writings during this period, in addition to his professional and personal activities, are multifaceted and very complex. He was primarily a pure philosopher although he did participate in discussions and debates about national ideology. It is important to point out that there can be no easy judgments either condemning him for fanatical nationalism or dismissing a political criticism altogether. Rather, as Pierre Bourdieu suggests in his discussion of *The Political Ontology of Martin Heidegger*,[10] who was similarly involved in a philosophical worldmaking which became entangled with fascist political ideology before World War II, there may be no such thing as autonomous philosophy independent of a socio-political environment so that it is necessary to recognize a dual reading of Nishida: the primary one philosophical, and the secondary one ideological. Furthermore, the distinction between an existential and a political criticism is not so clear-cut, because some of the Buddhist criticism has also focused on political issues, ranging from a right-wing perspective in the prewar writings of Tanabe, who at that time may have felt that Nishida was not sufficiently supportive of nationalism, to a left-wing perspective in the prewar work of Ichikawa Hakugen and the recent methodology known as Critical Buddhism *(hihan bukkyô),* both of which challenge the tacit complicity of Kyoto School thinkers with the emperor system.

In the next two sections, I will explain the formation of Nishida's philosophy of the place of absolute nothingness and assess the various criticisms, Buddhist and non-Buddhist, which suggest that Nishida portrays place in a way that is alternatively either too abstract or too specific. In the concluding section, I argue that the limitation in Nishida's philosophical worldmaking is not so much based on existential or political grounds, which reflect contemporary issues, but rather on the way he overlooks or at least chooses not to use key elements of the traditional Zen Buddhist discursive style, such as ironic wordplays, tautologies, and paradoxes, although he seeks to articulate Zen thought in modern perspectives. The medieval Zen records often include what can be referred to as rhetorical safeguard devices against overly literal or transcendental interpretations of sacred space by employing a paradoxical methodology of at once evoking and refuting, or constructing and deconstructing, supernatural imagery from an ironic standpoint.

II

THE FORMATION OF NISHIDA'S PHILOSOPHY OF PLACE

Nishida's thought developed through four stages of a complex, lifelong philosophical project, with the philosophy of place emerging prominently in the final two stages. The underlying goal of his project is a systematic disclosure of the unified ground of all forms of experiential reality, encompassing the intuitive and rational, aesthetic and moral, contemplative and active, religious and secular, and metaphysical and mathematical. This ground is disclosed in a manner that attempts to be faithful to Japanese spirituality, particularly Zen, yet borrows from Western logical rigor, especially Aristotelian logic and Kantian epistemology. Although references to Western thought, from the classics through medieval and modern philosophers, are actually frequently moreabundant than Buddhist sources, it is clear from both the philosophical content of his work and recorded private remarks to colleagues that Zen meditation lies at the root of Nishida's philosophy. Yet Nishida is by no means a Zen apologist. Nor does he engage in comparative philosophy as an end in itself or to assert the supremacy of Buddhism—a delicate but critical standpoint not always perfectly upheld by his disciples. Rather, comparison is used as a philosophical methodology for uncovering the universal logical-ontological foundations of the multiple manifestations and dimensions of the unity of experience.

The initial stage of Nishida's philosophy is manifested in his first major work, *An Inquiry into the Good* (1911),[11] which analyzes reality in terms of the notion of pure experience, the direct and immediate givenness or presentness of reality. Pure experience, identified with the 'good' *(zen)* as a unity of will and spirit, knowledge and action, is the fundamental moment of perception prior to thought, reflection, or judgment. It is the universal intentionality, not a passive perception, to 'know events as they truly are' without hesitation or deliberation. In this work, Nishida is influenced by William James's radical empirical methodology which seeks to get at things as they are, though with mystical or contemplative implications based on a sense of primordial harmony, rather than James's pragmatist moral imperative. The next stage, *Intuition and Reflection in Self-Consciousness* (1917),[12] marks an attempt, later acknowledged by Nishida to be unsuccessful, to overcome the psychologism or overtly subjectivistic tone of the earlier work. Here, Nishida seeks to escape from referring primarily to the self or the human subject and to find a neutral vantage point that encompasses subject and object, self and other, without giving priority to either side. He synthesizes Henri Bergson's 'pure duration' with neo-Kantian categories to eliminate psychological terminology and formulate an epistemological notion of self-consciousness as a transcendental ego at the foundation of experience.

The third stage, beginning with *From the Acting to the Seeing* (1927), marks Nishida's breakthrough or radical reversal from the subjectivist tendencies of his previous writings toward a neutral determination of reality beyond subject/object, internal/external, psychological/metaphysical dichotomies. This results in the logic of place of absolute nothingness, or, rather, in a topological or contextual logic articulating the meaning of nothingness. This can also be referred to as the 'logic of truly Subjective Self-awakening,' keeping in mind that '(t)he logic of place, however, neither confronts objective logic nor excludes it.'[13] According to one interpreter, 'The logic of place enabled [Nishida] to organize the whole of the efforts of philosophy—perceptual judgment, phenomenology of consciousness, enlightenment—in a single systematic whole . . .'[14]

Absolute nothingness is rooted in the Mahayana Buddhist doctrine of emptiness as the nondifferentiable and nonsubstantive ground of reality. Genuine emptiness or nothingness, though unsupported by any prior ontological condition, remains the basis of all phenomena, in contrast to the Western category of mere nonexistence or absence, for which the Japanese term *kyomu* (literally 'hollow nothingness') is used. According to Nishida, Western thought, with the exception of Neo-Platonic mystics like Meister Eckhart, Nicholas Cusanus, and Jakob Boehme, has generally been preoccupied with the opposition between being *(u)* and nonbeing *(kyomu)* and has failed to penetrate to absolute nothingness. Place is influenced by Plato's concept of *topos* as the 'receptacle of ideas' as well as Husserlian phenomenology and perhaps even quantum physics, the latter two representing modern standpoints that view the world from a synthetic and dynamic contextual perspective. The notion of place *(basho)* highlights the Zen emphasis that emptiness not be seen as an abstract transcendental realm detached from concrete existence but as perpetually realized in the ever-varying manifestations of the fullness of being, thus according with the famous *Heart Sutra* dictum: 'Form is none other than emptiness; emptiness is none other than form.'

Place as a unifying principle can be understood provisionally in terms of three dimensions. The first dimension is the physical world of objectifiable being corresponding to the noematic realm in Husserl's terminology. The second is the world of human reality, the subjective or noetic aspect of experience, that is, the realm of consciousness which perceives and evaluates objective entities. This realm was given priority in Nishida's early writings, but is seen now as an aspect of the topological self-determination of nothingness on a relative level which is experienced as a no-thing that makes possible our perception of and judgments concerning objects. The third dimension is the intelligible world of absolute nothingness, the nonsubstantive synthetic context for all appearances and judgments encompassing but unrestricted by the noetic and noematic, which are not independent entities linked together but a single inseparable event. The intelligible world is the basis of the good, the true, and the beautiful, and it is realizable only through the 'dazzling obscurity' of sudden and selfless illumination. Here, Nishida's work has significant affinities with a variety of sources which function on the fringes of mainstream Western discourse, including mystics who experience the unity-in-differentiation of the Godhead as expressed in Gnostic, Neo-Platonic, or Kabbalistic writings, and modern poststructuralist and deconstructive philosophers who seek to overcome logocentric tendencies in conventional Western thought and language by highlighting the infinite variety of signifiers without a single, transcendental signified standing substantively in the background.

The final stage of Nishida's work, culminating in his last major essay written at the end of World War II just before his death, 'Topological Logic and the Religious Worldview' (1945),[15] is a clarification of the central tenets of the previous stage in terms of two interrelated topics: the spiritual or existential in addition to the metaphysical or epistemological implications of place; and the temporal-historical foundations of culture and, in particular, the distinctiveness of Japanese culture in contrast to the West. Nishida shows that place is not a simple oneness but the dialectical interplay of antithetical, contradictory forces manifested in time as the Eternal Now embracing past/future in the absolute presencing of each and every complete moment. Religion, the cultural dimension that alone deals with the ultimate concern of life and death, can be transformed into a new foundation for world society through a synthesizing of Christian morality and Buddhist meditation on the basis of absolute nothingness that allows for the integrity and self-determination of each tradition as oppositions that are reconciled as part of the principle of contradictory self-identity. But during this last stage, perhaps under pressure from the government which he may or may not have been trying to resist,[16] and despite an otherwise international perspective, Nishida rather chauvinistically stresses how the unique features of Japanese spirituality realized in the imperial state are necessary for the overcoming of the Western scientific, mechanistic worldview. For example, Nishida suggests that the superiority of the imperial system over its Western rivals is due to the governing of the Japanese nation on the principle of nothingness rather than being.

III

NISHIDA'S CRITICS

Nishida's philosophy of place, or the unity of subject and object in the acts of perception and judgment, has clearly dominated Japanese thought for the last two-thirds of the twentieth century, but, like any prevailing perspective, it has received criticism from a variety of sources, including his own disciples and other Zen Buddhist scholars and thinkers, as well as non-Buddhist philosophers, particularly Marxists and poststructuralists. This criticism was initiated before the Second World War, while Nishida was alive and at the peak of his creativity and influence on Japanese society. It continues to the present time as questions are increasingly being raised about the prewar role of Nishida and the Kyoto School as a whole, which is accused of contributing to nationalist ideology and political fanaticism in a way that recalls the questions raised about the involvement of Heidegger, de Man, and Eliade in European Nazism and Fascism.

Kyoto School Criticism: Tanabe and Nishitani

The philosophy of Tanabe Hajime developed both under the sway of and as a critical response to Nishida's thought. Tanabe considered Nishida overtly mystical or contemplative in tone, neglecting the importance of social experience or one's interaction with the Thou (both vertically with God and horizontally with community). Tanabe's standpoint was influenced by his training in the other-power *(tariki)* tradition of Pure Land Buddhist faith rather than the self-power *(jiriki)* path of Zen meditation. He was also affected by the personal experience of his wife's sacrificial suicide on his behalf and the need to reconcile and redeem his own philosophical development in light of the Japanese military defeat and subsequent antinationalist criticism. Whereas Nishida identifies absolute nothingness with the transcendental good as the logical-ontological unity of opposites, Tanabe views nothingness in terms of the spiritual power of love in the social-ethical mission of repentance *(zange)* and resurrection. Nishida stresses action-intuition operating logically in the Eternal Now, while Tanabe focuses on the perpetual existential function of action-faith through the blind alleys and fundamental ignorance of the pathways of history.

The prewar critique of Nishida by Tanabe, whose earliest work was in the field of mathematics, is based on the notion of the 'logic of species' *(shu no ronri)* as a correction of topological logic or logic of place. According to Tanabe, Nishida's philosophy emphasizes the primacy of the universal encompassing the particular, or of the individual subsumed by the universal, and overlooks the crucial intermediary role of the category of species operating in logic and history. During this stage, Tanabe more or less equated species with the state and became known as the most virulent Kyoto School supporter of imperialism, a view for which he was attacked by progressive and later felt a deep sense of remorse.

At the end of the war, Tanabe responded to this challenge by formulating the philosophy of continuing self-criticism or absolute criticism, a total self-negation that can only come from the side of the Absolute, which appears as the power of self-negating love. In *Philosophy as Metanoetics* (1946, but written in 1944)[17] and other works, he argues that absolute criticism requires a transformational or profound change-of-heart experience based on a spiritual turning, metanoesis *(zangedô)*, or repentance. Metanoesis, in turn, involves a resurrection through existential dying or relinquishing of one's former self to be reawakened on the basis of nothingness-as-love. In this light, Tanabe reinterprets the Zen doctrine of the 'identity of life-death' *(shôji ichinyo)* as the unified experiential moment of simultaneous self-negation and redemption in an age in which the total destruction of and by humankind has become a real, if not necessarily imminent, possibility. In the last but no doubt most important stage of his career, Tanabe bypasses the debate between place and species, and his criticism of Nishida seems to be that if these notions are left, even if unintentionally, on a strictly metaphysical level of discourse, rather than brought to an intensely existential level of personal repentance, they will fail to penetrate to the fundamentally experiential realm of absolute nothingness.

Nishida's second main disciple, Nishitani Keiji, who was purged after the war and regained prominence beginning in the mid-1950s as the head of the Philosophy Department of Kyoto University, continues some of the nationalist tendencies in both Nishida and Tanabe as well as the existentialist critique of Nishida by Tanabe. However, in contrast to Tanabe's Pure Land-based approach, Nishitani seeks to deepen Kyoto School philosophy based on Zen meditation and Mahayana Buddhist compassion. Nishitani critically reviews 'the criticisms of Nishida's philosophy by Tanabe from the standpoint of the logic of species, by Takahashi [Satomi] from the perspective of finitude and becoming, and by Yamanouchi [Tokuryû] from the claims of a process dialectic . . .'[18] Like these critics, Nishitani feels that Nishida overlooks the process-oriented quality of the unfolding of history that characterizes the absolute, and he directs his attention to an overcoming of the nihilistic and scientific trends in the modern era. Nishitani's approach to the connection between philosophy and religion seems to bear an inverse relation to Nishida's concerns and methods. The starting point for Nishida is the philosophical query, 'What is the nature of pure experience?,' that eventually led him to proclaim that mystical insight alone discloses the fundamental structure of the topological logic of reality. Nishitani's leading question is 'What is religion?' (the title of one of his main works published in 1961 and translated under the title, *Religion and Nothingness*[19]), which involves an examination of the metaphysical foundations of religious experience. Both thinkers, however, appear to view the relationship between absolute and relative, I and Thou, subject and object, not from the standpoint of one side or the other of an irreconcilable opposition, but from the transcendental perspective of the 'and,' which constitutes the conjunctive process itself. The self-negating 'and' represents the place or context of absolute nothingness.

On the other hand, Nishitani, influenced by Nietzsche and Heidegger, is not so much interested in defining the nature of place as in using absolute nothingness as a tool by which to criticize and overcome the nihilistic tendencies in modern Western science which have infected the globe with a world-weary destructiveness and the potential for a catastrophic conflagration. Nishitani employs a threefold distinction in this cultural-epistemological critique: being, relative nothingness, and absolute nothingness. He accuses modern science of a fixation on the realm of being which belies an underlying fascination with nonbeing in the sense of hollowness or absence as well as an inability to understand genuine nothingness. This deficiency is based in part on the way science absorbs and reacts against the Christian monotheistic ideal in which humans gain fulfillment only through a self-negation of their humanity when contrasted with the divinity of God, a view that reinforces the scientific tendency to be oblivious to human needs. Yet science, which lacks a theological, or a teleological, background for its stance is, according to Nishitani, less in tune with the meaning of nothingness than is Christianity. Nishitani maintains that numerous Western thinkers, especially

Western mystics and modern existentialists (he seems to prefer Nietzsche's 'innocence of becoming' to the analysis of nothingness in Heideggerian or Sartrean phenomenology), have realized the standpoint of relative nothingness, a partial understanding limited by the attempt to conceptualize nonbeing as an antithesis to being. Absolute nothingness overcomes this duality, but for Nishitani this overcoming can only by attained by virtue of a bodhisattva-like change-of-heart rather than through logical analysis, as in the case of Nishida (at least prior to his final essay on **'Topological Logic and the Religious Worldview'**).

Other Buddhist Criticisms: Critical Buddhism

Criticism of the nationalist implications in Nishida's philosophy of place from within the Zen sect stem from the 1930s writings of Ichikawa Hakugen, who remained a forceful critic of the militarist-nationalist trends in samurai-influenced Zen practice through the Vietnam War period by both highlighting the ideals and exposing the weakness of traditional Sino-Japanese recorded sayings of the great masters.[20] Another Zen-based critique which sets up a contrast between the Kyoto School and the doctrines of early Buddhism expressed in Indian Sanskrit sources has come from the recent Critical Buddhism methodology,[21] which to some extent can be seen as a Tokyo-based effort of the Sôtô Zen sect to challenge the philosophical dominance of the Kyoto thinkers including Nishida and Nishitani who are associated with the Rinzai Zen sect. The Critical Buddhists make a refutation of Nishida's notion of place part of a larger criticism of an underlying problematic standpoint in Mahayana Buddhist metaphysics in China and Japan, leading to the contemporary problems of social discrimination and extreme nationalism.

First, the Critical Buddhists are deeply troubled by the Zen sect's discriminatory practices against outcastes (the so-called *burakumin* or special status community who often work in occupations involving some form of death, which is considered impure, such as crematorium workers, butchers, leather workers, etc.). One of the main social functions of Zen is the performance of funeral ceremonies for the lay community, including *burakumin*, who are given ceremonial names that reveal their outcaste status while Zen rhetoric continues tostress nonduality, nondiscrimination, and harmony. In order to understand this dilemma, the Critical Buddhist thinkers set up a contrast between two forms of Buddhism: critical philosophy based on a realization of the early Buddhist doctrine of moral causality (karma) liberated from substantiality; and the substantive, logocentric (which they term '*dhatu-vada*') or topological philosophy that violates causality by seeking a single source or locus of reality. They argue that Nishida's doctrine of 'place' is a throwback to medieval 'original enlightenment' (*hongaku*) thought, which, by denying causality, tends to foster a false sense of equality that mitigates the need for social responsibility. Original enlightenment and related doctrines such as the universal Buddha-nature (*busshô*)

espouse an uncritical tolerance and syncretism that fosters in the name of universal love such problematic viewpoints as the notion of demanding societal harmony (*wa*) at the expense of individuality and a tacit compliance with militarism. These attitudes are in turn supported politically by totalitarian and nationalist ideologies as well as intellectually by *nihonjinron* (cultural exceptionalism or 'Japanese-ism') rhetoric that ends up abetting social discrimination.

The basic weakness of original enlightenment thought is that because, ontologically, it does not allow for the existence of the Other since all things are considered to arise on the basis of the single, undifferentiated primordial 'dhatu' (place or locus), epistemologically and ethically it is rendered incapable of dealing with the inevitably complex manifestations of otherness that force concrete ethical choices. That is, the original enlightenment-influenced topological, *dhatu-vada* doctrines lack a basis and precedent for developing a mechanism for situationally specific, ethically evaluative judgments, and the result is an unreflective endorsement of the *status quo*. According to Hakamaya Noriaki's Critical Buddhist analysis of how epistemological non-discrimination (*musabetsu*) results in social discrimination (*sabetsu*), 'although some interpret the doctrine of original enlightenment as a theory of equality because it claims to recognize the fundamental universal enlightenment of all people, in reality . . . the doctrine of original enlightenment, which in a facile way requires seeking out the fundamental unified ground of enlightenment, must be considered the primary source of [social] discrimination.'[22] In Japan, this results in an acceptance and even support, rather than resistance, for the 'myth of Japanese uniqueness' and related nationalist and nativist ideology that has pervaded post-Tokugawa, especially prewar, intellectual life.[23] Zen, in particular, has often hidden its support for the status quo behind what becomes an elitist aestheticism based on the notion that everything reflects the Buddha Dharma.[24] The criticism suggested here is that Nishida's philosophy of place is one more example of asserting a logocentric basis of reality that renders various individuated appearances somewhat illusory and devalued,thereby resulting in an indifference to and even exploitation of the plight of outcastes who are seen as merely a part of the illusory realm.

Non-Buddhist Criticism: Asada Akira

Leftist criticism of Nishida's philosophy of place as a right-wing ideology began as early as 1932, the year after the Manchurian incident, when the term Kyoto School (Kyoto *gaku-ha*) was coined by Tosaka Jun.[25] From Tosaka's anti-nationalist perspective, recalling Ichikawa's Buddhist criticism, Nishida and his disciples were reactionary romantics idealizing the Japanese tradition while remaining blind to—or even covertly (and by the war more overtly) supporting—the hegemony of imperial ideology (*tenno ideorogii*). This criticism recalls a comment by Michel Serres that any theory of the priority of a single space is imperialistic. Tosaka acknowledged that there was a left-wing slant to some of the Kyoto School thinkers, but he felt that the orientation of the entire group drifted drastically to the right as the wartime approached, ensnaring even the progressives.

A more recent leftist critique of the Kyoto School is suggested by Asada Akira, who gained instant fame (referred to as the 'AA phenomenon') in the early 1980s for his book, *Structure and Power: Beyond Semiotics,*[26] which introduced French poststructuralist theories to Japan from a Marxist perspective. Asada points out that in the prewar work, *The Problems of Japanese Culture,* Nishida distinguishes between two forms of national power: power based on being *(u)* reflected in European kings and nations, which contains conflict between individuals and the whole; and power based on nothingness *(mu)* as in the case of the Japanese emperor which, via the principle of absolute contradictory self-identity, unifies particularism and universalism, atomism and holism from a 'holonic' *(zentaishi)* standpoint ever capable of harmonizing differences. Ironically, the political power of the place of nothingness, according to Asada's critique, is perhaps best symbolized by the 'empty space' of the imperial palace gardens in central Tokyo. Asada remarks that Nishida's philosophy seems at first to be peaceful and pluralistic. But, he argues sardonically, 'When this [power of place] spontaneously spreads, the "Great East Asian Co-Prosperity Sphere"—is this the absolute contradictory self-identity between liberation from European imperialism and aggression by Japanese imperialism—will be formed.'[27]

It must be pointed out, however, that by no means all scholars and commentators on the Kyoto School agree with Asada's view of Nishida. Some view Nishida as a pure philosopher uninvolved in politics, whereas Michiko Yusa argues that Nishida was actually working effectively behind the scenes to challenge militarist orthodoxy. According to Yusa, 'Far from being a recluse or anarmchair philosopher, [Nishida] was actively involved in the preservation of freedom of learning and education in opposition to the domestic policies of the nationalistic and militaristic government. . . . which had no little impact on the public.'[28] The questions raised in this debate, as in the controversies involving the participation by Heidegger, Paul de Man, and Mircea Eliade in European Nazi and Fascist ideology, are whether a thinker can be judged and held accountable for every possible implication, consequence, or by-product in his thought or methods. Furthermore, how can he be forgiven for past indiscretions, misjudgments, or mistakes? While a fuller analysis of these issues is beyond the scope of the present paper, it is important to point out that, unlike Nishitani and Heidegger, Tanabe, at least on a philosophical level, did offer a repentance for his pre-war activities, but Nishida died before he had the opportunity to explain and reckon with his own understanding of the relation between his philosophy and politics. Yet, Bourdieu's suggestion, mentioned above, of a dual reading that is simultaneously and ambiguously philosophical and ideological, seems as relevant to the case of Nishida and Japan as it is to Heidegger and the West.

IV

CONCLUSIONS: WHITHER PLACE

The criticisms of Nishida's philosophy of place have focused primarily on two issues. Kyoto School disciples, who are either Zen or Pure Land Buddhists, suggest that Nishida overlooks the meaning of time in the sense of the unfolding processes of history, which demand personal decision-making or existential choice in the encounter with human destructiveness and nihilism. For Tanabe, coming to terms with this issue is the key to understanding the error of excessive support for nationalism he felt that he and his colleagues committed before the war. Non-Buddhist leftist arguments deal mainly with the issues of militarism and imperialism, and offer a critical voice which in some cases also comes from Buddhists, including the postwar Tanabe as well as Ichikawa and Critical Buddhism. This criticism maintains that Nishida posits the category of place as an independent (non-)entity that is nevertheless located in a particular space, the contradictory space-less space of the imperial palace. Both Buddhists and leftists agree that the social aspect of Nishida's thought is not as well developed as the metaphysical dimension. For the Buddhists, especially Critical Buddhism, correcting Nishida requires rethinking the meaning of tradition and recovering the doctrine of moral causality or karma that was subverted by East Asian notions of original enlightenment. For the non-Buddhists, particularly Asada, the task is to deconstruct the power relations underlying Nishida's ideology.

However, I will point to a problem in Nishida's philosophy from a different angle, which pertains to the question of his use of language and rhetoric in constructing the world based on place, in particular, to his overreliance on Western-style logical formulations at the expense of losing touch with the style of discourse in the Zen Buddhist tradition. As indicated above, some of his translators and interpreters have probably done Nishida a disservice in misrepresenting 'topological logic' as the 'logic *of* place,' thereby hypostatizing the 'where' of nothingness. But part of the problem lies in Nishida's preoccupation with developing a Western logic that lacks some key discursive elements, particularly the use of irony and paradoxical wordplay, in the tradition of medieval Zen records, which he is trying to recapture in a contemporary context. In discussions of sacred places in medieval Zen texts, the commentators move in two directions simultaneously, both of which are generally missing in Nishida's texts (except when he cites these sources) as well as the texts of other Kyoto School thinkers: an ironic refutation of supernatural beliefs concerning the sacrality of space, which is intertwined with a rhetorical flirtation with those same beliefs. Medieval Zen in China and Japan developed in an intellectual climate of competing with popular religions, especially Taoism, Shinto, and folk beliefs, for defining the meaning of spaces populated by local demonic and protective gods or dominated by universal principles such as causality.[29] The Zen rhetorical strategy is to explore yet avoid a commitment to either perspective—that is, either to a popular belief in deities or to a philosophical view of causality—through the construction and deconstruction, mythologization and demythologization that continually plays the opposing beliefs off of one another.

A key example is a Zen *kôan* (spiritual puzzle) record concerning the pilgrimage site of Mt. Wu-t'ai, one of four sacred mountains in medieval China where bodhisattvas were said to appear to those who came seeking visions. This mountain was the abode of the bodhisattva Manjusri, who revealed himself in visions and performed miracles for devout pilgrims. Generally, the Zen anti-ritual, demythological approach shunned such popular symbols, and Rinzai, the founder of one of the main sub-sects within Zen, directly refuted and forbade Mt. Wu-t'ai pilgrimages.[30] Yet, other Zen records are less severe than Rinzai's, and make their point by a playful and ironic rhetorical style. In the *Blue Cliff Record kôan* collection commentary (case no. 35), monk Wu Cho is said to visit the mountain and engage in a dialogue with Manjusri, who, like a typical Zen master, outsmarts the pilgrim. Manjusri asks the monk about the size of the congregations in his monastery, and Wu Cho offers a literal response, 'Some are three hundred, some are five hundred.' When asked the same question in return, Manjusri resorts to a Zen tautology, 'In front, three by three; in back, three by three.' Manjusri, a supernatural ruler of the sacred mountain,'wins' this round of the dialogue, but the commentary makes it clear that we are not to take too seriously his exploits.

According to the verse commentary:

> Extending throughout the world is the beautiful monastery:
> The Manjusri that fills the eyes is the one conversing.
> Not knowing to open the Buddha-eye at his words,
> (Wu Cho) turned his head and saw only the blue mountain crags.[31]

The final line can be read as a criticism of the monk for not paying attention to the vision and words of the bodhisattva who 'fills the eyes' and ears, but it can also be interpreted as a simple, descriptive expression of nature that counteracts the supernatural claims: the mountain crags alone make up the universal/local place of nothingness for Wu Cho, who no longer needs to rely on visions or dialogues with other-worldly beings to experience the true nature of the world. The effectiveness of the last line lies in a double-edged quality that has been deleted in Nishida's attempt at logical worldmaking, even in his unique topological logic. The passage in the Zen record reflects an ability to construct and deconstruct the multiple meanings of place, perhaps thereby leaving less of a target for criticism.

Therefore, this example of traditional Zen discourse points out a limitation in Nishida's philosophical worldmaking that has been overlooked by his critics based on the role of language in expressing the meaning of nothingness. Nishida has chosen a metaphor, the image of place, to represent the function of nothingness. His critics, whether on philosophical or political grounds, suggest that place is something static and objectifiable. However, the problem is not with the metaphor of place *per se,* but rather with the fact that Nishida has not built into his analysis of place an ironic sense of displacement or self-negation of the metaphor. He examines the place of nothingness but does not convey the nothingness of place. One of Nishida's Kyoto School disciples, Masao Abe, has argued that nothingness, which is fundamentally nonconceptualizable and inexpressible, could be written with an X appearing over it, much as Heidegger has done in some writings with the word Being *(Sein).* Such a device might insure that readers would not understand the term as a objectifiable entity. But traditional Zen discourse makes this point even more effectively by referring to the sacred mountain as 'only the blue mountain crags.' It seems that the notion of place could rise above criticism if Nishida had developed a way of simultaneously deconstructing and constructing its metaphorical status.

NOTES

[1] Robert E. Carter, *The Nothingness Beyond God: AnIntroduction to the Philosophy of Nishida Kitarô* (New York: Paragon House, 1989), p. 1. This idea is conveyed in a wordplay suggested by Stephane Mallarmé, 'Nothing shall have taken place but place,' cited in Jonathan Z. Smith, *To Take Place: Toward Theory in Ritual* (Chicago: University of Chicago Press), p. 96.

[2] Nishida Kitaro, *Last Writings: Nothingness and the Religious Worldview,* trans. David A. Dilworth (Honolulu: University of Hawaii Press, 1987), p. 61; see n. 16 below.

[3] Dogen, *Shobogenzo* 'Uji,' trans. in Steven Heine, *Existential and Ontological Dimensions of Time in Heidegger and Dôgen* (Albany: SUNY Press, 1985), p. 160.

[4] Carter, *The Nothingness Beyond God,* p. 84.

[5] Nishida, *Last Writings,* p. 62 (parenthesis on last sentence deleted).

[6] Andrew Feenberg and Yoko Arisaka, 'Experiential Ontology: The Origins of the Nishida Philosophy in the Doctrine of Pure Experience,' *International Philosophical Quarterly* 30/2 (1990): 196.

[7] Smith, *Map is Not Territory: Studies in the History of Religions* (Leiden: Brill, 1978).

[8] Gaston Bachelard, *The Poetics of Space,* trans. Maria Jolas (Boston: Beacon, 1969).

[9] This comment requires two qualifications: first, 'logic of place' is technically an accurate translation, though

somewhat misleading in this particular context; second, I am referring primarily to Nishida's final philosophical essay written before his death in 1945 (see n. 16 below), although there are exceptions to this usage in his writings.

[10] Pierre Bourdieu, *The Political Ontology of Martin Heidegger,* trans. Peter Collier (Cambridge: Polity Press, 1991), esp. p. 3: 'Thus we must abandon the opposition between a political reading and a philosophical reading, and undertake a simultaneously political and philosophical dual reading of writings which are defined by their fundamental *ambiguity,* that is, by their reference to two social spaces, which correspond to two mental spaces.'

[11] There are several English translations, including *An Inquiry into the Good,* trans. Masao Abe and Christopher Ives (New Haven: Yale University Press, 1990).

[12] Nishida, *Intuition and Reflection in Self-Consciousness,* trans.Valdo Viglielmo, Takeuchi Yoshinori, and Joseph S. O'Leary (Albany: SUNY Press, 1987).

[13] Abe, 'Nishida's Philosophy of 'Place,'' *International Philosophical Quarterly* 28/4 (1988): 371.

[14] James W. Heisig, 'The Religious Philosophy of the Kyoto School: An Overview,' *Japanese Journal of Religious Studies* 17/1 (1990): 69.

[15] This essay, 'Bashoteki ronri to shukyoteki sekaikan,' is in Nishida's 19-volume collected works, *Nishida Kitaro zensho* (Tokyo: Iwanami shoten, 1979), 11:371-464. The two translations are: 'The Logic of *Topos* and the Religious Worldview,' trans. Michiko Yusa, *Eastern Buddhist* 19/2 (1986): 1-29, and 20/1 (1987): 81-119; and *Last Writings: Nothingness and the Religious Worldview,* trans. Dilworth, pp. 47-123.

[16] Pierre Lavelle, 'The Political Thought of Nishida Kitarô,' *Monumenta Nipponica* 49/2 (1994): 139-65.

[17] Tanabe Hajime, *Philosophy as Metanoetics,* trans. Takeuchi Yoshinori, Valdo Viglielmo, and James W. Heisig (Berkeley: University of California Press, 1986).

[18] Nishitani Keiji, *Nishida Kitaro,* trans. Yamamoto Seisaku and James W. Heisig (Berkeley: University of California Press, 1991), p. 228. Takahashi and Yamanouchi were both considered Kyoto School philosophers though the former taught at Tohoku University rather than Kyoto University.

[19] Nishitani, *Religion and Nothingness,* trans. Jan van Bragt (Berkeley: University of California Press, 1982).

[20] Ichikawa Hakugen, *Bukkyosha no senso-sekinin* (Tokyo: Shunjusha, 1970).

[21] See Heine, 'Critical Buddhism and the Debate Concerning the 75-Fascicle and 12-Fascicle Shobogenzo Texts,' *Japanese Journal of Religious Studies* 21/1 (1994): 37-72.

[22] Hakamaya Noriaki, *Hongaku shiso hihan* (Tokyo: Daizô shuppan), p. 142.

[23] See Peter N. Dale, *The Myth of Japanese Uniqueness* (New York: St. Martin's Press, 1986).

[24] Hakamaya, *Hihan bukkyo* (Tokyo: Daizo shuppan, 1990), pp. 47-92, esp. 77-80.

[25] Heisig, 'The Religious Philosophy of the Kyoto School,' p. 52.

[26] Asada Akira, *Kozo to chikara: kigoron o koete* (Tokyo: Keiso shobo, 1983).

[27] Asada, 'Infantile Capitalism and Japan's Postmodernism: A Fairy Tale,' in *Postmodernism and Japan,* eds. Masao Miyoshi and H. D. Harootunian (Durham: Duke University Press, 1988), p. 277.

[28] Yusa, 'Nishida and the Question of Nationalism,' *Monumenta Nipponica* 46/2 (1991): 204.

[29] See Bernard Faure, *Chan Insights and Oversights: An Epistemological Critique of the Chan Tradition* (Princeton: Princeton University Press, 1993), pp. 155-74.

[30] *Rinzai roku,* ed. Iriya Yoshitaka (Tokyo: Iwanami shoten, 1991), p. 65; Robert M. Gimello, 'Chang Shang-ying on Wu-t'ai Shan,' in *Pilgrims and Sacred Sites in China,* eds. Susan Naquin and Chün-fang Yü (Berkeley: University of California Press, 1992), pp. 119-24.

[31] *The Blue Cliff Record,* 3 vols., trans. Thomas and J. C. Cleary (Boulder: Shambala, 1977), 1:219-20; original in *Taishô shinshû daizôkyô* (Tokyo: 1905-12), 48:174a.

FURTHER READING

Criticism

Carter, Ronald E. *The Nothingness Beyond Good. An Introduction to the Philosophy of Nishida Kitaro.* New York: Paragon House, 1989, 191 p.

> Explains the fundamental tenets of Nishida's philosophy.

Dilworth, David A. "Nishida's Final Essay: *The Logic of Place and a Religious World-view,*" *A Quarterly of Asian and Comparative Thought* XX, No. 4 (October 1970): 355-67.

> Examines the significance of Nishida's last essay, *The Logic of Place and a Religious World-view,* as a successful synthesis of Nishida's thought.

————. "The Concrete World of Action in Nishida's Later Thought." In *Japanese Phenomenology. Phenomenology as the Trans-cultural Philosophical Approach,* edited by Yoshihiro Nitta and Hirotaka Tatematsu, pp. 249-70. Dordrecht, Holland: D. Reidel Publishing Company, 1979.

    Outlines major themes in the two essays that comprise Nishida's *Fundamental Problems of Philosophy: The World of Action* and *The Dialectical World.*

Kracht, Klaus. "Nishida Kitaro (1870-1945) as a Philosopher of State." In *Europe Interprets Japan,* edited by Gordon Daniels, pp. 198-203. Kent, England: Paul Norbury Publications, 1984.

    Uses Nishida's diaries and letters as well as his essays to discuss him as a political philosopher.

Luther, Arthur R. "Original Emergence in Heidegger and Nishida." *Philosophy Today* XXVI, No. 4 (Winter 1982): 345-56.

    Attempts "to clarify . . . original emergence in Heidegger and Nishida and draw some implications respecting the similarities in their approaches to origins."

Maraldo, John C. "Translating Nishida." *Philosophy East and West* 39, No. 4 (October 1989): 465-96.

    Analyzes various major English translations of Nishida's writings and notes difficulties in translating his works.

Masao Abe. "Introduction." In *An Inquiry into the Good* by Nishida Kitaro, translated by Masao Abe and Christopher Ives, pp. vii-xxvi. New Haven and London: Yale University Press, 1990.

    Provides an overview of the development of philosophy in Japan and positions Nishida in that tradition.

Matao, Noda. "East-West Synthesis in Kitaro Nishida." *Philosophy East and West* IV, No. 4 (January 1955): 345-59.

    Surveys Nishida's philosophy and his impact on Japanese thought.

Nishitani Keiji. *Nishida Kitaro.* Translated by Yamamoto Seisaku and James W. Heisig. Berkeley: University of California Press, 1991, 238 p.

    Examines both Nishida's thought and his personality; Nishitani was a student of Nishida's.

Mário de Sá-Carneiro

1890-1916

Portuguese dramatist, poet, short story writer, and novelist

INTRODUCTION

Considered one of the greatest poets of nineteenth-century Portugal, Sá-Carneiro is one of the initiators of Primeiro Modernismo, that country's avant-garde movement. During his brief life, Sá-Carneiro wrote poetry and novellas that are renowned for their intensely original imagery. The complex, obsessive overtones of his work, influenced by the writings of French symbolist poets Charles Baudelaire and Arthur Rimbaud, are thought to mirror Sá-Carneiro's own tragic life and ultimate suicide. His themes include the division of the soul and the struggle between human instincts and spiritual elevation. Though his literary forms are traditional, Sá-Carneiro's language, despite its message of despair, is considered musical and innovative.

Biographical Information

Sá-Carneiro was born into an affluent Lisbon family. However, his father was a reckless businessman who lost the family fortune when Sá-Carneiro was young. About the same time, his mother passed away, and her loss strongly influenced the desolate tone of his writing. After completing secondary school, Sá-Carneiro moved to Paris in 1912, where he enrolled at the Sorbonne. He never attended class, though, choosing instead to write dramas, poetry and novellas. Between 1912 and 1916, Sá-Carneiro composed extensively and also developed an editorial interest. With his friend, the renowned Portuguese poet Fernando Passoa, Sá-Carneiro edited the highly respected poetry journal *Orpheu*. Though his creative state increased, his mental state weakened, and his work became deeply macabre and depressed. In 1916, Sá-Carneiro swallowed a fatal dose of strychnine.

Major Works

Despite the brevity of his career, Sá-Carneiro wrote several works that are considered landmarks of Portuguese literature. These include the novella *Principio,* the novel *A Confissão de Lúcio* and the poetry volume *Dispersão.* Though their genres vary, vibrant imagery and symbolism prevail. In all his writings, Sá-Carneiro utilized a number of distinctive literary devices. *Paülismo* juxtaposes the abstract and concrete with the subjective and objective, while *interseccionismo* refers to the intersection of lines that intertwine the future and past. Prevalent thematic strains included despair, decadence and the search for identity. In his final poems, Sá-Carneiro abandoned his obsessive, alienated tone to return to a more colloquial, less symbolic style. Here, the constant mention of death foreshadows his own demise. After his death, the literary journal *Presença* paid tribute to Sá-Carneiro's aesthetic goal—to produce an art form devoted solely to creativity, free of political content.

Critical Reception

Though little English-language criticism exists about Sá-Carneiro, several recent translations indicate growing interest in his writings and his role in Portuguese literature. In particular, critics point to his innovative use of language and literary devices. They also praise his ability to meld the conventional and the absurd.

PRINCIPAL WORKS

Amizade [with Tomas Cabreira, Jr.] (drama) 1912
Principio (novellas) 1912
A Confissão de Lúcio [*Lucio's Confession,* 1993] (novel) 1913
Dispersão (poetry) 1914
Ceu em fogo (short stories) 1915
Indicios de ouro (poetry) 1937; published in journal *Presença*
Obras completas de Mário de Sá-Carneiro (correspondence, drama, novellas, novel, poetry, and short stories) 1945-59
Cartas a Fernando Pessoa (correspondence) 1958-59
The Great Shadow, and Other Stories (short stories) 1997

CRITICISM

John M. Parker (essay date 1960)

SOURCE: "Mário de Sá-Carneiro, Poesias," in *Three Twentieth-Century Portuguese Poets,* Witwatersrand University Press, 1960, pp. 20-31.

[*Parker discusses the techniques Sa-Carneiro utilizes in* Dispersão *and* Indícios de ouro *and notes that these poetic cycles reflect the author's personal sense of misery and despair.*]

The short life of [Mário de Sá-Carneiro] and particularly the brevity of his literary life, make it possible to give a fuller picture of his poetry. Mário de Sá-Carneiro was born in Lisbon in 1890. His father was then an officer in the Portuguese military engineers. At an early age he lost his mother, who was by all accounts an angelic creature; her death was perhaps the most tragic event in the poet's life, for though his early years were surrounded by the comforts of a well-to-do household, he missed the unselfish tenderness of a mother's love, a tenderness which he so often transposed nostalgically in his works. He had a distinguished school record in both arts and science subjects, and apparently began his university course at Coimbra University, but left within a short while for Paris, where he went ostensibly to study law, a course which he never followed. He had already turned to literature while still at school, and published a play and one book of short stories before his departure for Paris in October 1912. In Paris he lived at intervals until 1916, when he took his own life with four phials of strychnine. A spoilt child, coming from a rich family which suffered a reverse in fortunes, he was unfitted for any remunerative occupation, as well as being a social misfit. This he transposed onto a spiritual plane, and together with his constant financial worries, it forms a basis of his tragedy.

To enter into the atmosphere of Sá-Carneiro's poetry is to enter into a rarefied atmosphere, with its strange mixture of 'decadentism,' auto-psychoanalysis, surrealism and Kafka-like other-worldliness. At first a prose writer, and convinced that poetry was for him a mere relaxation, in the early part of 1913 he suddenly found himself a poet and taxed with the intolerable burden of a type of poetry perfectly fitted to the equally intolerable burden of his own personality. The poems which constitute his first book of poetry were written, with one exception, in the short space of a fortnight. A little before this he had completed two prose poems, entitled **"Além" ("Beyond")** and **"Bailado" ("Dance")**, in which the basis of nearly all his future poetry, spiritually and technically, is given form. In **"Além,"** with its unsuccessful dream attempt to possess beauty, and in **"Bailado,"** with its incipient surrealism and its fantastic dynamism we find the germ of the poetry which was soon to appear in published form.

To his first book of poetry Sá-Carneiro gave the name *Dispersão,* which is also the title of one of the poems, and which indicates the disintegration of personality. The first poem of the cycle, like the early poems of Alvaro de Campos, is an expression of the poet's enthusiastic aspirations and stands in direct contrast to all the poems which followed it. Originally the second part of a longer poem, in which Sá-Carneiro intended to contrast the bourgeois existence which could be his and the extraordinary life of the poet which he chose instead, **"Partida" ("Departure")**, as the poem is called, is a dramatization of the poet's moment of decision. Not possessing the simple virtues which would make everyday life tolerable, having no accepted faith, he strives to substitute for it the beauty which he is convinced is inside him, and which he hopes to transmute into great poetry. In this poem the mixture of medieval, religious and natural imagery which was to be pursued and expanded in his future poems is already present.

DEPARTURE

When I see life in its untroubled waters
Trickle on in human way, I hesitate,
And sometimes halt uncertain in the torrent
Of the things of genius on which I meditate.

I am assailed by a desire to flee
The mystery which is mine, by which I am seduced.
But at once I vanquish my weakness. This light
There are but few who can reflect its rays.

My soul, proud soul nostalgic for beyond,
Is shrouded yet again in sombre shade,
And to my glazed eyes the tears rise
But I have strength to conquer them as well.

For I react, react with force. Life, nature,
What are they for the artist? Not a thing.
What we must do is leap into the mist,
Run in search of beauty in the blue.

We must climb, climb beyond those skies
Our souls have merely accumulated,
And prostrate pray, in dreams, to the God
Our hands crowned with a halo there.

We must set off against the mountain without fear
Girt with the armour of chimera and the unreal;
Brandish the fulvous, mediaeval sword,
Taking with every hour a Spanish fort.

We must shake up colours in a maddened whirl,
Be the clenched fist that conquers worlds,
And, in a last sacrament of soul now more than soul,
Travel other senses, other lives.

Be a column of smoke, a star astray,
Force a winged way through whirling winds,
Be a palmtree's branch, be water at its source,
Be a taut-strung bow of gold and flame . . .

A distant wing whipping up insanity,
A precocious cloud of subtle mist,
Desire stirred up with mystery and perfume,
Shadow, dizziness, ascension—Height!

And I give myself, my all, this dying afternoon
To the whirlwind which bears me to the peaks.
Mad with sphynxes the horizon burns, but I,
Mid lightning flash and thunder bolt, remain
    unharmed! . . .

A blood-red mirage with enchanted halo—
I feel my eyes becoming space!
I advance, I conquer, attain and pass beyond;
I am labyrinth, unicorn, I am acanthus.

I know distance, I understand the Air;
I am a shower of gold, a spasm of light;
I am a glass goblet thrown out to sea,
Diadem and crown, royal helm and cross . . .

. . . . .

The band of chimeras appears afar . . .
What great apotheosis in the heavens!

Colour is no more colour—it is sound and aroma!
I am assailed by the nostalgia of having been God . . .

Onwards then, on to the greater triumph!
My destiny is different—it is lofty and rare.
Only the price to pay is very high:
The sadness of our never being two . . .

Dispersão is a drama in twelve poems. After **"Partida"** the remaining poems relate the poet's failure to realize his ambitious dreams. The title of the collection and of the next poem quoted indicates the tragic fault in the poet's character: the disintegration of his personality. This is explored in the remaining poems: his inability to concentrate himself, and therefore his efforts, on the profusion of wondrous things out of which he desires to build his monument to Beauty is analysed in terms of physical inner emptiness, inbetweenness, duality, Narcissism, his sense of failure, nostalgia for the life he had left behind, and the inevitable relapse into the impotence of *tédio* and passivity. All these are present in the poem **"Dispersão"** (**"Dispersion"**):

I lost the way within myself
Because I was a labyrinth,
And now when I feel myself
It is with nostalgia of what I was.

I passed through my life
A star gone mad with dreams.
In my desire to pass beyond,
I was quite blind to my life . . .

For me it is always yesterday
I have no to-morrow, no to-day:
The time which for others speeds by
Falls on me made into yesterday.

(Sunday here in Paris
Reminds me of the lost one
And how moved he was by his feelings
For Sundays here in Paris:

For Sunday means the family,
Means well-being and simplicity,
And those who look upon beauty
Can have no well-being, no family.)

The poor boy with his longings . . .
You, yes, you were somebody!
And it was because of this
That you lost yourself in longings.

The great golden bird
Flapped his wings towards the heavens,
But closed them sated with boredom
On seeing he would reach the heavens.

Just as one weeps for a lover,
So I weep for myself:
I was a fickle lover
Who betrayed no one but myself.

The space I enfold I feel not
Nor the lines which I project:
If I look in a mirror, I'm mistaken—

I am not in the face I project.

I return to within myself
But nothing speaks to me, nothing!
I have my soul all shrouded,
Quite dry, within myself.

I have not lost my soul,
I have it still, but lost.
So my tears are for a soul
That is dead, though I still live.

With yearning I remember
A gentle companion whom
In the whole of my life
I never saw, but remember

Remember her golden mouth
And her body with passion fainting,
In a lost breath that reaches me
In the dusk of a golden evening.

(All my deepest yearnings
Are for things I never possessed.
Oh, how I feel this yearning
For the dreams I have never dreamed! . . .)

And I sense that my death—
My total disintegration—
Exists far away, in the north,
In some great capital.

I can see my last day of life
Painted in coils of smoke,
And all blue my cry of death
As in shadow and beyond I vanish.

Tenderness become yearning,
I kiss my own white hands . . .
I am full of love and pity
As I look at these white hands . . .

Sad hands, long and beautiful
They were made to give themselves . . .
No one would ever press them . . .
Sad hands, long and beautiful . . .

For myself I am full of pity,
Poor fairy-tale child . . .
What was missing after all?
A link? A path? . . . Poor me! . . .

Twilight has fallen on my soul;
I was someone who passed by.
I shall be, but am no longer me;
I am not live, I am sleeping the twilight.

The alcohol of an autumn sleep
Has seeped gently throughout my body,
Wafting my sleeping bones
Upon the autumn mist.

I have lost both life and death,
And, mad, I do not go mad . . .
The hour is lived and escapes
I follow it, yet remain here . . .

. . . . .

Castles stand in ruins,
Winged but maneless lions ...

. . . . .

The remaining poems emphasize in turn individual aspects of the poet's disillusions which have already been stated in general terms in the poem **"Dispersão,"** which was in fact the poem which followed **"Partida"** chronologically, though in the order of publication other poems precede it, making it more of a central point in the sequence. In the poem **"Quase"** (**"Almost"**) Sá-Carneiro recounts how near he was to realizing his ambition, how little separated him from his goal, and expresses the anguished wish that he had not made the attempt.

A little more sun—and I would be live coal,
A little more blue and I would be beyond.
To reach it I needed one more flap of wings ...
If only I might at least stay where I was ...

Wonderment or peace? In vain ... All swept away
In a treacherous shallow sea of foam;
And the fine dream born to life in mist,
The fine dream—oh agony!—almost lived ...

Almost love, almost triumph, almost flame,
Almost the beginning and the end—almost
    expansion ...
But in my soul everything overflows ...
And there was nothing, mere illusion!

Everything had a beginning ... and all went wrong ...
—Oh the grief of being almost, grief without end ...—
I failed before the world and failed myself,
A bird that left the nest but did not fly ...

Moments of greatness that I squandered ...
Temples where I never placed an altar ...
Rivers which I lost before they reached the sea ...
Longings which existed but which I did not hold ...

If I search myself I find only vestiges ...
Windows facing the sun—I see them closed;
And the hands of a hero without faith, cowardly
    hands,
Set railings along the top of the precipices ...

In a diffuse impetus of desperate force
I grasped at everything and nothing could possess ...
To-day all that is left of me is the disenchantment
Of the things I kissed but did not live ...

. . . . .

A little more sun, I would have been live coal,
A little more blue, I would have been beyond.
To reach it I needed one more flap of wings ...
If only I had at least stayed where I was before ...

The cycle draws to a close on a note of utter ennui, recalling the failure of early promise, in the poem **"Além-Tédio"** (**"Ultra-taedium"**), and the finishing touch, in the poem **"A Queda"** (**"The Fall"**), is a poetical suicide, in an attempt to resolve the duality constantly present in Sá-Carneiro's works.

After a short interval during which he dedicated himself to prose writing, producing in a short time the strange short novel *A Confissão de Lúcio (The Confession of Lúcio)* and a number of the stories which later went to make up his volume of stories *Céu em Fogo (Sky in Flames),* Sá-Carneiro began to write the poems not to be published as a volume until 20 years after his death, when the magazine *Preseneç* offered them to the public. These were the poems entitled *Indícios de Ouro (Traces of Gold).*

The poetical suicide of **"A Queda"** had marked an end, but not *the* end. After his disastrous failure to unify his personality in ordinary surroundings, the poet withdraws into a world of dreams, a world in which his ambitions should be realizable. The series opens with a sequence of poems notable for the poet's use of exotic imagery. This exoticism can be divided into three main aspects: eroticism, medievalism and what I call 'otherness,' or if you like 'other-worldliness,' from the poet's frequent use of the word *outro* (other). It is a world of kings and princesses, of Sleeping Beauties, of Salomes, and of Caesars and slave-girls. All this is an expression of the poet's soul projected onto other planes, presenting a contrast with the world of ordinary humans in which he had failed so miserably. But even in the dream world the poet fails to hold his personality together, the complete and utter disintegration of which he expresses magnificently in the hallucinatory poem **"O Resgate"** (**"Liberation"**), in which his own disintegration is symbolized in terms of a castle which crumbles into detailed ruins. The next poem, of which my translation is but the palest reflection, shows the poet looking back to the past of **"Partida"** with nostalgic regret. Here you will find examples of the 'otherness' I mentioned, and which might be defined as distance from the present or the actual in both time and place. The poem is called **"Distante Melodia"** (**"Distant Melody"**).

In a dream of Iris, dying in gold and flames,
Memories come to me, of another Time all blue
When I was balanced between veils of tulle—
A light and slender time, time-in-Wing.

My senses then were colours, and my desires,
Eager and burning, were in a garden born,
In my soul there were Other distances—
Distances which my following them was flowers ...

Gold showered down if my thoughts were Stars,
The moon's rays fell on my withdrawing ...
—Nights-ponds, how beautiful you were
Beneath water-lily-terraces of my remembrance! ...

A waking age of Inter-dream and Moon,
When the flying hours were ever jade,
When the morning mist was wistful yearning,
And the light—desires of a naked Princess ...

Balusters of sound, arches of Loving,
Bridges of brightness, ogives of perfume ...
Realm inexpressible of Opium and fire
Where never more, in colour, I shall dwell ...

Carpets from other Persias more Orient . . .
Curtains from Chinas yet more ivory . . .
Golden Temples for rituals of satin . . .
Fountains running shade, smooth and quiet . . .

Domes-Pantheons of my nostalgic sighs,
Cathedrals of Myself out over the sea . . .
Stairways of honour, stairs only, up in the air . . .
New Byzantiums of Soul, other Turkeys . . .

Fluid memories . . . Ashes of brocade . . .
Anil unreality which undulates in me . . .
—Around myself I am a king in exile,
A wanderer in a mermaid's dream . . .

In this poem we have an example of that *paülismo* which
I mentioned earlier, and also of a further development of
it which Pessoa and Sá-Carneiro called *interseccionismo*.
Sá-Carneiro is, as you have seen, an intensely subjective
poet. It was his instinctive belief that man is the centre of
the universe. Thus everything exists in function of himself, and disintegration of his own personality means disintegration of the universe. So external elements are
fused with his personality, since they exist in function of
it, and are used to convey that personality. *Paülismo* is a
fusion of the abstract and the concrete, of the subjective
and the objective which in Sá-Carneiro's poetry defeats
our attempts to seize it completely and produces the aesthetic emotion known contemptuously as the 'little sensation.' *Paülismo* aimed at vagueness in the over-all effect
of a poem, and at subtlety and complexity in the individual lines of poetry and the combinations of abstract
and concrete within those lines. *Interseccionismo* was
applied to the sequence of the lines, so that the images
contained in the lines should 'intersect' one another. In
the poem quoted above there is no logical moving forward from a beginning to an end. Within a static framework, a mass of varied imagery is made to intersect in
associations which the poet's memory and imagination
relate in the absence of any conscious link.

Soon after this poem, the vein of exoticism in Sá-
Carneiro's poetry begins to give way to a return to the
imagery of everyday life, though without banishing the
preciosity of abstract-concrete image combinations. It is
as if the poet becomes aware that the myriad facets of the
real world about him are as susceptible of transmuting his
inner yearning, hopes and despair as those of his imaginary world. The tone of his remaining poems is mainly
elegiac and self-ironical, with the latter gradually pre-
dominating. Development is continuous in the incredibly
brief span of Sá-Carneiro's literary life and the small
number of his poems. The next poem, *"O Lord,"* shows
a simplification of poetic method. It is based on a single
symbol-image followed through with something like a
logical development, and is representative of a later tendency of Sá-Carneiro, and foreshadowing a type of poem
which was finding favour in modern European poetry.

THE LORD

Lord of the Highlands in a different life
Now I drag my decadence through this,

Stripped of my shining coach and liveried train.
A Lord reduced to living from cheap pictures,
Stopping by windows full of costly jewels,
With nebulous desires—in an illusion of doubt . . .
(—For this my rage so ill-concealed,
—For this my eternal impatience.)

He eyes the Squares, walks round them . . .
Who knows if he sometime did not possess
Such Squares as this, and palaces and columns—
Extensive lands, full fields,
Yachts out at sea,
Mountains and lakes, forests and sandy shores . . .

(—Hence the sensation so long rooted in my mind
Of having lost somewhere a great inheritance;
Hence my high desire of unlimited luxury—
The Colour in my Works is all the spell has left . . .)

Following a similar tendency is the extremely beautiful
poem **"Ápice" ("Moment")** with which I shall finish this
brief survey of Sá-Carneiro's poetry. Fernando Pessoa
was fond of this poem, and it is little wonder, because it
is close in feeling and technique to many of his own
poems in which he attempted to fix the fleeting sensation
into something more lasting, by fusing it with emotion.

MOMENT

That ray of the evening sun
Reflected
In an indifferent moment
By a window lost in time—
Burns,
A faded recollection,
In my memory to-day,
Suddenly . . .

Its ephemeral shudder
Zigzags, undulates, shoots
Across my remembrance . . .
—Yet not to be able to divine
The mystery of why it is evoked,
This fleeting idea,
So faint that it scarce touches me! . . .

-—Ah, I know not why, but surely
That falling ray
Was something in my fate
Which it crossed in its course . . .

So much secret in the destiny of a life . . .

It is like the idea of North,
Preconceived,
Which has always accompanied me . . .

Pamela Bacarisse (essay date 1975)

SOURCE: "Sá-Carneiro and the Conte Fantastique," in
Luso-Brazilian Review, Vol. 12, No. 1, Summer, 1975,
pp. 65-79.

[*Bacarisse compares the incredible elements of Sá-
Carneiro's work to the fantasy writings of nineteenth-
century French writers.*]

An important and obvious facet of both the poetry and the prose of Sá-Carneiro is his fascination for the incredible, the impossible, in fact for the *fantastique* so dear to the *conteurs* of the 19th century in France and to the sources of inspiration of so many of them, E. T. A. Hoffmann and Edgar Allan Poe. This legacy from the Romantic movement is manifested over and over again in narrative action and the experiences of his protagonists, in his imagery and, not unexpectedly, in his own consciousness as a storyteller. *Impossível, incrível, bizarro, estranho, fantástico, inexplicável, mágico, esquisito, extraordinário, estrambótico, nimbado, singular, inexprimível, perturbador, quimérico, mistério, segredo, sonho, enigma, sombra, além, visão, encanto, milagre* and many other similar words appearing with very great frequency in his writings, even in his surviving correspondence,[1] bear witness to his narrator's awareness of this aspect of his work: he points out in his story **"O Incesto"**, for example, that a character's eyes "cintilaram num fulgor extranho";[2] among the thousand enigmas of *A Confissão de Lúcio* he comments on the "coisa bizarra" that "no seu corpo [that of one of the minor characters] havia mistério", the same man has an "estranho perfil" and sports a "chapéu [. . .] esquisito";[3] the enigmatic stranger of "O Homen dos Sonhos" "tinha opiniões bizarras, ideias estranhas—como estranhas eram as suas palavras, estravagantes os seus gestos";[4] Marta, in *A Confissão de Lúcio,* is referred to as "essa mulher de sombra" (p. 85); in "A Grande Sombra", we learn that "o enigma continuava" and then the storyteller muses, "Ah! se enfim eu estivesse na posse dum Segredo . . ."[5] In a letter to Fernando Pessoa dated 23 August, 1915, Sá-Carneiro describes a story he is planning as an "enredo complicado e bizarro" (vol. II, p. 68); an earlier letter (10 May, 1913) refers to the "singular turbilhão das coisas esplêndidas e bizarras" in one of his poems (vol. I, pp. 122-123); even earlier (21 January, 1913), he plans a story which will include "sensações estranhas e deliciosas, voluptuosidades ignoradas [. . .] delícias irreais" and so on (vol. I, p. 58). As for his imagery, there is no shortage of examples, especially in the poetry: in the first of the **"Sete Canções de Declínio"** we find "a fantástica bandeira sem suporte";[6] in **"Rodopio"**, "Planos, quebras e espaços/Vertiginam em segredo" (p. 76); in **"Ângulo"** the poet asks, "Que oceano vos dormiram de Segredo?" (p. 108); in **"Distante Melodia"** is found the "Domínio inexprimível de Ópio e lume" (p. 99); in **"Abrigo"** is a "Milagroso carroussel" (p. 131); in **"Partida"** the "Miragem roxa de nimbado encanto" (p. 53). In the prose we hear, for example, of the "mão brônzea, incrível, dum gigante" which seems to have descended on the back of the protagonist's neck (in the short story **"A Grande Sombra"**);[7] in **"Asas"**, Sá-Carneiro describes the "círculos enclavinhados, impossíveis" of vertigo;[8] **"O Fixador de Instantes"** involves a description of the beloved in which she is anointed by "sombras aureoladas, transparentes d'alma, sombras que ela mesma, da sua carne-luz, suscitava em miragem velada".[9] Everything is odd, worrying, even incomprehensible both to author and reader, and the incidence of the *merveilleux* in narrative action, too, is fre-

quent and striking: characters appear from nowhere, disappear as surprisingly, create other people out of thin air, have a sixth sense, bear uncanny resemblances to each other, go to other worlds, die from no apparent physical cause. In fact, the author makes use of the ideas found so often in the realm of the *conte fantastique,* a realm which obviously fascinated him (although he was not interested in reproducing or elaborating on folk tales or traditional myths in the style of Perrault). For us, this part of his work can be helpful both towards understanding the author and in placing his writings in some sort of literary perspective.

In his book *Le Conte fantastique en France de Nodier à Maupassant,*[10] Pierre-Georges Castex describes the technique of the French *conteurs* who follow the age-old tradition of treating as fact "un univers imaginaire"; the difference in the works of Mário de Sá-Carneiro is a subtle one—he is concerned with what he calls "a realidade inverosímil",[11] (though for him it does not differ from "a verdade simples").[12] The problem that faces him, and us, is the incredibility of the facts, or what Ione de Andrade has called "o fantástico oculto na própria realidade".[13] In the stories of say, E. T. A. Hoffmann (whom I propose to consider together with the French *conteurs* for the purposes of my argument), the reverse is the case. The complaisant reader suspends his disbelief and enjoys the impossible as though it were real. The difference between the approach typified by Hoffmann and that found in Sá-Carneiro is one that came about by means of a gradual but by no means consistent process, full of exceptions to the general tendency. Even today, for example, the works of Tolkien stand as a clear indication of the survival of the older view of the fantastic; conversely, writers such as Charles Nodier with his "histoire fantastique vraie" category—the "Histoire d'Hélène Gillet" is one—and Edgar Allan Poe were precursors of Sá-Carneiro and all those who favour the "realidade inverosímil" approach. But allowing for inconsistencies and exceptions, there was clearly, as the 19th century progressed, a growing awareness among the authors of the *conte fantastique* that they could no longer depend on the gullibility of their readers. Rightly or wrongly, they suspected that the reader would see himself as the author's dupe, and for this reason—and others, such as a growing contempt for Romantic preoccupations—began to show greater respect for the concept of common sense and the rational. The way out was the device of the "rational explanation", making "plausible l'oeuvre tout entière. À l'attrait de l'histoire marveilleuse se juxtapose l'interêt réaliste". Edgar Allan Poe was greatly admired in France, as Castex says, because his stories were almost invariably logical,[14] but I shall have more to say on the subject of logic later. The "rational explanation" itself could be produced in one of several ways. The first is perhaps more insulting to the intelligence of the reader than to expect him to accept, for example, that an unknown faerie child appears out of the blue to two young children playing in the woods;[15] it consists of producing a complete set of (often unconvincing) facts at the very last moment to explain away, somewhat after the manner of the detective story, the previously puzzling phenomena of the narrative. In many cases it turns out that there has been some sort of deliberate deception of the protagonist, sometimes for rather shady reasons. An example of this category is Horace Raisson's tale "L'Elixir de jeunesse",[16] where a magic rejuvenating philtre is presented to the heroine by a strange man in gratitude for her hospitality; when the disappearance of her chambermaid coincides with the sudden appearance of a baby in the house, she assumes that the magic potion has done its work, albeit accidentally and on the wrong person. Any belief the reader may have had in the liquid's supernatural powers is completely dispelled when the *dénouement* reveals, with the arrival ten years later of the chambermaid and the stranger in search of their child, that the whole episode had been contrived in order to get rid of an unwanted baby on a gullible and rich woman. Guy de Maupassant is an example of an author who actually changed a short story from its original version, in which no rational explanation was given, to its second: his macabre "La Main d'écorché" (1875)[17] presents the "fact" of the hand of a dead man kept by the protagonist as a morbid souvenir disappearing overnight, leaving the marks of its fingers on his throat and being found later by a gravedigger who has just come across a skeleton; in the second version, now called only "La Main" (1885),[18] the original owner of the hand was not, it seems, actually dead and has reclaimed his property. The more charitable among us may allow that praiseworthy motives lay behind the popularity of this sort of explanation among authors, a kind of respect for the reading public, but there can be little doubt that in many cases these ingenious solutions add little to the stories' artistic value and they are often far from convincing. Another way of making the incredible credible was to place an episode, an experience or, indeed, the whole tale in the world of dreams; or there were those authors who clarified all mysteries by revealing, either sooner or later, that the protagonist's "experiences" were the outcome of drug taking or intoxication. Finally, there are many cases where insanity, either temporary, as in Guy de Maupassant's "Lui?",[19] or permanent and congenital, convinces the victim that his hallucinations were real experiences. Each of these methods presupposes, of course, the credulity of the protagonist, who because of some sort of defect in his equilibrium is prepared to accept as plausible circumstances which his common sense should see as impossible. If the causes of his deception are not obviously external (drugs, alcohol) and are to be found within him (mental instability, stupidity), it is a different task altogether to determine whether they are genetic or environmental. The fact remains, however, that there *is* a deception, and the omniscience of the author in the face of the hero's confusion can lead to an unsympathetic or even scornful attitude: this fool, he seems to be saying, thought this was the case, but in fact I know—and shortly you will know too—where the truth lies. The relationship between the storyteller and a protagonist who is, to all intents and purposes, normal and who experiences something strange and inexplicable is surely a more appealing one. Even if

the "normality" we assume in a protagonist—in the absence of evidence to the contrary—is threatened by exceptional circumstances, such as the tremendous grief of the comte d'Athol at the death of his beloved wife in Villiers de L'Isle—Adam's "Véra",[20] it is more satisfying, it seems to me, to have our fears for his emotional stability allayed at the end of the story when we are given material proof of the impossible: the key of his dead wife's tomb, left on the nuptial bed, shows that her visit was not just a figment of a deranged imagination. To sum up, there are two clear forms of treatment of the supernatural in the *conte fantastique*: either the incredible is presented as the truth, with no embellishment or apology, or as the appearance of truth, and a rational explanation is given in order to reveal the reality behind appearances. Sometimes, it should be added, the tales which belong to this second category are loaded with symbolism and have an obvious homiletic purpose. Perhaps a preference for one method as opposed to the other is no more than a question of subjective taste on the part of the reader, but for the authors concerned there may have been motives other than those based on mere caprice. Nodier shows his disapproval of explanations by heading the final chapter of "La Fée aux miettes"[21] "Conclusion. Qui n'explique rien et qu'on peut se dispenser de lire". That he has already given a kind of "explanation" by making the storyteller, Michel, a lunatic in a Glasgow asylum is relatively unimportant for two reasons. Firstly, Nodier's attitude towards "les lunatiques" is a very special one: he claims that "il est absurde d'en conclure [from the fact that we cannot understand them] que leurs idées manquent de sens et de lucidité".[22] At one point he wonders if they are aware of "une révélation instinctive de supériorité morale",[23] and he is not above the odd wry joke which makes his point of view quite clear, for example, the heading of Chapter III of "La Fée aux miettes": "Comment un savant, sans qu'il y paraisse, peut se trouver chez les lunatiques, par manière de compensation des lunatiques que se trouvent chez les savants".[24] Secondly, the story's final chapter, far from explaining anything, adds new material just as incredible as the existence of a fairy, of a magic plant, of the Queen of Sheba, a magic portrait and all the phenomena made use of by Nodier. Prosper Mérimée hardly ever dispensed entirely with the supernatural element in his *contes* either: the phenomenon of the evil eye in *La Guzla*[25] for example, is no more acceptable at the end than at the beginning. Neither is the king's macabre, prophetic vision in "La Vision de Charles XI",[26] nor the statue's power in "La Vénus d'Ille",[27] in fact, the most famous story in which the author does tie up the loose ends (using the dream device), "Djoûmane", may be seen as one of his weakest.[28] That the storyteller himself is, or claims to be, entirely sure that there is no "answer" to his puzzles, no meaning to be attributed to them even, is probably of little importance where literary criticism in general is concerned, but for the present study this *is* relevant: neither Nodier nor Mérimée offers to tie up the loose ends of their fictional worlds. As we have already seen, E. T. A. Hoffmann, too, eschewed any clarification devices: he would happily use, for example, the word "merveilleux" in the literal sense, as in the "merveilleux orfèvre Léonard" of "Le Choix d'une fiancée",[29] without deeming any explanations necessary. This is not to say that he was not conscious of the incredible nature of his material; often other characters will point out the unacceptability of the facts as presented by the protagonist, equally often suggesting the excuses used by later writers as explanations—you've had a strange dream, they say, you're insane, you're obsessed by some superstition, you're covering up the truth, you drank a little more than you're used to.[30] In some cases, such as Villiers de L'Isle-Adam's "Claire Lenoir",[31] we are confronted by a matter-of-fact, pedestrian character who stands in contrast to the abstractions of the supernatural. This is one way in which the storytellers who present the incredible as reality may pander to the reader, making it easier for him to accept the bizarre phenomena being described. Another is the "realistic" technique used by so many of them to lull him into acceptance through recognition, recognition of landscape, states of mind, conversations, social attitudes and behaviour. This is a characteristic that becomes more and more evident. The reproduction of states of mind by these writers was a superficial one, and it was not until authors were influenced by Poe, with his psychological verisimilitude, that they discovered a wish to really plumb psychological depths in their characters. This is not to say, of course, that psychological verisimilitude and realistic description are mutually exclusive (though the one may edge the other out within the limited confines of one short story): Maupassant is renowned for his perspicacious pictures of society and landscape, yet it is undeniable that his investigations into the impossible are largely investigations into human behaviour and the human mind.

We have, then, two traditions. How does Sá-Carneiro solve the problem of whether or not to explain away the inexplicable phenomena of his stories? We have already decided that he is not concerned with the realistic presentation of "un univers imaginaire" but with the unrealistic, unacceptable, incredible nature of the facts. He is, therefore, on the horns of a dilemma. To explain away the *fantastique* using one of the many methods we have already considered would be to defeat his own object: he would be admitting that everything is possible and acceptable if you have the key to the puzzle, and that won't do. On the other hand, to leave the mysteries unexplained—though a possible and, in the past, often successful technique,—obviously did not appeal to him, possibly on aesthetic grounds. The answer he found is a technique which is both successful and revealing: successful because it goes some way towards filling the need for novelty in the realm of the *merveilleux,* and revealing because it gives his readers an insight into his personality and traumata. It is perhaps paradoxical that there should be any need for novelty in tales of the supernatural, that the fantastic can pall and the astonishing cease to astonish. Yet this is the case, for the reader, because of familiarity with supernatural manifestations in literature, can stop reacting in the desired fashion. Authors were, of course, aware of this, and Sá-Carneiro remedies it with a

technique which is exciting and appealing, even if it cannot be claimed that it was entirely original. His answer, as we shall see, was to give an explanation, an explanation not devoid of internal logic, but which in fact is as irrational as the mysteries it purports to clarify. As we have noticed, the logic of Edgar Allan Poe was admired in France, and we know too that Sá-Carneiro was an admirer of Poe.[32] But in both cases the presence of logic is irrelevant to the question of plausibility. Baudelaire was certainly right to see in Poe a taste for "une difficulté vaincue" or "une énigme expliquée",[33] neither could the truth of his summing up of the climate of the short stories—"l'absurde s'installant dans l'intelligence et la gouvernant avec une épouvantable logique"[34]—be faulted. Yet where plausibility is concerned, the "épouvantable logique" is as much a red herring in Poe as in Sá-Carneiro, and the absurdity and incredibility of the stories is always evident. Our actual enjoyment is no less, perhaps, for our inability to take "William Wilson"[35] as a factual sequence of events, though in say, "The Spectacles"[36] I should have thought that it is. The first story deals with the physical manifestation of the protagonist's "other half" in the form of a double who haunts and torments him. Eventually, in a drunken fury of desperation, he kills him, thus condemning himself to a living death, for it was only through the now destroyed good half of his personality that he had really lived before. What is interesting is that it was not a question of a hallucination on the part of the principal character, for the double actually existed and acted independently of him, other people knew him and he had a personality of his own: it is not then an allegory but a tale of mystery and imagination. It is one of Poe's best stories, to my mind, and it has served as an inspiration to later writers, but it *is* incredible. "The Spectacles" may well be one of Poe's worst and silliest tales, though the protagonist's family names do suggest that it was meant to be funny. (The previous generations of his family were called Froissart, Croissart, Voissart and Moissart.) The story tells of a young man so shortsighted that he falls madly in love with his own great-grandmother: in mitigation, it should be added that they had never before met, and that she failed to recognise his name because he had recently changed it, while she bore the name of her most recent husband. On any level, it is virtually impossible to suspend one's disbelief when faced with a narrative of this kind. When we consider the Portuguese writer, we are tempted to believe—at a first glance—that his "explanations" are no more than formal, rhetorical devices on a par with say, the technique of beginning stories with "The strangest thing happened to me . . ." or "I'm sure you will find this difficult to believe, but . . ." (both of which expressions he does, in fact, use), but the interesting realisation soon dawns that in all cases the stories actually pivot on these explanations.

The very title of Sá-Carneiro's story **"A Estranha Morte do Professor Antena"**[37] reveals a great deal about what is to follow, and the reader is already aware of the mystery element. The general tone of the title is reminiscent of the detective or suspense story, the Professor's name suggests science fiction, and the adjective *estranha* hints at the possibility (though on the evidence of the title alone we cannot yet be sure of this) of the intervention of the supernatural. This is perhaps the ideal work to illustrate my point. An eccentric scientist has died in mysterious circumstances and his favourite disciple now puts forward a new theory to explain the death, a theory based on documents that he has recently acquired. Instead of the implausible hit-and-run car accident which he had hitherto claimed was the cause of the Professor's death, he demonstrates how all the bizarre elements of the case fit neatly and logically together to give a totally different—and far less plausible—answer. He had actually witnessed the Professor's inexplicable end, and in fact no car had been involved, though the type of fearful injuries sustained out of the blue by the dead man did suggest a collision. He had previously insisted on the story of the car accident because he judged the facts too incredible to be accepted ("a alucinadora verdade" he calls them [p. 234]). Now, he recounts how the Professor had told him something of his latest fantastic discovery shortly before his sudden death, adding that soon he would be in a position to provide more details: he had been working in the field of reincarnation, or at least, rebirth from one world to another, convinced that the organism is *sensível* to only one world at a time. Therefore, he had argued, if the senses and organs can be artificially "disadapted" from their current environment (epileptics were cited as examples of those to whom this happens involuntarily), another world can be entered. And this is what he had achieved: he had entered another world by adapting himself to it, and it was there, in another world, that he had been struck down by a car or whatever fantastic vehicles they used, his mutilated body manifesting itself in *this* world only when he died. The "explanation" is evidently intended to be logical, and the tale is embellished with a quasi-scientific formula which serves the dual purpose of furnishing the right sort of background for the defunct Professor and of persuading the reader of the ineluctable rationality of his disciple's sequence of thought. So the mystery is solved, but the solution is as meaningless in our material world as the Professor's empty formula. The scientific jargon is part of the so-called rational explanation, but based as it is on groundless theories, it explains nothing. The "explanation" is important, however, both as a pivot for the narrative (the story would be singularly unsatisfying if we were told only that an eccentric professor's death cannot be explained) and, as we shall see, for some understanding of the author. We should perhaps see **"A Estranha Morte do Professor Antena"** as a continuation of the French *contes métaphysiques,* and an interesting avenue of exploration is suggested by the image of the physical manifestations of violence, like stigmata, on a man who has travelled to another world, though the journey was a scientific experiment and not a mystical quest.

The scientific veneer of **"A Estranha Morte"** does tend to make it unusual for Sá-Carneiro; more typical of his metaphysical preoccupations is **"O Homem dos Sonhos".**[38] Again mystery is present right throughout the story, from the title and the very first sentence to the flash of inspiration, like a "relâmpago de claridade",[39] in which the "truth" is revealed to the narrator. Sá-Carneiro described this tale as "uma história de *além*-vida, de *além*-terra; desenvolve-se," he affirmed, "noutros mundos, noutros sentimentos".[40] The story is a simple one: an enigmatic acquaintance of the narrator recounts some of his bizarre experiences to him one day, experiences that he has had in pursuit of the Ideal, reminding us of Gérard de Nerval. That this is not the only point of similarity between Sá-Carneiro and Nerval will soon become clear. Two days later they meet again, the strange man ruefully admits that he has now discovered what he was looking for and that it was not as exciting as he had hoped and imagined. He changes the subject and refuses to return to this fascinating topic. At the end of the evening, the two men separate and he is never seen again. The "explanations" in this story are, in a way, twofold. The stranger himself is mysterious, but clarifies everything by means of his confessions to the narrator. Now in fact, nothing is clear for his revelations simply deepen the mystery, and it is up to the narrator, with his "relâmpago de claridade", to sort it all out: and he does so. What are these two sets of "explanations"? Firstly, the stranger confides that he is a supremely happy man because he has discovered how to avoid life's pedestrian monotony: he actually controls his dreams and travels to other worlds, enjoying new experiences, seeing darkness, breathing music, encountering beings with visible souls and invisible bodies, investigating emotions that do not exist, and so on. Secondly, the narrator—with no documentary evidence to help him this time—works out for himself that this imprecise, vague and unreal character is, in fact, a creature out of a dream, though he is at the same time a real person. Making these two statements logically compatible gives the answer to the puzzle: "o homem estranho sonhava a vida, vivia o sonho. [. . .] Ele derrubara a realidade, condenando-o ao sonho. E vivia o irreal."[41] This second solution seems to me more logical than that to the enigma of **"A Estranha Morte do Professor Antena"**. And yet, of course, from a common sense standpoint, it is meaningless and as unhelpful as the revelations made by the strange man himself earlier in the story.

Sá-Carneiro's short novel *A Confissão de Lúcio* abounds with mystery and evidence of the supernatural: there are sudden manifestations and disappearances and an apparently inexplicable murder for which the narrator, now protesting his innocence, served a ten-year sentence in prison. In this case, as in **"A Estranha Morte do Professor Antena"** and **"O Homem dos Sonhos",** the object of the narrator is to present the facts, however strange they may seem—or as he says, may be. In each story, he is in a position to do this by means of information which had hitherto been unavailable: either documents have only recently come to light, as in **"A Estranha Morte"**, or he alone has vital knowledge which he is now prepared to divulge—only he was present at Antena's death, at Ricardo's death in *A Confissão de Lúcio,* only he was told about the strange man's experiences in **"O Homem** dos Sonhos" ("nunca dissera a ninguém o meu segredo," the man had said before recounting them).[42] *A Confissão de Lúcio,* like Villiers de L'Isle-Adam's "Claire Lenoir", is a story of marital infidelity, but in both cases this is no more than the tip of the iceberg, and the metaphysical concerns of the authors are evident most of the time. Lúcio Vaz, the narrator of the Sá-Carneiro novel, is surprised when after a year's separation from his intimate friend, Ricardo Loureiro, he discovers that Ricardo has married, and intrigued by the sensation that Marta—Ricardo's wife—has appeared from nowhere, without past, friends or background. Lúcio's intimacy with Marta grows until, with what seems like a certain amount of tacit encouragement from Ricardo, they become lovers. Lúcio's jealousy when he becomes sure of her unfaithfulness to him, together with a certain inexplicable physical revulsion for her, leads him to break off the relationship. Some time later, when he meets Ricardo again, his erstwhile friend is hysterical and insists on revealing what the circumstances of the whole affair were: he—that is, Ricardo—had *created* Marta as an extension of himself, not married her as he had said. By means of her, his love for Lúcio had been consummated. But he had brought about his own downfall through greed: his inability to resist the temptation of taking, through her, a second lover had ruined his relationship with Lúcio, and Lúcio was the only one he really cared for. Insanely furious that the woman whom he has actually fabricated for love of Lúcio should be the cause of their separation, Ricardo bursts into the room where she is sitting, takes out a revolver and shoots her. When Lúcio looks down aghast, the corpse is that of Ricardo, not Marta.[43] We have a narrative mystery yet again, full of other puzzling details such as Lúcio's discovery that Ricardo and Marta had met not in Lisbon, as he had supposed, but in Paris, where the two men had been enjoying the most intimate of friendships, without Lúcio's ever meeting her. Where did Marta come from? At the same time, we are confronted with psychological mysteries: why does Lúcio feel repugnance towards his mistress? Why is Ricardo so full of *tédio?* What lies behind his alienated attitude to people and love? And once again, thanks to the special knowledge of the narrator, these problems are cleared up . . . and at the same time, nothing is cleared up. Although *A Confissão de Lúcio* has suffered from critical neglect, as Dieter Woll points out,[44] there have been several different readings of it. In other words, the superficial puzzle is solved in a superficial way, but the real mystery is far from superficial and is open to varying interpretations.

In Sá-Carneiro, manifestations of the supernatural are evidence of the element of mystery which is thematically a cornerstone of his writings. They are, on a narrative level, reflections of a preoccupation with the unknown: "Afronta-me um desejo de fugir/Ao mistério que é meu e me seduz", he says in the poem **"Partida"**,[45] and it is obvious that there is not only a fascination with mystery in Sá-Carneiro's works but also that his relationship with it is a love-hate one: "o medo é Mistério", we find in **"Nao"**;[46] in *A Confissão de Lúcio* he says "O mistério

era essa mulher. Eu só amava o mistério . . .";[47] in **"A Grande Sombra"**, Sá-Carneiro talks of his "atracção de Mistério"[48] and later in the same story reveals his desire to one day "sugar [. . .] o gosto roxo e macerado do Mistério", adding how, if he were a millionaire or a prince, he would build his "domínio de Mistério".[49] The very frequency of the word "mistério" is evidence of his obsession with the concept. Therefore there are two levels: first, the narrative puzzle to be solved, a puzzle created by the intervention of the supernatural, and second, the idea of the unknown presiding over everything, which pervades Sá-Carneiro's thought and which the particular puzzles of the narrative represent. In the stories where there is no narrative puzzle, the emphasis falls directly on mystery with no intermediary, as it were. In *Princípio,* for example, we have psychological mysteries based on obsession, fear, sixth sense; John Parker claims that all the themes of the stories "could be reduced to one central theme or attitude: obsession", and he maintains that "this is true also of *A Confissão de Lúcio* and *Céu em Fogo".*[50] To all intents and purposes, the literary situation is the same in both types of story, for narrative puzzles are not really explained in those stories where they are a feature, and in those where mystery is investigated directly, without the metaphor of the question/answer device, we learn nothing. In fact, Parker sees the element of mystery as an end in itself, a means of escaping from everyday life: for Sá-Carneiro, "only the unknown is worth knowing".[51] This is the philosophy of many of the Sá-Carneiro protagonists—for example, the hero of the short story in *Princípio,* **"Página dum Suicida",** who commits suicide because "a única coisa interessante que existe actualmente na vida, é a morte!" (p. 174). But here again the mystery is not solved, for the tale ends with the disappearance of the hero, and obviously the new experience that is his is not shared with the reader.

The third level on which the *contes fantastiques* of Sá-Carneiro can be taken is the one which reveals part of his own personality and problems, and it is on this level that we catch a glimpse of one of the causes of his personal tragedy and his suicide. It is, it seems to me, the uselessness of his "omniscience". The hero's new experience after death in **"Página dum Suicida"** is not shared with the reader, but neither is it shared with the author. When we remember the explanations in *A Confissão de Lúcio,* **"O Homem dos Sonhos"** and **"A Estranha Morte do Professor Antena",** we find them irrational.[52] How can Ricardo "create" Marta in *A Confissão* for example? And Sá-Carneiro doesn't know the answer either. This is by no means the first time that authors have explained mysteries with mysteries, or just left them unsolved. But though other authors may have used similar techniques to that of Sá-Carneiro, it is unlikely that they all suffered the same bewilderment as he did. What I have called Sá-Carneiro's "bewilderment" is different and possibly more intense than that of others, such as Nodier or Villiers de L'Isle-Adam, for a fairly obvious reason. Sá-Carneiro does not write about Man but about a man—himself. He writes not about Death, but about his death. He deals not with universals, but with one personality and its problems. His works may be seen as constituting a psychiatric document, and though he may appear bright-eyed for a moment in his role as author as he ties up loose ends, this means nothing: his loose ends make an irrational tangle, he is not omniscient but ignorant, and the mysteries are no less oppressive or obsessive for having been put into another key. The Portuguese author's fantastic stories are not an expression of human truth in general, but of personal truth, unlike Villiers de L'Isle-Adam, for example, whose stories "Claire Lenoir" and "L'Intersigne" were quite rightly headed "faire penser" on their first publication by the *Revue des Lettres et des arts.* Villiers had something to say about life, literature and philosophy. Sá-Carneiro's escapism into the world of mystery is a reaction to personal preoccupations. The *conte fantastique* was a therapeutic exercise and an escape valve for groups of writers—the so-called 1830 Generation in France in particular—because of their disillusionment with religion, science, politics and society in general.[53] Their stimulus came partly from within, of course, but was also largely external. Sá-Carneiro's stimulus comes almost exclusively from within himself, and even those who see one of the sources of his problems as the absence of any religious faith do not suggest that he was intellectually disenchanted with the worldly manifestations of organised religion.[54] Like many others, he is conscious of what Guy de Maupassant called a "mal [. . .] inconnu",[55] and Sainte-Beuve's aphorism when assessing Mérimée applies equally well to Sá-Carneiro: "Mérimée," he wrote, "ne croit pas que Dieu existe, mais il n'est pas bien sûr que le diable n'existe pas".[56] So although the traumata of the French *conteurs* were by no means exclusively confined to reactions to the ways of society, the proportion of personal *Angst* to social disenchantment was different in them. Perhaps Sá-Carneiro has more in common with Gérard de Nerval than with any of the others. A lengthy comparison would be out of place at this point, but it is interesting to note some similarities between these two. In life, they both lost their mother at an early age, they both lived disordered (even Bohemian in the case of Gérard de Nerval) lives in Paris, they both delighted in shocking the bourgeoisie, both suffered financial disaster following the founding of a literary journal, they both liked travel and, of course, their ultimate suicide links them yet again. Many areas of common ground can be found in literary attitudes too: the stimulus from within, a largely a-sociological attitude to their writing, the invariably sterile, often fatal nature of love in their works. As we have already seen, they were dreamers of the impossible, the Ideal, striving—as the French writer puts it—to capture the ineffable ("fixer mon idéal", he says in *Sylvie*). Sá-Carneiro struggles, too, to "fixar" everything: his yearnings, in the poem **"Quase"** (*Poesias,* p. 69); the moment (in both **"A Grande Sombra"** and **"O Fixador dos Instantes"**, both in *Céu em Fogo*). And their imagery is similar: mysterious cities, the concept of the double, and so on. Urbano Tavares Rodrigues' assertion that Sá-Carneiro wrote "contos [. . .] sem parentesco, a não ser estilístico, na nossa prosa de ficção"[57] may well be true as far as Por-

tuguese literature is concerned, but they are not without "parentesco" in the realms of French and English literature.[58] M.-J. Durry sees Nerval's writings as a revelation of his soul, and this is true too for Sá-Carneiro. If Nerval's use of myth is "l'explication poétique du monde",[59] Sá-Carneiro's treatment of the unknown is the "explication poétique" of Sá-Carneiro. He is incapable of any sort of self-understanding and he is isolated. The mystery explained by a mystery is a metaphor for the literature that he wrote—itself a kind of irrational explanation of himself. He deals with the possible, not the impossible, and this is terrifying. As Villiers said of the "facts" of "Claire Lenoir", "la seule idée de *leur simple possibilité* est tout aussi terrible que le pourrait être leur authenticité démontrée et reconnue".[60] The "incredibility of the facts" is intolerable.

NOTES

[1] The largest and most revealing collection of Sá-Carneiro's letters is *Cartas a Fernando Pessoa,* Lisbon, vol. I: 1958, vol. II: 1959. Other *cartas inéditas* have been published from time to time, including, most recently, by François Castex in *Colóquio. Letras,* no. 7, Lisbon, May, 1972.

[2] In *Princípio,* Lisbon, 1912, p. 297.

[3] *A Confissão de Lúcio,* Lisbon, 1969, p. 20.

[4] In *Céu em Fogo,* Lisbon, s.d., p. 157.

[5] *idem,* p. 78.

[6] In *Poesias,* Lisbon, 1946, p. 119.

[7] *Céu em Fogo,* p. 98.

[8] *idem,* p. 198.

[9] *idem,* pp. 264-265.

[10] Pierre-Georges Castex, *Le Conte fantastique en France de Nodier à Maupassant,* Paris, 1951, p. 5.

[11] *A Confissão de Lúcio,* p. 17.

[12] *idem,* p. 15.

[13] Ione de Andrade, "Realismo Fantástico e Simbolismo dos Trajes na 'Confissão de Lúcio'", in *Bulletin des Études portugaises,* 1967-8, xxviii-xxix, pp. 337-354.

[14] Pierre-Georges Castex, *op. cit.,* pp. 70 and 399.

[15] As in E. T. A. Hoffmann's story "L'Enfant étranger", in *Contes Fantastiques,* vol. I, Paris, 1964, pp. 105-144. This is the translation by Loève-Veimars.

[16] In *L'Artiste,* vol. II, 1833. The story is recounted by P.-G. Castex, *op. cit.,* p. 71.

17 In *L'Almanach de Pont-à-Mousson*, 1875, under the pen-name of Joseph Prunier.

18 In *Contes du Jour et de la nuit*, Paris, 1885. Reprinted 1922, pp. 157-170.

19 In *Gil Blas*, 3 July, 1883 under the pen-name of Maufrigneuse. Reprinted in the *Oeuvres Complètes* ("Les Soeurs Rondoli. Le Baiser"), Paris, 1924, pp. 91-106.

20 In *La Semaine parisienne*, 7 May, 1874. Reprinted in Villiers de L'Isle-Adam, *Contes Fantastiques*, Paris, 1965, pp. 141-156.

21 In *Oeuvres*, vol. IV, Paris, 1832. Reprinted in Charles Nodier, *Contes* (ed. Pierre-Georges Castex), Paris, 1961, pp. 167-329.

22 *idem*, p. 176.

23 *idem*, p. 179.

24 *idem*, p. 185.

25 Prosper Mérimée, *La Guzla*, Paris, 1827, especially the introduction to "Sur le mauvais oeil": in the 1908 edition, pp. 196-199.

26 Prosper Mérimée "Vision de Charles XI" in *Revue de Paris*, July, 1829. Reprinted in *Colomba*, Paris, 1872, pp. 271-278.

27 Prosper Mérimée, "La Vénus d'Ille", in *Revue des Deux mondes*, 15 May, 1837. Reprinted in *Colomba*, Paris, 1872, pp. 152-185.

28 Prosper Mérimée, "Djoûmane", in *Dernières Nouvelles de Prosper Mérimée*, Paris, 1873.

29 E. T. A. Hoffman, *op. cit.*, vol. I, p. 157.

30 All these suggestions are made in the one Hoffmann story, "Le Choix d'une fiancée", *op. cit.*, vol. I, pp. 145-199.

31 In the *Revue des Lettres et des arts*, 13, 20, 27 October, 3, 10, 17, 24 November and 1 December 1867. Reprinted in the *Contes Fantastiques*, pp. 9-140.

32 See, for example, François Castex, *Mário de Sá-Carneiro e a Genese de "Amizade"*, Coimbra, 1971, p. 60: "as suas preferências vão para Stefan Zweig, Oscar Wilde e sobretudo Edgar Poë".

33 Charles Baudelaire, "Edgar Poe—sa vie et ses oeuvres", in *Curiosités. L'Art romantique*, Paris, 1962, p. 615.

34 *idem*, p. 616.

35 Edgar Allan Poe, *Tales of Mystery and Imagination*, London, 1908. In the 1971 edition, pp. 3-20.

36 *idem*, pp. 333-355.

37 In *Céu em Fogo*, pp. 225-256.

38 *idem*, pp. 157-170.

39 *idem*, p. 167.

40 *Cartas*, I, p. 57.

41 *Céu em Fogo*, p. 168.

42 *idem*, p. 159.

43 H. Houwens Post, "Mário de Sá-Carneiro, premier poète surréaliste portugais", in *Neophilologus*, Groningen, 1965, gives a summary of this story which is factually incorrect. Not content with misreading and misrepresenting it on this occasion, the author does so again in "Cinetism in the Imagery of Mário de Sá-Carneiro's Modernista Poetry", in *Ocidente*, no. 419, vol. LXXXIX, March, 1973, pp. 161-168, which is a reprint of a paper read at the F.I.L.L.M. Congress, Cambridge, 22 August, 1972.

44 Dieter Woll, "Decifrando 'A Confissão de Lúcio'", in *Miscelânea de Estudos em Honra do Prof. Vitorino Nemésio*, Lisbon, 1971, pp. 425-438.

45 *Poesias*, p. 51.

46 *idem*, p. 89.

47 *A Confissão de Lúcio*, p. 92.

48 *Céu em Fogo*, p. 49.

49 *idem*, pp. 54 and 64.

50 John Parker, *The Life and Works of Mário de Sá-Carneiro*, (unpublished thesis, Cambridge University, 1959), p. 392. I cannot agree that the concepts of "theme" and "attitude" are as interchangeable as Parker would appear to suggest: see my article "Arcadia Revisited: Recent Work on Luis Cernuda", in *Forum for Modern Language Studies*, vol. IX, no. 3, July, 1973, pp. 301-309.

51 *idem*, p. 401.

52 These are not, of course, the only examples of this in the works of Sá-Carneiro, e.g. the suicide of the protagonist of "O Sexto Sentido" (in *Princípio*)—which is recounted, in fact, in another story—has been motivated by the unhappiness caused by the possession of sixth sense; the inexplicable disappearance of Zagoriansky's poem in "Asas" (*Céu em Fogo*) was caused by its very perfection: the words no longer obey the laws of gravity and have floated away; perhaps the oddest explanation of all is found in "A Grande Sombra" (*Céu em Fogo*), where the important and enigmatic character, Lord Ronald Neville, turns out to *be* the death of the narrator's murdered mistress.

53 "Le thême l'effet maléfique des sciences a fair couler beaucoup d'encre de la plume de Nodier tout au long de sa carrière littéraire," says Miriam Hamenachem, *Charles Nodier. Essai sur l'Imagination mythique,* Paris, 1972, p. 32. She also maintains that he was impelled to create the "côté noir de son univers" by his witnessing the horrors of the French Revolution (p. 10). Pierre-Georges Castex, *op. cit.,* points out that "la plupart des écrivains fantastiques [were] des contempteurs du monde moderne", and shows how similar are the ideologies of Nodier and Villiers de l'Isle-Adam despite the fifty years between them (p. 400).

54 For example, M. A. Antunes, "A Poesia Modernista. De *Orpheu a Altitude*", in *Brotéria,* vol. XXXI, Lisbon, October, 1940, pp. 300-320.

55 Guy de Maupassant, "Le Horla", in *Gil Blas,* 26 October, 1886. Reprinted in *Le Horla,* Paris, 1909; p. 6: "ce pressentiment qui est sans doute l'atteinte d'un mal encore inconnu, germant dans le sang et dans la chair". "Le Horla" is a fascinating example of a story with many features in common with the works of Sá-Carneiro. For example, compare the protagonist's musings regarding the limitations of this world in the former with the opinion of the "homen dos sonhos" of the latter: "Pourquoi pas un de plus?" asks the Maupassant character, referring to an "être nouveau", "Pourquoi pas aussi d'autres arbres aux fleurs immenses, éclatantes et parfumant des régions entières? Pourquoi pas d'autres éléments que le feu, l'air, la terre et l'eau? [. . .] Comme tout est pauvre, mesquin, misérable!" (p. 41). The stranger in the Portuguese story says, "A vida, no fundo, contém tão poucas coisas, é tão pouco variada . . . [. . .] Por toda a banda o mesmo cenário, os mesmos acessórios: montanhas ou planícies, mares ou pradarias e florestas—as mesmas cores . . ." (pp. 158-159).

56 *Portraits Contemporains,* Paris, 1855, vol. III, quoted by P.-G. Castex, *op. cit.,* p. 248.

57 Urbano Tavares Rodrigues, Introduction to Mário de Sá-Carneiro, *Cartas a Fernando Pessoa,* vol. I, p. 19.

58 See my article, *"A Confissão de Lúcio:* Decadentism *aprés la lettre",* in *Forum for Modern Language Studies,* vol. X, no. 3, July, 1964. Although this deals exclusively with *A Confissão de Lúcio* as far as Sá-Carneiro's works are concerned, it can easily be seen that *Princípio, Céu em Fogo* and the poetry could have been compared with French Decadentism and English Aestheticism.

59 M.-J. Durry, *Gérard de Nerval et le mythe,* Paris, 1956, p. 80.

60 *op. cit.,* p. 12. The italics are the author's.

William W. Megenney (essay date 1976)

SOURCE: "This World and Beyond: Mário de Sá-Carneiro's Struggle for Perfection," in *Hispania,* Vol. 59, No. 2, May, 1976, pp. 258-67.

[*In the following essay, Megenney says that Sá-Carneiro's poetry reflects his search for the ideal in a tortured, tumultuous universe.*]

Portugal has produced many outstanding poets over the centuries. One of the most gifted of the twentieth century was Mário de Sá-Carneiro, who, with Fernando Pessoa, represents the apex of the Modernist movement in Portugal—a movement which sprang from a general feeling of anguish present during the turn of the century in Europe and in most of the world. Other writers who formed part of the Portuguese Modernist current and who emphasized notes of despair, solitude, and anxiety in their poetry include Antônio Botto, José Régio, Adolfo Casais Monteiro, and Miguel Torga. This movement in Portugal is paralleled chronologically and thematically in such Spanish poets as Antonio Machado and Juan Ramón Jiménez. Essential themes present in their poetry revolve around sensations of anguish produced by the uncertain and temporal nature of existence and the search for Beauty which is, supposedly, the font of all truth. There are also thematic links between Portuguese Modernism and the movement in Spanish America as exemplified in the works of such poets as Julián del Casal, Manuel Gutiérrez Nájera, and José Asunción Silva. These themes also emphasize the same anguish and despair that was present during this time in history. These are the thematic elements, then, which we will attempt to study in this article as we assess Mário de Sá-Carneiro's role in the Portuguese Modernist Movement.

Critics agree that the ultimate preoccupation in the poetry of Mário de Sá-Carneiro was a struggle to discover some meaning in life and to put his thoughts together in a coherent mental balance. *Dispersão* or dispersion, breakup, was the keynote of the poet's literary production. A complete state of dispersion or separation between the poet and the world, the poet and life, and the poet and himself, is summed up in Sá-Carneiro's poem **"Dispersão."** Two metaphors used in this poem, namely "Castelos desmantelados," and "Leões alados sem juba . . ."[1] express very well the resultant state of dispersion that the poet experiences because of his deep anguish. This theme, which is so predominant here, occurs frequently in the three genres used by Sá-Carneiro to record his thoughts. Throughout the author's poetry, short stories, and letters to Fernando Pessoa, there are allusions to a lack of stabilization in time, space and psyche. The poet confesses that he is torn apart by some mysterious force and hurled in many different directions simultaneously.

This cleavage in Sá-Carneiro's poetry is the result of his anxiety to comprehend entirely all which is perfect in life, and to be able, in turn, to create this perfection through literature.

In Sá-Carneiro's poem **"Dispersão,"** a feeling of complete disorientation in life is very evident:

Perdi-me dentro de mim
Porque eu era labirinto,
E hoje, quando me sinto,
É com saudades de mim.

Passei pela minha vida
Um astro doido a sonhar.
Na ânsia de ultrapassar,
Nem dei pela minha vida . . .

Para mim é sempre ontem,
Não tenho amanhã nem hoje:
O tempo que aos outros foge
Cai sobre mim feito ontem.

(p. 61)

Sá-Carneiro exists within an ambiguous juggling of time which he cannot define as being past, present, or future. He is unable to move forward in a natural progression of time sequences and therefore feels trapped inside something which he can only call "past" or "yesterday." This incarceration within one particular time period naturally creates the invention of a method for escape into another world or dimension in time and space. The method is manifest in a confession in which Sá-Carneiro refers to himself as a "crazy star, dreaming his life away" while, all the time, he was losing contact with the world of reality. It is imperative for him to escape, however, even though he is fully aware at this stage of his writing (from 1913 to 1916) that he has been dreaming and that this form of flight has been the reason for his inability to create his own perfect work of art.

The necessity for escape is obvious since the bulk of Sá-Carneiro's poetry and prose is concerned with ways of living in the unclear realms of otherworldliness. João Gaspar Simões, in his introduction to volume II of the **Obras completas de Mário de Sá-Carneiro,** states that "a obra de Sá-Carneiro é uma tentativa de fuga por inadaptação" (p. 24). This is precisely why Sá-Carneiro adapted so well to the Portuguese Modernist movement, the tonalities of which were strikingly similar to those of the romantics, the symbolists, and the Spanish American Modernists. Sá-Carneiro, through Portuguese Modernism, could live in his own imagination and attempt to experience the world which his own conscience wished to create.

Sá-Carneiro's inadaptability to reality made him fit perfectly into the literary currents of his day. He was, however, unable to come to terms with himself. As João Gaspar Simões writes, "pode dizer-se que no caso de Sá-Carneiro existe apenas objecto—falta o sujeito" (p. 27). In other words, his anxiety to create the perfect work of art was constantly frustrated because of the mental dispersion which he suffered.

Some indications of a desire to produce the impossible may be found in the excerpts that follow. In **"Partida,"** the first poem of **Dispersão,** the use of the direct object pronoun where it ordinarily is not found in Portuguese suggests that the poet wants to project himself beyond what he is: "Mas logo *me* triunfo" (p. 51). Upon saying this, Sá-Carneiro expresses the fact that he can escape and go beyond reality into a dream world. He can change himself by altering his artistic creation:

Porque eu reajo. A vida, a natureza,

Que são para o artista? Coisa alguma.
O que devemos é saltar na bruma,
Correr no azul à busca da beleza.

("Partida," p. 52)

It would appear that Sá-Carneiro is merely attempting to find Rubén Darío's blue happiness of never-never land where he could enjoy the rare sensations of a Parnassian *ars gratia artis.* However, these verses, placed in the context of the whole poem and then in that of the poet's complete works, indicate that Sá-Carneiro goes farther than such a Baudelairian search for sensuous correspondences. The twentieth-century Portuguese artist wants to become powerful enough to achieve the ultimate creation. This causes him to have delusions of grandeur. Psychologically trapped in the past, he envisions himself in a quasi-Platonic philosophy of having existed as God before he was born: "Vêm-me saudades de ter sido Deus . . ."[2] ("Partida," p. 54).

Farther along in **Dispersão,** Sá-Carneiro reiterates the idea of leaving this world and going into another. In this journey, he refers several times to *beleza,* and obviously wants to attain it in some way. One method of reaching it might be to induce *beleza* to dream about the poet. Sá-Carneiro suggests that this happens as a step toward achieving the realization of his desires to escape: "—P'ra que me sonha a beleza" ("Vontade de Dormir," p. 60). But what is *beleza* and what would Sá-Carneiro gain from being dreamed by it? *Beleza* is perfection in nature and in humanity as a part of nature. It is what the poet wants to become completely engulfed in so that he can understand it fully and thus create it. If he can be in its dreams, he can be a part of it, and thus, eventually, be able to use it for artistic purposes.

In his search for this mysterious element which the poet wants so desperately to comprehend, he reveals through the written word certain suppressed emotions. These emotions are the clues which point toward the reasons why the author yearned so to grasp this *beleza.*

A lack of family warmth during Sá-Carneiro's childhood forced him to seek love outside the bounds of parental relationships. This becomes clear in the fifth strophe of the poem **"Dispersão,"** when Sá-Carneiro recalls what Sundays used to be like in Paris:

Porque um domingo é família,
É bem-estar, é singeleza,
E os que olham a beleza
Não têm bem-estar nem família.

(p. 62)

Further evidence of the vacuum which resulted from not having any love from either mother or father can be found in the poem titled **"Como Eu não Possuo"** of **Dispersão.** The poet confesses that he does not have the capabilities to experience the pleasures that most people enjoy every day:

Olho em volta de mim. Todos possuem—

Um afecto, um sorriso ou um abraço.
Só para mim as ânsias se diluem
E não possuo mesmo quando enlaço.

(p. 70)

Sá-Carneiro cannot feel the total beauties of nature and therefore is unable to reproduce them in the perfect artistic form. This is the beginning of his frustration:

Roça por mim, em longe, a teoria
Dos espasmos golfados ruivamente;
São êxtases da cor que eu fremiria,
Mas a minh'alma pára e não os sente!

(p. 70)

The poet has never been able to find himself as a whole person belonging in the world in which he was born. Therefore, he must either escape to another world or be forever condemned to suffer the consequences of not having control of his own senses:

Quero sentir. Não sei . . . perco-me todo . . .
Não posso afeiçoar-me nem ser eu:
Falta-me egoísmo para ascender ao céu,
Falta-me unção p'ra me afundar no lodo.

Não sou amigo de ninguém. P'ra o ser
Forçoso me era antes possuir
Quem eu estimasse—ou homem ou mulher,
E eu não logro nunca possuir! . . .

(p. 70)

The fact that Sá-Carneiro expresses the desire to have either a man or a woman to "possess," reveals the poet's extraordinary longing for human communication. He simply cannot discover how to love and be loved by the human race.

As he continues to wish for spiritual contact in "Como Eu não Possuo," exclaiming how much he would love to possess a feminine passer-by that he sees in the street, he again confesses his impotency. Even though the ardent desire is present, the poet must confess that he becomes *retado*[3] when attempting to find the perfect link with humanity:

De embate ao meu amor todo me ruo,
E vejo-me em destroço até vencendo:
E que eu teria só, sentindo e sendo
Aquilo que estrebucho e não possuo.

(p. 72)

Sá-Carneiro therefore recognizes his deplorable state and weeps for himself because of the terrible sensation of fatality that this frustration produces:

Como se chora um amante,
Assim me choro a mim mesmo:
Eu fui amante inconstante
Que se traiu a si mesmo.

("Dispersão," p. 62)

This seemingly outward confession to narcissism is actually an admission of being incapable of communicating with nature. The poet says that he betrayed himself as an unsteadfast lover because he is unable to partake of love or beauty from the standpoint of an ideal to be fulfilled. He does not say that he loves himself nor that he ever did love himself. He says only that he attempted to love and that he betrayed himself because his efforts did not come to fruition. In fact, if he had loved himself and had been a narcissist, he would have had himself as the object of his love and should have established the perfect union with beauty through this self-love. Since he confesses his own imperfection, however, this love would have been impossible because the poet, in his literature, is constantly striving for absolute perfection.

It may be possible that Sá-Carneiro contemplated at some time the idea of searching for this magic link with beauty within himself as a form of narcissism. He writes, for example, in **"Dispersão,"** the following:

Regresso dentro de mim
Mas nada me fala, nada!
Tenho a alma amortalhada.
Sequinha, dentro de mim.

(p. 63)

This testifies to the poet's unsuccessful plunge within himself to find himself. Since there is no life inside of him, however, he cannot remain there and must search elsewhere for the living water that he so desperately needs.

As Sá-Carneiro continues to wish for the ability to understand nature fully, he again expresses what on the surface appears to be narcissism:

Ternura feita saudade,
Eu beijo as minhas mãos brancas . . .
Sou amor e piedade
Em face dessas mãos brancas . . .

Tristes mãos longas e lindas
Que eram feitas p'ra se dar . . .
Ninguém mas quis apertar . . .
Tristes mãos longas e lindas . . .

(p. 64)

Upon closer observation and within the context of all of Sá-Carneiro's writings, one realizes that these lines evoke images representing perfection. Adjectives such as "white," and "beautiful," which reappear with relative frequency throughout Sá-Carneiro's poems, are words generally used by Latin nations to describe the perfect qualities of humanity. The poet kisses his own hands not as a gesture of self-love but rather as a means to attain a basic understanding of what true beauty is and of how to interpret that beauty artistically.

It follows, then, that the verses "Sou amor e piedade / Em face dessas mãos brancas . . ." imply that the author momentarily approaches love, which is beauty (*beleza*), because at the instant of looking at and kissing his hands, he forces himself mentally to approach love, beauty, and humanity, as they merge into one entity. At the same time, the lines indicate juxtaposition of sentiments since a feeling of pity is also present at this moment of deep metamorphic contemplation—pity for himself because he knows that he will never be able to experience the perfection of this mysterious trinity. The metamorphosis from an imperfect human state to a perfect spiritual one cannot be completed. For this reason, his suffering is two-fold since he is very much aware of the reason for his dilemma and yet can do nothing but pretend to produce what he knows he is not capable of realizing. This is a terrible state of mind. It is in essence, the same type of anguish that we find expressed by Fernando Pessoa as Álvaro de Campos:

> Mal sei como conduzir-me na vida
> Com este mal-estar a fazer-me pregas na alma!
> Se ao menos endoidecesse deveras!
> Mas não: é este estar entre,
> Este quase,
> Este poder ser que . . .
> Isto.
>
> Um internado num manicómio é, ao menos,
> alguém,
> Eu sou um internado num manicómio sem
> manicómio.
> Estou doido a frio,
> Estou lúcido e louco,
> Estou alheio a tudo e igual a todos:
> Estou dormindo desperto com sonhos que são
> loucura
> Porque não são sonhos.[4]

In the same spirit as Álvaro de Campos, Sá-Carneiro writes:

> Perdi a morte e a vida,
> E, louco, não enlouqueço . . .
> A hora foge vivida
> Eu sigo-a, mas permaneço . . .
>   ("**Dispersão**," p. 65)

This soul-crushing predicament continues to rend the poet's heart as he faces reality by saying that no one wanted to fondle his hands. Herein, once again, we find the emptiness in Sá-Carneiro's soul due to a lack of parental love and to the misfortune of never having been able to communicate successfully with the beauty of life. This is why his hands are sad. They cannot find what they want because they cannot be what they want to be, namely, hands which have the power to create true beauty in a meaningful way.

All hope of ever being able to unite himself to life as the person he wanted to be has tumbled down and left Sá-Carneiro only with the consolation of knowing that he is going to die. He writes, in **"Além-Tédio":**

> E só me resta hoje uma alegria:
> É que, de tão iguais e tão vazios,
> Os instantes me esvoam dia a dia
> Cada vez mais velozes, mais esquios . . .
>   ("**Dispersão**," p. 74)

He dreams of royal palaces and "gold" (*ouro*), which represent his ideal, for they are "Poeira de amor . . ."

("**Não**," of *Indícios de Ouro*, p. 88) and encompass the *beleza* for which Sá-Carneiro searches.

The poet's ideal is also a Queen who lives in the Palace, but the Queen is old and paralyzed and serves no purpose. This is Sá-Carneiro, who knows that he can no longer struggle to attain his ideal. The last verses of **"Não"** are a confession of his impoverished state of mind:

> —A Rainha velha é a minha Alma—
> exangue . . .
> —O Paço Real o meu génio . . .
> —E os dragões são o meu sangue . . .
>
> (Se a minha alma fosse uma Princesa[5] nua
> E debochada e linda . . .)
>   (p. 91)

Here reality is seen allegorically in the first three verses, and unfulfilled hopeful wishing in the two in parentheses. Sá-Carneiro wants his soul to be a beautiful, nude Princess. But since reality for him is stronger than the world of fantasy which he has written about, he suffers mental dispersion and is unable to face reality because reality is not what he wants. As a result, he breaks up and instead of turning in the direction of communicative possibilities with beauty, he disintegrates and heads for oblivion which is the ultimate step along the road of *dispersão*.

This same Princess, which is Sá-Carneiro's *beleza*, becomes idealized and incarnate at the same time in several of the poet's journeys into his self-made dream world. Perhaps one of the best examples of this is found in the poem titled **"Certa Voz na Noite Ruivamente,"** in *Indícios de Ouro*:

> Esquivo sortilégio o dessa voz, opiada
> Em sons cor de amaranto, às noites de incer-
> teza,
> Que eu lembro não sei de Onde—a voz duma
> Princesa
> Bailando meia nua entre clarões de espada.
>
> Leonina, ela arremessa a carne arroxeada;
> E bêbeda de Si, arfante de Beleza,
> Acera os seios nus, descobre o sexo . . . Reza
> O espasmo que a estrebucha em Alma copulada . . .
>
> Entanto nunca a vi mesmo em visão. Sòmente
> A sua voz a fulcra ao meu lembrar-me. Assim
> Não lhe desejo a carne—a carne inexistente . . .
>
> É só de voz-em-cio a bailadeira astral—
> E nessa voz-Estátua, ah! nessa voz-total,
> É que eu sonho esvair-me em vícios de mar-
> fim . . .
>   (pp. 92-93)

As the poem so graphically indicates, and as may be seen throughout the book, *Indícios de Ouro* (the title itself divulges the contents), Sá-Carneiro is able to experience quick flashes of ecstasy because his imagination is sparked by unclear sights and sounds which enable him mentally to enjoy rare sensations of a spiritually elevated tone as he strives for the ideal state-of-being which he knows he can never reach.

The highly suggestive and subjective aspect of the images which the poet paints can be seen in the use of synesthesia (*sons cor de amaranto*), in the selection of descriptive words (*incerteza*), in the frequency of allegorical allusions (*Onde, Princesa, Si, Beleza, Alma*), and in the very nature of the source of the poet's vision: a voice coming from an unknown place in the darkness of night, tainted with opium. The ideality of the vision is called to mind not only by the perfidious dancer and what she is and does, but also by the use of the adverb *ruivamente* in the title of the poem; this automatically suggests a sandy color which, in turn, represents a fair, blonde Princess, the ideal model, as we have said, according to Latin tastes. This entire idea is completed by the inclusion of the amaranth, a very beautiful and colorful imaginary flower that never dies.

Yet, alas, in the word "imaginary" we have hit upon the crux of the poet's problem:—*a carne inexistente*. He knows that the ideal goal of understanding and creating perfect beauty is just that—ideal, and ideals like this one, which are contrary to the poet's nature, are never attained. This is why he says "Não lhe desejo a carne—," because once again, in the midst of his fantastic dream, he awakes to reality, and reality is what tortures him to such an extreme degree.

In spite of the torture, however, Sá-Carneiro is able to find flashes of exaltation and can grasp them for a longer period of time than if they were only the ethereal mist of which reveries are made. He achieves this elation by resorting to the creation of Parnassian figures so that his intangible visions become solidified. The "Voice-in-heat," which is the "heavenly dancer," turns into a "voice-Statue," a "totalvoice," with which Sá-Carneiro longs to communicate. The suggestion evoked by *Estátua* with a capital "E" is two-fold: it is the poet's ideal in his dream world, and an ideal which has taken on a very solid form, one which the poet can "feel," and which, as he evanesces farther and farther into his momentary realm of ideal sensations, he can almost enjoy as an experience of attaining perfection, as the entire image envelops him in a pleasant tactile hedonism of ivory. The sensation never reaches perfection, however, because Sá-Carneiro is too much aware of the real world and of what he is in this life.

Sá-Carneiro's poetry, especially in *Indícios de Ouro*, is pregnant with descriptive words, and one can cite many examples of the poet's use of a highly suggestive vocabulary that calls to mind the kinds of techniques used by the "school" of Spanish American Modernists inspired by the *Azul* and *Prosas profanas* periods of Rubén Darío. These Spanish American Modernists, as does Sá-Carneiro, strive for a perfect synthesis of form and meaning in poetry. They both emphasize words and phrases evoking sensations and aesthetic and physiological "correspon-dences." Their use of synesthesia is one example of this. The preoccupation with creating images which are full of light, colors, sounds, odors, and tastes is another common denominator. Just as the Spanish American Modernists struggled in their minds to reach exotic lands, so Sá-Carneiro longs to venture forth spiritually in order to find happiness (for example, in **"Distante Melodia"**). Certain word-symbols relished by the Modernists in Spanish America, such as "iris," "princess," "palace," "gold," and "satin," are used to full advantage by Sá-Carneiro.

There are also certain psychological parallelisms between Darío's and Sá-Carneiro's works which are interesting to note: both needed to escape reality, albeit for different reasons, and both were destined to wake up to reality and find that they really preferred their self-fabricated worlds of non-reality. Darío, abandoning, for the most part, the exterior pomp of his literary style, becomes highly sensitive to metaphysical doubt. His *Cantos de vida y esperanza* and the other poems after 1905 exemplify this attitude. The Nicaraguan poet becomes fully aware that the ideal creation in life can never be attained. He confesses, in the poem "Yo soy aquel . . ." that his thirst for illusions can never be quenched, "y una sed de ilusiones infinita."[6] Darío, like Sá-Carneiro, sought escape through the blue vastness of space, only to plummet to earth without any sense of direction. He writes, in "Lo fatal," "y no saber adónde vamos, / ni de dónde venimos! . . ." (*Azul . . .*, p. 168). Sá-Carneiro, in turn, says, "Não sei aonde vou, nem vejo o que persigo . . ." (***Indícios de Ouro,*** "16," p. 96). For both poets, reality is a stumbling block which impedes the attainment of perfection. Darío writes, "Bosque ideal que lo real complica" (*Azul . . .*, p. 114), and Sá-Carneiro:

> Parti. Mas logo regressei à dor,
> Pois tudo me ruiu . . . Tudo era igual:
> A quimera, cingida, era real,
> A própria maravilha tinha cor!
> (***Dispersáo,*** **"Além-Tédio,"** p. 74)

Both poets' gardens of potential ideal creativity become impossible places of refuge for them. Darío refers to his poetry as his "jardín de sueño" (*Azul . . .*, p. 113), in which "la adusta perfección jamás se entrega, / y el secreto ideal duerme en la sombra" (*Azul . . .*, p. 115). Sá-Carneiro expresses this idea by writing, "—O pântanos de Mim—jardim estagnado! . . ." (***Indícios de Ouro,*** **"Apoteose,"** p. 97).

Sá-Carneiro, taking full stylistic advantage of "ivory-tower" aesthetics, especially in ***Indícios de Ouro,*** laments over and over again his destiny as he foresees his own downfall, knowing that he can never reach the ideal point of perfect creativity:

> Há sempre um grande Arco ao fundo dos
> meus olhos . . .
> A cada passo a minha alma é outra cruz,
> E o meu coração gira: é uma roda de cores . . .
> Não sei aonde vou, nem vejo o que persigo . . .
> (***Indícios de Ouro,*** "16," p. 96)

On the twenty-sixth of April, 1915, we find Sá-Carneiro seated alone in a Parisian café taking another mental trip through the portal of his imagination:

> Na sensação de estar polindo as minhas unhas,
> Súbita sensação inexplicável de ternura,
> Todo me incluo em Mim—piedosamente.
> *(Últimos Poemas,* "Manucure," p. 169)

As he includes himself in Himself, that is, his flesh and blood self into the Ideal he would become, he cries because he knows that these sensations are ethereal and unreal. Because he is tortured by the imperfection of reality, he continues to suffer:

> E eu sempre na sensação de polir as minhas
>   unhas
> E de as pintar com um verniz parisiense,
> Vou-me mais e mais enternecendo
> Até chorar por Mim . . .
> **("Manucure,"** p. 170)

The poet's life-long experiences are expressed in this same poem, as the unattainment of the goal foreshadows self-destruction:

> É lá, no grande Espelho de fantasmas
> Que ondula e se entregolfa todo o meu passado,
> Se desmorona o meu presente,
> E o meu futuro é já poeira . . .
> **("Manucure,"** p. 170)

Here, the "Espelho de fantasmas" refers to the imaginative world that Sá-Carneiro built around himself and which is the ultimate cause of his death.[7]

It is at this point in Sá-Carneiro's life (May 1915) that he experiences one last surge of ecstasy as the Ideal now appears floating in the air in different shapes of various objects and in diverse sounds. Realizing that achieving his goal is definitely impossible, he adjusts all his efforts to the task of finding pleasure in another form of Ideal. The poet then attempts to refind himself:

> Deponho então as minhas limas,
> As minhas tesouras, os meus godets de verniz,
> Os polidores da minha sensação-
> E solto meus olhos a enlouquecerem de Ar!
> **("Manucure,"** p. 171)

The poet momentarily concentrates his energy on absorbing, as he states, this new found *Beleza,* which for him represents a form of escape from the spiritual and physical tortures that the struggle to gain the Ultimate produced. Here Sá-Carneiro has affirmed the fact that the *Beleza* he seeks is the Platonic one[8] in the strict sense of the word, which can be attained through the complete contemplation of *beleza* as it exists in the physical world in the form of numbers and letters as well as all sorts of shapes and sounds of various dimensions. In other words, the poet now wants to allay his former suffering by concentrating his sights on the ultimate *Beleza* as it reflects itself in those physical entities which are perfect.[9] He writes:

> Avido, em sucessão da nova Beleza atmosférica,
> O meu olhar coleia sempre em frenesis de
>   absorvê-la
> À minha volta.
> **("Manucure,"** p. 173)

It is evident in this outburst of literary production that Sá-Carneiro longs to be free and he attempts to find this freedom in the air which, according to him, will enable his body and soul to be caught up into a perfect *Beleza* where he will encounter complete liberty. He writes in the poem titled **"Apoteose"**:

> Eu próprio sinto-me ir transmitido pelo ar, aos
>   novelos!
>   (p. 177)
>
>   . . . . .
>
> Tudo isto, porém, tudo isto, de novo eu refiro ao Ar
> Pois toda esta Beleza ondeia lá também:
> Números e letras, firmas e cartazes—
> Altos relevos, ornamentação! . . . —
> Palavras em liberdade, sons sem-fio,
>
>   . . . . .
>
>   (p. 181)

Nevertheless, at the end of this poem Sá-Carneiro awakens to reality and losing all of his sanity in one final explosion, confesses that he will never attain the beauty he spent so much time and energy searching for:

> Levanto-me . . .
> —Derrota!
>
>   . . . . .
>
> —O sonho desprendido, o luar errado,
> Nunca em meus versos poderei cantar,
> Como ansiara, até ao espasmo e ao Oiro,
> Toda essa Beleza inatingível,
> Essa Beleza pura!
>   (p. 182)

Sá-Carneiro then ends the poem with a firing of onomatopoetic words indicating the sounds of complete destruction as the dispersion which constantly threatened him draws near its consummation.

Mário de Sá-Carneiro's ardent desires to reach Beauty reappear in July and August of 1915 when he writes in "2" of **"Sete Canções de Declínio"** (*Indícios de Ouro*):

> Quero ser Eu plenamente:
> Eu, o possesso do Pasmo.
> —Todo o meu entusiasmo,
> Ah! que seja o meu oriente!
>   (p. 120)

Here, he is saying that he wants to be the ideal *Eu,* which is not the real *eu* that exists physically. In order to become this new *Eu,* he must be totally enveloped by the Ideal, the Ultimate-State-of-Being, the Good in Plato's realm of the eternal, or Nirvana in Buddha's philosophy. And, as in the Platonic allegory, since this Ideal gives meaning to all of the other "layers" in life, the destruction of or the inability to reach the Ideal would mean the dissolution of Sá-Carneiro himself, since he is part of the world which depends for its existence on the Ideal. Destroy the Ideal and you have destroyed Sá-Carneiro. Since the poet knows that he can never attain the Ideal because of his innate lack of ability to do so, he automatically destroys the Ideal, and so he destroys himself. This paradoxical situation is given expression in a frequently quoted stanza of **"Dispersão"**:

> A grande ave doirada
> Bateu asas para os céus,
> Mas fechou-as saciada
> Ao ver que ganhava os céus.
>
> (p. 62)

The same admission of the impossibility of attaining the Ideal is expounded in **"Sete Canções de Declínio,"** where the poet, absolutely cognizant of the fact that his perfect treasure in life is only a dream, reiterates, as it were, the principal theme of his entire corpus of poetry:

> Mistério duma incerteza
> Que nunca se há-de fixar . . .
> Sonhador em frente ao mar
> Duma olvidada riqueza . . .
>
> (p. 121)

The Unbearable Torment of not fulfilling his dream of understanding completely and of being unable to create the perfect form of Beauty and thereby escape the desperation which engulfed him because of a lack of communication with humanity and with himself, helped provoke his suicide on April 26, 1916. If it had not been for Sá-Carneiro's literary creation, through which he found a way of continuing the quest for the perfect creation, he probably would have expired earlier in life.[10] The strain on the poet caused by an impossible task of creativity, coupled with an unexpected financial crisis, completed the process of dispersion in Sá-Carneiro's life and brought about his demise.

By way of a concluding note I would recall two of the metaphors mentioned at the beginning of this article ("Castelos desmantelados" and "Leões alados sem juba . . .") and suggest that they may now be understood in a deeper sense. After having examined the problem of the struggle for perfection as it appears in Sá-Carneiro's poetry, we should now realize that the winged lions, which can fly, are incomplete, as the poet is, since they have no manes (an image connoting the absence of maleness, i.e., impotency) and therefore serve no purpose as they lift off into the air and float around with no fixed destination. Sá-Carneiro's demolished castles are, of course, his splendid dreams of attaining perfection which have crumbled down around him as he becomes aware of his true incapabilities. It is easy for us to see, then, how Sá-Carneiro's life and works abound in negative elements, and how and why these elements finally destroyed him. His inability to endure against these forces with which life countered him made Sá-Carneiro an excellent example of the human suffering which was outstanding in so many writers of his time.

NOTES

[1] *Obras completas de Mário de Sá-Carneiro,* II (Lisbon: Edições Ática, 1946), p. 65. Further references to pages in this collection will be given in the text.

[2] Ricardo Gullón, in *Direcciones del modernismo* (Madrid: 1971) presents an excellent analysis of the theories and beliefs of the major exponents of Pythagoreanism, Buddhism, and Christianity. Herein is explained in a very concise and succinct manner the principal concepts of "metamorphosis, the eternal recurrence, and the circular and cyclical conception of existence . . ." (pp. 132-33), especially as it is manifested in the Modernist movement.

[3] The word *retado* is a non-translatable slang expression approaching the connotation of "frustrated" or "not being able to climax," especially in sexual contexts. It is used here because it expresses the exact state in which the poet finds himself.

[4] *Obras completas de Fernando Pessoa,* II (Lisbon: Edições Ática, 1964), pp. 52-53. Further references to pages in this collection will be given in the text.

[5] The word *Princesa* appears with a capital "P" here because ideality and reality are juxtaposed. The poet wants to attain his Ideal in life which is the creation of the perfect form of beauty. This, of course, is impossible since the Ideal itself (cf. Platonic philosophy) and the concrete realization of that Ideal are diametrically opposed as they are mutually exclusive, the one belonging to the world of the spirit or mind and the other to the world of the material. It is precisely this impossibility of joining these two worlds into one that causes Sá-Carneiro's deep frustration.

[6] Rubén Darío, *Azul . . . , El salmo de la pluma, Cantos de vida y esperanza, Otros poemas* (México: Editorial Porrúa, S.A., 1965), p. 114. Further references to *Azul . . .* will be given in the text.

[7] This same kind of objectification of sentiments which torture the body and the soul to the point of extinction can be found in the Mexican Modernist, Manuel Gutiérrez Nájera. It is possible that Sá-Carneiro may have drawn some of his thematic as well as spiritual inspiration from this nineteenth-century poet since in both we find the same types of metaphors used to express states of very deep emotion. One good example of this in Gutiérrez Nájera may be found in the poem entitled "Mis enlutadas":

> Descienden taciturnas las tristezas
> al fondo de mi alma,
> y entumecidas, haraposas brujas,
> con uñas negras
> mi vida escarban.
>
> . . . . .

Abrese a recibirlas la infinita
tiniebla de mi alma,
y van prendiendo en ella mis recuerdos
cual tristes cirios
de cera pálida.

(Julio Caillet Bois, *Antología de la
poesía hispanoamericana,* Madrid:
Aguilar, 1956, p. 727.)

[8] The scheme of Plato's four stages of cognition is found in the *Republic,* and is elaborated upon in the *Phaedrus,* and in the *Symposium.* Sá-Carneiro, at this stage of his striving for metamorphic transcendence, attempts to reach the Good through the mathematical objects of the intelligible world which serve as a link with the visible things of the world of appearances. By doing this, the poet hopes to establish a bridge between the two worlds and thus escape the torture of the physical world by entering the spiritual and eventually attaining what Plato designates as *noesis* or Intelligence.

This same notion is also expressed in Ricardo Gullón's essay, *Pitagorismo y modernismo* (op. cit.). Gullón's closing sentence summarizes Sá-Carneiro's state of mind at this particular moment of time: "No se olvide que para el budismo y el pitagorismo seguir viviendo es una condena; la vida, y más cuanto más baja sea, aleja y hace imposible ese extraño paralelo del paraíso que es el nirvana" (p. 136). As in Plato's philosophy, Pythagoras also sought to bridge the gap between worlds with numbers, as Sá-Carneiro. Gullón further writes: "El pitagorismo fue visto como un sistema concebido para poner orden en el caos; los números son cifras mágicas que revelan—si acaso no ocultan—la significación secreta de las cosas" (pp. 108-09).

[9] This momentary change in the direction the poet seeks for an escape can be compared to the dichotomy of the universe as it is explained by Arthur Ganz in his article "Human and Suprahuman: Ambiguity in the Tragic World of Jean Giraudoux" (*PMLA,* 87 [March 1972], p. 284).

That is to say, the new *Beleza* which Sá-Carneiro hopes to attain is, at this particular moment of his life, no longer a part of the human, flesh and blood side of existence, but rather "that great Romantic image of a beauty, power, and mystery that lies beyond the range of human experience." Just as the typical Giraudoux character when he sees that reality is too tragic to bear, Sá-Carneiro also at this point in time "steps aside and continues his quest for that vision which, though its pursuit may involve his own destruction, is more tempting, more satisfying than the pain and coarseness of ordinary existence." Sá-Carneiro here, too, is the victim of the "ambiguity of that Romantic ideality" (p. 288) for which he searches.

[10] In the historical anthology *Presença da literatura portuguêsa* (III, *Simbolismo e Modernismo*) compiled and edited by Antônio Soares Amora, Massaud Moisés, and Segismundo Spina (São Paulo, 1961), p. 233, the fact of the poet's very heavy dependence upon literature for everyday survival is stated: "uma vida que só existe como Literatura no bom e no mau sentido, pela exacerbação da fantasia apoiada numa imaginação sem limites, exótica, levando-o a planos neuróticos, arrancando o Poeta do solo já frágil sob dos pes. Sua vida é sua poesia, de forma que esta documenta um ser que se procura inùtilmente porque necessita de um "suporte" para evitar a "dispersão" interior, e, quem diz interior, diz total."

Interestingly enough, this same concept of attaining an ideal through the medium of literature, and especially poetry, was very prevalent among the Modernists. Ricardo Gullón (op. cit.) informs us that "Lo sustancial de la doctrina (of pythagoras) consistía en una concepción rítmica del universo y de la vida que los modernistas no sólo aceptaron sino convirtieron en idea central determinante de la creación poética. La poesía se les aparecía como articulación rítmica de intuiciones; el ritmo y la armonía que de él se deriva son claves de la belleza" (p. 108).

Twentieth-Century
Literary Criticism

Cumulative Indexes
Volumes 1-83

How to Use This Index

The main references

Calvino, Italo
1923–1985 .... CLC 5, 8, 11, 22, 33, 39,
73; SSC 3

list all author entries in the following Gale Literary Criticism series:

BLC = Black Literature Criticism
CLC = Contemporary Literary Criticism
CLR = Children's Literature Review
CMLC = Classical and Medieval Literature Criticism
DA = DISCovering Authors
DAB = DISCovering Authors: British
DAC = DISCovering Authors: Canadian
DAM = DISCovering Authors: Modules
      DRAM: Dramatists Module; **MST**: Most-Studied Authors Module;
      MULT: Multicultural Authors Module; **NOV**: Novelists Module;
      POET: Poets Module; **POP**: Popular Fiction and Genre Authors Module
DC = Drama Criticism
HLC = Hispanic Literature Criticism
LC = Literature Criticism from 1400 to 1800
NCLC = Nineteenth-Century Literature Criticism
PC = Poetry Criticism
SSC = Short Story Criticism
TCLC = Twentieth-Century Literary Criticism
WLC = World Literature Criticism, 1500 to the Present

The cross-references

See also CANR 23; CA 85-88;
   obituary CA116

list all author entries in the following Gale biographical and literary sources:

AAYA = Authors & Artists for Young Adults
AITN = Authors in the News
BEST = Bestsellers
BW = Black Writers
CA = Contemporary Authors
CAAS = Contemporary Authors Autobiography Series
CABS = Contemporary Authors Bibliographical Series
CANR = Contemporary Authors New Revision Series
CAP = Contemporary Authors Permanent Series
CDALB = Concise Dictionary of American Literary Biography
CDBLB = Concise Dictionary of British Literary Biography
DLB = Dictionary of Literary Biography
DLBD = Dictionary of Literary Biography Documentary Series
DLBY = Dictionary of Literary Biography Yearbook
HW = Hispanic Writers
JRDA = Junior DISCovering Authors
MAICYA = Major Authors and Illustrators for Children and Young Adults
MTCW = Major 20th-Century Writers
NNAL = Native North American Literature
SAAS = Something about the Author Autobiography Series
SATA = Something about the Author
YABC = Yesterday's Authors of Books for Children

20/1631
See Upward, Allen
A/C Cross
See Lawrence, T(homas) E(dward)
Abasiyanik, Sait Faik 1906-1954
See Sait Faik
See also CA 123
Abbey, Edward 1927-1989 .... **CLC 36, 59**
See also CA 45-48; 128; CANR 2, 41
Abbott, Lee K(ittredge) 1947- .... **CLC 48**
See also CA 124; CANR 51; DLB 130
Abe, Kobo 1924-1993**CLC 8, 22, 53, 81; DAM NOV**
See also CA 65-68; 140; CANR 24, 60; DLB 182; MTCW 1
Abelard, Peter c. 1079-c. 1142 ...... **CMLC 11**
See also DLB 115
Abell, Kjeld 1901-1961 .... **CLC 15**
See also CA 111
Abish, Walter 1931- .... **CLC 22**
See also CA 101; CANR 37; DLB 130
Abrahams, Peter (Henry) 1919- .... **CLC 4**
See also BW 1; CA 57-60; CANR 26; DLB 117; MTCW 1
Abrams, M(eyer) H(oward) 1912- .... **CLC 24**
See also CA 57-60; CANR 13, 33; DLB 67
Abse, Dannie 1923- . **CLC 7, 29; DAB; DAM POET**
See also CA 53-56; CAAS 1; CANR 4, 46; DLB 27
Achebe, (Albert) Chinua(lumogu) 1930-**C L C 1, 3, 5, 7, 11, 26, 51, 75; BLC 1; DA; DAB; DAC; DAM MST, MULT, NOV; WLC**
See also AAYA 15; BW 2; CA 1-4R; CANR 6, 26, 47; CLR 20; DLB 117; MAICYA; MTCW 1; SATA 40; SATA-Brief 38
Acker, Kathy 1948-1997............. **CLC 45, 111**
See also CA 117; 122; 162; CANR 55
Ackroyd, Peter 1949-.................... **CLC 34, 52**
See also CA 123; 127; CANR 51; DLB 155; INT 127
Acorn, Milton 1923- ....**CLC 15; DAC**
See also CA 103; DLB 53; INT 103
Adamov, Arthur 1908-1970**CLC 4, 25; DAM DRAM**
See also CA 17-18; 25-28R; CAP 2; MTCW 1
Adams, Alice (Boyd) 1926-**CLC 6, 13, 46; SSC 24**
See also CA 81-84; CANR 26, 53; DLBY 86; INT CANR-26; MTCW 1
Adams, Andy 1859-1935 .... **TCLC 56**
See also YABC 1
Adams, Brooks 1848-1927 .... **TCLC 80**
See also CA 123; DLB 47
Adams, Douglas (Noel) 1952- .... **CLC 27, 60; DAM POP**
See also AAYA 4; BEST 89:3; CA 106; CANR 34, 64; DLBY 83; JRDA
Adams, Francis 1862-1893 .... **NCLC 33**
Adams, Henry (Brooks) 1838-1918 **TCLC 4, 52; DA; DAB; DAC; DAM MST**
See also CA 104; 133; DLB 12, 47, 189

Adams, Richard (George) 1920-**CLC 4, 5, 18; DAM NOV**
See also AAYA 16; AITN 1, 2; CA 49-52; CANR 3, 35; CLR 20; JRDA; MAICYA; MTCW 1; SATA 7, 69
Adamson, Joy(-Friederike Victoria) 1910-1980 **CLC 17**
See also CA 69-72; 93-96; CANR 22; MTCW 1; SATA 11; SATA-Obit 22
Adcock, Fleur 1934- .... **CLC 41**
See also CA 25-28R; CAAS 23; CANR 11, 34, 69; DLB 40
Addams, Charles (Samuel) 1912-1988**CLC 30**
See also CA 61-64; 126; CANR 12
Addams, Jane 1860-1945 .... **TCLC 76**
Addison, Joseph 1672-1719 .... **LC 18**
See also CDBLB 1660-1789; DLB 101
Adler, Alfred (F.) 1870-1937 .... **TCLC 61**
See also CA 119; 159
Adler, C(arole) S(chwerdtfeger) 1932- . **C L C 35**
See also AAYA 4; CA 89-92; CANR 19, 40; JRDA; MAICYA; SAAS 15; SATA 26, 63, 102
Adler, Renata 1938- ....**CLC 8, 31**
See also CA 49-52; CANR 5, 22, 52; MTCW 1
Ady, Endre 1877-1919 .... **TCLC 11**
See also CA 107
A.E. 1867-1935 .... **TCLC 3, 10**
See also Russell, George William
Aeschylus 525B.C.-456B.C. ..**CMLC 11; DA; DAB; DAC; DAM DRAM, MST; DC 8; WLCS**
See also DLB 176
Aesop 620(?)B.C.-564(?)B.C. .... **CMLC 24**
See also CLR 14; MAICYA; SATA 64
Affable Hawk
See MacCarthy, Sir(Charles Otto) Desmond
Africa, Ben
See Bosman, Herman Charles
Afton, Effie
See Harper, Frances Ellen Watkins
Agapida, Fray Antonio
See Irving, Washington
Agee, James (Rufus) 1909-1955 **TCLC 1, 19; DAM NOV**
See also AITN 1; CA 108; 148; CDALB 1941-1968; DLB 2, 26, 152
Aghill, Gordon
See Silverberg, Robert
Agnon, S(hmuel) Y(osef Halevi) 1888-1970 **CLC 4, 8, 14; SSC 30**
See also CA 17-18; 25-28R; CANR 60; CAP 2; MTCW 1
Agrippa von Nettesheim, Henry Cornelius 1486-1535 .... **LC 27**
Aherne, Owen
See Cassill, R(onald) V(erlin)
Ai 1947- .... **CLC 4, 14, 69**
See also CA 85-88; CAAS 13; CANR 70; DLB 120
Aickman, Robert (Fordyce) 1914-1981 **C L C 57**
See also CA 5-8R; CANR 3, 72
Aiken, Conrad (Potter) 1889-1973**CLC 1, 3, 5, 10, 52; DAM NOV, POET; SSC 9**
See also CA 5-8R; 45-48; CANR 4, 60; CDALB 1929-1941; DLB 9, 45, 102; MTCW 1; SATA 3, 30
Aiken, Joan (Delano) 1924- .... **CLC 35**
See also AAYA 1, 25; CA 9-12R; CANR 4, 23, 34, 64; CLR 1, 19; DLB 161; JRDA; MAICYA; MTCW 1; SAAS 1; SATA 2, 30, 73
Ainsworth, William Harrison 1805-1882 **NCLC 13**
See also DLB 21; SATA 24
Aitmatov, Chingiz (Torekulovich) 1928-**C L C 71**
See also CA 103; CANR 38; MTCW 1; SATA 56
Akers, Floyd
See Baum, L(yman) Frank
Akhmadulina, Bella Akhatovna 1937-**CLC 53; DAM POET**
See also CA 65-68
Akhmatova, Anna 1888-1966**CLC 11, 25, 64; DAM POET; PC 2**
See also CA 19-20; 25-28R; CANR 35; CAP 1; MTCW 1
Aksakov, Sergei Timofeyvich 1791-1859 **NCLC 2**
See also DLB 198
Aksenov, Vassily
See Aksyonov, Vassily (Pavlovich)
Akst, Daniel 1956-............................. **CLC 109**
See also CA 161
Aksyonov, Vassily (Pavlovich) 1932-**CLC 22, 37, 101**
See also CA 53-56; CANR 12, 48
Akutagawa, Ryunosuke 1892-1927 **TCLC 16**
See also CA 117; 154
Alain 1868-1951 .... **TCLC 41**
See also CA 163
Alain-Fournier .... **TCLC 6**
See also Fournier, Henri Alban
See also DLB 65
Alarcon, Pedro Antonio de 1833-1891**NCLC 1**
Alas (y Urena), Leopoldo (Enrique Garcia) 1852-1901 ....
TCLC 29
See also CA 113; 131; HW
Albee, Edward (Franklin III) 1928-**CLC 1, 2, 3, 5, 9, 11, 13, 25, 53, 86, 113; DA; DAB; DAC; DAM DRAM, MST; WLC**
See also AITN 1; CA 5-8R; CABS 3; CANR 8, 54; CDALB 1941-1968; DLB 7; INT CANR-8; MTCW 1
Alberti, Rafael 1902- .... **CLC 7**
See also CA 85-88; DLB 108
Albert the Great 1200(?)-1280 ...... **CMLC 16**
See also DLB 115
Alcala-Galiano, Juan Valera y
See Valera y Alcala-Galiano, Juan

See Prado (Calvo), Pedro

Angelique, Pierre
See Bataille, Georges

Angell, Roger 1920- .... **CLC 26**
See also CA 57-60; CANR 13, 44, 70; DLB 171, 185

Angelou, Maya 1928-CLC 12, 35, 64, 77; BLC 1; DA; DAB; DAC; DAM MST, MULT, POET, POP; WLCS
See also Johnson, Marguerite (Annie)
See also AAYA 7, 20; BW 2; CA 65-68; CANR 19, 42, 65; CLR 53; DLB 38; MTCW 1; SATA 49

Anna Comnena 1083-1153 .... **CMLC 25**

Annensky, Innokenty (Fyodorovich) 1856-1909 **TCLC 14**
See also CA 110; 155

Annunzio, Gabriele d'
See D'Annunzio, Gabriele

Anodos
See Coleridge, Mary E(lizabeth)

Anon, Charles Robert
See Pessoa, Fernando (Antonio Nogueira)

Anouilh, Jean (Marie Lucien Pierre) 1910-1987 **CLC 1, 3, 8, 13, 40, 50; DAM DRAM; DC 8**
See also CA 17-20R; 123; CANR 32; MTCW 1

Anthony, Florence
See Ai

Anthony, John
See Ciardi, John (Anthony)

Anthony, Peter
See Shaffer, Anthony (Joshua); Shaffer, Peter (Levin)

Anthony, Piers 1934- .... **CLC 35; DAM POP**
See also AAYA 11; CA 21-24R; CANR 28, 56; DLB 8; MTCW 1; SAAS 22; SATA 84

Anthony, Susan B(rownell) 1916-1991 **TCLC 84**
See also CA 89-92; 134

Antoine, Marc
See Proust, (Valentin-Louis-George-Eugene-) Marcel

Antoninus, Brother
See Everson, William (Oliver)

Antonioni, Michelangelo 1912- .... **CLC 20**
See also CA 73-76; CANR 45

Antschel, Paul 1920-1970
See Celan, Paul
See also CA 85-88; CANR 33, 61; MTCW 1

Anwar, Chairil 1922-1949 .... **TCLC 22**
See also CA 121

Apess, William 1798-1839(?)**NCLC 73; DAM MULT**
See also DLB 175; NNAL

Apollinaire, Guillaume 1880-1918**TCLC 3, 8, 51; DAM POET; PC 7**
See also Kostrowitzki, Wilhelm Apollinaris de
See also CA 152

Appelfeld, Aharon 1932- .... **CLC 23, 47**
See also CA 112; 133

Apple, Max (Isaac) 1941- .... **CLC 9, 33**
See also CA 81-84; CANR 19, 54; DLB 130

Appleman, Philip (Dean) 1926- .... **CLC 51**
See also CA 13-16R; CAAS 18; CANR 6, 29, 56

Appleton, Lawrence
See Lovecraft, H(oward) P(hillips)

Apteryx
See Eliot, T(homas) S(tearns)

Apuleius, (Lucius Madaurensis) 125(?)-175(?) **CMLC 1**

Aquin, Hubert 1929-1977 .... **CLC 15**
See also CA 105; DLB 53

Aragon, Louis 1897-1982 .. **CLC 3, 22; DAM NOV, POET**
See also CA 69-72; 108; CANR 28, 71; DLB

72; MTCW 1

Arany, Janos 1817-1882 .... **NCLC 34**

Arbuthnot, John 1667-1735 .... **LC 1**
See also DLB 101

Archer, Herbert Winslow
See Mencken, H(enry) L(ouis)

Archer, Jeffrey (Howard) 1940- ..... **CLC 28; DAM POP**
See also AAYA 16; BEST 89:3; CA 77-80; CANR 22, 52; INT CANR-22

Archer, Jules 1915- .... **CLC 12**
See also CA 9-12R; CANR 6, 69; SAAS 5; SATA 4, 85

Archer, Lee
See Ellison, Harlan (Jay)

Arden, John 1930-CLC 6, 13, 15; DAM DRAM
See also CA 13-16R; CAAS 4; CANR 31, 65, 67; DLB 13; MTCW 1

Arenas, Reinaldo 1943-1990 . **CLC 41; DAM MULT; HLC**
See also CA 124; 128; 133; DLB 145; HW

Arendt, Hannah 1906-1975 .... **CLC 66, 98**
See also CA 17-20R; 61-64; CANR 26, 60; MTCW 1

Aretino, Pietro 1492-1556 .... **LC 12**

Arghezi, Tudor 1880-1967 .... **CLC 80**
See also Theodorescu, Ion N.
See also CA 167

Arguedas, Jose Maria 1911-1969 **CLC 10, 18**
See also CA 89-92; DLB 113; HW

Argueta, Manlio 1936- .... **CLC 31**
See also CA 131; DLB 145; HW

Ariosto, Ludovico 1474-1533 .... **LC 6**

Aristides
See Epstein, Joseph

Aristophanes 450B.C.-385B.C.**CMLC 4; DA; DAB; DAC; DAM DRAM, MST; DC 2; WLCS**
See also DLB 176

Arlt, Roberto (Godofredo Christophersen) 1900-1942 .... **TCLC 29; DAM MULT; HLC**
See also CA 123; 131; CANR 67; HW

Armah, Ayi Kwei 1939- .. **CLC 5, 33; BLC 1; DAM MULT, POET**
See also BW 1; CA 61-64; CANR 21, 64; DLB 117; MTCW 1

Armatrading, Joan 1950- .... **CLC 17**
See also CA 114

Arnette, Robert
See Silverberg, Robert

Arnim, Achim von (Ludwig Joachim von Arnim) 1781-1831 ...... **NCLC 5; SSC 29**
See also DLB 90

Arnim, Bettina von 1785-1859 .... **NCLC 38**
See also DLB 90

Arnold, Matthew 1822-1888**NCLC 6, 29; DA; DAB; DAC; DAM MST, POET; PC 5; WLC**
See also CDBLB 1832-1890; DLB 32, 57

Arnold, Thomas 1795-1842 .... **NCLC 18**
See also DLB 55

Arnow, Harriette (Louisa) Simpson 1908-1986 **CLC 2, 7, 18**
See also CA 9-12R; 118; CANR 14; DLB 6; MTCW 1; SATA 42; SATA-Obit 47

Arouet, Francois-Marie
See Voltaire

Arp, Hans
See Arp, Jean

Arp, Jean 1887-1966 .... **CLC 5**
See also CA 81-84; 25-28R; CANR 42

Arrabal
See Arrabal, Fernando

Arrabal, Fernando 1932- .... **CLC 2, 9, 18, 58**
See also CA 9-12R; CANR 15

Arrick, Fran .... **CLC 30**

See also Gaberman, Judie Angell

Artaud, Antonin (Marie Joseph) 1896-1948 **TCLC 3, 36; DAM DRAM**
See also CA 104; 149

Arthur, Ruth M(abel) 1905-1979 ...... **CLC 12**
See also CA 9-12R; 85-88; CANR 4; SATA 7, 26

Artsybashev, Mikhail (Petrovich) 1878-1927 **TCLC 31**

Arundel, Honor (Morfydd) 1919-1973**CLC 17**
See also CA 21-22; 41-44R; CAP 2; CLR 35; SATA 4; SATA-Obit 24

Arzner, Dorothy 1897-1979 .... **CLC 98**

Asch, Sholem 1880-1957 .... **TCLC 3**
See also CA 105

Ash, Shalom
See Asch, Sholem

Ashbery, John (Lawrence) 1927-CLC 2, 3, 4, 6, 9, 13, 15, 25, 41, 77; DAM POET
See also CA 5-8R; CANR 9, 37, 66; DLB 5, 165; DLBY 81; INT CANR-9; MTCW 1

Ashdown, Clifford
See Freeman, R(ichard) Austin

Ashe, Gordon
See Creasey, John

Ashton-Warner, Sylvia (Constance) 1908-1984 **CLC 19**
See also CA 69-72; 112; CANR 29; MTCW 1

Asimov, Isaac 1920-1992 **CLC 1, 3, 9, 19, 26, 76, 92; DAM POP**
See also AAYA 13; BEST 90:2; CA 1-4R; 137; CANR 2, 19, 36, 60; CLR 12; DLB 8; DLBY 92; INT CANR-19; JRDA; MAICYA; MTCW 1; SATA 1, 26, 74

Assis, Joaquim Maria Machado de
See Machado de Assis, Joaquim Maria

Astley, Thea (Beatrice May) 1925- ... **CLC 41**
See also CA 65-68; CANR 11, 43

Aston, James
See White, T(erence) H(anbury)

Asturias, Miguel Angel 1899-1974 **CLC 3, 8, 13; DAM MULT, NOV; HLC**
See also CA 25-28; 49-52; CANR 32; CAP 2; DLB 113; HW; MTCW 1

Atares, Carlos Saura
See Saura (Atares), Carlos

Atheling, William
See Pound, Ezra (Weston Loomis)

Atheling, William, Jr.
See Blish, James (Benjamin)

Atherton, Gertrude (Franklin Horn) 1857-1948 **TCLC 2**
See also CA 104; 155; DLB 9, 78, 186

Atherton, Lucius
See Masters, Edgar Lee

Atkins, Jack
See Harris, Mark

Atkinson, Kate .... **CLC 99**
See also CA 166

Attaway, William (Alexander) 1911-1986 **CLC 92; BLC 1; DAM MULT**
See also BW 2; CA 143; DLB 76

Atticus
See Fleming, Ian (Lancaster); Wilson, (Thomas) Woodrow

Atwood, Margaret (Eleanor) 1939-CLC 2, 3, 4, 8, 13, 15, 25, 44, 84; DA; DAB; DAC; DAM MST, NOV, POET; PC 8; SSC 2; WLC
See also AAYA 12; BEST 89:2; CA 49-52; CANR 3, 24, 33, 59; DLB 53; INT CANR-24; MTCW 1; SATA 50

Aubigny, Pierre d'
See Mencken, H(enry) L(ouis)

Aubin, Penelope 1685-1731(?) .... **LC 9**
See also DLB 39

Auchincloss, Louis (Stanton) 1917-CLC 4, 6,

See also AITN 1; CA 41-44R; 151; CANR 37; DAM POET; MTCW 1

Brodsky, Joseph 1940-1996 **CLC 4, 6, 13, 36, 100; PC 9**
See also Brodskii, Iosif; Brodsky, Iosif Alexandrovich

Brodsky, Michael (Mark) 1948- .... **CLC 19**
See also CA 102; CANR 18, 41, 58

Bromell, Henry 1947- .... **CLC 5**
See also CA 53-56; CANR 9

Bromfield, Louis (Brucker) 1896-1956 **T C L C 11**
See also CA 107; 155; DLB 4, 9, 86

Broner, E(sther) M(asserman) 1930- **CLC 19**
See also CA 17-20R; CANR 8, 25, 72; DLB 28

Bronk, William 1918- .... **CLC 10**
See also CA 89-92; CANR 23; DLB 165

Bronstein, Lev Davidovich
See Trotsky, Leon

Bronte, Anne 1820-1849 .... **NCLC 71**
See also DLB 21, 199

Bronte, Charlotte 1816-1855 **NCLC 3, 8, 33, 58; DA; DAB; DAC; DAM MST, NOV; WLC**
See also AAYA 17; CDBLB 1832-1890; DLB 21, 159, 199

Bronte, Emily (Jane) 1818-1848 **NCLC 16, 35; DA; DAB; DAC; DAM MST, NOV, POET; PC 8; WLC**
See also AAYA 17; CDBLB 1832-1890; DLB 21, 32, 199

Brooke, Frances 1724-1789 .... **LC 6**
See also DLB 39, 99

Brooke, Henry 1703(?)-1783 .... **LC 1**
See also DLB 39

Brooke, Rupert (Chawner) 1887-1915 **T C L C 2, 7; DA; DAB; DAC; DAM MST, POET; PC 24; WLC**
See also CA 104; 132; CANR 61; CDBLB 1914-1945; DLB 19; MTCW 1

Brooke-Haven, P.
See Wodehouse, P(elham) G(renville)

Brooke-Rose, Christine 1926(?)- .... **CLC 40**
See also CA 13-16R; CANR 58; DLB 14

Brookner, Anita 1928- **CLC 32, 34, 51; DAB; DAM POP**
See also CA 114; 120; CANR 37, 56; DLB 194; DLBY 87; MTCW 1

Brooks, Cleanth 1906-1994 **CLC 24, 86, 110**
See also CA 17-20R; 145; CANR 33, 35; DLB 63; DLBY 94; INT CANR-35; MTCW 1

Brooks, George
See Baum, L(yman) Frank

Brooks, Gwendolyn 1917- **CLC 1, 2, 4, 5, 15, 49; BLC 1; DA; DAC; DAM MST, MULT, POET; PC 7; WLC**
See also AAYA 20; AITN 1; BW 2; CA 1-4R; CANR 1, 27, 52; CDALB 1941-1968; CLR 27; DLB 5, 76, 165; MTCW 1; SATA 6

Brooks, Mel .... **CLC 12**
See also Kaminsky, Melvin
See also AAYA 13; DLB 26

Brooks, Peter 1938- .... **CLC 34**
See also CA 45-48; CANR 1

Brooks, Van Wyck 1886-1963 .... **CLC 29**
See also CA 1-4R; CANR 6; DLB 45, 63, 103

Brophy, Brigid (Antonia) 1929-1995 **CLC 6, 11, 29, 105**
See also CA 5-8R; 149; CAAS 4; CANR 25, 53; DLB 14; MTCW 1

Brosman, Catharine Savage 1934- ..... **CLC 9**
See also CA 61-64; CANR 21, 46

Brossard, Chandler 1922-1993 .... **CLC 115**
See also CA 61-64; 142; CAAS 2; CANR 8, 56; DLB 16

Brother Antoninus
See Everson, William (Oliver)

The Brothers Quay
See Quay, Stephen; Quay, Timothy

Broughton, T(homas) Alan 1936- ..... **CLC 19**
See also CA 45-48; CANR 2, 23, 48

Broumas, Olga 1949- .... **CLC 10, 73**
See also CA 85-88; CANR 20, 69

Brown, Alan 1950- .... **CLC 99**
See also CA 156

Brown, Charles Brockden 1771-1810 **N C L C 22**
See also CDALB 1640-1865; DLB 37, 59, 73

Brown, Christy 1932-1981 .... **CLC 63**
See also CA 105; 104; CANR 72; DLB 14

Brown, Claude 1937- **CLC 30; BLC 1; DAM MULT**
See also AAYA 7; BW 1; CA 73-76

Brown, Dee (Alexander) 1908-.. **CLC 18, 47; DAM POP**
See also CA 13-16R; CAAS 6; CANR 11, 45, 60; DLBY 80; MTCW 1; SATA 5

Brown, George
See Wertmueller, Lina

Brown, George Douglas 1869-1902 **TCLC 28**
See also CA 162

Brown, George Mackay 1921-1996 **CLC 5, 48, 100**
See also CA 21-24R; 151; CAAS 6; CANR 12, 37, 67; DLB 14, 27, 139; MTCW 1; SATA 35

Brown, (William) Larry 1951- .... **CLC 73**
See also CA 130; 134; INT 133

Brown, Moses
See Barrett, William (Christopher)

Brown, Rita Mae 1944- **CLC 18, 43, 79; DAM NOV, POP**
See also CA 45-48; CANR 2, 11, 35, 62; INT CANR-11; MTCW 1

Brown, Roderick (Langmere) Haig-
See Haig-Brown, Roderick (Langmere)

Brown, Rosellen 1939- .... **CLC 32**
See also CA 77-80; CAAS 10; CANR 14, 44

Brown, Sterling Allen 1901-1989 **CLC 1, 23, 59; BLC 1; DAM MULT, POET**
See also BW 1; CA 85-88; 127; CANR 26; DLB 48, 51, 63; MTCW 1

Brown, Will
See Ainsworth, William Harrison

Brown, William Wells 1813-1884 ...**NCLC 2; BLC 1; DAM MULT; DC 1**
See also DLB 3, 50

Browne, (Clyde) Jackson 1948(?)- .... **CLC 21**
See also CA 120

Browning, Elizabeth Barrett 1806-1861 **NCLC 1, 16, 61, 66; DA; DAB; DAC; DAM MST, POET; PC 6; WLC**
See also CDBLB 1832-1890; DLB 32, 199

Browning, Robert 1812-1889 **NCLC 19; DA; DAB; DAC; DAM MST, POET; PC 2; WLCS**
See also CDBLB 1832-1890; DLB 32, 163; YABC 1

Browning, Tod 1882-1962 .... **CLC 16**
See also CA 141; 117

Brownson, Orestes Augustus 1803-1876 **NCLC 50**
See also DLB 1, 59, 73

Bruccoli, Matthew J(oseph) 1931- ... **CLC 34**
See also CA 9-12R; CANR 7; DLB 103

Bruce, Lenny .... **CLC 21**
See also Schneider, Leonard Alfred

Bruin, John
See Brutus, Dennis

Brulard, Henri
See Stendhal

Brulls, Christian
See Simenon, Georges (Jacques Christian)

Brunner, John (Kilian Houston) 1934-1995

CLC 8, 10; DAM POP
See also CA 1-4R; 149; CAAS 8; CANR 2, 37; MTCW 1

Bruno, Giordano 1548-1600 .... **LC 27**

Brutus, Dennis 1924- **CLC 43; BLC 1; DAM MULT, POET; PC 24**
See also BW 2; CA 49-52; CAAS 14; CANR 2, 27, 42; DLB 117

Bryan, C(ourtlandt) D(ixon) B(arnes) 1936- **CLC 29**
See also CA 73-76; CANR 13, 68; DLB 185; INT CANR-13

Bryan, Michael
See Moore, Brian

Bryant, William Cullen 1794-1878 . **NCLC 6, 46; DA; DAB; DAC; DAM MST, POET; PC 20**
See also CDALB 1640-1865; DLB 3, 43, 59, 189

Bryusov, Valery Yakovlevich 1873-1924 **TCLC 10**
See also CA 107; 155

Buchan, John 1875-1940 ..... **TCLC 41; DAB; DAM POP**
See also CA 108; 145; DLB 34, 70, 156; YABC 2

Buchanan, George 1506-1582 .... **LC 4**
See also DLB 152

Buchheim, Lothar-Guenther 1918- .... **CLC 6**
See also CA 85-88

Buchner, (Karl) Georg 1813-1837 . **NCLC 26**

Buchwald, Art(hur) 1925- .... **CLC 33**
See also AITN 1; CA 5-8R; CANR 21, 67; MTCW 1; SATA 10

Buck, Pearl S(ydenstricker) 1892-1973 **CLC 7, 11, 18; DA; DAB; DAC; DAM MST, NOV**
See also AITN 1; CA 1-4R; 41-44R; CANR 1, 34; DLB 9, 102; MTCW 1; SATA 1, 25

Buckler, Ernest 1908-1984 .... **CLC 13; DAC; DAM MST**
See also CA 11-12; 114; CAP 1; DLB 68; SATA 47

Buckley, Vincent (Thomas) 1925-1988 **CLC 57**
See also CA 101

Buckley, William F(rank), Jr. 1925- **CLC 7, 18, 37; DAM POP**
See also AITN 1; CA 1-4R; CANR 1, 24, 53; DLB 137; DLBY 80; INT CANR-24; MTCW 1

Buechner, (Carl) Frederick 1926- **CLC 2, 4, 6, 9; DAM NOV**
See also CA 13-16R; CANR 11, 39, 64; DLBY 80; INT CANR-11; MTCW 1

Buell, John (Edward) 1927- .... **CLC 10**
See also CA 1-4R; CANR 71; DLB 53

Buero Vallejo, Antonio 1916- ..... **CLC 15, 46**
See also CA 106; CANR 24, 49; HW; MTCW 1

Bufalino, Gesualdo 1920(?)- .... **CLC 74**
See also DLB 196

Bugayev, Boris Nikolayevich 1880-1934 **TCLC 7; PC 11**
See also Bely, Andrey
See also CA 104; 165

Bukowski, Charles 1920-1994 **CLC 2, 5, 9, 41, 82, 108; DAM NOV, POET; PC 18**
See also CA 17-20R; 144; CANR 40, 62; DLB 5, 130, 169; MTCW 1

Bulgakov, Mikhail (Afanas'evich) 1891-1940 **TCLC 2, 16; DAM DRAM, NOV; SSC 18**
See also CA 105; 152

Bulgya, Alexander Alexandrovich 1901-1956 **TCLC 53**
See also Fadeyev, Alexander
See also CA 117

Bullins, Ed 1935- **CLC 1, 5, 7; BLC 1; DAM DRAM, MULT; DC 6**

MTCW 1

Chabon, Michael 1963- .... **CLC 55**
See also CA 139; CANR 57

Chabrol, Claude 1930- .... **CLC 16**
See also CA 110

Challans, Mary 1905-1983
See Renault, Mary
See also CA 81-84; 111; SATA 23; SATA-Obit 36

Challis, George
See Faust, Frederick (Schiller)

Chambers, Aidan 1934- .... **CLC 35**
See also AAYA 27; CA 25-28R; CANR 12, 31, 58; JRDA; MAICYA; SAAS 12; SATA 1, 69

Chambers, James 1948-
See Cliff, Jimmy
See also CA 124

Chambers, Jessie
See Lawrence, D(avid) H(erbert Richards)

Chambers, Robert W(illiam) 1865-1933
TCLC 41
See also CA 165; DLB 202

Chandler, Raymond (Thornton) 1888-1959
TCLC 1, 7; SSC 23
See also AAYA 25; CA 104; 129; CANR 60; CDALB 1929-1941; DLBD 6; MTCW 1

Chang, Eileen 1920-1995 .... **SSC 28**
See also CA 166

Chang, Jung 1952- .... **CLC 71**
See also CA 142

Chang Ai-Ling
See Chang, Eileen

Channing, William Ellery 1780-1842. **N C L C 17**
See also DLB 1, 59

Chaplin, Charles Spencer 1889-1977 **CLC 16**
See also Chaplin, Charlie
See also CA 81-84; 73-76

Chaplin, Charlie
See Chaplin, Charles Spencer
See also DLB 44

Chapman, George 1559(?)-1634 **LC 22; DAM DRAM**
See also DLB 62, 121

Chapman, Graham 1941-1989 .... **CLC 21**
See also Monty Python
See also CA 116; 129; CANR 35

Chapman, John Jay 1862-1933 .... **TCLC 7**
See also CA 104

Chapman, Lee
See Bradley, Marion Zimmer

Chapman, Walker
See Silverberg, Robert

Chappell, Fred (Davis) 1936- ..... **CLC 40, 78**
See also CA 5-8R; CAAS 4; CANR 8, 33, 67; DLB 6, 105

Char, Rene(-Emile) 1907-1988 **CLC 9, 11, 14, 55; DAM POET**
See also CA 13-16R; 124; CANR 32; MTCW 1

Charby, Jay
See Ellison, Harlan (Jay)

Chardin, Pierre Teilhard de
See Teilhard de Chardin, (Marie Joseph) Pierre

Charles I 1600-1649 .... **LC 13**

Charriere, Isabelle de 1740-1805 .. **NCLC 66**

Charyn, Jerome 1937- .... **CLC 5, 8, 18**
See also CA 5-8R; CAAS 1; CANR 7, 61; DLBY 83; MTCW 1

Chase, Mary (Coyle) 1907-1981 .... **DC 1**
See also CA 77-80; 105; SATA 17; SATA-Obit 29

Chase, Mary Ellen 1887-1973 .... **CLC 2**
See also CA 13-16; 41-44R; CAP 1; SATA 10

Chase, Nicholas
See Hyde, Anthony

Chateaubriand, Francois Rene de 1768-1848
NCLC 3

See also DLB 119

Chatterje, Sarat Chandra 1876-1936(?)
See Chatterji, Saratchandra
See also CA 109

Chatterji, Bankim Chandra 1838-1894 **NCLC 19**

Chatterji, Saratchandra .... **TCLC 13**
See also Chatterje, Sarat Chandra

Chatterton, Thomas 1752-1770 . **LC 3; DAM POET**
See also DLB 109

Chatwin, (Charles) Bruce 1940-1989 **CLC 28, 57, 59; DAM POP**
See also AAYA 4; BEST 90:1; CA 85-88; 127; DLB 194

Chaucer, Daniel
See Ford, Ford Madox

Chaucer, Geoffrey 1340(?)-1400 **LC 17; DA; DAB; DAC; DAM MST, POET; PC 19; WLCS**
See also CDBLB Before 1660; DLB 146

Chaviaras, Strates 1935-
See Haviaras, Stratis
See also CA 105

Chayefsky, Paddy .... **CLC 23**
See also Chayefsky, Sidney
See also DLB 7, 44; DLBY 81

Chayefsky, Sidney 1923-1981
See Chayefsky, Paddy
See also CA 9-12R; 104; CANR 18; DAM DRAM

Chedid, Andree 1920- .... **CLC 47**
See also CA 145

Cheever, John 1912-1982 **CLC 3, 7, 8, 11, 15, 25, 64; DA; DAB; DAC; DAM MST, NOV, POP; SSC 1; WLC**
See also CA 5-8R; 106; CABS 1; CANR 5, 27; CDALB 1941-1968; DLB 2, 102; DLBY 80, 82; INT CANR-5; MTCW 1

Cheever, Susan 1943- .... **CLC 18, 48**
See also CA 103; CANR 27, 51; DLBY 82; INT CANR-27

Chekhonte, Antosha
See Chekhov, Anton (Pavlovich)

Chekhov, Anton (Pavlovich) 1860-1904 **TCLC 3, 10, 31, 55; DA; DAB; DAC; DAM DRAM, MST; DC 9; SSC 2, 28; WLC**
See also CA 104; 124; SATA 90

Chernyshevsky, Nikolay Gavrilovich 1828-1889
NCLC 1

Cherry, Carolyn Janice 1942-
See Cherryh, C. J.
See also CA 65-68; CANR 10

Cherryh, C. J. .... **CLC 35**
See also Cherry, Carolyn Janice
See also AAYA 24; DLBY 80; SATA 93

Chesnutt, Charles W(addell) 1858-1932
TCLC 5, 39; BLC 1; DAM MULT; SSC 7
See also BW 1; CA 106; 125; DLB 12, 50, 78; MTCW 1

Chester, Alfred 1929(?)-1971 .... **CLC 49**
See also CA 33-36R; DLB 130

Chesterton, G(ilbert) K(eith) 1874-1936
TCLC 1, 6, 64; DAM NOV, POET; SSC 1
See also CA 104; 132; CDBLB 1914-1945; DLB 10, 19, 34, 70, 98, 149, 178; MTCW 1; SATA 27

Chiang, Pin-chin 1904-1986
See Ding Ling
See also CA 118

Ch'ien Chung-shu 1910- .... **CLC 22**
See also CA 130; MTCW 1

Child, L. Maria
See Child, Lydia Maria

Child, Lydia Maria 1802-1880 ... **NCLC 6, 73**
See also DLB 1, 74; SATA 67

Child, Mrs.

See Child, Lydia Maria

Child, Philip 1898-1978 .... **CLC 19, 68**
See also CA 13-14; CAP 1; SATA 47

Childers, (Robert) Erskine 1870-1922 **T C L C 65**
See also CA 113; 153; DLB 70

Childress, Alice 1920-1994 **CLC 12, 15, 86, 96; BLC 1; DAM DRAM, MULT, NOV; DC 4**
See also AAYA 8; BW 2; CA 45-48; 146; CANR 3, 27, 50; CLR 14; DLB 7, 38; JRDA; MAICYA; MTCW 1; SATA 7, 48, 81

Chin, Frank (Chew, Jr.) 1940- .... **DC 7**
See also CA 33-36R; CANR 71; DAM MULT

Chislett, (Margaret) Anne 1943- ...... **CLC 34**
See also CA 151

Chitty, Thomas Willes 1926- .... **CLC 11**
See also Hinde, Thomas
See also CA 5-8R

Chivers, Thomas Holley 1809-1858 **NCLC 49**
See also DLB 3

Chomette, Rene Lucien 1898-1981
See Clair, Rene
See also CA 103

Chopin, Kate **TCLC 5, 14; DA; DAB; SSC 8; WLCS**
See also Chopin, Katherine
See also CDALB 1865-1917; DLB 12, 78

Chopin, Katherine 1851-1904
See Chopin, Kate
See also CA 104; 122; DAC; DAM MST, NOV

Chretien de Troyes c. 12th cent. - .. **CMLC 10**

Christie
See Ichikawa, Kon

Christie, Agatha (Mary Clarissa) 1890-1976
CLC 1, 6, 8, 12, 39, 48, 110; DAB; DAC; DAM NOV
See also AAYA 9; AITN 1, 2; CA 17-20R; 61-64; CANR 10, 37; CDBLB 1914-1945; DLB 13, 77; MTCW 1; SATA 36

Christie, (Ann) Philippa
See Pearce, Philippa
See also CA 5-8R; CANR 4

Christine de Pizan 1365(?)-1431(?) .... **LC 9**

Chubb, Elmer
See Masters, Edgar Lee

Chulkov, Mikhail Dmitrievich 1743-1792 **LC 2**
See also DLB 150

Churchill, Caryl 1938- ..... **CLC 31, 55; DC 5**
See also CA 102; CANR 22, 46; DLB 13; MTCW 1

Churchill, Charles 1731-1764 .... **LC 3**
See also DLB 109

Chute, Carolyn 1947- .... **CLC 39**
See also CA 123

Ciardi, John (Anthony) 1916-1986 . **CLC 10, 40, 44; DAM POET**
See also CA 5-8R; 118; CAAS 2; CANR 5, 33; CLR 19; DLB 5; DLBY 86; INT CANR-5; MAICYA; MTCW 1; SAAS 26; SATA 1, 65; SATA-Obit 46

Cicero, Marcus Tullius 106B.C.-43B.C.
CMLC 3

Cimino, Michael 1943- .... **CLC 16**
See also CA 105

Cioran, E(mil) M. 1911-1995 .... **CLC 64**
See also CA 25-28R; 149

Cisneros, Sandra 1954- **CLC 69; DAM MULT; HLC; SSC 32**
See also AAYA 9; CA 131; CANR 64; DLB 122, 152; HW

Cixous, Helene 1937- .... **CLC 92**
See also CA 126; CANR 55; DLB 83; MTCW 1

Clair, Rene .... **CLC 20**
See also Chomette, Rene Lucien

Clampitt, Amy 1920-1994 ..... **CLC 32; PC 19**
See also CA 110; 146; CANR 29; DLB 105

See also CA 5-8R; 41-44R; CANR 8, 59; DLB 77; MTCW 1

Crebillon, Claude Prosper Jolyot de (fils) 1707-1777 .... LC 28

Credo
See Creasey, John

Credo, Alvaro J. de
See Prado (Calvo), Pedro

Creeley, Robert (White) 1926-CLC 1, 2, 4, 8, 11, 15, 36, 78; DAM POET
See also CA 1-4R; CAAS 10; CANR 23, 43; DLB 5, 16, 169; DLBD 17; MTCW 1

Crews, Harry (Eugene) 1935- CLC 6, 23, 49
See also AITN 1; CA 25-28R; CANR 20, 57; DLB 6, 143, 185; MTCW 1

Crichton, (John) Michael 1942-CLC 2, 6, 54, 90; DAM NOV, POP
See also AAYA 10; AITN 2; CA 25-28R; CANR 13, 40, 54; DLBY 81; INT CANR-13; JRDA; MTCW 1; SATA 9, 88

Crispin, Edmund .... CLC 22
See also Montgomery, (Robert) Bruce
See also DLB 87

Cristofer, Michael 1945(?)- .... CLC 28; DAM DRAM
See also CA 110; 152; DLB 7

Croce, Benedetto 1866-1952 .... TCLC 37
See also CA 120; 155

Crockett, David 1786-1836 .... NCLC 8
See also DLB 3, 11

Crockett, Davy
See Crockett, David

Crofts, Freeman Wills 1879-1957 .. TCLC 55
See also CA 115; DLB 77

Croker, John Wilson 1780-1857 .... NCLC 10
See also DLB 110

Crommelynck, Fernand 1885-1970 .. CLC 75
See also CA 89-92

Cromwell, Oliver 1599-1658 .... LC 43

Cronin, A(rchibald) J(oseph) 1896-1981C L C 32
See also CA 1-4R; 102; CANR 5; DLB 191; SATA 47; SATA-Obit 25

Cross, Amanda
See Heilbrun, Carolyn G(old)

Crothers, Rachel 1878(?)-1958 ...... TCLC 19
See also CA 113; DLB 7

Croves, Hal
See Traven, B.

Crow Dog, Mary (Ellen) (?)- .... CLC 93
See also Brave Bird, Mary
See also CA 154

Crowfield, Christopher
See Stowe, Harriet (Elizabeth) Beecher

Crowley, Aleister .... TCLC 7
See also Crowley, Edward Alexander

Crowley, Edward Alexander 1875-1947
See Crowley, Aleister
See also CA 104

Crowley, John 1942- .... CLC 57
See also CA 61-64; CANR 43; DLBY 82; SATA 65

Crud
See Crumb, R(obert)

Crumarums
See Crumb, R(obert)

Crumb, R(obert) 1943- .... CLC 17
See also CA 106

Crumbum
See Crumb, R(obert)

Crumski
See Crumb, R(obert)

Crum the Bum
See Crumb, R(obert)

Crunk
See Crumb, R(obert)

Crustt

See Crumb, R(obert)

Cryer, Gretchen (Kiger) 1935- .... CLC 21
See also CA 114; 123

Csath, Geza 1887-1919 .... TCLC 13
See also CA 111

Cudlip, David 1933- .... CLC 34

Cullen, Countee 1903-1946TCLC 4, 37; BLC 1; DA; DAC; DAM MST, MULT, POET; PC 20; WLCS
See also BW 1; CA 108; 124; CDALB 1917-1929; DLB 4, 48, 51; MTCW 1; SATA 18

Cum, R.
See Crumb, R(obert)

Cummings, Bruce F(rederick) 1889-1919
See Barbellion, W. N. P.
See also CA 123

Cummings, E(dward) E(stlin) 1894-1962CLC 1, 3, 8, 12, 15, 68; DA; DAB; DAC; DAM MST, POET; PC 5; WLC 2
See also CA 73-76; CANR 31; CDALB 1929-1941; DLB 4, 48; MTCW 1

Cunha, Euclides (Rodrigues Pimenta) da 1866-1909 .... TCLC 24
See also CA 123

Cunningham, E. V.
See Fast, Howard (Melvin)

Cunningham, J(ames) V(incent) 1911-1985 CLC 3, 31
See also CA 1-4R; 115; CANR 1, 72; DLB 5

Cunningham, Julia (Woolfolk) 1916-CLC 12
See also CA 9-12R; CANR 4, 19, 36; JRDA; MAICYA; SAAS 2; SATA 1, 26

Cunningham, Michael 1952- .... CLC 34
See also CA 136

Cunninghame Graham, R(obert) B(ontine) 1852-1936 .... TCLC 19
See also Graham, R(obert) B(ontine) Cunninghame
See also CA 119; DLB 98

Currie, Ellen 19(?)- .... CLC 44

Curtin, Philip
See Lowndes, Marie Adelaide (Belloc)

Curtis, Price
See Ellison, Harlan (Jay)

Cutrate, Joe
See Spiegelman, Art

Cynewulf c. 770-c. 840 .... CMLC 23

Czaczkes, Shmuel Yosef
See Agnon, S(hmuel) Y(osef Halevi)

Dabrowska, Maria (Szumska) 1889-1965CLC 15
See also CA 106

Dabydeen, David 1955- .... CLC 34
See also BW 1; CA 125; CANR 56

Dacey, Philip 1939- .... CLC 51
See also CA 37-40R; CAAS 17; CANR 14, 32, 64; DLB 105

Dagerman, Stig (Halvard) 1923-1954 T C L C 17
See also CA 117; 155

Dahl, Roald 1916-1990CLC 1, 6, 18, 79; DAB; DAC; DAM MST, NOV, POP
See also AAYA 15; CA 1-4R; 133; CANR 6, 32, 37, 62; CLR 1, 7, 41; DLB 139; JRDA; MAICYA; MTCW 1; SATA 1, 26, 73; SATA-Obit 30

Dahlberg, Edward 1900-1977 .. CLC 1, 7, 14
See also CA 9-12R; 69-72; CANR 31, 62; DLB 48; MTCW 1

Daitch, Susan 1954- .... CLC 103
See also CA 161

Dale, Colin .... TCLC 18
See also Lawrence, T(homas) E(dward)

Dale, George E.
See Asimov, Isaac

Daly, Elizabeth 1878-1967 .... CLC 52
See also CA 23-24; 25-28R; CANR 60; CAP 2

Daly, Maureen 1921- .... CLC 17
See also AAYA 5; CANR 37; JRDA; MAICYA; SAAS 1; SATA 2

Damas, Leon-Gontran 1912-1978 .... CLC 84
See also BW 1; CA 125; 73-76

Dana, Richard Henry Sr. 1787-1879NCLC 53

Daniel, Samuel 1562(?)-1619 .... LC 24
See also DLB 62

Daniels, Brett
See Adler, Renata

Dannay, Frederic 1905-1982 . CLC 11; DAM POP
See also Queen, Ellery
See also CA 1-4R; 107; CANR 1, 39; DLB 137; MTCW 1

D'Annunzio, Gabriele 1863-1938TCLC 6, 40
See also CA 104; 155

Danois, N. le
See Gourmont, Remy (-Marie-Charles) de

Dante 1265-1321 .... CMLC 3, 18; DA; DAB; DAC; DAM MST, POET; PC 21; WLCS

d'Antibes, Germain
See Simenon, Georges (Jacques Christian)

Danticat, Edwidge 1969- .... CLC 94
See also CA 152

Danvers, Dennis 1947- .... CLC 70

Danziger, Paula 1944- .... CLC 21
See also AAYA 4; CA 112; 115; CANR 37; CLR 20; JRDA; MAICYA; SATA 36, 63, 102; SATA-Brief 30

Dario, Ruben 1867-1916 .... TCLC 4; DAM MULT; HLC; PC 15
See also CA 131; HW; MTCW 1

Darley, George 1795-1846 .... NCLC 2
See also DLB 96

Darrow, Clarence (Seward) 1857-1938T C L C 81
See also CA 164

Darwin, Charles 1809-1882 .... NCLC 57
See also DLB 57, 166

Daryush, Elizabeth 1887-1977 ...... CLC 6, 19
See also CA 49-52; CANR 3; DLB 20

Dasgupta, Surendranath 1887-1952TCLC 81
See also CA 157

Dashwood, Edmee Elizabeth Monica de la Pasture 1890-1943
See Delafield, E. M.
See also CA 119; 154

Daudet, (Louis Marie) Alphonse 1840-1897 NCLC 1
See also DLB 123

Daumal, Rene 1908-1944 .... TCLC 14
See also CA 114

Davenport, Guy (Mattison, Jr.) 1927-CLC 6, 14, 38; SSC 16
See also CA 33-36R; CANR 23; DLB 130

Davidson, Avram 1923-
See Queen, Ellery
See also CA 101; CANR 26; DLB 8

Davidson, Donald (Grady) 1893-1968CLC 2, 13, 19
See also CA 5-8R; 25-28R; CANR 4; DLB 45

Davidson, Hugh
See Hamilton, Edmond

Davidson, John 1857-1909 .... TCLC 24
See also CA 118; DLB 19

Davidson, Sara 1943- .... CLC 9
See also CA 81-84; CANR 44, 68; DLB 185

Davie, Donald (Alfred) 1922-1995 . CLC 5, 8, 10, 31
See also CA 1-4R; 149; CAAS 3; CANR 1, 44; DLB 27; MTCW 1

Davies, Ray(mond Douglas) 1944- ... CLC 21
See also CA 116; 146

Davies, Rhys 1901-1978 .... CLC 23

See also CA 9-12R; 81-84; CANR 4; DLB 139, 191
Davies, (William) Robertson 1913-1995 **C L C 2, 7, 13, 25, 42, 75, 91; DA; DAB; DAC; DAM MST, NOV, POP; WLC**
See also BEST 89:2; CA 33-36R; 150; CANR 17, 42; DLB 68; INT CANR-17; MTCW 1
Davies, W(illiam) H(enry) 1871-1940**TCLC 5**
See also CA 104; DLB 19, 174
Davies, Walter C.
See Kornbluth, C(yril) M.
Davis, Angela (Yvonne) 1944- **CLC 77; DAM MULT**
See also BW 2; CA 57-60; CANR 10
Davis, B. Lynch
See Bioy Casares, Adolfo; Borges, Jorge Luis
Davis, Harold Lenoir 1896-1960 ...... **CLC 49**
See also CA 89-92; DLB 9
Davis, Rebecca (Blaine) Harding 1831-1910 **TCLC 6**
See also CA 104; DLB 74
Davis, Richard Harding 1864-1916**TCLC 24**
See also CA 114; DLB 12, 23, 78, 79, 189; DLBD 13
Davison, Frank Dalby 1893-1970 ..... **CLC 15**
See also CA 116
Davison, Lawrence H.
See Lawrence, D(avid) H(erbert Richards)
Davison, Peter (Hubert) 1928- .... **CLC 28**
See also CA 9-12R; CAAS 4; CANR 3, 43; DLB 5
Davys, Mary 1674-1732 .... **LC 1**
See also DLB 39
Dawson, Fielding 1930-........................ **CLC 6**
See also CA 85-88; DLB 130
Dawson, Peter
See Faust, Frederick (Schiller)
Day, Clarence (Shepard, Jr.) 1874-1935 **TCLC 25**
See also CA 108; DLB 11
Day, Thomas 1748-1789 .... **LC 1**
See also DLB 39; YABC 1
Day Lewis, C(ecil) 1904-1972 . **CLC 1, 6, 10; DAM POET; PC 11**
See also Blake, Nicholas
See also CA 13-16; 33-36R; CANR 34; CAP 1; DLB 15, 20; MTCW 1
Dazai Osamu 1909-1948 .... **TCLC 11**
See also Tsushima, Shuji
See also CA 164; DLB 182
de Andrade, Carlos Drummond
See Drummond de Andrade, Carlos
Deane, Norman
See Creasey, John
de Beauvoir, Simone (Lucie Ernestine Marie Bertrand)
See Beauvoir, Simone (Lucie Ernestine Marie Bertrand) de
de Beer, P.
See Bosman, Herman Charles
de Brissac, Malcolm
See Dickinson, Peter (Malcolm)
de Chardin, Pierre Teilhard
See Teilhard de Chardin, (Marie Joseph) Pierre
Dee, John 1527-1608 ....**LC 20**
Deer, Sandra 1940- .... **CLC 45**
De Ferrari, Gabriella 1941- .... **CLC 65**
See also CA 146
Defoe, Daniel 1660(?)-1731 **LC 1; DA; DAB; DAC; DAM MST, NOV; WLC**
See also AAYA 27; CDBLB 1660-1789; DLB 39, 95, 101; JRDA; MAICYA; SATA 22
de Gourmont, Remy(-Marie-Charles)
See Gourmont, Remy (-Marie-Charles) de
de Hartog, Jan 1914- ....**CLC 19**
See also CA 1-4R; CANR 1
de Hostos, E. M.

See Hostos (y Bonilla), Eugenio Maria de
de Hostos, Eugenio M.
See Hostos (y Bonilla), Eugenio Maria de
Deighton, Len .... **CLC 4, 7, 22, 46**
See also Deighton, Leonard Cyril
See also AAYA 6; BEST 89:2; CDBLB 1960 to Present; DLB 87
Deighton, Leonard Cyril 1929-
See Deighton, Len
See also CA 9-12R; CANR 19, 33, 68; DAM NOV, POP; MTCW 1
Dekker, Thomas 1572(?)-1632 .. **LC 22; DAM DRAM**
See also CDBLB Before 1660; DLB 62, 172
Delafield, E. M. 1890-1943 .... **TCLC 61**
See also Dashwood, Edmee Elizabeth Monica de la Pasture
See also DLB 34
de la Mare, Walter (John) 1873-1956**TCLC 4, 53; DAB; DAC; DAM MST, POET; SSC 14; WLC**
See also CA 163; CDBLB 1914-1945; CLR 23; DLB 162; SATA 16
Delaney, Franey
See O'Hara, John (Henry)
Delaney, Shelagh 1939-**CLC 29; DAM DRAM**
See also CA 17-20R; CANR 30, 67; CDBLB 1960 to Present; DLB 13; MTCW 1
Delany, Mary (Granville Pendarves) 1700-1788 **LC 12**
Delany, Samuel R(ay, Jr.) 1942-**CLC 8, 14, 38; BLC 1; DAM MULT**
See also AAYA 24; BW 2; CA 81-84; CANR 27, 43; DLB 8, 33; MTCW 1
De La Ramee, (Marie) Louise 1839-1908
See Ouida
See also SATA 20
de la Roche, Mazo 1879-1961 .... **CLC 14**
See also CA 85-88; CANR 30; DLB 68; SATA 64
De La Salle, Innocent
See Hartmann, Sadakichi
Delbanco, Nicholas (Franklin) 1942- **CLC 6, 13**
See also CA 17-20R; CAAS 2; CANR 29, 55; DLB 6
del Castillo, Michel 1933- .... **CLC 38**
See also CA 109
Deledda, Grazia (Cosima) 1875(?)-1936 **TCLC 23**
See also CA 123
Delibes, Miguel ....**CLC 8, 18**
See also Delibes Setien, Miguel
Delibes Setien, Miguel 1920-
See Delibes, Miguel
See also CA 45-48; CANR 1, 32; HW; MTCW 1
DeLillo, Don 1936- **CLC 8, 10, 13, 27, 39, 54, 76; DAM NOV, POP**
See also BEST 89:1; CA 81-84; CANR 21; DLB 6, 173; MTCW 1
de Lisser, H. G.
See De Lisser, H(erbert) G(eorge)
See also DLB 117
De Lisser, H(erbert) G(eorge) 1878-1944 **TCLC 12**
See also de Lisser, H. G.
See also BW 2; CA 109; 152
Deloney, Thomas (?)-1600 .... **LC 41**
See also DLB 167
Deloria, Vine (Victor), Jr. 1933- ..... **CLC 21; DAM MULT**
See also CA 53-56; CANR 5, 20, 48; DLB 175; MTCW 1; NNAL; SATA 21
Del Vecchio, John M(ichael) 1947- ... **CLC 29**
See also CA 110; DLBD 9
de Man, Paul (Adolph Michel) 1919-1983

CLC 55
See also CA 128; 111; CANR 61; DLB 67; MTCW 1
De Marinis, Rick 1934- .... **CLC 54**
See also CA 57-60; CAAS 24; CANR 9, 25, 50
Dembry, R. Emmet
See Murfree, Mary Noailles
Demby, William 1922-**CLC 53; BLC 1; DAM MULT**
See also BW 1; CA 81-84; DLB 33
de Menton, Francisco
See Chin, Frank (Chew, Jr.)
Demijohn, Thom
See Disch, Thomas M(ichael)
de Montherlant, Henry (Milon)
See Montherlant, Henry (Milon) de
Demosthenes 384B.C.-322B.C. ...... **CMLC 13**
See also DLB 176
de Natale, Francine
See Malzberg, Barry N(athaniel)
Denby, Edwin (Orr) 1903-1983 .... **CLC 48**
See also CA 138; 110
Denis, Julio
See Cortazar, Julio
Denmark, Harrison
See Zelazny, Roger (Joseph)
Dennis, John 1658-1734 .... **LC 11**
See also DLB 101
Dennis, Nigel (Forbes) 1912-1989....... **CLC 8**
See also CA 25-28R; 129; DLB 13, 15; MTCW 1
Dent, Lester 1904(?)-1959 .... **TCLC 72**
See also CA 112; 161
De Palma, Brian (Russell) 1940- .... **CLC 20**
See also CA 109
De Quincey, Thomas 1785-1859 ...... **NCLC 4**
See also CDBLB 1789-1832; DLB 110; 144
Deren, Eleanora 1908(?)-1961
See Deren, Maya
See also CA 111
Deren, Maya 1917-1961 .... **CLC 16, 102**
See also Deren, Eleanora
Derleth, August (William) 1909-1971**CLC 31**
See also CA 1-4R; 29-32R; CANR 4; DLB 9; DLBD 17; SATA 5
Der Nister 1884-1950 .... **TCLC 56**
de Routisie, Albert
See Aragon, Louis
Derrida, Jacques 1930- .... **CLC 24, 87**
See also CA 124; 127
Derry Down Derry
See Lear, Edward
Dersonnes, Jacques
See Simenon, Georges (Jacques Christian)
Desai, Anita 1937-**CLC 19, 37, 97; DAB; DAM NOV**
See also CA 81-84; CANR 33, 53; MTCW 1; SATA 63
de Saint-Luc, Jean
See Glassco, John
de Saint Roman, Arnaud
See Aragon, Louis
Descartes, Rene 1596-1650 .... **LC 20, 35**
De Sica, Vittorio 1901(?)-1974 .... **CLC 20**
See also CA 117
Desnos, Robert 1900-1945 .... **TCLC 22**
See also CA 121; 151
Destouches, Louis-Ferdinand 1894-1961**CLC 9, 15**
See also Celine, Louis-Ferdinand
See also CA 85-88; CANR 28; MTCW 1
de Tolignac, Gaston
See Griffith, D(avid Lewelyn) W(ark)
Deutsch, Babette 1895-1982 .... **CLC 18**
See also CA 1-4R; 108; CANR 4; DLB 45; SATA 1; SATA-Obit 33
Devenant, William 1606-1649 ....**LC 13**

Devkota, Laxmiprasad 1909-1959 . **TCLC 23**
See also CA 123

De Voto, Bernard (Augustine) 1897-1955
TCLC 29
See also CA 113; 160; DLB 9

De Vries, Peter 1910-1993 **CLC 1, 2, 3, 7, 10, 28, 46; DAM NOV**
See also CA 17-20R; 142; CANR 41; DLB 6; DLBY 82; MTCW 1

Dexter, John
See Bradley, Marion Zimmer

Dexter, Martin
See Faust, Frederick (Schiller)

Dexter, Pete 1943- ... **CLC 34, 55; DAM POP**
See also BEST 89:2; CA 127; 131; INT 131; MTCW 1

Diamano, Silmang
See Senghor, Leopold Sedar

Diamond, Neil 1941- .... **CLC 30**
See also CA 108

Diaz del Castillo, Bernal 1496-1584 .... **LC 31**

di Bassetto, Corno
See Shaw, George Bernard

Dick, Philip K(indred) 1928-1982**CLC 10, 30, 72; DAM NOV, POP**
See also AAYA 24; CA 49-52; 106; CANR 2, 16; DLB 8; MTCW 1

Dickens, Charles (John Huffam) 1812-1870
NCLC 3, 8, 18, 26, 37, 50; DA; DAB; DAC; DAM MST, NOV; SSC 17; WLC
See also AAYA 23; CDBLB 1832-1890; DLB 21, 55, 70, 159, 166; JRDA; MAICYA; SATA 15

Dickey, James (Lafayette) 1923-1997 **CLC 1, 2, 4, 7, 10, 15, 47, 109; DAM NOV, POET, POP**
See also AITN 1, 2; CA 9-12R; 156; CABS 2; CANR 10, 48, 61; CDALB 1968-1988; DLB 5, 193; DLBD 7; DLBY 82, 93, 96, 97; INT CANR-10; MTCW 1

Dickey, William 1928-1994 .... **CLC 3, 28**
See also CA 9-12R; 145; CANR 24; DLB 5

Dickinson, Charles 1951- .... **CLC 49**
See also CA 128

Dickinson, Emily (Elizabeth) 1830-1886
NCLC 21; DA; DAB; DAC; DAM MST, POET; PC 1; WLC
See also AAYA 22; CDALB 1865-1917; DLB 1; SATA 29

Dickinson, Peter (Malcolm) 1927-**CLC 12, 35**
See also AAYA 9; CA 41-44R; CANR 31, 58; CLR 29; DLB 87, 161; JRDA; MAICYA; SATA 5, 62, 95

Dickson, Carr
See Carr, John Dickson

Dickson, Carter
See Carr, John Dickson

Diderot, Denis 1713-1784 .... **LC 26**

Didion, Joan 1934-**CLC 1, 3, 8, 14, 32; DAM NOV**
See also AITN 1; CA 5-8R; CANR 14, 52; CDALB 1968-1988; DLB 2, 173, 185; DLBY 81, 86; MTCW 1

Dietrich, Robert
See Hunt, E(verette) Howard, (Jr.)

Difusa, Pati
See Almodovar, Pedro

Dillard, Annie 1945- .. **CLC 9, 60, 115; DAM NOV**
See also AAYA 6; CA 49-52; CANR 3, 43, 62; DLBY 80; MTCW 1; SATA 10

Dillard, R(ichard) H(enry) W(ilde) 1937-
CLC 5
See also CA 21-24R; CAAS 7; CANR 10; DLB 5

Dillon, Eilis 1920-1994 .... **CLC 17**
See also CA 9-12R; 147; CAAS 3; CANR 4,

38; CLR 26; MAICYA; SATA 2, 74; SATA-Obit 83

Dimont, Penelope
See Mortimer, Penelope (Ruth)

Dinesen, Isak .... **CLC 10, 29, 95; SSC 7**
See also Blixen, Karen (Christentze Dinesen)

Ding Ling .... **CLC 68**
See also Chiang, Pin-chin

Disch, Thomas M(ichael) 1940- ....**CLC 7, 36**
See also AAYA 17; CA 21-24R; CAAS 4; CANR 17, 36, 54; CLR 18; DLB 8; MAICYA; MTCW 1; SAAS 15; SATA 92

Disch, Tom
See Disch, Thomas M(ichael)

d'Isly, Georges
See Simenon, Georges (Jacques Christian)

Disraeli, Benjamin 1804-1881 .... **NCLC 2, 39**
See also DLB 21, 55

Ditcum, Steve
See Crumb, R(obert)

Dixon, Paige
See Corcoran, Barbara

Dixon, Stephen 1936- .... **CLC 52; SSC 16**
See also CA 89-92; CANR 17, 40, 54; DLB 130

Doak, Annie
See Dillard, Annie

Dobell, Sydney Thompson 1824-1874 **NCLC 43**
See also DLB 32

Doblin, Alfred .... **TCLC 13**
See also Doeblin, Alfred

Dobrolyubov, Nikolai Alexandrovich 1836-1861
NCLC 5

Dobson, Austin 1840-1921 .... **TCLC 79**
See also DLB 35; 144

Dobyns, Stephen 1941- .... **CLC 37**
See also CA 45-48; CANR 2, 18

Doctorow, E(dgar) L(aurence) 1931- **CLC 6, 11, 15, 18, 37, 44, 65, 113; DAM NOV, POP**
See also AAYA 22; AITN 2; BEST 89:3; CA 45-48; CANR 2, 33, 51; CDALB 1968-1988; DLB 2, 28, 173; DLBY 80; MTCW 1

Dodgson, Charles Lutwidge 1832-1898
See Carroll, Lewis
See also CLR 2; DA; DAB; DAC; DAM MST, NOV, POET; MAICYA; SATA 100; YABC 2

Dodson, Owen (Vincent) 1914-1983 **CLC 79; BLC 1; DAM MULT**
See also BW 1; CA 65-68; 110; CANR 24; DLB 76

Doeblin, Alfred 1878-1957 .... **TCLC 13**
See also Doblin, Alfred
See also CA 110; 141; DLB 66

Doerr, Harriet 1910- .... **CLC 34**
See also CA 117; 122; CANR 47; INT 122

Domecq, H(onorio) Bustos
See Bioy Casares, Adolfo; Borges, Jorge Luis

Domini, Rey
See Lorde, Audre (Geraldine)

Dominique
See Proust, (Valentin-Louis-George-Eugene-) Marcel

Don, A
See Stephen, SirLeslie

Donaldson, Stephen R. 1947- **CLC 46; DAM POP**
See also CA 89-92; CANR 13, 55; INT CANR-13

Donleavy, J(ames) P(atrick) 1926-**CLC 1, 4, 6, 10, 45**
See also AITN 2; CA 9-12R; CANR 24, 49, 62; DLB 6, 173; INT CANR-24; MTCW 1

Donne, John 1572-1631**LC 10, 24; DA; DAB; DAC; DAM MST, POET; PC 1**
See also CDBLB Before 1660; DLB 121, 151

Donnell, David 1939(?)- .... **CLC 34**

Donoghue, P. S.
See Hunt, E(verette) Howard, (Jr.)

Donoso (Yanez), Jose 1924-1996**CLC 4, 8, 11, 32, 99; DAM MULT; HLC**
See also CA 81-84; 155; CANR 32; DLB 113; HW; MTCW 1

Donovan, John 1928-1992 .... **CLC 35**
See also AAYA 20; CA 97-100; 137; CLR 3; MAICYA; SATA 72; SATA-Brief 29

Don Roberto
See Cunninghame Graham, R(obert) B(ontine)

Doolittle, Hilda 1886-1961**CLC 3, 8, 14, 31, 34, 73; DA; DAC; DAM MST, POET; PC 5; WLC**
See also H. D.
See also CA 97-100; CANR 35; DLB 4, 45; MTCW 1

Dorfman, Ariel 1942- ...... **CLC 48, 77; DAM MULT; HLC**
See also CA 124; 130; CANR 67, 70; HW; INT 130

Dorn, Edward (Merton) 1929- ... **CLC 10, 18**
See also CA 93-96; CANR 42; DLB 5; INT 93-96

Dorris, Michael (Anthony) 1945-1997 .. **C L C 109; DAM MULT, NOV**
See also AAYA 20; BEST 90:1; CA 102; 157; CANR 19, 46; DLB 175; NNAL; SATA 75; SATA-Obit 94

Dorris, Michael A.
See Dorris, Michael (Anthony)

Dorsan, Luc
See Simenon, Georges (Jacques Christian)

Dorsange, Jean
See Simenon, Georges (Jacques Christian)

Dos Passos, John (Roderigo) 1896-1970 **C L C 1, 4, 8, 11, 15, 25, 34, 82; DA; DAB; DAC; DAM MST, NOV; WLC**
See also CA 1-4R; 29-32R; CANR 3; CDALB 1929-1941; DLB 4, 9; DLBD 1, 15; DLBY 96; MTCW 1

Dossage, Jean
See Simenon, Georges (Jacques Christian)

Dostoevsky, Fedor Mikhailovich 1821-1881
NCLC 2, 7, 21, 33, 43; DA; DAB; DAC; DAM MST, NOV; SSC 2; WLC

Doughty, Charles M(ontagu) 1843-1926
TCLC 27
See also CA 115; DLB 19, 57, 174

Douglas, Ellen .... **CLC 73**
See also Haxton, Josephine Ayres; Williamson, Ellen Douglas

Douglas, Gavin 1475(?)-1522 .... **LC 20**
See also DLB 132

Douglas, George
See Brown, George Douglas

Douglas, Keith (Castellain) 1920-1944**T C L C 40**
See also CA 160; DLB 27

Douglas, Leonard
See Bradbury, Ray (Douglas)

Douglas, Michael
See Crichton, (John) Michael

Douglas, (George) Norman 1868-1952**T C L C 68**
See also CA 119; 157; DLB 34, 195

Douglas, William
See Brown, George Douglas

Douglass, Frederick 1817(?)-1895**NCLC 7, 55; BLC 1; DA; DAC; DAM MST, MULT; WLC**
See also CDALB 1640-1865; DLB 1, 43, 50, 79; SATA 29

Dourado, (Waldomiro Freitas) Autran 1926-
CLC 23, 60
See also CA 25-28R; CANR 34

Dourado, Waldomiro Autran
See Dourado, (Waldomiro Freitas) Autran

Feldman, Irving (Mordecai) 1928- ..... **CLC 7**
See also CA 1-4R; CANR 1; DLB 169
Felix-Tchicaya, Gerald
See Tchicaya, Gerald Felix
Fellini, Federico 1920-1993 .... **CLC 16, 85**
See also CA 65-68; 143; CANR 33
Felsen, Henry Gregor 1916- .... **CLC 17**
See also CA 1-4R; CANR 1; SAAS 2; SATA 1
Fenno, Jack
See Calisher, Hortense
Fenton, James Martin 1949- .... **CLC 32**
See also CA 102; DLB 40
Ferber, Edna 1887-1968 .... **CLC 18, 93**
See also AITN 1; CA 5-8R; 25-28R; CANR 68;
DLB 9, 28, 86; MTCW 1; SATA 7
Ferguson, Helen
See Kavan, Anna
Ferguson, Samuel 1810-1886 .... **NCLC 33**
See also DLB 32
Fergusson, Robert 1750-1774 .... **LC 29**
See also DLB 109
Ferling, Lawrence
See Ferlinghetti, Lawrence (Monsanto)
Ferlinghetti, Lawrence (Monsanto) 1919(?)-
CLC 2, 6, 10, 27, 111; DAM POET; PC 1
See also CA 5-8R; CANR 3, 41; CDALB 1941-
1968; DLB 5, 16; MTCW 1
Fernandez, Vicente Garcia Huidobro
See Huidobro Fernandez, Vicente Garcia
Ferrer, Gabriel (Francisco Victor) Miro
See Miro (Ferrer), Gabriel (Francisco Victor)
Ferrier, Susan (Edmonstone) 1782-1854
NCLC 8
See also DLB 116
Ferrigno, Robert 1948(?)- .... **CLC 65**
See also CA 140
Ferron, Jacques 1921-1985 .... **CLC 94; DAC**
See also CA 117; 129; DLB 60
Feuchtwanger, Lion 1884-1958 .... **TCLC 3**
See also CA 104; DLB 66
Feuillet, Octave 1821-1890 .... **NCLC 45**
See also DLB 192
Feydeau, Georges (Leon Jules Marie) 1862-
1921 .... **TCLC 22; DAM DRAM**
See also CA 113; 152; DLB 192
Fichte, Johann Gottlieb 1762-1814 **NCLC 62**
See also DLB 90
Ficino, Marsilio 1433-1499 .... **LC 12**
Fiedeler, Hans
See Doeblin, Alfred
Fiedler, Leslie A(aron) 1917- . **CLC 4, 13, 24**
See also CA 9-12R; CANR 7, 63; DLB 28, 67;
MTCW 1
Field, Andrew 1938- .... **CLC 44**
See also CA 97-100; CANR 25
Field, Eugene 1850-1895 .... **NCLC 3**
See also DLB 23, 42, 140; DLBD 13; MAICYA;
SATA 16
Field, Gans T.
See Wellman, Manly Wade
Field, Michael 1915-1971 .... **TCLC 43**
See also CA 29-32R
Field, Peter
See Hobson, Laura Z(ametkin)
Fielding, Henry 1707-1754 **LC 1; DA; DAB;
DAC; DAM DRAM, MST, NOV; WLC**
See also CDBLB 1660-1789; DLB 39, 84, 101
Fielding, Sarah 1710-1768 .... **LC 1, 44**
See also DLB 39
Fields, W. C. 1880-1946 .... **TCLC 80**
See also DLB 44
Fierstein, Harvey (Forbes) 1954- ... **CLC 33;
DAM DRAM, POP**
See also CA 123; 129
Figes, Eva 1932- .... **CLC 31**
See also CA 53-56; CANR 4, 44; DLB 14
Finch, Anne 1661-1720 .... **LC 3; PC 21**

See also DLB 95
Finch, Robert (Duer Claydon) 1900- **CLC 18**
See also CA 57-60; CANR 9, 24, 49; DLB 88
Findley, Timothy 1930- . **CLC 27, 102; DAC;
DAM MST**
See also CA 25-28R; CANR 12, 42, 69; DLB
53
Fink, William
See Mencken, H(enry) L(ouis)
Firbank, Louis 1942-
See Reed, Lou
See also CA 117
Firbank, (Arthur Annesley) Ronald 1886-1926
TCLC 1
See also CA 104; DLB 36
Fisher, M(ary) F(rances) K(ennedy) 1908-1992
CLC 76, 87
See also CA 77-80; 138; CANR 44
Fisher, Roy 1930- .... **CLC 25**
See also CA 81-84; CAAS 10; CANR 16; DLB
40
Fisher, Rudolph 1897-1934 **TCLC 11; BLC 2;
DAM MULT; SSC 25**
See also BW 1; CA 107; 124; DLB 51, 102
Fisher, Vardis (Alvero) 1895-1968 ...... **CLC 7**
See also CA 5-8R; 25-28R; CANR 68; DLB 9
Fiske, Tarleton
See Bloch, Robert (Albert)
Fitch, Clarke
See Sinclair, Upton (Beall)
Fitch, John IV
See Cormier, Robert (Edmund)
Fitzgerald, Captain Hugh
See Baum, L(yman) Frank
FitzGerald, Edward 1809-1883 .... **NCLC 9**
See also DLB 32
Fitzgerald, F(rancis) Scott (Key) 1896-1940
**TCLC 1, 6, 14, 28, 55; DA; DAB; DAC;
DAM MST, NOV; SSC 6, 31; WLC**
See also AAYA 24; AITN 1; CA 110; 123;
CDALB 1917-1929; DLB 4, 9, 86; DLBD 1,
15, 16; DLBY 81, 96; MTCW 1
Fitzgerald, Penelope 1916- ... **CLC 19, 51, 61**
See also CA 85-88; CAAS 10; CANR 56; DLB
14, 194
Fitzgerald, Robert (Stuart) 1910-1985 **CLC 39**
See also CA 1-4R; 114; CANR 1; DLBY 80
FitzGerald, Robert D(avid) 1902-1987 **CLC 19**
See also CA 17-20R
Fitzgerald, Zelda (Sayre) 1900-1948 **TCLC 52**
See also CA 117; 126; DLBY 84
Flanagan, Thomas (James Bonner) 1923-
CLC 25, 52
See also CA 108; CANR 55; DLBY 80; INT
108; MTCW 1
Flaubert, Gustave 1821-1880 **NCLC 2, 10, 19,
62, 66; DA; DAB; DAC; DAM MST, NOV;
SSC 11; WLC**
See also DLB 119
Flecker, Herman Elroy
See Flecker, (Herman) James Elroy
Flecker, (Herman) James Elroy 1884-1915
TCLC 43
See also CA 109; 150; DLB 10, 19
Fleming, Ian (Lancaster) 1908-1964 . **CLC 3,
30; DAM POP**
See also AAYA 26; CA 5-8R; CANR 59;
CDBLB 1945-1960; DLB 87, 201; MTCW
1; SATA 9
Fleming, Thomas (James) 1927- .... **CLC 37**
See also CA 5-8R; CANR 10; INT CANR-10;
SATA 8
Fletcher, John 1579-1625 .... **LC 33; DC 6**
See also CDBLB Before 1660; DLB 58
Fletcher, John Gould 1886-1950 .... **TCLC 35**
See also CA 107; 167; DLB 4, 45
Fleur, Paul

See Pohl, Frederik
Flooglebuckle, Al
See Spiegelman, Art
Flying Officer X
See Bates, H(erbert) E(rnest)
Fo, Dario 1926- . **CLC 32, 109; DAM DRAM**
See also CA 116; 128; CANR 68; DLBY 97;
MTCW 1
Fogarty, Jonathan Titulescu Esq.
See Farrell, James T(homas)
Folke, Will
See Bloch, Robert (Albert)
Follett, Ken(neth Martin) 1949- ..... **CLC 18;
DAM NOV, POP**
See also AAYA 6; BEST 89:4; CA 81-84; CANR
13, 33, 54; DLB 87; DLBY 81; INT CANR-
33; MTCW 1
Fontane, Theodor 1819-1898 .... **NCLC 26**
See also DLB 129
Foote, Horton 1916- **CLC 51, 91; DAM DRAM**
See also CA 73-76; CANR 34, 51; DLB 26; INT
CANR-34
Foote, Shelby 1916- **CLC 75; DAM NOV, POP**
See also CA 5-8R; CANR 3, 45; DLB 2, 17
Forbes, Esther 1891-1967 .... **CLC 12**
See also AAYA 17; CA 13-14; 25-28R; CAP 1;
CLR 27; DLB 22; JRDA; MAICYA; SATA
2, 100
Forche, Carolyn (Louise) 1950- **CLC 25, 83,
86; DAM POET; PC 10**
See also CA 109; 117; CANR 50; DLB 5, 193;
INT 117
Ford, Elbur
See Hibbert, Eleanor Alice Burford
Ford, Ford Madox 1873-1939 **TCLC 1, 15, 39,
57; DAM NOV**
See also CA 104; 132; CDBLB 1914-1945;
DLB 162; MTCW 1
Ford, Henry 1863-1947 .... **TCLC 73**
See also CA 115; 148
Ford, John 1586-(?) .... **DC 8**
See also CDBLB Before 1660; DAM DRAM;
DLB 58
Ford, John 1895-1973 .... **CLC 16**
See also CA 45-48
Ford, Richard 1944- .... **CLC 46, 99**
See also CA 69-72; CANR 11, 47
Ford, Webster
See Masters, Edgar Lee
Foreman, Richard 1937- .... **CLC 50**
See also CA 65-68; CANR 32, 63
Forester, C(ecil) S(cott) 1899-1966 ... **CLC 35**
See also CA 73-76; 25-28R; DLB 191; SATA
13
Forez
See Mauriac, Francois (Charles)
Forman, James Douglas 1932- .... **CLC 21**
See also AAYA 17; CA 9-12R; CANR 4, 19,
42; JRDA; MAICYA; SATA 8, 70
Fornes, Maria Irene 1930- .... **CLC 39, 61**
See also CA 25-28R; CANR 28; DLB 7; HW;
INT CANR-28; MTCW 1
Forrest, Leon (Richard) 1937-1997 .. **CLC 4;
BLCS**
See also BW 2; CA 89-92; 162; CAAS 7; CANR
25, 52; DLB 33
Forster, E(dward) M(organ) 1879-1970 **C L C
1, 2, 3, 4, 9, 10, 13, 15, 22, 45, 77; DA; DAB;
DAC; DAM MST, NOV; SSC 27; WLC**
See also AAYA 2; CA 13-14; 25-28R; CANR
45; CAP 1; CDBLB 1914-1945; DLB 34, 98,
162, 178, 195; DLBD 10; MTCW 1; SATA
57
Forster, John 1812-1876 .... **NCLC 11**
See also DLB 144, 184
Forsyth, Frederick 1938- **CLC 2, 5, 36; DAM
NOV, POP**

See also BEST 89:4; CA 85-88; CANR 38, 62; DLB 87; MTCW 1
Forten, Charlotte L. .... **TCLC 16; BLC 2**
See also Grimke, Charlotte L(ottie) Forten
See also DLB 50
Foscolo, Ugo 1778-1827 .... **NCLC 8**
Fosse, Bob .... **CLC 20**
See also Fosse, Robert Louis
Fosse, Robert Louis 1927-1987
See Fosse, Bob
See also CA 110; 123
Foster, Stephen Collins 1826-1864 **NCLC 26**
Foucault, Michel 1926-1984 . **CLC 31, 34, 69**
See also CA 105; 113; CANR 34; MTCW 1
Fouque, Friedrich (Heinrich Karl) de la Motte 1777-1843 .... **NCLC 2**
See also DLB 90
Fourier, Charles 1772-1837 .... **NCLC 51**
Fournier, Henri Alban 1886-1914
See Alain-Fournier
See also CA 104
Fournier, Pierre 1916- .... **CLC 11**
See also Gascar, Pierre
See also CA 89-92; CANR 16, 40
Fowles, John (Philip) 1926- **CLC 1, 2, 3, 4, 6, 9, 10, 15, 33, 87; DAB; DAC; DAM MST**
See also CA 5-8R; CANR 25, 71; CDBLB 1960 to Present; DLB 14, 139; MTCW 1; SATA 22
Fox, Paula 1923- .... **CLC 2, 8**
See also AAYA 3; CA 73-76; CANR 20, 36, 62; CLR 1, 44; DLB 52; JRDA; MAICYA; MTCW 1; SATA 17, 60
Fox, William Price (Jr.) 1926- .... **CLC 22**
See also CA 17-20R; CAAS 19; CANR 11; DLB 2; DLBY 81
Foxe, John 1516(?)-1587 .... **LC 14**
See also DLB 132
Frame, Janet 1924- **CLC 2, 3, 6, 22, 66, 96; SSC 29**
See also Clutha, Janet Paterson Frame
France, Anatole .... **TCLC 9**
See also Thibault, Jacques Anatole Francois
See also DLB 123
Francis, Claude 19(?)- .... **CLC 50**
Francis, Dick 1920- **CLC 2, 22, 42, 102; DAM POP**
See also AAYA 5, 21; BEST 89:3; CA 5-8R; CANR 9, 42, 68; CDBLB 1960 to Present; DLB 87; INT CANR-9; MTCW 1
Francis, Robert (Churchill) 1901-1987 **C L C 15**
See also CA 1-4R; 123; CANR 1
Frank, Anne(lies Marie) 1929-1945 **TCLC 17; DA; DAB; DAC; DAM MST; WLC**
See also AAYA 12; CA 113; 133; CANR 68; MTCW 1; SATA 87; SATA-Brief 42
Frank, Bruno 1887-1945 .... **TCLC 81**
See also DLB 118
Frank, Elizabeth 1945- .... **CLC 39**
See also CA 121; 126; INT 126
Frankl, Viktor E(mil) 1905-1997 ...... **CLC 93**
See also CA 65-68; 161
Franklin, Benjamin
See Hasek, Jaroslav (Matej Frantisek)
Franklin, Benjamin 1706-1790 .. **LC 25; DA; DAB; DAC; DAM MST; WLCS**
See also CDALB 1640-1865; DLB 24, 43, 73
Franklin, (Stella Maria Sarah) Miles (Lampe) 1879-1954 .... **TCLC 7**
See also CA 104; 164
Fraser, (Lady) Antonia (Pakenham) 1932- **CLC 32, 107**
See also CA 85-88; CANR 44, 65; MTCW 1; SATA-Brief 32
Fraser, George MacDonald 1925- ...... **CLC 7**
See also CA 45-48; CANR 2, 48

Fraser, Sylvia 1935- .... **CLC 64**
See also CA 45-48; CANR 1, 16, 60
Frayn, Michael 1933- **CLC 3, 7, 31, 47; DAM DRAM, NOV**
See also CA 5-8R; CANR 30, 69; DLB 13, 14, 194; MTCW 1
Fraze, Candida (Merrill) 1945- .... **CLC 50**
See also CA 126
Frazer, J(ames) G(eorge) 1854-1941 **TCLC 32**
See also CA 118
Frazer, Robert Caine
See Creasey, John
Frazer, Sir James George
See Frazer, J(ames) G(eorge)
Frazier, Charles 1950- .... **CLC 109**
See also CA 161
Frazier, Ian 1951- .... **CLC 46**
See also CA 130; CANR 54
Frederic, Harold 1856-1898 .... **NCLC 10**
See also DLB 12, 23; DLBD 13
Frederick, John
See Faust, Frederick (Schiller)
Frederick the Great 1712-1786 .... **LC 14**
Fredro, Aleksander 1793-1876 .... **NCLC 8**
Freeling, Nicolas 1927- .... **CLC 38**
See also CA 49-52; CAAS 12; CANR 1, 17, 50; DLB 87
Freeman, Douglas Southall 1886-1953 **T C L C 11**
See also CA 109; DLB 17; DLBD 17
Freeman, Judith 1946- .... **CLC 55**
See also CA 148
Freeman, Mary Eleanor Wilkins 1852-1930 **TCLC 9; SSC 1**
See also CA 106; DLB 12, 78
Freeman, R(ichard) Austin 1862-1943 **T C L C 21**
See also CA 113; DLB 70
French, Albert 1943- .... **CLC 86**
See also CA 167
French, Marilyn 1929- **CLC 10, 18, 60; DAM DRAM, NOV, POP**
See also CA 69-72; CANR 3, 31; INT CANR-31; MTCW 1
French, Paul
See Asimov, Isaac
Freneau, Philip Morin 1752-1832 ... **NCLC 1**
See also DLB 37, 43
Freud, Sigmund 1856-1939 .... **TCLC 52**
See also CA 115; 133; CANR 69; MTCW 1
Friedan, Betty (Naomi) 1921- .... **CLC 74**
See also CA 65-68; CANR 18, 45; MTCW 1
Friedlander, Saul 1932- .... **CLC 90**
See also CA 117; 130; CANR 72
Friedman, B(ernard) H(arper) 1926- **CLC 7**
See also CA 1-4R; CANR 3, 48
Friedman, Bruce Jay 1930- ...... **CLC 3, 5, 56**
See also CA 9-12R; CANR 25, 52; DLB 2, 28; INT CANR-25
Friel, Brian 1929- . **CLC 5, 42, 59, 115; DC 8**
See also CA 21-24R; CANR 33, 69; DLB 13; MTCW 1
Friis-Baastad, Babbis Ellinor 1921-1970 **C L C 12**
See also CA 17-20R; 134; SATA 7
Frisch, Max (Rudolf) 1911-1991 **CLC 3, 9, 14, 18, 32, 44; DAM DRAM, NOV**
See also CA 85-88; 134; CANR 32; DLB 69, 124; MTCW 1
Fromentin, Eugene (Samuel Auguste) 1820-1876 .... **NCLC 10**
See also DLB 123
Frost, Frederick
See Faust, Frederick (Schiller)
Frost, Robert (Lee) 1874-1963 **CLC 1, 3, 4, 9, 10, 13, 15, 26, 34, 44; DA; DAB; DAC; DAM MST, POET; PC 1; WLC**

See also AAYA 21; CA 89-92; CANR 33; CDALB 1917-1929; DLB 54; DLBD 7; MTCW 1; SATA 14
Froude, James Anthony 1818-1894 **NCLC 43**
See also DLB 18, 57, 144
Froy, Herald
See Waterhouse, Keith (Spencer)
Fry, Christopher 1907- **CLC 2, 10, 14; DAM DRAM**
See also CA 17-20R; CAAS 23; CANR 9, 30; DLB 13; MTCW 1; SATA 66
Frye, (Herman) Northrop 1912-1991 **CLC 24, 70**
See also CA 5-8R; 133; CANR 8, 37; DLB 67, 68; MTCW 1
Fuchs, Daniel 1909-1993 .... **CLC 8, 22**
See also CA 81-84; 142; CAAS 5; CANR 40; DLB 9, 26, 28; DLBY 93
Fuchs, Daniel 1934- .... **CLC 34**
See also CA 37-40R; CANR 14, 48
Fuentes, Carlos 1928- **CLC 3, 8, 10, 13, 22, 41, 60, 113; DA; DAB; DAC; DAM MST, MULT, NOV; HLC; SSC 24; WLC**
See also AAYA 4; AITN 2; CA 69-72; CANR 10, 32, 68; DLB 113; HW; MTCW 1
Fuentes, Gregorio Lopez y
See Lopez y Fuentes, Gregorio
Fugard, (Harold) Athol 1932- **CLC 5, 9, 14, 25, 40, 80; DAM DRAM; DC 3**
See also AAYA 17; CA 85-88; CANR 32, 54; MTCW 1
Fugard, Sheila 1932- .... **CLC 48**
See also CA 125
Fuller, Charles (H., Jr.) 1939- **CLC 25; BLC 2; DAM DRAM, MULT; DC 1**
See also BW 2; CA 108; 112; DLB 38; INT 112; MTCW 1
Fuller, John (Leopold) 1937- .... **CLC 62**
See also CA 21-24R; CANR 9, 44; DLB 40
Fuller, Margaret .... **NCLC 5, 50**
See also Ossoli, Sarah Margaret (Fuller marchesa d')
Fuller, Roy (Broadbent) 1912-1991 **CLC 4, 28**
See also CA 5-8R; 135; CAAS 10; CANR 53; DLB 15, 20; SATA 87
Fulton, Alice 1952- .... **CLC 52**
See also CA 116; CANR 57; DLB 193
Furphy, Joseph 1843-1912 .... **TCLC 25**
See also CA 163
Fussell, Paul 1924- .... **CLC 74**
See also BEST 90:1; CA 17-20R; CANR 8, 21, 35, 69; INT CANR-21; MTCW 1
Futabatei, Shimei 1864-1909 .... **TCLC 44**
See also CA 162; DLB 180
Futrelle, Jacques 1875-1912 .... **TCLC 19**
See also CA 113; 155
Gaboriau, Emile 1835-1873 .... **NCLC 14**
Gadda, Carlo Emilio 1893-1973 .... **CLC 11**
See also CA 89-92; DLB 177
Gaddis, William 1922- **CLC 1, 3, 6, 8, 10, 19, 43, 86**
See also CA 17-20R; CANR 21, 48; DLB 2; MTCW 1
Gage, Walter
See Inge, William (Motter)
Gaines, Ernest J(ames) 1933- **CLC 3, 11, 18, 86; BLC 2; DAM MULT**
See also AAYA 18; AITN 1; BW 2; CA 9-12R; CANR 6, 24, 42; CDALB 1968-1988; DLB 2, 33, 152; DLBY 80; MTCW 1; SATA 86
Gaitskill, Mary 1954- .... **CLC 69**
See also CA 128; CANR 61
Galdos, Benito Perez
See Perez Galdos, Benito
Gale, Zona 1874-1938 **TCLC 7; DAM DRAM**
See also CA 105; 153; DLB 9, 78
Galeano, Eduardo (Hughes) 1940- ... **CLC 72**

See also CA 29-32R; CANR 13, 32; HW
Galiano, Juan Valera y Alcala
See Valera y Alcala-Galiano, Juan
Galilei, Galileo 1546-1642 .... LC 45
Gallagher, Tess 1943- ...... CLC 18, 63; DAM
POET; PC 9
See also CA 106; DLB 120
Gallant, Mavis 1922- ... CLC 7, 18, 38; DAC;
DAM MST; SSC 5
See also CA 69-72; CANR 29, 69; DLB 53;
MTCW 1
Gallant, Roy A(rthur) 1924- .... CLC 17
See also CA 5-8R; CANR 4, 29, 54; CLR 30;
MAICYA; SATA 4, 68
Gallico, Paul (William) 1897-1976 ..... CLC 2
See also AITN 1; CA 5-8R; 69-72; CANR 23;
DLB 9, 171; MAICYA; SATA 13
Gallo, Max Louis 1932- .... CLC 95
See also CA 85-88
Gallois, Lucien
See Desnos, Robert
Gallup, Ralph
See Whitemore, Hugh (John)
Galsworthy, John 1867-1933TCLC 1, 45; DA;
DAB; DAC; DAM DRAM, MST, NOV;
SSC 22; WLC 2
See also CA 104; 141; CDBLB 1890-1914;
DLB 10, 34, 98, 162; DLBD 16
Galt, John 1779-1839 .... NCLC 1
See also DLB 99, 116, 159
Galvin, James 1951- .... CLC 38
See also CA 108; CANR 26
Gamboa, Federico 1864-1939 .... TCLC 36
See also CA 167
Gandhi, M. K.
See Gandhi, Mohandas Karamchand
Gandhi, Mahatma
See Gandhi, Mohandas Karamchand
Gandhi, Mohandas Karamchand 1869-1948
TCLC 59; DAM MULT
See also CA 121; 132; MTCW 1
Gann, Ernest Kellogg 1910-1991 ...... CLC 23
See also AITN 1; CA 1-4R; 136; CANR 1
Garcia, Cristina 1958- .... CLC 76
See also CA 141
Garcia Lorca, Federico 1898-1936TCLC 1, 7,
49; DA; DAB; DAC; DAM DRAM, MST,
MULT, POET; DC 2; HLC; PC 3; WLC
See also CA 104; 131; DLB 108; HW; MTCW
1
Garcia Marquez, Gabriel (Jose) 1928-CLC 2,
3, 8, 10, 15, 27, 47, 55, 68; DA; DAB; DAC;
DAM MST, MULT, NOV, POP; HLC; SSC
8; WLC
See also AAYA 3; BEST 89:1, 90:4; CA 33-
36R; CANR 10, 28, 50; DLB 113; HW;
MTCW 1
Gard, Janice
See Latham, Jean Lee
Gard, Roger Martin du
See Martin du Gard, Roger
Gardam, Jane 1928- .... CLC 43
See also CA 49-52; CANR 2, 18, 33, 54; CLR
12; DLB 14, 161; MAICYA; MTCW 1;
SAAS 9; SATA 39, 76; SATA-Brief 28
Gardner, Herb(ert) 1934- .... CLC 44
See also CA 149
Gardner, John (Champlin), Jr. 1933-1982
CLC 2, 3, 5, 7, 8, 10, 18, 28, 34; DAM NOV,
POP; SSC 7
See also AITN 1; CA 65-68; 107; CANR 33;
DLB 2; DLBY 82; MTCW 1; SATA 40;
SATA-Obit 31
Gardner, John (Edmund) 1926-CLC 30; DAM
POP
See also CA 103; CANR 15, 69; MTCW 1
Gardner, Miriam

See Bradley, Marion Zimmer
Gardner, Noel
See Kuttner, Henry
Gardons, S. S.
See Snodgrass, W(illiam) D(e Witt)
Garfield, Leon 1921-1996 .... CLC 12
See also AAYA 8; CA 17-20R; 152; CANR 38,
41; CLR 21; DLB 161; JRDA; MAICYA;
SATA 1, 32, 76; SATA-Obit 90
Garland, (Hannibal) Hamlin 1860-1940
TCLC 3; SSC 18
See also CA 104; DLB 12, 71, 78, 186
Garneau, (Hector de) Saint-Denys 1912-1943
TCLC 13
See also CA 111; DLB 88
Garner, Alan 1934-CLC 17; DAB; DAM POP
See also AAYA 18; CA 73-76; CANR 15, 64;
CLR 20; DLB 161; MAICYA; MTCW 1;
SATA 18, 69
Garner, Hugh 1913-1979 .... CLC 13
See also CA 69-72; CANR 31; DLB 68
Garnett, David 1892-1981 .... CLC 3
See also CA 5-8R; 103; CANR 17; DLB 34
Garos, Stephanie
See Katz, Steve
Garrett, George (Palmer) 1929-CLC 3, 11, 51;
SSC 30
See also CA 1-4R; CAAS 5; CANR 1, 42, 67;
DLB 2, 5, 130, 152; DLBY 83
Garrick, David 1717-1779 ....LC 15; DAM
DRAM
See also DLB 84
Garrigue, Jean 1914-1972 .... CLC 2, 8
See also CA 5-8R; 37-40R; CANR 20
Garrison, Frederick
See Sinclair, Upton (Beall)
Garth, Will
See Hamilton, Edmond; Kuttner, Henry
Garvey, Marcus (Moziah, Jr.) 1887-1940
TCLC 41; BLC 2; DAM MULT
See also BW 1; CA 120; 124
Gary, Romain .... CLC 25
See also Kacew, Romain
See also DLB 83
Gascar, Pierre .... CLC 11
See also Fournier, Pierre
Gascoyne, David (Emery) 1916- .... CLC 45
See also CA 65-68; CANR 10, 28, 54; DLB 20;
MTCW 1
Gaskell, Elizabeth Cleghorn 1810-1865NCLC
70; DAB; DAM MST; SSC 25
See also CDBLB 1832-1890; DLB 21, 144, 159
Gass, William H(oward) 1924-CLC 1, 2, 8, 11,
15, 39; SSC 12
See also CA 17-20R; CANR 30, 71; DLB 2;
MTCW 1
Gasset, Jose Ortega y
See Ortega y Gasset, Jose
Gates, Henry Louis, Jr. 1950-CLC 65; BLCS;
DAM MULT
See also BW 2; CA 109; CANR 25, 53; DLB
67
Gautier, Theophile 1811-1872 .. NCLC 1, 59;
DAM POET; PC 18; SSC 20
See also DLB 119
Gawsworth, John
See Bates, H(erbert) E(rnest)
Gay, Oliver
See Gogarty, Oliver St. John
Gaye, Marvin (Penze) 1939-1984 ..... CLC 26
See also CA 112
Gebler, Carlo (Ernest) 1954- .... CLC 39
See also CA 119; 133
Gee, Maggie (Mary) 1948- .... CLC 57
See also CA 130
Gee, Maurice (Gough) 1931- .... CLC 29
See also CA 97-100; CANR 67; SATA 46, 101

Gelbart, Larry (Simon) 1923- .... CLC 21, 61
See also CA 73-76; CANR 45
Gelber, Jack 1932- .... CLC 1, 6, 14, 79
See also CA 1-4R; CANR 2; DLB 7
Gellhorn, Martha (Ellis) 1908-1998 CLC 14,
60
See also CA 77-80; 164; CANR 44; DLBY 82
Genet, Jean 1910-1986CLC 1, 2, 5, 10, 14, 44,
46; DAM DRAM
See also CA 13-16R; CANR 18; DLB 72;
DLBY 86; MTCW 1
Gent, Peter 1942- .... CLC 29
See also AITN 1; CA 89-92; DLBY 82
Gentlewoman in New England, A
See Bradstreet, Anne
Gentlewoman in Those Parts, A
See Bradstreet, Anne
George, Jean Craighead 1919- .... CLC 35
See also AAYA 8; CA 5-8R; CANR 25; CLR 1;
DLB 52; JRDA; MAICYA; SATA 2, 68
George, Stefan (Anton) 1868-1933TCLC 2, 14
See also CA 104
Georges, Georges Martin
See Simenon, Georges (Jacques Christian)
Gerhardi, William Alexander
See Gerhardie, William Alexander
Gerhardie, William Alexander 1895-1977
CLC 5
See also CA 25-28R; 73-76; CANR 18; DLB
36
Gerstler, Amy 1956- .... CLC 70
See also CA 146
Gertler, T. .... CLC 34
See also CA 116; 121; INT 121
Ghalib .... NCLC 39
See also Ghalib, Hsadullah Khan
Ghalib, Hsadullah Khan 1797-1869
See Ghalib
See also DAM POET
Ghelderode, Michel de 1898-1962CLC 6, 11;
DAM DRAM
See also CA 85-88; CANR 40
Ghiselin, Brewster 1903- .... CLC 23
See also CA 13-16R; CAAS 10; CANR 13
Ghose, Aurabinda 1872-1950 .... TCLC 63
See also CA 163
Ghose, Zulfikar 1935- .... CLC 42
See also CA 65-68; CANR 67
Ghosh, Amitav 1956- .... CLC 44
See also CA 147
Giacosa, Giuseppe 1847-1906 .... TCLC 7
See also CA 104
Gibb, Lee
See Waterhouse, Keith (Spencer)
Gibbon, Lewis Grassic .... TCLC 4
See also Mitchell, James Leslie
Gibbons, Kaye 1960-CLC 50, 88; DAM POP
See also CA 151
Gibran, Kahlil 1883-1931 . TCLC 1, 9; DAM
POET, POP; PC 9
See also CA 104; 150
Gibran, Khalil
See Gibran, Kahlil
Gibson, William 1914- .. CLC 23; DA; DAB;
DAC; DAM DRAM, MST
See also CA 9-12R; CANR 9, 42; DLB 7; SATA
66
Gibson, William (Ford) 1948- ... CLC 39, 63;
DAM POP
See also AAYA 12; CA 126; 133; CANR 52
Gide, Andre (Paul Guillaume) 1869-1951
TCLC 5, 12, 36; DA; DAB; DAC; DAM
MST, NOV; SSC 13; WLC
See also CA 104; 124; DLB 65; MTCW 1
Gifford, Barry (Colby) 1946- .... CLC 34
See also CA 65-68; CANR 9, 30, 40
Gilbert, Frank

See De Voto, Bernard (Augustine)

Gilbert, W(illiam) S(chwenck) 1836-1911
TCLC 3; DAM DRAM, POET
See also CA 104; SATA 36

Gilbreth, Frank B., Jr. 1911- .... **CLC 17**
See also CA 9-12R; SATA 2

Gilchrist, Ellen 1935-**CLC 34, 48; DAM POP;
SSC 14**
See also CA 113; 116; CANR 41, 61; DLB 130;
MTCW 1

Giles, Molly 1942- .... **CLC 39**
See also CA 126

Gill, Eric 1882-1940 .... **TCLC 85**

Gill, Patrick
See Creasey, John

Gilliam, Terry (Vance) 1940- .... **CLC 21**
See also Monty Python
See also AAYA 19; CA 108; 113; CANR 35;
INT 113

Gillian, Jerry
See Gilliam, Terry (Vance)

Gilliatt, Penelope (Ann Douglass) 1932-1993
CLC 2, 10, 13, 53
See also AITN 2; CA 13-16R; 141; CANR 49;
DLB 14

Gilman, Charlotte (Anna) Perkins (Stetson)
1860-1935 ....
TCLC 9, 37; SSC 13
See also CA 106; 150

Gilmour, David 1949- .... **CLC 35**
See also CA 138, 147

Gilpin, William 1724-1804 .... **NCLC 30**

Gilray, J. D.
See Mencken, H(enry) L(ouis)

Gilroy, Frank D(aniel) 1925- .... **CLC 2**
See also CA 81-84; CANR 32, 64; DLB 7

Gilstrap, John 1957(?)- .... **CLC 99**
See also CA 160

Ginsberg, Allen 1926-1997**CLC 1, 2, 3, 4, 6, 13,
36, 69, 109; DA; DAB; DAC; DAM MST,
POET; PC 4; WLC 3**
See also AITN 1; CA 1-4R; 157; CANR 2, 41,
63; CDALB 1941-1968; DLB 5, 16, 169;
MTCW 1

Ginzburg, Natalia 1916-1991**CLC 5, 11, 54, 70**
See also CA 85-88; 135; CANR 33; DLB 177;
MTCW 1

Giono, Jean 1895-1970 .... **CLC 4, 11**
See also CA 45-48; 29-32R; CANR 2, 35; DLB
72; MTCW 1

Giovanni, Nikki 1943-**CLC 2, 4, 19, 64; BLC
2; DA; DAB; DAC; DAM MST, MULT,
POET; PC 19; WLCS**
See also AAYA 22; AITN 1; BW 2; CA 29-32R;
CAAS 6; CANR 18, 41, 60; CLR 6; DLB 5,
41; INT CANR-18; MAICYA; MTCW 1;
SATA 24

Giovene, Andrea 1904- .... **CLC 7**
See also CA 85-88

Gippius, Zinaida (Nikolayevna) 1869-1945
See Hippius, Zinaida
See also CA 106

Giraudoux, (Hippolyte) Jean 1882-1944
TCLC 2, 7; DAM DRAM
See also CA 104; DLB 65

Gironella, Jose Maria 1917- .... **CLC 11**
See also CA 101

Gissing, George (Robert) 1857-1903**TCLC 3,
24, 47**
See also CA 105; 167; DLB 18, 135, 184

Giurlani, Aldo
See Palazzeschi, Aldo

Gladkov, Fyodor (Vasilyevich) 1883-1958
TCLC 27

Glanville, Brian (Lester) 1931- .... **CLC 6**
See also CA 5-8R; CAAS 9; CANR 3, 70; DLB
15, 139; SATA 42

Glasgow, Ellen (Anderson Gholson) 1873-1945
TCLC 2, 7
See also CA 104; 164; DLB 9, 12

Glaspell, Susan 1882(?)-1948 .... **TCLC 55**
See also CA 110; 154; DLB 7, 9, 78; YABC 2

Glassco, John 1909-1981 .... **CLC 9**
See also CA 13-16R; 102; CANR 15; DLB 68

Glasscock, Amnesia
See Steinbeck, John (Ernst)

Glasser, Ronald J. 1940(?)- .... **CLC 37**

Glassman, Joyce
See Johnson, Joyce

Glendinning, Victoria 1937- .... **CLC 50**
See also CA 120; 127; CANR 59; DLB 155

Glissant, Edouard 1928- . **CLC 10, 68; DAM
MULT**
See also CA 153

Gloag, Julian 1930- .... **CLC 40**
See also AITN 1; CA 65-68; CANR 10, 70

Glowacki, Aleksander
See Prus, Boleslaw

Gluck, Louise (Elisabeth) 1943-**CLC 7, 22, 44,
81; DAM POET; PC 16**
See also CA 33-36R; CANR 40, 69; DLB 5

Glyn, Elinor 1864-1943 .... **TCLC 72**
See also DLB 153

Gobineau, Joseph Arthur (Comte) de 1816-
1882 .... **NCLC 17**
See also DLB 123

Godard, Jean-Luc 1930- .... **CLC 20**
See also CA 93-96

Godden, (Margaret) Rumer 1907- ... **CLC 53**
See also AAYA 6; CA 5-8R; CANR 4, 27, 36,
55; CLR 20; DLB 161; MAICYA; SAAS 12;
SATA 3, 36

Godoy Alcayaga, Lucila 1889-1957
See Mistral, Gabriela
See also BW 2; CA 104; 131; DAM MULT;
HW; MTCW 1

Godwin, Gail (Kathleen) 1937- **CLC 5, 8, 22,
31, 69; DAM POP**
See also CA 29-32R; CANR 15, 43, 69; DLB
6; INT CANR-15; MTCW 1

Godwin, William 1756-1836 .... **NCLC 14**
See also CDBLB 1789-1832; DLB 39, 104, 142,
158, 163

Goebbels, Josef
See Goebbels, (Paul) Joseph

Goebbels, (Paul) Joseph 1897-1945**TCLC 68**
See also CA 115; 148

Goebbels, Joseph Paul
See Goebbels, (Paul) Joseph

Goethe, Johann Wolfgang von 1749-1832
**NCLC 4, 22, 34; DA; DAB; DAC; DAM
DRAM, MST, POET; PC 5; WLC 3**
See also DLB 94

Gogarty, Oliver St. John 1878-1957**TCLC 15**
See also CA 109; 150; DLB 15, 19

Gogol, Nikolai (Vasilyevich) 1809-1852**NCLC
5, 15, 31; DA; DAB; DAC; DAM DRAM,
MST; DC 1; SSC 4, 29; WLC**
See also DLB 198

Goines, Donald 1937(?)-1974**CLC 80; BLC 2;
DAM MULT, POP**
See also AITN 1; BW 1; CA 124; 114; DLB 33

Gold, Herbert 1924- .... **CLC 4, 7, 14, 42**
See also CA 9-12R; CANR 17, 45; DLB 2;
DLBY 81

Goldbarth, Albert 1948- .... **CLC 5, 38**
See also CA 53-56; CANR 6, 40; DLB 120

Goldberg, Anatol 1910-1982 .... **CLC 34**
See also CA 131; 117

Goldemberg, Isaac 1945- .... **CLC 52**
See also CA 69-72; CAAS 12; CANR 11, 32;
HW

Golding, William (Gerald) 1911-1993**CLC 1,
2, 3, 8, 10, 17, 27, 58, 81; DA; DAB; DAC;**
DAM MST, NOV; WLC
See also AAYA 5; CA 5-8R; 141; CANR 13,
33, 54; CDBLB 1945-1960; DLB 15, 100;
MTCW 1

Goldman, Emma 1869-1940 .... **TCLC 13**
See also CA 110; 150

Goldman, Francisco 1954- .... **CLC 76**
See also CA 162

Goldman, William (W.) 1931- .... **CLC 1, 48**
See also CA 9-12R; CANR 29, 69; DLB 44

Goldmann, Lucien 1913-1970 .... **CLC 24**
See also CA 25-28; CAP 2

Goldoni, Carlo 1707-1793**LC 4; DAM DRAM**

Goldsberry, Steven 1949- .... **CLC 34**
See also CA 131

Goldsmith, Oliver 1728-1774**LC 2; DA; DAB;
DAC; DAM DRAM, MST, NOV, POET;
DC 8; WLC**
See also CDBLB 1660-1789; DLB 39, 89, 104,
109, 142; SATA 26

Goldsmith, Peter
See Priestley, J(ohn) B(oynton)

Gombrowicz, Witold 1904-1969**CLC 4, 7, 11,
49; DAM DRAM**
See also CA 19-20; 25-28R; CAP 2

Gomez de la Serna, Ramon 1888-1963**CLC 9**
See also CA 153; 116; HW

Goncharov, Ivan Alexandrovich 1812-1891
NCLC 1, 63

Goncourt, Edmond (Louis Antoine Huot) de
1822-1896 ....
NCLC 7
See also DLB 123

Goncourt, Jules (Alfred Huot) de 1830-1870
NCLC 7
See also DLB 123

Gontier, Fernande 19(?)- .... **CLC 50**

Gonzalez Martinez, Enrique 1871-1952
TCLC 72
See also CA 166; HW

Goodman, Paul 1911-1972 ...... **CLC 1, 2, 4, 7**
See also CA 19-20; 37-40R; CANR 34; CAP 2;
DLB 130; MTCW 1

Gordimer, Nadine 1923-**CLC 3, 5, 7, 10, 18, 33,
51, 70; DA; DAB; DAC; DAM MST, NOV;
SSC 17; WLCS**
See also CA 5-8R; CANR 3, 28, 56; INT CANR-
28; MTCW 1

Gordon, Adam Lindsay 1833-1870 **NCLC 21**

Gordon, Caroline 1895-1981**CLC 6, 13, 29, 83;
SSC 15**
See also CA 11-12; 103; CANR 36; CAP 1;
DLB 4, 9, 102; DLBD 17; DLBY 81; MTCW
1

Gordon, Charles William 1860-1937
See Connor, Ralph
See also CA 109

Gordon, Mary (Catherine) 1949-**CLC 13, 22**
See also CA 102; CANR 44; DLB 6; DLBY
81; INT 102; MTCW 1

Gordon, N. J.
See Bosman, Herman Charles

Gordon, Sol 1923- .... **CLC 26**
See also CA 53-56; CANR 4; SATA 11

Gordone, Charles 1925-1995**CLC 1, 4; DAM
DRAM; DC 8**
See also BW 1; CA 93-96; 150; CANR 55; DLB
7; INT 93-96; MTCW 1

Gore, Catherine 1800-1861 .... **NCLC 65**
See also DLB 116

Gorenko, Anna Andreevna
See Akhmatova, Anna

Gorky, Maxim 1868-1936**TCLC 8; DAB; SSC
28; WLC**
See also Peshkov, Alexei Maximovich

Goryan, Sirak
See Saroyan, William

Gosse, Edmund (William) 1849-1928**TCLC 28**
  See also CA 117; DLB 57, 144, 184
Gotlieb, Phyllis Fay (Bloom) 1926- .. **CLC 18**
  See also CA 13-16R; CANR 7; DLB 88
Gottesman, S. D.
  See Kornbluth, C(yril) M.; Pohl, Frederik
Gottfried von Strassburg fl. c. 1210- **CMLC 10**
  See also DLB 138
Gould, Lois ....**CLC 4, 10**
  See also CA 77-80; CANR 29; MTCW 1
Gourmont, Remy (-Marie-Charles) de 1858-1915 .... **TCLC 17**
  See also CA 109; 150
Govier, Katherine 1948- .... **CLC 51**
  See also CA 101; CANR 18, 40
Goyen, (Charles) William 1915-1983**CLC 5, 8, 14, 40**
  See also AITN 2; CA 5-8R; 110; CANR 6, 71; DLB 2; DLBY 83; INT CANR-6
Goytisolo, Juan 1931- . **CLC 5, 10, 23; DAM MULT; HLC**
  See also CA 85-88; CANR 32, 61; HW; MTCW 1
Gozzano, Guido 1883-1916 .... **PC 10**
  See also CA 154; DLB 114
Gozzi, (Conte) Carlo 1720-1806 .... **NCLC 23**
Grabbe, Christian Dietrich 1801-1836**NCLC 2**
  See also DLB 133
Grace, Patricia 1937- .... **CLC 56**
Gracian y Morales, Baltasar 1601-1658**LC 15**
Gracq, Julien .... **CLC 11, 48**
  See also Poirier, Louis
  See also DLB 83
Grade, Chaim 1910-1982 .... **CLC 10**
  See also CA 93-96; 107
Graduate of Oxford, A
  See Ruskin, John
Grafton, Garth
  See Duncan, Sara Jeannette
Graham, John
  See Phillips, David Graham
Graham, Jorie 1951- .... **CLC 48**
  See also CA 111; CANR 63; DLB 120
Graham, R(obert) B(ontine) Cunninghame
  See Cunninghame Graham, R(obert) B(ontine)
  See also DLB 98, 135, 174
Graham, Robert
  See Haldeman, Joe (William)
Graham, Tom
  See Lewis, (Harry) Sinclair
Graham, W(illiam) S(ydney) 1918-1986**CLC 29**
  See also CA 73-76; 118; DLB 20
Graham, Winston (Mawdsley) 1910- **CLC 23**
  See also CA 49-52; CANR 2, 22, 45, 66; DLB 77
Grahame, Kenneth 1859-1932**TCLC 64; DAB**
  See also CA 108; 136; CLR 5; DLB 34, 141, 178; MAICYA; SATA 100; YABC 1
Grant, Skeeter
  See Spiegelman, Art
Granville-Barker, Harley 1877-1946**TCLC 2; DAM DRAM**
  See also Barker, Harley Granville
  See also CA 104
Grass, Guenter (Wilhelm) 1927-**CLC 1, 2, 4, 6, 11, 15, 22, 32, 49, 88; DA; DAB; DAC; DAM MST, NOV; WLC**
  See also CA 13-16R; CANR 20; DLB 75, 124; MTCW 1
Gratton, Thomas
  See Hulme, T(homas) E(rnest)
Grau, Shirley Ann 1929-.. **CLC 4, 9; SSC 15**
  See also CA 89-92; CANR 22, 69; DLB 2; INT CANR-22; MTCW 1

Gravel, Fern
  See Hall, James Norman
Graver, Elizabeth 1964- .... **CLC 70**
  See also CA 135; CANR 71
Graves, Richard Perceval 1945- .... **CLC 44**
  See also CA 65-68; CANR 9, 26, 51
Graves, Robert (von Ranke) 1895-1985 **CLC 1, 2, 6, 11, 39, 44, 45; DAB; DAC; DAM MST, POET; PC 6**
  See also CA 5-8R; 117; CANR 5, 36; CDBLB 1914-1945; DLB 20, 100, 191; DLBD 18; DLBY 85; MTCW 1; SATA 45
Graves, Valerie
  See Bradley, Marion Zimmer
Gray, Alasdair (James) 1934- .... **CLC 41**
  See also CA 126; CANR 47, 69; DLB 194; INT 126; MTCW 1
Gray, Amlin 1946- .... **CLC 29**
  See also CA 138
Gray, Francine du Plessix 1930-..... **CLC 22; DAM NOV**
  See also BEST 90:3; CA 61-64; CAAS 2; CANR 11, 33; INT CANR-11; MTCW 1
Gray, John (Henry) 1866-1934 ...... **TCLC 19**
  See also CA 119; 162
Gray, Simon (James Holliday) 1936- **CLC 9, 14, 36**
  See also AITN 1; CA 21-24R; CAAS 3; CANR 32, 69; DLB 13; MTCW 1
Gray, Spalding 1941-**CLC 49, 112; DAM POP; DC 7**
  See also CA 128
Gray, Thomas 1716-1771**LC 4, 40; DA; DAB; DAC; DAM MST; PC 2; WLC**
  See also CDBLB 1660-1789; DLB 109
Grayson, David
  See Baker, Ray Stannard
Grayson, Richard (A.) 1951- .... **CLC 38**
  See also CA 85-88; CANR 14, 31, 57
Greeley, Andrew M(oran) 1928-..... **CLC 28; DAM POP**
  See also CA 5-8R; CAAS 7; CANR 7, 43, 69; MTCW 1
Green, Anna Katharine 1846-1935 **TCLC 63**
  See also CA 112; 159; DLB 202
Green, Brian
  See Card, Orson Scott
Green, Hannah
  See Greenberg, Joanne (Goldenberg)
Green, Hannah 1927(?)-1996 .... **CLC 3**
  See also CA 73-76; CANR 59
Green, Henry 1905-1973 .... **CLC 2, 13, 97**
  See also Yorke, Henry Vincent
  See also DLB 15
Green, Julian (Hartridge) 1900-
  See Green, Julien
  See also CA 21-24R; CANR 33; DLB 4, 72; MTCW 1
Green, Julien .... **CLC 3, 11, 77**
  See also Green, Julian (Hartridge)
Green, Paul (Eliot) 1894-1981**CLC 25; DAM DRAM**
  See also AITN 1; CA 5-8R; 103; CANR 3; DLB 7, 9; DLBY 81
Greenberg, Ivan 1908-1973
  See Rahv, Philip
  See also CA 85-88
Greenberg, Joanne (Goldenberg) 1932- **CLC 7, 30**
  See also AAYA 12; CA 5-8R; CANR 14, 32, 69; SATA 25
Greenberg, Richard 1959(?)- .... **CLC 57**
  See also CA 138
Greene, Bette 1934- .... **CLC 30**
  See also AAYA 7; CA 53-56; CANR 4; CLR 2; JRDA; MAICYA; SAAS 16; SATA 8, 102
Greene, Gael .... **CLC 8**

See also CA 13-16R; CANR 10
Greene, Graham (Henry) 1904-1991**CLC 1, 3, 6, 9, 14, 18, 27, 37, 70, 72; DA; DAB; DAC; DAM MST, NOV; SSC 29; WLC**
  See also AITN 2; CA 13-16R; 133; CANR 35, 61; CDBLB 1945-1960; DLB 13, 15, 77, 100, 162, 201; DLBY 91; MTCW 1; SATA 20
Greene, Robert 1558-1592 .... **LC 41**
  See also DLB 62, 167
Greer, Richard
  See Silverberg, Robert
Gregor, Arthur 1923- .... **CLC 9**
  See also CA 25-28R; CAAS 10; CANR 11; SATA 36
Gregor, Lee
  See Pohl, Frederik
Gregory, Isabella Augusta (Persse) 1852-1932 **TCLC 1**
  See also CA 104; DLB 10
Gregory, J. Dennis
  See Williams, John A(lfred)
Grendon, Stephen
  See Derleth, August (William)
Grenville, Kate 1950- .... **CLC 61**
  See also CA 118; CANR 53
Grenville, Pelham
  See Wodehouse, P(elham) G(renville)
Greve, Felix Paul (Berthold Friedrich) 1879-1948
  See Grove, Frederick Philip
  See also CA 104; 141; DAC; DAM MST
Grey, Zane 1872-1939 .. **TCLC 6; DAM POP**
  See also CA 104; 132; DLB 9; MTCW 1
Grieg, (Johan) Nordahl (Brun) 1902-1943 **TCLC 10**
  See also CA 107
Grieve, C(hristopher) M(urray) 1892-1978 **CLC 11, 19; DAM POET**
  See also MacDiarmid, Hugh; Pteleon
  See also CA 5-8R; 85-88; CANR 33; MTCW 1
Griffin, Gerald 1803-1840 .... **NCLC 7**
  See also DLB 159
Griffin, John Howard 1920-1980 ..... **CLC 68**
  See also AITN 1; CA 1-4R; 101; CANR 2
Griffin, Peter 1942- .... **CLC 39**
  See also CA 136
Griffith, D(avid Lewelyn) W(ark) 1875(?)-1948 **TCLC 68**
  See also CA 119; 150
Griffith, Lawrence
  See Griffith, D(avid Lewelyn) W(ark)
Griffiths, Trevor 1935- .... **CLC 13, 52**
  See also CA 97-100; CANR 45; DLB 13
Griggs, Sutton Elbert 1872-1930(?)**TCLC 77**
  See also CA 123; DLB 50
Grigson, Geoffrey (Edward Harvey) 1905-1985 **CLC 7, 39**
  See also CA 25-28R; 118; CANR 20, 33; DLB 27; MTCW 1
Grillparzer, Franz 1791-1872 .... **NCLC 1**
  See also DLB 133
Grimble, Reverend Charles James
  See Eliot, T(homas) S(tearns)
Grimke, Charlotte L(ottie) Forten 1837(?)-1914
  See Forten, Charlotte L.
  See also BW 1; CA 117; 124; DAM MULT, POET
Grimm, Jacob Ludwig Karl 1785-1863**NCLC 3**
  See also DLB 90; MAICYA; SATA 22
Grimm, Wilhelm Karl 1786-1859 .... **NCLC 3**
  See also DLB 90; MAICYA; SATA 22
Grimmelshausen, Johann Jakob Christoffel von 1621-1676 .... **LC 6**
  See also DLB 168
Grindel, Eugene 1895-1952

BLC 2; DAM MULT, POET; PC 16
See also DLB 31, 50

Hammond, Keith
See Kuttner, Henry

Hamner, Earl (Henry), Jr. 1923- ...... **CLC 12**
See also AITN 2; CA 73-76; DLB 6

Hampton, Christopher (James) 1946- **CLC 4**
See also CA 25-28R; DLB 13; MTCW 1

Hamsun, Knut .... **TCLC 2, 14, 49**
See also Pedersen, Knut

Handke, Peter 1942-**CLC 5, 8, 10, 15, 38; DAM DRAM, NOV**
See also CA 77-80; CANR 33; DLB 85, 124; MTCW 1

Hanley, James 1901-1985 ..... **CLC 3, 5, 8, 13**
See also CA 73-76; 117; CANR 36; DLB 191; MTCW 1

Hannah, Barry 1942- .... **CLC 23, 38, 90**
See also CA 108; 110; CANR 43, 68; DLB 6; INT 110; MTCW 1

Hannon, Ezra
See Hunter, Evan

Hansberry, Lorraine (Vivian) 1930-1965**CLC 17, 62; BLC 2; DA; DAB; DAC; DAM DRAM, MST, MULT; DC 2**
See also AAYA 25; BW 1; CA 109; 25-28R; CABS 3; CANR 58; CDALB 1941-1968; DLB 7, 38; MTCW 1

Hansen, Joseph 1923-......................... **CLC 38**
See also CA 29-32R; CAAS 17; CANR 16, 44, 66; INT CANR-16

Hansen, Martin A(lfred) 1909-1955**TCLC 32**
See also CA 167

Hanson, Kenneth O(stlin) 1922- .... **CLC 13**
See also CA 53-56; CANR 7

Hardwick, Elizabeth (Bruce) 1916- **CLC 13; DAM NOV**
See also CA 5-8R; CANR 3, 32, 70; DLB 6; MTCW 1

Hardy, Thomas 1840-1928**TCLC 4, 10, 18, 32, 48, 53, 72; DA; DAB; DAC; DAM MST, NOV, POET; PC 8; SSC 2; WLC**
See also CA 104; 123; CDBLB 1890-1914; DLB 18, 19, 135; MTCW 1

Hare, David 1947-......................... **CLC 29, 58**
See also CA 97-100; CANR 39; DLB 13; MTCW 1

Harewood, John
See Van Druten, John (William)

Harford, Henry
See Hudson, W(illiam) H(enry)

Hargrave, Leonie
See Disch, Thomas M(ichael)

Harjo, Joy 1951- .... **CLC 83; DAM MULT**
See also CA 114; CANR 35, 67; DLB 120, 175; NNAL

Harlan, Louis R(udolph) 1922- .... **CLC 34**
See also CA 21-24R; CANR 25, 55

Harling, Robert 1951(?)- .... **CLC 53**
See also CA 147

Harmon, William (Ruth) 1938-......... **CLC 38**
See also CA 33-36R; CANR 14, 32, 35; SATA 65

Harper, Daniel
See Brossard, Chandler

Harper, F. E. W.
See Harper, Frances Ellen Watkins

Harper, Frances E. W.
See Harper, Frances Ellen Watkins

Harper, Frances E. Watkins
See Harper, Frances Ellen Watkins

Harper, Frances Ellen
See Harper, Frances Ellen Watkins

Harper, Frances Ellen Watkins 1825-1911
TCLC 14; BLC 2; DAM MULT, POET; PC 21
See also BW 1; CA 111; 125; DLB 50

Harper, Michael S(teven) 1938-....**CLC 7, 22**
See also BW 1; CA 33-36R; CANR 24; DLB 41

Harper, Mrs. F. E. W.
See Harper, Frances Ellen Watkins

Harris, Christie (Lucy) Irwin 1907- **CLC 12**
See also CA 5-8R; CANR 6; CLR 47; DLB 88; JRDA; MAICYA; SAAS 10; SATA 6, 74

Harris, Frank 1856-1931 .... **TCLC 24**
See also CA 109; 150; DLB 156, 197

Harris, George Washington 1814-1869**NCLC 23**
See also DLB 3, 11

Harris, Joel Chandler 1848-1908 ... **TCLC 2; SSC 19**
See also CA 104; 137; CLR 49; DLB 11, 23, 42, 78, 91; MAICYA; SATA 100; YABC 1

Harris, John (Wyndham Parkes Lucas) Beynon 1903-1969
See Wyndham, John
See also CA 102; 89-92

Harris, MacDonald .... **CLC 9**
See also Heiney, Donald (William)

Harris, Mark 1922- .... **CLC 19**
See also CA 5-8R; CAAS 3; CANR 2, 55; DLB 2; DLBY 80

Harris, (Theodore) Wilson 1921- ..... **CLC 25**
See also BW 2; CA 65-68; CAAS 16; CANR 11, 27, 69; DLB 117; MTCW 1

Harrison, Elizabeth Cavanna 1909-
See Cavanna, Betty
See also CA 9-12R; CANR 6, 27

Harrison, Harry (Max) 1925- .... **CLC 42**
See also CA 1-4R; CANR 5, 21; DLB 8; SATA 4

Harrison, James (Thomas) 1937- **CLC 6, 14, 33, 66; SSC 19**
See also CA 13-16R; CANR 8, 51; DLBY 82; INT CANR-8

Harrison, Jim
See Harrison, James (Thomas)

Harrison, Kathryn 1961- .... **CLC 70**
See also CA 144; CANR 68

Harrison, Tony 1937- .... **CLC 43**
See also CA 65-68; CANR 44; DLB 40; MTCW 1

Harriss, Will(ard Irvin) 1922- .... **CLC 34**
See also CA 111

Harson, Sley
See Ellison, Harlan (Jay)

Hart, Ellis
See Ellison, Harlan (Jay)

Hart, Josephine 1942(?)-**CLC 70; DAM POP**
See also CA 138; CANR 70

Hart, Moss 1904-1961**CLC 66; DAM DRAM**
See also CA 109; 89-92; DLB 7

Harte, (Francis) Bret(t) 1836(?)-1902**TCLC 1, 25; DA; DAC; DAM MST; SSC 8; WLC**
See also CA 104; 140; CDALB 1865-1917; DLB 12, 64, 74, 79, 186; SATA 26

Hartley, L(eslie) P(oles) 1895-1972**CLC 2, 22**
See also CA 45-48; 37-40R; CANR 33; DLB 15, 139; MTCW 1

Hartman, Geoffrey H. 1929- .... **CLC 27**
See also CA 117; 125; DLB 67

Hartmann, Sadakichi 1867-1944 ... **TCLC 73**
See also CA 157; DLB 54

Hartmann von Aue c. 1160-c. 1205**CMLC 15**
See also DLB 138

Hartmann von Aue 1170-1210 ...... **CMLC 15**

Haruf, Kent 1943-............................... **CLC 34**
See also CA 149

Harwood, Ronald 1934-.........**CLC 32; DAM DRAM, MST**
See also CA 1-4R; CANR 4, 55; DLB 13

Hasegawa Tatsunosuke
See Futabatei, Shimei

Hasek, Jaroslav (Matej Frantisek) 1883-1923
TCLC 4
See also CA 104; 129; MTCW 1

Hass, Robert 1941- ... **CLC 18, 39, 99; PC 16**
See also CA 111; CANR 30, 50, 71; DLB 105; SATA 94

Hastings, Hudson
See Kuttner, Henry

Hastings, Selina .... **CLC 44**

Hathorne, John 1641-1717 .... **LC 38**

Hatteras, Amelia
See Mencken, H(enry) L(ouis)

Hatteras, Owen .... **TCLC 18**
See also Mencken, H(enry) L(ouis); Nathan, George Jean

Hauptmann, Gerhart (Johann Robert) 1862-1946 .... **TCLC 4; DAM DRAM**
See also CA 104; 153; DLB 66, 118

Havel, Vaclav 1936- ... **CLC 25, 58, 65; DAM DRAM; DC 6**
See also CA 104; CANR 36, 63; MTCW 1

Haviaras, Stratis .... **CLC 33**
See also Chaviaras, Strates

Hawes, Stephen 1475(?)-1523(?) .... **LC 17**
See also DLB 132

Hawkes, John (Clendennin Burne, Jr.) 1925-1998 .. **CLC 1, 2, 3, 4, 7, 9, 14, 15, 27, 49**
See also CA 1-4R; 167; CANR 2, 47, 64; DLB 2, 7; DLBY 80; MTCW 1

Hawking, S. W.
See Hawking, Stephen W(illiam)

Hawking, Stephen W(illiam) 1942- .**CLC 63, 105**
See also AAYA 13; BEST 89:1; CA 126; 129; CANR 48

Hawkins, Anthony Hope
See Hope, Anthony

Hawthorne, Julian 1846-1934 .... **TCLC 25**
See also CA 165

Hawthorne, Nathaniel 1804-1864 **NCLC 39; DA; DAB; DAC; DAM MST, NOV; SSC 3, 29; WLC**
See also AAYA 18; CDALB 1640-1865; DLB 1, 74; YABC 2

Haxton, Josephine Ayres 1921-
See Douglas, Ellen
See also CA 115; CANR 41

Hayaseca y Eizaguirre, Jorge
See Echegaray (y Eizaguirre), Jose (Maria Waldo)

Hayashi, Fumiko 1904-1951 .... **TCLC 27**
See also CA 161; DLB 180

Haycraft, Anna
See Ellis, Alice Thomas
See also CA 122

Hayden, Robert E(arl) 1913-1980 .**CLC 5, 9, 14, 37; BLC 2; DA; DAC; DAM MST, MULT, POET; PC 6**
See also BW 1; CA 69-72; 97-100; CABS 2; CANR 24; CDALB 1941-1968; DLB 5, 76; MTCW 1; SATA 19; SATA-Obit 26

Hayford, J(oseph) E(phraim) Casely
See Casely-Hayford, J(oseph) E(phraim)

Hayman, Ronald 1932- .... **CLC 44**
See also CA 25-28R; CANR 18, 50; DLB 155

Haywood, Eliza 1693(?)-1756 .... **LC 44**
See also DLB 39

Haywood, Eliza (Fowler) 1693(?)-1756**LC 1, 44**

Hazlitt, William 1778-1830 .... **NCLC 29**
See also DLB 110, 158

Hazzard, Shirley 1931- .... **CLC 18**
See also CA 9-12R; CANR 4, 70; DLBY 82; MTCW 1

Head, Bessie 1937-1986 **CLC 25, 67; BLC 2; DAM MULT**
See also BW 2; CA 29-32R; 119; CANR 25;

Author Index

NCLC 23
See also DLB 39

Lentricchia, Frank (Jr.) 1940- .... **CLC 34**
See also CA 25-28R; CANR 19

Lenz, Siegfried 1926- .... **CLC 27**
See also CA 89-92; DLB 75

Leonard, Elmore (John, Jr.) 1925-**CLC 28, 34, 71; DAM POP**
See also AAYA 22; AITN 1; BEST 89:1, 90:4; CA 81-84; CANR 12, 28, 53; DLB 173; INT CANR-28; MTCW 1

Leonard, Hugh .... **CLC 19**
See also Byrne, John Keyes
See also DLB 13

Leonov, Leonid (Maximovich) 1899-1994
CLC 92; DAM NOV
See also CA 129; MTCW 1

Leopardi, (Conte) Giacomo 1798-1837**NCLC 22**

Le Reveler
See Artaud, Antonin (Marie Joseph)

Lerman, Eleanor 1952- .... **CLC 9**
See also CA 85-88; CANR 69

Lerman, Rhoda 1936- .... **CLC 56**
See also CA 49-52; CANR 70

Lermontov, Mikhail Yuryevich 1814-1841
NCLC 47; PC 18

Leroux, Gaston 1868-1927 .... **TCLC 25**
See also CA 108; 136; CANR 69; SATA 65

Lesage, Alain-Rene 1668-1747 .... **LC 28**

Leskov, Nikolai (Semyonovich) 1831-1895
NCLC 25

Lessing, Doris (May) 1919-**CLC 1, 2, 3, 6, 10, 15, 22, 40, 94; DA; DAB; DAC; DAM MST, NOV; SSC 6; WLCS**
See also CA 9-12R; CAAS 14; CANR 33, 54; CDBLB 1960 to Present; DLB 15, 139; DLBY 85; MTCW 1

Lessing, Gotthold Ephraim 1729-1781 . **LC 8**
See also DLB 97

Lester, Richard 1932- .... **CLC 20**

Lever, Charles (James) 1806-1872 **NCLC 23**
See also DLB 21

Leverson, Ada 1865(?)-1936(?) ...... **TCLC 18**
See also Elaine
See also CA 117; DLB 153

Levertov, Denise 1923-1997**CLC 1, 2, 3, 5, 8, 15, 28, 66; DAM POET; PC 11**
See also CA 1-4R; 163; CAAS 19; CANR 3, 29, 50; DLB 5, 165; INT CANR-29; MTCW 1

Levi, Jonathan .... **CLC 76**

Levi, Peter (Chad Tigar) 1931- .... **CLC 41**
See also CA 5-8R; CANR 34; DLB 40

Levi, Primo 1919-1987 . **CLC 37, 50; SSC 12**
See also CA 13-16R; 122; CANR 12, 33, 61, 70; DLB 177; MTCW 1

Levin, Ira 1929- .... **CLC 3, 6; DAM POP**
See also CA 21-24R; CANR 17, 44; MTCW 1; SATA 66

Levin, Meyer 1905-1981 . **CLC 7; DAM POP**
See also AITN 1; CA 9-12R; 104; CANR 15; DLB 9, 28; DLBY 81; SATA 21; SATA-Obit 27

Levine, Norman 1924- .... **CLC 54**
See also CA 73-76; CAAS 23; CANR 14, 70; DLB 88

Levine, Philip 1928- ... **CLC 2, 4, 5, 9, 14, 33; DAM POET; PC 22**
See also CA 9-12R; CANR 9, 37, 52; DLB 5

Levinson, Deirdre 1931- .... **CLC 49**
See also CA 73-76; CANR 70

Levi-Strauss, Claude 1908- .... **CLC 38**
See also CA 1-4R; CANR 6, 32, 57; MTCW 1

Levitin, Sonia (Wolff) 1934- .... **CLC 17**
See also AAYA 13; CA 29-32R; CANR 14, 32; CLR 53; JRDA; MAICYA; SAAS 2; SATA

4, 68

Levon, O. U.
See Kesey, Ken (Elton)

Levy, Amy 1861-1889 .... **NCLC 59**
See also DLB 156

Lewes, George Henry 1817-1878 ... **NCLC 25**
See also DLB 55, 144

Lewis, Alun 1915-1944 .... **TCLC 3**
See also CA 104; DLB 20, 162

Lewis, C. Day
See Day Lewis, C(ecil)

Lewis, C(live) S(taples) 1898-1963**CLC 1, 3, 6, 14, 27; DA; DAB; DAC; DAM MST, NOV, POP; WLC**
See also AAYA 3; CA 81-84; CANR 33, 71; CDBLB 1945-1960; CLR 3, 27; DLB 15, 100, 160; JRDA; MAICYA; MTCW 1; SATA 13, 100

Lewis, Janet 1899- .... **CLC 41**
See also Winters, Janet Lewis
See also CA 9-12R; CANR 29, 63; CAP 1; DLBY 87

Lewis, Matthew Gregory 1775-1818**NCLC 11, 62**
See also DLB 39, 158, 178

Lewis, (Harry) Sinclair 1885-1951 . **TCLC 4, 13, 23, 39; DA; DAB; DAC; DAM MST, NOV; WLC**
See also CA 104; 133; CDALB 1917-1929; DLB 9, 102; DLBD 1; MTCW 1

Lewis, (Percy) Wyndham 1882(?)-1957**TCLC 2, 9**
See also CA 104; 157; DLB 15

Lewisohn, Ludwig 1883-1955 .... **TCLC 19**
See also CA 107; DLB 4, 9, 28, 102

Lewton, Val 1904-1951 .... **TCLC 76**

Leyner, Mark 1956- .... **CLC 92**
See also CA 110; CANR 28, 53

Lezama Lima, Jose 1910-1976**CLC 4, 10, 101; DAM MULT**
See also CA 77-80; CANR 71; DLB 113; HW

L'Heureux, John (Clarke) 1934- .... **CLC 52**
See also CA 13-16R; CANR 23, 45

Liddell, C. H.
See Kuttner, Henry

Lie, Jonas (Lauritz Idemil) 1833-1908(?)
TCLC 5
See also CA 115

Lieber, Joel 1937-1971 .... **CLC 6**
See also CA 73-76; 29-32R

Lieber, Stanley Martin
See Lee, Stan

Lieberman, Laurence (James) 1935- **CLC 4, 36**
See also CA 17-20R; CANR 8, 36

Lieh Tzu fl. 7th cent. B.C.-5th cent. B.C.
CMLC 27

Lieksman, Anders
See Haavikko, Paavo Juhani

Li Fei-kan 1904-
See Pa Chin
See also CA 105

Lifton, Robert Jay 1926- .... **CLC 67**
See also CA 17-20R; CANR 27; INT CANR-27; SATA 66

Lightfoot, Gordon 1938- .... **CLC 26**
See also CA 109

Lightman, Alan P(aige) 1948- .... **CLC 81**
See also CA 141; CANR 63

Ligotti, Thomas (Robert) 1953-**CLC 44; SSC 16**
See also CA 123; CANR 49

Li Ho 791-817 .... **PC 13**

Liliencron, (Friedrich Adolf Axel) Detlev von 1844-1909 .... **TCLC 18**
See also CA 117

Lilly, William 1602-1681 .... **LC 27**

Lima, Jose Lezama
See Lezama Lima, Jose

Lima Barreto, Afonso Henrique de 1881-1922
TCLC 23
See also CA 117

Limonov, Edward 1944- .... **CLC 67**
See also CA 137

Lin, Frank
See Atherton, Gertrude (Franklin Horn)

Lincoln, Abraham 1809-1865 .... **NCLC 18**

Lind, Jakov .... **CLC 1, 2, 4, 27, 82**
See also Landwirth, Heinz
See also CAAS 4

Lindbergh, Anne (Spencer) Morrow 1906-
CLC 82; DAM NOV
See also CA 17-20R; CANR 16; MTCW 1; SATA 33

Lindsay, David 1878-1945 .... **TCLC 15**
See also CA 113

Lindsay, (Nicholas) Vachel 1879-1931 **TCLC 17; DA; DAC; DAM MST, POET; PC 23; WLC**
See also CA 114; 135; CDALB 1865-1917; DLB 54; SATA 40

Linke-Poot
See Doeblin, Alfred

Linney, Romulus 1930- .... **CLC 51**
See also CA 1-4R; CANR 40, 44

Linton, Eliza Lynn 1822-1898 .... **NCLC 41**
See also DLB 18

Li Po 701-763 .... **CMLC 2**

Lipsius, Justus 1547-1606 .... **LC 16**

Lipsyte, Robert (Michael) 1938-**CLC 21; DA; DAC; DAM MST, NOV**
See also AAYA 7; CA 17-20R; CANR 8, 57; CLR 23; JRDA; MAICYA; SATA 5, 68

Lish, Gordon (Jay) 1934- .. **CLC 45; SSC 18**
See also CA 113; 117; DLB 130; INT 117

Lispector, Clarice 1925(?)-1977 .... **CLC 43**
See also CA 139; 116; CANR 71; DLB 113

Littell, Robert 1935(?)- .... **CLC 42**
See also CA 109; 112; CANR 64

Little, Malcolm 1925-1965
See Malcolm X
See also BW 1; CA 125; 111; DA; DAB; DAC; DAM MST, MULT; MTCW 1

Littlewit, Humphrey Gent.
See Lovecraft, H(oward) P(hillips)

Litwos
See Sienkiewicz, Henryk (Adam Alexander Pius)

Liu, E 1857-1909 .... **TCLC 15**
See also CA 115

Lively, Penelope (Margaret) 1933- .. **CLC 32, 50; DAM NOV**
See also CA 41-44R; CANR 29, 67; CLR 7; DLB 14, 161; JRDA; MAICYA; MTCW 1; SATA 7, 60, 101

Livesay, Dorothy (Kathleen) 1909-**CLC 4, 15, 79; DAC; DAM MST, POET**
See also AITN 2; CA 25-28R; CAAS 8; CANR 36, 67; DLB 68; MTCW 1

Livy c. 59B.C.-c. 17 .... **CMLC 11**

Lizardi, Jose Joaquin Fernandez de 1776-1827
NCLC 30

Llewellyn, Richard
See Llewellyn Lloyd, Richard Dafydd Vivian
See also DLB 15

Llewellyn Lloyd, Richard Dafydd Vivian 1906-
1983 ....
CLC 7, 80
See also Llewellyn, Richard
See also CA 53-56; 111; CANR 7, 71; SATA 11; SATA-Obit 37

Llosa, (Jorge) Mario (Pedro) Vargas
See Vargas Llosa, (Jorge) Mario (Pedro)

Lloyd, Manda

See Heinlein, Robert A(nson)
Macdonald, Cynthia 1928- .... **CLC 13, 19**
See also CA 49-52; CANR 4, 44; DLB 105
MacDonald, George 1824-1905 .... **TCLC 9**
See also CA 106; 137; DLB 18, 163, 178;
MAICYA; SATA 33, 100
Macdonald, John
See Millar, Kenneth
MacDonald, John D(ann) 1916-1986 **CLC 3,
27, 44; DAM NOV, POP**
See also CA 1-4R; 121; CANR 1, 19, 60; DLB
8; DLBY 86; MTCW 1
Macdonald, John Ross
See Millar, Kenneth
Macdonald, Ross .... **CLC 1, 2, 3, 14, 34, 41**
See also Millar, Kenneth
See also DLBD 6
MacDougal, John
See Blish, James (Benjamin)
MacEwen, Gwendolyn (Margaret) 1941-1987
CLC 13, 55
See also CA 9-12R; 124; CANR 7, 22; DLB
53; SATA 50; SATA-Obit 55
Macha, Karel Hynek 1810-1846 .... **NCLC 46**
Machado (y Ruiz), Antonio 1875-1939 **T C L C
3**
See also CA 104; DLB 108
Machado de Assis, Joaquim Maria 1839-1908
TCLC 10; BLC 2; SSC 24
See also CA 107; 153
Machen, Arthur .... **TCLC 4; SSC 20**
See also Jones, Arthur Llewellyn
See also DLB 36, 156, 178
Machiavelli, Niccolo 1469-1527 **LC 8, 36; DA;
DAB; DAC; DAM MST; WLCS**
MacInnes, Colin 1914-1976 .... **CLC 4, 23**
See also CA 69-72; 65-68; CANR 21; DLB 14;
MTCW 1
MacInnes, Helen (Clark) 1907-1985 **CLC 27,
39; DAM POP**
See also CA 1-4R; 117; CANR 1, 28, 58; DLB
87; MTCW 1; SATA 22; SATA-Obit 44
Mackay, Mary 1855-1924
See Corelli, Marie
See also CA 118
Mackenzie, Compton (Edward Montague)
1883-1972 .... **CLC 18**
See also CA 21-22; 37-40R; CAP 2; DLB 34,
100
Mackenzie, Henry 1745-1831 .... **NCLC 41**
See also DLB 39
Mackintosh, Elizabeth 1896(?)-1952
See Tey, Josephine
See also CA 110
MacLaren, James
See Grieve, C(hristopher) M(urray)
Mac Laverty, Bernard 1942- .... **CLC 31**
See also CA 116; 118; CANR 43; INT 118
MacLean, Alistair (Stuart) 1922(?)-1987 **C L C
3, 13, 50, 63; DAM POP**
See also CA 57-60; 121; CANR 28, 61; MTCW
1; SATA 23; SATA-Obit 50
Maclean, Norman (Fitzroy) 1902-1990 **C L C
78; DAM POP; SSC 13**
See also CA 102; 132; CANR 49
MacLeish, Archibald 1892-1982 **CLC 3, 8, 14,
68; DAM POET**
See also CA 9-12R; 106; CANR 33, 63; DLB
4, 7, 45; DLBY 82; MTCW 1
MacLennan, (John) Hugh 1907-1990 **CLC 2,
14, 92; DAC; DAM MST**
See also CA 5-8R; 142; CANR 33; DLB 68;
MTCW 1
MacLeod, Alistair 1936- **CLC 56; DAC; DAM
MST**
See also CA 123; DLB 60
Macleod, Fiona

See Sharp, William
MacNeice, (Frederick) Louis 1907-1963 **C L C
1, 4, 10, 53; DAB; DAM POET**
See also CA 85-88; CANR 61; DLB 10, 20;
MTCW 1
MacNeill, Dand
See Fraser, George MacDonald
Macpherson, James 1736-1796 .... **LC 29**
See also Ossian
See also DLB 109
Macpherson, (Jean) Jay 1931- .... **CLC 14**
See also CA 5-8R; DLB 53
MacShane, Frank 1927- .... **CLC 39**
See also CA 9-12R; CANR 3, 33; DLB 111
Macumber, Mari
See Sandoz, Mari(e Susette)
Madach, Imre 1823-1864 .... **NCLC 19**
Madden, (Jerry) David 1933- .... **CLC 5, 15**
See also CA 1-4R; CAAS 3; CANR 4, 45; DLB
6; MTCW 1
Maddern, Al(an)
See Ellison, Harlan (Jay)
Madhubuti, Haki R. 1942- **CLC 6, 73; BLC 2;
DAM MULT, POET; PC 5**
See also Lee, Don L.
See also BW 2; CA 73-76; CANR 24, 51; DLB
5, 41; DLBD 8
Maepenn, Hugh
See Kuttner, Henry
Maepenn, K. H.
See Kuttner, Henry
Maeterlinck, Maurice 1862-1949 ... **TCLC 3;
DAM DRAM**
See also CA 104; 136; DLB 192; SATA 66
Maginn, William 1794-1842 .... **NCLC 8**
See also DLB 110, 159
Mahapatra, Jayanta 1928- .... **CLC 33; DAM
MULT**
See also CA 73-76; CAAS 9; CANR 15, 33, 66
Mahfouz, Naguib (Abdel Aziz Al-Sabilgi)
1911(?)-
See Mahfuz, Najib
See also BEST 89:2; CA 128; CANR 55; DAM
NOV; MTCW 1
Mahfuz, Najib .... **CLC 52, 55**
See also Mahfouz, Naguib (Abdel Aziz Al-
Sabilgi)
See also DLBY 88
Mahon, Derek 1941- .... **CLC 27**
See also CA 113; 128; DLB 40
Mailer, Norman 1923- **CLC 1, 2, 3, 4, 5, 8, 11,
14, 28, 39, 74, 111; DA; DAB; DAC; DAM
MST, NOV, POP**
See also AITN 2; CA 9-12R; CABS 1; CANR
28; CDALB 1968-1988; DLB 2, 16, 28, 185;
DLBD 3; DLBY 80, 83; MTCW 1
Maillet, Antonine 1929- .... **CLC 54; DAC**
See also CA 115; 120; CANR 46; DLB 60; INT
120
Mais, Roger 1905-1955 .... **TCLC 8**
See also BW 1; CA 105; 124; DLB 125; MTCW
1
Maistre, Joseph de 1753-1821 .... **NCLC 37**
Maitland, Frederic 1850-1906 .... **TCLC 65**
Maitland, Sara (Louise) 1950- .... **CLC 49**
See also CA 69-72; CANR 13, 59
Major, Clarence 1936- **CLC 3, 19, 48; BLC 2;
DAM MULT**
See also BW 2; CA 21-24R; CAAS 6; CANR
13, 25, 53; DLB 33
Major, Kevin (Gerald) 1949- .. **CLC 26; DAC**
See also AAYA 16; CA 97-100; CANR 21, 38;
CLR 11; DLB 60; INT CANR-21; JRDA;
MAICYA; SATA 32, 82
Maki, James
See Ozu, Yasujiro
Malabaila, Damiano

See Levi, Primo
Malamud, Bernard 1914-1986 **CLC 1, 2, 3, 5,
8, 9, 11, 18, 27, 44, 78, 85; DA; DAB; DAC;
DAM MST, NOV, POP; SSC 15; WLC**
See also AAYA 16; CA 5-8R; 118; CABS 1;
CANR 28, 62; CDALB 1941-1968; DLB 2,
28, 152; DLBY 80, 86; MTCW 1
Malan, Herman
See Bosman, Herman Charles; Bosman, Herman
Charles
Malaparte, Curzio 1898-1957 .... **TCLC 52**
Malcolm, Dan
See Silverberg, Robert
Malcolm X .... **CLC 82; BLC 2; WLCS**
See also Little, Malcolm
Malherbe, Francois de 1555-1628 .... **LC 5**
Mallarme, Stephane 1842-1898 **NCLC 4, 41;
DAM POET; PC 4**
Mallet-Joris, Francoise 1930- .... **CLC 11**
See also CA 65-68; CANR 17; DLB 83
Malley, Ern
See McAuley, James Phillip
Mallowan, Agatha Christie
See Christie, Agatha (Mary Clarissa)
Maloff, Saul 1922- .... **CLC 5**
See also CA 33-36R
Malone, Louis
See MacNeice, (Frederick) Louis
Malone, Michael (Christopher) 1942- **CLC 43**
See also CA 77-80; CANR 14, 32, 57
Malory, (Sir) Thomas 1410(?)-1471(?) **LC 11;
DA; DAB; DAC; DAM MST; WLCS**
See also CDBLB Before 1660; DLB 146; SATA
59; SATA-Brief 33
Malouf, (George Joseph) David 1934- **CLC 28,
86**
See also CA 124; CANR 50
Malraux, (Georges-)Andre 1901-1976 **CLC 1,
4, 9, 13, 15, 57; DAM NOV**
See also CA 21-22; 69-72; CANR 34, 58; CAP
2; DLB 72; MTCW 1
Malzberg, Barry N(athaniel) 1939- ... **CLC 7**
See also CA 61-64; CAAS 4; CANR 16; DLB
8
Mamet, David (Alan) 1947- **CLC 9, 15, 34, 46,
91; DAM DRAM; DC 4**
See also AAYA 3; CA 81-84; CABS 3; CANR
15, 41, 67, 72; DLB 7; MTCW 1
Mamoulian, Rouben (Zachary) 1897-1987
CLC 16
See also CA 25-28R; 124
Mandelstam, Osip (Emilievich) 1891(?)-1938(?)
TCLC 2, 6; PC 14
See also CA 104; 150
Mander, (Mary) Jane 1877-1949 ... **TCLC 31**
See also CA 162
Mandeville, John fl. 1350- .... **CMLC 19**
See also DLB 146
Mandiargues, Andre Pieyre de .... **CLC 41**
See also Pieyre de Mandiargues, Andre
See also DLB 83
Mandrake, Ethel Belle
See Thurman, Wallace (Henry)
Mangan, James Clarence 1803-1849 **NCLC 27**
Maniere, J.-E.
See Giraudoux, (Hippolyte) Jean
Mankiewicz, Herman (Jacob) 1897-1953
TCLC 85
See also CA 120; DLB 26
Manley, (Mary) Delariviere 1672(?)-1724 **L C
1**
See also DLB 39, 80
Mann, Abel
See Creasey, John
Mann, Emily 1952- .... **DC 7**
See also CA 130; CANR 55
Mann, (Luiz) Heinrich 1871-1950 ... **TCLC 9**

CANR 21, 50; DLB 6, 173; MTCW 1; SATA 27

Maturin, Charles Robert 1780(?)-1824**NCLC 6**
See also DLB 178

Matute (Ausejo), Ana Maria 1925- .. **CLC 11**
See also CA 89-92; MTCW 1

Maugham, W. S.
See Maugham, W(illiam) Somerset

Maugham, W(illiam) Somerset 1874-1965
CLC 1, 11, 15, 67, 93; DA; DAB; DAC; DAM DRAM, MST, NOV; SSC 8; WLC
See also CA 5-8R; 25-28R; CANR 40; CDBLB 1914-1945; DLB 10, 36, 77, 100, 162, 195; MTCW 1; SATA 54

Maugham, William Somerset
See Maugham, W(illiam) Somerset

Maupassant, (Henri Rene Albert) Guy de 1850-1893 ....
NCLC 1, 42; DA; DAB; DAC; DAM MST; SSC 1; WLC
See also DLB 123

Maupin, Armistead 1944-**CLC 95; DAM POP**
See also CA 125; 130; CANR 58; INT 130

Maurhut, Richard
See Traven, B.

Mauriac, Claude 1914-1996 .... **CLC 9**
See also CA 89-92; 152; DLB 83

Mauriac, Francois (Charles) 1885-1970 **C L C 4, 9, 56; SSC 24**
See also CA 25-28; CAP 2; DLB 65; MTCW 1

Mavor, Osborne Henry 1888-1951
See Bridie, James
See also CA 104

Maxwell, William (Keepers, Jr.) 1908-**CLC 19**
See also CA 93-96; CANR 54; DLBY 80; INT 93-96

May, Elaine 1932- .... **CLC 16**
See also CA 124; 142; DLB 44

Mayakovski, Vladimir (Vladimirovich) 1893-1930 .... **TCLC 4, 18**
See also CA 104; 158

Mayhew, Henry 1812-1887 .... **NCLC 31**
See also DLB 18, 55, 190

Mayle, Peter 1939(?)- .... **CLC 89**
See also CA 139; CANR 64

Maynard, Joyce 1953- .... **CLC 23**
See also CA 111; 129; CANR 64

Mayne, William (James Carter) 1928-**CLC 12**
See also AAYA 20; CA 9-12R; CANR 37; CLR 25; JRDA; MAICYA; SAAS 11; SATA 6, 68

Mayo, Jim
See L'Amour, Louis (Dearborn)

Maysles, Albert 1926- .... **CLC 16**
See also CA 29-32R

Maysles, David 1932- .... **CLC 16**

Mazer, Norma Fox 1931- .... **CLC 26**
See also AAYA 5; CA 69-72; CANR 12, 32, 66; CLR 23; JRDA; MAICYA; SAAS 1; SATA 24, 67

Mazzini, Guiseppe 1805-1872 .... **NCLC 34**

McAuley, James Phillip 1917-1976 .. **CLC 45**
See also CA 97-100

McBain, Ed
See Hunter, Evan

McBrien, William Augustine 1930- .. **CLC 44**
See also CA 107

McCaffrey, Anne (Inez) 1926-**CLC 17; DAM NOV, POP**
See also AAYA 6; AITN 2; BEST 89:2; CA 25-28R; CANR 15, 35, 55; CLR 49; DLB 8; JRDA; MAICYA; MTCW 1; SAAS 11; SATA 8, 70

McCall, Nathan 1955(?)-.................... **CLC 86**
See also CA 146

McCann, Arthur
See Campbell, John W(ood, Jr.)

McCann, Edson
See Pohl, Frederik

McCarthy, Charles, Jr. 1933-
See McCarthy, Cormac
See also CANR 42, 69; DAM POP

McCarthy, Cormac 1933- **CLC 4, 57, 59, 101**
See also McCarthy, Charles, Jr.
See also DLB 6, 143

McCarthy, Mary (Therese) 1912-1989**CLC 1, 3, 5, 14, 24, 39, 59; SSC 24**
See also CA 5-8R; 129; CANR 16, 50, 64; DLB 2; DLBY 81; INT CANR-16; MTCW 1

McCartney, (James) Paul 1942- **CLC 12, 35**
See also CA 146

McCauley, Stephen (D.) 1955- .... **CLC 50**
See also CA 141

McClure, Michael (Thomas) 1932-**CLC 6, 10**
See also CA 21-24R; CANR 17, 46; DLB 16

McCorkle, Jill (Collins) 1958-........... **CLC 51**
See also CA 121; DLBY 87

McCourt, Frank 1930- .... **CLC 109**
See also CA 157

McCourt, James 1941- .... **CLC 5**
See also CA 57-60

McCoy, Horace (Stanley) 1897-1955**TCLC 28**
See also CA 108; 155; DLB 9

McCrae, John 1872-1918 .... **TCLC 12**
See also CA 109; DLB 92

McCreigh, James
See Pohl, Frederik

McCullers, (Lula) Carson (Smith) 1917-1967
CLC 1, 4, 10, 12, 48, 100; DA; DAB; DAC; DAM MST, NOV; SSC 9, 24; WLC
See also AAYA 21; CA 5-8R; 25-28R; CABS 1, 3; CANR 18; CDALB 1941-1968; DLB 2, 7, 173; MTCW 1; SATA 27

McCulloch, John Tyler
See Burroughs, Edgar Rice

McCullough, Colleen 1938(?)- **CLC 27, 107; DAM NOV, POP**
See also CA 81-84; CANR 17, 46, 67; MTCW 1

McDermott, Alice 1953- .... **CLC 90**
See also CA 109; CANR 40

McElroy, Joseph 1930- .... **CLC 5, 47**
See also CA 17-20R

McEwan, Ian (Russell) 1948- .... **CLC 13, 66; DAM NOV**
See also BEST 90:4; CA 61-64; CANR 14, 41, 69; DLB 14, 194; MTCW 1

McFadden, David 1940- .... **CLC 48**
See also CA 104; DLB 60; INT 104

McFarland, Dennis 1950- .... **CLC 65**
See also CA 165

McGahern, John 1934-**CLC 5, 9, 48; SSC 17**
See also CA 17-20R; CANR 29, 68; DLB 14; MTCW 1

McGinley, Patrick (Anthony) 1937- . **CLC 41**
See also CA 120; 127; CANR 56; INT 127

McGinley, Phyllis 1905-1978 .... **CLC 14**
See also CA 9-12R; 77-80; CANR 19; DLB 11, 48; SATA 2, 44; SATA-Obit 24

McGinniss, Joe 1942- .... **CLC 32**
See also AITN 2; BEST 89:2; CA 25-28R; CANR 26, 70; DLB 185; INT CANR-26

McGivern, Maureen Daly
See Daly, Maureen

McGrath, Patrick 1950- .... **CLC 55**
See also CA 136; CANR 65

McGrath, Thomas (Matthew) 1916-1990**CLC 28, 59; DAM POET**
See also CA 9-12R; 132; CANR 6, 33; MTCW 1; SATA 41; SATA-Obit 66

McGuane, Thomas (Francis III) 1939-**CLC 3, 7, 18, 45**
See also AITN 2; CA 49-52; CANR 5, 24, 49; DLB 2; DLBY 80; INT CANR-24; MTCW 1

McGuckian, Medbh 1950- ..... **CLC 48; DAM POET**
See also CA 143; DLB 40

McHale, Tom 1942(?)-1982 .... **CLC 3, 5**
See also AITN 1; CA 77-80; 106

McIlvanney, William 1936- .... **CLC 42**
See also CA 25-28R; CANR 61; DLB 14

McIlwraith, Maureen Mollie Hunter
See Hunter, Mollie
See also SATA 2

McInerney, Jay 1955-**CLC 34, 112; DAM POP**
See also AAYA 18; CA 116; 123; CANR 45, 68; INT 123

McIntyre, Vonda N(eel) 1948- .... **CLC 18**
See also CA 81-84; CANR 17, 34, 69; MTCW 1

McKay, Claude**TCLC 7, 41; BLC 3; DAB; PC 2**
See also McKay, Festus Claudius
See also DLB 4, 45, 51, 117

McKay, Festus Claudius 1889-1948
See McKay, Claude
See also BW 1; CA 104; 124; DA; DAC; DAM MST, MULT, NOV, POET; MTCW 1; WLC

McKuen, Rod 1933- .... **CLC 1, 3**
See also AITN 1; CA 41-44R; CANR 40

McLoughlin, R. B.
See Mencken, H(enry) L(ouis)

McLuhan, (Herbert) Marshall 1911-1980
CLC 37, 83
See also CA 9-12R; 102; CANR 12, 34, 61; DLB 88; INT CANR-12; MTCW 1

McMillan, Terry (L.) 1951- **CLC 50, 61, 112; BLCS; DAM MULT, NOV, POP**
See also AAYA 21; BW 2; CA 140; CANR 60

McMurtry, Larry (Jeff) 1936-**CLC 2, 3, 7, 11, 27, 44; DAM NOV, POP**
See also AAYA 15; AITN 2; BEST 89:2; CA 5-8R; CANR 19, 43, 64; CDALB 1968-1988; DLB 2, 143; DLBY 80, 87; MTCW 1

McNally, T. M. 1961- .... **CLC 82**

McNally, Terrence 1939-.... **CLC 4, 7, 41, 91; DAM DRAM**
See also CA 45-48; CANR 2, 56; DLB 7

McNamer, Deirdre 1950- .... **CLC 70**

McNeile, Herman Cyril 1888-1937
See Sapper
See also DLB 77

McNickle, (William) D'Arcy 1904-1977 **C L C 89; DAM MULT**
See also CA 9-12R; 85-88; CANR 5, 45; DLB 175; NNAL; SATA-Obit 22

McPhee, John (Angus) 1931- .... **CLC 36**
See also BEST 90:1; CA 65-68; CANR 20, 46, 64, 69; DLB 185; MTCW 1

McPherson, James Alan 1943-.. **CLC 19, 77; BLCS**
See also BW 1; CA 25-28R; CAAS 17; CANR 24; DLB 38; MTCW 1

McPherson, William (Alexander) 1933-**C L C 34**
See also CA 69-72; CANR 28; INT CANR-28

Mead, Margaret 1901-1978 .... **CLC 37**
See also AITN 1; CA 1-4R; 81-84; CANR 4; MTCW 1; SATA-Obit 20

Meaker, Marijane (Agnes) 1927-
See Kerr, M. E.
See also CA 107; CANR 37, 63; INT 107; JRDA; MAICYA; MTCW 1; SATA 20, 61, 99

Medoff, Mark (Howard) 1940- ... **CLC 6, 23; DAM DRAM**
See also AITN 1; CA 53-56; CANR 5; DLB 7; INT CANR-5

Medvedev, P. N.
See Bakhtin, Mikhail Mikhailovich

Meged, Aharon
See Megged, Aharon
Meged, Aron
See Megged, Aharon
Megged, Aharon 1920- .... **CLC 9**
See also CA 49-52; CAAS 13; CANR 1
Mehta, Ved (Parkash) 1934- .... **CLC 37**
See also CA 1-4R; CANR 2, 23, 69; MTCW 1
Melanter
See Blackmore, R(ichard) D(oddridge)
Melies, Georges 1861-1938 .... **TCLC 81**
Melikow, Loris
See Hofmannsthal, Hugo von
Melmoth, Sebastian
See Wilde, Oscar (Fingal O'Flahertie Wills)
Meltzer, Milton 1915- .... **CLC 26**
See also AAYA 8; CA 13-16R; CANR 38; CLR
13; DLB 61; JRDA; MAICYA; SAAS 1;
SATA 1, 50, 80
Melville, Herman 1819-1891NCLC 3, 12, 29,
45, 49; DA; DAB; DAC; DAM MST, NOV;
SSC 1, 17; WLC
See also AAYA 25; CDALB 1640-1865; DLB
3, 74; SATA 59
Menander c. 342B.C.-c. 292B.C. ..... **CMLC 9;
DAM DRAM; DC 3**
See also DLB 176
Mencken, H(enry) L(ouis) 1880-1956 **TCLC
13**
See also CA 105; 125; CDALB 1917-1929;
DLB 11, 29, 63, 137; MTCW 1
Mendelsohn, Jane 1965(?)- .... **CLC 99**
See also CA 154
Mercer, David 1928-1980CLC 5; DAM DRAM
See also CA 9-12R; 102; CANR 23; DLB 13;
MTCW 1
Merchant, Paul
See Ellison, Harlan (Jay)
Meredith, George 1828-1909 . **TCLC 17, 43;
DAM POET**
See also CA 117; 153; CDBLB 1832-1890;
DLB 18, 35, 57, 159
Meredith, William (Morris) 1919-CLC 4, 13,
22, 55; DAM POET
See also CA 9-12R; CAAS 14; CANR 6, 40;
DLB 5
Merezhkovsky, Dmitry Sergeyevich 1865-1941
TCLC 29
Merimee, Prosper 1803-1870NCLC 6, 65; SSC
7
See also DLB 119, 192
Merkin, Daphne 1954- .... **CLC 44**
See also CA 123
Merlin, Arthur
See Blish, James (Benjamin)
Merrill, James (Ingram) 1926-1995CLC 2, 3,
6, 8, 13, 18, 34, 91; DAM POET
See also CA 13-16R; 147; CANR 10, 49, 63;
DLB 5, 165; DLBY 85; INT CANR-10;
MTCW 1
Merriman, Alex
See Silverberg, Robert
Merriman, Brian 1747-1805 .... **NCLC 70**
Merritt, E. B.
See Waddington, Miriam
Merton, Thomas 1915-1968 CLC 1, 3, 11, 34,
83; PC 10
See also CA 5-8R; 25-28R; CANR 22, 53; DLB
48; DLBY 81; MTCW 1
Merwin, W(illiam) S(tanley) 1927- CLC 1, 2,
3, 5, 8, 13, 18, 45, 88; DAM POET
See also CA 13-16R; CANR 15, 51; DLB 5,
169; INT CANR-15; MTCW 1
Metcalf, John 1938- .... **CLC 37**
See also CA 113; DLB 60
Metcalf, Suzanne
See Baum, L(yman) Frank

Mew, Charlotte (Mary) 1870-1928 .. **TCLC 8**
See also CA 105; DLB 19, 135
Mewshaw, Michael 1943- .... **CLC 9**
See also CA 53-56; CANR 7, 47; DLBY 80
Meyer, June
See Jordan, June
Meyer, Lynn
See Slavitt, David R(ytman)
Meyer-Meyrink, Gustav 1868-1932
See Meyrink, Gustav
See also CA 117
Meyers, Jeffrey 1939- .... **CLC 39**
See also CA 73-76; CANR 54; DLB 111
Meynell, Alice (Christina Gertrude Thompson)
1847-1922 .... **TCLC 6**
See also CA 104; DLB 19, 98
Meyrink, Gustav .... **TCLC 21**
See also Meyer-Meyrink, Gustav
See also DLB 81
Michaels, Leonard 1933- CLC 6, 25; SSC 16
See also CA 61-64; CANR 21, 62; DLB 130;
MTCW 1
Michaux, Henri 1899-1984 .... **CLC 8, 19**
See also CA 85-88; 114
Micheaux, Oscar 1884-1951 .... **TCLC 76**
See also DLB 50
Michelangelo 1475-1564 .... **LC 12**
Michelet, Jules 1798-1874 .... **NCLC 31**
Michener, James A(lbert) 1907(?)-1997 **C L C
1, 5, 11, 29, 60, 109; DAM NOV, POP**
See also AAYA 27; AITN 1; BEST 90:1; CA 5-
8R; 161; CANR 21, 45, 68; DLB 6; MTCW
1
Mickiewicz, Adam 1798-1855 .... **NCLC 3**
Middleton, Christopher 1926- .... **CLC 13**
See also CA 13-16R; CANR 29, 54; DLB 40
Middleton, Richard (Barham) 1882-1911
TCLC 56
See also DLB 156
Middleton, Stanley 1919- .... **CLC 7, 38**
See also CA 25-28R; CAAS 23; CANR 21, 46;
DLB 14
Middleton, Thomas 1580-1627 **LC 33; DAM
DRAM, MST; DC 5**
See also DLB 58
Migueis, Jose Rodrigues 1901- .... **CLC 10**
Mikszath, Kalman 1847-1910 .... **TCLC 31**
Miles, Jack .... **CLC 100**
Miles, Josephine (Louise) 1911-1985CLC 1, 2,
14, 34, 39; DAM POET
See also CA 1-4R; 116; CANR 2, 55; DLB 48
Militant
See Sandburg, Carl (August)
Mill, John Stuart 1806-1873 .... **NCLC 11, 58**
See also CDBLB 1832-1890; DLB 55, 190
Millar, Kenneth 1915-1983 .... **CLC 14; DAM
POP**
See also Macdonald, Ross
See also CA 9-12R; 110; CANR 16, 63; DLB
2; DLBD 6; DLBY 83; MTCW 1
Millay, E. Vincent
See Millay, Edna St. Vincent
Millay, Edna St. Vincent 1892-1950TCLC 4,
49; DA; DAB; DAC; DAM MST, POET;
PC 6; WLCS
See also CA 104; 130; CDALB 1917-1929;
DLB 45; MTCW 1
Miller, Arthur 1915-CLC 1, 2, 6, 10, 15, 26, 47,
78; DA; DAB; DAC; DAM DRAM, MST;
DC 1; WLC
See also AAYA 15; AITN 1; CA 1-4R; CABS
3; CANR 2, 30, 54; CDALB 1941-1968;
DLB 7; MTCW 1
Miller, Henry (Valentine) 1891-1980CLC 1, 2,
4, 9, 14, 43, 84; DA; DAB; DAC; DAM
MST, NOV; WLC
See also CA 9-12R; 97-100; CANR 33, 64;

CDALB 1929-1941; DLB 4, 9; DLBY 80;
MTCW 1
Miller, Jason 1939(?)- .... **CLC 2**
See also AITN 1; CA 73-76; DLB 7
Miller, Sue 1943- .... **CLC 44; DAM POP**
See also BEST 90:3; CA 139; CANR 59; DLB
143
Miller, Walter M(ichael, Jr.) 1923-CLC 4, 30
See also CA 85-88; DLB 8
Millett, Kate 1934- .... **CLC 67**
See also AITN 1; CA 73-76; CANR 32, 53;
MTCW 1
Millhauser, Steven (Lewis) 1943-CLC 21, 54,
109
See also CA 110; 111; CANR 63; DLB 2; INT
111
Millin, Sarah Gertrude 1889-1968 ... **CLC 49**
See also CA 102; 93-96
Milne, A(lan) A(lexander) 1882-1956TCLC 6;
DAB; DAC; DAM MST
See also CA 104; 133; CLR 1, 26; DLB 10, 77,
100, 160; MAICYA; MTCW 1; SATA 100;
YABC 1
Milner, Ron(ald) 1938-CLC 56; BLC 3; DAM
MULT
See also AITN 1; BW 1; CA 73-76; CANR 24;
DLB 38; MTCW 1
Milnes, Richard Monckton 1809-1885N C L C
61
See also DLB 32, 184
Milosz, Czeslaw 1911- CLC 5, 11, 22, 31, 56,
82; DAM MST, POET; PC 8; WLCS
See also CA 81-84; CANR 23, 51; MTCW 1
Milton, John 1608-1674 LC 9, 43; DA; DAB;
DAC; DAM MST, POET; PC 19; WLC
See also CDBLB 1660-1789; DLB 131, 151
Min, Anchee 1957- .... **CLC 86**
See also CA 146
Minehaha, Cornelius
See Wedekind, (Benjamin) Frank(lin)
Miner, Valerie 1947- .... **CLC 40**
See also CA 97-100; CANR 59
Minimo, Duca
See D'Annunzio, Gabriele
Minot, Susan 1956- .... **CLC 44**
See also CA 134
Minus, Ed 1938- .... **CLC 39**
Miranda, Javier
See Bioy Casares, Adolfo
Mirbeau, Octave 1848-1917 .... **TCLC 55**
See also DLB 123, 192
Miro (Ferrer), Gabriel (Francisco Victor) 1879-
1930 ....
TCLC 5
See also CA 104
Mishima, Yukio 1925-1970CLC 2, 4, 6, 9, 27;
DC 1; SSC 4
See also Hiraoka, Kimitake
See also DLB 182
Mistral, Frederic 1830-1914 .... **TCLC 51**
See also CA 122
Mistral, Gabriela .... **TCLC 2; HLC**
See also Godoy Alcayaga, Lucila
Mistry, Rohinton 1952- .... **CLC 71; DAC**
See also CA 141
Mitchell, Clyde
See Ellison, Harlan (Jay); Silverberg, Robert
Mitchell, James Leslie 1901-1935
See Gibbon, Lewis Grassic
See also CA 104; DLB 15
Mitchell, Joni 1943- .... **CLC 12**
See also CA 112
Mitchell, Joseph (Quincy) 1908-1996CLC 98
See also CA 77-80; 152; CANR 69; DLB 185;
DLBY 96
Mitchell, Margaret (Munnerlyn) 1900-1949
TCLC 11; DAM NOV, POP

Author Index

13, 33
See also CA 85-88; DLB 40
Porter, William Sydney 1862-1910
See Henry, O.
See also CA 104; 131; CDALB 1865-1917; DA;
DAB; DAC; DAM MST; DLB 12, 78, 79;
MTCW 1; YABC 2
Portillo (y Pacheco), Jose Lopez
See Lopez Portillo (y Pacheco), Jose
Post, Melville Davisson 1869-1930 **TCLC 39**
See also CA 110
Potok, Chaim 1929- ... **CLC 2, 7, 14, 26, 112;
DAM NOV**
See also AAYA 15; AITN 1, 2; CA 17-20R;
CANR 19, 35, 64; DLB 28, 152; INT CANR-
19; MTCW 1; SATA 33
Potter, (Helen) Beatrix 1866-1943
See Webb, (Martha) Beatrice (Potter)
See also MAICYA
Potter, Dennis (Christopher George) 1935-1994
CLC 58, 86
See also CA 107; 145; CANR 33, 61; MTCW 1
Pound, Ezra (Weston Loomis) 1885-1972
**CLC 1, 2, 3, 4, 5, 7, 10, 13, 18, 34, 48, 50,
112; DA; DAB; DAC; DAM MST, POET;
PC 4; WLC**
See also CA 5-8R; 37-40R; CANR 40; CDALB
1917-1929; DLB 4, 45, 63; DLBD 15;
MTCW 1
Povod, Reinaldo 1959-1994 .... **CLC 44**
See also CA 136; 146
Powell, Adam Clayton, Jr. 1908-1972**CLC 89;
BLC 3; DAM MULT**
See also BW 1; CA 102; 33-36R
Powell, Anthony (Dymoke) 1905-**CLC 1, 3, 7,
9, 10, 31**
See also CA 1-4R; CANR 1, 32, 62; CDBLB
1945-1960; DLB 15; MTCW 1
Powell, Dawn 1897-1965 .... **CLC 66**
See also CA 5-8R; DLBY 97
Powell, Padgett 1952- .... **CLC 34**
See also CA 126; CANR 63
Power, Susan 1961- .... **CLC 91**
Powers, J(ames) F(arl) 1917-**CLC 1, 4, 8, 57;
SSC 4**
See also CA 1-4R; CANR 2, 61; DLB 130;
MTCW 1
Powers, John J(ames) 1945-
See Powers, John R.
See also CA 69-72
Powers, John R. .... **CLC 66**
See also Powers, John J(ames)
Powers, Richard (S.) 1957- .... **CLC 93**
See also CA 148
Pownall, David 1938- .... **CLC 10**
See also CA 89-92; CAAS 18; CANR 49; DLB
14
Powys, John Cowper 1872-1963**CLC 7, 9, 15,
46**
See also CA 85-88; DLB 15; MTCW 1
Powys, T(heodore) F(rancis) 1875-1953
TCLC 9
See also CA 106; DLB 36, 162
Prado (Calvo), Pedro 1886-1952 ... **TCLC 75**
See also CA 131; HW
Prager, Emily 1952- .... **CLC 56**
Pratt, E(dwin) J(ohn) 1883(?)-1964 **CLC 19;
DAC; DAM POET**
See also CA 141; 93-96; DLB 92
Premchand .... **TCLC 21**
See also Srivastava, Dhanpat Rai
Preussler, Otfried 1923- .... **CLC 17**
See also CA 77-80; SATA 24
Prevert, Jacques (Henri Marie) 1900-1977
CLC 15
See also CA 77-80; 69-72; CANR 29, 61;
MTCW 1; SATA-Obit 30

Prevost, Abbe (Antoine Francois) 1697-1763
LC 1
Price, (Edward) Reynolds 1933-**CLC 3, 6, 13,
43, 50, 63; DAM NOV; SSC 22**
See also CA 1-4R; CANR 1, 37, 57; DLB 2;
INT CANR-37
Price, Richard 1949- .... **CLC 6, 12**
See also CA 49-52; CANR 3; DLBY 81
Prichard, Katharine Susannah 1883-1969
CLC 46
See also CA 11-12; CANR 33; CAP 1; MTCW
1; SATA 66
Priestley, J(ohn) B(oynton) 1894-1984**CLC 2,
5, 9, 34; DAM DRAM, NOV**
See also CA 9-12R; 113; CANR 33; CDBLB
1914-1945; DLB 10, 34, 77, 100, 139; DLBY
84; MTCW 1
Prince 1958(?)- .... **CLC 35**
Prince, F(rank) T(empleton) 1912- .. **CLC 22**
See also CA 101; CANR 43; DLB 20
Prince Kropotkin
See Kropotkin, Peter (Aleksieevich)
Prior, Matthew 1664-1721 .... **LC 4**
See also DLB 95
Prishvin, Mikhail 1873-1954 .... **TCLC 75**
Pritchard, William H(arrison) 1932-**CLC 34**
See also CA 65-68; CANR 23; DLB 111
Pritchett, V(ictor) S(awdon) 1900-1997 **C L C
5, 13, 15, 41; DAM NOV; SSC 14**
See also CA 61-64; 157; CANR 31, 63; DLB
15, 139; MTCW 1
Private 19022
See Manning, Frederic
Probst, Mark 1925-............................. **CLC 59**
See also CA 130
Prokosch, Frederic 1908-1989 ...... **CLC 4, 48**
See also CA 73-76; 128; DLB 48
Prophet, The
See Dreiser, Theodore (Herman Albert)
Prose, Francine 1947- .... **CLC 45**
See also CA 109; 112; CANR 46; SATA 101
Proudhon
See Cunha, Euclides (Rodrigues Pimenta) da
Proulx, Annie
See Proulx, E(dna) Annie
Proulx, E(dna) Annie 1935-... **CLC 81; DAM
POP**
See also CA 145; CANR 65
**Proust, (Valentin-Louis-George-Eugene-)
Marcel** 1871-1922 **TCLC 7, 13, 33; DA;
DAB; DAC; DAM MST, NOV; WLC**
See also CA 104; 120; DLB 65; MTCW 1
Prowler, Harley
See Masters, Edgar Lee
Prus, Boleslaw 1845-1912 .... **TCLC 48**
Pryor, Richard (Franklin Lenox Thomas) 1940-
CLC 26
See also CA 122
Przybyszewski, Stanislaw 1868-1927**TCLC 36**
See also CA 160; DLB 66
Pteleon
See Grieve, C(hristopher) M(urray)
See also DAM POET
Puckett, Lute
See Masters, Edgar Lee
Puig, Manuel 1932-1990**CLC 3, 5, 10, 28, 65;
DAM MULT; HLC**
See also CA 45-48; CANR 2, 32, 63; DLB 113;
HW; MTCW 1
Pulitzer, Joseph 1847-1911 .... **TCLC 76**
See also CA 114; DLB 23
Purdy, A(lfred) W(ellington) 1918- **CLC 3, 6,
14, 50; DAC; DAM MST, POET**
See also CA 81-84; CAAS 17; CANR 42, 66;
DLB 88
Purdy, James (Amos) 1923- **CLC 2, 4, 10, 28,
52**

See also CA 33-36R; CAAS 1; CANR 19, 51;
DLB 2; INT CANR-19; MTCW 1
Pure, Simon
See Swinnerton, Frank Arthur
Pushkin, Alexander (Sergeyevich) 1799-1837
**NCLC 3, 27; DA; DAB; DAC; DAM
DRAM, MST, POET; PC 10; SSC 27;
WLC**
See also SATA 61
P'u Sung-ling 1640-1715 ....**LC 3; SSC 31**
Putnam, Arthur Lee
See Alger, Horatio, Jr.
Puzo, Mario 1920-**CLC 1, 2, 6, 36, 107; DAM
NOV, POP**
See also CA 65-68; CANR 4, 42, 65; DLB 6;
MTCW 1
Pygge, Edward
See Barnes, Julian (Patrick)
Pyle, Ernest Taylor 1900-1945
See Pyle, Ernie
See also CA 115; 160
Pyle, Ernie 1900-1945 .... **TCLC 75**
See also Pyle, Ernest Taylor
See also DLB 29
Pyle, Howard 1853-1911 .... **TCLC 81**
See also CA 109; 137; CLR 22; DLB 42, 188;
DLBD 13; MAICYA; SATA 16, 100
Pym, Barbara (Mary Crampton) 1913-1980
CLC 13, 19, 37, 111
See also CA 13-14; 97-100; CANR 13, 34; CAP
1; DLB 14; DLBY 87; MTCW 1
Pynchon, Thomas (Ruggles, Jr.) 1937-**CLC 2,
3, 6, 9, 11, 18, 33, 62, 72; DA; DAB; DAC;
DAM MST, NOV, POP; SSC 14; WLC**
See also BEST 90:2; CA 17-20R; CANR 22,
46; DLB 2, 173; MTCW 1
Pythagoras c. 570B.C.-c. 500B.C. . **CMLC 22**
See also DLB 176
Q
See Quiller-Couch, SirArthur (Thomas)
Qian Zhongshu
See Ch'ien Chung-shu
Qroll
See Dagerman, Stig (Halvard)
Quarrington, Paul (Lewis) 1953- ..... **CLC 65**
See also CA 129; CANR 62
Quasimodo, Salvatore 1901-1968 ..... **CLC 10**
See also CA 13-16; 25-28R; CAP 1; DLB 114;
MTCW 1
Quay, Stephen 1947-........................... **CLC 95**
Quay, Timothy 1947-......................... **CLC 95**
Queen, Ellery .... **CLC 3, 11**
See also Dannay, Frederic; Davidson, Avram;
Lee, Manfred B(ennington); Marlowe,
Stephen; Sturgeon, Theodore (Hamilton);
Vance, John Holbrook
Queen, Ellery, Jr.
See Dannay, Frederic; Lee, Manfred
B(ennington)
Queneau, Raymond 1903-1976 **CLC 2, 5, 10,
42**
See also CA 77-80; 69-72; CANR 32; DLB 72;
MTCW 1
Quevedo, Francisco de 1580-1645 .... **LC 23**
Quiller-Couch, SirArthur (Thomas) 1863-1944
TCLC 53
See also CA 118; 166; DLB 135, 153, 190
Quin, Ann (Marie) 1936-1973 .... **CLC 6**
See also CA 9-12R; 45-48; DLB 14
Quinn, Martin
See Smith, Martin Cruz
Quinn, Peter 1947-............................. **CLC 91**
Quinn, Simon
See Smith, Martin Cruz
Quiroga, Horacio (Sylvestre) 1878-1937
TCLC 20; DAM MULT; HLC
See also CA 117; 131; HW; MTCW 1

Shamlu, Ahmad 1925- .... **CLC 10**
Shammas, Anton 1951- .... **CLC 55**
Shange, Ntozake 1948-**CLC 8, 25, 38, 74; BLC
3; DAM DRAM, MULT; DC 3**
See also AAYA 9; BW 2; CA 85-88; CABS 3;
CANR 27, 48; DLB 38; MTCW 1
Shanley, John Patrick 1950- .... **CLC 75**
See also CA 128; 133
Shapcott, Thomas W(illiam) 1935-... **CLC 38**
See also CA 69-72; CANR 49
Shapiro, Jane .... **CLC 76**
Shapiro, Karl (Jay) 1913-... **CLC 4, 8, 15, 53**
See also CA 1-4R; CAAS 6; CANR 1, 36, 66;
DLB 48; MTCW 1
Sharp, William 1855-1905 .... **TCLC 39**
See also CA 160; DLB 156
Sharpe, Thomas Ridley 1928-
See Sharpe, Tom
See also CA 114; 122; INT 122
Sharpe, Tom .... **CLC 36**
See also Sharpe, Thomas Ridley
See also DLB 14
Shaw, Bernard .... **TCLC 45**
See also Shaw, George Bernard
See also BW 1
Shaw, G. Bernard
See Shaw, George Bernard
Shaw, George Bernard 1856-1950**TCLC 3, 9,
21; DA; DAB; DAC; DAM DRAM, MST;
WLC**
See also Shaw, Bernard
See also CA 104; 128; CDBLB 1914-1945;
DLB 10, 57, 190; MTCW 1
Shaw, Henry Wheeler 1818-1885 .. **NCLC 15**
See also DLB 11
Shaw, Irwin 1913-1984 **CLC 7, 23, 34; DAM
DRAM, POP**
See also AITN 1; CA 13-16R; 112; CANR 21;
CDALB 1941-1968; DLB 6, 102; DLBY 84;
MTCW 1
Shaw, Robert 1927-1978 .... **CLC 5**
See also AITN 1; CA 1-4R; 81-84; CANR 4;
DLB 13, 14
Shaw, T. E.
See Lawrence, T(homas) E(dward)
Shawn, Wallace 1943- .... **CLC 41**
See also CA 112
Shea, Lisa 1953- .... **CLC 86**
See also CA 147
Sheed, Wilfrid (John Joseph) 1930-**CLC 2, 4,
10, 53**
See also CA 65-68; CANR 30, 66; DLB 6;
MTCW 1
Sheldon, Alice Hastings Bradley 1915(?)-1987
See Tiptree, James, Jr.
See also CA 108; 122; CANR 34; INT 108;
MTCW 1
Sheldon, John
See Bloch, Robert (Albert)
Shelley, Mary Wollstonecraft (Godwin) 1797-
1851**NCLC 14, 59; DA; DAB; DAC; DAM
MST, NOV; WLC**
See also AAYA 20; CDBLB 1789-1832; DLB
110, 116, 159, 178; SATA 29
Shelley, Percy Bysshe 1792-1822 . **NCLC 18;
DA; DAB; DAC; DAM MST, POET; PC
14; WLC**
See also CDBLB 1789-1832; DLB 96, 110, 158
Shepard, Jim 1956- .... **CLC 36**
See also CA 137; CANR 59; SATA 90
Shepard, Lucius 1947- .... **CLC 34**
See also CA 128; 141
Shepard, Sam 1943- **CLC 4, 6, 17, 34, 41, 44;
DAM DRAM; DC 5**
See also AAYA 1; CA 69-72; CABS 3; CANR
22; DLB 7; MTCW 1
Shepherd, Michael

See Ludlum, Robert
Sherburne, Zoa (Morin) 1912- .... **CLC 30**
See also AAYA 13; CA 1-4R; CANR 3, 37;
MAICYA; SAAS 18; SATA 3
Sheridan, Frances 1724-1766 .... **LC 7**
See also DLB 39, 84
Sheridan, Richard Brinsley 1751-1816**NCLC
5; DA; DAB; DAC; DAM DRAM, MST;
DC 1; WLC**
See also CDBLB 1660-1789; DLB 89
Sherman, Jonathan Marc .... **CLC 55**
Sherman, Martin 1941(?)- .... **CLC 19**
See also CA 116; 123
Sherwin, Judith Johnson 1936- .... **CLC 7, 15**
See also CA 25-28R; CANR 34
Sherwood, Frances 1940- .... **CLC 81**
See also CA 146
Sherwood, Robert E(mmet) 1896-1955**TCLC
3; DAM DRAM**
See also CA 104; 153; DLB 7, 26
Shestov, Lev 1866-1938 .... **TCLC 56**
Shevchenko, Taras 1814-1861 .... **NCLC 54**
Shiel, M(atthew) P(hipps) 1865-1947**TCLC 8**
See also Holmes, Gordon
See also CA 106; 160; DLB 153
Shields, Carol 1935- .... **CLC 91, 113; DAC**
See also CA 81-84; CANR 51
Shields, David 1956- .... **CLC 97**
See also CA 124; CANR 48
Shiga, Naoya 1883-1971 ...... **CLC 33; SSC 23**
See also CA 101; 33-36R; DLB 180
Shilts, Randy 1951-1994 .... **CLC 85**
See also AAYA 19; CA 115; 127; 144; CANR
45; INT 127
Shimazaki, Haruki 1872-1943
See Shimazaki Toson
See also CA 105; 134
Shimazaki Toson 1872-1943 .... **TCLC 5**
See also Shimazaki, Haruki
See also DLB 180
Sholokhov, Mikhail (Aleksandrovich) 1905-
1984 .... **CLC 7, 15**
See also CA 101; 112; MTCW 1; SATA-Obit
36
Shone, Patric
See Hanley, James
Shreve, Susan Richards 1939- .... **CLC 23**
See also CA 49-52; CAAS 5; CANR 5, 38, 69;
MAICYA; SATA 46, 95; SATA-Brief 41
Shue, Larry 1946-1985**CLC 52; DAM DRAM**
See also CA 145; 117
Shu-Jen, Chou 1881-1936
See Lu Hsun
See also CA 104
Shulman, Alix Kates 1932- .... **CLC 2, 10**
See also CA 29-32R; CANR 43; SATA 7
Shuster, Joe 1914- .... **CLC 21**
Shute, Nevil .... **CLC 30**
See also Norway, Nevil Shute
Shuttle, Penelope (Diane) 1947- .... **CLC 7**
See also CA 93-96; CANR 39; DLB 14, 40
Sidney, Mary 1561-1621 .... **LC 19, 39**
Sidney, Sir Philip 1554-1586 **LC 19, 39; DA;
DAB; DAC; DAM MST, POET**
See also CDBLB Before 1660; DLB 167
Siegel, Jerome 1914-1996 .... **CLC 21**
See also CA 116; 151
Siegel, Jerry
See Siegel, Jerome
Sienkiewicz, Henryk (Adam Alexander Pius)
1846-1916 ....
TCLC 3
See also CA 104; 134
Sierra, Gregorio Martinez
See Martinez Sierra, Gregorio
Sierra, Maria (de la O'LeJarraga) Martinez
See Martinez Sierra, Maria (de la O'LeJarraga)

Sigal, Clancy 1926- .... **CLC 7**
See also CA 1-4R
Sigourney, Lydia Howard (Huntley) 1791-1865
NCLC 21
See also DLB 1, 42, 73
Siguenza y Gongora, Carlos de 1645-1700**LC
8**
Sigurjonsson, Johann 1880-1919 ... **TCLC 27**
Sikelianos, Angelos 1884-1951 .... **TCLC 39**
Silkin, Jon 1930- .... **CLC 2, 6, 43**
See also CA 5-8R; CAAS 5; DLB 27
Silko, Leslie (Marmon) 1948-**CLC 23, 74, 114;
DA; DAC; DAM MST, MULT, POP;
WLCS**
See also AAYA 14; CA 115; 122; CANR 45;
65; DLB 143, 175; NNAL
Sillanpaa, Frans Eemil 1888-1964 ... **CLC 19**
See also CA 129; 93-96; MTCW 1
Sillitoe, Alan 1928- ... **CLC 1, 3, 6, 10, 19, 57**
See also AITN 1; CA 9-12R; CAAS 2; CANR
8, 26, 55; CDBLB 1960 to Present; DLB 14,
139; MTCW 1; SATA 61
Silone, Ignazio 1900-1978 .... **CLC 4**
See also CA 25-28; 81-84; CANR 34; CAP 2;
MTCW 1
Silver, Joan Micklin 1935- .... **CLC 20**
See also CA 114; 121; INT 121
Silver, Nicholas
See Faust, Frederick (Schiller)
Silverberg, Robert 1935- **CLC 7; DAM POP**
See also AAYA 24; CA 1-4R; CAAS 3; CANR
1, 20, 36; DLB 8; INT CANR-20; MAICYA;
MTCW 1; SATA 13, 91
Silverstein, Alvin 1933- .... **CLC 17**
See also CA 49-52; CANR 2; CLR 25; JRDA;
MAICYA; SATA 8, 69
Silverstein, Virginia B(arbara Opshelor) 1937-
CLC 17
See also CA 49-52; CANR 2; CLR 25; JRDA;
MAICYA; SATA 8, 69
Sim, Georges
See Simenon, Georges (Jacques Christian)
Simak, Clifford D(onald) 1904-1988**CLC 1, 55**
See also CA 1-4R; 125; CANR 1, 35; DLB 8;
MTCW 1; SATA-Obit 56
Simenon, Georges (Jacques Christian) 1903-
1989 .. **CLC 1, 2, 3, 8, 18, 47; DAM POP**
See also CA 85-88; 129; CANR 35; DLB 72;
DLBY 89; MTCW 1
Simic, Charles 1938-.... **CLC 6, 9, 22, 49, 68;
DAM POET**
See also CA 29-32R; CAAS 4; CANR 12, 33,
52, 61; DLB 105
Simmel, Georg 1858-1918 .... **TCLC 64**
See also CA 157
Simmons, Charles (Paul) 1924- .... **CLC 57**
See also CA 89-92; INT 89-92
Simmons, Dan 1948- ..... **CLC 44; DAM POP**
See also AAYA 16; CA 138; CANR 53
Simmons, James (Stewart Alexander) 1933-
CLC 43
See also CA 105; CAAS 21; DLB 40
Simms, William Gilmore 1806-1870 **NCLC 3**
See also DLB 3, 30, 59, 73
Simon, Carly 1945- .... **CLC 26**
See also CA 105
Simon, Claude 1913-1984 .. **CLC 4, 9, 15, 39;
DAM NOV**
See also CA 89-92; CANR 33; DLB 83; MTCW
1
Simon, (Marvin) Neil 1927-**CLC 6, 11, 31, 39,
70; DAM DRAM**
See also AITN 1; CA 21-24R; CANR 26, 54;
DLB 7; MTCW 1
Simon, Paul (Frederick) 1941(?)- ..... **CLC 17**
See also CA 116; 153
Simonon, Paul 1956(?)- .... **CLC 30**

Sommer, Scott 1951- .... CLC 25
See also CA 106
Sondheim, Stephen (Joshua) 1930- . CLC 30,
39; DAM DRAM
See also AAYA 11; CA 103; CANR 47, 68
Song, Cathy 1955- .... PC 21
See also CA 154; DLB 169
Sontag, Susan 1933-CLC 1, 2, 10, 13, 31, 105;
DAM POP
See also CA 17-20R; CANR 25, 51; DLB 2,
67; MTCW 1
Sophocles 496(?)B.C.-406(?)B.C. ... CMLC 2;
DA; DAB; DAC; DAM DRAM, MST; DC
1; WLCS
See also DLB 176
Sordello 1189-1269 .... CMLC 15
Sorel, Julia
See Drexler, Rosalyn
Sorrentino, Gilbert 1929-CLC 3, 7, 14, 22, 40
See also CA 77-80; CANR 14, 33; DLB 5, 173;
DLBY 80; INT CANR-14
Soto, Gary 1952- CLC 32, 80; DAM MULT;
HLC
See also AAYA 10; CA 119; 125; CANR 50;
CLR 38; DLB 82; HW; INT 125; JRDA;
SATA 80
Soupault, Philippe 1897-1990 .... CLC 68
See also CA 116; 147; 131
Souster, (Holmes) Raymond 1921-CLC 5, 14;
DAC; DAM POET
See also CA 13-16R; CAAS 14; CANR 13, 29,
53; DLB 88; SATA 63
Southern, Terry 1924(?)-1995 .... CLC 7
See also CA 1-4R; 150; CANR 1, 55; DLB 2
Southey, Robert 1774-1843 .... NCLC 8
See also DLB 93, 107, 142; SATA 54
Southworth, Emma Dorothy Eliza Nevitte
1819-1899 ....
NCLC 26
Souza, Ernest
See Scott, Evelyn
Soyinka, Wole 1934-CLC 3, 5, 14, 36, 44; BLC
3; DA; DAB; DAC; DAM DRAM, MST,
MULT; DC 2; WLC
See also BW 2; CA 13-16R; CANR 27, 39; DLB
125; MTCW 1
Spackman, W(illiam) M(ode) 1905-1990C L C
46
See also CA 81-84; 132
Spacks, Barry (Bernard) 1931-......... CLC 14
See also CA 154; CANR 33; DLB 105
Spanidou, Irini 1946- .... CLC 44
Spark, Muriel (Sarah) 1918-CLC 2, 3, 5, 8, 13,
18, 40, 94; DAB; DAC; DAM MST, NOV;
SSC 10
See also CA 5-8R; CANR 12, 36; CDBLB 1945-
1960; DLB 15, 139; INT CANR-12; MTCW
1
Spaulding, Douglas
See Bradbury, Ray (Douglas)
Spaulding, Leonard
See Bradbury, Ray (Douglas)
Spence, J. A. D.
See Eliot, T(homas) S(tearns)
Spencer, Elizabeth 1921- .... CLC 22
See also CA 13-16R; CANR 32, 65; DLB 6;
MTCW 1; SATA 14
Spencer, Leonard G.
See Silverberg, Robert
Spencer, Scott 1945- .... CLC 30
See also CA 113; CANR 51; DLBY 86
Spender, Stephen (Harold) 1909-1995CLC 1,
2, 5, 10, 41, 91; DAM POET
See also CA 9-12R; 149; CANR 31, 54; CDBLB
1945-1960; DLB 20; MTCW 1
Spengler, Oswald (Arnold Gottfried) 1880-1936
TCLC 25

See also CA 118
Spenser, Edmund 1552(?)-1599LC 5, 39; DA;
DAB; DAC; DAM MST, POET; PC 8;
WLC
See also CDBLB Before 1660; DLB 167
Spicer, Jack 1925-1965 CLC 8, 18, 72; DAM
POET
See also CA 85-88; DLB 5, 16, 193
Spiegelman, Art 1948-........................ CLC 76
See also AAYA 10; CA 125; CANR 41, 55
Spielberg, Peter 1929- .... CLC 6
See also CA 5-8R; CANR 4, 48; DLBY 81
Spielberg, Steven 1947- .... CLC 20
See also AAYA 8, 24; CA 77-80; CANR 32;
SATA 32
Spillane, Frank Morrison 1918-
See Spillane, Mickey
See also CA 25-28R; CANR 28, 63; MTCW 1;
SATA 66
Spillane, Mickey .... CLC 3, 13
See also Spillane, Frank Morrison
Spinoza, Benedictus de 1632-1677 .... LC 9
Spinrad, Norman (Richard) 1940- ... CLC 46
See also CA 37-40R; CAAS 19; CANR 20; DLB
8; INT CANR-20
Spitteler, Carl (Friedrich Georg) 1845-1924
TCLC 12
See also CA 109; DLB 129
Spivack, Kathleen (Romola Drucker) 1938-
CLC 6
See also CA 49-52
Spoto, Donald 1941- .... CLC 39
See also CA 65-68; CANR 11, 57
Springsteen, Bruce (F.) 1949- .... CLC 17
See also CA 111
Spurling, Hilary 1940- .... CLC 34
See also CA 104; CANR 25, 52
Spyker, John Howland
See Elman, Richard (Martin)
Squires, (James) Radcliffe 1917-1993CLC 51
See also CA 1-4R; 140; CANR 6, 21
Srivastava, Dhanpat Rai 1880(?)-1936
See Premchand
See also CA 118
Stacy, Donald
See Pohl, Frederik
Stael, Germaine de 1766-1817
See Stael-Holstein, Anne Louise Germaine
Necker Baronn
See also DLB 119
Stael-Holstein, Anne Louise Germaine Necker
Baronn 1766-1817 .... NCLC 3
See also Stael, Germaine de
See also DLB 192
Stafford, Jean 1915-1979CLC 4, 7, 19, 68; SSC
26
See also CA 1-4R; 85-88; CANR 3, 65; DLB 2,
173; MTCW 1; SATA-Obit 22
Stafford, William (Edgar) 1914-1993 CLC 4,
7, 29; DAM POET
See also CA 5-8R; 142; CAAS 3; CANR 5, 22;
DLB 5; INT CANR-22
Stagnelius, Eric Johan 1793-1823 . NCLC 61
Staines, Trevor
See Brunner, John (Kilian Houston)
Stairs, Gordon
See Austin, Mary (Hunter)
Stannard, Martin 1947- .... CLC 44
See also CA 142; DLB 155
Stanton, Elizabeth Cady 1815-1902TCLC 73
See also DLB 79
Stanton, Maura 1946- .... CLC 9
See also CA 89-92; CANR 15; DLB 120
Stanton, Schuyler
See Baum, L(yman) Frank
Stapledon, (William) Olaf 1886-1950 T C L C
22

See also CA 111; 162; DLB 15
Starbuck, George (Edwin) 1931-1996CLC 53;
DAM POET
See also CA 21-24R; 153; CANR 23
Stark, Richard
See Westlake, Donald E(dwin)
Staunton, Schuyler
See Baum, L(yman) Frank
Stead, Christina (Ellen) 1902-1983 CLC 2, 5,
8, 32, 80
See also CA 13-16R; 109; CANR 33, 40;
MTCW 1
Stead, William Thomas 1849-1912 TCLC 48
See also CA 167
Steele, Richard 1672-1729 .... LC 18
See also CDBLB 1660-1789; DLB 84, 101
Steele, Timothy (Reid) 1948- .... CLC 45
See also CA 93-96; CANR 16, 50; DLB 120
Steffens, (Joseph) Lincoln 1866-1936 T C L C
20
See also CA 117
Stegner, Wallace (Earle) 1909-1993CLC 9, 49,
81; DAM NOV; SSC 27
See also AITN 1; BEST 90:3; CA 1-4R; 141;
CAAS 9; CANR 1, 21, 46; DLB 9; DLBY
93; MTCW 1
Stein, Gertrude 1874-1946TCLC 1, 6, 28, 48;
DA; DAB; DAC; DAM MST, NOV, POET;
PC 18; WLC
See also CA 104; 132; CDALB 1917-1929;
DLB 4, 54, 86; DLBD 15; MTCW 1
Steinbeck, John (Ernst) 1902-1968 CLC 1, 5,
9, 13, 21, 34, 45, 75; DA; DAB; DAC; DAM
DRAM, MST, NOV; SSC 11; WLC
See also AAYA 12; CA 1-4R; 25-28R; CANR
1, 35; CDALB 1929-1941; DLB 7, 9; DLBD
2; MTCW 1; SATA 9
Steinem, Gloria 1934- .... CLC 63
See also CA 53-56; CANR 28, 51; MTCW 1
Steiner, George 1929- ... CLC 24; DAM NOV
See also CA 73-76; CANR 31, 67; DLB 67;
MTCW 1; SATA 62
Steiner, K. Leslie
See Delany, Samuel R(ay, Jr.)
Steiner, Rudolf 1861-1925 .... TCLC 13
See also CA 107
Stendhal 1783-1842NCLC 23, 46; DA; DAB;
DAC; DAM MST, NOV; SSC 27; WLC
See also DLB 119
Stephen, Adeline Virginia
See Woolf, (Adeline) Virginia
Stephen, SirLeslie 1832-1904 .... TCLC 23
See also CA 123; DLB 57, 144, 190
Stephen, Sir Leslie
See Stephen, SirLeslie
Stephen, Virginia
See Woolf, (Adeline) Virginia
Stephens, James 1882(?)-1950 .... TCLC 4
See also CA 104; DLB 19, 153, 162
Stephens, Reed
See Donaldson, Stephen R.
Steptoe, Lydia
See Barnes, Djuna
Sterchi, Beat 1949- .... CLC 65
Sterling, Brett
See Bradbury, Ray (Douglas); Hamilton,
Edmond
Sterling, Bruce 1954- .... CLC 72
See also CA 119; CANR 44
Sterling, George 1869-1926 .... TCLC 20
See also CA 117; 165; DLB 54
Stern, Gerald 1925- .... CLC 40, 100
See also CA 81-84; CANR 28; DLB 105
Stern, Richard (Gustave) 1928- .... CLC 4, 39
See also CA 1-4R; CANR 1, 25, 52; DLBY 87;
INT CANR-25
Sternberg, Josef von 1894-1969 .... CLC 20

See also CA 81-84

Sterne, Laurence 1713-1768**LC 2; DA; DAB; DAC; DAM MST, NOV; WLC**
See also CDBLB 1660-1789; DLB 39

Sternheim, (William Adolf) Carl 1878-1942 **TCLC 8**
See also CA 105; DLB 56, 118

Stevens, Mark 1951- .... **CLC 34**
See also CA 122

Stevens, Wallace 1879-1955 **TCLC 3, 12, 45; DA; DAB; DAC; DAM MST, POET; PC 6; WLC**
See also CA 104; 124; CDALB 1929-1941; DLB 54; MTCW 1

Stevenson, Anne (Katharine) 1933-**CLC 7, 33**
See also CA 17-20R; CAAS 9; CANR 9, 33; DLB 40; MTCW 1

Stevenson, Robert Louis (Balfour) 1850-1894 **NCLC 5, 14, 63; DA; DAB; DAC; DAM MST, NOV; SSC 11; WLC**
See also AAYA 24; CDBLB 1890-1914; CLR 10, 11; DLB 18, 57, 141, 156, 174; DLBD 13; JRDA; MAICYA; SATA 100; YABC 2

Stewart, J(ohn) I(nnes) M(ackintosh) 1906-1994 .... **CLC 7, 14, 32**
See also CA 85-88; 147; CAAS 3; CANR 47; MTCW 1

Stewart, Mary (Florence Elinor) 1916-**CLC 7, 35; DAB**
See also CA 1-4R; CANR 1, 59; SATA 12

Stewart, Mary Rainbow
See Stewart, Mary (Florence Elinor)

Stifle, June
See Campbell, Maria

Stifter, Adalbert 1805-1868**NCLC 41; SSC 28**
See also DLB 133

Still, James 1906- .... **CLC 49**
See also CA 65-68; CAAS 17; CANR 10, 26; DLB 9; SATA 29

Sting 1951-
See Sumner, Gordon Matthew
See also CA 167

Stirling, Arthur
See Sinclair, Upton (Beall)

Stitt, Milan 1941- .... **CLC 29**
See also CA 69-72

Stockton, Francis Richard 1834-1902
See Stockton, Frank R.
See also CA 108; 137; MAICYA; SATA 44

Stockton, Frank R. .... **TCLC 47**
See also Stockton, Francis Richard
See also DLB 42, 74; DLBD 13; SATA-Brief 32

Stoddard, Charles
See Kuttner, Henry

Stoker, Abraham 1847-1912
See Stoker, Bram
See also CA 105; 150; DA; DAC; DAM MST, NOV; SATA 29

Stoker, Bram 1847-1912**TCLC 8; DAB; WLC**
See also Stoker, Abraham
See also AAYA 23; CDBLB 1890-1914; DLB 36, 70, 178

Stolz, Mary (Slattery) 1920- .... **CLC 12**
See also AAYA 8; AITN 1; CA 5-8R; CANR 13, 41; JRDA; MAICYA; SAAS 3; SATA 10, 71

Stone, Irving 1903-1989 .. **CLC 7; DAM POP**
See also AITN 1; CA 1-4R; 129; CAAS 3; CANR 1, 23; INT CANR-23; MTCW 1; SATA 3; SATA-Obit 64

Stone, Oliver (William) 1946- .... **CLC 73**
See also AAYA 15; CA 110; CANR 55

Stone, Robert (Anthony) 1937-**CLC 5, 23, 42**
See also CA 85-88; CANR 23, 66; DLB 152; INT CANR-23; MTCW 1

Stone, Zachary

See Follett, Ken(neth Martin)

Stoppard, Tom 1937-**CLC 1, 3, 4, 5, 8, 15, 29, 34, 63, 91; DA; DAB; DAC; DAM DRAM, MST; DC 6; WLC**
See also CA 81-84; CANR 39, 67; CDBLB 1960 to Present; DLB 13; DLBY 85; MTCW 1

Storey, David (Malcolm) 1933-**CLC 2, 4, 5, 8; DAM DRAM**
See also CA 81-84; CANR 36; DLB 13, 14; MTCW 1

Storm, Hyemeyohsts 1935- ...... **CLC 3; DAM MULT**
See also CA 81-84; CANR 45; NNAL

Storm, (Hans) Theodor (Woldsen) 1817-1888 **NCLC 1; SSC 27**
See also DLB 129

Storni, Alfonsina 1892-1938 . **TCLC 5; DAM MULT; HLC**
See also CA 104; 131; HW

Stoughton, William 1631-1701 .... **LC 38**
See also DLB 24

Stout, Rex (Todhunter) 1886-1975 ..... **CLC 3**
See also AITN 2; CA 61-64; CANR 71

Stow, (Julian) Randolph 1935- .. **CLC 23, 48**
See also CA 13-16R; CANR 33; MTCW 1

Stowe, Harriet (Elizabeth) Beecher 1811-1896 **NCLC 3, 50; DA; DAB; DAC; DAM MST, NOV; WLC**
See also CDALB 1865-1917; DLB 1, 12, 42, 74, 189; JRDA; MAICYA; YABC 1

Strachey, (Giles) Lytton 1880-1932 **TCLC 12**
See also CA 110; DLB 149; DLBD 10

Strand, Mark 1934- **CLC 6, 18, 41, 71; DAM POET**
See also CA 21-24R; CANR 40, 65; DLB 5; SATA 41

Straub, Peter (Francis) 1943- . **CLC 28, 107; DAM POP**
See also BEST 89:1; CA 85-88; CANR 28, 65; DLBY 84; MTCW 1

Strauss, Botho 1944-.......................... **CLC 22**
See also CA 157; DLB 124

Streatfeild, (Mary) Noel 1895(?)-1986**CLC 21**
See also CA 81-84; 120; CANR 31; CLR 17; DLB 160; MAICYA; SATA 20; SATA-Obit 48

Stribling, T(homas) S(igismund) 1881-1965 **CLC 23**
See also CA 107; DLB 9

Strindberg, (Johan) August 1849-1912**T C L C 1, 8, 21, 47; DA; DAB; DAC; DAM DRAM, MST; WLC**
See also CA 104; 135

Stringer, Arthur 1874-1950 .... **TCLC 37**
See also CA 161; DLB 92

Stringer, David
See Roberts, Keith (John Kingston)

Stroheim, Erich von 1885-1957 ..... **TCLC 71**

Strugatskii, Arkadii (Natanovich) 1925-1991 **CLC 27**
See also CA 106; 135

Strugatskii, Boris (Natanovich) 1933-**CLC 27**
See also CA 106

Strummer, Joe 1953(?)- .... **CLC 30**

Stuart, Don A.
See Campbell, John W(ood, Jr.)

Stuart, Ian
See MacLean, Alistair (Stuart)

Stuart, Jesse (Hilton) 1906-1984**CLC 1, 8, 11, 14, 34; SSC 31**
See also CA 5-8R; 112; CANR 31; DLB 9, 48, 102; DLBY 84; SATA 2; SATA-Obit 36

Sturgeon, Theodore (Hamilton) 1918-1985 **CLC 22, 39**
See also Queen, Ellery
See also CA 81-84; 116; CANR 32; DLB 8;

DLBY 85; MTCW 1

Sturges, Preston 1898-1959 .... **TCLC 48**
See also CA 114; 149; DLB 26

Styron, William 1925-**CLC 1, 3, 5, 11, 15, 60; DAM NOV, POP; SSC 25**
See also BEST 90:4; CA 5-8R; CANR 6, 33; CDALB 1968-1988; DLB 2, 143; DLBY 80; INT CANR-6; MTCW 1

Su, Chien 1884-1918
See Su Man-shu
See also CA 123

Suarez Lynch, B.
See Bioy Casares, Adolfo; Borges, Jorge Luis

Suckow, Ruth 1892-1960.................... **SSC 18**
See also CA 113; DLB 9, 102

Sudermann, Hermann 1857-1928 .. **TCLC 15**
See also CA 107; DLB 118

Sue, Eugene 1804-1857 .... **NCLC 1**
See also DLB 119

Sueskind, Patrick 1949- .... **CLC 44**
See also Suskind, Patrick

Sukenick, Ronald 1932- .... **CLC 3, 4, 6, 48**
See also CA 25-28R; CAAS 8; CANR 32; DLB 173; DLBY 81

Suknaski, Andrew 1942- .... **CLC 19**
See also CA 101; DLB 53

Sullivan, Vernon
See Vian, Boris

Sully Prudhomme 1839-1907 .... **TCLC 31**

Su Man-shu .... **TCLC 24**
See also Su, Chien

Summerforest, Ivy B.
See Kirkup, James

Summers, Andrew James 1942- .... **CLC 26**

Summers, Andy
See Summers, Andrew James

Summers, Hollis (Spurgeon, Jr.) 1916-**CLC 10**
See also CA 5-8R; CANR 3; DLB 6

Summers, (Alphonsus Joseph-Mary Augustus) Montague 1880-1948 .... **TCLC 16**
See also CA 118; 163

Sumner, Gordon Matthew .... **CLC 26**
See also Sting

Surtees, Robert Smith 1803-1864 .. **NCLC 14**
See also DLB 21

Susann, Jacqueline 1921-1974 .... **CLC 3**
See also AITN 1; CA 65-68; 53-56; MTCW 1

Su Shih 1036-1101 .... **CMLC 15**

Suskind, Patrick
See Sueskind, Patrick
See also CA 145

Sutcliff, Rosemary 1920-1992**CLC 26; DAB; DAC; DAM MST, POP**
See also AAYA 10; CA 5-8R; 139; CANR 37; CLR 1, 37; JRDA; MAICYA; SATA 6, 44, 78; SATA-Obit 73

Sutro, Alfred 1863-1933.................... **TCLC 6**
See also CA 105; DLB 10

Sutton, Henry
See Slavitt, David R(ytman)

Svevo, Italo 1861-1928 . **TCLC 2, 35; SSC 25**
See also Schmitz, Aron Hector

Swados, Elizabeth (A.) 1951- .:.......... **CLC 12**
See also CA 97-100; CANR 49; INT 97-100

Swados, Harvey 1920-1972 .... **CLC 5**
See also CA 5-8R; 37-40R; CANR 6; DLB 2

Swan, Gladys 1934- .... **CLC 69**
See also CA 101; CANR 17, 39

Swarthout, Glendon (Fred) 1918-1992**CLC 35**
See also CA 1-4R; 139; CANR 1, 47; SATA 26

Sweet, Sarah C.
See Jewett, (Theodora) Sarah Orne

Swenson, May 1919-1989**CLC 4, 14, 61, 106; DA; DAB; DAC; DAM MST, POET; PC 14**
See also CA 5-8R; 130; CANR 36, 61; DLB 5; MTCW 1; SATA 15

Wallace, Irving 1916-1990 **CLC 7, 13; DAM NOV, POP**
See also AITN 1; CA 1-4R; 132; CAAS 1; CANR 1, 27; INT CANR-27; MTCW 1

Wallant, Edward Lewis 1926-1962**CLC 5, 10**
See also CA 1-4R; CANR 22; DLB 2, 28, 143; MTCW 1

Walley, Byron
See Card, Orson Scott

Walpole, Horace 1717-1797 .... **LC 2**
See also DLB 39, 104

Walpole, Hugh (Seymour) 1884-1941**TCLC 5**
See also CA 104; 165; DLB 34

Walser, Martin 1927-.......................... **CLC 27**
See also CA 57-60; CANR 8, 46; DLB 75, 124

Walser, Robert 1878-1956 **TCLC 18; SSC 20**
See also CA 118; 165; DLB 66

Walsh, Jill Paton .... **CLC 35**
See also Paton Walsh, Gillian
See also AAYA 11; CLR 2; DLB 161; SAAS 3

Walter, Villiam Christian
See Andersen, Hans Christian

Wambaugh, Joseph (Aloysius, Jr.) 1937-**C L C 3, 18; DAM NOV, POP**
See also AITN 1; BEST 89:3; CA 33-36R; CANR 42, 65; DLB 6; DLBY 83; MTCW 1

Wang Wei 699(?)-761(?) .... **PC 18**

Ward, Arthur Henry Sarsfield 1883-1959
See Rohmer, Sax
See also CA 108

Ward, Douglas Turner 1930- .... **CLC 19**
See also BW 1; CA 81-84; CANR 27; DLB 7, 38

Ward, Mary Augusta
See Ward, Mrs. Humphry

Ward, Mrs. Humphry 1851-1920 .. **TCLC 55**
See also DLB 18

Ward, Peter
See Faust, Frederick (Schiller)

Warhol, Andy 1928(?)-1987 .... **CLC 20**
See also AAYA 12; BEST 89:4; CA 89-92; 121; CANR 34

Warner, Francis (Robert le Plastrier) 1937-**CLC 14**
See also CA 53-56; CANR 11

Warner, Marina 1946-........................ **CLC 59**
See also CA 65-68; CANR 21, 55; DLB 194

Warner, Rex (Ernest) 1905-1986 ...... **CLC 45**
See also CA 89-92; 119; DLB 15

Warner, Susan (Bogert) 1819-1885 **NCLC 31**
See also DLB 3, 42

Warner, Sylvia (Constance) Ashton
See Ashton-Warner, Sylvia (Constance)

Warner, Sylvia Townsend 1893-1978 **CLC 7, 19; SSC 23**
See also CA 61-64; 77-80; CANR 16, 60; DLB 34, 139; MTCW 1

Warren, Mercy Otis 1728-1814 ..... **NCLC 13**
See also DLB 31, 200

Warren, Robert Penn 1905-1989**CLC 1, 4, 6, 8, 10, 13, 18, 39, 53, 59; DA; DAB; DAC; DAM MST, NOV, POET; SSC 4; WLC**
See also AITN 1; CA 13-16R; 129; CANR 10, 47; CDALB 1968-1988; DLB 2, 48, 152; DLBY 80, 89; INT CANR-10; MTCW 1; SATA 46; SATA-Obit 63

Warshofsky, Isaac
See Singer, Isaac Bashevis

Warton, Thomas 1728-1790 .....**LC 15; DAM POET**
See also DLB 104, 109

Waruk, Kona
See Harris, (Theodore) Wilson

Warung, Price 1855-1911 .... **TCLC 45**

Warwick, Jarvis
See Garner, Hugh

Washington, Alex

See Harris, Mark

Washington, Booker T(aliaferro) 1856-1915 **TCLC 10; BLC 3; DAM MULT**
See also BW 1; CA 114; 125; SATA 28

Washington, George 1732-1799 .... **LC 25**
See also DLB 31

Wassermann, (Karl) Jakob 1873-1934**T C L C 6**
See also CA 104; DLB 66

Wasserstein, Wendy 1950- ... **CLC 32, 59, 90; DAM DRAM; DC 4**
See also CA 121; 129; CABS 3; CANR 53; INT 129; SATA 94

Waterhouse, Keith (Spencer) 1929- . **CLC 47**
See also CA 5-8R; CANR 38, 67; DLB 13, 15; MTCW 1

Waters, Frank (Joseph) 1902-1995 .. **CLC 88**
See also CA 5-8R; 149; CAAS 13; CANR 3, 18, 63; DLBY 86

Waters, Roger 1944- .... **CLC 35**

Watkins, Frances Ellen
See Harper, Frances Ellen Watkins

Watkins, Gerrold
See Malzberg, Barry N(athaniel)

Watkins, Gloria 1955(?)-
See hooks, bell
See also BW 2; CA 143

Watkins, Paul 1964- .... **CLC 55**
See also CA 132; CANR 62

Watkins, Vernon Phillips 1906-1967 **CLC 43**
See also CA 9-10; 25-28R; CAP 1; DLB 20

Watson, Irving S.
See Mencken, H(enry) L(ouis)

Watson, John H.
See Farmer, Philip Jose

Watson, Richard F.
See Silverberg, Robert

Waugh, Auberon (Alexander) 1939- .. **CLC 7**
See also CA 45-48; CANR 6, 22; DLB 14, 194

Waugh, Evelyn (Arthur St. John) 1903-1966 **CLC 1, 3, 8, 13, 19, 27, 44, 107; DA; DAB; DAC; DAM MST, NOV, POP; WLC**
See also CA 85-88; 25-28R; CANR 22; CDBLB 1914-1945; DLB 15, 162, 195; MTCW 1

Waugh, Harriet 1944- .... **CLC 6**
See also CA 85-88; CANR 22

Ways, C. R.
See Blount, Roy (Alton), Jr.

Waystaff, Simon
See Swift, Jonathan

Webb, (Martha) Beatrice (Potter) 1858-1943 **TCLC 22**
See also Potter, (Helen) Beatrix
See also CA 117

Webb, Charles (Richard) 1939- .... **CLC 7**
See also CA 25-28R

Webb, James H(enry), Jr. 1946- .... **CLC 22**
See also CA 81-84

Webb, Mary (Gladys Meredith) 1881-1927 **TCLC 24**
See also CA 123; DLB 34

Webb, Mrs. Sidney
See Webb, (Martha) Beatrice (Potter)

Webb, Phyllis 1927- .... **CLC 18**
See also CA 104; CANR 23; DLB 53

Webb, Sidney (James) 1859-1947 .. **TCLC 22**
See also CA 117; 163; DLB 190

Webber, Andrew Lloyd .... **CLC 21**
See also Lloyd Webber, Andrew

Weber, Lenora Mattingly 1895-1971 **CLC 12**
See also CA 19-20; 29-32R; CAP 1; SATA 2; SATA-Obit 26

Weber, Max 1864-1920 .... **TCLC 69**
See also CA 109

Webster, John 1579(?)-1634(?) ... **LC 33; DA; DAB; DAC; DAM DRAM, MST; DC 2; WLC**

See also CDBLB Before 1660; DLB 58

Webster, Noah 1758-1843 .... **NCLC 30**

Wedekind, (Benjamin) Frank(lin) 1864-1918 **TCLC 7; DAM DRAM**
See also CA 104; 153; DLB 118

Weidman, Jerome 1913- .... **CLC 7**
See also AITN 2; CA 1-4R; CANR 1; DLB 28

Weil, Simone (Adolphine) 1909-1943**TCLC 23**
See also CA 117; 159

Weininger, Otto 1880-1903 .... **TCLC 84**

Weinstein, Nathan
See West, Nathanael

Weinstein, Nathan von Wallenstein
See West, Nathanael

Weir, Peter (Lindsay) 1944- .... **CLC 20**
See also CA 113; 123

Weiss, Peter (Ulrich) 1916-1982**CLC 3, 15, 51; DAM DRAM**
See also CA 45-48; 106; CANR 3; DLB 69, 124

Weiss, Theodore (Russell) 1916-**CLC 3, 8, 14**
See also CA 9-12R; CAAS 2; CANR 46; DLB 5

Welch, (Maurice) Denton 1915-1948**TCLC 22**
See also CA 121; 148

Welch, James 1940- ..... **CLC 6, 14, 52; DAM MULT, POP**
See also CA 85-88; CANR 42, 66; DLB 175; NNAL

Weldon, Fay 1931- . **CLC 6, 9, 11, 19, 36, 59; DAM POP**
See also CA 21-24R; CANR 16, 46, 63; CDBLB 1960 to Present; DLB 14, 194; INT CANR-16; MTCW 1

Wellek, Rene 1903-1995 .... **CLC 28**
See also CA 5-8R; 150; CAAS 7; CANR 8; DLB 63; INT CANR-8

Weller, Michael 1942-.................. **CLC 10, 53**
See also CA 85-88

Weller, Paul 1958-................................ **CLC 26**

Wellershoff, Dieter 1925-................... **CLC 46**
See also CA 89-92; CANR 16, 37

Welles, (George) Orson 1915-1985**CLC 20, 80**
See also CA 93-96; 117

Wellman, John McDowell 1945-
See Wellman, Mac
See also CA 166

Wellman, Mac 1945-............................ **CLC 65**
See also Wellman, John McDowell; Wellman, John McDowell

Wellman, Manly Wade 1903-1986 .... **CLC 49**
See also CA 1-4R; 118; CANR 6, 16, 44; SATA 6; SATA-Obit 47

Wells, Carolyn 1869(?)-1942 .... **TCLC 35**
See also CA 113; DLB 11

Wells, H(erbert) G(eorge) 1866-1946**TCLC 6, 12, 19; DA; DAB; DAC; DAM MST, NOV; SSC 6; WLC**
See also AAYA 18; CA 110; 121; CDBLB 1914-1945; DLB 34, 70, 156, 178; MTCW 1; SATA 20

Wells, Rosemary 1943-...................... **CLC 12**
See also AAYA 13; CA 85-88; CANR 48; CLR 16; MAICYA; SAAS 1; SATA 18, 69

Welty, Eudora 1909- **CLC 1, 2, 5, 14, 22, 33, 105; DA; DAB; DAC; DAM MST, NOV; SSC 1, 27; WLC**
See also CA 9-12R; CABS 1; CANR 32, 65; CDALB 1941-1968; DLB 2, 102, 143; DLBD 12; DLBY 87; MTCW 1

Wen I-to 1899-1946 .... **TCLC 28**

Wentworth, Robert
See Hamilton, Edmond

Werfel, Franz (Viktor) 1890-1945 ... **TCLC 8**
See also CA 104; 161; DLB 81, 124

Wergeland, Henrik Arnold 1808-1845**N C L C 5**

Wersba, Barbara 1932-..................... **CLC 30**

Literary Criticism Series
Cumulative Topic Index

This index lists all topic entries in Gale's *Classical and Medieval Literature Criticism, Contemporary Literary Criticism, Literature Criticism from 1400 to 1800, Nineteenth-Century Literature Criticism,* and *Twentieth-Century Literary Criticism.*

Topic Index

Twentieth-Century Literary Criticism
Cumulative Nationality Index

TCLC-83 Title Index

ISBN 0-7876-2738-0

90000

9 780787 627386